ENGLAND

THE BLUE GUIDES:

BLUE GUIDE

ENGLAND

Edited by
STUART ROSSITER
M.A.

With 81 Maps and Plans
by JOHN FLOWER

LONDON
ERNEST BENN LIMITED
RAND McNALLY & COMPANY
CHICAGO, NEW YORK, SAN FRANCISCO

FIRST EDITION 1920
SECOND EDITION 1924
THIRD EDITION 1930
FOURTH EDITION 1939
FIFTH EDITION 1950
SIXTH EDITION 1957
SEVENTH EDITION 1965
EIGHTH EDITION (new format) 1972
NINTH EDITION 1980

Published by Ernest Benn Limited
25 New Street Square, London EC4A 3JA
and Sovereign Way, Tonbridge, Kent

Rand McNally & Company
Chicago, New York, San Francisco

Printed in Great Britain

ISBN *Library* 0 510–01618–9
528–84627–2 (USA)
ISBN *Paperback* 0 510–01619–7
528–84626–4 (USA)

PREFACE

This is the ninth edition of the Blue Guide to England. It remains an attempt in one handy volume to guide the traveller to whatever is most worth seeing while calling to his attention also the characteristics past and present of each region. It thus concerns architecture, archaeology, and landscape; the arts and inventions; the heritage of influential men, stirring or uncommon events, and memorable ideas; institutions which visually or intellectually improve the quality of life; and anything of interest which differentiates England from other lands.

The country is described according to a system of routes and sub-routes, in most instances using long-established roads since it is on these that all places of old foundation stand. It is not suggested that these are necessarily the 'best' ways—whether by this is meant the least crowded, the most beautiful, or the fastest—of making the journey between the terminal points of their titles. The routes do, however, have the merit of grouping places in a logical topographical order, which is impossible in the gazetteer-type guide and much more imperfect when every route takes the form of a 'suggested outing' with some particular aspect in view. It should serve equally the habitual traveller who has to go from one major centre to another by bringing to his notice what on the way can relieve his journey; while, by its emphasis in description, it shows the leisurely tourist those things most worth his attention or diversion. A very detailed index provides flexibility of use.

With every edition of the Blue Guide to England the scope of what is considered notable has been widened. Whereas in 1920 gothic architecture, 'beauty spots', and literary association almost alone attracted description, these have been joined by innumerable other attractions, from Roman remains to Victorian follies, from nature reserves to industrial archaeology. While the balance of fashion constantly changes, relative intrinsic values change somewhat less, and every attempt has been made in widening the scope to ensure that the mere proliferation of modern leisure pursuits does not unbalance the description.

The book does not attempt to catalogue every country mansion, historic inn, Roman road, museum of local bygones, bird sanctuary, 'safari park', sports centre, steam railway, rural custom, or alternative route. The reader should not expect to find in it at local level where to fish, to shop, to play golf, to watch boxing, or to have a drink. Comprehensive—that word beloved of blurb writers—it does not attempt to be save in the variety of its scope, and then without descent to the trivial.

It credits the traveller with some sensibility, some powers of observation, and some previous knowledge of the country's past. Every experienced traveller will know some delightful spot, some splendid view, some interesting local fact that has been omitted. How could it be otherwise given the richness of England's heritage and the diversity of the landscape? Many readers with a favourite 'stately home' write to say that this one is inadequately described. This is true of all of them. In order to put the best of England into one manageable volume, it must always be true. Pevsner found that sometimes he could not manage just the architecture of one county in a single volume.

The art of the guide-book is the art of selection: not to include everything in surfeit, not to omit anything that will be conspicuous by its absence (except perhaps deliberately!); not to make a rigid choice; above all to leave the reader with the pleasure of discovering that there is more to a place than the description specifies. The Editor assumes the reader to have bought a guide as a way of asking informed advice. It is the Editor's duty to give informed advice: he has not been hired to make the traveller's decisions nor to feel his emotions for him.

We live in an increasingly restless age. The privilege—unknown in the past save to the very rich, but become almost universal in a single generation—of going at will by personal transport is accepted as merely the opportunity to gratify a mannerless urge to be faster or go farther than the man in front. The obvious or most advertised tourist attractions are now more crowded than ever, for the crowds have come greater distances: where a majority of visitors to York once came from Leeds or Harrogate, they now come from London or Bristol, Amsterdam or Oslo. Alas, the 'approach by motorway' robs every 'centre' of its true relationship with what it is the centre of, if indeed (as, for example, at Leicester) the veritable centre itself has not, by planning, been rendered unrecognisable. A more thorough exploration of a smaller region or the choice of less obvious destinations can only be advantageous to all.

Because of its obvious attractions London is always bursting at the seams: a far less harassed time may be had almost anywhere else in England. Furthermore, contrary to apparent belief, it is not the only city that has concerts, theatre, opera, good shops, festivals, night clubs, or restaurants. Windsor and Stratford are not unrivalled for historic tradition. There seems to be no very good reason why Oxford gets more visitors than Cambridge. Canterbury and York, Devon and the Lake District are not the only other goals. Among places that will stand comparison in their special ways with anything Europe has to offer are (in no particular order) Durham, Norwich, Ely, Wells, Southwell, Beverley, Fountains, Compton Wynyates, Castle Howard, Penshurst, Althorp, and any one of a hundred more 'stately homes', Bury St Edmunds, Leeds Castle, Berkeley Castle, the Roman Wall, the Cotswolds, the North York Moors, and the Peak District.

The repercussions of the 1973 administrative changes are endless, making many previously useful and universally accepted descriptive statements about places technically incorrect. As far as possible, where the bureaucratic nonsense is a hindrance rather than a help, it has been ignored. On arrival in the characteristic centre of a country town, it is no help to know that it is in one region for electricity, another for the health service, and a third for railways, while for tourism its regional head-quarters are elsewhere again; that the postal code shows routing through one county and the telephone prefix numbers routing through another; that the inhabitants pay rates to one authority and your parking fees go to another. Camford may no longer be correctly described as a 'county town'. The former corporation of Camford has been replaced by the amorphous 'Borough of South Camfordshire'. Camford is not the largest town in its county, nor arguably the most important. How simply is one to emphasise its central historical place in county history? If purists detect residual technical errors of this sort, we shall be in the good company of the majority of our citizens faced with such strange juxtapositions as Warrington, Cheshire or Slough, Berks.

The Editor knows the limitations of the professional traveller including his own, and marvels at the riches of England still largely untapped by even those who consider themselves knowledgeable. He does not think that many people will exhaust the resources of this book. But he will be the first to welcome constructive suggestions for its improvement.

CONTENTS

II SOUTH-WESTERN ENGLAND

III CENTRAL ENGLAND

IV EASTERN ENGLAND

V NORTHERN ENGLAND

MAPS AND TOWN PLANS

GROUND PLANS

EXPLANATIONS

TYPE. The main routes are described in large type, smaller type being used for branch-routes and excursions, for historical and preliminary paragraphs, and (generally speaking) for descriptions of less importance or immediacy.

ASTERISKS indicate points of special interest or excellence; two asterisks are used sparingly implying worth travelling the length of the country to see.

POPULATIONS are given, for towns only, according to the census of 1971 (approximated to the nearest hundred). Though these figures are now out-of-date, they have the merit of indicating roughly the comparative sizes of places and the facilities that can consequently be expected.

DISTANCES are given cumulatively from the starting-point of the route or sub-route. Road straightening, one-way systems, and by-passes ensure that these are at best approximate.

OPENING HOURS. The expression 'or dusk' always implies closure at an earlier hour in winter, *not* opening to a later hour in summer.

PLANS. Double-page town plans are gridded with numbered squares, referred to in the text thus: (Pl. 1–16). On the cathedral plans figures or letters have their own key; where necessary the same reference appears in the text.

ABBREVIATIONS. In addition to generally accepted and self-explanatory abbreviations, the following occur in the Guide:

A.A. = Automobile Association
Abp. = Archbishop
Adm. = Admission, Admiral
BH. = Bank Holiday
Bp. = Bishop
B.R. = British Rail
c. = circa (about)
C = century
Dec. = Decorated
E.E. = Early English
exc. = except
fl. = floruit (flourished)
H.M.S.O. = Her Majesty's Stationery
                       Office
incl. = including
m. = mile(s)
min. = minutes

N.T. = National Trust
Perp. = Perpendicular
Pl. = plan
pron. = pronounced
R.A.C. = Royal Automobile Club
Rest. = restaurant
Rfmts = refreshments
Rte = Route
seq. = sequentia, etc. (following)
SS = Saints
St = Saint
St. = Street
tel. = telephone
Trans. = Transitional
Y.H. = Youth Hostels
Y.M.C.A. = Young Men's Christian
                          Association

PRACTICAL INFORMATION

This has been provided mainly for the benefit of visitors from overseas and may be safely ignored by most residents of Britain.

I APPROACHES TO ENGLAND

Travellers coming from overseas have the choice of innumerable air and sea services, and though the majority of these have as their destination London, it is by no means essential to begin a tour in the capital. Indeed travellers bringing their own transport are better advised not to make straight for London. Some of the busiest **Places of Arrival** are listed below with their principal connecting facilities.

Airports. World-wide international services arrive at Heathrow; many direct international flights land at Gatwick, Birmingham, and Manchester. Other airports have only limited international traffic.

LONDON (Heathrow). Frequent regular connecting coaches to *Victoria Air Terminal*, Buckingham Palace Rd.; to *Feltham Stn.* (trains to London, Waterloo); to *Woking Stn.* (trains to Portsmouth, Winchester, Southampton, Salisbury, etc.); to *Reading Stn.* (trains to Exeter, Bristol, Gloucester, S. Wales, etc.): to *Watford Junction* (trains to Birmingham, Liverpool, Manchester, N. Wales, Scotland): to *Luton Stn.* (trains to Leicester, Nottingham, Sheffield).—Underground (Piccadilly Line). Local buses to Hounslow, etc.

London (Gatwick). Airport Stn. with direct trains (every 20 min.) to *London* (*Victoria*); also to Brighton.

BIRMINGHAM. Local bus to Station St. Trains from *Birmingham International* to *Coventry* and *London* (*Euston*).

MANCHESTER. Local bus to Charlton St. Bus Stn.

BRISTOL (from Channel Is., Paris). Local bus to Marlborough St. Bus Stn.

SOUTHEND (from Ostend, Le Touquet). Until the Airport Stn. is completed (?1980), Airport coach in 5 min. to Rochford Stn., whence rail connection (every 20 min.) to *London* (*Liverpool St.*).

SOUTHAMPTON (from Channel Is., Paris). Trains from Airport Stn. to Southampton Central and to *London* (*Waterloo*).

BOURNEMOUTH, EXETER, and NORWICH also have some international services.

LIVERPOOL (from Channel Is., Paris, Dublin). Local bus to Lime St. Stn. and Pier Head.

LUTON (mainly charter flights). Bus to railway stn. whence trains to *London* (*St Pancras*) and the Midlands.

STANSTED (mainly charter flights). Bus to Bishop's Stortford Stn., frequent trains to *London* (*Liverpool St.*), and to Cambridge.

Seaports (passenger). Travellers by liner from Australia or the Americas arrive at Tilbury, Southampton, or Liverpool; from the Continent by steamer at various ports listed below:

TILBURY (also from Leningrad). Boat trains to *London* (*Fenchurch St.*).

SOUTHAMPTON (also from Le Havre, Cherbourg, Lisbon). Boat trains from Docks to *London* (*Waterloo*); direct services from Central Stn. to Salisbury and Bristol.

LIVERPOOL (also from Belfast, Dublin). Local buses from Pierhead to Lime St. Stn., whence express train service to principal cities.

LONDON (British and Foreign Wharf). Jetfoil from Ostend.

DOVER (from Boulogne, Calais, Dunkirk, Ostend, Zeebrugge). Boat trains from Marine Stn. to *London (Victoria)*.

FOLKESTONE (from Boulogne, Calais). Boat trains from Harbour Stn. to *London (Victoria)*.

NEWHAVEN (from Dieppe). Boat trains from Harbour Stn. to London (Victoria).

WEYMOUTH (from Channel Is., Cherbourg). Boat trains to London (Waterloo).

PLYMOUTH (from St Malo, Roskoff, Santander). Trains to London (Paddington), Bristol, Birmingham, York, Newcastle, etc.

SHEERNESS (from Flushing). Train or coach to London (Victoria).

FELIXSTOWE (from Rotterdam, Gothenburg). Local trains to Ipswich, change for Norwich, London (Liverpool St.).

HARWICH (from Ostend, Hook of Holland, Esbjerg, Kristiansand). Boat trains from Parkeston Quay to *London (Liverpool St.)*, also to Sheffield and Manchester. Also (from Hamburg, Bremerhaven): special bus from Harwich Town to London (Liverpool St.).

IMMINGHAM (from Gothenburg, Amsterdam). Special coach from Dock to London (Kings Cross Coach Stn.).

HULL (from Rotterdam, Gothenburg). Special bus from King George Dock to Railway Stn., whence trains to Doncaster and *London (Kings Cross)*.

NEWCASTLE (from Esbjerg, Stavanger, Bergen, Kristiansand, Gothenburg, Oslo). Local bus from Tyne Commission Quay to Central Stn., thence by train to principal cities.

Hovercraft Terminal. RAMSGATE (from Calais). Special connecting bus service to London (Victoria Coach Stn.).

Arrival by Car (Air Ferry). The only airports of entry are SOUTHEND, see Rte 47, and STANSTED. From the Hovercraft Terminal at RAMSGATE, see Rte 4.

(Sea Crossing). The following ports have facilities for landing cars; drivers setting off from these ports should consult the routes indicated below:

DOVER, see Rte 2, 5
FELIXSTOWE, see Rte 47
FOLKESTONE, see Rte 5
HARWICH, see Rte 47
HULL, see Rte 70B
IMMINGHAM, see Rte 57B
LIVERPOOL, see Rte 59
NEWCASTLE, see Rte 71
NEWHAVEN, see Rte 7B
PLYMOUTH, see Rte 22
PORTSMOUTH, see Rte 10
SHEERNESS, see Rte 2
SOUTHAMPTON, see Rte 11, 13
WEYMOUTH, see Rte 13B, 14

Arrival by Motor-Coach. Scheduled Continental services arrive at Victoria Coach Station, London.

Health. Vaccination certificates are not normally required by visitors arriving direct from Europe, Canada, U.S.A., Australia, or New Zealand.

Foreign Exchange. Most airports and seaports of entry are equipped with Bureaux de Change, which are open during the period of arrival of international services. Elsewhere exchange may be effected at most banks during normal banking hours (see p. 26). Eurocheque cards are generally accepted. At other times the larger hotels normally change certain currencies and travellers' cheques for their clients. In London an increasing number of bureaux are open all day (see 'Blue Guide to London').

The **British Tourist Authority**, 64 St James's St., London, S.W.1, founded with the object of promoting tourism in Britain, issues a monthly journal 'In Britain' with announcements of 'coming events', as well as a wide range of tourist literature. The ENGLISH TOURIST BOARD, 4 Grosvenor Gardens, London, S.W.1 (Tel. 01-730 3400) is responsible to it for tourist facilities and services and for sponsoring Regional Tourist Boards, which run information offices up and down the country. The B.T.A. has offices in New York (680 Fifth Ave.), Chicago, Los Angeles, Dallas, Sydney, Toronto, Johannesburg, Tokyo, Sao Paolo, Buenos Aires, and most W. European capitals. Telephone enquiries to the London Tourist Board (Tel. 01-730 0791).

Travellers who wish to save the bother of making their own arrangements will be advised to do so through a **Travel Agent,** choosing a reputable member of the Association of British Travel Agents. These organizations, for a small fee, obtain travel tickets, make hotel reservations, and, if desired, arrange tours for individuals or parties. A selection of agents in London is given below; several of them have branches in other towns.

Thomas Cook & Son, 45 Berkeley St., W.1, and many branches; *American Express* 6 Haymarket, S.W.1, 89 Mount St., W.1; *Dean & Dawson*, 81 Piccadilly, W.1.

II HOTELS AND RESTAURANTS

In the text the existence of **Hotels** has been indicated topographically merely as a quick indication of the likelihood of finding overnight accommodation of good quality, but names and details have been omitted. It was felt that there are now sufficient annual publications (comp. below) listing and evaluating hotels and restaurants, and that touring motorists are seldom without at least one of them. In addition many large towns have information services which help find rooms for travellers; most municipal councils issue free or at very small cost detailed local lists; and some of the larger hotel chains have central booking bureaux in London.

'Hotels and Restaurants in Great Britain', the official annual publication of the British Tourist Authority, gives a selected list "based solely upon the principle of suitability for visitors from overseas"

Both the principal motoring organizations publish annually excellent detailed guides to their recommended hotels and restaurants, and Ashley Courtenay's 'Let's Halt Awhile' is an independent hotel guide.

In addition there may be mentioned 'Egon Ronay's Guide' and the 'Good Food Guide' of the Consumers' Association, unofficial and often stringently critical surveys of the state of gastronomy in Britain.

In most cities, with notable exceptions, there are well-established large hotels and an increasing number of newly-built establishments (augmented by motels on the outskirts), offering a standard of comfort that compares favourably with that of their counterparts elsewhere. In country towns older inns, often of architectural distinction and with historical associations, have generally been discreetly modernized and afford comfortable accommodation on a more traditional pattern at somewhat lower cost.

Country House Hotels, converted from private mansions, standing in spacious grounds, are generally well-appointed and often have facilities for country sports. The B.T.A. publishes a list of 'Commended Country Hotels, Guest Houses, and Restaurants'. Many of these and their historic urban counterparts are mentioned in the text as worthy of a visit for their architecture or association with the past.

Nearly every small town has modest *Inns* where adequate accommodation for the night may be found. In many villages the local 'pub' (comp. below) has a few modest rooms, almost invariably clean, and often makes up for lack of luxury by a more personal welcome.

In cities and the principal tourist centres advance booking is always advisable; during July, August, and September, and at holiday weekends, this applies almost everywhere, except in recognized touring areas where many local hotels will not book single nights in advance. A booking service is provided by *Hotel Bookings International Ltd.*, at Heathrow and Gatwick Airports; *Hotel Booking Service Ltd.*, 137 Regent St., London, W.1 (Tel. 01-437 5052); *Hotelguide*, 8-10 Charing Cross Road (Tel. 01-836 5561), and others.

Hotels in Britain have neither official categories nor nationally standardized prices, but they are now obliged by law to produce a precise statement of charges. Breakfast is now not always included in the cost of the room, but no extra charge is made for baths taken in a public bathroom.

A service charge of 10, 12½, or 15 per cent is now often added to or included in the bill; in such circumstances additional tipping is necessary only for exceptional personal service or where porterage is specifically not included. Where no percentage is added, equivalent remuneration should be divided among individual staff who have given service. Normally visitors are required to vacate their rooms before 12 noon.

The average costs experienced by the editor during the compilation of this edition range for a single room from:

country districts from £5.50
towns and tourist centres £9–£13.50
big industrial cities and central London £12–£25 upward
London Airport £13.50–£25

It should be emphasized that these prices imply a reasonable degree of comfort; it is possible to find good cheaper accommodation in many places (though not easy in the larger provincial cities). On the other hand luxury may cost considerably more. In some seaside and holiday resorts prices vary with the season, the highest charges being effective in July–August and at the Christmas and Easter holidays.

Most hotels have restaurants which, with the exception of some in seaside towns during the summer season, are open to non-residents. In most places dining hours extend to at least 9.30, but in smaller hotels and remoter places it may be difficult to dine after 8 or 8.30.

Guest Houses. Visitors who propose to spend more than a week or two at any of the chief health or seaside resorts will find guest-houses or

'Boarding-houses' considerably cheaper than hotels. These usually charge by the week, but often provide only supper, bed, and breakfast. At *Furnished Apartments* the hirer may arrange either to do his own catering or to have it done for him by the landlady. Inquiries for accommodation of this type should be made locally.

Public Houses vary considerably with the district in which they are situated. The best, especially in country districts and market towns, are respectable, even family establishments, many supplying good food at moderate prices. Most 'pubs' are 'tied' to a particular brewery, which controls the brew (and sometimes the brands of liquor) it sells; a 'Free House' is not so tied. In general the Public Bar (or its regional equivalent: smoke-room, tap, vaults, etc.) is less well appointed and a fraction cheaper, and is patronized by the regular locals (male) and may be the scene of darts-playing, etc.; the Saloon, Private Bar, Lounge, are progressively more select (and usually less animated). Children under 14 years old are not admitted and those under 18 allowed only non-alcoholic drinks (except that those over 16 may have certain types of alcoholic drink with a meal). Unaccompanied ladies are discouraged in some city houses. 'Off-licences' sell liquor for consumption off the premises where their function has not been taken over by supermarkets or wine shops.

Licensing Hours. The 'permitted hours' during which alcoholic liquor may be supplied at restaurants or public houses vary in different districts, but the total number of such hours on weekdays is 8, unless specially extended to $8\frac{1}{2}$. Generally speaking, it is not possible to purchase liquor before 11 a.m., or between 3 and 5.30, or after 10.30 p.m. On market days in country towns special (longer) hours may apply. Restaurants may supply liquor for consumption with a meal for one hour after the ordinary hours. On Sundays the sale of liquor is permitted from midday to 2 p.m. and 7 to 10.30. These restrictions do not apply within their own hotels to travellers staying overnight.

Youth Hostels. The cheapest way of seeing the English countryside is to travel on foot or bicycle from Youth Hostel to Youth Hostel. The *Youth Hostels Association* (national office, Trevelyan House, St Albans, Herts), founded in 1930, runs c. 200 hostels in all parts of England, occupying buildings of many different characters, each in charge of a warden. Membership of the association costs 85p per annum for those from 5 to 15, £1.50 for those over 16 and under 21, and £2.50 for those of 21 or over (family membership £5). Accommodation is simple, but at most hostels hot morning and evening meals and packed lunches are provided at a low cost. All hostels are closed from 10 a.m. to 5 p.m. Members are required to do their share of the housework and to observe a few simple rules, which are detailed in the Y.H.A. Handbook (free to members, 30p post free to non-members).
Members of foreign Youth Hostels Associations need not join the English Y.H.A.; foreign visitors who are not already members may take out International Membership for £5. The *Y.H.A. Travel Bureau* at 29 John Adam St., London, W.C.2, will give advice.

Restaurants of reasonable quality are now to be found all over England. A handful of superb restaurants, often deep in the country or in small country towns, equal in quality and in price the best to be found on the Continent, and their number is increasing. Some are set in baronial luxury, some are adjuncts of hotels, but many others concentrate on haute cuisine in quite homely surroundings. Wine has of late become increasingly expensive, and as a proportion of the bill looms surprisingly large. More modest establishments generally serve a table d'hôte or set lunch (and sometimes dinner), providing an adequate if unimaginative meal for about £2.75. Grills and steak bars are becoming commonplace; the more pretentious are not necessarily the best. The English Tourist Board's booklet 'A Taste of England' lists 750 restaurants offering traditional English dishes.

Midday meals, often cheaper, can be had in pubs, many of which have good cold buffet counters supplemented by one or two modest dishes of the day; some pubs, however, do not serve food on Saturdays or Sundays.

In the less enterprising towns and in some industrial cities meals are still best taken at a hotel, although in nearly all large towns will be found good foreign restaurants, particularly Italian and Chinese. Local inquiry will often lead to the discovery of good food outside, but within easy motoring distance, of a large town.—The facilities at service areas on the motorways are much inferior to their counterparts in Italy or the United States.

Tea Shops, a peculiarly English phenomenon, which survive in the cathedral cities and country towns but to a decreasing extent elsewhere, are renowned for good home cooking, often served in buildings of character and historical interest. Substantial 'cream teas' are a speciality, but some also provide modest lunches. The tea 'hour' extends from about 3.30 to 5 or 5.30.

III   TRANSPORT

Motoring. To import a car for tourist use into the United Kingdom for a period not exceeding 12 months, no formalities are necessary except the possession of (a) a valid National Driving Licence or International Driving Permit; (b) an International Motor Insurance Card (Green Card) valid for the U.K. (otherwise British Insurance must be effected immediately). No one under 17 years of age may drive a motor-car in Great Britain, and no one under 16 may ride a motor-cycle.

CAR HIRE. When hiring a car, visitors must present a valid driving licence free from endorsement (and, usually, have had driving experience for at least a year). Hire companies usually stipulate that the hirer of a self-driven car must be between 21 and 65 years old. Charges vary according to season, length of hire (daily, weekly, or—cheaper—for longer periods), make and size of vehicle, etc. Most of the International Car Hire firms have agents at the main airports in England. Information may be obtained at the motoring organizations. For example, the A.A. (see below) issues, for a small fee, a comprehensive booklet 'Car Hire in Great Britain' with hire firms arranged by town alphabetically. Cars may also be hired through the American Express, B.E.A., and the Car Hire Centre International, Swallow St., Piccadilly.

The rule of the road throughout the United Kingdom is 'keep to the left and overtake on the right', which is the reverse of the procedure in most parts of Europe and in America. There is a general speed limit of 30 miles per hour on roads in built-up areas (i.e. those areas with street lighting), except where otherwise indicated; and a maximum speed limit on all roads and motorways of 70 m.p.h. Penalties for driving under the influence of alcohol or drugs have recently been increased. For all information on road conduct motorists should consult 'The Highway Code' (H.M.S.O.).

Motorists are strongly advised to join one or other of the national motoring organizations: the *Automobile Association of Great Britain* (A.A.), Head Office: Fanum House, Leicester Square, London, W.C.2; or the *Royal Automobile Club* (R.A.C.), Head Office: 85 Pall Mall, London, S.W.1. A slight reduction in the membership fee is granted to members of affiliated overseas organizations such as the American Automobile Association, and free reciprocal membership is offered in some cases to Commonwealth visitors.

Roads in Great Britain are divided into four categories: 'Class 1' ('A' roads), 'Class 2' ('B' roads), 'Class 3' ('C' roads), and 'Unclassified' roads. The 'A' and 'B' roads are numbered, the class and number usually shown on the direction signs. This classification is used in our descriptions of road routes throughout the guide. 'Unclassified' roads are not numbered and are of minor importance. As a general rule, it may be taken that 'A' roads are better than 'B' roads, though the heaviest traffic is likely to be found on 'A' roads. Secondary and minor roads are generally surfaced to the standard of main roads, but are narrower and more winding. On motorways, motor bicycles under 50 c.c., learner drivers, etc. are forbidden.

Some important roads, e.g. Watling Street, Foss Way, etc., run along the line of old Roman roads with their characteristic straightness. A few important thoroughfares, however (notorious among which is the A6), are still comparatively narrow and winding, sharp corners being by no means uncommon, and vision is impeded by the hedges or walls which are still usual, except in moorland and forest districts. Dangerous cross-roads, corners, bridges, hills, etc., are indicated by conventional signs, more judiciously placed in some counties than in others.

Main-road hills are not usually severe and the tendency is to 'by-pass' even quite moderate ascents, e.g. Dashwood Hill (1 in 10) on the London–Oxford road. The E. side of England, particularly East Anglia, Cambridgeshire, and Lincolnshire, is generally flat, though isolated hills, as at Lincoln, are not unknown even here. Many parts of Yorkshire, Durham, and Northumberland are hilly, Yorkshire especially having a number of very severe short hills (e.g. near Whitby), as well as long, fairly easy gradients over the moors. The Peak District and the Lake District possess very little level ground, but the worst hills are usually off the beaten track, the severest main-road hill in the Lake District being Honister Pass (1 in 4). The hilliest region in England is in W. Somerset, Dorset, and Devonshire, where 'single-figure' gradients are common, though the roads do not usually rise very high above sea-level. The stiffest main road in England is probably Porlock Hill (1 in 4–8; 3 m. long), in Somerset. Cornwall, the Cotswolds, the Chilterns, the Malvern Hills, and the Kentish Weald all yield their crop of gradients more or less severe.

Though Britain has been threatened for years with a change from miles to kilometres, at present all signposting is in miles and British-made cars have mileometers and speedometers reading m.p.h. It was thought therefore that to provide distances in both measurements would clutter every page with figures to no good purpose. Miles remain an integral part of the British (and American) scene, and Continental readers hardly need to be reminded that 5 miles are almost exactly equal to 8 kilometres.

CYCLING. The *Cyclists' Touring Club* (13 Spring Street, London, W.2) issues a useful handbook.

CAMPING AND CARAVANNING. Information can be obtained from the Camping Club of Great Britain and Ireland, East Grinstead House, East Grinstead, W. Sussex. The B.T.A. publishes a comprehensive list of sites and their facilities: the R.A.C. and A.A. also publish useful handbooks.

Walking. A feature of the English countryside that is shared by few other countries is the incidence of rights-of-way: footpaths through privately owned land where (subject only to the laws against damage, trespass, or misuse) the pedestrian has a legal right of passage. Recording and signposting of such paths has much improved of late and, in areas designated as National Parks, the system has been extended to provide magnificent opportunities for long walking tours away from populated regions. Among the longest and most beautiful long-distance footpaths are the South Downs Way, the Ridgeway Path from the Chilterns to the Berkshire Downs, the Cleveland Way, the Cotswold Way (100 m.) from Chipping Campden to Bath, and the Pennine Way, the last of which extends for 250 miles down the spine of England. Though detailed descriptions are beyond the scope of this volume, indications of some of their finest stretches are given at relevant points. Detailed guides to individual parks and paths are published by H.M.S.O. Walkers will find it useful to join the Ramblers' Association, 1/4 Crawford Mews, York St., London W.1

Maps. The *Ordnance Survey* issues a number of excellent series of maps. A catalogue may be had free on request to the Ordnance Survey, Romsey Road, Maybush, Southampton, SO9 4DH. The most useful of these for those exploring in any depth are the series at a scale of 1:50,000 (190 sheets for Great Britain; £1 each). An attractive 'Tourist' series (same scale) for the most-visited areas is now available for Cambridge, Dartmoor, Exmoor, Lake District, New Forest, North York Moors, and the Peak District in England. Walkers in country areas may prefer the $2\frac{1}{2}$ inches to 1 m. series. There is a special map also at 2 inch scale for Hadrian's Wall. For the motorist the series of quarter-inch maps (17 for Great Britain) are the most practicable. Before setting out on a trip, the Route Planning map of Great Britain is helpful. All the above are marked with the 'National Grid', which is marked also for convenience of cross-reference on our planning maps (between pp. 32 and 33). A 'Historical Series' includes maps, each with admirable explanatory text, of 'Roman Britain', 'Monastic Britain', etc. Numerous good commercial maps and road atlases, based on the O.S., are available. Among these may be mentioned good coverage of the Inland Waterways, the Broads, and the Thames, by Edward Stanford Ltd., of Long Acre, London. For motorists the series published by the R.A.C. is particularly clear and accurate.

Railways. The 'Inter-City' trains of British Rail provide a service between the principal cities that for speed (averaging 80 m.p.h. or more) and frequency (often hourly or better at regular intervals) is now probably unmatched. London has been brought within $1\frac{1}{2}$–2 hours of Southampton, Norwich, Bristol, and the main Midland towns; within 3 hours of Newcastle, Lancashire and Yorkshire; and within 5 hours of places as far distant as Edinburgh and Penzance. This has been achieved only at the expense of closing many intermediate stations and most country branch lines, so that overall journey times to smaller places are considerably longer and involve changes to buses.

The services are divided into Regions: Western, Southern, Eastern, and Midland, but their timetables are now amalgamated (published annually). Fares now vary according to area and frequency of service. Return tickets usually cost double the single fare, although some 3-month returns are considerably cheaper, and cheap day returns are sometimes available.

Britrail passes, bargain tickets allowing unlimited travel on all British Rail services, are available in most countries throughout the world. They must be bought before arrival in Britain and cover 8, 15 or 22 days, or one month. In Britain, Railrover tickets are on sale, allowing the holder unlimited travel for 7 or 14 days.

Motorail (car-carrier expresses, mostly with sleeping-cars) connect London with Newcastle, with Carlisle, and with various places in Devon and Cornwall, Birmingham (Sutton Coldfield), Carlisle, and Newcastle are similarly linked with Bristol and the s.w. Various services also connect England with Scotland and Wales.

For tabulated services from London the 'ABC Rail Guide' may be purchased; similar simplified tables are also published for various other cities.

Buses. There is a large and well-developed network of long-distance express coach services, run by the National Bus Company, which issue the 'Express Coach Guide' twice a year. The cost is generally less than by rail or air.

Overseas visitors may obtain a Coach Master ticket valid for 8 days (£24) which gives unlimited travel on the main express routes, and day tours in England. The main interchange points in England are London (Victoria Coach Station), Preston, Leeds, Manchester, Liverpool, Nottingham, Birmingham, Cambridge, Cheltenham, Oxford, Exeter, and Bournemouth. Details of other coach tours may be obtained from travel agents.

LOCAL BUSES serve the country districts, replacing many former railway branch lines. Municipal services reach a high standard of frequency and are increasingly being given special road 'lanes' to reduce timings and eliminate delays.

Internal Air Services. London is well connected with the principal centres of population, which are themselves, however, with the exception of the Midlands (Birmingham *Elmdon* and E. Midlands *Castle*

Donington), better connected with Scotland, Ireland, and the Channel Is. than with one another. There are however services between Bristol and Leeds/Bradford (Severn Airways) and between Gatwick and Plymouth (Brymon Airways).

IV GENERAL INFORMATION

Season and Plan of Tour. July, August, and September, especially the weeks of the long school holiday, are the popular travelling months in England, when 'tourist facilities' are in full operation; hotels are then at their fullest and the main roads overcrowded. In the latter half of May and in June, travelling is more comfortable, and October is often a month of fine weather and beautiful atmospheric and foliage effects. The chief characteristic of the climate is changeability, both from day to day and from place to place. Although long periods of fine weather occur each year, their incidence cannot usually be forecast with accuracy, and a little rain may be experienced at any season. Really hard winters (Jan–Feb) with considerable snowfall do occur, but seldom more than once a decade.

Of the summer resorts that fringe the long coast-line, those in Sussex, Devon, Cornwall, and Yorkshire mostly offer the additional attraction of picturesque hill-scenery. The flat E. coast generally affords sandier beaches and safer bathing, and has a more bracing climate. The s.w. coast, from the Isle of Wight to Land's End, is apt to be warm at midsummer but offers good winter quarters. The w. coast is the rainiest at any season. The leading inland health resorts include Bath, Harrogate, Buxton, Leamington, Cheltenham, Malvern, and Droitwich. Among tourist districts especially favoured for walking, cycling, and motor tours are the Lake District (where the mountaineer will find good rock-climbing), the Peak District, the Yorkshire Dales, Devon and Cornwall, Exmoor, the North and South Downs, and the New Forest. Boating-parties may make for the beautiful scenery of the Thames and Wye and the Norfolk Broads. Interest of a different kind is offered by the Shakespeare Country, 'Wordsworthshire' (i.e. the Lake District), the 'Wessex' of Thomas Hardy, the Constable Country, and the regions associated with the Brontës, Dickens, Hampden, Lincoln, and Washington. A tour of the cathedrals should include at least Canterbury, Winchester, Salisbury, Wells, Gloucester, Lichfield, Southwell, York, Durham, Lincoln, Peterborough, and Ely, and visits to Oxford and Cambridge should not be omitted. But the historic England, with its ruined castles and abbeys, its old towns and villages, its stately mansions and peaceful farms, is to be found in almost any county, and will richly reward those who quit the crowded main roads for the lanes and by-roads that add to the charm of the English countryside.

The **National Trust** FOR PLACES OF HISTORIC INTEREST OR NATURAL BEAUTY ('N.T.' in the text; 42 Queen Anne's Gate, London, S.W.1), founded in 1895, acts as trustee of properties acquired by the nation to be preserved intact for future generations. It preserves from destruction and damage some 400 m. of coastline and an ever-increasing number of national treasures. The minimum subscription is £7 (£3 under 23), allowing free access to N.T. properties where a charge is normally made. There are no standard hours of admission to N.T. properties.

Many other historic monuments have been scheduled for preservation by Act of Parliament, and numerous ancient buildings are under the efficient care of the **Department of the Environment** (AMHB/P, Room G1, 25 Savile Row, London, W.1). Admission fees range from 5p to 80p; season tickets are available (see below).

The STANDARD HOURS OF ADMISSION to the Ministry's monuments are as follows:

	Weekdays	*Sundays*
March, April, and October	9.30 a.m.—5.30 p.m.	2.00—5.30 p.m.
May to September	9.30 a.m.—7.00 p.m.	2.00—7.00 p.m.
November to February	9.30 a.m.—4.00 p.m.	2.00—4.00 p.m.

though they vary slightly on summer Sundays (see text).

National Parks (*Nat. Park* in text) are areas of fine natural beauty designated to preserve the landscape and promote facilities for open-air recreation. Visitors should keep in mind that farmland, although within Nat. Park limits, is nevertheless still private property.

NATURE RESERVES (Nat. Res. in text) are managed by the Nature Conservancy to protect areas of unusual scientific interest, and to provide controlled opportunities for study and research (flora, fauna, etc.). In some instances previous permission to visit a reserve must be obtained.

The **Gardens** of many country houses are thrown open to the public on certain days in summer (usually 11–7, Sun 2–7; adm. fee). The resultant funds are administered by the Queen's Institute of District Nursing, for the Retired District Nurses' Benefit Fund and the National Trust and Royal Horticultural Society Gardens Scheme. Particulars from the National Gardens Scheme, 57 Lower Belgrave St., London, S.W.1, which publishes an annual illustrated guide.

The **British Waterways Board** own and manage c. 2000 miles of canals and rivers in Great Britain. Information about the Board's waterways is obtainable from the General Manager, Melbury House, Melbury Terrace, London, N.W.1. The Board also publishes maps and cruising guides to its waterways. The *Inland Waterways Association*, 114 Regent's Park Road, London, N.W.1, an unofficial body of enthusiasts, champions the use of waterways for pleasure purposes. Information on the hire of boats may be obtained from (and bookings made through) *Boat Enquiries Ltd.*, 7 Walton Well Rd., Oxford.

Admission Fees to museums, monuments, and houses vary and tend, year by year, to rise. Precise sums have not been indicated in the text unless they are exceptionally large, but the existence of a charge has generally been indicated by the word 'fee'. Season tickets are available for properties of the Department of the Environment at £3 per annum; membership of the N.T. gives free entrance to its properties. Privately-owned 'stately homes' have, of course, complete freedom to vary their opening hours (which should always be checked) and often separate charges for their various attractions; inquiry is advisable about inclusive tickets.

An 'Open to View' season ticket is now available for overseas visitors (obtainable from Thos. Cook & Son Ltd. in the U.S.A., Canada, and Australia), entitling the holder to free admission to all properties owned by the Dept. of the Environment, the N.T., and also some 100 privately-owned houses.

The annual Index Publications: 'Historic Houses, Castles, and Gardens' and 'Museums and Galleries' (available from booksellers) are useful in providing up-to-date information about opening hours.

The **Civic Trust**, an independent and unofficial body, was founded in 1957 to encourage high quality in architecture and planning; to preserve buildings of artistic distinction or historic interest; to protect the beauties of the countryside; to eliminate and prevent ugliness, whether from bad design or neglect; and to stimulate public interest in the good appearance of town and country and to inspire generally a sense of civic pride. Its initial success in getting unsightly modern accretions removed from medieval Norwich has been followed by many practical schemes and reports advising local bodies, among the most important being saving the centre of Warwick and a project for turning the Lea Valley into a regional park. Its headquarters are at 79 Buckingham Palace Road, London, S.W.1.

Public Reference Libraries. All large towns in England maintain a Reference Library, where information of a local or general nature may be sought. In towns where a separate NATIONAL TOURIST INFORMATION CENTRE (symbol 'i') or a CIVIC INFORMATION BUREAU is not indicated in the text inquiries should be made at the Central Library.

Sports Centres. Most towns of any size now have a Municipal sports centre (open to all) and few towns do not have open and covered swimming pools.

Summer Time. A brief flirtation with Central European Time having proved unacceptable, Britain reverted to the general use of Greenwich Mean Time in 1971. From about mid-April to mid-September the clocks are advanced one hour to give 'Summer Time'.

Business is suspended all over England on Good Friday and Christmas Day and also on *Bank Holidays*, viz. New Year's Day, Easter Monday, May Day, Whit Monday or an alternative Mon in spring, the last Monday in August, and Boxing Day. On bank holidays, however, museums, public galleries, and places of amusement may close, whereas private collections are sometimes open. It is wisest to telephone beforehand. *Saturday* is a business half-holiday or holiday in the larger towns; but shops are more often open on Saturday and closed on Wednesday or Thursday after 1 p.m. On *Sunday* museums, collections, and pleasure-resorts are almost invariably closed in the morning.—*Market Days* in country towns, though in their way characteristic of English life, are on the whole to be avoided if possible, especially by the motorist. Local market days are indicated in some of the motor handbooks.

Money. In 1971 a decimal system was adopted in Britain which left the exchange value of £1 sterling unaltered, while redividing it into 100 new pence. The denominations of 'silver' coins are 50p, 10p, and 5p; and of copper coins 2p, 1p, and ½p. The former silver sixpence (6*d*) still circulates with an equivalent value of 2½p. Old shilling and two-shilling pieces are equal to 5p and 10p respectively. Four values of notes exist: £20 (rarely seen), £10, £5, and £1. Notes and coins issued in Scotland, the Isle of Man, and the Channel Is., though officially equal in value, do not circulate freely in England and are best exchanged at a bank.

BANKS are open Mon–Fri 9.30–3.30; also 4.30–6 on one night a week, the day being decided on a local basis according to demand.

Tipping. In a restaurant, according to the quality of the service, the waiter should be rewarded with 10–12½ per cent of the bill; somewhat less where a considerable proportion of the bill is for a single bottle of wine. Cloak-room attendants expect to be tipped unless a charge is made. Taxi-drivers expect about 20 per cent of their fare (minimum 10p); barbers and hairdressers 20–30 per cent on their charges. Barmen in pubs (unlike those in hotel cocktail bars), usherettes at cinemas and theatres, and attendants in public lavatories are not tipped.

Postal Rates. All letter-post to the continent of Europe (incl. Turkey and Cyprus) goes by airmail without surcharge.

Telephones. Call-boxes take 2p and 10p coins. The subscriber trunk dialling (S.T.D.) system whereby 2p (in the case of coinboxes; 3p with a different scale of charges from private lines) buys time according to distance now covers the greater part of Britain; it is also available to the main cities of most of Europe and the U.S.A. Charges can be transferred (reversed) to Canada and the U.S.A. Calls are cheaper after 6 p.m. and all day Saturday and Sunday.

SOVEREIGNS OF ENGLAND

Anglo-Saxons

827–836	EGBERT
837–858	ETHELWULF
866–871	ETHELRED I
871–899	ALFRED THE GREAT
899–925	EDWARD THE ELDER
925–940	ATHELSTAN
959–975	EDGAR
978–1016	ETHELRED II (THE UNREADY)
1016	EDMUND IRONSIDE
[1016–1035	CANUTE THE DANE
1035–1040	HAROLD I
1041–1042	HARDICANUTE]
1042–1066	EDWARD THE CONFESSOR
1066	HAROLD II

Normans

1066–1087	WILLIAM I (THE CONQUEROR)
1087–1100	WILLIAM II (RUFUS)
1100–1135	HENRY I
1135–1154	STEPHEN

Plantagenets

1154–1189	HENRY II
1189–1199	RICHARD I
1199–1216	JOHN
1216–1272	HENRY III
1272–1307	EDWARD I
1307–1327	EDWARD II
1327–1377	EDWARD III
1377–1399	RICHARD II

Lancastrians

1399–1413	HENRY IV
1413–1422	HENRY V
1422–1461	HENRY VI

Yorkists

1461–1483	EDWARD IV
1483	EDWARD V
1483–1485	RICHARD III

Tudors

1485–1509	HENRY VII
1509–1547	HENRY VIII
1547–1553	EDWARD VI
1553–1558	MARY I
1558–1603	ELIZABETH I

Stuarts

1603–1625	JAMES I
1625–1649	CHARLES I
[1649–1660	COMMONWEALTH]
1660–1685	CHARLES II
1685–1688	JAMES II
1688–1694	WILLIAM III AND MARY II
1694–1702	WILLIAM III
1702–1714	ANNE

Hanoverians

1714–1727	GEORGE I
1727–1760	GEORGE II
1760–1820	GEORGE III
[1810–1820	REGENCY]
1820–1830	GEORGE IV
1830–1837	WILLIAM IV
1837–1901	VICTORIA

House of Saxe-Coburg

1901–1910	EDWARD VII

House of Windsor

1910–1936	GEORGE V
1936	EDWARD VIII
1936–1952	GEORGE VI
1952–	ELIZABETH II

DIMENSIONS OF ENGLISH CATHEDRALS

(Measurements, given in feet, are internal, except for the Towers)	Total Length	Length of Nave	Width of Nave (incl. Aisles)	Height of Nave	Length of Transept	Height of Central Tower	Height of West Towers	Total Area in Sq. ft.[1]
BRISTOL	300	125	69	52	115	107	123	22,556
CANTERBURY	517	188	72	80	156[2]	235	178	43,294
CARLISLE	204	39½	62	72[3]	121	110	—	15,270
CHESTER	345	150	73	73	182	127	—	31,550
CHICHESTER	376	155	90	61	130½	271	92	28,500
DURHAM	469½	205	80	72¾	172	218	144½	44,602
ELY	521	248	78	86	178½	170	215	46,000
EXETER	383	150	72	68	140	145	—	29,600
GLOUCESTER	420	180	86	68	149	225	—	30,600
GUILDFORD	365	160	66	65	100	156	—	31,060[13]
HEREFORD	342	158½	73½	64	146	140	—	33,318
LICHFIELD	371	173	67	57	149	258	198	27,720
LINCOLN	481	215	80	82	223[4]	271	206	57,200
LIVERPOOL[5]	500	363[7]	88	120	199	331	(200[6])	104,275
LONDON[12]	463	180	125	92½	227½	355½	212½	87,400
NORWICH	399	253	72	69½	173	313	—	34,800
OXFORD	179	102	53	41½	115	144	—	12,915
PETERBOROUGH	426	230	81	80½	182	124	177[8]	39,591
RIPON	270	133	87	94	133	121	121	25,280
ROCHESTER	305½	118	63	55	120[9]	156	—	23,300
ST ALBANS	520	275½	77¾	70	175½	144	—	39,200
SALISBURY	449	195	82	81	206[10]	404	130	43,515
SOUTHWELL	318	185	72	70	128	105	149	26,000
TRURO	275	135	62	70	111	250	204	23,200
WELLS	383	161	82	67	135	165	125	29,070
WINCHESTER	526	250	88	78	208	150	—	53,480
WORCESTER	400	178	75	68	126[11]	196	—	33,200
YORK	486	212	104½	99½	223½	213	202	60,952

[1] Mainly from Lord Grimthorpe's 'A Book on Building' (1880).—[2] E. Transept 172 ft.—[3] Choir.—[4] W. Transept 127 ft.—[5] Unfinished.—[6] As designed.—[7] Incl. central space.—[8] N.W. Spire 170 ft.—[9] E. Transept 88 ft.—[10] E. Transept 143 ft.—[11] E. Transept 120 ft.—[12] From Poley's 'St Paul's Cathedral' (1927).—[13] Estimated.

ARCHITECTURAL PERIODS

The following chronological table of English architectural periods gives in round figures the dates corresponding to the 'period names' mentioned in the text, which, though they are objected to by some present-day authorities, may be justified on the grounds of convenience and general usage. The word 'prehistoric' is employed in a special sense applicable to England.

Periods	*Approximate Dates*
Pre- and Proto Historic:	
Neolithic	3000?–1800 B.C.
Bronze Age	1800–500 B.C.
Early Iron Age and Late Celtic Period	500 B.C.–A.D. 100
Romano-British	A.D. 43–400
Romanesque	
Anglo-Saxon	400–1066
Early Norman	1050–1100
Mature Norman	1100–1150
Transitional	1150–1190
Gothic:	
Early English	1190–1280
Decorated	1280–1380
Perpendicular	1380–1550

PLANNING MAPS
see overleaf

HISTORIC ENGLISH COUNTIES

Key to Numbers
1 Bedfordshire
2 Berkshire
3 Buckinghamshire
4 Cambridgeshire
5 Cheshire
6 Cornwall
7 Cumberland
8 Derbyshire
9 Devon
10 Dorset
11 Durham
12 Essex
13 Gloucestershire

14 Hampshire
15 Herefordshire
16 Hertfordshire
17 Huntingdon
18 Kent
19 Lancashire
20 Leicestershire
21 Lincolnshire
22 Norfolk
23 Northamptonshire
24 Northumberland
25 Nottinghamshire
26 Oxfordshire
27 Rutland

28 Shropshire
29 Somerset
30 Staffordshire
31 Suffolk
32 Surrey
33 Sussex
34 Warwickshire
35 Westmorland
36 Wight Isle of
37 Wiltshire
38 Worcestershire
39 Yorkshire
40 Isle of Man

New Boundaries

Avon — New Counties

––––– Old Boundaries

Towns shown have Plans ■

SCOTLAND

NORTH SEA

24

Newcastle
Cleveland
11
Durham
Tyne-and-Wear

7
Cumbria
35

40

North Yorkshire
39
York
Humberside
Hull

IRISH SEA

19
West Yorkshire
Leeds

Merseyside
LIVERPOOL
MANCHESTER
South Yorkshire
Sheffield

Gt. Manchester
Chester
5

8

25

21
Lincoln

Nottingham

30

King's Lynn
22
Norwich

Shrewsbury
28
West Midlands
BIRMINGHAM
Coventry
34

Leicester
20
27
Stamford

17
4

31

WALES

Worcester
38
Hereford
15

Stratford

23

1
Cambridge
Ipswich
Colchester
12

13
Gloucester

26
3
Oxford

16
St. Albans

London
London
Medway Towns
18
Canterbury
Dover
Folkestone

Bristol
Bath
Avon
37

2

32

29

Salisbury
14
Winchester
West
33
East

9
Exeter

10
Southampton
Bournemouth
Portsmouth
Brighton

36

ENGLISH CHANNEL

SCILLY
ISLES

6
Plymouth

Key page to Planning Maps

ENGLAND

I SOUTH-EASTERN ENGLAND

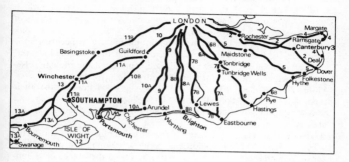

The area between the Lower Thames and the South Coast comprised in this section is bounded on the w. by the Southampton road, and includes the counties of Kent, Surrey, Sussex, and the greater part of Hampshire. It is given its general character by the North and South Downs, parallel chalk ridges which, though nowhere exceeding 900 feet, are marked by short and often sharp ascents. Between them lies the Weald, alternately pastoral and wooded. All roads from London to the Coast must surmount both lines of Downs. With one or two busy exceptions, roads running E. and W. tend to be minor, narrow, and indirect.

Kent has been called the 'Garden of England' from the fruit orchards which are a conspicuous feature, especially in the blossoming season (April–May). The Hop Gardens are noticeable at all times, but particularly so when "the hop that swings so lightly, the hop that shines so brightly" is hanging in golden clusters from the poles, strings, or wires on which it is trained. The 'oast houses', for drying the hops, with their pointed ventilating cowls, are characteristic. In 1940–45 Kent received the full brunt of the German air-attack, and won the nickname of 'Bomb Alley'. Natives of the county are divided in local rivalry into 'Men of Kent' and 'Kentish Men', the former born to the E. and the latter to the w. of the Medway. William Caxton, father of English printing, was a native of the Kentish Weald. The *North Downs* overlook the Thames Valley and eventually meet the sea in the famous chalk cliffs to continue beyond the Straits of Dover in the Pas de Calais. Kent can be stormy in winter: great damage was suffered in 1953 and 1978.

Surrey, one of the 'Home Counties' (Kent, Surrey, Middlesex, Essex, and Hertford), becomes ever smaller as its N. parts are encroached upon by the spread of the Greater London Council. But farther s., e.g. about Leith Hill, Box Hill, Hindhead, etc., are charming tracts of unspoilt scenery, as well as many historic mansions. The *North Downs*, with the Pilgrims' Way, traverse the county from E. to w.

Sussex, though divided administratively into E. and w. (with county towns respectively at Lewes and Chichester), geographically is divided N. to S. The N. part is occupied by the well-wooded *Weald*, which extends far into Kent, and was once covered by the immense forest of *Andredsweald*, of which the main relic is *Ashdown Forest*. Sussex oak was long held the best timber for shipbuilding, and for five centuries the forests yielded fuel for an important iron forging and smelting industry, until early in the 19C the use of pit-coal transferred the industry elsewhere. Farther S. Sussex is traversed from w. to E. by the *South Downs*, "blunt, bow-headed, whale-backed downs", once famous for their sheep. Sussex suffered heavily from German air-attacks in 1940–45, and the coast, strongly fortified, became a 'prohibited area' occupied by the Services.

Hampshire, or **Hants,** a county of low hills, rolling downs, and fertile valleys, is famous for its woodland scenery, culminating in the New Forest. Yew trees are so numerous as to be called the 'weeds of Hampshire'. Except in the **Isle of Wight,** historically included in the county, though made separate in 1974, the coast is comparatively tame. Hants, containing the ancient capital of Winchester, was the original Wessex, the nucleus of the future kingdom of England. Izaak Walton is an immortal memory along the river-banks of Hampshire; it is the county of Gilbert White; and it claims to be the birthplace of cricket. In 1974 it lost the area w. of the Avon, including Bournemouth, to Dorset.

1 LONDON

LONDON, the capital, is situated in S.E. England, about 40 m. from the mouth of the *Thames*, which winds through it from w. to E. dividing it roughly into halves. The N. half is by far the more important for the tourist; and in both halves the interest diminishes in the inner suburbs as we recede from the river. The *Greater London Council* has jurisdiction over 7 million inhab. in an irregular area of c. 620 sq. miles that includes outer suburbs that were formerly in the Home Counties. A loosely defined 'Outer Metropolitan Area' contains a further 5 million. London is fully described in the **'Blue Guide to London',** and the following condensed information is intended for visitors whose object is not London for itself but London as a brief stage in the exploration of England.

Railway Termini. The following is an alphabetical list of the chief London termini, all of which are directly connected by passages or subways with the system of Underground Railways within London: CHARING CROSS, West End terminus of the Southern Region.—EUSTON, terminus of the London Midland Region, serving Liverpool and Manchester.—FENCHURCH STREET, city terminus of the Eastern Region, with trains from Tilbury.—KING'S CROSS, terminus of the Eastern Region, and services from Newcastle and Hull.—LIVERPOOL STREET, terminus of the Eastern Region (E. lines).—PADDINGTON is the terminus of the Western Region.—VICTORIA, the chief West End terminus of the Southern Region, is the station for the Continental routes viâ Folkestone, Dover, etc.—WATERLOO is another terminus of the Southern Region, where the boat-trains for Southampton start.

Hotels (often full in summer). Many, but not all, hotels of the highest class are to be found in Mayfair and Piccadilly, and in Kensington. Other first-class hotels are in the Strand, and in Bloomsbury, where there are also many less expensive ones. Accommodation is still virtually non-existent on the South Bank but increasing on the ᴇ. fringes of the City, and there is an increasing number of small private hotels in suburban areas.

Restaurants. The fashionable eating areas are still in St James's, Mayfair, and the West End, though better value gastronomically is often to be found in the less pretentious restaurants of Soho, Chelsea, or the Charlotte St. area. Many of the suburbs, such as Hampstead, Wimbledon, and Richmond are now also well provided with restaurants.

Buses serve most areas in London, including the inner suburbs, although some services are infrequent, or irregular. 'Red Arrow' single-decker buses connect the main railway stations.—**Coaches.** The environs of London with a radius of c. 35 m. are served by Green Line Coaches, which pick up passengers in London at fixed points only. In summer there are coach excursions to points of interest around London, and 'Seeing London' drives are organized by London Transport throughout the year, and by the principal tourist agencies.

Underground Railways, beneath the most frequented parts of London, provide an efficient and convenient method of transit. At their points of intersection the lines are connected with one another by subways, and they communicate directly with most of the railway termini.

River excursions in summer from Westminster Pier to Kew, Richmond, and Hampton Court; also downstream to Greenwich.

HOURS OF ADMISSION TO THE PRINCIPAL SIGHTS

	Weekdays	Sundays	Notes
Apsley House	10–6	2.30–6	
British Museum	10–5	2.30–6	
Carlyle's House	11–1, 2–6	2–6 or dusk	Closed on Mon & Tues
Chelsea Hospital	10–4.30	—	Closed 12–2
Chiswick House	9.30–4, 5.30, or 7	9.30–4, 5.30, or 7	Closed Mon & Tues, Nov–Feb
Courtauld Institute	10–5	2–5	
Dickens House	10–5	—	
Dulwich Gallery	10–4, 5, 6	2–5, 6	Closed on Mon, & on Sun in winter
Geffrye Museum	10–5	2–5	Closed on Mon
Ham House	2–6	2–6	Closed Mon; Oct–March, 12–4
Hampton Court	9.30–4, 5, 6	2–4, 5, 6	
Hayward Gallery	10–8	12–6	Closed 6 on Sat
Johnson's House	11–5, 5.30	—	
Keats's House	10–6	2–5	
Kensington Palace	10–4, 6	2–4, 6	
Kenwood	10–dusk	2–dusk	
Kew Gardens	10–dusk	2–dusk	
Museum of London	10–6	2–6	
National Gallery	10–6	2–6	

HOURS OF ADMISSION TO THE PRINCIPAL SIGHTS

	Weekdays	Sundays	Notes
National Maritime Museum	10–5 or 6	2.30–6	
National Portrait Gallery	10–5 or 6	2–6	Sat 10–6
Natural History Museum	10–6	2.30–6	
Osterley House	2–6	2–6	Closed Mon Oct–March, 12–4
Parliament, Houses of	10–4	—	Sat only. Also BH., & Mon, Tues & Thurs in Aug & Sept
Queen's Gallery	11–5	2–5	Closed Mon
Record Office Museum	1–4	—	Closed on Sat
Royal Academy	10–6	2–6	
Royal Mews	2–4	—	Wed & Thurs only
St Paul's Cathedral	8–5, 7	Services	
Science Museum	10–6	2.30–6	Library weekdays 10–5.30
Soane Museum	10–5	—	Closed on Mon, & Aug
Syon House	2–4.15	1–5	April–July, closed Sat & Sun; Aug–Oct, closed Fri & Sat
Tate Gallery	10–6	2–6	
Tower of London	9.30–4, 5	2–5 in summer	
Victoria & Albert Museum	10–6	2.30–6	
Wallace Collection	10–5	2–5	
War Museum	10–6	2–6	
Wesley's House	10–4	—	Closed 1–2
Westminster Abbey	8–6	Services	Chapels 10–4, Fri till 3, Wed also 6–8, Sat 9.30–2, 3.45–5; Chapter House 10.30–4, 6.30; Museum 9.30–5; all closed Sun
Westminster Hall	10–4	—	
Zoological Gardens	9, 10–dusk or 7	9, 10–dusk or 7	

ADMISSION. Most of the privately-owned houses and galleries charge an admission fee. State-owned collections and galleries are generally free.

Amusements are advertised in the newspapers (and in *What's on in London* and *Time Out*) and by posters. The WEST END THEATRES are mostly situated in or near Piccadilly Circus and the Strand. Tickets may be obtained in advance at the box-office (no extra charge) or at one of the numerous ticket agents' offices (commission). Opera and ballet are given at *Covent Garden* and also at *Sadler's Wells Theatre* and the *Coliseum*.—The leading VARIETY THEATRES are the *Palladium*, near Oxford Circus and *Victoria Palace*, near Victoria Station.—CONCERTS are given in the *Royal Festival Hall*, the *Queen Elizabeth Hall*, *Royal Albert Hall*, *Wigmore Hall*, W.1, etc. For these and for numerous ART EXHIBITIONS the newspapers should be consulted.—Among other places of amusement are *Mme Tussaud's Waxworks*, and the *Planetarium*, near Baker Street Station, and numerous *Cinemas*.

Post Office. Letters addressed 'Poste Restante', without mention of any special post office, should be called for at the *General Post Office* in King Edward St., E.C.1.—*Trafalgar Square Post Office* (William IV St.) is open day and night.

American Embassy, 1 Grosvenor Square, W.1. Irish Embassy, 17 Grosvenor Place, S.W.1.—High Commissioners of the British Commonwealth: *Australia*, Australia House, Strand, W.C.2; *Canada*, Canada House, Trafalgar Square, S.W.1; *India*, India House, Aldwych, W.C.2; *New Zealand*, New Zealand House, Haymarket, S.W.1; *Pakistan*, 35 Lowndes Sq., S.W.1.

Tourist Agents. *Thomas Cook & Son*, 45 Berkeley St., W.1, 11 Gt. Cumberland Place, W.1, Ludgate Circus, E.C.4, 125 Pall Mall, S.W.1, 378 Strand, W.C.2, 145 Oxford St., W.1, 123 High Holborn, W.C.1; *Dean & Dawson*, 81 Piccadilly, and 163 Fenchurch St., E.C.3; *American Express*, 6 Haymarket, S.W.1; *Frames' Tours*, 25 Tavistock Place, W.C.1; *Sir Henry Lunn*, Marble Arch House, Edgware Rd., W.2.

Police Headquarters. New Scotland Yard, near St James's Park Station. *Lost Property Office*, 15 Penton St., N.1; articles left in buses or the Underground should be applied for at 200 Baker St.

For the purposes of the tourist, London N. of the Thames (apart from the outlying regions) may be regarded as comprising three districts: *Westminster and the West End*, to the w. of Charing Cross and Regent St. and extending into Kensington and Chelsea; the *City and East End*, to the E. of Temple Bar and Gray's Inn Road; and between these a *Central District*, extending N. from the Strand to Soho and Bloomsbury. Through these districts two main thoroughfares run from w. to E. to converge at St Paul's Cathedral. The first, beginning at Hyde Park Corner, follows the line of Piccadilly to the E., trends to the s. by Regent St. or Haymarket to Charing Cross, and there resumes its E. direction viâ the Strand and Fleet St. The other, a little to the N., leads E. to St Paul's from Marble Arch by the once continuous line of Oxford St., Holborn, and Newgate St., a way of Roman origin now somewhat distorted in the interest of traffic flow.

A drive on the top of a bus going E. by the Piccadilly route (No. 9), and returning by the other (No. 7, 8, or 25) is an excellent introduction to the exploration of London.

WESTMINSTER AND THE WEST END. To the N. of Charing Cross opens *Trafalgar Square*, with the tall *Nelson's Column*. On the N. side of the square is the ****National Gallery,** in which the representation of the various schools of painting (except the Early British School) is probably the most choice and thorough in the world. Behind, opposite the church of *St Martin in the Fields* (1721–26), is the **National Portrait Gallery,** with an extensive and valuable collection of British historical portraits. On the w. side of the square is Canada House.—To the w. from Charing Cross, beyond the statue of Charles I, the *Admiralty Arch* admits to the

MALL, bordered on the left by *St James's Park* and (r.) by *Carlton House Terrace, Marlborough House, St James's Palace,* and *Clarence House.* At the end is **Buckingham Palace,** the London residence of the Queen. The *Queen's Gallery* (on the l., in Buckingham Gate) has exhibitions of paintings from the royal collections.

Whitehall and its continuation, Parliament St., leading S. from Trafalgar Square towards Westminster, are flanked on the W. side by a continuous row of *Government Offices,* punctuated half-way down by the *Horse Guards,* and, beyond, by *Downing Street,* the residence of the Prime Minister. On the E. side of Whitehall, between two buildings of the Ministry of Defence, stands the ***Banqueting House,** the only relic of the old Whitehall Palace, with a ceiling by Rubens. At the beginning of Parliament St. rises the ***Cenotaph,** commemorating in dignified simplicity the Glorious Dead of 1914–18 and 1939–45.

**Westminster Abbey, dating as it stands mainly from the 13C, is one of the most beautiful examples of Gothic architecture in England, but is still more famous as the burial-place of the illustrious dead of many ages, including the Unknown Warrior. *Poets' Corner* is in the S. transept, but the finest monuments are in the *Choir Chapels,* culminating in the **Chapel of Henry VII* (built in 1503–19), with its superb fan-vaulting, the most sumptuous example in England of late-Perpendicular Gothic. The *Cloisters,* with the *Chapter House* and *Chamber of the Pyx* should also be visited.

To the N. of the Abbey is *St Margaret's Church* and immediately opposite rise the ***Houses of Parliament,** by Sir Charles Barry (1840–50), a stately and extensive pile in a late-Gothic style, with a terrace on the river, three towers, and an elaborately decorated interior. A flag on the noble **Victoria Tower* (336 ft; at the S.W. angle) by day and a light in the *Clock Tower* (320 ft) by night indicate that Parliament is sitting. The term 'Big Ben' refers strictly to the hour-bell, not the clock. The venerable **Westminster Hall* (now part of the Houses of Parliament), in which Charles I was condemned, dates from 1097 but received its present form and its magnificent oaken roof from Richard II in 1399 (restored in 1914–23; damaged in 1940–41 and since restored).

Millbank leads S. from Westminster Abbey and along the river-bank to the ***Tate Gallery** of painting and sculpture with a fine collection of British painting from the 16C to the present day and 19–20C foreign works; while Victoria St. leads S.W. to *Victoria Station,* passing near the large Rom. Cath. ***Westminster Cathedral,** a notable building (1895–1903) by J. F. Bentley, with a square campanile (284 ft) and a sumptuous interior. From Victoria Station, Buckingham Palace Road leads S.W. towards *Chelsea,* with *Chelsea Royal Hospital,* a picturesque home for veteran soldiers, *Carlyle's House,* and the self-consciously 'arty' atmosphere of the King's Road.

From Piccadilly Circus, *Piccadilly* leads S.W., passing *Burlington House* (the home of the Royal Academy of Arts and the ethnographical *Museum of Mankind*), and skirting the S. side of *Mayfair,* to Hyde Park Corner, whence Knightsbridge and Kensington Road continue its line along the S. side of *Hyde Park* and *Kensington Gardens.* Behind the *Royal Albert Hall,* in Kensington Road, is a remarkable and important group of institutions devoted to science and art, including the *Royal College of Music,* the

Imperial College of Science, the **Science Museum*, the **Geological Museum*, the **Natural History Museum*, and the ****Victoria & Albert Museum,** containing perhaps the largest and finest collections of applied art in the world, beautifully displayed. At the w. end of Kensington Gardens is *Kensington Palace*, containing the *State Apartments.*

Regent Street leads N. from Piccadilly Circus to *Regent's Park*, in which are the **Zoological Gardens.*—A little s. of the park and to the N. of Oxford St. is the ****Wallace Collection,** the most important single art collection in London (paintings, French furniture, Sèvres porcelain, arms and armour, bronzes, miniatures, ivories, enamels, etc.). Also in this area are the *Post Office Tower* (580 ft) and the *Planetarium* and *Madame Tussaud's* waxworks.

CENTRAL DISTRICT. To the E. of Regent St., between *Oxford Street* on the N. and *Leicester Square* on the s., extends SOHO, a region of narrow streets with many foreign residents, numerous theatres, and many restaurants. It is intersected by *Shaftesbury Avenue* and by *Charing Cross Road,* and provides a characteristic kaleidoscope of exotic but not always reputable entertainment.

From Charing Cross the busy *Strand*, containing several theatres, leads E. towards the City, with interesting districts on both sides. On the right, near its w. end, Adam St. leads to the *Adelphi*, a district named after the Scottish brothers Adam who designed it, but now largely rebuilt; and on the left, Southampton St. leads to *Covent Garden*, with one of the world's famous opera houses. The former market for fruit, vegetables, and flowers has been moved to Battersea and its attractive setting will be put to other uses. Savoy St., to the right, leads to the *Chapel of the Savoy*, erected c. 1505 on the site of the ancient Savoy Palace. Farther on in the Strand we pass **Somerset House** (the registrar-general's office; with a stately river-façade), built in 1777–80 on the site of another old palace. In the middle of the street, almost opposite the new façade of *King's College*, which occupies the E. wing of Somerset House, rises the church of *St Mary le Strand* (1714). On the left is the huge *Bush House*, farther on is *Australia House*, and just beyond it is *St Clement Danes* (1681), burned in 1941, now restored as the headquarters church of the Royal Air Force. The Strand next passes the **Royal Courts of Justice,** an imposing Gothic pile dating from 1874–82, and ends at *Temple Bar*, where Fleet St. and the City begin (see below). Immediately N. of the Courts of Justice lies *Lincoln's Inn*, one of the four great Inns of Court or legal corporations, adjoined on the w. by *Lincoln's Inn Fields* (1618), one of the largest squares in London, with the *Royal College of Surgeons* on the s. side and **Sir John Soane's Museum* on the N. side. North of Holborn, on the w. side of Gray's Inn Rd., is *Gray's Inn*, another of the Inns of Court, largely rebuilt since the bomb damage of 1940–41.

Westward from Gray's Inn Rd. to Tottenham Court Rd., and to the N. of New Oxford St. and High Holborn, extends *Bloomsbury*, a region of formal streets and squares laid out in the 18–19C, the large houses of which have been absorbed by business and London University. Its principal building is the ****British Museum,** unsurpassed in the world for the value and variety of its contents. The **British Library** continues to share the building. Just behind are administrative buildings and other institutions of the

University of London, begun in 1933; and farther N., in Gower St., is *University College.*

THE CITY AND EAST END. *Fleet Street*, with its memories of Dr Johnson, and long association with the Press, leads E. from Temple Bar to St Paul's. From its w. end Chancery Lane, passing the *Public Record Office* (contents partly dispersed to Kew), with an interesting little museum, runs N. to Holborn, while on its s. side lies the **Temple,** a name covering two Inns of Court, the *Middle* and *Inner Temple.* The restored *Temple Church* is the largest and most important of the five remaining round churches in England, and the *Middle Temple Hall* (badly damaged in 1941; restored 1949) is a stately Elizabethan chamber of 1562–72, in which Shakespeare is said to have acted. Off the N. side of Fleet St. farther on is *Gough Square* with *Dr Johnson's House.* To the s. is seen the beautiful spire of *St Bride's Church.*

St Paul's Cathedral, the masterpiece of Sir Christopher Wren, with its famous dome unequalled for beauty of outline, stands at the top of Ludgate Hill and can best be seen from Cannon Street. The monument to Wellington (who, with Nelson, is buried in the crypt), the memorials to many other famous men, and the 'Whispering Gallery' are among the chief points of interest.—To the E. of St Paul's is the busiest part of the City. Many of its churches and most of the halls of the Livery Companies were severely damaged by air-raids; nearly all have been restored, though some were entirely destroyed. *Cheapside*, with *Bow Church*, on the right, passes a little s. of the **Guildhall**, the seat of the Corporation of the City of London, with its fine Gallery, hall, and library; to the l. is *St Lawrence Jewry.* The **Bank of England** (1732; greatly enlarged in 1924–38), one of the most important banks in the world, the former **Royal Exchange** (1842–44), and the **Mansion House** (1739–53), the official residence of the Lord Mayor, are grouped around a triangular space, the heart of the City, whence many important streets radiate.

THREADNEEDLE ST. is continued N. by BISHOPSGATE, with the church of *St Helen*, 'the Westminster Abbey of the City', towards Shoreditch.—CORNHILL is continued E. to Aldgate by LEADENHALL ST., with *Leadenhall Market* on the right, and *Lloyd's* farther E.—LOMBARD ST. passes the church of *St Mary Woolnoth* (r.), and is prolonged likewise to Aldgate by FENCHURCH ST. In Rood La. (N.) is the well-restored church of *St Margaret Pattens.* In Hart St., leading E. from Mark Lane (s. of Fenchurch St.), is *St Olave's* (beautifully restored), the church of Samuel Pepys, the diarist.—To the E. of Aldgate lie the 'East End' districts of *Whitechapel* and *Bethnal Green.*

From the Bank, King William St. leads s.E. to the *Monument* (202 ft high), which commemorates the Great Fire of 1666, and to the new *London Bridge.* Until 1739 Old London Bridge was the only bridge over the Thames at London. Descending the steps at the N. end of the bridge to Lower Thames St., we follow the latter E., past *Billingsgate Market* and the *Custom House* to the church of *All Hallows by the Tower* (beautifully restored), with its interesting crypt, and to Tower Hill. The *Tower of London* is one of the most famous as well as most interesting buildings in the metropolis. The *White Tower*, the oldest part, dates from soon after the Conquest, while most of the other fortifications are due to Henry III. The Norman chapel, the collection of armour, and the crown jewels are perhaps the chief points of interest. Within the gardens of Trinity Square, N.W. of Tower Hill, is the site of the ancient

scaffold; and adjoining are the offices of the *Port of London Authority.*
To the N.E. of Tower Hill is the old *Royal Mint.* Immediately below the
Tower the Thames is spanned by the imposing **Tower Bridge** (1886–94), and
thence down the river extend the **Docks,** nearly all on the N. bank. ST
KATHARINE DOCK, with the *World Trade Centre,* is now a marina.

To the N. of Holborn and Newgate St. and to the E. of Gray's Inn Rd. lie
the districts of Smithfield and Clerkenwell. Newgate St. passes close to the
Post Office Headquarters, and at its w. end is the *Central Criminal Court*
('Old Bailey'), on the site of Newgate Prison. Giltspur St. leads thence N.,
passing *St Sepulchre's Church* (l.) and *St. Bartholomew's Hospital* (r.) to
Smithfield, with its large meat-market. In the E. corner of Smithfield is the
entrance to *St Bartholomew the Great,* which, next to the chapel in the
Tower, is the oldest church in London. Beyond Aldersgate St. to the E. rise
the multi-story buildings of the *Barbican,* an ambitious scheme, centring
on St Giles Cripplegate, with a lake and an arts centre, preserving a corner
tower and stretches of the *Roman Wall* of the City. Here is the splendid
Museum of London. A little to the N. is the *Charterhouse* (restored after
war damage), founded as a convent in the 14C, but since 1611 a hostel for
poor gentlemen. *St John's Gate* (1504), spanning St John's Lane, w. of the
Charterhouse, is a relic of a wealthy priory; near by is the fine crypt of the
ancient priory church.

SOUTH OF THE THAMES. To the N. of the Houses of Parliament
Westminster Bridge (1862) crosses the Thames to Lambeth. Just below
it, on the right bank, is *County Hall* (1922), administrative headquarters
of the Greater London Council. Beyond, between Waterloo Station and
the river, on the 'South Bank' site of the 1951 Exhibition, are the *Royal
Festival Hall,* the *Queen Elizabeth Hall,* and the *Hayward Gallery,* in
a harsh 20C idiom and linked by an exposed tangle of concrete walk-
ways. The viewing platform of the Shell Centre affords a fine view.
Under the graceful *Waterloo Bridge* is the *National Film Theatre,* and
beyond rises a new *National Theatre* for the company that formerly used
the 'Old Vic' in Waterloo Road, and the London Television Centre.
Farther E. is industrial *Bankside,* once noted for its theatres and pleasure
resorts. Here is moored *H.M.S. 'Belfast',* a floating naval museum.
Southwark Cathedral (13–19C), at the s. end of London Bridge, is the
finest Gothic building in London after Westminster Abbey. A little to the s.
is *Guy's Hospital.*

Just above Westminster Bridge is *St Thomas's Hospital,* on the Albert
Embankment. **Lambeth Palace,** the London residence of the Archbishops of Canterbury for seven centuries, several times struck by
bombs, has a Chapel of c. 1250, the Lollards' Tower (1434–45), and a
valuable Library.—In Lambeth also, in the former buildings of Bethlem
Hospital, is the *Imperial War Museum,* including a remarkable
collection of paintings.

For numerous other places of interest in and near London, such as *Chiswick
House, Hampstead Heath, Kenwood,* and *Keats's House, Harrow,* the *R.A.F. Museum,
Hendon,* the *National Maritime Museum* at *Greenwich, Eltham Palace, Dulwich,
Hampton Court Palace, Richmond, Kew Gardens,* the mansions of *Ham, Syon,* and
Osterley, Epping Forest, Waltham Abbey, Dulwich, Kew Gardens, etc., see the 'Blue
Guide to London'.

2 LONDON TO DOVER VIÂ CANTERBURY

ROAD, (71 m.) A 2. 4 m. *New Cross.*—A 207. 16 m. *Dartford.*—A 2. 28 m.
Rochester.—29½ m. *Chatham.*—39 m. *Sittingbourne.*—45 m. *Ospringe* (**Faversham**).
—55 m. **Canterbury.**—71 m. **Dover.**—MOTORWAY, see Rte 4.

RAILWAY, 77¼ m. in 1¾ hrs from *Victoria*, viâ *Bromley South*, to *Chatham* in ¾ hr;
to *Canterbury* in 80 min.— Principal Stations: 17¾ m. *Swanley* (junction for Maidstone).— 33¾ m. *Rochester.*— 34½ m. **Chatham.**— 36 m. *Gillingham.*— 44½ m.
Sittingbourne (junction for Sheerness).— 52 m. *Faversham* (see Rte 4).— 62 m.
Canterbury (East).—72 m. **Shepherdswell** (for Barfreston).—77¼ m. **Dover**
(Priory).— *Rochester* and *Chatham* may be reached also by the Thames-side route
(2 m. shorter, but slower) from Charing Cross, Cannon Street, and London Bridge,
viâ *Gravesend* (28¼ m.) *Higham*, and (31¼ m.) *Strood.* To Canterbury viâ
Ashford, see Rte 5.

A2 quits London by the Old Kent Road, New Cross, and (7 m.)
Blackheath. It then avoids the centres of Bexleyheath and Dartford by
Rochester Way, a long urbanized bypass, continued by quasi-motorway.
Watling Street (A207), the old Dover road since Roman times, shorter and
for those with a sense of the past interesting *per se*, climbs straight up
Shooters Hill and down through Bexleyheath.—At (14 m.) *Crayford* we
bear right.— 16 m. **Dartford,** a busy town on the Darent, has a fine galleried
inn of 1703. Wat Tyler's rising probably originated in the town, and
another inn (renamed after him) in the High St. claims to be a meeting-
place of his insurgents. The *Church*, on the river, has a strong Norman
tower with 14C upper story.

The interior, spacious but over-restored, contains a late-15C wall-painting of St
George and the Dragon. The Spilman tomb, with inscriptions in German, was
erected to his wife (d. 1607) by Sir John Spilman or Spielmann (d. 1626), who came
from Lindaü on the Lake of Constance and built at Dartford one of the earliest
paper-mills in England; according to popular belief 'foolscap' paper was so called
from a jester ('Spielmann') forming part of his arms and used by him as a water-
mark. A tablet in the s. aisle commemorates Richard Trevithick (1771–1833), who
died in poverty at the Bull inn and was carried to his grave by his workmates at
Hall's engineering works.—The works, by the railway, hide remains of Dartford's
once famous priory of Dominican nuns.

Beyond the town A 207 passes over the approach to the Dartford–
Purfleet tunnel ½ m. before the A 2 (here motorway in everything but name)
comes in from the right to regain its Roman alinement.

An alternative road (A 226) from Dartford to Rochester diverges left from
Watling Street, ¾ m. from the church. This follows the course known to both
Shakespeare and Dickens when the Roman road had decayed.—2 m. *Horns Cross*,
in a region of chalk pits and cement works. A little to the left, looking out across
the Thames is *Stone Church*, a beautiful building of c. 1245 with a chancel higher
than its nave. The richly sculptured interior of the chancel, with exquisite windows
and blind arcading, has many features in common with contemporary work at
Westminster Abbey. The Wylshire chantry (N.E.) is a 16C addition; the vault is a
successful restoration by G. E. Street.—3 m. *Greenhithe*, with a quaint river-front,
was the scene of the departure in 1845 of the ill-fated polar voyage of Sir John
Franklin. *Ingress Abbey* (by Chambers; 1772) was enlarged with stone from old
London Bridge. It became the last home of 'H.M.S. Worcester', a nautical training
college founded in 1862 at Blackwall and disbanded in 1972.—5 m. *Northfleet* has
a large 14C church on a bluff, with a contemporary rood screen.

7 m. **Gravesend** (Hotel), a famous Thames-side port (54,000 inhab.), is the pilot
station for vessels using the Port of London. It still maintains a traditionally maritime appearance with old inns and some weather-boarded houses in its narrow High
Street. From the *Town Pier* a steam ferry for passengers plies at frequent intervals
to Tilbury (p. 476); the car ferry, superseded by the Dartford Tunnel (see above),
was discontinued in 1965. The *Terrace Pier* is used by pilots. The views of the

Thames from near the piers or (better) from Gordon Terrace, farther E., are famous. The gardens here mark the site of Fort House, the residence of Gen. Gordon in 1865–71. A statue, and windows in *St George's* church, W. of the piers, commemorate the burial here of Pocahontas (d. 1617), the Indian princess who saved the life of Capt. John Smith, the colonizer of Virginia. Leonard Calvert (son of Lord Baltimore, the founder of Maryland) set sail from here in 1633; so also did George Fox, the Quaker (1671), and John and Charles Wesley (1735) on their American journeys. A tablet on the pier recalls Strindberg's residence here in 1839.

At (10 m.) *Chalk* are the house where Dickens spent his honeymoon and a forge popularly identified with Joe Gargery's. The road descends *Gad's Hill* (wide view from Sir John Falstaff Inn) where Falstaff encountered the 'rogues in buckram' ('Henry IV', Pt I, ii, 4). At *Gad's Hill Place* an 18C red-brick house now a school, opposite the inn, Dickens lived from 1857 till his death in 1870. Part of the garden, known as the 'Wilderness', is reached by a tunnel under the road. The railway passes beneath the ridge in a tunnel (3909 yds) built in 1819–24 for a canal. We rejoin the Roman road in Strood.—15 m. **Rochester**, see below.

On the peninsula lying between Thames and Medway to the E. of Chalk, are (3 m.) *Higham* church (14C *Door, screen, and pulpit) and (5 m.) *Cooling Castle*, with a 14C gatehouse, the home of Sir John Oldcastle, the supposed original of Falstaff. The opening scenes of Dickens's 'Great Expectations' are laid in the marshes which stretch N. to the Thames and are well seen from near the large 13C church of *Cliffe* (mural of life of St Edmund). The peninsula ends as the *Isle of Grain*, with a huge oil refinery.

A 2 crosses the Gravesend–Wrotham road 4 m. N. of *Meopham* (pron. 'Meppam'), the birthplace of John Tradescant (1608–62), the naturalist, where the large church of 1325 has a late-14C aisle, and a pulpit (1682) from St Margaret's Westminster. We skirt *Cobham Park* (r.), landscaped by Repton.

Cobham Hall (now a girls' school; adm. Sun, Wed, & Thurs in Aug; fee), an imposing and predominantly Elizabethan mansion, with a centre block of 1662–72 and archaizing alterations by the Reptons, was the home of the Duke of Richmond and his duchess ('La Belle Stuart'), and later the seat of the Earls of Darnley. At the s.w. entrance to the park is the village of *Cobham*, the church of which has the largest collection of brasses in England (14–16C). Close to the Leather Bottle Inn (Dickens relics) Mr Pickwick discovered his wonderful inscribed stone. The College Almshouses evolved in 1598 from a college founded in 1362. Owletts (adm. Apr–Oct, Wed & Thurs, 2–5; fee), a Carolean house at the w. end of the village, was presented to the Nat. Trust by Sir Herbert Baker.

At 26 m. the M 2 proper diverges right (comp. Rte 4).—28 m. *Strood* is linked to Rochester by three parallel bridges; Temple Manor (daily, Sun from 2, fee), a 13C hall of the Knights Templar, with 16C additions, is in Priory Rd., s.w. of the High Street.

28½ m. **ROCHESTER,** an ancient town (55,500 inhab.) dating from pre-Roman times, was known to the Romans as *Durobrivæ*, to the Saxons as *Hroffeceaster*, and has been an episcopal see since the 7C. It is adjoined without break by Chatham on the E. and that again by Gillingham, the three 'Medway Boroughs' thus forming practically one town with a total population of 199,000. Strood and Frindsbury, beyond the Medway, are virtually suburbs.

Parking. Arrival by car from the London direction necessitates a short 'one-way' detour to reach the Esplanade car park.

Railway Stations. *Rochester* and *Chatham*, ½ m. apart; the faster trains stop only at *Chatham*.

Hotels and CAFÉS in High Street, Rochester; also in Gillingham.—**Restaurant** in Chatham.

Post Office, High St.—INFORMATION BUREAU, Central Library, Northgate.

Buses from Frindsbury and Strood through Rochester and Chatham to Gillingham and Rainham, etc.—LAUNCHES from Sun Pier in summer.

Theatre. Medway Little Th., High St.

Charles II spent a night at Rochester in 1660 on his way from Dover, and here James II took up his escape in 1688. Rochester was the scene of some of the earliest adventures of Mr Pickwick and it is the Cloisterham of 'Edwin Drood'.

The *Esplanade* on the E. bank of the Medway is balustraded with stone from the 14C bridge, demolished in 1856. Here stands *Bridge Chapel* (1387; visitors ring), rebuilt in 1737, and now the board-room of the Bridge Wardens. The **Castle** is approached by an archway (imitation Norman) in the ragstone enceinte built by Bp. Gundulf c. 1087 but partly rebuilt in the 14C. Within stands the huge square *KEEP (adm. daily; fee; closed Sun in winter till 2; *View) of coursed rubble, erected after 1127 by Wm. de Corbeuil, Abp. of Canterbury. One of the finest specimens of Norman military architecture in England, it is 120 ft high and has walls averaging 12 ft in thickness.

The **Cathedral**, modest in size, originally dedicated to St Andrew and since the Dissolution to Christ and the Virgin, dates mainly from the 12–14C, and resembles Canterbury Cathedral in having double transepts, a raised choir and presbytery, forming a relatively long E. arm, and a large crypt under the presbytery. The N. side is open to the High Street, from which Gundulf's Tower is well seen. The Norman West Front, with its elaborate recessed *Doorway (1160), perhaps the finest of its kind in England, is the most striking feature of the exterior. The tympanum and the figures on the shafting of the door (Solomon and the Queen of Sheba) were added in c. 1175. The figures of Bishops Gundulf and John of Canterbury, in the niches flanking the arch, are modern.

HISTORY. Of the original Saxon church, founded c. 604, when the first bishop was consecrated by Augustine, a few foundations were found in 1889. Its Saxon successor, remains of which were identified below the N. transept in 1968, was in ruins at the Conquest. Gundulf, the second Norman bishop (who built the White Tower at London), began a new church in 1082 and replaced the secular clergy by Benedictine monks. Gundulf's work may be traced in the nave aisle walls, in the arches of the nave arcade (s. side), in the crypt, and in the ruined N. tower (95 ft high; originally detached). The so-called second Norman church, consecrated in 1130 (completed in 1160), was merely a re-casing of Gundulf's arcades and a rebuilding of the upper stages, the N. arcades, and the W. front (which, with part of the nave, remains). About 1200, or earlier, a rebuilding in the pointed style was begun; the E.E. presbytery and the E. transepts were erected round the Norman presbytery previous to its demolition; the choir, separated by solid walls from its aisles (comp. below), was then remodelled by Prior William de Hoo, and the whole covered with fine sexpartite vaulting (1227). The N. main transept (E.E.) dates from c. 1250, the S. transept (early Dec.) from c. 1280, the two E. bays of the nave from c. 1300. The central tower and spire were completed c. 1343. Late in the 15C the great Perp. window was inserted in the W. front. In 1904 the central tower, rebuilt in the 19C, was replaced by the present tower and spire (156 ft high), completed in accordance with the 14C originals.

Interior. The six W. bays of the sombre NAVE are Norman. Lines on the pavement at the N.W. angle mark the probable site of the E. wall or apse of the Saxon church. The elaborately adorned triforium passage opens on both nave and aisles. In the same stage the junction with the 14C work (E. bays and tower-arch) is remarkable, the later builders having rebuilt a triforium arch on each side in the Norman style. The windows are Perp. Off the s. aisle is the *Lady Chapel* of c.1490, its great arch into the transept now closed by a modern altar screen. In the S. TRANSEPT are a brass memorial to Dickens and the monuments of Richard Watts (p. 46) and Dean Hole (d. 1904). The N. TRANSEPT was

the entrance lobby of approach through the choir aisle to the shrine of
St William (see below).

A peculiarity of the raised E.E. CHOIR is the absence of aisle-arcades.
The figures on the *Choir Screen* are a memorial to Dean Scott (1811–87),
of Liddell and Scott's famous Greek lexicon. The details of the corbels
and the shafts of Petworth marble are noteworthy. The *Stalls* and
monks' benches (with modern book-desks) are probably the oldest work
of the kind in England (13C; comp. p. 114), but were disastrously restored c. 1870. Opposite the episcopal throne (modern) is part of a mural
painting of the Wheel of Fortune (13C). The N. CHOIR TRANSEPT was
formerly the *Chapel of St William of Perth*, a Scottish baker murdered
in 1201 when on a pilgrimage to Canterbury; the shrine became so
popular that the rebuilding of the choir is said to have been defrayed by

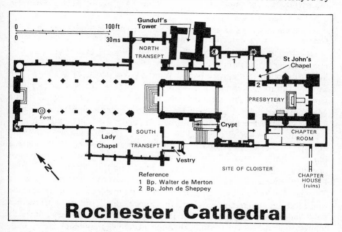

Rochester Cathedral

Reference
1 Bp. Walter de Merton
2 Bp. John de Sheppey

the offerings of the pilgrims to it. Under the windows is the much-
restored tomb of Bp. Walter de Merton (d. 1277), founder of Merton
College, Oxford, with an Elizabethan effigy in alabaster. To the E. is
St John's Chapel, with the supposed tomb of St William, removed from
the centre of the transept. In the arch between this chapel and the
presbytery is the tomb, with coloured effigy, of Bp. John de Sheppey
(d. 1360), discovered in the wall in 1825. The S. CHOIR TRANSEPT contains the remarkable Dec. *Doorway (c. 1340) leading to the CHAPTER
ROOM, which contains the *Library*. The figures (carefully restored in
1825) represent the Synagogue and the Church, the four great Church
Fathers, and a soul rising from Purgatory. The apparent oak carving of
the door itself is a lead casting (c. 1826).—To the E. of the choir is the
PRESBYTERY, with tombs of 12–13C bishops.

From the s. aisle of the choir a flight of steps descends to the *CRYPT, which is
one of the largest and most beautiful in England (fine E.E. vaulting, with great
variety of spans and many graffiti on the piers). The two w. bays, with piers of
tufa and Barnack rag and ribless quadripartite vaulting, are Gundulf's work. The
ancient glass in the E. windows probably came from Canterbury. In a case are
exhibited Cromwellian uniforms and equipment.—To the s. of the choir are the

ruins of the *Chapter House* (c. 1215), entered by a doorway of c. 1140, and remains of the unusually placed Norman cloister. The ruined 14C *Bishop's Gate* was the w. entrance to the cloister.

From the precincts we pass through the 15C *Prior's Gate*, and turn left past the 19C buildings of the *King's School*, refounded by Henry VIII on the dissolution of the Benedictine priory (see above). Beyond this we turn to the right, and then proceed to the left, beneath the splendid avenue of *The Vines*, an oasis of greenery (the site of the monks' vineyard), emerging in Maidstone Rd. Opposite is the handsome Tudor mansion known as *Restoration House* (adm. April–Sept, first Thurs in month, 10–2, also BH; fee), where Charles II perhaps slept in 1660, generally held to be the 'Satis House' of 'Great Expectations'. Maidstone Rd. descends to the High St. into which we turn right. On the left stands the Elizabethan *Eastgate House* (the 'Nuns' House' of 'Edwin Drood'), now enlarged to house a museum (open 2–5.30, closed Fri).

It accommodates the Swiss chalet used as a study at Gad's Hill (see above) by Charles Dickens, to whom it was given in 1865 by the actor, Charles Fechter.

Opposite the museum is a gabled Tudor building claiming to be that occupied by Uncle Pumblechook and Mr Sapsea, in 'Great Expectations' and 'Edwin Drood' respectively. What Dickens calls "the silent High Street—full of gables with old beams and timbers" leads N.W. (1.) back towards the river. The demolition of Free School Lane (r.; including the Mathematical School, at which David Garrick was a pupil) has revealed a long stretch of the old city wall with a corner bastion; while an alley on the opposite side of the High St. affords access to a garden alongside another stretch of the Roman and medieval wall. Beyond *La Providence* (r.), a rebuilt group of almshouses now belonging to the Huguenot Society, is (No. 97 High St.) the gabled building known as *Watts' Charity*, founded in 1579 by the will of Richard Watts "for Six Poor Travellers, who, not being rogues or proctors, may receive gratis for one night lodging, entertainment, and fourpence each", but discontinued in 1947 (adm. weekdays 2–5). On the left is the *College Gate*, Jasper's 'Gatehouse' in 'Edwin Drood', through which we may reach Boley Hill, s.w. of the cathedral, with the *Old Hall* and *Satis House* (the home of Richard Watts), two fine Tudor houses, with 18C alterations. On the right of High St., farther on, are the old *Corn Exchange* (1706) "oddly garnished with a queer old clock, as if Time carried on business there", and the *George Inn*, with a 14C undercroft (shown on request). The 17C *Guildhall*, with a fine plaster ceiling, contains portraits, including Queen Anne by Kneller and Sir Cloudesley Shovel (d. 1707), M.P. for Rochester.

The Elizabethan *Upnor Castle* (3 m. down the Medway; launches, see above) was built in 1563 to guard the approach to Chatham (adm. daily, Sun from 2; fee). A little farther down river is moored the 'Arethusa', a training ship of the Shaftesbury Homes.—At *Borstal*, 1 m. s. of Rochester, is a prison-reformatory (1902) for criminals under 21, which has given a generic name to others of its kind.

29½ m. **Chatham** (56,900 inhab.; Restaurant), on the Medway, long one of the chief naval stations of Great Britain, is also a centre of military engineering.

Henry VIII was the first to use Chatham for naval purposes, and by the time of Charles II it had become the chief naval station of the kingdom. In 1667 De Ruyter ascended the Medway to Chatham, where he destroyed some ships but did not damage the town. The 'Chatham Lines' of 1758–1807 were later reinforced by outlying forts, now disused. Dickens's childhood homes, after leaving Portsmouth, were first in The Brook (house demolished); then in Ordnance Terrace, on a height above Chatham station. Lt Thos. Waghorn, RN (b. Chatham; 1800–50), who pioneered the overland mail route to India, is buried at Snodland, 4 m. S.

In Chatham High St., which prolongs that of Rochester, is the *Sir John Hawkins Hospital*, founded in 1596 and rebuilt in the 19C; opposite is a restored Norman chapel, once part of a leper hospital. Medway St. bears left to the *Town Hall*, in front of which lawns extend to the river (view of Rochester). Behind rise the derelict 'Great Lines', where a path ascends to the *Naval War Memorial*, by Lorimer (1924) and Maufe (1952), giving a wide view of the Medway Towns. Dock Road continues above the Medway to *St Mary's* (usually locked), a 19C church on an ancient site (Norman details) containing the brass of Stephen Borough (d. 1584), pioneer of the sea-route to Archangel. Opposite is a mounted statue of Lord Kitchener (d. 1916), removed from Khartoum in 1958. Farther on is the ROYAL NAVAL DOCKYARD, with shipbuilding, repair, and conversion yards, a technical college (900 apprentices) founded in 1843, and the contiguous 'H.M.S. Pembroke', headquarters of the Flag Officer Medway.

Through the *Main Gate* (1720; fine Royal Arms on both faces; no adm.) can be seen the *Dockyard Church* (1808), but access (guided tours daily 9.45, 10.45, & 2.45, free) is by *Pembroke Gate*, ¾ m. farther on, opposite the gate of the Royal Naval Barracks, where *St George's* (1905) has its E. end arranged as a war memorial (by Maufe; stained glass by Easton). The tour generally includes visits to workshops, a refitting dry dock, and one of the basins (good views of H.M. ships and of Upnor Castle across the river), but not the Georgian Ropery and Sail Loft or Brunel's steam saw mills, all nearer the main gate.

The road opposite the main gate ascends to *Brompton Barracks*, a well-designed early-19C quadrangle facing which are memorials to the Royal Engineers and a statue of General Gordon (d. 1885), on camelback, by E. Onslow Ford (1890).

These lie within the boundaries of **Gillingham** (pron. 'Jillingham'; Hotel), the largest borough (86,700 inhab.) in Kent, with paper-making works. Its fine Perp. church, N. of the centre, has a good E. window and a Norman font.

At the top of the long Chatham Hill a memorial clock (l.) commemorates Will Adams (d. 1620), the Gillingham sailor who founded Japan's sea-power.—33½ m. *Rainham* has a good 14C church tower.—36 m. *Newington*, in a famous cherry-growing district, has a church with a Tudor font-cover and brasses. At *Lower Halstow*, 2 m. N., the Saxon church, remodelled in the 13C, has a leaden *Font of c. 1150.—37 m. *Key Street* crossroads.

A 249 diverges left for the ISLE OF SHEPPEY, crossing the Swale, an arm of the Thames (now bordered by paper mills), in which St Augustine baptized 10,000 persons in 597. Road and railway are carried by Kingsferry Bridge (lifting).—7 m. (l) *Queenborough*, a decayed port, was named from Queen Philippa, wife of Edward III. The Flushing packet sailed hence in 1875–1916, with a few brief intervals.—10 m. **Sheerness** (31,500 inhab.; Hotel) a port at the mouth of the Medway, has a formerly important naval dockyard, where are preserved relics of fortifications and the dignified boatstore (1861), one of the first iron-framed buildings. James II embarked here in 1688 in an ineffectual attempt to escape from England. Car ferry services ply to Flushing and Dunkirk.—Offshore is *The Nore*, a sandbank buoyed for safety at least since the 16C, which gave name to a naval command until 1961. Here the pressed crews were brought to man the ships of the Royal Navy, and here they revolted in the Great Mutiny of 1797.

A road runs E. across Sheppey to (9 m.) *Leysdown*, on the estuary of the Thames. This passes (3¼ m.) *Minster-on-Sea*, with a golf course. The old *Abbey Church (with a Saxon window in the N. aisle) of SS. Mary and Sexburga was founded in 664. It contains the monument of Sir Robert Shurland (d. c. 1300), whose romantic story has been told in the 'Ingoldsby Legends' ('Grey Dolphin'), and the fine brasses (c. 1325) of Sir Roger de Northwode and his lady. The Abbey Gatehouse has been restored. The low clay cliffs to the E. are interesting to geologists. *Eastchurch* airfield, S.E. of Minster, was heavily attacked in the Battle of Britain, 1940. It is now an open prison. The desolate marshland on the S. of the island is given over to sheep and hares.

39 m. Sittingbourne, a paper-, brick-, and cement-making town (30,900 inhab.), is adjoined on the N. by the ancient borough of *Milton Regis* (1 m.), with a small museum in the old Court Hall and a good 17C building housing the Post Office. The large 14C church, ¾ m. out on the Sheppey road, has a massive tower. The *Dolphin Sailing Barge Museum* was opened in 1970 on Bourne Creek. *Bredgar*, 4 m. s.w. beyond the motorway, has a Dec. collegiate church and chantry cottages of c. 1392.—42 m. *Teynham* (l.) is traditionally the first place where cherries and apples were grown in· Kent.—45 m. *Ospringe* has two medieval houses above a 13C undercroft of a 'Maison Dieu' (daily, Sun from 2, fee). We diverge (l.; 1 m.) for Faversham.

Faversham (Hotels) is an ancient town (14,800 inhab.) and a former seaport. James II was detained here after his abortive flight from Sheerness. George Finlay (1799–1875), the historian, was a native. In the Market Place is a quaint *Guildhall* (1574) on timber arches. The splendid *ABBEY ST., largely 16–18C and restored with taste, affords occasional glimpses of the creek and its timberyards. At the far end is the *House of Thomas Arden* (1540), whose murder here by his wife was dramatized in the play 'Arden of Feversham'. The site of the Cluniac abbey, founded here by King Stephen, and the base of his tomb, were located in 1965. A path from Abbey Close leads back past the *Old Grammar School* (1567), now Freemasons' Hall (adm. by appointment), to the *Parish Church*, enlarged with aisled transepts in 1305 (contemporary pillar *Paintings) and given its unexpected Grecian nave in 1754.

At *Davington*, N.W. of the town beyond the creek, is the plain Norman church of a small nunnery founded in 1153, while farther on (r.) *Chart Gunpowder Mill* has been restored as a memorial to three centuries of explosives manufacture (ended in 1935). The church of *Preston*, just beyond the station, contains an alabaster monument (1629) to the parents of the 1st Earl of Cork.

At (47½ m.) *Brenley Corner*, junction with the M 2 (Rte 4), by-roads (r.) lead to (1 m.) *Boughton-under-Blean*, where the Hawkins monument in the church has vigorous reliefs by Evesham (1618); and to (2½ m.) *Selling*, with a church containing good E.E. glass.—50½ m. *Dunkirk* (Hotel). At (53½ m.) *Harbledown* (*View) is the Hospital of St Nicholas, founded for lepers by Abp. Lanfranc, with an 11C chapel and rebuilt almshouses. The hill to the S. is crowned by a Belgic fort.—55 m. **Canterbury**, see Rte 3.

To the left of Harbledown, on St Thomas's Hill (so named from a vanished chapel dedicated to Becket) stands the *University of Kent*, founded in 1962.

To the left of (58 m.) *Bridge* is *Patrixbourne* church with a *Doorway of c. 1175 and 16–17C Swiss glass; *Bekesbourne*, ½ m. farther on, has remains of an archiepiscopal palace.—Richard Hooker (1554–1600) lies in the church of (59½ m.) *Bishopsbourne*, of which he was rector from

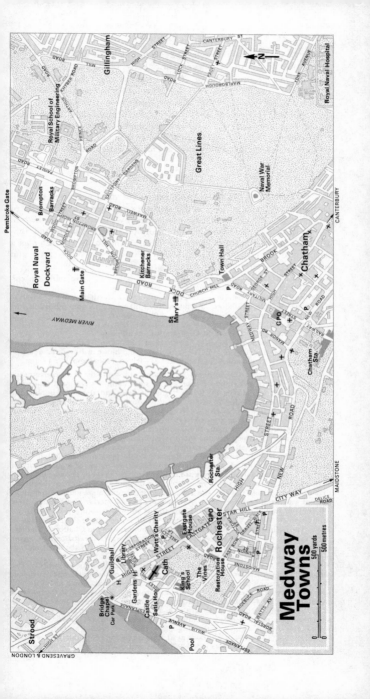

1595. 'Oswalds' (now the rectory) here was the home of Joseph Conrad (1857–1924) from 1919. *Bourne Park* (early 18C), near by, is a fine mansion in a beautiful setting. To the right diverges the Elham Valley road (p. 59), and farther on (64½ m.) the main Folkestone road (A 260). Between these two roads lies *Broome Park* (now a hotel), a house of 1635–38, once the seat of Lord Kitchener and probably the 'Tappington' of the 'Ingoldsby Legends'.—67½ m. *Lydden*, has a motor-racing circuit. —At (68 m.) *Temple Ewell* King John met Pandulf, the Pope's legate, preparatory to resigning his throne at Dover.—71 m. **Dover**, see Rte 5.

3 CANTERBURY

CANTERBURY (33,200 inhab.), one of the most venerated pilgrim-shrines in the Middle Ages, is the archiepiscopal see of the Primate of All England. The ancient city, dominated by the splendid cathedral, lies on the Stour, in a peaceful country of meadows, orchards, and hop-gardens. It retains many medieval features and in its character as a garrison town and as a prosperous country-town, with corn, cattle, and other markets, resembles its Roman predecessor.

Parking. Car Parks, open and multi-story, within the walls; also, more convenient for the cathedral, etc. in Broad St.
Railway Stations. *Canterbury East*, for London viâ Faversham and for Dover.— *Canterbury West*, for London viâ Ashford, for Folkestone, Dover, and Ramsgate.
Hotels and **Restaurants** (particularly good in Longport).
Post Office, St Peter's St.— INFORMATION CENTRE, Longmarket.
Buses from the Bus Station, St George's Rd., to all parts.
Amusements, *Marlowe Theatre,* St Margaret's St.—GOLF COURSE, 1½ m. E.— CRICKET WEEK in early Aug.—FESTIVAL of drama and music in July and August.— SWIMMING POOL (covered), Kingsmead Road.—RIVER TRIPS from The Friars.

History. The Roman *Durovernum,* a commercial post situated at the convergence of military roads from Lympne, Dover, and Richborough, was renamed *Cantwara-byrig* (borough of the men of Kent) by the Saxons, and about 560 became the capital of Ethelbert, King of Kent. To this court, where the Frankish Queen Bertha was already a Christian, St Augustine and his fellow-missionaries were welcomed in 597; the king granted to them and to Bertha the use of a church and was himself baptized with many of his subjects. Augustine founded (598) a Bene-dictine monastery, which became the revered burial-place of the kings and early sainted archbishops, afterwards named St Augustine's Abbey; and on his later return to England as 'bishop of the English' established another church which became the first cathedral; a monastery was afterwards organized as the priory of Christ Church by Lanfranc. It was not until the murder of Abp. Thomas Becket in 1170 and his canonization two years later that the fame of the cathedral eclipsed that of St Augustine's abbey and that the ecclesiastical supremacy of the arch-bishops was definitely established. As "the holy blissful martyr", St Thomas drew all England and many foreign pilgrims to his miracle-working shrine until its demolition by Henry VIII in 1538. Louis VII of France made the pilgrimage in 1179. The holiday aspect of the pilgrimages is immortalized in Chaucer's 'Canter-bury Tales' (c. 1387). The present archbishop, the *Most Reverend Donald Coggan,* D.D., translated from York in 1974, is the hundred and first (by the latest reckon-ing) in a series including many illustrious names.

Canterbury was wantonly attacked by German aircraft in May–June 1942. The cathedral escaped serious damage, but a large area S.E. of the centre was destroyed. This quarter was replanned disastrously in the styleless modern manner of the 50s with the eccentric conservation of a few church towers. Excavations in the bombed area unearthed the foundations of a Roman theatre (only the second to be identified in Britain). A pre-Roman settlement of c. 200 B.C. and a Saxon colony of the 5C have also been traced, proving a continuous occupation of 2000 years.

Canterbury often figures in the 'Ingoldsby Legends', whose author, the Rev. R. H. Barham (1778–1845), was born at 61 Burgate (destroyed; tablet). The birth-place of Christopher Marlowe (1564–93), poet and dramatist, at 57 St George's

St., was also destroyed in 1942. David Copperfield went to Dr Strong's school at Canterbury, and here lived Uriah Heep. Joseph Conrad is buried in the Roman Catholic cemetery.

The modern approach deviates from that of the old Dover Road, which passed through the city from N.W. to S.E., at the centre becoming the High Street (comp. below). RHEIMS WAY now channels traffic round the s. walls, passing (l.) *St Mildred's Church* (part Saxon; usually locked), and the massive keep of the *Castle* (c. 1175), and gives access to the centre through the rebuilt sector.

Mercery Lane, the regular pilgrims' approach to the cathedral, formerly lined with shops and booths for the sale of 'ampulles' of healing-water from Becket's Well in the crypt, medallions of St Thomas, and other memorials of pilgrimage, leads from High St. to the Butter Market. Here are the Canterbury War Memorial (by Pite, 1921), and *Christ Church Gate*, the main entrance to the cathedral precincts, a noble Perp. building (1520, not 1507) commemorative of Arthur, Prince of Wales (1486–1502). The gates are of c. 1662. It was restored in 1931–37. Beyond it we obtain an admirable view of the cathedral.

The magnificent **Cathedral (*Christ Church*) is, as it stands, the work of two detached centuries, for, though it was begun in 1070 and completed in 1503, little was contributed by the two centuries between 1180 and 1379. Though in area it ranks only ninth, and in length fourth, among English cathedrals, in its majestic proportions and the interest of its detail, it stands in the top rank. Externally its character is Perp. w. of the central tower and Norman at the E. end. The stained glass compares in quality with the best in France.

HISTORY. The oldest portions are fragments of the church raised by Lanfranc, first Norman archbishop (1070–89), on the ruins of Augustine's church, burned down in 1067. This hasty reconstruction proved too small for the devotions and accommodation of the monks of Lanfranc's priory, and his successor Anselm (1093–1109) decided to rebuild the E. end. Begun under Prior Ernulf in 1096, the work was promoted to a grander scale by Prior Conrad, who nearly doubled the area of the building. The 'glorious choir of Conrad' is immortal in the annals of architecture, though it stood for little more than half a century, having its middle part burned down in 1174, leaving the outer aisle walls. A French master-mason, William of Sens, was chosen for the rebuilding, which began in 1175. He, however, was crippled by a fall three years later, and, after directing the work from his bed until he had completed the E. transepts, gave it over to William the Englishman. Working, apparently, on the plans of French William, the English master-mason finished St Thomas's Chapel, Becket's Crown, and the Crypt beneath these (1179–84). The church remained thus for nearly 200 years, with Lanfranc's unambitious nave and transepts adjoining the rich and intricate E. end. Under Abp. Sudbury, Lanfranc's nave was pulled down, and the present nave and transepts built by Henry Yevele (1391–1405). Additional chapels were added, and, finally, between 1493 and 1505, *Bell Harry*, noblest of Perpendicular towers, was built by John Wastell in place of the original Angel Steeple. The N.W. tower of Lanfranc was replaced in 1834 by a copy of Thomas Mapilton's s.w. tower (1424–34). The sanctuary roof was restored after a fire in 1872. The central tower is shown Easter to Oct (not Sun; fee).

The principal entrance, the SOUTH PORCH (1418), probably commemorates the victory of Agincourt (1415). The old bas-relief over this represents the Altar of the Martyrdom, erected where Becket fell. The statues here, as on the w. front (1862), replace those destroyed at the Reformation.

Interior. The NAVE (c. 1380) is well-lighted and stately in design, but unfortunately has lost (except for some fragments collected in the

w. window) its fine old original stained glass. Under the N.W. tower is a memorial to Abp. Benson (1882–96). The vista from the w. end, closed by the flight of steps ascending to the choir-screen, through which a glimpse of a second flight to the altar is obtained, produces a noble and suggestive effect. The reticulated cross-pieces under the lantern are struts to support the piers under the enormous weight of the tower. They bear the rebus of Prior Goldstone, who completed the tower begun for Chillenden. In the N. aisle are the ornate font (1639) and (5th bay) the monument, by Stone, to Orlando Gibbons who died suddenly at Charles I's prenuptial celebration (p. 56). An elaborate 15C *Screen*, with six crowned figures (Henry V, Richard II, Ethelbert; Edward the Confessor, Henry IV, Henry VI), and its original iron gates, separates the nave from the choir. The great *Windows in the w. transepts are well seen from here; that in the N.W. transept, with its silvery colouring and its portrait-figures of Edward IV and his queen, was presented by that king (d. 1483); that in the s.w. transept has 15C tracery, filled with glass, mostly 15C, but with three 12C rows from the choir-clerestory.

The WEST or NAVE TRANSEPTS, like the nave, were rebuilt by Yevele, who left little of Lanfranc's work but the rough lower portion of the walls. The *N.W. Transept*, or *Martyrdom*, was the scene of Becket's murder (29 Dec 1170), and the door from the cloisters is in the same position as when the four knights entered by it to cut down "the turbulent priest". The spot where the archbishop is believed to have fallen is marked by a small slab of stone, replacing (according to tradition) a blood-stained fragment of the pavement cut out and sent to Rome as a relic. Under the Edward IV window are the tombs of Abp. Peckham (1279–92; the oldest effigy in the cathedral) and Abp. Warham (1504–32).—The *Lady Chapel*, to the E. of this transept, called also the *Deans' Chapel*, on account of the tombs it contains, is late-Perp. (1449–68), with a rich fan-vault.—The *S.W. Transept* (with the cathedral bookstall) has a corresponding chapel, known as *St Michael's* or the *Warriors' Chapel* (Perp.; c. 1420–28). In the centre stands the tomb erected by Margaret Holand (d. 1437) for herself and her two noble husbands. The N. wall is crowded with monuments, mainly good 17C work. At the E. end, projecting from the wall, is the stone coffin of Abp. Stephen Langton (1207–28), who assisted in extorting Magna Carta from King John.

In this chapel is the Roll of Honour of the Buffs (E., now Royal, Kent Regiment), a page of which is turned daily at 11 by a soldier of the regiment; the ship's bell of *H.M.S. Canterbury* just outside is struck every day at 11, as a memorial to men of the Navy. In All Saints Chapel above, a Norman arch of Lanfranc's church has been exposed.

On entering the CHOIR, one of the longest in England, we notice the peculiar contraction at the E. end. William of Sens drew in his building thus to preserve the two Norman side-chapels of St Anselm and St Andrew. The Transition style of the choir is seen in the juxtaposition of Norman and E.E. features. The choir of Sens Cathedral (finished in 1168) determined the form of Canterbury choir, which resembles the French model in many particulars, though irregularities, such as the mixture of round and pointed arch-forms and of Norman and E.E. decoration, seem to indicate an attempted compromise between French innovation and English tradition. The stalls at the w. end are attributed

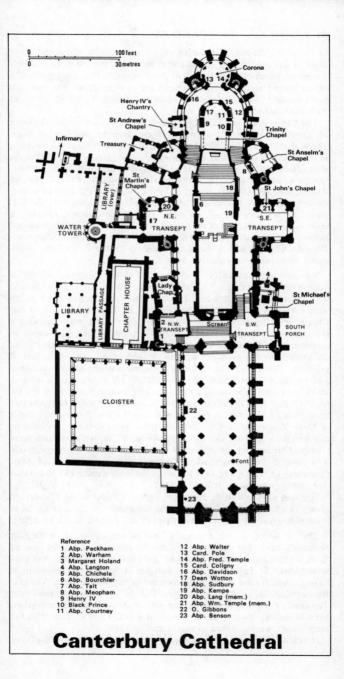

Reference
1 Abp. Peckham
2 Abp. Warham
3 Margaret Holand
4 Abp. Langton
5 Abp. Chichele
6 Abp. Bourchier
7 Abp. Tait
8 Abp. Meopham
9 Henry IV
10 Black Prince
11 Abp. Courtney
12 Abp. Walter
13 Card. Pole
14 Abp. Fred. Temple
15 Card. Coligny
16 Abp. Davidson
17 Dean Wotton
18 Abp. Sudbury
19 Abp. Kempe
20 Abp. Lang (mem.)
21 Abp. Wm. Temple (mem.)
22 O. Gibbons
23 Abp. Benson

Canterbury Cathedral

to Grinling Gibbons. The diaper work on the s. wall, above the lower flight of stairs to the altar, should be noted. This, though more probably a remnant of sedilia, may be part of the shrine of St Dunstan (c. 909–88), which ranked second only to Becket's shrine in sanctity. The beautiful and unusual *Screens* between the choir and its aisles (1304–05) alternate with canopied tombs.

The CHOIR AISLES and EAST or CHOIR TRANSEPTS are mainly the work of Ernulf and Conrad, altered and enriched by William of Sens. Through the N. door of Prior Eastry's screen we enter the *N. Choir Aisle*, in the windows of which is some fine medallion glass of c. 1200. On the wall adjoining the N.E. transept is a 15C fresco of the vision of St Eustace. On the s. side are the canopy-tombs of Abp. Bourchier (1454–86) and Abp. Chichele (1414–43), the latter kept in repair by All Souls College, Oxford.—In the *N.E. Transept* the circular window preserves its late-12C glass. *St Martin's Chapel*, on the E. side of the transept, contains a restored glass medallion of the saint. Abp. Lanfranc (d. 1089) is buried below. The ashes of Abp. Lang (d. 1945) lie in the adjoining *St Stephen's Chapel*. At the E. end of the N. choir-aisle is *St Andrew's Chapel* (Norman), retaining some coloured decoration.

The part of the cathedral to the E. of the choir was erected wholly in honour of St Thomas. TRINITY CHAPEL, behind the high altar and approached by steps, retains the name of a chapel burned down along with Conrad's choir, though it was built by English William as the Chapel of St Thomas; and in this chapel, from 1220 (when the saint's remains were translated from the original tomb in the crypt) down to its destruction by Henry VIII in 1538, stood his sumptuous shrine, its site marked by the pavement in opus alexandrinum worn by the feet of pilgrims. The coupled columns of coloured marbles are noteworthy, and beautiful stained-glass *Windows (1220–30) depict the miracles of St Thomas. Between the N. piers is the resplendent tomb of Henry IV (d. 1413) and Joan of Navarre (d. 1437), his second wife. Adjacent has been placed a tiny 18C organ. Next comes the fine Renaissance tomb of Dean Wotton (d. 1567). Between the s. piers is the effigy-tomb in copper gilt of Edward the Black Prince (d. 1376), with reproductions (1954) of his surcoat, gauntlets, helmet, shield, and scabbard (originals in a case in the s. choir-aisle). To the E. is the monument of Abp. Courtenay (d. 1396), and next to that is the leaden coffin of Card. Odet de Coligny, who died a refugee in 1571.

Opening off the aisle to the N. of Trinity Chapel is the *Chantry of Henry IV*, dedicated to St Edward the Confessor; in the aisle to the s. is the oldest tomb in the cathedral, that of Abp. Hubert Walter (d. 1205).

The *CORONA, at the extreme E. end of the cathedral, is English William's work, but evidently of French design. It is known also as 'Becket's Crown', because, it is said, the skull of St Thomas was preserved here. *St Augustine's Chair*, possibly of Roman workmanship in Saxon times, is used at the enthronement of the archbishops. The last Roman Catholic archbishop, Cardinal Pole (d. 1558), lies on the N. side. The centre *Window dates from the 13C, with a modern interpolation, hard to detect. Two beautiful panels of a 13C Jesse window, lost for many years, were restored to this chapel in 1954.

In the *S. Choir Aisle* are the monuments of Abp. Simon of Sudbury

(1375–81), Abp. Stratford (1333–48), and Abp. Kempe (1452–54). The main windows contain 13C French medallions set in modern grisaille (1960). *St Anselm's Chapel*, at the E. end, is mainly Ernulf's work, though the S. window is Dec. (1336) with modern glass (Stammers, 1959) in honour of Abp. Anselm, who is buried behind the altar. The 12C wall-painting of St Paul at Malta was brought to light in 1888. The screen of the chapel is formed by the beautiful tomb of Abp. Meopham (1329–33). The so-called 'Watching Chamber', above this chapel, overlooks Trinity Chapel.—The *S.E. Transept* contains the so-called 'Corinthian Throne', by Grinling Gibbons, presented in 1704 by Abp. Tenison. The four south windows (Bossanyi, 1960) are striking. The *Chapel of St John the Evangelist* was restored in 1951 as a memorial to Abp. Wm. Temple (1881–1944). On the S. wall of the aisle is the recumbent figure of Prior Eastry (d. 1322).

The spacious *CRYPT, dedicated to the Virgin, is entered from the S.W. transept. It is mainly the work of Ernulf and Conrad, and the *Capitals of the pillars and some ornamental shafts are vigorous examples of Norman stone-carving. Especially fine is the central pillar of the chapel at the S.E. corner, dedicated to St Gabriel; the apse preserves its *Paintings of c. 1130. A chapel of the S. aisle is walled off to form a '*Temple*' for the French Protestants, who have worshipped here since 1568 (service in French on Sun at 3 p.m.). The French church includes the beautiful *Black Prince's Chantry*, by which he 'paid' for marriage with his cousin, the Fair Maid of Kent, in 1363, giving, too, the graceful screen of the *Chapel of Our Lady in Crypta*, in which are the grave of Card. Morton, archbishop in 1486–1500, and a 17C ivory Madonna (Portuguese), presented in 1949.—The graceful late-12C *Crypt* under the Trinity Chapel and Corona includes the site of the chapel where St Thomas was first buried. Here culminated the long-drawn act of penance enjoined on Henry II. On the W. wall is a graffito, and at the sides are two 7C columns and (in a case farther W.) fragments of a Saxon cross from Reculver.

Precincts. On the N. side of the cathedral are the extensive monastic buildings. The Benedictine monastery founded by St Augustine was enlarged and converted into a priory by Lanfranc, and much altered and rebuilt by later archbishops.

The GREAT CLOISTER (1397–1414) is entered from the N.W. transept. Though mainly Perp., it incorporates some fine Norman work and beautiful E.E. arcading, in the N. walk, cut into by the Perp. vaulting. The painted vault-bosses, which include 40 shields, are noteworthy. In the E. walk a boss portrays Yevele, the architect. Opening off the E. walk is the spacious CHAPTER HOUSE, the lower part of which is the work of Prior Eastry (1304–20), completed by Chillenden when he began the cloisters. T. S. Eliot's 'Murder in the Cathedral' was commissioned for performance here in 1935. To the N.E. is the rebuilt *Chapter Library* (1954), replacing a building destroyed in 1942. In the *Dark Entry*, between this and the chapter house, are two fine ranges of pillars of Lanfranc's time, some with incised decoration; these and the pillar-bases in the lawn beyond the modern arcade of the library were part of the sub-vault of the *Dormitory*. We emerge in the *Infirmary Cloister*, passing on the right a door into the crypt and a stair to the N.E. transept. On the left is the elaborate Norman sub-vault of the *Lavatory Tower*, part of the ingenious water-supply system of Prior Wibert (1151–67); the upper floor is Perp. The cloister is continued by the 13C sub-vault of the *Prior's Chapel* (chapel replaced after 1660 by the brick Howley Library).

The infirmary cloister is prolonged N. by a passage below the Wolfson Library (1966) to *Prior Sellingegate* (c. 1480) and the Green Court. On the E. side of this square stands the *Deanery*, mixed medieval and 16C; and in the S.W. corner is the *Archdeaconry* with a curious wooden pentice (1390) in its garden. To the E. of this the *Larder Gate Building* (1951) incorporates a 15C archway and part of the monastic kitchens. This, with all the remaining buildings in the square, belongs to the **King's School**, a monastic foundation of the 7C, installed on this site by Henry VIII as a grammar school for 50 (now 700) boys. Linacre, Marlowe, Thurlow, Harvey, Robert Boyle, and Somerset Maugham were pupils here. The monastic *Brewhouse* and *Bakehouse* (1303) are incorporated in the N. range. In the N.W. corner of the Green Court the exterior *Norman Staircase* (by Wibert, 1151–67) leading to the hall is unique and still supremely beautiful, despite the modern roof. Through the adjacent *Court Gate* we enter the *Mint Yard*, the former Almonry. Hence the North Gate opens on Palace St., named from the Archbishop's Palace destroyed in the primacy of Laud (traces visible in Walpole House). From that time until the completion of the present modest palace on the old site in 1901, the archbishops had no official residence in Canterbury.

Returning to the Prior's Chapel, we turn E. where a stately row of Norman arches marks the hall of the *Infirmary*. The more ornate arches, still farther E., are remains of the *Infirmary Chapel*. On the right of the hall is the arcaded Norman *Treasury*, while the *Choir School* on the left, incorporates a refectory of 1343. Passing round the unfinished exterior of the Corona, we join the path skirting the S. side of the cathedral. This leads across the former lay cemetery, which extended from the South Porch to the exquisitely arcaded *St Anselm's Tower* and was there divided by a wall from the monks' cemetery. The grandeur and fine colouring of the S.E. transept are very striking from this point. Opposite the E. end of the cathedral is a garth, long the private pleasance of the Dean and Chapter, by whom it was resigned as a site for the *Kent War Memorial* (by Sir Herbert Baker). On its E. side is a bastion of the old city wall, transformed into a chapel of silence, with a cenotaph, flags, and inscriptions. A gate opens into Broad St.

In Broad St., E. of the precincts, a fine stretch of the medieval city wall is visible. Lady Wooton's Green leads thence to ST AUGUSTINE'S COLLEGE, founded in 1848 for missionaries, and reorganized in 1952 as a training college for Anglican clergy. It occupies part of the site of *St Augustine's Abbey, the excavated ruins of which (adm. daily, fee; closed Sun in winter till 2) are reached by a path to the left of the main gate.

The original Abbey of SS Peter & Paul founded by St Augustine in 598 had three separate 7C churches in line. In 978 St Dunstan rededicated the abbey to the founder, and in 1049–59 Abbot Wulfric began to link the two W. churches by a rotunda on the model of Saint-Benigne at Dijon. All this work was demolished by the first Norman abbot, who in 1073 started a new church, completed c. 1120. The abbey, which to the time of Becket ranked as the second Benedictine house in Europe, was destroyed in 1538 and a royal posting-house built on the site. This was visited by Elizabeth I, Charles I (who received his bride here in June 1625), and Charles II.

We approach by the cloister garth. On the right beneath a low protective roof lies the N. part of the first church (SS Peter & Paul) in which King Ethelbert, Queen Bertha, St Augustine, and at least eight of his early successors were buried. The first tombs of SS Lawrence, Mellitus, and Justus have been identified. The massive octagonal foundations of *Abbot Wulfric's Rotunda* are prominent to the S.E. Of the *Norman Church* the N.W. wall of the nave still stands, with Tudor additions of the 'King's House', and much of the crypt of the absidal choir (service on 29 June). *St Pancras*, the easternmost of the three 7C churches, built of Roman bricks, had its E. end altered c. 1387.

The COLLEGE (adm. Wed & Thurs, 2–4; museum of Saxon finds) incorporates *Fyndon's Gate* (1300–9), the great gate of the monastery, as its main entrance; parts of the guest hall and, farther s., the *Cemetery Gate* (1390; badly restored). The remaining buildings, following the medieval plan are the first major work of Wm. Butterfield.—To the N. of the excavations is *Christ Church College*, a teacher's training college (1964).

We next follow Longport E. past (l.) the *County Gaol* (1808) and (r.)

Canterbury

N

| 0 | | 300 yards |
| 0 | | 300 metres |

RAMSGATE & MARGATE

St. Dunstan's ← LONDON

'Roper Arch'

Barracks

ST. MARTIN'S HILL

St. Martin's †

SPRING LANE

DOVER & FOLKESTONE

Hospital

Barton Court Tech. Coll. (Girls)

Playing Fields

Prison

Session Ho.

St Augustine's Abbey

St Augustine's College

Abbey Ch (ruins)

Tech. College (Boys)

Coach Park

ALBERT RD.

NEW DOVER ROAD

Telephone House

LOWER CHANTRY LANE

UPPER CHANTRY LANE

LONGPORT

MONASTERY STREET

IVY LANE

Christ Church College

ST. GREGORY'S ROAD

NORTH HOLMES ROAD

EDGAR ROAD

College Road

ST. MARTIN'S ROAD

PRETORIA ROAD

VICTORIA ROAD

MILITARY ROAD

BROAD STREET

NORTHGATE

HAVELOCK STREET

OLD RUTTINGTON LANE

LANE

UNION ST.

ARTILLERY ST.

KNOTT LANE

City Wall

War Memorial

Deanery Wall

Staircase

Kings School

Chap. House

Cathedral

Christ Church Gate

City War Mem.

St. Alphege's

Blackfriars Priory

Beaney Art Coll. Inst.

Weavers'

Guildhall

Tower

BURGATE

St. Paul's †

CHURCH ST.

LOWER BRIDGE ST.

ST. GEORGE'S PLACE

Baptist

Cinema

DOVER STREET

VERNON PLACE

OLD DOVER ROAD

R.C. Church

Tower

ST. GEORGE'S STREET

Bus Station

H

Police

Riding Gate

UPPER BRIDGE STREET

GRAVEL WALK

Car Park

ROSE LANE

WATLING STREET

Marlowe Theatre

H

MERCERY LANE

ST. MARGARET'S ST.

PARADE

HIGH STREET

THE FRIARS

ORANGE ST.

PALACE STREET

ST. PETER'S STREET

MILL LANE

KING STREET

THE BOROUGH

ST. RADIGUND STREET

DUCK LANE

ALMA ST.

STOUR STREET

HAWKS LANE

JEWRY LANE

BEER CART LANE

STOUR STREET

WHITE HORSE LA.

ST. MARY'S ST.

ADELAIDE PLACE

MARLOWE AV.

GAS STREET

Municipal Buildings

Dane John

City Wall

RHODAUS TOWN

RHODAUS TOWN

Meat Market

WORTHGATE PLACE

CASTLE STREET

Castle

St Andrew's

WINCHEAP

WINCHEAP GROVE

STATION ROAD EAST

Footbridge

St. Mildred's †

WAY

RHEIMS

Tannery

Great Stour River

RHEIMS WAY

GORDON RD.

WHITEHALL ROAD

ORCHARD STREET

NEW STREET

ST. DUNSTAN'S STREET

STATION ROAD WEST

KIRBY'S LANE

NORTH LANE

POUND LANE

ST. PETER'S LANE

ST. PETER'S GROVE

BLACK GRIFFIN LANE

GRIFFIN PLACE

Grey Friars

Poor Priests' Hosp.

Hospital of St. Thomas

GPO

St. Thomas

St. Peter's

Cinema

West Gate

Holy Cross

Westgate Gardens

Roper's Inn

QUEEN'S AVENUE

LAKE

ASHFORD

LONDON →

ASHFORD →

the *Hospital of John Smith* (1657), to ($\frac{1}{2}$ m.) ***St Martin's Church,** in use
for Christian services before the coming of St Augustine, possibly on the
site of a Romano-British church.

St Martin's Hill was occupied by Roman villas in the 4C, and possibly part of a
pre-Christian building exists in the w. part of the chancel s. wall, especially the
square-headed archway; the round-headed doorway is probably early Saxon. The
nave, of Kentish rag, is plastered in the Roman fashion; the tower is 14C. Within,
the 13C chancel arch and subsequent restorations obscure the antiquity of what is
one of the earliest extant churches in Europe. A Norman piscina at the S.E. corner
of the nave is beautiful in its simplicity, but most interesting is the tub-shaped
*Font, the lower part possibly of Saxon origin, but too late to be that in which
Ethelbert was baptized. On the N. wall is a 16C carving of St Martin.

We re-enter the Walls by Burgate. To the left, amid the Longmarket
shopping precinct, which covers the remains of a *Roman House* (adm.
daily, Sun from 2; fee), stands the tower of the bombed church of
St George, where Marlowe was baptized (tablet). St George's St. continues as High Street. On the left side is *Queen Elizabeth's Guest
Chamber*, a splendid Tudor house (1573), with colourful pargetting, now
a tea-shop. Farther, on the right, is the *Beaney Institute*, housing the
Free Library, the *Slater Art Gallery*, and the *Museum*, the last containing
a fine collection of Roman and other antiquities, including a silver
hoard (5C) uncovered in 1962 and the 13C Burghmote horn.

Off Stour St., leading to the left, in a garden on the Stour, is *Greyfriars* (Easter–
Oct, 1.30–5.30; fee), part of the first Franciscan friary in England (founded 1267,
consecrated 1325), afterwards occupied for a time by Richard Lovelace (1618–58).
Farther on are the 14C buildings, much altered, of the *Poor Priests' Hospital*, now
occupied by a clinic and the regimental museum of The Buffs (adm. weekdays 2–4
or 5, also 10–1 in summer; fee).

Best Lane, opposite, leads to the 13–14C refectory and undercroft of *Blackfriars*.
Now adapted as a Christian Science church, the refectory was for a time used as a
Baptist chapel, in which Defoe is said to have preached.

Beyond the Post Office is the *Hospital of St Thomas*, or *Eastbridge
Hospital*, a well-preserved hostel founded in 1180 for poor pilgrims
(visitors admitted), with a fine chapel and crypt, and a hall with an early
13C Christ in Majesty, in tempera. The main street here crosses a
branch of the Stour, and on the left, overlooking the river, are the Tudor
houses (fee) occupied by the Huguenot weavers who settled in Canterbury after the revocation of the Edict of Nantes (1685). At the end
of St Peter's Street, with (r.) *St Peter's Church* (13C), we see the imposing
West Gate, the only survivor of the seven city gates, which was built
probably by Henry Yevele (1375–81; view from the top). In the guard-
chamber is a collection of arms and armour, fetters, a scold-bridle, etc.
(adm. daily; fee). The church of the *Holy Cross*, also built about 1380,
is just inside the gate, and to the left are the attractive riverside *Westgate
Gardens*, with a tower of the city wall.

Outside the gate, the old London road, here called St Dunstan's St.,
passes on the right the old *Falstaff Inn*, now a restaurant, and, farther
on, a 16C house (l.; facing Station Rd.), which was a hostelry for pilgrims
arriving after the city gates were closed; it claims to be the house of
Agnes Wickfield, in 'David Copperfield'. Beyond, (l.) is *St Dunstan's
Church* (13C), with the Roper vault containing the head of the sainted
Sir Thomas More (1478–1535), given to his daughter Margaret Roper
after 14 days' exposure on London Bridge. A brick archway opposite
the end of Orchard St., is the only relic of the Ropers' house.

At the s. end of the town are the pleasure grounds of the *Dane John*, partly enclosed by the (refaced) city walls (*View of the cathedral). The obelisk on the Dane John itself (an unexplained tumulus 80 ft high) commemorates the laying out of the gardens in 1790. Within the Riding Gate, where the Roman road from Dover entered the city, is the 'Invicta' locomotive (Stephenson, 1830) of the Canterbury and Whitstable Railway.

Beyond Palace St. (see above), Northgate leads past (r.) the *Institute of Heraldic and Genealogical Studies* (display open free) and *St John's Hospital*, founded by Lanfranc in 1084, with a picturesque gatehouse and chapel (11C).

FROM CANTERBURY TO FOLKESTONE by the Elham Valley, 20 m., a winding but pretty road (B 2065).—To (5½ m.) *Bishopsbourne*, see Rte 2. B 2065 skirts *Charlton Park* as it branches right from A 2.—7¾ m. *Barham* (Hotels).— 12½ m. *Elham* (pron. 'Eelam'; Hotels). The fine church in a pretty square dates from the 12–15C. Among the interesting contents are: a 15C alabaster triptych (one panel restored), 15C and 16C stained glass, and some good 20C fittings. The Abbot's Fireside (1614; now a hotel), has an elaborate carved fireplace (1624).— Just one mile farther on, a by-road (l.) leads in 1 m. to *Acrise Place* (adm. Easter–Sept, Thurs & Sun, 3–5), the 16C house of the Papillons, enlarged in the 17–18C, which contains a display of costumes. The church (key at the house), is part-Norman.—At (13¾ m.) *Lyminge*, the church (c. 965) adjoins the foundations of a 7C nunnery church founded by Eadburg (Ethelburga), daughter of Ethelbert.— 20 m. *Folkestone*, see Rte 5.—The direct road from Canterbury to Folkestone (A 260; 17 m.) diverges from the Dover road beyond Broome Park and crosses the pleasant upland common called *Swingfield Minnis*.

FROM CANTERBURY TO MARGATE (16 m.; A 28) and RAMSGATE (16½ m.).—To the s. of (2½ m.) *Sturry* is *Fordwich* (Restaurant), the old port of Canterbury when the Stour was navigable, where the Caen stone for the Cathedral was landed. The ancient town hall contains a ducking-stool.—Beyond a small colliery and (6½ m.) *Upstreet* is (r.) *Grove Ferry* (Hotel). At (9 m.) *Sarre* (Hotel) A 253 diverges r. for *Ramsgate* (Rte 4), passing 1 m. N. of *Minster* (Hotel), where the grand *Church (often locked) has a fine Norman tower and nave and an E.E. chancel. Near by is Minster Abbey (now occupied by Benedictine nuns; adm. daily, exc. Sun). The w. range dates from the late 11C or early 12C, and this incorporates the w. end of the church (with a spiral staircase in the tower); excavations revealed the plan of the church, which can be seen marked out in the ground. A groin-vaulted passage and chapel are also shown. The Margate road (A 28) joins A 299 beyond (l; 10 m.) *St Nicholas-at-Wade*, the church of which has E.E. carving on Norman arches. Thence to (16 m.) *Margate*, see Rte 4.

4 LONDON TO MARGATE AND RAMSGATE

ROAD (and MOTORWAY), 80 m. To (26 m.) *Cobham Park*, see Rte 2.—M 2 branches r. to (51 m.) *Brenley Corner*.—A 229 bears left, skirting *Whitstable* and *Herne Bay* and joining (68 m.) A 28.—71½ m. *Birchington*.—76 m. **Margate**.— 80 m. **Ramsgate**.

RAILWAY, 79¼ m. from *Victoria* and *Cannon Street* in 1¾–2 hrs; to (74 m.) *Margate* in 1½–1¾ hrs. Principal Stations: To *Faversham*, see Rte 2.—58½ m. *Whitstable*.—62½ m. *Herne Bay*.—70½ m. *Birchington*.—72 m. *Westgate*.—74 m. **Margate**.—77 m. *Broadstairs*.—79¼ m. **Ramsgate**.—For another route, viâ *Ashford* (slower), see Rte 5.

From London to (26 m.) Cobham Park, see Rte 2. The M 2 branches right, crossing the Medway by a high bridge (1963), the longest pre-stressed concrete span in the world. The motorway, with open views, climbs to the N. Downs, crossing the Rochester–Maidstone road at Bluebell Hill (p. 65).—At (51 m.) *Brenley Corner*, the huge junction with the A 2, we quit the Dover road. Our road, no longer motorway, continues as A 299, by-passing (56 m.) *Whitstable* and (62 m.) *Herne Bay*, two seaside resorts.

Whitstable (25,400 inhab.; Hotel), noted for its oysters ('natives'), faces the Isle of Sheppey. **Herne Bay** (Hotels), with 25,100 inhab., has a more attractive sea-front with an esplanade of 1830. The pier was wrecked by storm in 1978. **Reculver**, the site of the Roman fort of *Regulbium*, lies 3½ m. E. along the coast, surrounded by a hideous caravan site. The Church, erected within the castrum in 669, stood here until it was demolished in 1809; only the twin w. towers (12C) were preserved as a sea-mark (adm. daily; fee) and a little sculpture was removed to Canterbury Cathedral (p. 51). The plan of the Saxon church can still be seen.

We join A 28 near (68 m.) *St Nicholas-at-Wade* (see above).—71½ m. *Birchington* (Hotels) and (73 m.) *Westgate-on-Sea* (Hotels), are resorts, both now joined to Margate (see below).

The 13–14C church of *Birchington* has brasses in the Quex chapel; also the Crispe mural monument (1651) with its six busts by J. Marshall, and a bust of Gertruy Crispe by W. Palmer. D. G. Rossetti, who died here in 1882 in a house pulled down in 1963, is commemorated by a Celtic cross in the churchyard (by Madox Brown), and a window beside the s. porch. Half a mile S.E. lies *Quex Park* (1813), which William III used as a stage on his journeys to and from Holland. In the grounds are two 19C tower follies, and the Powell-Cotton Museum of natural history and ethnography (adm. Thurs 2.30–6; Apr–Sept also Wed & Sun; Aug daily from 2.30 exc. Mon & Sat; fee). At *Acol*, ⅓ m. farther s., is the chalk-pit of 'The Smuggler's Leap' ('Ingoldsby Legends').—Behind Westgate is the 15C gate-tower of the former manor-house of *Dandelion*.

The N.E. corner of Kent, N. of the Stour, is known as the ISLE OF THANET, famous for its bracing air, 'with nothing between it and the North Pole'. The vanished w. boundary of the 'isle' was the Wantsum, an ancient navigable channel beginning on the s. at Rutupiæ (Richborough) and forming part of the regular water-route from Bononia (Boulogne) to London. Its N. mouth was at Regulbium (Reculver), and this and Richborough were two of the chief Roman forts guarding the Saxon Shore from pirates. The former advanced R.A.F. airfield of *Manston*, in the centre of the 'isle', temporarily put out of action in the Battle of Britain (1940), was later the saving of many crippled aircraft limping home.

76 m. **MARGATE** (50,100 inhab.), frequented for bathing since 1753, when the bathing-machine made its first appearance, remains one of the most popular seaside resorts in England, enjoying fine sands and the fresh breezes off the North Sea.

Hotels on the sea-front from Westbrook to Cliftonville.
Post Office, Cecil Square.—INFORMATION BUREAU, Marine Terrace.
Buses to *Ramsgate*, to *Westgate* and *Birchington*, to *Herne Bay*, to *Dover*, to *Deal*, to *Canterbury*, etc.—BOAT day-trips to *Boulogne* or *Calais* (summer only).
Amusements. *Winter Gardens Pavilion, Dreamland Park, Queen's Centre* (shows, dancing, etc.), Marine Terrace.—*Tennis* in Dane Park, Hartsdown Park, and Palm Bay, Cliftonville.—*Golf Links* (18 holes) at Westgate, Birchington, and the North Foreland, 2½ m. E.—*Swimming Pools:* Lido, Walpole Bay at Cliftonville, and at Margate.

History. Once a packet station for Flushing, Margate saw the embarkation of the Elector Frederick V (King of Bohemia) and Elizabeth Stuart after their marriage in 1613; and William III and Marlborough frequently used its harbour. In 1588 Lord Howard of Effingham and Sir Francis Drake wrote despatches from 'Meregate' after the rout of the Spanish Armada.

The handsome quarter on the cliffs E. of the old town is known as *Cliftonville*, while to the w. is *Westbrook*. A favourite resort, beside the sands and sea-front, is the *Jetty* (1240 ft long). The *Pier* (760 ft) by Rennie (1810–15) was totally destroyed in the great storm of Jan 1978. In the old town is the flint church of *St John* (partly 12C), rich in brasses, with no less than 20 hatchments. In King St. is a restored early-16C timbered house. Inland, near Dane Park, a 19C *Grotto* or *Catacomb* (fee) is fantastically decorated with shells.

Kingsgate (Hotel), 3 m. E., is where Charles II landed in 1683 on his way from London to Dover, and here an imitation Norman castle (now flats), was built by Lord Holland in 1760 and once occupied by Lord Avebury, who died here in 1913. Beyond, across the bay, is the *North Foreland* (lighthouse), the *Promontorium Acantium* of the Romans, off which Monk defeated De Ruyter in 1666.

From Margate to *Canterbury*, see Rte 3.

About 3 m. S.E. of Margate is **Broadstairs** (Hotels), a quiet holiday resort, but an expanding residential town (20,000 inhab.). Many of the larger houses are now used by Preparatory schools. Harbour St. leads down to the sea through *York Gate*, a flint arch erected in 1540 to protect the 'stair' or gap in the low white cliffs.

Dickens described Broadstairs as "one of the freest and freshest little places in the world"; tablets mark the houses associated with him: in one of these, in Harbour St., he wrote part of 'Barnaby Rudge'; and in *Bleak House*, on top of the cliff above the pier, he planned the novel from which the house was later named. *Dickens House*, at the w. end of Victoria Parade, has been identified with the home of Miss Betsey Trotwood, though in 'David Copperfield' it is transferred to Dover. At *Pierremont Hall*, now the Council offices, Queen Victoria stayed in 1829. *St Peter's*, 1¼ m. W.N.W., has a church of the 12C with a 16C flint tower.

80 m. **RAMSGATE** (39,500 inhab.), a seaport and bathing resort spreading over two chalk cliffs and the 'gate' or valley between them, has a south aspect and is thus more sheltered than Margate.

Hotels on the sea-front.
Post Office, High Street.—INFORMATION BUREAU, 24 King Street.
Amusements. *Granville Theatre*, on the E. Cliff; *Royal Victoria Pavilion* (variety) *Merrie England* (shows, dancing, etc.), near the harbour.—*Golf* at St Augustine's, 2½ m. w.—*Tennis* at Spencer Sq., E. Cliff, and St Lawrence.
Buses to *Canterbury*, *Margate*, *Sandwich*, *Dover*, etc.—Pleasure trips by boat to N. Foreland and Pegwell Bay in summer.
Hoverport (with Regional Information Centre) see below.

History. Heine stayed here in 1827, Elizabeth Fry died here in 1845, and Van Gogh taught in a school here in 1876. In 1914–18 Ramsgate came next after Dunkirk and Calais as a target for German bombardment (119 air-raids), while in 1940 it was one of the chief bases for the evacuation of the British Army from Dunkirk.

The *Harbour*, with an obelisk (1821) recording the departure from Ramsgate of George IV to Hanover, is of growing commercial importance, especially for the import of cars, and it also has berths for 100 yachts.

At the end of W. Cliff is the Rom. Cath. church of *St Augustine*, considered by A. W. N. Pugin to be his best work (1845–50); it was made monastic after his death and provides a fitting burial-place. Next door is the *Grange*, also designed by him, where he died. On E. Cliff is the early 19C Wellington Crescent, the gigantic Granville Hotel by E. W. Pugin, and, at the end of the sea-front, the King George IV memorial park. *St George* (1824–27), off High St., has a conspicuous tower and light interior.

FROM RAMSGATE TO DOVER, 20¼ m. (A 256, A 258); railway, 22 m. in 40 min.—Beyond *St Lawrence* with a 13–15C church and Norman tower, we skirt *Pegwell Bay* (Motel), with the world's first international 'hoverport' (1968–69; flights to Calais in 40 min).

Beside the road is a Danish longship which was built and sailed in 1949 to celebrate the 1500th anniversary of the landing of Hengist and Horsa at Ebbsfleet (see below). Half a mile farther, a by-road (r.) leads to (1 m.) *St Augustine's Cross*, erected in 1884 to commemorate his landing in 596 (however the exact landing-place may have been at the now vanished *Stonar* across the Stour from Sandwich).

Beyond (4 m.) *Ebbsfleet* is the huge power station (1963), and, in the bend of the Stour, the extensive war-transport depot of *Richborough*, created in 1916, which is now an industrial estate. We cross the river by a toll bridge (1797) into (7 m.) **Sandwich** (Hotels; 4500 inhab.), a charming medieval town, largely contained within its ancient limits. It was one of the original Cinque Ports, though now 2 m. from the sea. Becket landed here in 1170 after his self-imposed exile in France, as did Richard Cœur-de-Lion in 1194 after his Austrian imprisonment. Thomas Paine lived in New Street for a year as a master stay-maker.

On the Quay (car parking) are part of the town walls (continued farther w.; fine raised promenade) and the *Fisher Gate*. The Tudor gate-tower gave name to the *Barbican* theatre. The attractive UPPER STRAND STREET has the Old Customs House and, at the end, a large house (1911) designed by Lutyens. We may turn r. to reach *St Clement's*, on higher ground, an E.E. church with a low arcaded Norman tower and many interesting internal features. The fine HIGH STREET leads back towards the centre and (l.) *St Peter's*, which dates from the end of the 13C, with later additions. Beyond is the Cattle Market (car parking) with the *Guildhall*, much extended in 1910. It contains a 17C court-room and a museum (adm. weekdays, 10.30–12.30, 2–4; fee). Farther N., in STRAND STREET, is *St Mary's* founded in the early 12C (restored). The *King's Arms* is a timber-framed house of 1592. Beyond is *Manwood Court* (c. 1580), the fine former grammar school building. The school was moved to the outskirts in 1894.

A 257 leads out of Sandwich past a windmill and in half a mile, a by-road (r.) leads to (1 m.) *Richborough Castle*, on the Stour. This is probably where the Romans landed in A.D. 43. A fort was built here to guard *Rutupiæ*, the chief Roman port on the E. coast of England until the end of the occupation. In the late 3C it became an important fort of the 'Saxon Shore'. The ruins (adm. daily; fee) include the S., W., and N. walls of the Saxon Shore Fort, in places 25 ft high. At the W. Gate, Watling Street, the Roman road from Canterbury, enters the fort. Within the walls are remains from Roman and Saxon times (1C–3C A.D.), including the cruciform foundations of a large monument built to commemorate the final con-quest of England in A.D. 81–96, a Saxon church dedicated to St Augustine, and defensive ditches, etc. A small museum contains interesting objects found during excavations.—To the S. is the site of a Roman amphitheatre.

By the sea, to the E. of Sandwich is (2½ m.) *Sandwich Bay* (Hotel), to the N. of which, among the sandhills, are the magnificent *Royal St George's* and the *Prince's Golf Links*. Farther N., at the mouth of the Stour is *Shellness* nature reserve.

12½ m. **Deal** (25,400 inhab.; Hotels), a 'limb' of the Cinque Ports, is a quiet coastal town with excellent streets of 18C housing, parallel to the sea. *Old* or *Upper Deal* with St Leonard's church (late Norman aisled nave), lies inland. Deal or its immediate vicinity is believed to be the scene of Julius Caesar's landing in 55 B.C., and Wm. Penn sailed hence in 1682 on his first voyage to America. *Deal Castle* (adm. daily; fee) is the most intricate of three castles built here by Henry VIII for coast defence to protect the safe anchorage of the Downs (see below). It is well preserved with good vaulted chambers and galleries. The Earl of Ypres (1852–1925), who died at Deal Castle, was born and is buried at *Ripple*, 2½ m. w. The scant remains of *Sandown Castle* lie to the N., and beyond, the famous *Royal Cinque Ports Golf Course*.

Off the coast lie the GOODWIN SANDS, a series of dangerous sandbanks about 10 m. in length, marked by lightships and exposed at low water. According to the legend, these were once the fruitful island of Lomea, which was submerged by a furious storm in the 11C, owing to the fact that the stones intended to strengthen its sea-wall were used by the abbot of St Augustine's for the tower of Tenterden Church. The Downs, the famous roadstead between the Goodwin Sands and the coast, form a natural refuge, not too safe in strong gales from the s., when the traditional hardihood of the Walmer lifeboatmen is often called upon to succour ships in distress. In the great storm of Nov 1954, the South Goodwin lightship was lost and in that of Jan 1978 Deal was extensively flooded. There is a coastguard station permanently manned at Deal.

13½ m. *Walmer* (Hotel), with the depot of the Royal Marines (to close by 1981), adjoins Deal on the s. *Walmer Castle*, the third built in this area by Henry VIII, was converted c. 1730 into the official residence of the Lord Warden of the Cinque Ports (in 1941–65 Sir Winston Churchill). William Pitt was once Warden, and the Duke of Wellington succeeded Lord Liverpool in that office in 1829 and died here in 1852 (room with his camp-bed, etc.). Adm. daily when the Lord Warden (in 1979 H.M. Elizabeth The Queen Mother) is not in residence.— 20½ m. *Dover*, see Rte 5.

At 17¾ m. B 2058 diverges l. for (1¾ m.) St Margaret's Bay (Hotel), situated on precipitous wooded cliffs, in the lee of the S. Foreland. *Martin Mill* station is 2 m. N.W. The old church, in the landward part of the village, is a good example of Norman work. On the E. horn of St Margaret's Bay stands the *Dover Patrol Monument*, a tall granite obelisk unveiled in 1921. Companion monuments have been erected on Cap Blanc Nez and in New York Harbour. Pleasant cliff-walk back to Walmer (4 m.) viâ *Kingsdown*.

5   LONDON TO DOVER VIÂ FOLKESTONE

ROAD, 78 m. (A 20).—4 m. *New Cross.*—17 m. *Swanley* (by-pass).—27½ m. *Wrotham Heath.*—35 m. **Maidstone** (by-passed by using M 20).—54 m. **Ashford** (by-pass).—66 m. **Hythe.**—71½ m. **Folkestone.**—78 m. **Dover.**—MOTORWAY (M 20) on a similar course (in construction) from Swanley to Folkestone.

RAILWAY, 77½ m. in 1½–2½ hrs from *Charing Cross, Waterloo,* or *Cannon Street.* This is one route (the other is viâ Chatham and Canterbury) of the Continental boat-trains (from *Victoria*) on the Boulogne, Calais, and Ostend services, and the Dover–Dunkirk ferry.—Principal Stations: 22 m. **Sevenoaks.**—29½ m. **Tonbridge.**—34½ m. *Paddock Wood.*—56 m. **Ashford,** where we join the lines from Maidstone and Canterbury.—70 m. **Folkestone Central.**—77½ m. **Dover** (Priory).

Quitting London by the Old Kent Rd. (A 2), New Cross, where A 20 diverges r., and (4 m.) Lewisham, we traverse a suburban district, by-passing Eltham and Sidcup, and also (17 m.) *Swanley.*—19 m. *Farningham* (r.; Hotel), a charming 18C village on the Darent, has an E.E. church with a Perp. tower.

A 225 (r.) runs from Farningham to (9 m.) Sevenoaks through typical Kentish scenery viâ (1 m.) *Eynsford,* with the well-preserved ruins of a Norman pre-keep castle; it retains a high curtain-wall of c. 1100 (adm. daily; closed Sun morn. in winter; fee. Excavations were continued in 1971). Opposite Eynsford church (part-Norman), a by-road crosses the Darent by a stone bridge and passes under a graceful railway viaduct to (¾ m.) *Lullingstone Roman Villa (adm. daily; fee). This is one of the most spectacular Roman villas in England, well-desplayed with finds from the site in situ and covered by a protective building. Excavations in 1949 disclosed fine mosaic pavements, with inscription, and three marble busts, now in the British Museum. The painted wall-plaster, pieced together, has revealed the existence of the earliest known place of Christian worship in Britain (4C). On a hillside above the site an important Romano–British pagan funerary temple of c. A.D. 300 was found in 1958. A private road continues to *Lullingstone Castle* (May–Sept, Wed, Sat, Sun, & BH, 2–6; fee), a Queen

Anne house with a Tudor gatehouse and an interesting church, which has been the home of the Hart Dyke family since c. 1500. The first game of lawn tennis was played here in 1873, with rules drafted by Sir Wm. Hart Dyke.—4 m. *Shoreham* has a late Perp. church.—At (5½ m.) *Otford* are the remains of a 16C manor-house of the Abps. of Canterbury. To the left runs the so-called *Pilgrims' Way* (fine views), originally a British track followed the s. slope of the Downs.

A 225 (l.) descends the Darent valley for (3 m.) *Sutton-at-Hone*, where the church has a monument to Sir Thomas Smyth (1558?–1625), "Governor of the East Indian and Other Companies, Treasurer of the Virginian Plantation and sometime Ambassador to the Emperor and Great Duke of Russia and Muscovy". The house of St John's Jerusalem (12–18C) embodies the 13C chapel of a Commandery of the Knights Hospitallers (N.T.; chapel and garden Wed 2–6; fee). The 10–12C church of *Darenth* (¾ m. N.E.), partly constructed of Roman materials, has a priest's chamber above the vaulted chancel and a curious font of c. 1140.

A 20 passes near (21½ m.; l.) *Brands Hatch* motor racing circuit, and at 25 m. descends the notorious Wrotham Hill.—26 m. *Wrotham* (r.; Hotels), pronounced 'Rootam', is an attractive village with an early 14C church.

A 227 leads r. to (1 m.) *Borough Green* railway station and (2 m.) *Ightham* (pron. 'Item'), with interesting monuments in the church. *Oldbury* (N.T.), ½ m. w. is a large hill-fort (1C A.D.). *Ightham Mote (Fri 2–dusk or 5; fee), 2½ m. s., a charming old manor-house enclosing a court and surrounded by a moat, dates from the early 14C, but possesses a late 15C gate-tower and an admirable specimen of a Tudor domestic chapel (c. 1530).—We return to A 227 where a by-road (l.) leads in ¾ m. to the pleasant village of *Plaxtol.* 1¾ m. E. is *Old Soar Manor* (N.T.; April–Sept daily, Sun from 2; fee), a fine example of the solar end of a knight's house of c. 1290, now attached to an 18C house.—A 227 continues s. passing (l.) the 18C house and grounds of *Fairlawne.*— 5 m. *Shipbourne*, a village of considerable character, was the birthplace of Christopher Smart (1722–71), the poet.

At (27½ m.) *Wrotham Heath* beyond a junction with the M 20 we join the road from Sevenoaks.—29½ m. *West Malling* (r.; Hotel) a pleasant 18C village, preserves the ruins, including the w. front, of a Benedictine abbey (adm. on request, but with the restrictions of a closed Order), founded in 1090 by Bishop Gundulf of Rochester; a new abbey church was consecrated here in 1966. *St Leonard's Tower*, beyond the end of the high street, dates from c. 1100. About 1 m. w. is *Offham*, with the only quintain on the green in England.

Leybourne Castle (now the wing of a 20C house), ½ m. N. on A 228, was the home of William de Leybourne (d. 1310), England's first admiral (tablet in the church).— *Clare House* (1793), in an attractive park is on the old road linking West Malling with *East Malling* (2 m.), which has a 14–15C church, and an important Fruit Research Station (adm. by appointment Mon–Fri) in Bradbourne House (rebuilt 1715).

31½ m. *Ditton.* B 2011 (narrow bridge) leads l. for Aylesford (see below), while, just beyond, the M 20 may be joined to by-pass Maidstone.

35 m. **Maidstone** (Hotels), the congested county town and agricultural centre of Kent, with paper-mills and breweries (70,900 inhab.), lies on both banks of the Medway. It is an important shopping centre; some streets off the High Street, all with interesting old houses, have been closed to traffic. On the E. bank, a little s. of the bridge, is the fine large church of *All Saints* (Perp.), chiefly built by Abp. Courtenay (d. 1396) in connection with a secular *College* (suppressed in 1547), which can be seen to the s. through a vaulted gate-tower. The church contains good sedilia and stalls (with misericords), a carved chancel screen (1886), the canopied tomb of Dr Wotton, first Master of the College (1417), with

a wall-painting of him being presented to the Virgin by Saints and a memorial (s. wall) to Laurence Washington (d. 1619), a collateral ancestor of George Washington. The existing *Palace*, N. of the church, is Perp. with an Elizabethan E. front. Near the road is a small 13C house, now the Department of Weights and Measures. Across Bishop's Way is a 14C *Tithe Barn* (adm. weekdays, 10–1, 2–5; fee), with a fine roof, containing a splendid collection of carriages (17–19C), many of them royal. The *Museum and Art Gallery* (weekdays, 10–5 or 6), with relics of William Hazlitt, a native of Maidstone, and a county collection, occupies *Chillington Manor House*, an admirable 16C mansion in St Faith's St. near the East Station. In the 18C *Town Hall* hangs a portrait of Disraeli, who held Maidstone as his first parliamentary seat.

3 m. S.E. is *Otham* with good timber-framed houses, notably Wardes and Stone-acre, a 16C yeoman's house (N.T.; adm. by written application only).—*Boughton Monchelsea Place* (adm. April–Oct, 2.15–6, Sat, Sun, & BH, Wed also in Aug; fee; teas), 5 m. s., is a 16C mansion in a fine park. The church has a lych-gate of 1470.

A pleasant walk or boat-trip may be taken down the river to (2 m.) *Allington* and (3 m.) *Aylesford*. *Allington Castle* (conducted visits daily 2–4; fee), a restored building of the late 13C, with Tudor additions, was the early home of Sir Thomas Wyatt (1503–42), the poet, and from here his son Sir Thomas (1521–54) set out on the ill-starred rebellion against Queen Mary's Spanish marriage. It now belongs to the Carmelites and is used for retreats.—*Aylesford*, with a 14C bridge and a fine river frontage, has a lovely old inn, and the noble monument of Sir Thomas Cole-peper (d. 1604) in its church. Sir Charles Sedley (1639–1701), the poet and wit, was born in *The Friars* (¼ m. w.), which incorporates much of one of the earliest Carme-lite foundations in England (1240). In 1949 the Carmelites reoccupied the buildings, this being the first occasion in England for a dispossessed Order to regain its old home; the relics of St Simon Stock (d. 1265), the first prior, were translated from Bordeaux, and in 1958–61 a new Shrine Church (for open-air services) was built by Adrian Gilbert Scott on the site of the sanctuary of the priory church (adm. free daily; rfmts.).—About 2 m. N.E. of Maidstone viâ *Penenden Heath*, the assembly-ground of the Men of Kent since Saxon times, is *Boxley*, in the partly Norman church of which is a memorial to Sir Francis Wyatt, Governor of Virginia in 1621 et seq.

FROM MAIDSTONE TO CHATHAM, 8 m. A 229 leads N., crossing the by-pass at Sandling, where (l.) a road leads to *Cobtree Manor*, said to be the original of Mr Wardle's house at 'Dingley Dell'.—4 m. Pratling St. (l.) leads in half a mile to a footpath signposted to *Kit's Coty House* (¼ m. farther), a huge dolmen with a capstone 11 ft long, the long barrow of which existed up to the 18C. It stands in a magnificent position.—The Roman road ascends Bluebell Hill, and climbs the N. Downs, crossing the M 2 motorway, into *Chatham*.

FROM MAIDSTONE TO RYE, 30 m. A 274 leads S.E. through typical orchard country, across the Quarry Hills, famous for 'ragstone'.—5¾ m. *Sutton Valence*, with a boys' public school (1578).—9 m. *Headcorn* on the main Tonbridge to Ashford railway, has some fine old timbered houses.—13 m. *Biddenden* has a half-timbered village street. We join the A 262.—16¼ m. *High Halden* (l.), with a splendid timber belfry.—A 28 continues to (20 m.) **Tenterden** (Hotels), a dignified little town (5900 inhab.) with a broad High St., and a noble Perp. tower. Here the resuscitated Kent & East Sussex Light Railway uses steam locomotives to Bodiam. *Hales Place* has an Elizabethan garden. A 28 goes on to Hastings, see p. 77.—B 2082 leads s., passing (22½ m.) *Smallhythe Place* (N.T.; March–Oct, 2–6 or dusk, exc. Tues & Fri; fee), an early 16C house, which was the last home of Ellen Terry (1847–1928), and is preserved as a memorial of the great actress.—We pass (27 m.) *Stocks Windmill* (1781), and soon descend to the marshes.—30 m. *Rye*, see Rte 6.

FROM MAIDSTONE TO TONBRIDGE, 14 m. (A 26), through a pleasant reach of the Medway valley. 2 m. *East Barming* has a Norman church with sculptured bench-ends c. 1300.—4 m. *Teston*, with a medieval bridge, was the home of Adm. Lord Barham (1726–1813). *West Farleigh*, on the s. bank, has a well-preserved early Norman church and some large 18C houses.—5 m. *Wateringbury*. One mile left at *Nettlestead*, the tiny church has a fine series of windows.—6¼ m. *Mereworth Castle* (no adm.), was built in 1720–23 by Colen Campbell, modelled on Palladio's Villa Rotonda, near Vicenza.—10 m. *Hadlow* has a church with a Saxo-Norman w. end, and the remains of a castle built by Walter Barton May (c. 1830), including a tower 170 ft high.—14 m. *Tonbridge*, see Rte 6.

A 2020 runs E. out of Maidstone past Mote Park and in 4 m. crosses B 2163. A mile left is *Hollingbourne*, a charming village on the Pilgrims' Way, with the fine tomb of Lady Elizabeth Culpeper (d. 1638), by E. Marshall, in its church. *Eyhorne Manor* (15C) is open at weekends in summer. Just beyond the junction between A 20 and M 20, the main road skirts the extensive grounds of *Leeds Castle* (adm. from B 2163, r.; Apr–Sept, Tues, Wed, Thurs, Sun & BH, 1–5.30; fee), the typical moated castle of romance, standing in a small lake and dating partly from the 13C. This was the home of Lord Culpeper, Governor of Virginia in 1680–83, and belonged to his grandson Lord Fairfax (1692–1782), who migrated to Virginia c. 1746.—42 m. *Harrietsham* has a Norman font and, in East St., a fine 16C wealden house.—44 m. *Lenham* is well-grouped round the church which has a rare armchair sedile. Sir Henry Wotton (1568–1639), poet, diplomat, and wit, was born at *Boughton Malherbe*, 2½ m. s.w. beyond *Chilston Park*, praised by Evelyn in 1666.—48 m. *Charing* (Hotel) retains, beside the noble church, the remains of a manor house of the Abps. of Canterbury.

Otterden Place (adm. 2–4, Wed & Thurs, May–Sept; fee) 3½ m. N., is a pleasant Tudor and Georgian house beside a church rebuilt in 1753, having a fine monument of 1620.

54 m. **Ashford** (Hotels), with 35,600 inhab., an ancient market town, was an important centre of steam locomotive building. The church, surrounded by charming old houses, has a Perp. tower and contains monuments and brasses, including that of Elizabeth, Countess of Atholl (1375). Replanning has not been kind to the rest.

Godinton, 2 m. N.W., a house of 1628–31, has contemporary woodwork and fine gardens (adm. June–Aug and at Easter, Sun & BH, 2–5; fee).
FROM ASHFORD TO CANTERBURY, 14 m. A 28 leads N.E. following the Stour valley.—3 m. *Kempe's Corner*. To the right (1 m.) beyond Ashford racecourse, lies *Wye* (Restaurant), perhaps the birthplace of Aphra Behn (1640–89), dramatist, novelist, and spy. Wye College (1892), the agricultural school of London University, is the successor of a school and college founded in 1447 by Abp. Kempe. The crown cut in the chalk downs (r.) commemorates the coronation of Edward VII. *Brook*, 2½ m. S.E., has an agricultural museum (adm. Wed in summer, 2–5) and a Norman church containing wall-paintings.—4 m. (l.) *Boughton Aluph* church (being restored 1971) has fine 14C nave arcades and contemporary stained glass. In the beautiful surrounding country is *Eastwell Park* (2000 acres; lake) traversed by the Pilgrims' Way; Richard Plantagenet, natural son of Richard III lived here after Bosworth Field, working as a bricklayer until his death in 1550.— 6 m. *Godmersham* has an unusual apsidal church with a Norman tower and a 12C relief of an Archbishop. At Godmersham Park (backed by fine woods), Jane Austen frequently visited her brother, Edward Knight (monument in church).— 9 m. **Chilham** (Hotel), a pretty feudal village with a flint church, is compactly placed at the gates of a 'castle', of which the octagonal Plantagenet keep survives. In the present 'castle', a mansion (1616; by Inigo Jones?), was born Governor Edward Digges of Virginia (1655–58). The park (adm. May–Oct, closed Mon & Fri, 2–6; fee) was landscaped by Capability Brown, and public banquets are held in the great hall.—11 m. *Chartham* church has a fine chancel with stained glass, and 'Kentish' tracery, and good brasses (one of 1306 being the oldest in Kent). It has an original timber roof.—14 m. *Canterbury*, see Rte 3.

The road passes between (57 m.) *Mersham* (pron. 'Merzam'), where the church has monuments by Evesham and N. Stone and *Mersham le Hatch*, an Adam house of 1766. For a brief period in 1511–12 Erasmus held the living of *Aldington*, 3 m. s.e.—60 m. *Sellindge* church, with a Norman tower.—At (63 m.) *Newingreen* (Motel) a road climbs right to Lympne Castle (1 m.; see below). To the l. the Roman 'Stone Street' leads N. to Canterbury, passing (l.) *Westenhanger* racecourse and the remains of a 14C fortified manor house. A 20 bears to the l. for Folkestone, viâ (65½ m.) *Sandling Park* (adm. to garden Sun in May 10–6; fee); A 261 leads r. for Hythe and Sandgate.

66 m. **Hythe** (11,900 inhab.; Hotels), one of the Cinque Ports, is divided in two by the Royal Military Canal, built in 1804–6 (23 m. long, connecting Hythe with Rye). The old village on the hillside has some interesting houses, and an E.E. church with a fine raised chancel above a vaulted processional path, containing numerous skulls and other human bones, believed to have been brought from the old churchyard (14–15C). Lionel Lukin (1742–1834), inventor of the lifeboat (1785) is buried in the church. Many important historic documents relating to the Cinque Ports may be seen on application at the Town Clerk's office, and the municipal *Museum* (closed Tues aft.) contains medieval seals and official weights and measures. The unpretentious sea-front has three Martello towers, built to counter the threat of invasion by Napoleon.

A walk may be taken along the canal to (3 m.) *Stutfall Castle* (no adm.) the scanty remains of the castrum of the Roman Portus Lemanis. The Roman name is preserved in *Lympne Castle* (pron. 'Lim'; adm. April–Oct, Wed, Sun & BH, July–Sept daily; fee) on the scarp above, 2 m. w. of Hythe (bus). The 14–15C fortified mansion was the residence of the Archdeacons of Canterbury until 1860. The square tower survives from an earlier 12C building and the new w. wing was added during Sir Robert Lorimer's restoration. The church, probably built by Lanfranc (d. 1089) has been much restored. To the w. lies an airfield.—Scarcely 1 m. N. of Hythe is the well-preserved *Saltwood Castle* (adm. June–Aug, Sun & BH, 2–5.30), where the murderers of Becket met for their journey to Canterbury.— MINIATURE RAILWAY (at Easter and in summer) to *Dymchurch* and *New Romney*.— 69 m. **Sandgate** (Hotels) forms, with *Seabrook* (Hotel), a small resort, below Shorncliffe camp famed in 1914–18. The road ascends past the inconspicuous Sandgate Castle one of Henry VIII's coast defences, into Folkestone.

71½ m. **FOLKESTONE** (43,800 inhab.), a well-situated and fashionable resort, is an ancient town once a 'limb' of the Cinque Ports, with a large harbour carrying on active passenger traffic with the Continent. It is divided in two by the Foord valley, across which the railway is carried by Cubitt's fine viaduct (1843).

Railway Stations. *Central*, the main station; *Harbour*, for cross-Channel passengers only; *West*, for local traffic.

Hotels mostly on or near the Leas.

Post Office, Bouverie Place.—INFORMATION OFFICES, Harbour St. and Civic Centre, Castle Hill Avenue.

Amusements. *Leas Pavilion*, repertory; *Leas Cliff Hall, Marine Pavilion*, concerts and other entertainments.—GOLF COURSE (18 holes), Sene valley.—TENNIS at Radnor Park, Cheriton Road, East Cliff, and Sandgate, etc.—BATHING POOL, Marine Gardens.—CRICKET (County Matches) at the Sports Ground, Cheriton Rd.—RACE MEETINGS (June to September), at *Westenhanger*, 7m. N.W.

Ships to *Boulogne* daily in summer (day excursions).

The chief resort of visitors is the *LEAS, a wide grassy promenade extending along the top of the cliff for over a mile, with views of the sea and the coast of France, 22 m. distant. Striking new buildings are being added to the impressive mid-19C terraces. More sheltered walks are afforded by the shrub-grown paths on the face of the beautifully planted cliff (lift). At the w. end of the Leas the *New Metropole Arts Centre* (adm. daily exc. Mon from 10.30, Sun from 2; fee) holds temporary exhibitions of painting and sculpture. A '*Road of Remembrance*' planted

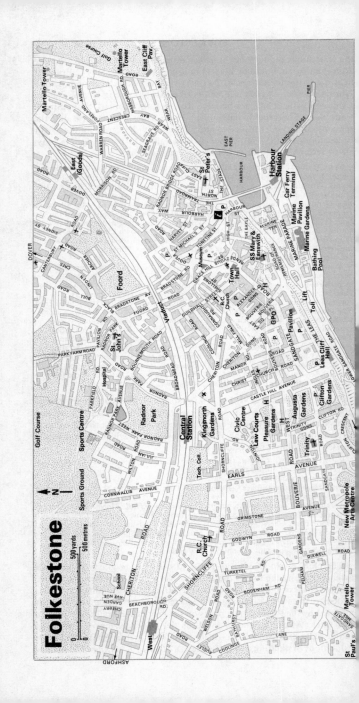

Folkestone

0   500 yards

0   500 metres

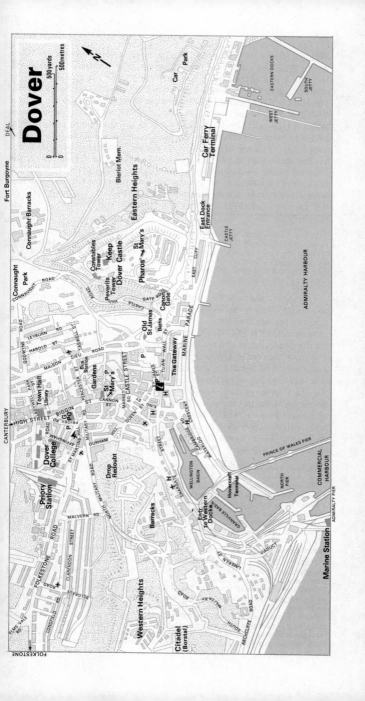

with rosemary, descending to the harbour, commemorates the First World War, and a toll road runs along the base of the cliff to Sandgate. Near the E. end of the Leas is the church of *SS Mary & Eanswith*, largely rebuilt since its foundation in 1137 on the site of an 11C nunnery church. The Harvey Aisle (added in 1874) and the w. window, presented by over 3000 medical men, as well as a statue (1881) on the Leas, commemorate William Harvey (1578–1657), discoverer of the circulation of the blood, who was born at Folkestone. In the chancel is a 14C canopied tomb with effigy. The site of Folkestone's ancient castle may be determined by *The Bayle* and *Bayle Pond*, near the church. In Grace Hill is the *Museum* (adm. weekdays) with collections of local interest, including finds from two Roman villas excavated near the road to the Warren. Only a few narrow streets leading down to the lively harbour survived the bombing of 1941–44, but the district still retains a marine atmosphere.

To the E. beyond the harbour is the East Cliff, with a sandy beach and pleasant gardens, and farther on (1½ m. E.) is the *Warren*, a rough expanse of tumbled chalk between the cliffs and the shore, of interest to the botanist, entomologist, and fossil-gatherer.—On the N. rise the *Sugar Loaf, Caesar's Camp*, and other chalk hills.—From Folkestone to *Canterbury*, see Rte 3; to *Sandgate, Hythe*, etc., see above.

The Dover road climbs steeply above the Warren and crosses open downland (stormy in winter), while the railway threads three long tunnels through the cliffs.

78 m. **DOVER** (34,300 inhab.), one of the chief embarkation points for the Continent, is also a military base and is visited as a seaside resort. The town, flanked E. and w. by fortified heights, lies on the low ground at the mouth of the Dour and extends up its narrow valley, which here interrupts the line of the famous white cliffs. DOVER HARBOUR includes the old *Commercial Harbour* (three basins; 75 acres), the *Eastern and Western Docks*, the *Hoverport*, and the *Admiralty Harbour*, abandoned as a naval base in 1923. The last (1½ m. by ¾ m.), enclosed by massive breakwaters constructed in 1898–1909, was of great naval importance during the First World War. The town suffered from air-raids and shell-fire in 1940–44.

Railway Stations. *Priory*, for all services; *Marine* (Western Docks), for cross-Channel services only.

Hotels on the sea front, and in Folkestone Rd., Castle St., etc. in the town.

Post Office, Biggin St.—INFORMATION OFFICE, Town Hall, High St.

Buses from Pencester Rd. to all destinations.

Ferries. From the train-ferry berth at Marine Station (W. Docks) to *Dunkirk* (with cars) and to *Ostend* (passengers only) nightly in 3 hrs 45 min., and to *Calais* (passengers only) in 1½ hrs.—CAR FERRY TERMINAL, Eastern Docks, to *Calais* (1½ hrs), *Zeebrugge* (4 hrs), *Ostend* (3¾ hrs), and *Boulogne* (1½ hrs).—HOVERCRAFT from Seaspeed Terminal, Western Docks to *Calais* and *Boulogne* in 35 min.

History. Dover (the Roman *Dubræ* or *Dubris*), in all ages a landing-place of consequence, was the starting-point of Watling Street, the great Roman road to London viâ Canterbury, and in the 3C–4C was a fortress guarding the 'Saxon Shore', which extended from The Wash to Spithead. Though there is evidence of an Iron Age settlement on the site, it has only a shadowy connection with Hengist and Horsa (or even, according to Camden, with King Arthur). It emerges into historical importance under the early Norman kings, and in 1190 Richard I assembled his knights here before starting on the 3rd Crusade. The castle came to be regarded as the 'Key of England', and in 1216, under Hubert de Burgh, successfully withstood a long siege by the Dauphin and King John's rebellious barons.

About 1295, however, the town was pillaged by the French. During the Civil War it was captured in 1642 by the Parliamentarians. In 1660 Charles II landed here at the Restoration. Allan Ramsay (1713–84), the painter, died here returning from a visit to Rome. Woodrow Wilson, the first President of the United States to visit England, landed at the Admiralty Pier on 26 Dec 1918, and departed thence on the 31st.

The STRAITS OF DOVER, 17 m. wide between Dover and Cape Gris Nez, are the narrowest part of the Channel. Here, within sight of the town, the Spanish Armada of 1588 received its first shattering blow. Capt. Webb swam from Dover to (21 m.) Calais in 1875 in 21 ¾ hrs, and more recently the Straits have been swum many times, mostly in the reverse direction (fastest time, Penny Dean, 7 hrs 40 min.). They were swum both ways in 1965 by E. Erickson in 30 hrs 3 min., and in 1970 Kevin Murphy was the first to swim the return journey non-stop (35 hrs 10 min.). The youngest to swim the straits is Marcus Hooper, aged 12, in 12 hrs 37 min. in 1979, and the first woman was Miss G. Ederle in 1926, in 14 hrs 34 min. Louis Blériot was the first man to fly an aeroplane across the Channel (25 July 1909), and the Hon. C. S. Rolls, the first to cross and recross in a single flight (1910), but they were preceded by François Blanchard, who flew from Dover to Guines in his dirigible balloon (7 Jan 1785).

In the First World War Dover was the headquarters of the *Dover Patrol*, the naval organization in which British and American destroyers combined to protect navigation against the German submarines and mines. It enabled 12,000,000 soldiers to pass in safety to the battlefield. Of 125,100 vessels passing through the patrolled area (600 m. across) only 73 were lost. In the Second World War Dover played a prominent part in the evacuation of the British Army from Dunkirk, and was one of the first places to be attacked from the air (12 Aug 1940) in the Battle of Britain. From 1940 to 1944 the town was under continual shell-fire, the case-mates of the Castle providing shelter for the population.

Dover is the chief of the **Cinque Ports**, or five S.E. ports which, in return for various privileges and immunities, were formerly bound to furnish, when required, a certain number of ships for the royal fleets. The name dates from the time of Edward the Confessor, or earlier; and for centuries the maritime defence of the s. coast of England largely depended on this system. A charter was granted by Edward I. The original Cinque Ports were Dover, Sandwich, Hythe, Romney, and Hastings; Rye and Winchelsea were added as 'Ancient Towns', and various smaller ports as 'Limbs' or 'Members'. The ports are under a Lord Warden (comp. p. 63), who exercises a nominal jurisdiction and presides at occasional quaint 'courts', as well as at ordinary courts.

The main street of the town reaches the harbour at the Dover Stage Hotel. The well laid-out **Marine Parade** leads in front of *The Gateway* (1961), a long block of flats with interesting garden-mosaic, and continues to the *Eastern Docks*, passing monuments to Capt. Webb and C. S. Rolls.

From the Marine Parade a path ascends to the *Eastern Heights*. On *North Fall Meadow*, to the E. of the castle, a memorial marks the spot where Louis Blériot landed. The heights afford excellent views of the harbour and hoverport.

To the w., Waterloo Crescent with the White Cliffs Hotel leads to *Prince of Wales Pier*, below which passes King Charles's Walk, opened in 1960, the tercentenary of Charles II's landing. Beyond the Commercial Harbour lies *Admiralty Pier* with the Marine Station (1300 yds; fine views from raised promenade).

The main street runs inland to Market Square continuing N. as Cannon St. to *St Mary's Church*, with a remarkable Norman tower. It contains memorials to the actor Samuel Foote (1720–77) and the poet Churchill (1731–64; "the comet of a season"). Farther N. in Biggin St., is the *Town Hall* incorporating the fine *Maison Dieu Hall* (daily 10–5), a 14C enlargement of the pilgrims' hostel founded in c. 1221 by Hubert de Burgh; the restored 13C chapel at the E. end was changed in the 19C into a Sessions Hall. St Richard of Chichester died in the Maison Dieu.

Maison Dieu House, adjoining (now a public library), is an attractive mansion of 1665, built for the Agent Victualler of the Navy. The *Museum* (adm. daily, exc. Wed & Sun) is beside the Town Hall.

In Priory Rd., the tiny restored *Chapel of St Edmund*, consecrated in 1253 by St Richard, was formerly attached to the Maison Dieu; dissolved in 1544, it was reconsecrated in 1968. Near Priory Station is *Dover College*, the buildings of which include the refectory, dormitory, and gatehouse of *St Martin's Priory*, a Benedictine foundation of 1132.

*Dover Castle, the chief interest to most visitors, picturesquely crowns the summit of the cliff (375 ft) to the E. of the town, and is open daily, Sun from 2 (May–Sept, Sun from 9.30). It is approached by motorists from Castle Hill Rd., through *Constable's Tower* (1227), passing 'Queen Elizabeth's Pocket Pistol', a bronze cannon, 23 ft long, presented by Charles V to Henry VIII (it was cast in Utrecht in 1544 and bears a Low Dutch inscription), to the car park. Pedestrians approach from the bombed Norman church of St James at the beginning of Castle Hill Rd., through *Canon Gate*. The *Pharos*, perhaps the oldest standing building in England (c. A.D. 50), is a relic of the original Roman fortress (the octagonal belfry was added by Humphrey of Gloucester); the ancient church of *St Mary de Castro*, built of Roman bricks, is Saxon (badly restored in 1860); while the keep (83 ft high, with walls 17–22 ft thick) built by Henry II (1181–87), and other towers are late Norman. The KEEP (Sun in winter from 2; *View) contains an armoury and a late Norman chapel. In many of the rooms are inscriptions scratched by prisoners of war during Marlborough's campaigns. From the top story a well descends into the thickness of the wall and down into the cliff for 289 ft.—The underground passages and casemates (fee) are open at the same hours.

THE WESTERN HEIGHTS, occupied by the *Citadel* (now a borstal) and other Napoleonic fortifications, contain near the summit (l. of road), the foundations of a *Church of the Templars* with a round apse, in which King John made submission to Pandulf, the Pope's legate, in 1213. A deep cleft separates the W. Heights from Shakespeare Cliff (350 ft; footpath), so called from traditional association with a famous passage in 'King Lear' (IV, 6). It is approached direct from the town viâ Limekiln St. and Archcliff Rd.; the return may be made from its w. end by the beach (at low tide).

A cliff-walk from the E. Heights passes a conspicuous radar station to (3 m.) the *South Foreland* (lighthouse) and (4 m.) *St Margaret's Bay* (p. 63). The road from Dover to St Margaret's passes *Connaught Barracks* and the *Duke of York's Military School* for soldiers' sons.

About 3 m. N.W. of Dover are the extensive and romantic ruins of *St Radegund's* or *Bradsole Abbey* (Premonstratensian, 1191; no adm.), reached from the Canterbury road at *River*. B 2060 runs along the next valley w. past the pleasant public parks of *Kearsney Abbey* (l.) and *Russell Gardens* (r.), to *Alkham*, with a beautiful 13C church with fine wall-arcading in the N. chapel.

FROM DOVER TO BARFRESTON, 10 m. Following the Canterbury road (Rte 2) to (6 m.) *Lydden*, we there turn r. for (7½ m.) *Coldred*, the church of which has an E.E. bell-gable. On the right is *Waldershare Park*, a Queen Anne mansion in a beautiful park; the church has interesting monuments.—9 m. *Eythorne*, with a lead font, is in the small E. Kent coalfield.—10 m. **Barfreston** has a small very ornate Norman *Church, probably built in 1170–80, with remarkable carvings.

From Dover to *Canterbury*, see Rte 2; to *Deal*, *Sandwich*, and *Ramsgate*, see Rte 4 (end).

6 LONDON TO HASTINGS

A Deviously viâ Westerham

ROAD, 71 m. To (10 m.) *Bromley*, see Rte 6B.—A 233. 20½ m. *Westerham.*—B 2026. 26 m. *Edenbridge.*—B 2027, 2176. 33 m. *Penshurst.*—38½ m. *Tonbridge.* To (71 m) Hastings, see Rte 6B.

RAILWAY. From *Charing Cross* to (29½ m.) **Tonbridge**, see Rte 5. From Tonbridge, branch-line to (4 m.) *Penshurst Station* and (9 m.) *Edenbridge.*

We follow A 21 to (10 m.) *Bromley* (see Rte 6B), where A 233 diverges right.—At 12 m. the road passes close to the site of a Roman villa.—14½ m. *Biggin Hill* airfield was a vital fighter station in the Battle of Britain. The road ascends (16½ m.) Westerham Hill (809 ft; view), the highest point in Kent, and descends to cross the Pilgrims' Way.—20½ m. Westerham.

Westerham (Hotels) is pleasantly situated near the source of the Darent. General Wolfe (1727–59) was born in the vicarage here, and spent his early boyhood in what is now known as *Quebec House* (N.T.; adm. daily exc. Thurs & Sat; March–Oct, 2–5 or 6; BH. 10–1, 2–6; fee). Some of his relics are preserved here, and also at *Squerryes Court* (adm. March–Oct, Wed, Sat, Sun, & BH, 2–6; fee), a 17C mansion s.w. of the town. Though he left Westerham at the age of eleven, Harry Warrington (in 'The Virginians') is represented as visiting him here. On the village green is a statue of Wolfe, by Derwent Wood (1911). That of Churchill by Oscar Nemon (1969) stands on a marble plinth given by Marshal Tito of Yugoslavia. *Pitt's Cottage*, now a restaurant, was for a time the country retreat of the younger Pitt. The parsonage of Mr Collins ('Pride and Prejudice') was at "Hunsford, near Westerham".

We leave Westerham by B 2026, passing (l.) wooded sandy hills stretching to Brasted (600 acres N.T. property; pleasant walks and drives).—22½ m. **Chartwell,** the home of Sir Winston Churchill in 1922–65, and now preserved as a memorial to him (N.T.; March–Nov; garden and studio, April–mid-Oct; Sat, Sun & BH 11–6, Tues–Thurs 2–6; fee).—23 m. *Crockham Hill*, with good views over the Weald. We cross the railway and the junction with B 2027 into (26 m.) *Edenbridge*, with some old buildings above the bridge. B 2027 leads E., passing (30 m.) a by-road r. for *Hever* (2 m.; Hotel), where the church with a fine shingled spire, has a beautiful tomb of Sir Thomas Boleyn (d. 1538), father of Anne, and a brass of Margaret Cheyne (d. 1419). *Hever Castle* (adm. Apr–Sept, Wed, Sun, & BH, 1.30–6.15; fee), the castellated mansion of the Boleyn family (14C), is interesting as the traditional meeting-place of Anne Boleyn (perhaps born here) and Henry VIII, who afterwards granted it to Anne of Cleves. It has a fine Italian garden.—30½ m. By-road (r.) for *Chiddingstone* (1½ m.), a charming group of half-timbered houses (N.T.). The *Castle* (adm. Easter–Oct daily, exc. Mon, 2–5,30, weekends from 11.30; fee), refaced in the 'Gothick' manner c. 1810, is notable for its 17C woodwork and collection of Stuart relics including Charles Edward's last letter before the '45 rebellion and Monmouth's plea for life written the day before his execution.

33 m. *Penshurst Station*. Here B 2176 leads s. to *Penshurst*, a delightful village, with many of the local buildings in the vernacular tradition by George Davey (c. 1850). It is dominated by ***Penshurst Place,** the splendid seat of Viscount De L'Isle, V.C. (adm. Easter–June, daily exc. Mon & Fri, 2–6; July–Sept 1–6; BH. 11.30–6; fee).

The house, approached by a path past the church (which contains Sidney monuments), is of various dates, but the characteristic feature is the fine hall of c. 1340–50, 64 ft long, with its open timber roof, 'Kentish' tracery, and central hearth. Penshurst has been in the possession of the Sidneys since 1552, and the most interesting of its contents are probably the portraits of that distinguished family, including those of Sir Philip Sidney (born here in 1554) and Algernon Sidney (1663); in the armoury are personal relics of Sir Philip, and of Lord Gort, V.C., father of the late Lady De L'Isle. Ben Jonson was the first of many visiting poets who have praised the charms and the hospitality of Penshurst. An avenue in the beautiful park is named 'Sacharissa's Walk' from Lady Dorothy Sidney (d. 1684), the 'Sacharissa' of Waller.

36 m. *Bidborough*, a pleasant village with a well-positioned church.— 38½ m. **Tonbridge** (Rte 6B).

B Viâ Sevenoaks

ROAD, 62 m. (A 21).— 10 m. *Bromley*.— 24 m. **Sevenoaks**.— 30 m. **Tonbridge** (both by-passed to the w.).— 55 m. *Battle*.— 62 m. **Hastings**.

RAILWAY, 62½ m. from *Charing Cross, London Bridge*, and *Cannon St*. in 1¼–1¾ hr; to *Tunbridge Wells*, 34½ m. in 50 min. Principal Stations: To (29½ m.) *Tonbridge*, see Rte 5.— 34½ m. **Tunbridge Wells**.—49¼ m. *Robertsbridge*.— 55½ m. *Battle*.— 61¾ m. **St. Leonards**.— 62½ m. **Hastings**.

We quit London by the Old Kent Road for New Cross and (4 m.) *Lewisham*. (From Lewisham to Badger's Mount there is a quicker alternative by A 20, A 224, viâ Orpington.) Here A 21 diverges on the right for (10 m.) *Bromley*.— 15 m. By-road (r.) for (3 m.) *Downe*.

The road, through pleasant country (footpaths), passes High Elms golf course. Half a mile s. of Downe is the Georgian *Down House* (adm. daily except Mon & Fri; fee), the family home of Darwin. It contains many of his possessions and works, and also paintings by Stubbs and Wright of Derby.

The road climbs the N. Downs to Badger's Mount and then descends into the Darent valley. At 20 m. it branches r. to by-pass Sevenoaks and Tonbridge, but we continue on A 2028.

B 2211 (r.) skirts *Chevening Park* (no adm.; being restored 1971), a mid-17C house by Inigo Jones (altered in 18C). In the fine wooded park is a lake where the inventive 3rd Earl Stanhope (d. 1816) launched 'the first little craft ever propelled by steam', and here his daughter, the eccentric Lady Hester Stanhope (1776–1839), was born.

22 m. *Riverhead*, with some pleasant 18C houses. Here A 25 diverges left.

At (2 m.) *Seal* (on A 25), the interesting church with a 16C tower, has a brass of 1395, and a bronze sculpture of a child (1908).— 6 m. *Ightham* (Ightham Mote, p. 64), whence we may reach (13½ m.) Tonbridge by A 227.

24 m. **Sevenoaks** (Hotels), a pleasant town of 18,200 inhab., has a large *School*, founded in 1432 (George Grote, the historian, was a pupil in 1800–4). The *Vine* is said to be the oldest cricket-ground in England, and William Pett (1710–86), the earliest known maker of cricket bats, lived at Sevenoaks. The High St. (s. end of the town) has some fine 17C houses, and a church with 13C nave arcades and a Perp. chancel (monuments). Donne was the pluralist rector in 1616–31.—*Solefields* (½ m. s.) is the site of the signal defeat of the Royalist troops by Jack Cade in 1450.

Entered from the top of the town is *Knole*, the seat of the Sackville family, one of the finest and largest baronial mansions in England, presented to the Nat. Trust in 1946. Partly built by Abp. Thomas Bourchier (d. 1486), the house belonged to the Archbishops of Canterbury until Cranmer resigned it to Henry VIII. Elizabeth I presented it to her cousin, Sir Thomas Sackville, in 1603. In its present form the house dates mainly from the time of James I and Charles I, and its internal fittings and furniture are practically unchanged. The house is shown on Wed, Thurs, Fri, Sat & BH., 10–12, 2–3.30 or 5; closed Dec–Feb. The rooms shown include the Great Hall (potraits by Van Dyck, etc.); the Great Staircase (c. 1604–8); the Brown Gallery (early English furniture and historical portraits); Lady Betty Germain's Rooms (English carpets); the Spangle Bedroom (17C Brussels tapestries); the Billiard Room (Charles I table); the Venetian Bedroom; the Leicester Gallery. The next three rooms have fine plasterwork ceilings, c. 1600. The Ball Room (portraits of the Sackvilles by Gainsborough, Van Dyck, Kneller, etc.); the Crimson Drawing Room (portraits by Reynolds); the Cartoon Gallery; the King's Bedroom, fitted up for James I, with magnificent Carolean silver furniture.— The finely wooded *Park* of c. 1000 acres (open to the public daily), commands a famous view of the Weald of Kent.

A 225 continues s. to rejoin A 21 just E. of *Sevenoaks Weald.* At the Long Barn here, Caxton is reputed to have been born and here in 1927 Virginia Woolf started 'Orlando' and Roy Campbell wrote 'The Georgiad'.

30 m. **Tonbridge** (Hotels) is a market town (31,000 inhab.) on the Medway. Among its ancient but fast disappearing timbered buildings are *Chequers Inn* (15C) and the portreeve's house (16C). The remains of the Norman *Castle* (adm. daily; fee), built by Richard de Clare, a kinsman of William the Conqueror, and enlarged in the 13C, stand above the river. *Tonbridge School* was founded in 1553 by Sir Andrew Judd, who placed it under the protection of the Skinners' Company of London. The Rev. George Austen, father of Jane, was a master here, and Adm. Sir Sidney Smith and Sir Herbert Baker are famous pupils.— *Tudeley* church, with stained-glass windows by Marc Chagall, lies c. 3 m. E.

The Hasting road turns l. in Tonbridge and, rejoined by the by-pass, ascends to (35 m.) *Pembury*.— 37 m. By-road leads (l.) for *Matfield* (1½ m.), with a fine group of houses (1728) on the green.

At 39 m., A 262 diverges left for Goudhurst and Tenterden.— 3 m. *Goudhurst* (Hotels), is a high-lying village with fine views and a church containing Colepeper monuments (1537) in coloured wood. *Finchcocks* (adm. July–Aug; Fri–Sun & BH, 2–6; fee) has a collection of keyboard instruments. Concerts are held here in the autumn. 1½ m. N.W., in an area famous for oaks, is *Horsmonden* church (early 14C), with a fine brass of 1340. *Pattyndenne Manor* (1470), a timber-framed house, is open Sun 2–5, May–Oct. *Bedgebury Pinetum* (2½ m. s.) belongs to the Royal Botanic Gardens (open daily).—At (8½ m.) *Wilsley Pound,* a road leads s. for (1 m.) **Cranbrook** (Hotels) with a steep High St., and the largest working windmill in England (1814). The grammar school, founded in 1576, was the birthplace of Phineas Fletcher (d. 1650); the present buildings are 18–20C. The Perp. church has some 16C stained glass, and wooden bosses (c. 1300) on the w. wall.— 10 m. (l.) *Sissinghurst Castle* (N.T.), a fragment of a Tudor mansion, where Gibbon once served as an officer in charge of French prisoners. Richard Church (1893–1972), poet and novelist, lived in the grounds. The charming gardens created by Victoria Sackville-West and Harold Nicolson, are open daily, April–mid-Oct.— 13½ m. *Biddenden,* where we join A 274 from Maidstone, see p. 65.

40 m. *Lamberhurst*, once the centre of the Wealden iron-smelting industry. 1½ m. w. is *Bayham Abbey* (no adm.), a ruined 13C Premonstratensian house.—A 21 continues s.e. passing (l.) *Scotney Castle*, beautifully landscaped, a 14C foundation with 17C additions (N.T.; adm. April–Oct, Wed–Sun & BH., 2–6; fee).—At (45 m.) *Flimwell*, we enter Sussex. About 3 m. E. on A 268 is *Hawkhurst* (Hotels), where William Penn once owned the ironworks; the good late-Dec. church, in the old village to the s., has been kindly treated in successive restorations.—48 m. *Hurst Green*.

A 265 leads s.w. past *Haremere Hall* (17C; l.; adm. BH weekends, 2.30–5.30), pleasantly sited on the steep hillside, to (2 m.) *Etchingham*, with a Dec. church with fine window tracery and fragments of the original stained glass. It also contains good stalls and a screen, and brasses.—6 m. *Burwash* has a pleasant High St., and a church with a Norman tower. *Batemans* (N.T.; adm. March–Oct; Mon–Thurs, 2–6; also 11–12.30 in June–Sept; Sat & Sun, 2–6; fee), a 17C ironmaster's house, was the home of Rudyard Kipling (d. 1936). Exhibits include his Nobel Prize citation (1907), the first time the award for literature was won by an Englishman. The surrounding country, with low undulating hills, is the scene of 'Puck of Pook's Hill'. At *Brightling*, 2 m. s. is the pyramid tomb of Mad Jack Fuller (d. 1834).

Between Hurst Green and (50 m.) *Robertsbridge* (known for its cricket bats), a by-road leads E. for Bodiam (3½ m.) in the Rother valley.

Near the bridge is *Bodiam Castle (N.T.; adm. April–Sept daily, Oct–March, weekdays only). This fine fortress, built by Sir Edw. Dalyngruge in 1386, and dismantled in the Civil War, though now a mere shell, is still surrounded by a wide moat filled with water-lilies. The great gateway, on the N. side, is flanked by machicolated turrets. The outer portcullis is still visible, and beyond are grooves for two more. The castle was carefully restored by Lord Curzon in 1925.—*Salehurst*, ½ m. E. of Robertsbridge, has a 13–14C church with a contemporary font and fragments of stained glass with birds.

At John's Cross we take the right fork (B 244) which leads due s. —55 m. **Battle** (Hotels), a pleasant small town, takes its name from the Battle of Hastings (1066), which was fought S.E. of the town. The fine *Church* (12–15C) has interesting pier capitals and fragments of 15C stained glass. There is also the handsome tomb of Sir Anthony Browne (see below) and his wife, a few brasses, and a memorial to Edmund Cartwright (1743–1823), inventor of the power-loom, who died at Hastings and is buried here. The incumbent enjoys the title 'Dean of Battle'. *Battle Abbey (of which the Abbot's Lodging is now a school) is approached through the gatehouse that dominates the Market Square.

BATTLE ABBEY was founded by William the Conqueror in fulfilment of a vow made before the fateful battle; it occupies the spot where Harold erected his royal standard and afterwards fell. The abbey was colonized by Benedictines from Marmoutier, near Tours, and the church was consecrated to St Martin in 1094. At the Dissolution (1539), the richly endowed abbey was given by Henry VIII to Sir Anthony Browne, Master of the Horse, who destroyed the church. The grounds and ruins are open to visitors daily, 10–4 or 6 (fee).
The imposing *Gatehouse (1339) is battlemented and turreted with Dec. arcading; the E. wing is 16C. In front as we enter are the inhabited parts of the abbey, including the *Abbot's Lodge* (no adm.) remodelled by Browne, and two towers (1540), all that remains of *Princess Elizabeth's Lodgings.* We follow the path to the left. The *Abbey Church*, 224 ft long, has practically disappeared, save for part of the undercroft of the 14C eastern extension, which had five chapels. The high altar was erected on the spot where Harold's body was found. The most impressive remains are those of the *Dormitory*, to the s. of the church, with its fine s. wall and lancet windows. The undercroft remains intact, with three beautiful E.E. vaulted chambers. The lower floor formed the E. side of the *Cloister*; the arcading of the w. side with Perp. tracery is incorporated into the School house (abbot's lodge). Scant remains of the *Parlour* may be seen adjoining the Dormitory to the N. Beyond these to the right, we reach a broad walk commanding a view of the battlefield, including the heights of Senlac and of *Telham* (across the valley), where the Normans encamped the night before the battle. Above the barrel-vaulted monastic cellars, which may be visited, Browne built a guest house, two turrets of which alone survive.—The famous 'Roll of Battle Abbey' was probably not meant to be a list of the individual Norman nobles who came over with the Conqueror but merely to enumerate the family surnames. It seems to have been compiled in the 14C and certainly contained many names of later settlement. The original document was probably burned at Cowdray in 1793.—At *Sedlescombe*, an attractive village 2 m. N.E., was founded, in 1960, a 'Pestalozzi Village' for refugee children. *Ashburnham* church (1665), 3 m. w. of Battle, contains interesting tombs and ironwork from a local industry that flourished until 1825. The Place, for c. 800 years until 1935 the home of the Ashburnham family, is now a Church of England College.

62¼ m. **HASTINGS** and the contiguous **St Leonards** (on the w.), well-found and comfortable sea-bathing resorts with a genial winter climate, form together a county borough (72,200 inhab.), which extends some way up the hills behind its sea-front of 3 m., with the ruined castle as a picturesque feature. Hastings is one of the Cinque Ports, and though its harbour has almost disappeared before the encroaching sea the *Old Town* is unusually well preserved. The Battle of Hastings (14 Oct 1066) was fought c. 10 m. N.W. In 1870 the Marine Hotel was the first refuge of Empress Eugénie and the Prince Imperial on their flight from France.

Railway Stations. *Hastings Central*, at the end of Havelock Rd.; *St Leonards Warrior Sq.*, at the end of King's Rd.; *West St Leonards*, at the w. end of the double town; *Ore*, 1 m. N.E., terminus of the electric line.

Hotels mainly on the sea-front.

Post Offices in Cambridge Rd., Hastings, and in London Rd., St Leonards.—INFORMATION BUREAU, 15 Wellington Place.

Buses from the Coach Station, Queen's Rd. to all destinations and in summer observation buses on the Circular Route, with good views from the ridge behind the twin towns (9 m. in ¾ hr).

Amusements. *White Rock* and *Pier Pavilions* (concerts, dancing, plays, etc.); *Stables Theatre*, the Bourne. Music Festival in March.—*Lawn Tennis* (tournaments in Aug) and *Bowls* are well provided for.—*White Rock Baths*, Hastings, with sauna and swimming baths; *Bathing Pool*, with squash courts, etc., at West Marina, St Leonards.

The sea-front from the w. end of Hastings to St Leonards, with substantial residences, public buildings and hotels, affords an interesting picture of 19C development. East of Harold Place is Pelham Crescent (1824) by Joseph Kay. West of Queen's Hotel is the crowded pier and White Rock Pavilion. St Leonards was laid out by James and Decimus Burton (1828–34). The Royal Victoria Hotel forms the centre of the composition which extends inland. In Hastings, Queen's Rd. leads N. to the pleasantly wooded *Alexandra Park* (100 acres), while Cambridge Rd., passing White Rock Gardens, leads to the *Museum and Art Gallery* (open daily; Sun, 3–5), with collections of Wealden pottery and Sussex ironwork and an Indian pavilion of 1886. Castle Hill Rd. (near the early 19C Wellington Sq.) climbs to the *West Hill* (also lift from George St.), on which stand the scanty ruins of the *Castle* (adm. daily; fee), possibly founded by William the Conqueror. *St Clement's Caves* (adm. daily, Sun from 2; fee), excavated on the E. slope of West Hill, are said to have been used by smugglers.

The E. end of Hastings, the old fishing-town, between the W. Hill and the E. Hill, retains its narrow streets and ancient houses though less and less of its old atmosphere. Here are the tall black storing-shreds for nets, a unique survival, and the '*Fishermen's Church*', now a fishing museum. The *East Hill* (250 ft; lift from Rock-a-Nore Rd.; fee), on which are traces of old earthworks, commands a good view, including (in clear weather) the coast of Picardy. The Perp. church of *St Clement*, near the s. end of High St., contains two brasses (1563 and 1601) and was the scene of the marriage of D. G. Rossetti (1860). Near by is the *Old Town Hall*, now a museum of local history (adm. daily in summer). At the other end of the attractive High St., with many fine houses, is the Rom. Cath. church of *St Mary Star of the Sea*, built mainly by the poet Coventry Patmore. Beyond are the old *Stables* (now a theatre) of c. 1700. To the E. is *All Saints'*, another Perp. church, at which Titus Oates (baptized here in 1660) was for a short time curate under his father (rector 1660–90). All Saints' St. contains more fine houses: No.

125 was frequently visited by Sir Cloudesley Shovel and Garrick often stayed in a house at the sea end.

The most attractive short walk from Hastings is that from the East Hill along the cliffs to (¾ m.) *Ecclesbourne Glen* and (1¾ m.) *Fairlight Glen*, where the cliffs rise to a height of 400 ft and the luxuriant trees descend almost to the sea. Beyond the head of the glen, ½ m. from the sea, we may join the road and return to (2¼ m.) Hastings viâ the suburb of *Ore*, high up on St Helen's Down.

FROM HASTINGS TO TENTERDEN, 21 m. A 28 leads N. to (5 m.) *Westfield*, with a Norman church. The road descends to cross the wide open valley of the Brede, and then climbs to (7 m.) *Brede*, where the church contains the well-carved tomb of Sir Goddard Oxenbridge (1537).— 12 m. *Northiam*, with weather-boarded houses, has a church with a fine Perp. spire and elegant piers carrying E.E. nave arcades. *Great Dixter*, ¾ m. N.W. (adm. April–Oct daily, exc. Mon; fee) is a 15C half-timbered house restored and with additions (and garden) by Lutyens (1910). We cross the Rother valley into Kent.— At (14 m.) *Newenden* the tiny church contains a carved late-Norman font. The road skirts the grounds of *Great Maytham Hall* (by Lutyens, 1909; adm. May–Sept, Wed & Thurs 2–4; fee) into (17 m.) *Rolvenden*, with a fine 14C church. To the w., beyond a windmill, is (2½ m.) *Benenden*, with a famous girls' public school, built in an Elizabethan style in 1859.— 21 m. *Tenterden*, p. 65.

FROM HASTINGS TO EASTBOURNE, 17 m. (A 259); railway, 16 m. in 30–40 min. The coast is lined with Martello towers.— 5 m. **Bexhill** (Hotels), a seaside resort (32,800 inhab.) with an esplanade and good public park, the De La Warr pavilion (1935), and a golf course. The church of *St Peter* at Old Bexhill dates back to 1070 and contains a unique Saxon tombstone. The *Manor House* was once a residence of the Bps. of Chichester. J. L. Baird (1888–1946), the pioneer of television, lived at No. 1 Station Rd. (plaque) from 1941.— 12½ m. *Pevensey* (Hotels), on Pevensey Bay, the landing-place of William the Conqueror in 1066. Beyond the E.E. church is ***Pevensey Castle** (adm. daily, Sun from 2; fee), a Norman castle, consisting of a keep begun c. 1080 and a gatehouse and inner bailey added in the 13C. It stands in the S.E. angle of an enclosure of about ten acres, surrounded by a Roman wall, strengthened by round towers and still at places 20 ft high. This was the Roman *Anderida*, one of the great fortresses of the 'Saxon Shore', which was taken in 491 by the Saxons, who "slew all that dwelt therein, nor was there one Briton left." The *Old Minthouse* (14C) opposite merits a visit.

FROM HASTINGS TO WINCHELSEA, RYE, AND FOLKESTONE, 37 m. (A 259). The road ascends N.E. through Ore.— 7¼ m. *Icklesham* has a fine Norman *Church with 14C chancel.

8 m. **Winchelsea** (Hotel) the smaller of the two 'Ancient Towns' added to the Cinque Ports (possibly by the Conqueror himself), lies on a knoll rising over the marshes and the river Brede. The original town and harbour were destroyed by the encroachments of the sea, and this 'new' Winchelsea was founded by Edward I in 1283, and rebuilt on the regular lines of a French 'bastide'. It has long since sunk to the dimensions of a village, but still retains edifices that "plead haughtily for honours gone". It is the opening scene of Thackeray's 'Denis Duval'.

The *Church, dedicated to St Thomas Becket and occupying one of the 'squares' laid out by Edward I, is the most important Dec. building in Sussex (begun c. 1300), though the nave has vanished or was never built. It contains beautiful sedilia and some very fine tombs of the Alards, 'England's first admirals' (14C). Part of the window-tracery is of the so-called 'Kentish' pattern. The modern glass is by Douglas Strachan (1928–33). The old *Court Hall*, opposite, contains a local museum (adm. daily Whitsun–Sept). Of the wall that once surrounded Winchelsea, *Strand Gate* is at the beginning of the road to Rye, and *Pipe Well*, or *Land Gate*, is to the N.W., while *New Gate* is now some distance s. of the village.

11 m. **Rye** (Hotels), the companion 'Ancient Town' of Winchelsea, stands also on an isolated hill, looking across the salt-marshes towards its neighbour, and its quiet cobbled streets retain many attractive houses of the 15–18C.

Like Winchelsea, it has lost most of its former importance through the alteration of the coast, but it keeps part of its trade and is in summer frequented by many golfing and other visitors. The Rye potteries are well known. The town was twice burned down by the French (1377 and 1448), and many of its inhabitants still bear the names of the Huguenot fugitives who took refuge here. John Fletcher, the dramatist, was born here in 1579 in a house in Lion St., now a tea-shop.

The approach at the N. end of the town is through *Land Gate*, the last of three in the wall erected by Edward III. On top of the hill is *St Mary's*, a Norman and E.E. church with Dec. and Perp. windows and good flying buttresses. The mahogany altar-table is alleged (wrongly) to have been made with wood from the Armada. The pendulum of the great clock (probably the oldest in England still at work with its original mechanism, 1561–2) swings inside the church. The w. window commemorates Abp. Benson (1829–96). No. 40 Church Sq., a small building of c. 1263, was a house of the *Friars of the Sack*, and to the s.E. is the turreted *Ypres Tower* (locally pronounced 'Wipers', a form made familiar by British soldiers in Flanders), built c. 1250 by Peter of Savoy and sold in 1430 to one John de Ypres. *Flushing Inn*, in a square N. of the church, has an interesting cellar and 16C mural painting. *Lamb House* (N.T.; adm. April–Oct, Wed & Sat 2–6), in West St., facing the w. end of St Mary's, was from 1898 to 1916 the home of Henry James (1843–1916) and afterwards of E. F. Benson. In the romantic Mermaid St., which leads off West St., is the early 16C *Mermaid Hotel*. In High St. is *Peacocke's School* building (1636), where Thackeray's 'Denis Duval' was a pupil. The *Monastery* in Conduit Hill, off High St., was originally part of a late-Dec. Augustinian Friary. At the *Rye Art Gallery* in East St. local exhibitions are held.

Rye Harbour, 1½ m. s., is now a quiet fishing port at the mouth of the Rother. Across the river towards *Camber* is the famous *Rye Golf Course*. At the beginning of the harbour road a footpath leads over the marshes to *Camber Castle*, one of Henry VIII's coast defences.

Beyond Rye, A 259 crosses the fertile pastures of Romney Marsh and enters Kent.—18 m. *Brookland* church has a detached pyramidal boarded steeple and Norman lead *Font. At 19 m., B 2080 leads l. for *Appledore* (4 m.), which has a good 14C church.—21 m. *Old Romney* has an un-restored 13C church with later additions.

About 3 m. s. (r.) is *Lydd* (Hotel), with the 'cathedral of Romney Marsh' (E.E. and Dec.); the chancel was destroyed by German bombs. The Perp. tower is particularly fine, with good vaulting. The interior incorporates remains of a Saxon church. The explosive lyddite takes its name from its development at the experimental ranges here. *Ferryfield Airport* is c. 1 m. E. of Lydd. A road goes on over the shingle flats to (3 m.) *Dungeness* (½ m. r.) on a bleak promontory with rough seas and good deep-sea fishing. It has two lighthouses, the new one begun in 1959 (130 ft high), and a huge nuclear power station. We may return along the coast through the week-end resorts of (6 m.) *Greatstone* and (7 m.) *Littlestone-on-Sea* (Hotel), with a golf course, rejoining the main road at (8 m.) New Romney.

23 m. **New Romney** (Hotels), one of the original Cinque Ports though its harbour was destroyed by a storm in the 13C, has a beautiful Norman and E.E. church with a memorial to E. Nesbit (1858–1924), the children's novelist, who died at Jesson, near here, and is buried at St Mary in the Marsh, 1¾ m. N. A celebrated miniature steam railway runs to Hythe and Dymchurch.—27 m. *Dymchurch*, a week-end resort, has a sea-wall 3 m. long protecting the marshes, heavily fortified in 1940. Here are two restored Martello towers, one of which has been turned into a Museum (adm. daily; fee). It is the 24th of 74 which originally extended along the coast from Folkestone to Seaford; only 27 now remain intact. They were built in 1803–8 to counter the threat of invasion by Napoleon. —32 m. *Hythe*, and thence to *Folkestone*, see Rte 5.

7 LONDON TO EASTBOURNE

A Viâ Tunbridge Wells

ROAD, 67½ m., longer but more attractive than the main road. To (30 m.)
Tonbridge, see Rte 6B.—A 26. 36 m. **Tunbridge Wells.**—A 267. 45 m. *Mayfield.*—
58 m. A 22.—63 m. *Polegate.*—67½ m. **Eastbourne.**

RAILWAY to *Tunbridge Wells*, see Rte 6; to *Eastbourne*, see Rte. 7B.

From London to (30 m.) *Tonbridge*, see Rte 6. A 26 keeps straight
on beyond the station.—32½ m. B 2176 leads r. for Penshurst, p. 73.
33½ m. *Southborough* (Hotel), with a pleasant common. *Speldhurst*, 2 m.
w., has fine windows by Burne-Jones and William Morris in its church.

36 m. **Tunbridge Wells** (c. 400 ft), an old-established inland health-
resort (44,500 inhab.), officially designated 'Royal' by Edward VII, lies
in an attractive hilly and moorland district where Kent and Sussex meet.

Railway Stations (¾ m. apart). *Central*, Mt. Pleasant, for Hastings, and London
viâ Sevenoaks; *West*, Eridge Road, for Brighton, and London viâ Oxted.

Many **Hotels** in pleasant positions facing the Common.

Post Office, Vale Rd., below the Central Station.—INFORMATION BUREAU, Assembly
Hall, Crescent Road.

Buses from Mount Pleasant to *Tonbridge, Penshurst, Mayfield, Crowborough,
Sevenoaks, Ightham, Uckfield*, etc.

Amusements. *Assembly Hall Theatre*, Crescent Rd.—Two *Golf Courses* (18 and
9 holes).—*Tennis Courts* in the Calverley Grounds, etc.; annual tournament in
July.—*Cricket Week* in June.

The mild chalybeate waters of Tunbridge Wells were first brought into notice
by Dudley, Lord North, in 1606, and after the Restoration they enjoyed a great
vogue, of which reflections may be found in the pages of Macaulay, Thackeray,
Meredith, and others. Local names such as Mount Sion, Mount Ephraim, and
perhaps Calverley (Calvary?), suggest a Puritanical strain in the patrons of the
place, and Tunbridge Wells long had the reputation of being pre-eminently the
watering-place of the serious-minded. 'Tunbridge Ware' is a kind of wood-mosaic,
produced from the 17C (originally at Tonbridge) to 1934.

At the town centre is an imposing group of buildings (1939), including
the *Town Hall, Assembly Hall*, and *Library* with the Museum (weekdays
10–5.50), illustrating local history; but the chief centre of interest is the
Pantiles, a short promenade first laid out in 1638 and named from the
original nature of its paving. On one side is a colonnade, and some fine
houses were added in the 18C and 19C. A recent development to the s.
blends well with the curve of the shop façades. At the Springs at the
N.E. end mineral water may be taken. Opposite the N. entrance to the
Pantiles is the church of *King Charles the Martyr* (1684) with a contemporary plaster ceiling. The Calverley estate was laid out by Decimus
Burton in 1828–52. To the w. and N. stretches the *Common* (170 acres),
with its gorse and bracken.

Short walks may be taken to *Rusthall Common*, 1 m. N.W., with the fantastic
Toad Rock; to the *High Rocks*, 1½ m. s.w., a group of curious sandstone rocks, and
thence by path near the Medway to the pretty village of (3½ m.) *Groombridge*, with
a chapel of 1625. The charming moated *Groombridge Place* (mid-17C; footpath
through the park) lies to the left of the road. ¾ m. N.W. is *Burrswood*, by Decimus
Burton (1831–38), now the Dorothy Kerin Home of Healing.

FROM TUNBRIDGE WELLS TO LEWES, 22 m. (A 26).—3 m. (l.) *Eridge Park* (Marquess of Abergavenny).—7 m. *Crowborough* (Hotels and Restaurant), a breezy
golfing resort, has an 18C church and vicarage. Sir Arthur Conan Doyle (1859–
1930) died here at the house called Windlesham, and Richard Jefferies lived at

Downs Cottage.—14 m. *Uckfield*, where we join A 22 (see Rte 7B), and continue into (22 m.) *Lewes*.

FROM TUNBRIDGE WELLS TO EAST GRINSTEAD, 15 m. (A 264).—4½ m. *Groom-bridge*, see above.—7 m. *Withyham* church has monuments of the Sackville family, including a fine *Tomb by C. G. Cibber (1677). To the s. are *Old Buckhurst*, the former seat of the Sackvilles (now flats), and *Duckings*, a fine timbered farmhouse. —12½ m. *Forest Row* and thence to *East Grinstead*, see Rte 7B.

A 267 ascends to the Weald, passing into Sussex.—45 m. **Mayfield,** a pleasant village with the fine Middle House hotel (1575), stands on high ground. Remains of the 14C *Old Palace* of the Abps. of Canterbury (adm. by appointment), form part of a convent school. It was the favourite archiepiscopal residence from the time of St Dunstan (d. 988) of whom some relics are shown. The medieval *Hall, carefully restored as a chapel by E. W. Pugin in 1863–66, has three huge stone arches on exquisite carved corbels, carrying a timber roof. The chapel contains a 14C crucifixion, a Madonna (c. 1460), and the decorated back to the original Archbishop's throne. *St Dunstan's Church* (13–15C) contains some iron tomb-slabs from local foundries in its pavement.—50 m. *Cross-in-Hand* is 1½ m. w. of *Heathfield*, an untidy village with the cenotaph (in the church) of Lord Heathfield (d. 1790), defender of Gibraltar. A pillar in the neighbouring hamlet of *Cade Street* marks the spot where Jack Cade was mortally wounded by Alexander Iden, sheriff of Kent, in 1450.—At 58 m. we join the A 22.

A 271 leads E. to (4 m.) *Herstmonceux* (Hotel at *Boreham Street*, 1½ m. E.), famous for its 'trugs' or wooden garden-baskets. *Herstmonceux Castle* (c. 1½ m. s.; adm. to park only, in summer), is a fortified and moated brick mansion of 1440, with a fine s. gatehouse, now restored and fitted up to accommodate the Royal Observatory transferred in 1948–49 from Greenwich. Well-placed within the park are six domes (1958) for telescopes. The 98 ft telescope, erected in 1965, is the largest in Europe. Opposite the entrance gate is a 12–13C church with a magnificent late 15C monument and fine brass of Wm. Fiennes (d. 1402).

We cross the Cuckmere, which 2 m. s.w. forms the moat of *Michelham Priory* (owned by the Sussex Archaeological Trust; adm. daily April–Oct; fee), the attractive remains of an Augustinian house founded in 1229. Of the 13C, the vaulted buttery, the lavatory arches (on the cloister wall), and the rebuilt refectory remain; the gate-tower by the wide moat dates from 1405. The Tudor wing, built by Herbert Pelham after 1587, contains interesting old furniture.

63 m. *Polegate* stands at the crossing of the A 27 and the railway from Hastings to Lewes. Pevensey Castle, p. 78, is 4½ m. E.—65 m. *Willingdon* (by-pass) has a 13C church with monuments and brasses.

67½ m. **EASTBOURNE**, a county borough with 166,000 inhab., is a prosperous and attractive seaside resort, sheltered by the South Downs and Beachy Head. The sea-front is 2½ m. long.

Many Hotels (prices reduced in winter).
Post Office, Upperton Rd., near the station.—INFORMATION BUREAU, 3 Cornfield Terrace.
Buses from Pevensey Rd. to all destinations; from Royal Parade to *Beachy Head.*
Amusements. Devonshire Park, with *Congress Theatre* (1963), *Winter Garden Pavilion* (excellent concerts, etc.), *Swimming and Sauna Baths, Tennis,* etc.; *Pier Pavilion*; *Redoubt* (open-air shows).—GOLF COURSES, to the N.W. of Compton Place; on the road to Willingdon; and on the Downs above the old town.—*County Cricket Ground* at The Saffrons, facing the Town Hall. Cricket Week in August.

Lewis Carroll spent summer vacations regularly at No. 7 Lushington Rd.; Sir C. Sherrington (1857–1952), the physiologist, died here.

The PARADE or ESPLANADE skirts the sea-front in terraces at different levels. Eastwards it extends past the *Pier* to (¾ m.) the *Redoubt*, once an anti-invasion fort, now accommodating a model village. Westwards it leads to (1½ m.) *Holywell*, with tea-gardens, near the foot of Beachy Head, passing the *Wish Tower* (1804), a restored Martello tower (the 73rd of 74) with a small museum (June–Sept, daily). It also has a garden, 'sun-lounge', and café. Just inland from this point is *Devonshire Park* (13 acres; see above), famous for its lawn-tennis tournaments (Sept), and near by is *Eastbourne College*, a well-known boys' school. In the old village, ½ m. farther inland, are the 18C *Manor House*, now containing the *Towner Art Gallery*, with a good collection of Sussex pictures (adm. weekdays 10–5 or 6, Sun from 2), and *St Mary*, a Trans. church with Dec. windows and Perp. tower. Beneath the 16C *Lamb Inn*, opposite, is an E.E. vaulted chamber. *Compton Place* (1726–27) by Colen Campbell, now a school, but until 1954 a seat of the Dukes of Devonshire, to whom Eastbourne owes much of its development, lies between the old and new towns. Fully 3 m. s.w. of the pier by the zigzag Duke's Drive (beginning just beyond Holywell) is *Beachy Head ('Beauchef'; 575 ft), a magnificent and precipitous chalk headland, with the Beachy Head Hotel. The ruined *Belle Tout Lighthouse*, erected in 1831 about 1 m. w. and rebuilt after war damage, was superseded in 1902 by a new lighthouse at the foot of the cliff.

The walk may be continued to (¾ m.) *Birling Gap* (Hotel), where the cable from France lands, beyond which are the cliffs known as the *Seven Sisters* (632 acres; N.T.). *Eastdean* (p. 85) is 1 m. inland. The Downs to the N.W. provide fine walks; points of interest include (3 m.) *Jevington*, which has a restored church with a massive tower; and *Wannock*, 1½ m. N. of Jevington, with its glen and its old mill. See also p. 85.

B   Viâ East Grinstead and Lewes

ROAD, 70 m. A 22. 14 m. *Purley.*—31 m. **East Grinstead.**—34 m. *Forest Row.*—37 m. *Wych Cross* (junction of alternative route viâ *Uckfield.*—A 275. 52 m. Lewes (by-pass; for *Newhaven*).—A 27. 65½ m. *Polegate.*—A 22. 70 m. **Eastbourne.** Green Line Coach 708 from Victoria to *East Grinstead*.

RAILWAY, 66 m. from Victoria or London Bridge in 1½–1¾ hrs. Principal Stations: To (38 m.) *Hayward's Heath*, see Rte 8.—50 m. **Lewes** (junction for Newhaven and *Seaford.*—61¾ m. *Polegate.*—66 m. **Eastbourne.**

Quitting London by the A 23 (Rte 8), we keep straight on at the end of the Purley Way in to (14 m.) *Purley.*—We continue s. on A 22 to by-pass (19 m.; r.) *Caterham*, and leave the suburbs of London.—21 m. *Godstone*, with a 16C inn (Restaurant). We traverse the busy A 25 which leads r. for Redhill (6 m.) and l. for Westerham (6 m.).

Bletchingley (1½ m. w., Hotel), has a 12–15C church with fine corbels, and a grandiose 18C Crashaw monument; to the N. is a half-timbered farmhouse of the 15C (at *Brewer Street*) and *Pendell Court*, a gabled mansion of 1624.

To the E., A 25 passes *Tandridge* golf course to (2¾ m.) *Oxted*, a 'dormitory' town and (3½ m.) *Limpsfield*, an attractive village below a pleasant common. The church (l.) has a Norman tower and three lancet windows in the chancel. In the churchyard is the grave of Frederick Delius (1863–1935), the composer. *Detillens* (adm. Sat & BH, 2–5, May–Sept; also Wed in July–Sept; fee), a 15C hall house, has a fine collection of Orders and Decorations.

24½ m. *Blindley Heath* (Hotel).—At (27½ m.) *New Chapel* rises the 160 ft steeple of a Mormon Temple (1958). 2 m. E. is *Lingfield*, with a racecourse and a large church, rebuilt in the 15C. It contains a fine monument to Sir Reginald de Cobham and his wife (1431), brasses, and carved stalls with misericords. 2 m. N. is *Crowhurst Place* a pink-coloured moated manor-house with an attractive gatehouse on the road. Crowhurst church (1 m. farther on) is E.E. with brass and iron tomb-slabs and a wooden steeple.—Beyond (29½ m.) *Felbridge* (Hotel), we enter Sussex.—31 m. **East Grinstead** (Hotels), is a pleasant town (18,600 inhab.), with a wide High St. containing timber-built houses. *Sackville College* (adm. 2–6, April–Sept; fee) is a Jacobean almshouse of 1619.—34 m. *Forest Row* (Hotels) in *Ashdown Forest*, a beautiful region of moorland and woods (fine walks). The house of an ancient British chief (50 B.C.) was found here in 1971. The Spring Hill Wildfowl Park (1½ m. s.w.) is open daily. In the grounds of the Bush-Davies School of Ballet stands the *Adeline Genée Theatre* (1967), named after the Danish-born ballerina (1877–1970). A plaque in the R.C. church records Pres. Kennedy's attendance at Mass in 1961. On the bank of the infant Medway are the ruins of the 'Jacobean' mansion of *Brambletye* (1631). Farther w. is the large Weir Wood reservoir.

West Hoathly, 3½ m. w., is an isolated village with a 13C church and a 16C Priest's House, now a Sussex Museum (adm. April–Sept daily except Fri, Sun from 2; fee). Near by is *Gravetye Manor* (now a hotel), with a late Elizabethan s. front, famous for the garden of William Robinson (1838–1935), a pioneer of modern gardening.

At (37 m.) *Wych Cross*, in the heart of the forest, A 22 bears left, offering an alternative approach to Eastbourne viâ (45 m.) the small town of *Uckfield* with the Maiden's Head, a fine Georgian inn. Near here (1½ m. w.) is *Pilt Down*, the site of a celebrated archaeological hoax. We follow A 275 to (40 m.) *Danehill*, where a road leads (r.) to (1½ m.) *Horsted Keynes*, with a Norman church and miniature 13C effigy. The station on the Bluebell Line (see below) is farther west.—At 41½ m., the road passes close to *Sheffield Park*, the mansion of Edward Gibbon's friend, the first Earl of Sheffield. The 16C house, remodelled in 1775–78, is open Easter–Oct, Wed, Thurs, & Sun, 2–5 (fee). The *Gardens (N.T.) are open Apr–Nov, Tues–Sun, 11–5 or 7; fee.

Just beyond is *Sheffield Park Station*, a terminus of the 'Bluebell Railway', 5 m. of an otherwise abandoned line running to Horsted Keynes through charming scenery. It runs several times daily June–Sept, and BH. Also, Wed, Sat, & Sun in May & Oct, and at weekends in winter.

Gibbon (1737–94) is buried in the church of *Fletching*, 2 m. E., which contains also the Dalyngridge brass (c. 1380) and a unique brass of a glover (1450).—At 44 m. we cross the A 272. To the west lies *Chailey North Common*, once owned by Anne of Cleves (now a nature reserve), with a windmill and the Heritage Crafts School for Crippled Children.

52 m. **Lewes** (Hotels), the ancient and attractive county town (14,000 inhab.) of East Sussex, stands mostly on the w. bank of the Ouse, surrounded by the South Downs. The High St., with few blemishes, provides a comprehensive survey of English domestic architecture.

The importance of Lewes dates from William de Warenne's foundation of the castle and priory (c. 1075–88). Henry III built the town walls, but in 1264 he was defeated by Simon de Montfort at the Battle of Lewes, fought on the slope of the Downs to the w. In 1555–57, near the present Town Hall, 17 Protestants were burnt at the stake (obelisk on Cliffe Hill). John Evelyn, the diarist, attended the Gram-mar School in 1630–37. George Baxter (1805–67), inventor of the colour-printing process named after him, was a native of the town. Guy Fawkes' Day is the occasion of great bonfires and firework displays, a tradition probably antedating the event of 5 Nov 1605.

On a height near the middle of the town stands the Norman *Castle* almost blocking the pass through the Downs. The fine Edwardian barbican (1334) is well preserved but Warenne's keep (weekdays 10–5.30, Sun from 2 in Easter–Sept only; fee; *View), on its motte, with 13C additions, is a ruin. In Barbican House, at the corner of Castle Gate, is the *Museum* of the Sussex Archaeological Society (weekdays, 10–6; fee). HIGH STREET rises to the w. On the right is the round 13C tower of *St Michael's.* Tom Paine (1737–1809) lived in 1768–74 in the 15C *Bull House* (adm. by arrangement with the restaurant) opposite. The Bookshop (also 15C) stands at the top of Keere St., down which survive portions of *Town Wall.* Shelley's Hotel dates from the 16C (flagged hall). Farther up, beyond more good houses, is *St Anne's Church*, mainly 12C, with a fine Norman font.

In or off the E. part of High St. are *Pelham House* (16C; 18C façade in St Andrew's Lane), the White Hart opposite the County Hall (1812), and the *Town Hall*, notable for a staircase of c. 1590 from Slaugham (p. 87). The Market Tower (1792) is unusual. To reach the suburb of *Southover*, on the s. side of the town, we descend the steep Southover High St. beside the Crown Inn, passing *Southover Grange* (1572), the home of Evelyn. The church of *St John* preserves, in the s. chapel (key at 4 St James's St.), the leaden coffins of Wm. de Warenne (d. 1088) and his wife (also her carved tomb-slab). The so-called *Anne of Cleves House* (adm. weekdays, 10–1, 2–6; fee), farther on, bears the date 1599, and contains good Sussex ironwork.

Behind the church, and bisected by the railway, lie the extensive but rather formless ruins of the *Priory of St Pancras*, once the most important Cluniac house in Britain, founded in 1075 and systematically demolished by Thomas Cromwell in 1539. Beneath the site of the high altar the coffins of the founders (see above) were discovered in 1845. A monument in the form of a medieval helmet by Enzo Plazzotta was placed here in 1965 to mark the 700th anniversary of the Battle of Lewes. The remains are best viewed from the recreation ground in Mountfield Rd.

On the Ouse bank, 1 m. N., is *South Malling* church (1627), where John Harvard, 'founder' of Harvard University, was married in 1636. Walks may be taken on the Downs: to *Mount Harry* (640 ft), 2½ m. N.W., above the racecourse; *Cliffe Hill* (golf course); *Mount Caburn* (490 ft; with a good British fort), 2½ m. S.E.

A 265 leads N.E. to (3 m.) *Ringmer*, with a village signpost recording its association with the wives of John Harvard and Wm. Penn. **Glyndebourne** (1 m. s.) is a mansion with lovely grounds and a famous opera-house, with restaurant, much frequented in summer. 1½ m. farther s. is *Glynde*, with the 16C *Place* (open May–Sept, Thurs, Sat, & Sun; 2.15–5.30; also Easter and BH.; fee), with Rubens' original sketch for the Whitehall Banqueting House ceiling.

FROM LEWES TO NEWHAVEN, 7 m. (A 275). Beyond (1½ m.) Kingston under Lewes, we pass close to (r.) *Swanborough Manor* (with part of a 13C hall, altered in the 15C). At (3½ m.) *Rodmell* was the home (Monk's House) of Leonard and Virginia Woolf and the scene of her death in the Ouse. The 17C house is to be opened to the public. The road keeps to the w. bank of the Ouse, passing the round church towers of *Southease* and *Piddinghoe*; the railway to the E.—7 m. **Newhaven**, a small port (10,000 inhab.), at the mouth of the Ouse. The fugitive Louis-Philippe landed here in 1848 and put up at the Bridge Hotel. The 'new' haven dates from 1570, when the Ouse mouth shifted from the E. to the w. side of the valley. The apsidal 12C church, high above the town, is a relic of the medieval village of Meeching. The coastal fort of 1685 is now a holiday centre.

The boat-trains and the car-ferry road run on to Newhaven Harbour whence passenger ships ply to (4 hrs) *Dieppe*. Other trains continue past the Harbour station to (2½ m. more) Seaford.—To *Brighton*, see Rte 8.

A 259 crosses the Ouse and, leaving on the left *Bishopstone*, with its little Norman church (part-Saxon), and remains of a Saxon village and cemetery discovered in 1968, reaches (11 m.) **Seaford** (Hotels), a bathing and golfing resort (16,200 inhab.). The church has Norman portions and a remarkable capital by the s. door, and a relief (c. 1130–40) of St Michael and the Dragon. A fine cliff walk leads E. over Seaford Head to *Cuckmere Haven* (2½ m.), while the road to Alfriston (3½ m.; see below) runs viâ 'High & Over' (or Hindover; *View).—At (13¾ m.) *Exceat* the road crosses the Cuckmere valley near the charming village of *Westdean*. The church here has two bronze busts: one of Sir Oswald Birley, the painter (1880–1952) by Clare Sheridan, and one of Lord Waverley (d. 1958) by Epstein. In a retired valley just to the N. is *Charleston Manor* (gardens open Apr–Oct, daily 11–6; house, Wed by appointment only; fee), originally a Norman house, but with Tudor and Georgian additions.—A 'festival' is held in the Tithe Barn in June–July.— 16½ m. *Friston* church has a Saxon window.— 17 m. *Eastdean* (½ m. r.), where the church has a Norman tower.— 20½ m. *Eastbourne*, see Rte 7A.

From Lewes A 27 leads E., passing beneath Mount Caburn (l.; see above).—55 m. By-road (l.) for Glynde and Glyndebourne, p. 84. To the right, beyond is *Firle Place* (adm. June–Sept; Wed & Thurs, 2.15–5.30; Sun & BH., 3–6; fee), seat of the Gage family since the 16C. General Gage was Commander of British forces at the beginning of the American War of Independence. He married Margaret Kemble of Boston, Mass. It contains good paintings, including the Cowper collection from Penshanger, and some notable Sèvres china. Behind rises *Firle Beacon* (718 ft; *View), peppered with Neolithic and Bronze Age barrows, and in *West Firle* church are Gage monuments (Sir John Gage, by Gerard Johnson; 1595).—61½ m. *Berwick* church (E.E.), has wall-paintings (1942–43), including a Crucifixion by Duncan Grant.

On the Cuckmere, 2 m. s., is **Alfriston** (good Inns and Restaurant), with an interesting Perp. church. (the 'Cathedral of the Downs') and the shaft of a market-cross. The 14C timber-built parsonage was the first building acquired by the N.T. in 1896 (adm. free daily, Apr–Christmas Eve, 11–6). The 16C Star Inn has quaint carvings. *Lullington*, beyond the river, has one of the smallest churches in England (16 ft sq.; in fact the chancel of a larger edifice).

63½ m. *Wilmington* has the scanty ruins of a *Benedictine Priory* (14C; adm. daily, Sun from 2; fee. A small museum contains collections illustrating rural life). In the face of the chalk downs on our right appears the *Long Man of Wilmington*, a figure 240 ft high, with a staff in each hand. Its origin and purpose are uncertain; but its age is at least medieval.—65½ m. *Polegate*, and thence to (70 m.) **Eastbourne**, see Rte 7A.

8 LONDON TO BRIGHTON

A Viâ Redhill

ROAD, 51 m. (Motorway, see Rte 8B). More attractive than Rte 8B.—A 23. 14 m. *Purley.*— 21 m. **Redhill.**— 25 m. *Horley.* — B 2036. 37 m. *Cuckfield.* — 51 m. **Brighton.**
RAILWAY, 51 m., from *Victoria* or *London Bridge* in 1–1½ hrs. Principal Stations: 10¼ m. *East Croydon.*— 20¾ m. *Redhill.*— 27 m. *Gatwick Airport.*— 29¼ m. *Three Bridges*, junction for Crawley.— 37¾ m. **Hayward's Heath.**— 49¼ m. *Preston Park.* — 50¼ m. **Brighton.**

We quit London viâ Vauxhall Bridge Rd., Streatham High Rd., and Purley Way (Croydon by-pass).— 14 m. *Purley.*— 15¼ m. *Coulsdon.* The road on the right ascends to the still-rural village of *Chipstead* (2 m.) with a 12–13C church. The isolated church of *Chaldon* lies c. 3 m. s.e., with a large and remarkable tempera painting of the 'Ladder of Human Salvation', ascribed to c. 1200. Beyond the present motorway exchange, we traverse the *North Downs*, which separate the London basin from the wealds of Kent and Sussex.— 18¾ m. *Merstham.*

To the right lies (1½ m.) *Gatton Park*, now occupied by the Royal Alexandra and Albert School. The house and grounds are strictly private, but a drive leads to the adjoining church, which contains exquisite woodwork from Belgium, France, and Germany, a little strange in this setting. From the church path can be seen the tiny 18C town hall. Beyond the park are 2000 acres of N.T. woodland.

21 m. **Redhill** (Hotel), an important railway junction, is an eastern extension of Reigate (Rte 8b).

The road to Godstone leads e. viâ (2 m.) *Nutfield* and (3 m.) Bletchingley (p. 82). At *Outwood*, 3 m. s.e., is a windmill of 1665, and 2000 acres of N.T. property.

On approaching (25 m.) *Horley* (Hotel), we take B 2036 to the left and soon after enter Sussex and the attractive Wealden country.—27 m. *Burstow* church (1 m. e.) is part-12C, and has a memorial to John Flamsteed (d. 1719), astronomer-royal, who was rector here from 1684.—29½ m. By-road (l.) to *Worth church. This large Saxon church retains its original plan and masonry, with an imposing chancel arch and rare two-light nave windows. The font is 13C.—Beyond (33 m.) *Balcombe* we see (l.) the lofty viaduct on which the railway crosses the Ouse valley.—37 m. *Cuckfield* (Hotels) lies on the Southern Forest Ridge. In the churchyard is the tomb of Henry Kingsley (1830–76). On leaving the village, the road passes the delightful gate-house of *Cuckfield Place* (ascribed to Flynton; see p. 87), a fine mansion of c. 1574 (altered in 1848) described in Harrison Ainsworth's 'Rookwood', though the 'Rookwood' of the tale is located in Yorkshire. *Legh Manor*, 1½ m. s., is a small 16C mansion with lovely gardens and interesting furniture (adm. by appointment, April–Oct daily, except Sat & Sun).

A 272 leads e. to (2 m.) the pleasant residential town of *Hayward's Heath* Hotels). *Lindfield* (Hotel), to the n., has some fine old houses (notably Old Place) in the well-preserved village street. At *Ardingly*, 2 m. farther n., is an Anglican school, one of a group which includes also Lancing, Hurstpierpoint, Cawston, and a girls' school at Bognor Regis. *Wakehurst Place*, 1½ m. n.w. (N.T.; gardens only open daily, hours vary, but always open 2–4), is administered by the Royal Botanic Gardens, Kew. The 460-acre park, created by the first Lord Wakehurst, a President of the Royal Horticultural Society, combines great scenic beauty with botanic interest.

41 m. *Burgess Hill* and (43½ m.) *Hassocks* are growing residential towns. To the e. is *Ditchling* (2 m.), an unusual village, where Sir Frank Brangwyn (1867–1956) died.—At (44½ m.) *Clayton* we reach the South Downs; on the right rises Wolstanbury Hill (677 ft), on the left Ditchling Beacon (812 ft; *View; N.T.), and two 19C windmills. Clayton church has an 11C chancel arch and *Wall-paintings c. 1140, very well-preserved. We soon join A 23 for (51 m.) **Brighton** (Rte 8b).

B Viâ Reigate

Road, 50 m. (A 217 and A 23).—21 m. **Reigate.**—29½ m. *Crawley.*—33½ m. *Handcross.*—44½ m. *Pyecombe.*—50 m. **Brighton.**—Green Line Coach 711 from

Trafalgar Sq. to *Reigate.*—In 1979 access to the MOTORWAY (M 23) was still from the Coulsdon Road (Rte 8A), affording a faster and well-landscaped alternative by-passing Reigate/Redhill and Crawley to the E.

Crossing the Thames at Putney Bridge, we traverse Wimbledon and Morden and take the Sutton by-pass (A 217) to the right, viâ (15 m.) *Banstead.* Beyond (16 m.) *Burgh Heath* we descend Reigate Hill (*View).

21 m. **Reigate** (Motel), a pleasant town (56,000 inhab. incl. Redhill), with a *Market House* (1708), lies at the S. base of the North Downs. In the Recreation Grounds N. of High St. are the earthworks that mark the site of *Reigate Castle*, slighted by the Parliamentarians in 1648. The gateway is a Gothic erection of 1777. The curious caverns in the depths of the mound were probably nothing but sand-pits, and their association with the Magna Carta barons is quite apocryphal. Lord Howard of Effingham (1536–1624), conqueror of the Spanish Armada (1588), is buried below the chancel of the large parish church of *St Mary Magdalen*, which stands at the E. end of the town. The nave-pillars date back to c. 1200.

To the W. of the town is *Reigate Priory*, occupying the site of an Augustinian foundation of the 13C and once the seat of Lord Howard of Effingham.—*Reigate Park*, a finely wooded ridge S. of the Priory, has been given to the town.—*Reigate Hill* (700 ft) and *Colley Hill* (763 ft), 1½ m. N. and N.W. of the town (128 acres, N.T.), command an extensive *View of the Weald.—Among other points within easy reach are *Leigh Church* (pron. 'Lye'; brasses), 3½ m. S.W., and *Charlwood Church* (13–15C wall-paintings; 15C screen), 6½ m. S.—The road to (7 m.) *Dorking* leads viâ *Buckland* (rebuilt church, with an old wooden belfry) and (2½ m.) *Betchworth* (Hotel); and a fine walk leads along the ridge of the N. Downs from Reigate Hill to Box Hill.

26½ m. *Gatwick*, with London's second airport, has a spur from M 23. We are now in Sussex.—29½ m. **Crawley** (Hotels), a 'satellite' town (67,600 inhab.) retaining an old centre, is by-passed to the W. We traverse Tilgate Forest and the South Downs appear ahead.— 33½ m. *Handcross* (by-pass). To the S.E. (½ m.) are the noted gardens of *Nymans* (N.T.; adm. April–Oct, daily except Mon & Fri, 2–7; fee). At *Slaugham Manor* (Hotel and Country Club), 1 m. S.W., are the ruins of a mansion probably built for Richard Covert (d. 1579), the ironmaster, and dismantled after 1735; it is perhaps by Flynton, who carved Richard's tomb in the church.— 39 m. *Hickstead*, famous venue of international showjumping.— 40½ m. *Sayers Common* (Hotel). As we approach the South Downs we pass near *Hurstpierpoint* (1 m. l.) with a boys' school.— 44½ m. *Pyecombe* lies in a gap between Wolstanbury Hill (l.; see above) and Newtimber Hill (N.T.; 660 ft). The central chancel arch of the church is Norman, and the interesting leaden font dates from the late 12C. On the W. side of Newtimber Hill is *Poynings* (2 m.), where the 14C church is on the plan of a Greek cross; and there is another lead font at *Edburton* (2 m. farther w.). Devil's Dyke is described on p. 92.—At (47 m.) *Patcham* (by-pass) we enter the surburbs of Brighton.

50 m. **BRIGHTON,** the largest town and most widely known seaside resort (166,000 inhab.) in southern England, owes its prosperity to the residents, and still more perhaps to the crowds of temporary visitors, who are attracted by its bright and bracing air, as well as by the abundant arrangements for their comfort and amusement. The borough, whose area was more than trebled in 1929, stretches inland for 3½ m. towards the

Brighton

0	300 yards
0	300 metres

South Downs, and eastward for 3½ m., while its sea-front, from **Hove** (an independent borough with 72,700 inhab.) to beyond Rottingdean, is over 7 m. long.

Railway Stations. *Central*, at the N. end of Queen's Rd., for all trains; *Hove*, for Worthing trains; *Preston Park*, for the N. side of town; *London Road*

Hotels on or near the sea-front. YOUTH HOSTEL at *Patcham*, 3½ m. N.

Post Office, Ship St.—INFORMATION BUREAUX: Old Steine; on the sea-front between the piers; Brooker Hall, Hove.

Buses. BUS STATION at Pool Valley. Local buses run from *Old Steine* and *Pool Valley* to Central Station, sports grounds, etc. From *Old Steine* E. along the coast to *Eastbourne*, viâ *Rottingdean*, *Peacehaven*, and *Seaford*; from *Pool Valley* W. along the coast to *Littlehampton*, viâ *Hove* and *Shoreham*. Open-top summer services along the sea-front from *Hove* to *Rottingham*, viâ *Palace Pier.*—ELECTRIC RAILWAY (Volk's 1883; first electric railway in England) along the beach from Palace Pier to the Children's Playground and *Black Rock* (summer only).

Amusements. THEATRES: *Royal*, New Road; *Dome* (variety); *Palace Pier* (repertory in summer); *Gardner Centre*, Univ. of Sussex.—AQUARIUM, Marine Parade.—SWIMMING POOLS at Black Rock and Rottingdean (open-air); indoor pool, King Alfred, Hove (also sauna baths); Saltdean Lido (children's pool).—TENNIS in most parks.—GOLF on the Downs (3 courses) and at the municipal courses of Hollingbury, Waterhall, and The Dyke.—COUNTY CRICKET GROUND, Hove.—FOOTBALL (Albion) at Goldstone Ground, Hove.—RACECOURSE, White Hawk Down.—GREYHOUND STADIUM, Nevill Rd., Hove.—ICE RINK, Top Rank Centre, King's Rd.—SPORTS ARENA, Tongdean Lane, see p. 92.

History. Brighton is mentioned in Domesday Book under the name of *Brighthelmston* or *Brithelmeston*, after a more or less mythical Bishop of Selsey; and the fishing-village of Domesday seems to have remained a fishing-village for about seven centuries. The one gleam of interest in its history is that Charles II spent a night here before his escape to France in 1651. The foundation of its modern prosperity was laid in the middle of the 18C by Dr Richard Russell of Lewes, who strongly recommended its bracing air and sea-bathing (tablet on the Albion Hotel). Miss Burney, Mrs Thrale, and Dr Johnson were among the early visitors (1770); and a decisive cachet of fashion was added when George IV, then Prince of Wales, came to live here in 1784 and built the Pavilion. Since then its growth has been very rapid. It is still 'fashionable', though not exclusively so; and its modern catholicity in summer is well summarised in its sobriquet of 'London by the Sea'.

Aubrey Beardsley (1874–98; born in Buckingham Rd.) and Roger Quilter (1877–1953) were natives of Brighton; Herbert Spencer (1820–1903), who lived at 5 Percival Terrace, Kemp Town, R. S. Surtees (1803–64), Hablot K. Browne ('Phiz'; 1815–82), Thomas Hughes (1822–96), and G. J. Holyoake (1817–1906), the social reformer, died here; while the list of distinguished residents includes George Canning (1770–1827; tablet on the Royal Crescent Hotel), Harrison Ainsworth (1805–82), and Richard Jefferies (1848–87). Rowland Hill (1795–1879), the originator of penny postage, was also chairman of the Brighton Railway, and was responsible for the introduction of express and excursion services. Lewis Carroll spent his Christmas holiday for 25 years at 11 Sussex Square, Kemp Town. William Friese-Greene (1855–1921), a pioneer of the cinema, had his workshop in Middle St.; Gladstone frequently spent his holidays at the former Lion Mansion Hotel; and Metternich stayed at 42 Brunswick Terrace in 1848–49. Sir Hamilton Harty (1880–1941) died at Hove, and Sir Winston Churchill was at school at Lansworth House, Brunswick Rd., in 1883–85.—Macaulay, Thackeray, Dickens, Conan Doyle, and Graham Greene have featured Brighton in their pages.—Mrs Pipchin's infantine boarding-house was in a steep by-street, but Dr Blimber's was a mighty fine house fronting the sea.

The centre of the town is the *Old Steine* (Pl. 11; pron. 'Steen'), an open garden-space believed to take its name from the stone on which the fishermen used to dry their nets.

The **Royal Pavilion** (adm. daily; fee), begun in 1786 by Henry Holland, was rebuilt after 1817 in an Oriental style by Nash for George IV (when Prince of Wales), who frequently resided here. No. 55 on the w. side of the Steine was the residence of his wife Mrs Fitzherbert (d. 1837, and buried in St John's, Kemp Town). Queen Victoria transferred her sea-side home to Osborne in 1845, and the building was sold to the town of Brighton for about £50,000 (a small fraction of the sums lavished in its erection). Its sumptuous apartments now display much of their Regency 'Chinese' decoration, while many of the original furnishings have been recovered.

In summer (July–Sept) a special Regency exhibition is usually held, while out of season the rooms are used for concerts, etc. In 1914–18 it was used as a hospital for Indian soldiers, and, in 1922, a Memorial Gateway (s.) was erected as a mark of India's gratitude to Brighton. The *Chattri* (1921), a domed building on the Downs N.E. of *Patcham*, 3 m. N., marks the site of the burning ghât where the bodies of Sikhs and Hindus who died in the hospital were burned. The statue of George IV at the N. end of the Pavilion Gardens is by Chantrey (1828).

The former royal stables, to the N., covered with a dome (80 ft in diameter), have been converted into a theatre, known as the *Dome*.—In Church St., adjoining, is the building containing the PUBLIC LIBRARY, MUSEUM, & ART GALLERY (adm. daily, Sun from 2).

The **Museum** is interesting for its Sussex Room, illustrating the archaeology and history of Sussex, and contains the well-known Willett Collection of English pottery. The **Art Gallery**, with 18C furniture (made for Stanmer House) and silver (by Lamerie and Paul Storr), has a representative collection of British paint-ing of the 19C and early 20C, fine water-colours, and some Old Masters.

The old town between the Old Steine, West St., and North St. (the main shopping street), contains THE LANES (Pl. inset), a quarter of narrow alleys, with many antique shops. Brighton Square is a successful new addition to this pedestrian precinct. The area to the N. right up to Trafalgar St. and bounded W. and E. by Queen's Rd. and the Victoria Gardens is developing a similar character.

A broad ESPLANADE stretches the whole length of the sea-front. East of the Old Steine and Palace Pier runs Marine Parade, with attractive early 19C terraces, squares, and crescents, to (1 m.) *Kemp Town*. On the level of the beach is the wide and well-sheltered *Madeira Drive*, skirted by Volk's Electric Railway, and bordered by a covered walk ½ m. long, above which is a sheltered promenade on the cliff-side. The Drive ends at *Black Rock*, where a large marina caters for pleasure boats. An undercliff walk continues to Rottingdean and Saltdean.

The *Palace Pier* (1710 ft long) and the *West Pier* (1866), 1100 ft long are popular rendezvous. The Palace Pier replaces the *Chain Pier*, the first of its kind (1823), which stood a few yards farther E. until it was destroyed in a December storm in 1896. For many years it was the terminus of a regular cross-Channel service to Dieppe, and Queen Victoria and the Prince Consort disembarked here in 1843.

West of Palace Pier, King's Road runs to (1 m.) **Hove,** and is pro-longed to Kingsway, separated from the beach by well-kept lawns and skirting charming squares and terraces. Regency Square and Brunswick Square and Terrace are notable examples of early 19C architecture. Adelaide Crescent (1830–50) and Palmeira Square are also attractive. Hove *Museum* is in Brooker Hall, New Church Rd.

'*King Alfred*', on the front at Hove, a swimming and bathing establishment, served in 1939–45 as 'H.M.S. King Alfred', the chief war-time training centre for officers of the Royal Navy.

At the start of London Rd. (N. of Old Steine) is *St Peter's* (Pl. 7), the parish church of Brighton since 1873, a conspicuous Perp. building by

Barry (1824). The former parish church of *St Nicholas* (in Dyke Rd., reached viâ the central station and Queen's Road), was built in 1380, and largely rebuilt in 1853. The font (c. 1170) has good carvings of the Last Supper, and Baptism of Christ, and the Legend of St Nicholas. The font cover (now at w. end of N. aisle) is an elaborate memorial to the Duke of Wellington (1853). On the N. wall (E. end), near what used to be the Thrale pew, is a tablet recording that Dr Johnson used to worship here. In the churchyard (S. of chancel) lies Nicholas Tettersell, captain of the ship that bore Charles II from Shoreham in 1651 (see below). Near by (E.) is the tomb of Martha Gunn (1727–1815), most famous of Brighton 'bathing-women'.

In Preston Rd. (a continuation of London Rd.) is *Preston Park*, with beautifully laid-out gardens and Preston Manor House (1739). Here is the *Thomas-Stanford Museum* (adm. daily, Sun from 2; fee), with a collection of furniture and silver and a Sussex library. To the left, beyond, Tongdean Lane leads to the *Sports Arena*.

Dyke Road (Pl. 1) runs N.w. past (1 m.) the *Booth Bird Museum* (adm. daily), in which about 250 species are shown in surroundings illustrating their natural habitat, to (5½ m.) Devil's Dyke.

The *Devil's Dyke is a deep and narrow hollow in the Downs. The top of the dyke hill (697 ft; bus), since 1928 the property of Brighton, affords an extensive *View. The Dyke is a good starting-point for walks on the Downs. A pleasant descent may be made N.E., viâ the pretty hamlet of *Saddlescombe*, to (½ hr) Poynings (p. 87).

The road from Brighton to Lewes (9 m.), viâ (4½ m.) *Falmer*, skirts *Stanmer Park*, occupied since 1961 by the **University of Sussex**, with new buildings towards Falmer, designed by Sir Basil Spence; the Gardner Centre for the Arts holds music and drama events. The public still have access to the beautiful park (535 acres) and to part of Stanmer House, begun by Nicolas Dubois in 1772.

FROM BRIGHTON TO NEWHAVEN, 9 m. Marine Parade leads E. to Black Rock (see above), where A 259 continues, passing *Roedean*, a well-known school for girls founded in 1885, and the home and training establishment (1939) of *St Dunstan's*, primarily for blinded ex-service men.—3 m. **Rottingdean** (Hotels) lies at the mouth of a 'dean' or combe in the chalk cliffs, and still preserves its old village street. The church contains windows by Sir E. Burne-Jones (1833–98), who is buried in the churchyard, at the S.w. corner of the church. Close by is the grave of William Black (1841–98). Rudyard Kipling lived for a time at 'The Elms', and Burne-Jones at North End House. The *Grange* (adm. daily, Sun from 2) contains a good collection of toys, Sussex antiquities, and Kipling relics. *Ovingdean* (1 m. N.W.) has a church (St Wulfran) with an 11C chancel and a manor-house celebrated by Ainsworth in 'Ovingdean Grange'. The cliff road goes on to (9 m.) Newhaven viâ the villa-resorts of (4¾ m.) *Saltdean* and (6 m.) *Peacehaven*.

FROM BRIGHTON TO WORTHING, 10½ m., A 259 or A 27 (railway in 20 min.).—1 m. *Hove.*—2 m. *Portslade* and (3½ m.) *Southwick* are connected by a line of wharves. At the foot of the Downs, above Southwick, is an interesting Roman villa.—5 m. **Shoreham-by-Sea** (18,800 inhab.), still important as a port. From the small harbour Charles II escaped to Fécamp in 1651. *St Mary de Haura (i.e. of the harbour), has a fine Trans. choir with E.E. vaulting. The tower arches have unusually large capitals. Near by, in High St., is *The Marlipins*, a small 12–14C chequer-board house (now a museum; May–Oct, 10–12.30, 2–5). In Old Shoreham, 1 m. up the Adur, just below a conspicuous new bridge, is the Norman church of *St Nicholas*, with a contemporary tower, and a part-Saxon w. end. To *Horsham*, see p. 95.—We cross the Adur.—

7¼ m. *Lancing* has a partly Norman church. Lancing College, on the r., has a dominant Gothic *Chapel, begun in 1868 and completed with a huge rose-window in 1977. The 'central minster of the Woodward Foundation' (comp. p. 86), it is open daily to the public.—10½ m. *Worthing*, see Rte 9.

9 LONDON TO WORTHING

ROAD, 57 m. (A 243 and A 24).—19 m. *Leatherhead* (by-pass).—22½ m. *Burford Bridge* (Box Hill).—24 m. Dorking (by-pass).—37½ m. Horsham (by-pass).—49¼ m. *Washington*.—57 m. Worthing.

RAILWAY viâ Hove, 60 m. from Victoria or London Bridge in 80–90 min. Principal Stations: To (49½ m.) *Preston Park*, see Rte 8.—51½ m. Hove.—55¾ m. **Shoreham**.—60 m. **Worthing** (Central).—61 m. *West Worthing.*—Places between London and Horsham are served by the Arundel line (Rte 11A).—Trains from Waterloo for Box Hill (*Boxhill and Westhumble* station) and Leith Hill (*Holmwood* station).

We quit London by Putney Bridge and the Kingston by-pass, and at (14 m.) *Hook Corner* turn left on A 243.

An alternative route from London (A 24) runs viâ Morden to (15 m.) EPSOM (72,000 inhab.; Hotels), 1½ m. N.W. of *Epsom Downs*, where the 'Derby' and the 'Oaks' (instituted in 1780 and 1779) are run in May or June. The parish church contains monuments by Flaxman and Chantrey. The mineral springs that gave name to 'Epsom Salts' were discovered in 1618, but are no longer in vogue. *Durdans*, a mansion where the fifth Earl of Rosebery (1847–1929), Prime Minister and winner of the Derby, died, lies ¾ m. s., adjoining *Woodcote Park*, with the country club of the R.A.C.—At (17½ m.) *Ashtead*, where the church has a stained-glass window (c. 1500) brought from Herck in Belgium, George MacDonald died in 1905. A 24 joins our route at (19½ m.) *Leatherhead*.

On the right at (15½ m.) *Chessington* is a popular Zoo and amusement park.—19 m. **Leatherhead** (40,100 inhab.; Hotel), with a large boys' school (St John's), is on the Mole. It is one of the claimants to be the 'Highbury' of Jane Austen's 'Emma'. Anthony Hope (Sir Anthony H. Hawkins; 1863–1933) is buried in the churchyard; while the Council Offices are on the site of Kingston House, in which John Wesley preached his last sermon (23 Feb 1791).

A 246 runs hence along the N. ridge of the Downs to Guildford (11½ m.) viâ *Great Bookham*, *Effingham* (4½ m), and *East Horsley* (5½ m.; Hotel), where the church has an 11C tower and good brasses. At *Clandon Park* (8½ m.; r.) is a mansion built by Giacomo Leoni c. 1733. The magnificent interior (N.T.; adm. Apr–mid-Oct, 2–6; closed Mon & Fri; fee. Restaurant) has been redecorated (1970) by John Fowler, and contains the fine Gubbay collection of furniture and china.

21 m. *Mickleham* (l.; Restaurant) has a church in which Fanny Burney was married in 1793 and George Meredith in 1864. To the left (N.E.) is *Cherkley Manor*, where Lord Beaverbrook died (1879–1964; memorial window in church). A path leads across the Mole and through *Norbury Park*, famous for its beeches and for the yews in the 'Druids' Grove', rejoining the road near Burford Bridge. *Juniper Hall*, 1 m. S.E., now a field-study centre, was once occupied by a group of French refugees, one of whom (Gen. d'Arblay) married Fanny Burney.—22½ m. *Burford Bridge* spans the Mole at the foot of Box Hill. At the hotel, Keats finished 'Endymion' (room shown) and R. L. Stevenson stayed four times in 1878–86

*Box Hill (596 ft; view. Station 5 min. walk), including c. 900 acres of N.T. property, is a spectacular expanse of down and woodland with numerous box trees from which it takes its name. A fine walk leads along the s. face following the

Pilgrims' Way, viâ Pebble Coombe to (6 m.) Reigate; or the ridge may be followed N. across Mickleham Downs (N.T.) to (4 m.) Leatherhead.—A little above Burford Bridge is *Flint Cottage*, the home from 1867 of George Meredith (1828–1909), who is buried in Dorking Cemetery. At the top of the steep garden is the chalet built by Meredith as a study and bedroom in 1877. A later occupant of the cottage was Max Beerbohm, a refugee in the Second World War from Rapallo, and from his bombed cottage at Abinger.

24 m. **Dorking** (Hotels), an ancient market-town (22,400 inhab.), is a favourite centre for walks. It gives its name to an old-fashioned breed of five-toed fowls. The former King's Head inn in North St. is supposed to be the original of the 'Marquis of Granby' in 'Pickwick'. Ralph Vaughan Williams lived for 20 years at 'White Gates'.

On the by-pass to the E. of Dorking, is the site (now occupied by railway offices) of *Deepdene*, a once famous mansion where Disraeli wrote most of 'Coningsby'. Beyond are *Glory Woods* (r.) and the golf course (l.). A pleasant walk to the N.W. of Dorking leads over *Ranmore Common* (views) to (5 m.) *Great Bookham* viâ (3 m.) ***Polesden Lacey** (N.T.), a mansion of 1824 by Cubitt, in beautiful grounds (900 acres), bequeathed in 1942 by Mrs Ronald Greville with its collection of paintings and other works of art. The grounds are open daily, 11–dusk; the house from April–Oct, daily exc. Mon & Fri, 2–6 or dusk; also Sat & Sun in Mar & Nov; fee. Plays are staged outdoors here in July. King George VI spent part of his honeymoon in the mansion. Sheridan lived for some years in a previous house on the site.

*Leith Hill (965 ft), the highest point in S.E. England, c. 4½ m. s.w. of Dorking, commands an extensive ***View**, including (on a clear day) St Paul's in London and the Channel, with ships passing Shoreham Gap. The surrounding woods (750 acres, N.T.) are noted for bluebells and rhododendrons. It is approached by several pleasant footpaths from the Guildford road between Westcott and Wooton Hatch, or from Holmwood station. Motorists may leave Dorking by South St., and ascend to (3½ m.) *Coldharbour*, a hamlet lying at the foot of *Anstiebury Camp* (l.; no adm.), with its double trench, the finest prehistoric camp in Surrey. Beyond (4 m.) Coldharbour church, the road traverses a beautifully wooded stretch, and passes just below the conspicuous tower on the top of the hill, and a hotel. Farther on, we take the road to the right for (7½ m.) *Abinger*, with an 11C church (restored), a manor-house with a Jacobean porch, and the old stocks (on the green). About ¾ m. E. is *Friday Street*, a picturesque hamlet of red cottages faced by a large mere. 1 m. s.w. lies *Pasturewood*, opened as an educational centre in 1947 in memory of Beatrice Webb, Lady Passfield (1858–1943), and 1 m. farther on, the charming village of *Holmbury St Mary* beneath *Holmbury Hill* (857 ft). We join the A 25 to Guildford due N. of Abinger at (8½ m.) *Manor Farm*.—A pleasant walk may be taken from the summit of Leith Hill N. to (c. ½ hr) Friday Street, and thence down the w. bank of the brook to (1 m.) Wooton House, on the Guildford road.

FROM DORKING TO GUILDFORD, 12 m., A 25. We leave Dorking by West St. and beyond (1¼ m.) *Westcott* and *The Rookery* (l.), birthplace of Malthus (1766–1834), ascend to (2¾ m.) *Wotton*. To the right, below the road, we see the church in which John Evelyn (1620–1706), the diarist, is buried in the family chapel. Hard by (l.) is *Wotton House* (no adm.), Evelyn's home; parts of the surrounding fine woods date from his planting. Shortly beyond the second side road on the left (leading to Leith Hill, see above), we pass *Crossways Farm* ('Diana of the Crossways'), and (4½ m.) *Abinger Hammer*, a village named after an old iron furnace. E. M. Forster (1878–1969) lived here at West Hackhurst (no adm.), which adjoins Piney Copse ('Forster's Wood'), left to the N.T. on his death.—5 m. *Gomshall Station*. An attractive road leads s. to *Peaslake* (2½ m.; Hotel) and thence almost to the top of *Coneyhurst Hill* (844 ft), the w. summit of the Leith Hill greensand ridge. The thickly wooded ridge to the N. (*Hackhurst Downs, Netley Heath*; 270 acres N.T.) is traversed by steep and remote lanes, some of them accessible to cars.—6½ m. *Shere*, on the Tillingbourne, perhaps the prettiest village in Surrey, is by-passed by the main road, and has a well-restored church (12–15C).

The road to the left at the next fork (A 248) is an alternative route to Guildford viâ *Albury* (1½ m.) and *Chilworth* (2½ m.) to the N. of *Blackheath* (N.T.), a tract of open heathland. *Albury Park* (now flats; adm. to reception rooms May–Sept; Wed & Thurs, 2–4) contains some fine pictures. In the lovely grounds, laid out by John Evelyn, is a large Catholic Apostolic Church (or 'Cathedral'), an edifice in a Perp. style, erected in 1840 by Mr Henry Drummond, who converted the old church, with its early-Norman tower, into a mortuary chapel. A new chapel (1939), by Edward Maufe, commemorates the eighth Duke of Northumberland.— About 1 m. N. of Chilworth is *St Martha's Hill* (720 ft), with the lonely *Chapel of St Martha* (*View), on the Pilgrims' Way. The Norman fabric was largely rebuilt in 1848.

A 25 ascends to (8½ m.) *Newlands Corner* (500 ft), on the summit of the chalk ridge, affording a famous *View. Part of the Pilgrims' Way is traceable on the Downs, and to the s. appears St Martha's Chapel. The road goes on, over *Merrow Downs*, to (10 m.) *Merrow*, and thence to the left to (12 m.) *Guildford* (Rte 10B).

A pleasant walk leads back from Newlands Corner to (8 m.) *Dorking* along the crest of the North Downs, viâ Netley Heath and Ranmore Common.

We skirt *Holmwood Common* (N.T.; 630 acres) and enter Sussex, leaving the Arundel road (A 29) on the right. About 1½ m. s.w. of (35 m.) *Warnham* is *Field Place*, where the poet Shelley (1792–1822) was born and wrote his 'Queen Mab'.

37½ m. **Horsham** (by-pass; Hotels), a market-town (26,400 inhab.) and railway junction. Many old houses are to be seen in The Causeway, at the end of West St.; among them the gabled 16C *Museum* (Tues–Sat, 1–5) with the old stocks, bull-ring, and whipping-post. At the end is the E.E. *Church*, with Perp. windows and a shingle spire, containing interesting monuments. Horsham stone, easily split, is a traditional material for roof-slabs throughout Sussex.

About 2 m. s.w. are the large but somewhat ineffective red brick buildings of **Christ's Hospital**, the famous 'Blue Coat School', founded in London by Edward VI in 1552 and removed hither in 1902. The boys still wear the ancient costume of blue gowns, knee breeches, and yellow stockings. This was the school of Charles Lamb, Coleridge, Leigh Hunt, and Constant Lambert, and among earlier pupils were Camden, Stillingfleet and Middleton. In the dining hall is a large painting by Verrio depicting the Endowment of the Royal Mathematical School in 1672 (to which Peter the Great came for young astronomers); and in the chapel are paintings by Brangwyn.

From Horsham to Shoreham, 21 m.—7 m. *Cowfold*. The Perp. church surrounded by pretty cottages, has a fine tower and contains the splendid brass, 10 ft long, of Prior Nelond (1433).—Beyond (8¼ m.) *St Hugh's Charterhouse*, established by monks from the Grande-Chartreuse (1877–83; male visitors admitted 10–3, exc. Sun), we turn right and cross the Adur beyond (9½ m.) *Partridge Green*.—At (12 m.) *Ashurst* 'Michael Fairless' (Margaret Fairless Barber; d. 1901), author of 'The Roadmender', is buried. She died at Mock Bridge House, near Shermanbury, 1½ m. E. on the Henfield road.—16 m. **Steyning** (Hotels), a pleasant little town with an old grammar school at the foot of the Downs, has a *Church founded by St Cuthman. Its most striking feature is the series of enriched late-Norman arches in the nave (c. 1150). The plain E. arches of the nave and aisles are 100 years older. Near the Purbeck marble font is the 'Steyning Stone', probably of pre-Christian origin, rediscovered in 1938 in the churchyard. In the house on Chantry Green Yeats wrote many of his later poems. About 2 m. w. rises *Chanctonbury Ring* (783 ft), a conspicuous summit crowned with ancient entrenchments and a circle of beeches. Glorious walks may be taken from Steyning along the Downs to (5 m.) the Devil's Dyke on the E., or to (10 m.) Amberley on the w.—17 m. *Bramber* has a little Norman chapel with interesting capitals beside fragments of a castle (N.T.), including part of the tower-keep, 76 ft high, erected to guard the estuary of the Adur. *St Mary's* is a 15C house with period rooms (adm. daily except Mon, 11–6, Sun from 2; fee), and the House of Pipes, a museum of smoking, is open daily. At *Botolphs* and at *Coombes*, 1 and 2 m. s., are quaint little churches of 11C foundation, with mural paintings (c. 1100).—21 m. *Shoreham*, see p. 92.

From Horsham to *Guildford*, see p. 105; to *Arundel*, etc., see Rte 10A.

43½ m. *West Grinstead* (l.) has a partly Norman church. In West Grinstead Park is 'Pope's Oak', under which Pope is said to have composed the 'Rape of the Lock' at the suggestion of his host, John Caryll.

On the right are the ruins of *Knepp Castle* and *Knepp Park*, with a lake 1 m. long.—49½ m. *Washington*, where John Ireland died in 1962, lies below Chanctonbury Ring (see above) and a fine road leads w. beneath the South Downs to *Storrington* (2½ m.; Hotels, and at *Thakeham*, 2 m. N.E.) and Amberley (6 m.; Rte 10A).—52½ m. *Findon* (by-pass) is the nearest village to Cissbury Ring (see below). A 280, the 'Long Furlong' with splendid views, leads r. for Arundel.

57 m. **Worthing** (Hotels mainly on the front, and restaurants), is a popular seaside resort (88,200 inhab.) and place of retirement, with a mild climate. There are swimming baths and superb gardens, but the beach is shingly except at low tide. In Chapel Rd. are the *Post Office* and the *Town Hall* and *Museum* (weekdays 10–5 or 7) with a good collection of Roman remains, English water-colours, dolls, etc. and in Union Place, nearly opposite, is the *Connaught Theatre*. Concerts are held in the Pier Pavilion.

Worthing is a good starting-point for visits to the South Downs and several interesting churches.—The Transitional Norman church of *Broadwater*, a suburb 1 m. N., contains old brasses and monuments. In the cemetery, a few yards w., lie Richard Jefferies (see below) and W. H. Hudson (1841–1922), the naturalists.—The Norman *Church of *Sompting*, 2 m. N.E., has a Saxon tower with the single example in England of a 'Rhenish helm' roof. Many of the other features, such as the vaulted sanctuary off the s. chapel, and various sculpture fragments, are of much interest, and the church has been described as "the greatest architectural curiosity in the county". Near by is the cottage where Edward Trelawny, Shelley's friend, died in 1881.—*West Tarring*, 1½ m. N.W., has some late-15C cottages (adm. April–Oct, daily from 2, exc. Sun & Mon) and an E.E. church with a Perp. tower, Italian mosaics (1885), and a tablet to John Selden (1584–1654), who was born at *Salvington*, 1 m. farther N., in a cottage still extant (with a Latin inscription over the door). The famous Fig Garden at Tarring is said to have been originally planted by Becket. High Salvington has a post-mill of 1700, recently restored.—*Cissbury Hill* (603 ft; N.T.), 3 m. N., is crowned by the largest entrenchment on the South Downs (c. 300 B.C.).

FROM WORTHING TO CHICHESTER by the coast road, 25 m. (A 259; bus) passing a succession of seaside resorts.—At (2½ m.) *Goring-by-Sea* Richard Jefferies died in 1887.—3½ m. *Ferring* (Hotel).—6 m. *Angmering* (Hotels). The Pigeon House, in the village 2 m. N., is an interesting medieval house (adm. by appointment).—10 m. Littlehampton (Hotels), with good sands and a golf course at the mouth of the Arun.—12 m. *Climping* (Hotel) has a 13C church with a tower of 1170. To the N. is *Ford*, with an open prison and a tiny Norman church.—At (16½ m.) *Felpham*, now a suburb of Bognor, are a cottage occupied by William Blake in 1801–4 and the house of William Hayley (1745–1820), the poet, who is buried in the church.

18 m. **Bognor Regis** (Hotels), a bathing-resort (34,400 inhab.) with a sandy beach, owes its surname 'Regis' to the fact that Craigweil House (demolished) at *Aldwick*, 1½ m. w., was occupied by George V during his convalescence in 1929. We join A 29 for (25 m.) *Chichester*, see Rte 10A.

10 LONDON TO PORTSMOUTH

A Viâ Arundel

ROAD, 87 m. To (24 m.) *Dorking*, see Rte 9.—A 29. 43½ m. *Billingshurst*.—48½ m. *Pulborough*.—57½ m. **Arundel**.—A 27. 68½ m. **Chichester** (by-pass).—85½ m. **Portsmouth**.

RAILWAY, 87½ m. from Victoria or London Bridge in 2¼ hrs. Principal Stations: 13¾ m. *Sutton.* —16 m. *Epsom.* —25½ m. *Dorking North.* —39 m. **Horsham.**—51¼ m. *Pulborough.* —58½ m. **Arundel**, junction for *Littlehampton.* —62 m. *Ford*, junction for *Littlehampton.* —63¾ m. *Barnham*, junction for **Bognor Regis** (3½ m.; through trains).—71 m. **Chichester.**—73¾ m. *Bosham.* —78 m. *Emsworth.* —79¾ m. *Havant*, and thence to **Portsmouth**, see Rte 10B. Some trains run to Horsham viâ East Croydon, Three Bridges, and Crawley (2 m. shorter).

From London to (24 m.) *Dorking*, see Rte 9.—At (28½ m.) *Beare Green*
A 29 bears to the right.—Near (32 m.) *Ockley* (Hotel) the Danes were
defeated with great slaughter in 851 by Ethelwulf of Wessex. On the
right rises Leith Hill (p. 94).—At (38½ m.) *Roman Gate* begins a long
section of the Roman *Stane Street*, leading from London to Chichester.
—43½ m. *Billingshurst*, with a 16C half-timbered inn. At *Coolham*, 3 m.
s.e., is the curiously named 'Blue Idol', an old Quaker meeting-house
(now a guest-house) associated with William Penn. *Shipley* church, 2 m.
farther, is Norman; the windmill has associations with Hilaire Belloc
(1870–1953), who lived in the house near by. *Wisborough Green*, 2 m.
w. of Billingshurst on the Petworth road, is a charming village on the
verge of some of the best country in Sussex.—48½ m. **Pulborough**
(Hotels), on the Arun, has a large E.E. and Perp. church (brasses), and
a good golf course.

At *Bignor*, 7 m. s.w. (2 m. w. of Bury, see below), in a pleasant position at the
foot of the Downs, is a fine *Roman Villa (adm. March–Oct, Tues–Sun; also Mon
in Aug, & Sun in Nov; fee). It was inhabited in the 2–4C, and first excavated in
1811–19, when the rustic buildings covering important mosaics (mostly 4C), were
erected. A museum contains finds from more recent excavations.—A footpath
leads along the Arun from Pulborough to *Wiggonholt*, 2 m. s.e., while *West
Chiltington*, 3 m. e., has its stocks and whipping-post and a good 12C church with
contemporary wall-paintings. *Parham*, 4 m. s.e. of Pulborough, is a stately
mansion of 1577, with interesting furniture and portraits (adm. April–Oct, Wed,
Thurs, Sun, & BH., 2–5.30; fee).

From Pulborough to Midhurst, 12 m.—1 m. *Stopham*, with a 14C bridge over
the Arun.—2½ m. *Fittleworth* (Hotel).—5 m. *Petworth* (Hotel), with narrow streets
and picturesque houses, lies close beside Petworth House (adm. April–Oct, Wed,
Thurs, Sat, & BH., 2–6, also 1st and 3rd Tues in each month; fee). The mansion
(1688–96), presented to the N.T. by Lord Leconfield in 1947, contains some
exquisite carvings by Grinling Gibbons, Roman and Greek sculpture, and a
notable collection of pictures. Turner, who was a frequent visitor here, is particularly well represented. The fine chapel dates from the 13–17C. The *Park*, landscaped by Capability Brown, is open daily to the public (no cars).—12 m. **Midhurst**
(Hotels), a charming old town on the Rother, is interesting for the imposing
remains of *Cowdray House*, a Tudor mansion destroyed by fire in 1793, in Cowdray
Park, which is open to the public (polo matches). Cobden and H. G. Wells were
pupils at the 17C Grammar School (altered in 18C). The church of *Easebourne*
(pron. 'Ezburn'), 1 m. n.e. contains an effigy of Sir David Owen (d. 1535), uncle of
Henry VII, and adjoins the buildings of a 13C priory of Augustinian nuns (now
the church hall and vicarage). About 1 m. s. of Midhurst an obelisk commemorates Richard Cobden (1804–65), who built *Dunford House* (adm. by appointment),
near by, on the site of his birthplace; he is buried at *West Lavington*, ¾ m. s.e.
Trotton, 3½ m. w., was the birthplace of Thomas Otway (1652–58); the church contains a wall-painting of the Last Judgment c. 1380, and impressive brasses to
members of the Camoy family (one of 1310 is the earliest brass in England to a
lady).

We cross the Arun, which meanders through rich water-meadows.—
49½ m. *Hardham* has a church with 12C wall-paintings.—53½ m. *Bury*,
2 m. from Bignor (see above), with the country house of John Galsworthy
(d. 1933), lies opposite *Amberley*, a charming *Village with a ruined castle
(no adm.) of the bishops of Chichester and a late-Norman church. At
the Arun bridge beside the station, 1 m. s., are pleasant garden cafés.—
55 m. *Whiteways Lodge* commands a fine *View, with Arundel park on
the left.

57½ m. **Arundel** (Hotels), a quiet country town (2400 inhab.), clusters
round the base of its Castle, which was founded at a very early period
to protect the gap here made by the Arun in the chalky South Downs.

Besieged by Henry I in 1102 and by Stephen in 1139, the castle was finally laid in ruins by the Parliamentarians in 1643–44. Now it is held in trust as a residence for the Earl Marshal, the Duke of Norfolk. The occupied part of the castle (adm. April–May, Mon–Thurs, 1–5; June–Sept, Mon–Fri, 12–5; also Sun in Aug; fee), rebuilt at the end of the 18C, was recast in the 13C style in 1890–1903. The ticket admits also to the ancient *Keep* (12C; restored) and the Fitzalan Chapel (see below). In the fine *Park* is *Swanbourne Lake* with a Wildfowl Trust centre (open daily).—The parish church of *St Nicholas* (c. 1380) has a rare pre-Reformation pulpit and 14C mural paintings. The *Fitzalan Chapel*, behind the altar and separated from the rest of the building by an ancient iron grille protected by plate glass, is the property of the Duke of Norfolk (who is a Roman Catholic). It was originally founded (1380) as the chapel of the College of the Holy Trinity, and contains fine *Monuments of the Fitzalans, previous holders of the earldom of Arundel, which passes with the property and was acquired by the Howard family through marriage in 1580. The 15th duke (1847–1917) restored the chapel and also built the conspicuous Roman Catholic cathedral church of *St Philip Neri, with a slender flèche (by J. A. Hansom; 1869–76). George MacDonald was pastor of the Tarrant St. chapel in 1850.— In the High St. are the Information Centre and *Potter's Museum of Curiosity*, a Victorian museum of taxidermy (open daily, Easter–Oct) formerly at Bramber.

Charming walks ascend both banks of the Arun to (3 m.) *Amberley Bridge* (w. bank) and to (2 m.) *Burpham* (E. bank), at the foot of the S. Downs, with a Norman and E.E. church and a notable promontory-fort, probably built to resist Danish sea-raiders.—For *Littlehampton* (4 m.; p. 96) we cross the Arun and bear right beyond Arundel station.

The Chichester road (A 27) runs w. from Arundel, crossing the Bognor road (A 29). To the r. (½ m.) is *Slindon*, where Abp. Stephen Langton died in 1228 (memorial in the church), with 3500 acres of N.T. land above it.—62¼ m. *Fontwell Park* racecourse (steeplechases).—65¼ m. Opposite *Tangmere*, with an R.A.F. station, is *Boxgrove*, ¼ m. N. of the main road. The interesting Benedictine *Priory Church here is notable for its late-Norman and E.E. work recalling that of Bp. Seffrid at Chichester. The w. end of the nave is now in ruins. The pretty ceiling was painted by Lambert Barnard in 1530. The De La Warr chantry is an elaborate work of 1532. Of the monastic buildings to the N., only the ruined Guest House (c. 1300) and a fragment of the Cloister survive.

68½ m. **CHICHESTER** (pleasant large Hotels), a charming cathedral city (20,500 inhab.) and the administrative centre of West Sussex, pre-serves an unusual number of 18C houses, both large and small. It is the ancient *Regnum*, called *Cisseceaster* in the Saxon Chronicle, and betrays its Roman origin in its four main streets, meeting at right angles in the centre of the town. Here stands the ornate *Market Cross* (1501), sur-mounted by a cupola put up in 1724. On the E. side is a good bronze bust of Charles I.

The *Cathedral (Plan, opposite) is predominantly a Norman building, with few though important alterations and additions. Unenclosed on the N. flank, it dominates West St., and seen from afar provides a constant focus to the town. The *Bell Tower* (c. 1400–36) is the only remaining English example of a detached belfry adjoining a cathedral. Visitors enter by the E.E. west porch.

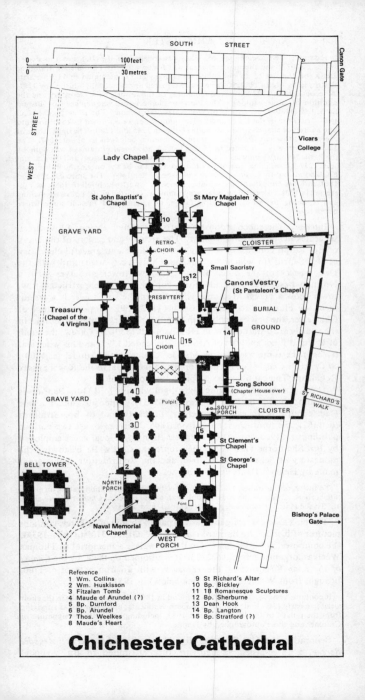

SOUTH STREET

0 _____ 100 feet
0 _____ 30 metres

WEST STREET

Canon Gate

Vicars College

Lady Chapel

St John Baptist's Chapel

St Mary Magdalen's Chapel

GRAVE YARD

10

8

RETRO-CHOIR

CLOISTER

9   11

Small Sacristy

13 12

Canons Vestry (St Pantaleon's Chapel)

PRESBYTERY

BURIAL GROUND

Treasury (Chapel of the 4 Virgins)

14

RITUAL CHOIR   15

7

Song School (Chapter House over)

ST RICHARD'S WALK

GRAVE YARD

4

Pulpit

6

SOUTH PORCH

CLOISTER

3

5

St Clement's Chapel

St George's Chapel

BELL TOWER

2

NORTH PORCH

Font   1

Bishop's Palace Gate →

Naval Memorial Chapel

WEST PORCH

Reference
1 Wm. Collins
2 Wm. Huskisson
3 Fitzalan Tomb
4 Maude of Arundel (?)
5 Bp. Durnford
6 Bp. Arundel
7 Thos. Weelkes
8 Maude's Heart

9   St Richard's Altar
10 Bp. Bickley
11 18 Romanesque Sculptures
12 Bp. Sherburne
13 Dean Hook
14 Bp. Langton
15 Bp. Stratford (?)

Chichester Cathedral

HISTORY. The ancient see of Selsey (established in the 7C) was transferred hither c. 1072; and the new cathedral was begun after 1091 by Bishop Ralph de Luffa (on the site of an old collegiate church) and consecrated in 1108. Partly destroyed by fire in 1114, it was at once repaired and practically finished by 1184. A second fire in 1187 led to the rebuilding of the inside of the clerestory and the addition of stone vaulting. The Norman chancel-apse was replaced by Bishop Seffrid II (1180–1204) by the present square retro-choir. The three porches and the sacristy are of the E.E. period. The outer aisles were formed by throwing into one a series of chapels originally added between 1245 and 1280. The upper stage of the central tower, with its plate-tracery windows, belonged to about 1247. The Lady Chapel was completed in 1288–1304. A good deal of damage was done by the Parliamentary iconoclasts in 1643. The bell-tower, the cloister, and the graceful spire (277 ft), recalling that of Salisbury and said to be the only cathedral spire in England visible from the sea, were built soon after 1400. The spire collapsed in 1861 and was almost at once rebuilt. The N.W. tower, which fell in 1635, was re-erected in 1901. A careful ten-year programme was started in 1964 of strengthening and repairing the whole cathedral fabric, using imported French stone where necessary.

Interior. The sober proportions are extremely pleasing; a low screen separates the nave from the choir. The arcades and gallery of the NAVE of Bp. Ralph contrast effectively with the light and graceful clerestory of Bp. Seffrid (in which Purbeck marble is freely used) and with the Dec. tracery of the outer aisles. The S.W. tower preserves its fine Norman base with E.E. additions, copied in the reconstructed N.W. tower (now a Naval Memorial Chapel). In the s.w. tower is a monument, by Flaxman, to William Collins (1721–59), the poet, a native of Chichester, the best example of this sculptor's work in the cathedral. In the N. aisle are a statue of Wm. Huskisson (d. 1830), by Carew; the tomb of Richard Fitzalan, Earl of Arundel (beheaded 1397) and his wife; and (E. bay) the tomb ascribed to Maude, Countess of Arundel (c. 1300). *St George's Chapel* has been restored as a memorial to the Royal Sussex Regiment. The cantilevered pulpit dates from 1966.

The S. TRANSEPT has a fine seven-light window (c. 1330). Beneath is the canopy-tomb of Bp. Langton (1305–37). Opposite, under a fine Dec. canopy is an expressive effigy, probably that of Bp. Stratford (d. 1362); the tomb-chest dates from 1846. Here, also, are two curious paintings (1519; restored) by Lambert Barnard, a local artist employed by Bp. Sherborne (1508–36); they represent Ceadwalla bestowing the monastery of Selsey on St Wilfrid, and the confirmation of this grant made by Henry VIII to Bp. Sherborne.

To the w. of this transept is the E.E. *Sacristy*, with fine vaulting resting on exquisite corbels. It is now the song-school, with a 15C panelled *Chapter House* above it. To the E. is *St Pantaleon's Chapel* (Trans.), now a vestry.

The N. TRANSEPT, long used as the parish church of St Peter, contains pictures of bishops by Barnard (see above). Gustav Holst (1874–1934), the composer, is buried here. On the w. wall is a memorial to Thomas Weelkes, organist here in 1602–23. It is adjoined on the E. by the *Chapel of the Four Virgins*, now the *Treasury*, with an iron gate of c. 1700, brought from Westgate House (see below) in 1951.

It contains vessels, rings, etc. (13C), found in 1829 in bishops' tombs in the choir aisles; an early 13C chest; some fine modern vestments; and a few books surviving from the pillage of the library here in 1643, including one with the signature of Cranmer and three autographed by Donne.

Separating the nave from the slightly raised choir is the *Bell-Arundel Screen*, a three-aisled vaulted structure attributed to Bp. Arundel

(1459–78). Taken down in 1860, this fine Perp. screen was stored in the bell-tower until its re-erection in 1961 as a memorial to Bp. Bell (1929–58), whose portrait in bronze is affixed to the s. of it.

In the CHOIR, the *Stalls*, partly modernized, date from c. 1335 and have well-carved misericords. A tapestry designed by John Piper (1966) covers the oaken *Altar Screen*. In the s. aisle are two interesting sculptured *Panels (c. 1140) of particularly refined workmanship and design, representing the Raising of Lazarus and Christ at the Gate of Bethany. Between them is the tomb of Bp. Sherborne (d. 1536), and, opposite, that of Dean Hook (d. 1875), a good work by Gilbert Scott.—The *RETRO-CHOIR, completed by Bp. Seffrid in 1199, is a charming example of the final transition from the massive Norman to the lighter Gothic style. The interval between the fine Purbeck marble piers and their detached shafts is wider than in any other known example. The sculptural decoration in the triforium is noteworthy. On the s. side is the fragment of a 2C Roman mosaic (glassed over), found under the foundations in 1969.

Here stood the shrine of the sainted bishop Richard de la Wych (d. 1253), which attracted many pilgrims. The gates of the Lady Chapel are a relic of the grille that surrounded the raised platform, on which stands his altar (1930).

Of the long and narrow LADY CHAPEL, the two w. bays belonged to the original Norman church, while the two E. bays were added between 1288 and 1304. In the first two bays are traces of the paintings by Barnard (see above) which once covered the vaults throughout the church. Here is the simple tomb of Bp. Ralph de Luffa.

THE CLOISTERS, entered by the beautiful E.E. South Porch, are 15C, and irregular both in position and form. There is no N. walk. The garth is known as the Paradise. From the s. walk a passage called St Richard's Walk leads to *Canon Lane*. In front is the *Deanery* (1725); to the right the lane ends at the 14C gateway of the *Bishop's Palace*, half of which is now a theological college. Its chapel and kitchen-walls are of the 13C, the remainder 14–18C. The chapel (entered opposite the s.w. tower) has fine vaulting and corbels, and an exquisite painted tondo (c. 1250). At the other end of the lane, beyond the 15C *Vicar's Close*, is the 16C *Canon Gate* into South St. By another entrance to the precincts, a few yards to the left along South St., is a 12C vaulted undercroft (now a café) beneath the *Vicars Hall and Parlour* (14C).

From the Market Cross, North Street, the finest in the city and predominantly Georgian, leads past (r.) *Market House* (1807) by Nash, and the former church of *St Olave* (now a bookshop), with early Norman features. On the outside wall of the *Council Chambers* (1731–33; interior shown when not in use) is a Roman inscription recording the erection of a temple to Neptune and Minerva. The stone was dug up in 1723 on this site. We follow Lion St. (r.) to the quiet St Martin's Square, a delightful group of houses. Here is *St Mary's Hospital (adm. Tues–Sat, 11–12, 2–4 or 5; donation), founded c. 1158 for the care of the sick but since 1528 an almshouse for the aged. The *Great Hall*, formerly the infirmary but since 1680 occupied by small dwellings, has a magnificent timber roof reaching at the sides to within 6 ft of the floor; it is separated by a carved oaken screen from the *Chapel*, which has good stalls and misericords, so that patients could hear mass from their beds (an arrangement unique in England; but comp. Beaune in France). Except for the partitions and chimneys, the whole dates from c. 1290. To the N. is the well-kept *Priory Park*, with the E.E. choir of the *Grey Friars'

Church, later used as an assize court, and now the GUILDHALL MUSEUM (June–Sept, Tues–Sat, afternoon 1–5). Here William Blake was tried for sedition in 1804 (he had ejected a soldier from his garden at Felpham). The park also contains the motte of Chichester castle, and is surrounded by part of the CITY WALLS. These rest on Roman foundations and indicate the extent of the Roman town. The North and East Walls have pleasant raised footpaths.

Farther N., in Broyle Rd. (the continuation of North St.) is the cantilevered *Festival Theatre* (1962) by Powell and Moya, with an open stage. The dramatic productions during the Festival Theatre Season (usually May–Sept) are important.

In Little London, leading out of Priory Rd., the CHICHESTER DISTRICT MUSEUM is housed in an 18C corn-store (adm. daily, Tues–Sat).

Here are Prehistoric remains, and Roman finds from the town cemetery; wood-carving from The Grange, a mansion demolished in 1962, and from the Oliver Whitby School (founded in 1712, merged in Christ's Hospital in 1951); and rooms devoted to the Royal Sussex Regiment. Frequent exhibitions are held. The fitting sculpture by John Skelton, outside, dates from 1964. If we continue s. across East St., and then turn right, we reach *St John's Church* (1812) with an interesting octagonal Low Church plan and monumental three-decker pulpit. At No. 11 Eastgate Sq., farther on, Keats began 'The Eve of St Agnes' in 1819.

The area s.e. of the Market Cross is known as THE PALLANT, with four streets (N., S., E., and W. PALLANT), intersecting the Palatinate or Archbishop's 'Peculiar', a sort of miniature city within the city. It contains some very fine 18C and 19C buildings, among them Pallant House (c. 1712).

West St., opposite the Cathedral, has more 18C houses. Leading from it is Chapel St., where further Roman remains came to light in 1971. West St. continues past a well-placed church by R. C. Carpenter (1848–52) to the striking *Westgate House* (1696), now the county record office. The modern *County Hall* behind, is a worthy pendant, although recent extensions in Tower St. are far less harmonious. Farther w., off Westgate, in Mount Lane is the new extension to the Theological College, well landscaped beside ilexes. Westgate Fields afford good views of the cathedral and walls, despite the intrusion of a new College and the by-pass.

Just 1¼ m. w. is *Fishbourne Roman Palace* (adm. Mar–Apr & Oct–Nov 10–4; May & Sept 10–6; June–Aug daily 10–7; closed Dec–Feb; fee), excavated in 1961–69. The largest single Roman building so far found in Britain, it vies in size and grandeur with the imperial palaces of Rome itself. The MUSEUM contains many objects, well-displayed, found during the course of excavations.

The Palace is believed to have belonged to Cogidubnus, a Roman citizen, who was ruling as king in the Chichester area at the time of the Roman invasion by Vespasian. It is thought that Fishbourne could have been the base and supply depot for the Roman army in A.D. 43. Two large wooden store-houses of this period have been discovered, and evidence of a harbour. Although a large house was built in A.D. 50–59, the main palace and gardens were constructed c. A.D. 75. Remains of the N. wing of this palace are now covered by a pleasant protective building, and mosaics of this period are the finest examples yet discovered in Britain. Parts of the w. and e. wings have also been uncovered, and the extensive garden has been replanted on the lines of the bedding-trenches found during excavations. The southern part of the garden and s. wing lie under modern houses and the A 29 road. Early in the 2C, part of the palace was demolished, new mosaics were laid, and central heating installed. In A.D. 285, the whole palace was destroyed by fire, evidence of which can be seen in the N. wing.

For several weeks in the year Chichester may be said to lose its dignity of cathedral town and become merely a starting-point for the fashionable races held on the racecourse in *Goodwood Park* (views; Hotel at the S. Gate), 4½ m. N.; there is also an airfield, motor circuit, and golf course. **Goodwood** itself, the seat of the Duke of Richmond, was built by James Wyatt (1780–1800). It contains a fine collection of pictures (adm. Sundays & some Mon in summer; fee). The park is open daily, and is noted for its cedars. Overlooking the racecourse is the prominent *Trundle*, a prehistoric earthwork, on *St Roche's Hill* (667 ft), at the foot of which is the *Weald and Downland Open Air Museum* (Apr–Sept, daily exc. Mon, 11–6; also Wed, Thurs & Sun in Oct, 11–5; in winter Sun only, 11–4) with 14–19C houses. Farther N. is *Singleton*, a secluded village with a Norman church, containing an unusual pulpit incorporated into the side of the chancel arch with two lancet openings.—The church of *Appledram*, 1½ m. s.w. of Chichester, has the sides of its chancel occupied by graduated triplets (windows), a rare feature that it shares with Brecon Priory in Wales.

FROM CHICHESTER TO SELSEY, 8 m. This road traverses the fertile peninsula of Selsey ('seal's island'), the main interest of which lies in the fact that here St Wilfrid established Christianity among the S. Saxons (681). St Wilfrid was followed by a long line of bishops, until the Conqueror transferred the see to Chichester.—4 m. *Sidlesham*. At *Pagham*, an untidy seaside village, 2 m. E. by footpath (the approach by-road is from Hunston, 3 m. N.), has a finely proportioned E.E. church with lancet windows, dedicated to St Thomas Becket.—6⅓ m. By-road (l.) for *Church Norton* (1 m.). Here, overlooking Pagham Bay with its nature reserve (700 acres), is the romantic St Wilfrid's Chapel. The simple 13C chancel is all that remains of the church which was moved in 1866 to Selsey.—8 m. *Selsey* (Hotel) is visited for sea bathing. The church built in 1865 incorporates the fine nave arcades of the old church (see above). To the s. projects the headland of *Selsey Bill*, and along the sandy shore to the w. are the bungalow resorts of *Bracklesham Bay* and *East Wittering*.

From Chichester to *Bognor* and *Brighton*, see p. 96.

71½ m. **Broadbridge**. About ½ m. s. is *Bosham* (pron. 'Bozzam'; Hotel), a pretty village and yachting centre on Chichester Harbour. The small *Church of singular interest appears in the Bayeux Tapestry, where Harold is shown on his way to hear mass before his ill-starred visit to Normandy. The tower, the w. part of the chancel with the fine chancel arch, and possibly the nave (aisles later), date from the time of Edward the Confessor. The chancel (good lancet E. window) was extended in the early-Norman and again in the E.E. period.

Tradition alleges that a young daughter of King Canute was buried in this church, and a small stone coffin was found at the required spot in 1865. Some think Bosham the scene of Canute's command to the waves (comp., p. 124). From here a road leads to a ferry for *West Itchenor*, a picturesque yachting village.

At (75½ m.) *Emsworth*, we enter Hampshire. The Isle of Wight comes into view on the left.—77½ m. *Havant*, a rapidly developing town (109,000 inhab.), has almost trebled its population in twenty years.

To the s. (buses from Havant) lies *Hayling Island*, 4 m. long and 2 m. broad, with (2½ m.) *North Hayling* and the sea bathing and golfing resort of (4½ m.) *South Hayling* (Hotel). The E.E. church of St Mary at S. Hayling has good sculptures and fine lancet-windows. In the churchyard is a yew 31 ft in circumference. The defunct branch line (Havant to Hayling) is commemorated at the *Hayling Billy* nn, named from the locomotive preserved outside.

Skirting the shallow *Langstone Harbour*, we reach (85½ m.) **Portsmouth** Rte 10B).

B Viâ Petersfield

ROAD, 72 m. A 3. 29 m. **Guildford**. N.B. From the entrance to Guildford a by-pass on the right avoids the old town, passes under the Hog's Back (Farnham road) in a cutting, and rejoins the old road at Milford.—33 m. *Godalming.*—35¾ m. *Milford.*—42¼ m. **Hindhead.**—54 m. **Petersfield.**—72 m. **Portsmouth.**

RAILWAY, 74½ m. from Waterloo in 95 min. Principal Stations: 12 m.
Surbiton.—19¼ m. *Weybridge* (junction for Virginia Water).—24 m. **Woking**—
30¼ m. **Guildford**, junction for Farnham, Aldershot, etc.—34½ m. *Godalming.*—
43 m. **Haslemere.**—55 m. *Petersfield.*—66½ m. *Havant*, junction for Chichester.—
73 m. *Fratton.*—73¾ m. **Portsmouth & Southsea.**—74½ m. **Portsmouth Harbour.**

Leaving London by Putney Bridge, we join the A 3 (from Elephant and
Castle) at Putney Heath. The modern road now by-passes Kingston, Esher,
and Cobham, joining the old Portsmouth Road at (20¼ m.) *Pain's Hill.*

The old Portsmouth road traversed Kingston upon Thames (see 'Blue Guide to
London') and, beyond *Sandown Park* racecourse, became the High Street of (16 m.)
Esher, with pleasant greens. Of Esher Place, built by Waynflete in 1477–86 and
occupied by Wolsey, the sole original relic is the gatehouse (Wolsey's Tower), altered
by William Kent. From Esher roads run N.W. towards the Thames at Walton,
Weybridge, and other places described in Rte 28B. To the s. lies *Claremont*, now a girls'
school (adm. first Sat and following Sun in each month, Feb–Nov, 2–5; fee), a mansion
built by 'Capability' Brown in 1768–72 for Lord Clive, which has been occupied in turn
by Princess Charlotte (d. 1817) and her husband Leopold I of Belgium, Louis-Philippe
(who died here in 1850), and the Duchess of Albany (d. 1922).
From Pain's Hill A 245 runs s.e. to Leatherhead (6¼ m.) through Cobham village,
with the grave of Lord Ligonier (d. 1770), where Cedar House (N.T.) has a fine 15C hall
(shown on application). Peter II of Yugoslavia acceded to his throne in 1934 while a
schoolboy at Cobham.—At (2¾ m.) *Stoke d'Abernon* the church (Saxon and E.E.)
contains the earliest *Brass in England (to Sir John d'Abernon, 1277), that of his son (d.
1327), and Flemish 14–16C glass.

22 m. *Wisley Common* (Hotel) with the pretty Bolder Mere is 1 m. s.
of *Wisley*, where the *Gardens of the Royal Horticultural Society are
open on weekdays (10–7 or sunset; fee). *Ockham*, 1 m. s., has a 7-light
E. window in its church.—24 m. *Ripley* (Restaurant), is now by-passed to
the s. Off the old road lie the 13C ruins of *Newark Priory* (Augustinian;
c. 1190), near a charming stretch of the Wey (comp. p. 259).

Also off the old road, c. 2 m. farther w., A 247 diverges right, viâ *Old Woking*, on the
Wey, with an interesting church, for (3¾ m.) **Woking** (Hotel at Horsell, 1 m. N.), a
thriving 'dormitory' town (75,800 inhab.).

29 m. **GUILDFORD** (Hotels in the High St. and on the Epsom Rd.;
Restaurants), a cathedral city and the county town (56,900 inhab.) of
Surrey, is attractively situated on the Wey and bounded on the N.E. by
Stoke Park, venue of the Surrey show. The town is first mentioned as a
borough in 1131, but its records go back to the time of King Alfred
(900). The steep *HIGH STREET descends to the w., with many old
and picturesque buildings. Near the top of High St. (l.) the *Royal
Grammar School* retains its 16C main building, with a library founded
in 1573 by Bp. Parkhurst, a native of Guildford, and containing 89
chained books (adm. on Sat and in vacation). Across the street farther
on is *Archbishop Abbot's Hospital*, a Jacobean brick building founded
in 1619 for a master, twelve brethren, and ten sisters (adm. 11–12 &
3–4; donation). It contains a wealth of contemporary carved oak, a
portrait group by John Russell (a native of Guildford; 1745–1806),
stained glass (1621; in the chapel), and portraits of Calvin, Wyclif, and
Foxe. The chimneys should be noted. *Trinity Church*, opposite,
rebuilt in the 18C, contains the monument of Abp. Abbot (d. 1633;
from an earlier church) and the cenotaph of Speaker Onslow (d. 1768;
buried at Merrow). Near the middle of the street (r.) is the *Town Hall*,
a brick and timber building of 1682, identified by its projecting clock.
Below the noted *Angel Hotel* are groined 13C cellars.

Lower down, QUARRY STREET, with old houses, leads to the left, passing the unusual church of *St Mary*, which dates largely from the late-Norman period (1160–80; central tower probably pre-Norman).

Within should be noted the curious splayed openings (Saxon) above the later tower-arches, the corbels in the aisles, a piscina in the s. aisle, the square 'low side' window at the w. end of the N. aisle, and the 15C screen incorporated in the organ-case.

A little way beyond St Mary's is the *Castle Archway*, admitting to the public gardens in which, on an artificial mound, stands the keep of the Norman CASTLE (c. 1150; view from the top), which is 70 ft high and has walls 10–14 ft thick. Adjoining the Castle Archway is a small *Museum* (weekdays 11–5) of Surrey antiquities, ironwork, and needlework; also relics of 'Lewis Carroll' (C. L. Dodgson; 1832–98), who is buried in Guildford cemetery and whose house in Quarry St. ('The Chestnuts') survives.

Mill Lane descends to the *Yvonne Arnaud Theatre*, in meadows by the Wey (here overlooked by the picturesque backs of Quarry St.). The church of *St Nicholas*, beyond the river, incorporates the 15C *Loseley Chapel*, with monuments of the Mores of Loseley. Beyond the Bus Stations is the fine *Sports Centre* (1971) with three swimming pools.

On Stag Hill, N.W. of the town, stands the **Cathedral**, by Sir Edward Maufe, of the diocese of Guildford, created in 1927. Begun in 1936, the building was consecrated in 1961 and completed in 1964. The plain exterior is built in local brick, relieved only by sculptured allegorical figures. The interior, austerely effective in a modern Gothic style, is faced in stone with concrete vaults. The furnishings throughout are designed with consistent simplicity. The N. transeptal chapel is dedicated to the Queen's Royal Surrey Regiment.

The N. side of the hill is occupied by the *University of Surrey*, constituted in 1966 from the former Battersea Polytechnic and moved to this site.

Just s. of Guildford, on the Wey, is *St Catherine's Hill* (view), crowned with the ruins of an early 14C chapel.—*Loseley House* (adm. June–Sept 2–5 Wed–Sat, & BH.; fee), 2 m. s.w. in a finely wooded park, is an admirable example of an Elizabethan manor-house (1560–69); the so-called 'Nonsuch' panels of Henry VIII's reign (? by Toto del Nunziata) were probably painted for the king's tents. The Norman *Church of Compton*, 1¼ m. w. of Loseley (3 m. from Guildford), with its Saxon cells and tower, is unique in having a chapel above its low vaulted sanctuary. The wooden rail of this chapel is probably the oldest woodwork in England. On the chancel arch is an incised figure of a Norman soldier. G. F. Watts (1817–1904), the painter, long lived at *Linnerslease*, ½ m. N. of Compton; and his memory is kept green here by the *Watts Picture Gallery* (daily except Thurs, 2–4 or 6, also Wed & Sat 11–1; free). The *Mortuary Chapel* in the new graveyard is adorned with symbolical terracotta work executed by the villagers, directed by Mrs Watts (d. 1939).

Other interesting points within easy reach of Guildford are *St Martha's Chapel* (p. 95), 2¼ m. s.E. viâ Chantry Woods; and *Godalming*, 4 m. s. (pleasant path along the Wey). Also in the neighbourhood are several fine mansions: *Sutton Place* (no adm.), a beautiful Tudor work of brick and terracotta (c. 1525), 3½ m. N.; *Clandon Park* (see p. 93), 2¼ m. E., and *Hatchlands*, 3½ m. E. (N.T.; adm. 2–5.30, Wed & Sat, Apr–Sept; fee).

Two roads run from Guildford to Horsham, dividing at (1½ m.) *Shalford*. A 281 (19 m.) traverses (3 m.) *Bramley* (Hotel); B 2128 runs through (3 m.) *Wonersh* (Restaurant), with its old manor-house, (4 m.) *Shamley Green*, and (7¼ m.) *Cranleigh* (Restaurant), with a fine 14C church and a well-known boys' school (1863).

From Guildford to Farnham, Alton, and Winchester, see Rte 11A.

The Portsmouth road ascends the Wey.—33 m. **Godalming** (Hotels), an old town (18,600 inhab.) with narrow streets, an elegant little market-house, and half-timbered and decorated brick houses (17C), was formerly a centre of the Surrey wool industry. Here was born Aldous Huxley (1894–1963), the novelist. The large church of *SS. Peter & Paul*, near the station, is mainly Norman and 13C. The Meath Home for Epileptics, close to the station, occupies the house of General Oglethorpe (1696–1785), founder of the State of Georgia.

To the N. of the town are the imposing buildings of *Charterhouse School*, by Hardwick, Blomfield, and others, including a large War Memorial chapel and the so-called Founder's Tower (130 ft). The school (over 600 boys), founded in London by Thomas Sutton in 1611, was removed to Godalming in 1872. An old archway, carved with the names of former Carthusians, was brought from London. Among famous pupils are Crashaw, Lovelace, Barrow, Roger Williams (of Rhode Island), Steele, Addison, Wesley, Blackstone, Ellenborough, Thomas Day (author of 'Sandford and Merton'), Grote, Thirlwall, Havelock, Leech, Thackeray, Baden-Powell, Vaughan Williams, and Max Beerbohm. The library contains many of Leech's drawings for 'Punch' and the MS. of 'The Newcomes' by Thackeray.— *Eashing Bridges* (1½ m. w.; N.T.), (B 2130) to *Hascombe*, 4 m. s.e., is (3 m.) the *Winkworth Arboretum* (N.T.; adm. free), a hillside planted with rare trees and shrubs.

At (35¾ m.) *Milford* (Hotel; Restaurant), with well grouped domestic buildings and the 11C refectory (restored) and dovecot of a convent, the Guildford by-pass rejoins the old road. Milford and Witley commons include 377 acres of N.T. property.

Two roads here diverge on the left for Chichester.—A 283 (24¼ m.) running viâ Petworth, A 286 (26¼ m.) viâ Haslemere and Midhurst. A 283 passes (1½ m.) *Witley*, with an E.E. church, where (at 'The Heights'; now 'Rosslyn Court') George Eliot lived from 1877 till her death in 1880, and (2½ m.) *Chiddingfold* with the medieval Crown Inn, a characteristic Weald village, formerly engaged in making glass and iron (Restaurant). *Hambledon* (1 m. N.E.), with its two fine churchyard yews, lies beneath *Hydon's Ball* (593 ft; N.T.), a wooded hill crowned by a monument to Octavia Hill (1838–1912) the social reformer.
A 286 traverses (7 m.) **Haslemere**, with two old coaching hotels, agreeably situated (c. 500 ft) between the heathery heights of Blackdown and Hindhead. This market-town (13,300 inhab.), now the centre of a rambling residential district, dates its popularity from 1887, when Prof. Tyndall (1820–93) came to live on Hindhead. The *Dolmetsch Musical Festival*, held in July (commemorating a later resident, Arnold Dolmetsch; 1858–1940), is noted for medieval music played on old instruments. The *Educational Museum* in High St. (Tues–Sat 10–4 or 5, fee; Sun 2–5, Apr–Oct) is arranged on the 'space for time' principle and contains also a collection illustrating peasant arts, and a bird-protection exhibit. George Eliot lived for some time (1871) at Brookbank at *Shottermill*, 1 m. s.w.
Blackdown (918 ft), rising 2½ m s. of Haslemere, commands an admirable view of the Weald—Tennyson's "Green Sussex fading into blue, with one gray glimpse of sea." To reach it we leave Haslemere by Tennyson's Lane (N.T.) and ascend to the right. Tennyson died in 1892 at *Aldworth*, a house built by him on the E. slope in 1868–69 and named from Lady Tennyson's ancestral connection with Aldworth in Berks.

The Portsmouth road rises through heathy country.—37¾ m. *Thursley*, to the right of the road, has a church with a tub-font, three windows of c. 1030, and a fine timber-framed belfry.—42¼ m. **Hindhead** (Hotels) rising N. of Haslemere is the scene of an enormous car and motor-cycle traffic at week-ends. Over 2000 acres of the common are N.T. property. The summit (895 ft) is marked by a granite cross and a pillar with an indicator showing the chief points in the magnificent *View.

The name of *Gibbet Hill*, attached to the summit, refers to the murder of a sailor (1786) on the old road road skirting the edge of the *Devil's Punch Bowl, a curious depression on the N. side, where a memorial stone recounts the fact and the fate of the assassins—an inscription listened to by Smike "with greedy interest" when Nicholas Nickleby read it to him. From Hindhead to *Farnham*, see Rte 11A.

We enter Hampshire before (46½ m.) *Liphook* (Hotel), a good centre for walks (e.g. in *Wolmer Forest*, to the N.W.). Sidney Webb, Lord Passfield (1859–1947), Fabian philosopher, died here, at Passfield Corner.—54 m. *Petersfield* (Hotels) is a country town (9000 inhab.) with a part-Norman church (restored) and a leaden equestrian statue of William III (1724).

Bedales, 1½ m. N., is a well-known co-educational school, and 2 m. N. is *Steep*, with the cottage of Edward Thomas (1885–1917), the poet, killed in action in France (memorial on the hill opposite). About 2½ m. s. of Petersfield is *Buriton*, where the manor-house was the early home of Gibbon, and 4 m. S.E. is *Harting*, where Card. Pole was rector in 1526–51, and Anthony Trollope lived in 1880–82. *Elsted* church, 2 m. farther E., has a 13C chancel built on a Saxon nave with herringbone masonry. Roofless for 100 years, it was skilfully restored in 1952.—About 1½ m. s. of Harting is *Uppark* (1690; N.T.; adm. Easter–Sept. Wed, Thurs, Sun & BH; fee), notable for its 18C furnishings.

We cross the South Downs beside Butser Hill (889 ft) and beyond (62 m.) *Horndean* and Waterlooville reach the boundary of Portsmouth. On the steep ridge of Portsdown (400 ft) we pass (67 m.) Christ Church, in which two windows commemorate the Second Army's part in the invasion of Normandy (1944). From the road along the ridge (leading r. to Southwick; 2¾ m.) an extensive view is obtained of Portsmouth and its harbours.—At (69 m.) *Hilsea* we cross the M 27 motorway and reach Portsea Island, on which the main part of Portsmouth city stands.

72 m. **PORTSMOUTH** (197,000 inhab.), with a magnificent harbour entered from the famous roadstead of Spithead, is the chief naval station ('Pompey') of England. The city includes **Southsea**, the most attractive residential district, western and Old Portsmouth, and the dockyard. *Gosport* on the other side of the harbour, though an independent borough, is closely associated with Portsmouth.

Hotels in Pembroke Park, on The Hard, and in Southsea; **Restaurants** also in Southsea.

Railway Stations. *Portsmouth & Southsea*; *Portsmouth Harbour* for the Isle of Wight steamers.

Post Office, Commercial Rd.—INFORMATION BUREAU, Castle Bldgs, Clarence Esplanade.

Country Buses from Hyde Park Road. EXCURSIONS in summer from South Parade Pier.

Ferries. To *Ryde*, from Harbour Stn, no cars, hourly; to *Fishbourne*, from Broad St., cars, hourly, week-end every 2 hrs. Also by hovercraft to Ryde, from Harbour Stn and Clarence Pier, no cars, frequently.—To *Gosport*, from Harbour Stn, no cars, continuous.—In summer, steamer excursions from South Parade and Clarence Piers.

Amusements. *South Parade* and *Clarence Piers*. King's Theatre, Albert Rd. CONCERTS in the *Guildhall*.—GOLF at Gt Salterns and Croakhorn Lane. *Cricket* at the United Services ground and various parks. *Tennis*, etc. in Southsea.— SWIMMING POOLS: *Hilsea Lido* (open air); *Victoria Park* (covered).

History. A small town existed at the mouth of Portsmouth Harbour soon after the Conquest, but the real importance of Portsmouth may be dated from the reign of Henry VII, who established the first dry dock and declared Portsmouth a Royal dockyard and garrison. Remains of later Tudor fortifications are still an outstanding feature. Charles II was married here, in Government House, to Catherine of Braganza in 1662.—The distinguished natives of Portsmouth include Charles Dickens (1812–70; see below), whose father was a clerk in the dockyard; George Meredith (1828–1909); Sir Walter Besant (1835–1901); Isambard Kingdom

Brunel (1806–59), the engineer; Jonas Hanway (1712–86), the philanthropist; and John Pounds (1766–1839), the crippled cobbler who established the first 'ragged school' (1819). Its associations with Lord Nelson and other naval heroes are innumerable; and it frequently appears in the novels of Capt. Marryat. Mr Crummles (in 'Nicholas Nickleby') lived in St Thomas's St.; Nicholas and Smike in two small rooms, up two pairs of stairs and a ladder, at a tobacconist's shop on the Common Hard. Fanny Price, heroine of 'Mansfield Park', had her first home here. Conan Doyle here practised as a doctor and wrote his first Sherlock Holmes story, 'A Study in Scarlet'. H. G. Wells in 'Kipps' describes his years in Portsmouth. The city suffered heavily from air-raids in 1941–44, and was one of the main 'D'-day assembly areas.

At the centre of the city is the main railway station. Adjacent is the CIVIC CENTRE, with the Victorian *Guildhall* (gutted by fire 1941, restored 1959), the *Central Library*, and the civic offices. To the N. lies the main shopping area. All this district is being altered to a new plan involving realinement of roads and the creation of pedestrian zones. To the s.w. of the Civic Centre lies Old Portsmouth; to the s.e., Southsea; and to the w. the Dockyard. Between Old Portsmouth and the Dockyard is the United Services Recreation Ground, entered by two former town-gates, the *King James Gate* (1687) in Burnaby Road and the Land Port (1698) in its original position in St¹ George's Road.

At 393 Commercial Rd. the *Dickens Museum* (Adm. daily 10–4 or 6; fee) occupies the house in which Charles Dickens was born in 1812.

On Portsea Hard is the main entrance to the **Royal Dockyard** (visitors admitted to 'H.M.S. Victory' and museum only, 10–5; Sun 1–5). This, a town in itself, covers an area of over 300 acres and comprises 15 dry docks, 62 acres of fitting and repairing basins, 6000 yds. of wharfage, 10 miles of railway, some fine 18C houses, including the former Navigation School ('H.M.S. Dryad') and Admiralty House (the office of the Commander-in-Chief). Just inside the entrance is the 'quarter-deck', with the figurehead of H.M.S. 'Benbow' (1813) and the dockyard muster-bell, used from 1791 to 1922. In the *Old* or *King Charles's Dock* (1648) straight in front of the dockyard entrance is ***H.M.S. Victory**, which was moored in the harbour until 1921 and has been restored and fitted out almost to her appearance as at Trafalgar. Adm. free, but donation expected. Visitors are shown the spot where Nelson fell and the cockpit where he breathed his last. Before Trafalgar the 'Victory' was the flagship of Keppel, Kempenfelt, Howe, Hood, and Jervis, and afterwards of Saumarez; she still wears the flag of the Commander-in-Chief, Naval Home Command.

Facing the 'Victory' is the **Portsmouth Royal Naval Museum** (adm. fee), with an interesting collection of Nelson and other naval relics, and a Trafalgar panorama by W. L. Wyllie.— To the N. of the dockyard is *Whale Island*, occupied by the *Naval Gunnery School* ('H.M.S. Excellent). At the s. end of Portsea Hard is the castellated entrance to the *Gun Wharf*, with the Torpedo and Anti-Submarine School ('H.M.S. Vernon).

HIGH STREET, the chief street of Old Portsmouth, was devastated in 1941. The *Grammar School* founded in 1732, is largely contained in a former barracks with a fine Georgian façade. Among the few surviving old houses is *Buckingham House* (tablet), formerly the Spotted Dog Inn, where the first Duke of Buckingham (the 'Steenie' of James I) was assassinated by John Felton in 1628. Later (1634–35) the house belonged to John Mason, founder of New Hampshire and captain of Southsea Castle. The George Hotel, where Nelson spent the night before embark-

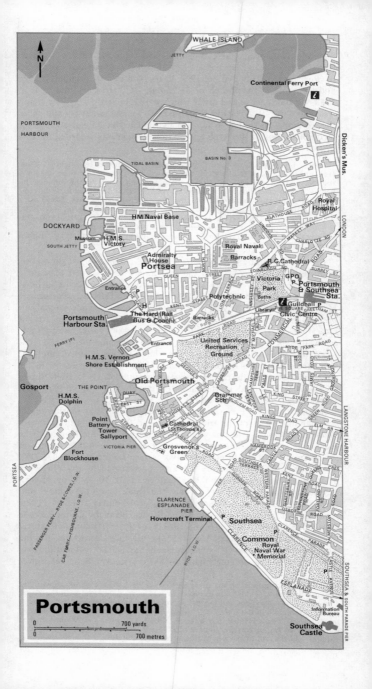

Portsmouth

WHALE ISLAND

JETTY

Continental Ferry Port

PORTSMOUTH
HARBOUR

TIDAL BASIN

BASIN No. 3

DICKEN'S Mus.

LONDON

Royal
Hospital

FLATHOUSE ROAD

LINDEN RD

MARKET WAY

CHARLOTTE RD

DOCKYARD

Museum

South Jetty

H.M.S.
Victory

HM Naval Base

Admiralty
House

Portsea

Royal Naval
Barracks

R.C. Cathedral

SURREY ST

EDINBURGH
ROAD

GPO

Victoria
Park

Portsmouth
& Southsea
Sta.

QUEEN

STREET

NORTH

Entrance

P

Baths

GREETHAM ST

H

Polytechnic

Library

Guildhall P
Civic Centre

KENT

STREET

Barracks

The Hard (Rail
Bus & Coach)

PARK

ROAD

Portsmouth
Harbour Sta.

COMMERCIAL

ROAD

HYDE

PARK

ROAD

FERRY (P)

Entrance

United Services
Recreation
Ground

H.M.S. Vernon
Shore Establishment

ST MICHAEL'S

HAMPSHIRE

TERRACE

GEORGE'S

ST JAMES'S ROAD

Gosport

THE POINT

Old Portsmouth

Grammar
Sch

KING

STREET

GREEN ROAD

LANGSTONE HARBOUR

H.M.S.
Dolphin

QUAY

EAST ST

ST THOMAS'S STREET

Cathedral
(St Thomas's)

KINGS

ROAD

ELM GR

Point
Battery
Tower
Sallyport

MUSEUM ROAD

HAMBROOK

ST

CASTLE

PORTSEA

Fort
Blockhouse

VICTORIA PIER

Grosvenor's
Green

PIER

ROAD

SOUTHSEA
TERRACE

WESTERN PARADE

KENT

ROAD

OSBORNE

ROAD

CLARENCE
ESPLANADE
PIER

P

Southsea

GROSVENOR

ST

CLARENCE

PARADE

PALMERSTON ROAD

PASSENGER FERRY—RYDE & COWES, I.O.W.

CAR FERRY—FISHBOURNE, I.O.W.

Hovercraft Terminal

P

Common
Royal
Naval War
Memorial

CLARENCE

SOUTHSEA & SOUTH PARADE PIER

CASTLE

AVENUE

RYDE I.O.W.

ESPLANADE

Information
Bureau

Southsea
Castle

0 ————— 700 yards
0 ————— 700 metres

N

ing on his last voyage (tablet on a new block), and Meredith's birthplace
(No. 73) have been destroyed. The unfinished **Cathedral** of the diocese
of Portsmouth, founded in 1927, incorporates the original chancel
and transepts of the church of *St Thomas of Canterbury*, dating from
1188–96, and its nave and tower which were rebuilt c. 1693. The cupola
was added in 1703. The old church now forms the sanctuary and choir;
the nave and aisles, begun in 1935 by Sir Charles Nicholson, are still
incomplete though the resolve to complete them was recorded in stone
in 1966.

The s. presbytery aisle (c. 1185) contains a monument by Nicholas Stone
(1631) to the Duke of Buckingham (see above), and the s. choir-aisle, known as
the 'Navy Aisle' (rededicated 1938), serves as a memorial to the innumerable
heroes of the Royal Navy. Here hangs a model (1929) of the 'Mary Rose' of 1669.
The choir, with a w. gallery of 1707, contains the Corporation Pew of 1693 and a
wall-painting of the Last Judgment (c. 1250) on the N.E. wall. In the nave is the
'Golden Barque', which served as a weather-vane'on the tower (1710–1954). The
new N. tower-transept contains a Della Robbia plaque of the Madonna.
    Several old houses survive in St Thomas's St., N. of the cathedral, with the
Cathedral House (1955), and in Lombard St.

Broad St., passing (l.) the *Sally Port*, the classic embarkation-point
of Britain's naval heroes, and the 15C *Round Tower* (open May–Sept,
10–sunset), runs N.W. to the *Point*, on the narrow entrance to the harbour.
Here a few alleys characteristic of the old town still survive. **Portsmouth
Harbour**, less than 300 yds wide at its entrance, expands into a vast
basin, 4 m. long and 2 m. broad, affording secure anchorage for the
largest vessels. Eastwards from the Round Tower a raised rampart and
sea-wall walk extends much of the way to Clarence Pier. Below the
ramparts, on Governor's Green, is the *Garrison Church*, an E.E.
structure originally a hospital ('Domus Dei'), with the patients in the
nave and a chapel in the choir; the nave was gutted in 1941. Gen. Napier
(1782–1853) is buried in the churchyard. Farther on, in Pembroke
Gardens, is a statue of Nelson (by F. B. Hitch; 1951).

Beyond Clarence Pier we reach **Southsea**, a popular seaside resort
commanding views of the Isle of Wight and the shipping in Spithead.
Southsea Common, laid out with *Gardens, extends the length of the
Esplanade. Among the memorials on the Esplanade are the anchor of
the 'Victory', and the large *Naval War Memorial* (comp. pp. 47, 218).
Southsea Castle, built by Henry VIII and now restored, houses a museum
of local archaeology and military history (daily 10–4, 6, or 9; fee).
Beyond are the Information Bureau, the Rock Garden Pavilion, and
South Parade Pier, one of the centres of local holiday activity. A few
yards farther is the 'D'-day Memorial Stone. Near the Canoe Lake is
Cumberland House Museum (daily 10–4, 6, or 9; free), mainly of natural
history. The former Officers' Mess (1868) of Eastney Barracks houses the
Royal Marines Museum (10–4, closed Sat & Sun at 12; free) and *Eastney
Beam Engine House* with machinery of 1887 is open Apr–Sept, Sat, Sun &
BH.

Opposite Portsmouth, on the other side of the harbour (ferry, see above), lies
Gosport, a town of 75,900 inhab., many of whom are connected with the *Royal
Clarence Victualling Yard* and the *Royal Naval Armament Depot*. Near Gosport
Hard is the church of the *Holy Trinity*, containing an organ brought from Canons,
in Middlesex, where Handel may have played on it. *Haslar Bridge* (no vehicles)
leads hence to *Haslar Hospital* (façade of 1746–62), with accommodation for 2000
patients. At the end of the Sea Wall are *H.M.S. 'Dolphin'*, the submarine base,

and *Fort Blockhouse* at the entrance to the harbour. From Gosport buses run to *Fareham*, to *Alverstoke* (Hotel), a seaside resort 1 m. s.w., and to *Lee-on-the-Solent*, a bathing resort with a naval air station (H.M.S. 'Daedalus'), 3 m. w.

FROM PORTSMOUTH TO SOUTHAMPTON, 21 m. (railway in c. 50 min.).—We skirt the base of *Portsdown*, with Portsmouth Harbour on the left.—7¼ m. **Portchester**, i.e. *Portus Castra*, was the site of a Roman *Fortress (Portus Adurni) guarding the Saxon shore, the superb bastions of which are second alone in interest to Hadrian's Wall. Current excavations (not always visible) are now revealing also extensive Saxon occupation. In the N.W. angle of the Roman fortress, remarkably well preserved, Henry II built a *Castle (adm. daily; closed Sun in winter till 2; fee) in 1160–72, which was extended by Edward II and Richard II; here Henry V mustered his Agincourt expedition. The roof of the Keep commands the entire harbour. The *Church, in the s.e. angle, was founded by Austin Canons in 1133.· On Portsdown is a *Nelson Monument* (150 ft) erected by his comrades at Trafalgar.—10½ m. **Fareham** (Hotels), a busy market town (80,300 inhab.) with a fine High St., is also on A 32, the road to Gosport (5 m. s.) and to the Meon Valley and Alton (see Rte 11A). *Boarhunt*, with a late-Saxon church, is 3 m. N.E.—11 m. *Titchfield* has a large church (Saxon to Perp.) with a splendid monument of the Southampton family by Gerard Johnson (1594), and the remains of *Titchfield Abbey* (daily, Sun from 2; fee) built by the first Earl of Southampton in 1542 on the site of and incorporating the nave of the abbey church (1232–38). Here Margaret of Anjou, just landed at Southampton, was married to Henry VI in 1445, and here Charles I was arrested in 1647 before his imprisonment in Carisbrooke.—21 m. *Southampton*, see Rte 11.

From Portsmouth to *Chichester*, see Rte 10A; to the *Isle of Wight*, see Rte 12.

11 LONDON TO SOUTHAMPTON

A Viâ Alton and Winchester

ROAD, 78½ m. From London to (29½ m.) *Guildford*, see Rte 10B.—A 31. 39½ m. *Farnham.*—48½ m. *Alton.*—65½ m. *Winchester.*—A 33. 77½ m. **Southampton**.

RAILWAY, 47 m. From Waterloo to Alton, electric service in c. 70 min. Principal stations: To (24½ m.) *Woking*, see Rte 10B.—34½ m. *Farnham.*—38½ m. **Aldershot**.— 47 m. *Alton*. Bus from Alton to Winchester. A private company intends to reopen the former rail link to Winchester (comp. p. 113). Main line, see Rte 11B.

From London to (29 m.) the beginning of the Guildford by-pass, see Rte 10B. After 3 m. more we ascend to the right on to A 31, which follows the chalk ridge known as the HOG'S BACK (350–500 ft; Hotel near w. end), a favourite excursion spot, with wide views.

39½ m. **Farnham** (Hotels) is a thriving town (31,200 inhab.) with good Georgian houses. Since 688 the manor has belonged to the Bishops of Winchester, and their princely *Castle dominates the town. The ruined moated keep (adm. Apr–Sept, daily, Sun from 2; fee) was erected in 1160–75 by Bp. Henry of Blois after an earlier tower had been slighted (its deep well-shaft has been exposed). The Centre for International Briefing occupies the domestic buildings (open to the public Wed, 2–4.30; fee) which owe their present form mainly to Bp. Morley (1662–84; fine staircase and chapel), though incorporating the Norman Great Hall, chapel, and kitchen; 'Fox's Tower', in fact the work of William of Wayneflete, is a notable example of early brickwork. Castle St., broad and dignified, descends. In the churchyard of the large *St Andrew's* is the tomb of William Cobbett (1763–1835), who was probably born in the house now the 'Jolly Farmer Inn'. The *Willmer House Museum* (38 West St.; Tues–Sat 11–5, Sun 2.30–5) is devoted to local history and Cobbett mementoes. Charles I spent a night on his way to trial in London at the house now occupied by the Library.

Sir Walter Scott is said to have taken the name of his first novel from *Waverley Abbey* (founded in 1129), the earliest Cistercian house in England, the ruins of which (1203–31) lie in the lovely valley of the Wey, 2 m. s.e. of Farnham, by the Godalming road. The ruins are unsafe and are closed for repairs (1971). Beyond the river is *Moor Park* (now an Anglican education centre), where Swift, as secretary to Sir Wm. Temple, first met Stella (Esther Johnson) in 1697; 'Stella's Cottage' is a little to the N.—*Crondall*, 4 m. N.W. of Farnham, has a fine Norman church with a good brass of a priest.

From Farnham an attractive road (bus) runs s. to (8½ m.) Hindhead, across *Frensham Common* (665 acres N.T.), passing (4½ m.) *Frensham Pond* (Hotel). The three "rather squat sugar-loaf hills", c. 2 m. e., are known as the *Devil's Jumps*. The easternmost ('Stony Jump') is open to the public.—At (6 m.) *Churt* (Hotel) Lloyd George lived (at 'Bron-y-de') in 1925–44.

About 3 m. N. of Farnham lies **Aldershot** (Hotels), an inconsiderable village before the establishment of the MILITARY CAMP in 1855, but now having a total population of 33,300 (incl. the troops). The camp is c. 10 sq. m. in area, with its 'Lines', barracks, and military institutions of all kinds. On the w. of the town is an equestrian statue of Wellington, brought from London (Green Park Arch) in 1885, about 1 m. s. of which is the height known as *Caesar's Camp* (600 ft).

For the direct road to London viâ Farnborough and Bagshot, see Rte 11b.

Beyond Farnham we leave on the left A 325, which traverses *Alice Holt Forest* (200 acres) with the Forestry Commission's research station, and leads to *Bordon* (6½ m.), with its large artillery camp. We enter Hampshire.—At (46 m.) *Holybourne* Mrs Gaskell died in 1865.

48½ m. **Alton** (Hotels), with 12,700 inhab., has a mainly 13–15C *Church* (St Laurence) with a Norman crossing, a Saxon font, and a 15C pillar painting depicting Henry VI. The s. door was riddled with Parliamentarian bullets in 1643 when the Cavalier Col. Boles was shot in the pulpit. The *Curtis Museum* (adm. free weekdays, 10–5; closed on Wed), in the long and attractive main street, contains a remarkable collection of old farm and craftsmen's tools, and of domestic utensils. The *Museum Annexe and Allen Gallery*, in Church St. opposite, is open weekdays at the same hours.—*Selborne*, 5 m. s.e., a charming village, was the home of Gilbert White (1720–93), author of 'The Natural History of Selborne'. The Wakes (adm. daily, exc. Fri, 2.30–5.30; and 11–1 weekdays Apr–Oct), the house in which he was born and died (with a fine library of 40,000 vols.), is preserved as a memorial to him. There are also relics of Capt. Oates, the Antarctic explorer. The church has a Norman font and piers; in the churchyard, where White is buried, is a fine old yew. Selborne Common (250 acres) belongs to the N.T.

FROM ALTON TO FAREHAM, A 32 (25 m.).—At (12½ m.) *West Meon*, where Thomas Lord (p. 644) was buried, we reach the pleasant Meon Valley. *East Meon*, a delightful village 3 m. e., has a *Church with a Tournai font (comp. p. 116); its fine Norman tower makes a splendid group with the Court House (c. 1400; no adm.) opposite. A ridge road (*Views) running s. from West Meon to H.M.S. 'Mercury' (R.N. signal school) passes the Iron Age fort known as *Old Winchester Hill*.—15½ m. *Corhampton* has a remarkable late-Saxon church with a plain Norman font and an old stone chair in the sanctuary.—17 m. *Droxford* has a part-Norman church and an 18C rectory (N.T.). The railway station was the headquarters of the War Cabinet immediately before 'D' Day (1944). *Hambledon*, 3½ m. s.e., claims to be the birthplace of cricket (1774). Its church is of peculiar plan and of many periods.—21½ m. *Wickham*, birthplace of William of Wykeham (1324–1404), has a fine square and a flour mill made from the timbers of the 'Chesapeake'.—25 m. *Fareham*, see p. 111.

At (49½ m.) *Chawton* is the red-brick house (adm. daily 11–4.30; fee) occupied by Jane Austen in 1809–17, the period of her chief works.— 58½ m. *New Alresford* (Hotels) keeps its plan of 1200 in which a Broad St., perhaps the most attractive in the county, rises from a small lake towards the church tower. A tablet marks the birthplace of Mary R. Mitford (1787–1855), authoress of 'Our Village'. Steam trains run daily Mar–Oct to Ropley (3 m.); it is hoped eventually to reopen all the former 'watercress' line from Alton to Winchester. Admiral Rodney (d. 1792) is buried at *Old Alresford*, 1 m. N.—*Tichborne* (2 m. s.w.) is a pleasant village with a partly Saxon church (10–11C).

Just s. of an alternative road to Winchester (B 3047), viâ Itchen Abbas, is *Avington Park*, 4 m. N.E. of the city, a charming early 18C house (adm. 2.30–5.30, Sat, Sun, & BH, May–Sept; fee).

65½ m. **WINCHESTER**, one of the great historical cities of England (31,000 inhab.), once the capital of the kingdom, and famous for its cathedral and its school, is situated at the base and on the slope of a hill rising from the Itchen. As well as being a market centre and regimental depot, it is the assize and county town of Hampshire.

Car Parks in Middle Brook St., Tower St. (multi-story), etc.
Hotels in the precincts, in Southgate St., and St Peter St., etc.; **Restaurants**.
Post Office, Middle Brook St.—INFORMATION OFFICE, Colebrook St.
Bus Station, Broadway, for all destinations.—COACH STATION, Worthy Lane.

History. Winchester, which in 1897 celebrated the 1000th anniversary of its civic institutions, is the successor of the British settlement of *Caer Gwent*, the Roman town of *Venta Belgarum*, and the Saxon *Wintanceaster*, which became the capital of Wessex in 519 and saw Egbert crowned as first king of all England in 827. Christianity was introduced by Bp. Birinus in 634, though the bishopric was not founded till 40 years later. Winchester was the capital of Alfred and of many of his successors, including Canute and the Danish kings; Edward the Confessor was crowned in the Old Minster in 1043; and William the Conqueror made the city a joint capital with London and was crowned in both, an example followed by several of his successors. In commerce Winchester was long the rival of London, reaching its zenith in the 12C, but by the time of Henry VIII its famous wool industry had died out. Here Henry III (Henry of Winchester) was born in 1207, and here in 1100 Henry I, in 1402 Henry IV, and in 1554 Mary and Philip of Spain were married. In 1213, at the door of the cathedral, Abp. Stephen Langton absolved King John from excommunication. Winchester was captured by Cromwell in 1645, after the battle of Naseby. The unfinished palace adjoining the castle, begun by Wren for Charles II in 1683, was burned down in 1897.—The *Statute of Winchester* (1285) was a kind of early police act.—Keats wrote the 'Ode to Autumn' and possibly finished 'The Eve of St Agnes' at Winchester (1819).

Since 1953 demolition and rebuilding in Winchester have given occasion for an important programme of excavation N. of the Cathedral (site of the Roman Forum) and on various other sites. Sections of a Roman road have been discovered in St George's St., N. of the High St.; medieval town houses have been investigated in Lower Brook St.; and work continues on the Roman defences, the Norman bishop's palace at Wolvesey, and at the site of the new Law Courts. Some of the finds are on exhibition in the city museum, but many still await room for display. During the excavation season (June–Oct) tours and lectures on the sites take place daily.

The sharp curves of Magdalen Hill descend to *Soke Bridge* across the Itchen. On the right the *City Mill* (1744; N.T.), now a youth hostel, is open free on Mon, Tues, and Fri, also BH, 10–1. Flanking the BROADWAY are (l.) the *Abbey Grounds*, on the site of 'Nunnaminster', a convent for Benedictine nuns, founded by Alswitha, wife of King Alfred. A bronze statue of Alfred, by Hamo Thorneycroft, dominates the street. The *Guildhall* (1873) has been restored after a fire in 1969. Beyond *St John's Hospital* (13C chapel adjoining the Bus Stn; apply opposite), HIGH STREET (part closed to traffic in 1972) rises towards the West Gate. The tower of the demolished *St Maurice's Church* (l.) preserves a Norman doorway. The colonnaded *Pentice* has overhanging gables, barge-boards, and moulded ridge-tiles. The Butter Cross dates from the 15C (restored). A passage leads through *The Square* to the Cathedral precinct. The church of *St Laurence* probably occupies the site of the Conqueror's Chapel Royal. The City Museum (weekdays 10–4, 5, or 6; Sun 2–4; free) displays archaeological finds from Winchester and Hampshire. These include Belgic pottery; Roman mosaic floors and painted wall plaster; fragment of a carved Saxon cross-shaft; Saxon coins minted in Winchester; painted stone from the Saxon New Minster; 12C inscription commemorating King Alfred (from Hyde Abbey); and Wren's drawings for Charles II's palace.

The *Cathedral, dedicated to St Peter, St Paul, and the Holy Trinity, is a building of high architectural interest, though disappointing at first sight owing to its unimposing w. front and the absence of a lofty tower. It is the longest medieval church in Europe (526 ft; St Peter's at Rome 611 ft) and ranks fifth in point of area among English cathedrals. The *West Front* (by which we enter) is approached by a fine avenue of limes. Opposite are a War Memorial (by Herbert Baker), incorporating a stone from the Cloth Hall at Ypres, and a fine statue of a Rifleman (K.R.R.C.) by Tweed.

History. Excavations begun in 1961 to the N. of the existing cathedral located the Saxon Old Minster built by Cenwalh, king of Wessex, in 643–648 on the site of the Roman forum. Outside the w. door of this the original cathedral of Eastern Wessex, *St Swithin*, or Swithun, Bp. of Winchester, was buried in 862. On 15 July 971 his remains were transferred to a golden shrine within the church; and it is the legendary delay of this removal, caused by forty days of rain, that accounts for St Swithin's control of the weather after that date. The church was then given a w. extension to honour the original shrine and, in 980–994 extended to the E. To the N. of the Old Minster was the New Minster, an abbey founded by King Alfred and built by Edward the Elder in 903. This removed before 1110 outside the N. gate of the city (comp. p. 120). To the w. lay the Royal Palace. Of all this complex, comparable with that of Aachen, nothing is now visible.

The present fabric was begun by *Bp. Walkelin* "from the foundations" in 1079 and consecrated in 1093. Walkelin's superb Norman building received additions in the E.E. style from *Bp. Godfrey de Lucy* (1189–1204). *Bp. Edington* (1346–66) rebuilt the w. front and began the transformation of the nave from Norman to Perp., which was mainly carried on by the great *Bp. William of Wykeham* (1367–1404) but actually completed by *Bp. Waynflete* (1447–86). The arduous task of underpinning the foundations of the cathedral, which the original builders had not carried down to sufficiently firm ground, was satisfactorily accomplished in 1905–12 by Sir T. G. Jackson and Sir Francis Low.

The Southern Cathedrals Festival of music is held annually (in July) in rotation with Chichester and Salisbury (Winchester next in 1981).

Interior. The core of the interesting and imposing *Nave, with its thick walls, bold vaulting, and massive piers, is substantially the work of Walkelin. The two w. bays on the N. side and the w. bay on the s. side were rebuilt by Bp. Edington (see above), and the remainder, including the arcades, was transformed by Bp. Wykeham into the new Perp. style. This was done without pulling down the old 11C work; the Gothic mouldings of the s. piers are simply cut in the Norman stones. The main arcade and clerestory were greatly enlarged, while the triforium was reduced to the present beautiful little balcony. Most of the windows are very graceful. Fragments of 14C glass remain in the aisles and clerestory and in the great w. window. The magnificent lierne vault bears the arms of Edington and Wykeham. Against the w. wall are statues of James I and Charles I, by Le Sueur. In the s. arcade of the nave are the two earliest of an unsurpassed series of

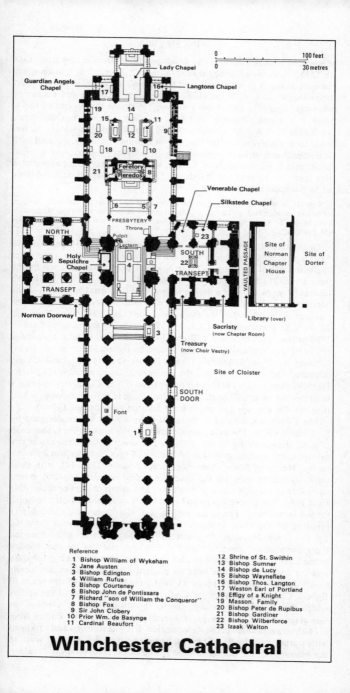

Reference
1 Bishop William of Wykeham
2 Jane Austen
3 Bishop Edington
4 William Rufus
5 Bishop Courteney
6 Bishop John de Pontissara
7 Richard "son of William the Conqueror"
8 Bishop Fox
9 Sir John Clobery
10 Prior Wm. de Basynge
11 Cardinal Beaufort

12 Shrine of St. Swithin
13 Bishop Sumner
14 Bishop de Lucy
15 Bishop Wayneflete
16 Bishop Thos. Langton
17 Weston Earl of Portland
18 Effigy of a Knight
19 Masson. Family
20 Bishop Peter de Rupibus
21 Bishop Gardiner
22 Bishop Wilberforce
23 Izaak Walton

Winchester Cathedral

Chantries, which illustrates the development of architecture from 1366 to 1555. *Edington's Chantry* is near the E. end. Succeeding it in date, and far surpassing it in splendour, is *Wykeham's Chantry*, in the fifth bay from the w. end, with the effigy of the great architect and statesman (d. 1404; figures in the niches restored, 1893). At the w. end of the N. aisle is a stone *Cantoria* or minstrel gallery, in which (May–Sept, weekdays 11–1 & 2.30–4, Sun 2.30–4.30; fee) is displayed notable silverware from the *Treasury*. On the wall of this aisle (which is covered with Riflemen's memorials), opposite the Wykeham Chantry, are a brass tablet and a window to Jane Austen, who lies beneath the pavement at this spot. In the next bay stands the *Font* (12C), carved with the story of St Nicholas of Myra.

This is one of seven fonts in England of dark Tournai marble, with rich carvings of Belgian workmanship (12–13C). The others are at Southampton (St Michael's), East Meon, St Mary Bourne, Lincoln (Cathedral), Thornton Curtis, and Ipswich (St Peter's).

Opposite Edington's Chantry is the Jacobean pulpit.—The massive *Transepts* remain much as Walkelin left them (1079–98) and represent the vast scale of his design. Later Norman work (distinguished by the finer masonry) is a rebuilding necessitated by the fall of Walkelin's central tower in 1107, popularly attributed to the burial beneath it of the heretical king William Rufus in 1100. Under the organ-loft of the N. transept is the *Chapel of the Holy Sepulchre* (12C; 13C *Wall Paintings of the Life and Passion of Christ). The w. aisle was screened off in 1908 as the *Epiphany Chapel* (Burne-Jones windows). The s. transept is rendered less impressive than the N. arm by the enclosure of the aisles, forming (E.) *Prior Silkstede's Chapel* (1524) and the *Venerable Chapel* (elaborate iron-work) and (w.) the *Treasury of Henry de Blois* (1129–71). Izaak Walton (1593–1683), who died at No. 7 The Close, lies beneath a tablet in Silkstede's Chapel. The s. choir aisle is entered through a 12C iron *Grille, that used to admit to St Swithin's shrine (see below).

The Choir is separated from the nave by an oak screen designed by Sir Gilbert Scott. The excessive stoutness of the tower-piers is the result of their strengthening after the fall of the tower. Under the tower is a marble tomb traditionally that of William Rufus but ascribed by some to Bp. Henry of Blois. The magnificent *Stalls (1305–10), with their vigorous misericords, are the oldest cathedral-stalls in England except some fragments at Rochester; the desks and stools of the upper tier date from 1540. The pulpit was given by Prior Silkstede (c. 1520); the bishop's throne is modern. The piers, arches, and clerestory of the *Presbytery* (prolonging the choir towards the E.) were rebuilt early in the 14C. Bp. Fox (1501–28) rebuilt the outer walls of the presbytery aisles, inserted the tracery of the clerestory and E. window, and put up the wooden lierne vault. To him are due also the screens between the presbytery and the aisles, which now bear six painted and gilded mortuary chests (four of 1525, and two copies, of 1661), made to contain the bones of Egbert, Canute, and other pre-Conquest monarchs. Two of the coffers which they contained stand in the N. choir aisle. The E. window has fine glass of c. 1525. The great *Reredos*, almost certainly dating from c. 1480, was mutilated at the Reformation, but was restored and equipped with statues in 1884–91. There is, however, some fine original work in the spandrels of the doors. On the E. side of the reredos is the *Feretory*,

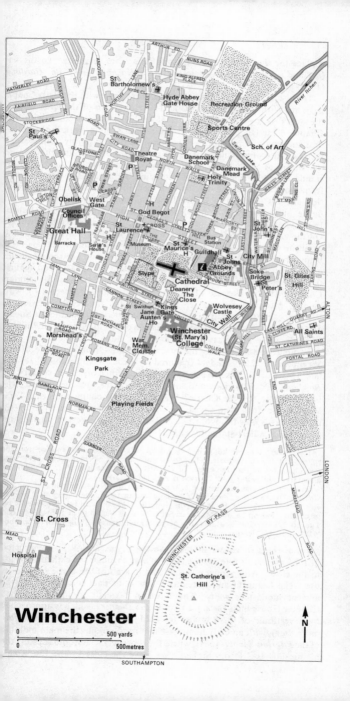

Winchester

| 0 | 500 yards |
| 0 | 500 metres |

N

SOUTHAMPTON

a place for the 'feretra' or shrines for the relics of saints. To the left (N.) and right (S.) of the feretory are the *Chantries of Bp. Gardiner* (1555) and *Bp. Fox* (1528).

To the E. is the large RETRO-CHOIR of three bays, with the Lady Chapel beyond. With the exception of the 15C elongation of the Lady Chapel the work is by Bp. de Lucy (1189–1204) and (together with the Chapel of the Holy Sepulchre) is the earliest Gothic work in the cathedral and (saving Lincoln choir) perhaps the earliest purely Gothic work in England (comp. Chichester). In the centre of the retro-choir stood the shrine of St Swithin. Here, above 13C encaustic floor-tiles, now stands a new shrine (1962) of the saint, by Brian Thomas, an iron framework supporting a canopy with medallions of the saint's consecration and his teaching of Prince Ethelwulf and, at the w. end, a relief figure of St Swithin in brass, with the first bridge over the Itchen. In the windows are panels of 13C grisaille glass (s. side) from Salisbury. On the E. wall of the feretory, at the w. end of the retro-choir, are nine exquisite niches, and below is the entrance to the 'Holy Hole', or vault below the feretory. In the retro-choir on either side are the *Chantries of Bp. Waynflete* (1486; N.) and *Cardinal Beaufort* (1447; s.), and against the N.E. pier is a wooden figure of *St Joan of Arc* (by Sir Ninian Comper; 1923). The late 12C *Chapel of the Guardian Angels* (N.), with painted *Roof-medallions (c. 1240), contains the tomb of Richard Weston, earl of Portland (d. 1635), a masterpiece ascribed to Le Sueur, and Queen Mary's Chair, used by the queen on her marriage with Philip II of Spain. The 15C glass in the E. window came from Salisbury. The admirable woodwork and the mural paintings from the 'Life of the Virgin' in the *Lady Chapel* (restored by Prof. Tristram, 1933–36) are late 15C work. The chapel to the 's. was fitted up as a chantry by *Bp. Langton* (1501); its woodwork is remarkable. At the entrance (l.) is a statuette, by Sir Charles Wheeler (1962), commemorating Wm. Walker, the diver who saved the cathedral from collapse in 1906–12, though this is now thought to be a likeness of Wm. West, his mate; and (r.) a fine headless statue (c. 1235).

The CRYPT (adm. weekdays in Aug & Sept; apply verger; fee), entered from the N. transept, is in three parts. The first two of these are Norman, of the same date and character as the transepts. In the first and larger is a *Well* of unknown antiquity. The rectangular E. crypt is E.E. (1189–1204).

Over the passage between the s. transept and the Norman arches of the old Chapter House is the *Library* (12C; reconstructed 1668), containing 4000 printed vols and some rare MSS. It is open (fee) 10.30–12.30 & 2.30–4.30 on weekdays (exc. Mon morn.) in mid-May–mid-Sept; Wed & Sat only in Sept–May (also Tues 10–12). Its chief treasures are a magnificent illuminated Vulgate in three folios (12C) and a 12C leather binding.

From the s.w. corner of the nave the *Slype*, a passage constructed in 1636 as a substitute for the right of way through the cathedral, leads to the close. Anagrams on the w. and E. arch of the Slype refer to its use. The beautiful and spacious CLOSE is in part surrounded by the ancient monastery walls. The Norman *Arcade of the demolished Chapter House links the s. transept to the *Deanery*, which is approached by a vestibule of three arches (c. 1225–50). The 14C *Pilgrims' Hall* (adm. free), with an early hammer-beam roof, adjoins the main building of the *Pilgrims School* (1687), where the choristers' classrooms occupy the picturesque 16C Priory Stables. We leave the close by the 13C *King's*

Gate, over which is the church of *St Swithun* (rebuilt in the 16C).

Kingsgate St. is lined with old houses, mostly belonging to the College; on No. 9 is a tablet to S. S. Wesley, the anthem composer, cathedral organist in 1849–64.

In College St., on the s. side, is the house in which Jane Austen died (tablet). On the same side farther on is the great gateway (1394–97; wood figure of the Virgin) of *Winchester College* or *St Mary's College*, founded by William of Wykeham in 1382 and the model for the great public schools of England. The first stone of the chapel was laid in 1387, and the buildings were occupied in 1394. The school is allied with New College at Oxford founded by Wykeham in 1379. Besides the 70 foundation scholars, who live in college, there are about 450 'commoners', living in masters' houses.

The chapel, the war memorial cloister, and, during term, the old cloisters and chantry, are open free 10–4 or 6 (Sun from 2); the college is open on Bank Holidays exc. 25–26 Dec). Conducted tours of the most interesting buildings (fee) are made exc. on Wed & on Sun mornings) at 10, 11.45, 2, 3, and (Apr–Sept only) 4.30. Tours start from Outer Gate in College St.
To the left of Outer Court are the *Warden's Lodgings*, with a frontage of 1833. Within the Middle Gate is Chamber Court. Here the *Chapel* retains its original fan-tracery ceiling of wood (by Hugh Herland, designer of the roof of Westminster Hall) and some original *Glass depicting Richard II from the E. window (now in the late 15C s. chapel). The *Dining Hall* has a fine oaken roof renewed in 1819. In the passage to the *Kitchen* is a curious figure of the 'Trusty Servant', placed there in 1809. The lavatory and boot-cleaning room are known as *Moab* and *Edom* (Ps. lx. 8; cviii. 9). In the middle of Wykeham's *Cloisters* is *Fromond's Chantry* (1420–45), with good glass of 1502. The ground floor serves as a chapel for the younger scholars; above is a library devoted to the history of the college. In the garth is buried Lord Wavell (1883–1950), while the cloister is carved with the names of Bp. Ken (1656) and many other notable Wykehamists. On the wall of 'School' (1683–87; not shown in term-time), usually ascribed to Wren, is the inscription 'aut disce, aut discede, manet sors tertia caedi' ('learn, leave, or be licked'). To the E, beyond the mill-stream, is the *New Hall* (1958–60), by P. Shepheard, lined with the oak panelling and screen (1680–82) formerly installed in Chapel. The beautiful *War Memorial Cloister* (adm. free, entrance in Kingsgate St.), by Sir Herbert Baker, commemorates over 500 Wykehamists who fell in 1914–18 and 270 who fell in 1939–45. The *College Sickhouse* dates from 1656. Use of the fine *Swimming Pool and Gymnasium* (1968) is not confined to the college.

Among famous Wykehamists may be mentioned Grocyn, Sir Henry Wotton, Sir Thomas Browne, Bp. Ken, Otway, Sydney Smith, Trollope, Dr. Arnold and Matthew Arnold, the Earls of Selborne, Lord Grey of Fallodon, Lord Wavell and Lord Dowding.

On the left (N.) side of College St. are the ruins of *Wolvesey Castle*, begun by Bp. Henry of Blois in 1129, and now under restoration. Of the medieval building, most of which was destroyed by Waller in 1646, the Perp. chapel survives, and the foundations of the huge Great Hall have been located. The castle grounds provide a playing field for the Pilgrims School.

A wing of the adjacent *Wolvesey Palace*, perhaps designed by Wren for Bp. Morley in 1684, is now the bishop's residence; the rest was pulled down in 1800.—College Walk is prolonged by a path along the Itchen that affords the most pleasant approach to St Cross (see below).

An attractive path between the *City Wall* and the Itchen leads back to Soke Bridge (comp. p. 113).

Beyond the bridge, at the corner of Cheesehill St., is a mid-15C house (now a restaurant) claiming to be the oldest in Winchester. *St John's Church*, ¼ m. N, is of various periods from the 12C to the 16C and has aisles wider than the nave. It contains 13C paintings discovered in 1958 in the embrasures of two lancet windows uncovered in the N. aisle. *St Peter's Church*, Cheese Hill (13–14C), has been con verted into a theatre club. The Norman font has been placed in *All Saints.—S Giles's Hill*, to the E., commands a good view.

Beyond the Butter Cross High St. continues the ascent past (r.) the *Manor of God Begot* (No. 101), a Tudor house with a modern half timbered façade, and (l.) the *Old Guildhall* (now a bank), with the curfew bell-tower and a clock (1713) commemorating the Treaty of Utrecht, to the *West Gate*. A good specimen of medieval military architecture (archway 13C; upper part c. 1380), it contains a small museum (adm 10–4, 5, or 6; Sun 2–4.30; fee; free Thurs) with a fine array of medieval weights, the 13C moot horn, and the city champion's costume. Castle Hill (l.) leads to the *Great Hall* (adm. weekdays 10–4, 4.30 or 5, free; Sur in summer 2–4.30, fee) of the castle begun by William the Conqueror and enlarged and altered by Henry III in 1222–36. Here Raleigh was tried in 1603 beneath its clustered columns of Purbeck marble and beautiful two-light windows. At the w. end, above the remains of the royal dais hangs the so-called 'Round Table of King Arthur' (18 ft in diameter) known to have been here in 1400 and scientifically dated in 1976 to the 14C it was painted in 1522 for a visit of the Emp. Charles V (repainted 1789) Adjoining the Great Hall rise the new *Law Courts*. To the N. are the buildings of *County Hall* (1959–60) with a well-designed multi-story car park adjoining in Tower St.

The *Royal Greenjackets Museum* (adm. Mon–Fri, 10 or 10.30–12.30 & 2–4 o 4.30, Sat in Apr–Sept only, 2.30–4.30) is in Romsey Road. Tower St or Jewry S and its prolongation Hyde St, in which are some fine 17C houses, lead to ($\frac{1}{2}$ m. the gatehouse, the sole surviving relic of *Hyde Abbey*. This house, originally known as the *New Minster* (comp. p. 114), removed to its present site c. 1110. The monk brought with them the body of King Alfred, but its resting-place is now unknown —Near by is *St Bartholomew's Church*, with some Norman fragments. Farthe on is *North Walls Recreation Ground*.

Southgate St., opposite Jewry St., retains an 18C appearance. Beyond the Southgate Hotel (1715) is *Serle's House*, with the Royal Hampshire Regiment Museum (Mon–Fri 10–12.30 & 2–4, free). About 1 m farther on, reached by St Cross Rd (on foot, see above), stands the venerable **Hospital of St Cross* (adm. weekdays, summer 9.30–12 & 2–5, winter 10–11.30 & 2–3.30; fee). Visitors are conducted by a brother.

This was founded by Bp. Henry of Blois for 13 poor brethren in 1136, and second foundation (of 'Noble Poverty') was added by Card. Beaufort in 1446 The brethren of the first foundation wear a black gown, with a Jerusalem cross while the others have a red gown bearing a cardinal's hat. Passing through the outer court, we take our tickets at the *Beaufort Tower*, where the 'Wayfarer' Dole' of bread and ale is supplied to all applicants. In the inner court are the *Brethren's Houses* (c. 1445), the *Refectory*, the *Kitchen*, the *Master's House*, the *Infirmary*, and the **Church*, a fine example of its period (1136–c. 1250). The unusual lectern dates from 1510, and in front of the altar is the brass of a Master of the Hospital (1410). The triptych in the s. chapel is attributed to Mabuse (1470–1532 'The Warden', by Trollope, and 'Brother Copas', by Quiller-Couch, undoubtedly refer to St Cross.
Across the river, to the E., rises *St Catherine's Hill* (255 ft), commanding fine view. At the top are a clump of trees, an Iron Age fort, the foundations of medieval chapel, and a 'mizmaze' cut in the turf. *Chilcomb* (1 m.), in the valley to the N., has a very early little Norman church.

FROM WINCHESTER TO FAREHAM, A 333, 19$\frac{3}{4}$ m.—Beyond (3$\frac{1}{2}$ m.) *Twyford*

(d. 1572), was famous for its stout resistance, under the fifth marquess, to the Parliamentarians for two years, finally yielding to Cromwell himself (1645) when Inigo Jones was one of the prisoners taken. Little remains intact except the 16C gatehouse and dovecote (adm. March–Oct daily 10–6; Sun 2–6; fee).—A 30 avoids Basingstoke by a by-pass (l.).

46 m. **Basingstoke** (Hotels), with a growing 'overspill' population, is a thriving modern town (52,500 inhab.). Close to the station, in an old 'liten' or graveyard said to owe its origin to the Interdict of 1207, which closed the ordinary graveyards, are the ruins of the *Holy Ghost Chapel* (1525). *St Michael* is a good 16C town church. In New St. the *Willis Museum* (10–12.30, 1.30–5.30, exc. Mon morn.) has local collections.

About 3 m. N. is *The Vyne*, a mansion of c. 1520, enlarged by John Webb and much altered inside after 1754, with a chapel much lauded by Horace Walpole (early 16C glass and tiles from Flanders). It is now N.T. property and is open Easter–Sept, Wed & BH 11–1, 2–6, Thurs, Sat & Sun 2–6 (fee; teas).

An alternative route to Winchester, 1 m. longer than the main road, runs viâ (4 m.) *Farleigh Wallop*, with Farleigh House, rebuilt by the first earl of Portsmouth (c. 1750).—At (9½ m.) *Chilton Candover* the crypt of the destroyed Norman church has been excavated.

From Basingstoke to *Salisbury*, etc., see Rte 14.

Beyond (61 m.) *King's Worthy* the Winchester by-pass diverges left. *Headbourne Worthy* (r.) has important Saxon work in its church, notably a fine but damaged *Rood.—63½ m. **Winchester** and thence to Southampton, see Rte 11A. The new road avoids the villages.

75½ m. **SOUTHAMPTON** (214,800 inhab.), a great seaport with many historic associations and interesting ancient remains, is finely situated at the head of Southampton Water, the estuary of the Test, on a peninsula bounded on the E. by the river Itchen. The harbour, one of the best natural harbours in England, has the advantage of a double tide, first viâ the Solent and then (two hours later) viâ Spithead. A notable feature of the city is the provision of many parks and gardens.

Airport, 3½ m. N. of the centre, with services to Manchester, Glasgow, Dublin, Jersey, Guernsey, Alderney, Paris, etc.
Railway Stations. Central (Rfmts), for all through services; several local stations, including Southampton Airport, served by London trains. Special trains to docks for some steamer sailings.
Hotels in the High St., near the Civic Centre and near the New Docks.
Post Office, 59 High St.—INFORMATION BUREAU, The Junction, Above Bar St.
Travel Agents. *American Express*, E. Jones, Queensway; *Thos. Cook & Son*, 31 Oxford St.
Buses. Long distance, from Bedford Place and near Civic Centre.—CITY AND DOCKS TOURS, from Civic Centre (summer only; times from Inf. Bureau).
Ferries. To *Cowes*: steamer from Royal Pier, cars, frequent; hydrofoil from Royal Pier, no cars, frequent; hovercraft from Crosshouse Rd., no cars, frequent.— To *Hythe*, steamer from Town Quay, no cars, half-hourly.—Continental and Morocco car ferries, mainly from Princess Alexandra Dock.—STEAMER CRUISES from Royal Pier to view docks, liners, Esso oil refinery; also from Hythe Pier at 2.30 p.m. every weekday in summer.
Amusements. THEATRES. *Nuffield Theatre* at the university; *Gaumont*, Commercial Rd. Concerts, etc., at *Guildhall*, Civic Centre.—SWIMMING. *Central Baths* (Olympic with 10-metre diving-stage), *Lido* (open air), both Western Esplanade.—BOWLS. 'Old Green', near God's House Tower, claims to be the oldest in England (1299) and is the scene every Aug of the Knighthood Contest (dating from 1776). Extensive facilities for many other sports at the SPORTS CENTRE, Lordswood.

History. The Saxon town of *Hamwih* (still being excavated) superseded the Roman *Clausentum* (now Bitterne) on the other side of the Itchen. Both already had overseas trade, and it is said that at Hamwih Canute administered the famous rebuke to his courtiers (comp. p. 103). After the Norman Conquest the Continental trade of Southampton became of great importance. The town had a piped water supply by 1290. Part of Richard Cœur-de-Lion's crusading fleet sailed from Southampton in 1189; in 1345 and 1415 the armies that conquered at Crécy and Agincourt took ship here; and in modern times it has continued to be the principal port of embarkation for troops on foreign service down to 1914 and again in 1944. The most notable of many hostile descents was that of 1338, when a large French, Spanish, and Genoese fleet plundered the town. In the 15C it was the chief centre of trade with Mediterranean ports. The Pilgrim Fathers initially sailed for America from Southampton in 1620 in the 'Speedwell' (which had brought some of them from Holland) and the 'Mayflower'. The rise of Portsmouth and a terrible visitation of the plague (1665) conspired with other causes to diminish the prosperity of Southampton, but a new era of advance was ushered in by the creation of a spa and the Napoleonic wars. This was confirmed by the coming of the railway (1840) when Southampton replaced Falmouth as mail packet station for the Mediterranean and (later) N. America, with construction of the docks. In 1940–41 the town suffered heavily from air-raids. In the 1930s it was in the forefront of flying-boat design and operation, and more recently here the hovercraft was invented.

John Alden (1599–1686), a pilgrim father and the hero of 'The Courtship of Miles Standish', was an artisan of Southampton. Natives of the town were Isaac Watts (1674–1748), writer of hymns; Charles Dibdin (1745–1814), composer of sea songs; father and son Walter Taylor (18C), makers of the first reliable machine tools; Sir John Millais (1829–96), painter; George Saintsbury (1845–1933), historian and critic; and Lord Jellicoe (1859–1935), naval commander. 'Artemus Ward' (C. F. Browne) died here in 1867; and here R. J. Mitchell worked on the Schneider Trophy seaplanes which led to the 'Spitfire'. Southampton is the 'Bevishampton' of Meredith's 'Beauchamp's Career'.

The **Civic Centre**, E. of *Central Station*, is an imposing group of municipal buildings by E. B. Webber (1932–39), surmounted by a clock tower (182 ft). The *ART GALLERY (weekdays 10–7, Sun 2–5), in the N. wing, contains works by Reynolds, Romney, Gainsborough, Richard Wilson, and John Opie. The collection of 20C English painters is outstanding; particularly well represented are the Camden Town Group and Graham Sutherland, but there are also good examples of John Piper, Paul Nash, Matthew Smith, Augustus John, and Stanley Spencer. The earliest Continental painting is a 14C triptych by A. Nuzi, and there is another triptych by Goossen van der Weyden and works by Van Dyck, Jordaens, and Nic. Maes. Later painters represented include Utrillo, Renoir, Corot, Sisley, C. Pissarro, the surrealist Delvaux, and the French 'Primitive' painters Rousseau and Vivin. The sculpture includes small bronzes by Maillol, Degas, Gaudier-Brzeska, and Epstein.

Opposite the gallery extends *West Park*, the first of the **Parks** that are so pleasant a feature of the city; it centres on a statue of Isaac Watts, whose hymns are said to have been first sung in Above Bar Congregational Chapel (destroyed). A War Memorial by Lutyens faces across London Road to *East Park*, with a memorial to the engineers who perished in the 'Titanic' (1912). The lawns are continued s. and E. by *Palmerston Park*, adorned with a statue of Lord Palmerston (1784–1865), and *Hoglands*.

In Kingsbridge Lane the old Marlands Entertainments Hall has been converted into the *R. J. Mitchell Memorial Hall* to house the Spitfire Museum. Here also is his Supermarine S6B aircraft which won the Schneider Trophy in 1931.

We turn into Above Bar St., unimaginatively rebuilt. Portland St. (r.) has good examples of early 19C houses and Portland Terrace, beyond, bold redevelopment in 20C styles. HIGH STREET, anciently known as English St., continues Above Bar to the Town Quay. At its head is the **Bargate**, the old N. gate of the city which still shows on the N.

its 13C drum towers, as well as the 15C projection with machicolated parapet. This is enlivened by 17C armorial decorations and guarded by leaden lions of 1743. The battlemented s. front retains three arches of the 13C; the taller flanking arches were pierced in 1764 and 1774. The statue above is of George III. The windows were gothicized in 1865 after the former *Guildhall* of c. 1400 had been made a court of justice in 1852. It now houses a museum of local history (weekdays 10–12, 1–5, Sun 2.30–4.30). Among the exhibits are the oak panels, repainted in the 17C (formerly on the Bar Gate), of Sir Bevis of Southampton, the legendary hero of the town, and the giant Ascupart whom he conquered; and the D-day embroidery. Beyond, on the E. side of High St., are the *Star* and the bow-windowed *Dolphin*, rebuilt as Georgian coaching inns but both of 15C origin.

In St Michael's Sq., r. of this part of High St., is the church of *St Michael*, unhappily modernized in 1828. The low central tower rests on early Norman arches but bears a disproportionately lofty 18C spire. The elaborate font (12C), of dark Tournai limestone, resembles that of Winchester Cathedral. The screens are excellent modern ironwork and the Lady Chapel has the earliest brass lectern in England (14C Flemish).—*Tudor House* (weekdays 10–5, Sun 2.30–4.30), a handsome timber-framed house on the w. side of the square, with a fine banqueting hall, is a period museum. In the garden, abutting on the ramparts, is a rare example of a Norman merchant's house built in c. 1150–75 and once known erroneously as *King John's Palace*. Against the E. wall is a Norman chimney (c. 1200; not *in situ*). In Bugle St., to the s., is the *Duke of Wellington Inn*, rebuilt c. 1490 on 12C foundations and admirably restored in 1963; farther s. is the *Wool House* (see below).

To the s. of the Dolphin the ruined *Holy Rood* church forms a memorial to men of the Merchant Navy killed in 1939–45. Here in 1554 Philip II of Spain heard his first mass in England before riding to his wedding. Farther s. in Lower High St. is the *Red Lion Inn* with a Norman cellar and 'King Henry V's courtroom'. Farther on, in Porter's Lane (r.), are the remains of a long Norman house erroneously known as *Canute's Palace*. To the left in Winkle St. stands *God's House* or the *Hospice of St Julian*, founded in the 12C, granted to Queen's College, Oxford in 1343, and now harbouring four 'brothers' and four 'sisters' (cottages rebuilt 1861).

The chapel (key from God's House Tower), which has been drastically restored, was assigned to Walloon refugees in 1567 and is now occupied by a congregation using the Anglican service in French. It contains the remains of Richard, earl of Cambridge, Lord Scrope, and Sir Thomas Grey, who were executed outside Bar-gate in 1415 for treason ('Henry V', ii. 2). Against the s. wall is a strange memorial to the first Walloon minister (1569).

Beyond are *God's House Tower* and *God's House Gateway* at the s.E. angle of the walls. The early 15C tower now houses a *Museum of Archaeology* (weekdays 10–5, Sun 2.30–4.30) with local Prehistoric, Roman, Saxon, and medieval finds, including pottery to the late 17C. We pass beneath the gateway to Town Quay. To the left Platform Road skirts *Queen's Park* to the main gates of the extensive **Docks**, which occupy the lower end of the town's peninsula.

Opened in 1842 and purchased in 1892 by the L. & S. W. Railway, they have been since 1950 administered by British Transport through the Docks Board, while the harbour has its own board. They are among the best equipped in the world (bus tours from Civic Centre), with a fine *Ocean Terminal* (1950; Rest.) for trans-atlantic passengers and a tower 100 ft high. On No 4 Dock Gate a plaque records the embarkation of the 'Old Contemptibles' in 1914. *New Docks,* see below.—

Canute Road continues E. to the *Floating Bridge* across the Itchen, just N. of which is the *Hovercraft Terminal*.

To the w. TOWN QUAY passes the fine *Wool House* (14C), afterwards used as a gaol and known as the French Prison. It retains its original Spanish chestnut roof and was restored in 1966 as a maritime museum (weekdays 10–5, Sun 2.30–4.30). From the *Royal Pier* depart dock cruises, etc., see above. Beyond is *Mayflower Park*. On Western Esplanade, opposite, stand the *Pilgrim Fathers' Memorial* (1913), commemorating the sailing of the 'Mayflower' on 15 Aug 1620, and a fountain honouring a stewardess heroine of the 'Stella' lost in 1899. Two pillars of Tudor brick in Cuckoo Lane, behind, are remnants of the house of the Wriothesley earls of Southampton.

Farther w. on reclaimed land extend the *New Docks* (1934), the terminal for S. African and Australian traffic, with the Skyway Hotel and a heliport near the gates, and the King George V Graving Dock, 1200 ft long, 135 ft wide, and 59 ft deep, the largest commercial dry dock in England. Behind lies a huge factory estate with much of Southampton's heavy industry.

The ancient **Walls* of Southampton, dating from Norman times but later rebuilt, are almost intact (in part restored) on the w. side. Forming a circuit of c. 1¼ m., they stood 25–30 ft high and were defended on the N. and E. by a double moat and on the s. and w. by the then more extensive estuary of the Test. They were strengthened by towers and had seven principal gates. A flight of steps ascends to Rampart Walk, soon blocked by the 17C 'Guard Room'. This adjoins the *West Gate* (14C), once giving directly on to West Quay, the actual embarkation point of 1620 and probably also of 1415. To the N. begin the external arcades, with arrangements for showering missiles on assailants, by which the Norman walls were strengthened after the French raid of 1338. The conspicuous gunports in the converted wall of the Norman merchant's house (comp. above) are reputedly the earliest of their kind in Great Britain. A medieval postern opens into Blue Anchor Lane. Opposite the *Central Baths* opens Simnel St., with an early-14C *Undercroft*. To the N. a tall block of flats marks the site of the once important *Castle*, the 12C curtain-wall of which was incorporated in the town circuit. The Forty Steps mount to the rampart walk between *Catchcold Tower* (15C) and the *Arundel* or *Windwhistle Tower* at the N.W. corner.

Bargate St., with further fragments of wall, marks the line of the town moat; beyond Bargate the N.E. corner is marked by the ruined *Polymond Tower*.—The line of the E. wall (fragmentary remains) is indicated by the street name Back of the Walls.

London Rd. and The Avenue lead to **Southampton Common*, a fine natural park of 350 acres, with a *Zoo*, a cemetery (s.w. corner; grave of 'Lord Dundreary' Sothern, d. 1881), and the County Cricket Ground.—At *Highfield*, c. 1 m. E. of the Common, is **Southampton University**, with the Sims Library, a zoological museum, and five halls of residence. There are c. 5000 students in seven faculties and an associated School of Navigation (at Warsash, see below). The educational institute opened here in 1862 as a result of a bequest from H. R. Hartley, a Southampton wine-merchant, was incorporated in 1902 as a university college, and received its charter as a university in 1952. The most striking building is the copper-covered *Nuffield Theatre*, by Sir Basil Spence, used for both lectures and drama (public admitted).

At *Maybush*, 3 m. N.W. on the Romsey road, is the headquarters of the Ordnance Survey, established in 1791 and moved to Southampton in 1841.

Netley Abbey, 3 m. S.E.. may be reached by railway, by water, or by bus from

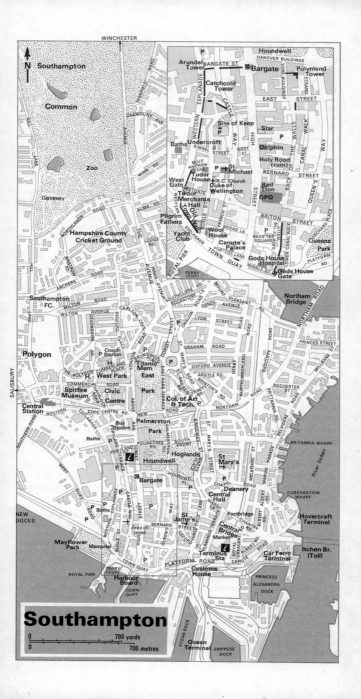

Southampton

| 0 | | | | | 700 yards |
| 0 | | | | | 700 metres |

Woolston. Netley Station is 1 m. from the Abbey, the boat-landing ½ m. The usual way is to cross by the floating bridge (toll) to *Woolston*, 2 m. from the abbey. *Netley Abbey (adm. daily; Sun from 2; fee) was a Cistercian foundation of Henry III (1239), originally occupied by monks from Beaulieu. The picturesque ruins include the church, the cloisters, the chapter house, and some domestic buildings. Netley Castle (19C) is now a convalescent home.—*Hamble*, 1½ m. farther, is a well-known yachting centre, with a good church (Norman and E.E.), on the w. shore of the Hamble estuary. On the E. side is *Warsash*.

FROM SOUTHAMPTON TO LYNDHURST (A 35), 10 m. Commercial Rd. runs behind the New Docks on reclaimed land along the estuary of the Test, crossing the river at *Redbridge*. At (4 m.) *Totton* A 36 bears right for Salisbury (17 m.) viâ Ower (p. 135); A 336 goes straight on for Cadnam (4½ m.; p. 135); we keep left on A 35, entering the New Forest near (7¼ m.) *Lyndhurst Road Station* (Hotel).—10 m. *Lyndhurst*, see Rte 13A.

B 3053 runs S.E. from Totton to (6½ m.) *Hythe* (Hotels; ferry to Southampton), (9½ m.) *Fawley* (Hotel) with a Norman church damaged in 1940 and a huge oil refinery, and (11½ m.) *Calshot Castle*, one of Henry VIII's coast defences, at the mouth of Southampton Water.

From Southampton to *Portsmouth*, see p. 111; to the *Isle of Wight*, see below.

12   ISLE OF WIGHT

There are three regular ports of entry to the island: Ryde, Cowes, and Yarmouth, approached respectively by ship (rail connections from London) from Portsmouth, Southampton, and Lymington. Ferries run every half hour or every hour all the year round; booking is advisable in summer.— FROM PORTSMOUTH HARBOUR TO RYDE OR FISHBOURNE. Car ferry in 45 min. to Fishbourne (2 m. w. of Ryde). Hovercraft from Southsea (Clarence Pier) to Ryde (passengers only) in 7 min.— FROM SOUTHAMPTON TO COWES. Car ferry in 55 min.; hovercraft (from near Woolston Floating Bridge) and hydrofoil (from Royal Pier; both passengers only) in 15–20 min.— FROM LYMINGTON TO YARMOUTH. Car ferry in 35 min. (connecting trains for passengers, see Rte 13A).

The *Isle of Wight is separated from Hampshire (in which it was long administratively included) by the *Solent* (2–4 m. wide) on the N.W. and *Spithead* (1½–4 m. wide) on the N.E. The odd-looking tower in the midst of Spithead is *The Nab* (now a lighthouse), built as an anti-submarine device in 1918 and placed here in 1920. The beautiful island, of an irregular lozenge shape, is about 23½ m. long from E. to W. and 13¾ m. wide from N. to S. Its area is 147 sq. m., or about two-thirds of that of the Isle of Man. It is divided into two 'hundreds' or 'liberties', named *East* and *West Medina*, by the river Medina, which furnishes also a title (Earl of Medina) of the Marquess of Milford Haven. The population numbers 109,300.

The island attracts thousands of visitors annually by its fine and varied scenery its many pleasant seaside resorts, and its mild climate. In August and the first half of September it is necessary to book hotel accommodation well in advance. The great variety of scenery is mainly due to the curiously abrupt geological formations: the grand headland overlooking the Needles, the unique Undercliff, and the Landslip contrast with the downs inland.—The National Trust owns c. 2000 acres on the island.

History. In A.D. 43 the Isle of Wight was conquered by the Romans, by whom it was known as *Vectis* or *Ictis*, and after 449 it seems to have been settled by the Jutes. Relics of both these occupations have been found. Annexed to Wessex in 661 and christianized in the next half-century, it was the headquarters of the Danes at the end of the 10C. William the Conqueror bestowed the lordship of the island on William Fitz-Osbern, from whom it passed to the family of Redvers, Earls of Devon. In 1293 it was repurchased by the Crown and it was governed by 'captains', from 1509 to 1642, and by governors thereafter. It is now a county in itself.

BUSES serve almost every place in the island, and coaches radiate in the season from all the chief centres to places of interest. The RAILWAY now operates with former London Transport underground stock only from Ryde to (8½ m.) Shanklin, viâ (4¾ m.) Brading and (6½ m.) Sandown. BOAT excursions operated in summer from Ryde.—The island has many well signposted public footpaths and nature trails. The coast may be followed by walkers almost continuously for the whole of its length of c. 65 miles.

The usual gateway to the island is **Ryde**, a lively and popular town (23,200 inhab.) on a hillside, well seen from the sea.

Railway Stations. *Pier Head* and *Esplanade* at either end of the pier.
Many Hotels.
Post Office, Union St.—INFORMATION BUREAU, Western Gardens.
Amusements. *Esplanade Pavilion* (variety, concerts, etc.); orchestra (twice daily in season) in *Eastern Gardens.* GOLF, LAWN TENNIS and BOWLS in various parks. YACHT RACING in June, July, and August at Ryde and Seaview.
Car ferries and hovercraft services to Portsmouth, see above.

The main development of Ryde was in the early 19C, and many of its Regency and Victorian buildings remain. *All Saints* (1868–72) by Gilbert Scott, with a high steeple, is the most conspicuous of the many churches built at that time. At the w. end of the fine *Esplanade* (1¾ m.) is the *Royal Victoria Yacht Club* (regatta the week after Cowes). From the *Pier* (c. ½ m.) a magnificent view of Spithead and its shipping is enjoyed.

Binstead Church (1 m. w.), mainly rebuilt, has an E.E. chancel with some earlier herring-bone work; over the plain Norman door serving as a gateway is a grotesque figure. The fine wood panelling comes from Winchester College Chapel, and the carved altar panelling is late 16C Flemish work. A mile farther on are the scanty ruins of *Quarr Abbey*, a Cistercian house founded by Baldwin de Redvers for Savigny monks in 1131, taking its name from the adjacent quarries of fine limestone (used in Winchester and Chichester cathedrals). The estate was purchased by the Benedictines of Solesmes in 1907, and Dom Paul Bellot built a remarkable brick *Church in 1911–12 (approached from Fishbourne road; open to visitors).
—The walk may be continued to (3 m.) *Fishbourne*, with the car ferry slip, at the mouth of the attractive wood-girt *Wotton Creek*; and the return may be varied by crossing the creek (ferry) to (1 m. farther) *Wotton Church* (Norman door), whence Ryde is 4 m. by the main Newport road.

To the E. of Ryde is the attractive small yachting village of (2½ m.) **Seaview** (Hotels), reached by the sea-wall and footpath, or by a toll-road. We may go on to (2 m. more) *St Helen's*, another sailing centre, with the Duver (N.T. common) along the coast and the old tower of St Helen's church (now a sea-mark). *Bembridge* (see below) is reached from here by ferry (¾ m.) or toll-road (2 m.).

FROM RYDE TO NEWPORT, 8 m. The main road is dull and it is preferable to take a road to the S. viâ (3½ m.) *Mersley Down* (413 ft) and (5 m.) *Arreton Down* (444 ft), a route of noble views. Below Mersley Down, S. of the road, is *Newchurch*; the church, with an 18C wooden tower, has a gilded 'pelican in her piety' (actually an eagle with her young) as a lectern. Below Arreton Down is *Arreton Manor* (adm. April–Oct; daily, Sun from 2.30; also Nov–March, Wed, Thurs, & Sun, 2–dusk; fee; rfmts.), a Jacobean house with period furniture and fine panelling and a charming museum of dolls, toys, domestic bygones, etc. A footpath leads to the 12–16C *Church* which has a beautiful s. chapel.

FROM RYDE TO VENTNOR, A 3055, 12 m.—3 m. *Brading* is a decayed little town at the foot of Brading Down (407 ft; view) and at the head of a once navigable inlet. The fine church (1150–1250) has a tower of which the lower stage is open. The monuments in the Oglander Chapel (15C) include two wooden effigies. On the floor of the sanctuary is an incised slab of 1441. The 16C timber-framed house opposite now houses a wax museum. Under the old Town Hall are kept the stocks and whipping-post, and at the cross-roads is the ring once used in bull-baiting.

About 1 m. s.w. are the remains of a *Roman Villa (adm. April–Oct; daily, Sun from 2), including mosaic pavements, heating arrangements, and objects discovered during excavation (1880).—About ¾ m. w. is *Nunwell* (adm. June–Sept; Sun–Thurs; 2–5.30; fee), the seat of the Oglanders, who have been one of the leading families of the island since the 11C.

From Brading to Bembridge, 3½ m.—1 m. *Yaverland* (r.; signpost to Sandown) has a Jacobean manor-house next to a church with a late-Norman door and chancel arch, and a well-carved modern reredos.—3½ m. *Bembridge* (Hotel), a yachting resort, lies at the mouth of the shallow *Brading Harbour* (ferry to St Helen's). The Ruskin Gallery at Bembridge School contains a large collection of pictures and MSS. by Ruskin and his contemporaries (adm. by previous appointment). The windmill (N.T.; adm. May–Oct daily from 11; fee) of c. 1700 is the last to survive on the island. Bembridge airport is used by private aircraft and charter services.—A charming coast-walk may be taken to (5 m.) *Sandown* (see below), viâ the *Foreland* (the e. point of the island), *Whitecliff Bay* (geologically interesting) and *Culver Cliff* (254 ft), the seaward end of *Bembridge Downs* (343 ft; view), with its old fort, and monument to Lord Yarborough (d. 1846).

7 m. **Sandown**, a flourishing bathing resort with a long esplanade and a pier, lies between the white Culver Cliff and the dark-red promontory of *Dunnose*. It is now administratively combined with Shanklin, with a population of 15,800.

Hotels mostly open in summer only.
Post Office, St John's Rd.
Amusements. *Theatre* on pier. Golf Course (18 holes), near the airport. *Zoo* at Granite Fort, open April–Oct, daily. *Sandham Castle Pleasure Centre*, with tennis courts.
Airport, for private planes and charter services.

The sands are particularly fine; and the cliff-walk to Shanklin commands an excellent view of the bay. In the Public Library is the *Museum of Isle of Wight Geology* (April–Sept; daily exc. Sun & Wed), with a unique collection of fossils.

9 m. **Shanklin**, one of the best-known summer resorts in the island, is built mainly on the high ground away from the sea, but has an esplanade, a good sandy beach, and a pier. The Hotels are mostly closed in winter. In the High St. are the Post Office and the Theatre.

At its s. end is the 'Old Village', with a few thatched cottages and rich vegetation. Above a fountain, near the Crab Inn, are some lines written by Longfellow when staying here in 1868. Keats's visit in 1819 is recorded by a plaque on Eglantine Cottage. Close by is the upper entrance of *Shanklin Chine*, a narrow wooded fissure in the sandstone, above which are the attractive *Rylstone Gardens* with splendid views from the cliffs.

A pleasant walk leads to (3 m.) Ventnor viâ (¾ m.) the head of the small *Luccombe Chine*, (1½ m.) *the Landslip*, and (2¼ m.) *Bonchurch*.

The road ascends sharply over Shanklin Down, then descends above the Landslip.—11 m. *Bonchurch* (Hotels) is a pretty village beneath the towering Downs. The tiny old church has some slight Norman remains (c. 1170). In the new churchyard (higher up) is buried A. C. Swinburne (1837–1909), who used to spend his boyhood holidays at East Dene (close by); now a hostel.

12 m. **Ventnor** (6900 inhab.), a noted health-resort with a mild winter climate, is well situated on a series of terraces above the sea and under the steep face of St Boniface Down.

Hotels, some in pleasant grounds.
Post Office, Church St.
Amusements. *Cascadia* and *Pier* for summer entertainments.—Cricket Week in August.—Golf Course (9 holes) on Rew Down.

The road descends steeply to the little esplanade and pier. From the charming Park, reached by the St Lawrence road, there is a cliff-walk along the so-called *Undercliff, a fine stretch of cliff and terrace ¼–1 m. in width, consisting of a huge mass of chalk and limestone which has slipped off the blue clay beneath.—*St Boniface Down* (787 ft; N.T.) is the highest point in the island (*View).

FROM VENTNOR TO FRESHWATER AND ALUM BAY viâ CHALE, 23 m. We pass (r.) *St Lawrence Hall*, once Lord Jellicoe's home.—2 m. *St Lawrence*, see below. The road is bordered on the right by precipitous cliffs (200 ft; fine walk along the top); the Undercliff proper is below us.—We turn inland for (4 m.) *Niton*, a pleasant village with a 13C church, and a good centre for walks. Below us, to the left, is *St Catherine's Lighthouse*, on the s. extremity of the island, with one of the most powerful coast-lights in the world (open 1 p.m.–1 hr before sunset, provided not in operation).—5½ m. *Blackgang Chine*, 400 ft in depth, is practically bare of vegetation.—Behind (6½ m.) *Chale* (Hotel) lies *St Catherine's Hill* (781 ft), crowned by the remains of a 14C beacon, known as the 'Pepper Pot'. From the E.E. church the so-called 'Military Road' runs straight along the coast to (10 m.) Freshwater; it is one of the few roads of the island commanding wide sea views. The more interesting route turns inland and runs viâ (8 m.) *Chale Green* and (9½ m.) *Kingston* to (11½ m.) *Shorwell*, a pretty village. The 15C church, with an early 13C door, contains a delightful wall-painting of St Christopher (c. 1440), a medieval pulpit, entered through a pillar, with a canopy of 1620 and hour-glass, a 16C brass of a priest, and many 17C Leigh monuments. Close by are three great manor-houses: *Northcourt* (1615), with beautiful terraced grounds; *Westcourt*, ½ m. w. (1579); and *Wolverton*, ½ m. s.w. (c. 1600).—13½ m. *Brighstone*, another stone-built village; the church has a late-13C chancel and Jacobean pulpit.—15 m. *Mottistone* has a church with coloured pillars and a memorial chapel to Lord Mottistone (1868–1947), whose home was the fine manor-house of 1567. The adjoining woods are N.T. property (footpath).—20 m. *Freshwater* and thence to (23 m.) *Alum Bay*, see below.

FROM VENTNOR TO FRESHWATER viâ NEWPORT, 9 m. Beyond (1¼ m.) *St Lawrence* (Hotels), the old church of which is one of the smallest in England (25 ft by 11 ft), we turn inland.—2¾ m. *Whitwell* church (SS. Mary & Radegund) has two chancels, originally separate chapels.—5¼ m. *Godshill*. The attractive old village is on a hill beside a stately Perp. church containing a rare *Wall-painting of Christ hanging from a foliated cross, and a painting of Daniel in the Lions' Den, a composition by Rubens and probably painted by his School. The monuments are to the Worsleys of Appuldurcombe, including Sir Richard (d. 1805), historian of the island, and a rich one to Sir John Leigh (c. 1520). The remains of *Appuldurcombe* lie 2 m. s.e. (adm. daily, Sun from 2; fee). The pleasing exterior was built c. 1710.—7¼ m. *Rookley*. To the right is *Merstone*, with a Jacobean manor-house. To the left, in Gatcombe Park, is *Gatcombe Church* (13C), with a wooden effigy of a knight. The stained *Glass (1865–66) in the chancel windows is by Morris, Rossetti, Ford Madox Brown and Burne-Jones.—Whitecroft Hospital, with a conspicuous tower, lies ½ m. N.

11 m. **Newport** (Hotels), the capital (22,300 inhab.) of the island, situated above the Medina, is an attractive, busy town, with several monuments honouring Queen Victoria. In the High St. are some charming 18C houses, notably No. 97, next to the post office. In St James's Square is the *Guildhall* (1819) by Nash, near an Art Nouveau monument of 1901. The Jacobean *Grammar School* (now a youth club) in St James's St. was the lodging of King Charles during the conference of 1648, while the Parliamentary Commissioners were housed at the Bugle Inn. The church of *St Thomas* (1854) preserves its Victorian interior, and

contains a monument commissioned by Queen Victoria to Princess Elizabeth (see below), who is buried in the vault below. This, and a plaque to Prince Albert are fine works by Marochetti. Relics from the old church include the elaborate pulpit (1636), an alabaster effigy of 1582, and a 17C font. Behind, in St Thomas Square, is *God's Providence House* (1701; now a restaurant). Beyond, in Pyle St., is the former Victoria Methodist Church (fine façade), now a theatre. The County Hall was built in 1938. In Avondale Rd. (on the right of the Shanklin road) is a *Roman Villa* (adm. June–Sept; Mon, Tues, Wed & Fri; 2.30–5; or by appointment, apply at the Town Hall; fee) of the second to fourth century.

From Newport to *Ryde*, see p. 129; to *Cowes*, see p. 133.

About 1 m. s.w. of Newport is *Carisbrooke Castle (adm. daily, Sun from 2; fee), situated on a hill ½ m. s. of the village.

The castle was founded on the site of a Roman fort in early Norman times for the defence of the island, and was always important as a fortress. Its chief interest, however, is the imprisonment here of Charles I from Nov 1647 to Sept 1648. From it he was removed to Newport Grammar School, and then to Hurst Castle. His daughter Elizabeth (1635–50) died here a prisoner.

The outer entrance consists of an archway of 1598, beyond which we cross a stone bridge and pass through a noble 14C *Gatehouse*, with a 15C upper stage and inner doors. To the right is the rebuilt *Chapel of St Nicholas*. The former *Governor's Lodging*, the range of domestic buildings (restored) facing the gatehouse, consists of the *Great Hall*, with a chimneypiece of 1390, the remains of a chapel (c. 1270) with an interesting wall-painting, and the *Great Chamber* (no adm.). The *Museum* here includes a well-displayed archaeological collection, local antiquities, a 16C parish gun, and Charles I's nightcap and other relics. Among the pottery are some very early Neolithic examples from Niton. There is a section devoted to children (16–19C); and the oldest chamber organ in working order in Britain (1602). To the s. is the *Well House* (16C), where the water from the well is drawn by a donkey treading inside a large wheel. Beyond is the lofty *Keep* (mid-12C) with a well, 160 ft deep. A pleasant walk may be taken along the 12C *Ramparts*, from which Roman earthworks to the s. can be seen.

Carisbrooke has a Priory Church with the finest tower in the island (1474). The 12C arcade survives but the chancel was pulled down by Sir Francis Walsingham, Elizabeth I's secretary of state. On the tomb (16C) of Lady Margaret Wadham, aunt of Jane Seymour, are interesting carvings. The sculpture of the Madonna and Child (1969) is by John Skelton.—We follow the Yarmouth road to (16 m.) the *Calbourne* cross-roads. In the village (l.) the pleasing rebuilt church contains a brass of a knight (1379); the road goes on over the downs (516 ft) to Brighstone (4½ m.; p. 131). We turn right for (17¾ m.) *Shalfleet* where the church has a huge square Norman tower, a Norman doorway with tympanum, a good roof, and unusual window-tracery. The remarkable s. arcade dates from the 13C. *Newtown*, 1¼ m. N.E., is a silted former port (footpath to quay), with a little town hall built in 1699 (N.T.; adm. May–Sept, Tues, Wed, Thurs & Sun; daily in Aug; fee), and a chapel (1835) by A. F. Livesay (N.T.). In the estuary is a nature reserve and an oyster fishery (N.T.).

21 m. **Yarmouth** (Hotels), a small port (ferries, see p. 128) and a yachting centre, is a tiny but ancient town, once a parliamentary borough. Near the George Hotel, which was the Governor's Lodging, are the remains of a *Castle* of Henry VIII (adm. daily, Sun from 2; fee). The 17C *Church* contains a statue of Admiral Sir Robert Holmes (d. 1692),

who took New York from the Dutch in 1664. The figure was begun as Louis XIV by a French sculptor, and was captured at sea.

About 1 m. beyond Yarmouth a road on the right leads viâ (3 m.) *Colwell Bay* and (5 m.) *Totland Bay*, a pleasant little bathing resort with a pier, to (7 m.) *Alum Bay* (see below).

23½ m. *Freshwater*, the birthplace of Robert Hooke (1653–1703), the physicist, has a rebuilt church with a Norman doorway and memorials to Thackeray's daughter Lady Ritchie (d. 1919) and to Lord Tennyson (1892). Lady Tennyson (d. 1896) is buried in the churchyard.—24½ m. **Freshwater Bay** (Hotels) is a sea-bathing resort, where G. F. Watts and Ellen Terry spent their honeymoon in 1864.

About ¾ m. N.W. is *Farringford* (now a hotel), a mansion leased by Tennyson in 1853 and purchased by him in 1855 out of the profits of 'Maud'. He wrote 'Crossing the Bar' while crossing the Solent on one of his annual journeys between this home and Aldworth (p. 106).—To the E. is *Afton Down* (golf course) and the walk may be continued to (3 m.) *Brook*, with its lifeboat station and submerged forest.

Between Freshwater Bay and the Needles (3 m.) are the imposing **Freshwater Cliffs*, rising to a height of c. 400 ft. They are best seen from the sea, and motor-boats from Yarmouth and Totland piers make the trip to the Needles and Alum Bay, passing *Lord Holmes's Parlour* (cave) and the recessed arch at *Scratchell's Bay*. The walk along the top of the downs above the cliffs commands a series of grand views, and *Tennyson Down* (485 ft; N.T.) is surmounted by the Tennyson Monument. The view near the *Needles Fort* is very striking, but the remarkable contrast between the white cliff on the s. side of Alum Bay and the many-coloured sands towards its centre should be seen from a boat.

*Alum Bay, named after the alum formerly obtained here from the clay, is famed for the brilliant hues of the vertical strata of sandstone. A granite memorial marks the site of the first permanent wireless station (1897–1900), from which, in 1898, Lord Kelvin sent the first paid marconigram. At the s. extremity of the bay are the three isolated and pointed masses of chalk known as the **Needles* (100 ft high; lighthouse on the outermost).

FROM NEWPORT TO COWES, 4½ m. The road keeps to high ground w. of the Medina, passing Parkhurst, a convict prison. At (2½ m.) *Northwood* is the mother-church of Cowes, with a Norman doorway and a Jacobean pulpit.

Cowes (Hotels), a busy little port (18,900 inhab.), with the best harbour in the island, is the chief yachting centre in the country. Regattas are frequent in summer and autumn, culminating in the expensive 'Cowes Week' (1st week in Aug). In the days of sail it was a packet station of some importance, and it is still a boat-building centre.

The older part of Cowes, or *West Cowes*, on the left bank of the Medina, has a winding and hilly High St (one-way, N. to S.), running parallel to the shore, with some quaint old shops. At the N. end is the Parade, where a tablet commemorates the departure of the 'Ark' and 'Dove' with the founders of Maryland on 22 Nov 1633. Jefferson landed here in 1784 and 1789 on his way to and from his embassy in Paris. *Cowes Castle* (farther N.) has been rebuilt, but was originally one of Henry VIII's defences; since 1856 it has been the headquarters of the *Royal Yacht Squadron*, the most exclusive yacht club in the world.

Hard by is the Royal London Yacht Club. At the other end of High St., and in its continuation, Birmingham Rd., are shipbuilding, engineering and hovercraft works, and Westbourne House, where Dr Arnold of Rugby was born (tablet). The newer part, along the Solent shore, has a long esplanade opened by George VI in 1926, extending w. beyond *Egypt Point* to (1 m.) *Gurnard*, a popular seaside resort. At *East Cowes*, on the other side of the Medina (ferry; toll) are *Norris Castle* (by J. Wyatt; 1799), where Queen Victoria spent some youthful holidays, and *St James's Church* with the grave of John Nash (d. 1835).

About ¾ m. s.e. is *Osborne House (adm. April–Oct; Mon–Fri; 11–5; fee), built in an Italianate style in 1846 by Prince Albert and Thomas Cubitt, and long the seaside home of Queen Victoria, who died here in 1901. King Edward presented it to the nation in 1902, as a memorial of his mother, and one wing was made into a convalescent home for officers and civil servants. The rooms, preserved as they were on the death of the Queen, present a vivid picture of Victorian life.

The State Apartments include the Durbar Room, decorated in an elaborate Indian style by J. Lockwood Kipling, father of Rudyard. The Private Suite is above. The *Swiss Cottage* (¾ m. e.; bus), used by the Royal children, adjoins a small museum of objects collected by the Royal family on their travels. Queen Victoria's bathing machine is exhibited near by.—Much of the beautiful *Park* was planted by the Prince Consort.

On the high bank of the river, ¾ m. s. of Osborne, stands *Whippingham Church* (1854–62), a strange medley of English and German architecture, said to have been designed by Prince Albert.

13 WINCHESTER TO SWANAGE AND WEYMOUTH. THE NEW FOREST

A Viâ Lyndhurst and Bournemouth to Swanage

ROAD, 66 m. A 31. 10 m. **Romsey.**—16 m. *Cadnam* (faster alternative to Cadnam by A 33 and M 27).—A 337. 20 m. *Lyndhurst.*—A 35. 34 m. *Christchurch.*—40 m **Bournemouth.**—45 m. *Poole.*—A 35, A 351. 55 m. *Wareham.*—66 m. **Swanage.**

RAILWAY to Weymouth (76¼ m. in c. 2¼ hrs; through-trains from Waterloo in 1 hr more, comp. Rte 11B). Principal Stations: 12½ m. *Southampton.*—19¾ m. *Lyndhurst Road.*—21½ m. *Beaulieu Road.*—26 m. **Brockenhurst,** junction for Lymington.—31¾ m. *New Milton.*—37½ m. *Christchurch.*—41 m. **Bournemouth.**—47 m. *Poole.*—54 m *Wareham,* bus to (6 m.) *Corfe* and (11 m.) *Swanage.*—Trains continue to (76¼ m.) **Weymouth.**

A 31 climbs out of Winchester.—At (4 m.) *Hursley* is the grave (in the churchyard) of John Keble (1792–1866), vicar of the parish for about 30 years. The church was rebuilt from the proceeds of 'The Christian Year'. *Hursley House* replaces Merdon Manor, the home of Richard Cromwell (d. 1712), who, with several members of his family, is buried in the church.

10 m. **Romsey** (Hotel), a small town (10,100 inhab.) on the Test, is famous for its **ABBEY CHURCH, which presents the aspect of a purely Norman conventual church more completely than any building of equal size in England (263 ft long, 86 ft wide; transepts 131 ft). In its present form it dates mainly from about 1130, but remains of the earlier Saxon church (967) of the Benedictine nunnery of SS. Mary and Ethelfleda (founded c. 907) have been discovered beneath the flooring (trap-door in N. Transept). The first abbess seems to have been St Elfleda, daughter of Edward the Elder. The w. bays of the nave are E.E., made to assimilate

with the older work, on the foundations of which they evidently rest.
There is no w. door. The aisles of the choir end in apses (square externally); the E. side of the transepts is also adjoined by circular chapels.
The two great E. windows are 14C insertions. The N. aisle and transept
were long used as a parish church, and the reredos here preserves
notable paintings of c. 1500 (Resurrection and saints). The beautiful
mouldings and original Norman triforium and clerestory of the choir
deserve special attention. At the E. end of the s. choir-aisle is a carved
Saxon crucifix; and outside the s. or Abbess's Door is another Saxon
*Rood now ascribed to the 11C.

The so-called *King John's Hunting Box*, just E. of the abbey, is a small 13C house
with interesting inscriptions of 1306 in the upper room. In the market-place are the
White Horse Hotel with Tudor wall-paintings; a wrought-iron sign bracket from
which two of Cromwell's soldiers were hanged; and a statue of Lord Palmerston,
whose home, *Broadlands*, now the seat of the Mountbatten family, adjoins the
town on the s.—Florence Nightingale (1820–1910) is buried at *East Wellow*, 3 m. w.
Embley House, on the road from Romsey, was her family home in winter in 1825–96.

At (14 m.) *Ower* (Motel) our road coincides for ½ m. with A 36, here
linking Salisbury with Southampton, and at (16 m.) *Cadnam* (Hotel)
we quit A 31 (comp. Rte 11B), bearing s.

20 m. **Lyndhurst** (Hotels), the 'capital of the New Forest', is the best
headquarters for visitors. The elaborate *Church* (1858–70) contains a
painting by Lord Leighton and windows by Morris and Burne-Jones; and
in the churchyard is buried Mrs Reginald Hargreaves, the original of
'Alice in Wonderland'. Adjoining the *King's House*, formerly the residence of the Lord Warden of the New Forest, is a hall used by the Forest
Court, or Court of Swainmote, which meets every 40 days. Over the
chimneypiece hangs the so-called 'William Rufus's stirrup-iron' (in
reality of the 17C).

The *New Forest, occupying the s.w. corner of Hampshire, between Southampton
Water and the Avon, covers about 93,000 acres, of which about 67,000 acres
belong to the Crown (28,000 of which are reserved for the commercial growth of
timber), the remainder being disafforested and in private hands. The Court of
Verderers includes a Chief Verderer, five verderers elected by the commoners
and four appointed. The forest existed as such in 1016, but the name 'New Forest'
dates from 1079, when William the Conqueror, who "loved the tall deer as if he were
their father", set it apart as a hunting-ground, with less ruthlessness and under a
less severe forest-code than was long popularly believed. It is a 'forest' only in the
sense of being an uncultivated region used as a royal hunting-ground (just as 'chase'
is a similar tract not belonging to the Crown) and its fine stretches of ancient oaks,
beeches, yews, and hollies are diversified by wide expanses of heath, farm-land,
and fir-plantations. A few red deer, many fallow deer, and roe deer survive, but
the hardy and active New Forest ponies (descended from an indigenous wild
breed), and the commoners' cattle and donkeys are more in evidence. Badgers are
numerous near Boldrewood. Adders and lizards are not uncommon, the insect
life is varied, and botanists may find rare plants. The more accessible parts of the
forest are crowded in summer with motorists and other visitors, but its attractive
inner recesses are open to the pedestrian only, whose best plan, perhaps, is to follow
the water-courses. *Marryat's* 'Children of the New Forest' and *Blackmore's*
'Cradock Nowell' have their scenes in the forest. Arnewood Tower (1879–85) at
Sway, a site-cast concrete 'folly' (218 ft), is the most conspicuous landmark.—
Permits for camping are obtained from the Deputy Surveyor, Queen's House,
Lyndhurst.

FROM LYNDHURST TO BROCKENHURST, BEAULIEU, AND BACK, 17 m.,
an easy round giving a fair deal of New Forest scenery.—A 337 leads
s. past the *Balmer Lawn Hotel* into (4 m.) **Brockenhurst** (Hotels), a
popular starting-point for excursions.

From Brockenhurst a road and a branch-line run s. to (4¾ m.) **Lymington** (Hotels), a picturesque old port and yachting station (35,600 inhab.) at the mouth of the Lymington River, which flows into the Solent. King Henry II landed here in 1154 on the way to his coronation. Paul Verlaine was an usher in 1879 at a school next to the church, his last post in England. In the isolated church of *Boldre*, 2 m. N.E., which has a wide nave with simple Norman arcades, Southey married his second wife in 1839. Here also is a memorial to the men of H.M.S 'Hood' killed in action against the 'Bismarck' in 1941, and a beautiful E. window (1967; by Alan Younger). The train, crossing the river, runs on to (½ m.) *Lymington Pier*, whence ferries (cars carried) ply to Yarmouth in the Isle of Wight (see Rte 12).

The Beaulieu road runs E. through attractive woodland and heath to (10 m.) *Beaulieu* (Hotel), pron. 'Bewley', a pleasant village in a lovely situation at the head of the tidal Beaulieu River.

*Beaulieu Abbey, a wealthy and powerful Cistercian house, founded by King John in 1204, stood on the E. side of the river. The chief relic of the extensive buildings is the old E.E. refectory, now the *Parish Church*, with fine lancet windows, roof-bosses, and a beautiful reader's *Pulpit. Other remains (adm. daily; inclusive ticket to Abbey ruins, Palace house and Motor Museum; rfmts), are the ruined cloisters, three arches of the chapter house, and the lay brothers' dormitory. Only the s. wall of the large church survives; the foundations are marked out by stones. Margaret of Anjou, wife of Henry VI, here sought sanctuary with her son Prince Edward in 1471 after the battle of Barnet, and here also Perkin Warbeck found a brief refuge in 1497.

The *Palace House* (open daily, April–Oct, 10–6; in winter 10–5; fee), representing the old gatehouse, is now the residence of Lord Montagu. Approached through forest from the Lyndhurst road is the *National Motor Museum with the Transport Library; in a superb display by Sir Hugh Casson is one of the finest collections of veteran and vintage cars and motor-cycles in the world.—A pleasant walk may be taken down the creek to (2¼ m.) *Buckler's Hard*, a pretty waterside hamlet famous for its shipbuilding yards in the days of oaken ships. The *Maritime Museum* is open daily, April–Oct, 10–6 or 9, Nov–March, 10–4.30; fee. *Exbury Gardens*, 4 m. S.E. of Beaulieu, are sometimes open in May or June.

The return to Lyndhurst leads N.W. viâ (13½ m.) *Beaulieu Road Station.*—17 m. *Lyndhurst*, see above.

Some of the chief points in the N. part of the New Forest may be included, as follows, in a round of about 11 m. from Lyndhurst. We ascend Lyndhurst Hill to the W., and, leaving A 35 at the top, bear right through *Emery Down*, with its large village green, and then left on an unfenced road. We proceed viâ (3 m.) *Mark Ash, with the finest beeches in the forest, and (1½ m.) *Boldrewood*, with the 'King' oak and many fine fir trees. On reaching (½ m.) the Ringwood–Southampton main road, we keep to the right and proceed to (2¼ m.) *Stoney Cross* (370 ft.; Hotel), a good centre. About ¾ m. E., a little N. of the road, is the *Rufus Stone*, on the probable site of the tree from which glanced the arrow that slew William Rufus in 1100. According to one account the king was accidentally killed by Sir Walter Tyrrel, according to another he was murdered by a dispossessed Saxon; all that is known for certain is that he was killed by an arrow in the forest and was hastily interred at Winchester. From Stoney Cross we descend viâ the pretty village of (2 m.) *Minstead*, where Conan Doyle is buried, to Lyndhurst, 2 m. farther on. The fine gardens of *Furzey*, near Minstead, are open daily, fee.

We quit the New Forest at (30½ m.) *Hinton* (Hotel), with the quaint Cat & Fiddle inn.

Highcliffe (Hotel), 1¼ m. s., is a small seaside resort.

The coast road running E. passes the seaside resorts of (2 m.) *Barton-on-Sea* (Hotels), and (5½ m.) *Milford-on-Sea* (Hotels), with good bathing. *Hurst Castle* (adm. daily, Sun from 2; fee), built by Henry VIII to guard the w. entrance to the Solent, stands 2½ m. from Milford, at the extremity of a bar of shingle resembling Chesil Bank. Charles I was confined here for 18 days before his removal to Windsor in 1648.

34 m. **Christchurch** (Hotel) is an ancient town (31,400 inhab.), at the head of Christchurch Harbour, between the Avon and the Stour

(boating and fishing). Once known as *Twineham*, the town derives its present name from its magnificent *PRIORY CHURCH, now the longest parish church in England (312 ft). The late 15C w. tower is 120 ft high (view). The beautiful Norman work on the exterior of the N. transept should be noted. We enter by the large *North Porch* (c. 1300); under the tower is a monument to Shelley by H. Weekes (1854). The *Nave*, built by Bp. Flambard of Durham about 1093, is a fine specimen of Norman architecture, especially the triforium; the clerestory is E.E. and the vaulting by Garbett (1819). The aisles are Norman work, recast in the 13C. The 14C rood-screen was radically restored in 1848. The *Choir* is for the most part late 15C; the stalls have quaint misericords (1200–1500), but the chief feature is the stone *Reredos (Dec.), representing the Tree of Jesse. The *Chantry of the Countess of Salisbury* (beheaded 1541), the *Lady Chapel* (c. 1405), *St Michael's Loft*, the *Draper Chantry*, E. end of s. aisle (1529), and the characteristic group by Flaxman, should not be overlooked.

Opposite the King's Arms, N. of the church, are the ruins of the *Castle* (adm. daily, Sun from 2) and of the *Norman House*. The Georgian *Red House* in Quay Rd., contains a small museum of local interest (11–1, 2.15–5 or 6, Sun from 2.15; fee).—About 2 m. s. is *Hengistbury Head*, commanding fine sea views, and 2 m. s.e. is *Mudeford* (Hotel), with a sandy beach.

40 m. **BOURNEMOUTH**, a 'city set in a garden' (153,400 inhab.) described by Thomas Hardy in 'Tess of the D'Urbervilles' under the name of 'Sandbourne' as 'a Mediterranean lounging-place on the English Channel', is a favourite summer resort and a frequented winter residence for invalids. Its popularity dates from c. 1810, and is due in great part to the enterprise of its municipality and to its beautiful situation on Poole Bay, at the mouth of a central valley (that of the little river Bourne). The characteristic features of Bournemouth are its pinewoods, and the beautiful 'chines' that interrupt the line of cliffs. To the E., *Boscombe*, *Pokesdown*, and *Southbourne* extend to Christchurch; to the w., *Westbourne*, *Branksome Park*, and *Canford Cliffs* join Bournemouth to Poole. All are now in Dorset.

Airport, at *Hurn*, 4 m. N. (services to Paris and Channel Islands).

Hotels and Restaurants. Many, throughout the town; details from the Information Bureau.

Post Office, off Old Christchurch Rd.—INFORMATION BUREAU, Westover Rd.

Buses. Local buses from the Square; Country services from Bus Station just s. of the Square.—SEA TRIPS in summer from Jetty and Pier to *Isle of Wight*, *Poole*, and *Swanage*.

Amusements. *Pavilion*, with theatre, ballroom, and restaurants; *Winter Gardens*, in which first-class Sun evening concerts are given by the Bournemouth Symphony Orchestra; *Pier Theatre*, Westover Rd.—*Rowing Boats* and *Motor Boats* for hire. —*Tennis Courts* in the parks.—*Cricket* at Dean Park, Meyrick Park, etc.—*Golf Courses* at Meyrick, Queen's Park, Boscombe, and Parkstone.—*Swimming Pool*, sauna and Turkish baths, opposite the Pier.—*Ice Rink*, Westover Rd.

Bournemouth is well provided with the attractions of a high-class resort, including a pier, pleasant overcliff and undercliff drives, and good bathing; it has about 2000 acres of public parks and gardens. The banks of the Bourne are attractively laid out, and behind the extensive *Meyrick Park* stretch the remains of the *Talbot Woods*, with fragrant pine trees. On the E., dividing Bournemouth from Boscombe, lies *Boscombe Chine*, while on the w. are *Durley Chine*, the less sophisticated *Middle* and *Alum Chines*, and *Branksome Chine.* — In the graveyard of *St Peter's* are the tombs of William Godwin (d. 1836), his wife Mary Wollstonecraft (d. 1797), and his daughter Mary Shelley (d. 1851). The *Russell-Cotes Art Gallery & Museum* (10–5 or 6; Sun 2.30–5) has interesting paintings (R. Wilson, Morland, and many of the later Victorians).

There are examples of the arts of Japan and Burma; ceramics; a room devoted to Irving, and ethnography collections. The Museum buildings themselves are noteworthy.—In Bath Rd. near by is the *Rothsay Museum* (adm. as above), with the Lucas Collection of Italian painting and pottery, English furniture, pottery and porcelain; Victorian bygones; armour; rooms devoted to the sea and ships, and one to New Zealand.—Paul Verlaine taught at St Aloysius College in 1875–76. R. L. Stevenson lived at Bournemouth in 1884–87, but the house ('Skerryvore', Alum Chine Rd.) where he spent the last two years and completed 'Kidnapped' and 'Dr Jekyll' was destroyed in 1940; the site is occupied by a Memorial Garden. Sir Hubert Parry (1848–1918) was a native, and John Keble (1792–1866) died at Bournemouth.

To the w. of Branksome Chine are *Canford Cliffs*, with the magnificent gardens of Compton Acres (April–Nov, daily; fee), and (5 m.) the bathing resort of *Sandbanks* (Hotels) on Poole Harbour, connected by floating bridge with Studland and Swanage (toll).

From Bournemouth to *Salisbury*, see Rte 14; A 350 leads N.W. to *Blandford* and *Shaftesbury*, see pp. 151, 155.

Passing through the suburban districts of *Branksome* and *Parkstone*, we skirt Poole Park with a salt-water lake of 60 acres. The imposing Italianate church (1905) of St Osmund, at Parkstone, has 17C ironwork from St Mary-le-Bow.—45 m. **Poole** (Hotel) is an ancient and still active seaport (106,700 inhab., including Branksome), with a quay lined with old warehouses, the *Custom House*, and potteries (*Poole Pottery* open daily Mon–Sat; tours, Mon–Fri; fee). In High St., *Scaplen's Court* incorporates a 14C house of the Guild of St George; it is arranged as a small museum (weekdays, 10–5; Sun from 2), which includes a Bronze Age canoe dredged out of Poole Harbour in 1964. The *Guildhall* (same hours) dates from 1761. The quay faces POOLE HARBOUR a capacious and almost landlocked bay, with an oyster fishery, surrounded by heaths and favoured by yachtsmen.

Within the narrow mouth of the harbour lies *Brownsea Island* (N.T., April–Sept, daily, 10–dusk, passenger ferry; fee) with a bird sanctuary, and a castle begun by Henry VIII, now a private holiday centre. The Boy Scout movement began in a trial camp here in 1907.

Our road skirts Hole's Bay, a branch of Poole Harbour, with its huge power station, and beyond (50 m.) *Lytchett Minster* bears left. (A 35 continues to Bere Regis, comp. Rte 13B.)—55 m. **Wareham** (Hotels), an ancient and interesting little town (4400 inhab.) on the navigable Frome, is built within an enceinte of massive Anglo-Saxon earthworks ('the Walls'), with its four main streets intersecting at right angles. *Lady St Mary's Church* contains a stone coffin traditionally connected with King Edward the Martyr; the unusual shape may derive from Saxon burial customs. There is also an hexagonal leaden font, and two remarkable little chapels. *St Martin's*, a small church on the walls, is partly Saxon and has Norman wall-paintings (badly damaged). The fine monument to T. E. Lawrence (see below) is by Eric Kennington.

The road now crosses the so-called *Isle of Purbeck*, a bold promontory of downs and heath, of great interest to geologists and yielding potter's clay and the shelly limestone, known as Purbeck marble. The scenery

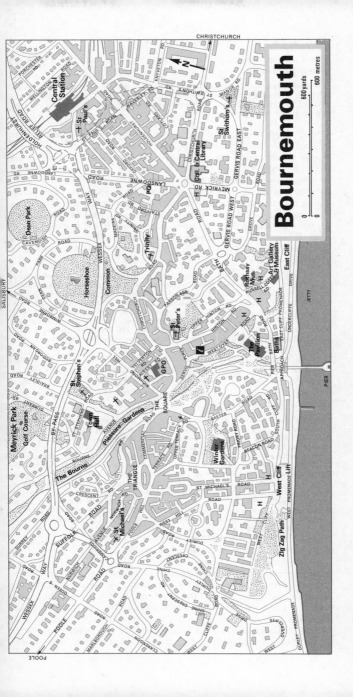

is beautiful and varied, although access to much of the lovelier stretches is restricted because of use by the army.—56 m. *Stoborough*.

A road runs s. to (2½ m.) the Tudor and William & Mary *Creech Grange* (closed in 1971). Beyond, the road climbs a ridge of the Purbeck Hills to (½ m.) the summit (*View). The road farther on, when open (usually at weekends), affords a beautiful approach to Kimmeridge (see below).

60 m. *Corfe Castle*. Above this pretty village, boldly situated on an isolated hill in the centre of a gap in the Downs, are the striking ruins of *Corfe Castle (open daily; fee), famous for its gallant defence for six weeks in 1643 by Lady Bankes against 600 Parliamentary troops. In 1646, however it was seized by strategem and deliberately reduced to its present curiously shattered condition by gunpowder. The castle, dating mainly from the Norman period, occupies the site of a Saxon stronghold of King Edgar (950), at the gate of which King Edward the Martyr was murdered by his step-mother Elfrida in 978 to clear the way to the throne for her son Ethelred. It was a favourite residence of King John; and Edward II was imprisoned here in 1326, just before his death at Berkeley Castle.

At *Kingston*, 2 m. s., in a fine position high on the Downs, is a sumptuous church built by Street in 1880; the vaulting and the apsidal chancel are particularly noteworthy. Lord Chancellor Eldon (d. 1838 at Encombe, 1½ m. s.w.) is buried in the old parish church. The area abounds in small Purbeck marble quarries. *Church Knowle*, 1½ m. s.w. of Corfe has a painted triple chancel arch, and a wall-tomb of 1572. The tiny village of *Kimmeridge* lies 2½ m. farther s.w., near *Smedmore Manor* (adm. June–Sept, Wed, 2.30–5; fee), a fine 18C house, containing antique dolls. An estate road (toll) runs to the secluded *Kimmeridge Bay* (footpaths).

66 m. **Swanage** (Hotels), a pleasant seaside resort (8550 inhab.), stands on a fine bay. The façade of the Town Hall was designed by Wren and originally belonged to the Mercers' Hall in London; the clock-tower, near the pier, was first erected in honour of the Duke of Wellington at the s. end of London Bridge.

A road runs on to (½ m.) Peveril Point and the coastguard station. Another road runs s. to (1¼ m.) *Durlstone Head*, with a stone terrestrial globe 10 ft in diameter and weighing 40 tons, and on to the *Tilly Whim Caves* (fee), once used by smugglers. From here a spectacular walk may be taken w. along the cliffs past (1½ m.) *Dancing Ledge* (so called from the motion of the waves of the making tide), to (4½ m.) *St Aldhelm's Head*, with a Norman chapel, and (5½ m.) the lovely little bay of *Chapman's Pool*. The Dorset Coast Path continues w. to Weymouth (comp. below). The return to (6 m.) Swanage may be made viâ *Worth Matravers*, with its Norman church (impressive s. door and chancel arch), and *Langton Matravers*, with a church tastefully rebuilt in 1875.—About 3 m. N. of Swanage is the charming village of *Studland* (Hotels), with a tiny Norman church, on a pretty bay with good bathing. On the moor, 1 m. N.W. of Studland, is a curious perched block of ferruginous sandstone (16½ ft high; c. 400 tons), known as the *Agglestone*. The road goes on to (3 m. more) the floating bridge for Sandbanks and Bournemouth.

FROM WAREHAM TO WEYMOUTH, 19 m. We ascend the valley of the Frome.—5 m. *Wool*, a pretty village with Woolbridge Manor (now a hotel; approached by a fine bridge), which belonged to the Turbervilles, and was where Tess and Angel Clare spent their wedding night. The romantic, but scant, ruins of the Cistercian *Bindon Abbey* (adm. daily; fee) lie c. ½ m. E. It was founded by Robert de Newburgh in 1172, and retains large fishponds surrounded by fine woods. About 2 m. N. is *Bovington Camp*, the original headquarters of the Royal Tank Corps (Tank Museum, open Mon–Fri, 10–12.30, 2–4.45, Sat, Sun & BH,

10.30–12.30, 2–4). To the right farther on is *Winfrith Heath*, with its atomic energy plant.

T. E. Lawrence of Arabia (1888–1935) is buried at *Moreton*, 3½ m. N.W. His cottage (N.T.) at *Clouds Hill*, on the Puddletown road N. of Bovington Camp, is open Apr–Sept, Wed–Fri, Sun & BH, 2–5; Oct–March, Sun only, 1–4; fee. *Lulworth Cove*, 5 m. s. of Wool, beyond *West Lulworth* (Hotels), is a little summer resort. The Cove proper is a remarkable circular bay, about 500 yds in diameter, almost completely landlocked by tall oolite and chalk hills. At *East Lulworth*, 2¼ m. N.E., is *Lulworth Castle* (16–17C), the square feudal-looking seat of the ancient Roman Catholic family of Weld, where Charles X of France found shelter for a time after 1830. It contains a fine collection of pictures removed from Ince Blundell Hall, Lancs., in 1960 (adm. sometimes granted on application.)—A fine walk leads w. along the cliffs to (10 m.) *Weymouth* (Rte 14); to the E. the *Dorset *Coast Path* leads along beautiful cliffs to Lulworth and Kimmeridge. It passes through military ranges and is closed during firing (notice board in w. Lulworth), but usually open at weekends (the path was closed for 59 years and off it unexploded missiles have not been cleared).

At 11½ m. the Weymouth road leaves the Dorchester road on the right and crosses the Downs. To the right beyond (14½ m.) *Osmington* is an equestrian figure cut in the chalk, supposed to represent George III (see 'The Trumpet Major').—19 m. **Weymouth**, see Rte 14.

B Viâ Ringwood and Wimborne to Weymouth

ROAD, 64 m. A 31.—16 m. *Cadnam*, see Rte 13A.—A 31. 27 m. Ringwood.— 35 m. Wimborne.—46 m. *Bere Regis*.—A 35. 56 m. *Dorchester*, and 64 m. *Weymouth*, see Rte 14.

To (16 m.) *Cadnam*, see Rte 13A. We continue on A 31, leaving the New Forest shortly before (27 m.) **Ringwood** (Hotels), a town on the Avon, where an interesting market is held on Wednesday. A road descends the Avon valley to Christchurch (10 m.) viâ *Avon* (6 m.; Hotel). Farther on a new road (A 338) provides a fast approach to Bournemouth. At (31 m.) *Trickett's Cross*, an alternative route to Bere Regis (c. 2 m. longer) diverges (l.) to join the A 35 (Rte 13A) just inland of Poole.— 32 m. *Ferndown* is a villa colony with hotels.— 35 m. **Wimborne** (Hotel), an ancient town (5000 inhab.) on the Allen at its confluence with the Stour, has a fine **MINSTER*, or collegiate church, with a noble Trans. Norman tower of red sandstone over the crossing and a Perp. tower (1448) at the w. end. The most interesting features of the somewhat crowded interior are the central lantern, the E. window filled with 15C Flemish glass, the monument of the Duke of Somerset (d. 1444) and his wife, the chain library, and the late 16C clock in the w. tower. To the s. of the church is the *Priest's House Museum* (April–Oct, Mon–Fri; 10.30–12.30, 2.30–4.30).

Canford School (removed from Weston-super-Mare in 1923), a mansion by Barry, beyond the Stour, was formerly the seat of Lord Wimborne. Outside the adjoining church of Canford Magna (12C) is the tomb of Sir A. Henry Layard (1817–94), the excavator of Nineveh. About 2 m. N.W. is *Kingston Lacy* (1663), the seat of the Bankes family. The site of a large Roman fort was recently discovered 1 m. s.w. of Wimborne at Lake Farm. Blandford is 10 m. N.W. by B 3082 viâ (4 m.) *Badbury Rings* (view), an Iron Age fort and reputed site of Mons Badonicus, Arthur's last great battle; the Romans made it one of their main road junctions. Poole is 6 m. s. of Wimborne.

We follow A 31 up the Stour, passing (at 40 m.) the prominent Lion Lodge and Stag Gate of Charborough Park. At (43 m.) *Winterborne Tomson* the tiny apsidal church (14 ft by 23) has beautiful early 18C oak fittings.—46 m. *Bere Regis*, where we join A 35 (comp. Rte 13A), is the 'Kingsbere' of Hardy's 'Tess', and the interesting church, which has a good carved timber ceiling, contains the burial-chapel of the Turbervilles. *Woodbury Hill*, close by, is the scene of a once-famous fair (18 Sept), the Greenhill Fair of 'Far from the Madding Crowd'.—49 m. *Tolpuddle* is noted for its 'Martyrs', five agricultural labourers sentenced to transportation in 1834 for 'forming an illegal union', now regarded as pioneers of the Trade Union movement in England.—50¼ m. The fine medieval *Athelhampton Manor* with its gardens, is open April–Sept, Wed, Thurs & Sun & BH, 2–6; fee; teas.—51 m. *Puddletown*, and thence to (56 m.) *Dorchester*, and (64 m.) *Weymouth*, see Rte 14.

II SOUTH-WESTERN ENGLAND

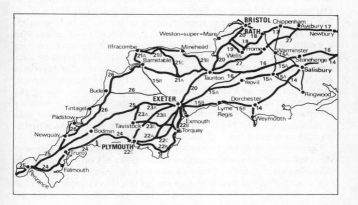

The region here described, lying w. of Hampshire's border and s. of the Great West Road, comprises roughly speaking the whole of five counties and part of the newly formed county of Avon.

Wiltshire, or **Wilts,** is an inland agricultural county, noted for its dairy farming (chiefly in the N.), its sheep, and its bacon. Three-fifths of its area is occupied by Salisbury Plain (including the Marlborough Downs on the N.), a spacious chalk upland, whose pastoral solitude has been invaded by military requirements. Wilts is the county of Stonehenge and Avebury, and none is richer in prehistoric remains (200 round barrows and 80 long barrows). The natives are nicknamed 'Moonrakers' from an old story of rustic simplicity.

Dorsetshire, or **Dorset,** a hilly county partly occupied by chalk downs, is mainly pastoral and agricultural, noted for its dairy farms in the *Vale of Blackmore* and other fertile valleys, yielding the famous Dorset butter, though the stone quarries of Purbeck and Portland are also important. Its prehistoric and Roman remains are interesting. Dorset forms the main part of the Wessex of Thomas Hardy, though hardly of history. Its dialect may be studied in the poems of William Barnes. In 1974 it acquired greater Bournemouth from Hampshire.

Somerset, formerly one of the larger English counties, has lost the territory between the Mendips and Bristol (including Weston and Bath) to Avon. The coast-line of the Bristol Channel is of less interest than the inland districts of Exmoor Forest, the Mendips, and the Quantocks. The rest is predominantly agricultural, with a well-marked dialect of its own ('Zummerzetsheer'), and produces excellent cheese (cheddar) and cider. It contains some of the most historically interesting towns in the country, and it is noted for its beautiful Perp. church towers.

Avon, formed in 1974 from roughly equal parts of Somerset and Gloucestershire either side of the eponymous river, has Bristol at its centre and borders the Severn from Weston-super-Mare nearly to Berkeley. Its boundaries include the ancient city of Bath.

Devonshire, or **Devon,** one of the most beautiful of English counties and, in the spacious days of Elizabeth I, one of the most famous, ranks in size next to Yorkshire and Lincolnshire. The moorland scenery of Dartmoor and Exmoor occupies a considerable part of its hilly surface, but the remainder, except some districts in the N., is well wooded. South Devon is renowned for its mild climate, its rich vegetation, with a wealth of ferns and wild flowers, its luxuriant hedgerows, its deep winding lanes, and its lovely combes. The s. coast, interrupted by estuaries, presents vivid contrasts of red rocks, blue seas, and verdant woods; while the N. coast has bold cliffs cleft by narrow ravines. Devonshire cider and clotted cream are highly esteemed. During the high season 'beauty spots' are apt to be crowded and caravan sites are embarrassingly prominent. Motorists should drive with special care in the narrow lanes. The South Hams district was turned into a battle-training ground by the U.S. military forces in 1942–44.

Cornwall is strictly speaking a 'duchy' and not a county or shire, and the eldest son of the sovereign, as hereditary Duke of Cornwall, possesses valuable rights. Whether Cornwall was ever visited by the Phoenicians is a moot point, but that it was known to the Greeks more than four centuries before our era is certain. The *Cassiterides,* mentioned by Herodotus as yielding tin, undoubtedly included the peninsula as well as the Scilly Isles. Fishing (pilchards) has always been important in Cornwall, and china-clay, granite, and slate are yielded in large quantities. Most of the tin and copper mines have long been shut down and many Cornish miners emigrated to America and South Africa. The duchy remained Celtic long after the rest of England was Saxon, and traces of a Celtic origin are seen in the dark hair and complexions of many of the present inhabitants, while the ancient 'Cornish' language did not become extinct as a spoken dialect until the second half of the 19C. It is still preserved in a few printed books and survives also in place and personal names. The frequently recurring prefixes 'Tre', 'Ros', 'Pol', 'Lan', 'Caer' and 'Pen' mean respectively 'dwelling', 'heath', 'pool', 'church', 'town' or 'fort', and 'summit' or 'headland'. Wrestling, a traditional Cornish sport, may be seen at Summercourt Fair (p. 234) on 25 September. The famous cliff scenery of the rugged coast is seen at its best between Newquay and Boscastle, at Land's End, and in the Lizard. The heathy interior abounds with prehistoric antiquities, and is comparatively treeless; but it is a libel to say that "Cornwall does not grow wood enough to make a coffin." The climate is mild; sub-tropical plants flourish and early flowers and vegetables are grown in large quantities in the s.w.—In 1549 the 'Western Rising', an anti-Reformation movement, was suppressed at Launceston, but in 1688 the Cornishmen gave enthusiastic support to Bp. Trelawny against James II. The humours and traits of the 'Delectable Duchy' are portrayed in many stories by 'Q' (Sir Arthur Quiller-Couch).

14 LONDON TO SALISBURY AND WEYMOUTH

ROAD (131 m.), A 30, A 354.—To (46 m.) *Basingstoke*, and for the alternative approach by M 3, see Rte 11B.—67½ m. *Stockbridge.*—82½ m. Salisbury.—105 m. *Blandford Forum.*—123 m. *Dorchester.*—131 m. Weymouth.

RAILWAY to *Salisbury* (83¾ m.) every two hrs from Waterloo in c. 1½ hrs.—To *Weymouth*, from Paddington viâ Westbury, in c. 3¼ hrs; for the better route viâ Southampton (in 2¾ hrs), see Rte 11B and 13.

From London to (46 m.) *Basingstoke*, see Rte 11B. A 30 by-passes Basingstoke to the s.—Just before (53 m.) *Popham*, where we meet the end of the M 3 motorway, A 33 forks left for Winchester (see Rte 11B). At *Steventon*, 2½ m. N.W., Jane Austen (1775–1817) was born and spent her first 25 years.—At 56½ m. the junction of the Andover road (Rte 16), we fork left. The road traverses rich agricultural downlands to (66 m.) *Woolbury Ring* (N.T.; l.), an Iron Age hill-fort (views), and drops in to the valley of the Test at (67½ m.) *Stockbridge* (Hotels), centre of the fishing on this famous chalk stream. The town was a notorious 'Rotten Borough'.

A 3057 follows the Test s. to (10 m.) *Romsey*, passing (6½ m.; r.) *Mottisfont*, where the church has a Norman font and chancel arch, and 15C glass. Mottisfont Abbey (N.T.; mainly 18C; adm. April–Sept, Wed & Sat 2.15–6; fee) occupies the nave and part of the cloister of a 12–13C Austin priory. The drawing-room is decorated by Rex Whistler.—The Iron Age hill-fort of *Danebury* (fine views) is 3 m. N.W. of Stockbridge.

70½ m. We cross a tributary of the Test. *Nether Wallop* church, 1 m. r., has a 15C painting of St George and the Dragon.—At (74½ m.) *Lopcombe Corner* we join the main road from Andover (A 343; 10 m.), and enter Wiltshire.—At (75½ m.) the Pheasant Inn (Hotel), formerly 'The Hut', about 2 m. N. of *Winterslow*, Hazlitt wrote the 'Winterslow Essays' and was frequently visited by Charles and Mary Lamb.—Just below (78½ m.) *Figsbury Ring* (N.T.; r.), an Iron Age camp commanding a fine view of Salisbury, we cross the prominent line of the Roman road from Winchester to Old Sarum (a splendid walk; 21½ m.).

82½ m. **SALISBURY** (35,300 inhab.), cathedral city of a diocese, is attractively situated among level meadows, mainly on the N. bank of the Avon, which is here joined by the Bourne and Nadder. It is partly laid out in squares known as 'chequers', and well provided with excellent hotels and restaurants. Its prosperous but uneventful history begins in 1220, when the see of Old Sarum was transferred to it. Salisbury is mainly an agricultural centre, and is the 'Melchester' of Hardy's Wessex novels.

Extensive **Car Parks** on the Avon meadows, N.W. of the Centre, reached from Castle St. or Fisherton St.

Hotels (see plan).

Post Office, Castle St.

Bus Station in Endless St.

Theatre. *Playhouse,* Fisherton St.

Boats on the Avon (attractive) obtained at 91 Castle St.

Golf Courses, 1½ m. s. and 2½ m. N. of the Cathedral.—SWIMMING POOL, off Castle St.

The most striking approach to the cathedral is by *St Ann's Gate*, which admits to the North Walk of the precincts and gives us our first complete view from the N.E. The tranquil **Close* (closed to traffic on Sat & Sun), with its spacious greensward, noble trees, and dignified old houses, forms a charming setting for the great church. The Avon marks the western limit of the precincts, the other three sides being bounded by a wall built in the 14C of stone from Old Sarum (p. 150). At the s.w. angle is *Harnham Gate*; and to the N.W. is *North* or *High St Gate*.

The pretty public garden beside Fisherton Mill on the Nadder, reached by the old Crane Bridge, affords a charming view of the cathedral.

The ***Cathedral**, dedicated to St Mary, was begun by Bp. Poore in 1220 and consecrated in 1258 under Bp. Giles de Bridport. It was built on a virgin site and, alone among English medieval cathedrals, is of uniform design (E.E.), for though the graceful **Spire* (the loftiest in England) was the daring addition of a century later (c. 1320), it is the consummation of the original pyramidal conception. The apex of the spire (404 ft) is 2½ ft out of the perpendicular. A local rhyme ascribes to the cathedral as many pillars, windows, and doors as the year has hours, days, and months. The usual entrance is by the N. porch.

Perfectly proportioned, restrained in ornament, of exquisitely precise workmanship, built of material so well chosen that seven centuries have but added a little beauty of tint to the stone, Salisbury Cathedral is a classic of architecture. It expresses the renewal of national spirit realized in the 13C, and its square E. end, following the model of the later church at Old Sarum (one of the earliest instances of the departure from the Norman tradition of the apsidal end), became the norm for future English choirs. The w. front, contemporary with the spire, seems to have been intended to present a great drama of sculpture (comp. Exeter and Wells); its present sculptures, representing the Te Deum, are recent (1838–76). The detached bell-tower, which stood about 200 ft N. of the nave, was removed by Wyatt.

The **Interior**, in spite of its fine proportions and the harmony of the design, is scarcely so satisfying as the exterior. The chilliness of effect has been increased by the ruthless way in which Wyatt (1788–89) removed screens and chapels and rearranged the monuments in tidy rows. Motley found Salisbury "too neat", and Henry James inappositely calls it "a blonde beauty among churches". The restoration begun by Sir Gilbert Scott in 1859 tries to minimize the damage done by Wyatt, and recent repainting of tombs has restored some colour to the aisles.

The NAVE, perhaps rather narrow for its height, is divided into ten bays by clustered columns of polished Purbeck marble. The fine triforium has characteristic E.E. plate-tracery. In the w. triple lancet window is a patchwork of old glass (13–15C; some from Dijon), and the 3rd window from the w. in the s. aisle contains a 14C **Tree of Jesse*. At the w. end of the aisles is some 13C grisaille glass of lovely quality. The **Clock Movement* at the w. end of the N. aisle, probably the oldest surviving mechanism in Europe (1386), has been put in working order (1956). Nearly above it hang colours of the Wiltshire Regiment.

Among the monuments may be mentioned the following (beginning to the right of the entrance and following the s. aisle): 1. Oldest monument in the church, brought from Old Sarum (possibly *Bp. Herman*, d. 1078); 2. *Bp. Roger* of Old Sarum (d. 1139); 3. *Bp. Jocelin* of Old Sarum (d. 1184); 5. *Bp. Beauchamp* (d. 1482); 6. *Robert, Lord Hungerford* (d. 1459; elaborate effigy); 7. Base of the 13C *Shrine of St Osmund* (see below; the holes are the 'foramina' into which the sick were thrust to be healed); 8. *Bp. de la Wyle* (d. 1271); **9. William Longespée* (d. 1226), first Earl of Salisbury, son of Henry II and (?) Alix de Porhoët (fine effigy, once brilliantly coloured). We cross to the N. aisle. **10. Sir John Cheney* (d. 1509), a gigantic knight of the bodyguard of Henry VII, who fought at Bosworth; 11. *Walter, Lord Hungerford* (d. 1449), a hero of Agincourt; 14. *Sir John de Montacute* (d. 1390), a hero of Crécy, with elaborate gauntlets; 17. *William Longespée*, second Earl of Salisbury, killed by the Saracens near Cairo (1250); 18. Diminutive effigy, probably enclosing the heart of *Bp. Poore* (d. 1237).

The WEST TRANSEPTS resemble the nave; the Perp. arches at the crossing were inserted by Bp. Beauchamp (1450–81) to strengthen the original

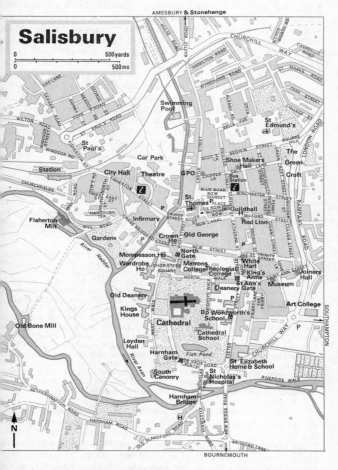

arches against the lateral thrust of the tower and spire. In the N.W. arm is a bust of Richard Jefferies (d. 1887); in the s.w. arm is a War Memorial chapel.—In general design the CHOIR and PRESBYTERY differ little from the nave; they suffered from the drastic clearing of Wyatt, bent on obtaining a vista from end to end of the church. The paintings on the vault are repaintings (c. 1870) of defaced 13C originals. The stalls have been freely restored. The throne is by Scott, but most of his furnishings were replaced in 1959 by Lord Mottistone. In front of the altar are buried the Earls of Pembroke, and a diamond-shaped stone is inscribed "near this spot lies Sidney's sister, Pembroke's mother". On the N. side of the second bay from E. is the *Chantry of Bp. Audley* (d. 1524; fine late Perp.), and opposite it is the *Hungerford Chantry* (c. 1429), an important example of early iron work.—In the N.E. TRANSEPT are portions of the original screen (13C) and the unusual 14C *Brass of Bp. Wyvill (d. 1375). In the aisle, near Audley's chantry, is the cenotaph of Bp. Bingham (d. 1246), and farther E. are the lavish monuments to Sir Thomas Gorges (d. 1610) and his wife, builders of Longford Castle and that of Bp. Wordsworth (d. 1911), with a silver plaque presented by the Abp. of Uppsala; also a 16C 'memento mori'. The LADY CHAPEL to the E., is the earliest part of the building (1220–26); it is divided into nave and aisles by graceful clustered shafts and slender single pillars; here is some 13C, 14C, and 16C glass. In the centre stood the *Shrine of St Osmund* (d. 1099), Bp. of Old Sarum; his grave-slab, on the s. side marks the spot where his body was first reburied after the building of the cathedral. At the E. end of the s. aisle is the imposing monument of Edward, Earl of Hertford (d. 1621), and his wife Lady Catherine (d. 1568), sister of Lady Jane Grey. Also in the s. choir aisle are the finely-sculptured tomb of Bp. Bridport (d. 1262) and the Mompesson tomb (1627); two windows here are of the Pre-Raphaelite school, and in the s.E. transept is some 13C grisaille glass and a 14C cope-chest. The tomb of Bp. Mitford (d. 1407), farther w., also has some delicate sculpture.

From the s.w. transept we enter the well-preserved *CLOISTERS (c. 1270) begun by Bp. de la Wyle, unusually large for a non-monastic church, which are separated from the cathedral itself by a passage known as the Plumberies. Above the E side is the LIBRARY (adm. free Mon & Fri 2–3.30), built in 1446 and devoted to its present purpose in 1756. It contains an Anglo-Saxon liturgy with finely drawn capitals, a late-11C St Augustine, perhaps written by St Osmund, one of the four original copies of Magna Carta, and other interesting books and MSS. The octagonal *CHAPTER HOUSE (52 ft high), entered from the E. walk, was built a little after the cloisters. The sculptures (scenes from Genesis and Exodus) are notable late 13C work. Many houses in the Close, old and new alike, merit attention. Among the finest, both in Choristers' Square, are the gabled *Wardrobe* (mainly 15C) and *Mompesson House* (1701; N.T.) with fine panelling and exquisite interior decoration (adm. May–Sept, Wed & Sat 2.30–6; winter by appointment; fee). The mainly 13C Old *Deanery* (adm. in Aug, Tues–Sat 2–5; fee) and the late 14C *King's House* in the West Walk, both now used by a diocesan training college, and the old *Bishop's Palace* (13–18C), now the Cathedral School, to the s.E., are notable.

We leave the close, past the charming *College of Matrons* (1682) on the right), by the *North* or *High St. Gate*, on the inner side of which is a figure of Edward VII, succeeding earlier figures of Henry III and James I or Charles I. Beyond we pass (r.) the *Old George*, with a remarkable old rose-tree and a room in which Pepys slept. Old George Mall behind, is a cleverly harmonized pedestrian precinct. Silver St., farther on to the right, ends at the hexagonal *Poultry Cross* (15C). Adjacent the large civic church of *St Thomas* of the 15C, with a carved roof and painting of the Last Judgment (restored) over the chancel arch. In the MARKET PLACE, to the E., stands a statue of Lord Herbert of Lea (1810–61; by Marochetti); another, of Professor Fawcett (1833–84), the blind statesman, faces Blue Boar Row, in which he was born.

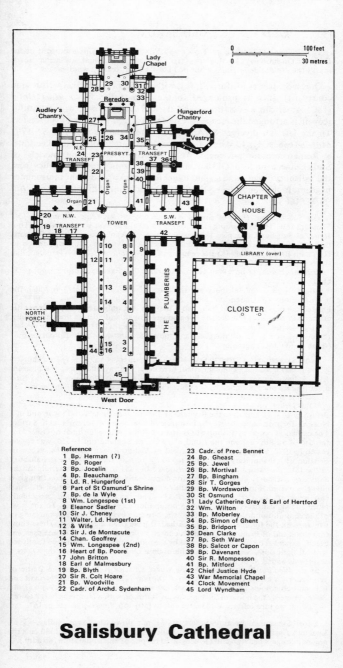

Lady Chapel

28 29 30 31 32 33

Reredos

Audley's Chantry

27 25 26 34 35

Hungerford Chantry

Vestry

N.E. TRANSEPT 24

23 PRESBYT 37 36 S.E. TRANSEPT

22 38 40 39

Organ Organ Organ

Organ 21 41 43

N.W. TOWER S.W. TRANSEPT

P 20 19 18 17 TRANSEPT

CHAPTER HOUSE

42

LIBRARY (over)

10 8 9

12 11 7 6 5 THE PLUMBERIES

13 4

14

CLOISTER

NORTH PORCH

15 3 2

44 16

45 1

West Door

0 ———————————— 100 feet
0 ———————————— 30 metres

Reference

1 Bp. Herman (?)
2 Bp. Roger
3 Bp. Jocelin
4 Bp. Beauchamp
5 Ld. R. Hungerford
6 Part of St Osmund's Shrine
7 Bp. de la Wyle
8 Wm. Longespee (1st)
9 Eleanor Sadler
10 Sir J. Cheney
11 Walter, Ld. Hungerford
12 & Wife
13 Sir J. de Montacute
14 Chan. Geoffrey
15 Wm. Longespee (2nd)
16 Heart of Bp. Poore
17 John Britton
18 Earl of Malmesbury
19 Bp. Blyth
20 Sir R. Colt Hoare
21 Bp. Woodville
22 Cadr. of Archd. Sydenham
23 Cadr. of Prec. Bennet
24 Bp. Gheast
25 Bp. Jewel
26 Bp. Mortival
27 Bp. Bingham
28 Sir T. Gorges
29 Bp. Wordsworth
30 St Osmund
31 Lady Catherine Grey & Earl of Hertford
32 Wm. Wilton
33 Bp. Moberley
34 Bp. Simon of Ghent
35 Bp. Bridport
36 Dean Clarke
37 Bp. Seth Ward
38 Bp. Salcot or Capon
39 Bp. Davenant
40 Sir R. Mompesson
41 Bp. Mitford
42 Chief Justice Hyde
43 War Memorial Chapel
44 Clock Movement
45 Lord Wyndham

Salisbury Cathedral

The *Guildhall* (1788–95), by Taylor and Pilkington, contains a portrait of the Duke of Queensberry, by Raeburn. To the s., in New Canal, a cinema façade masks the *Hall of John Halle*, built in 1470–83 by a wealthy woolstapler.

Queen St. passes Milford St. (l.), with the *Red Lion Hotel* (picturesque courtyard), then is prolonged to the s. past the *White Hart Hotel* (18C; American associations) and the old *King's Arms*, where faithful Royalists arranged the escape of Charles II after the Battle of Worcester. To the left (E.) diverges St Ann's St., where the *Salisbury & S. Wilts Museum* (weekdays 10–4 or 5; fee) has excellent archaeological collections, a Roman mosaic pavement from Downton, relics and models of Stonehenge, a model of Old Sarum, English ceramics, medieval relics from the Salisbury streets, and a giant figure formerly carried in the midsummer pageant. In the same street is the fine timbered front of the old *Joiners' Hall* (N.T.; 16C).

The *Shoemakers' Hall*, of similar date, stands in Salt Lane, behind the 15C Pheasant Inn. Henry Fielding (1707–54), who is said to have written part of 'Tom Jones' at Salisbury, occupied a house just s. of St Ann's Gate. Exeter St. leads thence to the pleasant *Riverside Walk* (l.); while St Nicholas Rd. (r.) goes on to Harnham Bridge, passing (l.) the remains of *St Nicholas's Hospital*, founded, like the bridge, by Bp. Bingham.
Britford church, 1¼ m. s.e. of Harnham bridge, has Saxon sculptures on the N.E. arch of the nave.
About 2½ m. E. of Salisbury are the ruins of *Clarendon Palace*, in which the 'Constitutions of Clarendon' were enacted in 1164. Excavations in 1934–37 located the dais of the great hall, and a tile-kiln, the only medieval non-monastic example in England; but the site is again overgrown and visitors are unwelcome. —At *Bemerton*, 1½ m. w. of Salisbury, George Herbert (1593–1633) spent the last three years of his life in "the good and more pleasant than healthful parsonage" (tomb in old 14C church).

From Salisbury to Stonehenge, 10½ m. The direct road (A 345; 1 m. shorter) is less pretty than the secondary road, here described, which follows the pleasant Avon valley. We leave Salisbury by Castle St.—1½ m. *Stratford-sub-Castle*, with a manor-house once occupied by the elder Pitt, who first entered Parliament in 1735 as member for Old Sarum.
*Old Sarum, on a low hill to the E. of the village, is the site successively of a British earthwork known to the Romans as *Sorviodunum*, of a Saxon town, and of a Norman fortress. About 1078 the bishopric of Sherborne was translated to Sarum. The cathedral begun by Bishop St Osmund (p. 148), whose 'Ordinal of Offices for the use of Sarum' became the ritual of all South England until 1550, was consecrated in 1092, and subsequently enlarged by Bishop Roger, Osmund's successor. Friction with the military authorities led to the transference of the see to Salisbury in the 13C, the cathedral at Sarum was razed in 1331 to provide materials for the Salisbury cathedral close, and the town gradually became deserted, though a chapel survived until the 16C, and the 'rotten borough' of Old Sarum returned two members to Parliament until 1833.—The remains excavated are chiefly Norman; almost no traces of Roman occupation have been found. To the N.W. of the central mound, on which stood the Norman castle (closed Sun morning in winter; fee), the foundations of the cathedral have been marked out. These show that the E. end of Bishop St Osmund's church which terminated in three apses was greatly extended by Bishop Roger, and by the middle of the 12C had been furnished with straight outer walls. At the same time a cloister, adjoined on the w. by a crypt, was added N. of the choir.
5½ m. *Woodford*, with *Heale House* where Charles II hid after the Battle of Worcester. A bridge crosses the Avon to *Durnford* (1½ m.) where the Norman and E.E. church adjoins an early earthwork known as *Ogbury Camp*.—Beyond (7 m.) *Lake*, reputedly the home of Sir Lancelot, is *Wilsford*, with a Norman church tower. —At 9 m. we turn left on A 303 (Rte 16), to (10½ m.) *Stonehenge*, see p. 167.

From Salisbury to Bournemouth, 31 m., down the Avon valley.—3 m. Longford Castle (Earl of Radnor) was built by Sir Thomas Gorges c. 1580 on a triangular design which can still be recognized in spite of much alteration (no adm.).—

6 m. *Downton* (l.; Hotel), with a part-Norman church, preserves a 'Moot' (no adm.), or mound, used for meetings of the Saxon hundred-moot. *Trafalgar House*, c. 1½ m. N., built in a classical style in 1733 (with later additions), was given to Nelson's family by the nation after the battle of Trafalgar.—At (9 m.) *Breamore* (pron. 'Bremmer') the 10–11C *Church retains a contemporary West Saxon inscription and a fine Rood. *Breamore House* (adm. April–Sept daily exc. Mon & Fri, but incl. BH, 2–5.30; rfmts; fee), home of the Hulse family, dates from 1583.—11 m. *Fordingbridge* (Hotel), where Augustus John (1878–1961) died (bronze group by I. Roberts-Jones), has a 13–15C church.—17 m. *Ringwood* and thence to (31 m.) *Bournemouth*, see p. 141.

The Weymouth road (A 354) crosses Harnham New Bridge and turns r. (s.w.). At (85 m.) *Combe Bissett* we cross the Ebble, 5 m. up the valley of which is *Broadchalke*, where Maurice Hewlett (1861–1923) died in a house formerly occupied by John Aubrey (1626–97). We enter Dorset, crossing at 92 m. Bokerley Dyke, where we briefly join the line of the Roman road, leaving it again before (94 m.) *Handley Hill*, where we cross the Shaftesbury–Ringwood road.

98 m. *Chettle*, to the right, has a mansion of c. 1711 attr. to T. Archer (adm. on application). To the left lies *Crichel Down*, notorious as the scene of one of the more arbitrary examples of land requisitioning by a Government department.—105 m. **Blandford Forum** (Hotels), a market town on the Stour (3600 inhab.), was burned down four times between 1579 and 1731, and has some fine buildings of 1735–40 by John and William Bastard, notably the town hall and church. The pulpit is from the destroyed Wren church of St Antholin in London. Alfred Stevens, the sculptor (1818–75), was a native.

Bryanston, 1 m. N.W., has a mansion built by Norman Shaw, now a boys' school. It is well seen from (but not approached by) the Shaftesbury road (A 350), to the w. of which at 3½ m. rises *Hod Hill*, an important example of a prehistoric 'summit-fort', enclosing a permanent Roman fort in its N.W. corner, and at 4½ m. *Hambledon Hill* (622 ft), a Neolithic earthwork affording an even better view.—At (6 m.) *Iwerne Minster*, with a good church spire, is Clayesmore School.

About 7 m. s.w. is *Milton Abbas*, a 'model' village dating from about 1786, when the old village was removed from beside *Milton Abbey*, an imposing mansion built for the first Earl of Dorchester by Sir Wm. Chambers on the site of a monastic house and church founded by Athelstan (938). The stately Abbot's Hall (1498; adm. daily in school Easter and summer hols; fee) is incorporated in the house (now a school). The noble *Abbey Church* (open daily) consists of choir and transepts (14C) with a 15C pinnacled tower (101 ft high). Within are a rich altar-screen of 1492, an elaborate wooden tabernacle (15C), two paintings referred to the reign of Edward IV, interesting tombs, and a brass (1565) of Sir John Tregonwell. The tiny chapel of St Catherine on the hillock above was begun by Athelstan, and restored under the Normans and again in the 16C.—*Tarrant Crawford*, 3 m. s.e. of Blandford, has an unspoilt 13C church, with *Wall-paintings (mainly 14C) of the life of St Margaret of Antioch, and the coffin slab of Bp. Poore (p. 146), a native.

118 m. *Puddletown* has an interesting Norman font and a fine group of 14–16C monuments in its church. *Waterston Manor*, 2 m. w., was Bathsheba's home ('Weatherbury') in 'Far from the Madding Crowd'.

123 m. **Dorchester** (Hotels), the pleasant county town (13,700 inhab.) of Dorset, was the Roman *Durnovaria*, the line of the old walls of which are now marked by the avenues known as 'The Walks'; a fragment of the w. wall is left. Excavations at Colliton Park during the building of the new County Hall, at the top of the town, revealed a wealth of Roman remains. The *Dorset County Museum* (weekdays, 10–1, 2–5; fee), in High West St., contains good collections of fossils, of natural history, and of British and *Roman antiquities, including a fine mosaic from Hinton St Mary (discovered 1963) with a representation of the

head of Christ (late 4C), a figure of a Thracian horseman, and a hoard of 22,000 silver coins. Here are also many relics of William Barnes and of Thomas Hardy (1840–1928), including his reconstructed study, and the MS. of 'The Mayor of Casterbridge' (i.e. Dorchester).

Hardy, commemorated by a statue (by Eric Kennington, 1931), near the County Hall, died at 'Max Gate', a house built by himself, on the Wareham road. His heart is buried in the church of *Stinsford* ('Mellstock'), 2 m. N.E., in the parish of which he was born at the hamlet of *Higher Bockhampton* (cottage, N.T.; adm. to exterior daily 11–6; interior by appointment; fee).

In the 15C church of *St Peter*, with a s. doorway of 1206, near which is buried the Rev. John White (d. 1648), founder of Dorchester in Massachusetts, are a monument to Denzil Holles (d. 1680), two 14C effigies (in the Hardy Chapel), and an effective 19C reredos. Wm. Barnes (p. 155) is commemorated by a statue outside the church and a plaque on No. 40 South St., where he lived in 1847–62, after 10 years' residence in a house almost opposite. In 1862–86 he was rector of *Winterborne Came*, 2 m. S.E. *Napper's Mite*, a 17C almshouse here, has been well restored and adapted as a restaurant. In High West St., opposite St Peter's, is the traditional lodging (now a café) of Judge Jeffreys during the 'Bloody Assize' of 1685, when 74 of Monmouth's adherents were here sentenced to death and 175 to transportation. His Court Room is now part of the *Antelope Hotel*.

The *Dorset Military Museum* (weekdays 9–5, closed at 12 on Sat, Oct–June; fee) has an unusually good collection of local and other military relics.— *Wolfeton House*, off the A 37, 1½ m. N.W., is a fine manor house (open May–Sept, Wed, Sat & BH, 2–6).
On the s. edge of the town are *Maumbury Rings* (218 ft long, 163 ft wide), the largest and most perfect Roman amphitheatre in the country. To the N.W. is the British or Roman camp of *Poundbury*, and on a conspicuous hill (432 ft), 2 m. s., is *Maiden Castle, one of the finest prehistoric forts in England, covering 115 acres and at one point showing eight lines of defence. Excavations in 1934–38 have shown that the hill was first occupied in c. 2000 B.C. and again from 500 B.C. In the 1C B.C. the majority of the great defence works were built, only to be stormed by Vespasian in A.D. 43. The latest building was a Roman temple of the 4C near the top of the hill.
From Dorchester to *Exeter*, see Rte 15B; to *Wimborne* (Bournemouth), see Rte 13B.

The Weymouth road ascends s. to the Ridgeway, with Maiden Castle on the r., then descends through (127 m.) *Upwey*.— V. L. Cameron (1844–94), the African explorer, was born at (129 m.) *Radipole*.

131 m. **WEYMOUTH,** a popular and old-established coastal town (42,300 inhab.), is situated on both sides of the *Nothe*, a promontory laid out with gardens, which, with the harbour below, divides the beautiful bay into Weymouth Bay (N.) and Portland Roads (s.).

Railway Stations. *Town*, for London, etc.; *Quay*, for Channel Islands boat-trains, at the harbour mouth.
Hotels on the Esplanade.
Post Office, St Thomas St.
Buses from Edward St. to *Dorchester; Portland Bill; Abbotsbury* and *Bridport;* and to the other main centres of interest N. and E. of the town.
Ferries to the *Channel Islands.*—*Regatta* of the Royal Dorset Yacht Club in August.—CONCERTS at the Alexandra Gardens; *Pavilion Theatre*, with ballroom and restaurant.

John Endicott sailed from Weymouth in 1628 to found the plantation of Salem. It was a favourite resort of George III, who lived at Gloucester House (now a hotel); and a contemporary statue of him stands at the s. end of the Esplanade. T. L. Peacock (1785–1866) and H. G. W. Moseley (1887–1915), the X-ray chemist (killed at Suvla Bay), were both born here. Weymouth has a long history as a military port, and from here the American assault force of 'D' day was launched in 1944 (commemorative column).

The old town of Weymouth lies s. of the little river Wey, the mouth of which forms the harbour. Some Tudor cottages in Trinity St. have been fitted with 17C furnishings (adm. Easter–Oct, Wed, Sat & BH; 2.30–5; fee). The newer town to the N., with the stations, late-Georgian esplanade, hotels, and principal shops, is *Melcombe Regis*, on a peninsula between Weymouth Bay and Radipole Lake, an expansion of the Wey, now a bird-sanctuary. *St Mary's Church* has an altarpiece by Sir James Thornhill (1675–1734), a native of Melcome Regis, which he represented in Parliament for 12 years. A large holiday camp has been erected at *Bowleaze Cove*, 2 m. N.E.

The Isle of Portland (12,300 inhab.), a rocky limestone peninsula (4¼ m. long, 1¾ m. wide), is reached by frequent bus services from Weymouth (40–45 min. to Portland Bill). The island, called by Hardy 'the Gibraltar of Wessex' and figuring in his novel 'The Well-Beloved' as 'the Isle of Slingers', is famous for its building-stone (five quarries are still operative). It has been a royal manor since William the Conqueror and still holds a royal court leet to apportion the royalties from the quarries between the Crown and the tenants of the seven villages. The island is connected with the mainland by the *Chesil Bank*, a remarkable stretch of shingle, 30 ft high and 200 yds wide, which extends as far w. as Bridport (18 m.). The pebbles gradually decrease in size from E. to w.—The road, viâ the suburban village of *Wyke Regis*, reaches the island at (3½ m.) *Chiswell* (Hotel) and forks left to *Castletown*, with *Portland Castle* (adm. daily April–Sept, Sun from 2; fee), built by Henry VIII in 1520; his other blockhouse, *Sandsfoot Castle*, on the opposite shore, is in ruins. *Portland Breakwater*, c. 6000 ft long, constructed by convict labour in 1849–72, encloses the largest harbour in the kingdom (2107 acres) and is an important naval base (with heliport), and underwater weapons establishment, made notorious in 1960 by the 'Portland Spy case'. An inner harbour, protected by 'Mulberry' prefabricated units, was constructed in 1947.—7¼ m. *Easton*, with St George's church (1754–66), is the chief village of the island. On the coast to the E. is the prison, now a Borstal institution, while just to the S., in Wakeham Rd., is the 17C *Avice's Cottage*, now a 'bygones' museum (adm. daily exc. Sun, 10–5; closed Tues & Fri in winter). *Pennsylvania Castle* here was built by James Wyatt c. 1800 for John Penn, governor of the island and a grandson of the founder of Pennsylvania; it is now a restaurant and the grounds, with *Rufus Castle* (late 11C), are shown on request. A footpath descends to Church Ope Cove (good swimming) with a ruined watch-tower contemporary with Portland Castle.—9¼ m. *Southwell* is the last village before the small hamlet of (10½ m.) *Portland Bill*, a fine mass of rock with an old lighthouse, and a dangerous 'race' offshore. Most of the area is now Ministry of Defence property.

B 3157, with good views of the Chesil Bank (see above) leads from Weymouth to (17½ m.) *Bridport*, viâ (9 m.) *Abbotsbury*, with the ruins of a Benedictine abbey (noble 15C barn) and a swannery (c. 800 birds; decoys; adm. May–Sept, weekdays 10–4.30, Sun if fine; fee) and fine sub-tropical gardens (weekdays April–Sept 10–4.30, Sun, April–Aug 2–6; fee). On a height to the s. stands *St Catherine's Chapel* (Perp.; key at 3 Back St.; fee), with a singular stone roof.

From Weymouth to *Bournemouth*, see Rte 13A.

15 LONDON TO EXETER
A Viâ Salisbury and Yeovil

ROAD, 170 m. (A 4 and A 30), congested at summer week-ends.—To (82½ m.) Salisbury, see Rte 14.—85½ m. *Wilton.*—102 m. *Shaftesbury.*—118 m. *Sherborne.*—123 m. *Yeovil.*—132 m. *Crewkerne.*—140 m. *Chard.*—153½ m. *Honiton* (by-pass).—170 m. *Exeter.*

RAILWAY, 171¾ m. from Waterloo in 3¼–4 hrs. To (83½ m.) *Salisbury*, see Rte 14.—105½ m. *Gillingham* (bus for Mere and Shaftesbury).—118½ m. *Sherborne.*—123 m. *Yeovil Junction.*—131¾ m. *Crewkerne.*—144¾ m. *Axminster.*—155 m. *Honiton.*—171¾ m. *Exeter* (Central).—173 m. *Exeter* (St David's).

From London to (82½ m.) *Salisbury*, see Rte 14.—85½ m. **Wilton** (Hotels) is a carpet-making town (3800 inhab.) with a remarkable *Church* (by T. H. Wyatt; 1844) in Italianate Romanesque style, lavishly adorned with marble and mosaics and with 12–16C stained glass from various sources. **Wilton House** (adm. April–Sept, Tues–Sat & BH, 11–6, Sun from 2; fee), the magnificent seat of the Earl of Pembroke, begun in the time of Elizabeth I, was provided with an Italian s. front (by I. de Caus; 1633) on the advice of Charles I, and restored in 1649–52 by Inigo Jones and his nephew-in-law, John Webb. 'Gothicized' by James Wyatt, it has been purified by 20C modifications.

The 'Holbein Porch' (late-16C) is now a pavilion in the garden. The 'Palladian Bridge' in the park was built by the 9th Earl (d. 1751). The art-treasures include paintings by Richard Wilson and Rembrandt, and portraits by Van Dyck, in the splendid 'Double Cube' room, with decorations by Edw. Pierce the Elder (c. 1650) and Emm. de Critz. De Critz's dado in the 'Single Cube' room illustrates Sidney's 'Arcadia', much of which was written here. Shakespeare is believed to have acted in 'As You Like It' in the great hall, and the names of Spenser, Ben Jonson, and Massinger are likewise associated with Wilton.

FROM WILTON TO BATH, 35½ m. (A 36), ascending the Vale of Wylye. The river, though close, is largely hidden, and the prettier scenery along the s. bank is on a by-road more suited to cycling than motoring. At (11½ m.) *Codford St Peter*, the church has a 9C cross-shaft, excellently carved.—At (13½ m.) *Heytesbury* are an imposing church (12–15C), restored by Butterfield, and a Tudor almshouse faithfully rebuilt c. 1769. At Heytesbury House, his home, died Siegfried Sassoon (1886–1967). *Scratchbury* and *Battlesbury*, two large Iron Age forts, to the r. of the road farther on, afford wide panoramas.—17½ m. **Warminster** (Hotels), with 13,600 inhab., the half-way point just below the Downs, where we cross the Chippenham–Shaftesbury road (p. 174), preserves good coaching inns in its wide Georgian main street. The early 14C *Church* has an organ once in Salisbury cathedral. The *Lord Weymouth School* was founded by the Thynne family (comp. below) in 1707 (portal by Wren) and had Arnold of Rugby as a pupil.

A 362 runs w. to Frome (5 m.). Below (2½ m.) *Cley Hill* (784 ft), another conspicuous Iron Age hill-fort, is the entrance to *Longleat (adm. daily exc. Christmas Day, 10–4 or 6; fee; restaurant), the seat of the Marquess of Bath, one of the most splendid country houses in England, erected in 1559–80 by Sir John Thynne. The grounds are an outstanding example of 'Capability' Brown's landscape gardening. The Stable Court (1801–11) was added by Wyatville, who also transformed much of the interior and designed the main staircase. The Old Library, where Bp. Ken wrote the Divine Poems, is not shown, but selected treasures are displayed from the library, which includes superb copies of the first folio Shakespeare and the 1462 Fust & Schoeffer Bible, as well as MS. letters of Elizabeth I and a charter granted to Glastonbury Abbey in 681, and an important collection of books on Revolutionary France. Among other precious relics is Talleyrand's desk, on which the Treaty of Vienna was signed in 1815. Hitler forms the subject of a more recent collection. Most notable of many fine paintings are the portraits, and a series of sporting scenes by Wootton (mid-18C), and a Holy Family by Titian. In special enclosures in the park roam the 'Lions of Longleat' and other exotic fauna.—At *Horningsham*, 1 m. s., the thatched Meeting House, built (1566) by Thynne for his

Scottish Presbyterian masons, is the oldest Dissenting place of worship in England. A 36 runs N.W., rejoined at (24½ m.) *Beckington* by the road from Frome (comp. Rte 27), then turns N. to (30 m.) *Limpley Stoke* (p. 194) and descends the Avon to (35½ m.) *Bath*.

At (92½ m.) *Fovant* the chalk downs are carved with the emblems of the troops quartered there in 1914–18.

In the Nadder Valley (2 m. N.) lies *Dinton*, where Hyde's House (1725), next the church, probably occupies the site of the birthplace of Edward Hyde, earl of Clarendon, the historian (1609–74). Philipps House (N.T.), built by James Wyatt in 1813–16, is shown on Wed (2–4 or 6; fee). Little Clarendon (N.T.), a late 15C house, is shown on application; the adjoining cottage (no adm.) was the birthplace of Henry Lawes (1596–1662), the composer, Milton's friend. *Tisbury*, 5 m. w. of Dinton, has a large cruciform church (12–13C), with a fine 15C roof. At *Place House*, an ancient abbey grange, is a huge 15C tithe-barn (188 ft long). *Wardour Castle*, 2½ m. s.w., by James Paine (1769–76), now a girls' school (adm. 2.30–6, Mon, Wed, Fri, Sat in Aug; fee), has a richly decorated chapel by Quarenghi enlarged by Soane (1788) and containing in its sacristy the finest private collection of medieval embroideries in the country. It was the home of the Lords Arundell of Wardour, whose old castle (1393; blown up after a siege in 1643) is ¾ m. s.e. (adm. daily, Sun from 2; fee). *Pyt House* (adm. 2–5, Wed & Thurs in summer; fee) dates from 1805.

102 m. **Shaftesbury** (Hotels), an ancient town with 4000 inhab., strikingly situated on a spur (700 ft), is traditionally one of the oldest towns in England ('Palladour'). In 880 Alfred founded here an important house for Benedictine nuns. The *Abbey Ruins* (open Easter–Sept, 10–12.30, 2–6, Sun 2–6; fee), though scanty, are beautifully laid out; the ground plan of the large church has been revealed by excavation; and there is an interesting little museum. The empty tomb of Edward the Martyr (d. 978) was found in 1861 on the N. side of the altar, and in 1931 a casket was unearthed near by containing bones which may be those of the Martyr. King Canute died here in 1035. *St Peter's* church has a good 15C N. parapet and 16C w. porch. The *Grosvenor Hotel* has the remarkable carved 'Chevy Chase' sideboard. A cottage *Museum* (adm. 3–5 daily Easter–Oct; fee), at the top of the steep Gold Hill, contains a selection of buttons (once the town's chief manufacture) and a 14C Nottingham alabaster (Burial of St Catherine). A good description of Shaftesbury under its old name of 'Shaston' is found in Hardy's 'Jude the Obscure'.

FROM SHAFTESBURY TO RINGWOOD, B 3081 (23 m.), a fine scenic road traversing Cranborne Chase. A zigzag climbs Charlton Down to 862 ft.— 7 m. *Tollard Royal* was King John's seat for the hunting of Cranborne Chase.— Beyond (10½ m.) *Sixpenny Handley* where the ancient church has 13C wall-paintings we cross the Salisbury–Blandford road (Rte 14), then the prominent Roman *agger* of Ackling Dyke.— 15 m. *Cranborne* (l.) is a small town with a charming manor-house (Tudor with Jacobean porches) of the Marquess of Salisbury (*Gardens open occasionally). St Giles House (no adm.) at *Wimborne St Giles*, 1½ m. s.w., is the Jacobean home of the Earls of Shaftesbury. We cross Ringwood Forest.— 23 m. *Ringwood*, see Rte 13B.

At (112 m.) *Henstridge* a maid, alarmed by the smoke from his pipe, threw a tankard over Sir Walter Raleigh as he sat outside the Virginia Tavern.

To the s. A 357 traverses the *Blackmore Vale*, with centres at *Stalbridge* (3½ m. s.), with a tall market-cross, and *Sturminster Newton* (8½ m. s.), the chief cattle-market. William Barnes (1801–86), the Dorset poet, was born at *Rushay* between Sturminster and Stalbridge.

113½ m. *Purse Caundle Manor* (l.; adm. Mar–Oct, Wed, Thurs, Sun and BH, 2–5; fee) is a picturesque medieval house with Tudor additions and an attractive garden.—The church of (115 m.) *Milborne Port* is notable for its early-Norman crossing and other details.

118 m. **Sherborne** (Hotels) is a lively stone-built town (7300 inhab.), with ancient houses. In 705 it became the seat of a bishopric, removed in 1078 to Old Sarum. The *ABBEY CHURCH, as it stands, is one of the finest extant examples of the Perp. style.

The Saxon minster, from 909 the church of a Benedictine abbey, was entirely rebuilt after 1122, and of this Norman church the s. porch and the tower arches survive. Early in the 15C the nave was recast and the choir rebuilt. The details of the external ornamentation are admirable, and the design of the choir approaches perfection.

Within, the effect of the interior, with its magnificent fan-vaulting, is of great richness. At the w. end of the N. aisle an early-11C doorway of the last Saxon church is sheltered by a modern porch. In the N. transept a stone marks the probable grave of the poet Sir Thos. Wyatt (d. 1542); in the adjoining chapel is the tomb of Sir John Horsey (d. 1546), who sold the church to the town at the Dissolution, and of his son (d. 1564). The chapel beyond is a 13C addition, as is the Lady Chapel, which served as the headmaster's house in 1560–1860 and was restored and enlarged (by Caröe) in 1921–34. The s.E. or Bow Chapel is a mixture of 14C, 15C, and 16C work. In the s. transept is the monument (1698), signed by John Nost, to George, 3rd Earl of Bristol, while St Katherine's chapel, beyond, contains the 16C Leweston tomb and good heraldic glass. The central tower may be ascended on weekdays at 3 and 4.

Sherborne School, an important public school (540 boys), refounded by Edward VI in 1550, incorporates the 15C Abbot's Hall and other monastic buildings (adm. free in school holidays). *Foster's School* and *Lord Digby's School* are likewise of old foundation. The *Hospital of SS John the Baptist and the Evangelist* (1437) is a two-storied medieval hospital with a notable painted wooden altarpiece in its chapel.

On the s. side of the Yeo are the ruins of the bishops' *Castle* (c. 1100), with a Norman gatehouse and keep, and the present *Sherborne Castle* (adm. Easter–Sept, Thurs, Sat, Sun & BH, 2–6; fee; rfmts), part of which was built by Sir Walter Raleigh in 1594. The park is crossed by a public footpath (views).—The Tudor manor-house at *Sandford Orcas*, 3 m. N., is open daily 11–5.30. At *Trent* manor-house, 3½ m. N.W., Charles II lay hidden for a fortnight after the battle of Worcester.— *Cerne Abbas* (Hotel), 11 m. s. on the Dorchester road, is a charming village, preserving the beautiful 15C gatehouse of a Benedictine abbey. The church has 14C wall-paintings and a 15C screen. Above it is the *Cerne Giant* (N.T.), a figure 180 ft long, cut in the chalk.

Leaving on the left the road to *Bradford Abbas*, where the church has a notable w. front, stone screen, font, and bench-ends (15C), we cross the Yeo and enter (123 m.) **Yeovil** (Hotels), a bustling old town (25,500 inhab.) amid pleasant surroundings. It manufactures gloves, sailcloth, and helicopters and has milk and cheese factories. The beautiful Perp. *Church is "one grand harmonious whole, truly the work of real artistic genius" (Freeman). William Dampier (1652–1715), the navigator, was born at *East Coker*, 3 m. s.s.w. and T. S. Eliot (1888–1965) is buried here.

FROM YEOVIL TO ILMINSTER (A 3088).—2 m. *Brympton d'Evercy* (1; adm. Easter & May–Sept, daily exc. Thurs & Fri, 12–6; fee) has 16–17C state-rooms and an agricultural museum.—4 m. **Montacute**, built of local Ham Hill stone, has a church (Norman and Perp.) with a fine tower, and a splendid Elizabethan *Mansion built by

Sir Edward Phelips in 1580–1601, which contains a good collection of furniture, tapestry, and needlework, also paintings loaned by the National Portrait Gallery (N.T.; adm. Easter–Sept, daily exc. Tues, 12.30–6; also Sat & Sun, 2–6 or dusk in Mar, Oct & Nov; fee).—At (5½ m.) *Stoke-under-Ham*, a charming village, the church is of outstanding interest, and the Priory (15C) has a fine hall (N.T.; adm. daily 10–4 or 6). The Fleur-de-Lis Inn has a fives court built in 1760. *Ham Hill*, with famous limestone quarries, has been fortified since Neolithic times. *Norton-sub-Hamdon*, 1 m. s., is dominated by its church tower.—At 7 m. we join A 303 (Rte 16) for (14 m.) *Ilminster*.

FROM YEOVIL TO DORCHESTER (A 37), 21½ m. (railway from Pen Mill station in ½ hr).—8 m. *Melbury House* (1547, with Carolean additions), to the right, is the seat of the Earl of Ilchester (no adm.; but footpath across the park to *Melbury Sampford* church, with good 15C tombs). The remote church of *Melbury Bubb* (to the left of our road) has a very early Norman carved *Font.—The church at *Cattistock*, 1 m. N. of (13½ m.) *Maiden Newton*, has a carillon of 35 bells cast at Louvain in 1882.—21½ m. *Dorchester*, see Rte 14.

A 30 continues through (126 m.) *West Coker* and (127½ m.) *East Chinnock*, both with hotels, and beyond (130 m.) *Haselbury Plucknett* crosses the infant Parrett, crossed also (by-road, r.) by a 15C bridge.— 132 m. **Crewkerne** (Hotels), a market town (4800 inhab.) with a long history of flax weaving and sailcloth making, has a richly decorated 15C church, a grammar school founded in 1499, and almshouses of 1604 and 1707. *Hinton St George*, 3 m. N.W. has Poulett monuments in its church.

From Crewkerne a bus runs in 50 min. to (12 m.) *Bridport* (Rte 15B) viâ (6 m.) **Beaminster** (pron. 'Bemminster'), the 15C church of which has a stately Perp. tower, adorned with sculptures. Thomas Hollis, the patriot and benefactor of Harvard University (1720–74), lived and died at *Corscombe*, 3 m. N.E.; and Thomas Fuller, the divine (1608–61), was rector of *Broadwindsor*, 3 m. N.W. To the w. of Beaminster rise *Lewesdon Hill* (894 ft; N.T.) and *Pilsdon Pen* (909 ft), the highest hill in Dorset (*View); Wordsworth lived in 1795–97 at *Racedown Lodge*, on the Lyme Regis road, below the latter hill. *Parnham*, ⅓ m. s., on the Bridport road (adm. Wed, Sun & BH, 10–5, Apr–Oct; fee), and *Mapperton* (2 m. s.E.) are fine Tudor mansions.—On the Dorchester road, which commands wide views, is the Wessex Division War Memorial (1952).

A 30 climbs above 750 ft (view), then descends Windwhistle Hill between a noble avenue of beeches, skirting the grounds of Cricket House, built for Adm. Hood in 1804, and now having a wild-life park. 140 m. **Chard** (Hotels) is a lace-making town (7900 inhab.) with the former Court House (1590; opposite the Town Hall of 1834), where Jeffreys sat at the 'Bloody Assize'. Margaret Bondfield (1873–1953), the first woman cabinet minister, was born at Chard; Lucien Pissarro (1863–1944), the painter, died at South Chard.

In the rich green valley of the Axe, 3½ m. s.E., is *Forde Abbey* (adm. Wed, Sun & BH, May–Sept, 2–6; fee; rfmts in undercroft), a mansion incorporating the beautiful remains of a Cistercian monastery, built in 1138, reconstructed in 1528, and altered by Inigo Jones c. 1658. It was rented in 1814–17 by Jeremy Bentham. In the large saloon hang the famous Mortlake tapestries after Raphael's Cartoons. The lovely gardens cover 25 acres.

Axminster (Hotels), a pleasantly situated little town, 7 m. s. of Chard, is known for its carpet industry, re-established in 1937 after a lapse of a century. Probably *Great Trill* and not *Ashe House*, near *Musbury*, 2 m. s.w., was the birthplace of the Duke of Marlborough (1650–1722). In Musbury church are the *Drake Monument with three pairs of polychrome stone figures (1558–1636), including the grandparents of the Duke of Marlborough.

The Exeter road becomes very hilly, rising beyond Snowdon Hill to 733 ft. Entering Devon, we cross the Yarty valley and climb past (146½ m.) *Yarcombe* to 874 ft before joining A 303.—153½ m. **Honiton**

(Hotels) has a harmonious 18C High St. with coaching inns, and is frequented for trout-fishing in the Otter. Honiton lace is now made chiefly in the neighbouring villages. A 375 diverges on the left for Sidmouth (Rte 15B).

A 30 passes 1½ m. N. of (158 m.) **Ottery St Mary** (Hotels) to which the diversion (1 m. farther) is well worth while. The town (5800 inhab.) has a notable E.E. and Dec. *Church, of which the transeptal towers and other features were copied by Bp. Grandison from Exeter Cathedral. The Dorset aisle (1504–30) has fine fan-vaulting, and the *Clock retains its original works of Elizabethan date. The weather-vane (1335) is the oldest still working in England; the stocks still stand in the churchyard. Ottery was the birthplace of S. T. Coleridge (1772–1834), and it is the 'Clavering St Mary' ('Pendennis') of Thackeray, who used to spend his Charterhouse holidays in the neighbourhood. *Cadhay Manor* (adm. 2–6, Wed & Thurs mid-July–Aug & BH; fee) is a house of 1550 with good gardens (1 m. N. of Ottery).—At (164 m.) *Clyst Honiton* is Exeter Airport.—170 m. **Exeter,** see Rte 15B.

B Viâ Dorchester

ROAD, 177 m. To (123 m.) *Dorchester*, see Rte 14.—A 35. 138½ m. *Bridport*—148 m. *Lyme Regis.*—A 3052. 163 m. *Sidford.*—177 m. *Exeter.*

From London to (123 m.) *Dorchester*, see Rte 14. A 35 runs due w. across the Dorset Downs, with fine views.—135 m. *Kingston Russell* (r.), a manor-house where Adm. Sir Thomas Hardy (1769–1839) was born and John Lothrop Motley (1814–77) died (tablet). A monument (1844) to Adm. Hardy crowns *Blackdown Hill* (776 ft), 3 m. S.E. *Littlebredy* and other pretty villages to the s. merit a detour.—138½ m. **Bridport** (Hotels), the 'Port Bredy' of Hardy's Wessex novels, is an agreeable small town (6400 inhab.), 1½ m. N. of its tiny harbour and bathing-beach at *West Bay*. Noted for its ancient manufactures of ropes, twines, nets, etc. (a 'Bridport dagger' is a hangman's halter), the town has an attractive main street with an 18C town hall; near the church (mainly Perp.), in South St., is a 16C stone house, now a museum.—The road becomes very hilly, with some gradients of 1 in 5.—141½ m. *Chideock* (Hotels) is a charming village affording access to fine cliff scenery (N.T.).—145½ m. *Charmouth* (Hotels) is a pleasant little seaside resort with a steep street. Both here and at Bridport Charles II was nearly taken by the Parliament men on his flight from Worcester.

The church (Norman to Perp.) of *Whitchurch Canonicorum*, 2¼ m. N.E., contains the little shrine of St Candida, the only one in England (save that of Edward the Confessor at Westminster) to survive the Reformation unplundered.

A 35 bears right for Axminster (6 m.; p. 157); we follow A 3052.— 148 m. **Lyme Regis** (Hotels, numerous but small) is a charming old fishing town (5400 inhab.) and bathing resort with steep streets and an abiding 'Regency' atmosphere. It withstood a siege of two months by the Royalists in 1644. The stone pier, known as the 'Cobb', on which the Duke of Monmouth landed in 1685, is perhaps better known as the scene of Louisa Musgrove's accident in Jane Austen's 'Persuasion'. The church contains a 16C tapestry, commemorating the marriage of Prince Arthur and Catherine of Aragon. Sir George Somers (1554–

1610), who first settled the Bermudas ('Somers Islands'), Capt. Coram (1668–1751), founder of the London Foundling Hospital, and Eleanor Coade (1733–1821), inventor of 'Coade stone', were natives of Lyme Regis.

The blue lias cliffs of the neighbourhood abound in fossils, and here Mary Anning (1799–1847) discovered the ichthyosaurus in 1811. About 3½ m. w. is the *Dowlands Landslip* (fee), where 40 acres of ground slipped down from the cliff in 1839. There is a good golf course on the Charmouth road.

155 m. *Colyford* is 1¾ m. N. of Seaton (see below) and 1 m. s. of *Colyton* (Hotel) which has a fine church with a 15C octagonal lantern, notable monuments, and an early 10C cross.

Seaton (Hotels), a breezy little bathing-resort with a shingle beach (4100 inhab.) at the mouth of the Axe, is best approached along the E. bank of the river viâ *Axmouth*, 1 m. E. of which is the unusual 15C tower-house of *Bindon*. Delightful walks lead along the coast E. to the Landslip (see above) and w. viâ (1 m.) *Beer* (Hotels), a fishing-village with old quarries, and (3 m.) *Branscombe Mouth*. The good church of the romantic village of *Branscombe* (Hotels) lies 1½ m. from the sea. Over 300 acres of the Branscombe estate including medieval farmhouses, a forge and a bakery are N.T. property.

At (163 m.) *Sidford* (Hotel) we cross the Honiton–Sidmouth road, c. 2 m. N. of Sidmouth.

Sidmouth (many Hotels), a dignified seaside resort (12,000 inhab.) with a shingle beach and a golf course, is delightfully situated between fine reddish cliffs; protected on the N. by a circle of hills, it is apt to be sultry in summer. The town retains many Regency villas. Queen Victoria lived at Woolbrook Cottage (now Royal Glen Hotel) as a baby, and her father died here in 1824. *Woolcombe House* (adm. daily July–Sept; Thurs, Sat, Sun only in winter) is a medieval hall, now a museum. The *Norman Lockyer Observatory* (1912) was attached to Exeter University in 1948.
A pleasant road leads s.w. from Sidmouth to (4 m.) *Otterton*, near the favourite bathing-beach of *Ladram Bay*, (4¾ m.) *East Budleigh*, and (6½ m.) **Budleigh Salterton** (Hotels), at the mouth of the Otter, once occupied in salt-extraction and now an attractive bathing-resort, with golf course. Near East Budleigh are *Bicton Park* (1 m. N.; adm. 10–6, June–Sept; 2–6 in Apr, May, & Oct; fee), with fine gardens and arboretum, a countryside museum, and a miniature railway; and *Hayes Barton*, 1 m. w., the birthplace of Sir Walter Raleigh (1552–1618).

A 3052 crosses the Otter at (166 m.) *Newton Poppleford*; beyond the river A 376 leads l. for Budleigh Salterton (4½ m.) and Exmouth (10 m.).

177 m. **EXETER** (95,600 inhab.), the county town of Devon, is a historic city, with a beautiful cathedral and considerable remains of its medieval walls. It lies on rising ground on the left (N.E.) bank of the Exe, and is connected also with the tidal estuary of that river at Topsham by a ship canal (5 m. long), begun in 1563. The irregular orientation of many of the old churches is evidently determined by the Roman lines of the old streets.

Railway Stations (Rfmts at the first two). *St David's* (Pl. 10), N.W. of the city, nearly 1 m. from the cathedral; *Central* (Pl. 6), near the Castle and ½ m. from St David's; *St Thomas's* (Pl. 13), for local (s. Devon) trains.
Airport at Clyst Honiton, 6 m. E.
Hotels in the town (see plan), also at *Pinhoe*; MOTELS on by-pass.
Post Office (Pl. 11), Bedford St.—INFORMATION BUREAU (Pl. 10), 18 Queen St.
Bus Station (Pl. 10), Paul St., for services to all destinations.
Amusements. *Northcott Theatre*, Exeter University.—GOLF COURSE, on the Topsham road.—SWIMMING BATHS, Heavitree Rd.—RACE MEETINGS at *Haldon*, c. 6½ m. s., Aug and Sept.—BOATS at Exe Bridge (Pl. 13) and The Quay (Pl. 14).

History. Exeter was the *Isca Dumnoniorum* of the Romans, stretches of whose masonry (c. 200) survive in the town walls, and the *Escancestre* of the Saxons. A monastery with a Saxon abbot was in existence at Exeter by 680. The town was stormed by the Danes in 876, and, though walls were built by Athelstan c. 932, it was again plundered in 1003. In 1050, however, the bishopric of Devon and Cornwall was transferred from Crediton, for its greater security, to Exeter. In 1068 the town submitted to William the Conqueror only after a long siege, and the castle was begun. The first mayor was appointed in 1205. Exeter has frequently been besieged. Though occupied by Parliament at the onset of the Civil War, it was later held for the King until 1646. Princess Henrietta (1644–70), daughter of Charles I and wife of Philippe d'Orléans, was born at Exeter. William III was proclaimed here in 1688. The city was wantonly attacked from the air in 1942, when 40 acres, including many ancient buildings, were destroyed.—Sir Thomas Bodley (1545–1613), Abp. William Temple (1881–1944), and probably Nicholas Hilliard (1537–1619), were born here. The *University of Exeter*, founded in 1865 and incorporated as the University College of South-West England in 1922, received its charter in 1955. It has faculties of arts, law, science, and social studies.

HIGH STREET (Pl. 10), largely rebuilt since the German bombing, retains a Roman course, continued by Fore St. down to the *Exe Bridge* (Pl. 13; 1905). Broadgate, on the left beyond the Guildhall (see below), is the best approach to the cathedral.

The *Cathedral (Pl. 10), dedicated to St Peter, is a comparatively small but admirable building of the Geometrical Decorated period, with Norman towers.

HISTORY. The conventual church founded by Athelstan c. 932, which probably served as the earliest cathedral, was superseded by a Norman edifice built in 1112–1206. Of this the only important remains are the massive transeptal towers (to which the battlements and turrets were added in the 15C), the only transeptal towers in England, except those copied from them at Ottery St Mary. The transformation of the Norman church was begun (from the E. end) c. 1270 by Bp. Bronescombe (d. 1280) and was continued by Bps. Quivil (d. 1291), Bitton (d. 1307), Stapeldon (d. 1326), and Grandison (d. 1369). The w. façade is decorated with sculptured figures forming a well-ordered scheme, the central subject being the Enthronement, flanked in the upper tier by Apostles, Evangelists, Patriarchs, and Prophets, while in the lower tier are the chief persons of the royal line of Judah. The lower figures appear to belong to the time of Bp. Grandison, the upper figures are much later (possibly late 15C). The numerous flying buttresses contrast agreeably with the solid Norman towers. The curfew is rung from the North Tower on 'Great Peter', a bell of over 6 tons.

*Interior. The most striking characteristic is the uniformity of design, each detail marked by purity of style (Dec.) and answering to its counterpart with unfailing symmetry. The unbroken stretch of vaulted roof, over 300 ft in length, is most impressive, with good bosses. There is a lofty clerestory, but the triforium is represented by a small blank arcade. At the w. end of the N. aisle is the *Chapel of St Edmund*, dedicated to the Devonshire Regiment, adjoined by a tablet to Richard Blackmore (1825–1900). To the s. of the central door, in the thickness of the w. wall, is a chantry constructed by Bp. Grandison (c. 1360).

The most notable single feature of the NAVE, with its fine Purbeck marble pillars, is the *Minstrels' Gallery* (by Bp. Grandison) on the N. side, with angels playing on various musical instruments. Near the w. end of the s. wall is the sledging flag of Captain Scott (1868–1912), given by his mother in 1922.

The TRANSEPTS, with their beautiful window-tracery and exquisite triforium gallery, were reconstructed by Bps. Bronescombe and Quivil under the Norman towers. In the N. transept are the *Sylke Chantry*, founded in 1508, a 15C wall-painting of the Resurrection, an interesting

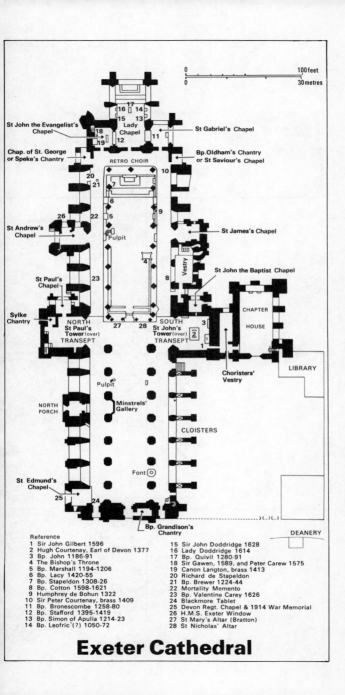

0 100 feet
0 30 metres

St John the Evangelist's Chapel

St Gabriel's Chapel

16 17 14
15 13

Lady Chapel

18
19 **12** **11**

Chap. of St. George or Speke's Chantry

Bp.Oldham's Chantry or St Saviour's Chapel

RETRO CHOIR

20
21 **10**

7

26 **6**

9

St Andrew's Chapel

22 **5**

Pulpit

St James's Chapel

4

23 Vestry

St John the Baptist Chapel

St Paul's Chapel

8

Sylke Chantry

CHAPTER HOUSE

NORTH St Paul's Tower (over) TRANSEPT

SOUTH St John's Tower (over) TRANSEPT

27 28 **3**
2
1

Choristers' Vestry

LIBRARY

Pulpit

NORTH PORCH

Minstrels' Gallery

CLOISTERS

St Edmund's Chapel

Font (○)

25 **24**

Bp. Grandison's Chantry

DEANERY

Reference
1 Sir John Gilbert 1596
2 Hugh Courtenay, Earl of Devon 1377
3 Bp. John 1186-91
4 The Bishop's Throne
5 Bp. Marshall 1194-1206
6 Bp. Lacy 1420-55
7 Bp. Stapeldon 1308-26
8 Bp. Cotton 1598-1621
9 Humphrey de Bohun 1322
10 Sir Peter Courtenay, brass 1409
11 Bp. Bronescombe 1258-80
12 Bp. Stafford 1395-1419
13 Bp. Simon of Apulia 1214-23
14 Bp. Leofric¹(?) 1050-72

15 Sir John Doddridge 1628
16 Lady Doddridge 1614
17 Bp. Quivil 1280-91
18 Sir Gawen, 1589, and Peter Carew 1575
19 Canon Langton, brass 1413
20 Richard de Stapeldon
21 Bp. Brewer 1224-44
22 Mortality Memento
23 Bp. Valentine Carey 1626
24 Blackmore Tablet
25 Devon Regt. Chapel & 1914 War Memorial
26 H.M.S. Exeter Window
27 St Mary's Altar (Bratton)
28 St Nicholas' Altar

Exeter Cathedral

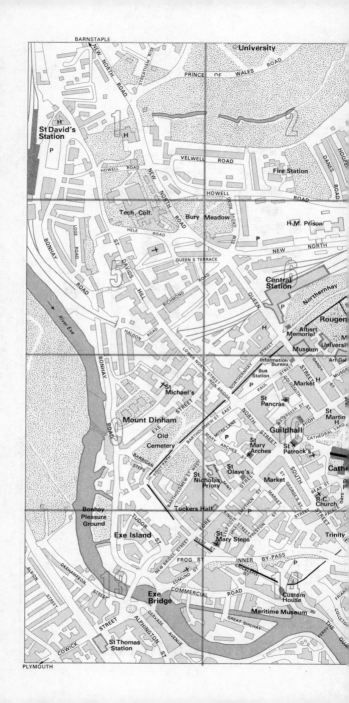

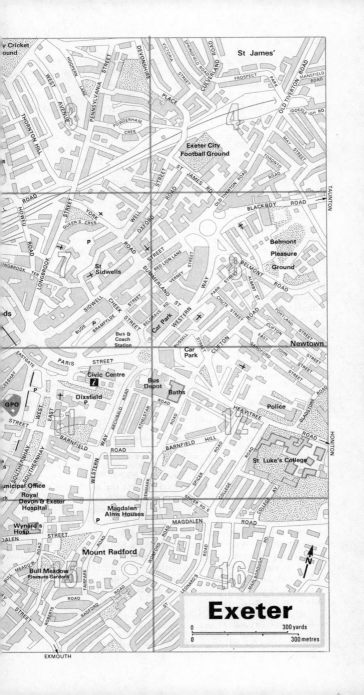

Exeter

| 0 | | | 300 yards |
| 0 | | | 300 metres |

*Clock of 1423, and a statue of Northcote, the painter (1746–1831), by Chantrey. The s. transept contains the tomb of Hugh Courtenay, Earl of Devon (d. 1377), and his wife. In the s.w. corner is the entrance to a vestry (c. 1500–1640, the Chapel of the Holy Ghost), to the s. of which stands the CHAPTER HOUSE (E.E. & Perp.; ceiling of 1465–78), shown by a verger.

The CHOIR is separated from the nave by a triple-arched screen erected by Bp. Stapeldon (d. 1326), with paintings of the 17C. Henry de Bracton (p. 206) was buried near here in 1268.—Noteworthy monuments are those of Bp. Marshall (d. 1206) and Bp. Stapeldon (both on the N. side; Pl. 5 & 7). The *Stalls* and *Reredos* are of the 19C, but the former have E.E. misericords, and the oaken *Bishop's Throne* and stone *Sedilia* are exquisite works of the early 14C. The E. window (Perp.) contains glass of the 14C. Three of the small chapels opening off the choir-aisles are closed by early 15C stone screens; the others have 16C screens. *St James's Chapel* (s.), destroyed by a German bomb in May 1942, has been beautifully rebuilt; in emulation of the medieval spirit the corbels are topical. *St Andrew's Chapel* (N.) has a memorial window (1948) to the men of H.M.S. 'Exeter', sunk in the Java Sea in 1942. *Bp. Oldham's Chantry* (1519), in the s.E. corner, is decorated with owls, in punning reference to the founder's name. At the s. side of the Lady Chapel entrance is a *Wall-painting of the Assumption and Coronation of the Virgin* (c. 1500).—The LADY CHAPEL is mainly the work of Bp. Bronescombe, with four interesting episcopal tombs, notably that of Bronescombe himself (1329), intricately decorated, with the gilding and colour well restored.

On the s. side part of the *Cloister* has been rebuilt in the original (Dec.) style.—A wing of the *Bishop's Palace* (rebuilt) is occupied by the CATHEDRAL LIBRARY (open on Tues, Wed, & Fri, 10–1, 2.30–5; entrance Palace Gate), which includes some Saxon MSS., the Exeter Domesday MS., and the 'Codex Exoniensis' (10C), a famous collection of early Anglo-Saxon poetry. The former palace chapel (partly 13C) serves as vestries.

In the CATHEDRAL CLOSE are several interesting old houses: next *St Martin's Church* (15C and 17C), in the N. corner, is *Mol's Coffee House* (1596; now an art-shop), in which a fine oak-panelled room is shown; No. 5 has a 15C hall (adm. free); the *Law Library* (No. 8) occupies a 14C hall (adm. 10–1 on application); and farther on a stone archway, with a Jacobean oak door, admits to a charming little quadrangle. To the N. of the cathedral is a statue of Richard Hooker (1554–1600), a native of Heavitree (the E. suburb), by Alfred Drury.

We return to High St., leaving on the left the much altered church of *St Petrock* (Pl. 10), with a tower of pre-Norman days. The *Guildhall* (Pl. 10), dating from 1330, is conspicuous by reason of its pillared façade (added in 1593) projecting over the pavement. The Hall (open to visitors) has a fine roof (1464), with corbels showing the 'bear and ragged staff' of Warwick the Kingmaker, and panelled walls (1594) ornamented with the arms of the trade-guilds, mayors, etc. It contains several portraits: Princess Henrietta, and General Monk, both by *Lely*, Chief Justice Pratt, by *Hudson*. From the roof hangs the ensign of H.M.S. 'Exeter', flown at the River Plate (1939). The city regalia is shown on request.

In Waterbeer St., which may be reached by the narrow alley called Parliament 'Street' (s. of the Guildhall), is a tessellated pavement (covered) which may mark the site of the Roman Prætorium. Close by is *St Pancras Church* (Pl. 10), with a Norman font, an E.E. chancel and piscina, and a holy-water stoup.

Farther up High St. is *St Stephen's* (r.; Pl. 10), rebuilt c. 1665 with an elevated chancel on an old arch called 'Stephen's Bow', behind which is a quiet little square. Hence Bedford St. leads to *Southernhay*, a charming street with Georgian houses. On the w. side of Southernhay a fine section of the **City Wall** with bastions, revealed by bombing, is well seen.

Traversing the area within the wall that was devastated in 1942 is Princesshay, a new footway which leads back to the top of High St. In Eastgate (r.; Pl. 11) is the entrance to the medieval *Underground Passages* (adm. 2–5 in summer), probably conduits for the city's water supply.

In Castle St. (Pl. 6), diverging right from High St., are *Rougemont House*, containing Roman antiquities (adm. on application to museum, see below), and the beautiful **Rougemont Gardens**, which contain the scanty remains of *Rougemont Castle*, erected by William the Conqueror and mentioned by Shakespeare in 'Richard III' (iv. 2). Beyond Castle Yard, in which stands the *County Assize Court* (Pl. 6; 1774) and a *Museum* of local history, extends another attractive park, *Northernhay* (Pl. 6), in which part of the old *City Wall* is visible; the *Prison* (1853) is prominent to the N. beyond the railway.

The w. portion of the wall may be reached viâ Northernhay St. and Bartholomew St. (Pl. 9), which brings us to a footpath on top of the wall, above the *Old Cemetery* (opened in 1637); thence Bartholomew St. leads to Fore St. (see below).

From the w. exit from Northernhay Queen St. leads to the left to High St., passing the ROYAL ALBERT MEMORIAL (Pl. 6), a group of buildings including an overcrowded *Museum* (natural history, local silver and pottery, and good costumes from 1750); a *Picture Gallery* (works by Reynolds, Turner, Opie, etc.; weekdays, 10–5.30); and the *Art School* of the University.

In the other direction Queen St. passes *Central Station* (Pl. 6), whence the line descends one of the steepest railway gradients in England to *St David's Station* (Pl. 1). Exeter University occupies several fine mansions in beautiful grounds and new buildings by Holford in Prince of Wales Road (Pl. 2). Northcott Theatre was opened in 1967.

We descend High St. to Fore St., off which, on the r., is the church of *St Mary Arches* (Pl. 10), with a norman nave and Jacobean monuments. *St Olave's* (Pl. 10), in Fore St., is an ancient edifice singularly unorthodox in plan. In The Mint, diverging right, is the Benedictine *Priory of St Nicholas (Pl. 10; adm. fee; weekdays 10–1 and 2–5.30, April–Sept; closed Sun). Visitors are shown the Norman Undercroft (c. 1087), Kitchen (13C and 15C), Tudor Room with plaster ceiling, Guest Hall and Tower (15C), with the Prior's Solar and Cell. In the garden is a 7C Celtic cross, attached for 200 years to a pier of the Exe bridge. The Mint takes its name from the small assay-furnaces formerly in the Undercroft.—Lower down (r.) is *Tucker's Hall* (Pl. 10), the guildhouse of the 'weavers, fullers, and shearmen', with fine roof (1471) and oak panelling (1634). It is open in summer 2.30–4.30 Tue, Thu, & Fri; in winter 11–1 on Fri; gratuity.

We descend the steep West St. (Pl. 14), on the l., to visit the interesting church of *St Mary Steps* (Pl. 14), with its Norman font, fine rood-screen, and curious clock (c. 1656). Next door are some 16C houses including one moved on rollers in 1961 from farther w. Opposite the church stood the West Gate and a little farther on was the Water Gate (s.e. angle); on the Quay is the *Custom House* (1678–81).

Hence the wall runs N.E. to the South Gate (removed in 1819) and along Southern-hay (comp. p. 162).—In Magdalen St. is *Wynard's Hospital* (Pl. 15), founded c. 1430, with a chapel, sympathetically restored in Victorian times, containing an arch and window of the 15C.

About ¼ m. N. of the Cullompton road, near (1½ m.) *Polsloe Bridge Halt*, are the 13C remains of *Polsloe Priory*, now used as a store.

FROM EXETER TO EXMOUTH, 10½ m. (railway from Central Sta.). Leaving by South St. (Pl. 10) and passing (1 m.) the County Hall, we cross the by-pass just above the 16C *Countess Wear Bridge* over the Exe (widened 1937).—4 m. **Topsham** (Motel), formerly the port of Exeter and now a lively yachting centre, has several Dutch-style houses, in the charming Strand, built of Dutch bricks (ferry for Exminster and Turf).—5½ m. *Clyst St George* is 2 m. N.W. of *Woodbury*, the birthplace of Nicholas Stone (1586–1647).—10½ m. **Exmouth** (Hotels) is a popular seaside resort (25,800 inhab.) enjoying a fine view across the mouth of the Exe, with a sandy beach, esplanade, and golf links. Ferry to *Starcross*; excursion steamers in summer. The road goes on to Budleigh Salterton (p. 159).

FROM EXETER TO BARNSTAPLE, 40 m. (A 377); railway in 1–1½ hr. A 377 ascends the Creedy valley.—5 m. *Newton St Cyres* has notable monuments in its church.—8 m. **Crediton** (5100 inhab.; Hotel), the birthplace of St Boniface or Winfrid (680–755), was the original seat of the episcopal see of Devon and Cornwall (909–1050). A statue of the Saint (by Alan Durst) was unveiled in 1960. The cruciform sandstone church, once collegiate, was founded in the 12C, but dates mainly from the 15C; it contains two good 17C tombs.—At (14¼ m.) *Morchard Road Station* the Bideford road (B 3220) diverges to the left; A 377 descends to the beautiful valley of the Taw (good fishing).—17 m. *Lapford* church (r.) has a wealth of fine woodwork.—21 m. *Eggesford* (Hotel; fishing) has the fine Chichester monuments in its church, while *Chawleigh*, 2 m. N.E., and *Chulmleigh*, 2½ m. N., have good rood-screens.—32 m. *Umberleigh* (Hotel; fishing) lies 2¼ m. S.E. of the noble *Tower (1520) of *Chittlehampton* church (dedicated to the local virgin martyr Urith), and 1¼ m. E. of *Atherington*, with a famous rood-screen in its interesting church.—At 36 m. where our road crosses the Taw a lane goes straight on to *Tawstock* *Church (14C; 1½ m.) with notable monuments and one of the most elaborate pews in the country.—40 m. *Barnstaple*.

From Exeter to *Tiverton* and *Exmoor*, see Rte 21C; to *Taunton* and *Bristol*, see Rte 20; to *Torquay*, *Plymouth*, and the w., see Rte 22.

16   LONDON TO TAUNTON

ROAD, 143 M.—To (46 m.) *Basingstoke*, see Rte 11B.—A 30, A 303. 65 m. *Andover* (by-pass).—79 m. **Amesbury**.—119½ m. We branch right on A 372.—130 m. **Langport**.—A 378. 143 m. **Taunton**. This road forms yet another approach to Exeter (169 m.), viâ Ilminster (comp. below).

RAILWAY TO **Taunton**, 143 m. from Paddington in 2 hrs. 10 min. Route viâ *Reading* to (61½ m.) *Hungerford*, see Rte 17. Thence viâ (95½ m.) *Westbury*.

From London to (46 m.) *Basingstoke*, see Rte 11B. From the end of the by-pass we follow A 30 (comp. Rte 14), at 56 m. branching right on to A 303.—65 m. *Andover* (see below) is well by-passed to the s.

A much prettier road from Basingstoke (B 3400; 1 m. shorter) follows the upper Test valley.—3½ m. *Oakley* (Hotel).—7 m. *Overton*, in the rolling chalk-hill country extolled by Cobbett.—8½ m. *Laverstoke* is a model village where the paper for Bank of England notes was made for over 200 years.—11 m. *Whitchurch*, see p. 121.—18 m. **Andover** (Hotels), an ancient town (25,500 inhab.) unattractively 'redeveloped', now shows few signs of its past. In 994 King Olaf of Norway was baptized here by St Alphege.

We cross the chalk ridges on the edge of Salisbury Plain to (79 m.) **Amesbury** (Hotels) in the valley of the Hampshire Avon. The large abbey-church (Norman and E.E.) is a successor of "the holy house at Almesbury" where the penitent Guinevere sought refuge. Here in 1292 died Eleanor of Provence. At *Amesbury Abbey*, then the seat of the Duke of Queensberry, Gay wrote the 'Beggar's Opera' (1727). To the N.W. are the prehistoric earthworks known as *Vespasian's Camp*, and at *Durrington*, 2 m. N., is *Woodhenge*, consisting of six concentric rings originally marked by wooden posts (now replaced by concrete pillars), the whole encircled by a mound and a ditch.

Salisbury Plain is an undulating expanse about 20 m. long by 10 m. wide, which has lost much of its former loneliness through the advance of tillage and the formation of many permanent military camps. Among these are *Bulford* (artillery), *Netheravon* (R.A.F.), *Upavon* (R.A.F.), *Larkhill* (artillery), and *Tidworth*.—The characteristic flint and stone banding of the local churches is well seen at *Tilshead*, 7 m. N.W. of Stonehenge.

81 m. ****Stonehenge** ('Stanhengist', 'hanging stones') is a circular group of huge standing stones, formerly the most elaborate and perhaps the latest monument of the kind in England (adm. daily, Sun in winter from 2; fee; car park across the Shrewton road). The first view is apt to be disappointing—Emerson thought that it "looked like a group of brown dwarfs on the wide expanse"—but a closer acquaintance reveals its mysterious dignity. When complete, it appears to have consisted of two circles and two horseshoes of upright stones, concentric and enclosed by an earthen rampart (300 ft in diameter) outside which stood a single upright stone. The so-called 'Aubrey Holes', now marked by white patches inside the rampart, each apparently indicated a burial-site, or a ritual pit. The monument is approached on the N.E. by an avenue, flanked by earthworks; and air photographs have revealed two branches converging upon this, one from the nearest point on the course of the Avon, the other, to the N., from an earthwork (the Cursus), perhaps a racecourse.

The larger circle at Stonehenge, 108 ft in diameter, consisted of a series of 30 huge monoliths bearing large lintel stones morticed to them, a form unrepresented elsewhere in western Europe, but recalling the megalithic construction at Mycenae. Of these, sixteen uprights and five imposts remain in position. The inner circle, c. 90 ft in diameter, was formed of smaller and less perfectly hewn stones, eighteen of which remain. Inside this was a horseshoe of five huge trilithons formed by ten monoliths with their imposts (two still perfect), and within this again was a smaller horseshoe of 19 stones. Of the three standing trilithons, one, which fell in 1797, was re-erected in 1958. The larger circle and horseshoe are made of sarsen sandstone, found in the neighbourhood (resembling the 'Grey Wethers' mentioned on p. 223); the smaller circle and horseshoe consist of so-called 'foreign' or 'blue' stones, a kind of granite quarried in the Preseli Hills in Pembrokeshire, and brought hither overland or perhaps partly by water (comp. above).—In the centre lies a slab of micaceous sandstone (perhaps from Milford Haven) named the Altar Stone (15 ft long), across which one of the huge uprights has fallen. The largest standing trilithon is 21 ft high (above ground) and extends 8½ ft below ground. The isolated block of unhewn sarsen stone, outside the earthen circle, is known as the 'Hele Stone', or 'Friar's Heel'. The so-called Slaughter Stone, a prostrate block at the N.E. opening of the circle, perhaps brought but not required for the outer circle of trilithons, does not appear to have been connected with the Hele Stone.—Although the purpose of Stonehenge is still doubtful, it is now believed that there were three successive monuments on the site: the oldest, of which the Hele Stone and Aubrey Holes are relics, dates from c. 1850 B.C.; the second, a circle of 60 'Blue Stones' (c. 1700 B.C.), was partially demolished and reset to form part of the third monument, c. 1500 B.C. Several of the sarsen stones bear incised drawings of axes and daggers (? of Helladic type) visible only with difficulty.

The fact that the sun on midsummer day rises over the Hele Stone, on the axis of the avenue, has long been used as an argument that Stonehenge was a temple of the sun, the slight deviation now noticeable being due to a change in the relative position of the earth. This, however, need not affect the belief that, like other stone circles, it was at least in part a sepulchral monument. The numerous barrows and tumuli scattered round it have doubtless some connection with it. It is differentiated from other British circles by having hewn stones, cap stones, tenons, and sockets, evidence of much greater sophistication in its builders. Recent measurements of its orientation have suggested to some scholars that it was erected as a device to predict astronomic occurrences.

Beyond Stonehenge the right fork (A 360) leads across the Plain to (4 m.) *Shrewton*, there dividing for (18 m.) *Devizes* (r.) viâ Tilshead (comp. above) and (l.) for (17 m.) *Warminster*, viâ Heytesbury.

87 m. *Yarnbury Castle* (r.) is a prehistoric hill-fort. The road descends to (89 m.) *Wylye* in its river valley, where the church has a 17C pulpit.— At (94 m.) *Bishop's Fonthill* (1 m. s.) are the remains of *Fonthill Abbey* the fairy palace built in 1796–1812 by James Wyatt for Wm. Beckford **(1760–1844)** author of 'Vathek'. Tisbury, p. 155, lies c. 3 m. s.e.—We descend to (103 m.) **Mere** (Hotels), recently by-passed. Charles II rested at the Talbot Inn, on his flight after the battle of Worcester, and William Barnes, the Dorset poet, kept school here for 12 years. The large Dec. church has 15C stalls and screens.— 105½ m. *Zeals.*

To the N. (1½ m.) is *Stourton*, an attractive village with the mansion of **Stourhead**, built mainly in 1720–24 by Colen Campbell for Henry Hoare (N.T.; adm. Wed, Sat, Sun, & BH, 2–6; Tues–Sun Easter–Sept; closed Dec–Feb; fee). The house contains notable paintings, sculpture, and furniture. Its magnificent *Pleasure-grounds* (open daily 11–7 or dusk; fee) are landscaped round a lake (1 m. walk) with the old High Cross of Bristol (14C), brought here in 1763. *Alfred's Tower* (damaged by an aircraft in 1944; on a ridge 800 ft high; view) lies to the N. (c. 2 m.) of the park, and was built in 1772 to mark the supposed site where in 879 Alfred rallied his army to repel the Danes.

110½ m. **Wincanton** (Hotels, also at Holbrook House, 1½ m. w.), an old coaching town (by-passed), is at the head of the broad *Blackmore Vale*, with its rich pasture-lands. In the church porch is a curious relief of the legend of St Eligius, the patron saint of smiths.

Two roads run N. from Wincanton to Shepton Mallet. On the one lies (4½ m.) **Bruton**, a charming old town with a Perp. church (18C chancel), the King's School dating from 1519, and a packhorse bridge (Bruton Bow). Sexey's Hospital (1638) adjoins the Court House (1684), now a school. The road continues viâ (8 m.) *Evercreech*, with one of the best church towers in Somerset, to (11½ m.) *Shepton Mallet*, p. 245.—Another road from Wincanton (1½ m. longer) passes east of the fine churches of (6 m.) *Alford* (Perp. with good stained glass) and (8 m.) *Ditcheat*.

The Taunton road runs s.w. and at 116 m. passes between *North Cadbury* (r.), with a fine church and manor-house, and *Cadbury Castle* (l.), an Iron Age hill-fort 18 acres in area, the most likely claimant to be the *Camelot* of the Arthurian legend. Excavations since 1966 have proved the existence of a fortress dating from c. A.D. 500.—117½ m. *Sparkford*, at the junction of the road from Frome to Yeovil. *Queen Camel*, 1½ m. s.w., has another fine church (late-14C).

FROM SPARKFORD TO EXETER, 51⅓ m. Following the Taunton road for 3 m. we then bear left on A 303 past *Yeovilton* naval air-station, where some Fleet Air Arm planes are preserved in a *Museum.—5½ m. *Ilchester* (Hotel; by-pass), a once important town on the Foss Way, was the Roman Lendiniæ, and the birthplace of Roger Bacon (1214–94). A unique 13C mace in the town hall is the sole relic of its

medieval importance.— 7½ m. *Tintinhull* (l.). Tintinhull House (N.T.; 1700) has a
famous formal garden (adm. April–Sept, Wed, Thurs, Sat & BH, 2–6; fee).—We pass s.
of the attractive little towns of *Martock* (good 14C church with tie-beam *Roof) and
South Petherton (also with a good church, and a manor-house 2 m. N.), and quit the
Foss Way.—At (18 m.) *Ilminster* (Hotels), the church has a noble Perp. central tower
and contains the tomb of Nicholas and Dorothy Wadham (d. 1609 and 1618), founders
of Wadham College, Oxford. The grammar school, now a girls' school, dates from 1586
(restored). Jordans, on the Taunton road, was the home of J. H. Speke (1827–64), the
discoverer of Victoria Nyanza, the source of the Nile. *Dillington House* (16C; altered in
19C), 1 m. N.E., now the Somerset College for Adult Education, was the residence of
Lord North while Prime Minister. *Barrington Court* (N.T.), 3½ m. N.E., is a Tudor
mansion (adm. Wed 10.15–12.15, 2–6; 2–4 Oct–Easter; fee). Ilminster makes a good
centre for visiting the fine churches of *Stocklinch, Dowlish Wake,* and *Donyatt.*—We
approach hilly country and enter Devon, soon after (30 m.) joining A 30. Thence to
(51½ m.) *Exeter,* see Rte 15B.

At 122¼ m. we cross the Foss Way. *Lyte's Cary* (N.T.; adm. March–Oct,
Wed & Sat 2–6; fee), c. 1 m. N., is a notable 14–15C mansion, well restored.
Keinton Mandeville, birthplace of Sir Henry Irving (Henry Brodribb;
1838–1905), is 4 m. farther N. From *Barton St David,* 1 m. beyond, the first
member of the presidential family of Adams emigrated to the United States
(tablet in the church).— 126½ m. *Long Sutton,* with an interesting church
and court-house. *Somerton,* c. 2½ m. N.E., is an old-fashioned little town
with a fine Dec. church and a 17C market cross. It was once the capital of
Somerset and the residence of the West Saxon kings.—At (129½ m.) *Huish
Episcopi,* the church has one of the finest towers in Somerset, a Norman
doorway, and glass by Burne-Jones (1899). *Kingsbury Episcopi,* 4 m. s., has
another lavishly decorated tower.— 130 m. *Langport* (Hotel), overlooking
the marshes of the Parrett, was the birthplace of Walter Bagehot (1826–77).
It has a fine Perp. church with good stained glass, and an interesting
Norman carving over the s. door.

The so-called 'Hanging Chapel', an ancient Perp. chapel above an archway near
the church, is now a masonic temple. About 1 m. s. is *Muchelney,* with a 14C
priest's house (N.T.; adm. by written appointment; fee), and the mainly 15C
remains of an abbey of Saxon foundation (adm. daily, Sun from 2; fee).—*Low
Ham* and *High Ham,* 1¾ and 3 m. N. of Langport, both have notable churches, the
one a 17C Gothic work with many strange features, the other containing splendid
woodwork.

132 m. *Curry Rivel* church (Perp.) has good parclose screens. On the
right are *Red Hill* (N.T.), with a view over the marshes, and the *Park-
field Monument,* 140 ft high, erected by the Earl of Chatham to Sir
Wm. Pynsent who bequeathed to him the neighbouring mansion of
Burton Pynsent.—135 m. *Fivehead* (l.).

The *Church of *Ile Abbots,* 2 m. s., has a fine tower with original sculptures, and
beautiful sedilia and piscina.
In the drained marshes on the right is the *Isle of Athelney,* where King Alfred
gathered his forces for the final struggle with the Danes in 878 (memorial pillar).
The scene of the burned cakes is laid here, and Alfred's Jewel (now at Oxford)
was found in the vicinity.

143 m. **Taunton,** see Rte 20.

17 LONDON TO BATH AND BRISTOL

ROAD, 118 m. A 4. From London by the Great West Rd. to (26½ m.) *Maidenhead*, see Rte 28.— 38½ m. **Reading.**— 56 m. *Newbury.*— 74½ m. *Marlborough.*— 93 m. *Chippenham.*— 106 m. **Bath.**— 118 m. **Bristol.** Frequent coaches from Victoria Coach Stn. in 2¼–4½ hrs.—MOTORWAY (M 4) passing s. of Reading, N. of Newbury, and only just s. of Swindon, approaches Bristol (M 32 spur) from the N.E.
RAILWAY, 118½ m. from Paddington in 1½–1¾ hr. (viâ Swindon). To Bath (107 m.) in 70–90 min. *Newbury* and *Hungerford* have stations on the line to Westbury and Taunton, which leaves the Bristol line at Reading.

From London to (26½ m.) *Maidenhead*, see Rte 28. We continue on A 4.— Beyond (28½ m.) *Maidenhead Thicket* is The Stubbings (r.), the home of Queen Wilhelmina of the Netherlands in 1941–45. We pass (34½ m.) between Wargrave (r.) and *Twyford* (l.), near which, at *Ruscombe*, William Penn died in 1718.

38½ m. **READING** (Hotels), the county town of Berkshire, is situated on the Kennet, but though close to the Thames is cut off from it by the railway. A centre of the medieval cloth trade, it is now an important industrial town (132,000 inhab.) and railway headquarters, with a university but little that merits a special diversion. Its biscuit manufacture is famous.

In the old centre of the town is the church of *St Laurence*, rebuilt but still imposing, with a good font in which was baptized Abp. Laud (1573–1645), a native of Reading. Adjoining is the *Museum & Art Gallery* (weekdays 10–5.30), notable for *Finds from Silchester (see below), a unique collection illustrating the everyday life of a country town in Roman Britain, and for finds of all ages from the river Thames, including a magnificent gold *Torc (mid-Bronze Age) from Moulsford. It also houses the notable collection of Baxter prints.

Of the famous Benedictine *Abbey* (reached viâ Forbury), founded by Henry I in 1121 and once ranking as third in all England, only scanty ruins are left. A tablet in the chapter house commemorates the fact that the canon 'Sumer is icumen in', the earliest known piece of music for several voices, was composed by one of the monks here about 1240. A memorial stone marks the grave of Henry I (d. 1135). The gatehouse was once occupied by the *Abbey School*, where Jane Austen was a pupil in 1786. In *Reading Gaol*, adjoining the ruins, Oscar Wilde wrote 'De Profundis' (1897); the 'Ballad of Reading Gaol' is later. A new *Shire Hall* is sited between Forbury Gardens and the Kennet. Some medieval portions have been preserved in the churches of *Greyfriars* and *St Mary* (N. door and s. arcade brought from the abbey), both a little farther w.

Watlington St., to the s.E., leads past the 18C *Watlington House* (garden front of 1688) to the *Royal Berkshire Hospital* with an Ionic façade of 1839. In *White-knights Park* (300 acres), 1½ m. s. on the Shinfield Rd., new buildings for the *University* (c. 2000 students), originally established in London Rd., have been erected including an Arts Building (1957), a Physics Laboratory (1960), and a Library (1964). The university received its charter in 1926 and has faculties of Letters, Science, and Agriculture, Horticulture, and Dairying (research farm at Shinfield). In the mansion is the *Museum of English Rural Life* (adm. 10–1, 2–4.30, exc. Sun, Mon, & BH) with an admirable collection of farm tools, carts, and other material illustrating country life.—Miss Mitford (see below) lived in London Rd. (tablet) in 1847. The ancient *Grammar School* (Reading School), of which Laud was a pupil, occupies 19C buildings in Erleigh Road.

At *Caversham*, the suburb on the N. bank, where William Marshal, the great earl of Pembroke, died in 1219, is Queen Anne's School for girls. A pleasant walk leads thence to Mapledurham (3 m.; p. 260).

Three Mile Cross, 3½ m. s. of Reading, is the scene of 'Our Village', by Miss Mitford, who is buried at *Swallowfield*, 2½ m. farther s.E.—From Three Mile Cross a road leads s.w. to (4¾ m.) *Mortimer Common* and (l.) to (8 m.) **Silchester,** identified with *Calleva Atrebatum*, a flourishing Roman (and pre-Roman) town, which seems to have contained several dyeworks. The site of the ancient town is enclosed by walls fully 1½ m. in circuit and at places still 12–14 ft high (s. side). Here, too, a building, almost certainly a 4C church, has been excavated. The little *Calleva Museum* (adm. free daily; contributions welcome), near the rectory, serves as an excellent introduction to the greater collection at Reading. The interesting *Parish Church* (1 m. E. by footpath; 2 m. by road) lies just inside the E. gate; and 150 yds from the N.E. corner of the enceinte are the earth-banks of a Roman *Amphitheatre.—Stratfield Saye House* (3½ m. E. of Silchester church, and 1½ m. s. of Swallowfield), presented by the nation to the first Duke of Wellington in 1815, contains relics of the Duke, pavements from Silchester, and portraits (adm. Easter–Sept, daily 11–5.30 exc Fri). 'Copenhagen', the Duke's favourite charger, is buried in an adjoining paddock. On the E. side of the park is the *Wellington Monument*, with a bronze statue by Marochetti (1866).

From Reading to *Wokingham* and *Ascot* (London), see Rte 11B.

We quit the Thames valley and ascend the tributary vale of the Kennet.—42½ m. *Theale* has a large church (1820–22) modelled on Salisbury Cathedral. About 3¼ m. N.W., beyond *Englefield*, the last home and burial-place of the fifth Marquess of Winchester (d. 1675), is *Bradfield College* (St Andrew's College; founded in 1850), a public school noted for the Greek plays performed by the boys every third year in an open-air 'Greek' theatre in an old chalk-pit.—47 m. *Aldermaston* station.

A by-road on the left leads to (1¼ m.) *Padworth*, with a small Norman church, ¾ m. E. of which is *Ufton Court*, an Elizabethan mansion, once the home of Arabella Fermor, the lovely heroine of 'The Rape of the Lock'.—*Aldermaston*, 1½ m. s.w. of its station, has a 14C wall-painting and a fine monument to Sir George Forster (d. 1526), in its church. The Atomic Weapons Research Establishment here was the scene of an annual political protest in the 1950s and 60s.

From (48½ m.) *Woolhampton* a road ascends N. to *Douai Abbey*, a Benedictine house (1903) with a boys' school transferred from Douai in France, and to (3 m.) *Bucklebury Common*, an open sandy heath. The Old Vicarage gardens contain sculptures by Moore and other contemporary artists.

56 m. **Newbury** (Hotels) is a thriving town (23,700 inhab.), once a centre of the cloth trade. The Jacobean *Cloth Hall* is now a museum (adm. 10–12.30, 1.30–4 or 5, exc. Wed aft.) containing Civil War relics; its curious galleried extension, known as the Granary, now serves as part of the bus-station. 'Jack of Newbury' (John Smallwood, afterwards Winchcombe; d. 1520) was a patriotic clothier, who led 150 men to Flodden in 1513, and his brass is to be seen in the church of *St Nicholas*, which he rebuilt. Benj. Woodridge, the first graduate of Harvard, was rector of Newbury. The disused Kennet and Avon canal has been restored for pleasure cruising for some miles W. of the town.

The N. end of Newbury, on the main road, called *Speenhamland*, has given its name to the 'Act' of the Berkshire magistrates who here, in 1795, first applied the allowance system of poor relief to supplement low wages.

During the Civil War two indecisive battles were fought near Newbury: the first in 1643, at which the "blameless and the brave" Lord Falkland was killed (monument 1 m. s.w. of the town); the second in 1644, near the 14C gatehouse of *Donnington Castle* (no adm. to interior), 1 m. N.W. Newbury racecourse is c. ½ m. S.E.

B 4000 leads N.W. from Newbury up the beautiful valley of the Lambourn.—
11 m. *Lambourn* is an old town with a late-Norman church with an alabaster relief of Charles I. It is the 'Maryland' of 'Jude the Obscure' and now has important training-stables, separated by the Lambourn Downs from the Vale of the White Horse.—15 m. *Ashdown House* (N.T.) is a tall late-17C building of unusual design (garden open 2–6 May–Sept, on Wed & 1st and 3rd Sat; April, Wed only; with access to house-roof; fee),

built by Lord Craven and dedicated to Elizabeth of Bohemia. Above the park is *Alfred's Castle*, an Iron Age fort. Near by Alfred fought the Danes in 871.—17½ *Ashbury* has a part-Norman and E.E. church.—At (20 m.) *Shrivenham* we join A 420 (p. 293).

A 343 runs s.w. to (15 m.) Andover, passing at 6 m. just E. of *Ashmansworth*, where the church has a tablet to Gerald Finzi (d. 1956) by Reynolds Stone, his next-door neighbour.—10 m. *Hurstbourne Tarrant* church has early 14C mural paintings. At *St Mary Bourne*, 3½ m. s.E., is a Tournai marble font.

FROM NEWBURY TO OXFORD, 25 m. (A 34).—Beyond (9 m.) *East Ilsley*, once an important downland sheep-market, we descend into the Vale of the White Horse, passing (l.) the Harwell Research Establishment (p. 292) and crossing A 417.— 15½ m. *Steventon* is an attractive village with pargeted houses.—19 m. *Abingdon* and thence to Oxford, see Rte 11A.

From Newbury to *Whitchurch* and *Winchester*, see p. 121.

57 m. *Speen* stands on the site of the Roman station of *Spinis*.—62 m. (l.) *Avington*, a quiet village on the Kennet, preserves its Norman church.—64 m. *Hungerford*, was John of Gaunt's fief town, to which he gave its fishing rights on the Kennet; it remains an angling resort. John's horn is preserved in the Town Hall, and to this day a red Lancastrian rose is presented to any sovereign passing through the town. A cheerful Hocktide Festival is celebrated here (2nd Tues after Easter) when the 'tutti-men' trade kisses for oranges.

Littlecote (adm. Easter–Sept, Sat, Sun, & BH, 2–6; fee), 3 m. N.W., is a mansion of c. 1500 with fine panelling and plasterwork ceilings and a 17C armoury. *Inkpen*, 3½ m. s., a pretty village, has a church used by the Templars, who are reputed to have imported the tulips and lilies that now grow wild in the area. Le Nôtre (1613– 1700) stayed at the rectory and designed its gardens. *Inkpen Beacon* (954 ft), and *Walbury Hill* (974 ft), the loftiest chalk down in England, both with fine views, lie to the s.

Ramsbury, 5 m. N.W. on the Kennet, once a market town, with an unusually large 13C church, shows little trace of its importance in the 10C, when it was the seat of the bishops of Wiltshire, except some remarkable monuments of the period. The by-road up the valley goes on to (11½ m.) Marlborough viâ (10 m.) *Mildenhall* (pron. 'Minall'), the Roman *Cunetio*, where the church, with Saxon and Norman details, is notable for its early-19C woodwork.

Beyond (67 m.) *Froxfield*, with the prominent Somerset Hospital (17–18C), we skirt the N. edge of *Savernake Forest*, a beautiful sylvan tract of oaks and beeches (16 m. round). The domain of the Marquess of Ailesbury, it is the only English forest not belonging to the Crown. Here charcoal burning had a fillip in the Second World War in the manufacture of gas-masks.

74½ m. **Marlborough** (Hotels) is an attractive town (6000 inhab.) with a broad old High Street, largely colonnaded and tile-hung on one side, and closed at either end by church towers. To the w. of the town, spanning the main road, is *Marlborough College*, one of the leading English public schools, founded in 1843, where William Morris was a pupil. In the grounds is Castle Mound, the traditional burial-place of Merlin. *Castle House* set the graceful architectural style of the well-grouped buildings. Built c. 1700–20 for the 6th Duke of Somerset (d. 1748), it was for a century a famous coaching-inn (comp. Stanley Weyman's 'The Castle Inn'); in this house the poet Thomson, while the guest of the Countess of Hertford, wrote part of his 'Spring' (1727). The White Horse to the s. was cut by schoolboys in 1804.

An attractive walk of 6 m. from Marlborough to Avebury (comp. below) leads viâ *Manton*, famous for its training-stables, and (3 m.) the great dolmen known as the *Devil's Den*, and thence over the downs, sprinkled with *Grey Wethers* or 'sarsen stones', curious boulders left isolated by the denudation of softer strata.

A 346 leads s. to Andover viâ (5½ m.) *Burbage*, where, at Wolf Hall, Jane Seymour (1509?–37) was born and celebrated her marriage feast with Henry VIII. —A 345, viâ (7 m.) *Pewsey*, leads to Amesbury past (9½ m.; r.) *Manningford Bruce* with an early-Norman church. Along the N. side of the downs between Marlborough and Pewsey runs the *Wansdyke*, probably a post-Roman border-entrenchment, extending, with many gaps, from beyond Savernake Forest to Dundry Hill, s. of Bristol. The *White Horse*, N.W. of Pewsey, was cut on the downs in 1785 (recut 1937).

At (80 m.) *West Kennett* B 4003 (r.) leads in 1 m. to Avebury (see below) and we approach one of the most remarkable groups of prehistoric antiquities in England.—80¾ m. *Silbury Hill* (130 ft high) is the largest artificial mound in Europe, the purpose of which is still uncertain. Constructed c. 2660 B.C., it would have taken 700 men ten years to build. To the s. of the road (footpath, ½ m.) is *West Kennett Long Barrow*, a chambered tomb of c. 3250 B.C., with c. 46 burials associated in timespan with the use of Windmill Hill; the finds of the 1955–56 excavations are in Devizes Museum.—81½ m. *Beckhampton* stands at the junction of the Bath road with the Swindon–Devizes road (Rte 27). Some 400 yds of Roman road are preserved alongside the Devizes road, to the s.w.

Just to the N. the village of *Avebury* (Hotel; bus from Swindon or Devizes) is situated in the centre of **Avebury Circle** (N.T., with 900 acres), a henge monument of 2450–2200 B.C. "as much surpassing Stonehenge", says Aubrey, "as a cathedral doth a parish church".

Visitors should first turn down the village Street to the *Church*, which preserves a reworked Saxon nave, a Saxo-Norman tub font, a rood-loft of 1460, and a squint. At the gates of the late-16C *Manor House* (adm. May–Aug daily exc. Tues 2–6; April & Sept, Sat, Sun; BH, 10–6; fee), with good panelling and plasterwork, a *Museum* of finds from Avebury and Windmill Hill (adm. daily, closed Sun in winter till 2; fee) provides a superbly illuminating introduction to the monuments. The remains at Avebury consist mainly of a massive circular earthwork, ¾ m. round and about 15 ft high, with a fosse (originally 30 ft deep) on its *inner* side, thus suggesting a religious rather than a defensive object for the entrenchment. Fringing the inner edge of the fosse stands, in part, a gigantic circle of unhewn megaliths and in the centre of the enclosed area were two smaller concentric circles. The largest stones weigh about 60 tons. From the circle an avenue of stones (many re-erected) led s.E., beyond West Kennett, to a group of small stone and timber circles, called the Sanctuary, long since vanished, and now marked out on the ground.—To the N.W. (1½ m. viâ Avebury Trusloe) is *Windmill Hill* (N.T.), with a Neolithic causewayed enclosure built c. 3250 B.C. and used until c. 2000.

The Bath Road ascends over the downs; on the left are seen the Lansdowne Column (c. 1843) and a White Horse, cut in the turf in 1780.— 87½ m. *Calne* (9700 inhab.; Hotel), noted for Wiltshire bacon since the first factory was set up here c. 1770, has a 12C church, much altered. Dr Pristley lived here in 1770–80, Coleridge in 1814–16.—93 m. **Chippenham** (Hotels) is a busy country town (18,700 inhab.) on the Avon. John Wood the Younger built the church of Hardenhuish ('Harnish'), 1 m. N.W., in 1779.

About 3½ m. s.E. (2 m. s.w. of Calne) is *Bowood Park* (no adm.), with a s. range by Robert Adam. One of the earliest experiments in steam central heating was carried out in the library in 1790. The magnificent park has fine rhododendrons (walk open in season) and a mausoleum (1765) by Adam. At Sloperton Cottage, near *Bromham*, 3 m. s. of Bowood, the poet Thomas Moore (1779–1852) passed most of the last 35 years of his life; a Celtic cross marks his grave in the churchyard. At Battle House, in the village, his friend Sir William Napier wrote the first 3 vols of his 'History of the Peninsular War' from 1826.—About 2½ m. N.W. at *Kington St Michael*, John Aubrey was born in 1626.

Farther w. (6 m.) lies *Castle Combe* (Hotels), a pretty village with a 13C market cross and the ruins of a Saxon castle. In the church is the fine tomb of Walter de Dunstanville (d. 1270).

FROM CHIPPENHAM TO SHAFTESBURY, 33 m. (A 350).—3½ m. *Lacock* (Hotel) is a very attractive village (N.T.) with a fine late-Perp. chapel in its church. On the Avon is *Lacock Abbey* (N.T.; adm. to house and cloisters April–Oct daily exc. Mon & Tues 2–6; fee), founded for Augustinian canonesses in 1229–32, and presenting one of the most perfect remaining examples of conventual arrangements, with fine 13–14C cloisters. The private residence built round it in 1540 (altered 1753 and 1828) was the scene of William Fox Talbot's early experiments in photography (c. 1835).

7 m. *Melksham* is an agricultural town (9800 inhab.), with a restored church, originally Norman.—11 m. By-road (l.) for *Steeple Ashton* (1½ m.), once an important wool-market, which preserves its lock-up and charter cross. The church has a fine late-Perp. *Nave (1480) with curious corbels, and fine vaulting, and a good wool-merchant's house (restored) remains in the street.—16 m. Westbury, an old town (6500 inhab.), with a handsome Perp. church, is an important railway junction. The White Horse of Westbury (see p. 245) is seen on the downs to the E.—20 m. *Warminster*, see p. 154.—27½ m. *East Knoyle* was the birthplace of Sir Christopher Wren (1632–1723).—33 m. *Shaftesbury*, see Rte 15A.

From Chippenham to *Faringdon*, see Rte 30B.—An alternative route direct to (22 m.) Bristol (A 420) runs w. over the Cotswolds, viâ (9 m.) the high-lying town of *Marshfield* (633 ft), 3 m. S.E. of Dyrham Park (p. 194).

At (97 m.) *Corsham* (Hotel) are some fine houses, a large church, and *Corsham Court*, the seat of Lord Methuen, in part of which is accommodated the Bath Academy of Art.

The Elizabethan mansion (1582), altered in 1760–75 by 'Capability' Brown for Paul Methuen, is open April–Oct, Wed, Thurs & Sun; July–Sept daily exc. Mon & Fri; Sun & BH, throughout the year; 11–12.30, 2–6 (4.30 in Oct); fee. It contains notable paintings: *Van Dyck*, The Betrayal; *Filippo Lippi*, Annunciation; *Andrea del Sarto*, St John the Baptist; *Correggio*, the Pandolfini cartoon; portraits by *Gainsborough*, *Reynolds*, and *Romney*; and many other fine works.

Neston Park, 1¾ m. S.W., was the scene of Speke's fatal accident in 1864 (comp. p. 169).

A long hill leads down past (r.) the entrance to *Box Tunnel*, the longest railway tunnel in the world when it was built in 1837 by Brunel, to (100 m.) *Box*. The subterranean quarries of 'Bath stone' were used in 1939–45 both as an aircraft factory and to house treasures from the national museums. *Colerne*, 2 m. N., has a broken 9C cross-shaft in its 13–14C church.

106 m. **Bath**, see Rte 18. We cross the Avon.—At (113 m.) *Keynsham* is *Somerdale*, with Messrs. J. S. Fry & Sons' cocoa and chocolate factory.—An alternative road on the N. bank of the Avon passes (112½ m.) *Bitton*, with a notable church, while the church at *Oldland Common*, just to the N.W., has an Ecce Homo, by Murillo.

118 m. **BRISTOL** (425,200 inhab.), a famous old city and seaport, an important manufacturing town, and the see of a bishop, is situated on the Avon, about 7 m. from the Bristol Channel. The city formed a county in itself from 1373 to 1974; previously the N. bank of the Avon was in Gloucester, the S. in Somerset, now both are in the county of Avon. Long famous for 'Bristol Milk' (in which connection Thomas Fuller observed that "as many Elephants are fed as Cows grazed within the walls of this city"), it has imported wine from Bordeaux since the 12C and from Spain since the 15C. In the 17C and 18C Bristol was especially noted for its trade with the Americas (comp. Thackeray's 'Virginians') and still carries on important Atlantic trade, importing grain, provisions, timber, tobacco

leaf, etc., although larger vessels now dock at Avonmouth and the goods are transported to Bristol warehouses by road and canal. The city's early association with powered flight (Bristol Boxkite, 1910) has continued with the manufacture of aero engines, and in 1969 the Anglo-French Concorde. Despite war damage and strenuous redevelopment, the city preserves a number of 17C houses, some gracious 18C and early-19C terraces and splendid examples of Victorian industrial architecture.

Railway Stations. *Temple Meads* (Pl. 15) the principal station. Local stations (Clifton Down, etc.) on the Avonmouth line.— *Parkway* on the London–South Wales line is near *Mangotsfield*, 5 m. N.E. with access to M 4 and M 5 motorways.

Airport at *Lulsgate*, on A 38 (the Bridgwater road), 8 m. S.W.

Hotels and Restaurants in Bristol and Clifton.

Post Office (Pl. 7), Small St.

Buses traverse the city and suburbs and run also from the *Bus and Coach Station* (Pl. 3) to *Avonmouth*; *Bath*; *Gloucester*; *Cheltenham*; *Malmesbury* and *Cirencester*; *Bridgwater*, *Cheddar*, *Wells*, and *Glastonbury*; *Chippenham*; also to the airport.

Steamers in summer daily at 3 from the Neptune Statue (Pl. 10) to *Hanham* and *Keynsham*.

Theatres. ARTS CENTRE (Pl. 11): *Royal* Theatre, *New Vic*, and *Cooper's Hall* (to be completed, 1972).—CONCERTS, and *Little* Theatre in Colston Hall (Pl. 6).

History. Of probably late-Saxon foundation, Bristol was the centre of the pre-Conquest trade in English slaves, as it was to become, in the 18C, the chief centre of the African slave-trade. At the time of the Domesday Survey it already ranked next after London, York, and Winchester. In the 12C the town is described by William of Malmesbury as full of ships from every part of Europe, which ascended the tidal Avon to the very doors of the merchants. The castle, at the junction of the Avon and Frome, was rebuilt in 1126 by Robert, Earl of Gloucester, and here King Stephen was held prisoner for nine months in 1141. The summary execution of Richard II's followers before the castle was to give Bristol its only scene in Shakespeare. The growing trade in cloth and wine favoured maritime daring and led to the founding of the Merchant Venturers' society. On 24 June 1497, John Cabot and his son Sebastian, who had sailed from Bristol in the 'Matthew', discovered the mainland of America, and in the following year Sebastian Cabot explored the American coast from Newfoundland to Florida. During the Civil War, Bristol was captured by Prince Rupert in 1643 and became the chief Royalist stronghold in the West; but in 1645 it was stormed by the Parliamentarians under Fairfax and in 1655 its castle was 'slighted' by order of Cromwell. During the Reform riots of 1831 two sides of Queen Sq., with the Mansion House, custom house, bishop's palace, and gaol, were burned. In 1838 the 'Great Western', Isambard Kingdom Brunel's first steam ship and pioneer of the transatlantic steam traffic, was launched at Bristol. In 1940–41 Bristol was heavily attacked from the air with great loss of life and property, and work of rebuilding still continues.— Defoe is believed to have met Alexander Selkirk (or to have heard his story) at Bristol. Sir Thomas Lawrence, P.R.A. (1769–1830), was the son of an innkeeper in Redcross St. (Pl. 8). 'Perdita' Robinson (1758–1800) was born in a house adjoining the cathedral, Robert Southey (1774–1843), the son of a mercer, was born in Wine St. Samuel Plimsoll (1824–98), 'the sailors' friend', was born at No. 9 Colston Parade (Pl. 15); John Addington Symonds (1840–93) at 7 Berkeley Sq. (Pl. 5). W. G. Grace (1848–1915) was born at Downend, near Mangotsfield, 3 m. N.E., and lived at 15 Victoria Square. College St. (Pl. 10), now demolished, was the birthplace of W. Friese-Greene (1855–1921), pioneer of the cinema, and here Coleridge and Southey lived in 1794–95. Elizabeth Blackwell (1821–1910), the first woman on the British medical register, was born in Countership (Pl. 10).

The focus of movement in present-day Bristol is the **Centre** (Pl. 6), an ornamental open space, known to the natives as 'The Silly Isles', formed in 1893 by covering over part of an arm of the Floating Harbour (see below). The statues are of Edmund Burke (replica in Washington), M.P. for Bristol in 1774–80, and Edward Colston, and at the s. end, dockyard cranes rise behind a figure of Neptune. Baldwin St. leads E. to Bristol Bridge, but we turn s. and traverse a Georgian quarter, partly rebuilt, bounded on three sides by the Floating Harbour. In King St., are the *Merchants' Almshouses* (1699), well restored since the bombing that destroyed the adjoining Hall. The Merchant Venturers' society is traceable back to the reign of Henry II. Also in this street are an employment centre occupying the old *Free Library*, founded in 1613 but removed to the Central Library in 1906; the **Theatre Royal* (Pl. 10), modelled on Wren's Drury Lane theatre in London, opened in 1766, the home of the Bristol Old Vic since 1946; *Coopers' Hall*, with a classical front (1744) by Halfpenny; the *St Nicholas Almshouse* (1656; rebuilt 1961); the splendid *Llandoger Trow* inn, and other fine 17C houses. The *Old Granary* in Little King St. (now a night-club) is an entertaining piece of Victorian architecture. The new Redcliffe Way runs diagonally across Queen Sq. (Pl. 10), scene of the riots of 1831, past an equestrian statue of William III by Rysbrack. At No. 16 David Hume was a merchant's clerk in 1734; at No. 37 was the first American Consulate in Europe (1792).

By a bridge across the Floating Harbour we approach **St Mary Redcliffe* (Pl. 15), described by Queen Elizabeth I as "the fairest, the goodliest, and most famous parish church in England". The present magnificent and harmonious Perp. structure replaces an earlier church of the 12C, and was built mainly between 1325 and 1375, the s. side being older than the N.; but the tower is of the mid-13C in its lower stories, early-14C above. The church owes much to the munificence of Wm. Canynge the elder (d. 1396) and his grandson Wm. Canynge the younger (1399?–1474), two famous mayors of Bristol. The whole was extensively restored in 1930–33. The chief features of the exterior are the massive tower, with its rich decoration of pinnacles and ball-flower ornamentation, and a spire 285 ft high (upper portion recent); and the hexagonal **North Porch* (late 13C), most unusual in ground-plan and execution, with an elaborately carved door and an inner porch of 1180. The South Porch dates from c. 1325.

The INTERIOR, 240 ft in length and 117 ft wide across the transepts, with elaborate vaulting, large windows, and stellate tomb-recesses, produces a general impression of lightness and loftiness, richness of decoration, and harmony of proportions. There is no triforium, and the want of a horizontal string-course is noticeable. The aisled transepts are a feature unusual in parish churches and rare even in cathedrals. The chapel under the tower (N.W.; American Chapel) has some old stained glass, a fine grille (1710) by William Edney, and the so-called rib of the dun cow slain by Guy of Warwick (really a whale-bone, said to have been presented to the church by Cabot in 1497). Here too is a wooden figure of Elizabeth I (c. 1574). In the s. transept are the monuments of Canynge the younger and his wife, and another Canynge, as Dean of Westbury College (see p. 185). The tomb-slab of Adm. Sir Wm. Penn (d. 1670), captor of Jamaica and father of the founder of Pennsylvania, is at the entrance to this transept; his classical monument, with his armour, is high up at the w. end of the nave. The canopied monuments of the Medes (c. 1475), and an interesting brass of their son, are in the N. choir aisle. The Lady Chapel has two bays, one 25 years older than the other (1375–1400) and stained glass (1959–65) by H. J. Stammers.

There are good brasses (kept covered) to Sir John Inyn (d. 1439), in the Lady

Chapel, and, in front of the high altar, to John Brooke (d. 1512) and his wife Johanna, daughter of Mayor Richard Ameryk, patron of John Cabot and a claimant to be the 'godfather' of America.

Above the N. porch (the interior of which deserves careful examination) is a muniment room where the boy-poet Thomas Chatterton (1752–70) pretended to have discovered the Rowley MS. in an old chest. Chatterton, who was the nephew of the sexton of St Mary's, was born near by, and educated at Colston's School (in the dress of which he is represented on the poor monument in the churchyard; family gravestone on the s. side of the church). His birthplace in Redcliffe Way is open on application. Southey and Coleridge were married in this church to Edith and Sara Fricker in 1795.

To the E. of St Mary Redcliffe are *Temple Meads Station* (Pl. 16) and the ruined *Temple Church* (Pl. 12), a large Perp. building with a tower 5 ft out of the perpendicular, on the site of a church of the Knights Templar. Close by are the Shakespeare Inn (1636) and the church of *St Thomas* (Pl. 11), of 1792–95 by J. Allen, with an earlier reredos (1716) and *Organ-loft (1730). On the other side of Redcliffe Hill is the *Shot Tower* where in the 18C William Watts first made spherical shot by dropping molten lead from a height into water.

To the w., in Wapping Dry Dock (Pl. 9; well signposted) where she was built, lies Brunel's **'*Great Britain*', the first ocean-going iron ship with screw propulsion (adm. daily 10–8; fee; rfmts). She made her maiden voyage to New York in 1845. Towed home, a hulk, in 1970 from the Falkland Is, where she was wrecked in 1886, she is slowly being restored; on the dock is a museum of relics of her history.

Redcliffe St. leads N. from St Mary Redcliffe to ($\frac{1}{2}$ m.) *Bristol Bridge* (Pl. 7), built in 1768 to replace an original structure of 1247. It spans the *Floating Harbour* formed in 1803–9 by furnishing a section of the Avon 2 m. long with a lock at either end and diverting the tidal river to a new channel. On the left, in Baldwin St., is *St Nicholas* (Pl. 7), a 'Gothick' church of 1762, with a 14C crypt (now a medieval local museum). To the N. of the bridge lies the old central part of the city.

The 'Cross', the junction of the four streets here (High St., Wine St., Broad St., and Corn St.), was marked until 1733 by the High Cross (c. 1373; now at Stourhead). On the E. (r.), at the corner of Wine St., is *Christ Church*, rebuilt by Paty in 1786–90, with two Quarter Jacks (1728; exterior) from the old church, a striking rood-screen, and a 17C font from St Ewen's (now replaced by the Old Council House), in which Southey was baptized.

On the left, at the corner of Corn St., stood the bookshop of Joseph Cottle, the friend and publisher of Coleridge, Wordsworth, and Southey, while at the opposite corner is the *Old Council House* (Pl. 7), by Smirke (1827), containing portraits (Earl of Pembroke, by Van Dyck; James II, by Kneller) in the *Old Council Chamber, shown on request. In *All Saints* (Pl. 7), a good 15C church with two Norman bays, is the monument, by Gibbs and Rysbrack, of Edward Colston (1636–1721), the most princely benefactor of a city noted for its public spirit. The Exchange (Pl. 7; 1743), by the elder Wood, is now a corn-market, in front of which are the 'Nails', four bronze tables from the old Tolsey, formerly used by the merchants for their cash transactions (whence, perhaps, 'to pay on the nail'). Corn St. is continued by Clare St., to the right of which, just before the Centre, rises the elaborate tower (133 ft) of *St Stephen's* (Pl. 7), a church of 1450–90. Within are some good late-medieval tomb recesses and two quaintly-carved monuments of 1617 and 1627. The iron gates and *Sword Rest, by Edney, are from St Nicholas.

Beyond the Cross, High St. is continued by Broad St., on the left of which is the *Guildhall* (Pl. 7; 1843), now used as law courts. The Bank of England (1845) is by Cockerell. Farther down (r.) the façade of a 19C printing house is decorated with brightly coloured tiles. Spanning the end of the street is *St John's Gate*, with statues of Brennus and Belinus, mythical founders of Bristol, surmounted by the spire of St John's (Pl. 7), a 14C church on two levels (key at 23 Broad St.).

Wine St., greatly rebuilt, leads N.E. from the Cross. On the right a new block masks the tower of St Mary-le-Port beyond which is the ruined church of St Peter. The area between is designated for a new museum building.

Union St. leads N. to *St James's* (Pl. 3), the nave of a late-Norman priory church built in 1130 by Robert, earl of Gloucester (d. 1157), whose tomb is here preserved. In the w. front is a rose window of unique design.

Newgate, straight on, keeps the name of the former prison in which Richard Savage, the poet, died in 1743. To the right is the site of the *Castle*. Off Merchant St. farther on is (r.) *Quakers' Friars* (Pl. 4, 8), a quiet square with the relics of a 13C Dominican friary. Rebuilt to serve as the *Cutlers' Hall* and *Bakers' Hall*, the upper floor is devoted to a Planning Exhibition (free weekdays 1–4.30). Adjoining on the E., the *Register Office* occupies the old Friends' Meeting House (1747), on a site occupied by the Quakers in 1670–1956. Here Penn married his second wife in 1696. To the w. lies a quarter of popular modern shops, suburban in character apart from the *Merchant Taylors' Almshouses* (1701; now a bank) in Merchant St., and, in Broad Mead, the early-19C *Greyhound Hotel*. Nearly opposite the last is the entrance to the oldest Methodist chapel in England, the '*New Room*' built by John Wesley in 1739, and well restored in 1930. His statue, by A. G. Walker (1933), stands in the courtyard, and his rooms are shown from 10 to 4 (closed Sun & Wed).

Nelson St. leads back from Broad Mead to the Centre. On the right Christmas St., with the 13C porch of the vanished *St Bartholomew's Hospital* (r.), leads to *Christmas Steps*, a quaint byway climbing up to Colston St. At the top are some stone seats (l.), an old inscription, and *Foster's Almshouses* (rebuilt 1861–84), with a 16C chapel dedicated to the Three Kings of Cologne. Higher up is *St Michael's* (Pl. 6), of 1774, with a 15C tower; and above that again are the more attractive *Colston's Almshouses*, founded in 1691.

St Augustine's Parade leads s. from the Centre to COLLEGE GREEN (Pl. 10), the former burial-ground of the abbey.

The *Cathedral (Pl. 10), originally the church of an abbey founded in 1148 for Augustinian canons by Robert Fitzhardinge, provost of Bristol, was built on the traditional site of Augustine's Oak, where St Augustine conferred with the British Christians.

HISTORY. Of the Norman buildings the chief relics are the chapter house and the two precinct gateways. The choir was rebuilt in 1298–1363, mainly by Abbot Knowle (1306–32), who connected with his choir the previously detached Elder Lady Chapel (c. 1215), erected by Abbot David. The transepts were mainly rebuilt after 1463, on the model of the older work. The Norman nave, half rebuilt at the Dissolution, was allowed to fall into ruin, and the church remained naveless until 1868–88, when the present nave, with its two w. towers, was built by G. E. Street, on the lines of Knowle's choir, with slight modifications. The central tower dates from c. 1450. After the Dissolution the abbey church became the cathedral of the new see of Bristol, created in 1542. From 1836 to 1897 this see was united with that of Gloucester.

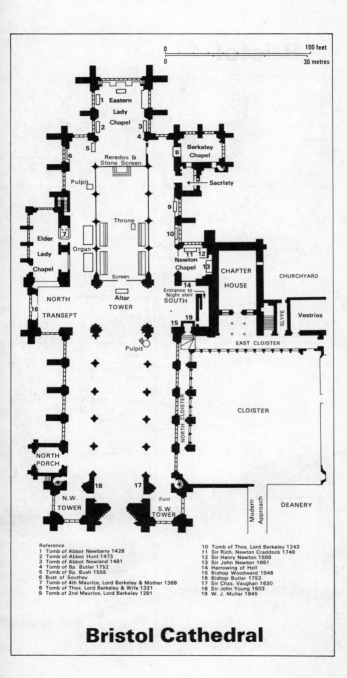

0   100 feet

0   30 metres

Eastern
Lady
Chapel

Berkeley
Chapel

Reredos &
Stone Screen

Sacristy

Pulpit

Throne

CHAPTER
HOUSE

CHURCHYARD

Elder
Lady
Chapel

Organ

Newton
Chapel

Screen

SLYPE

Vestries

NORTH
TRANSEPT

Altar
TOWER

Entrance to
Night stair
SOUTH

EAST CLOISTER

Pulpit

NORTH CLOISTER

CLOISTER

NORTH
PORCH

N.W.
TOWER

Font
S.W.
TOWER

Modern Approach

DEANERY

Reference
1 Tomb of Abbot Newberry 1428
2 Tomb of Abbot Hunt 1473
3 Tomb of Abbot Newland 1481
4 Tomb of Bp. Butler 1752
5 Tomb of Bp. Bush 1558
6 Bust of Southey
7 Tomb of 4th Maurice, Lord Berkeley & Mother 1368
8 Tomb of Thos. Lord Berkeley & Wife 1321
9 Tomb of 2nd Maurice, Lord Berkeley 1281

10 Tomb of Thos. Lord Berkeley 1243
11 Sir Rich. Newton Craddock 1748
12 Sir Henry Newton 1599
13 Sir John Newton 1661
14 Harrowing of Hell
15 Bishop Woodward 1946
16 Bishop Butler 1752
17 Sir Chas. Vaughan 1630
18 Sir John Young 1603
19 W. J. Muller 1845

Bristol Cathedral

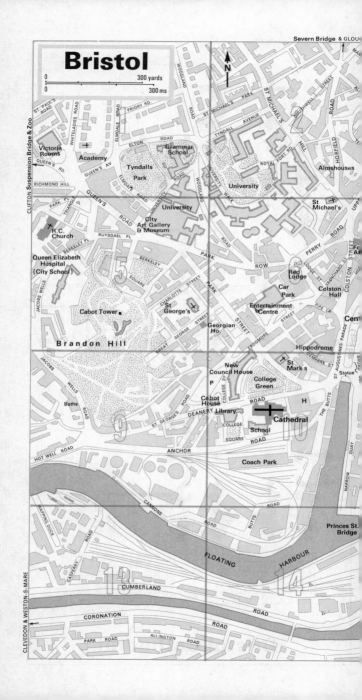

Bristol

0 — 300 yards
0 — 300 ms

N

Severn Bridge & GLOU

CLIFTON Suspension Bridge & Zoo

ST. PAUL'S ROAD
WHITELADIES ROAD
PRIORY RD
ELMDALE ROAD
WOODLAND ROAD
ST. MICHAEL'S PARK
ST. MICHAEL'S HILL
SOUTHWELL STREET
HORFIELD ROAD
AL

Victoria Rooms
QUEEN'S RD
RICHMOND HILL

ELTON ROAD
Academy
QUEEN'S AV

Grammar School
TYNDALL AVENUE

Tyndalls Park
ELMDALE ROAD

ROYAL FORT RD
University

Almshouses

PARK PL
TRIANGLE
QUEEN'S ROAD
UNIVERSITY ROAD
WOODLAND ROAD
UNIVERSITY WALK

University
City Art Gallery & Museum

St Michael's

UPP

R.C. Church
BERKELEY PL
RUYSDAEL PL

PARK ROAD

ROW
PERRY ROAD
LODGE ST
ST. RICHMOND ST
COLSTON STREET

Fo
Al

Queen Elizabeth Hospital (City School)
JACOBS WELLS
BERKELEY SQUARE
CHARLOTTE STREET

PARK STREET

Red Lodge

Car Park

Colston Hall

PIPE LA
HIGH

Cabot Tower
St George's
GREAT GEORGE STREET

Georgian Ho.
FROGMORE STREET

Entertainment Centre

ST AUGUSTINES PARADE
PARADE

Cen

Brandon Hill

Hippodrome

JACOBS WELLS ROAD

New Council House
COLLEGE STREET
COLLEGE GREEN

St Mark's
DENMARK ST

Statue

P

Baths

ST GEORGE'S ROAD
DEANERY ROAD
Cabot House
Library
COLLEGE ROAD
COLLEGE SQUARE
COLLEGE GREEN ROAD

School
ROAD

Cathedral

H

THE BUTTS

QUAY

HOT WELL ROAD

ANCHOR ROAD

Coach Park

NARROW

WAPPING DOCK
GASFERRY ROAD
CANNONS ROAD
BUTTS ROAD
ROAD

Princes St. Bridge

CLEVEDON & WESTON-S-MARE

FLOATING HARBOUR

CUMBERLAND ROAD

CORONATION ROAD
PARK ROAD
ALLINGTON ROAD
ROAD

Interior. The chief feature of the interior is the absence of triforium and clerestory, the aisles, nave, and choir being of equal height, with pier arches rising to the full height of the building. In the aisles of the NAVE Street has copied the extraordinary vaulting of the choir; at the w. end is the tomb of Sir John Young (d. 1603) and his wife Joan, with the arms of Wadham College. The N. TRANSEPT, with rich lierne vaulting probably due to Abbot Newland or Nailheart (1481–1515), contains a beautiful window and a monument to Bp. Butler (d. 1752), with an inscription by Southey. The *ELDER LADY CHAPEL is pure E.E. in style, with Dec. vaulting and E. window and a beautiful arcade with grotesque carvings. On the s. side is the tomb of the 9th Lord Berkeley (d. 1368) and his mother.

The *CHOIR, in an early Dec. style unparalleled elsewhere, has lierne vaulting, the earliest in England, and foliage capitals of great beauty. The canopied stalls (given by Abbot Elyot, 1515–26) have been restored; the misericords and pew-ends are interesting. The organ-case and front pipes date from 1685, being part of Renatus Harris's organ, the best stops of which still survive. The reredos (1899) is by Pearson. The choir-aisles are noteworthy for two almost unique features: the skeleton vaulting, which recalls timber rather than stone construction; and the stellate tomb-recesses, paralleled only at St Mary Redcliffe and St David's Cathedral. The E. windows of the choir-aisles, of enamelled glass, were presented by Dean Glemham (1661–67). In the N. choir-aisle, the earlier of the two, are a tablet to Hakluyt, prebendary at Bristol in 1586–1616, a 13C coffin cover with Lombardic inscription, the tomb of Bp. Bush (d. 1558), with a 'cadaver', and a bust of Southey by Baily. The EASTERN LADY CHAPEL behind the chancel has a beautiful Dec. *East Window, with some original glass of c. 1340 (notable heraldry) and other glass of the same date in the s.w. window. The reredos is partly Knowle's but with cresting added by Abbot Burton (1526–39). The chapel contains beautiful sedilia (restored), and tombs of Abbots Newbury (1428–73), builder of the tower, Hunt (1473–81), and Newland (1481–1515), coloured according to the original scheme. A tablet marks the grave of Bp. Butler. In the s. choir-aisle, with Berkeley monuments in the tomb-recesses, is the beautiful Dec. entrance to the monastic *Sacristy*, with detached vaulting and fine bosses, a recess for banner-staves, and a hearth for the baking of the sacramental bread. Off it opens *Berkeley Chapel*, which contains a gilt brass *Chandelier (1450) from the Temple Church. Note the decoration of ammonites (?) and medlars on the entrance-arch. The *Newton Chapel*, entered from the w. end of the s. choir-aisle, late Dec. in style, contains 17–18C tombs of the Newton family.

The S. TRANSEPT, with a groined roof by Abbot Hunt (1473–81), contains a sculptured coffin-lid (c. 1000), of the Hereford school, found under the chapter house and representing the 'Harrowing of Hell'. In the Norman s. wall is the entrance to the night stair which descended from the dorter.

A door in the w. wall of the s. transept leads to the scanty remains (restored), of the CLOISTERS (c. 1480). Off the E. Walk (with fragments of old glass, documents etc.) opens the *CHAPTER HOUSE, a relic of Fitzhardinge's building, late Norman in style. Entered through a vaulted vestibule, it is rectangular, like other early chapter houses, and is enriched with zigzag and cable mouldings and interlaced arches. The E. wall was rebuilt after the 1831 riots. The series of vestries, etc. erected in 1923 as a memorial to H. O. Wills, founder of Bristol University, occupy the site of the ancient Dorter. The doorways of the slype and the day stair are preserved. At the end is the 14C doorway of the former bishop's palace (no adm.).

To the W. of the cathedral, leading from College Green to College Sq., is the late Norman *Abbey Gateway*, with receding orders enriched by zigzag mouldings. The upper part of the gate is Perp., by Abbot Elyot. In Cloister Court, to the left within the gate, a 13C gateway was the entrance to the Refectory, now part of the Cathedral School (refounded 1542); and lower down, in College Sq. is another Norman gateway which led to the abbot's lodgings. Adjoining the gateway, the *Central Library* (by Holden; 1906) contains a chimneypiece (first floor) by Grinling Gibbons, from the old library in King St.

On the W. side of the green is the *New Council House* (1935–55), by Vincent Harris. The statue, by Wheeler, of an Elizabethan seaman, commemorates John Cabot. On the N.E. side ***St Mark's** or the *Lord Mayor's Chapel* (Pl. 10; open daily, exc. Fri 10–4), a gem of Gothic architecture, was founded c. 1230 by Maurice de Gaunt, grandson of Fitzhardinge.

Originally the chapel of a hospital for the support of a chaplain and the relief of 100 poor daily, it was taken over in 1541 by the Corporation. The hospital buildings were used as a school: for *Queen Elizabeth's Hospital* (see below) until 1732, then for *Bristol Grammar School* (p. 184) up to 1877. On the hospital estate was also the *Red Maids' School* (founded 1621; now at Westbury-on-Trym), so named from the 'Bristol red' uniform of the girls. From 1687 the chapel was used by a Huguenot congregation until 1722, when it became the official chapel of the Corporation.

The nave and transept arches belong to the original 13C chapel (16C roof), but the N. transept dates from a 19C rebuilding. The aisle, with wagon-shaped roof, was added c. 1260; the chancel, chapels and tower in the late 15C. The French and Flemish stained glass (16–17C) mostly came from Fonthill and Ecouen. The fine monuments include those of the founder; his nephew Robert de Gournay (d. 1269); his brother Henry, first Master of the hospital; and Sir Maurice Berkeley (d. 1464). The reredos and *Sedilia* were restored c. 1500; the sword-rest (1702) was made by Edney for the Temple Church. Painted stones in the aisle are probably relics of a former chantry. The **Poyntz Chapel* (S.E.) is a notable late-Perp. chantry (c. 1520), with early glass and 16C Spanish tiles.

From College Green PARK STREET (Pl. 6) ascends towards Clifton. At No. 43 Hannah More and her sisters kept a boarding-school (1767–74) where 'Perdita' Robinson was a pupil. At No. 7 Great George St. (l.) is *Georgian House* (open weekdays 11–5), a dignified merchant's house of 1789, with appropriate furnishings. The classical *St George's* (Pl. 5; closed), opposite, is by Smirke (1823). *Brandon Hill* (260 ft), beyond, is crowned with the *Cabot Tower* (Pl. 5; 105 ft high), erected in 1897–98, the quatercentenary of John Cabot's expedition. On the N.W. slope of the hill is *Queen Elizabeth's Hospital* (Pl. 5), a blue-coat school founded in 1590.

The *Red Lodge* (Pl. 6; open weekdays 1–5), in Park Row, E. of Park St., was built in 1578–90 and contains fine carved woodwork and stone-carving of the 16C and 18C, as well as an interesting museum with contemporary furnishings.

In QUEEN'S ROAD, at the top of Park St., is a group of imposing, though ill-assorted buildings. The **City Art Gallery** (Pl. 5; open weekdays 10–5.30) houses also the **City Museum** which formerly occupied the Venetian Gothic building adjoining, now the University refectory.

The Museum includes historical relics of all periods, with emphasis on the West of England, and a good transport section (full-size replica of the 1910 Bristol Boxkite biplane). The Gallery contains the great *Altarpiece by *Hogarth* from St Mary Redcliffe, and the *Withypool Triptych, by *Andrea Solario* (signed and dated 1514), as well as works by *Constable, Gainsborough, Reynolds, Ibbetson, Lawrence* and *Wilson*; and paintings of great topographical interest, by local artists, including *W. J. Müller* (1812–45) and *Francis Danby* (1793–1861). The representative collection of European paintings (subject to alteration) includes: *Lucas Cranach,* Luther; *B. van Orley,* Portrait; *Giov. Bellini,* Christ's Descent into Hell; *Carpaccio,* Portrait; *A. Brouwer,* Tavern Scene; *Jan Steen,* Sleeping Toper; *Pittoni,* Winter; works by *Taddeo Gaddi, M. le Nain, Hubert Robert,* and *Corneille de Lyon.* Later artists include *Courbet, Forain,* and the Impressionists. There are also a contemporary collection of painting and sculpture; Bristol glass and delft ware; the Schiller Collection of *Chinese ceramics and glass, and *Chinese ivories.

On the right rises the commanding Gothic tower (1925), by Oatley, of **Bristol University** (Pl. 1, 5), incorporated in 1909, which owes its existence chiefly to the generosity of the Wills family. It comprises faculties of Arts, Theology, Science (Fruit Research Institutes at Long Ashton and Campden; Royal Agricultural College, Cirencester), Medicine, Veterinary Science, and Engineering.

In Tyndall's Park, behind, are the *Grammar School* (Pl. 1), founded by Robert and Nicholas Thorne in 1532, transferred hither in 1879, and many new buildings of the university, which has extended E. beyond Woodland Rd. In this road is the *Baptist College* (Pl. 1), originally established in 1720 in Stokes Croft. It possesses a miniature of Cromwell and a unique copy of Tyndale's New Testament (1526). In Cotham Rd., a little to the N.E., is the *Western Congregational College,* founded by the Independents in 1752 and transferred from Plymouth in 1901.

Farther on in Queen's Rd., opposite the Garden Centre and the *Victoria Rooms* (Pl. 1; 1840), a well-proportioned classical building, by Dyer, now the University Club Rooms, is the *Royal West of England Academy.*

We are now in **Clifton,** the high-lying residential quarter at the w. end of Bristol with a few 18C mansions and many gracious early-19C villas and terraces. From the Victoria Rooms, bus No. 18 ascends to (½ m.) Clifton Down viâ Queen's Rd. and Clifton Down Rd. *Clifton Down* and *Durdham Down,* farther N., together form a limestone plateau c. 500 acres in area and 250–300 ft above the level of the city. On the w. they are bounded by the impressive gorge of the Avon, which is here crossed by the lofty and graceful *Clifton Suspension Bridge* (toll), begun by Brunel in 1831 but not completed till 1864. The chains once formed part of the old Hungerford Bridge in London. It is 1352 ft in total length (702 ft between the piers), 31 ft wide, and 245 ft above high tide. The bridge commands a splendid *View of the gorge, marred at low water by the muddy bed of the river. On the opposite side are the beautiful *Nightingale Valley* and the hanging *Leigh Woods* (159 acres; N.T.).

On the hill above the E. end of the bridge is an 'observatory' with a camera obscura (fee), whence access may be obtained also to a cave (fee) in *St Vincent's Rocks.*—From the E. end of the bridge a zigzag footpath descends to the 18C quarter environing the *Hotwells,* a spa which attracted crowds of visitors in the 18C (comp. 'Humphrey Clinker' and 'Evelina'). The long Hotwell Rd. leads back to College Green, passing (l.) *Holy Trinity,* a church (1828–30) by C. R. Cockerell, gutted in 1941, and charmingly refitted by T. Burrough (1959).

Clifton Down Rd. (bus 83) leads on from near the bridge to the *Zoological Gardens* (adm. 9–dusk, Sun 10 or 11–dusk; fee), noted for their carnivora. Close by is *Clifton College,* founded in 1862 and now one of the great public schools. Earl Haig (statue in the quadrangle), Sir A. Quiller-Couch, Sir Henry Newbolt, and Roger Fry were educated here. The College was U.S. 1st Army H.Q. under Gen. Omar Bradley (1943–44). Bus No. 17 returns to the Centre.

At **Westbury-on-Trym** (bus No. 1, 84, or 85), 3 m. N. of central Bristol, where Southey wrote 'Madoc' (1798), is the 15C tower gatehouse (N.T.) of a college of secular clerks, of which Wyclif was a prebendary, founded on the site of a 10C Benedictine monastery. The former collegiate church (of older foundation) has some E.E. features, but is principally Perpendicular. The monument of Bp. Carpenter (d. 1477) who was responsible for the rebuilding, lies near the Sanctuary. No. 38 Church Rd., another 15C building, probably formed part of the college. Mrs Indira Gandhi attended Badminton School here. Near *Henbury*, 1¼ m. N., with a golf course, is *Blaise Castle House*, a mansion of 1795 in a fine park, now a *Folk Museum* (adm. 2–5 or 5.30, Sun 3–5; closed Dec–Feb; fee), illustrating the crafts of workshop, farm and home. Outdoor exhibits include the 18C Stratford Mill (from the 'drowned' Chew valley), a thatched dairy, etc. Blaise Castle itself is a 'sham' built in 1766; Blaise Hamlet is a 'rustic' fancy by Nash. To the W., at Lawrence Weston, is a *Roman Villa* (key at 17 Hopewell Gdns.), with mosaic pavements; while farther S. at *Sea Mills*, are foundations of the Roman port of *Abonae*. *Kings Weston* house was begun in 1710 by Vanbrugh. On Henbury Hill is *Didsbury Methodist College*, removed from Manchester in 1945. *New Passage* reached from Westbury in ½ hr by bus, is a good place to see the Seven 'bore'. The *Severn Tunnel* (4 m. 638 yds), the longest tunnel in Britain, by which the railway crosses the Severn Estuary, was built in 1873–86 by Charles Richardson, a pupil of Brunel. *Aust*, 4½ m. farther N., has a good view of the *Severn Bridge* (com. p. 363), which carries the M 4 to the Welsh bank of the Estuary.—The fine Perp. church tower built by the Merchant Venturers in 1483 on *Dundry Hill*, 4½ m. s. of Bristol, commands an extensive *View.

At **Avonmouth** (Hotel), 5 m. N.W. of central Bristol (Bus No. 28, 29, or railway) are the major *Docks* of the Corporation of Bristol, including a large oil basin. Other imports include grain, molasses, bananas, timber, tobacco and chemicals. The town itself has hardly developed since the 19C, but industrial works are springing up on the outskirts. On the way is (3½ m.) *Shirehampton*, with a fine public park (N.T.) and golf course. The third limb of Bristol Docks is at **Portishead** (bus) on the Severn Estuary (11½ m. w. of Bristol), whose chief imports are phosphate and timber. An expanding town with a National Nautical School, it is becoming less dependent on Bristol. Buses run from Portishead to (6 m.) *Clevedon* (see below) viâ (2¾ m.) *Weston-in-Gordano*, where the church has a unique 'Palm Sunday' gallery.

From Bristol to *Exeter*, see Rte 20; to *Birmingham*, see Rte 35.

FROM BRISTOL TO CLEVEDON, 13 m. (A 369; or B 3128 viâ the Yeo valley); railway to Yatton in ¼ hr., with bus connection to Clevedon. We follow A 369 viâ (6 m.) *Portbury*, with its large part-Norman Church, and the pleasant Gordano valley.—8½ m. *Portishead* (see above).— 13 m. **Clevedon** (Hotels) is a quiet watering-place (14,300 inhabit.), attractively situated on the Severn estuary at the foot of *Dial Hill* (296 ft; view). In Old Church Rd., near the station, is a cottage (tablet), doubtfully identified as the 'pretty cot' to which S. T. Coleridge brought his bride, Sara Fricker, in 1795; and in the 'old church' of *St Andrew* are buried Arthur Hallam (1811–33), the subject of Tennyson's 'In Memoriam', and his father Henry Hallam (1777–1859), the historian.

*CLEVEDON COURT (adm. April–Sept, Wed, Thurs, Sun, & BH 2.30–5.30; fee), long the seat of the Elton family and the home of Arthur Hallam's maternal grandparents, an interesting building of 1320 with Elizabethan and later alterations. 'Castlewood' in Thackeray's 'Esmond' was drawn from Clevedon Court, though located in 'county Hants'.—At *Tickenham*, 3½ m. E., are a fine manor-house, partly of the 15C, and a church dedicated to SS Quiricus and Julietta. On the hill above (391 ft) is *Cadbury Camp*, an entrenchment of 7 acres, with a double rampart.

FROM BRISTOL TO WESTON-SUPER-MARE, 20¾ m. (A 370); railway in 25–35 min.—At (4 m.) *Long Ashton* is an important Fruit Research

Station, founded in 1903.—12½ m. *Congresbury* (pron. 'Commsbury') has a vicarage built in 1445 and an E.E. church with a fine stone spire. At *Yatton*, 1¼ m. N., is another good church (12–15C), with a Friends' Meeting House of 1729 at *Claverham*, adjoining on the N.E.—20¾ m. **Weston-super-Mare** (many Hotels), a frequented seaside resort (50,800 inhab.) on the Bristol Channel, has a Winter Garden, an esplanade, a sandy beach, and two piers, one leading to the rocky islet of *Birnbeck*. It is built partly on the slopes of *Worlebury Hill* (357 ft; views), encircled by a toll-road. On top are the remains of a British camp. Off the coast are the islets of *Steep Holme* and *Flat Holme*.

About 4 m. N. are the remains of *Woodspring Priory* together with 435 acres extending to the coast acquired by the N.T., founded as an expiatory chapel in honour of Thomas Becket, by a grandson of Reginald Fitzurse, one of his murderers, and 2 m. s. is the ruined *Uphill Old Church.*—On the opposite side of the Axe (ferry) is *Brean Down*, a bird sanctuary.

Excursion-steamers ply in summer to points of interest along the coast, and there are services to Cardiff several times daily.

From Bristol to Gloucester, 35 m. (A 38). Railway from Temple Meads Station in c. 45 min.—At (4 m.) *Filton* are the works of the Bristol Aeroplane Co., with huge hangars and 1¾ m. runway.—9½ m. *Alveston* (Motel).—10½ m. *Thornbury*, the early home of Dr W. G. Grace (1848–1915) and his brothers, has a Perp. church and a justly famous restaurant in a large late-Tudor mansion. We cross the South Wales motorway.—We leave on the left several roads leading to *Berkeley*, conveniently visited from Gloucester (Rte 30B), and pass (17 m.) *Newport Towers Hotel*, and (19 m.) *Berkeley Road Station*, with (r.) the road to *Dursley* (3 m.), a small machinery-making town. William Tyndale (1484–1536), translator of the Bible, is claimed as a native of *Nibley*, 2 m. s.—35 M. *Gloucester*, see Rte 30B.

From Bristol to Cirencester, 38 m. B 4058 leads to (6½ m.) *Winterbourne*, where the much restored church has interesting effigies and a brass of 1370.— 9½ m. *Iron Acton* has a 15C memorial cross in the churchyard. Beyond (17½ m.) *Wotton-under-Edge* (Hotel), a pleasant small town, we ascend the wooded slopes of the Cotswolds. To the right lies *Newark Park* (N.T.), with a footpath to *Ozleworth*, where the early Norman church has an hexagonal tower. The substantial houses of *Alderley*, 2 m. down the valley, recall the prosperous wool traders of the 16–18C. At the top of the ridge (21½ m.) we join A 4135 for (28 m.) *Tetbury*. Thence to *Cirencester*, see Rte 30B.

18   BATH

BATH (84,500 inhab.), whose natural hot springs have made it a fashionable spa since Roman times, retains a celebrated 18C atmosphere. The Roman Baths are one of the most important remains of the period in England. The town is situated on the winding Avon, in a cup or bowl surrounded by wooded downs, up the steep sides of which its buildings climb in tier upon tier of crescent, terrace, and square. These, built in a dignified Palladian style, give Bath an architectural character quite its own, as a unique and harmonious creation of the 18C.

Railway Station. *Spa* (Pl. 15), facing Manvers St.

Hotels of good quality are fewer than might be expected. Good **Restaurants.**— CARAVAN PARK, Brassmill Lane.

Post Office (Pl. 7), New Bond St.—INFORMATION BUREAU, with accommodation service (Pl. 11), Abbey Churchyard.

Buses. For the hurried visitor a frequent bus service runs in summer between the Pump Room and the Assembly Rooms.—BUS STATION (Pl. 11), Manvers St. Services to *Lansdown*, *Colerne*, and *Castle Combe*; *Bradford-on-Avon* and *Trowbridge*; *Devizes* and *Salisbury*; *Bristol*; *Radstock* and *Wells*; *Frome*, etc.—In summer CIRCULAR TOURS by coach include a round of the City; *Cheddar, Glastonbury,* and *Wells, Salisbury* and *Stonehenge, Tintern* and *Wye Valley,* etc.

Theatre. *Theatre Royal,* Sawclose (Pl. 10).

Music. A small orchestra plays in the Pump Room during morning coffee (aft. tea on Sun). During the summer season, afternoon concerts in Parade Gardens.—The annual 'Bath Festival' particularly noted for musical events, is held in May or June.

Golf Courses at *Sham Castle,* to the S.E.; *Lansdown* to the N.; and *Victoria Park* (approach courses).—RACING at *Lansdown.* —SPORTS CENTRE, North Parade Road.

Baths. The Hot Springs Physical Treatment Centre gives all recognized forms of hydrotherapy and physiotherapy, including free treatment under the National Health Service. The baths are open weekdays 9–6 (Sat 9–1; shown to visitors at 2.15).—Swimming Baths. *Beau St. Bath* (Pl. 11), open 8–7.15, Sat to 5.30, Sun to 11. *Royal Bath,* Hot Bath St. (Pl. 11), same hours (but subject to alteration). Both are warm (21–27°C), and covered. *Cleveland Open Air Pool,* Bathwick (Pl. 4).

Boating, on the Avon. Boats may be hired at Bathwick (Pl. 4) and Newbridge.—*Canal trips* at weekends in summer.—FISHING on the Avon and Kennet & Avon Canal, by licence.

Combined tickets for Pump Room, Roman Baths, Assembly Rooms, and Museum of Costume (30 p.); with No. 1 Royal Crescent, and Holburne of Menstrie Museum (50 p.).

History. According to the legend, Bath was founded by the British swineherd-prince Bladud (father of King Lear), expelled from court as a leper, who, imitating his leprous swine, regained health by rolling in the warm mud where the mineral waters stagnated. More probably the first discoverers were the Romans, who about A.D. 54 here established an elaborate system of baths. The name of the Roman settlement was *Aquæ Sulis,* from Sul, a local deity, also identified with Minerva. By the Saxons, who captured Bath in 577, it was known at first as *Akemanceaster* and later as *Æt Bathum.* About 1090 the see established at Wells was transferred to Bath by Bp. John de Villula, but about 1206 it was restored to Wells, though the bishops are still known as Bishops of Bath and Wells. In the Middle Ages Bath was a centre of the cloth-trade, and Chaucer's 'Wife of Bath' surpassed "them of Ypres and of Gaunt" in cloth-making. The Hospital of St John the Baptist, founded 1174 and rebuilt 1573, has as its successor the *Royal National Hospital for Rheumatic Diseases,* in Upper Borough Walls, built (as the Royal Mineral Water Hospital) by the elder Wood in 1738–42, and greatly extended since. The zenith of Bath's prosperity as a fashionable watering-place coincides with the 18C, during which it was visited by almost everyone of account in literature, politics, or society (see below). In the same century a new city was designed and built by the two John Woods, father and son (d. 1754 and 1782), supported by Ralph Allen (1694–1764), the wealthy Mæcenas of Prior Park (p. 193) and the original of Squire Allworthy in Fielding's 'Tom Jones', who exploited the rich quarries of Bath stone. Beau Nash (1674–1762), appointed Master of Ceremonies in 1704, introduced order and method into the gaieties and social life of the place, of which pictures have been drawn for us by innumerable authors—Smollett, Sheridan, Fanny Burney, Jane Austen, Thackeray, and (for a later period) Dickens. Nor should Christopher Anstey's amusing satire 'The New Bath Guide' (1766) be forgotten. The Woods' successors carried on their tradition up to c. 1800. In 1942 Bath was attacked from the air, with considerable loss of life and damage to many historic buildings. Plans have been approved to divert through traffic in the city by means of tunnels.

Many houses associated with illustrious names of the past are marked by mural tablets (historic map by T. S. Cotterell). At the Garrick's Head (now a storehouse), beside the theatre in Sawclose (Pl. 10), lived *Beau Nash* in 1705–61. *General Wolfe* left 5 Trim St. (Pl. 10) in 1759 to take command of the force against Quebec. At Rosewell House in Kingsmead Sq. (Pl. 10) *Bp. Butler* died in 1752. No. 41 Gay St. (Pl. 6) was the residence of *Fanny Burney,* who is buried in Walcot Cemetery (Pl. 3); at No. 8 lived *Mrs Piozzi;* No. 34 was *Friese-Greene's* first photographic studio (1874–84). In the Circus (Pl. 6): at Nos. 7 and 8, in 1753–63, *Wm. Pitt,* Earl of Chatham, who represented Bath in Parliament; at No. 13, *Livingstone;* at No. 14, *Clive,* broken in health, in 1774; at No. 17, *Gainsborough,* who here won his early fame; at No. 27, *Parry,* the Arctic voyager. At 35 St James's Sq. (Pl. 2) Dickens, Forster, and Maclise were the guests of *Landor* in 1840. *Wm. Beckford* lived at 20 Lansdown Crescent (Pl. 2) in 1822–44.. No. 9 New King St. (Pl. 10) was the residence of *Sheridan,* No. 22 that of *W. H. Hudson,*

Bath

0 _____ 400 yards
0 _____ 400 ms

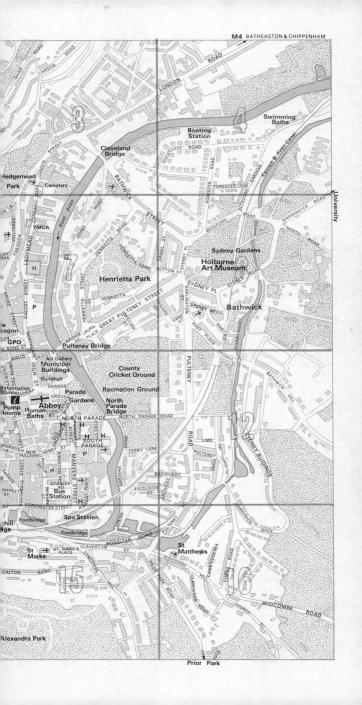

and at No. 19 the planet Uranus was discovered in 1781 by *Sir Wm. Herschel*, then organist of the Octagon (a fashionable proprietary chapel in Milsom St.; see p. 192). No. 11 North Parade (Pl. 11) was the residence of *Burke*, and *Goldsmith* stayed here in 1771; No. 9 was visited by *Wordsworth*. To No. 2 Pierrepont St. (Pl. 11) came *Nelson* in 1780 after the expedition to Central America; at No. 4 *James Quin*, the actor, was visited by Handel. At 15 Johnstone St. (Pl. 7) lived *Wm. Pitt* the younger in 1802. At 6 South Parade (Pl. 11) *Scott* lived in early youth with his uncle (1777); at No. 9 *Lord Roberts*, 'the idol of Bath'; No. 14 was a residence of *Fanny Burney* (see above); *Jane Austen* lived at 4 Sydney Place (Pl. 8) in 1801–5. *Dr Johnson* and *Boswell* put up in 1776 at the 'Three Cups' in Walcot St. (demolished) and *Mrs Thrale* married Mr Piozzi in St James's Church (Pl. 11; destroyed by fire) in 1784. *Mrs Siddons* dwelt for some years at 33 The Paragon and achieved her first real stage success in 1775 in the Bath Theatre (now Freemasons' Hall in Old Orchard St.). At No. 19 Bennett St. (Pl. 6) *Adm. Phillip* (1738–1814), first Governor of N.S.Wales, spent his last years. From No. 11 Royal Crescent in 1772 *Elizabeth Linley* eloped with Sheridan; *Frederic Harrison* died at No. 10 in 1923, and *Geo. Saintsbury* at No. 1 in 1933. A tablet on No. 10 New Bond St. commemorates *John Rudge* and *Wm. Friese-Greene*, originators of cinematography in England. *C. P. Scott* (1846–1932), editor of the 'Manchester Guardian' 1872–1929, was born in Bath. *Haile Selassie*, emperor of Ethiopia, lived at Fairfield House, on Newbridge Hill (A 431), during his exile (1936–40).

Bath has given its name to bath-chairs, Bath stone, Bath chaps, Bath buns, and Bath Oliver biscuits; but not Bath brick (comp. p. 200).

The **Abbey Church** (Pl. 11), situated in an attractive paved piazza called *Abbey Churchyard*, is a cruciform building in a consistent late-Perp. style. The w. front has a magnificent window of seven lights, flanked by turrets on which are carved ladders with angels ascending and descending, commemorating a vision that led Bp. King to build the church. The central tower (162 ft high), oblong in plan, and the flying buttresses may be noted also.

HISTORY. A nunnery founded at Bath in 676 was converted into a Benedictine monastery by King Edgar, crowned there in 973. John de Villula rebuilt the church (1107), but his Norman structure fell into ruin after the bishopric was restored to Wells, and on its site the smaller present church was begun in 1499 by Bp. Oliver King. The dissolution of the monasteries delayed its completion, and it was not consecrated until 1616, so that it may be regarded as the last of the great English pre-Reformation churches. It was restored in 1951–60.

Interior. The spacious church is remarkable for the size and number of its windows, which have earned for it the title of 'Lantern of the West'. The glass is nearly all modern. There is no triforium and the clerestory windows are unusually high. The rich fan-tracery roof, originally confined to the choir, was extended by Scott over the nave. At the s.e. angle of the choir is the small chantry of Prior Bird, begun in 1515 but completed only in recent years; it is notable for its exquisite stone carving. The aisle walls are encrusted with unworthy monuments ("Messieurs, vous voyez très bien ici Que ces eaux ne sont pas d'eaux de vie"). On the N. side of the nave is the altar-tomb of Bp. Montagu (d. 1618).

Among the important persons commemorated in the abbey are: Thomas Robert Malthus (d. 1834), political economist (in the porch); Sir Isaac Pitman (d. 1897), inventor of modern shorthand; Thomas Pownall (d. 1805), governor of Massachusetts and S. Carolina. S. aisle: Hon. Wm. Bingham (d. 1804), American senator, by Flaxman; Beau Nash (d. 1762). S. transept: Lady Waller (d. 1633), wife of the Parliamentary general. (In the N. transept the wrought-iron screen of 1725, was presented by Gen. Wade.) N. choir aisle: James Quin (d. 1766), with inscription by Garrick. S. choir aisle: Dr Sibthorp (d. 1796), with epitaph quoted from Dryden; Wm. Hoare (d. 1792), portrait-painter, by Chantrey.

The **Grand Pump Room** (Pl. 11; open 9–5 or 6, Sun from 11 or 2;

fee, inclusive ticket for Roman Baths and Assembly rooms), on the s. side of Abbey Churchyard, was rebuilt in the classical style by Thomas Baldwin and John Palmer in 1792–96, bears on its architrave the Pindaric motto *ΑΡΙΣΤΟΝ ΜΕΝ ΥΔΩΡ* ('water best of elements'). Inside we pass a fine concert hall, a series of reading rooms, and a terrace restaurant (overlooking the Roman Great Bath), to reach the handsome *Pump Room* itself, a favourite resort of visitors where coffee (with a morning concert) and tea (concert on Sun) may be taken. A statue of Beau Nash, usually attrib. to Prince Hoare (though probably by John Plura) surmounts the Tompion clock mentioned in 'Pickwick'. A fountain supplies mineral water for drinking, and a window commands a view of the *King's Bath*, fashionable in the 17C and 18C, with the main hot spring in the centre.

The MINERAL SPRINGS, three in number, to which Bath owes its name and its prosperity, are the only really hot springs in Britain and yield over half a million gallons per day, at a temperature of 49° C. They are available for patients at the various Bathing Establishments belonging to the Corporation, which are fitted up with every comfort and even luxury as well as with every scientific requirement. The highly radioactive waters contain metallic sulphates and chlorides, as well as other salts. Used for both bathing and drinking, they are beneficial in all forms of rheumatism and gout, nervous and digestive disorders, tropical and skin diseases, anæmia, and for restoring muscular tone after wounds and injuries.

At the far end of the room we descend a modern staircase to the *Roman Baths (another entrance is in Stall St.). The Baths were in use from the 1C to the 4C, during which time many alterations and extensions were carried out. A temple dedicated to Sulis Minerva is known to have existed in the area (now under the Pump Room) to the N. of the main spring, and fragments are preserved in the museum. Excavations were begun in 1755 (although the most important discoveries were made after 1878), and still continue in the temple area and to the s. of the Great Bath. An excellent Guide Book is available.

At the bottom of the stairs we pass first a hypocaust and flue, part of the heating arrangements for a tepid room in a system of 'Turkish' baths. Turning in to the main bath complex, we see (l.) the King's Bath, which lies above the Roman reservoir (see below). The viewing platform which would have provided a vista across the sacred spring to the temple beyond, remains. The *Circular Bath*, inserted early in the 2C A.D. into the original entrance hall, was the cold bath in a series of 'Sauna' baths.

The *Great Bath*, which once occupied a pillared hall 110 ft by 68 ft, measures 83 ft by 40 ft at its surface, below which six steps descend to the bottom. It is in a remarkable state of preservation, with the original pavements, exedræ or recesses, and flooring of lead from the Mendips (weighing 40 lb per ft), and the twelve great piers that once supported the roof. Some of the lead piping of the drainage system remains in place. On the terrace above are 19C statues of famous Romans. The architectural fragments displayed round the sides include part of the roof vaulting constructed in the 3C with hollow tiles.

The E. group of baths include the rectangular *Lucas Bath*, which preserves fragments of a second floor which was added with a mortar base. The semicircular bath to the N. has seats for the immersion of the patient's body. Beyond are further remains of baths and culverts.

The MUSEUM contains part of the pediment of the temple of Sulis Minerva. The striking design with a gorgon's head is an engaging example of Romano-British art. Two corner shafts of the temple altar are preserved, also an inscribed base of a statue, and fragments of a façade. Other objects found during excavations include a superb bronze head of Minerva, sculptural fragments (note the relief of a hound carrying a stag), and votive objects (a series of engraved gems, a tin mask, a curse scratched on lead, etc.).—The overflow conduit from the reservoir retains its Roman masonry, and the culvert can be seen beneath the museum floor.

Across Abbey Churchyard is the *City Department of Architecture and Planning* (open weekdays 8.45–1, 2.15–5.30), with a model of the city.

BATH STREET (Pl. 11) is a perfect colonnaded thoroughfare. The delightful *Cross Bath* (1787; by Baldwin), at the end, was fashionable in the 18C. *Hetling House* (Pl. 10; now the Abbey Church House), beyond, is one of the few Elizabethan houses in Bath (1570; restored 1954). In Sawclose (Pl. 10) is the *Theatre Royal*, with a façade (1804–5) by George Dance the Younger.

In Terrace Walk, s. of Orange Grove, the open space E. of the Abbey, stood the Old Assembly Rooms, the scene of Beau Nash's glory. Opposite are the pleasant *Parade Gardens*, entered from North Parade, at the w. end of which (backing on York St.) is *Ralph Allen's Town House*, rebuilt by the elder Wood (1727), with good E. façade. Near North Parade Bridge is the so-called *Sheridan's Grotto*, a stone alcove once used as a 'post-office' for lovers' clandestine letters.

High St. leads N. from the Abbey to Bridge St., passing the MUNICIPAL BUILDINGS (Pl. 11), the nucleus of which is the *Guildhall*, built by Baldwin in 1768–75 and containing a great *Banqueting Room* (adm. Mon–Fri 9–5; Sun in summer 2.30–4) in the Adam style with Whitefriars chandeliers of 1778, and portraits including George III and Queen Charlotte by Reynolds. In the N. wing is the *Public Library* and *Victoria Art Gallery* (weekdays 10–6), with the Bath Abbey Library of Bp. Lake (1619), some views of Old Bath, a good show of Bohemian glass, and a small collection of paintings, mainly by 19C local artists, but including the Adoration of the Magi, by *Van der Goes* (15C).

Off High St. is a covered market place (r.), and attractive alley-ways of colourful shops (l.), among them the Corridor (1825), Northumberland Place, and Union Passage.

Pulteney Bridge (Pl. 7; 1769–74), by Robert Adam, a charming little bridge flanked with shops, crosses the Avon enhanced in 1972 by a new weir, part of flood protection works. New buildings will include a hotel and car park. The long Great Pulteney Street, designed by Baldwin, and unbroken on the l. except for a terrace overlooking Henrietta Park (with a garden for the blind) leads on to the HOLBURNE OF MENSTRIE ART MUSEUM (Pl. 8; weekdays 11–5; closed 1–2 in winter; Sun 2.30–6; fee), built as a hotel in 1796–97 by C. H. Masters.

The collections, formed by Sir Thos. Holburne (d. 1874) and bequeathed to the town by his sister in 1882, include paintings and miniatures of the English School (good examples of Gainsborough and Allan Ramsay), and 15C Dutch, Flemish, and German works, china, gold- and silver-plate, Italian Renaissance bronzes, a small library of rare books, etc.—Behind the museum lie the shady *Sydney Gardens*, laid out in 1795, formerly the 'Vauxhall' of Bath.

In the N.W. residential quarter we find 18C Bath, with its characteristic architecture practically unaltered. Off *Milsom Street* (Pl. 7), a fine shopping street, is the *Octagon*, built by Lightoler as a chapel in 1767 and now used by the Royal Photographic Society. Quiet St. leads to Queen Sq., Gay St., and the Circus, all the work of the elder Wood, who himself lived and died in Queen Sq., though at No. 15 not No. 24 (plaque). On the w. side of Queen Sq., is the *Reference Library* (Mon–Fri 10–8; Sat 9.30–6) with many incunabula, a unique collection of books, prints, etc. relating to Bath (shown on request), exhibition rooms, and a fine geological collection. Off Gay St., in George‵St., is the re-

nowned Hole in the Wall restaurant. The ingenious planning of the
*CIRCUS (Pl. 6), with a true crescent facing each of its three approaches,
should be noted. Close by (E.) in Bennett St., are the **Assembly Rooms**
(Pl. 6; adm. 9.30 or 10–5 or 6; Sun from 11; fee, combined ticket, see
p. 187), built by the younger Wood (1771), gutted by fire in 1942,
restored and reopened in 1963. The ballroom and state rooms are
decorated in late-18C style by Oliver Messel. The rooms house a
*Museum of Costume from 1580 to the present, with some charming
tableaux, Byron's Albanian dress (1809), baby clothes, footwear, under-
wear (including 'patriotic corsets' of the First World War), etc. To the
w. is Wood's chef-d'œuvre (1769), the monumental *ROYAL CRESCENT
(Pl. 6), the segment of an ellipse over 600 ft in length. It was here that
Mr Winkle, on a famous occasion, found himself on the wrong side of
the door. No. 1, bought and beautifully restored and furnished by the
Bath Preservation Trust, is open Mar–Oct, Tues–Sat, 11–5, Sun from
2 (fee). It was built for Wood's father-in-law, Thomas Brock, in 1776.
Thence we may make our way N. to the high-lying Lansdown Crescent
(by J. Palmer; 1789–93); Somerset Place (c. 1790); and Camden Crescent
(c. 1788), both by Eveleigh, all commanding fine views of the city.—
Of the numerous parks and gardens of Bath the largest is the charming
Victoria Park (Pl. 1, 5; 50 acres), with a botanic garden.

ENVIRONS. The best near view of the city is obtained from *Beechen Cliff
(Pl. 15), a finely wooded escarpment on the s., 390 ft above the river, reached by
crossing the Southgate Footbridge (Pl. 15) and thence either viâ Holloway or by the
steps ascending from Lyncombe Hill.—To the N.W. of Bath rises Lansdown (813 ft)
with Kingswood School, founded by Wesley in 1748 and transferred from Bristol in
1851. Beckford's Tower (2 m.), a classical structure 150 ft high, recently restored,
commands one of the finest prospects in the West Country. Adjacent is the tomb of the
eccentric millionaire (d. 1844). About 2½ m. N. was fought the battle of Lansdown, in
which Sir Bevil Grenville (monument) defeated Waller in 1643, but was himself killed.
From *Prospect Stile, 2 m. w. of the tower and situated on a well-defined Roman road,
both Bath and Bristol are visible.—Another favourite viewpoint is Sham Castle, on
Bathwick Hill, 1 m. E., an artificial ruin built in 1760 by Ralph Allen. Farther N. is
Bathampton, where W. R. Sickert (1860–1942) died at St George's Hill House. In the
churchyard is the grave of Adm. Phillip (p. 190). Hampton Down (672 ft), above, and
Little Solsbury (625 ft; N.T.) across the river, both crowned by 'camps', are good
points of view. About 1 m. S.E. of Bath is *Prior Park (bus), the magnificent Palladian
masterpiece of the elder Wood, built in 1743 for Ralph Allen, who here entertained
Pope, Fielding, and other distinguished men. The mansion, impaired by fire and
alterations, but retaining a fine chapel, is now a Catholic school (adm. May–Sept, Tues
3–6, Wed 2–6; fee). The fine grounds with a notable Palladian bridge contain a
monument to General Wade, Allen's father-in-law; his son-in-law and successor was
Bp. Warburton, who erected the memorial tower. We may continue to the top of Combe
Down (550 ft; view) and return (on foot) by 'Pope's Walk' and Widcombe Church, close
to which was the house in which Fielding wrote part of 'Tom Jones' (1749). Widcombe
Manor (c. 1727) was the home of the novelist H. A. Vachell in 1927–52. Or we may
drive on to Englishcombe with a fine tithe-barn and a church with grotesque Norman
sculpture (N. side) and an unexpected figure of a swaddled child above the chancel
arch.—Other walks may be taken viâ Bathford to the tower known as 'Brown's Folly'
on the top of Kingsdown (620 ft), or viâ Batheaston (Hotel) to (4½ m. N.E.) St
Catherine's, with the remains of a 16C grange and a church of 1490 with contemporary
glass.

Bradford-on-Avon, 9¼ m. S.E. of Bath (bus) should on no account be overlooked.
It may be pleasantly reached by the *Avon valley viâ Bathwick Hill (Pl. 12) and
(2½ m.) Claverton, where the manor-house (1819–20; by Wyatville) contains an
American Museum (April–Oct daily exc. Mon, but incl. BH, 2–5; rfmts). It has
domestic interiors (17C–early-19C) imported from America, a 'Shaker' room and a
'Pennsylvania Dutch' room, pewter, glass, and folk-art (both European and
American-Indian); also a plaque recording Sir Winston Churchill's first political

speech, made here in 1897. Ralph Allen is buried in the churchyard.—Above on Claverton Down, is *Bath University of Technology*, founded in 1966; but we cross the river at (5 m.) *Limpley Stoke* (Hotels) where the screen adventures of the 'Titfield Thunderbolt' were enacted.—In **Bradford-on-Avon** (Hotel), a little stone-built town (8000 inhab.), is the early Romanesque **Church of St Laurence*. To the level of the string-course the church probably dates from Aldhelm's foundation of c. 705, the arcading above from the end of the 10C. The flying angels over the chancel arch are noteworthy examples of Saxon sculpture. The nave is only 26 ft in length. *Kingston House*, or 'The Hall' (c. 1600), recalling the style of Longleat (p. 154), is "full of beautiful Italian feeling in an English environment" (W. D. Howells); its lovely gardens are usually open to visitors on application. The *Town Bridge* is 17C (with two 13C arches), and has an almost unique 'lock-up' created out of an old bridge chapel (comp. Wakefield, p. 563). The *Parish Church* (Norman, Dec., and Perp.) has some interesting details. *Barton Farm*, to the s., has a remarkable tithe-barn, 168 ft long (early 14C; key at farmhouse). At *South Wraxall*, 3½ m. N., is a fine 15C manor, and at *Great Chalfield*, 3 m. N.E., is another fine house of the same period (N.T.; May–Oct, Wed 12–1, 2–5; fee) and a church with 15C wall-paintings. This last may be reached viâ (2½ m.) *Holt*, where The Courts (N.T.; adm. to gardens only April–Oct, Mon–Fri 2–6; fee; or on prior request) is a notable house of c. 1700, with William IV associations. *Westwood*, 1½ m. s.w. of Bradford, has another good manor-house (N.T.; adm. April–Sept, Wed, 2.30–6; fee) built in 1400–1620, and a church with a notable tower and glass of c. 1520.—The return to Bath may be made viâ (3 m. s.w.) the ruined *Farleigh Castle* (1383; adm. daily, Sun from 2; fee), with a chapel containing Hungerford tombs; the church (1443) has a stained-glass portrait of Sir Thomas Hungerford (d. 1398), first recorded Speaker of the House of Commons; *Norton St Philip* (2 m. farther), where the picturesque George Inn (15C; Restaurant), occupies a former guest-house of the abbot of Hinton Charterhouse, and (3 m. more) *Wellow*, probable birthplace of the composer John Bull (?1562–1628), which has a faith-fully restored church of 1372 with a fine roof and a unique fresco of c. 1500.

Dyrham Park (N.T.; adm. daily, exc. Mon & Tues, 2–6; Oct–Nov, Sat & Sun only, 2–dusk; BH, 12–6; closed Dec–March; rfmts; fee), c. 8 m. N. of Bath on A 46, is a mansion with a garden front of 1692 by Hauduroy, and a main extension built by Talman in 1698–1704 for William Blathwayt (d. 1717). It contains a Renaissance chimneypiece (brought from Rushbrooke, Suff.) and paintings by *Murillo* (Peasant woman) and by Dutch masters, notably a perspective view by *S. van Hoogstraeten*, once in the possession of Pepys's friend Thomas Povey, Blathwayt's uncle.

From Bath to *Wells*, see Rte 19; to *London* and *Bristol*, see Rte 17; to *Salisbury*, see p. 154.

19   BATH TO WELLS AND THE MENDIP HILLS

ROAD, 24 m., A 367. 9 m. *Radstock*.—B 3139. 24 m. Wells.—Shorter, but less interesting, is the direct road (A 39; 20 m.) viâ *Farrington Gurney* and *Chewton Mendip*.

The Foss Way climbs out of Bath on the line of a pre-Roman Hollo-way.—9 m. *Radstock*, with the adjoining town of *Midsomer Norton* (together 15,200 inhab.), is the chief centre of a coalfield. Beyond the town the road, now on a markedly Roman alinement, leaves a more direct road to Wells on the right.—At (13½ m.) *Stratton-on-theFosse*, a community, expelled from Douai in 1793, founded in 1814 the Benedictine abbey of *Downside*. The buildings include a beautiful church (1874–1935), with the shrine of the Blessed Oliver Plunket, and a well-known boys' school.—We ascend the Mendip Hills to a height of 889 ft and descend to (18 m.) *Shepton Mallet* (see Rte 27). A 371 runs w. down the pretty Sheppey valley.—20½ m. *Croscombe* has good Jacobean woodwork in its church.

24 m. **WELLS** (Hotels), a quiet and beautiful cathedral city and market town (8600 inhab.), is finely situated at the foot of the Mendip Hills. Wholly ecclesiastical in origin and development, Wells retains much of

its medieval character. The best view of the city is obtained from *Milton Hill*, 1 m. N.W.

The irregular market place is enclosed by the 17C *Crown Hotel*, a *Town Hall* of 1779, and a N. side (altered) built by Bp. Beckington c. 1450. The *Bishop's Eye* leads to the episcopal palace, and *Penniless Porch* (where alms were distributed) to the cathedral close, rivalled in its calm beauty only by that at Salisbury. This, however, is better entered by *Browne's Gate*, or the *Dean's Eye*, in Sadler St., where the astonishing façade of the cathedral bursts on the view. All these gates were built by Bp. Beckington (1443–65).

The **Cathedral**, one of the smaller but certainly one of the most beautiful of English cathedrals, is complete in all its parts and is "the best example to be found in the whole world of a secular church, with its subordinate buildings" (Freeman).

HISTORY. Tradition says that a church of St Andrew was founded by King Ine in 704 near the springs which have given the city its name. In 909 Wells became the seat of the new bishopric of Somerset, but John de Villula, the 16th bishop (1088–1122), transferred the see to the walled town of Bath. Under Bp. Savary (1192–1205) the title of the see was 'Bath and Glastonbury'. Bp. Jocelin (1206–42) returned to Wells and in 1219 surrendered the claim to Glastonbury, retaining the title 'Bath'. His successors ever since 1244 have been bishops of 'Bath and Wells', and the monks of Bath and the canons of Wells had equal voices in the election of the bishops until the suppression of the Abbey of Bath in 1539.

The present cathedral was begun under Bishop Reginald (1174–91) about 1176. The three W. bays of the choir, the transepts, and the E. bays of the nave were probably finished soon after 1200. The N. porch was built for Bp. Jocelin (see above), who also saw completed the nave, and the famous W. front designed by Thomas Norreys (fl. 1229–49). The church was consecrated in 1239. To the Decorated style belong the chapter house (1293–1319), with its staircase and earlier undercroft (1286), and the central tower, raised to its present height in 1321. The present 'Lady Chapel behind the high altar' (as it was called to distinguish it from an earlier 'Lady Chapel next to the cloister'), the three E. bays of the choir, and the retro-choir were rebuilt under Dean Godelee and completed about 1325. The Perp. w. towers, designed by William de Wynford (fl. 1360–1403), were built from the legacies of Bp. Harewell (d. 1386; s.w. tower) and Bp. Bubwith (d. 1424; N.w. tower). The cathedral has suffered from Puritan vandalism, damage done by Monmouth's rebels in 1685 (comp. *Conan Doyle's* 'Micah Clarke'), and the restorations of Ferrey (1842), who substituted Kilkenny marble for the blue lias shafts on the w. front, and Salvin (1848–54). In 1978 the whole façade was hidden by scaffolding and many statues being replaced.

Exterior. The **WEST FAÇADE**, of pure E.E. work, challenges comparison with Reims and Amiens. The w. towers, Perp. in their upper parts, are not in continuation of the aisles but, unusually for England, stand beyond them; thus is provided a vast screen, 147 ft wide and divided vertically by six buttresses, on which is carved "a magnificent Te Deum in stone". The superb **Statuary** and exquisite sculptural detail were created by a local school of craftsmen. There were originally over 400 figures in full colour, an epitome of sacred and profane history, carried in six tiers across the whole façade and round the sides of the w. towers. Over 300 remain, about half of them life-size or larger, to form the finest collection of medieval sculpture in England. Traces of the original polychrome colouring are still visible. The statues have suffered from weather and iconoclasm and identification in many cases is doubtful. In the tympanum of the main portal are the seated Virgin and Child; in the niche above, the Coronation of the Virgin. In the gable are the nine orders of angels, the twelve apostles, and the Saviour (highest of all; figure mutilated).

On the N. side of the nave we note the Trans. Norman walls with their elegant Dec. parapet (c. 1326) and Perp. window-tracery. The *North Porch*, unspoilt by restoration, was built c. 1213 for Bp. Jocelin. The exquisite carving of the Martyrdom of St Edmund (on the capitals of the E. side) and the other details, of a most delicate and refined workmanship, merit careful examination. On the N. transept, which is similar in style, is the dial of the 14C clock (see below), with two *Figures in armour striking the quarters with their battle-axes, probably the oldest clock-jacks in the country. The *Chain Gate*, an elegant Perp. bridge built for Bp. Beckington (1443–65), connects the chapter house with the Vicars' Close.

Interior. As we enter from the w. end our eye is at once attracted to the remarkable double straining arch erected to support the tower soon after its completion (c. 1322). Over this arch stands the Rood, replaced in this position in 1920, after the lapse of 400 years. The rich Transitional architecture of the NAVE makes it look higher than it is (67 ft), and the unbroken row of lancets in the triforium greatly increases its apparent length. The chief decorations are the elaborate *Capitals, and the medallions and carvings in the spandrels of the lancets in the triforium. In the s. clerestory is an early Perp. music-gallery, and below the triforium are carved brackets, probably supports for an early organ. On the N. side is the hexagonal Perp. chantry of Bp. Bubwith (d. 1424), with an alabaster panel of the Ascension, and opposite is that of Treasurer Hugh Sugar (d. 1489), with a stone pulpit of 1540 attached. The imposing lectern (1660) was a gift of Bp. Creyghton; and in the w. window the side-lights contain remains of enamel-painted glass (1670–72) presented by him.

The aisled TRANSEPTS are somewhat earlier in date than the nave, but some at least of the *Capitals may have been finished later; several on the w. side are said to refer to the cures of toothache for which the tomb of Bp. William Bytton II (see below) became famous. In the N. transept (fee) is the *Clock, probably erected in 1388–92, which retains its contemporary astronomical indications and tournament of knights (original works in the Science Museum in London). Below is a striking Crucifixion in yew by E. J. Clack (1955). The space beneath the tower, which is E.E. with fan-tracery vaulting, is bounded on three sides by 'scissors' arches (see above). On the fourth side is the screen (14C), altered by Salvin in order to carry the organ. In the s. transept are the *Chapel of St Calixtus* (see Pl.), containing the *Monument of Dean Husee (?; c. 1400), with unique representations of medieval choir vestments and alabaster *Panels of the Annunciation and the Trinity, and the *Chapel of St Martin* (see Pl.), refitted as a War Memorial by Sir Chas. A. Nicholson (1922), with the tomb of Chancellor William Biconyll (d. 1448). By the s. wall of the transept are the brass of Viscountess Lisle (d. 1464; Pl. 4) and the tomb of Bp. William of March (d. 1302); Pl. 3). The position of the font (? 12C, with Jacobean cover) is unusual.

In the s. choir aisle are the tombs of Bp. Wm. Bytton II (d. 1274; Pl. 10), with the oldest incised slab in England, and Bp. Beckington (d. 1465; Pl. 13), with an exquisite canopy and iron screen and a

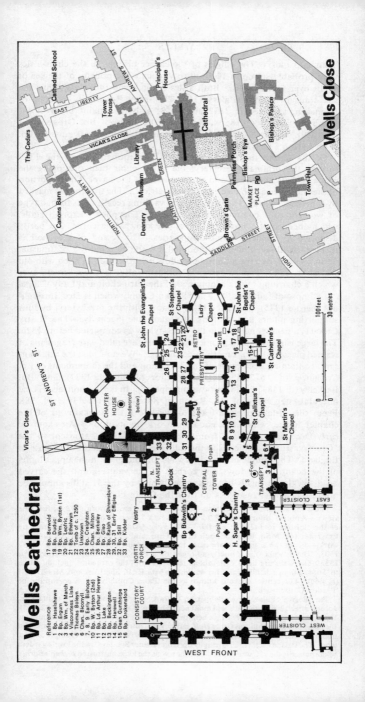

Wells Cathedral

Reference
1 Bp. Haselshawe
2 Bp. Ergum
3 Bp. Wm. of March
4 Viscountess Lisle
5 Thomas Boleyn
6 Chan. Biconyll
7, 8, 9 Early Bishops
10 Bp. W. Bytton (2nd)
11 Bp. Ld. Arthur Hervey
12 Bp. Lake
13 Bp. Beckington
14 Bp. Harewell
15 Dean Gunthorpe
16 Bp. Drokensford
17 Bp. Burwold
18 Bp. Duduc
19 Bp. Wm. Bytton (1st)
20 Bp. Leofric
21 Bp. Ethelwyn
22 Tomb of 1250
23 Unknown
24 Bp. Creighton
25 Chan. Milton
26 Bp. Berkeley
27 Bp. Giso
28 Bp. Ralph of Shrewsbury
29, 30, 31 Early Effigies
32 Bp. Still
33 Bp. Kidder

WEST FRONT

Wells Close

'memento mori'. The effigies of the earlier bishops in the choir-aisles were probably set up in 1220–30 to vindicate the priority of the see of Wells over that of Bath. Both aisles retain some 14C glass, while the s.e. transept contains glass (1500–25) from Rouen, by Arnold of Nijmegen, acquired in 1812 and 1953; also the quaint brass of Sir Humphrey Willis (1618; w. wall) and the effigy of Bp. Drokensford (d. 1329). In the s.e. chapel is the chantry-like tomb assigned to Bp. Wm. Bytton I (d. 1264).

Of the CHOIR the first three bays (Transitional, end of the 12C) formed the original presbytery, the ritual choir then occupying the space beneath the tower and the first bays of the nave. The e. portion of the choir is in a rich Dec. style (Geometrical). The triforium is masked by tabernacle work. The lierned stone vaulting recalls in its form a type of wooden roof common in the county. The poor Victorian stalls, which incorporate, however, 64 of the old *Misericords, are partly disguised by modern heraldic tapestries. The e. end of the choir is formed by three arches surmounted by the e. window, of unusual design, which, like the adjoining window on either side, is filled with old *Glass (c. 1340; Tree of Jesse). Behind the altar is a low screen, over which a charming *Vista is obtained of the retro-choir and Lady Chapel ("a glimpse of fairyland"). The *RETRO-CHOIR, which is Dec. throughout (before 1325), unites the Lady Chapel with the presbytery, by four supporting pillars and vaulting of remarkable ingenuity.—The *LADY CHAPEL, a pentagonal apse in the Dec. style, was completed before 1326. The large windows, with geometrical tracery, are filled with fragments of stained glass (c. 1330), superb in colouring.—We now pass the N.E. transept, containing a sculpture of the Ascension and the monuments of Bp. Creighton (d. 1672; Pl. 24), Chancellor Milton (d. 1337), and Bp. Berkeley (d. 1581; Pl. 26; curious inscription). In the N. choir-aisle is the fine alabaster effigy of Bp. Ralph of Shrewsbury (d. 1363; Pl. 28). From this aisle a passage leads to the late E.E. UNDERCROFT of the chapter house, which has good ironwork on its door.—An exquisite early-Dec. staircase leads from the e. aisle of the N. transept to the *CHAPTER HOUSE, which is in the full Dec. style, the finest of its date in England. The double-arched doorways, the old glass in the upper lights of the beautiful windows, the corbels of the vaulting and the carved heads on the springers of the arcade formed by the 51 stalls should be noticed. The staircase goes over the Chain Gate.

FROM the s. transept a staircase ascends the CENTRAL TOWER (182 ft; fee; fine view).—Another doorway leads to the CHAPTER LIBRARY, built over the e. walk of the cloisters in 1425. It contains 3000 vols. (Aldine Aristotle, annotated by Erasmus; 14C MS.), the papal bull to Bp. Giso, and a crozier with 13C Limoges work.—From the s. transept we enter the three-sided CLOISTERS, rebuilt c. 1425–1508. The e. walk was formerly adjoined by a Perp. Lady Chapel, destroyed in 1552. The walls are lined with tablets removed from the cathedral, including one to Thos. Linley (d. 1795) and his daughters Mrs R. B. Sheridan and Mrs Tickell (e. side). The central space is known as the 'Palm Churchyard', a corruption of 'Pardon Churchyard'.

The *Bishop's Palace (grounds open on Thurs & Sun aft. in summer) was built by Bp. Jocelin after 1206, with walls and moat added by Bp. Ralph of Shrewsbury (1329–63). Here the swans occasionally ring a bell for their dinner. Beyond the 14C gatehouse are the ruins of the magnificent *Great Hall*, built by Bp. Burnell (1274–92) and dismantled under Bp. Barlow (1549–54). The *Chapel* (Bp. Burnell) is a beautiful example of Dec. work. The Palace itself (13C) is usually open on summer Sundays. In the lovely gardens of the palace is the 15C well-house.—To the s.w. is the long, buttressed *Bishop's Barn*, a perfect specimen of the early 15C.—Rounding the s. side of the moat a path leads back to the road, from which we obtain a good view of the finest E. end in England, with the Dec. central tower, octagonal chapter-house (fine gargoyles), and pentagonal Lady Chapel standing clear of the choir.

On the N. side of the Cathedral Green is the *Deanery*, partly rebuilt by Dean Gunthorpe in 1472–98. Adjoining it is the *Museum* (weekdays 10–6; in winter 2–4; July–Sept Sun 2.30–5.30; fee), the rebuilt Chancellor's House, with finds from Wookey Hole and local antiquities. Next comes the *Theological College*, incorporating the hall of the Archdeaconry, dating from c. 1280 but modernized. It is now used as a library and has a 15C timber roof.

Farther E. and connected with the N. side of the cathedral by the bridge over the Chain Gate, lies the unique *Vicars' Close*, built by Bp. Ralph (c. 1348) and his successors for the College of Vicars Choral, the deputies of the canons, and now partly occupied by theological students. It consists of two rows of 21 houses, altered but retaining their original charm. At the entrance is a much-copied oriel window and the common dining hall, with a pulpit and an interesting painting. At the farther end of the close is the tiny chapel, altered by Bp. Beckington. Beyond the Close is *Tower House* (14–16C), opposite which is the *Prebendal House*, assigned to the principal of the college, a 15C house with a beautiful porch.

In East Liberty and North Liberty notable domestic buildings of many periods form components of Wells Cathedral School.

The civic church of *St Cuthbert* has an assertive Perp. tower of the Somerset type, and contains two well-carved, though mutilated, reredoses (one a Jesse Tree) in the transepts. Close by are *Bp. Bubwith's Almshouses* (1436, with 17C additions).

BUSES to *Wookey Hole, Glastonbury, Cheddar*, etc.—Glastonbury (Rte 27) lies 6 m. S.W. by A 39.

Wells makes an excellent centre for excursions in the **Mendip Hills**. The hills, a limestone chain about 25 m. long, running from N.W. to S.E., with many caves and 'swallet holes' and with numerous traces of Roman lead-mines, culminate in *Blackdown* (1065 ft), 3 m. N. of Cheddar.—*Wedmore*, 4 m. s. of Cheddar, has given its name to the peace concluded in 878 between King Alfred and Guthrum the Dane after the battle of Ethandune (p. 246). The church has a fine 12C portal and a 15C St Christopher overpainted c. 1520.

A 371 (the road to Weston-super-Mare) leads N.W. along the foot of the hills towards Cheddar (8 m.) and Axbridge. In the outskirts of Wells a by-road (r.) leads in 2 m. to *Wookey Hole* (fee) said to be the oldest known bone cavern in Britain, whence the river Axe gushes forth. Three caverns are shown; twelve more have been explored. A swimming-pool and other popular attractions are provided in summer. A steep by-road climbs the hills to (5 m.) *Priddy* (789 ft), with a noted restaurant, a little higher N. of which we join B 3135. The road now descends *Cheddar Gorge*, a narrow winding cleft over 2 m. long between perpendicular limestone cliffs, rising to 430 ft above the floor of the gorge. The rock-scenery is striking and the cliffs are perforated with caves having stalactites of unusual delicacy. *Cox's Cavern* and *Gough's Cavern*, which is the larger and was inhabited in the Stone Age, are open to the public (fees).—11½ m. *Cheddar* (Hotels), a considerable village, commercialized and congested in summer, is situated at the mouth of the gorge. It has given name to a type of Somerset cheese now made, but rarely equalled, elsewhere.

13½ m. *Axbridge*, with a long plain street and a commanding church (nave roof of 1636), is the centre of a strawberry-growing area and its fruits are justly renowned.—We join A 38 (comp. Rte 20) for c. 1 m., then diverge left to visit (15½ m.) *Winscombe* and (17 m.) *Banwell*, both with fine Perp. towers and good glass; the roofs and screen of 1522 at

Banwell show excellent workmanship. A 368 now runs E. along the N. flank of the Mendips to (23 m.) *Burrington*. Here B 3134 climbs *Burrington Combe*, a smaller gorge, less frequented than Cheddar, in one of whose cleft rocks, while sheltering from a thunderstorm, Augustus Toplady was inspired to write 'Rock of Ages'. The road passes just below Blackdown and the centre of Roman lead mining near *Charterhouse*, with a road that led eventually to the Solent. Later mining was centred on Priddy and over the whole upland area there are open trenches (or 'scruffs') and spoil heaps.—At (31 m.) *Green Ores* we turn S. down A 39, on which (½ m. farther on) is a monumental Romulus and Remus carved by an Italian prisoner of the Second World War.—35 m. *Wells*.

An alternative route from Burrington follows A 368 through woodland to (1 m.) *Blagdon*, overlooking a lake-reservoir, then continues along the foot of the Mendips with fine views and good churches at (4½ m.) *Compton Martin* (Norman) and (10 m.) *Chewton Mendip* (tower, 126 ft); hence A 39 leads direct to (16 m.) Wells.

20   BRISTOL TO EXETER

ROAD, 76 m. (A 38).—33 m. *Bridgwater.*—44 m. **Taunton.**—51 m. *Wellington.*—63 m. *Cullompton.*—76 m. **Exeter.**—MOTORWAY (M 5) on a roughly similar line.
RAILWAY, 75½ m. in 80–100 min. Intermediate stations: 19 m. *Weston-super-Mare.*—27 m. *Highbridge*, for *Burnham.*—33 m. *Bridgwater.*—44¾ m. **Taunton.**—60¾ m. *Tiverton Junction*, for Tiverton (5 m.; see Rte 21c).—75½ m. **Exeter** (St David's).

Leaving Bristol by Redcliffe St. and Bedminster, the road ascends, with Dundry Hill and tower on the left.—5½ m. *Barrow Gurney*, with reservoirs.

To the left B 3130 leads to (4½ m.) *Chew Magna* and (6 m.) *Stanton Drew*, with three remarkable stone circles and the 'Cove' of three standing stones; also a fine medieval parsonage; while just over 1 m. S.W., near a huge reservoir (trout-fishing), is the charming village of *Chew Stoke*. Near *Stowey*, 2 m. S.E., is *Sutton Court*, partly built by 'Bess of Hardwick' and often visited by John Locke.
About 1½ m. N.W. of A 38, 4½m. farther on, is *Wrington*, with perhaps the finest of the celebrated Perp. church towers of Somerset. This was the birthplace of John Locke (1632–1704); tablet in the churchyard wall); Sir Walford Davies (1869–1941) died here, and in the churchyard lies Hannah More (1745–1833). *Barley Wood*, the pretty cottage (now modernized and enlarged), to which Hannah More removed in 1800 from *Cowslip Green* on the main road, is c. 1 m. N.E.

Beyond (12 m.) *Langford* we thread the W. outliers of the Mendips, leaving on the right at 14½ m. *Winscombe* (1 m.) and *Banwell* (3 m.; comp. Rte 19) and on the left at 15¾ m. the road to Wells, then descend to the rich grazing flats or 'levels' of N. Somerset between the Axe and the Parrett.—23½ m. The isolated *Brent Knoll* (457 ft) breaks the monotony of the landscape, affording a fine *View from a summit crowned with Iron Age fortifications. The church in the village on its farther side is Norman with Perp. additions and has satirical bench-ends and a monument to John Somerset (d. 1663).—At (26 m.) *Highbridge* a road leads (r.) for (1¾ m.) *Burnham*.

Burnham-on-Sea (Hotels) is a golfing resort (12,300 inhab.) at the mouth of the Parrett. In the church is a white marble altarpiece carved by Grinling Gibbons as part of Wren's refurbishing of the chapel of Whitehall Palace in 1686.

33 m. **Bridgwater** (Hotels) is a busy red-brick town (26,600 inhab.) on the Parrett, whose capture by Fairfax in 1645 was a heavy blow to the Royalists. 'Bath brick', named after its maker, not the city, is

manufactured only at Bridgwater, from the clay and sand deposited by the Parrett, here tidal. The *Market Hall* (1834), with a curved colonnade, faces Cornhill. Behind it in a quiet setting, is *St Mary's*, with wide Dec. transepts and a slender spire 174 ft in height, built in 1366 by Nicholas Waleys; the 15C chancel roof, the Perp. pulpit, and the Jacobean screen (s. transept) are notable. A statue in Cornhill commemorates Adm. Blake (1599–1657), who was born in a house in Blake St., to the s., now a *Museum* (adm. free weekdays 10–1, 2–5, closed Tues afternoon) with important relics of the Admiral and of the battle of Sedgemoor. West Quay and Castle St. preserve some attractive houses.

At SEDGEMOOR, in the marshes 3 m. s.E. (1 m. N. of *Weston Zoyland*), the Duke of Monmouth's rebellion was crushed on 6 July 1685, a fortnight after he had been proclaimed king at Bridgwater. A flagstaff and a stone of memory, with four 'stedale' stones, mark the 'graveyard' field where the slain lie buried, and a memorial in Weston church (which has a fine roof, c. 1500, put up by Abbot Bere of Glaston), recalls the temporary imprisonment here of 500 rebel peasants, some score of whom were hanged in chains from the belfry battlements.

FROM BRIDGWATER TO MINEHEAD, 25½ m. (A 39), bus in 2 hrs.—4 m. *Brymore House*, birthplace of John Pym (1584–1643).—8½ m. **Nether Stowey**, birthplace of the Jesuit Robert Parsons (1546–1610). Coleridge occupied a cottage here (adm. Apr–Sept, Sun–Thurs, 2–6; fee) in 1797–1800, and in 1797 he was joined by Wm. Wordsworth (com. below). As a result of their constant companionship, by which Wordsworth was profoundly influenced, the 'Lyrical Ballads' (to which Coleridge contributed 'The Ancient Mariner') were produced. Nether Stowey is a stag- and fox-hunting centre and a good starting-point for walks in the Quantock Hills (comp. Rte 21B). *Stogursey*, 3 m. N., has a notable Norman priory church and at *Hinkley Point*, 3 m. farther, on the coast, is a nuclear power station (1957).— 10 m. *Dodington* (r.) has a beautiful Elizabethan manorhouse.—Near (11½ m.) *Holford*, another good centre for walks, is *Alfoxton House*, occupied by Wordsworth in 1797, and now a hotel.—From (13½ m.) *East Quantoxhead*, a charming village, a coastal path leads along the cliffs to Watchet.—At (15 m.) *West Quantoxhead* we descend to (17 m.) *Williton* where we join the road from Taunton (Rte 21B).

36 m. *North Petherton* has a fine church tower and (38 m.) *Thurloxton* church (r.) wood furnishings of 1634.

44 m. **TAUNTON** (good Hotels), the county town (37,400 inhab.) of Somerset, lies in the beautiful valley of *Taunton Dean*, noted for its apples and cider. A flourishing market town, it is provided with good communications.

History. Founded c. 705 by Ine, king of the West Saxons, as a stronghold against the Celts, Taunton remained a fortified seat of the Bishops of Winchester for more than a thousand years. The castle dates from early in the 12C. Here in 1497, after his unsuccessful rebellion, Perkin Warbeck was examined by Henry VII. Heroically defended by Blake, the castle withstood three sieges by Royalist forces in 1644–45, during which two-thirds of the town was destroyed by fire. On 20 June 1685, James, Duke of Monmouth, was proclaimed king in the market place. After the battle of Sedgemoor swift retribution fell on the inhabitants, who suffered the cruelties of 'Kirke's Lambs', and Judge Jeffreys' 'Bloody Assize'. The Devon & Somerset Stores in Fore St. occupy the site of the White Hart inn, from the signboard of which Col. Kirke hanged captured rebels. Sydney Smith made his famous speech on Reform in Taunton in 1831.

The road from Bridgwater leads past the thatched *St Margaret's Almshouses* (rebuilt), formerly a leper hospital, and viâ East Reach and *Gray's Almshouses* (1635) to the market place, now called Fore St., the triangular centre of the town. To the left is the *Tudor House* (1578; now a restaurant) where Judge Jeffreys lodged. Beyond the Municipal Buildings, which incorporate the old *Grammar School* (now known as

King's College and situated s. of the town), we turn into Castle Green. The *Castle*, founded in the 12C and much restored, contains the Somerset County Museum (weekdays 10–4 or 5.30; fee), with a good prehistoric collection, a fine late Roman *Mosaic from Low Ham, and a portrait of Jeffreys.

Passing under the outer gate by Castle Bow, we cross Fore St. to Hammet St., its Georgian symmetry recently and unpardonably spoiled. It was designed as a plain but dignified approach to *St Mary Magdalen's* one of the largest Perp. churches in England, with a magnificent, richly sculptured tower, 163 ft high, reconstructed in 1858–62. The church has double aisles, figures of angels between the clerestory lights, and a glorious oak roof. *St James's* (rebuilt) has a good font and a fine tower faithfully reconstructed in 1870. *Wilton House*, at the top of High St., was the birthplace of the historian A. W. Kinglake (1809–91). *Taunton School* (1847) lies N. of the town; *Queen's College* (1843), to the s. Both are important schools, founded by Dissenters.

Trull, 2 m. s., has a small church with much 16C woodcarving including a remarkably fine pulpit; and *Kingston St Mary*, 3 m. N., has a fine Perp. church tower.

From Taunton to *Minehead* and to *Barnstaple*, see Rte 21; to *Wells*, see Rte 27; to *London*, see Rte 16.

51 m. *Wellington* (Hotels) is a woollen-making town (9300 inhab.) from which the great duke derived his title. In the church is the tomb of Sir John Popham (d. 1607), the judge who tried Raleigh.

Nynehead, 2 m. N., has a church with sculptures by the Della Robbia and other Italian artists, beside a manor of 1675.—To the s. rise the *Blackdown Hills*, crowned by (2½ m.) the Wellington Monument (900 ft). *Culmstock Beacon* (819 ft), at their w. extremity, preserves a stone-built fire turret.—*Cothay Manor*, at *Greenham*, 5 m. w., survives largely unaltered as a 15C manor-house, preserving even its wall-paintings, and has lovely gardens on the Tone (open occasionally or by written permission). In *Holcombe Rogus*, c. 1½ m. farther w., is Holcombe Court (adm. by prior application) with a s. front of c. 1520.

We soon enter Devonshire, and at (58 m.) *Waterloo Cross* leave the Tiverton road on the right. On the left is the Culm valley, ascending to *Hemyock* (7 m.) at the s. foot of the Blackdowns. We descend the river past (63 m.) *Cullompton* (Hotels), where the fine Perp. *Church has a richly carved roof, a magnificent tower, and the beautiful vaulted Lane Aisle (16C). The Old Priest's House, with fine hall and gallery, is open daily on previous application.—At (68½ m.) *Beare* we enter a large and finely wooded N.T. property (10 sq. m.), including *Killerton House* (r.), the gardens of which are open daily (fee).—71 m. *Broadclyst* has a notable church.—At (73 m.) *Pinhoe* (Hotel) we reach the outskirts of (76 m.) **Exeter.**

21 TAUNTON TO BARNSTAPLE AND ILFRACOMBE. EXMOOR
A Viâ Bampton

ROAD (50 m.), A 361. 20 m. *Bampton.*—38 m. *South Molton.*—50 m. **Barnstaple.**—63½ m. **Ilfracombe.**

A 361, the most direct road, winds through magnificent scenery to the s. of Exmoor.—2 m. *Norton Fitzwarren* has a good church screen of 1509.—The fine Perp. church at (7 m.) *Milverton* has carved woodwork.—11 m. *Wiveliscombe.*—We enter Devon before (20 m.) *Bampton* (Hotel), where the chief fair for Exmoor ponies is held (last Thurs in Oct). The small town has good Georgian houses.

A 396 runs down the Valley of the Exe. Northwards, see Rte 21c.—7 m. **Tiverton** (Hotels) is an old market and lace-making town (15,500 inhab.) on the Exe, with a truncated *Castle* (14C gateway) and old almshouses. The fine 15C *Church* (freely restored) contains the richly carved Greenway Chapel (1517) and an organ of 1696 by Father Smith. *Blundell's School* (founded in 1604) occupies Victorian quarters w. of the town, but the old buildings (N.T.) still stand on the bank of the Loman. Here John Ridd (in 'Lorna Doone', like his creator, went to school, as did also Richard Cosway and Wm. Temple, Abp of Canterbury 1896–1902. The 19C *Knightshayes Court*, a house by Burges of 1870 (N.T.; adm. Apr–Oct, Sun–Thurs 2–6; fee) lies 1½ m. N.E. of Tiverton.—11¾ m. *Bickleigh Bridge* (Hotel) dates from 1640. *Bickleigh Castle*, ½ m. s., has a Norman chapel and a 15–17C gatehouse (open mid-week aft. in summer).—21½ m. **Exeter,** see Rte 15.

We cross the Exe valley (Rte 21c).—38 m. *South Molton* has a pleasant market place; from it a road crosses Exmoor to (11 m.) Simonsbath, and another leads N. to (24 m.) Ilfracombe, passing (6 m.) *Charles,* with the rectory where R. D. Blackmore (1825–1900) spent his boyhood.—Just before (42 m.) *Filleigh* the splendid mansion of Castle Hill (1684, rebuilt after fire in 1934; no adm.) is prominent on the right.—45 m. *Swimbridge* church has a notable rood screen.

50 m. **BARNSTAPLE** (Hotels; Restaurant), a decayed seaport but still a busy town (17,300 inhab.) with 1000 years of corporate history, lies at the head of the Taw estuary. It is a good centre for the exploration of N. Devon. 'Barum Ware' still enjoys a certain reputation. The Taw is here crossed by a bridge of 16 arches (15C; widened 1796 and 1962), and there is a pleasant riverside promenade. *Queen Anne's Walk* is a colonnade of 1796–98 with a statue of Queen Anne (1708). *St Peter's* church (restored), dating in part from the 14C, has a crooked leaden spire and contains interesting monuments. *Horwood's Alms-houses* and the *Maids' School,* near by, and the *Penrose Almshouses* in Litchdon St., E. of the Square, are typical of 17C Barnstaple. Bp. Jewel (1522–71) and John Gay (1685–1732; a native) were educated in the *Grammar School,* formerly in *St Anne's Chapel* (1330; now a museum). W. R. Lethaby (1857–1931) was born here.

The railway station (trains from Exeter, see Rte 15b) is beyond the river (connecting buses to Ilfracombe).—Opposite the former 'Town' station is the motte of the *Castle* and ½ m. N. is the church of *Pilton* (good woodwork).

FROM BARNSTAPLE TO LYNTON viâ BRATTON FLEMING, 19 m. Walkers may follow the course of the old railway between Chelfham and Blackmoor Gate (views). As far as (5 m.) *Chelfham* we ascend the valley of the Yeo which is comparatively tame, but farther on the scenery is very attractive.—7 m. *Bratton Fleming.*—At (11 m.) *Blackmoor Gate* we join the main road (A 39; 10 m.), which runs viâ (3¾ m.) *Shirwell Cross* and passes (6½ m.; r.) *Arlington Court* (N.T.; 1820–23); the house and grounds are open daily 11–12.30, 2–5.30 (April–mid-Oct); fee; Restaurant.

A 361 continues on the right bank of the Taw estuary, passing (53½ m.; l.) *Chivenor R.A.F. Station.* The church of *Heaton Punchardon* (½ m. r.) contains a sumptuous tomb of 1523, and in the churchyard are buried airmen from the Dominions who lost their lives in 1939–45.—56½ m. *Braunton* has a church dedicated to St Brannock, with an early tower, and good bench-ends and other woodwork. To the s.w. is the 'Great Field' (over 300 acres) still cultivated on the medieval strip system;

beyond it lie *Braunton Burrows*, a happy hunting-ground for the botanist, with a Nature Reserve (over 500 acres), and *Saunton Sands* (2 m.; Hotels), with a notable golf course.—We ascend gradually and at the summit (662 ft) leave the Mortehoe road (see below) on the left.

63½ m. **ILFRACOMBE** (9800 inhab.) is beautifully situated on the s. shore of the Bristol Channel. Once a fishing port, it acquired its character in late Victorian times as a well-to-do summer resort, but lost its elegance after the First World War. It is well supplied with public gardens, and with charming woods and glens inland.

Numerous **Hotels**, many of them inexpensive, most closed in winter.
Amusements. *Victoria Pavilion*, *Gaiety Theatre*, on Promenade; *Alexandra Theatre*, Market St.—GOLF COURSE at Hele, 1½ m. E.—TENNIS at Bicclescombe Park, and Torrs and Larkstone Sports Grounds.—Zoo at Comyn Hill, 1 m. s., on Old Barnstaple Road.
Bathing at *Rapparee Cove*, *Tunnels Beaches*, and *Hele*.—SWIMMING POOLS at the Tunnels, and on the Promenade (covered).
Buses from Wilder Rd. to *Barnstaple*; to *Woolacombe*; to *Newquay* viâ Bude; to *Minehead* viâ Simonsbath; from Marlborough Rd. to *Lee*; to *Combe Martin* and *Lynton*.
Steamers in summer to *Swansea, Cardiff, Bristol, Minehead, Clevedon,* etc.; 2 or 3 times weekly to *Lundy* viâ Clovelly. Cruises along the coast; also to *Lynmouth*.

The steep turnings on the seaward (N.) side of High St. lead to *Wildersmouth Beach*, with the prominent *Capstone Hill* (181 ft; view), at the foot of which is the *Victoria Pavilion*; while just to the w. are the *Tunnels Beaches*, approached through tunnels in the rock. To the s.e. of the Capstone are the *Harbour* and *Pier*, sheltered on the N. side by *Lantern Hill*, with the remains of the 13C *Chapel of St Nicholas* on its crest. Farther s.e. is the sheltered *Rapparee Cove* beneath the lofty *Hillsborough* (447 ft; view). The medieval *Chambercombe Manor*, 1 m. s.e., is open Easter–Sept, Sun aft. & Mon–Fri, 11–1, 2–5.30; fee.

To the w. of the town is the *Torrs Walk, a zigzag 'corniche' path affording a series of charming seaward views. Thence it is a fine walk, passing *Flat Point* (N.T., 92 acres), to (3 m.) Lee (Hotel, summer only), a pretty village, famous for its fuchsias, a little inland from *Lee Bay*. From Lee Bay a hilly footpath leads to (5 m.) *Bull Point Lighthouse* (r.; 154 ft; adm. weekdays from 1 p.m.). Thence we may follow the road to (6½ m.) **Mortehoe** (Hotels; all closed in winter). The E.E. church, with a 14C tower, contains the tomb of William de Tracey (1321), a former vicar sometimes confounded with the murderer of Thomas Becket. *Morte Point*, a rock-bound headland 1 m. w., commands a wild and wide view. The road goes on s. past (7 m.) *Barricane Bay*, with its beach of minute shells, to (7½ m.) **Woolacombe** (Good Hotels, closed in winter), with golf links and a sandy beach noted for surf-bathing. The Nat. Trust owns over 1200 acres on Morte Point, behind Woolacombe Sands, and on Baggy Point to the s. The return to Ilfracombe may be made viâ (2 m.) Mortehoe station.

Lundy (the terminal 'y' means 'island'), a granite islet (3 m. long; ½–¾ m. broad) in the Bristol Channel, with about 40 inhab., lies 12 m. off Hartland Point. It contains some curious rock-formations and is the breeding-place of innumerable puffin, etc. Near the quay are the remains of *Marisco Castle* (335 ft), the stronghold of an early piratical ruling family, and down to the reign of Queen Anne the island was a nest of pirates. The *Shutter Rock*, off the s.w. end, so called because it is believed that it would exactly fill the rifted opening of the adjacent *Devil's Lime Kiln*, was the scene of the wreck of the 'Santa Catharina' in 'Westward Ho!' The 19C buildings include a church, an inn, and three lighthouses. The island was bought in 1969 by the National Trust.

B Viâ Minehead

ROAD, 62½ m. A 358. 15½ m. *Williton.*—A 39. 22 m. **Dunster.**—24 m. **Minehead.**
—41 m. **Lynmouth.**—A 399. 58 m. *Combe Martin.*—62½ m. **Ilfracombe.**

The road crosses the Taunton by-pass (A 361) and skirts the s.w. flank of the QUANTOCK HILLS (300 acres N.T.), which extend from Taunton to the sea. With their clear springs, wild red deer, heather, and bilberries, they culminate in *Will's Neck* (1261 ft) 2 m. s.w. of Crowcombe. A magnificent walk (c. 12 m.) may be taken along the ridge from Kingston St Mary (p. 202) to West Quantoxhead (p. 201).—5 m. *Bishop's Lydeard* has a Perp. church (good wood-carving) and a 14C churchyard cross.—At (6¾ m.) *Combe Florey* (l.) Sydney Smith was rector from 1829 to 1845. Near *Tolland*, 3 m. farther w., *Gaulden Manor* (adm. 2–6, May–Aug, Thurs, Sun & BH; fee), partly 12C, was once the home of the Turbervilles. On the left appear the *Brendon Hills.*—9 m. *Crowcombe* (r.) has a Perp. church with good bench-ends and two crosses (12C and 14C). A fine scenic road crosses the Quantocks to Nether Stowey (p. 201).—13 m. *Bicknoller* church has a carved screen and Tudor bench-ends. *Stogumber*, 2 m. s.w., has attractive cottages and a Perp. church with a good 17C monument to Sir George Sydenham. The priest who prosecuted Joan of Arc came from Stogumber.—At (15½ m.) *Williton* (Hotel) we join A 39 from Bridgwater (Rte 20). The buses make a detour to *Watchet*, a small port on the Bristol Channel, 2 m. N.—17¼ m. *Washford* (Hotels) lies just N. of the remains of **Cleeve Abbey*, founded for Cistercian monks in 1188 (adm. daily, Sun from 2; fee), which include the gatehouse (c. 1530), the excellently preserved dormitory (E.E.) and **Refectory* (15C), with a fine timber roof. The numerous fine doorways and tiled pavements should be noticed.—18½ m. *Carhampton*, with a fine rood-screen, is 1 m. s. of *Blue Anchor* (Hotel), a bathing resort.

22 m. **Dunster** (Hotel), a quaint and attractive old town, has among many interesting buildings the *Yarn Market* (c. 1590) and the *Luttrell Arms*, altered in the 17C, with a 15C hall. The large *Priory Church* (1150; with enlargements of the 13C and 1443) has a good roof, a **Screen* of 1500, and Luttrell monuments. **Dunster Castle* (N.T.), a splendid castellated mansion, built by Mohun, earl of Somerset, c. 1070, and held by the Luttrells since 1376, dates in its present form from the 13–18C with embellishments by Salvin; it was held in 1645 by Col. Wyndham for 160 days against Blake's Parliamentarians.

The castle (fee) and grounds are open daily exc. Sat & Mon, 11–5 in Apr–Sept; Tues, Wed & Sun, 2–4, in March & October. Among the notable portraits is one by Eworth (1550) of Sir John Luttrell, emblematic of his captivity in Scotland; and the late-17C plasterwork and wood-carving, and a unique series of Dutch embossed leather hangings (mid-17C) are outstanding. *Conygar Hill*, conspicuous on the left, is a landmark for sailors.
A 396 ascends the wooded valley of the Avill to (5 m.) *Timberscombe* and (8¼ m.) *Wheddon Cross* (comp. Rte 21C).

24 m. **MINEHEAD** (Hotels), a popular summer resort (8100 inhab.) with a picturesque quay and harbour at the w. end, beneath the old village where steep lanes lead up to the 14C church (good screen). In the centre of the lower town is a statue of Queen Anne (1719). The attractions include beautiful environs, a mild climate, a swimming pool, and a golf course; and there is a large 'holiday camp' at the E. end. The

Market House in the Parade is the Information Centre for Exmoor National Park.

The wooded cliffs to the N.W. afford pleasant walks; and a road climbs North Hill to (3½ m.) *Selworthy Beacon* (see below). *Dunkery Beacon* (2½–3 hrs) and many other points on Exmoor may be visited from Minehead; and to the W. is *Bratton Court* (1½ m.), perhaps the birthplace of Henry de Bracton, 'Father of the Common Law' (d. 1268).—STEAMERS to *Lynmouth, Ilfracombe, Clevedon, Cardiff, Bristol,* etc.—From Minehead to Lynton by the coast, see below.

The road undulates along the N. verge of Exmoor, passing just s. of *Selworthy*, a pretty village with a tithe-barn and a fine Perp. church, and (28 m.) *Allerford*, which has a two-arched pack-horse bridge.

*Exmoor Forest, a tract of high moorland about 120 sq. m. in area, lies wholly in Somerset. Geologically it is Devonian, and its slate and sandstone summits are less rugged than the granite tors of Dartmoor. It is mentioned as a royal forest in a charter of King John, but was disafforested by Act of Parliament in 1819. Large tracts are still uncultivated and covered with colourless tussocky grass, prickly grey furze, or heather. The wild red deer (otherwise extinct in England) is still regularly hunted on Exmoor, and its pastures support also a hardy race of horned sheep. The native Exmoor pony may sometimes be seen on the last Thurs in Oct, at Bampton Fair. Excellent fishing is afforded by the streams. The highest summit is *Dunkery Beacon* (1705 ft), but many other hills are over 1500 ft. A large part of Exmoor is included in the 13,710 acres of N.T. property which comprises Winsford Hill, Tarr Steps, Selworthy, Bossington Hill, and the Holnicote estate, and the region is designated a National Park.

30 m. **Porlock** (Hotels), the 'enclosed port', is a charming village in a fertile vale. In the little 13C church of *St Dubricius* is the sumptuous tomb of Baron Harington (d. 1418) and his wife. The county library occupies Doverhay Manor, with a fine 15C window.

It was in a "lonely farmhouse between Porlock and Lynton" that Coleridge is said to have had the vision which resulted in 'Kubla Khan' (1798); and 'Southey's chimney-corner', in the picturesque Ship Hotel, is pointed out as the place where that poet wrote the lines on Porlock's 'verdant vale'.—About 1½ m. W. is the pretty little harbour of *Porlock Weir* (Hotels).

Dunkery Beacon (1705 ft; N.T.), the highest hill on Exmoor, rises about 4 m. s. of Porlock. It is a dark brown moorland hill, "whose Celtic name has an appropriate sound among the remains of primeval times with which it is crowned" (E. A. Freeman). Motorists may drive nearly all the way to the top, either viâ *West Luccombe* or viâ the *Horner Woods* and *Cloutsham*, where the opening meet of the Devon and Somerset Stag Hounds is held annually, early in August. The *View on a clear day may extend from Brown Willy in Cornwall (s.) to the Malvern Hills (N.), and includes 120 m. of the Bristol Channel. The descent may be made s.e. to (3½ m.) *Wheddon Cross* (see below), or N.E. to (3 m.) *Wootton Courtenay* (Hotel); while the narrow and winding road s. of Cloutsham goes on to (4 m.) *Exford* (p. 209).

The long ascent of *Porlock Hill* (1 in 4; dangerous bends) can be avoided by an easier toll road to the right, which rejoins A 39 just before (33 m.) *Oare Post*. Here a by-road diverges (l.) to *Oareford* (1½ m.; see below). A little farther on we reach the summit (1378 ft) and begin a gentle descent through the woods of Culbone Hill; fine views of the sea. On the left a by-road leads s. to (1 m.) *Oare Church*, where Lorna Doone was married to John Ridd and shot by Carver Doone. At (36½ m.) *County Gate* (1059 ft) we enter Devon. Malmsmead (see below) is c. ¾ m. s. (footpath). To the right rises the *Old Barrow* (1135 ft). *Black Gate* and *White Gate* are both entrances to Glenthorne (see below).— Beyond (39 m.) *Countisbury* (866 ft; Inn) the road descends Countisbury Hill (1 in 4½; fine views). To the right diverges a path for *Sillery Sands.*— 40½ m. *Lynmouth.*

LYNTON and **LYNMOUTH** are two popular summer-resorts, with good hotels. Lynmouth lies on the shore at the point where the deep wooded valleys of the East and West Lyn converge and discharge their waters into the sea. Lynton stands on the edge of the cliff, 430 ft above. The two are united by steep roads and a cliff railway. As headquarters for excursions in the charming environs, there is little to choose between them. Lynmouth offers sea-bathing; Lynton, on the other hand, has the finer views.

Southey found Lynmouth the finest spot he ever saw "except Cintra and the Arrabida". Shelley, who spent some time at Lynmouth in 1812 after his marriage with Harriet Westbrook, in a 'myrtle-twined' cottage (rebuilt), was another enthusiastic admirer of the twin villages. In 1952 devastating floods wrought havoc on Lynmouth, with tragic loss of life.

The best general views of the two villages are obtained from *Hollerday Hill* (w. of Lynton) and *Summerhouse Hill* (850 ft), ascended by a zigzag path beginning near the parish church in Lynmouth. Near the bridges, in Lynmouth, is the entrance to *Glen Lyn* (fee), revealing the romantic cascades and fern-clad banks of the lower course of the West Lyn.

Other favourite excursions from Lynton and Lynmouth are indicated in Rte 21c. **Buses** from Lynton to *Ilfracombe* viâ Combe Martin; to *Barnstaple*; from Lynmouth to *Minehead* viâ Porlock.—**Steamers** to *Ilfracombe* and *Lundy*; to *Weston*, *Cardiff*, *Clevedon*, and *Bristol*; and to *Swansea*.—**Tennis Courts**, Lee Rd. —**Fishing Tickets** (trout, salmon) from Handicraft shop, Lydiate Lane, Lynton.

A splendid *Walk follows the coast from Lynton to Minehead (18–19 m.). We ascend to (1½ m.) *Countisbury* and then follow the cliff-path, passing the church. On nearing (2½ m.) *Foreland Point* (lighthouse) the path turns E., and we cross (3 m.) a deep combe. We then follow a rough cart-track leading towards the shore for about ¼ m. and leave it for a higher path on the right, which crosses the ridge and descends to a gate. Here we keep to the right. At (4¾ m.) the next fork we take the lower path, and follow it past numerous combes (some of them richly wooded) to (5¾ m.) a small iron gate admitting to the beautiful grounds of *Glenthorne*, through which walkers are allowed to pass.

On emerging from the grounds, we cross a small field and follow a road running towards the shore till we reach an iron railing. At the various forks, keep to the right and avoid descents. We soon reach a wooded combe, where we take the middle path. This crosses the combe at a wooden railing, and brings us to a cart-track, which ascends and crosses a small brook. The path to the right leads through woods to (9½ m.) *Culbone Church*, the smallest in England in regular use with both nave and chancel (33 ft by 12 ft).—The coast or landslip path, though rough, is now more easily traced. From (11 m.) *Porlock Weir* a road leads to (12½ m.) *Porlock* (see above). The coast walk is continued by proceeding N.E. from Porlock to (13½ m.) *Bossington*, and ascending (14½ m.) *Selworthy Beacon* (1014 ft; *View). Hence we follow the ridge road all the way to (18 m.) *Minehead*, or (by a detour of ½ m. to the left) we may descend to *Greenaleigh* and follow the coast.

To **Watersmeet and Rockford**, 4 m. Leaving Lynmouth by Tors Rd. we quickly reach the path on the right bank of the East Lyn, which here forces its way through the narrow Watersmeet Valley with sides rock-strewn or thickly wooded. Beyond (1½ m.) *Myrtleberry Tea Gardens* we either cross the wooden bridge or go along the same side to (1¾ m.) *Watersmeet* (N.T., 366 acres; tea) where the East Lyn (known above the confluence as the Brendon Water) receives the Hoar Oak Water. Our path follows the left bank of the valley, rising considerably above the stream. Passing through Nutcombe Wood, we emerge (3 m.) on the hillside, but soon re-enter the woods by a small gate (good retrospect). Various paths lead right to the *Long Pool* (with its fall). Regaining the main path, we soon reach (4 m.) a bridge by which we cross the stream to *Rockford Inn*. The road back to (3⅓ m.) Lynmouth leads w. to (¼ m.) *Brendon Church* and (1¼ m.) *Hillsford Bridge*, and thence descends (A 39) by the valley of the East Lyn. For the walk from Rockford Inn to Malmsmead, etc., see below.

To the **Doone Valley**. The shortest road route (9 m.) is viâ Countisbury, Leeford, and Malmsmead. The most attractive route for walkers (10¼ m.) is viâ Watersmeet, Leeford, and Malmsmead.—From Watersmeet to *Rockford Inn*, see above. Thence we follow the road to (5 m.) *Leeford* (Inn), where the road from Countisbury comes in on the left. Opposite (r.) is a lane leading to (6 m.) *Cross Gate* (1055 ft), whence a track leads along Tippacott Ridge to (8½ m.) the *Doone Valley*, steering s. for the first mile, then trending s.e., and finally turning almost due e. From Leeford it is more interesting to follow the road to (7 m.) *Malmsmead*, where a road from *Oare* (1 m.; see above) comes in on the left. From Malmsmead a track ascends along the w. side of the valley of the *Badgworthy Water* for about ¾ m. This is continued by a footpath which brings us to (1 m.) a side-stream (r.) identified with the *Waterslide*, up which little John Ridd struggled in the pages of Blackmore's 'Lorna Doone'. About ⅓ m. farther on, on the same side, opens the **Doone Valley** itself, the scenery of which is neither so wild nor so romantic as readers of 'Lorna Doone' may have been led to expect. The Doones (according to tradition) were a little band of outlaws who terrorized the countryside at the close of the 17C, making their headquarters in this valley until a particularly atrocious act of cruelty nerved the inhabitants to exterminate the pest. Blackmore, whose grandfather was rector of the adjoining parish of Oare, adapted the legend in his well-known novel, using a romancer's privilege to heighten the colours a little. The only trace of the Doone settlement consists of the foundations of some huts. Doone Valley is 5 m. from Simonsbath (see Rte 21c) by a rough moorland route. Good walkers, who wish to see a really wild bit of Exmoor before returning to Lynmouth, may proceed (s.e.) from the Badgworthy valley for 1½ m., turn e. for (2½ m.) the *Chalk Water*, and make their way down this stream to (6½ m.) *Oareford*, whence they follow the road downstream to Oare and (8½ m.) Malmsmead.

Coast Road to Combe Martin, 12½ m. The road (toll) passes inland of Hollerday Hill into the *_Valley of Rocks_ (walkers may take the cliff path called the *_North Walk_ to seaward of the hill). Passing *Lee Abbey* and *Lee Bay*, the road, affording exquisite views, drops steeply above (3½ m.) *_Woody Bay_ (Hotels), a tiny seaside resort enclosed by abrupt and richly wooded cliffs. A wide sweep, high above the sea (views), follows through (4½ m.) *Martinhoe*, then a steep descent to (6¾ m.) the *Hunters' Inn*, delightfully situated in the valley of the Heddon, about 1 m. above its mouth. From here a path on either side of the Heddon leads in 1½ m. to *Heddon's Mouth*, a small cliff-girt cove connected by a beautiful cliff path with Woody Bay (2 m. more). The road now winds up (*Views) above *Trentishoe* (1 m. r.), with a full view of the sea, to reach (9½ m.) a summit (989 ft) between Trentishoe Barrows (l.; 1060 ft) and Holdstone Down (r.; 1145 ft), before descending to (10¾ m.) *Stony Corner* (844 ft) where several roads meet. On the coast (r.) are the *Great Hangman* (1043 ft) and the *Little Hangman* (716 ft), the e. pillar of Combe Martin Bay. A steep hill joins A 399 at the s.e. end of (12½ m.) *Combe Martin*.

The main road ascends the East Lyn viâ Hillsford Bridge (comp. above), crosses Beggars Roost (947 ft), and drops down to (46½ m.) *Barbrook Mill* to meet the more direct exits from Lynton and Lynmouth up the charming valley of the West Lyn. By *Dean Steep* we climb again to a summit of 1013 ft at *Martinhoe Cross*.—50 m. *Parracombe* (Hotel), at the foot of a steep hill (by-pass), has a disused church with a Georgian interior.—At (52¼ m.) *Blackmoor Gate* (Hotel), we turn right on A 399.

A 39 continues to (62 m.) *Barnstaple*.—The road to the left crosses Exmoor to (8½ m.) *Simonsbath* (comp. below), passing between the *Chapman Barrows* (1574 ft) and *Shoulsbarrow Castle* (1553 ft), a prehistoric earthwork, 1½ m. n. and s. respectively of (3½ m.) *Challacombe* (Hotel).

58 m. **Combe Martin** (Hotels) straggles along the road for 1½ m. to the sea. The 15C *Church*, with an E.E. chancel, has a fine tower (99 ft high) and contains a well-sculptured effigy of 1634. The *Pack of Cards Inn*

was reputedly built by a gambler. Farther on (l.) is a road to (½ m.)
Berrynarbor, the birthplace of Bp. Jewel (1522–71), with a beautiful
Perp. tower.—59¾ m. *Watermouth* has a 19C Gothic castle and two
caves.—61¼ m. *Hele* stands beyond the charming little sandy bay of that
name.—62½ m. **Ilfracombe**, see Rte 21A.

C Exmoor and the Upper Exe

ROAD from Lynmouth, A 39, B 3223. 9 m. *Simonsbath.*—B 3224. 14 m.
Exford.—19 m. *Wheddon Cross.*—A 396, B 3222. 29¼ m. *Dulverton.*—37 m.
Bampton.

We follow A 39 up the East Lyn to (2½ m.) *Hillsford Bridge* (comp.
p. 208), turning s. on B 3223, and soon reach open moorland. The road
ascends steadily to (6 m.) *Brendon Two Gates* (1379 ft; now one gate
only), where we enter Somerset and *Exmoor Forest* proper (see above).
To the right rises *Chains Barrow* (1561 ft; 2½ m.). A little N.E. is the head
of the Doone Valley. About 1¼ m. farther on our road crosses the Exe
near its source, and soon after begins the descent (S.E.) to (9 m.)
Simonsbath (Hotel), so named from a pool in the Barle above the
bridge. A minor road goes on s.w. to (20 m.) *South Molton* (p. 203),
passing *Span Head* (1618 ft). Our road turns E.—13 m. *White Cross.*
Here the pleasant B 3223 diverges (r.) across *Winsford Hill* (1405 ft;
N.T.; 1288 acres) direct to Dulverton (9½ m.; see below), affording
access to the pretty Barle at *Withypool* (2½ m.; Hotels) and at *Tarr Steps*
(3½ m.; N.T.; Hotel), where the prehistoric clapper bridge (180 ft long)
swept away by floods in 1952 has been rebuilt.

14 m. *Exford* (Hotels) is a fishing resort on the Exe, with the kennels
of the Devon and Somerset stag-hounds. A mile farther on a by-road
(r.; shorter by 3 m.) rejoins the Exe above *Winsford* (4 m.; Hotel),
a hunting and fishing resort in charming surroundings, and the birthplace of Ernest Bevin (1881–1951). The main road continues E. to
(19 m.) *Wheddon Cross* lying between Dunkery Beacon and the Brendon
Hills. Here it joins A 396 from Dunster (p. 205), turning s. up the tributary Quarme to its confluence with the Exe a mile below Winsford at
(23½ m.) *Coppleham Cross.* A 396 now follows the lovely VALLEY OF THE
EXE nearly all the way to Exeter.

At (28 m.) *Hele Bridge* the Exeter road keeps straight on down the
river, but a pleasant route turns r. for (29¼ m.) **Dulverton** (Hotels),
another fishing resort and centre for walking in the charming Barle
valley, 5 m. below Tarr Steps.—Beyond (30½ m.) *Brushford* (Hotels),
the Barle joins the Exe, and beyond (32¼ m.) *Exebridge* we rejoin the
main road.

About half-way between Exebridge and Hele Bridge, a by-road ascends a side
valley E. to *Bury* (¾ m.) with its narrow hump-backed bridge.

Just below Exebridge we may branch left on B 3222 direct to Bampton
(3 m. shorter), or follow the river to approach it from the s.—37 m.
Bampton, and thence to *Exeter*, see Rte 21A.

22 EXETER TO PLYMOUTH
A Viâ Ashburton

Road, 43 m. (A 38).—9½ m. *Chudleigh.*—19 m. *Ashburton.*—21½ m. *Buckfast leigh.*—32 m. *Ivybridge.*—43 m. **Plymouth.** A 38 (dual-carriageway throughout) by passes all towns, which are approached individually by short surviving stretches of th old road.

Crossing the Exe Bridge, we turn sharp left, and at (1½ m.) *Alphington* the church of which has a notable font of c. 1140, leave the coast road on our left.—3½ m. *Kennford.* We join A 38 at the end of the Exeter by-pass.—At 5½ m. we bear right, ascend the steep Haldon Hill (view) and pass (l.) Haldon racecourse.—9½ m. *Chudleigh,* with the picturesque *Chudleigh Rock.*

A pleasant road ascends the Teign valley to (7½ m.) *Dunsford* (p. 223). Above the E. side of the valley are *Higher Ashton,* where the 15C *Church has fine roo and parclose screens (painted), and *Doddiscombsleigh,* noted for the wealth of 14C stained glass in its church (6 m. and 8 m. from Chudleigh respectively).

Leaving on the right roads to Bovey Tracey and Moretonhampstead (Rte 23c), and on the left to Newton Abbot and Torquay (see below) we cross the Teign and Bovey and come into view of Dartmoor. The road forms the s. boundary of the National Park through (19 m. **Ashburton** (p. 224).—We cross (20¾ m.) *Dart Bridge* and turn r. fo (½ m.) **Buckfast Abbey,** founded by Canute in 1018, refounded fo Cistercians by Stephen in 1147, and colonized by French Benedictine in 1882.

Nothing remains of the original building but a 12C undercroft and the 14C Abbot's Tower. The present cruciform church (adm. daily), modelled on Kirkstal and Fountains, with a square central tower, was built by the monks with thei own labour in 1907–38 on the old foundations. The dignified interior has a magnifi cent mosaic pavement; an altar, font, and corona modelled on German Roman esque works; and two candelabra and a plaque to Abbot Vonier (d. 1938) b Benno Elkan.—*Hembury Castle,* an Iron Age camp, lies 1 m. N.W., surrounded b woodland (374 acres, N.T.).

From Dart Bridge the road goes on to (21½ m.) *Buckfastleigh* (Hotel a small market town (2700 inhab.), once famous for woollens. The late Perp. church has good monuments.—At (23½ m.) *Dean Prior* Herrick (1591–1674) was rector in 1629–47 and again from 1662, and here he i buried (tablet and window in the church).—The road passes (25 m. *Syon Abbey,* a Bridgettine nunnery since its foundation by Henry V i 1414 (formerly at Isleworth), to reach (26½ m.) *South Brent* (r.) with Norman church tower and font. *Brent Hill* (1019 ft), 1 m. N., is a goo point of view and the romantic scenery of the *Dean Burn Valley,* 3 m N., repays a visit. For the upper Avon valley, see Rte 23c.

32 m. **Ivybridge,** a well-situated village, derives its name from the 13C bridge over the Erme. It is convenient for excursions on S. Dartmoor

Pleasant walks may be taken in the beautiful *Ivybridge Woods* and to (2 m. *Hanger Down,* (1½ m.) *Western Beacon* (1088 ft), or (2 m.) *Harford Bridge.* Fro *Harford Church* (Perp.) a fine moorland walk leads along the right bank of th Erme to (3 m.) the *Stall Moor Circle.* Higher up the valley are some good example of hut circles.—The road from Ivybridge to (8 m.) *Shaugh Prior* (Rte 23B) leads t (3 m.) *Cornwood* and thence N.W., viâ (5 m.) *Tolch Moor Gate,* with the fine height of *Pen Beacon* (1407 ft) and *Shell Top* (1546 ft) on the right.—To *Two Bridges* ove the moor, see p. 226.

38 m. *Plympton* (Hotel, 4 m. N.E.), a 'Stannary' town (p. 223), is th

birthplace of Sir Joshua Reynolds (1723–92), with the old grammar school (1664) attended by him and his brother-artists Haydon (1786–1846) and Northcote (1746–1831); the church of St Mary is noteworthy. Saltram lies 2 m. w. (p. 220). Crossing the Plym we leave A 38 (Plymouth by-pass) on the right.—43 m. **Plymouth,** see Rte 22c.

B Viâ the Coast Road

Road, 70½ m. (A 379).—13 m. *Dawlish.*—16 m. *Teignmouth.*—24 m. **Torquay.** —27 m. **Paignton.**—35 m. **Dartmouth.**—49½ m. *Kingsbridge.*—57¾ m. *Modbury.*— 63½ m. *Yealmpton.*—70½ m. **Plymouth.**—The direct road to Torquay (22½ m.) runs viâ Newton Abbot.

Railway to Kingswear, 34¾ m., B.R. to Paignton; Dart Valley Line (summer only) to Kingswear. Principal stations: To (20 m.) *Newton Abbot*, see Rte 22c.—25¾ m. **Torquay.**—28 m. **Paignton.**— 31 m. *Churston*, for *Brixham* (2 m.).— 34¾ m. **Kingswear** (ferry to *Dartmouth*, 10 min.).

Taking A 38 we diverge l. at (1½ m.) *Alphington.*—At (7¾ m.) *Kenton* the church (1360) has a wonderful rood-screen (c. 1480; loft partly modern). On the left in a large deer park is *Powderham Castle* (adm. June–late-Sept, Sun–Thurs 2–5.30, also Sun, Easter–Oct; fee), the seat of the Earl of Devon. Largely 18C in appearance, with fine plaster decoration of 1739–69, it retains a tower built c. 1390–1400 by Sir Philip Courtenay, ancestor of the present owner.—From (9 m.) *Starcross* a ferry plies to Exmouth (see p. 166). The tower of a pumping house of Brunel's experimental 'atmospheric railway' survives here.— 13 m. **Dawlish** (Hotel is a seaside resort with 9500 inhab. laid out in 1803, sheltered by the *Haldon* range (821 ft), with the railway (successor to Brunel's 'atmospheric') skirting the beach on a viaduct. It was the birthplace of Nicholas Nickleby. Dawlish Warren, 1½ m. N.E., has a good sandy beach, and a golf course.— 16 m. **Teignmouth** (pron. 'Tinmouth'; Hotels) frequented for sea-bathing since the 18C (12,600 inhab.), with a sandy beach and a pier, is well situated at the mouth of the Teign. Andrew Patey of Exeter built the fine classical *Den Crescent* (1826), and *St Michael's* (1823), in an extravaganza of styles. Keats stayed here in 1818, correcting the proofs of 'Endymion'. Local clays are shipped from the ancient little harbour.

The walk by the *Sea Wall* (N.) to (2 m.) the curiously formed red rocks known as the *Parson and Clerk* should be taken, and also that to (2 m.) *Little Haldon* (811 ft; bus), with golf course.—A 381 ascends the Teign to (6 m.) Newton Abbot (Rte 22c), leaving on the right (2½ m.) *Bishopsteignton*, with a Perp. church (Norman doorway and 13C tympanum).

A long bridge (557 yds) crosses the estuary to *Shaldon* (Hotels), with some charming Regency houses, situated under a bold headland called the *Ness.* The hilly Torquay road skirts the cliffs above Babbacombe Bay (see below).

24 m. **TORQUAY,** administratively part of the new county borough of Torbay (108,900 inhab.), is charmingly situated on seven hills rising from the N. shore of *Tor Bay*, at the convergence of two valleys. The beauty of its position, the luxuriance of its semi-tropical vegetation, the equability of its climate, its protection against all winds except those from the genial south, and its attractive environs, have won for "la coquette ville de Torquay" (as Max O'Rell calls it) a high reputation as a health-resort and winter residence. Mrs Bröwning (before her marriage) lived in 1838–41 at Bath House, now the Regina Hotel; Dame Agatha

Christie (1890–1976) was born here; and Sean O'Casey (1880–1964) died in a Torquay nursing-home.

Many good **Hotels** near the harbour and sea-front (prices lower out of season); also at Babbacombe and St Marychurch.

Post Office, Fleet Street.

Buses from the Strand and the Station to *Babbacombe, Paignton, Newton Abbot, Brixham*; from the Strand to *Teignmouth* viâ Maidencombe and Shaldon; from Torwood St. Coach Sta. to *Exeter*; from Castle Circus and Station to *Totnes* and *Plymouth*.—COACH TOURS (Grey Cars) from Torwood St.

Motor Launches from Princess Pier to *Brixham* every ¾ hr; from Haldon Pier to the *River Dart*, and along the coast.

Bathing from numerous beaches and coves.—*Swimming and Medical Baths*, Marine Spa.

Amusements. *Pavilion, Princess Theatre*, both at the harbour; *Babbacombe Theatre* at Babbacombe Beach.—CONCERTS at the *Princess Pier Hall*, at the theatres on Sun, and at the *Marine Spa* (11 a.m.). DANCING at the *Spa Ballroom*, etc.— REGATTAS are held in August.—TENNIS COURTS in Abbey Gardens, Upton, Cary Park, and Palace Hotel (covered).—GOLF at Petitor, Preston, and Churston.

Torbay Road leads E. from the station at the s.w. end of the town, passing *Torre Abbey* (with its attractive gardens), a 17–18C house built on to the remains of a Premonstratensian abbey founded in 1196. The house is now the Art Gallery (adm. daily 10–1, 2–5.30; fee; closed in winter on Sat and Sun). Of the monastic buildings, the chapter-house doorway (c. 1200), the 14C gatehouse and the guest hall remain, also a fine tithe barn. The road ends at (c. 1 m.) the *Inner Harbour*, the N.E. side of which is skirted by the *Strand*. The *Outer Harbour*, bounded on the N. by the Princess Gardens, with the *Pavilion*, is protected on the W. side by the *Princess Pier*, and on the s.E. side by the *Haldon Pier*. Near the latter are the *Aquarium* (fee), the *Marine Spa* (with warm swimming-bath) and the *Royal Torbay Yacht Club*. The Strand is continued N.W. by Fleet St. and Union St., the main thoroughfare of the town. The characteristic terraces of Torquay were designed by Jacob Harvey and his sons John and William in 1811–53. *St John's* is a striking church (1861–71), by G. E. Street, decorated by Burne-Jones.

From the Strand, Torwood St. and Babbacombe Rd. lead N.E., passing the *Museum* (weekdays 10–5; fee), which contains remains found in Kent's Cavern, local bygones, etc. At Wellswood (c. 1 m.) we diverge to the right on Ilsham Rd. to visit *Kent's Cavern* (open 10–5 or 8; fee), a stalactite cave in which important discoveries of bones and flint implements were made.

From the cavern we make our way N. to (½ m.) Anstey's Cove, a pretty little bay, and return by the Bishop's Walk (cliff path; *View) and Marine Drive, on which is *Ilsham Manor*, part of a 15C grange of Torre Abbey. Passing below *Lincombe Gardens* we descend to (2 m.) *Meadfoot Beach*, whence we may reach (¾ m.) the harbour across the elevated *Daddy Hole Plain* (view).

Nearly 2 m. N. of the harbour, by the winding Babbacombe road or over *Warberry Hill* (448 ft), lies **Babbacombe**, a suburb of Torquay, above *Babbacombe Bay*, notable for its lovely colouring. A good view of the coast is obtained from Babbacombe Down. Near a miniature *Model Village* (fee), a cliff railway (summer only) descends to Babbacombe and Oddicombe Beaches. Beyond Babbacombe is *St Marychurch*, where the old parish church, retaining a 12C font, has been well restored after bomb damage in 1943. From *Petitor* (golf course) a fine walk leads along the cliffs to (1¼ m.) *Watcombe*, with its *Giant Rock*, and to (2 m.) *Maidencombe*, going on to (3 m.) *Labrador*, and Shaldon.

Among the points of interest W. of Torquay are (1 m.) *Cockington*, with its Perp. church, 16–17C manor house, old forge, and thatched cottages; *Marldon* (3 m.), in the Perp. church of which are monuments of the Gilberts of Compton, one of whom (Sir Humphrey) was half-brother of Sir Walter Raleigh and coloniser of Newfoundland (1583); and (4 m.) *Compton Castle* (N.T.), a fortified house of the 14–16C (restored). The courtyard, great hall, chapel, and kitchen are shown April–Oct, Mon, Wed & Thurs 10–12, 2–5 (fee).

Almost continuous with Torquay is (27 m.) **Paignton** (Hotels), a residential seaside resort in the middle of Tor Bay, with fine sands, a small harbour, and a pier. The *Church* has a Norman doorway, the Kirkham chantry (c. 1526) with a fine *Screen, and an old stone pulpit. The 14C Coverdale Tower is a fragment of a palace of the bishops of Exeter and has no association with Miles Coverdale; near by is the 15C *Kirkham House* (adm. April–Sept, weekdays 9.30–5.30 or 7; Sun from 2.30; fee). Beautiful grounds surround the Municipal Offices. *Oldway Mansion*, now the Civic Centre, was built by Paris Singer, son of the American sewing machine millionaire. The famous *Zoo* and *Botanical Gardens* (adm. daily; fee) are on the Totnes Road. To the s. are *Goodrington Sands.* — 30½ m. *Churston Ferrers* (Hotels), with an 18-hole golf course. The E. window of the church was a gift of Agatha Christie.

Brixham (Hotels), 1½ m. E., is a fishing port with an attractive harbour long noted for its trawlers and a busy fish-market. William of Orange landed here in 1688, an event recalled by a statue and by the preservation of the stone on which he stepped from his boat (at the pier). The Rev. H. F. Lyte (d. 1847), who wrote 'Abide with me' at Berry Head House, is commemorated by the bells of *All Saints*. Off Mount Pleasant Rd. are prehistoric caves with stalactites and stalagmites (floodlit).

From (34½ m.) *Kingswear* (Hotel), we cross the Dart by ferry to **Dartmouth** (Hotels), the 'Dertëmouthe' of Chaucer's Prologue, a beautifully situated and ancient port on a safe and land-locked *Estuary (regatta in Aug), from which embarked Crusaders, in 1147 and 1190, and American troops in 1944. Thomas Newcomen (1663–1729), inventor of the atmospheric steam engine, was born here, and is commemorated by one of his engines (1725; altered 1821) re-erected by the Newcomen Society in 1964. The church of *St Saviour*, altered c. 1630, has a handsome rood-screen (15C), a carved stone pulpit, and a gallery of 1633 bearing the arms of the merchant families. A brass (1408) to John Hawley (probably Chaucer's 'Schipman') and the ironwork on the s. door are noteworthy. The fine *Butterwalk* (1635–40; restored) with carved overhangs, includes a small museum (adm. weekdays; fee). At Bayard's Cove are ruins of a castle of 1537; and at the mouth of the harbour are *St Petroc's Church* (Norman font) and *Dartmouth Castle*, begun in 1481 (fee), opposite *Kingswear Castle* (1491–1502). On Mount Boone, to the N., is the *Royal Naval College*, by Aston Webb.

The favourite trip ascends the river *Dart* to (10 m.) *Totnes* (steamer in summer in 1½ hr.). Opposite (3 m.) *Dittisham* (right bank) is *Greenway*, the birthplace of Sir Humphrey Gilbert (1539?–83); car ferry in summer. In the stream, visible at low water, is the *Anchor Rock*, on which (according to tradition) Sir Walter Raleigh used to smoke his pipe. Beyond (6 m.) *Stoke Gabriel* (left bank; Hotel) we skirt the hanging woods of *Sharpham* (right bank). The landing-place at Totnes is short of the bridge and c. 1 m. from the station.

Beyond Dartmouth A 379 climbs steeply, passes (36¾ m.) *Stoke Fleming* (Hotel) with its conspicuous church, and reaches the shore at *Blackpool* (good bathing).—39 m. *Strete*. The road follows a strip of shingle separating the sea from *Slapton Ley*, a narrow freshwater lagoon 2 m. long (Nature Reserve). It is divided by the road to *Slapton* (with the scant remains of a chantry; 13.72), which starts beside an obelisk erected by the U.S. Army (see p. 144)—At (42½ m.) *Torcross* (Hotel) the road turns abruptly inland.

From Torcross good walkers may follow the coast (fine cliff scenery) to (4 m.) *Start Point* (lighthouse and radio station), *Prawle Point* (9 m.), and (14½ m.) *Portlemouth* (ferry to Salcombe, fee). From Chillington *Portlemouth* may be reached also by road (c. 8 m.) viâ (4 m.) *South Pool*, a charming village, or (4 m.) *Chivelstone*, both of which have interesting churches.

49½ m. **Kingsbridge** (Hotels), at the head of the land-locked *Kingsbridge Estuary*, is a busy little market town, with the colonnaded Shambles (1585; upper story added in 1796). The church has a good monument by Flaxman.

Salcombe (Hotels), 6½ m. s., is a delightful holiday resort amid charming scenery, with luxuriant vegetation. Once a notable ship-building port, it is now a fine sailing centre. J. A. Froude (see below) is buried in the churchyard. A fine walk leads viâ (2 m.) *Bolt Head* to (8 m.) *Bolt Tail* and *Hope Cove* (Hotels), a little bathing resort. This magnificent stretch of *Coast belongs to the N.T.—About 4 m. w. of Kingsbridge is **Thurlestone** (Hotels), a bathing and golfing resort, with the Old Rectory Garden (adm. April–Oct daily).

At (53½ m.) *Aveton Gifford*, where the fine church was almost destroyed in the Second World War, the Plymouth road crosses the Avon.— 57¾ m. *Modbury* (Hotel) is a severe little town with steep streets and slate-hung houses.

Off *Bigbury-on-Sea* (Hotels), 5 m. s. at the mouth of the Avon, is the tidal *Burgh Island* with a restaurant.

At 59 m. we cross the Erme. The churches of *Ermington* (1 m. N.) and *Holbeton* (1½ m. s.) have similar twisted spires and good screens.— 63½ m. *Yealmpton* (pron. 'Yampton'), at the head of the Yealm estuary.

A thatched cottage here claims to be that of 'Mother Hubbard,' said to have been housekeeper at *Kitley*, where her story was rhymed (1805) by Sarah Martin, the squire's sister-in-law.

By bus, or preferably by boat, we may descend the Yealm to (4 m.) *Newton Ferrers* (Hotels), an attractively situated village. The coastal scenery, to the s., with the ruined church of *Revelstoke*, is magnificent.

70½ m. **Plymouth**, entered by Laira Bridge, see Rte 22c.

C Viâ Newton Abbot and Totnes

ROAD, 48½ m. A 380.— 16 m. *Newton Abbot* (by-pass).—A 381. 24½ m. *Totnes.*— A 385. 32 m. junction with A 38; thence to **Plymouth**, see Rte 22A.
RAILWAY, 52 m., in 1¼–1½ hrs. Principal Stations: 12 m. *Dawlish.*— 15 m. *Teignmouth.*— 20 m. **Newton Abbot**, junction for **Torquay**, etc. (Rte 22B).—28¾ m. **Totnes.**— 52 m. *Plymouth.*

From Exeter we follow A 38 for 5½ m., then bear left and ascend Telegraph Hill (763 ft; 1 in 7).— 16 m. **Newton Abbot** (Hotels), a railway centre (19,400 inhab.), is pleasantly situated near the confluence of the Teign and the Lemon. Near the station, on the Torquay road, is *Ford House* (1610; fee), visited by Charles I (1625) and by William of Orange (1688), and in the centre of the town is *St Leonard's Tower* (14–15C) where William is said to have been proclaimed king. To the w. is *Bradley Manor* (15C; N.T.; adm. Wed in summer 2–5), with a Perp.

chapel, and 2 m. N.W. is the *Seale Hayne Agricultural College. Sandford
Orleigh* was the home of Sir Samuel Baker (1821–93), the African explorer.

B 3195 leads E. to Shaldon viâ (3 m.) *Combeinteignhead*, in pleasant country.—
The church at *Haccombe* (E.E.; c. 1240), 3 m. E.S.E., has interesting effigies and
brasses (15–17C) of the Carew family. *Lindridge Mansion*, 4 m. N.E., a late-17C
house with fine grounds incl. a swimming pool, is open occasionally.—A 382
which ascends the Teign valley, affords an approach to Dartmoor from the Torbay
coast, past Newton Abbot golf course to (6 m.) *Bovey Tracey* and (12½ m.)
Moretonhampstead (see p. 225).

A 380 continues to Torquay. We take A 381 s. to (19 m.; r.) *Ipplepen*,
with a 15C church. At *Torbryan*, with Church House Inn (1500), 1 m. W.,
the *Church contains a screen of c. 1430 and old glass.—22½ m. *Little
Hempston* (r.) has a 14C parsonage (now a farmhouse), enclosing a square
court and containing a fine hall.

24½ m. **Totnes** (Hotels), one of the oldest boroughs in England
(5800 inhab.), lies on the side of a hill. It consists mainly of one long
congested *Street with many old houses with interesting interiors, which
leads from Bridgetown across the Dart and up to the keep of the Norman *Castle* (adm. daily, Sun from 2; fee). A walk round the upper
circular story affords a good *View. The *Church* of 1432–60, has a
noble red tower, a coloured and gilt stone *Rood Screen, formerly
ascended by a unique stone staircase on the N. side, good parclose
screens, and a stone pulpit. To the N. is the quaint pillared *Guildhall*
(16–17C). The Butterwalk drops down the hill towards the *East Gate*
(rebuilt c. 1500); by the Dart is a monument to W. J. Wills (1834–61),
one of the first explorers to cross Australia. Parts of the 12C *Town Hall*
survive near the East Gate. Salmon and trout fishing is good (permits
from the Dart Angling Assoc., Totnes).

About 2½ m. E. is **Berry Pomeroy Castle**, a picturesque ruin, dating largely from
the 16C, with some 14C remains (great gateway).—J. A. Froude (1818–94) was
born at *Dartington*, 2 m. N. of Totnes. *Dartington Hall* is a restored 14C manor-
house. The estate is now a trust, with agricultural and other commercial enter-
prises. Here, too, are a well-known school, a College of Arts, and an Adult
Education centre. The fine grounds include terraces overlooking the old tiltyard,
on one of which is a statue by Henry Moore. Parties may view the hall and some
of the departments on written application to the Public Relations Office.
From Totnes by-roads ascend the pretty valley of the Dart to (9½ m.) *Ashburton*
viâ (3¼ m.) *Staverton*, noted for its picturesque bridge, and (7 m.) *Buckfastleigh*.
Steamer to *Dartmouth*, see p. 213.—The fine *Dart Valley Railway* from Totnes to
Buckfastleigh (station at Staverton, for Dartington Hall) is owned privately and
has a steam train service.

At (30 m.) *Avonwick* we cross the Avon and 1½ m. farther on we join
A 38. Thence to (48¼ m.) *Plymouth*, see Rte 22A.

PLYMOUTH, one of the chief seaports of England, stands in a
dramatic position at the mouths of the Plym and Tamar and at the head
of Plymouth Sound, a splendid natural haven hemmed in with islands
and promontories. The contiguous **Stonehouse** and **Devonport**, the
naval quarter since 1691, were combined with Plymouth in 1914, and
the 'Three Towns' became a city in 1928. The joint population is 239,300
(incl. the garrison). It is a fortress of the first rank and as an arsenal
it is second to Portsmouth alone. Its port carries on a large foreign
and coasting trade, mainly in china-clay.

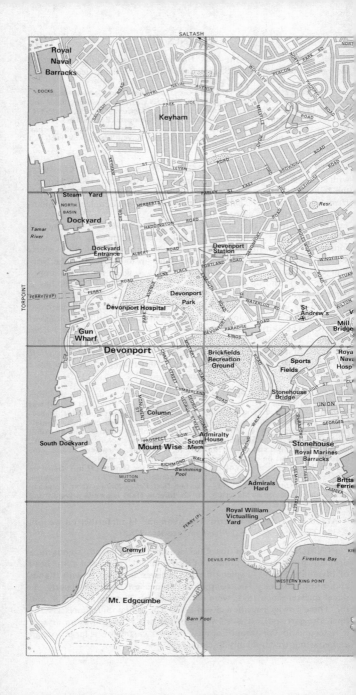

TAVISTOCK & EXETER

Plymouth

0 _____ 800 yards
0 _____ 800 metres

N

3
Football Ground
Skate Park
VENN LANE
FLORA
BARN PARK ROAD
HIDE PARK ROAD
GLENDOWER ROAD

4
COMPTON AVENUE
MANNAMEAD ROAD
SEYMOUR ROAD
ELM ROAD

Mayflower Sports Centre
Swimming Bath
Central Park
Cemetery

7
DELA WAY AVENUE
WHITTINGTON STREET
CENTRAL PARK AVENUE
FORD
DALE ROAD
ROAD
SEATON AV.
LIPSON
ALEXANDRA ROAD
BELGRAVE ROAD

8
GREENBANK ROAD
CLIFTON PLACE
General Hospitals
TOTHILL ROAD

Plymouth Station
NORTH ROAD

PLYMOUTH
PORTLAND SQ.
NORTH CROSS
SALTASH RD.

Polytechnic
Library Museum Art Gallery
EBRINGTON
DRAKE CIRCUS
TAVISTOCK

R.C. Church
NGHAM STREET
NORTH

Beaumont Park
BEAUMONT ROAD

11
APPROACH
MAYFLOWER
CORNWALL STREET
NEW GEORGE STREET
Pannier Market
ARMADA WAY
WESTERN APPROACH

Charles Ch (ruins)
EXETER STREET
GPO
Bus Sta
NEW QUAY

PO
Civic Centre
DERRY'S CROSS
ROYAL PARADE
ST ANDREWS CROSS
Guildhall
Law Courts
St Andrew's

12
Custom House
SUTTON POOL
GASCDOWN ROAD
DARTMOUTH

ILLBAY ROAD
CRESCENT
CITADEL ROAD
Rec Ground

NOTTE STREET
NEW ST.
BABBICAN
THE BARBICAN

Hoe Park
THE PROMENADE
The Hoe
CLIFF RD.
GRAND PARADE
CITADEL ROAD
LAMBHAY ST

Citadel

Phoenix Wharf

Tower
Marine Lab
Royal Yacht Club
WEST HOE PIER
GT WESTERN RD.
MADEIRA RD.

HOE RD.
Swimming Pool

Deadmans Bay
FISHERS NOSE
FERRY (P)
BEAR'S HEAD
Cattewater

15
YMOUTH SOUND

DRAKE'S ISLAND

14
MOUNT BATTEN BREAKWATER
Mount Batten
Clovelly Bay

Railway Station. *North Road* (Pl. 7).

Hotels on and near the Hoe, and in Millbay Rd.—YOUTH HOSTEL at *Stoke*.

Post Office (Pl. 11), Tavistock Rd.—INFORMATION BUREAU, in the Civic Centre.

Bus Station (Pl. 12) in Union St. for all country services; suburban services start from the City Centre.

Ferries. For cars: from Ferry Rd. (Pl. 5) to *Torpoint* (every ¼ hr.).—For passengers: from *Admiral's Hard* (Pl. 10) every ½ hr. to *Cremyll* (Mt. Edgcumbe; bus in connection to *Cawsand*); from *Phœnix Wharf* (Pl. 12) to *Turnchapel* (every ½ hr.) and *Oreston* (4 times daily).—MOTOR LAUNCHES from the *Barbican* (Pl. 12) to *Cawsand* and to *Bovisand* and *Drake's Island*, and from the Barbican or Phœnix Wharf round the warships and dockyard.

Steamers in summer from the Phœnix Wharf to *Looe, Fowey, Salcome, Dodman Point*, etc.

Amusements. *Athenæum Theatre, Hoe Theatre* (revue, etc.). TENNIS, PUTTING, and BOWLS on the Hoe, in Central Park, etc.—BATHING in swimming-pools beneath the Hoe (Pl. 15) and at Mount Wise (Pl. 9).—BOATS for hire at W. Hoe Pier.

History. Plymouth, known to Domesday Book as Sutton, received its charter and its present name in 1439, was fortified soon after, and has ever since played an important part in the maritime history of England. Catherine of Aragon landed here in 1501. The town supplied seven ships to fight the Armada (1588), and in Plymouth Sound the English fleet awaited the arrival of the Spaniards. It was the starting-point of many of the expeditions of Drake, Humphrey Gilbert, Cook, and Hawkins (a native of the town), and was the last port touched by the Pilgrim Fathers on their way to America (comp. p. 124); and here, standing on the 'Mayflower' slab (see below), the mayor welcomed, in June 1919, the crew of the American seaplane NC 4, the first aircraft to cross the Atlantic (viâ the Azores). In the Civil War Plymouth sided with the Parliamentarians, and was the only town in s.w. England to escape capture by the Royalists. In 1913, at the Wesleyan Methodist Conference at Plymouth, the suggestion was first made that resulted in the union of the three Methodist Churches in 1932. Capt. R. F. Scott (1868–1912), the Antarctic explorer, born at Devonport, is commemorated by monuments on Mount Wise and in St Mark's church, Ford (Keyham), where he served as a choir-boy. In 1941 the city was severely damaged from air attacks, and the new city centre has been thoughtfully re-built. A tablet beneath the great bridge at the old Saltash Ferry commemorates the embarkation of U.S. troops on 'D' Day, 1944.

From St Andrew's Cross, where Exeter St. meets Old Town St. (from Tavistock), ROYAL PARADE, the main thoroughfare of the new city centre, runs w. to Derry's Cross (see below). Half-way along, where the broad ARMADA WAY cuts a swathe s. to the Hoe, stands a flagstaff based on a bronze representation of Drake's drum. The restored *Guildhall* (Pl. 11), to the E., built in 1870–74 and reopened in 1959, has a hall 148 ft long with historical windows by F. H. Coventry and a huge but incongruous Gobelins tapestry representing the Miraculous Draught of Fishes. Opposite, across the Great Square with ornamental pools, rises the lofty *Civic Centre* (1962) with a restaurant and belvedere on the 14th floor (lift; *View). Armada Way leads between the Council house and the *Law Courts* (1963; with a striking entrance-panel by P. Fourmaintreaux) to the Hoe. Farther N. is the colourful *Pannier Market* (1960), with an aluminium-covered roof.

The *Hoe (Pl. 11) is a fine elevated esplanade with extensive lawns overlooking the Sound, on which Drake is said to have been playing bowls when the Spanish Armada hove in sight. Here stand the unsatisfactory *Armada Tercentenary Memorial* (1890), the *Naval War Memorial* (comp. p. 47), a statue of *Sir Francis Drake* (1884; a replica of that at Tavistock), and *Smeaton's Tower* (adm. in summer), the upper part of the third Eddystone Lighthouse (comp. below). The striking view from the Hoe (best from Smeaton's Tower) extends in clear weather to the Eddystone, 14 m. s. To the E., below the walls of the Citadel, are the *Marine Biological Laboratory*, with an aquarium (open weekdays; fee), and, near by, the *Royal Marine War Memorial*.

The *Citadel* (Pl. 12), erected in 1666, with a fine gateway and a statue of George II in Roman costume, is occupied by the military; the ramparts and chapel may be seen (12–6) on application to the guard commander. To the N. lies the old quarter of Plymouth and Sutton Pool with the quay known as the *Barbican* (Pl. 12), where the trawlers land their fish. The sailing hence of the 'Mayflower' in 1620 is commemorated on the pier by a stone slab, an arch, and an inscription. Another slab refers to 'NC 4' (see above). Among the ancient buildings near by may be noted the remains of the gatehouse of the 14C *Castle* (foot of Lambhay St.) and the *Old Custom House* (Pl. 12; 1586). In New St., off the Barbican, is an Elizabethan house (adm. weekdays 10–1, 2.15–6 or dusk, also Sun in summer 3–5). In Southside St. the refectory (c. 1425) survives of a Dominican monastery (visitors welcome; apply at distillery). The Pilgrim Fathers gathered here before their voyage, and in 1672 it became the meeting place of the Plymouth Nonconformists. We continue viâ Notte St. and St Andrew's St., to **St Andrew's** (Pl. 11), the mother church of Plymouth, a 15C structure with a good tower.

The nave, burned by enemy action in 1941, was reconsecrated in 1957, with a w. window by John Piper and Patrick Reyntiens. The head, by Chantrey, of Zachariah Mudge (d. 1769) survived the fire. The entrails of Sir Martin Frobisher (d. 1594) and of Admiral Blake (1599–1657) are interred in or near the chancel, and here was baptized Wm. Bligh of the 'Bounty'. Behind St Andrew's is *Prysten House*, a late 15C monastic hostel with a galleried courtyard. The doorway leading to the cemetery has been restored as a 'Door of Unity' and a memorial to two American officers killed in the war of 1812–13. To the N.E. Exeter St., carried over the *Bus Station* (Pl. 12) by a viaduct, leads to the 17C *Charles Church*, retained as a ruin.

In Drake Circus (Pl. 8) are the *Public Library* (1956) and *Museum & Art Gallery* (daily 10–6, Sun 3–5), noted for relics of Reynolds, Old Master drawings, Plymouth and Bristol porcelain, the first Eddystone Lighthouse modelled in silver as a table salt, and the silver gilt Drake Cup (by Gessner of Zürich, 1571), presented to Drake by Elizabeth I after his circumnavigation. Here also are Scott's skis and Epstein's bronze 'Deirdre'. The best items from the Clarendon Collection of portraits are at Buckland Abbey (p. 224; administered by the curator).

Beyond the *Railway Station* (Pl. 7) extends the large *Central Park*, where are the Football Ground and *Mayflower Sports Centre* (indoor Swimming Pool).

Devonport (Pl. 4) lies w. and N. of Stonehouse Creek and is easily reached by bus. From *Derry's Cross*, named from a Clock Tower (1862) to the s.w., Union St. traverses STONEHOUSE, on the s. promontory of which stands the *Royal William Victualling Yard* (Pl. 14; no adm.; best seen from Mount Wise), an immense establishment, 13 acres in extent, laid out by Rennie in 1826–35 and containing everything necessary for the commissariat of the navy; the gate is surmounted by a colossal statue of William IV. Near *Admiral's Hard* (Pl. 10) are the *Royal Marine Barracks* (begun 1784). Beyond Stonehouse Bridge rises (l.) *Mount Wise* (Pl. 9), where stand the official residences of the General in Command

and the Port Admiral, and the Scott Monument (1925; view to Stone-house and Mt. Edgcumbe). Richmond Walk, below, leads to *Mutton Cove*.

The *Devonport Column*, adjoining the former *Guildhall* (Pl. 9; 1821–23), commemorates the change of name from 'Plymouth Dock' to Devonport (1824); both are by John Foulston, a local architect. Since 1960 much of the old centre has been lost to the S. dockyard. The *Sailors' Rest*, with accommodation for 1000 men, was founded by Agnes Weston (d. 1918).

The DOCKYARD (Pl. 5; adm. by Albert Road gate, Mon–Thurs at 10, 11, 2, & 3, Fri 10 & 11; British subjects only) covers 300 acres and fronts on the *Hamoaze*, or estuary of the Tamar, which is reserved as a harbour for vessels of war, including Nuclear Fleet submarines. The S. dockyard and the *Gun Wharf* (Pl. 5), built by Vanbrugh (1718–25), are connected with the *Keyham Steam Yard* (Pl. 5; the part shown) by railway tunnel. Here the largest vessels can be refitted.

The return may be made across *Devonport Park*. St Andrew's, *Stoke Damerel* (Pl. 6), the mother church of Devonport, was enlarged in 1750, with ships' masts as roof-piers. Here was baptized John Macarthur (1767–1834), the 'father of New South Wales'. Immediately opposite, Devonport High and Tamar Secondary Schools occupy the former *Station Hospital* (1797). We leave Victoria Park and North Road (see above) on the left. The *Royal Naval Hospital* (Pl. 10) dates from c. 1762. In Wyndham St. is the *Roman Catholic Cathedral* (Pl. 7), a 19C Gothic building with a lofty spire.

The granite *Breakwater* (1812–41), 1 m. long, protecting the entrance of Plymouth Sound may be visited (2¼ m.) by small boat, passing *St Nicholas* or *Drake's Island* (Pl. 15; N.T.; boat trips June–Aug, Tues, Wed, & Thurs 11–6), where John Lambert, Cromwell's general, was confined from 1664 till his death in 1683. The island is now an Adventure Training Centre.

The *Eddystone Lighthouse*, 14¼ m. S. (135 ft high), was built by Sir James Douglas in 1878–82; its light (two flashes every ¼ min.) is visible for 17 m. Of its predecessors, the first built by Winstanley in 1696–99, was swept away by a storm in 1703; the second, of wood, by Rudyerd (1706–8), was destroyed by fire in 1755, and the third, Smeaton's lighthouse of 1759 (94 ft high), was removed in 1882 owing to the action of the sea on the reef supporting it.

On the Cornish peninsula opposite Stonehouse (ferry, see p. 218) is *Mount Edgcumbe* (Pl. 13), the seat of the Earl of Mount Edgcumbe. The 16C mansion (May–Sept, Mon & Tues 2–6; fee), gutted in 1941, was restored by A. Gilbert Scott in 1960. The finely wooded park, commanding beautiful views, is open daily. From Cremyll a bus climbs to (2½ m.) the twin fishing villages of *Kingsand* and *Cawsand* (Hotels). A fine cliff walk goes on thence viâ Penlee Point to *Rame Head* (2½ m.), with the Chapel of St Michael (15C).

Saltram (N.T.; adm. April–Oct daily 11–12.30, 2–5.15; fee; teas), 3½ m. E. of Plymouth, is the largest house in Devon. Rebuilt after 1750 by John Parker (d. 1768), ancestor of the Earls of Morley, and richly decorated, it contains a saloon and a dining-room by Robert Adam (1768) with ceilings by Zucchi, furniture and china, and 14 portraits by Sir Joshua Reynolds, a frequent visitor (special bus on Wed, Sat, and BH in summer, to the house). The kitchen remains in full working order. The riverside amphitheatre (c. 1750) is to be used as a summer open-air theatre.

The attractive excursion up the *Tamar* to (19 m.) *Weir Head* takes c. 5½ hrs by boat from Phœnix Wharf. Steering through the *Hamoaze* between Devonport (r.) and Torpoint (l.) we leave the mouth of the Lynher (p. 227) on the left, and enter the Tamar proper, the boundary between Devon and Cornwall. We pass under the *Royal Albert Bridge* of the railway (built by Isambard Kingdom Brunel in 1859; nearly ¼ m. long, 100 ft clearance) and then the *Tamar Suspension Bridge* (p. 227). At the W. or Cornish end of these lies (4 m.) *Saltash*. Above the bridges the river expands into a lake ¾ m. wide, with the Tavy estuary to the right and Great Mis Tor visible in the distance to the N. At *Landulph* (l.) is the tomb of Theodore Palæologus (d. 1636), a descendant of the Byzantine emperors. On the same side, round the next bend, is *Pentillie Castle*, with its charming grounds.—14 m. *Calstock*, see p. 223. The river makes a wide loop (3 m.) to the right to (17 m.) *Morwellham Quay*, about 1 m. short of the *Morwell Rocks* (r.; 300 ft). At

(19 m.) *Weir Head* we are within 4 m. of Tavistock (Rte 23A; to the N.E.). The fine scenery higher up is accessible by small boat only.—For *Antony House* beyond the Tamar, see Rte 24.

Among the pleasant bays to the S.E. are *Bovisand*, reached by water (p. 218), *Heybrook* and *Wembury* (bus from Plymouth), where the 15C church (with 17C Hele and Calmady tombs) overlooks the *Great Mew Stone*. The Hele almshouses date from 1682, and the coast W. to *Warren Point*, on the Yealm estuary, is N.T. land.

From Plymouth to *Truro* and *Penzance*, see Rte 24; to *Princetown* (Dartmoor), see Rte 23B.

23 DARTMOOR

DARTMOOR is broken granite table-land in Devonshire rather over 300 sq. m. in extent, measuring 23 m. from N. to S., and 10–12 m. from E. to W. The mean elevation is about 1200 ft, but some of the hills are over 1800 ft high and two of them exceed 2000 ft. The masses of granite known as 'Tors', which crown many of the hills, are characteristic features. The streams are many, bright, and rapid, with numerous pools and 'stickles', and afford good trout fishing. Cattle and sheep are pastured on Dartmoor during summer, and the semi-wild Dartmoor ponies roam over it all the year round. The central portion (about 50,000 acres) forms what was anciently the royal 'Forest of Dartmoor,' and is an appanage of the Duchy of Cornwall. Henry III gave it to his brother Richard, and it then became a 'chase' (comp. p. 135), though it is still always referred to by its ancient title. The air on Dartmoor is pure and bracing, the scenery wild and romantic, and its antiquities include the rude stone remains of a Bronze Age population, traces of 7C Saxon immigration, vestiges of the 'tinners', and stone crosses indicating the way to former religious houses on its borders. The area is now a National Park; information offices at Two Bridges Hotel (April–Sept), and County Hall, Exeter.

Two main roads, intersecting at Two Bridges, cross the moor; one leading from Tavistock to Ashburton, and the other from Plymouth to Moretonhampstead. It is to the N. and S. of the district through which these roads run that the wilder parts of Dartmoor are situated. Walkers are advised to carry a good map and compass; to refrain from attempting to cross swampy spots (beware of bright green grass); to make for a valley if overtaken by a mist; and to remember that recent heavy rain is apt to make the streams impassable. Most of the N. section is used as an artillery range; the boundaries are indicated by red and white posts. For information on access restrictions, apply to HQ Devon & Cornwall, Crownhill Fort, Plymouth (Tel. 72312); or Southern Command Battle Camp, Okehampton (Tel. 244).—H.M.S.O. publish a useful handbook on the National Park.

A From Exeter to Tavistock viâ Okehampton

ROAD, 38½ m. (A 30 & A 386).

A 30 runs W.—8 m. *Tedburn St Mary* (Hotel).—Beyond (11 m.) *Cheriton Bishop* (r.), with a good font and woodwork in its church, we follow the N. boundary of the National Park.—At (13 m.) *Crockernwell*, a by-road (l.) leads viâ Drewsteignton to *Castle Drogo* (2 m.; N.T.), a fortified mansion designed by Lutyens in 1910–30 for Julius Drewe in his ancestral parish. Built in local granite in a Tudor style recalling college architecture, it is elegantly massed above the Teign. The comfortably grand interior is lit by huge windows.—A 382 from Moretonhampstead (Rte 23c) joins from the left at (16½ m.) *Whiddon Down.*—18½ m. *South Zeal*, a former copper-mining village with a 16C inn, lies beneath *Cosdon* or *Causand Beacon* (1799 ft; view). *South Tawton*, 1 m. N., one of John Wesley's regular preaching stations, has a 15C granite church beside a 16C church-house.—At (19½ m.) *Sticklepath* an old forge on the Taw houses a Museum of Rural Industry. An attractive by-road ascends the valley for

1¾ m. to *Belstone* (Hotel), 3¼ m. from Okehampton, with fine tors and river scenery.

22½ m. **Okehampton** (Hotel) stands at the confluence of the East and West Okement, and is a good centre for exploring North Dartmoor when the military danger-zone is accessible (inquire at Post Office). The *Castle*, in a fine position on the river to the s., has some late-Norman work in the keep (adm. daily, Sun from 2; fee). The *Pine Valley Wildlife Park* is 2½ m. N.

Yes Tor (2028 ft; *View) and *High Willhays* (2039 ft; highest point on Dartmoor), c. 4 m. s., may be ascended in 2–3 hrs. A red flag on Yes Tor indicates danger from artillery practice.—From Meldon Viaduct, 2½ m. s.w. of Okehampton, a pleasant walk ascends the w. Okement to (2 m.) the *Island of Rocks*, just above which is a fine cascade. Only the E. side of the river is in the military zone.—*Cranmere Pool* (3 m. s., in the military zone) is now drained and simply a boggy hollow. It lies 1½ m. beyond the end of the Row Tor road (to the left, 1 m. s. of the station).

FROM OKEHAMPTON TO CHAGFORD, 11 m. Diverging on the right from the Exeter road beyond (3 m.) *Sticklepath*, we round the base of Cosdon Beacon (see above). —6¼ m. *Throwleigh* is a remote parish with a fine 15–16C church and ancient farmhouses. Beyond the many hut-circles on the moor above, is a spectacular stone-circle, with a diameter of 80 to 90 ft.—From (7½ m.) *Moortown* we go on s. to (8½ m.) *Gidleigh* (p. 225) and (11 m.) *Chagford*.

FROM OKEHAMPTON TO BARNSTAPLE, 29 m. B 3217 descends the w. Okement valley to (12 m.) *Dowland*, where the little church has an early-16C oaken arcade.— 13½ m. *Dolton* church contains a strange font made up of two blocks of a 10C cross. We ascend to cross the Exeter–Torrington road.—20½ m. *High Bickington* is notable for the *Bench-ends in its part-Norman church.—Beyond (22½ m.) *Atherington* (p. 166) we join the main Barnstaple road.—An alternative route (A 386; 32 m.) runs viâ Hatherleigh, Merton, and Torrington (p. 243).

The remote but lovely 14C church at *Bratton Clovelly* lies 7½ m. w. of Okehampton, off the Holsworthy road.—From Okehampton to *Launceston*, etc., see Rte 25.

At 25½ m. we leave on the right the main road to Cornwall, and continue s. on A 386.—31 m. *Dartmoor Inn*. About 1½ m. s.w. is **Lydford** (Hotel), now a mere village, but an important town, with a mint, in Saxon times and preserving a ruined Norman *Keep* (1195), built as the 'Stannary' prison (see below). Here the Forest Courts were believed to act in accordance with the maxim "first hang and draw, and then hear the cause, is Lydford Law". In the 16C the town imprisoned their M.P. Richard Strode for introducing an unpopular bill. This incident led to the establishment of Parliamentary Privilege. From *Lydford Gorge* (N.T.; 37 acres; adm. daily April–Oct; fee), a steep walk leads to the spectacular *Cascade* (90 ft high; reached also from the former Lydford Station road).

To reach *Tavy Cleave, a deep rocky valley on Dartmoor, with bold tors on its w. side, we follow a green path leading E. across the common behind the Dartmoor Inn. We cross the Lyd (2¼ m.; beware danger signals) by stepping-stones and proceed E. to (3 m.) *Doe Tor* and s.E. to (3¼ m.) *Hare Tor*, whence we descend s.E. to (4¼ m.) the Cleave.—Another pleasant walk, crossing the Lyd ½ m. N.E. of the Dartmoor Inn (stepping-stones), ascends to (1 m.) *Brat Tor*, which is in full view from the stream. This walk may be extended to (1 m. N.E.) *Great Links Tor* (1924 ft). From Lydford to *Merrivale* viâ Peter Tavy, see Rte 23C.

To the right of (35 m.) *Mary Tavy* (Hotel and Restaurant) rises Brent Tor (see below) and just short of Tavistock is *Kelly College*, a boys' school founded in 1877.

38½ m. **TAVISTOCK** (Hotels), a grey-stone market town on the Tavy, offers excellent headquarters for the exploration of w. Dartmoor. Of its Benedictine *Abbey* (founded 981) the chief remains amid the

Victorian gothic benefactions of the 7th Duke of Bedford are the main gatehouse (restored), a fragment of the cloister (in the churchyard), the infirmary hall (now the Unitarian chapel), and the Still Tower(by the river) and west gateway. The last is in the vicarage garden, in which also are three inscribed stones (? 6C), one with ogams. The church of *St Eustachius* (15C) contains the fine monument of Sir John Glanville (d. 1600).

Tavistock, the centre of a once important mining district (tin, copper, and manganese), Chagford, Ashburton, and Plympton were the four 'Stannary' towns appointed by charter of Edward I for the weighing and stamping of tin and the holding of monthly mining courts. The title of Lord Warden of the Stannaries is still· borne by the chief member of the Duke of Cornwall's Council.—A canal, once used for ore transport, leads to the edge of the Tamar gorge (4 m.), 240 ft above *Morwellham Quay* (p. 220). The barges were hauled up by a winch driven by a water-wheel.

About ½ m. s., on the Yelverton road, is a statue (by Boehm) of Sir Francis Drake (1542–96), who was born at *Crowndale*, ½ m. farther down the Tavy (house pulled down; tablet on near-by farmhouse).—The conical *Brent Tor* (1100 ft; view), with its 13C chapel of St Michael, is 4 m. N. of Tavistock. *Peter Tavy* is 2¼ m. N.E.

The road from Tavistock to *Liskeard* (A 390; 18½ m.) crosses the Tamar by the medieval New Bridge to (4½ m.) *Gunnislake*. *Calstock*, 2¼ m. s., has a graceful railway viaduct. The noble church of *Bere Ferrers* lies c. 3½ m. farther s., across the Tamar. *Cotehele House*, c. 2 m. s. of Gunnislake viâ *Albaston* (bus from Tavistock), is a finely preserved medieval mansion of 1435–1539 (N.T.; adm. April–Oct daily, exc. Mon 11–12.30, 2–5.30; rfmts; fee) still equipped with its 17–18C tapestries and furniture lent by Lord Mount Edgcumbe. Notable features are the original chapel with a clock of 1489 and the Bronze Age horns in the Great Hall.—Passing *Kit Hill* (1094 ft; r.), we reach (10 m.) *Callington*, with a noble church.—18½ m. Liskeard, see p. 227.

B   From Exeter to Plymouth viâ Princetown

ROAD, 40½ m. (A 30, B 3212, A 386).

We follow A 30 for over 1 m. from the Exe Bridge and then ascend left on B 3212. Farther on a descent leads into the attractive upper valley of the Teign, with the pretty village of (6 m.; r.) *Dunsford*. We enter the National Park, and cross the river at (6¾ m.) *Steps Bridge*. —12 m. **Moretonhampstead** (Rte 23c). We cross the Bovey before (15 m.) *Beetor Cross* (p. 225). One mile farther on the road climbs the shoulder of *Shapley Common* (l.; 1075 ft; viewpoint).

A track leads s. to (1½ m.) *Grimspound*, a good example of a Bronze Age walled settlement. A wide wall encloses an area of 4 acres with the remains of 24 huts. Outside the pound the old field pattern can be traced. Across the valley (½ m. due w.) is the *Challacombe Stone Row*, three rows leading up to a menhir (also approached from Warren House Inn).

The road passes between tors with hut circles, stone rows, and disused mines; footpaths from (18 m.) *Warren House Inn*.—20 m. *Postbridge*, with an admirable example of a 'clapper', or rude stone, bridge over the E. Dart.

The valley abounds in prehistoric remains, reached only by foot. *Broadun Ring* and *Pound* are c. 1 m. N. (w. bank of river), while the *Grey Wethers*, the two largest Bronze Age stone rings on the Moor, are across the valley, 2 m. farther N.— For the footpaths from *Chagford*, see p. 225.

We cross the Torquay–Tavistock road at (24 m.) *Two Bridges* (p. 226). —25½ m. (r.) **Princetown** (1409 ft) owes its existence to the *Prison* opened in 1809 at the instigation of Sir Thomas Tyrwhitt, Lord Warden of the Stannaries, for French and (after 1813) American prisoners of war, the total number at one period being over 9000. The church was built and fitted up by the prisoners (1814), and a memorial window (1910) and gateway (1928) commemorate the 218 Americans who died on the Moor. In 1850 the building was reopened as *Dartmoor Convict Prison*, and in a mutiny in 1932 a part of the buildings was burned down. Some of the adjacent moorland was brought under cultivation by convict 'hard labour' before this was abolished.— 30 m. *Dousland* (Hotel) is ½ m. s. of *Walkhampton*, with its 16C church-house and conspicuous church tower. *Yannadon Down* (r.) commands a view with a particularly fine grouping of the tors around Burrator reservoir (see below).

31½ m. **Yelverton** (Hotels) lies on the edge of *Roborough Down* (golf links), and is now a dormitory suburb for Plymouth.

A lane near the Rock Hotel leads E.S.E. to (1½ m.) *Meavy*, with an old village cross and an oak 25 ft in girth. Hence we proceed E. to (2½ m.) *Sheepstor*, with its 15C priest's house, the tomb of Sir James Brooke, Rajah of Sarawak (d. 1868), and his nephew (d. 1917), and an ancient bull-ring. In the s. side of the tor (845 ft) that gives name to the village is the '*Pixies' Cave*'. About 2 m. S.E. are the *Drizzlecombe Antiquities* (see p. 226). To the N.W. of Sheepstor is the beautiful *Burrator Reservoir* (150 acres), the largest in Devon, which we leave to the right. At the w. end of the dam we turn to the left and follow the road past *Yennadon Down* to (4¾ m.) *Dousland* (see above).

*Buckland Abbey (N.T.; adm. Easter–Sept daily 11–6, Sun 2–6; winter, Wed, Sat, Sun 3–5; fee), c. 2½ m. w., founded by the Cistercians in 1278, was most probably the birthplace of Sir Richard Grenville (1542–91) and was purchased in 1581 by Sir Francis Drake. Remains of the original buildings include the tithe barn and the church tower, which is incorporated in the present house. This is now a Drake, Naval, and West Country museum. Among Elizabethan portraits from the Clarendon Collection is one of Sir John Hawkins, by Zuccari. About 1 m. N. is the village of *Buckland Monachorum*, with the Garden House (adm. to garden, Wed 3–7, April–Sept; fee), and a fine Perp. church with a monument to Lord Heathfield, d. 1790, the defender of Gibraltar.

We continue s. on A 386.—At (35½ m.) *Roborough*, a road (l.) leads to *Bickleigh* (1½ m.).

To the N.E. (c. 1½ m.) is *Shaugh Bridge*, at the junction of the Meavy and the Plym, below which is the wooded *Bickleigh Vale*, normally accessible to walkers as far as *Plym Bridge* (c. 4 m.). Above Shaugh Bridge is the fine cliff on the Plym known as the *Dewerstone* and about 1 m. S.E. lies *Shaugh Prior*. Thence to Ivybridge (8 m.) see p. 210.

36½ m. *Plymouth Airport.*—At (38 m.) *Crownhill*, we cross A 374. On the right is *Manadon House* (1680), now occupied by the *Royal Naval Engineering College.*—40½ m. **Plymouth.**

C From Torquay to Tavistock

ROAD, 40½ m. (A 380, A 383, A 38, A 384).

From Torquay we take A 380 to (6 m.) *Newton Abbot* (p. 215), and there continue on A 383 which joins A 38 (Rte 22c) before (12½ m.) **Ashburton** (Hotels). A 'Stannary' town (comp. p. 223; 3500 inhab.), with many old houses and a fine 14–15C church, it is a good starting-point for the moor E. of the Dart.

The lovely woods of *Holne Chase* are open to the guests of Holne Chase Hotel.— A pleasant short round from Ashburton (c. 9 m.) skirts the Chase. We follow the Tavistock road N.W. for c. ¾ m., then take the r. branch at the fork.—2½ m. *Ausewell Cross*; keep left.—At 4 m. we reach *Buckland-in-the-Moor* (E.E. church, with Perp. screen and Norman font), at the foot of *Buckland Beacon* (1282 ft; view). We then descend (l.) to (4½ m.) *Buckland Bridge*, where the *Webburn* joins the Dart, ½ m. above the crag called the *Lovers' Leap*. Hence we follow the road to the s.w., with the Dart on our left, to (5½ m.) the *New Bridge*. Crossing this we proceed E. (r. for Holne village, p. 226) to (6¾ m.) *Holne Bridge*, 2 m. from Ashburton.

FROM ASHBURTON TO CHAGFORD AND BACK, 37½ m.—We ascend to the right off the Tavistock road for (2 m.) *Ausewell Cross*, there keeping to the right past *Buckland Beacon* (1281 ft; view to the w.) for (4¾ m.) *Hemsworthy Gate*, with *Rippon Tor* (1563 ft), studded with cairns, on the right.—Leaving the double-headed *Hay Tor* (1490 ft; good view) on the left, where the tracks of a Granite Railway opened in 1820 and operated by horses can still be seen, we reach (5¼ m.) **Haytor** (Hotels). The 14–15C parish church is at *Ilsington*, 1½ m. S.E., and 1½ m. s. is *Bagtor*, birthplace of John Ford (1586–1640?), the dramatist.—The descent passes Yarner Wood (l.), on the left beyond which (6½ m.) is the road to *Becka Falls* (3 m.) and *Manaton* (4 m.), a delightful village near Lustleigh Cleave (see below).—10 m. **Bovey Tracey** (Hotels), affords good headquarters for excursions in S.E. Dartmoor and the lower Teign Valley (E.). The Perp. church, dedicated to St Thomas Becket, contains a remarkable coloured stone screen and pulpit.

John Cann's Rocks, 1 m. N.W., and *Bottor Rock*, 1½ m. N.E., are two good points of view.

From Bovey Tracey we go N.W. by the main road (A 382), and turn left for (13½ m.) **Lustleigh**, with its interesting church and famous *Cleave*, a moorland valley over 1 m. w.

On the first tor reached along the path to the Cleave is a rocking-stone known as the *Nutcrackers*, about 1 m. w. by N. of which is *Little Silver*, a thatched cottage in a charming nook, whence a path leads up through the wood to (¾ m.) *Manaton* (see above).—Steep moorland tracks can be followed N.W. to Moretonhampstead.

Returning to A 382, we follow the valley to (17 m.) **Moretonhampstead** (Hotels), a pleasant little town, with a colonnaded almshouse (1637), a starting-point for the moorlands near the Teign. *North Bovey* (Hotel, with golf course, 1 m. N.W.), 1¾ m. S.W., is a lovely village above the Bovey, with an oak-shaded green. For the Exeter–Tavistock road, see Rte 23A.—At (20 m.) *Easton*, we turn l. for (21½ m.) **Chagford** (many Hotels), an old 'Stannary' town (comp. p. 223) of quiet charm, and a good starting-point for excursions on N. or E. Dartmoor.

WALKS. A pleasant round may be taken viâ *Teigncombe*, 2½ m. w., to (4 m.) the stone remains near *Kes Tor* (1433 ft), and thence N. to (5 m.) the *Scorhill Circle* and *Wallabrook Clapper*, and back viâ (6 m. N.E.) *Gidleigh*, with a fortified mansion of c. 1300.—A steep by-road leads to *Batworthy*, 3 m. w., the nearest point to *Shovel Down* (½ m. farther), with five stone rows. The walk may be continued s.s.w., keeping to the w. of *Fernworthy Forest*, viâ the Grey Wethers (p. 173) to *Postbridge* on B 3212 (Rte 23B).—Other points of interest are (3 m. N.E.) *Cranbrook Castle* (an Iron Age fort) and (4 m.) *Fingle Bridge*; the Drewsteignton Dolmen, c. 2½ m. N., and *Castle Drogo* (p. 221).

We turn S. over Meldon Hill to cross the Moretonhampstead–Two Bridges road at (24 m.) *Beetor Cross*, and continue s. on B 3344.—At 26 m. we turn r., leaving on the l. a road to N. Bovey (1½ m.; see above), and, passing some fine tors, reach (29 m.) **Widecombe-in-the-Moor** (Hotel), a beautifully situated village (crowded in the summer season) associated with the song 'Widdicombe Fair'. Its 14–16C church with a tower 120 ft high, is known as the 'Cathedral of Dartmoor'; the church-house (N.T.) dates from the 15C. The fair is still held on 2nd Tues in Sept.—We cross the Webburn and return (E.) to (31 m.) *Hemsworthy Gate*, and thence S. to (37½ m.) *Ashburton.*

We leave Ashburton by A 384 and cross the Dart on the medieval *Holne Bridge* and (16 m.) *New Bridge*, skirting the edge of Holne Chase (see above).—19½ m. **Dartmeet*, where the E. and W. Dart unite, is 1¼ m. N.E. of *Hexworthy* (Hotel), a fine view-point.

FROM HEXWORTHY TO SOUTH BRENT, partly on foot. We follow the road S.E. above the right bank of the Dart to (4 m.) *Holne*, a picturesque village, the birthplace of Charles Kingsley (1819–75), 2¼ m. from Holne Bridge, beyond the *Moor Gate*, and 4 m. by road from Buckfastleigh (see Rte 22A). Walkers, however, proceed S.W. across the common to (5½ m.) the *Mardle*. We cross the stream and strike S. to (6 m.) *Pupers Hill* and (7½ m.) *Hickaton Hill*, with its fine pounds and hut circles. To the S. of the hill, crossing the Abbot's Way (see below), flows the Avon (here dammed to form a small reservoir), which we take as our guide to (9½ m.) **Shipley Bridge*. Hence a lane descends the valley to (12 m.) *South Brent*, on A 38 (Rte 22A).

23½ m. **Two Bridges** (Hotel), at the crossing of the two main roads across the moor, lies just below the confluence of the West Dart and the Cowsic. The Cowsic valley is particularly charming, and a Lich Way may be followed from Lydford Tor (2½ m. up the valley) to Peter Tavy (c. 6 m. W.; see below). On the Dart, 1¾ m. N., is *Wistman's Wood*, one of the few old groves of stunted oaks that still linger on the Moor. About ¾ m. N.E. is *Crockern Tor* (1391 ft), where the 'Tinners' Parliament' was attended until 1730 by representatives of the four original 'Stannary' towns.

Another excursion may be made from *Tor Royal*, 1½ m. S.W., to *Nun's Cross*, 3½ m. S., thought to have been used as a boundary mark for the Forest of Dartmoor in 1204 (mentioned in 1240), and bearing the inscriptions 'Siward' and 'Boc Lond'. Good walkers may proceed by (4½ m.) an old mine on *Harter Tors*, to (5¼ m.) the *Drizzlecombe Antiquities*, on the Plym, which include two fine menhirs, and thence W. to (7 m.) *Sheepstor* (see p. 224).

From Nun's Cross an old track, known as Abbot's Way, running first S.E. and thence S.W., leads to (1¼ m.) a ford on the Plym. The path on the other side is ill-defined, but a S.E. course will bring us to (2½ m.) *Erme Head* (c. 1530 ft), with its mining remains. Descending the left bank of the Erme, we reach (3½ m.) a stream coming from some clay-works. Crossing this and keeping S.E., we reach the old railway track, which we follow S. to (6 m.) the slope of *Three Barrows* (1522 ft; view) and (8 m.) a point c. ¾ m. E. of Harford church. About ¼ m. farther on we descend S.S.W. to a gate, from which a lane leads in the same direction to (10 m.) *Ivybridge* (p. 210).

From Two Bridges to *Princetown* and *Plymouth*, see Rte 23B.

At (25½ m.) *Rendlestone* we join a road from Princetown.—27½ m. *Merrivale* (Hotel), on the Walkham. Above the E. bank of the stream are many hut-circles, a menhir, and two double stone rows.

An easy walk to Lydford (9 m.) leaves the Tavistock road c. 1 m. W. at a point where a water-course runs under the road. We strike N.N.W. over the common for (2 m.) *Cox Tor* (1452 ft; view). A lane on the N. side of the hill on which the tor stands leads to (2¾ m.) a farmhouse whence a path runs W. to (3¼ m.) **Peter Tavy Combe*, with its charming cascades. About ½ m. from the lower end of the combe is the village of *Peter Tavy*, from the church of which a lane runs N. to (4¾ m.) *Mary Tavy*. Beyond this village we follow the road N. through Blackdown for c. 1¼ m., and then take a rough track to the left, which crosses the shoulder of *Gibbet Hill* (1159 ft) to (7½ m.) a gate near the old Lydford station. Here we turn (r.) into a road running N.E. to (9 m.) *Lydford.*

Beyond Merrivale Bridge conspicuous tors rise on either hand before the final descent to (40½ m.) **Tavistock** (p. 222).

24 PLYMOUTH TO PENZANCE

ROAD, 79 m. A 38. 4 m. *Tamar Suspension Bridge.*—16½ m. **Liskeard** (by-pass).—
A 390. 27½ m. *Lostwithiel.*—35½ m. *St Austell* (by-pass).—49 m. **Truro.**—A 39, A 394.
66 m. *Helston.*—79 m. **Penzance.**—RAILWAY, see Rte 25.

AN ALTERNATIVE ROUTE (A 374; 19 m.) crosses the Hamoaze from Devonport
by floating bridge (car toll) to (3¼ m.) *Torpoint*, in Cornwall.— 5 m. *Antony House*
(1711–21; N.T.; open April–Oct, Tues, Wed, Thurs, & BH, 2–6; fee) contains
original panelling and furniture.—8½ m. *Sheviock*, with a 13C church (Courtenay
monuments), is 1 m. N.E. of *Portwrinkle* (Hotel), with golf course and a long sandy
beach, extending E. ro Rame Head.—11 m. *Polbathic.*
Here the road on the right leads in 1 m. to *St Germans*, where the striking church,
with two W. towers and a deep-set Norman *Porch, served as the cathedral of
Cornwall until c. 1049. Adjoining is the mansion of *Port Eliot* (1802–29). To the
W. are the picturesque 17C Moyle Almshouses.—About 3 m. S.W. of Polbathic is
Downderry (Hotels), a seaside resort, with good bathing and a large holiday camp.
Leaving on our left, at 12 m., the direct road to Looe (7 m.; see below), we join
A 38 5½ m. short of Liskeard.

From the centre A 388 runs N.W. to (4 m.) *St Budeaux*, there joining
A 38 (which now by-passes Plymouth on the N.). The church (1563)
of this large suburb (on A 38) saw the marriage of Sir Francis Drake
(1569) and contains the tomb of Sir Ferdinando Gorges (d. 1647), first
governor of Maine. The old village lay 1¼ m. N. on the creek leading to
Tamerton Foliot, still with attractive waterside scenery.—We ascend to
cross the Tamar, alongside the Royal Albert Bridge (p. 220), by the
*TAMAR SUSPENSION BRIDGE (1959–61; toll), by Mott, Hay, and
Anderson, with towers 250 ft high. It replaces the ferry to *Saltash* (l.),
an old borough (9900 inhab.) beneath the railway bridge, now by-
passed by the main road. *Trematon Castle*, with 13C keep and gatehouse,
lies 1½ m. S.W., and *Ince Castle* (c. 1550), 2½ m. farther on, overlooks the
beautifully wooded Lynher.—A 38 crosses the Lynher and the Tiddy,
and at 10 and 11 m. is joined by roads from St Germans and Polbathic
(comp. above).

16½ m. **Liskeard** (Hotel s. of town), a market town (5300 inhab.)
with a large Perp. church and a spacious square, once returned Gibbon
to Parliament (1774), and, with Lostwithiel, Truro, and Helston, is
one of the four 'Stannary' towns of Cornwall (comp. p. 223).

About 2½ m. N. on the s. edge of Bodmin Moor lies *St Cleer* (fine view), with its
holy well and inscribed *Doniert Stone* (9C). Near by are the striking *Trethevy
Quoit* (1 m. E.), the three imperfect stone circles known as the *Hurlers* (2 m. N. of
the Trethevy Quoit), and the *Cheesewring*, a singular pile of weathered granite slabs
about 30 ft. high (½ m. farther on).—The fine 15C church of *St Neot*, about 5 m.
N.W. of Liskeard, has a good series of stained-glass windows (1400–1532; partly
restored). *Dozmary Pool* is about 4 m. N.

FROM LISKEARD TO LOOE AND POLPERRO, 13½ m. B 3254 descends the Looe
River.—3 m. *St Keyne's Well* was the subject of a humorous ballad by Southey.—
4½ m. *Duloe*, with a 13C church and a stone circle.—9 m. **Looe** (Good Hotels),
a historic little port and former haunt of smugglers, is a popular seaside resort
(4100 inhab) on both banks of its river. It is a centre of shark fishing.—13½ m.
Polperro (small Hotels), farther w., a quaint and popular fishing-village in a narrow
ravine, was another nest of smugglers. Hence a road leads w. to (10½ m.) *Bodinnick
Ferry* opposite Fowey (see below).—A hilly road goes N.W., viâ (c. 6 m.) *Lanreath*
(Hotel), with good stalls in its church, and (8½ m.; r.) *Boconnoc*, where Chatham
spent his boyhood, to (11 m.) Lostwithiel.
From Liskeard to *Tavistock*, see Rte. 23A.

From (19½ m.) *Dobwalls* we bear left off the Bodmin road and cross
the Fowey at (27½ m.) **Lostwithiel** (Motel; Hotel), the 13C capital of
Cornwall, once represented in Parliament by Addison. The *Church*

has a striking spire, a fine E. window and *Font. The medieval *Fowey Bridge* and *Stannary Court*, and the *Guildhall* of 1740 are of interest. *Restormel Castle*, high above the river, 1 m. N., was reconstructed c. 1300 by either Richard, earl of Cornwall (Henry III's brother) or his son Edmund.

About 2 m. beyond Lostwithiel B 3269 turns S. for (5¼ m.) **Fowey** (pron. 'Foy'; Hotels), a quaint and characteristically Cornish little seaport at the mouth of the lovely estuary of the Fowey. It is the 'Troy Town' of Sir A. Quiller-Couch (1863–1944), who resided here at 'The Haven'. It was once one of the foremost seaports of the kingdom, and the achievements of the 'Gallants of Fowey' rank with those of the 'Sea-Dogs of Devon'. Its harbour admits vessels of 12,000 tons, and china-clay is exported; oysters are also bred here. Many old and picturesque houses survive. The 13–15C church of *St Finnbarus* has a rich tower, Norman font, good monuments, and a waggon roof. Above is *Place*, the ancestral mansion of the Treffrys. *St Catherine's Fort* (Henry VIII) is now in ruins. Ferries cross the river to *Polruan* and to *Bodinnick* (toll; Hotel). The boating is good and safe; a pleasant boat-trip may be made to (1½ m. S.) *Pridmouth*, just inland of which is *Menabilly*, with a 'grotto' and an inscribed stone (6–7C.; from Castle Dore) at the E. gate. From Bodinnick ferry walkers should ascend to the *Hall Walk* (N.T.; *View; memorials to 'Q' and to the Second World War). Thence they may continue along the river to Pont, then s. to *Lanteglos* (old church), returning to Fowey viâ Polruan (3½ m. in all). Many acres of the cliffs between Polruan and Polperro are protected by the N.T.—*Castle Dore*, a gorse-clad mound 2½ m. along the Lostwithiel road, is believed to be the palace of King Mark, while *Golant*, with its old church (notable woodwork) on the river to the E., was the scene of the romance of Tristram and Iseult. Here *Penquite House*, birthplace of J. W. Peard ('Garibaldi's Englishman'), is a field study centre of the Y.H.A.

At (31½ m.) *St Blazey* we approach the rather dreary china-clay country. To the N., however, is the wooded *Luxulyan Valley*, rich in ferns and spanned by the lofty Treffry Viaduct (c. 1830) with its aqueduct still in use under disused railway track. Just to the S. is *Par*, a china-clay and granite shipping port, the railway junction for Newquay, and beyond it is the golfing resort of *Carlyon Bay* (Hotels).—35½ m. **St Austell** (Hotels), the centre of the kaolin or china-clay industry, the refuse heaps of which mar the adjoining district, has a church with a good Perp. tower embellished with statues and a Norman font. *Duporth Bay*, 1¾ m. S.E., has a hotel and holiday camp.

B 273 runs S. to (5½ m.) *Mevagissey* (Hotels), an attractive fishing port of cottages and a fine harbour; the church has a 17C monument with an amusing epitaph. A by-road continues to (8 m.) *Gorran Haven*, pretty and unspoilt, and *Dodman Point* (the 'Dead Man's Rock' of 'Q'), a lovely gorse-covered promontory (400 ft; N.T.).

FROM ST AUSTELL TO ST MAWES, 18 m. Following the Truro road for 3 m., we then turn l. on B 3287 and on A 3078. Lanes on the left lead to (11½ m.) *Portloe* (Hotel) and to (12 m.) *Veryan* (Hotel) with its early 19C 'round houses'. Between them on the coast is *Nare Head* (N.T.).—11½ m. *Ruan High Lanes*.—At (14 m.) *Trewithian* the left hand road leads to (18 m.) *St Anthony-in-Roseland*, with an attractive 12–13C church, viâ (15½ m.) the seaside village of *Portscatho* (Hotels) connected by bus with *Percuil*, for the Falmouth ferry. The right branch goes on viâ (16¼ m.) *St Just-in-Roseland*, with a lovely churchyard set in a cove off the Fal estuary, to (18½ m.) *St Mawes* (Hotels; ferry to St Anthony and Percuil; to Falmouth, see p. 230), a fashionable resort, with one of Henry VIII's coast castles (adm. daily, Sun in winter from 2), opposite Pendennis (fine view).

The road on the right at Ruan High Lanes affords a pleasant alternative route to Falmouth (14¼ m.), passing Polsue Manor Hotel and (2½ m.) *Philleigh*. We cross the Fal estuary by (4½ m.) *King Harry Ferry* (cars; toll). On the w. bank is *Trelissick* with its wooded grounds and flowering shrubs (N.T.; adm. March–Oct, 11–6, Sun from 2), beyond which a lane leads l. to the pretty village of *Feock* (1½ m.) and the Friends' Meeting House (1709) in the form of a thatched cottage at *Come-to-Good*.—At 7¼ m. we join A 39 c. 4 m. S. of Truro. Thence to Falmouth, see below.

41 m. *Grampound*, on the Fal, with its wide and dignified street, was once notorious as a 'rotten borough'. It was John Hampden's first parliamentary seat (1621).—43½ m. *Probus* has a beautiful late Perp. church-tower (123½ ft). On the left is *Trewithen* (adm. on Thurs, May–Sept, 2–4.30; fee), a mansion of c. 1715 by Thos. Edwards.

49 m. **TRURO** (Hotels; good Restaurants), a market town (14,800 inhab.) and the seat of a bishop, lies on the Truro River, a branch of the

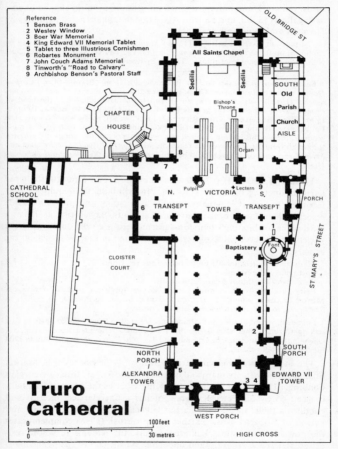

Reference
1 Benson Brass
2 Wesley Window
3 Boer War Memorial
4 King Edward VII Memorial Tablet
5 Tablet to three Illustrious Cornishmen
6 Robartes Monument
7 John Couch Adams Memorial
8 Tinworth's "Road to Calvary"
9 Archbishop Benson's Pastoral Staff

OLD BRIDGE ST

All Saints Chapel

CHAPTER HOUSE

Sedilia   Sedilia

SOUTH
Old
Parish
Church
AISLE

Bishop's
Throne

Organ

CATHEDRAL
SCHOOL

8
7
N.   Pulpit   VICTORIA   ✝Lectern   9
6   TRANSEPT   TOWER   TRANSEPT   S.

PORCH

ST MARY'S STREET

CLOISTER
COURT

Baptistery

1
Font

2

NORTH
PORCH
/
ALEXANDRA
TOWER

5

3 4

SOUTH
PORCH

EDWARD VII
TOWER

**Truro
Cathedral**

0   100 feet
0   30 metres

WEST PORCH

HIGH CROSS

Fal. Its prosperity in the 18–19C is attested by the Georgian terraces in Boscawen St. and Lemon St. and by fine houses in Prince's St. and Trafalgar Row. When the see of Cornwall, after eight centuries of union with that of Devon, was reconstituted in 1876, Truro was chosen as the cathedral city. The **Cathedral**, a most effective E.E. structure by J. L. Pearson, was built in 1880–1910 on the site of the Perp. church

(16C) of St Mary, the s. aisle of which survives as an additional s. aisle to the choir. The satisfactory interior contains several monuments from St Mary's Church, a lofty carved reredos, and a memorial to 'Q'. The circular *Baptistery* is a memorial of Henry Martyn (1781–1812), the missionary, a native of Truro. The *Chapter House* was completed in 1967. Samuel Foote (1720–77) was also born here. The *Museum and Art Gallery* (10–4 or 5, weekdays), in River St., contains Cornish birds, minerals, and antiquities, including an ingot of tin shaped like an astragalus (158 lb.), and an Iron Age wooden tankard; also paintings by Hogarth and Opie and drawings.

The pleasant riverside drive to (1¾ m.) *Malpas* (pron. 'Mopus'; ferry) may be continued on foot to (2½ m.) *St Clement*, with a 13C church, s. of which is a stone with Latin and Ogam inscriptions. Thence by lane to (4 m.) Truro.

FROM TRURO TO FALMOUTH. BY ROAD (A 39), 11 m. Beyond (4 m.) *Carnon Downs* we cross Restronguet Creek and ascend a side valley to (5 m.) *Perranarworthal* (Hotel).—8¼ m. *Penryn*, an ancient town (5100 inhab.) at the head of *Penryn Creek*, is built of the granite for which it is famous.—BY RIVER, 10 m. in 1¼ hr. The boat descends Truro River to (1¾ m.) *Malpas*, below which it enters the Fal proper. To the left is *Tregothnan* (Viscount Falmouth), with its charming grounds. Below this is *King Harry Reach*, with a ferry and the woods of *Trelissick* (l.; see above). Farther down we reach the wide *Carrick Roads*. Restronguet and *Mylor Creeks* are on the right, and beyond *Trefusis Point* the boat enters *Falmouth Harbour*.

11 m. **FALMOUTH** (17,900 inhab.) overlooks its beautiful sheltered harbour opening off Carrick Roads. It maintains well-equipped port facilities, though it is equally notable as a sunny and popular seaside resort. Three sandy beaches are on Falmouth Bay, facing s. It is an ideal place for boating excursions, the numerous creeks offering a great variety of scenery; while oysters are cultivated in several places on the estuary.

Many good Hotels, mostly on or behind the sea front.
Post Office, The Moor.
Buses from The Moor to all destinations.
Ferry (weekdays only in winter) to *St Mawes*; to *Percuil* and *St Anthony*.—MOTOR BOATS in summer to *Helford* and *Port Navas*; to *Portloe*; to *Mylor*; to *St Mawes*; to *St Just-in-Roseland*; and to *Truro*.

Falmouth served as the chief Atlantic packet station from 1689 to 1840, at first serving Corunna and, after 1702, the West Indies. The road from Exeter, viâ Okehampton, Launceston, St Columb, and Truro to Falmouth was devised in 1704 for the Falmouth mails.

The most interesting part of the town is by the harbour; in Market St. and Church St. are many old houses and the Royal Hotel, a Georgian building. The church, dedicated to King Charles the Martyr, was built in 1662–65 by Sir Peter Killigrew; it has a fine classical interior and contains a tablet to the 14th Earl of Glencairn (d. 1791), the friend and patron of Robert Burns. Farther on an obelisk (1738) commemorates the powerful but extinct Killigrew family, the remains of whose residence, *Arwenack House*, stand opposite. At the end of the peninsula is **Pendennis Castle** (200 ft; view; fee; closed Sun morning in winter), built by Henry VIII and taken by the Parliamentarians in 1645 after a five months' siege. A beautiful road leads round the promontory. The *Custom House* is one of several early-19C buildings in the Doric style; near it is the 'King's Pipe', the chimney used for burning contraband tobacco.

The ferry to *St Mawes* (see above) affords access to the charming peninsula of Roseland; motorists must go round by the ferry over King Harry Reach (see above).—The lovely subtropical gardens of *Penjerrick*, 3 m. s.w. of Falmouth, are open to visitors occasionally. The boat trip to Flushing (ferry from Prince of Wales pier) may be recommended. *Mylor* church (1½ m. N.) has Norman details, a good screen, and the tallest cross in Cornwall.

The ROAD to the Lizard passes (6½ m.) *Constantine*, a charming village; (9 m.) *Gweek*, at the head of *Helford River* (in which oyster-farming is carried on); and (10½ m.) *Mawgan*, with a Perp. church. Near the last is *Trelowarren Park*, the beautifully wooded estate of the Vyvyans.—Good walkers will find the COAST ROUTE to the Lizard (c. 23 m.) very interesting; a bus runs viâ (2½ m.) *Maenporth* (Hotels) and (4 m.) *Mawnan Smith* (Hotel), whence a fine walk may be taken to *Rosemullion Head* (N.T.), and (4½ m.) the subtropical *Glendurgan Gardens* (N.T.; adm. Mon, Wed, 10.30–4.30, April–Sept, Fri also April–May; fee) to (5½ m.) *Helford Passage* (Hotel and golf course), where the estuary is ferried to Helford (p. 233).

From Truro we follow the Falmouth road and after 6½ m. diverge to the right on A 394.—66 m. **Helston** (Hotels) is a lively and attractive little town (9800 inhab.), once one of the Duchy's 'Stannary Towns' as the name of Coinagehall St. suggests, pleasantly situated above the Looe valley. It is connected by bus with Camborne and Redruth. The church of 1756–62 is by Thos. Edwards. On 8 May large crowds are annually attracted hither to see the 'Furry Dance', in which couples, moving to a tune probably as old as the fête itself, solemnly dance along the streets and through the houses and gardens. About 1½ m. s. are the beautiful grounds of *Penrose* (open weekdays 8–8; walkers only), on the bank of *Loe Pool* (which disputes with Dozmary the possession of Excalibur), and 1 m. farther on is *Loe Bar*, formed of stones thrown up by the sea.

Godolphin House (adm. 2–5 on Thurs, June–Sept; Tues also in Aug–Sept; fee), a 16–17C mansion with a fine colonnaded range of 1635, lies 5 m. N.W. viâ Breage.

The strenuous coast walk to Penzance (17½ m.) leads viâ (2½–3 m.) *Porthleven*, a quaint village with a considerable harbour, (5 m.) *Trewavas Head*, (6½ m.) *Praa Sands* (Hotels), a fine bathing beach, near the ruined *Pengersick Castle*, (10½ m.) *Cudden Point*, and (14 m.) *Marazion*. On the E. side of Cudden Point is *Prussia Cove*, once a haunt of smugglers.

On the main road is (69½ m.) *Breage*, where the church contains late 15C mural paintings (St Christopher, etc) and a 3C Roman milestone.—75½ m. *Marazion* or *Market Jew* (Hotel), served by bus from Penzance, is important only as the starting-point for St Michael's Mount. Its names have nothing to do with 'Jews' or 'Zion', but seem connected with the old Cornish word for 'market' ('marghas').

*St Michael's Mount (c. 200 ft), a precipitous mass of granite and slate resembling a smaller Mont St Michel, is connected with the shore by a causeway (500 yds) uncovered at low tide for 3 hrs. At other times it is reached by boat from Penzance or Marazion. It is identified with the Roman *Ictis* and has been associated with Christianity possibly from the 5C (St Keyne) and certainly from the 11C (1047), when Edward the Confessor established a chapel here and placed it under the Benedictine abbey of Mont St Michel in Normandy. The Mount was presented to the Nat. Trust in 1953 and the castle still belonging to the St Aubyn family (Lord St Levan), is open to the public on Mon, Wed & Fri (fee; conducted parties at 11, 12, 2, 3, & 4 in Nov–March; 10.30–4.45 in Apr–October). The drawing room, formed from the Lady Chapel, the refectory (altered in the 17C), and armoury are among the rooms shown, as well as the 14–15C chapel (service on Sun at 11). Refreshments available.

The church of *St Hilary*, 2 m. E. of Marazion, has a Dec. spire and two inscribed stones (one 4C Roman, the other 6–7C).

Beyond Marazion station we join A 30.—79 m. **Penzance,** see Rte 25.

The Lizard

The Cornish peninsula to the s. of Helford River is now generally known as the **Lizard,** from the headland at its s. extremity. Its N. part was formerly called *Meneage.* It consists of a tableland of serpentine, 200–370 ft in height, the breezy *Goonhilly Downs* on which the Post Office radio telescope (1962) and satellite communications centre are prominent. The Cornish heath (*Erica vagans*), however, grows in profusion; but the main attraction for the tourist lies in the striking cliff-scenery and delightful beaches of the coast-line.

A frequent bus service connects Helston with (10½ m.) *Lizard Town* in c. 1 hr., viâ Poldhu and Mullion; but good walkers will prefer the coast route, either all the way (14 m.) or from Poldhu (see below; 6½ m.). Other services (not Sun) go from Helston to Ruan Minor and Kuggar; to Coverack, St Keverne, and Port-hallow; and to Manaccan and Gillan.

From *Helston* (see above) the main road runs s.e., passing 'H.M.S. Seahawk', a huge naval air station. At (2½ m.) *Dodson's Gap* the road to Coverack, etc. (see below), diverges left. The right-hand turning, c. 1¾ m. farther on, goes to Poldhu and Mullion (see below), rejoining the main road at (7 m.) *Penhale.* Beyond (8¼ m.) *Ruan Major,* the road to *Ruan Minor* and Cadgwith (see below) diverges on the left.

10½ m. **Lizard Town** (Hotels), a straggling village, lies ¾ m. inland from *Lizard Point* (the *Ocrinum* of Ptolemy), the southernmost point of England (49° 57′ 32″ N. lat.), marked by two powerful lighthouses (adm. afternoons). To the E. of the lighthouses is *Housel Bay,* with the bathing-beach.

For the COAST ROUTE from Helston to the Lizard we skirt the w. side of *Loe Pool* to reach the sea at (2½ m.) *Loe Bar,* whence we follow the coastguard path to the left.—5½ m. *Gunwalloe* has a 15C church with a detached belfry, and 125 acres (N.T.) of cliff and dune.—6 m. *Poldhu Cove* (Hotel). A monument, set up by the Marconi Co., marks the site of the wireless station (demolished 1933) from which the first wireless signals to cross the Atlantic were transmitted in Dec 1901.

From this point a road runs inland to (1 m.) *Mullion,* the Perp. church of which is noted for its carved bench-ends. The road goes on to (2¼ m.) *Penhale* (see above).

The next point on the coast is (6¾ m.) *Polurrian Cove* (Hotel), with a good sandy beach. This is followed by (7½ m.) *Mullion Cove (N.T.; Hotel, Café), the wonderful caves of which may be visited at low tide (best at new moon or full moon; *View of Mullion Island, etc., from a tunnel connecting two parts of the cave).—The path goes on viâ *Predannack Head, Vellan Head,* and *Gew Graze* to (12½ m.) **Kynance Cove** (N.T.), with its richly coloured serpentine cliffs, its fantastic rock-formations, and its silvery sands. On the w. side is *Asparagus Island,* where, when the tide is making, clouds of spray rise from the *Devil's Bellows.* The cave here is called the *Devil's Throat* or *Drawing Room,* while the two on the shore are known as the *Kitchen* and *Parlour.*—We may now turn inland for (14 m.) *Lizard Town* (see above) or con-tinue along the coast past *Yellow Carn Cliff, Caerthilian Cove,* and *Pistol Meadow,* where the bodies washed ashore from the wreck of the 'Despatch' were buried (1809), to (14 m.) *Lizard Point* and *Lighthouse* (see above).

The coast walk goes on beyond the *Bumble Rock*, the W. horn of *Housel Bay*, with the huge cavity known as the *Lion's Den*. Rounding *Bass Point*, we begin to follow the E. side of the peninsula. Beyond *Hot Point* we pass *Kilcobben Cove*, with the Lizard lifeboat station. Inland is *Landewednack* (with the parish church of Lizard Town). The *Dolor Hugo* and other caves on this part of the coast are best explored by boat.—2 m. The *Devil's Frying Pan* is another circular hollow like the Lion's Den.—2¼ m. *Cadgwith* is a picturesque little fishing village.—Beyond the glade of *Poltesco* and (3½ m.) the broad *Kennack Sands*, we round (7 m.) *Black Head*, famous for its serpentine, and reach (8½ m.) *Coverack* (Hotel), a charming little place (road, see above).—Just beyond *Manacle Point*, nestling in a cove, is (11½ m.) *Porthoustock*.

Offshore are the dangerous *Manacle Rocks* and 1 m. inland is *St Keverne*, with the largest church in W. Cornwall.

From (13 m.) *Porthallow*, a little fishing village, or from (14½ m.) *Gillan* we may return to Helston by bus. The latter route passes (16½ m.) *Manaccan* (Hotel), with an interesting church.

A road runs N. from Manaccan to *Helford* (1½ m.) on Helford River (p. 231) across which walkers may ferry to join the Falmouth road (bus) at Helford Passage.

25 EXETER TO BODMIN AND PENZANCE

ROAD, 110 m. A 30. To (22½ m.) **Okehampton,** see Rte 23A.—41 m. **Launceston** (by-pass).—63½ m. *Bodmin* (by-pass).—76¼ m. *Fraddon* (l. after 1 m. for Truro and the Lizard).—93½ m. *Redruth.*—97 m. *Camborne* (both by-passed to the N. by the new alignement of A 30).—110 m. **Penzance.**

RAILWAY, 131½ m. in 3¼–4 hrs. Principal stations: To (52 m.) *Plymouth*, see Rte 22.—56¼ m. *Saltash.*—69¾ m. **Liskeard,** junction for **Looe** (8¾ m.).—78¾ m. *Bodmin Road*, bus connection to *Padstow* (16 m.).—82¼ m. *Lostwithiel*, bus connection to *Fowey* (5½ m.).—86½ m. **Par,** junction for **Newquay** (20¾ m.).—91 m. *St Austell.*—105½ m. **Truro,** junction for **Falmouth** (11¾ m.).—114¾ m. *Redruth.*—118¼ m. *Camborne.*—125¾ m. *St Erth*, junction for **St Ives** (4¼ m.).—131½ m. **Penzance.**

From Exeter to (22½ m.) *Okehampton*, see Rte 23A. We bear right after 3¾ m. for (32½ m.; l.) *Lew Trenchard*, the rectory of the Rev. Sabine Baring-Gould (1834–1924) for 43 years. The fine early-17C mansion of *Sydenham* (shown in school holidays) lies c. 2½ m. S.W. on the Lyd.—Beyond (37 m.) *Lifton* (Hotel), we cross the Tamar and enter Cornwall.

41 m. **Launceston,** a pleasant town of 4700 inhab., anciently known as *Dunheved* ('hill-head'), rises between two hills. On the summit of one is a ruined Norman *Castle* (adm. daily, Sun from 2; fee), the chief relic of which is the fine circular keep. George Fox was imprisoned here in 1656. On the other is a public park; both command views. The *South Gate* is the only remaining town-gate. **St Mary Magdalene* (14C tower) has elaborate carving on the exterior (1510–24), notably on the S. porch; *St. Thomas* preserves a Norman font. A Norman arch from an Augustinian priory is now the entrance to the White Hart Hotel, while the large Georgian Lawrence House (N.T.) in Castle St. is now a local museum (April–Sept, Mon, Wed, & Thurs 2.30–4.30; winter Wed only). The Kensey is crossed by two fine old bridges (one a footbridge, 1 m. E.).

46 m. *Polyphant*, a small quarrying village which has supplied stone for many of the Duchy's churches.—49½ m. *Five Lanes* is ½ m. S. of

Altarnun, with a pretty village street, and the 14C church of St Nonna, notable for its font and its woodwork. *Laneast* church, with notable bench-ends is 1½ m. farther N.—We cross the wild Bodmin Moor, dotted with ancient stones, circles, and crosses. At (53½ m.) *Bolventor,* with the famous Jamaica Inn, we pass about 1½ m. N.W. of *Dozmary Pool* (890 ft), where "the waves wap and the winds wan", the lake into which Sir Bedivere threw Excalibur at King Arthur's behest. The spirit of Tregeagle, an unjust steward of Lanhydrock, is doomed in popular belief to empty the pool with a leaky limpet shell. About 3 m. N.W. rise *Brown Willy* (1377 ft), the highest hill ('Bryn Whelli') in Cornwall, and its twin summit, *Rough Tor* (1311 ft; war memorial to Wessex Regiment on the top; 174 acres N.T.).—59½ m. *Blisland* (1½ m. N.), with a pleasant green and the part-Norman church of SS. Protus and Hyacinth. The moor to the N. has some fine scenery; 2 m. *Hantergantick* valley (E. of the quarries), and, c. 3 m. more, *Hannon* valley, with the 'Devil's Jump'.—63½ m. **Bodmin** is the county town of Cornwall (9200 inhab.). The church (15C; restored) is the largest old church in Cornwall; it contains a *Font of c. 1200, a moveable piscina (1495), interesting woodwork, and the remarkable tomb of Prior Vivian (d. 1533).

Lanhydrock House, 2½ m. S.W., approached by an avenue of sycamores (1648), has a fine 17C gatehouse and gallery (N.T.; April–Oct, daily 11–12.30, 2–5.30; fee), while c. 4½ m. N.E. lies *Cardinham,* with a good 15C church (bench-ends) and a Celtic cross. At *Washaway,* 4 m. N.W., off the Wadebridge road, *Pencarrow House* (18C) is open Easter–Sept, Tues, Wed, Thurs, & Sun, 1.45–5; also BH from 11 (fee; rfmts).

We now enter the china-clay country, and the conical white waste dumps are seen on all sides.—66½ m. *Lanivet* has many carved and inscribed stones (6–10C) in its churchyard.—At (71 m.) *Roche* (1 m. S.) a chapel (1409) is built into an unusual outcrop of granite rocks; *Hensbarrow* (1027 ft; view) rises behind.—We pass (r.) *Castle-an-Dinas* (703 ft), a large Iron Age fort, to reach (75¾ m.) *Indian Queens,* where the Newquay road bears off to the right and (76¼ m.) *Fraddon* where A 39, from N. Cornwall, comes in, to diverge left, 1 m. farther on, for Truro.—78½ m. *Summercourt,* famous for its fair (p. 144).—At 87 m. we cross the road from Truro to Perranporth, see Rte 26. The newly alined A 30 (shorter) by-passes both Redruth and Camborne.—93½ m. **Redruth,** in the midst of the tin and copper district, with the Mining Exchange, has been the Cornish mining centre since the mid-19C when it was one of the most important areas in the world for copper. It is now incorporated with Camborne (42,000 inhab.). The house of Wm. Murdock (1754–1839), discoverer of gas as an illuminant, etc., has been restored as a memorial to him and to Richard Trevithick (1771–1833), the engineer, who made a steam vehicle for passengers in 1801.

At *Gwennap Pit,* a grassy hollow 1¼ m. S.E., Wesley used to preach to large congregations of miners, and huge Methodist gatherings still take place at Whitsun. To the S.W. is *Carn Brea* (738 ft), occupied from Neolithic times to the Middle Ages, with the Dunstanville monument (1836).

From *Portreath,* a small resort 4 m. N.W. of Redruth (bus), the coast road (B 3301) runs S.W. to (5½ m.) *Gwithian,* skirting as many miles of seal-haunted cliff, owned by the N.T., including *Godrevy Point,* the E. horn of St Ives Bay.

At (97 m.) **Camborne** is the School of Metalliferous Mining, with the Hunt Memorial Museum (minerals; weekdays 9–4.30; closed Sat). Trevithick was born at Pool, between Redruth and Camborne, and lived for 25 years at Penponds, w. of Camborne, where his cottage survives; the *Cornish Engines Museum* (N.T.; April–mid-Oct, Mon–Fri 11–1, 2–5.30; fee) is at East Pool.—103½ m. *Hayle* is a small port on the estuary at the head of St Ives Bay, opposite Lelant. About 1 m. farther on diverges the road to St Ives (4½ m; r.).

The intervening places are the seaside and golfing resorts of (1 m.) *Lelant*, with the mother church of St Ives, and (3 m.) *Carbis Bay* (Hotels, mostly closed in winter). The Knill Monument, erected in 1782 by a mayor of St Ives who was a smuggler turned lawyer, 1 m. w. of Carbis Bay, is the scene of a bizarre ceremony every fifth year (next in 1982).

St Ives (Hotels), on one of the most charming bays in England, has a long record as a pilchard-fishing town (9,700 inhab.) but is now rather a popular seaside-resort (fine sandy beach) and a haunt of artists; and paintings to suit all tastes may be viewed in the gallery of the Penwith Society of Arts (1961) and in the Museum, which covers also local crafts. The parish church (15C; good bench-ends), in the old part of the town, is dedicated to St Ia, an Irish saint believed to have suffered martyrdom here in the 5C. It contains a Madonna by Barbara Hepworth, and by the s. porch is a 15C cross.—The conspicuous *Trencrom Hill* (N.T.; view) lies 3 m. s.—*Towednack*, 3 m. s.w. on a lane off the Zennor road, has a plain little church with a 13C chancel arch.—There are fine points on the coast s.w. of St Ives, but the road viâ *Zennor* (4 m.), *Morvah* (8 m.), and *St Just* (12 m.) to (18 m.) *Land's End* is hilly and not very interesting (see p. 236).

110 m. **PENZANCE** (i.e. 'holy headland'), a seaport (19,400 inhab.) delightfully situated on *Mount's Bay*, may be considered, owing to its mild climate and charming surroundings, the capital of what is some-what ambitiously styled the 'Cornish Riviera'. Its fisheries and its market gardens are important. Penzance is the best headquarters for excursions in the Land's End district, and the archæologist will find many interesting monuments within reach. John Davidson (1857–1909), the Scottish poet, drowned himself here.

Hotels on the front, and in Chapel St.; some closed in winter.
Post Office, Market Jew St.—INFORMATION BUREAU, 104 Market Jew St.
Buses from the Station to the Esplanade; *Land's End; St Just; Gurnard's Head* and *Zennor; St Ives; Lamorna* and *Treen; Mousehole; Helston* and *Falmouth; Truro* and *Plymouth*.
Steamer and Air Service to the *Scilly Islands*, see p. 237.
Bathing Pool at Battery Rocks, E. end of Promenade.

We enter the town from the E., alongside the station. Thence Market Jew St. ascends to the *Market House* (1836), in front of which is a statue of Sir Humphry Davy (1778–1829), a native of the town. A tablet on the Union Hotel, w. of the harbour, records that the first announcement of the victory of Trafalgar was made from the minstrel gallery here. From the Market House or from Alverton St. several streets lead down to the sea-front, passing the *Morrab Gardens* (sub-tropical vegetation), with the *Penzance Library* (rare Cornish books and prints). In the attractive *Penlee Park*, off Morrab Rd., are the interesting *Museum* (12.30–4.30) of natural history and Cornish antiquities and the ancient *Market Cross*, and in Alverton St. is the *Royal Geological Society Museum* (10–5). On the N. side of the town, not far from the station, are the remains of *Lescudjack Castle*, an ancient hill-fort (view).

Among the interesting points in the nearer environs are *Gulval*, 1 m. N.E., with luxuriant graveyard and vicarage garden; *Bleu Bridge*, 1½ m. N., a slab-bridge with an inscribed stone (?7C); *Madron*, 2 m. N.W., the mother church of Penzance (view of Mount's Bay), with a ruined baptistery and well, 1 m. farther N. To the left lies *Trengwainton*, with a notable garden (N.T.; adm. March–Sept, Wed–Sat, & BH, 11–6; fee).—*Castle-an-Dinas* (765 ft; view), lies to the left of the uninteresting St Ives road.—St Michael's Mount (p. 231) may be reached by boat.

The Esplanade goes on to (1 m.) **Newlyn** (Hotels), a fishing village which has given name to a school of 'open-air' artists. Here are the *Passmore Edwards Art Gallery* (weekdays 10–1, 2–5; fee) and *St Peter's Church*, with fittings (1937–41) by Newlyn artists. The road ends at (3 m.) **Mousehole** (pron. 'Mowsal'; Hotel), a picturesque fishing village, with the fine Elizabethan Keigwin Arms. *Paul Church*, ½ m. inland, is the burial-place of Dolly Pentreath (d. 1777), usually described as the last person who spoke Cornish.—From Mousehole we may follow the coast footpath to (5½ m.) *Lamorna Cove* (Hotels). Near *Boleigh*, 1½ m. inland, are two menhirs and a stone circle, known as the *Pipers* and the *Merry Maidens*. The cliff walk may be prolonged to (13 m.) the *Logan Rock* (see below).

The Land's End District

The S.W. peninsula of Cornwall, which terminates in **Land's End**, presents on its coast some of the finest cliff-scenery in England, while the interior abounds in ancient stone monuments. It is here described in a series of routes radiating from Penzance. St Ives offers alternative headquarters for the N. portions.

FROM PENZANCE TO LAND'S END

Bus direct (10 m.) in ¾ hr.; or coach viâ the Logan Rock (13 m.; comp. below).

We leave Penzance by Alverton St. (A 30) and soon the road to St Just diverges right. At (2½ m.) *Drift* the road on the right leads to *Sancreed* (with two fine churchyard crosses; 1½ m.), and at (3¼ m.) *Catchall* our road keeps to the right. Just before the top of Tregonebris Hill, on the right, is a menhir known as the *Blind Fiddler*, while on the left stands *Boscawen-noon* (the Nine Maidens), a circle 80 ft in diameter, consisting of 19 stones around a menhir. At (5½ m.) the village of *Crows-an-Wra* is an old cross. Farther on we are joined (r.) by a road from St Just. Beyond (8¾ m.) *Sennen* (Hotels), with the misnamed 'First & Last House Hotel', the buses go on to (10 m.) *Land's End* (Hotel). In fact the last house in England is a cottage dispensing refreshments.

*Land's End (5° 41′ 31″ w. long.), the westernmost point of England, known to the ancients as *Bolerium* and in Cornish as *Penwith*, is a huge, turf-topped mass of granite, 60 ft in height, from which a narrow ridge juts out into the sea. The *View extends 25 m. w. to the Scilly Isles and is bounded on the N. by Cape Cornwall and the Brisons rocks. Immediately in front is the *Longships Lighthouse*. To the right (N.) and left (s.) are the rocks known as the *Irish Lady* and the *Armed Knight*. About 8 m. s. is the *Wolf Rock Lighthouse*.

FROM PENZANCE TO THE LOGAN ROCK, 9 m. (bus to Treen). At (3¼ m.) *Catchall* (see above) we keep left, and 2 m. farther on we reach *St Buryan*, with a conspicuous 15C granite church tower (90 ft high) and a good rood-screen (restored). From (8¼ m.) *Treen* we may visit the headland fort of *Treryn Dinas* and the *Logan Rock*, ¾ m. s. (N.T.).

This huge mass of stone (65 tons) is so delicately balanced that it can be moved with trifling exertion. It has, however, never rocked or 'logged' so well since it was idly overset in 1824, with the aid of a friend, by Lieut. Goldsmith (the poet's nephew), who had to replace it at a cost of c. £125.

By following the coast westward to (5½ m.) Land's End viâ (¾ m.) *Porthcurno*, with the Minack Cliff Theatre, and (2 m.) the small church of *St Levan* (E.E. and Perp.), with a good screen and bench-ends, walkers may see some of the finest rock-scenery in England, including the bold headlands of *Tol Pedn Penwith* and *Pardenack*. At Porthcurno Cove is the main landing station of deep-sea cables.

FROM PENZANCE TO ZENNOR, 7 m. (bus). We follow the road up the vale of *Trevaylor*, passing (1½ m.) *Bleu Bridge* (r.; see above). Beyond (3 m.) *Newmill* we may diverge (r.) to visit (4½ m.) the hut-village (c. 100 B.C.) of *Chysauster* (adm. daily, closed Sun morning in winter; fee). To the left of the road, 1 m. farther on, is the *Mulfra Quoit* dolmen. A path on the left, just short of (5½ m.) the coast road, leads to the fine beehive hut at *Bosporthennis*. *Gurnard's Head*, a bold promontory, lies ¾ m. straight ahead from the junction with the coast road. We turn right for (7 m.) *Zennor*, with a half-fallen dolmen of unusual size (18 ft by 9½ ft), on the moor to the s. (r.), and the Wayside Museum (10.30–6, Whitsun–Oct). St Ives is 4 m. E. (bus).

FROM PENZANCE TO MORVAH AND ST JUST, 10 m. (bus). The road runs N.W., passing (2 m.) *Madron*. Beyond (4 m.) *Lanyon Quoit* dolmen a path leads in ¾ m. to the *Ding Dong Mine*, almost certainly worked before the Christian era. On the moors to the N.W. are the *Mên-an-Tol* ('holed stone') and the *Mên Scryfa* ('written stone'). A little farther E. are the remains of a stone circle called the *Nine Maidens* (1 m. w. of Mulfra, see above). From our road, 1 m. beyond the Lanyon Quoit, a track on the left brings us in 1¼ m. to the late Iron Age hill-fort known as *Chûn Castle*, with two concentric walls, and a fine dolmen.—We join the coast road just short of (6 m.) *Morvah*.—10 m. **St Just-in-Penwith** (Hotel) is a small town (3600 inhab.) with a 15C church (interesting interior). The St Just Round or Amphitheatre was used for Cornish miracle and mystery plays.

On the coast, 1½ m. N.W., is the *Botallack Mine*, the workings of which extend a long way under the sea (no adm.), and 1 m. farther on is the *Levant Mine*. About 1¼ m. w. of St Just is *Cape Cornwall* (view), whence good walkers may follow the coast to (6¼ m.) Land's End.

The Scilly Isles

The R.M.S. 'SCILLONIAN', of the Isles of Scilly S.S. Co., leaves from the s. pier at Penzance to (39 m.) *Hugh Town*, on St Mary's, taking 2¾ hrs. Daily sailings, 15 May–11 Sept, Mon–Sat (twice on Sat); 11 Sept–11 Oct, Mon–Fri; other seasons on Tues, Thurs, & Sat only. The passage, which is apt to be rough, affords good views of the coast. About half-way we pass the *Wolf Rock Lighthouse* (l.).

Frequent HELICOPTER SERVICE (no flights on Sun) from Penzance (Eastern Green; connecting bus from railway station) to St Mary's in 25 min.

AIR SERVICES in summer from Exeter, Newquay, or Plymouth.

MOTOR LAUNCH on weekdays from St Mary's to *Tresco*, *Bryer*, and *Samson*; to *St Martin's*; and to *St Agnes*.

The **Scilly Isles** are an archipelago of about 150 islands, islets, and rocks, 28 m. s.w. of Land's End, forming an outlying portion of the granitic mass of Cornwall. The name, taken from Scilly Isle, one of the smallest of the group, is somewhat of a mystery, and their former exclusive identification with the Cassiterides or 'Tin Islands' of Herodotus has been abandoned. According to legend they are the only visible relic of *Lyonesse*, the land of the Arthurian legends, which lies, forty fathoms deep, between them and Cornwall. The innumerable 'passage graves' and other Bronze Age remains give colour to the supposition that the isles were the 'Highlands' adjoining the low alluvial plain of Lyonesse. The total population is 2400, confined to the five islands of *St Mary's, St Martin's, Tresco, Bryher,* and *St Agnes.* The climate is very mild (mean winter temp. 8 C., summer 14 C.), and the chief occupation of the inhabitants is now the growing of early flowers for the London market. Fishing also is carried on. Seals are numerous on the smaller islands. Since 1337 the islands have belonged to the Duchy of Cornwall.

St Mary's, the largest island (2¼ m. by 2 m.), contains more than half of the population. On its w. coast lies *Hugh Town* (Hotels, closed in winter), with a pleasant main street, the capital of the group. Among the chief points (all on the coast) are *Porth Hellick* (E. side), the cliff-fort known as *Giant's Castle* (close by), *Old Town Bay* (with the graves of 120 persons lost in the 'Schiller' in 1875), *Pulpit Rock,* and *Peninnis Point* (lighthouse). Near the last is a 'logan rock', weighing over 300 tons. The best views are from *Garrison Hill* (s.w.), with *Star Castle* (1593; now a Hotel), and *Telegraph Hill* (N.W.).—**Tresco** (Hotel), lies about 1 m. N.W. of St Mary's. Here (½ m. inland) is *Tresco Abbey,* the residence of the Dorrien-Smith family, with its wonderful sub-tropical *Gardens (adm. weekdays 10–4; fee) with the 13C ruins of a Benedictine priory; also the *Valhalla Museum* (fee) of figureheads of ships lost on the Scilly Rocks. Near the N. end of the island is the so-called *Cromwell's Castle* (c. 1650)—a name commemorating the fact that the isles, the last stronghold of the Royalists, were subdued by the Cromwellians under Adm. Blake. There are also remains of a castle of Henry VIII, and a fort of c. 1600. On the N. coast is *Piper's Hole,* a narrow shaft running underground for 600 ft.—**Bryher,** w. of Tresco, repays a visit by its rocky coast, especially at *Shipman Head* and *Hell Bay.*—**St Martin's,** to the N.E., contains Bronze and Iron Age remains.—**St Agnes** has some good barrows, a curiously perched boulder called the *Punch Bowl,* and the old sacred well of *Sancta Warna.* On the downs is an ancient maze, set in pebbles and known as 'Troy Town'.—**Samson,** to the s. of Bryher, is the scene of Sir Walter Besant's 'Armorel of Lyonesse'; it is now uninhabited. On **St Helen's,** N.E. of Tresco, are the scanty remains of an early medieval church and of a Celtic monastery, probably connected with St Elidius, of whose name that of the island seems a corruption.

On the *Bishop Rock,* c. 4 m. s.w. of St Agnes and accessible only on calm days, Adm. Sir Cloudesley Shovel perished in a wreck in 1707, before the lighthouse were erected. His ship, H.M.S. Association, was located on the Gilstone Ledge in 1967. Treasure from the 'Hollandia' which foundered in 1743 off *Gunners Rock* yielded (1971) previously unknown Spanish-American coins and many Mexican 'pieces of eight'.

26 NORTH CORNWALL
From Penzance to Barnstaple

North Cornwall has some of the most striking scenery in England and many of the finest beaches, washed by Atlantic rollers. It also includes a region closely associated with the legendary history of King Arthur. The traveller who has reached Land's End viâ the s. coast of Devon and Cornwall is strongly advised to return by the N. coast, making his way from Penzance to Newquay by road and proceeding thence by the fine route to Clovelly and Bideford. The energetic walker may advantageously make several of the stages on foot.

DIRECT ROAD FROM PENZANCE TO BARNSTAPLE (A 30 and A 39), 107 m. To (35 m.) Fraddon, where we take A 39 (l.), see Rte 25.—38 m. *St Columb Major.* [**Newquay** 32 m. from Penzance, may be included by diverging l. on A 3075, and rejoining the main route at (39 m.) St Columb Major.] From (40 m.) *Winnard's Perch,* B 3274 runs l. to **Padstow** (4 m.).—46 m. **Wadebridge.**—56½ m. *Camelford.*—63½ m. *Tresparrett Posts.* [Or from Camelford l. by B 3266 and B 3263 to (6 m.) **Tintagel.**—10 m. *Boscastle.*—14 m. Tresparrett Posts.].—74½ m. *Stratton* (**Bude,** 1½ m. w.).—78 m. *Kilkhampton.*—88 m. *Clovelly Cross,* 1 m. s. of **Clovelly.**—95 m. *Ford.*—98 m. *Bideford.*—107 m. **Barnstaple.** The distances in the text below have been cumulated to include the major coastal diversions.

Railway from London. Newquay is reached from Paddington (281 m. in 5¾–6¼ hrs) viâ Exeter, Plymouth, and Bodmin Road (where a change is made); hence there is also a connecting bus to *Padstow*.

From Penzance to (16½ m.) *Redruth*, see Rte 25. We continue on A 30 for 5 m., crossing a road to St Agnes, then branch left on A 3075. By-roads lead left to Perranporth (4 m.).

Perranporth (Hotel) is a seaside resort on Perran Bay, noted for surf-bathing. About 1½ m. N. are the remains of the small *Oratory of St Piran*, restored to the light of day in 1835, after having been buried in the sand for upwards of 700 years. It is believed to have been erected over the tomb of St Piran in the 7C. The 11C church, with its cross, a little inland, was also engulfed by the sands. About 1½ m. E. of Perranporth is the ancient amphitheatre of *St Piran's Round*, 130 ft. in diameter.—*St Agnes*, 4 m. S.W., was the birthplace of John Opie (1767–1807; at *Mithian* hamlet), the painter. Hotels at Trevaunance Cove, 1 m. N.; at Mithian, 1½ m. E.—*Porthtowan*, 2½ m. farther S.W., is a popular little bay. *St Agnes Beacon* (699 ft; view) and 363 acres of coastland between St Agnes and Porthtowan are N.T. property.

32 m. **NEWQUAY**, a highly popular seaside and golfing resort (15,000 inhab.), with excellent hotels, lies on a magnificent coast. It is well provided with local bus and coach services, and may be reached by train and (in summer) by air from most cities in Britain.

The town lies parallel with the coast, at the landward end of the promontory ending in *Towan Head*, which separates Newquay Bay, with the little harbour, from Fistral Bay, overlooked by the golf course and *Pentire Point* (bus). The cliffs both to E. and W. are fine and the bathing is good, though dangerous in places (warning notices); and visitors should beware of taking long walks along the beaches when the tide is making.

Trerice (N.T.; adm. April–Oct, daily, 11–1 & 2–6; rfmts; fee), a manor-house of 1571, lies 3 m. S.E.—A good walk crosses the *Gannel* to the S. of Newquay and leads viâ *Crantock* (2 m.; font recarved in 1473) to (4 m.) *Kelsey Head* (N.T.; 305 acres) and (5½ m.) *Holywell Bay*, 2 m. N. of St Piran's Church. *Cubert*, 1½ m. S. of Crantock, has a curious church in a wild, windswept setting above Penhale Sands.

From Newquay to Padstow by the Coast Road, 13 m. B 3276, winding, hilly, and often narrow, quits Newquay viâ *Porth*, the original settlement, then hugs the coast along *Watergate Bay* (Hotel).—At (5 m.) *Mawgan Porth*, a road leads up the *Vale of Mawgan to *St Mawgan* (2 m.), a lovely village where the 13–15C church has a fine tower and a wealth of woodcarving (1450–1550) and a 14C cross in the churchyard. *Lanherne* (façade of 1580), close by, once the manor house of the Arundells, is now a nunnery and has a 10C cross by the gate.—Beyond (7½ m.) *Bedruthan Steps*, with magnificent rock *Scenery (especially in rough weather), we follow the coast to (9 m.) *Porthcothan Bay*, then turn inland viâ *St Merryn* for (13 m.) *Padstow*. The lovely coast round Trevose Head (comp. below) is approached by a maze of lanes and paths.

Padstow ('Petrock's Stow'; Hotels), a decayed port administratively linked with Wadebridge, stands on the lovely Camel estuary and is famous for its Hobby Horse festivities on May Day. The cluster of colour-washed cottages on the quay is attractive. The church has an E.E. tower, a 15C font, and the 17C Prideaux monument. Prideaux Place, with an Elizabethan façade, stands opposite.

A ferry crosses the Camel to *Rock* (see below).—*Stepper Point*, 2½ m. N. (footpath viâ St George's Well), commands a fine view of the coast.—About 2–2½ m. N.W. are the bathing resorts, with fine sands, of *Trevone* (Hotel) and *Harlyn Bay* (Hotel) with prehistoric burials and a museum. From the cliffs above is quarried catacleuse slate, used in local church building. About 2 m. farther is *Trevose Head* (lighthouse; good view) with *Constantine Bay* (Hotel) and a golf course on its W. side. Superb sands extend S. to *Treyarnon Bay* (Hotel) with particularly fine surfing.

From Newquay we take A 392 and pass just S. of (34 m.) *St Columb Minor*, with a late-Dec. tower, then branch left on A 3059, skirting the airport (St Mawgan).—38½ m. *St Columb Major*, where we join A 39, has a prominent Dec. and Perp. church with a crudely carved font (c. 1300). The lofty earthwork of *Castle-an-Dinas*, 2 m. S.E., has been damaged by a wolfram mine. The high-lying road, commanding wide views down to the sea, crosses the St Austell–Padstow road at (40½ m.) *Winnard's Perch*, then passes the 'Nine Maidens', a line of standing stones (r.), and crosses *St Breock Downs*, on the N. side of which are the *Pawton* dolmen and the inscribed stone of *Nanscow*.

48 m. **Wadebridge** (Hotel), a market town on the Camel estuary, is noted for its fine bridge dating from 1485 (320 ft; 15 arches; widened in 1847 and 1963). *Egloshayle* (E.E. and Perp. church) stands on the right bank.

A 389 crosses the uplands to (6¾ m.) Padstow (see above), viâ (3½ m.) *St Issey*, where the church has a fine carved reredos (c. 1400) in catacleuse stone. Much shorter and more attractive is the derelict railway line along the Camel, once followed by the 'Atlantic Coast Express'.

TO ROCK AND POLZEATH. Beyond the river we branch left on B 3314 and cross an arm of the Camel estuary.—2½ m. *Chapel Amble* (1½ m. E.) with the Walmsley Bird Sanctuary (geese and waders). A by-road (l.) leads in 3 m. to **Rock** (Hotels), frequented for golf and small-boat sailing and connected by ferry with Padstow, opposite. **Polzeath** (Hotels), 3 m. farther on, a sandy seaside resort with *Pentire Point* (N.T.) to the N. and adjoined on the S. by *Trebetherick* and *Daymer Bay*. Between Trebetherick and Rock, on the *St Enedoc* golf course, is a 15C church recovered from the sand in 1863.

B 3314 (comp. above) runs N., then turns parallel to the coast to (6¼ m.) *St Endellion*, where the church has a shrine carved in catacleuse by the same hand as the St Issey reredos. *Port Isaac* (Hotels), 2 m. N., is a delightful fishing village much frequented in summer on a little cove separated by a headland from the smaller cove of *Port Gaverne* (Hotels). A magnificent stretch of coast (cliff path and 510 acres N.T.) extends W. by *Portquin* to (c. 6 m.) Pentire Point.—From (8 m.) *Pendoggett*, B 3267 leads r. to St Teath and Camelford; our road passes below *Tregeare Rounds*, an Iron Age fort with three rings of earthworks (view).—12 m. *Delabole*, the 'St Tid' of Eden Philpotts, has quarries of roofing-slate which have been worked for four centuries. We join the Tintagel road (comp. below) just before (14 m.) the derelict railway station of Camelford.

51½ m. *St Kew Highway*. The village church, over 1 m. N., has 15C stained glass and an Ogam stone.—55 m. *St Teath* (l.).—58 m. **Camelford** (Hotel) is a dull town; its mother church, with another inscribed Saxon stone, is at *Lanteglos*, 1½ m. S.W.

The main road ascends to 1000 ft, with wide but dreary views towards Brown Willy (Rte 25), then descends to (7 m.) *Tresparrett Posts* (comp. below).

About 1 m. short of Camelford we diverge left on B 3266 for Camelford station (disused). *Slaughter Bridge* (on a by-road; r.) was the scene of a battle between Britons and Saxons in 823, but not of Arthur's death (Camelford was once regarded as Camelot). B 3263 now runs N.W., passing just inland of *Trebarwith Strand*, where Gull Rock rises out of the fine bay.

63 m. **Tintagel** (Hotels)—"wild Tintagel by the Cornish seas"—
is one of the most famous places in Cornwall. On the coast, ½ m. from
the little village (once called *Trevena*), and rising above a narrow cove
surrounded by sombre cliffs of slate, is *Tintagel Head*, a promontory
connected with the mainland by a rocky neck. Here, partly on the
'island' portion and partly on the mainland, are ruins of the *Castle*
(fee; closed Sun morn. in winter) which the early chroniclers and modern
poetry conspire to accept as the birthplace of King Arthur, son of
Uther Pendragon and Ygrayne. The castle was a stronghold of the
Earls of Cornwall from c. 1150 and the keep (on the mainland) dates
from c. 1236–72, but excavations have revealed traces of a Celtic monastery occupied from c. 500 to c. 850. A steep railed path mounts to the
summit, on which are the remains of a small chapel of the 13C (perhaps
incorporating some Saxon work), a spring of fresh water, and a natural
cavern.—The striking *View from the headland (N.T.) comprises the
wild and rocky shore from Trevose Head (s.) to Hartland Point (N.).

The *Parish Church* (SS. Materiana and Marcelliana), on the cliffs w. of the village, contains traces of Saxon (?) work (N. wall of nave and chancel), a curious
Norman font, and a stone altar in the little Lady Chapel. In the village is the *Old
Post Office* (N.T.; adm. April–Oct, daily 11–1, 2–6 or dusk; Sun 2–6; fee), a 14C
house which handled the mail in 1844–92.—*Bossiney*, which adjoins Tintagel on the
N., had Sir Francis Drake as its M.P. Just to the N. is *Rocky Valley*, a beautiful
walk that leads (l.) to the sea or (r.) to *St Nectan's Kieve*, a pretty waterfall.

66½ m. **Boscastle** (Hotel) is a small village, the chief interest of which
is its intricate little *Harbour* (disused), flanked by formidable cliffs
(N.T.). The name is a corruption of *Bottreaux Castle*, now vanished.
The mother church of Boscastle is at *Minster*, 1½ m. inland; nearer is
that of *Forrabury*, close to the soaring headland of *Willapark*.

A walk may be taken N. to (1 m.) *Pentargon Bay*, with its waterfall, and thence
along the cliffs to (5½ m.) *Crackington Haven*.—*St Juliot's*, 2½ m. from Boscastle
up the valley of the Valency, is the 'Endelstow' in 'A Pair of Blue Eyes' by Thomas
Hardy, who was employed as architect on the restoration of the church (1872).

The road from Boscastle rejoins A 39 at (70 m.) *Tresparrett Posts*,
whence a lane descends to Crackington Haven (2½ m.; see above).—
76 m. **Bangors Cross** is ¾ m. E. of *Poundstock*, where the church and 14C
Guildhall make an attractive group, and Penfound Manor, an Elizabethan house, has origins in a manor of Edith, wife of Edward the
Confessor.—The road divides: the left branch goes to Bude (1 m.),
while the main road keeps straight on through (82 m.) Stratton (see
below), administratively part of Bude (together 5600 inhab.).

Bude (Hotels) is a favourite summer and golfing resort with fine sands,
and magnificent coast scenery both N. and s. *Bude Haven* is protected
by a breakwater terminating in the *Chapel Rock*. *Compass Point*, to
the w., and *Efford Beacon*, to the s.w., afford good views. *Ebbingford
Manor* (12C) is open certain days in summer.

A pleasant walk leads s. to (4 m.) *Widemouth Bay* viâ (1½ m.) *Upton*; buses run to
all points in the neighbourhood.
Morwenstow (Inn), of which R. S. Hawker was vicar from 1834 to 1875, lies
7½–8 m. N. of Bude. To reach it we follow the coast N. past *Menachurch Point* to
(4 m.) the *Duck Pool*, at the mouth of the *Coombe Valley* (see below), and hence
either continue to follow the coast, viâ (1 m.) the *Lower* and (1½ m.) *Higher Sharp-
nose Point*, or turn inland for ½ m. and then follow the road. The church of Morwenstow has an early-Norman font and Norman arches with beautiful zigzag
moulding. Over the door of the vicarage, built by Hawker, is a quaint inscription

in rhyme. *Tonacombe*, just to the s., is a Tudor house, the home of Eustace Leigh in 'Westward Ho!'—Good walkers may extend their coast walk N. viâ (7 m.) *Hartland Quay* to (9 m.) *Hartland Point*, passing on the way the lofty *Hennacliff* and *Embury Beacon*.—From Duck Pool (see above) we may ascend the *Coombe Valley*, passing the woods of *Stow* (the site of Sir Richard Grenville's house described in 'Westward Ho!'), to (3½ m.) Kilkhampton, whence we may return by road to (5½ m.) Bude viâ (4 m.) Stratton.

FROM BUDE TO EXETER, 50 m.   A 3072 runs E.—2 m. *Stratton* (Hotels), where we cross A 39, has a fine Perp. church containing the tomb of Sir John Arundell (1561). Just to the N.W. is *Stamford Hill*, where the Parliamentarians were defeated in 1643 "by the valour of Sir Beville Grenville and ye Cornish army". *Launcells* church, 1 m. E., has notable 15C woodwork and tiles.—Farther on we cross the Tamar and the disused *Bude Canal* (1825), on which inclined planes take the place of locks, and enter Devon.—9 m. *Holsworthy* (Hotels), at the junction of the road from Launceston to Bideford, has a massive Perp. tower, whose bells inspired a well-known hymn tune.—11 m. *Stapledon* (l.) was the birthplace of Walter de Stapledon (1261–1326), founder of Exeter College, Oxford.—22 m. *Hatherleigh* (Hotel), on the Lew, is on the road from Okehampton to Torrington. The church of *Northlew*, 4½ m. S.W., contains good 16C woodwork.—Following B 3216, we cross the Okement 5 m. N. of Okehampton.—28½ m. *Sampford Courtenay* is a charming village with a Perp. church (good roofs). Here began the 'Western Rising' of 1549 (comp. p. 144).—We cross the Taw, by-passing *North Tawton* (Hotel), join B 3215, and at (38 m.) *Copplestone* A 377. Thence to (42 m.) *Crediton* and (50 m.) *Exeter*, see p. 166.

Beyond Stratton we follow A 39 northwards.—86½ m. **Kilkhampton** has a Norman and Perp. *Church* with good carved bench-ends and the tomb of Sir Bevil Grenville (d. 1643).—At 91 m. we enter Devon and soon reach the West Country Inn.—At (96½ m.) *Clovelly Cross* we turn left for **Clovelly**.

Motorists must park at the main car park, whence luggage is conveyed on donkey-back or by jeep (down the rough lane w. of the village).

Clovelly (Hotels), a fishing village, is so delightfully and uniquely situated, in a narrow rift in the cliffs, that it has become only too popular a resort both for tourists and for painters. The best description of this most quaint and charming of villages is that by Dickens in 'A Message from the Sea'. The main street, far too steep for wheeled traffic, descends in steps and stages from a height of 400 ft to the little cove and pier (1587) at the foot, and no two of the white-washed houses gay with flowers are on the same level. The *View from the sea is particularly charming. Steamers in the season to *Lundy* (fee) and to *Ilfracombe*.—On the N.W. side of the village are the charming grounds of *Clovelly Court*, entered by *Yellary Gate* 250 yds w. of the Hobby Drive (pedestrian entrance only; see below). The prime beauty spot is *Gallantry Bower* (c. 1¼ m.), which rises sheer from the sea for 387 ft and affords a superb view. The walk is generally extended for ½ m. to *Mouth Mill*, a picturesque rocky cove. We may direct our return so as to pass near *Clovelly Court* (only the 14C wing of which survived a fire in 1943). The *Church* of Clovelly, with monuments of the Carys and Hamlyns, contains a memorial to Charles Kingsley, who spent his boyhood at the rectory.

From Clovelly Cross, beside which there is a fine Iron Age camp, we turn W. for (4 m.) the village of *Hartland* and go on viâ (5½ m.) *Stoke*, with the large and interesting 14C parish church (striking rood-screen, font, and roof), to (6½ m.) *Hartland Quay* (Hotel with swimming-pool), a secluded hamlet, noted for its contorted slate rocks. *Hartland Point* (350 ft; lighthouse), 4½ m. N., is the N.W. extremity of Devon (fine cliff scenery; 160 acres N.T.).

A 39 continues eastwards, passing the *Hobby Drive, a splendid alternative approach (toll for cars) to Clovelly commanding fine views of Lundy and Bideford Bay.—From (99 m.) *Buck's Cross* a lane descends to *Buck's Mills* (1 m.), a charming fishing hamlet.—103¾ m. *Abbotsham Cross*. Here B 3236 runs N. to Westward Ho (3 m.) through *Abbotsham* (Hotel), where the small 13C church has a Norman font and good bench-ends.

106 m. **Bideford** (pron. 'Biddy-'; Hotels), an ancient seaport (11,800 inhab.) the "little white town" of 'Westward Ho!' is charmingly situated on **two** hills rising from the Torridge, here spanned by a bridge of 24 arches (1460; widened in 1925). The rebuilt *Church* contains a Norman font and a monument of 1513. The Grenvilles obtained a charter for the town in 1573 and the 'Revenge' was crewed by Bideford men "at Flores in the Azores". A Red Indian, perhaps brought home by Sir Richard Grenville and baptized here as Christian Rawley in 1588, is believed to have been the first of his race to visit England. The Quay and Bridgeland Road have prosperous merchants' houses of c. 1690. Facing the quay is a statue of Charles Kingsley (1819–75), who wrote part of 'Westward Ho!' in the Royal Hotel (room shown), and eight old Spanish cannon are preserved in the Borough Park. *Chudleigh's Fort* (1630–43), part of the Town War Memorial, is on the right bank ($\frac{1}{4}$ hr above the station) and affords a good view.

There are occasional steamers in summer from Bideford to Ilfracombe. Buses go from the quay via ($1\frac{3}{4}$ m.) *Northam* to (3 m.) *Appledore*, a quaint little port, or to (3 m.) **Westward Ho!** (Hotel), a bathing resort, named after Kingsley's novel (1855). Its famous golf links lie to the N., separated from the sea by the curious *Pebble Ridge*, 20 ft high and 2 m. long. Kipling's 'Stalky & Co.' is believed to describe life at the United Services College, a school formerly at Westward Ho! In the lonely country S.W. of Bideford are several churches worth visiting, notably at *West Putford* ($11\frac{1}{2}$ m.) and *Sutcombe* ($16\frac{1}{2}$ m.).

A pleasant road ascends the Torridge.—At the Norman font of (2 m.) *Landcross* Gen. Monk was baptized, while *Orleigh Court*, c. 3 m. w., was the birthplace of J. H. Speke (p. 169).—4 m. **Weare Gifford** (l.; beyond the river) has an interesting church and a fine 15C manor house.—7 m. **Great Torrington** (Hotels) is well situated above the Torridge. Fairfax routed the Royalists close by in 1646. Gen. Monk (1608–70), Duke of Albemarle, was born at *Great Potheridge* (rebuilt c. 1660), 4 m. s. off the Hatherleigh road. *Merton*, 2 m. farther on, was the birthplace of Walter de Merton, founder of Merton College, Oxford.

A 39 descends the E. bank of the river, passing *Tapeley Park* where John Christie, creator of Glyndebourne, was born; the gardens are open May–September.—109 m. *Instow*, facing Appledore (passenger ferry) at the confluence of the Torridge and the Taw, has wide sands at low water.—115 m. **Barnstaple**, see Rte 21.

27   TAUNTON TO MARLBOROUGH

ROAD, $72\frac{1}{2}$ m. A 361.—$19\frac{1}{2}$ m. *Street.*—21 m. **Glastonbury.**—$29\frac{1}{4}$ m. *Shepton Mallet.*—40 m. *Frome.*—$47\frac{1}{2}$ m. *Trowbridge.*—$58\frac{1}{4}$ m. **Devizes.**—$65\frac{1}{2}$ m. *Beckhampton.*—A 4. $72\frac{1}{2}$ m. *Marlborough.* (A 361, continuing N. via Swindon, Burford, and Chipping Norton to Banbury forms an attractive link between the W. Country and the Midlands.)

A 38 from the centre or A 361 from N. of the station coincide 3 m. N.E. of Taunton.—4 m. *Walford Cross.* We leave A 38 (p. 201) turning E,

A by-road runs s. to (2 m.) *Creech St Michael* church, with interesting 13C details, and a fine wagon roof. From here we may follow the s. bank of the Tane via ($5\frac{1}{2}$ m.) *North Curry* where the imposing church is framed by a medley of fine houses, to (8 m.) *Stoke St Gregory* church (c. 1300, with Perp. additions). We rejoin the main road at (12 m.) Burrow Bridge.

9 m. *Burrow Bridge*, where the hillock called *Burrow Mump*, the probable site of Alfred's fort in 879 (comp. p. 169), rises above the fens. —11 m. *Othery* church has a Perp. central tower. We cross King's

Sedge Moor, and at 16¼ m. join A 39 from Bridgwater (see p. 201).—
19¼ m. *Street* (Hotels), a shoemaking town since 1822, with 8200
inhab., depends largely on its one industry, whose Nonconformist
family owners exercise enlightened quasi-feudal sway.

21 m. **GLASTONBURY** (Hotels), an ancient town (6600 inhab.) at
the base of Glastonbury Tor, owes its origin and its fame to its celebrated abbey.

The *Abbey (adm. 9.30 or 10 to 6, 7, or 8; fee), "the first and greatest
house of the oldest and most famous monastic order", entered by the
Abbot's Gate in the market place, represents the earliest Christian
foundation in England, which survived the storms of Saxon, Danish,
and Norman conquest and presents a continuity of religious life elsewhere unparalleled.

According to the romantic legend, St Joseph of Arimathea with eleven com-
panions brought to Glastonbury the chalice of the Last Supper (or, according to
another tradition, the phials that held the blood of the Crucifixion; comp. Abbot
Bere's shield in St Benedict's Church, p. 245); and here, in the Druidic Isle of
Avalon or Ynyswytryn, the 'Blessed Isle', built the 'Vetusta Ecclesia', or primitive
church of wood and wattle-work. Refounded by Pope Eleutherius in A.D. 166,
the settlement was visited by St Patrick (who, according to one legend, died here
in 463) and by St Bridget (488). Larger churches, always with the careful inclusion
of the Vetusta Ecclesia, were raised successively by Ine, King of the West Saxons,
in 708; by St Dunstan (d. 988), who was born and educated at Glastonbury; and by
Thurstin and Herlewin, the first Norman abbots after the Conquest. Under Dunstan, who became abbot in 940 and introduced the Benedictine rule, the abbey
became a centre of light and learning and gave England many great ecclesiastics.
The Saxon kings Edmund the Magnificent (d. 946), Edgar (d. 975), and Edmund
Ironside (d. 1016) were buried in this sacred spot. Until 1154, when precedence
was given to St Albans, the mitred abbot of Glastonbury was the premier abbot of
England. The remains of King Arthur and Guinevere, reputed to have been discovered here in 1191, were finally reinterred in front of the high altar in 1276, in the
presence of Edward I.

In 1184 the whole abbey, including the Vetusta Ecclesia, was burned to the
ground. The rebuilding was begun at once and was completed in 1303 (except
for a few later additions). The first part to be finished (1186) was the Lady Chapel
(often called St Mary's Chapel), on the exact site of the old wooden chapel and
(so it is said) in strict fidelity to the ancient plan. The abbey was suppressed in
1539, the last Abbot, Richard Whiting, being executed on the Tor (see below).
After the Reformation the buildings were neglected and until about 1830 they were
used as the stone-quarry of the neighbourhood. The ruins were bought for the
Church of England in 1908 and vested in trustees, since when much notable excavation work was carried out by F. Bligh Bond (1864–1945).

Of the vast Church the sole remains, "appalling in their dead elo-
quence," are the two E. piers of the central tower (with portions of the
transeptal walls attached), one of the N. transeptal chapels (with groups
of floor-tiles), parts of the S. aisle walls of the nave and choir, and the
w. door. The last leads into the 13C Galilee connecting the church with
the *Lady Chapel* (walls still standing), "a jewel of late-Romanesque,"
with rich carvings and interlacing arcades. Beneath is a 15C *Crypt*
connecting with a well of unknown antiquity. The length of the whole
range of buildings was proved to be c. 590 ft by the discovery (1909) of
the apsidal *Edgar Chapel*, built by Abbot Bere, at the extreme E. end.
The foundations of *St Dunstan's Chapel*, at the extreme W., and of the
North Porch and the *Loretto Chapel* (N. side of nave) are marked on
the ground, as are the sites of the *Chapter House*, *Cloisters*, and the sub-
vaults of the *Refectory* and *Dormitory*.

Within the Abbey enclosure is the *Abbot's Kitchen* (14C), with a high octagonal stone roof and lantern; it contains a small museum of Abbey antiquities. The 15C *Lower Gateway*, formerly an inn, was restored in 1928. In Bere Lane (to the N.E.) is the *Abbot's Barn* (late 14C), with symbols of the Evangelists and a fine collar-beam roof.

The *Almshouses*, founded by Abbot Bere, with their chapel (1512), lie behind the Abbot's Gate. On the left in High St. are the *George and Pilgrims' Inn* (1470; now a hotel), and the *Abbot's Tribunal* (adm. daily, Sun from 2; fee), with fine old woodwork, which houses the *Lake Village Museum* (daily 10–1, 2.15–5.15; fee) with interesting finds from the lake villages of Meare and Glastonbury. The Church of *St John the Baptist* (1465), has a fine tower and a 15C sarcophagus from the abbey. *St Benedict's* (St Benignus), built on older foundations by Abbot Bere, lies w. of the market place.

The Tor (550 ft), crowned with the tower of a chapel of *St Michael* (destroyed by a landslip in 1271), commands a famous *View of Glastonbury, Wells, and the Bristol Channel.—At the foot of Tor Hill, in the garden of Chalice Well, is the chalybeate *Blood Spring*, formerly of repute for its healing virtues.—On Wyrral Hill, w. of the town, grew the original '*Glastonbury Thorn*' (Cratægus præcox), which sprang from St Joseph's staff. The tree was hacked down by the Puritans, but offshoots, with the unimpaired virtue of blossoming at Christmas-tide, may be seen in the abbey grounds and in St John's churchyard.—*Sharpham* (2 m. s.w.), a manor-house built by Abbot Bere and the scene of Abbot Whiting's arrest, was the birthplace of Henry Fielding (1707–54).—At *Butleigh*, 4 m. s. of Glastonbury, Adm. Lord Hood (1724–1816) was born (monument in church, with epitaph by Southey).—*Meare*, 3½ m. N.W., has the Fish House and Manor of the abbots of Glastonbury (both 14C) and the remains of ancient lake-dwellings.

A 361 divides again from A 39.— 27 m. *Pilton*, with a fine part-Norman church and a Georgian manor-house, is built on a steep hill.—29½ m. **Shepton Mallet** (Hotels) with 5900 inhab., has a market place with the 15C Shambles and a cross of 1500, and a good panelled wagon *Roof in the church. The grounds of the Bath and West Agricultural Show (early June), lie to the s.E.— 31 m. *Doulting* provided the stone for Wells cathedral; the attractive church has good ceilings in the transepts.— 37 m. (l.) *Nunney*, with a well-designed moated castle of 1373 in a pleasant setting. *Cloford* church, 1 m. s.w. of the main road, has 17C Horner monuments.— 38½ m. our road skirts Marston Park with the church of *Marston Bigot* which has 16C German glass.— 40 m. **Frome** (pron. 'Froom'; Hotels) is a cloth and carpet-making town (13,400 inhab.), solidly built in stone with steep and narrow streets and a thriving market. The paved Cheap St., above the market, has a central water-course. The parish church of the 13C and late 14C, was restored in 1866. Outside the E. end is the tomb of the outspoken Bp. Ken (1637–1711), who died at Longleat.

Excursions may be made to the noteworthy church of (2½ m. N.) *Lullington*, with a Norman font and N. doorway, and (3½ m. w.) the attractive village of *Mells*, with a beautiful Perp. *Church (memorials by Burne-Jones and Munnings). The restored 16C manor-house belongs to the Horner family, of which 'Little Jack Horner' is said to have been a member. *Witham Friary*, 5 m. s. of Frome, was the site of one of the first Carthusian monasteries in England (1178–79; founded by Henry II in expiation of Becket's murder), of which the lay-brothers' church is still in use. The Little Cloister of the Domus Superior (the first home of St Hugh of Lincoln) was unearthed in 1965.—*Longleat* (p. 154), lies c. 4½ m. s.E.

B 3098 runs E. for 19 m. to join A 342 c. 4 m. s.E. of Devizes (see below).—6 m. *Westbury*, see p. 174. We skirt the edge of Salisbury Plain, passing (7½ m.) under the White Horse of Westbury. Its present outline dates from 1873; but a similar figure is recorded in the 18C.—9½ m. *Edington*, probably the former Ethandune, site of Alfred's victory of c. 878, has a 14C *Priory Church, a beautiful example of the transition from Dec. to Perp. (good monuments including two from the abandoned church of *Imber*, now in the military zone to the S.E.). A festival of liturgical music is held in the 3rd week of August.—The road crosses A 360 (p. 167) at (14 m.) *West Lavington*, with Dauntsey's School.—At (18 m.) *Urchfont*, the church has a fine chancel.

At (42½ m.) *Beckington* we cross A 36 (comp. p. 155).—44 m. *Rode Manor* has a collection of tropical birds.—47½ m. **Trowbridge** is a cloth-making town (19,200 inhab.) in which are the County Offices for Wilt-shire. It has a number of streets (the Parade, Fore St., Roundstone St., etc.) of prosperous merchants' houses. George Crabbe was rector of the restored 15C church from 1813 till his death in 1832 (tomb in the chancel). *Bradford-on-Avon* (p. 194) is 3 m. N.W.—At (51 m.) we cross A 350 from Chippenham to Shaftesbury, see p. 174.—58½ m. **Devizes** (Hotels), formerly called *Ad Divisas* ('on the borders'), stands at the mouth of the Vale of Pewsey; it was once an important cloth-making town and is now a large corn-market and the chief town of North Wilts (10,200 inhab.) with many dignified houses of the 18C and a *Town Hall* (1806–8) by T. Baldwin. *St John's*, with a fine tower, and *St Mary's* were founded by Roger of Salisbury c. 1150, the former for the castle (which has been replaced), the latter for the town; both were enlarged in the 15C. The inscription on the market cross (1814) should be noted.

The *Museum* of the Wiltshire Archaeological Society (adm. Tues–Sat 11–4 or 5; fee) contains important antiquities from the Wiltshire barrows and the 'Marl-borough Bucket', a Belgic wooden vat, with bronze reliefs (1C B.C.). Sir Thomas Lawrence, the painter, spent his boyhood at the Bear, where his father was land-lord. To the w. of the town (1–2 m.) the Kennet and Avon canal descends by a flight of 29 locks.—At *Potterne*, 2 m. S., are a good E.E. church and the 15C Porch House (adm. Wed in summer 2–5; fee).—*Roundway Down*, 2½ m. N., is where the Parliamentarians were defeated in 1643; *Oliver's Castle*, an Iron Age hill-fort, over-looks the scene.

FROM DEVIZES TO ANDOVER (A 342), 26 m.—2 m. (r.) *Stert*, a pleasant hamlet.—At 4 m. we join B 3098 from Frome (see above).—5 m. (l.) *Chirton*, where the church has a Norman doorway—9 m. *Upavon* church has a (restored) Norman chancel and font. The village is situated at the head of the Avon valley which divides Salisbury Plain from N. to S. Here is H.Q. Air Support Command of the R.A.F.; *Casterley Camp*, an Iron Age hill-fort, lies 1½ m. S.W.—18 m. *Ludgershall*, with the fine Brydges monument (c. 1558) in its church. *Tidworth*, 2½ m. W., is an important military camp.—26 m. *Andover*, p. 166.

At (65½ m.) *Beckhampton* crossroads, just s. of Avebury, we join A 4; thence to (72½ m.) *Marlborough*, see Rte 17.

III CENTRAL ENGLAND

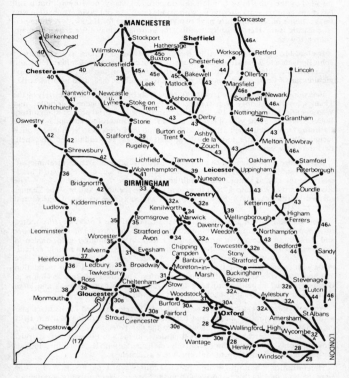

Central England, as described in this section, comprises some sixteen ancient counties of diverse character, which may be grouped very roughly for convenience into regions: the CHILTERNS (Bucks, Herts, Beds); the THAMES VALLEY (Berks, Oxon) bordered to the W. by the COTSWOLDS, VALE OF SEVERN, and SHAKESPEARE COUNTRY (Glos, and the s. portions of Worcs and Warwicks); the WELSH MARCHES (Herefordshire, Salop, Cheshire); the West Midlands and BLACK COUNTRY (much of it comprising Greater Birmingham); and the East Midlands including the SHIRES and PEAK DISTRICT (Northants, Leics, Rutland, Derbyshire, and Notts).

Buckinghamshire, or **Bucks**, an agricultural and pastoral county, contains several famous mansions and many interesting villages and churches. About the middle extends the fertile *Vale of Aylesbury* and in the s.w. are the *Chiltern Hills*. The S.E. side has been invaded by London's suburbs. The Chiltern beech-woods where once the lonely 'bodger' made his 'Windsor' chairs, now provide material for the factory-made furniture at High Wycombe. The literary and historical associations of the country are numerous: the names of Hampden, Penn, Burke, Disraeli, Milton, Cowper, Gray, Waller, and Shelley all figure in its annals. In 1974 Bucks lost a small area adjoining the Thames s. of Slough to Berkshire.

Hertfordshire, or **Herts,** was a favourite county of Charles Lamb, who refers to it as "hearty, homely, loving Hertfordshire". This pleasant, undulating, district is invaded by the suburbs of London and obscured by many 'new towns', but it still has many country seats alternating with arable land. An old saying runs: "He who buys a home in Hertfordshire pays two years' purchase for the air." A characteristic feature is the Hertfordshire 'needle', the unusually small spire crowning many church towers.

Bedfordshire, or **Beds,** watered by the tortuous Ouse, is famous as the county of John Bunyan and John Howard. Though it includes part of the Chiltern Hills and the greensand ridge with open agricultural landscape, it has been called the least picturesque of English counties, and much of its surface is disfigured by brickworks.

Berkshire (pron. 'Barkshire'), or **Berks,** previously bounded on the N. entirely by the Thames, lost its pleasant N.W. part (including Wallingford, Abingdon, Faringdon, and Wantage) to Oxfordshire in 1974, gaining instead the industrial area of Slough from Bucks. It comprises the Vale of Kennet, on the s., once famous for elmwood bowls; the Berkshire Downs, with their attractive villages, and the Forest District in the E., which includes Windsor Castle, but it has large built-up areas in Reading and Bracknell. Berkshire hogs have long been famous.

Oxfordshire contains many churches and mansions of great architectural interest. It saw several of the early contests in the Civil War, when, as the Royalist headquarters, the city of Oxford added military importance to its academic fame. The scene of Scott's 'Woodstock' is in this county, and in the upper valley of the Thames roamed Matthew Arnold's 'Scholar Gipsy'. It gained a large section of agricultural Berks in 1974.

Gloucestershire, with the contrasting landscapes of the *Cotswold Hills* (noted for sheep and for charming stone-built villages) and the fertile *Vales of Gloucester* and *Berkeley*, is a county of great beauty. Except in the mining region, hidden in the *Forest of Dean* beyond the Severn estuary, its occupations are mainly agricultural. The renowned cheeses—'double Gloucester' and 'single Gloucester'—are made with cream and without cream respectively. Two cities of Roman foundation and numerous villa sites lie within the boundaries. The adage "as sure as God is in Gloucestershire" is believed to refer to the number of wealthy abbeys and large churches in the county. It lost some s. lands to Avon in 1974.

Worcestershire, intersected from N. to s. by the Severn, is noted for its black and white houses, its pretty villages, and pastoral scenery. The striking Malvern Hills on its s.w. border are in marked contrast to the flat *Vale of Evesham,* or valley of the Avon, rich in orchards and market-gardens, in the S.E. Pre-eminently a fruit-growing county, it has been administratively amalgamated with Herefordshire, though the absurd idea of calling them Malvernshire was scotched.

Herefordshire, a beautiful, mainly pastoral county is bisected by the Wye, at one time the boundary between the Welsh and the Saxons. Herefordshire is noted for its breed of store-cattle and, as Fuller puts it, "this shire better answereth (as to the sound thereof) the name of Pomerania than the dukedom of Germany so called, being a continued orchard of apple-trees, whereof much cider is made." Its cider and perry are still famous.

Warwickshire, the most central county in England, was formerly considered to consist of the 'Woodland' portion to the N. and the 'Felden' (or champaign) district to the s. The former included the ancient 'Forest of Arden', which gave the county its sobriquet of 'Woody' or 'Leafy Warwickshire'. The name of Shakespeare survives here, but its bearers seem to have no connection with the poet. Besides the overwhelming interest of the 'Shakespeare Land', Warwickshire has a secondary literary interest in the neighbourhood of Coventry and Nuneaton, which may fairly be termed the 'George Eliot County'. It is more pastoral than ever since 1974 when its huge industrial areas were joined with others from Staffs and N. Worcs to form, with Birmingham at the heart, the county of **West Midlands.** This corresponds almost exactly with the so-called Black Country.

Shropshire, or **Salop,** is the largest inland county of England and a border-county towards Wales, which latter fact enlivened its early history. The portions next to Wales are generally hilly or even mountainous, while to the N. and E. of the Severn extend fertile plains, in which the numerous meres are a characteristic feature. The region about Ludlow is celebrated in A. E. Housman's 'A Shropshire Lad'.

Cheshire, largely agricultural since in 1974 it lost its suburban fringes to Greater Manchester and Merseyside, is generally low and flat, though in *Macclesfield Forest* in the E. the scenery is hilly, attractive, and even wild. The county contains many old half-timbered houses as well as mansions with beautifully landscaped grounds. Cheshire has been noted for centuries for its cheese and for its salt (produced near Northwich). Silk is an old manufacture of Macclesfield. The *Wirral*, the W. peninsula between the Mersey and the Dee, is shared with Merseyside.

Staffordshire, or **Staffs,** rich in coal and other minerals, is pre-eminently an industrial county, with *The Potteries* in the N., though it shed its Black Country to West Midlands in 1974. But it contains also some magnificent scenery. Between Lichfield and Stafford stretches *Cannock Chase*; and in the N.W. is the attractive 'Moorlands' region, adjoining and resembling the Derbyshire Peak district. Staffordshire is the county of Dr Johnson and Izaak Walton; one side of Dovedale belongs to it.

Northamptonshire, or **Northants,** as Fuller, a son of the soil, pointed out, "bordereth upon more counties than any other in England, being nine in number". The number was reduced to six in 1974 when the Soke of Peterborough was confirmed in its adherence to Huntingdon as part of a greatly enlarged Cambridgeshire (comp. p. 438). It is especially noted for the manufacture of boots and shoes, for the somewhat disfiguring ironstone quarries, and, in reference to its many 'county' families and to the interesting and beautiful architecture of its churches, it has been called a land of 'squires, spires, and spinsters'. This is the county of the Spencers of Althorp, the Cecils of Burghley, and the Comptons of Castle Ashby, and it is the native county of John Dryden.

Though the adjoining county of **Leicestershire** includes several industrial centres (Leicester, Loughborough, Hinckley) as well as a small coalfield in the N.W., adjoining the wild heathlands of *Charnwood Forest*, it is best known for its famous grasslands (mainly in the E.), a classic region for fox-hunters. Leicestershire, Rutland, and Northamptonshire are sometimes spoken of as 'the Shires', but, more strictly, that term is reserved for the country hunted by the celebrated packs of foxhounds known as the Quorn, the Cottesmore, the Pytchley, the Woodland Pytchley, and the Belvoir, and thus excludes a considerable part of Northants while it includes a portion of Lincolnshire. Outside these limits are 'the Provinces'. In 1974 it absorbed **Rutland,** formerly the smallest county in England (152 sq. m.) and a famous fox-hunting district. Almost every village contains notable stone-built houses.

Derbyshire, with scenery varying from the bleak moors of the Peak to the pastoral meadows in the south, and from the crowded industrial area on the Notts border to the romantic loveliness of Dovedale, provides as many striking contrasts as any county in England. The chief rivers are the Derwent and the Dove, both tributaries of the Trent. The main industry is mining (coal and iron, with some lead and zinc), though Derby and some other towns are manufacturing centres of importance. Its boundary changes in 1974 were minor.

Nottinghamshire, or **Notts,** is the county of Lord Byron and Robin Hood. Its forests (including *Sherwood*) and streams, its uplands and fertile dales, its busy villages and towns, and its handsome parks are characteristically English. Its river is the navigable Trent. This county saw the beginning of the Civil War in 1642.

28 LONDON TO OXFORD. THE THAMES VALLEY
A By road viâ Windsor and Henley

ROAD, 60 m. (A 4, A 423). 19 m. *Colnbrook* roundabout, for Windsor (3½ m.).—26¼ m. *Maidenhead.*—35½ m. **Henley.**—51 m. *Dorchester.*—60 m. **Oxford.** The M 4 MOTORWAY, by-passing Slough and Maidenhead, affords an alternative (by junction 9 and A 423M) to Maidenhead Thicket. A spur from the Slough West exit (*View of the Castle) serves Windsor.
    Windsor is usually visited as an excursion from London, and alternative road and rail approaches are described in the 'Blue Guide to London'.—For the quickest road direct to Oxford, see Rte 30.

RAILWAY to Oxford (63½ m.), from Paddington, viâ Reading, approx. every hour in 60–70 min.

From London viâ the Great West Road (or motorway, comp. above) to (19 m.) *Colnbrook* ('Slough East' motorway exit), see the 'Blue Guide to London'. Here A 331 diverges left viâ Datchet to (3½ m.) Windsor.

WINDSOR (Hotels; 30,100 inhâb.), famous for its stately castle, which has been the chief residence of the sovereigns of England for 850 years, is situated on the right bank of the Thames and is connected by bridges with Eton and Datchet on the left bank. It was made a Royal Borough in 1922.

On the corner of Thames St., which ascends from the river, is a memorial (1937) to George V, by Lutyens. The street climbs round between the castle *Bastions and 18C houses refronted with shops. In High St., its continuation, beyond the statue of Queen Victoria at Castle Hill, is the *Guildhall* (adm. Apr–Oct daily 1–6; fee), designed in 1686 by Sir Thos. Fitch and completed by Wren (1707). It is adorned with statues of Queen Anne and Prince George of Denmark, and contains royal portraits, notably Prince Rupert, by D'Agar. The *Church*, farther on (rebuilt 1822) contains good carving perhaps by Grinling Gibbons; and there are a few interesting houses in Market St. and Church Street, both cobbled.

*Windsor Castle, on a chalk cliff rising abruptly above the Thames, was started in wood by William the Conqueror, continued in stone by Henry II, and though extended by Henry III and Edward III still preserves its original plan (two baileys and a mote-hill).

Henry I's marriage to Adeliza of Louvain (1121), was the first royal wedding to be celebrated here. Edward III was born here in 1312, and Henry VI in 1421, and three kings (David II of Scotland, John of France, and James I of Scotland) have been imprisoned within its walls; and from his cell window James first espied his future wife, Jane Beaufort. Edward III's queen, Philippa of Hainault, died in the castle in 1369. The present appearance of the building dates from the extensive restorations undertaken by Wyatville under George IV.

The *Lower Ward*, the *North Terrace*, and part of the *East Terrace* are open free daily 10–4 or dusk (Guards' band on the E. terrace, 2–4 on Sun in June–Aug). In the absence of the Court (inquire beforehand) the *State Apartments* are shown on weekdays 10.30–3 (to 5 during British Summer Time); also Sun in May–mid-Oct 1.30–5; fee. The *Round Tower* (Apr–Sept) and the *Albert Memorial Chapel* are open free weekdays 10–1, 2–3.45. *St George's Chapel* is open (exc. Jan) on weekdays 11–3.45 or 4 (Fri from 1), Sun from 2 or 2.15 (fee); free for services. The State Apartments are closed when the Queen is in residence; usually for c. 6 weeks at Easter and 3 weeks in June for the Ascot race-meeting.

On entering the Lower Ward from Castle Hill by *Henry VIII's Gateway*, we have in front of us the entrance to the *Horseshoe Cloisters*, built under Edward IV, at the N.W. angle of which stands the *Curfew Tower*, with a 13C interior. On the right are the houses of the *Military Knights of Windsor*.

This Order was founded by Edward III as the 'Poor Knights of Windsor' at the same time as the Order of the Garter; its present name was given by William IV in 1833.

St George's Chapel (fee), dedicated to the patron saint of the Order of the Garter, was begun c. 1478 by Henry Janyns for Edward IV and continued in 1503–11 by William Vertue. It is one of the most perfect specimens of 15–16C Gothic work, ranking with King's College Chapel at Cambridge and Henry VII's Chapel at Westminster. In the N.W. corner is the tomb, by Lutyens and Reid Dick, of George V (d. 1936) and Queen Mary (1953), with the theatrical tomb of Princess Charlotte (d. 1817), behind. The great W. window contains much fine glass of c. 1500, including a portrait of Vertue (N. bottom light).

In the corners of the nave, and in both choir-aisles, are a series of elaborate 16C chantries, many with contemporary tombs. The Bray chantry, near the S. door, contains the cenotaph of the Prince Imperial, son of Napoleon III, killed in S. Africa in 1879. The S.E. chapel, with the tomb of the Earl of Lincoln (d. 1585) is called the *Lincoln Chapel*, or *John Schorne's Tower*, front the relics of Sir John Schorne, brought here in 1478 from N. Marston in Bucks.

The *CHOIR is separated from the nave by a Gothic screen (c. 1785) by Henry Emlyn, who also added the Garter stalls. Within it are the stalls (late 15C) and banners of the Knights of the Garter, whose installations have taken place at Windsor since 1348. On the S. side of the altar is the tomb, by Mackennal, of Edward VII (d. 1910) and Queen Alexandra (d. 1925). To the N. of the altar is the Royal Pew, below which is a fine pair of iron gates, once part of Edward IV's tomb. In the N. choir aisle is the tomb of Edward IV, in the S. choir aisle is that of Henry VI, and in the vaults below are buried Henry VIII and Jane Seymour, Charles I, George III, George IV, William IV, George VI, and other royal personages.

The **Albert Memorial Chapel** was built by Henry VII as his burial-place, and afterwards assigned to Wolsey, whose magnificent tomb here was never occupied and was broken up during the Civil War. Queen Victoria caused the chapel to be converted into a splendid memorial for her husband (d. 1861). It contains the cenotaph of Prince Albert, by Baron Triqueti, and the tombs of the Duke of Clarence (d. 1892), the elder son of Edward VII, by Alfred Gilbert, and of the Duke of Albany (d. 1884), Queen Victoria's youngest son. The passage between the two chapels leads to the *Dean's Cloister* and the *Canons' Cloister* (no adm.). —To the left of the entrance to the N. terrace is the *Winchester Tower*, where Chaucer may have lived in 1390, when Master of the Works at Windsor.—A gateway leads on to the long *North Terrace* (*View of the Home Park, Eton, and Stoke Poges church).

Immediately below is *St George's School*, the choir school, in the building (1802) of *Travers College*, founded in 1795 from a bequest of Samuel Travers (d. 1725) for 'Naval Knights', an order corresponding to the Military Knights (see above) but disbanded in 1892.

From the North Terrace we enter the *State Apartments, which occupy the N. wing of the Upper Ward. These are used mainly for royal functions and contain many notable paintings from the royal collections, superb *Furniture, and other treasures.

From the China Gallery we ascend the GRAND STAIRCASE, with a statue of George IV, by *Chantrey*, and armour made for Henry VIII and the sons of James I. CHARLES II's DINING ROOM has a ceiling by *Verrio* and carvings by *Grinling Gibbons*. In the *KING's DRAWING ROOM, or RUBENS ROOM, is a series of noble works by *Rubens* (Holy Family, etc.) and a St Martin by *Van Dyck*. The STATE BEDCHAMBER contains a fine Louis Seize bed, and paintings by *Canaletto*; the adjoining DRESSING ROOM, or LESSER BEDCHAMBER, a painting by *Van Dyck* (Charles I, from three points of view for use in the execution of a bust), and many of the smaller *Paintings: portraits by *Clouet, Memling, Dürer*, and *And. del Sarto*; by *Rubens* (of himself and of Van Dyck); and by *Holbein*. In the KING'S CLOSET are Venetian views by *Canaletto* and portraits of David Garrick by *Hogarth* and *Reynolds*. The QUEEN'S DRAWING ROOM contains an unequalled array of *Portraits by *Van Dyck*: Charles I, Henrietta Maria, their children, and members of the court; also *Dobson*, James II as Duke of York; 17C French and English furniture.

We pass into an older wing (renewed by Charles II), where the QUEEN'S BALL-ROOM has more characteristic views by Canaletto. The QUEEN'S AUDIENCE CHAM-BER has *Gobelins* tapestries, and portraits of the Princes of Orange (by Honthorst) in frames carved by *Grinling Gibbons*; the QUEEN'S PRESENCE CHAMBER continues the series of tapestries. Both these rooms have ceilings by *Verrio* glorifying Queen Catherine of Braganza. Here also is a bust of Handel by *Roubiliac*. The QUEEN'S GUARD CHAMBER displays a fine suit of armour (1585), made for Sir Christopher Hatton, and busts (Philip II, Charles V) by *Leone Leoni*. Above busts of Marl-borough and Wellington hang the replica standards that constitute the annual rent paid for Woodstock and Stratfield Saye. A bust of Churchill was commis-sioned from *Oscar Nemon* (1953). The noble ST GEORGE'S HALL, 185 ft long, in which the festivities of the Order of the Garter are held, bears on the ceiling and walls the coats-of-arms of the knights since 1348. The portraits of English sover-eigns from James I to George IV are by *Van Dyck, Kneller*, etc. Among the parallel range of busts (by Nollekens, Chantrey, etc.), that by Roubiliac represents George II (*not* I). The GRAND RECEPTION ROOM has fine Gobelins tapestries; the THRONE ROOM or GARTER ROOM contains portraits of sovereigns in their Garter robes. The large *WATERLOO CHAMBER, constructed in 1830 inside a 12C court, contains portraits, mostly by *Lawrence*, of personages who were instrumental in the downfall of Napoleon. From the GRAND VESTIBULE beyond, with relics of Napoleon and the Japanese surrender sword (early 15C) of 1945, we descend by King John's Tower to the Quadrangle.

In a room to the left of the entrance is *Queen Mary's Dolls' House* (add. fee), designed by Sir Edwin Lutyens on the scale of an inch to a foot, and furnished and decorated on the same scale by 1500 eminent artists and craftsmen (1922–23). —Reached also from the entrance to the State Apartments is a splendid *Exhibition of Old Master Drawings* from the royal collection (add. fee), including works of Holbein, Leonardo da Vinci, Raphael, and Michelangelo, the French School (Claude, Poussin, etc.), and 17–19C British artists, notably Hogarth and Paul Sandby.

Between the Upper and Lower Wards rises the **Round Tower** or *Keep*, enlarged by Wyatville, which should be ascended (220 steps) for the extensive *View.—On the E. side of the Upper Ward (no adm.) are the *Private Apartments of the Queen*. The passage between the Round Tower and the Upper Ward leads through St George's Gateway to Castle Hill, near the entrance to the *Royal Stables*.

Immediately adjoining Windsor Castle on the N. and E. is the **Home Park**, in the s. part of which are *Frogmore House* and *Mausoleum*. The latter contains the remains of the Prince Consort and of Queen Victoria and is open to the public 11–4 on Whit Monday.—To the s. of Windsor lies **Windsor Great Park** (nearly 2000 acres), traversed by the road to Ascot and the *Long Walk*. The latter, a recently replanted avenue, stretches straight from the castle to (2¾ m.) *Snow Hill*, which bears a huge statue of George III ('the Copper Horse') by Westmacott. On the right of the Ascot road stood *Cranbourn Lodge* (demolished), where the great Duke of Marlborough died in 1722.

Still within the park, but best approached from Windsor viâ Old Windsor village, along the winding Crimp Lane and past the hamlet of Bishopsgate (where Shelley had a cottage in 1816), is (4½ m.) the *Savill Garden* (adm. daily 10–6, Mar–Oct, fee; Restaurant), 20 acres of lovely woodland garden, named after a former park ranger. Wick Lane goes on to *Englefield Green*, on the A 30 between Egham and Virginia Water. To the s. of the garden is Smith's Lawn, a polo ground, and beyond that the *Valley Gardens* (open all the year). These lie on the N. side of *Virginia Water*, comp. Rte 120.

From Windsor A 308 leads in 6¼ m. to Maidenhead (see below).

Beyond Windsor Bridge (no cars) begins the long street forming

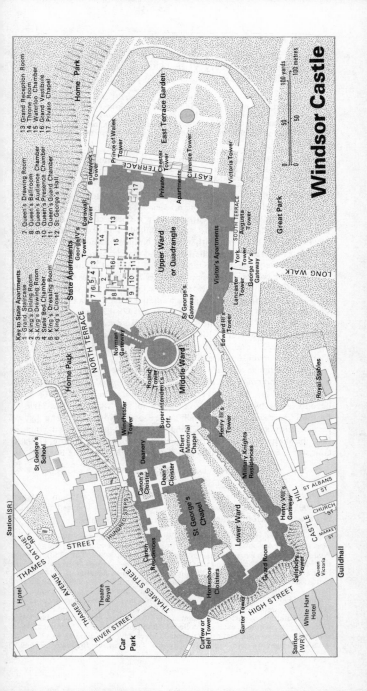

Windsor Castle

Key to State Apartments:

State Apartments
1 Grand Staircase
2 King's Dining Room
3 King's Drawing Room
4 State Bed Chamber
5 King's Dressing Room
6 King's Closet

7 Queen's Drawing Room
8 Queen's Ballroom
9 Queen's Audience Chamber
10 Queen's Presence Chamber
11 Queen's Guard Chamber
12 St George's Hall

13 Grand Reception Room
14 Throne Room
15 Waterloo Chamber
16 Grand Vestibule
17 Private Chapel

Station (SR)

Hotel

THAMES

THAMES AVENUE

River Street

THAMES STREET

DATCHET RD

Car Park

Theatre Royal

Home Park

St George's School

Hundred Steps

NORTH TERRACE

Canon Residences

Horseshoe Cloisters

Curfew or Bell Tower

Garter Tower

St George's Chapel

Canon's Cloister

Dean's Cloister

Deanery

Albert Memorial Chapel

Superintendent's Off.

Winchester Tower

Norman Gateway

Round Tower

Middle Ward

Edward III Tower

St George's Gateway

George IV's Gateway

Lancaster Tower

York Tower

Augusta Tower

SOUTH TERRACE

Visitor's Apartments

Upper Ward or Quadrangle

George IV's Tower

Cornwall Tower

Brunswick Tower

Prince of Wales Tower

Chester Tower

Clarence Tower

EAST TERRACE

East Terrace Garden

Victoria Tower

Private Apartments

Home Park

Home Park

Lower Ward

Henry III's Tower

Military Knights Residences

Guard Room

Salisbury Tower

Henry VIII's Gateway

Queen Victoria

White Hart Hotel

Station (WR)

HIGH STREET

CASTLE HILL

ST ALBANS ST

CHURCH ST

MARKET ST

Guildhall

LONG WALK

Great Park

Royal Stables

0   50   100 yards
0   50   100 metres

the small town of **Eton** (4000 inhab.) and leading to (⅜ m.) ***Eton College,** founded by Henry VI in 1440 and perhaps the most widely known of all English Schools.

On weekdays (unless required for school purposes) *School Yard* and *Cloisters* may be visited from noon (from 2 in summer) to lock-up (10–5 during holidays); the *Chapel, Upper School,* and *Lower School* are shown by a guide (fee) 11.30–12.30 and 2.30–5 or 2–6 (from 10.30 during holidays), on application at the School Office, just inside the main entrance. On Sundays the College is closed to visitors.

The pupils of Eton College consist of the 70 *Collegers,* representing the original foundation, who obtain scholarships by open competition, and about 1100 *Oppidans,* who live at the masters' houses. The boys wear broad collars, and tail-coats, the last replaced for boys below a certain height by short jackets.

The main block, of fine mellow red brick, includes two courts, or quadrangles, the larger of which, *School Yard,* contains a statue of Henry VI (1719). On the entrance side a frieze commemorates 1157 Etonians who fell in 1914–19 and 748 killed in 1939–45. Above is the *Upper School* (1689–94), with busts of eminent Etonians, damaged in 1941, but restored; the panelled walls and staircase are covered with the names of boys going on to King's (earliest 1577) cut in the wood. On the N. side of the courts is the *Lower School* (c. 1500), with wooden pillars of c. 1625. Opposite stands the **Chapel,* a Perpendicular structure begun in 1441, and completed (though on a smaller scale than was intended) by William Orchard for William Waynflete in 1479–83. It was given a new fan-vault by Sir Wm. Holford in 1958 and contains a series of wall-paintings (1479–88) of British workmanship, discovered in 1847 and restored in 1927, and a stained-glass E. window (1952) by Evie Hone. The clerestory windows are by John Piper.

A fine gatehouse of c. 1517, erected by Provost Lupton, admits to the original second court or *Cloisters,* with the Collegers' *Dining Hall* (1450) and the *College Library* (1725–29) above it.—In the playing fields beyond is the 'wall', which gives name to the 'wall-game', a style of football peculiar to Eton (chief game on 30 Nov). The long list of famous Etonian's includes Fielding C. J. Fox, the elder and younger Pitt, the Walpole brothers, Gray, Shelley, Wellington, Canning, Hallam, Gladstone, Rosebery, Roberts and King Leopold III of the Belgians.

The High Street of Eton is prolonged N. by Slough Rd., which crosses the M 4 for (2 m.) *Slough.*

The A 4 passes through the huge industrial town of (21 m.) **Slough** (86,800 inhab.), now part of Berkshire.—25 m. *Taplow* (r.), still in Bucks, has a well-known hotel and a church with 14–15C brasses.

FROM TAPLOW TO BEACONSFIELD, 8 m. (B 476). From the village the road rises steeply and soon skirts (l.) the beautiful woods of **Cliveden** (adm. March–Nov, Wed–Sun, 11–6.30, fee; mansion Apr–Oct, on Wed, Sat, & Sun, 2.30–5.30), given to the Nat. Trust in 1942 by Viscount Astor. The *Canadian Red Cross Memorial Hospital,* built in the woods in 1940 near the site of the Canadian hospital of 1914–18, was presented to the nation in 1946. The mansion, farther N., designed in 1849 by Sir Charles Barry, succeeds one built for the dissolute second Duke of Buckingham, who, after killing the Earl of Shrewsbury in a duel (1668), while the Countess, disguised as a page, held his horse, retired with her to this "bower of wanton Shrewsbury and of love". In this house the national air, 'Rule Britannia', by Dr Arne, was first performed on 1 Aug 1740. The place is now an extension college of Stanford University. The former Italian Garden contains a memorial (by Mackennal), erected by the Canadian Red Cross to 'Men who fought in France and died at Cliveden'. On the right is *Dropmore* (no adm.), an estate with magnificent gardens laid out in 1801–5 by Lord Grenville. To the E. of Dropmore, between the park and the fine wooded common of *Burnham Beeches* (see Rte 30), is *Dorneywood* (N.T.; normally open Sat in Aug–Sept, 2.15–6; fee) with fine grounds, presented to the national as an official residence for a Secretary of State.— Beyond (3½ m.) *Hedsor* we descend to join the Wycombe road at (5 m.) *Wooburn*, but keep r. on B 440 for (8 m.) *Beaconsfield.*

A bridge of 1772–77 carries the road across the Thames from Bucks to Berkshire.—26 m. **Maidenhead** (Hotels), with 45,300 inhab., at the beginning of a beautiful stretch extending to Marlow (7 m.), is perhaps the most animated of the 'up-river' summer resorts (comp. Rte 28B), especially during the week-ends.

'Oldfield', in Riverside, houses the *Henry Reitlinger Bequest* notable for Oriental ceramics and drawings (open Tues & Thurs, 10–12.30, 2.15–4.30).—In *Shottes-brook Park*, 4½ m. s.w., is a beautiful Dec. church.

FROM MAIDENHEAD TO HIGH WYCOMBE there are two roads. One (A 4094; 11½ m.) starts from the bridge; the other (A 308 and 404; 10½ m.) from the centre. The former passes Boulter's Lock (p. 260) and (3½ m.) **Cookham**, a pretty riverside village with the timbered *Bel & the Dragon* (c. 1417; Restaurant) and a monument to Fred Walker (1840–75). Here, too, was born Sir Stanley Spencer (1891–1959), who died at Taplow (see above). A gallery (10.30–7.30 Apr–Sept; fee) is devoted to loan collections of his paintings.—We cross the river to the large residential village of (4½ m.) *Bourne End.*—The other alternative crosses the river between (4¾ m.) Bisham and (5½ m.) Marlow. *Bisham Abbey* (no adm.), a Tudor mansion now a 'National Recreation Centre', incorporates the hall of an Augustinian priory. In the church are a monument to Sir Philip and Sir Thomas Hoby (d. 1558, 1566) and a fine armorial window of enamelled glass.—**Marlow**, where the river is crossed by a suspension bridge of 1831–36 by Wm. Tierney Clark, is a pleasant old town (11,700 inhab.) with many old houses and well-favoured hotels. Shelley and his wife visited Peacock here in 1816, and in 1817–18, when they occupied Albion House (now divided; tablet) in West St., Shelley composed the 'Revolt of Islam', and Mrs Shelley (Mary Wollstonecraft) wrote 'Frankenstein'. The monument of Sir Myles Hobart (d. 1632), in the parish church, is said to be the first monument in England erected at the public expense. In the Rom. Cath. church, built by A. W. Pugin, is preserved the hand of St James the Apostle, brought from Reading Abbey.

At Maidenhead Thicket A 423 bears to the right.—31 m. *Hurley* (Hotel), ½ m. from the river, has a restored Norman (partly pre-Conquest) church of a Benedictine priory, other remains of which are incorporated in an adjacent house.

35½ m. **Henley-on-Thames** (Hotels), a pleasant, well-built town (11,400 inhab.), has a handsome bridge (1786), with sculptured masks of the Thames and Isis by Mrs Damer. The course of the famous regatta (prices raised) begins about 350 yds below Temple Island and ends at (1 m. 450 yds) Poplar Point, immediately opposite which is *Phyllis Court*, a fashionable riverside club with a war memorial incorporating the 18C gates from Grosvenor House in London. On the Berkshire bank, close to the bridge, is the boathouse of the well-known *Leander Rowing Club*. In the exceptionally wide Dec. *Church* is the 17C Lady Periam monument; here also is buried Gen. Dumouriez (1739–1824), who died a refugee at Turville Park, 6 m. N. Next to the church is a 14C *Chantry House*, contemporary with the adjacent 'Red Lion'.

On a window of the 'Red Lion' Shenstone is said to have written his famous lines:

> "Whoe'er has travell'd life's dull round,
> Where'er his stages may have been
> May sigh to think he still has found
> The warmest welcome at an Inn."

In the grounds of *Park Place* (no adm.), below the town, stands the upper part of the original spire (by Wren) of St Bride's, Fleet St. About 5 m. N.W., in the Chilterns, is *Stonor* (Hotel). In the mansion of Lord Camoys here (restored and reopened to view in 1979) Edmund Campion (1540–81), the Jesuit martyr, set up his printing press. The chapel (open) has been in use for Mass without break for eight centuries. *Greys Court*, 3 m. w., is a ruined fortified mansion (c. 1350) enclosing a Jacobean house (N.T.). The gardens, the fortifications, and a donkey-wheel like that at Carisbrooke are open 2.15–6 on weekdays in Apr–Sept, fee (house Mon, Wed, & Fri only).

On the Berkshire bank of the Thames, 3¼ m. s. of Henley, is *Wargrave* (Hotel), a pretty riverside village much frequented by artists. The church, burned down by suffragettes in 1914, was rebuilt in 1916, when some fine Norman masonry was discovered beneath the 17C brick casing of the tower. It contains the monument of Thomas Day (1748–89), author of 'Sandford & Merton'. The sign-board of the George & Dragon was painted by Leslie and Hodgson, both Academicians.—At *Shiplake*, opposite, Tennyson was married in 1850.

The Oxford road now quits the Thames valley and ascends to (40½ m.) *Nettlebed* (Hotel), the gateway to some of the loveliest Chiltern country (see p. 289).—Beyond the summit (626 ft) we descend, past *Huntercombe* and its well-known golf course.

The main road now bears left from its natural course (which is blocked by Benson R.A.F. airfield) to (46½ m.) *Crowmarsh Gifford*, with its little Norman church, on the Thames opposite Wallingford. Jethro Tull (1674–1741), the pioneer of mechanized farming, lived at Howbery Park, between Crowmarsh and Benson. If we take this road we may visit Wallingford (see below) rejoining A 423 at Shillingford.

It is more attractive and no further to continue on the old road for 1½ m. and turn right viâ (46 m.) **Ewelme,** the prettiest of Chiltern villages, with a *Church, almshouse, and school of the 15C, a lovely group. Within the church are the *Tombs of Alice, Duchess of Suffolk (d. 1475; wife of the founder) and of her parents, Thomas Chaucer (supposed to be the son of the poet) and his wife. The Duchess wears the Order of the Garter on her left arm (one of the three effigies of ladies so decorated; comp. p. 262). On the floor are 15 brasses (1458–1517). The screens and roofs are notable and the font (c. 1480) has a magnificent pyramidal *Cover in carved wood; the head on the corbel above may represent Edward III.—48 m. *Benson* (Hotels), a large village was once a seat of the kings of Mercia. The airfield lies to the S.E.

We join the road from Crowmarsh Gifford, and at (49 m.) *Shillingford*, A 329 from Reading. In the pleasant village of *Warborough* (adjoining r.) there is a 13C lead font.

THE APPROACH FROM READING (19 m.) keeps near the s. bank of the Thames through one of the loveliest portions of its valley, even more pleasantly visited by river (see Rte 28B). At *Streatley* (9½ m. from Reading; Hotel), at the foot of the juniper-studded Berkshire Downs (*View from the top), the Port Way diverges to the w. Opposite is Goring-on-Thames (p. 261).
Aldworth, with the remarkable series of De la Beche effigies in its church, is 3¾ m. w. of Streatley. On the Icknield Way, 3 m. N.E. of Goring, is *Ipsden*, where Charles Reade (1814–84) was born. The *Oratory School*, a leading Roman Catholic boys' school, transferred from Birmingham to Caversham in 1922, was again removed, in 1942, to Woodcote House, 2¾ m. E. of Goring.
Wallingford (Hotels), 2 m. s. of Shillingford, is a historic town (6200 inhab.) encircled by earthen ramparts with narrow streets and a Town Hall of 1670. The medieval bridge was gracefully widened in 1809. In *St Peter's Church* is buried Sir Wm. Blackstone (d. 1780). The Treaty of Wallingford ended the strife between Stephen and Henry II. *North Moreton* church, 3 m. w., has fine 14C glass in the Stapleton chantry.

We cross the Thame.—51 m. **Dorchester** (Hotels), now a mere village of pleasant houses, was formerly a Roman station and an important Saxon town. From 634 to 705 it was the cathedral city of Wessex, and from 869 to 1072 that of Mercia. A priory of Austin canons was founded here in 1140. Near the bridge over the Thame is the *Abbey Church* of SS Peter and Paul, a remarkable Trans. Norman and Dec. building and a famous battleground of ecclesiologists. The ground-plan and proportions are most singular. Though 200 ft in length, it is of a purely parochial type. The nave and the w. end of the choir date from c. 1180. The round transeptal arches (like the tower) date only from the 17C. The nave and choir aisles are built in the geometrical Dec. style (1280–1320); note the unrivalled *Choir-arcades and the leaden font (1170–80), with figures of the Apostles. The E. end of the church dates from the close of the Dec. period, and has three unique windows, filled with tracery throughout and ornamented with sculptured figures. The painted glass is original. On the N. side is the celebrated *Jesse Window. Under the s. window are the beautiful sedilia and piscina; the old glass in the little triangular windows represents the life of St Birinus, the apostle of Wessex.

A new N. door (1963) leads to an 'Anglo-American' garden on the site of the cloister. A corbel (1970) on the w. front commemorates the responsible Bostonian benefactress, who also paid for the restoration of the E. window in memory of Sir Winston Churchill.
   Overy, across the fields to the s.e., has attractive thatched cottages.

A 423 (comp. below) runs direct to Oxford, but a diversion (c. 4 m. longer) may be made following the loop of the Thames to the w.— 3 m. *Clifton Hampden* (p. 261).—4½ m. *Culham* has a Church of England college for schoolmasters and an atomic energy research station.— 7 m. **Abingdon** (Hotel; bus to Oxford), a pleasant old town (18,600 inhab.), sprang up round a powerful Benedictine mitred abbey, founded in the 7C, and was until 1870 the county town of Berkshire. Appropriate modern building has enhanced its character. The rebuilt bridge affords a striking view, with the disused *Gaol* (1811), well-proportioned if forbidding, prominent in the foreground. On the right, by the river, are the surviving *Abbey* buildings (adm. daily 2–6 or dusk; closed Mon Oct–March; fee), including the *Checker Hall* (now fitted up as a theatre), the *Checker* (i.e. exchequer) itself, a fine 13C building with a vaulted undercroft and a rare contemporary chimney, and the 15–16C *Long Gallery*, recalling that at Newbury. A path alongside the Abbey Grounds leads through the *Abbey Gateway* (c. 1450), adjoining the 12–15C church of *St Nicholas*, to the Market Place. The 18C *Guildhall*, s. of the gatehouse, contains an art gallery (open daily) with civic plate, etc. It preserves traces of the abbey hospital and includes the old grammar school of 1563. Just down Bridge St., the *Crown and Thistle* has a picturesque courtyard. In the market-place stands the dignified *County Hall* (1677–80), the masterpiece of Christopher Kempster, Wren's master-mason, with an arcaded lower story. It contains the Borough Museum (daily 2–5). A pleasing shopping precinct runs N.W., while the attractive East St Helen St. leads to *St Helen's*, a noble Perp. church with a fine spire, double aisles, and a Jacobean pulpit. The churchyard is surrounded by almshouses, notably the picturesque *Christ's Hospital*, founded in 1553 in direct succession to the ancient Guild of the Holy Cross (hall shown on application).

The church at *Drayton*, 2½ m. s., has alabaster carvings of the 16C. That of *Sunningwell*, 3 m. N., has a classic seven-sided porch, added by Dr Jewel in 1552. Roger Bacon is said to have used the tower for astronomical observations.—At *Radley*, 2½ m. N.E., is a well-known boys' school, founded in 1847

From Dorchester A 423 runs N.W.—54 m. *Nuneham Courtenay*. The village and church were transferred to a position on the main road by Earl Harcourt in 1765. On the left the beautiful woods of *Nuneham Park* now belong to Oxford University (no adm.).—At the ring road (57 m.) we may turn left, then right to approach the city by Folly Bridge; or right towards *Cowley*, with the original works of Morris Motors, then left to enter by Magdalen Bridge across the Cherwell. *Iffley*, on the Thames between the two approach roads, has the best-preserved specimens of a small Norman parish *Church in England, built about 1170, with a fine low square tower, of which the top story is specially notable. The W. front has a beautifully ornamented recessed doorway. There are also good N. and S. doorways. The last bay of the chancel is E.E., and many of the windows were inserted in the 14–15C. The door-ways to the (former) rood-loft reveal elaborate groined archways.— 60 m. **Oxford,** see Rte 29.

B By River

The Thames above London is an ideal boating-river, for its commercial traffic is small, its current gentle (except after floods), and its varied scenery unsurpassed for quiet, typically English beauty: low hills and wooded cliffs, luxuriant meadows, handsome country-houses, and pretty bungalows with gardens and lawns sloping down to the river. Pleasant villages and quiet little towns stand on its banks, and comfortable and attractive inns and hotels are numerous (though rarely cheap). The finest stretches are those between Maidenhead and Marlow, Henley and Sonning, Mapledurham and Goring. Reading is the only industrial town between Kingston and Oxford. The closing down of most of the pedestrian ferries has lessened the opportunities for long Thames-side walks, but those demanding immediate access by car limit themselves to the most obvious and most crowded places.

Steamers. An excellent service of steamers is maintained during summer (mid-May to third week in September) by Salter Bros. of Oxford, twice daily in each direction between *Kingston Pier* and (91½ m.) *Oxford* (Folly Bridge). The steamers leave Kingston at 9 a.m. and 2.30 p.m. The journey takes 2½ days if started in the afternoon, or 3 days with a half-day rest if started in the morning, the nights being passed at either Windsor or Marlow and at Reading. Oxford is reached at 7 p.m. on the third day. Passengers may board or leave the steamers at any lock or regular stopping-place, at proportionate fares (cheap day return fares). Holders of through-tickets may break the journey. Combined railway and steamer tickets are issued at Paddington, Waterloo, and other stations. Children under 14 half-price. Luggage up to 112 lb free. Bicycles are carried at a special tariff, dogs by special arrangement only. Rfmts are obtainable, and the steamers stop for luncheon at Windsor, Marlow, or Benson.

Boating. Rowing-boats, punts, and canoes can be hired for the day at many points, and cabin-cruisers by the week from the many hire firms. The best punting waters are at Staines, Maidenhead, and Goring. The trip by cruiser from Kingston to Oxford and back may be comfortably accomplished with sightseeing within a fortnight.

A licence for cruising is obligatory and the 'Thames Conservancy Launch Digest', issued free with it, gives all necessary regulations about channels, buoys, etc., including dimensions of locks and headway of bridges. There are 31 locks between Kingston and Oxford, a few of which are equipped with rollers for small boats.

Salter's 'Guide to the Thames' (Salter Bros., Oxford) is recommended for detailed description.

Regattas. *Henley Royal Regatta*, held on four days in the first week of July, is the premier amateur regatta of the world (founded 1839) and is a very gay, crowded, and fashionable function. The chief events (open also to foreign and Commonwealth oarsmen) are the Grand Challenge Cup (eights), Stewards' Cup (fours), Silver Goblets (pairs), and the Diamond Sculls. The Ladies' Plate (eights) and Visitors' Cup (fours) are restricted to college and public school crews. Other rowing regattas are held (mostly in July and early August) at Molesey, Marlow, Kingston, Staines, Walton, Reading, Bourne End, and Goring. At these and at the minor regattas elsewhere visitors usually contribute to the expenses by buying little boat-flags.

In the following description the words 'right' and 'left' (r. and l.) refer to the journey upstream. For fuller details of the Thames below Walton Bridge, see the 'Blue Guide to London'.

Kingston-upon-Thames is reached by train from Waterloo. The principal landmarks going upstream are: 3 m. *Hampton Court*. On the right is the palace; on the left, the mouth of the *Mole*. Above *Tagg's Island*, a pleasure-resort, is *Hampton* (r.), with Garrick's Villa.—6 m. *Sunbury Lock.*—7½ m. *Walton Bridge*. The straight Desborough Channel here cuts off c. 1 m., but the river runs more pleasantly by *Lower Halliford* and *Shepperton* (r.) with a pleasing 17–18C village centre.—9½ m. *Shepperton Lock.*

On the left, at the mouth of the Wey, is **Weybridge** (Hotels), which preserves on its green the Seven Dials column (1794) from London. *Oatlands Park*, now a hotel, on the Walton road, was built in 1827 and succeeds a royal palace (destroyed in the Civil War) where Henry VIII married Catherine Howard.

Between Weybridge and Guildford (15 m.) the WEY NAVIGATION (N.T.) is available to pleasure-boats. It passes through a charming stretch of country at *Pyrford*, near Newark Priory and Old Woking, and skirts the grounds of Sutton Place.

Beyond *Chertsey Bridge* (1780–85) is (11½ m.) *Chertsey Lock*. Abbey Mead (l.) recalls the famous Benedictine abbey of **Chertsey**, founded in the 7C and refounded in 1110, of which almost nothing survives. It was known especially for its floor-tiles, which adorn many English churches. —At (12½ m.) *Laleham* (r.) Matthew Arnold (1822–88) was born and is buried beside the part-Norman church. Laleham Abbey was the home of Lord Lucan of Crimean War fame.—13½ m. *Penton Hook Lock*, with a marina.—15½ m. *Staines*, with two bridges across the Thames.—Just short of (16½ m.) *Bell Weir Lock*, we pass under the Staines by-pass; the *Colne* enters the Thames on the right. Upstream is the level meadow of *Runnymede* with (18 m.) *Magna Carta Island*. Above is *Cooper's Hill*, crowned by the *Commonwealth Air Forces Memorial.*—19½ m. *Old Windsor Lock*, at the entrance to one of three artificial cuts on the way to Oxford.—*Datchet*, facing the Home Park of Windsor (l.), lies between two bridges. Here Wm. Herschel moved after receiving a pension from George III; a visit to his observatory by Haydn is supposed to have inspired 'The Creation'.—22½ m. *Romney Lock.*—23 m. *Windsor Bridge* connects **Windsor** with **Eton**, comp. Rte 28A.

Most of the riverside towns and villages between Windsor and Oxford are more fully described on the road-routes (comp. the index).

Above Windsor is (24 m.; l.) *Clewer*, with the headquarters of the Clewer Sisterhood and a partly Norman church.—25 m. *Boveney Lock.* —27 m: *Down Place* (l.) was the residence of Jacob Tonson (d. 1736), the publisher, and a meeting-place of the Kit-Cat Club.—At (27½ m.) *Monkey Island* (Hotel), a popular resort, the stream is very swift. We pass under a bridge (1960–64), carrying the M 4.—28 m. *Bray Lock*. At the large village of *Bray* (Restaurants), ½ m. farther on, is the picturesque Jesus Hospital (1627). The fine half-timbered 15C mansion of *Ockwells* lies 2 m. w.

The notorious 'Vicar of Bray', who thrice changed his creed in order to keep his preferment, is commonly identified with one Simon Aleyn (d. 1588), who, however, flourished under the last four Tudor monarchs, and not "in good King Charles's golden days".

Passing under Brunel's railway bridge and (29½ m.) *Maidenhead Bridge* (1772) we reach **Maidenhead**, opposite *Taplow* (r.). Here begins one of the most beautiful (and most frequented) reaches of the Thames, especially near (30¼ m.) *Boulter's Lock*. On the right, for 2 m. above the lock, extend the *Cliveden Woods*, and to the E. of (32¼ m.) *Cookham Lock* stands *Hedsor*, on high ground. *Cookham*, with a bridge, lies on the left bank, ½ m. beyond the lock, and on the right, 1 m. farther, is *Bourne End*. The fine Quarry Woods (l.) begin just short of (36¼ m.) *Marlow Lock*. **Marlow** is on the right bank, with the grounds of Bisham Abbey opposite. Bisham church (comp. p. 255) can be reached from the river bank.—38 m. *Temple Lock*.—38½ m. *Hurley Lock*. About 1 m. farther on is (r.) *Medmenham Abbey*, a mansion occupying the site of a 13C Cistercian monastery.

The 'Monks of Medmenham', otherwise the 'Hell-Fire Club', a fashionable club founded here by Sir Francis Dashwood about the middle of the 18C, adopted the maxim 'Fay ce que voudras' ('do what you please'; still to be seen above the door) and were notorious for blasphemous orgies (probably exaggerated in the telling). Churchill, the poet, Whitehead, the dramatist, and John Wilkes (a guest only) were among the leading spirits.

Beyond *Aston Ferry* are (42 m.) *Hambleden Lock*, 1 m. s. of the village, and the grounds of *Greenlands* (r.), a 17C mansion presented in 1945 by Viscount Hambleden to serve as an Administrative Staff College. Then come *Temple Island* and the Henley Regatta course. *Fawley Court* (r.), designed by Wren, stands, opposite *Remenham* (Inn), on the boundary between Buckinghamshire and Oxfordshire.

44½ m. *Henley Bridge*. **Henley** is on the right (Oxford) bank.—45½ m. *Marsh Lock*. On the left is a picturesque backwater. Then comes *Wargrave* on the Berkshire bank.—48 m. *Shiplake Lock*, where the little river *Loddon* joins the Thames. *Shiplake* is on the right. On the left is *St Patrick's Stream*, a pleasant backwater.—The charming village of *Sonning* (Hotels), on the left, has an ancient bridge and a church containing eight brasses of the 15–17C.—51 m. *Sonning Lock*, is one of the prettiest on the river.—53½ m. *Caversham Lock*, beyond which are *Reading Bridge* and *Caversham Bridge*, connecting **Reading** with *Caversham*, its north-bank suburb.

About ½ m. below the lock the Thames is joined by the *Kennet*, which is navigable for c. 10 m. and is to be reopened to (18½ m.) *Newbury*.

The church of (57 m.) *Tilehurst* contains the splendid monument of Sir Peter Vanlore (d. 1627).— 58 m. *Mapledurham Lock*, with a much-painted mill and weir, inspired some of E. H. Shepard's drawings for 'Wind in the Willows'. Close by is *Mapledurham House* (adm. Easter-

Sept, Sat, Sun, & BH, 2.30–5; fee) the Tudor manor-house (1588–1606) of the Roman Catholic Blount family, of which Martha Blount, Pope's friend, was a member. Its splendid plaster ceilings have recently been restored. The s. aisle of the church is walled off as a family chapel (R.C.).—We now enter one of the finest reaches of the Thames. On the right is *Hardwick House*, delightfully situated.—60½ m. *Whitchurch Lock*, with a toll bridge connecting *Pangbourne* (l.) with *Whitchurch*. At *Pangbourne* (Hotels), is Church Cottage, where Kenneth Grahame lived from 1924 till his death in 1932. Pangbourne College, 1¼ m. s.w., founded as the Nautical College, no longer exclusively trains for the merchant marine.—Farther on is *Basildon* (l.), with its low-lying church and the former mansion of Viscount Fane (1770). On the r. is the lovely Hartslock Wood.—64½ m. *Goring Lock*, with a rebuilt bridge. At *Goring* (r.; Hotel) the ancient Icknield Way crosses the Thames. The church, with a tourelle on its Norman tower and Roman (?) tiles in the s. porch, contains remnants of the chapel of an Augustinian nunnery. Beyond the pretty Berkshire village of *Streatley* (see p. 256) both banks are now Oxfordshire.—65 m. *Cleeve Lock* (Inn).—Opposite (67 m.) *Moulsford* (Hotel) is *South Stoke*, with an E.E. church. Farther on, at *North Stoke*, was the residence of Dame Clara Butt (1873–1936), the singer.

70½ m. *Wallingford Bridge*, leading from **Wallingford** (l.) to *Crowmarsh Gifford*.—71½ m. *Benson Lock*. The twin *Sinodun Hills* or *Wittenham Clumps* (ancient encampment; fine walk from Day's Lock, see below) now come into view and remain in sight for the next 8 m.—72½ m. *Shillingford Bridge* (p. 256). Farther on is (74½ m.) the mouth of the river *Thame*. Above this point the Thames is known also (poetically but not locally) as the *Isis*.—75½ m. *Day's Lock*. On the left bank is *Little Wittenham*. On the right a footpath leads to (1 m.) *Dorchester* (p. 257), past the Dyke Hills, an old fortification extending from the Thame to the Thames. On the r., both with ancient inns, are (76¾ m.) *Burcot* and (78 m.) *Clifton Hampden*, with a church (12–14C) situated on a low cliff. —78½ m. *Clifton Lock*. On the backwater is the pretty village of *Long Wittenham*, the church of which has a sundial, a unique piscina (serving also as the founder's monument), and a leaden font of c. 1190. We pass next *Appleford* (l.) near the railway-bridge; Didcot power-station is all dominant.—81½ m. *Culham Lock*. Culham (r.) is connected by a bridge with *Sutton Courtenay*, a delightful old village on a *Backwater (reached from the far end of Culham Cut), with an interesting church. The Earl of Oxford and Asquith (1852–1928) died and is buried here. *Old Culham Bridge* (r.), farther on, on another backwater, dates from 1430. —**Abingdon** (p. 257) has a rebuilt bridge, ¼ m. below (84 m.) *Abingdon Lock*.—Beyond the railway-bridge begin (r.) the beautiful woods of *Nuneham Park*. Leaving *Radley* on the left, we arrive at (88½ m.) *Sandford Lock*, the deepest on the Thames, with the Radley College boathouse.—About ½ m. farther on we pass *Kennington Island* (Inn).—90 m. *Iffley Lock*. On the right is Iffley church. The reach between Iffley and (1½ m.) Folly Bridge is the scene of the 'Eights' and 'Torpid' boat-races. Opposite the 'New Cut', an artificial mouth of the *Cherwell*, is the University Boathouse, on the left. On the right survive a few college barges, behind which lies Christ Church Meadow. The steamer landing-place at (91½ m.) **Oxford** (Rte 29) is at Folly Bridge.

THE THAMES ABOVE OXFORD, known at Oxford as the 'Upper River', is much less frequented for boating, in spite of its beauty, as the headroom at Osney Bridge is only 7½ ft.—1 m. *Osney Lock.* On the right is the entrance to the *Oxford Canal*, which runs viâ *Banbury* (27¼ m.) and *Napton* (49 m; Warwick & Napton Canal) to *Longford* (78 m.; Coventry Canal).—2 m. *Medley.* On the right is *Port Meadow*, where the burgesses of Oxford have enjoyed the right of free pasture since the time of Edward the Confessor; on the left is *Binsey*, with St Frideswide's Well.—3¼ m. *Godstow Lock* (Restaurant), with the ruined Benedictine nunnery where Fair Rosamond was educated and was buried (c. 1176), though Hugh of Lincoln is said to have ordered the removal of her body from the church in 1191. To the left is *Wytham*, famous for its strawberries, with *Wytham Abbey*. The house, with surrounding woods, was presented to the University in 1943.—4½ m. *King's Lock*, with another entrance to the Oxford Canal. We pass (6 m.) the mouth of the *Evenlode* (r.).—7 m. *Eynsham Lock*, with *Swinford Bridge* (1777), leading to *Eynsham*, ¾ m. to the right.—8½ m. *Pinkhill Lock.*—11½ m. *Bablock Hythe*, celebrated in Matthew Arnold's 'Scholar Gipsy'. On the left a path leads to (1 m.) *Cumnor*, the scene of Amy Robsart's death. Cumnor Place is gone, but the church, with one of the two known contemporary statues of Elizabeth I and memorials of Amy Robsart, is interesting. To the right is (2 m.) *Stanton Harcourt*, the original seat of the Harcourts, with the gatehouse, 'Pope's Tower', and the kitchen of the old manor-house. The church contains perhaps the earliest chancel screen (E.E.) in England and the monument of Margaret Harcourt (1471), one of the three known effigies of ladies wearing the Order of the Garter (comp. p. 256).—12½ m. *Northmoor Lock.* A footpath runs s. to (1 m.) *Appleton*, with a church well known for change-ringing and a manor-house of c. 1190 (no adm.).—15 m. *New Bridge* (c. 1200; Hotel) disputes with Radcot Bridge the title of the oldest bridge on the Thames. Here the Windrush flows in. At the pretty village of *Longworth*, 1 m. from the river on the s. side, R. D. Blackmore was born in 1825.—17 m. *Shifford Lock*, the entrance to a cut; the backwater is crossed by a ford.—21 m. *Tadpole Bridge.*— 21½ m. *Rushy Lock.*—24 m. *Radcot Lock.*—26 m. *Radcot Bridge* (Hotel) is the best surviving medieval bridge (before 1312) over the Thames. Stone from Burford was shipped hence for St Paul's Cathedral in London. On the left is the church of *Eaton Hastings*; on the right, farther on, is (½ m.) *Kelmscott*, the country home of William Morris from 1871 till his death in 1896, bequeathed to Oxford University by his daughter in 1939, but now owned by the Society of Antiquaries of London. The house was restored in 1966–67 and is open to view occasionally. It gave name to the famous Kelmscott Press at Hammersmith. Morris is buried in the church-yard.—28½ m. *Hart's Weir Bridge.* The right bank now belongs to Gloucestershire. —29½ m. *Buscot Lock.*—30¼ m. *St John's Lock*, the first on the river.—31 m. Lechlade (p. 293) is the present head of the navigation, but plans are afoot to dredge at least to (32¼ m.) *Inglesham* at the entrance of the derelict *Thames & Severn Canal*. The church has a fine 14C tomb of Purbeck marble. On the right is *Kempsford*, with a beautiful church tower.—42¼ m. *Cricklade* (p. 295).

29   OXFORD

OXFORD (108,600 inhab.), a thriving city, an episcopal see, and the seat of an ancient university, is one of the most famous and interesting towns in Europe. The beautiful grouping of its spires and towers as seen from a distance is renowned, not less the noble architecture of its colleges, and the "streamlike windings" of its famous High Street. The Cherwell ('Char') joins the Isis (or Upper Thames) just below the town.

OXFORD UNIVERSITY has 34 colleges (5 founded for women), 164 professors, about 900 readers or lecturers, 735 fellows, and 10,700 students (7700 undergraduates, of whom c. 1500 are women).

From 1979 all former men's colleges except Oriel will accept women students, but only Lady Margaret Hall has decided to accept men.

The five Graduate Colleges of *Nuffield*, *St Anthony's*, *Linacre*, *St Cross*, and *Wolfson*, are all mixed colleges. *Wolfson College* (1966), founded by the Wolfson and Ford Foundations, incorporates *Iffley College* (1965). *Campion Hall*, *St Benet's Hall*, and *Greyfriars* are licensed as private halls for Jesuit, Benedictine, and Franciscan students respectively, and *Mansfield College* and *Regent's Park College* for Congregational and Baptist students respectively. Not incorporated with the University are *Ruskin College* and five theological institutions: *Ripon Hall, St Stephen's Hall, Wycliffe Hall, Manchester College, and Pusey House.*—The WOMEN STUDENTS of Oxford were admitted to full membership of the University in 1920, including the right to degrees. Their colleges are *Lady Margaret Hall* (1878); *Somerville College* (1879); *St Hugh's College* (1886); *St Hilda's College* (1893); and *St Anne's College* (1952), formerly *Oxford Home Students* (1897).

A unique feature of Oxford life is the body of *Rhodes Scholars* (nearly 180 in number), appointed under the will of Cecil Rhodes (d. 1902). They are now drawn from the U.S.A., South Africa, the Commonwealth, and Germany. The scholars are allowed to choose among the different colleges.

Car Parks near St Aldate's, near Magdalen Bridge, and (usually crowded), by the University Parks. In Broad St., St Giles, etc., parking is allowed for short periods only (disc obligatory; obtain from Information Centre).

Railway Station (Pl. 9), Botley Rd. (Bus No. 1 to Carfax and Magdalen); service to *London* (Paddington) in 1–1¼ hr.

Hotels in the town, and Iffley Rd. Pl. 16 (charges raised during Eights Week and Commemoration, when rooms must be booked in advance); Motel on by-pass to the N.—Excellent **Restaurants**.

Post Office (Pl. 14), St Aldate's.—INFORMATION CENTRE (Pl. 14) St Aldate's.—ENGLISH SPEAKING UNION, 19 Beaumont St.

Buses from Carfax to the station, Cowley, Headington, Iffley, Hinksey, etc. From Gloucester Green (Pl. 10) to all destinations outside the city. COACH to *London* in 2¾ hrs.

Theatres. *New* (Pl. 10), George St.; *Playhouse* (Pl. 10), Beaumont St.

Boating is very popular on the Thames and on the Cherwell. Boats may be hired from Salters, Folly Bridge, or Medley Boat Station, on the Thames, and from Faulkner, Howard, and the Cherwell Hotel on the Cherwell (punts and canoes are the most suitable craft for the Cherwell). Dinghy sailing is popular on the Upper Thames, and craft may be hired from Bossom's Boatyard, Port Meadow. Canal cruisers can be hired from British Waterways, Juxon St. Wharf.

River Bathing. In the Cherwell, reached from South Parks Rd. at Parson's Pleasure, for men only, and at Dame's Delight, mixed; in the Thames at Long Bridges, reached by towpath from Folly Bridge, and at Tumbling Bay, reached by towpath from Botley Rd., both mixed.—INDOOR BATHS at Temple Rd., Cowley.

Hints to Visitors. The best way of seeing Oxford is under the escort of a member of the University; but the colleges and most of the college gardens are open to the unaccompanied visitor except (in some cases) before 1.30 or 2 p.m. in term time. During the vacations, especially in 'the Long' or 'the Long Vac.' (from mid-June to mid-October), the characteristic University life ebbs, but the 'architectural' visitor finds compensation in the longer periods at which the colleges are accessible (unless given over to conferences). Each college displays a notice stating where visitors may go. To pay for wear to the fabric caused by an ever-increasing throng of sightseers, some colleges charge an entrance fee.—The chapels of New College, Magdalen, and Christ Church (Cathedral) are noted for their musical services.—In correct University parlance, High St. is always spoken of as 'the High' (similarly 'the Broad', 'the Corn', for Cornmarket St., 'the Turl', 'St Aldate's', 'Holywell', and 'Longwall'); in referring to the colleges the word 'college' is usually omitted except in the case of New College and should never be used of Christ Church.

History. Though J. R. Green (a native of the city; 1837–83) claims for Oxford that it had "five centuries of borough life before a student appeared in its streets", the first authentic mention of its name (the 'ford for oxen' over the Thames at Hinksey) occurs in the Anglo-Saxon Chronicle of 912. The University is first mentioned in the 12C, though there are picturesque legends that it was founded by the mythical British king Memphric or, at least, by Alfred the Great; it may have developed from the monastic schools of St Frideswide's priory or perhaps owed its origin indirectly to the expulsion of foreign students from Paris. The early students (c. 1000–1500 in number) who flocked to hear the lectures at Oxford found accommodation in the numerous 'Halls' (hostels kept by graduate principals). During the Middle Ages the 'Colleges', which came to be founded as corporate bodies with their own rules and privileges, were practically reserved for graduates (like All Souls today), so that it was not until the reign of Elizabeth that the whole body of undergraduates was admitted to the Colleges. The teaching body was in due time recognized as a 'studium generale' or university, with all the powers of a corporation. In 1214 the University received from Pandulf, the papal legate, its first legal privilege, conferring immunity from lay jurisdiction, which was the first stage in the long and often riotous struggle between 'Town' and 'Gown'. Oxford quickly became one of the intellectual centres of Europe and, with the aid of the Dominican and Franciscan friars, took a leading part in the development of scholastic philosophy, the revived study of Aristotle, and the beginnings of the experimental method. Her leading schoolmen were Grosseteste, Roger Bacon, Duns Scotus, Bradwardine, and Fitzralph. In the 14C important controversies were raised by the teachings of John Wyclif, while the 15C saw contacts with Italy, and there followed the advent of the Renaissance, associated especially with the names of Grey, Sellyng, Grocyn, Colet, Linacre, More, and Erasmus.

The Reformation was felt most severely at Oxford, and the successive changes of religion effectively emptied the University of students. The iconoclastic Calvinism of Edward VI's reign was followed by the Marian reaction and the execution of bishops. The Test Act of 1672 made Oxford an Anglican university, and until 1871 all members had to subscribe to the Thirty-nine Articles. Under the chancellorship of Laud the statutes were codified and public examinations instituted; the number of students rose to c. 3000. Always the "home of lost causes", the University espoused the Stuart cause at the outbreak of the Civil War, while the city declared for Parliament. Oxford became the headquarters of the king and court in 1642, but in 1646 yielded to Fairfax. After the Restoration the University settled down into the ease of the 18C, interrupted only by political disputes and the Methodist movement. Interesting events of the 19C were the Tractarian and Lux Mundi movements in the Anglican Church; and the beginning of the democratization of the University shown in the 'Extension' movement and the foundation of Ruskin College. In 1914–18 the number of undergraduates fell to about 350, and most of the colleges and University buildings were used as quarters for officer cadet battalions or as hospitals. The academic year 1919–20 saw three important changes: the dethroning of Greek as a necessary part of University education, the admission of women to degrees, and the acceptance of a Government grant (after 700 years of independence). In later years Oxford has become also an important industrial and commercial centre and there has been much rebuilding and expansion. In an attempt to preserve the traditional amenities of the place, its old buildings, open spaces, etc., the Oxford Preservation Trust has been formed. Among its successes has been the prevention of a by-pass through Christchurch Meadows. Architecturally some of the new foundations and the university buildings have been more successful than the additions to the older colleges.

University System. The distinguishing mark of Oxford and Cambridge, as compared with American, Continental, and even Scottish universities, is their combination of the communal life of the *Colleges* with the teaching and degree-conferring functions of the *University*. There is no University Building as such, the 'University' being the inward and spiritual grace of which the colleges are the outward and visible forms. Both University and colleges are corporate bodies with their own quite distinct endowments, and the colleges now contribute to the funds of the University. Each college has its own staff of tutors, enabling pupils to enjoy individual attention, but its members are entitled to attend also all University lectures. The Honours lectures of the colleges are open to all members of the University.

The college community consists of a Head, Fellows, and Undergraduates. The Head is known as *Master* (the almost invariable term at Cambridge), *Warden, President, Principal, Provost, Rector,* or (at Christ Church) *Dean.*—The *Fellows* are selected from distinguished graduates, not necessarily of the University in which they hold a fellowship. The Fellows and Tutors are popularly known as *Dons.*—The *Undergraduates* are either *Scholars* (who form part of the foundation) or *Commoners* (at Cambridge, *Pensioners*)—the great majority, including *Exhibitioners.* Some of the undergraduates live within the college, the others occupy approved ('licensed') lodgings in the town. They take meals together in the college hall, and must be in their rooms at the closing of the gates, not later than midnight. At lectures, at dinner in hall, in chapel, and at all official ceremonies, undergraduates wear 'academic dress,' viz. a black gown (dark blue at Caius and at Trinity, Cam.); the square cap is seldom seen except at official functions. At Oxford, Scholars wear longer gowns and Commoners shorter gowns than at Cambridge, where some colleges have a distinctive pattern of gown. At Cambridge on Sunday, white surplices take the place of gowns at the chapel services. At Oxford the white surplice is usually worn by Heads, Fellows, and Scholars only. Graduates wear fuller gowns, differing according to their degrees; the full dress of Doctors is mainly scarlet.

The ultimate governing authority of the University consists of the Masters of Arts, resident or non-resident, who have kept their names on the books, and is known at Oxford as *Convocation*, at Cambridge as the *Senate*. The Senate legislates by so-called 'graces', Convocation by 'statutes'. All legislation, however, is initiated by the *Council of the Senate* (Cam.) or the *Hebdomadal Council* (Ox.), small elected bodies consisting of University officials, heads of colleges, and other members of the Senate or Convocation. At Cambridge this Council is elected by the so-called *Regent House*, composed (roughly) of the resident part of the Senate; at Oxford all measures must be approved by the similar body known as *Congregation*, and under the statutes of 1926 these bodies can legislate without the consent of non-residents. The executive authority of the University rests in theory with the *Chancellor*, elected by the Senate or Convocation and usually a nobleman or statesman of high standing, but the duties are practically performed by the resident *Vice-Chancellor*, who is invariably one of the heads of colleges, nominated at Oxford by the Chancellor and elected at Cambridge by the Senate. The two *Proctors*, appointed yearly, have charge of University discipline and are assisted by Pro-Proctors and by servants popularly known as 'Bull Dogs'. From 1603 to 1950 the Universities of Oxford and Cambridge returned representatives (called 'burgesses') to Parliament, but this privilege was abolished by the Representation of the People Act of 1949.

Details as to the requirements for entry, the courses of study, the examinations, the degrees conferred, and the general life of the student may be most easily obtained from the *University Calendars* and the *Students' Handbooks* to the Universities. Most undergraduates read for an honours degree, usually Bachelor of Arts (B.A.). No additional examination is necessary at either University for the degree of *Master of Arts* (M.A.), which is merely a matter of standing and fee.— Both Universities confer the degrees of Bachelor and Doctor of Law (D.C.L. at Oxford, LL.D. at Cambridge), Medicine, Theology, Music, Science, and Letters. There are also Masters' degrees in various subjects, obtainable by research, as is the degree of Doctor of Philosophy (at Oxford D.Phil., at Cambridge Ph.D.).

The University year (not occupying more than seven months) is divided into three terms, known at Oxford as Michaelmas, Hilary, and Trinity, and at Cambridge as Michaelmas, Lent, and Easter Terms. *Commemoration* or the *Encaenia* is the week at the close of the summer term when honorary degrees are conferred and the colleges give their Commemoration Balls. At *Eights Week* at the end of May college boat-races and cricket matches are held. The boat-races begin at Iffley and finish near Folly Bridge. The inter-university boat-race, cricket and football matches, and athletic sports take place in London (see the 'Blue Guide to London').

'Undergraduate' should never be shortened to 'undergrad'. Men 'go up' to the university at the beginning of term, and 'go down' when they leave. To 'send down' means to expel definitively; to 'rusticate' is to expel temporarily. College menservants are 'scouts' at Oxford, 'gyps' at Cambridge; many of their functions have now been assumed by women bedmakers ('bedders'). A quadrangle is a 'quad' at Oxford, a 'court' at Cambridge.

CARFAX (Pl. 10; *quadrifurcus, quatre voies*), where four streets join, is the centre of the old city. The 14C tower, with archaic clock-jacks, at the N.W. angle is a relic of *St Martin's Church.* Here Shakespeare is said to have stood sponsor for the infant William Davenant, whose father was landlord of the Crown; and here Orlando Gibbons (d. 1625), the composer, was baptized in 1583.

The guest-chamber of the old *Crown Tavern*, where John Davenant may have entertained Shakespeare c. 1600, is at No. 3 Cornmarket, opposite. Now known as the *Painted Room*, it is occupied by the Oxford Preservation Trust (normally open Mon–Fri 9.30–12.30, 2.30–4.30; fee). The wall-paintings date from 1450 and 1550, the panelling from 1630. Similar paintings were discovered in 1948 in the *Golden Cross*, adjoining.

High Street leads eastward, but we proceed to the south down ST ALDATE'S (Pl. 14) passing between the Town Hall (l.) and the City Information Centre (r.). In this street is *St Aldate's Church* (14C; altered), behind which is Pembroke College, while opposite is the main front of Christ Church.

In Brewer St. (r.) are the *Cathedral Choir School* and *Campion Hall*, for Jesuit students (by Lutyens, 1936); and in Rose Place, farther on, is *Bishop King's Palace*, built in the 16C by Robert King, last abbot of Osney and first bishop of Oxford, but dating in its present form from 1628 (restored 1952) and now with its stark modern extension the home of the Roman Catholic Chaplaincy to the University.

No. 81 St Aldate's is the noted Elizabeth Restaurant and No. 83 the original of the shop in 'Through the Looking Glass'. Opposite is an entrance to Christ Church Meadow (p. 268), and farther on are the former buildings of *St Catherine's Society* (1936), by Worthington, occupied as *Linacre College* for postgraduates. The new courthouse of the city is in Speedwell St., opposite. St Aldate's descends to (¼ m.) *Folly Bridge* (rebuilt by Ebenezer Perry in 1825–27), on which stood a gatehouse said to have been used by Roger Bacon as an observatory.

Pembroke College (Pl. 14), founded in 1624 to supersede the ancient Broadgates Hall, is named after the Earl of Pembroke, chancellor at the time. The chapel (1732; re-decorated in 1884) has the most lavish classic interior in Oxford. The hall is a fine example of 19C work; to the N. the Besse Building and Beef Lane (now a paved footpath) and reconstructed 16C houses of Pembroke St. form a delightful quad. reminiscent of a small country-town square (1954–62).

FAMOUS MEMBERS: Bp. Bonner, Francis Beaumont, John Pym, and Sir Thomas Browne studied at Broadgates Hall; Samuel Johnson (who occupied the second floor rooms over the gateway), Shenstone, James Smithson (founder of the Smithsonian Institution at Washington), George Whitefield, Blackstone, and Lemprière at Pembroke. The library, the old refectory of Broadgates Hall, contains Johnson's desk; in the Senior Common Room are his portrait by Reynolds and his tea-pot.

*Christ Church (Pl. 15), known familiarly as 'the House' (Aedes Christi), is the largest college in Oxford (c. 360 undergraduates). 'Cardinal College', founded in 1525 by Wolsey, on the site of St Frideswide's priory, and refounded in 1532 by Henry VIII, was suppressed in 1546 and Christ Church was founded in its place. The throne of the Bp. of Oxford was placed in the church here in 1546, so that the college chapel is also the cathedral of Oxford, while the Dean (appointed for life by the Crown) is head both of the college and of the cathedral chapter. The 'Students' of Christ Church correspond to the 'Fellows' of other colleges.—In *Tom Tower*, built by Wren in 1681 over Wolsey's Gateway (statue of Wolsey, 1719), the main entrance, hangs 'Great Tom', a huge bell from Osney Abbey (6¼ tons; last recast in 1680), on which 101 strokes are sounded every evening at 9.5 (one for each member of the original foundation) formerly giving the signal for the closing of all college gates. The GREAT QUADRANGLE ('Tom Quad'; 264 ft by 261 ft), the largest in Oxford, originally intended by Wolsey as a cloister, was not finished until the Restoration. Adm. fees to some parts.

The pool in the centre, known as 'Mercury' from a 17C statue, since destroyed, was provided in 1928 with a copy of Giov. da Bologna's Mercury.

From the N.E. corner of Tom Quad Dr Fell's Tower (with an archway and passage called 'Kill-Canon' from their draughtiness), with statues of Dean John Fell (1660–86; "I do not like thee, Dr Fell") and Dean Liddell (1855–91), leads to PECKWATER QUADRANGLE, built in 1705 on the site of Peckwater Inn. Here (s. side) is the *Library* (1716–61), whose splendour was revealed by restoration in 1962–63. It normally contains a collection of interesting MSS. including John

Evelyn's Diary, and Wolsey's hat and chair. An extension to the college (1968) backs on to Blue Boar St.—CANTERBURY QUADRANGLE (1773–83), to the S.E., occupies the site of Canterbury College (belonging to the monks of Canterbury Cathedral), which had Sir Thomas More as a student. Here is the *Picture Gallery* (adm. daily, exc. Sun, 2–4.30), displaying the finest college collection of paintings and drawings (mostly 14–17C Italian) in Oxford.

In the S.E. angle of Tom Quad, beneath the massive bell-tower (1879), a staircase (1643), with a beautiful fan-tracery *Roof, last example of this style in England, leads to the *Hall* (2–4; or by arrangement with the Steward), the largest and finest in Oxford, completed by Wolsey in 1529. In this hall, 115 ft long, 40 ft wide, and 50 ft high, with an elaborately carved oaken roof, a notably early use was made of stage-scenery in a play acted before Elizabeth I in 1566. The splendid collection of *Portraits include those of Wolsey, ascribed to *Robert Greenbury*; Henry VIII, by *Sonmans*; Elizabeth I, by *Zucchero* (?); Bp. King, by *C. Johnson*; Locke and Atterbury, by *Kneller*; William Penn (copy of the portrait in Haverford College, U.S.A.); John Wesley and Sir Wm. Eden, by *Romney*; Canning, by *Lawrence*; Gladstone, by *Millais*; C. L. Dodgson ('Lewis Carroll'), by *Herkomer*; Dean Liddell, by *Watts*; and Bp. Strong, by *Orpen*. Outside the hall a staircase on the right descends to the *Kitchen* (adm. as for Hall), the oldest part of Wolsey's building, with vast fireplaces and a huge gridiron. An arch beneath the Hall staircase leads to *Dr Lee's Gallery* (usually closed), built in 1766 as an anatomy school.

FAMOUS MEMBERS: Sir Philip Sidney, Richard Hakluyt, Robert Burton, Richard Busby, William Penn ('sent down' for nonconformity, 1661), John Locke ('sent down' for sedition, 1684), Bolingbroke, John Wesley, Lord Mansfield, Canning, Sir Robert Peel, Gladstone, Ruskin, Pusey, Liddon, 'Lewis Carroll', Lord Salisbury, Lord Rosebery, Edward VII.

The *Cathedral, approached by an inconspicuous double gateway on the E. side of Tom Quad, has suffered from neglect and from restoration. Besides old glass (some by A. Van Linge) it has several windows designed by Burne-Jones and executed by William Morris. Adm. 11–5.

The church of a nunnery founded by St Frideswide in the 8C was rebuilt for secular priests in 1004 by Ethelred II, and became a church of Austin Canons in 1122; but the present late-Norman appearance dates from the restoration or rebuilding by Robert of Cricklade (1141–80). The three w. bays of the nave were pulled down by Wolsey, while the E. wall was entirely rebuilt and the w. front altered in 1870. The spire (144 ft) is one of the earliest in England (13C).

Interior. In the NAVE the massive pillars of the arcades are alternately round and octagonal. The arrangement by which the real arcade arch and the triforium in each bay are framed in what is apparently, though not really, the main arch of the arcade, is paralleled at Romsey and Jedburgh. The roof is good 16C woodwork, while the organ-screen and pulpit are Jacobean. On the N. side of the nave is the monument of Bp. Berkeley (d. 1753; "To Berkeley every virtue under heav'n"); in the pavement is a slab commemorating Dr Pusey (d. 1882).—The TRANSEPTS, like the lantern, have early 16C roofs. The s. end of the s. transept is a conjectural restoration by Scott, consisting of a slype surmounted by a gallery, which commands a good view of the whole interior. *St Lucy's Chapel*, now the baptistery, in the former E. aisle of this transept, has a flamboyant *East Window, with fine old glass (c. 1330), including a representation of Becket's martyrdom, from which the saint's head has been struck out.

The CHOIR has a rich and beautiful *Roof, which, like the clerestory windows, dates from c. 1490. In the s. choir-aisle are the tomb of Bp. King (d. 1557) and a 17C window commemorating him. On the N. side of the choir are three aisles, the two outermost being known as the *Lady Chapel* and the *Latin Chapel*. Between the N. choir-aisle and the Lady Chapel is the fragmentary base of the late 13C shrine of St Frideswide, once a resort of pilgrims, and opposite, between the Lady Chapel and the Latin Chapel, is the so-called 'Watching Chamber' of St Frideswide (Perp.).—The Latin Chapel (now called *St Catherine's Chapel*), mainly in the Dec. style and once used for divinity lectures, contains a 17C pulpit and has 14C glass in the side-windows. Here are also the fine tombs of Lady Furnival (d. 1353), Prior Sutton (d. 1316), and Sir George Nowers (d. 1425). Near the last is a tablet to Robert Burton (d. 1640; 'Democritus Junior'), author of the 'Anatomy of Melancholy'.

From the s. nave-aisle or the hall staircase we enter the small Perp. CLOISTER, the w. walk of which was destroyed by Wolsey. This was the scene of Cranmer's degradation. In the E. walk is the late-Norman doorway of the CHAPTER HOUSE (closed till 12 during term), a beautiful E.E. rectangular chamber, now a lecture room. On the s. side is the 'Old Library', now a lecture room and undergraduates' rooms, beneath which a passage leads to *Meadow Buildings* (1863).

Meadow Gate gives access to *Christ Church Meadow* (Pl. 15, Pl. 16; entered also from St Aldate's; see p. 265), across which the *New Walk* runs s. to the Isis, where are moored the gaily decorated *College Barges*, gradually being replaced by boathouses. The *Broad Walk*, with its avenue of elms, leads E. to the Cherwell and w. to St Aldate's. A path leads N. from the Broad Walk, crossing *Merton Field* and passing between Corpus (l.) and Merton (r.), with sections of the old city wall on either hand, to Merton St., one of the quaintest old streets of Oxford.

Corpus Christi College (Pl. 15) was founded in 1517 by Bp. Richard Foxe, who appointed university lecturers in Greek, Latin, and Hebrew, whence Erasmus named the college the 'bibliotheca trilinguis'.

The front quadrangle and the gateway, with its fine oriel and fan-vaulted roof, date from the founder's time. The remarkable sundial with its perpetual calendar was erected in 1581. The *Hall*, with a hammer-beam roof, is small but attractive; in the *Chapel* are a fine E. window and an altarpiece ascribed to Rubens; the rich *Library* is one of the most picturesque in Oxford. Foxe's pastoral staff is preserved in the *Buttery*. The *Turner Buildings* on the s. side date from 1706. Corpus still possesses its founder's plate, the finest in Oxford; it was the only college that did not melt down its plate for Charles I.

FAMOUS MEMBERS: Nicholas Udall, Bp. Jewel (fellow 1542–53), Richard Hooker, Gen. Oglethorpe, Thomas Day, John Keble, and Dr Arnold.

*Merton College (Pl. 15), in all essentials the oldest college in Oxford, though both University and Balliol were endowed a few years earlier, was founded by Walter de Merton in 1264 as a special training school for the secular as opposed to the monastic clergy. Its scholars are known as 'postmasters' (probably from Lat. 'portionista'). The organization was the model for subsequent Oxford and Cambridge colleges.

The irregular old buildings are among the most interesting in Oxford. The gateway tower was built in 1418. The front of the college was rebuilt by Sir Henry Savile in 1581. The *Hall* (much restored) has an old oak door with 13C ironwork. Between the front quadrangle and the picturesque 'Mob Quad' (both possibly c. 1308–9) is the curious *Treasury* or muniment room (1274), the oldest part of the college, with a high-pitched stone roof. The **Library* (2–4 or 5), in Mob Quad, is perhaps the most interesting medieval library in England; built in 1371–78, it was the first 'Renaissance' library in England, that is with books upright in shelves instead of presses; and it still retains many of its old fittings. Also in Mob Quad are two rooms of 'relics' of Max Beerbohm. The Dec. **Chapel* (1294–97), with a conspicuous Perp. tower added in 1450, never had a nave, and the transepts (14C) now form an antechapel, in which are a fine Dec. piscina, old glass, and the monuments of Sir Henry Savile (d. 1622), Sir Thomas Bodley (d. 1613; by Nicholas Stone), and Anthony Wood (d. 1695). Three arches of the screen designed by Wren are in the crossing (1960). The beautiful windows of the choir are filled with unique painted glass of c. 1300. In front of the high altar are two very fine brasses (1387 and 1471). The *Fellows' Quadrangle* (1608–10) is a good example of Jacobean architecture.—Adjoining the front quadrangle on the E. is St Alban Hall Quad (1905), occupying the site of *St Alban Hall* ('Stubbins'), which was founded in 1220 and amalgamated with Merton in 1881.

FAMOUS MEMBERS: Thomas Bradwardine and other notable 14C philosophers and mathematicians, and possibly Wyclif; and Sir Henry Savile. Other famous students are Thomas Carew, Richard Steele, Lord Randolph Churchill, Lord Halsbury, Saintsbury, Max Beerbohm, and T. S. Eliot. Massinger and Speaker Lenthall were members of St Alban Hall, and Newman was its vice-principal. During the Civil War William Harvey was warden, and Henrietta Maria lodged here while the King was at Christ Church.

At the W. end of Merton St. is Oriel St., with the Canterbury Gate of Christ Church and the main entrance to **Oriel College** (Pl. 15), founded as 'St Mary's College' in 1324 by Adam de Brome and refounded in 1326 by Edward II, to whom he was almoner. It was long known as 'the King's College'. It occupies the site of a building known as 'La Oriole' (probably from a projecting oriel window). Oriel was endowed with the patronage of St Mary's, and used the church for services in the Middle Ages. In the 19C it was the centre of the Tractarian movement.

The picturesque front quadrangle, a good example of 17C Gothic, with hall (fine hammer-beam roof) and chapel, was built between 1619 and 1642; the left quadrangle, with the library, in the 18C. Above the hall porch are statues of the Blessed Virgin and of two kings, perhaps Edward II and James I or Charles I. Adjacent on the N. is *St Mary's Hall* ('Skimmery'), absorbed by Oriel in 1902, with an attractive little hall and chapel (c. 1640). The new front (1909–11) of Oriel, in High St., was built by Basil Champneys from the bequest of Cecil Rhodes, whose statue it bears.

FAMOUS MEMBERS: Thos. Gascoigne, Sir Walter Raleigh, Wm. Prynne, Bp. Butler, Gilbert White, Bp. Wilberforce, Thomas Hughes, Whately, Keble, Dr Arnold, Newman, Pusey, H. and J. A. Froude, A. H. Clough, Matthew Arnold, Lord Bryce, and Cecil Rhodes.

At the N. end of Oriel St. we emerge in the famous but overcrowded ***High Street** (Pl. 11), leading from Carfax in a gentle curve to ($\frac{1}{2}$ m.) Magdalen Bridge. The unfolding of its charm is best seen early on Sun morning on the ascent by the N. side of the street from Magdalen to Queen's Lane.

St Mary's Church (Pl. 11) has a conspicuous Dec. *Spire (188 ft high). The chancel and nave, in the Perp. style, date from c. 1463–90. Facing the High is a picturesque Baroque porch (restored 1971) erected by Dr Morgan Owen, one of Laud's chaplains; the image of the Virgin and Child, by Stone, inspired one of the charges against the archbishop.

Since the 14C at least this has been used as the University Church, where the University Sermons are preached by 'select preachers' every Sun morning in term time and where the 'Bampton Lectures' are given. The sermons are preceded by the 'bidding prayer' for University benefactors. Abp. Cranmer was tried at St Mary's in 1555, and it was here, in the following year, that he publicly repudiated his recantation. Newman was vicar from 1828 to 1843. A slab in the choir records the burial of Amy Robsart (d. 1560). On the N. side is the tomb of Adam de Brome (1328). A tablet in memory of Dr John Radcliffe (1652–1714; see p. 274) was unveiled in 1953; and a plaque recalls the burial of John Aubrey here in 1697.— The *Old Congregation House*, N.E. of the nave, once housed the first University library, founded by Bp. Cobham in 1320, and now contains the original statues from the spire. The tower may be ascended daily; fee.

All Saints (Pl. 11; rebuilt 1706–8), at the corner of Turl St., became the City Church after the demolition of St Martin's, Carfax (now a library, see p. 275).

All Souls College (Pl. 11) was founded in 1438 by Henry Chichele, Abp. of Canterbury, as a chantry for the souls of those killed in the French wars of Henry V and Henry VI. It has a warden and 54 fellows, and until the foundation of Nuffield College was unique in having no undergraduates. The fine front and gateway facing the High St. and the first quadrangle are unspoiled 15C work.

From the N.W. angle of the quadrangle an exquisitely vaulted passage leads to the Perp. *Chapel*, which contains an 18C screen, a carved oak roof, and a beautiful stone *Reredos, restored in 1872–79 after being walled up for two hundred years. The statues are 19C, but the painting is original. Note the 15C *Glass in the antechapel. The second quadrangle, built by Hawksmoor in 1715–40, is debased in style, but "somehow or other the architect blundered into magnificence". On the N. side is the *Library* (200 ft long), founded by Christopher Codrington (d. 1710), governor of the Leeward Islands, containing 150,000 vols, and Wren's designs for the building of St Paul's.
FAMOUS MEMBERS: Linacre, Sheldon, Jeremy Taylor, Wren, Blackstone, Bp. Heber, Lord Salisbury, Max Muller, Lord Curzon.

University College (Pl. 11) lies a little farther down the High St., almost opposite All Souls. Though it nominally claims Alfred the Great as its founder and celebrated its millenary in 1872, it received its first endowment (1249) by bequest of William of Durham, and until 1280 was administered by the University. It removed to its present site about 1332.

The long curved front of the college, with its two tower-gateways, oriels, and ogee gables, is a good example of 17C Gothic. The w. gateway, with statues of Queen Anne (outside) and James II (inside), leads to the larger quadrangle (1635–74); the E. gateway, with statues of Queen Mary (outside) and Dr Radcliffe (inside), to the smaller quadrangle, built in 1716–19 from a bequest by Dr Radcliffe. The dark *Chapel* (begun 1637, consecrated 1666, and altered in 1800 and 1862) has a very fine set of 17C glass by A. Van Linge and a screen and cedar wainscoting by R. Barker. The *Library* was built by Scott in 1861, and the *Master's Lodge* in Logic Lane was added by Bodley in 1879.—A passage in the N.W. corner of the great quad (staircase 3) leads to the *Shelley Memorial* (adm. in term 2–4; vacation 10–6), a domed chamber containing the realistic marble figure of the drowned poet by Onslow Ford (1893). Shelley had rooms in 1810 on the first floor of the stair to the right of the Hall; he was 'sent down' after 11 months for publishing his pamphlet on 'The Necessity of Atheism'. To the s. between Logic Lane and the Examination Schools (see below) is the attractive Goodhart Quad (1962) with a copper roof and spire.
FAMOUS MEMBERS: Shelley, Lord Herbert of Cherbury, Dr Radcliffe, Sir Edwin Arnold, Prince Felix Youssoupoff (Rasputin's assassin), Lord Attlee, and, as fellows, Lord Eldon, Dean Stanley, Goldwin Smith, Conington, Viscount Cecil, and Lord Beveridge (master).

Nearly opposite University is the classical front of **The Queen's College** (Pl. 11), founded in 1340 by Robert de Eglesfield, chaplain to Queen Philippa, and favoured by her and other queens consort. The founder provided for a provost and twelve fellows to represent Our Lord and the Apostles, and seventy 'poor boys' as disciples, the first formal arrangement in Oxford for the education of undergraduates.

Several quaint customs are kept up at Queen's: the college is summoned to dinner by the sound of a trumpet; on Christmas Day the 'boar's head' dinner is celebrated; and on New Year's Day the Bursar presents to each guest at the 'gaudy' a needle and thread ('aiguille' and 'fil', a pun on the founder's name), with the words "Take this and be thrifty". The eight senior scholars are known as 'Taberdars'.

The college, the only one in Oxford entirely in the classical style, was mainly rebuilt in 1692–1716. The fine front quadrangle (1710) is mainly by Hawksmoor, with a statue of Queen Caroline under the entrance-cupola. The *Chapel* (good glass) and the *Hall* were designed by Wren. The *Library*, in the back quadrangle, is an ornate room containing 110,000 vols, with the finest collection of Slavonic literature in England. The founder's drinking-horn is still in use as a loving-cup.— Henry V is said to have lodged at Queen's. To the w. along Queen's Lane is the pleasant new Provost's Lodging (1959).

FAMOUS MEMBERS: Thomas Middleton, Wycherley, Joseph Addison and Wm. Collins (both of whom migrated to Magdalen from Queen's), Jeremy Bentham, Wm. Mitford, Francis Jeffrey, and Walter Pater.

At No. 83 High St. a tablet records that here in 1650 was established the first coffee-house in England (comp. p. 276).

From the corner of Queen's Lane the finest view of the grand curve of the High St. is obtained. Opposite, a little farther down, are the EXAMINATION SCHOOLS (Pl. 11; open 9.30–4 in vacation) built in 1876–82 by Sir T. G. Jackson. They are now used for lectures also. Within is a large collection of portraits of English composers of the 17–18C and several pictures from the Bodleian Library.

*Magdalen College (pronounced 'Maudlen'; Pl. 12), the most beautiful as well as one of the richest colleges in Oxford, was founded by William of Waynflete in 1458, but the buildings on the present site, once occupied by the Hospital of St John, were not completed till 1480. The scholars of Magdalen are called 'demies' (because they receive only half the allowances of a fellow). From the first Magdalen enjoyed a large share of royal favour, and it made great sacrifices for the royalist cause during Charles I's occupation of Oxford; but none the less in 1687–88 the fellows courageously resisted James II's unconstitutional attempt to force his nominee upon them as president.

The chief feature of the High St. front is the graceful Perp. *TOWER (view), 145 ft high, built in 1492–1505 as the bell-tower of the college chapel, though separated from it. According to tradition it was designed by Wolsey, who was bursar at the time. A 17C 'Eucharistic Hymn' is sung at the top of the tower at c. 6 a.m. on May morning. Entering by the modern gateway we have on the left *St Swithun's Quadrangle* (1880–84 and 1932), and straight in front is the President's House, to the left of which is the *Grammar Hall*, a restored fragment of Magdalen Hall. Immediately to our right are the open-air *Pulpit*, where a University sermon is preached on the Sunday after St John the Baptist's day (24 June), and the narrow entrance of the *Chaplain's Quadrangle*, with remains of St John's Hospital, including the blocked-up Pilgrims' Gate. The *Chapel* (entrance under the Muniment Tower, to the right) was finished before 1483, but the interior is now practically 19C work. The fine Lyttelton monument (1634) is by Nicholas Stone. Choral services on Tues–Sat in term are held at 6.15 p.m.; on Sun (adm. by fellow's order) at 6 p.m.; the choir is famous for its singing. Beyond the Muniment Tower is the *Founder's Tower* (no adm.), containing the State apartments, with a piece of tapestry representing the marriage of Prince Arthur to Catherine of Aragon. Beneath the Muniment Tower a passage leads to the picturesque *Cloisters*, dating from the founder's time but renewed in 1822. The grotesque figures (c. 1509) on the buttresses of the quad are known as the 'hieroglyphs'. A flight of steps in the S.E. corner leads to the *Hall*, with beautiful panelling, an oriel, a musicians' gallery on the top of a Jacobean screen, a number of fine portraits, and a modern oak roof. The old *Kitchen* was perhaps a part of the original hospital. The *Library* (partly housed also in the former buildings of Magdalen College School) contains illuminated MSS. and early printed books, incl. Wolsey's copy of the Gospels. The elegant *New Building*, beyond the lawn to the N. of the cloisters, dates from 1735. Beyond stretches the *Grove*, Magdalen's deer-park (no adm.). Thence a bridge crosses to a meadow encircled by the Cherwell and by the *Water Walks (Pl. 12), one of which (on the N.) is known as 'Addison's Walk'.

FAMOUS MEMBERS: Bp. Foxe, Grocyn (divinity reader), John Colet (?), William Lily (?), Wolsey (the 'boy bachelor'), Card. Pole, Foxe the martyrologist (fellow),

John Lyly, Prince Henry, eldest son of James I, John Mason (founder of New Hampshire), John Hampden, Prince Rupert, Joseph Addison, Henry Sacheverell, Wm. Collins, Gibbon ('sent down' for joining the Church of Rome), John Wilson ('Christopher North'), Charles Reade (fellow), Oscar Wilde, Compton Mackenzie, and Goldwin Smith.

Just beyond the college the stately *Magdalen Bridge* (Pl. 16; view), built by John Gwynn in 1772–79 and widened in 1883, crosses the Cherwell.

At the E. end of the bridge is the Waynflete Building (1961–63) of Magdalen; and in St Clement's St. (l. farther on) is *Stone's Hospital*, an almshouse of 1697–1700.

Opposite Magdalen is the *Botanic Garden* (Pl. 16), the oldest in England, founded in 1621, with a gateway by Nicholas Stone (c. 1630). The gardens are open free to the public (weekdays 8.30–5; Sun May–Sept 10–12, 2–6, Oct–April 10–12, 2–4.30; plant houses 2–4). Rose Lane (r.) leads into Merton Field and Christ Church Meadow.—Immediately beyond Magdalen Bridge, on the right, are *Magdalen College School*, and *St Hilda's College* (Pl. 16).

We now retrace our steps to Queen's Lane, a narrow and crooked roadway which we follow between high walls. On the right is **St Edmund Hall** (Pl. 12), the last survivor of the medieval Halls, founded c. 1220. Controlled by Queen's College from 1557 to 1937, it now enjoys full collegiate status. It is dedicated to St Edmund of Abingdon, Abp. of Canterbury, who taught at Oxford c. 1195–1200. The picturesque old quadrangle, dating in part from c. 1650, was completed in 1932–34. During the rebuilding a fragment of *White Hall*, a 15C hall formerly under the control of St Edmund's, was discovered. The tiny panelled 17C chapel contains an unusual altarpiece by Ceri Richards (1958).— A little farther on is *St Peter's in the East* (Pl. 11), an interesting old church with some 15C glass, a late-Norman chancel, s. door, and *Crypt (c. 1150), and the tomb of James Sadler (1753–1828), an assistant in the laboratory of the Old Ashmolean (p. 276), who made the first English balloon-ascent, from Oxford, in 1784.

New College Lane goes on to the modest entrance of *New College (Pl. 11), founded in 1379 by William of Wykeham, founder also of Winchester College. The figures over the gate are a rare example of pre-Reformation sculpture.

The buildings, completed about 1386, remain much as the founder left them, and are among the earliest and finest examples of the English Perp. style. The *Front Quadrangle* was sadly marred in 1675 by the addition of a third story and the modernization of the windows. The noble *Chapel* was restored in 1879 by Gilbert Scott, who, unfortunately, raised the roof. The *Glass in the antechapel is original 14C, except the great w. window, painted by Jervais from the designs of Reynolds (1777); the glass in the chapel itself dates from 1740 (s. side) and 1765–74. In the pavement is a fine series of 23 brasses, dating from 1403 to 1619. Epstein's statue of Lazarus stands in the antechapel. The reconstructed stalls retain their old misericords, including one of the founder (first stall on s. side). In a recess on the N. side of the altar is the founder's *Pastoral Staff; N. of this is St James, by El Greco. The choral services vie with those of Magdalen (Sun 6 p.m., weekdays exc. Wed 6.15 p.m.; sub-warden's order necessary on Sun in term). The quiet *Cloisters*, with remarkable wood vaulting, to the w. of the chapel, and the detached *Bell Tower* were completed in 1400. The *Hall*, adjoining the chapel, is the oldest and one of the finest halls in Oxford, with linenfold panelling ascribed to Abp. Warham and a modern oak roof. A passage on the E. side of the quad, under the *Library* (by Wyatt), leads to the picturesque *Garden Quadrangle*, built in 1684–1708. The chief feature of the extensive *Gardens* is a well-preserved remnant of the old *City Wall*, constructed in the reign of Henry III. The late-17C wrought-iron screen comes from Canons near Edgware. Facing Longwall St. is the long Sacher Building (1962).

FAMOUS MEMBERS: Chichele, William of Waynflete (?), Grocyn, Abp. Warham, Sir Henry Wotton, Bp. Ken, Sydney Smith, John Galsworthy, and A. P. Herbert, last independent M.P. for the University (1935–50).

We emerge in Catte St., opposite the Bodleian Library (see below). The bridge over the lane connects the old and the new buildings of **Hertford College** (Pl. 11), the successor of Hart Hall (founded in 1284), which afterwards became Hertford College (1740–1816) but was absorbed by Magdalen Hall in 1822, its endowments being applied to founding the Hertford University Scholarship. On the dissolution of Magdalen Hall in 1874, the college was refounded following a bequest by Charles Baring, the banker. The oldest part is the 16C library, formerly the hall.

FAMOUS MEMBERS: Of Hart Hall, John Selden; of the original Hertford College, Charles James Fox; of Magdalen Hall, William Tyndale, Thomas Hobbes, Lord Clarendon, Sir Matthew Hale, Sir Henry Vane, and Dr Wilkins; of the refounded Hertford College, Evelyn Waugh.

On the corner of Catte St. opposite the Bodleian Library Extension (see below) stands the classical *Clarendon Building* (Pl. 11), built by Hawksmoor under Vanbrugh's influence in 1713, partly from the profits of Lord Clarendon's 'History of the Rebellion'; it housed the Clarendon Press till 1830 and is now used for various University delegacies. Adjoining it in Broad St. is the splendidly restored **Sheldonian Theatre** (Pl. 11; open 10–1 & 2–4 or 5), holding 1500 spectators and built by Wren in 1664–68 at the expense of Abp. Sheldon, in imitation of the Theatre of Marcellus at Rome. The masks surmounting the piers of the external railings were renewed in 1971–72. Here is held the annual *Commemoration* or *Encænia* (20 June), commemorating benefactors of the University, when prize compositions are recited and honorary degrees are conferred. The octagonal cupola, reconstructed in 1838, commands an excellent view. Within, the ceiling-painting, 'Triumph of Truth and the Arts', is by Robert Streater (1669).

Behind the Sheldonian lies the OLD SCHOOLS QUADRANGLE, built in 1613–19 on the site of earlier schools of 1439. The Gate Tower on the E. side, built by Thomas Holt, is ornamented with columns of the five classical orders and a statue of James I. On the w. side is a bronze statue, by Le Sueur, of the Earl of Pembroke (see p. 266). The building is now occupied by the *Bodleian Library** (Pl. 11), which extends also over the upper story of the Divinity School and the Convocation House. The library, which is the oldest and one of the most important in the world, containing c. 2,500,000 printed books and c. 50,000 MSS., was founded in 1602 by Sir Thomas Bodley (1545–1613), who presented his magnificent collection to the University. Visitors are admitted on weekdays (except holidays and in the week beginning the first Mon in Aug) from 9.30 to 5, Sat 9.30–12.30; readers must be graduates or recommended by a 'don'. The older portion of the premises is in the form of the letter H, of which the central apartment, over the Divinity School, originally contained the library of Humphrey, Duke of Gloucester (1391–1447), dispersed in the reign of Edward VI; while the E. wing, or 'Arts End', was added by Bodley in 1612 and the w. wing (over the Convocation House) was built by the University for John Selden's books in 1636. The library is one of the six that enjoy a right to a copy of every book published in the United Kingdom. Extensive reconstruction was carried out in 1945–55.

Visitors enter behind Le Sueur's statue the basement story of Duke Humphrey's library, built c. 1430–90 by Richard Wynchcombe and others. Beyond the vestibule or *Proscholium*, used as a 'Pig Market' under Edward VI, we enter the *Divinity School, a noble room, with an elaborately vaulted and arched stone *Roof. Here Cranmer, Ridley, and Latimer were examined in 1555, and here the House of Commons met in 1681, while the Peers occupied the picture-gallery (see below). It was subsequently used as a storehouse for corn, but was restored at the beginning of the 18C by Wren, who designed the door on the N. side. It is now used for periodic book exhibitions. The door at the W. end leads into the *Convocation House*, an addition of 1634–37, with fine woodwork, where Convocation and Congregation meet. The *Apodyterium*, or robing-room, is used as the Vice-Chancellor's Court.

A door in the S.W. corner of the vestibule gives access to a staircase off which is an Exhibition Hall. At the top of the stairs is the entrance to Duke Humphrey's Library, the *Arts End* of which only may be visited by non-readers, but this affords an excellent view of the fine roof and the presses.

At the beginning of Broad St. is the **New Bodleian** (Pl. 11; entrance in Parks Rd.), a massive stonefaced block begun in 1935 by Sir Giles Scott, connected with the old library (see below) by an underground passage. Exhibitions of selected treasures of the library are held here (Mon–Fri 9–5, Sat 10–12.30).

The LOWER EXHIBITION ROOM is for temporary exhibitions. The *UPPER EXHIBITION ROOM shows many of the outstanding exhibits formerly in the old Bodleian. They include: Confirmation of Magna Carta by Edward I (14 Feb 1301), with the King's Great Seal; Latin exercise-book of Edward VI; Latin letter from Elizabeth I; draft letter of Charles I to Henrietta Maria; incunabula, including a 'Mazarine' Bible (1454–55); Biblia Pauperum (15C); Canon of the Mass (1457–58) by Fust and Schœffer; Caxton's Advertisement (1477); Caxton's 'Mirror of the World' (1481; first illustrated book printed in England). Numerous first and early editions are shown of works by Chaucer, Shakespeare, Bacon, Spenser, Marlowe, Jonson, Milton, Walton, Pope, and Swift, and a Bible of 1611 (first edn. of Authorized Version); Bay Psalm Book, the first English book printed in America (1640); Letters of Oliver Cromwell, Nelson, Wellington, Florence Nightingale, and George VI; Persian illuminated MSS. In this room also are Bodley's chest, and a chair made from the wood of Drake's ship the 'Golden Hind'. Portraits on the walls include one of Lord Burghley (1520–98), and Hugo Grotius (1583–1645; attrib. to J. A. Ravensteyn). Also exhibited (possibly only temporarily) are some MSS. formerly in the 'Arts End' of the Bodleian. These include 7C MS. of the Acts of the Apostles ('Codex E'), used by the Venerable Bede; King Alfred's translation of Gregory the Great's 'Pastoral Care' (c. 894); *Anglo-Saxon Chronicle (Peterborough Abbey, 1123); Cædmon's metrical translation of Genesis in Old English (c. 1000), with outline drawings of the Winchester School; Boccaccio's 'Filicopo' (1472); and illuminated Books of Hours.

In the square to the S. of the Old School rises the *Radcliffe Camera (Pl. 11), a handsome classical rotunda, with a dome on an octagonal base (100 ft in diameter, 140 ft high), the chef-d'œuvre of James Gibbs (1737–49). It was founded as a separate library by Dr Radcliffe, the court-physician, but is now part of the Bodleian.

On the W. side of Radcliffe Sq. is **Brasenose College** ('B.N.C.'; Pl. 11), founded in 1509 by Wm. Smyth, Bp. of Lincoln, and Sir Richard Sutton. The name is probably derived from the brazen knocker (a lion's head) of an older Hall, which was carried off to Stamford in 1334; this was recovered in 1890 and is kept in the college hall. Another derivation is from a supposed 'brasenhus' or brewery, on the site of the college.

The front quadrangle, with the entrance-tower and the *Hall*, entered by a curious porch, dates from the founder's time (a third story was added in the reign of James I). No. I˙ staircase led to the old chapel, now the *Common Room*. The present *Chapel* and the *Library* were built in 1656–66. The former, also with a curious vestibule, is noteworthy for its successful combination of classical and Gothic forms. Its fan-tracery ceiling is said to have been brought from St Mary's College. Beneath the library was formerly an open cloister. The uninspired High St. front is by Sir T. G. Jackson (1886–1909), but cleverly inserted w. of Jackson's Quad are sets of rooms by Powell and Moya (1959–61).

FAMOUS MEMBERS: John Foxe, Robert Burton, Elias Ashmole, John Marston, the dramatist, Bp. Heber, R. H. Barham of the 'Ingoldsby Legends', Walter Pater (fellow 1864), and Earl Haig. The 'Childe of Hale', whose name is borne by the Brasenose boat, was a giant visitor to the college when Pepys went there.

We now follow Brasenose Lane to reach **Lincoln College** (Pl. 11), founded in 1427 by Bp. Fleming of Lincoln as a counterblast to the Wycliffite movement. It was originally a college of priests attached to All Saints Church, which now forms its library.

The *N. Quadrangle* is a pleasing example of pre-Reformation architecture, marred by the addition of battlements. The *Hall* (1436) contains a portrait of John Wesley, whose pulpit is preserved in the **Chapel*, which, like most of the s. quad, was built by Bp. Williams of Lincoln in 1610–31. The cedar wainscoting, carved bench-ends, and contemporary stained glass by B. Van Linge of the chapel should be noted. The *Kitchen* is the oldest part of the college. *Wesley's Rooms* (restored 1928), over the passage between the quadrangles, with linen-fold oak panelling and period furniture, are shown on application to the porter.

FAMOUS MEMBERS: Sir Wm. Davenant; Dr Radcliffe (fellow); John Wesley (fellow, 1726–51), who here founded the society of 'Methodists'; Mark Pattison (rector 1861–84); and Lord Morley.

On the opposite (w.) side of the Turl is **Jesus College** (Pl. 10), the first post-Reformation college in Oxford, founded in 1571, nominally by Elizabeth I but in reality by Hugh Price, treasurer of St David's. The college has always had a very close connection with Wales.

The oldest part of the college is the Turl St. front, rebuilt in the Perp. style in 1856 by Buckler, who restored the chapel and the Market St. front also. The s. side of the front quadrangle, the chapel, and the principal's house were built by Sir Eubule Thelwall (principal in 1621–30). The picturesque back quadrangle, with the library (late 17C fittings), was mainly the work of Sir Leoline Jenkins, the 'second founder' (principal 1661–73). The *Chapel* is a good specimen of 17C Gothic, with barrel-vaulting and an E. end added in 1636. The service is in Welsh on St David's Day. The *Hall* (c. 1617) has a carved Jacobean screen and contains portraits of Elizabeth I, Charles I by Van Dyck, Charles II by Lely, and Nash the architect by Lawrence. In the *Common Room* is a fine original portrait of Elizabeth I by Zucchero.

FAMOUS MEMBERS: Bp. Lancelot Andrewes (fellow), Henry Vaughan, the 'Silurist', Beau Nash, J. R. Green, Sir John Rhys, and T. E. Lawrence.

Exeter College (Pl. 11), opposite Jesus, founded by Walter de Stapledon in 1314 and refounded by Sir Wm. Petre in 1566, is now one of the largest colleges in Oxford, extensively Victorianized, but partly remodelled in 1949 by T. H. Hughes.

The w. front and tower-gateway were rebuilt in 1671–1703 and again in 1834. The picturesque gabled house at the N.W. corner of the college is a relic of Rector Prideaux's buildings (1620). The old N. gate, or Palmer's Tower (1436), has a war memorial for 1939–45 in its lowest story. The *Hall* (1618; restored in 1818) contains a Jacobean screen with the earliest representation of a man smoking. The *Chapel*, an elaborate work by Gilbert Scott (1857), replaces a fine 17C chapel. It contains a tapestry by William Morris and Burne-Jones, whose college friend-ship led to the formation of the Pre-Raphaelite Brotherhood.

FAMOUS MEMBERS: John Ford, Sir John Eliot (1607), the first Earl of Shaftes-bury, Sir Chas. Lyell, J. A. Froude (fellow), F. D. Maurice.

At the corner of the Turl and Broad St. are the Exeter new buildings (1964), and just beyond is the lovely *Old Ashmolean Museum* (Pl. 11), now the MUSEUM OF THE HISTORY OF SCIENCE (weekdays 10.30–1, 2–4.30). Built in 1679–83 to receive the collections of Elias Ashmole, as well as the School of Natural History and a chemical laboratory, it was the first public museum in England. The nucleus of the present museum is the unrivalled Lewis Evans Collection of scientific instruments (1925) enriched by the Billmeir Collection (1957). Also shown are items relating to the history of pharmacy and medicine, among them the penicillin material.

We now cross Broad Street to visit **Trinity College** (Pl. 10), which lies some way back from the street. It was founded in 1555 by Sir Thomas Pope, a wealthy Oxfordshire landowner, on the site of Durham College (established in 1286 for students from the Benedictine monasteries at Durham and elsewhere in the North).

The buildings are among the most charming in Oxford. In the front quadrangle is the *Chapel*, rebuilt in 1691–94. It contains a carved cedar-wood screen and altarpiece by Grinling Gibbons; on the left of the altar is the tomb of the founder and his third wife. The *President's House* and the *New Buildings*, on the E. side of the front quadrangle, are by Sir T. G. Jackson (1883–87). On the S. side, facing the Broad, are a number of picturesque cottages, once students' halls, recently incor-porated in the college; next to them is *Kettell Hall*, built by Dr Kettell, president in 1599–1643. Parts of the small quadrangle beyond the chapel are relics of Durham College (e.g. the buttery, bursary, common room, and the E. side). The *Hall* was rebuilt in 1618–20 and contains a specially fine collection of portraits. The *Library*, opposite, contains some curious 14C glass. The War Memorial Library (1928, by J. Osborne Smith) is a small classical building. The *Garden Quadrangle* farther on, the N. block of which was built by Wren in 1665, is one of the first classical build-ings in Oxford. The *Gardens* are pleasant. Two new residential blocks have been built at either side of the rose garden.

FAMOUS MEMBERS: Lord Baltimore, one of the founders of Maryland (1594), Abp. Sheldon, Ireton, Sir John Denham, Chatham, Landor (1793), 'sent down' for firing at the rooms of the man opposite, Card. Newman, Professor Freeman, Sir Richard Burton (1840), 'sent down' for trying to fight a duel, Quiller-Couch, Elroy Flecker, and Lord Bryce.

To the w. lies **Balliol College** (Pl. 10), planned by John de Baliol, father of the Scottish king, as a penance imposed by the Bishop of Durham. It was established by his widow Devorguilla before 1266, at first merely as a hostel; the statutes date from 1282.

The buildings are almost entirely Victorian, but the ancient gates (1288) are now restored (N.W. of front quadrangle). The first quadrangle, into which the Broad St. entrance leads, contains the *Library* (opposite, on the left) and its reading-room (w. side; formerly the dining-hall), both dating from the 15C, but recast by Wyatt in the 18C. The *Chapel*, on the right of the library, was built by Butterfield in 1856 in place of the 16C chapel. Some Anglo-Flemish stained glass of 1528, discarded by Butterfield, was replaced in 1912; other windows contain glass of 1637 by A. Van Linge. The lectern dates from c. 1635.—Coffee was prob-ably first drunk in England by N. Kanopios, a Cretan student (1637).

FAMOUS MEMBERS: John Wyclif (master in 1364), Humphrey, Duke of Gloucester (?), John Evelyn, Adam Smith, Southey, Sir Wm. Hamilton, Card. Manning, A. H. Clough, both Abps. Temple (father and son), Matthew Arnold, Calverley ('sent down' in 1852), Swinburne, Andrew Lang, Arnold Toynbee, Lord Asquith, Lord Milner, Lord Curzon, Lord Grey of Fallodon, Vincent Massey, and King Olav of Norway. Benjamin Jowett was master in 1870–93.

Opposite the w. front of Balliol, is the *Martyrs' Memorial* (Pl. 10), erected in 1841 in the style of the 'Eleanor Crosses' from the design of

Sir G. G. Scott, with statues by Weekes of Cranmer, Ridley, and Latimer (burned at the stake in Broad St., at a spot marked by a cross in the roadway opposite Balliol College). Within the neighbouring church of *St Mary Magdalen* (Pl. 10) is preserved the oak door from Bocardo Prison (see below), in which the martyrs were incarcerated.

We now enter the broad tree-lined thoroughfare called *ST GILES. At the corner of Beaumont St. (Pl. 10) is an imposing building in the classical style, by C. R. Cockerell (1841–45). The E. wing, facing St Giles, is occupied by the TAYLOR INSTITUTION of modern languages, founded from the bequest of Sir Robert Taylor (d. 1788).

The central portion and the w. wing contain the ****Ashmolean Museum** (Pl. 10; 10–4, Sun 2–4), with the highly important art and archaeological collections of the University.

The nucleus of the Ashmolean Museum was 'Tradescant's Ark', collections formed by John Tradescant the elder (d. 1638) and his son. Settled by the latter upon Elias Ashmole, they were offered to the University which erected the 'Old Ashmolean' (see above) to receive them. The natural curiosities were later transferred to the University Museum and the ethnographical exhibits to the Pitt-Rivers Museum. The remainder was removed to a new building behind the University Galleries and the two institutions finally amalgamated under the title of the Ashmolean Museum of Art and Archaeology.

Ground Floor. To the left of the entrance is the RANDOLPH GALLERY, containing classical sculptures, Greek, Hellenistic, and Roman originals, and Roman copies, mainly from the *Arundel* or *Pomfret Marbles*, including a torso of c. 480 B.C., a pedimental sculpture embodying two linear measures (Aegean of 5C B.C.), and the fragment of a frieze of an Athenian temple. In the show-cases are fine temporary displays of individual facets of ancient art. To the w. are the *Petrie Room* of predynastic groups, mainly from Sir Flinders Petrie's Egyptian excavations; the *Chester Room*, with fine scarabs, beads, seals, papyri, etc.; and the *Egyptian Dynastic Gallery*, which includes furnishings, bronzes, and inscriptions, mostly from excavated sites. The Egyptian Sculpture Gallery (*Griffith Gallery*) contains the *Shrine of Taharqa from Kawa (7C B.C.) adorned with bas-relief, with wall-paintings from Tell el Amarna; finds from the Oxford excavations in Nubia; reliefs, stelae, and figures (Intermediate Period and Middle Kingdom); mummy cases and funerary furnishings; stone fragments from Tell el Amarna; masks (New Kingdom); and painted and sculptured fragments.

From here a passage leads to the *Marshall Room* with coloured Worcester porcelain (1750–83).

North of the Randolph Gallery, the MEDIEVAL ROOM contains the 'Alfred Jewel' (9C A.D.; comp. p. 167) perhaps the handle of an 'æstil' or pointer for following lines of illuminated MSS.; the similar 'Minster Lovell Jewel'; local pottery; brooches; a wooden 'Peg' tankard; medieval tiles; and the Odda stone, the foundation stone of 1056 of the Saxon chapel at Deerhurst; and objects of historical interest. In the lobby are Viking antiquities. To the right in the Medieval Room, the SUNKEN COURT, containing large numbers of Greek vases; open to students on request.

Opposite the main entrance is the well-arranged ***Department of Eastern Art**. In the *Vestibule* are examples of Gandhara sculpture and early

Chinese bronze. The Ingram Gallery of Chinese ceramics (400 B.C.–14C A.D.) contains also pottery tomb figures (A.D. 618–906) and a Sung gilt bronze Bodhisattva and 16C cast iron heads. The following rooms to right & left show Chinese porcelains 14–20C, and Chinese decorative arts. The end room is devoted mainly to Japanese and Persian ceramics and other decorative arts. The Screen gallery (l.) houses Japanese fine arts, and leads into the Tibetan Room. Beyond, the Temporary Exhibition Gallery is on the right (exhibitions here are usually changed monthly) and on the left stone, metal and terracotta works of India and South East Asia are displayed in two adjacent rooms.

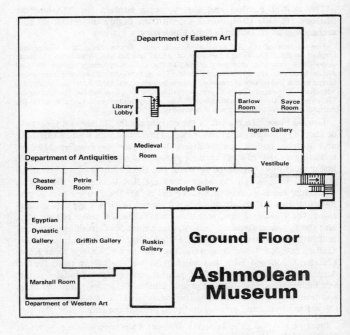

FIRST FLOOR. Passing through the small *Founder's Room* (exhibiting portraits of Elias Ashmole) we descend a few steps into the DEPARTMENT OF ANTIQUITIES, the many superb finds arranged for expert study rather than aesthetic appreciation. An exhibition in the corridor describes the early history of the Museum. The TRADESCANT ROOM exhibits objects from the original collections and historical relics, such as Guy Fawkes' Lantern, Bradshaw's hat, Powhatan's mantle etc. Displayed in the JOHN EVANS ROOM are gold ornaments and other objects of the European prehistoric periods with a large alcove for Italic and Etruscan antiquities. The Cretan collection in the ARTHUR EVANS ROOM, principally from the excavations of Sir Arthur Evans at Knossos, is of special importance, and includes pottery, Minoan seals, Linear B tablets, swords, jewellery, Cycladic finds from Phylakopi in Melos and from the Diktaean Cave. Beyond is the *Myres Room* of Cypriot antiquities, with seals, jewellery, sculpture, etc.; to the right is the *Drapers' Gallery* of finds from the Near East including "Luristan Bronzes" and objects from Jericho. To the left the BEAZLEY ROOM is devoted to Greek antiquities including Geometric, orientalising, black- and red-figure vases (note especially those with scenes of men at work: a shoemaker, potters in their workshop, and a helmet maker), bronzes, terracottas, gems and jewellery. The LEEDS ROOM houses finds from the Roman Empire and Europe during the Dark Ages, with particular reference to Britain. A staircase descends to the Viking Lobby.

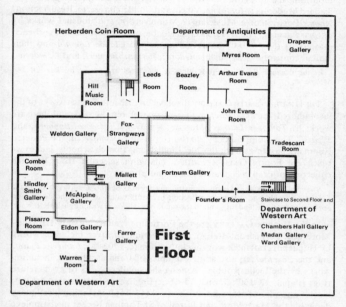

The *Hill Music Room* contains Italian and English stringed instruments (16C–18C) including 'Le Messie' by Stradivarius. The *Heberden Coin Room* (open 10–12.30 and 2–4) contains rich collections of Greek, Roman, Oriental, medieval European, and modern coins, and medals, a selection from all periods being on exhibition. Students may consult the main part of the collection by appointment only.

THE DEPARTMENT OF WESTERN ART occupies the remainder of the upper floors. Beyond the Founder's Room (see above) is the FORTNUM GALLERY, containing the well-known Fortnum collection of Renaissance bronzes, as well as a remarkably representative collection of Italian *Paintings of the 13–17C (see also below). *Orcagna*, Birth of the Virgin; *Bronzino*, Portrait of Giov. de' Medici as a boy; *Giac. Pacchiarotti*, Virgin and Child; *Christofano Allori*, Portrait; *And. Solario*, Ecce Homo; *Davide Ghirlandaio*, Saints; *Uccello*, Hunt in a Forest; *Lor. di Credi*, Madonna and Child; *Vitt. Crivelli*, St Catherine of Alexandria; *And. Vanni*, Virgin and Child; *Fra Filippo Lippi*, Meeting of Saints; *Ghirlandaio* (attrib.), Portrait of Young Man; *Piero di Cosimo*, Forest Fire; *Pinturicchio*, Virgin and Child; cartoons by *Raphael* and *Sodoma*.

At the end is the *Mallett Gallery* with tapestries and sculpture including busts of Cromwell and Wren by *Edward Pearce* (d. 1698), and of Marlborough by *Rysbrack*. The inlaid brass and tortoiseshell medailler is by *A.–C. Boulle*. Here also are a painted wooden statue of an acolyte (Netherlandish, c. 1470) and *Vay Dyck*, Deposition.

The Fox-Strangways Gallery contains small Netherlandish, German, Spanish, and Italian paintings, including some lovely primitives; *Giov. Bellini*, St Jerome; *Camillo Procaccini*, Rest on Flight; *Luis de Morales*, Virgin and Child; *Simon Marmion* (?), St Francis, Virgin mourning the Body of Christ; *Veronese*, Holy Family; *Giorgione*, The Tallard Madonna; *Montagna*, Virgin and Child; *Tintoretto*, Resurrection; *Anon.*, Portrait of a Musician (? Monteverdi); and unusual works by *Jacopo Bassano*. The Weldon Gallery beyond, is devoted to the French masters of the 16–18C, notably *Poussin* and *Claude Lorrain* and their Italian contemporaries such as *Guardi*, *Bernini*, *Barocci*, and *Canaletto*.

In the *Coombe Room* of Pre-Raphaelite paintings are works by *Rossetti* and *Millais*.

The Hindley-Smith Gallery displays English and French works of the last hundred years. *Courbet* and *Corot* are well represented, and there are works by *Toulouse-Lautrec*, *Matisse*, *Van Gogh*, *Pissarro*, *Bonnard*, and *Picasso*. The sculpture is by *Rodin*, *Degas* and *Daumier*. In the Pissarro Room are paintings from the 20C English and French Schools. Hence we reach the Eldon Gallery with a changing selection from the rich collection of drawings, watercolours and prints.

A vestibule at the far end containing drawings by Max Beerbohm, gives access to the *Fine Art Library* and reference collection of prints (adm. to ticket-holders or on application to the attendant), and to the small *Warren Room* with English Delft ware.

In the Farrer Gallery are the Fortnum ceramics, mainly Hispano-Moresque, Turkish and Italian, and collections of silver, including works by Huguenot craftsmen working in London (c. 1705–50; *Lamerie*, *Platel*, and the *Courtaulds*); also some examples of Italian sculpture, including works by the Della Robbia. Among the smaller works of art here are rings (Papal, 13–15C; Jewish 15–16C; English ecclesiastical, 13–17C); ivories and plaquettes; Limoges enamel (13–16C) including a reliquary depicting the Martyrdom and Burial of St Thomas Becket in champlevé enamel; and a fine display of *Timepieces (16–17C). Hence we may regain the Mallett Gallery.

Second Floor. Approached from the Mallett Gallery by a staircase showing examples of tapestry and needlework are the *Chambers Hall Gallery* devoted to the British School, including works by *Hogarth*, *Reynolds*, *Zoffany*, *Richard Wilson*, *Gainsborough*, *Constable*, *Romney*, *Samuel Palmer*, and *Bonington*; the *Madan Gallery* of Dutch and Flemish works of the 17C (works by *Rubens*, *Van Dyck*, *Van Goyen*, *Ruisdael*, *Paul Bril*, *David Teniers the Younger*, *Jan Van Huysum*) and the Marshall Collection of 17–18C glass; and the *Ward Gallery* of Dutch 17–18C paintings of flowers and still-life.

The Cast Gallery (Mon–Fri 10–1, 2–4) lies to the north of the Museum, approached from St John's St. It contains over 250 casts of Greek and Greco-Roman statuary, arranged in historical sequence.

Across St Giles is **St John's College** (Pl. 6), founded in 1555 by Sir Thomas White, a Reading clothier and Lord Mayor of London, on the site of the old Cistercian college of St Bernard (founded by Abp. Chichele in 1437).

The front and the W. side of the first quadrangle (to which a third story has been added) are remnants of St Bernard's College, and over the entrance are statues of St Bernard, Chichele, and White, and (inside) St John the Baptist, by Eric Gill. The *Hall* (c. 1502) and the *Chapel* (1530) have both been altered, the former in the 18C, the latter in 1843. The portraits in the hall include those of Henry Hudson, the navigator, and Sir Walter Raleigh. In the chapel rest the remains of the founder and Abps. Laud and Juxon. The E. side of the first quadrangle and the S. side of the second (Canterbury Quad) were put up in 1596–97. The remaining two cloistered sides of the second quadrangle were built in 1631–36 at the expense of Abp. Laud. The famous *Colonnades (resembling the Hospital at Milan) and the charming *Garden Front form an interesting blend of the traditional Gothic of Oxford with the classical style of Italy. The bronze statues of Charles I and Henrietta Maria on the gate-towers are by Le Sueur. The *Library*, on the S. and E. side of this qud, contains a portrait of Charles I, partly composed of psalms written in a minute hand; Laud's skull-cap, the staff he used at his execution, and MS. of his diary. The S. quadrangle (1950) is by Maufe, who also enlarged the 19C N. quadrangle (1933), which includes the 'Beehives', octagonal cell-like undergraduates' rooms (1958–60), one of the bolder new Oxford buildings. Behind is a further new quadrangle by Arup Associates. The *Gardens of St John's, laid out by 'Capability' Brown, are perhaps the most beautiful in the University.

FAMOUS MEMBERS: Edmund Campion, Abps. Laud and Juxon, James Shirley, A. E. Housman, and Gilbert Murray.

On the opposite side of St Giles are *Blackfriars Priory* (Dominican), and *Pusey House* (a High Church clergy-house). The yard of the Lamb & Flag leads into Museum St. with the fortress-like exterior of Keble's new extension. Farther N. in St Giles *St Benet's Hall* (Benedictine), faces Black Hall (Pl. 6), a 17C house, occupied as *Queen Elizabeth House*, a centre of Commonwealth studies (1935). Here the chief thoroughfares of the Victorian residential district of NORTH OXFORD, Banbury Rd. and Woodstock Rd. diverge, isolating *St Giles's Church* and the Old Parsonage (now a hotel), which dates from the 17C.

In BANBURY RD. are the *School of Engineering*, the nucleus of a new science area, and conspicuous because of the Engineering Science Lab. with its generator tower; *Wycliffe Hall*; and *St Hugh's College*. In Norham Gardens on the right is the beautifully situated *Lady Margaret Hall*, with a new library (1961) and Quadrangle (1967), a successful composition with clean lines. In Woodstock Rd. are (l.) the *Radcliffe Infirmary*, and the former Radcliffe Observatory (with 18C sculptures by John Bacon and others). The observatory has been transferred to South Africa. Beyond (r.) is *St Anne's College*, with the kitchens of the large, light, and graceful hall along Woodstock Rd. The hall (1959) is crowned with a small cupola. Adjacent is the white carved and balconied Wolfson Building (1964). Beyond is *St Antony's College* (comp. p. 262).

Little Clarendon St. leads w. past **Somerville College**, beyond which in Walton St. is the **Clarendon Press**, belonging to the University, founded in 1586 and removed hither from the Clarendon Building (p. 273) in 1830. For admission apply to the Printer. Farther N., where Walton St. is continued by Kingston Rd., a turning (l.) leads to *Port Meadow* for a favourite Oxford walk to Binsey or Godstow (p. 262). To the s. beyond Wellington Square (being developed by the University), runs St John's St. with its fine Regency terraces, off which is *Regent's Park College* (Baptist; 1938), which occupied Holford House in Regent's Park, London, in 1856–1927. Facing the end of the dignified Georgian Beaumont Street, with the appropriate façade of the *Playhouse* (by Maufe; 1938), is **Worcester College** (Pl. 10), once known from its remoteness as 'Botany Bay'. It was founded in 1714 by Sir Thomas Cookes, but the site had been occupied first by *Gloucester College* (founded in 1283), the general house of studies for English Benedictines, and after the Reformation by *Gloucester Hall*.

The main buildings are in the classical style of the 18C (1746–84). The *Chapel*, very dark, was elaborately decorated by Burges in 1866 with paintings and mosaics recalling his work in Cardiff Castle. On the left side of the quadrangle is a row of five small *Monastic Houses*, known as the 'Cottages', relics of the medieval Gloucester College, with the arms of Benedictine abbeys over the doorways. The *Gardens* are extensive and beautiful and contain a lake.

FAMOUS MEMBERS: Thomas Walsingham, the chronicler, member of the Benedictine house; Sir Kenelm Digby and Richard Lovelace of Gloucester Hall; and De Quincey (No. 10 staircase) of Worcester College.

A little to the N. is the building (1913) of **Ruskin College** (Pl. 6), founded in 1899 by Walter Vrooman and Charles Beard, American admirers of John Ruskin, to enable working men to study history, sociology, and economics in the academic atmosphere of Oxford. It has no official connection with the University.

Worcester St. leads s. to **Nuffield College**, endowed by Lord Nuffield in 1937 for postgraduate studies, with Cotswold-style buildings and a tower (1949–60), on the site of the former basin of the Oxford Canal. Across New Road the County Hall, Assize Court, and Prison occupy the site of the Norman and medieval *Castle* (Pl. 6), claimed as the birthplace in 1157 of Richard I, and the start of the romantic 'flight through the snow' of his grandmother, the Empress Matilda (1142). St George's tower and crypt and the mound (all early Norman) are the chief remains.

To the s. of the castle, *Paradise Square* (Pl. 14) occupies the site of the Franciscan house of which Roger Bacon was a member; tablet on the old city wall, in King's Terrace, off Penson's Gardens (Pl. 14), close to the site of his burial-place. The neighbouring church of *St Ebbe's* (Pl. 14) has a Norman w. doorway. A huge new *Shopping Precinct* is rising in the area.—Of the once rich and powerful *Osney Abbey* (Augustinian; founded 1129) nothing remains save a 15C archway near the cemetery w. of the railway (by Osney Lane); while a doorway in the railway goods-yard is the sole relic of the Cistercian *Rewley Abbey*.

To the N.E. of the Castle in New Inn Hall St. is **St Peter's College** (Pl. 10), founded in 1928, in memory of Bp. Chavasse of Liverpool, and incorporated by Royal Charter in 1961 as a fully independent college. It incorporates the old buildings of *New Inn Hall*, one of the old students' inns, used as a mint by Charles I, and absorbed by Balliol. The hall, fitted with new oak panelling, is the college dining-hall, and the adjoining church of *St Peter-le-Bailey* serves as the college chapel. New Inn Hall was for a time Hannington Hall, headquarters of the Oxford Missionary Union. Opposite St Peter-le-Bailey is the old gateway of *St Mary's College*, dissolved under Elizabeth I, where in 1498 Erasmus prepared his edition of the Greek Testament. The site of the hall is occupied by *Frewin Hall*, the residence of Edward VII during his year at Oxford (1860).

St Michael's St. leads back to Cornmarket St. (see below) past the premises of the **Oxford Union Society** (Pl. 10), founded in 1823 as a social and debating club for University men. Debates are held at 8 p.m. on Thurs, in term; visitors' tickets may be obtained through a member.

We may return to the centre by Magdalen St. which is continued s. to Carfax by CORNMARKET STREET (Pl. 10). Here, on the left, is *St Michael's* (Pl. 10); its gaunt tower, dating from before 1050 (restored in 1896), was once a watch-tower of the city-wall, defending the N. or *Bocardo Gate*, which used to span the street here. The church, damaged by fire in 1953, was restored with alterations (1956). The four figures in the E. windows are the oldest examples of stained glass in Oxford (c. 1290). Wm. Morris was married here in 1859. No. 28, just beyond, is a half-timbered house of c. 1450 (restored).

Those with time should go back along Broad St., famous for its bookshops (one under Trinity Quad), to the New Bodleian (p. 274).

A short way along Parks Rd. is **Wadham College** (Pl. 7), facing the gardens of Trinity. It was founded by Nicholas Wadham of Somerset and built in 1610–13 on the site of an Augustinian friary by his widow Dorothy.

The buildings, well restored, are in a noble and undecorated Perp. style, in no way debased in spite of their late date. Between the hall and the chapel, on the E. side, is a Jacobean porch, with statues of Nicholas and Dorothy Wadham. The *Chapel*, which was modified internally in 1834, has a Jacobean screen and stall-work, and good 17C stained glass (E. window by Bernard van Linge). The *Hall* has a hammer-beam roof, a Jacobean screen, and a large collection of portraits. The secluded *Gardens* give a lovely view of the garden-front. In the s. quadrangle is a pleasant copper-roofed block opened in 1953.

FAMOUS MEMBERS: Adm. Blake, Christopher Wren, Speaker Onslow, Dean Church, Sir T. G. Jackson, Sir Thos. Beecham and Cecil Day-Lewis. The ingenious Dr John Wilkins was Warden in Wren's time.

Opposite the New Bodleian, and now an extension to it, is a building of 1882, by Champneys, originally intended as an Indian Institute. *HOLYWELL STREET, an attractive and dignified old street, leads E. past the *Old Music Room* (l.), the first room to be built in Europe solely for musical purposes (1748). Bath Place (r.) is well known for the *Turf Tavern.*

In Mansfield Rd., leading from Holywell to the Parks, are *Manchester College* (Pl. 11) and *Mansfield College* (Pl. 7), two Nonconformist theological colleges. The former, built by T. Worthington in 1891–93, is intended chiefly for the training of Unitarian ministers; the chapel contains a series of windows by Burne-Jones and Morris; and some of the old houses in Holywell have been adapted to form a picturesque quadrangle. Mansfield College, by Champneys (1886–89), with an addition of 1960–61, is maintained by the Congregationalists.

At the corner where Longwall St. leads back to the High, we turn left into St Cross Rd. passing the tiny nucleus of *St Cross College*, adjacent to the church, which retains a 12C chancel-arch and 13C tower. In the cemetery behind are buried Walter Pater (1839–94) and Kenneth Grahame (1859–1932). Beyond, Holywell Manor with the new building opposite comprises Balliol and St Anne's Graduate Society. On the corner is the interesting library group for the faculties of Law and English and the Dept. of Statistics (designed by Sir L. Martin, 1964). Built low in brick with clean horizontal lines and cantilevered upper floors, it is attractively massed round a broad flight of steps.

Manor Rd. leads E. to St Catherine's College (1963), formerly a society for non-collegiate students founded in 1868, a special feature of which is the high percentage of science students. The college buildings, the gardens, and (notably) the furnishings are all designed by the Danish architect Arne Jacobsen (1960–64), and are the outstanding example of the 'new wave' in Oxford architecture.

St Cross Rd. continues between playing-fields to join South Parks Rd. with the huge Zoology block in stilted concrete on the corner. To the N. are the UNIVERSITY PARKS, 100 acres of playing-fields surrounded by a belt of shrubs. They contain the University Cricket Ground, and football, hockey, and lacrosse are played here in winter. To the r. is a pleasant walk along the bank of the Cherwell, beyond which the Parks have been extended, and on the s.e. begins a walk called *Mesopotamia*, leading between two branches of the river to (1¼ m.) Magdalen Bridge. We turn left past a number of well-equipped *Laboratories* devoted to University instruction and research in natural science, and the interestingly shaped Dyson Perrins Lecture Hall.

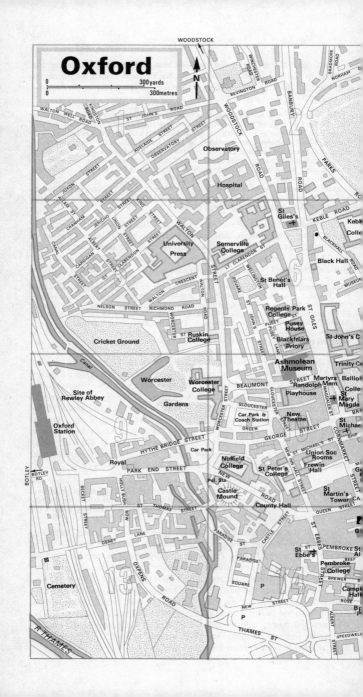

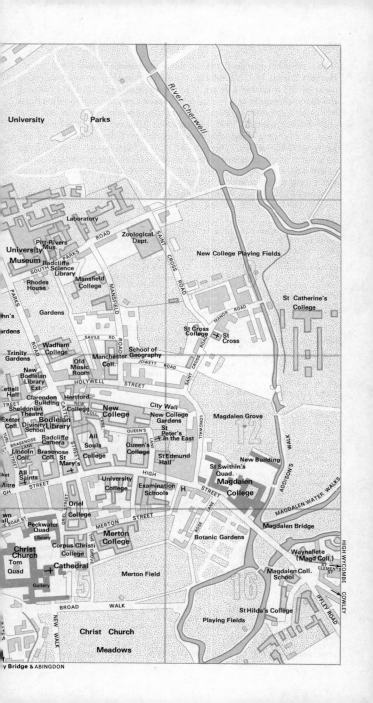

In a pleasant garden (l.) is the imposing **Rhodes House** (1929, by Sir Herbert Baker; Pl. 7), headquarters of the Rhodes Trust and a department of the Bodleian Library (Commonwealth and U.S.A.). Crowning the entrance-cupola is a bronze bird copied from the carved stone birds found at Zimbabwe in Rhodesia. On the opposite corner is the Radcliffe Science Library (1901–34), removed from the Radcliffe Camera in 1861. An underground extension lies beneath the forecourt of the **University Museum** (Pl. 7; open 10–4), built in 1855–60 in cast-iron Gothic style for the natural science collections of the University. At the N.E. corner of the central court is the entrance to the *Pitt-Rivers Museum (2–4), an interesting anthropological collection.

Across Parks Rd. is **Keble College** (Pl. 6), opened in 1870 as a memorial to the Rev. John Keble (1792–1866).

Originally governed by a council, the college became self-governing in 1952, and it has possessed Fellows since 1930; previously there were only tutors nominated by the Warden. The rooms are arranged in corridors instead of in staircases, and in the chapel all the seats face the E.

The brick buildings, designed by Butterfield, have been criticized for their lack of harmony with the spirit of Oxford architecture. The *Chapel* is richly decorated with wall-paintings and mosaics; the Liddon Chapel contains Holman Hunt's famous painting 'The Light of the World'. The *Hall* contains portraits of Keble (by Richmond), Dr Liddon, and others. In the *Library* are Sir Charles Brooke's collection of medieval illuminated MSS. and fine early printed books and bindings; also the 'Christian Year' and other MSS. of Keble.

Keble Rd. leads w. to Banbury Rd. whence we may return s. viâ St Giles and Cornmarket St. to the centre.

Among points of interest near Oxford are *Shotover* (4 m. E.) with a view of the city; *Boar's Hill*, 4 m. s., where Gilbert Murray (1866–1957) lived and died; and *Elsfield Manor*, 4 m. N.E., the home of John Buchan (Lord Tweedsmuir) in 1920–40 (his death). Besides the trips on the Thames, the excursions up the Cherwell to *Water Eaton* and *Islip* can be recommended.

FROM OXFORD TO EYNSHAM (Witney), 6¼ m. From the station Botley Road crosses the Thames to join A 4141, leaving on the right a road to Binsey and Wytham, on the left one to *North Hinksey* with the buildings (1955–60; by Lord Mottistone) of *Westminster College* (Methodist), removed from Horseferry Rd. in London. Passing (l.) the road to Cumnor (p. 262) we recross the Thames at (5 m.) *Swinford Bridge* (car toll) over 1 m. short of *Eynsham* and the junction with A 40 (see Rte 30A).

FROM OXFORD TO BANBURY, 22½ m. (A 423). Railway in ½–¾ hr (through-trains by this route from the South to Birmingham). This road is the same as the Bicester road (see below) for 5 m., then it bears left, keeping above the right bank of the Cherwell and the OXFORD CANAL (by Brindley; 1769–90), which is navigable to Braunston (p. 316) and Coventry.—12¼ m. *Hopcroft's Holt* (Hotel). The road on the r. leads in 1¼ m. to *Rousham*, a charming little village on the Cherwell adjoining the 17C mansion of the Cottrell-Dormers (adm. 2–5.30 Wed, Sun & BH, April–Sept; fee; gardens daily 10–6), with good family portraits and miniatures and grounds laid out by Kent in the Italian manner. The church has interesting Norman and Dec. features.— 13¼ m. *Steeple Aston* church (r.) possesses a famous embroidered cope of 1310–40.— 16¼ m. *Deddington* (Hotel) is a small decayed town, in the vanished castle of which Piers Gaveston was arrested in 1312. The church at *Somerton*, on the Cherwell 4 m. s.E., contains remarkable Fermor memorials (16C).—At (19¼ m.) *Adderbury* we join the main road from London (Rte 32A).

FROM OXFORD TO BICESTER, 13¼ m. (A 43, A 421). At first we follow the Banbury road. On the right at 4 m. is a lane leading to *Water Eaton* (1 m.), on the Cherwell, with an early Jacobean manor-house. At 5 m. we diverge r. and cross the Cherwell. Beyond the bridge (6 m.) is a road leading r. for *Islip* (1 m.), the birthplace of Edward the Confessor (1004). *Wood Eaton*, 1¾ m. s., preserves a painted rood-beam, rediscovered in the church in 1957. The church of *Charlton-on-Otmoor*,

2½ m. N.E., is a well-preserved example of the transitional style between Dec. and Perp., with a fine rood-screen and loft (c. 1500).—9 m. *Weston-on-the-Green*, where Weston Manor (15C hall) now a hotel, is at the Northampton road fork.—13¼ m. *Bicester*, see Rte 32A.

From Oxford to *Worcester*, see Rte 31; to *Stratford-on-Avon*, see Rte 34; to *Gloucester*, see Rte 30B.

30 LONDON TO GLOUCESTER
A Viâ Oxford and Cheltenham

ROAD, 104 m. (A 40).—25 m. *Beaconsfield.*—29 m. *High Wycombe.*—36¼ m. *Stokenchurch.*—54½ m. **Oxford** (Northern by-pass).—66 m. *Witney* (by-pass).—73 m. *Burford.*—82 m. *Northleach.*—95 m. **Cheltenham.**—104 m. **Gloucester.** Motor coach from Victoria; Green Line coach (711) from Oxford Circus to High Wycombe.—MOTORWAY (M40) from Denham to Wheatley.

From London, continuing the line of Marylebone Rd., A 40, at first partly elevated and designated as motorway, then as Western Avenue, runs N. of the old Uxbridge road.—Beyond (18 m.) *Uxbridge Common*, it crosses the Grand Union Canal in the Colne valley, and enters the Chiltern Hills (comp. p. 307).—At (19 m.) *Denham Roundabout* we are joined by the Uxbridge road and leave on our left the motorway and a busy road to Slough (A 412; 6½ m.). Just beyond, off to the right, is the charming old village street of *Denham*. The church contains a brass to Dame Agnes Jordan, abbess of Syon (1544), one of only two extant brasses to an abbess. Denham Place is a notable 17C house.— 21 m. *Gerrards Cross* (Hotels) is a residential district extending N. to Chalfont St Peter.

To the right are the roads (A 413 or A 332) viâ (2½ m.) *Chalfont St Peter* (Hotel; 14C) to (4½ m.) **Chalfont St Giles**, a pleasant village with the old cottage where Milton lived in 1665–66, while the plague was raging in London. 'Paradise Lost' was completed, 'Paradise Regained' begun here. The cottage contains a few relics of the poet (adm. daily, exc. Sun morn. and all Tues, 10–1, 2.15–6 or dusk; in Nov–Jan open only on Sun aft. and all Sat). A fine old lychgate leads to the church with its medieval wall-paintings. The road goes on to join Rte 32A at *Amersham* (p. 307).

About 2 m. S. of Chalfont St Giles is the old Quaker Meeting-house of *Jordans*, built in 1688 (adm. daily; service on Sun at 11). In the burial-ground lie William Penn (1644–1718), founder of Pennsylvania, his two wives, and five of his children; also Thomas Elwood (d. 1713), Milton's friend. Near by is the *Old Jordans Hostel*, occupying the farmhouse in which the Quakers met before the meeting-house was built. That the timbers of the 'Mayflower' were used in building the barn is an attractive but unlikely theory.

To the left at Gerrards Cross roads lead S. to the pretty village of *Fulmer* (2 m.), where the church of 1610 has a rare contemporary wooden font, and (2 m. farther) *Stoke Poges Church, with the beautiful churchyard in which Gray's immortal 'Elegy' was probably written. On our right is a monument to Thomas Gray (1716–71), and close to the E. wall of the church is the tomb of Gray's mother (epitaph by the poet) beneath which the poet himself rests. The church dates mainly from the 14C; the square manor pew beneath the tower is approached from the manor-house by a 'cloister' in which is the 'Bicycle Window' (1643), showing a hobby-horse. Gray's 'Ode on a Distant Prospect of Eton College' is said to have been written in his mother's garden at *Stoke Court*, 1 m. N. *Stoke Park*, to the W., belonged in 1760–1840 to the descendants of William Penn.—B 473 leads on W. to *Farnham Royal* (1½ m.), whence we may rejoin A 40 at Beaconsfield (5 m.), skirting *Burnham Beeches (444 acres) a magnificent tract of forest purchased in 1879 by the Corporation of London and added to since. At *East Burnham House*, S. of the Beeches, Sheridan spent his honeymoon in 1777, while in 1838 it was purchased by George Grote, who here wrote his 'History of Greece' and entertained many famous contemporaries, including Chopin, J. S. Mill, Jenny Lind, and Mendelssohn.

25 m. **Beaconsfield** (Hotels; 11,900 inhab.), with a fine wide street in Georgian brick, is famed for its associations with Edmund Burke (1729–97), Benjamin Disraeli, Earl of Beaconsfield (1808–81), and G. K. Chesterton (1874–1936; memorial in St Teresa's church). Burke is buried in the *Parish Church* and Edmund Waller, the poet, beneath a walnut tree (the family emblem) in the churchyard. The lodge of Hall Barn (no adm.), Waller's house, is panelled with medieval woodwork. In Warwick Rd., N. of the station, is the *Bekonscot Model Village* and garden (adm. daily 10–6.30 or 7; fee) with a model railway (working Sat, Sun, & BH, 2–6.30 Easter–Oct; daily 2–5 in Aug–Sept).

29 m. **High Wycombe** (Hotels), a flourishing town (59,300 inhab.) strung out along a valley, is specially noted for its chairs and other furniture. The lofty 13–16C *Parish Church* is the largest in the county. The *Guildhall* (1757) and the *Little Market House* (1761), close by, were designed by Henry Keene. *Wycombe Abbey* (c. 1870), once the seat of Lord Carrington and in 1942–45 headquarters of the U.S. 8th Army Air Force, is now a well-known girls' school. Hannah Ball opened the first Sunday School in England in St Mary's St. in 1769. Sir Wm. Ramsay, the chemist, died in 1916 at *Hazlemere*, on the Amersham road.

About 2½ m. N.E. lies *Penn*, the alleged ancestral home of the family of William Penn. The church has a good roof and contains a fine painted Doom of the 15C, a plain old leaden font (unique in England), and Penn brasses.—*Hughenden Manor*, 1½ m. N. (N.T.; adm. weekdays 2–6; Sat & Sun 12.30–6; closed Mon & Tues and Dec–Jan), was the home of Benjamin Disraeli, Earl of Beaconsfield, from 1847 till his death in 1881, and was opened in 1949 as a Disraeli Memorial Museum. He is buried in the churchyard, and in the church is a monument erected by Queen Victoria. An obelisk in the park commemorates his father, Isaac D'Israeli (1766–1848).

Roads to *Maidenhead*, see Rte 28.

FROM HIGH WYCOMBE TO AYLESBURY. The direct route (17¾ m.) is viâ West Wycombe (see below), but a more attractive route (18½ m.) runs N. from the Guildhall viâ (1½ m.) *Hughenden* (see above) and through the Chiltern Hills to (4½ m.) *Speen*, in undulating country, and (6½ m.) *Lacey Green*. These routes unite at Princes Risborough (see below).—Yet another route runs through a district closely associated with John Hampden (1594–1643), who was M.P. for Buckinghamshire. This passes (5½ m.) *Prestwood* (6½ m.), a stone cross marking the parcel of land for which Hampden refused to pay the illegal 'ship-money' tax of 20/-, and (7½ m) *Hampden House*, largely rebuilt in the 18C, long Hampden's residence and now a girls' school. Close by is the church of *Great Hampden*, where he is buried; it contains the tomb of his first wife (d. 1634), with a touching epitaph, and several re-used brasses of the Hampdens. Between Gt. Hampden and Lacey Green (see above) is a well-preserved stretch of *Grim's Dyke*, an ancient bank and ditch of uncertain purpose. Just below it, to the N.W., is the Pink & Lily inn, a favourite haunt of Rupert Brooke.—9½ m. *Chequers* (l.), a historic Tudor mansion (no adm.), was presented to the nation in 1917 by Lord Lee of Fareham for the use of the Prime Minister. Its collection of Cromwell portraits and relics is famous.—16½ m. *Aylesbury*, see Rte 32A.

31½ m. *West Wycombe*, a village of 16–18C houses (N.T.), has a curious 'classical' church, built on the hill (646 ft) above it in 1763–69 by Sir Francis Dashwood (Lord le Despencer, p. 260), with a tower surmounted by a gilded ball (no adm.) capable of holding 10 persons. At the E. end is a huge hexagonal mausoleum (1765), by John Bastard (adm. Sun and BH in summer, 2–7; fee), and below are artificial caves, quarried for road building and later adapted to the revels of the Hell-Fire Club (opened to the public in 1978). *West Wycombe Park*, built for Sir Francis in 1765 and visited by Benjamin Franklin in 1773, is now N.T. property, with extensive grounds (open in July–Aug, daily, exc. Sat, 2.15–6; also Mon–Fri in June; fee).

FROM WEST WYCOMBE TO AYLESBURY, 16 m. (A 4010).—1½ m. *Bradenham* has a Saxon church-doorway. Isaac D'Israeli (see above), who is buried in the church, lived in the manor-house from 1829 to 1848.—7 m. **Princes Risborough** (Hotel), a small town below the Chiltern Hills, has a 17–18C manor-house (N.T.; open Tues & Wed 2.30–4.30, free). It is so named as a royal possession in contra-distinction to (8 m.) *Monks Risborough*, a village with an interesting E.E. to Perp. church, which belonged to the Abp. of Canterbury.—Cut into the chalk hillside above Monks Risborough is the *Whiteleaf Cross* (80 ft by 70 ft), probably marking the intersection of the Icknield Way with another important road running N. to Oxford. *Bledlow*, a finely placed village 2 m. S.W. of Princes Risborough, has a notable Norman font in its church.—16 m. *Aylesbury*, see Rte 32A.

Beyond (36½ m.) *Stokenchurch*, with a Post Office radio tower, we reach the crest of the Chiltern ridge (787 ft; view) and descend a long hill into Oxfordshire.—40 m. **Aston Rowant** (Hotel) has a church (¾ m. r.), with early Norman details and a Purbeck marble font.

Watlington, 2¾ m. S.W., with a 17C market house, is 4 m. S.E. of *Chalgrove*, with the battlefield where Hampden was mortally wounded in 1643 (obelisk).—He died at Thame (Hotels), a market town (5900 inhab.), 6¼ m. N.W. of Aston Rowant. The large church contains a fine early 14C screen and the monument of Lord Williams (d. 1559) and his wife. The original Grammar School buildings (1575) adjoin; here John Hampden, Dean Fell, and Anthony Wood were educated. The Prebendal House close by has a fine E.E. chapel.

Some of the finest Chiltern scenery is reached by the roads running S. (l.) between Stokenchurch and Aston Rowant, and their branches. The Hambleden road traverses *Ibstone Common* (*Views), with its quaint little Norman church (r.) and old windmill, and descends to (4 m.) *Fingest*, where the church has a unique twin-gabled tower.—7 m. *Hambleden*, a charming village, is 1 m. from the Thames and c. 2 m. from Henley by road or footpath.—Another road farther w. follows the crest of the Chilterns to Nettlebed (8 m.; p. 256) viâ *Christmas Common* and (6 m.) *Cookley Green*. Just short of the latter a road branches l. for Stonor (3 m.; p. 256) viâ *Pishill*.

43 m. *Tetsworth* (Hotel).—45½ m. *Milton Common* (Hotel). The motorway rejoins A 40.—To the s. of (48¾ m.) *Wheatley*, on the Thame, is *Cuddesdon*, with the residence of the Bishop of Oxford and a theological training college.—50½ m. *Forest Hill* was the scene of Milton's unhappy first marriage (1643).—54½ m. **Oxford**, see Rte 29.

A 40 passes N. of the city, crossing the Banbury and Woodstock roads on the edge of North Oxford, and meeting the direct w. road from the city at (61½ m.) **Eynsham** (Hotels), which has an old village cross and scanty relics of a once-famous abbey.—65 m. **Witney** (12,500 inhab.; Hotel), on the Windrush, is noted for its blanket manufacture in well-built and harmonious 18C factory buildings. It possesses a butter-cross of 1683, a fine Town Hall, and a noble church (remodelled in the Perp. period), with a beautiful E.E. spire. The animal carvings on the porch, the Dec. N. window, and 15C monuments should be noted.

There are many interesting churches in the lowlands s. of Witney. On the Lechlade road (s.w.) are (4¼ m.) *Brize Norton*, with a Norman door and a fine screen; and (5¾ m.) *Black Bourton*, the birthplace of Maria Edgeworth (1767–1849), with wall-paintings of c. 1275 and another Norman door. Just off the route (4 m. N.E. of Lechlade) is *Langford*, with a very fine *Church, partly pre-Norman and partly of c. 1200. In the porch is a Saxon sculptured Rood. *Broadwell*, ¾ m. N., has another fine 11–13C church.—At *South Leigh*, 2¼ m. S.E. of Witney, where the church is notable for its 14–15C wall-paintings, John Wesley preached his first sermon (1725).—At *Bampton* (Hotel), 5½ m. s. of Witney (bus) and 2 m. N. of Tadpole Bridge (p. 262), is another noteworthy church (Norman; E.E. *Spire), and here the art of morris-dancing has never died out. The Whit Monday festival is characteristic.—*North Leigh* church, 2½ m. N.E. of Witney, contains a remarkable chantry chapel.

At (68 m.) *Minster Lovell* (Hotel), charmingly placed on the Windrush, are a good Perp. church and the ruins of a moated manor-house (fee, not Sun morn.), in which Francis, Lord Lovell, an adherent to Lambert Simnel, is said to have perished of starvation after the battle of Stoke, owing to the death of the servant who alone knew the secret of his hiding-place.— 72 m. We cross the road from Swindon to Banbury (A 361), on which (r.) stands **Burford** (Good hotels), a charming little place, once one of the principal Cotswold wool towns. The High St. drops steeply down the hillside to cross the Windrush by a fine old bridge and abounds in stone-built houses with spandrelled doorways and mullioned windows. It was the birthplace of Sir William Beechey, R.A. (1753–1839). The fine church of *St John the Baptist* (Norman, E.E., & Perp.) is notable for its many chapels. Speaker Lenthall, who died in 1662 at *Burford Priory* (rebuilt Elizabethan), is buried in the N. transept and John Meade Falkner (1858–1932), the author, in the churchyard; while a memorial to Christopher Kempster (1626–1709), one of Wren's master-masons, reminds us of the proximity of the best Cotswold stone-quarries (Taynton, Barrington, etc.).

On the N. bank of the Windrush, 2½ m. E., is *Swinbrook*, where the church contains monuments of the Fettiplaces, quaintly arranged in tiers, and grotesquely carved stalls. *Asthall*, across the river, has a fine manor-house and church.— *Shilton* church, 2½ m. S.E., has an early font, possibly of Saxon origin.—*Sherborne* on the N. bank of the Windrush, half-way between Burford and Northleach, has the fine monument of John Dutton (1661), by T. Burman, and other good tombs of the Dutton family, whose beautiful little hunting-lodge, *Lodge Park* (1655), lies 1½ m. s. of the main road.

At (81 m.) *Northleach* (Hotel) the 15C church has a noble *Porch and good brasses. Chedworth, see p. 304.—At (88 m.) *Andoversford* we cross the road (A 436) from Stow to Gloucester (p. 303). *Dowdeswell*, 1 m. w., has an Elizabethan manor-house.

94 m. **CHELTENHAM** (69,700 inhab.), a fashionable inland spa and an important centre of education and contemporary arts, is situated near the w. base of the Cotswold Hills. It is renowned for its charming late 18C and early 19C terraces, and is a favourite residence of retired officers and civil servants. Standing at the crossing of two trunk routes, it now suffers from traffic congestion. Charles Sturt (1795–1869), the Australian explorer, died at Cheltenham, and Gustav Holst (1874–1934), the composer, was born there.

Numerous good-sized **Hotels** throughout the town.
Post Office, Promenade (N. end).—INFORMATION BUREAU, 99 Promenade.
Bus Station in Royal Well Rd.
Theatre. *Everyman* (formerly the *Opera House*), Regent St.—MUSIC. *Annual Festival of Contemporary Music*, in July.
Racecourse at *Prestbury Park*, 1 m. N.E. (Nat. Hunt Steeplechases in winter; horse shows in summer).—GOLF at *Lilley Brook* (S.E.) on the Cirencester road, and at *Cleeve Hill* (N.E.) on the Winchcombe road.—CRICKET FESTIVAL (Aug) on the College Ground.—SWIMMING in Sandford Park or (indoors) Alstone Baths.— TENNIS in the parks.

Until 1718, when the purgative powers of the spring were discovered, Cheltenham was a small market town. A spa developed on which the seal of approval was set by George III's visit in 1788. The next forty years gave the town the opulent architectural character which survives to a great extent (though threatened) over a wide area today.—Tablets mark Jenner's house in St George's Rd. and the site of the stable (in Pittville St.) where Mrs Siddons played in her earliest days.

The backbone of Cheltenham is the HIGH STREET (1¾ m. long), running S.E. to N.W. In it is the 19C building of the *Grammar School* founded by Richard Pate in 1576, which includes Holst and R. S. Hawker among its famous pupils. *St Mary's Church*, though modernized, possesses many interesting features of early work, such as the tower and spire (Norman to Dec.), the late-Dec. wheel-window, the elaborate late-Perp. N. porch (now a baptistery), and a brass of 1513 (N. side of chancel). Near by in Clarence St. is the *Public Library, Museum, & Art Gallery*.

The well-shaded PROMENADE, given the illusion of greater length by clever perspective narrowing, leads s.w. from the High St. past a fine *Terrace of c. 1823 housing the *Municipal Offices*, in front of which stands a statue (by Lady Scott) of Dr E. A. Wilson (who perished with Scott in the Antarctic, 1912). *Cheltenham Ladies' College* (1853) is in Old Well Lane, to the w. Farther on, beyond the Town Hall (1901) and the fine *Queen's Hotel*, by the Jearred Brothers, are *Montpellier Gardens*. A bank now occupies the *Rotunda* (1817) of the original Montpellier Spa. *Cheltenham College*, a leading public school founded in 1841, is in the Bath Rd. to the s.E. Lord Morley and W. E. H. Lecky are among Old Cheltonians. Oriel Road and the associated streets off Bath Road have fine terraces and houses. *Sandford Park* has an open-air swimming pool.

The Evesham Road leads N.E. through Pittville, developed as an entity in 1820-30. In *Pittville Park* is the colonnaded *Pump Room* by John Forbes, restored in 1951-59 as an architecture school and concert hall.

A short excursion may be made to (6½ m.) Winchcombe viâ *Southam Delabere* (2¼ m.), with a manor-house of the late 15C (paintings in the chapel) and a good tithe-barn, at the foot of *Cleeve Hill* (1031 ft; view; Hotel). *Bishop's Cleeve*, 2 m. N.W., has a Norman *Church with a well-decorated W. front, a massive nave, and a superb Jacobean musicians' gallery. The fine monuments include one to Richard de la Bere (d. 1636) and his wife.

Winchcombe (Hotels) is an old-fashioned market town with a fine late-Perp. church (freely restored). *Hailes Abbey* (adm. daily, Sun from 2; fee), a Cistercian ruin (1246), 2 m. N.E., once famous for its relic of the Holy Blood (mentioned in Chaucer's 'Pardoner's Tale'), was the burial-place of its founder Richard, Earl of Cornwall and King of the Romans (1209-72), and of his son Henry (murdered at Viterbo in 1271). A small archaeological museum adjoins it. The parish church (1140) has wall-paintings of c. 1300 (*St Cecilia; fine heraldry). Henry VIII's widow, Catherine Parr (1512-48), who married Lord Seymour of Sudeley, is buried in the chapel adjoining *Sudeley Castle* (1 m. s.E.; adm. March–Oct daily, 12-5.30; fee). The 12C castle, rebuilt c. 1450 and dismantled in 1644, was restored in the 19C; it contains relics of Catherine Parr and interesting pictures, furniture, and royal relics; the gardens (open till 7) are fine.

Leckhampton Hill (978 ft), 2 m. s. of Cheltenham, has a view, while *Seven Springs*, 1½ m. farther s.E., among the Cotswold Hills, is the source of the Churn and considered by some the true head of the Thames.

A 40 descends to the Severn Vale and (103 m.) **Gloucester.**

B Viâ Cirencester

ROAD, 110½ m. To (47½ m.) *Wallingford*, see Rte 28A.—A 4130 and A 417. 60½ m. *Wantage.*—72½ m. *Faringdon.*—78½ m. *Lechlade.*—91½ m. **Cirencester.**— A 419. 110½ m. **Gloucester** (alternative route viâ Stroud, see p. 295).

An alternative approach to (56½ m.) Harwell can be made viâ Reading (comp. Rte 17) and the Thames-side road to (48 m.) *Streatley* (p. 256), there taking A 417. —53 m. *Blewbury*, 2½ m. s. of *Didcot*, has some chained books in its church. Here Sir William Nicholson (1872–1949), the painter, died.—54½ m. *Upton* has a small primitive Norman church.

RAILWAY, 113¾ m. from Paddington in c. 2½ hrs. Principal stations: To (53½ m.) *Didcot*, see Rte 28.—77½ m. **Swindon,** junction for the main lines to S. Wales and to Bristol.—91 m. *Kemble.*—102½ m. *Stroud.*—105 m. *Stonehouse.*—113¾ m. **Gloucester** (Eastgate). Most of the trains go on to (120½ m.) **Cheltenham Spa.**

From London viâ Henley to (47½ m.) *Wallingford*, see Rte 28A. A 4130 continues through (53 m.) *Didcot*, an important railway junction; *East Hagbourne*, 1½ m. s., is a notably pretty village. At (55½ m.) *Harwell*, an attractive village with a large 13–14C church, we join A 417 (the *Port Way*). The sprawling Atomic Energy Research Establishment is 2 m. s.w. beyond the A 34, which we cross.—57½ m. *East Hendred* has a church with an early 14C wooden lectern of unique two-tiered design, and a Perp. wayside chapel with priest's house attached. *Hendred House*, the seat of the Eyston family, contains relics of St Thomas More (cup; portrait by Holbein) and St John Fisher (staff used on the scaffold) and a private chapel (adm. on application) where Mass has been said since 1291.

60½ m. **Wantage** (8000 inhab.; Hotel), in the sheltered Vale of the White Horse, was the birthplace of Alfred the Great (849–99; statue in market place) and of Bp. Butler of the 'Analogy' (1692–1752). In the parish church are numerous fine brasses and the 14C tomb of Sir William Fitzwarren, who, with his wife Dame Alice, is a leading character in the pantomime 'Dick Whittington'. At *West Challow*, 2½ m. w., is a small 12C church, well restored, while *Childrey*, a little farther s., has a notable lead font and good brasses. At *Sparsholt*, a little w., the church has a 12C doorway and 14C knightly effigies in stone and oak. An ancient locomotive (1857) of the abandoned tramway from the town is preserved at Wantage Road station (closed) on the main line, 2½ m. N. of the town.

The VALE OF THE WHITE HORSE is bounded on the s. by the long line of the Berkshire *Chalk Downs, largely cultivated, but partly covered with springy turf. Thomas Hughes (1822–96), who was born at Uffington (see below), describes the vale in the opening chapters of 'Tom Brown's School Days'. Roughly parallel with the Port Way, along the breezy top of the Downs, runs the famous grass-grown British trackway known as the 'Ridgeway'. This magnificent right-of-way, affording superb walks, follows the curve of the Downs from Streatley to (14 m.) *Segsbury*, an Iron Age fort above *Letcombe Bassett* (2½ m. s.w. of Wantage), then to (20 m.) *Uffington Castle* (see below), (27½ m.) *Liddington Castle*, (32 m.) *Barbury Castle*, all similar earthworks; continuing along the ridge of *Hackpen Hill*, it crosses at 38 m. the upper Kennet valley, 1½ m. E. of Avebury (p. 173) and joins the Wansdyke. The Ridgeway was a favourite haunt of Richard Jefferies and figures in many of his writings.

Kingston Lisle, 5 m. w. of Wantage, lies beneath *White Horse Hill* (856 ft), with the sketchy figure of a horse (374 ft long) cut in the turf. The figure is now believed to be a work of c. 100 B.C., though popularly it is associated with the victory of King Alfred over the Danes at the battle of Ashdown, fought somewhere on these Downs in 871. A little s.w. of Kingston church (14C paintings) is the *Blowing Stone*, a famous perforated sarsen stone. The hollow on the w. side of the hill is known as the *Manger*, and a detached knoll on the w. side is the *Dragon's Hill*, where, according to local tradition, St George slew the dragon. From *Uffington Castle*, an oval earthwork (*View) on the top of White Horse Hill, the Ridgeway (see above) leads s.w. to (1½ m.) the dolmen known as *Wayland Smith's Cave*, a double burial-place reconstructed c. 2000 B.C., the legend attaching to which has been adapted in Scott's 'Kenilworth'.—*Uffington* church, 1½ m. N.w. of Kingston, is a fine E.E. building.

72½ m. **Faringdon** (Hotels), a well-grouped market town noted for its bacon and dairy produce, has an old market hall and three picturesque inns. The cruciform *Church*, with a Trans. Norman core (good clustered tower piers), preserves its original s. door and has many good details (sedilia, 6-light Perp. windows in N. aisle, monuments, organ of 1969). *Faringdon House* was built in 1780 by Henry Pye, the poet laureate, who planted the conspicuous 'Faringdon Clump'. The folly on the hill to the E. was built by Lord Berners in 1935, perhaps the last such edifice in England.

At *Great Coxwell*, 2 m. s.w., the great Cistercian *Tithe Barn (N.T.; early 13C) was called by Wm. Morris "the finest piece of architecture in England".—*Pusey House*, 4 m. E., was the birthplace of Dr E. B. Pusey (1800–82), the divine.

FROM FARINGDON TO CHIPPENHAM, 31 m. (A 420).—At (5½ m.) *Shrivenham* is the Royal Military College of Science, moved here from Woolwich in 1946.—12 m. **Swindon** (Hotels, Motel), a town of 90,800 inhab., was created by the establishment here of the locomotive and carriage works of the G.W.R., and has a *Museum* (weekdays 10–5, Sun 2–5; fee) illustrating the history of the Great Western Railway (in a former Methodist Chapel). It incorporated the market town of *Old Swindon*, on the hill 1 m. s. Richard Jefferies (1848–87) was born at *Coate Farm*, 1½ m. s.E., now a museum (adm. Wed, Sat, & Sun, 2–5; closed Sun in winter), and is buried in the disused Holy Rood churchyard. The church at *Lydiard Tregoz*, 6 m. w., contains notable memorials of the St John family, whose seat for 400 years was at *Lydiard Park* (adm. daily, exc. Mon & Tues, 10.30–12.30, 2–5 or 8, fee), a mansion rebuilt in 1743–49.—17 m. *Wootton Bassett* has a quaint half-timbered town hall. *Brinkworth*, 4 m. w., has a 15C church with contemporary wall-paintings; *Penn's Lodge* (rebuilt 1866), c. 1 m. N., was almost certainly not a residence of the Penn family, which in fact held property at *Minety*, 3 m. farther N. *Dauntsey*, 2 m. s.w. of Brinkworth, was a favourite resort of the poet George Herbert.—31 m. *Chippenham*, see Rte 17.

Beyond (76 m.) *Buscot Park* we cross the Thames and enter Gloucestershire. The mansion (1780; N.T.) has notable pictures and furniture and a saloon painted by Burne-Jones (adm. by appointment only, 2–6 Wed; fee).

78½ m. **Lechlade** (Hotel), a small market town with a large Perp. 'wool' church, is the present upper limit of navigation on the Thames. *Kelmscott*, see p. 262.—82¾ m. **Fairford** (Hotel), a small and attractive town on the Coln, famous for trout. The late-Perp. church of *St Mary*, decorated on the outside with sculpture, contains a wonderful array of 16C painted glass *Windows, probably from the same Anglo-Flemish workshop as those in King's College Chapel, Cambridge. The series of 28 is complete and tells the Christian story from the Creation to the Last Judgment. In the High St. are fine merchants' houses, and in

London Rd. the birthplace of John Keble (1792–1866). The British prototype 'Concorde' was tested at the R.A.F. airfield to the s., in 1969 and later.

A charming road ascends the Coln to two delightful villages, (2 m.) *Quenington* and (5 m.) *Bibury* (Hotel) with Arlington Row (N.T.), a noted example of the stone-built cottages of the Cotswold country. The road goes on upstream to join the Foss Way 2 m. E. of Chedworth (Rte 31).

91½ m. **Cirencester** (Hotels), the *Corinium* of the Romans and the *Cicester* of Shakespeare's 'Richard II' (locally called 'Ciren'), an attractive old market *Town on the Churn, with 13,000 inhab., is often called the 'Capital of the Cotswolds', from the hills amid which it lies. Its once considerable wool-trade gave it wealth to build well in the local stone. The *Parish Church*, one of the largest in England (180 ft long), with its fine w. tower (132 ft), is a Perp. structure incorporating Norman details. The three-storied s. porch dates from 1500. The most notable internal features are the Trinity Chapel (1430), with many brasses, the fan-vaulting of St Catherine's Chapel, and the pulpit (1515), one of the few pre-Reformation examples in the country. The *Corinium Museum* (weekdays 10–5 or 6; Sun from 2; closed Mon in winter) contains painted wall-plaster, mosaics, tombstones, a Christian 'acrostic', a 'pig' of lead (A.D. 79) from the Mendips, and other Roman antiquities.

In Spitalgate Lane are some arches of the *Hospital of St John*, founded by Henry I, but the only relic of the mitred (Augustinian) abbey, which he refounded, is a gateway in Grove Lane (farther on, to the right), apart from a range of the cloister, unearthed in 1964. Extensive excavation since 1960 in various outlying sites has revealed much of the street-plan of Corinium, as well as the foundations of the forum and basilica, the amphitheatre, a gateway. and 4C mosaic floors. Its predecessor, the oppidum of the Belgic Dobunni, has been excavated (1954–56) at *Bagendon*, 3 m. N.—To the w. of the town is *Cirencester Park* (Earl Bathurst), with a noble wooded park (open daily to walkers, Sun from 2), formerly called *Oakley Park* and often visited by Pope and Swift. Polo is played here on most Sun. aft. in summer. Adjoining on the Tetbury Rd. is the *Royal Agricultural College*, founded in 1842. Beyond the park (r. of the Stroud road) is *Sapperton*, with *Daneway*, a 14–17C manor-house.

BUSES to *Cheltenham*; *Gloucester*; *Cricklade* and *Swindon*; *Tetbury* and *Bristol.*

FROM CIRENCESTER TO BRISTOL, 36¾ m. A 429 follows the Roman *Foss Way* out of Cirencester, and bears left at 1½ m. for Malmesbury and Chippenham.

11½ m. **Malmesbury** (Hotel) is a pleasant little town (2500 inhab.) charmingly situated above the Avon, with a partly ruined *ABBEY CHURCH (1115–39), of which the most striking feature is the richly sculptured s. porch. Within are a little watching-chamber (14C) in the triforium, and the alleged tomb of King Athelstan (d. 940). The historian William of Malmesbury (d. about 1143) was a monk of the abbey (founded in 680), as was Oliver, who in the 11C made himself wings and jumped from the tower; miraculously his inability to fly only resulted in his laming. Thomas Hobbes, 'the philosopher of Malmesbury' (1588–1679), was born here; and Joseph Addison represented it in Parliament from 1710 to 1719. In the market-place is a fine market-cross (c. 1500) and at the foot of the hill is the late-12C *St John's Hospital*. About 2 m. N.E. is *Charlton Park*, often visited by Dryden; and 2 m. E. is *Garsdon*, the church of which contains Washington tombs.

From the Malmesbury road-fork the Bristol road (A 433) keeps to the right past *Thames Head*, generally regarded as the source of the Thames.—10¾ m. **Tetbury**, another small market town on a hill, has a quaint old town hall and a fine church (1777–81), with tall wooden pillars and contemporary pews and galleries. *Chavenage* (adm. Thurs 2–6 in May–Sept; fee) a 16C manor-house, lies 2 m. N.W.—13½ m. *Westonbirt* (Hotel) has a large girls' school in the former mansion of Sir George Holford. To the right is a fine Arboretum (open all day), founded in 1829.—Beyond (17½ m.) *Didmarton* is the Worcester Lodge of Badminton Park, a charming work by Kent (1745).—We join A 46 and continue s. to (23½ m.) *Old Sodbury* (Hotel), where we turn right on A 432 for (25 m.) *Chipping Sodbury* (Hotel), an old market town, as its name suggests, with a good church, and a splendid broad stone-built street. Tyndale translated the Bible in the 16C mansion-house of *Little Sodbury*, to the N., while the 12C hall of *Horton Court* (N.T.), farther N., is shown on Wed & Sat (April–Oct only, 2–6). Over 3 m. N.E. of Old Sodbury is *Badminton House*, the splendid Palladian mansion (1682) of the Duke of Beaufort, altered by Kent c. 1740 (adm. June–August, Wed 2.30–5; fee; teas). The church contains ducal monuments and the tomb of Lord Raglan (d. 1855). Badminton has given its name to a sporting library, a magazine, a London club, a well-known game, and a species of claret-cup. The Duke is Master of Horse to the Queen, and the challenging 'Three Day Event' Horse Trials are held here. *Dodington House* (adm. April–Sept daily; 11–5.30; fee; rfmts) the home of the Codringtons since 1578, is a dignified mansion (1796–1813) by James Wyatt, in fine grounds. Trips may be taken in some of the carriages from the Museum. It lies 2 m. S.W. of Old Sodbury. Dyrham (p. 194) is 3 m. farther S.—36¾ m. *Bristol*, see Rte 17.

Ermine Street, another Roman road, runs S.E. from Cirencester to (7½ m.) *Cricklade* (Hotel), on the Upper Thames (see p. 262), which has two interesting churches, one (St Mary's) mainly of the early 12C, the other (St Sampson's) E.E., Dec., and Perpendicular. *Purton*, 4 m. s., has one of the few parish churches in England (Perp.) with both a central and a w. tower. *Down Ampney*, 3 m. N.E., was the birthplace of Ralph Vaughan Williams (1872–1958).

The main road to (112½ m.) **Gloucester** follows the course of Ermine St. across the Cotswolds. To the right at (99½ m.) is *Elkstone* (½ m.), with a very fine Norman *Church, the best of a score or so in the district. —Beyond (102 m.) *Birdlip*, a sharp detour to the right avoids the steep descent of Birdlip Hill (*View).

Great Witcombe (l.), half-way down the hill, has a small part-Norman church. Near by is a Roman villa (adm. daily), with fine mosaic pavements in Witcombe Park.

A more interesting route runs due w. from Cirencester, descending into the Stroudwater valley, somewhat disfigured by cloth-factories, at (103¾ m.) *Chalford*.—105 m. **Stroud** (Hotels), the headquarters of the West of England cloth industry (19,100 inhab.), lies on the steep flank of a narrow valley, traversed by two canals.

A 46 runs s. viâ (2 m.) *Woodchester*, with its large Roman villa (occasionally uncovered) and a Dominican Priory, to (4¼ m.) *Nailsworth*, where the 'super-tramp' poet, W. H. Davies (1871–1940), died. *Nailsworth Ladder*, a local freak hill, has a gradient of 1 in 2¼. On the Tetbury road, 2½ m. farther, is *Avening*, with a partly Norman church.

Another road climbs steeply s. to (1½ m.) *Rodborough Common* with 840 acres of N.T. land, and runs thence viâ (3 m.) *Amberley* (Hotel), where Mrs Craik wrote 'John Halifax, Gentleman', to (4 m. S.W.) *Minchinhampton* (671 ft) with a pillared market-house and a famous golf course.

Stonehouse, 2½ m. w. of Stroud, has a 16C manor-house, and at *Frocester*, 2 m. farther s., are a 14C manor-house and barn.

An attractive winding road B 4066 leads s.w. from Stroud to Dursley (10 m.; p. 183) viâ (8 m.) *Uley*, before which (r.) on the hill-top is the noted Uley Tumulus, a 'long barrow' 180 ft long.

We follow A 46 to the N.W. up the Painswick valley. On the left rises *Haresfield Beacon* (N.T.; 834 ft; *View).—109¼ m. *Painswick* (Hotel), an unspoilt Cotswold town with typical stone-built houses, is noted for its churchyard containing 18C *Table-tombs and 99 trimmed yews. The *Old Court House*, with a court room panelled with a painted design, is open on Thurs 2–5, June–Sept (fee). *Painswick House*, ½ m. N., is a Palladian mansion enlarged by Basevi.—112 m. *Cranham Woods* lie beneath the earthwork called *Kimsbury Castle* (view).

In a hollow, to the left, lies *Prinknash Abbey*, an ancient residence of the abbots of Gloucester, occupied since 1928 by Benedictine monks from Caldey and greatly

enlarged. The foundation-stone of the church (by H. S. Goodhart-Rendel, and
F. G. Broadbent) was laid in 1939. To the right rises *Cooper's Hill* where, on Whit
Monday, the local villagers hold a cheese-rolling contest, said to date from the 15C.
At *Upton St Leonards*, 1½ m. N.W. of Prinknash, the church has a Norman doorway
and E.E. chancel.

Commanding fine views of the Vale of Gloucester and the Malvern
Hills, A 46 descends to join A 417 at (113½ m.) *Brockworth*, where we
turn left past a large aircraft works; for Cheltenham we keep straight on.

118 m. **GLOUCESTER** (pron. 'Glo'ster'; 90,000 inhab.), a bustling
county town and cathedral city, lies on rising ground near the left (E.)
bank of the Severn. Connected with the sea by a canal, it has a considerable trade in grain, timber, coal, and iron, while it carries on also match-
and toy-making, and the manufacture of aircraft components. Despite
much bad modern building, the cathedral still dominates the town and
the surrounding countryside.

Railway Station for London, Bristol, Cheltenham, Birmingham, and the North, for
S. Wales and Hereford.
Hotels in Northgate, Southgate, and Westgate.
Post Office, King's Sq.
Buses from the Bus Station, to all destinations.—STEAMERS on the Severn in
summer to *Deerhurst* and *Tewkesbury* on Thurs and Sun.
Swimming Pool, Barton St.; SPORTS STADIUM, Horton Rd.

History. Gloucester, the British *Caer Glou* and the Roman colonia *Glevum*,
commanded the lowest practicable crossing of the Severn. The Roman walls
and a Norman royal castle survived until 1663. According to E. A. Freeman,
"in the reign of Rufus almost everything that happened at all, somehow contrived
to happen at Gloucester", but the first extant charter dates from 1155. King John
is said to have "loved Gloucester better than London", and Henry III was crowned
here in 1216. The city sided with Parliament in the Civil War and successfully
resisted the Royal forces in 1643. Its fortifications were consequently dismantled
at the Restoration.—The 'worthies' of Gloucester include Robert Raikes (1735–
1811), the virtual founder of Sunday Schools, though Hannah Ball opened a Sunday
School at High Wycombe in 1769, eleven years before him; John Taylor (1580–
1653), the 'Water Poet'; Sir Charles Wheatstone (1802–75), the chief founder of
modern telegraphy; George Whitefield (b. 1714 at the Bell Inn, d. 1770 at
Newburyport, Mass.); Cardinal Vaughan (1832–1903), also born at the Bell Inn;
and W. E. Henley (1849–1903), poet and essayist, born at No. 2 Eastgate St.—The
Severn 'bore', a wave caused by the incoming tide, about the equinoxes usually
6–9 ft high, is better seen below Gloucester (at Minsterworth or Stonebench) than
in the city itself. The river is famous for its salmon and lampreys.

In the rectangular arrangement of its four main streets (*Northgate*,
Southgate, *Eastgate*, and *Westgate*) Gloucester reflects the Roman period
of its history, and the *Cross* at which they meet (crossless since 1745)
is the natural focus of the city's life, with the Perp. tower of *St Michael's*.

In Northgate St. is the *New Inn*, a half-timbered house erected c. 1450 by John
Twyning for the accommodation of pilgrims. Lady Jane Grey is said to have been
proclaimed queen in its yard in 1553. At the corner is a fine carved angle-post.—
St John's is a church of 1732–34, by the Woodwards.

From the Cross we proceed to the cathedral viâ Westgate St. and
College St. No. 24 Westgate St., known as *Maverdine House*, turns a
quaint façade towards the side-lane. At No. 99 Bp. Hooper (p. 301)
may have spent his last night; *Bishop Hooper's Lodging* and two adjacent
houses are occupied by a good local *Folk Museum* (weekdays 10–5.30),
containing also mementoes of Hooper. Next door, in another timber-
framed house, is the *Museum of the Gloucestershire Regiment.* Opposite is
the church of *St Nicholas*, with a tall Perp. spire and Norman s. door.

The *Cathedral, once the church of the Benedictine Abbey of St Peter, and since the Dissolution (1540) a cathedral church dedicated to the Holy Trinity, is a noble building, a splendid feature in both the city and the surrounding country.

HISTORY. The character of the foundation has varied. Beginning as a Benedictine house for men and women (681–790), it became in 823 a college for secular priests. These were replaced in 1022 by the Benedictines, who built the church and held it till Henry VIII returned it to the secular clergy, raising it to cathedral rank. The existing fabric was begun in 1089 by Abbot Serlo and dedicated in 1100. The building of the Norman nave soon afterwards completed, except for the Lady Chapel, the present plan of the church. In 1327 the body of the murdered Edward II (p. 301), refused burial at Bristol and Malmesbury, was enshrined at Gloucester and soon became a focus of miracles and pilgrimage. From the vast income thus derived the monks largely rebuilt both church and abbey, and by their ability to employ a Court mason to build in the new style, then being developed in London, made Gloucester the first major success of Perp. architecture. As a result the exterior is almost purely Perp., and in the choir a Perp. casing effectively disguises the Norman core. The choir vault dates from 1337–51, the cloisters from 1351–1412; the west façade and south porch (much restored) were built in 1420–37; the stately central tower (225 ft high), with its austerely fine decoration, replaced the 13C tower in 1450; and the beautiful Lady Chapel (1457–98) closed the work of the Gloucester masons. During the Commonwealth destruction, actually begun, was averted only by application to Cromwell, who, in 1657, granted the cathedral to the mayor and citizens. The organ (1665), by Thomas, father of Renatus Harris, was enlarged and restored in 1920. The tasteful revival of the colouring of the monuments in 1947–48 has set an excellent fashion throughout the country.

Interior. The NAVE, with the exception of the two w. bays (1421–37), is predominantly Norman in appearance, the great cylindrical pillars quite overpowering the effect of the triforium and the timidly designed E.E. clerestory and vaulting (1242–45). These uniquely tall pillars (30 ft 7 in high) were doubtless necessitated by the fact that the original cloister against the N. wall precluded low aisle-windows, and that high-set windows could light the nave only through a lofty pier-arcade. The support of the cloister preserved the N. aisle when the s. aisle became unsafe and had to be re-vaulted in 1318, the date, also, of the ball-flowered geometrical tracery of the s. aisle windows. In the N. aisle the Norman vaulting and carved capitals should be noted, also, at its E. end, the fine Perp. door to the cloisters. In the s. aisle is a monument to Sir Onesiphorus Paul (d. 1820), the prison-reformer; at its w. end is a tablet to Sir Hubert Parry (1848–1918), the composer. Near the w. door is a statue of Dr Jenner (d. 1823), a Gloucestershire man. The third and fifth windows from the w. end on the N. side contain old glass (restored). Flaxman's memorial to Mrs Morley (d. 1784) is a graceful design (N. aisle); here also is the tomb of Mayor Machen (d. 1614) and his wife. At the E. end are some good 18C stalls and a litany desk.

The *CHOIR (which projects one bay into the nave and is separated from it by a screen of 1820) is usually entered from the s. aisle, at the E. end of which is *Abbot Seabrook's Chantry* (1457). Choir and TRANSEPTS look pure Perp., the walls having been veiled with tracery and the massive piers whittled down, when the dim old Norman choir was transformed (1330–74). The latest part is the N. transept (restored 1368–74), which contains a beautiful piece of E.E. sculpture (c. 1240), possibly an Easter Sepulchre. On its E. side is the *Chapel of St Paul*, with a fine (restored) altar-screen.—The similar s. transept, which was remodelled in 1331–37, forestalls by some twenty years the evolution of the Perp. style elsewhere in England. On the E. wall is the quaint 'Prentice's

Bracket', and beside it the *Chapel of St Andrew*, with a huge diagonal strut and fine 14C glass (releaded).—From floor to vault the design of choir and transepts is a perfect unity. The tall clerestory windows; the rectilinear tracery necessitated by the size of the end-wall windows; the one-story design of the tracery, carried up on unbroken vaulting-shafts, that covers the Norman triforium and pier arcades; the lierne *Vaulting, whether in the complicated pattern of the choir roof, with its galaxy of angel-bosses, or in the simpler but more subtly skilled vaulting of the s. transept—these are the origin and inspiration of Perp. architecture. The great *East Window* (72 ft by 38 ft) was erected by Lord Bradeston in 1352 to commemorate the battle of Crécy. The light tone of the glass is as much an innovation as the architecture, and the walls have been made slightly wider than the chancel by tilting the walls outwards. The *Reredos* is Victorian (1873), as are the sub-stalls. The 14C *Stalls*, with their vigorous misericord grotesques, have been restored. The w. window—an unusual feature, due to the difference in height between nave and choir—contains some old glass from other windows. Of various noteworthy tombs in the choir the canopied *Tomb of Edward II*, erected by Edward III, is chief in beauty and interest. It stands under the N. arcade of the presbytery between the monument (Pl. 7; 16C) of King Osric, who founded the first abbey in 681, and the tomb prepared for Abbot Parker (1539), but occupied by two bishops. The bracket tomb on the s. (Pl. 9) has been assigned to Serlo (p. 297), but the figure with the church in its hand is probably Abbot Foliot (1228–43). In the centre of the presbytery is the tomb of Robert Curthose (d. 1134), eldest son of William the Conqueror, with a curious coloured effigy of bog-oak (c. 1290) resting on a mortuary chest of the 15C. Well-preserved encaustic tiles of 1455 in front of the altar differ markedly from the over-glazed, mechanically designed 'copies' in the choir-floor. In the N.E. chapel (*SS Edmund & Edward*), with good tiles and fragments of a reredos (c. 1450), is kept the roll of honour of the Gloucestershire Regt.; opposite, in the N. ambulatory, stands the small cross carved in 1951 by Col. Carne, V.C., during his captivity in Korea. At the w. end of the ambulatory is a small stone lectern of uncertain use. The s.E. chapel is dedicated to *St Stephen*.

The *Lady Chapel* was the last great work at Gloucester (1457–98). To avoid obscuring the E. window, the w. end diminishes in height and breadth to form a charmingly vaulted vestibule. Open tracery fills the upper part of the w. arch; and the exquisite lierne vaulting, with leaf-bosses, the admirable tracery of the windows and of the narrow wall-spaces between, the vaulting-shafts, the ruined reredos, the sedilia, and the remaining 15C tiles all contribute to the architectural harmony, and there are two charming Jacobean ladies' monuments. Side-chapels, with oratories or music chambers in the upper stories, are delicately vaulted. The nine-light E. window (late 15C) contains old glass, some of it not designed for this window, which represented the Stem of Jesse. At the w. end stands a lead font formerly in Lancaut church.

The CHOIR TRIFORIUM with a half barrel vault is reached from the s. transept. Exceptionally important, showing Perp. work imposed on the Norman structure, it affords a close view of the E. window. The E. chapel opens from the 'Whispering Gallery', even more remarkable before restoration than now for its acoustic qualities.

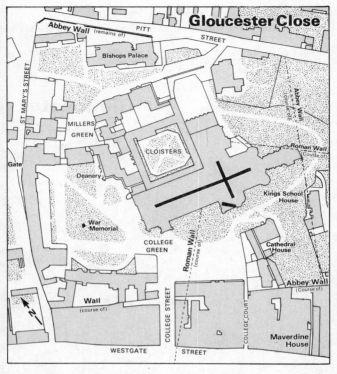

Gloucester Close

Abbey Wall (remains of) PITT STREET

ST MARY'S STREET

Bishops Palace

MILLERS GREEN

Gate

Deanery

CLOISTERS

Abbey Wall (course of)

Roman Wall (Course of)

Kings School House

War Memorial

COLLEGE GREEN

Cathedral House

Roman Wall (course of)

Abbey Wall (Course of)

Wall (course of)

N

COLLEGE STREET

COLLEGE COURT

Maverdine House

WESTGATE STREET

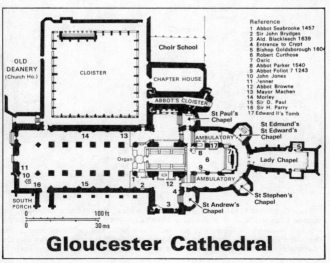

OLD DEANERY (Church Ho.)

CLOISTER

Choir School

CHAPTER HOUSE

ABBOT'S CLOISTER

St Paul's Chapel

Organ

AMBULATORY

St Edmund's St Edward's Chapel

Lady Chapel

AMBULATORY

St Stephen's Chapel

SOUTH PORCH

St Andrew's Chapel

Reference
1 Abbot Seabrooke 1457
2 Sir John Brydges
3 Ald. Blackleech 1639
4 Entrance to Crypt
5 Bishop Goldsborough 1604
6 Robert Curthose
7 Osric
8 Abbot Parker 1540
9 Abbot Foliot ? 1243
10 John Jones
11 Jenner
12 Abbot Browne
13 Mayor Machen
14 Morley
15 Sir O. Paul
16 Sir H. Parry
17 Edward II's Tomb

0   100 ft
0   30 ms

Gloucester Cathedral

The Norman *CRYPT, entered from the S. transept, consists of an apse and five chapels, with remains of piscina and altar-steps.

The CENTRAL TOWER (225 ft) commands a wide view. In the lower part hangs 'Great Peter' (c. 1420), weighing 65 cwt. The bells, four of which are pre-Reformation, play four tunes (at 1, 5, and 8 p.m.).

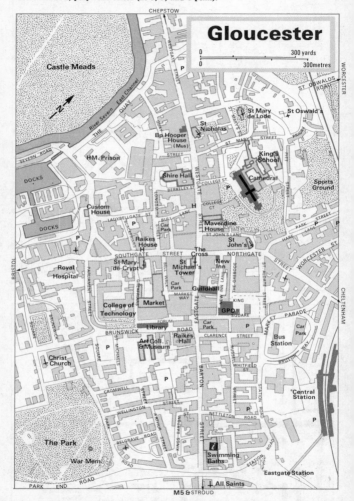

The *CLOISTERS (1351–1412), remarkable both in preservation and beauty, are entered from the N. aisle of the nave. The fan-tracery vaulting is claimed as an original device of the Gloucester masons. The S. side, with its 'carrel' recesses for desks and 16C heraldic glass from Prinknash, was the *Scriptorium*; on the N. is the *Lavatory*. The *Chapter House* on the E. is Norman (restored) with a Perp. E.

bay.—The *Library* (above, and in the N. choir triforium) includes among its treasures the finest existing copy of Coverdale's Bible (1535) and leaves of a 10C Anglo-Saxon MS.

Other remains of the monastery include the *Abbot's House*, of the 11–13C (no adm.), under which is the outer *Parlour*, a vaulted Norman passage leading from the s.w. corner of the cloisters. The *West Gate* (12C; restored 1916–19) in St Mary's St., is the best of the remaining precinct gates; it was probably used as the almonry. Thence we may walk round the N. side of the precincts, past the picturesque 'Little Cloister' and the ruined arcade of the Infirmary.

The 'Three Choirs Festival' is held yearly (Aug) in rotation at Worcester (1975), Hereford (1976), and Gloucester (1977). Charitable in object and continuous since 1724, the festival began at Gloucester c. 1715 as an informal 'Music Meeting', and is now one of the finest choral festivals in the world.

Opposite the West Gate (see above) is the *Memorial to Bp. Hooper*, who was martyred here in 1555, watched (so the story goes) by Bp. Bonner from the window over the gateway. The adjacent church of *St Mary-de-Lode*, with its low Norman chancel, stands on the site of a Roman building. A little N. four 11–12C arches mark the site of *St Oswald's Priory*, founded in 909 and destroyed in 1643.

Following Southgate St. from the Cross, we soon reach (l.) the church of *St Mary-de-Crypt*, a 12C building with later alterations, named from the two charnel-houses below it. It contains some good brasses and the tomb of Robert Raikes, whose house stands on the other side of the street. George Whitefield was christened and preached his first sermon in this church.

Behind St Mary's is the 13C *Greyfriars Church*, long disused, which the Franciscan Order proposes to rebuild; some remains of the *Blackfriars* monastery can be seen on the other side of Southgate St. In Brunswick Rd., at the end of Greyfriars, beyond the *Technical College*, a building houses the *College of Art*, the *Library*, and the **City Museum** (weekdays 10–5), enlarged in 1958, with a good collection of local antiquities, including a 1C bronze mirror from Birdlip with associated finds, a group of Romano-British sculptures (A.D. 100–250) from Lower Slaughter, and Roman altars from the city itself. Here also are natural history, costume, and pottery collections, furniture, silver, and glass.

In the s.w. quarter of the city lie the *Docks*. In the s. part of the city are also the *Spa Field* and the *Public Park* with a statue of Raikes. To the w. of the city, c. ¾ m. from the Cross, are the derelict remains of *Llanthony Abbey* (12C), a daughter house of the famous Welsh monastery.

FROM GLOUCESTER TO BERKELEY.—We follow the Bristol road for 14 m. then turn right.—15½ m. Berkeley (Hotel), a sleepy little town. *Berkeley Castle* (adm. Easter–Sept daily, exc. Mon 11 or 2–5; also BH, 11–5; in Oct, Sun only 2–4.30), home of the Berkeley family since 1153, is a little-altered feudal stronghold, entered by a bridge over the moat, with a circular keep (1155–60) and a 14C hall and gateway. Here Edward II was murdered in 1327. The fine E.E. *Church* has a good 15C screen and effigies of the Lords Berkeley. Dean Swift wrote the epitaph on Dicky Pearce, the jester (d. 1728), in the churchyard. Edward Jenner (1749–1823), introducer of vaccination, was born and died (in what is now the vicarage) at Berkeley. *Wanswell Court*, a farm 1½ m. N., is an unusually perfect small 15C manor-house with a later wing.—*Sharpness*, 1½ m. farther on, is the foreport of Gloucester, on the Severn and the *Gloucester & Berkeley Ship Canal* (17 m. long), which, N.W. of the road, passes (8 m.) *Slimbridge* and (11 m.) the charming village of *Frampton-on-Severn*, where the church has a Romanesque lead font, one of six identical ones in Gloucestershire. On the Severn shore, 1½ m. N.W. of Slimbridge are the grounds of the *Wildfowl Trust* (adm. daily exc. Sun morning; fee; rfmts), where many thousand waterfowl may be seen.

The winding road following the Severn from Frampton back to Gloucester passes (2½ m.) *Epney*, the chief place for the export of elvers to Holland, where they are cultivated and re-exported to the E. coast of England as full-grown eels. Farther on is (6½m.) *Elmore*, with the attractive 16–18C Elmore Court, 5 m. from Gloucester.

From Gloucester to Chepstow and the Forest of Dean (railway to Chepstow, 27½ m. in 30–40 min.). Crossing the Severn by A 40, we turn l. on A 48.—10 m. *Westbury-on-Severn* has a conspicuous detached 13C steeple and the fine Stuart water-garden of Westbury Court. *Flaxley*, 2¼ m. N.W., was the home of Sir Roger de Coverley's 'Widow Boevey', whose family occupied *Flaxley Abbey*. The mansion, partly Jacobean with additions of 1780, preserves the refectory (c. 1148) and the abbot's hall (c. 1350) of a Cistercian abbey.—At (12 m.) *Newnham*, a charming little town, Henry II and Strongbow embarked for Ireland in 1171. To the left is the widening Severn, to the right the Forest of Dean (for the E. part of which this is a good centre). The rebuilt church contains a 'Twelve Apostles' font of the Mitcheldean type. The road to Littledean (see below) affords fine views over the Forest and the Severn.—15¼ m. *Blakeney*.—19 m. *Lydney* (Hotel) has a fine 14C cross, 17½ ft high. In the grounds of *Lydney Park* (Viscount Bledisloe; open Sun aft in May) are the remains of a small 12C castle and of a Roman temple.—28½ m. *Chepstow* (see Rte 38); a road runs S.E. to a junction with M 4 which crosses the new Severn Bridge.

The Forest of Dean, extending N. for 20 m. from the junction of the Wye and the Severn, with an extreme width of 10 m., has been a royal forest from time immemorial. It now includes a National Forest Park of 34,000 acres and is an excellent area for walks, even though the woodland beauties are in places some-what marred by coal-workings. The iron mines, worked as early as Roman times, are now overgrown and rather add to the interest. The characteristic trees are oaks and beeches. The Forest is traversed by two roads from Gloucester to Monmouth (c. 25 m.), one viâ (11½ m.) *Mitcheldean*, where the 14–15C church has a fine oaken roof, a slender spire, and a 12C font with the Twelve Apostles; the other viâ (12½m.) *Littledean, Cinderford*, (17m.) *Speech House*, and (19m.) *Coleford*. The most central quarters for visitors are at the Speech House Hotel (1674; 566 ft), the seat of the Verderers' Court, surrounded by magnificent old holly woods. At *Blackpool Bridge*, 3 m. S.E., a considerable fragment of a Roman road is exposed. At *Newland* (4½ m. w.) the spacious church, the 'Cathedral of the Forest', has a Dec. tower and a famous brass depicting a 15C free miner. *St Briavels*, 5½ m. S.W., commanding views of the Wye Valley, has a part Norman church and a restored castle (now a youth hostel). *Ruardean Hill* (951 ft; 4 m.), in the N. part of the forest, is a good viewpoint. The Norman church of Ruardean has a notable carving of St George and the Dragon.

From Gloucester to Ledbury, 17 m.—Beyond the Severn B 4215 diverges r. from A 40 and ascends the Leadon valley through attractive country noted for its Norman village churches.—9 m. *Newent* is a little town with a good 16C market hall.—12¾ m. *Dymock*, with a large and interesting church (note the s. doorway of c. 1130), is famed for orchards and wild daffodils. The little Norman church of *Kempley*, 2 m. w., is decorated with a magnificent series of *Frescoes (c. 1150) on walls and vault.—B 4216 continues N. to (17 m.) *Ledbury*, see p. 358.

From Gloucester to *Birmingham*, see Rte 35; to *Bristol*, see Rte 17; to *Hereford*, see Rte 36; to *Worcester*, see Rte 35; to *Cheltenham* and *Oxford*, see 30A.

31   OXFORD TO WORCESTER

Road, 57 m. (A 34 and A 44). 8 m. *Woodstock.*—20 m. *Chipping Norton.*— 28 m. *Moreton-in-Marsh.*—36 m. *Broadway.*—42 m. *Evesham.*—48 m. *Pershore.* —57 m. **Worcester.** Motor-Coach in 2 hrs; from London (Victoria) in 3½ hrs. Railway, 57 m. in c. 1½ hr (through trains from London, 120½ m., in c. 2½ hrs). —Stations: 21½ m. *Kingham* (Hotels).—28½ m. *Moreton-in-Marsh.*—43½ m. **Evesham.**—57 m. **Worcester.**

We quit Oxford by A 34, the Woodstock road.—8 m. **Woodstock** (Hotels) is an attractive little town (1900 inhab.) noted for its gloves. Nothing remains of the royal manor-house built by Henry I, who enclosed a vast deer-park now represented by the park of Blenheim Palace. *Chaucer's House*, near the main entrance to the park, was the property of Thomas Chaucer, probably the son of the poet. *Fletcher's House* (in Park St., opposite the church) is devoted to the *Oxford City and County Museum*, which illustrates the way of life and history of the county. The *Town Hall* (1766) is by Sir W. Chambers.

Fair Rosamond is said to have lived here in a secluded bower built for her by Henry II. Edmund of Woodstock, second son of Edward I, and Edward the Black Prince and Thomas of Woodstock, sons of Edward III, were born here. Elizabeth was confined in the gatehouse by her sister Mary in 1554. Scott's novel of 'Woodstock', though an admirable picture of the manners of the period, is unhistorical in its facts.

In 1704 the royal manor was settled upon John Churchill, Duke of Marlborough, as a reward for his victory over the French and Bavarians at Blenheim. **Blenheim Palace**, the vast and heavy masterpiece of Vanbrugh, in the classical style, was begun in 1705 and finished after the duke's death in 1722. The total cost was £300,000, of which £250,000 was defrayed by Parliament. The main entrance to the park is by the triumphal arch a little beyond the church. The deer-park (2700 acres; model railway and lake cruises), always open to pedestrians, contains fine oaks and cedars, a lake formed by 'Capability' Brown, a column 134 ft high, erected in honour of the great duke, and 'Fair Rosamond's Well'. The trees around the column are planted in groups so as to form a plan of the battle of Blenheim. The palace (adm. mid-March–Oct, daily 11.30–5; fee; higher rates on Spring BH; restaurant; Son et Lumière), contains some good 17–18C portraits and in the chapel is the pompous marble tomb of the great duke and his duchess. Sir Winston Churchill (1874–1965) was born at Blenheim and lies beside his ancestors in the churchyard of *Bladon*, on the s.e. edge of the park.

To the N.W. of Woodstock is the Evenlode valley, with the little towns of *Charlbury* (Hotel) and *Shipton-under-Wychwood* (Hotel), 7 m. and 13½ m. from Woodstock. Above Charlbury is *Wychwood Forest*, a haunt of the 'Scholar Gipsy', now a nature reserve and closed to the public. *Cornbury Park*, s. of Charlbury, is on the site of the house where Leicester, the favourite of Elizabeth I, died in 1588 on his way north. It was later bought (1663) by Lord Chancellor Clarendon, and rebuilt by Hugh May.

14 m. *Kidlington. Ditchley Park*, 1¼ m. left, now an American Study Centre, is a mansion designed by Gibbs (1720–26) with decorations by Flitcroft and Cheere, and was long the home of the Lee family (adm. certain days in late July–early Aug; fee).—20 m. **Chipping Norton** (Hotels), locally called 'Chippy', with a tweed factory, has a fine church with several brasses, a row of 17C almshouses, and an 18C guildhall. The *Rollright Stones*, 3½ m. N. near the road to Stratford, are a small megalithic circle; across the road is the 'King's Stone', a coeval monument of doubtful significance.

Warren Hastings (1732–1818) was born at *Churchill*, 3 m. s.w., and died at *Daylesford House*, 3 m. w. He is buried in Daylesford churchyard. William Smith (1769–1839), 'father of British geology', was another native of Churchill. *Hook Norton* church, 5 m. N.E., contains a celebrated early 12C *Font with quaint carvings. At the charming village of *Great Tew*, 5 m. E., the park belonged to Lord Falkland (p. 171), who is buried in the church. The estate was purchased in 1816 by the son of Matthew Boulton, the famous engineer; and a characteristic figure by Chantrey commemorates Mrs Boulton (1795–1829).

FROM CHIPPING NORTON TO CHELTENHAM, 27½ m. (A 436), an elevated route across the Cotswolds. At 4 m. we branch left from the Worcester road and cross the Evenlode near Daylesford (comp. above).—At (7½ m.) *Oddington* the old church (restored) contains wall-paintings and Norman details.—9½ m. **Stow-on-the-Wold** (good Hotels), a small market town in the Cotswolds noted for antiques shops, stands on the Foss Way. A 14C cross stands in the large market-place and the old church contains a Crucifixion by Gaspard de Crayer (1610). To Cirencester, see below.—At (14½ m.) *Harford Bridge* we cross the Windrush.—At 21½ m. *Andoversford*, we join A 40 for *Cheltenham* (Rte 30A).

A little beyond (24 m.) the road to Stow, a turning on the left leads in 1¼ m. to *Chastleton House* (weekdays, exc. Wed, 10.30–1, 2–dusk or

5.30, Sun 2–dusk or 5; fee), a Jacobean mansion (1603) with an 18C box garden. The house contains fine furniture and tapestries, Jacobite glass, and the Bible given by Charles I on the scaffold to Bp. Juxon. —28 m. **Moreton-in-Marsh** (Hotels) is a small Gloucestershire market town, having the Foss Way as its High St. Charles I spent a night at the White Hart in 1644.

FROM MORETON-IN-MARSH TO CIRENCESTER, 23 m. (A 429), the Foss Way in its straightest Roman stride across undulating hills.—5 m. *Stow-on-the-Wold*, see above.—9½ m. **Bourton-on-the-Water** (l.) is a delightful stone-built *Village, with the Windrush flowing down its main street.—At 14 m. we cross A 40 just w. of *Northleach* (p. 290).—17 | m. *Fossebridge Hotel* stands a little N.W. of the ancient churches of *Coln St Denis* and *Coln Rogers*. Chedworth, 2 m. w., has a part-Norman church and the best *Roman Villa in England (N.T. 1½ m. N.; daily exc. Mon other than BH, 10–1, 2–7 or dusk, fee; closed Jan and first half Oct). The local tradition is that the countless lilies of the valley growing here were originally planted by the Romans.—23 m. *Cirencester*, see Rte 30B.

A 44 ascends through (30 m.) *Bourton-on-the-Hill* to (33½ m.) the crest of the Cotswolds. The COTSWOLD HILLS, a narrow limestone range, run from N.E. to s.w. across Gloucestershire, forming the water-shed between the Thames and Severn valleys. They reach a height of 1070 ft at Cleeve Cloud, near Cheltenham, and are renowned for their stone-built market towns and their rolling landscape. About 2 m. to the right (N.) is **Chipping Campden** (good Hotels), locally just 'Campden', an ancient *Town built entirely of stone, once the capital of the Cots-wold wool trade. In 'islands' in the broad HIGH STREET, with many delightful old houses once belonging to prosperous wool-merchants, are the *Town Hall* and the *Market Hall* (1627); *Woolstapler's Hall* (c. 1340) contains a fascinating collection of bygones (Apr–Sept, daily 11–6; fee). Farther to the s. are the *Grammar School* (founded 1487) and the stately Perp. church of *St James*, with its handsome tower. Within, the light proportions are more striking than the unorthodox detail. In the chancel of the church are a number of good brasses, including that of William Grevil (d. 1401), "flos mercatorum tocius Anglie"; beneath the tower, cope and altar hangings (15C); and in the s. chapel are the elaborate tombs of the Hicks and Noel families, includ-ing that of Sir Baptist Hicks (d. 1629), Viscount Campden, the remains of whose mansion are seen near the church. A little farther on are *Almshouses* of 1612.

Hidcote Manor (N.T.), 4 m. N.E. of Campden, has a notable garden (open April–Oct, daily exc. Tues and Fri, 11–7; fee).

We enter Worcestershire and descend Broadway Hill, passing Broad-way Tower, a folly built in 1800 by the Earl of Coventry. It and the adjacent country park are open daily 11–3 or 6 (fee).—36 m. **Broadway** (good Hotels) is a notably pretty village, with stone-built Elizabethan houses, its very charm often marred by the summer crowds. The *Lygon Arms*, a former manor-house, was used by both Charles I and Cromwell as the tide of battle flowed in the vicinity: it is now a noted hotel. The *Tudor House* (1660) is almost as fine and many others deserve detailed attention. *St Eadburgha's*, the medieval church, lies 1 m. s. nearly half-way to *Snowshill Manor* (N.T.; adm. Apr–Oct, Sat, Sun, & BH, 11–1, 2–6; also May–Sept, Wed & Thurs; fee), a typical 16C Cotswold house, refaced c. 1700, which contains an extraordinary eclectic collection of bygones (early bicycles; Japanese Samurai armour; 18C musical instruments, etc.).

Buckland, 2 m. s.w. off A 46, has England's oldest rectory with a 15C great hall (adm. May–Sept, Mon 11–4, also Fri in Aug; fee)—*Mickleton*, 6½ m. N.E. on the Stratford road, is a pretty village at the N. verge of the Cotswolds.

42 m. **Evesham** (Hotels), a town with 13,800 inhab., lies on the Avon in the fertile Vale of Evesham, a district of fruit and vegetable gardens, especially noted for plums. The river (boats for hire), pleasantly bordered by gardens, is navigable down to Tewkesbury and will shortly be made so to Stratford (comp. p. 335). In the Market Place are the '*Round House*', a large timbered building of the 15C, and the *Town Hall* (1586, remodelled 1885). All that remains of the once large and rich Benedictine *Abbey* (dating back to the 8C) is the Norman and Tudor gateway of the churchyard and a superb detached *Bell Tower (1533), of the best ornate Perp. work. Close by are the two churches of *St Lawrence* (16C) and *All Saints* (Perp. with E.E. remains), both notable for their fan-vaulted chapels. The Tudor *Almonry Museum* (adm. Good Friday–Sept, daily, exc. Mon & Wed, 2.30–6.30; fee) in Vine St., to the s., has a good historical collection. In the Battle of Evesham (1265) the Royalists under Prince Edward (Edward I) defeated Simon de Montfort. An obelisk of 1845 marks the battlefield N. of the town and a stone, erected in 1965 in Abbey Gardens, the site of the Abbey high altar where Simon was buried.

The composer Muzio Clementi (1752–1832) died at Evesham.—In the church of *Wickhamford*, 2 m. s.e., is the tomb of Penelope Washington (d. 1697), bearing the Washington arms.—About 2¼ m. N.W. of Evesham is *Wood Norton*, once the imposing English home of the Duc d'Aumale, and afterwards of his nephew, the Duc d'Orléans. It was briefly one of the dispersed outposts of the B.B.C. in 1939.

48 m. **Pershore** (Hotels), another town on the Avon, is noted for its Benedictine *Abbey Church, now the parish church of Holy Cross. It preserves the Norman crossing and s. transept (c. 1100), a fine lantern-tower (c. 1335), and a beautiful apsidal choir, with interesting vaults in the aisles and a combined triforium and clerestory (1239). The adjoining church of *St Andrew*, redesigned as a community centre, shows some Norman work. *Strensham*, 4½ m. s.w., was the birthplace of Samuel Butler (1612–80).—57 m. **Worcester**, see Rte 35.

32 LONDON TO BIRMINGHAM
A Viâ Bicester and Warwick

ROAD, 112 m. (A 41).—20 m. *King's Langley.*—39 m. *Aylesbury.*—56 m. *Bicester.*—71 m. Banbury.—90½ m. Warwick.—112 m. **Birmingham.** An interesting variation (10½ m. longer) can be made to take in **Stratford-on-Avon** by diverging from the above route 5 m. beyond Banbury. Alternative route to Aylesbury viâ *Amersham*, see below.

RAILWAY. From Marylebone to **Banbury**, 68¾ m. in c. 1¾ hr. Principal stations: 27¾ m. *High Wycombe.* — 36 m. *Princes Risborough*, junction for *Aylesbury* (7¼ m.).— 54¾ em. *Bicester.* Occasional trains through to Birmingham.— From Paddington viâ Oxford and Banbury to **Birmingham**, 135 m. in 2½ hrs. Principal stations: 86½ m. **Banbury.**— 106¼ m. **Leamington Spa.**—Some trains viâ (122½ m.) *Solihull* (4½ m. shorter); most viâ Coventry and Birmingham Airport to **Birmingham** (New St.).

From London A 41 cuts a swathe through the N.W. suburbs viâ *Swiss Cottage*, with the M 1 motorway affording it relief between (8 m.) *Mill Hill* and (15 m.) *Aldenham*.—At 12 m., between Elstree (r.) and Bushey (l.), we enter Hertfordshire. Haberdashers' Aske's and Aldenham Schools lie right of the road beyond Aldenham Reservoir. Leaving

Watford on our left, we join the line of the *Grand Union Canal* (comp. Rte 32B), just short of (20 m.) *King's Langley* (Hotel). Here the church contains the heraldic tomb used for Edmund de Langley, duke of York (born here, 1341; d. 1402) and his wife Isabella of Castile (d. 1394), though probably designed for Richard II, his brother. Richard lay buried elsewhere in the church in 1399–1413. Only a fragment remains of the Dominican friary where Piers Gaveston was buried in 1315. *Bedmond*, a hamlet 1 m. E., was the birthplace of Nicholas Breakspear (d. 1159), the only English pope (Adrian IV; tablet in the 12–13C church of *Abbot's Langley*, ½ m. s.).

At (21¼ m.) *Apsley*, with paper-mills, we reach the outskirts of **Hemel Hempstead** (Motel, Hotel), whose population (now 69,400) was trebled between 1949 and 1961. The successful new *Town Centre* has a fine water-garden. The good Norman church, with a leaden spire, adjoins the ancient High Street, 1½ m. N.E.

At *Piccotts End*, 1 m. farther on, a hall house (r.; adm. daily 10–6; Mar–Dec; fee) contains wall-paintings of the 15C.

27 m. **Berkhamsted** (6300 inhab.; Hotels) has a well-known boys' school, founded in 1541. To the right, beyond the Grand Union and the railway, are the scanty but extensive remains of a royal *Castle* (11C), where William the Conqueror received the submission of Edgar Atheling in 1066, and John II of France was imprisoned after Poitiers (1356). William Cowper (1731–1800) was born in the former rectory.

About 3 m. N. is **Ashridge Park**, a vast mansion built by Wyatt in 1808, now a Management Training Centre (open to view a few days a year). It succeeded a monastery of Bonhommes (1283), famous for its possession of a drop of Christ's blood. Here Princess Elizabeth (afterwards queen) was arrested in 1554 by order of Queen Mary. Much of the beautiful deer-park, with 3800 acres of downland, is N.T. property. The Corinthian column to the N.W. commemorates the 3rd Duke of Bridgewater (1736–1803), 'father of inland navigation'.

At (30 m.) *Cowroast Lock*, the summit lock of 44 from the Thames, we diverge from the Grand Union Canal.— 32 m. *Tring* (Hotel) is an ancient town (9200 inhab.) at the foot of the Chiltern Hills, 1¾ m. w. of its station, where the railway enters Robert Stephenson's great cutting (1834–38) through the summit. The town has a motorway by-pass (s.). The baptismal register of the handsome flint church (14–16C) contains entries referring to the Washington family.

Along Akeman St. is *Tring Park*, formerly a seat of the Rothschild family, and still containing an admirable *Zoological Museum* (adm. free weekdays in summer 2–5, in winter 1–4, Sun always 2–5) built by the late Lord Rothschild and now a department of the British Museum. About 1½ m. w. of Tring is *Drayton Beauchamp*, where the 'judicious' Hooker was rector in 1584–85 and where he was visited by his pupils, George Cranmer and Edwin Sandys, as related by Izaak Walton. The church has 14C glass in the E. window.—At *Aldbury*, a charming village 1 m. E. of Tring Station, Mrs Humphry Ward (1851–1920) is buried. Her residence (later that of Lord Grey of Fallodon) was at Stocks.

B 488 runs N.E. to Dunstable (10 m.), passing (3½ m.) *Ivinghoe* (Restaurant), whence Scott derived the title of 'Ivanhoe'. It has a striking 13–14C church and the oldest post windmill in Britain (N.T.; 1627, restored). The view from Ivinghoe Beacon (756 ft) across to Whipsnade is marred by a radio station.

35 m. *Aston Clinton* (Hotel) in Bucks.—39 m. **Aylesbury** (Hotels), the county town of Bucks, with 41,300 inhab., once best known for its ducks and dairy produce, is now an expanding centre of industry. It has been divisively replanned into old and new, in violent juxtaposition.

From the ring road, beneath a lumpy tower block, Gt Western St. passes beneath *Friar's Square* market, a new precinct in harsh and restless concrete, incorporating at different levels the Bus Station, the County Library, and new Municipal Offices, to emerge in the old *Market Square*. Here are statues of Hampden and Beaconsfield, the original *County Hall* (1723–40) by Thos. Harris (with contemporary Court Room), and the Bull's Head (15C interior); and just off it the *King's Head* (15C; N.T.) with a fine mullioned window. Many good houses of the 17–18C survive, notably in Temple St. and Church St., where the *County Museum* (weekdays 9.30–12.30, 1.30–5, free), in the former Grammar School (15C, rebuilt in 1730), has a good collection of Bucks antiquities. *St Mary's*, imposing if over-restored, in a peaceful square, contains a good Norman font.

Hartwell House, 2 m. s.w., now an international college (adm. 2–5, Wed in May–mid-July), was occupied by Louis XVIII in 1808–14, and at *Dinton*, 2¼ m. farther on, is a *Church with Norman s. door. At *Hardwick*, 3½ m. N. of Aylesbury, is the tomb of Sir Robert E. Lee (d. 1616), once incorrectly thought to be an ancestor of Gen. Robert E. Lee. *Nether Winchendon House* (adm. July–Aug, occasional Thurs 2–6; fee), in a pretty village 2¼ m. w. of Dinton, is a Tudor house with 18C additions, once the home of Sir Francis Bernard, Governor of New Jersey and Massachusetts (1760–61).

An alternative route to Aylesbury (40 m.) leaves London viâ Harrow and (20 m.) *Rickmansworth* (A 404); see the 'Blue Guide to London'.— Beyond (24½ m.) *Chenies* (Hotel and Restaurant), a 19C 'model' village with *Monuments of the dukes of Bedford (seen through screens) in its church, A 416 diverges r. for *Chesham* (3¾ m.; Hotel), a pleasant town (20,400 inhab.) in the charming valley of the Chess.

26½ m. **Amersham** (Hotels), an attractive old town (68,400 inhab.), has a brick market hall (1682) and almshouses (1657). The varied domestic architecture on the s. side of the *High Street includes the timbered King's Arms Hotel and fine 18C houses. In the church are monuments of the Curwen family, by John Clarke, and of the Drake fam ly, whose seat was at *Shardeloes*, an Adam mansion in a pleasant park (public paths). The modern sector of the place is *Amersham-on-the-Hill*, with the station, to the N.E. Edmund Waller (1606–87) was born at *Coleshill*, 2 m. s.

The road now crosses the beech-clad CHILTERN HILLS, a line of chalk downs (700–850 ft) affording delightful walks.

The only way in which a member of Parliament may voluntarily vacate his seat is by accepting an office of profit under the Crown, and the Stewardship of the Chiltern Hundreds (Stoke, Desborough, and Burnham) is the office for which application is usually made with that end. The nominal duty of the Steward is to protect wayfarers from bandits (who once lurked in the thick beech-forests), for which he is paid a nominal salary.

28¾ m. *Little Missenden* (l.) has a 12C church with 14C wall-paintings. —30¾ m. *Great Missenden* (Hotel), in a beautiful valley, is by-passed by the main road. Its Dec. and Perp. church has a monument to Lady Boys (1638) by Nicholas Stone.

Just beyond, a pleasant road (l.) ascends towards the Hampden country (l.; Rte 30A) and *Little Hampden* (r.; 3 m.), with a tiny church adorned with 14C wall-paintings, and a large common with fine beech-woods.

35 m. *Wendover* (Hotel), a charming village beautifully situated on the Icknield Way, is an admirable centre for walks. *Coombe Hill* (N.T.; 852 ft), the highest of the Chilterns, rises 1½ m. w.—We descend into the fertile *Vale of Aylesbury*, noted for its pastures and churches, with the R.A.F. training school of *Halton* conspicuous on the right. On the left

is the hospital for paraplegics at *Stoke Mandeville.*—40 m. *Aylesbury,* see above.

---

45 m. *Waddesdon* (Hotels), where the street broadens with a green at the gates of the sumptuous mansion of the Rothschilds. ***Waddesdon Manor** (N.T.; open Wed–Sun, Easter–Oct, 2–6; Good Fri & BH, 11–6; fee; Connoisseurs' Day Fri: extra; teas) contains one of the finest private art collections in the country, a worthy rival of the Wallace Collection.

Designed by G.-H. Destailleur for Baron Ferdinand de Rothschild, the mansion was built in 1880–89 in the style of a French château, with motives brought from Blois, Chambord, etc. It stands in splendid grounds landscaped by Lainé.

Among the *Collections, the furniture is mainly 18C French, with masterpieces (1777–90) made by *Riesener* for Marie Antoinette and Comte de Provence (Louis XVIII), and a bureau belonging to Beaumarchais (1779), with inlay alluding to his works. The Savonnerie carpets, Sèvres porcelain, sculpture (by *Lemoine, Clodion, Falconet* and others), snuff-boxes, musical instruments, etc., are of the same period. Many of the rooms have panelling brought from 18C French mansions. The collection of paintings includes (in the Morning Room) the Garden of Love, by *Rubens* (in fact, a group of portraits of himself and Helène Fourment); *P. de Hooch,* *Game of Ninepins; *Cuyp,* the Maas near Dordrecht; *Dou,* Girl leaning from a window; *Van der Heyden,* Quay at Amsterdam; notable paintings by *Metsu, Terborch,* and *Teniers*; *Gainsborough,* the 'Pink Boy' (Master Nicholls), the Duke of Hamilton, and his brother, Lord Archibald Hamilton. Elsewhere are paintings by *Watteau, Lancret, Pater,* and *Boucher* (Phillippe Egalité at the age of 2); *Reynolds,* Col. St Leger (unusually romantic), Duchess of Cumberland, Mrs Sheridon as St Cecilia; also *Romney,* Lady Hamilton and Mrs Jordan; and portraits of Perdita Robinson by both *Gainsborough* and *Reynolds.*

Open on Fri only is the *Mezzanine floor, with a notable collection of 16–17C armour; paintings and sculpture (15–17C); miniatures (including *Hilliard,* Anne of Denmark); Renaissance jewellery; 16–17C glass; Limoges enamel; and illuminated manuscripts. In the grounds is an *Aviary* of 18C design.

Quainton church (2½ m. N.) has many fine monuments. At *Quainton Road,* former depôt of the Great Central Railway, are preserved c. 30 steam locomotives. To the left farther on (3½ m. s.) appears the isolated hill of *Brill* (694 ft; *View), which has an interesting church (11–14C) and was the site of a hunting-lodge of Edward the Confessor. The 17C *Dorton House* (adm. May–July, Sat 2–5, fee), now a school, is 2 m. E. and a little N. of it *Wotton House* (adm. June–Sept, Wed 2–6; fee) is of the early 18C, remodelled by Soane c. 1820. *Boarstall Tower,* 2 m. w. of Brill, is a 14C fortified gatehouse.

We enter Oxfordshire before reaching (56 m.) **Bicester** (pron. 'Bister'; Hotel), a hunting centre (12,300 inhab.), with scanty remains of an Augustinian priory. Many of the churches in the neighbourhood are of great interest.—At (65 m.) *Aynho* (Hotel), a charming Northamptonshire village, built in creamy stone with apricots growing on its cottage walls, is *Aynhoe Park House* (adm. May–Sept, Wed & Thurs 2–4; fee), mainly by Sir John Soane. We cross the Cherwell to join the Oxford road at (67½ m.) *Adderbury,* a village with a fine *Church (14C; 15C chancel). Adderbury House was a residence of the Earl of Rochester (1647–80).

King's Sutton, 1½ m. E. across the Cherwell, has an elaborate Perp. steeple. *Bloxham*, 2 m. W., is a large and well-built village, with a boys' school (1860), and a magnificent *Church (mainly c. 1300) with a spire 198 ft high. A local jingle thus describes the spires: "Bloxham for length, Adderbury for strength, and King's Sutton for beauty." *South Newington* church, 1½ m. beyond Bloxham, has wall-paintings dating from c. 1360.

71 m. **Banbury** (Hotels), a busy town (19,100 inhab.), contains several old houses of the 16–17C and quaint lanes off the High St. It is famous for its cakes and ale and for 'Banbury Cross', destroyed by Puritans in 1602, but replaced by a new one in 1858. The large and imposing church (1790–1822) is by S. P. and C. R. Cockerell, the citizens having blown up the previous one with gunpowder.

Near Banbury are *Broughton Castle* (Lord Saye and Sele; shown Wed, April–Sept, 2–5.30; also Sun in June–Aug & BH; fee), 3 m. s.w., dating from the 14–16C and in the family since 1451 when it was inherited from William of Wykeham; *Chacombe Priory* (adm. April, May, & Sept on Sun; June & July, Sat & Sun; Aug, Fri–Sun; 2.30–6.30; fee), rebuilt in 1600; *Wroxton Abbey* (17C), 3 m. N.W., the 17C home of Lord North, prime minister during the American War of Independence, now a centre for American post-graduate studies; and *Warkworth* (2 m. E.), with the Lyons tomb (c. 1350) in its church. *Compton Wynyates* lies c. 9 m. w. (see p. 330).

*Sulgrave (7½ m. E.), the home of the Washington family (1539–1626), before they removed to Brington, is conveniently visited from Banbury by road. The manor-house here was purchased in 1539 and rebuilt by Laurence Washington (p. 394), the seventh ancestor in direct ascent of the famous President. In 1914, to commemorate the 100th anniversary of the Treaty of Ghent, the manor-house (afterwards a farmhouse), together with ten acres of land, was purchased by the British Peace Centenary Committee (afterwards reorganized as the Sulgrave Manor Board) and has been restored (w. wing rebuilt by Sir R. Blomfield) and equipped as a *Washington Museum* (daily exc. Wed 10.30–1, 2–4 or 5.30, closed Jan; fee). The porch bears the Washington coat-of-arms (dubiously regarded as the origin of the 'Stars and Stripes', described in heraldic language as "barry of four, gules and argent; on a chief azure three mullets of the second; crest, a demi-eaglet sable rising from an earl's coronet." The relics include portraits of Washington by Gilbert Stuart and Archibald Robertson, a chair from Mt. Vernon, etc. The village of *Sulgrave* has an interesting church, with memorial brasses of the first Laurence Washington (d. 1583) and his wife, which disappeared in 1834 but were restored to their place in 1924. The village stocks, removed in 1850, were replaced in 1933. —*Canons Ashby*, the 16C seat of the Drydens (no adm.), is 4½ m. N. of Sulgrave. The church is a relic of an Augustinian priory.

FROM BANBURY TO STRATFORD-ON-AVON. The direct road (A 422; 20 m.) runs viâ Wroxton and *Sunrising Hill* (1 in 6). Near the top is (8½ m.) *Upton House* (17–18C), presented to the Nat. Trust in 1948 by Lord Bearsted, with its *Collections of Dutch paintings (including the *Bosch* *Nativity) and 18–19C English paintings, furniture, tapestries, etc. (open Wed Oct–April, also Sat in May–Sept, 2–6; fee).—A better route follows the Birmingham road to (5½ m.) *Warmington*, there turning left.—Below (8 m.) *Edge Hill* (1 in 7) the first battle of the Civil War was fought in 1642 between Charles I and Essex, with indecisive results (memorials erected 1949).—10½ m. *Kineton* (Hotel).—12½ m. *Compton Verney* church contains tombs of the Verney family. We cross the Foss Way and, at (15 m.) *Wellesbourne*, join the route from Warwick.—20½ m. *Stratford-on-Avon* (Rte 34c).

FROM BANBURY TO COVENTRY, 27 m. (A 423).—4½ m. *Mollington*. At *Cropredy*, 2 m. E. on the Cherwell, Charles I defeated Waller in 1644.—6 m. *Farnborough*. The 17–18C Hall (N.T., adm. 2–6, Wed & Sat, April–Sept; fee) is noted for its plaster decorations and attractive grounds.—9 m. *Wormleighton* (1½ m. r.) has a fine church and remains of an early-17C manor-house, half destroyed after Prince Rupert's stay here before Edgehill.—14 m. *Southam* (Hotel) is a small town with an old bridge and 'Mint House'.—27 m. *Coventry*, see p. 316).

Beyond Banbury we soon enter Warwickshire.—76½ m. *Warmington* (see above).—On the right rise the *Dassett Hills* and farther on Chesterton Windmill is conspicuous. We cross the Avon on entering (90½ m.)

Warwick, which, with **Leamington** (1½ m. w.), is described in Rte 34.—
101½ m. *Knowle* (Hotels) has a long-bodied Perp. church.—104¼ m.
Solihull (Hotels), now a suburban community (107,000 inhab.) has a
13–15C church (restored). The flagrant destruction by a developer in
1966 of the 14C Solihull Hall, despite a preservation order, occasioned
an increase in the legal penalty for such offences.—112 m. **Birmingham,**
see Rte 33.

B Viâ Coventry

ROAD, 110 m. (A 5, A 45).—21 m. **St Albans.**—34 m. *Dunstable.*—53 m. *Stony
Stratford* (Milton Keynes).—61 m. *Towcester.*—69 m. *Weedon.*—73 m. *Daventry.*—
92 m. **Coventry** (by-pass).—110 m. **Birmingham.**
  MOTORWAY, M 1 and M 6 for Birmingham (118 m.); M 1 and M 45 (A 45)
for Coventry (96 m.).
  RAILWAY, 113¼ m. from Euston in c. 1½ hr, stopping only at (94 m.) **Coventry**;
most trains go on to Wolverhampton. Other principal stations on this line are
served by hourly trains from Euston to (82 m.) **Rugby** (viâ the Northampton loop):
17½ m. *Watford,* junction for *St Albans.*—40¼ m. *Leighton Buzzard.*—46¾ m.
Bletchley.—52¼ m. *Wolverton.*—Frequent local service between Coventry· and
Birmingham.

  The Edgware Road (A 5; Watling Street), scarcely deviating from its
Roman course, runs viâ Elstree and Radlett to St Albans (21 m.).
Longer but quicker is the modern route (A 41, A 1) entering Hertford-
shire just short of (15 m.) *South Mimms,* where we take A 6.—17¾ m.
Salisbury Hall.

  Salisbury Hall, a medieval manor-house on a moated site inhabited since Roman
times, was remodelled by Charles II in 1668 for Nell Gwynn. Hence the Kingmaker
marched to Barnet and here Sir Winston Churchill spent part of his boyhood.
The house (adm. Easter–Sept, Sun 2–6, also Thurs in July–Sept; BH, Mon 10.30–
5.30; fee) has a fine Tudor hall. In an outbuilding is the prototype of the de
Havilland Mosquito aircraft designed here in the Second World War, as were also
Sir Nigel Gresley's last Pacific locomotives during his residence.—Nicholas Hawksmoor (d. 1736), the architect, is buried in the churchyard of St Botolph's *Shenley,*
2 m. s.w.

  21 m. **ST ALBANS** is an ancient city (52,100 inhab.) on a hill above the
little river Ver. A bustling town having printing works and light industries
as well as a general market (Sat) and cattle market (Wed), it has been the
seat of a bishop since 1877.

  Railway Stations. *City,* with frequent service to London (St Pancras) in 20–40
min.; *Abbey,* local service to Watford Junction.
  Car Parks near the Civic Centre. For Verulamium, near St Michael's (best
approached from A 414).—INFORMATION BUREAU, Chequer St.
  Hotels, more numerous than expected, in the centre and periphery.
  Amusements. Abbey Theatre.—CONCERTS in *City Hall.*—SWIMMING POOLS
(covered and open-air).
  Bus Station, near St Peter's. GREEN LINE services and most buses also stop in St
Peter's St.

  History. St Albans is the successor of the important Roman-British town of
Verulamium (see below). It owes its name to St Alban, a Roman soldier and the
first Christian martyr in England, who was beheaded here in A.D. 303 for harbouring St Amphibalus, the priest who had converted him. Offa, King of Mercia,
founded a Benedictine abbey c. 793 in honour of St Alban, and this eventually rose
to great wealth and power, so that from 1154 to 1396 its mitred abbot was the
premier abbot in England. Matthew Paris (d. 1259) was a monk here and Robert
Fayrfax was organist from c. 1498 until his death in 1521. Dame Juliana Berners,
author of the 'Boke of St Albans' (printed at St Albans in 1486) was prioress c.

1400 of Sopwell Nunnery (p. 309). During the Wars of the Roses two important battles took place at St Albans: at the first (1455), fought near Holywell Hill, Henry VI was defeated and captured by the Duke of York and the Earl of Warwick; at the second (1461), on Barnard's Heath, N. of St Peter's Church, Warwick was defeated by Queen Margaret and Henry VI was released.—Sarah Jennings (1660–1744), duchess of Marlborough, was born at St Albans, and, until the erection of Blenheim Palace, frequently lived in Holywell House (now demolished), at the foot of Holywell Hill.—Cowper, the poet, spent eighteen months in St Albans in 1764–65, partly in an institution for the mentally afflicted in College St.

The *Clock Tower* (fee; view) in the High St., in the centre of the town, dates from 1411; in front stood an Eleanor Cross, destroyed in 1702. Thence the old French Row leads past a 15C inn to the *Old Town Hall* (1830). A bookshop (l.) occupies a 14C Moot Hall. The broad tree-shaded St Peter's St., site of the Sat market, goes on to *St Peter's*, a late-Perp. church with some old glass and a tablet to Edward Strong (d. 1723), Wren's master-mason.

Nearly opposite the w. end of St Peter's are *Pemberton's Almshouses* (1624); beyond is the Bus Station. In Hatfield Rd. to the E. is another fine group of alms-houses, founded by Sarah, Duchess of Marlborough, and facing the *Herts County Museum* (10–4, not Sun or Mon). A house at the end of Catherine St., now re-named *Bleak House*, has some claims to be the original house Dickens had in view in writing his novel.—Off St Peter's St. to the E. is the *Civic Centre* with the *City Hall* (1968).

Passages from High St. (or from Holywell Hill) lead to the **Cathedral*, built on higher ground (320 ft) than any other in England. In origin it is an early Norman building and the nave is the longest medieval nave in existence (275½ ft). The massive Norman tower, with its striking arcade, is (like the other Norman portions) largely constructed of Roman bricks and tiles. The ugly w. façade and the transeptal façades are for the most part 19C.

HISTORY. The central part of the cathedral is substantially the church built on the site of Offa's church in 1077–88 by Paul of Caen, the first Norman abbot, and dedicated in 1116. This seems to have ended, just E. of the present transepts, in seven apses, and the present E. end of the cathedral dates from the 13C (presbytery, etc.) and 14C (Lady Chapel). The w. bays of the nave were rebuilt in the early 13C. After the Dissolution the church became parochial. A restoration was begun under Sir Gilbert Scott in 1856, and subsequently Sir Edmund Beckett (afterwards Lord Grimthorpe) completed the work at his own expense and according to his own designs, often with questionable taste. In 1877 the church became the cathedral of a new diocese.—Biennial Organ Festival (next 1981).

Interior. The plain but graceful w. end of the NAVE is E.E., abruptly joining the severe early Norman work on the N. side and continued on the s. side by five Dec. bays erected in 1323. On the second pillar on the N. side is an inscription to 'Sir John Mandeville', the imaginary traveller, supposed to have been born at St Albans. Incongruously displayed are the wooden doors from the former Perp. w. front. On the w. and s. sides of the Norman piers are considerable remains of **Wall-paintings*. The Crucifixion, the westernmost of these, is probably by Walter of Colchester (c. 1220), called by Matthew Paris an incomparable painter.—A stone *Rood Screen* (c. 1350) separates the nave from the Norman ritual CHOIR, which is continued E. by the **PRESBYTERY*. The fine painted ceiling over the choir dates from the late 15C; the tower ceiling was renewed in 1952, when one original panel was removed to the N. aisle. A larger panel of c. 1530 representing the Martyrdom of St Alban from the N. transept is preserved in the s. choir-aisle. Most of the presbytery and of the retro-choir was rebuilt by Abbot de Hertford (1235–60); the unique wooden vault was painted c. 1450. The unfinished altarpiece (The Resurrection) is by Sir Alfred Gilbert. The stone *Altar Screen* (restored) was erected by Abbot Wm. de Wallingford (1476–84). On the N. side of the presbytery is the chantry of Abbot Thomas Ramryge (d. 1520), on the S. side the chantry of Abbot John Wheathampstead (d. 1464), now containing the large *Brass of Abbot Thomas de la Mare (d. 1375; best seen from the S. choir-aisle). In the aisle a beautiful 14C arched recess marks the tomb of two hermits.— The TRANSEPTS are the best preserved portions of the Norman church. The arches on their E. side led into apsidal chapels. In the N. transept is a 15C fresco (Incredulity of St Thomas) and a plan of the Abbey before the Dissolution. In the S. transept the blind *Triforium on the E. wall has arches separated by small circular shafts, fitted with Norman capitals and Norman bases, but usually accepted as relics of Offa's Saxon church. The S. wall was rebuilt by Lord Grimthorpe, who incorporated in it some late-Norman arcading and the doorway of the former slype. The Elizabethan dole-cupboards in the recess (w. wall) are still in use.

Immediately E. of the presbytery is ST ALBAN'S CHAPEL, in the middle of which is the elaborately carved marble base of *St Alban's Shrine*, pieced together from more than 2000 fragments in 1872. The so-called *Watching Loft*, on the N. side, in oak (c. 1400), with carvings of the Months on the back, consists of a relic cupboard (below) and (probably) an ordinary chantry (above). On the S. side is the *Monument of Humphrey, Duke of Gloucester (d. 1447), with a lofty canopy and statuettes of English kings and a grille of Sussex ironwork (c. 1290).— Beyond the retro-choir is the LADY CHAPEL, built by Abbot Hugh de Eversden (1308–26), freely restored; from the Reformation until 1870 it was used by the school.—In the N. presbytery aisle are fragments of the *Shrine of St Amphibalus*.

In 1978 excavations outside the S. Transept were uncovering the Chapter House.

A few yards w. of the cathedral is the *Abbey Gatehouse* (1361), a relic of the monastic buildings, now occupied by the *Grammar School*, which is perhaps 1000 years old. Thence a lane descends to a bridge over the Ver, beside which is the little *Fighting Cocks Inn*, probably built on the site of a boat-house of Offa's Saxon monastery.

Beyond the river and ornamental lake lies the site of **Verulamium**, the capital of Roman Britain, occupied by a fine *Park and the school playing-fields.

Succeeding a British (Belgic) town of the late 1C B.C., in Prae Wood on the hill to the s.w., Verulamium was founded soon after the Roman conquest of A.D. 43, and became a 'municipium' (the only one in Britain) two years later. In 61 it was sacked by Boadicea, but was rebuilt on a larger scale and flourished until c. 410.

The city *Wall*, portions of which remain on the S. side with towers, enclosed an area of over 200 acres, and much of the site has been excavated and filled in again. A hypocaust with mosaic floor (A.D. 150 and 300) has been roofed over *in situ*. Other floors and a splendid collection of finds from the site are housed in a *Museum*, near St Michael's Church (open 10–4 or 5.30, Sun from 2; Sat & Sun in May–Aug 2–8.30; fee). These include wall-paintings on plaster, large glass burial urns,

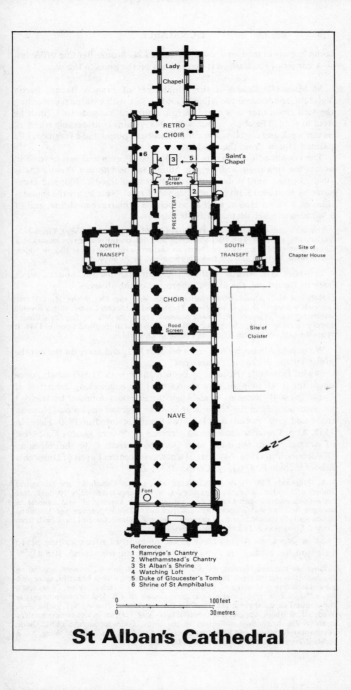

Lady
Chapel

RETRO
CHOIR

6   4   3   5 ← Saint's
                Chapel

Altar Screen

1   2

PRESBYTERY

NORTH
TRANSEPT

SOUTH
TRANSEPT

Site of
Chapter House

CHOIR

Rood
Screen

Site of
Cloister

NAVE

Font

Reference
1 Ramryge's Chantry
2 Whethamstead's Chantry
3 St Alban's Shrine
4 Watching Loft
5 Duke of Gloucester's Tomb
6 Shrine of St Amphibalus

0   100 feet
0   30 metres

St Alban's Cathedral

coffin burials in lead, and a well-preserved 2C bronze figurine of Venus. —A corner of the *Basilica* is marked out on the grass to the w.

St Michael's Church is the burial-place of Francis Bacon, Baron Verulam, and Viscount St Albans (1561–1626), with a statue representing the lord chancellor in a characteristic attitude ("sic sedebat"; 'thus he used to sit'). The church, founded in 948, retains considerable traces of Saxon work and contains a beautiful Jacobean pulpit and a fragment of a painted Doom, from the rood-loft.

The church adjoins the site of the Roman Forum and just beyond it, across the ring road, a drive gate admits to the *Roman Theatre (daily 10–dusk; fee), built c. 140 but soon altered, enlarged c. 300, and excavated by Kathleen Kenyon and Sheppard Frere. Near by are the foundations of a Town House, with an associated subterranean shrine, and of a wooden market destroyed by Boadicea.

The drive goes on to *Gorhambury* (Earl of Verulam; adm. May–Sept, Thurs 2–5; fee), an 18C mansion with Bacon's library and fine portraits and two remarkable Tudor enamelled glass windows from an earlier house (ruins near by), in which Bacon died. Notable also are two chimneypieces by Piranesi.

FISHPOOL ST., with several 15–16C inns and fine 18C houses, winds back to Romeland, the old burial-ground of the abbey.

Holywell Hill, also with attractive houses and the 15C White Hart Hotel, descends s. from High St. to the *Abbey Theatre* and the *Sports Centre*, with a covered swimming pool. The site of *Sopwell Nunnery* lies to the left. *St Stephen's Church* contains a lectern said to have been looted at Holyrood in Hertford's raid in 1544. It bears the name of George Crichton, Bishop of Dunkeld.

We quit St Albans by A 5, cross beneath M 1, and leave on the left the pretty village of (28¾ m.) *Flamstead*.

34½ m. **Dunstable** (Hotels), in Bedfordshire, with 31,800 inhab., once noted for its straw-plait, now shares the light engineering industries of Luton (p. 404). Remains of an Augustinian priory founded by Henry I are incorporated in the **Church of St Peter*, a grand example of Norman (nave and great portal) and E.E. (w. front), restored in 1850. Here, in 1533, Abp. Cranmer pronounced sentence of divorce against Catherine of Aragon. From the main road Queensway leads E. to the imposing *Queensway Hall* (1958–64), part of a new civic centre. Pupils of Dunstable School include F. J. (Gary) Cooper (1901–61).

At **Whipsnade** (700 ft), on the Chilterns, 3 m. s.w. of Dunstable, the Zoological Society of London has a *Zoological Park of 500 acres (adm. daily 10–dusk, fee; restaurants and car park), a pioneer venture in the keeping of wild animals in uncaged freedom within enclosures and paddocks. The Whipsnade and Umfolosi Steam Railway uses locomotives that once ran in Zululand. Green Line Coach from Central London in c. 1½ hr (summer only).

38 m. *Hockliffe* is important as the junction of roads leading w. to Leighton Buzzard (3¼ m.) and N.E. to Northampton (comp. Rte 43).

Leighton Buzzard (Hotel), an old town of 20,300 inhab., now incorporating *Linslade* (transferred from Bucks), has an E.E. church with a beautiful spire and good 13C ironwork on the w. door. The basilican **Church of *Wing*, 2½ m. s.w., has a Saxon apse, crypt, and nave-arches; among 16–17C Dormer monuments is the unusual classical tomb (1552) of Sir Robert. *Ascott House* (N.T.; adm. 2–6, Wed, Sat, & BH in Apr–Sept, also Sun in July–Aug; fee), set in a charming garden, contains the Rothschild collection of paintings (Gainsborough, Stubbs, Cuyp, Hobbema), furniture, and Chinese porcelain. *Stewkley*, 3 m. N.W. of Wing, has a richly decorated late-Norman *Church (c. 1150).

47½ m. *Fenny Stratford*, now incorporated in Milton Keynes (see below), has a marina on the Grand Union Canal. The curious little cannon ('Fenny Poppers') outside the church are discharged every year at Martinmas.

B 4034 runs w. through **Bletchley**, a thriving town (30,600 inhab.) of light industries (also part of Milton Keynes), which has trebled its population in twenty years.— 9½ m. *Thornborough Bridge* (14C; preserved r. of road); finds of the 2C from the two tumuli above the approach are in the Cambridge Museum of Archaeology.— 12 m. **Buckingham** (Hotels), a quiet old town (5100 inhab.), has long been superseded as county town by Aylesbury. Built round the market-place, with a Georgian town hall at the s. end and the 18C gaol farther N., it is notable for the 15C chantry chapel (Old Latin School; N.T.) with its Norman doorway. The high-lying parish church was built on a new site in 1777–81, and completely altered in 1862–65 from designs by Sir G. G. Scott, who was born at *Gawcott*, 1½ m. s.

The remote Perp. church of *Hillesden* (c. 1493), 2 m. s. of Gawcott, with Denton tombs, is one of the best in the county, and that of *Chetwode*, 4 m. farther w., with a 5-light window (1244), is the chancel of an Austin priory. Both display good stained glass.—*Maids' Moreton* church, 1½ m. N., is a beautiful example of 15C work (1450). Adm. Lord Keyes (1872–1945) and his son, Lt.-Col. Geoffrey Keyes, V.C., lived at *Tingewick House*, 2½ m. w., and are commemorated in the village church.

An avenue of elms leads N. from Buckingham to (3 m.) *Stowe*, once the princely seat (1697, remodelled in 1775) of the Temples, Dukes of Buckingham, whose title became extinct in 1889, but since 1923 a boys' school. The famous *Gardens (adm. daily during Christmas, Easter and Summer vacations; fee) were laid out in 18C taste, with numerous classical temples, etc., mainly designed by Gibbs for Sir Richard Temple, the friend of Pope; and their magnificence has been extolled by Pope, Thomson, Horace Walpole, and others. The chapel (1929) was designed by Sir Robert Lorimer. The Comte de Paris died here in 1894.

Near *Steeple Claydon*, 5 m. s., is *Claydon House* (N.T.; adm. 2–6 daily April–Oct, exc. Mon & Fri; fee), the seat of the Verneys, partly late-Tudor and partly built by Sir Thos. Robinson in 1760–80 for the 2nd Earl Verney. It contains many Rococo apartments designed by Lightfoot (otherwise unknown), including an amazing 'Chinese Chippendale' room; a magnificent staircase, with plaster-work by Rose; fine family portraits; and memorials of Florence Nightingale, who frequently visited her sister here. The adjoining church of *Middle Claydon* contains monuments of the Verneys (including a portrait-bust of Sir Edmund Verney, who fell at Edgehill) and of the previous owners, the Giffords.

A 422 runs w. to (21 m.) **Brackley** (Hotel), another pleasant old town (4600 inhab.) situated on A 43 half-way between Oxford and Northampton. *Magdalen College School*, founded by William of Waynflete in 1447, incorporates the old chapel of St John's Hospital. This, like the low-lying parish church of *St Peter*, retains 12C statues in the niches of its tower. The 18C *Town Hall* stands in the midst of the broad High St. The manor-house is now also a school.—31 m. *Banbury*, see Rte 32A.

At (53 m.) **Stony Stratford** (Hotels) Edward V and the Woodvilles were intercepted by Richard of Gloucester ('Richard III', II. iv). The jests interchanged by coaching travellers at the two inns are said to have given rise to the phrase 'a cock and bull story'. This town has also been absorbed by **Milton Keynes**, a planned city with a university and eccentric signposting. *Passenham* church, 1 m. s.w. contains remarkable stalls, dated 1628, and wall-paintings.

A 422 leads r. to (2 m.) *Wolverton*, an industrial town with railway carriage works.

We cross the Great Ouse and enter Northants, leaving on the right a road to Northampton (Rte 43), which passes close to Stoke Bruerne (see below), on the left a road to Buckingham (7 m.). The remnants of Whittlewood Forest lie to the w.

61 m. **Towcester** (Hotels), an ancient town of 21,000 inhab., on the site of Roman *Lactodorum*, has a prominent racecourse. Dean Swift was a

frequent guest at the Talbot inn. The church of *St Lawrence*, with a 13C crypt, contains the tomb of Archdeacon Sponne (d. 1449), a great benefactor of the town, and a carved organ (c. 1760) brought from Fonthill.

Easton Neston, to the E. (public drive to the church), is a notable mansion by Hawksmoor.—At *Stoke Bruerne* (4 m. E.), on the Grand Union Canal (comp. below) near the s. end of Blisworth Tunnel (3075 yds) is the **Waterways Museum** (adm. 10–12.30, 2–5, 6–8) with historical relics of the canal era. In Stoke Park (Sat & Sun 2–6, in July–Aug; fee) are two pavilions and a colonnade by Inigo Jones (1630). *Blisworth*, at the N. end of the tunnel, is on A 43 between Towcester (4 m.) and Northampton.

Slapton church, which contains remarkable 14C wall-paintings, lies 4 m. s.w. of Towcester; about 3 m. farther is the manor-house of *Astwell* (Tudor and earlier, the remains of which are now a Y.H.), the birthplace of Selina, Countess of Huntingdon (1707–91). At *Weedon Lois*, a little to the N., is the grave of Edith Sitwell (d. 1965).—*Silverstone* (4 m. s.), with a motor-racing track, is on the Brackley road (Hotel, at Brackley Hatch, 2 m. on).

At (69 m.) *Weedon* (Hotel), properly *Weedon Bec*, we leave Watling Street and turn left on A 45.

Here St Cadoc of Llancarfan (d. c. 570) was murdered while praying at the altar of the small monastic church of which he was bishop.—The churches of *Stowe Nine Churches* (Saxon tower), 2 m. s., and *Dodford*, 1¼ m. w., are noted for their monuments.

73 m. **Daventry** (Hotel), an ancient town (11,800 inhab.), where Charles I spent the week before Naseby at the Wheatsheaf Inn, has a handsome church of 1752–58 by David Hiorns and a prominent B.B.C. radio transmitter.

The Banbury road leads s. to (4½ m.) *Charwelton*, at the source of the Cherwell, which rises in the cellar of Cherwell House, an old farm. Close by is a picturesque 13C footbridge. The church (1 m. E.) contains the fine brasses and tombs of the Andrew family. A footpath leads N.E. to (1½ m.) *Fawsley* (public road through the fine park), the deserted Tudor seat of the Knightleys, where some of the Marprelate Tracts were printed.

76 m. *Braunston* (boats for hire) is known to cruising enthusiasts as an important inland waterway junction.

The **Grand Union Canal**, formed in 1929 by the union of the Grand Junction Canal, the Regent's, and six other canals, all of which remain navigable, connects Braunston with the Thames, the Nene, and the Trent, and with most centres of the Midlands. The *Grand Junction Canal*, built in 1793–1805, quits the Thames at Brentford and runs viâ Watford, Berkhamsted, Tring, Leighton Buzzard, and Wolverton (closely followed by the Midland Rly., p. 363) to (93¾ m.) Braunston, where it joins the Oxford Canal (p. 286). It has tunnels at Blisworth (comp. above) and at Braunston (2042 yds).—The old *Grand Union* (24½ m.; 1814), which now forms part of the 'Leicester Arm', connects the Grand Junction at *Norton* (4½ m. E. of Braunston) with the *Leicestershire and Northamptonshire Union Canal* at *Gumley* (threading *Crick* and *Husbands Bosworth* tunnels and descending Foxton Locks); hence the Trent may be reached.—The 'Birmingham Arm' of the Grand Union branches from the Oxford Canal at *Napton*, 5 m. w. of Braunston, to run viâ Kingswood (p. 339) and Warwick to Birmingham.

We enter Warwickshire.—81 m. *Dunchurch* (Hotel), still possessing its village stocks, lies 2¾ m. s. of Rugby (see Rte 39). Joining the M 45 (a link from the M 1 at Watford Gap) we ascend to the open Dunsmore Heath.—87 m. *Ryton*, with a Police College (1948).—At (89½ m.) *Willenhall* (Hotel), we approach the suburbs of Coventry. *Wolston* (Hotel), 3½ m. E., has a church with pre-Norman work, and some remains of an old priory.

92 m. **COVENTRY** (334,800 inhab.) is an ancient city important alike in history and in industry. Down to the close of the 17C it was the centre

of the English cloth industry, under the control of the 'Crafts' or City Companies. Afterwards it was famous for its ribbons, watches, and sewing-machines, and in 1870–1939 as the English headquarters of the cycle and motor-car industries. In 1914–18 and 1939–45 Coventry was a centre of war industry, and on the night of 14 Nov 1940, it suffered one of the most violent air-raids of the war, being damaged to such an extent as to provide a new verb in the German language. The centre has been planned anew within an American-style partly-elevated ring road, and the range of engineering, electrical, and chemical industries greatly increased. The *University of Warwick* stands 3 m. s.w. of the city.

Airport, 3 m. s. of the city.
Hotels in Broadgate and Warwick Rd; also MOTEL.—Several Restaurants.
Post Office, Hertford St.—INFORMATION BUREAU, 1 Union St.
Theatres. *Belgrade*, Corporation St.; *Coventry*, Hales St.; *College* (repertory), in the Technical College.
Buses from Pool Meadow to most Midland towns.
History. *Coventre*, the *Couentrev* of Domesday Book, may derive from a convent of the Saxon period; but its practical history begins with the foundation of a Benedictine priory in 1043 by Leofric, Earl of Mercia, and his wife Godgyfu. The legend, retold by Landor and by Tennyson, of how the Lady Godiva averted Leofric's anger from the town by riding naked through its streets is first found in permanent form in the 'Flores Historiarum' of 1235. The episode of 'Peeping Tom' dates from 1678 only. After the Conquest the lordship of Coventry passed to the earls of Chester, and in 1102–85 the priory church was the cathedral of the diocese of Coventry and Lichfield. The town prospered so greatly (in spite of conflicts between the 'Earl's Half' and the 'Prior's Half') that by 1377 it ranked in industrial importance next to London, York, and Bristol. In 1398 Coventry (Gosford Green; E. of the town) was the scene of the interrupted 'wager of battle' between Bolingbroke and Norfolk (Shakespeare's 'King Richard II'), and it was the meeting-place of the 'Parliamentum Indoctorum' (1404; so called on account of the exclusion of lawyers) and of the 'Parliamentum Diabolicum' (1458; so called from its numerous attainders). The priory was dismantled after 1539. The present bishopric dates from 1918. The popular phrase 'to send to Coventry' is of uncertain derivation. 'True as Coventry blue' was a tribute to its commercial honesty. The 'Coventry Plays' are one of four extant collections of medieval English miracle-plays (15C or 16C).—Dame Ellen Terry (1847–1928) was born in 'theatrical lodgings' in either Market St. or Smithford St. (both houses destroyed), and Sir Henry Parkes (1815–96), 'Father of the Australian Commonwealth', was born at *Canley*, 2 m. s.w. The future King Paul of the Hellenes lived here during part of his 12-years' exile, working incognito as a motor mechanic.

The centre of Coventry is the open space at Broadgate, laid out attractively as a garden with an equestrian statue of Lady Godiva, by Reid Dick (1949), where High St. and Hertford St. converge. At the entrance to the Bridge Restaurant under the *Godiva Clock* is a mosaic memorial by René Antonietti (1953) to 16C Coventry martyrs. The reliefs on the steel doors of the National Provincial Bank are notable. To the w. of Broadgate extends the *Shopping Precinct*, a disappointing realization of a bold plan.

To the E. rise two of Tennyson's "three tall spires" of Coventry. The nearer belongs to *Holy Trinity* (237 ft), a good Perp. church where William Siddons married Sarah Kemble (25 Nov 1773). The roof and tower-lantern (1667) are notable and the pulpit is a remarkable example of 15C stonework. The fine w. window (Christ in Majesty) is by Hugh Easton (1955). Priory Row, N. of the church, retains some pleasant old houses, and a curious wooden steeple of 1853.

Just to the s. rises the splendid steeple, with tower, octagon, and spire, 295 ft high, which survived undamaged the destruction of the old cathedral in 1940; its ruined shell has been rededicated as a memorial shrine and vestibule to the new *Cathedral. The moving desolation of its 14C walls is heightened by the two crosses on the altar, one of charred roof beams, one of nails, with the words 'Father forgive' carved on the E. wall. As a gesture of reconciliation the vestries were rebuilt as an international centre by German students and apprentices.

The new edifice, designed by Sir Basil Spence in modern idiom and materials and erected in 1954–62, extends towards the N. at right angles to the old. The EXTERIOR presents an alternating screen of wall (in uncoursed pink sandstone) and window, set saw-toothed to the line of the building, an arrangement which affords marked contrasts according to the viewpoint. A gilded bronze flèche (set in place by helicopter) surmounts the roof; it has been affectionately dubbed 'Radio Coventry' by the natives. Old and new are linked by a bold *Porch*, the extended roof of which binds the two together. The glass screen, by John Hutton, engraved with translucent figures of saints and angels, which takes the place of a 'w. wall', further emphasizes their unity. The porch is traversed by a ceremonial way (St Michael's Avenue), so that entrance can also be made from either side independently of the old cathedral. On the nave wall facing Priory St., at the head of a great flight of steps, is *St Michael subduing the Devil, a figure in bronze, 25 ft high, by Epstein.

In the angle of the old and new buildings, and connected with the latter by a short cloister, stands the *Chapel of Unity*, an undenominational place of worship for all Christians. It has the form of a crusader's tent with heavy buttresses. The mosaic floor was designed by the Swedish artist Einar Forseth, and the cost of the windows was defrayed by donors in the German Federal Republic.

INTERIOR. Beyond the screen the attention, undiverted by lateral windows which are hidden from view, is immediately drawn towards the altar by the immensity of Sutherland's tapestry. The nave, 270 ft long and 80 ft wide, has a floor of polished black and white marble contrasting with the plain plastered walls. The ceiling, borne on two rows of 7 slender concrete columns is made up of concrete ribs, forming an unbroken diamond pattern that extends to the chancel and is filled in with wooden louvres (the roof above is wholly borne by the outer walls). To the right the *Baptistery* takes the form of a shallow alcove bounded by an immense stained-glass **Window, by John Piper and Patrick Reyntiens, extending from floor to ceiling. The 195 lights, set in patterned mullions, represent in abstract form the glory of Baptism, the light of the Holy Spirit shining through the life of man. On a single step of marble in the centre of the alcove stands an unwrought sandstone boulder from the valley of Barakat, outside Bethlehem, in which a scolloped hollow serves as font.

As we advance, passing the carved stone *Tablets of the Word*, designed by Ralph Beyer, which adorn the foot of each section of wall, each pair in turn of the ten nave windows comes into view. They throw their light in the direction of the altar.

The windows were designed by Lawrence Lee, Geoffrey Clarke, and Keith New, and made in London. Each pair has a predominant colour and theme but an abstract form. The first pair (green) represents Beginnings; the second (red), God's intervention in His world; the third (multicoloured), Conflict; the fourth (blue and purple), Maturity; and the fifth (silver and gold), the Ultimate Realities.

The CHANCEL is not distinguished structurally from the nave but formed by the traditional placing of lectern, pulpit, and *Stalls*. These and the *Bishop's Throne*, on the left, have canopies suggesting (not too happily) flights of doves. The uncased *Organ* is built on either side against the end walls of the aisles. The stone *Altar*, 15 ft long and unadorned, stands alone in front of a huge silver-gilt cross by G. Clarke. Below it, work during the building uncovered the apse of the 12C cathedral (comp. above). Between the high altar and the 'E.' wall extends the *Lady Chapel*, its structural simplicity a foil for the vast *Tapestry*, by Graham Sutherland, which fills the whole of the wall.

The tapestry, woven in one piece at Felletin, near Aubusson, in Australian wool, is the largest in the world, measuring 74¾ ft by 34 ft. On a green background is displayed a figure of Christ in Glory with man between His feet. The composition was inspired by St John's vision: "On the throne sat one whose appearance was like the gleam of jasper and cornelian; and round the throne was a rainbow, bright as an emerald. And round about the throne were four beasts full of eyes before and behind" (Revelation, iv, 6–8). A lower panel (Christ crucified) gives the effect of a reredos to the Lady Chapel altar and, when seen from the nave, even to the High Altar, 48 ft farther forward.

To the right of the Lady Chapel is the theatrical *Chapel of Christ in Gethsemane*, separated from the aisle only by an iron screen, in the form of a crown of thorns, wrought and presented by the Royal Engineers. Behind the asymmetrically placed altar a kneeling angel, in bronze relief, holding a cup, is silhouetted against a rich gold mosaic.—A short passage leads to the *Chapel of Industry* (Christ the Servant), a separate circular structure, which from outside provides a graceful foil to the massive chancel. It combines the functions of the former guild chapels, and has windows of plain glass affording glimpses of industrial Coventry.

John F. Kennedy House, a residential youth centre in the precincts, was opened in 1965 by Herr Willy Brandt, chief burgomaster of Berlin.

To the s. of the cathedral is *St Mary's Hall*, founded in 1342 for the Merchant Guild, enlarged after 1394 for the Trinity Guild, and since 1552 the property of the Corporation. Above the kitchen and the vaulted crypt (now a magistrates' court) is the *Great Hall*, containing the celebrated Coventry Tapestry (Flemish, early 16C), probably commemorating the visit of Henry VII and Elizabeth of York in 1500. Off the hall open two small chambers with panelling from old Coventry inns. Adjoining on the s. rises *Caesar's Tower* (13C), perhaps built on a portion of the Earl of Chester's vanished castle; this was the only part of the building to be destroyed in 1940, and it has been reconstructed with the old material. On its second floor Mary, Queen of Scots, was imprisoned for a while in 1569.

Greyfriars Lane leads s. from High St. past *Ford's Hospital*, a half-timbered almshouse for five poor men and their wives (1509), restored, after bomb damage, in 1953. In Cow Lane (l.) the *Public Reference Library* finds a temporary home in a chapel of 1793. Farther s. is *Christ Church*, burned in 1940 except for the octagonal steeple (230 ft), a survival of the Grey Friars' monastery (demolished 1539), the third of the three spires of Coventry.

Warwick Rd. and Eaton Rd. go on to the *Station*, passing Greyfriars Green with its charming garden and a statue of Sir Thomas White (1492–1567), founder of St John's College, Oxford.—Also in the s. quarter of the city, in Cheylesmore, are the slight remains of *Cheylesmore Manor House*, the successor of that from which Godiva set out on her legendary ride. Little Park St., modern except for a mid-18C merchant's house, leads back to the High St.

In Jordan Well is the **Herbert Art Gallery and Museum** (weekdays 10–6, Sun 2–5; open till 8 on Tues & Wed).

ENTRANCE HALL. Alvis motor-car (1920); gold watch by Sam Watson (1690); steel sallet (15C N. Italian); glaze 'face' jug (13C; local).—To the left, archaeological finds from Town Wall excavations; pagan burial goods from the Baginton cemetery (Anglo-Saxon), including a

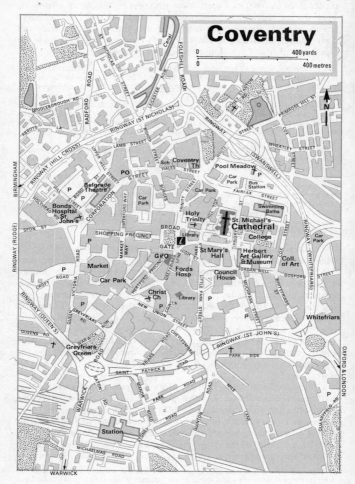

fine bronze bowl; part of Saxon cross-shaft (10C); local fauna.—Across the hall, vintage cars, motor-cycles, and engines since 1897; examples of silk-ribbon weaving and watch-making; old whipping-post.

FIRST FLOOR. Staircase (r.), copies on glass of local brasses. Vestibule: *Epstein*, bust of Tagore; *David Cox*, Kenilworth. ROOM I. Warwickshire water-colours,

1770–1960, including works by *Cox* and *Holman Hunt.*—R. II. Well-chosen collection of modern art with a good *Ruskin Spear* (London whelk-woman) and the Coventry Sculpture by *Peter Peri.* Temporary exhibitions are displayed in the remaining rooms on both floors. It is hoped that the Iliffe collection of cartoons and working drawings for Sutherland's tapestry will find a permanent home here.

By Whitefriars St. and a subway under the Ring Road, we reach the **Whitefriars,** comprising the E. cloister walk, chapter house, and dormitory of a Carmelite friary founded in 1342. The E. and w. walls of its former church, 303 ft apart, were located in 1962. The dormitory was opened in 1970 as a *Museum of Coventry History* (adm. free, Fri & Sat 10–6, Sun 2–5), displaying local finds, chiefly of medieval date.

In Priory St. flanking the cathedral rises *Lanchester College of Technology*, opened in 1960 and since made part of the University of Warwick, with a towering hall of residence. Beyond rises the graceful cantilevered roof of the *Swimming Pool* (1965).

In Hales St., N. of the centre, a section of the old *City Wall* (1356, dismantled 1662), skirted by a pleasant garden, connects two small gates, the *Swanswell Gate* and *Cook St. Gate*. At the other (w.) end of Hales St. is the old schoolroom of *King Henry VIII School*, founded by John Hales in 1545 and transferred to new buildings on the Warwick Rd. in 1885, where the stalls from the White Friars' church are preserved. Corporation St. continues s.w. past the *Belgrade Theatre*, whose name recalls the wartime exchange of aid between the two 'blitzed' cities. A picturesque survival of Coventry's medieval hospitals is *Bond's Hospital*, in Hill St., with the former buildings of *Bablake School* (1560; now in Coundon Rd.) adjoining. Close by is *St John's Church* (1344, restored), with a lantern tower. The Shopping Precinct (comp. above) leads back to the centre.

Important public buildings are the *Technical College* (1935), in The Butts; and the *War Memorial* (1927) in a fine park (121 acres) on the Kenilworth road.

Admirers of GEORGE ELIOT (p. 365) may well devote an extra day to the Coventry and Nuneaton district, which is intimately connected with her life and novels. In Coventry itself, which has been doubtfully identified with the 'Treby Magna' of 'Felix Holt' and with 'Middlemarch', Marian Evans was for a short time at the Misses Franklin's boarding-school (now 'Nantglyn', 29 Warwick Row, on the w. side of Greyfriars Green). Not far off is Cow Lane, where Mr Franklin (prototype of 'Rufus Lyon') used to preach in a chapel now used for other purposes. From 1841 to 1849 she lived with her father at 'Bird Grove' on the Foleshill road. The road from Coventry to Nuneaton affords access to other shrines (comp. also pp. 365, 401, 415).

Excursions from Coventry may be made to *Wyken Church* (c. 1100), with a 15C wall-painting of St Christopher, and the remains of *Caludon Castle* (14–16C), 2 m. N.E. (½ m. apart): to *Allesley Hall* and its park, 2 m. N.W., presented to the city by Lord Iliffe; and to *Whitley Abbey*, an Elizabethan mansion 1½ m. S.E. The church at *Baginton* (Inn, on the R. Sowe), 3 m. s. (near the Coventry airfield), contains the good brass of the Bagot (d. 1407) of 'King Richard II'. Bolingbroke lodged with him at Baginton Castle, while Norfolk was entertained at Caludon (see above). 'The Lunt', a 1C Roman fort, is being reconstructed from archaeological evidence as a museum.—About 4 m. E., in a well-wooded park, is *Combe Abbey* (no adm.), on the site of a Cistercian monastery (1150) and incorporating parts of its cloisters (13–15C). Princess Elizabeth, daughter of James I, was living here at the time of the Gunpowder Plot, and was transferred to Coventry in order to forestall any attempt of the conspirators to seize her.—*Stoneleigh Abbey* (p. 332) lies 4½ m. s.

From Coventry to *Warwick* and *Leamington*, see Rte 34.

The old Birmingham road passes Allesley (see above) and at (98 m.) *Meriden* (Rest.) passes the cross that is said to mark 'the centre of England'. Here also is a cyclists' war memorial. *Berkswell*, with its interesting church (Norman chancel and Saxon and Norman crypts), lies 2 m. s. *Great Packington*, 1 m. N.W., has a strange church of 1789, by J. Bonomi, on a Greek-cross plan.— 104 m. *Elmdon*, with the Birmingham airport, is near the new National Exhibition Centre. We approach Birmingham through the E. suburbs of Yardley and Small Heath.— 110 m. **Birmingham,** see below.

33 BIRMINGHAM

BIRMINGHAM, the foremost metal-working town in Britain and metropolis of an industrial region of two and a half millions, is the second city in Britain, with a population of 1,103,400; and it has a Roman Catholic archbishop, an Anglican bishop, two universities and two noted art-collections. It spreads over the heights (200–600 ft) and hollows of small tributaries of the Tame. A rich and energetic city, Birmingham has replaced much of its older housing by tower blocks and is in course of rebuilding its whole central area.

Railway Stations. *New Street*, for London (Euston) viâ Coventry; London (Paddington) viâ Leamington; Bristol, Derby, Liverpool, Manchester, Wales, and Scotland.— *Moor Street*, local services to Stratford and Leamington.— *Birmingham International*, 9 m. S.E., serves the National Exhibition Centre and the Airport.

Airport at Elmdon, 6 m. S.W., on the Coventry road. Services to London, Edinburgh, Belfast, Aberdeen, Glasgow, and Inverness.

Hotels in Hagley Rd., New Street, Smallbrook, etc.; also at Airport.

Restaurants. Mostly in hotels.

Baths. Among the city's many swimming pools and baths, there are Turkish and Russian baths at Erdington, Grove Lane, and Kent St., and Finnish Sauna baths at Bournville Lane.

Post Office, Victoria Sq.— INFORMATION BUREAU, Council House.

Amusements. THEATRES: *Repertory*, Station St. (to be moved); *Alexandra*, John Bright St.; *Birmingham Theatre*, Hurst St.; Midlands *Arts Centre*, Cannon Hill Park.— CONCERTS: City of Birmingham Symphony Orchestra in the Town Hall, at least twice weekly incl. Thurs at 7.30. Organ Recitals in Town Hall, Wed 1.15. Also chamber concerts at City Art Gallery.

History. Although Birmingham is primarily a modern city, *William de Bermingham*, Lord of the Manor, was able to show in 1309 that his ancestors had held a market and levied tolls here before the Conquest. The town became known for its workers in metal as early as 1538, when Leland wrote of 'Bremishcham' that "a great part of the towne is mayntayned by smithes, who have their yren out of Staffordshire and Warwickshire, and their sea-coale out of Staffordshire". In the Civil War Birmingham supplied the Parliamentarians with 15,000 swords, and was sacked by Prince Rupert. At the end of the 18C the town began its phenomenal recent growth due to abundant supplies of coal, iron, and wood in the vicinity, the multiplicity of trades, and the skill and energy of its inhabitants; in 1801 its population was 86,000, in 1851 233,000. Boulton and Watt, with the world-famous Soho Manufactory, at one time employing 1000 people, helped to establish Birmingham as a manufacturing centre, while Baskerville, the printer, Priestley, the chemist, and Murdock, the inventor of gas-lighting, gave an impetus to advance in science and learning, which even the fierce 'Church and King Riots' of 1791 could not seriously hamper. In 1835 De Tocqueville described the city as "an immense workshop, a huge forge, a vast shop. One only sees busy people and faces brown with smoke. One hears nothing but the sound of hammers and the whistle of steam escaping from boilers". Birmingham took a leading part in the Reform agitation of 1832 and in the Chartism of 1839; and its continued national importance is shown by the names of Joseph Sturge (1793–1859), John Bright (1811–89), and Joseph Chamberlain (1836–1914). Under Chamberlain's leadership Birmingham started its tradition of enlightened municipal enterprise, being described in 1890 by an American writer as "the best-governed city in the world". Among its many municipal activities are a Symphony Orchestra, and the unique Municipal Bank, founded by Neville Chamberlain, Lord Mayor 1915–17, Prime Minister 1937–40. For long a stronghold of Nonconformity and the chief centre of English Unitarianism, Birmingham's importance in another ecclesiastical sphere is attested by Cardinal Newman's work at the Oratory.

In Easy Row stood the "old red-brick house with three steps before the door" where Mr Pickwick tried in vain to mollify Mr Winkle, senior; this and the house where Washington Irving wrote 'Rip van Winkle' (1818) have been demolished. Birmingham, with the country to the w., is described in many of Brett Young's novels.

Birmingham is famous for being the home of the 'small master', with over 5000 factories and 1500 different trades. Practically everything made of metal from pen-nibs to railway carriages is turned out, and jewellery is important. During both world wars Birmingham was a major arms-manufacturing centre (and supplied 800,000 guns for the American Civil War), but now the vehicle-building industries predominate, employing over 120,000 people.

Inner Ring Road. Planned in the 1940s by Sir Herbert Manzoni, the new central road system is now being completed, at a cost of £33 million. The central area is tightly encircled by a ring ¾ m. by ½ m., with an additional cross link by Colmore Circus: construction has involved extensive alterations to much of the centre and threatened most of the rest. Pedestrian passage is restricted and the roads may only be negotiated viâ steps and tunnels, but 'piazzas' created by roundabouts and attractive works of art afford visual interest.

The centre of the city we may fix at VICTORIA SQUARE. On the w. side of this stands the **Town Hall**, a classical temple modelled on that of Castor and Pollux in Rome, with 40 Corinthian columns, started in 1832 by Joseph Hansom (of hansom-cab fame) and E. Welch. The large hall contains a fine organ, and here in 1846 was given the first perform-ance of Mendelssohn's 'Elijah'. Outside are statues of Queen Victoria (by Brock, 1899) and James Watt (1736–1819), a fine work by Alexander Munro.

On the N. side of the square, at the end of Colmore Row, is the COUNCIL HOUSE, erected 1874–79 in an elaborate Renaissance style, with a dome and a clock tower (160 ft), known locally as 'Big Brum'. A bridge over Edmund St. connects it with the classical Council House Extension, completed in 1919.

The upper part of both wings of the Council House are occupied by the ***Corporation Art Gallery and Museum** (open free weekdays 10–6, Sun 2–5.30). The collection, one of the most important in England outside London, is noted for its examples of David Cox and Burne-Jones (both born in Birmingham) and its Pre-Raphaelite paintings and drawings.

From the main entrance, opposite the Town Hall in Congreve St., visitors ascend to the ROUND ROOM. To the right are the collections of APPLIED ART (costumes, silver, ceramics); ahead, across a bridge-passage are the NATURAL HISTORY and ARCHAEOLOGICAL DEPARTMENTS; while a vestibule (r.) leads to the main PICTURE GALLERIES.

APPLIED ART. The Evans Collection of postage stamps takes second place only to the Tapling Collection in the British Museum, and the Kineton silver medal of 1643 is unique. The famous collection of silver plate ranges from the Holte dish of the Restoration period, the Osbaldestone cup and cover by *P. Lamerie* (1733–34), to the late 18C Kandler salver (1775–76), the Darwin tureen, and silver designed by *Matthew Boulton*, and contemporary works. The ceramics exhibits illustrate the manufacturing processes, and there are fine enamels, ivories, and embroidery, with a miniature by *Nicholas Hilliard*.

PAINTINGS. Old Masters: *Simone Martini*, Saint holding a book; *Boccaccio Boccaccino*, Madonna with saints and donors; *Botticelli*, Descent of the Holy Ghost; *Carlo Dolci*, St Andrew praying (1643); *G. Crespi*, Girl with a bird; *Garófalo*, Agony in the Garden; *Luca Giordano*, Dives and Lazarus; *Carlevaris*, Arrival in Venice of the Earl of Manchester (1707); *Guardi*, S. Maria della Salute; Triptychs by *Scoreel* (?), and *Isenbrandt*; *Rembrandt*, Artist's father; *Rubens*, Head of a bearded man; *Ochterveld*, Music Lesson; *M. Stomer*, Old woman and a boy; *Van Goyen*, Estuary; *Claude*, Ponte Molle, Embarkation of St Paul (1655; painted on copper); *Subleyras*, Blessed John of Avila; *Lely*, Portrait of Oliver

Cromwell, Susannah and the Elders. English 18C paintings include portraits by *Gainsborough* (Sir Charles Holte of Aston), *Reynolds* (fine group of the Roffey family), *Romney* (Lady Holte), *George Knapton* (the Walthen family), and *Francis Cotes*; an interesting *Hogarth* (The distressed poet); *Opie* (Detected correspondence); two typical theatre scenes by *Zoffany*; and landscapes by *Gainsborough* and *Richard Wilson* (Tivoli; Okehampton Castle). The magnificent collection of ENGLISH WATER COLOURS, augmented by the Leslie Wright collection of over 300 works, starts with the 18C masters.

Among examples of the 19C are *Turner*, St Gotthard Pass; *Constable*, Autumn on the Stour, Cloud study; *Crome*, Walnut-tree walk, View near Norwich; *David Roberts*, St Stephen's, Vienna; *Diaz*, Woodland scene; *C. Pissarro*, Rouen. The collection of Pre-Raphaelite paintings is outstanding and includes many famous and popular works. The Pre-Raphaelite drawings should be noted; also examples of *G. F. Watts*, a portrait, by *Watts*, of Burne-Jones, and a self-portrait (1845) by *Holman Hunt*. *Thomas Couture* (Manet's master) is represented by a portrait, and *Degas* by his Roman beggar woman.

Recent and contemporary paintings include works by *Fantin-Latour*, *L. Pissarro*, *Courbet* (Venus), *Sisley*, *Orpen* (Ray Lankester), *Wilson Steer*, *Tonks*, *Eves* (Thomas Hardy), *Sickert* (Street in Dieppe; Miner), *Vlaminck*, *Gertler*, *Gilman*, *Augustus John* (King Feisal; Canadian soldier), *Jongkind* (Landscape), *Ethel Walker*, *Mary Cassatt* (Portrait), *Peploe*, *Lowry*, *Pryde* (Beggar), *Paul Nash* (Oxenbridge pond), *Stanley Spencer* (an unusual landscape), *Matthew Smith*, and *Graham Sutherland*. Water-colourists of the period are fully represented.

There are examples of sculpture by *Donatello* and of the school of *Verrocchio*; also *Rodin*, Eve; *Renoir*, Bust of Mme Renoir; *Epstein*, Lucifer; *Henry Moore* The Warrior.

ARCHAEOLOGY. *Near East Room. Stone and Bronze Age finds from excavations (partly financed by the city) at Jerusalem and Jericho (reconstruction of a tomb of c. 1800 B.C.); from Cyprus; from Ur (engraved bronze *Coffin); and from Nineveh (inscribed slab of Ashur-Nasir-Pal from Temple of Ishtar); ivories from the royal palace at Nimrud. Objects from Egypt (late 18C dynasty limestone bust from Thebes), Etruria, Greece (red-figure stamnos of 470 B.C.), and Rome (head of a young girl, 1C A.D.). Far Eastern, Mexican, and Peruvian antiquities, and part of a frieze of the Nereid Monument from Xanthus in Lycia (c. 400 B.C.). British history of the Roman, Anglo-Saxon, and Medieval periods is illustrated by local finds of pottery, glasswork, and jewellery; notable are the Hilton hoard (7C B.C.) from Dorset, and a rare 14C pewter cruet from Weoley Castle. A remarkable ethnographic collection illustrates Pacific magic; and the natural history section includes the comprehensive Lysaght Collection of birds.

Beyond Paradise Circus BROAD STREET leads to the important office centre of Five Ways. On its N. side, on the corner, is the HALL OF MEMORY, erected in 1925 in memory of the 14,000 Birmingham men who fell in 1914–18. Behind is a garden, and, beyond, *Baskerville House* (1939) with corporation offices. On the s. side are the *Engineering and Building Centre*, with a permanent trade exhibition, the *Municipal Bank* (1933) and the *Register Office*, in front of which stands a bronze group, by William Bloye (1956), commemorating Boulton, Watt, and Murdock.

Behind Baskerville House a new housing scheme includes restored cottages and is attractively landscaped to the canal (see below). Nearer Broad St. is *Bingley Hall*, an exhibition centre, and the site for the new Repertory Theatre; and farther along is the *Church of the Messiah* (Unitarian), with a monument to Dr Joseph Priestley, whose house (with his library and chemical apparatus) was burned down by the rioters of 1791.

Opposite the church, off Gas St., access can be gained to the *Gas St. Canal Basin*, from which it is a short walk by towpath under Broad St. to Worcester Bar, the centre of the English canal system. One branch leads viâ the basin and the attractive wooded scenery of Edgbaston to *King's Norton tunnel* (1½ m. long) and Worcester; another N.E. to Fazeley in a dramatic stretch passing the city's *Brindley Walk* scheme (see above), 13 locks and the G.P.O. tower; and the straight 'main line' with two towpaths, completed by Telford in 1838, viâ Smethwick to Wolverhampton, with the loops of the previous 'contour' canal on either side.

Beside the Town Hall in Victoria Square, the *General Post Office* contains a

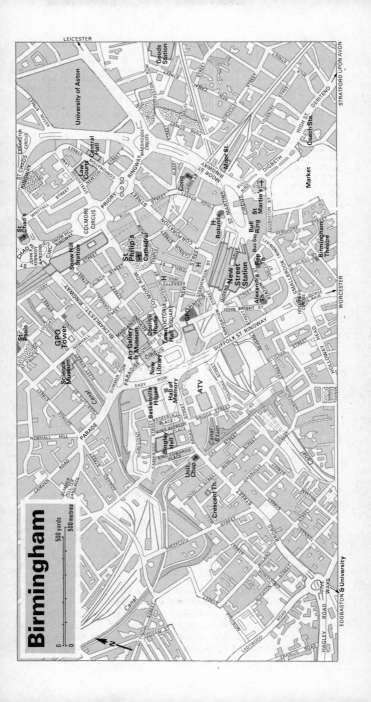

Birmingham

LEICESTER

STRATFORD UPON AVON

DERITEND

Goods Station

University of Aston

Market

WORCESTER

Coach Sta.

Central Hall

St Chad's
Circus

Law Courts

Corporation Street

Old Sq.

Masshouse Circus

Moor St.

Digbeth

St Chad's

Colmore Circus

Priory Ringway

Albert Street

Moor St. Ringway

Bull Ring

St Martins Circus

Bull Ring

St Martins

Pershore Street

Snow Hill Ringway

John Bright Street

Colmore Row

Snow Hill Station

St Philip's Cathedral

Rotunda

New Street Station

Birmingham Theatre

St Paul's

GPO Tower

Science Museum

Newhall

St Charles St. Ringway

Paradise Circus

Art Gallery & Museum

Council House

Town Hall

New Library

Victoria Square

GPO

Alexandra St. Rep Th.

Bus Sta.

Navigation Street

Suffolk St. Ringway

Smallbrook

Horse Fair

Canal

Easy Row

Baskerville House

Hall of Memory

ATV

Bath Row

Holloway Head

Parade

Newhall Hill

Bingley Hall

King Alfred's Place

King Edwards Place

Canal Basin

Bridge Street

Blucher Street

Gas Street

Granville Street

Oxford Street

Broad Street

Cambridge Street

Crescent

Unit. Chap.

Crescent Th.

Sheepcote

Camden Street

Canal

Ladywood

EDGBASTON & UNIVERSITY

HAGLEY ROAD

FRANCIS ROAD

ROAD WAYS

500 yards

500 metres

N

statue (by M. Noble) of Sir Rowland Hill (1795–1879), who was the son of a Birmingham schoolmaster. Behind, in Paradise Circus, the new Central Library and School of Music is under construction. The **Central Library** (800,000 vols) contains a Shakespeare Memorial Library (40,000 vols) and the important *Boulton and Watt Collection* of documents and engineering drawings. In Margaret St. beyond the Council House are the temporary premises of the **Birmingham and Midland Institute**, with a wide range of cultural activities, and a centre for Society meetings; it controls the *Birmingham Library*, a private subscription service founded in 1779.

In Newhall St., beyond Margaret St., at the corner of Fleet St. is the ***Museum of Science and Industry** (weekdays 10–5, Sat 10–5.30, Sun 2–5.30; 1st Wed in month 10–9) graphically illustrating the work of Birmingham engineers and craftsmen. It occupies an old factory next the canal. The large *Engineering Hall*, on the ground floor, with historic machines (beam-engines, turbines, glass-rolling mill, etc.) leads to the *Transport Section*, with a fine range of motor-cars from the 'Dog-cart' to John Cobb's Railton Mobil which attained a speed of 400 m.p.h. in 1947, Marshal Hindenburg's Benz car, and bicycles (from 1818) and motor-cycles. Other sections include machine tools, small arms (with historic rifles, pistols, and gunsmiths' tools), mechanical organs, the Charles Thomas Collection of writing implements, and an *Electrical Department* with control equipment.— The prominent *G.P.O. Tower* (1966; 350 ft: 498 ft with aerials) is near by in Lionel St. *St Paul's* to the N. in the old jewellery quarter, is an attractive church of 1779.

COLMORE ROW, lined with banking and insurance offices, leads N.E. from Victoria Sq. to the city's only central open space, *St Philip's Churchyard*. Here stands the Cathedral, by Thomas Archer, opened in 1715 as a parish church, with a good Baroque tower. The chancel was added by J. A. Chatwin in 1884 and the fine stained-glass windows are by Sir Edward Burne-Jones (1833–98), born in the neighbouring Bennett's Hill. The proposed widening of Colmore Row threatens the few remaining historic buildings here and in Waterloo St.

Beyond the gigantic new Colmore Circus, Snow Hill Ringway leads past the site of the former G.W.R. Station to St Chad's Circus, which contains a memorial to President Kennedy, with a mosaic by Kenneth Budd (1969; 300 ft by 16 ft). The near-by *St Chad's Roman Catholic Cathedral*, built in brick in a 14C Baltic style by A. W. Pugin in 1839–41, has a well-proportioned interior with a 16C oak pulpit from Louvain and 15C stalls from Cologne.

In Gosta Green, N.E. of the cathedral, and beyond the Inner Ring Road, is the **University of Aston in Birmingham**, formerly a College of Advanced Technology, chartered in 1966.

To the S. of St Philip's Churchyard attractive narrow streets lead to NEW STREET, the chief business street of Birmingham, which runs from Victoria Sq. to St Martin's Circus and the Bull Ring. At Stephenson Place under a modern tower block is the pedestrian access to the multi-level *New St. Station*.

CORPORATION STREET runs N. from this point, constructed through a slum district in 1875–82 for £1½ million. The original buildings have been replaced for the most part by post-war department stores, but at the N. end stand the red-brick *Victoria Law Courts* (1887–91), by Sir Aston Webb and Ingress Bell, and the *Methodist Central Hall* (1903, by E. and J. Harper), with a 200 ft tower. To the E., beyond High St., *Carr's Lane Congregational Church* has associations with John Angell James (1806–59), R. W. Dale (1859–95), and J. H. Jowett (1895–1911).

New St. meets High St. below a striking circular block of offices (1965, by J. Roberts), which adjoins the vast new BULL RING CENTRE. This is an air-conditioned multi-level shopping area of 23 acres, with markets, car parks, restaurants, and bus station. On a terrace above the open-air market stands Westmacott's bronze statue of Nelson (1809). To the S. is **St Martin's Church**, rebuilt in 1873–75 on the 14C plan. The spacious interior contains monuments of the De Bermingham family, and a window by Burne-Jones and Morris (s. transept).

From the E. end of St Martin's the oldest street in Birmingham runs S.E. The first section is called DIGBETH, and its continuation DERITEND, on the left side of which stands the *Old Crown House* (No. 188), a quaint medieval inn.

Among points of interest in the Eastern inner area are the fine Ionic portico of *Curzon St. Goods Station*, the original terminus from London, by Philip Hardwick, 1838; *St Alban's Church*, Conybere St. Highgate, an excellent example of J. L. Pearson's work (1881; 13C Gothic style), in one of the city's first post-war housing redevelopment areas, and near by in Stratford Place Bordesley, *Stratford House*, dating from 1601.

On the S.W. of the city is the spacious residential suburb of EDGBASTON. The N. part contains many early-19C houses, and in Hagley Rd., is the **Oratory of St Philip Neri**, established by Newman in 1847, the chief English home of the Congregation of the Oratory.

The memorial church of the *Immaculate Conception*, in an elaborate Baroque style, contains tablets to Cardinal Newman ('Ex umbris et imaginibus in veritatem') and his associates, and to alumni of the Oratory School (now at Goring) who fell in 1914–18. Newman (1801–90) is buried in the tiny graveyard adjoining the country-house of the Oratory Fathers on *Rednal Hill*, on the Bristol road.
A little s. of the Oratory is the *Botanical Garden* (weekdays 9–dusk, Sun from 10.30; fee). Hagley Rd. continues w. towards (1½ m.) *Lightwoods Park* (30 acres), which includes a 'Shakespeare Garden'. Adjoining is *Warley Park* (111 acres), a fine expanse of woodland, with a rose-garden, an old mansion known as 'Warley Abbey', and a golf-course.
Harborne, s.w. of Edgbaston, was the birthplace of the historian E. A. Freeman (1823–92), and in its churchyard is buried David Cox (1783–1859), the son of a Deritend blacksmith. *Harborne House* is now the residence of the Bishop of Birmingham.

In the suburb of Selly Oak, s. of Edgbaston and 3 m. from the centre of Birmingham, are the main buildings of **Birmingham University** (1909) from designs by *Sir Aston Webb* and *Ingress Bell*. The lofty central tower (325 ft) is a memorial of Joseph Chamberlain, first Chancellor of the University.

The University, incorporated in 1900, has about 7000 students, and succeeds *Mason College*, formerly in the city centre, endowed by Sir Josiah Mason in 1874–80 as a college of science. The buildings vary from the rigidly planned red-brick complex of 1909 to recent buildings which include a *Physical Education Centre*, by Chamberlain, Powell, and Bon, the *Arts and Commerce* tower by Arup Associates, and the *Refectory* and *Dept. of Education* by Casson and Conder who are also consultants for the overall plan. To the N.W., beyond the railway and canal, rises the large *Queen Elizabeth Hospital* (1938) with the Medical School.
Across Edgbaston Park Rd. are the buildings (1940) of **King Edward VI's School**, the successor of a foundation of 1552, moved from New St. in 1936. It is attended by 700 boys and there are over 3500 pupils in the other schools of the same foundation.

At the University's Edgbaston Park Rd. entrance is the **Barber Institute of Fine Arts**, founded by Lady Barber (d. 1933), widow of Sir Henry Barber. The building (1939), by *Robert Atkinson*, is preceded by an equestrian *Statue of George I (1722), by *Van Nost the Elder* (?), originally on Grattan Bridge in Dublin.

Within are a music room and a small but select *Art Collection (adm., on request at door, Mon–Fri 10–5). By the terms of the Trust ceramics are excluded, and any object of later date than 1900. The collection includes some fine Italian Renaissance bronzes, and sculptures by *Giov. Della Robbia, Barye, Rodin,* and *Degas*; a number of drawings and miniatures; and a choice collection of gold, silver, ivory, enamels, furniture, and tapestry. The superb collection of over 90 paintings of the European schools includes: Italian schools: *Giov. Bellini*, St Jerome, Portrait of a boy; *Matteo Giovanni*, Madonna; *Simone Martini*, St John the Evangelist; *Cima*, Crucifixion; and works by *Signorelli, Beccafumi, Dosso, Veronese*, and *Guardi*. Dutch and Flemish schools: *Rubens*, *Landscape; *Frans Hals*, Man holding a skull, an early work; *J. Ruysdael*, Landscape; *Van Dyck*, Ecce Homo; and works by *Steen, Cuyp*, and *Rembrandt* (?). The French school is represented by *Watteau*, Hurdy-gurdy man, a fine *Poussin*, an excellent *Claude* (landscape), a notable *Manet* (Carolus-Duran), a lovely landscape by *Monet* (Varengeville church), *Degas*, Racehorses, and typical works by *Courbet, Pissarro, Gauguin, Toulouse-Lautrec*, and *Bonnard*. English school: *Gainsborough*, The Harvest Wagon, and two fine portraits; *Reynolds, Romney*, and *Lawrence*, Portraits; landscapes by *Crome, Wilson*, and *Turner*; and works by *Sickert* and *Whistler*.

Out of the Quaker settlement for the study of ecclesiastical and social subjects established in 1903 at *Woodbrooke*, just beyond the University, has arisen the group of associated colleges of various denominations, known as the *Selly Oak Colleges*, with a common library named after J. Rendel Harris, director of Woodbrooke in 1903–18. To the w. are the remains of *Weoley Castle*, a 12–14C moated house, containing a good local museum (adm. Wed–Sun 2–5, Sat open at 10).

Bristol Rd. and the parallel Pershore Rd. pass a little to the w. of the *Warwickshire County Cricket Ground* (a test-match ground since 1957), and of *Cannon Hill Park* (81 acres), which is the most decorative of the Birmingham parks and contains a branch museum (weekdays 10–5, or 8; Sun from 2) with natural history collections and a Zoo. Here also are the 'Golden Lion', a half-timbered house (15–16C) brought from Deritend; and the modern buildings of the recently founded **Midland Arts Centre**, run by an independent education trust to introduce children and young people to the arts, which includes two theatres with a permanent company, art galleries, and studios, as well as sporting facilities. Beyond, in Moor Green, is *Highbury Park* (75 acres), long the home of Joseph Chamberlain.

In ASTON, on the N.E. side of the city, is *Aston Park* (49 acres), interesting chiefly for *Aston Hall (1618–35), a fine red-brick Jacobean house, the original of Washington Irving's 'Bracebridge Hall' (adm. weekdays 10–5, Sun in summer only, from 2; fee). The contents of special interest include the grand staircase, the long gallery, the room occupied by Charles I in 1642, and the Children's Museum. One room is fitted up with original panelling from the house in Old Square in which Dr Johnson used to visit his friend Edmund Hector. Lady Holte's drawing-room contains the 18C embroidered hangings made for it by a daughter of the house. —HANDSWORTH, adjoining Aston on the w., contained the famous *Soho Works* in which James Watt and Matthew Boulton demonstrated the powers of the steam engine (1775–1800). In 1848 the works were dismantled and the engine factory removed to Smethwick. Boulton, Watt, and Murdock all rest in *St Mary's Church*, the first with a monument by Flaxman, the other two with monuments by Chantrey. *Handsworth Park* (63 acres) is the venue of the autumn City of Birmingham Show. At *Perry Barr*, 3 m. N., is the church of *St Matthew's* (1964, by Robert Maguire and Keith Murray).

At *South Yardley*, 4 m. E. of the centre, is *Blakesley Hall, a half-timbered mansion of 1575, with a *Museum of Local History* (weekdays 9.30–6, Sun 2–5); and beyond the S.E. suburb of Sparkhill, is *Sarehole Mill*, once owned by Matthew Boulton (c. 1751–62), and fully operational, with a museum of agricultural history (daily in summer, 2–7, Sat 11–7).

About 4½ m. s. of Birmingham is **Bournville**, with the large cocoa and chocolate works of Messrs. Cadbury Brothers, a charming garden suburb, founded by George Cadbury in 1879 and placed under the Bournville Village Trust in 1900. With the declared object of "the amelioration of the condition of the working-class and labouring population, by the provision of improved dwellings", the 'model village' influenced municipal housing all over the country. On the estate two fine 14C houses of local type have been re-erected: *Selly Manor* and *Minworth Greaves* (adm. Tues, Wed, & Fri 1–5). The works and the housing estate may be visited on previous application to the Visitors' Department. The tower of the Day School contains one of the four British carillons (48 bells).—*King's Norton*, 1½ m. farther s., has an interesting church with a fine spire, a grammar school (partly 13C), an old half-timbered inn, used as church meeting-rooms, and the Serbian Orthodox church of St Lazar (1966).

FROM BIRMINGHAM TO LICHFIELD AND DERBY, 40 m. (railway from New St. to Lichfield in 40 min, to Derby viâ Tamworth in 40–60 min). A 38 runs N.E. through Aston and (5 m.) *Erdington*. About 1½ m. N.W. of the last is *Oscott College*, a Rom. Cath. seminary, of which Lord Acton (1834–1902) was a lay pupil.—7 m. **Sutton Coldfield** (Hotel; also at Walmley Golf Course), a pleasant residential town of 83,000 inhab., has a large rebuilt church retaining traces of E.E. work (Norman font; quaint monuments). *Old Moor Hall* (16C), the former residence of the bishops of Lichfield, and the *Moat House* and *Rectory* (by Sir Wm. Wilson, c. 1680) still survive; and *New Hall*, 1½ m. S.E., is a moated mansion dating in part from the 13C. *Sutton Park* (2090 acres) is very picturesque, with fine hollies. At 14 m. we cross Watling Street; c. 1 m. to the left is *Wall*, the Roman Letocetum, with remains of a Roman Bath (open daily, Sun from 2).—16 m. **Lichfield**, see Rte 39. We follow Icknield Street and beyond (21 m.) *Alrewas* (with an interesting church) we cross the Trent. Croxall and Elford (see p. 366) lie a short distance to the right, beyond the Tame.

28½ m. **Burton-upon-Trent** (by-pass; Hotel, also at Bretby, 3 m. E.), the metropolis of brewing (50,200 inhab.) is situated on the left bank of the Trent. It still preserves the very scanty remains of an 11C *Abbey*, to which it may owe its association with beer. Its six breweries produce about 3,000,000 barrels of beer annually, made with water from deep wells in the gravel beds above the town. About 6500 men in all are employed in the trade. The *Bass Museum of Brewing* occupies a tall joinery warehouse of 1866 within their brewery.

At (33½ m.) *Egginton Common*, beyond the Dove (here crossed by a 14C bridge), a road leads r. across the Trent for (2 m. S.E.) **Repton**, once the Mercian capital (*Hreopandum*), and seat of bishop. *St Wystan's Church*, with a lofty spire (210 ft), has a 10C chancel, below which and reached by two coeval staircases is a small crypt believed to go back to the 7C. *Repton School*, founded in 1557, is approached by the old gateway of a priory of Black Canons, parts of which are preserved.—At *Foremark*, 2 m. E., the church (1662) has outstanding early-Georgian ironwork by Bakewell; the Palladian Hall, by D. Hiorns is open daily 2.30–4.30, in late-June.—40 m. *Derby*, see Rte 43.

FROM BIRMINGHAM TO LEICESTER, 39½ m. (railway from New Street in c. 1 hr). A 47 runs E. through Saltley.—5 m. *Castle Bromwich* is the site of the annual British Industries Fair (May).—10 m. *Coleshill* has a Dec. and Perp. church with a fine spire (rebuilt 1887), a Norman font, and good monuments. *Maxstoke Castle* (no adm.), 2 m. E., is a fortified and moated mansion of 1346, containing the chair in which Henry VII was crowned on Bosworth Field. About 2 m. farther S. are the ruins of *Maxstoke Priory* (14C), now partly incorporated in a farm-house. —13 m. *Shustoke* was the birthplace of Sir Wm. Dugdale (1605–86), the antiquary, who is buried in the church.—At (14 m.) *Over Whitacre* we turn right and then left. —22 m. *Nuneaton* (Rte 39).—27 m. *Hinckley*, a hosiery and shoemaking town (48,000 inhab.) with a large church, lies c. 5 m. S.E. of Bosworth Field.—39½ m. *Leicester*, see Rte 43.

FROM BIRMINGHAM TO KIDDERMINSTER, 18¾ m. (railway from New Street in 40–45 min; not Sun). We follow Hagley Rd. (A 456) nearly due w.—9 m. *Halesowen* (54,000 inhab.) has a ruined abbey (13C) and the grave of the poet Shenstone (1714–63; in the churchyard).—11 m. The road skirts the beautiful park of *Hagley Hall*, the seat of the Lytteltons since the 13C, extolled by Horace Walpole and by James Thomson. Here, early in 1606, betrayed by a servant, John Winter, last survivor of the Gunpowder plotters, was captured. To the S. rise the *Clent Hills* (1035 ft; N.T.: view-indicator). About 2 m. N. is **Stourbridge** (Hotels; 54,300 inhab.), with iron works and fire-brick factories, and the centre of a glass-making industry introduced about 1556 by refugees from Hungary and Lorraine.—17 m. *Kidderminster*, see p. 347.

FROM BIRMINGHAM TO STRATFORD-ON-AVON, 28 m. (railway from Moor Street in 1 hr). A 34 runs S.E. through the suburbs of Sparkbrook and Hall Green.— 11 m. *Hockley Heath* (Motel). *Lapworth*, 1½ m. S.E., has a church with some very early details (possibly Saxon); *Packwood House*, 2 m. E., is a half-timbered mansion (partly 15C), with furniture and tapestry, and a 17C yew-garden (N.T.; open April–Sept, Tues, Wed, Thurs, Sat, & BH, 2–7, Sun from 2.30; Oct–March, Wed, Sat, & BH, 2–5, Sun from 2.30; fee).—16 m. *Henley-in-Arden*, a quaint little town in the *Forest of Arden*, has a Perp. church, an old Guildhall (1448; now in private occupation), the White Swan Hotel dating from the early 17C (restored; now a restaurant), and a 13C (?) market-cross.—28 m. *Stratford-on-Avon*, see Rte 34C.

From Birmingham to *London*, see Rte 32; to *Chester*, see Rte 41; to *Gloucester* and *Bristol*, see Rte 35; to *Shrewsbury*, see Rtes 41, 42; to *Worcester*, see Rte 35.

34 THE SHAKESPEARE COUNTRY

The three chief centres of the 'Shakespeare Country', all affording comfortable accommodation and plentiful means of communication are *Leamington*, *Warwick*, and *Stratford-upon-Avon* itself. Leamington offers the entertainments of an inland watering-place to fill up the hours not devoted to literary exploration; Warwick, only 2 m. from Leamington, what Sir Walter Scott describes as the "fairest monument of ancient and chivalrous splendour which yet remains uninjured by time"; and Stratford is the very heart and focus of the Shakespearian associations. All three are surrounded by charming country.

Road Routes. A good approach by road from London follows the Oxford and Worcester road (Rtes 30, 31) for 72 m. to a point c. 1¼ m. short of Chipping Norton. The Stratford road (A 34) there bears r., passing within ¾ m. of the Rollright Stones (p. 303).—76½ m. *Long Compton*.—82½ m. *Shipston-on-Stour* (Hotel) is about 5 m. w. of Compton Wynyates.

*Compton Wynyates (Marquess of Northampton) lies secluded in a richly wooded hollow (adm. 2–6, Easter weekend, Wed, Sat & BH, Apr–Sept, and Sun in June–Aug; fee). The beautiful Tudor mansion, a harmonious combination of brick, timber, and stone, is built around a courtyard entered by a porch over the door of which are the arms of Henry VIII. The interior, notable for the number of its rooms and its secret staircases and hiding-places, contains a fine panelled Great Hall, with a timber roof brought from Fulbrook Castle; a Chapel, divided by a carved oak screen; Henry VIII's Room; and a Council Chamber, in the great tower, above which is a Priest's Room, approached by three separate staircases. The gardens have fine topiary; the detached chapel, to the N., (1665) has mutilated 15–16C monuments and splendid hatchments.

Ilmington (Hotel), 4 m. N.W. of Shipston, has a good Norman church, while *Barcheston*, 1 m. S.E. of Shipston, with alabaster monuments in its church, was the original home of tapestry-weaving in England (16C) by Wm. Sheldon.—Our road descends the valley of the Stour, keeping near the river almost all the way to (93½ m.) **Stratford-upon-Avon**. Thence to *Warwick* and *Leamington*, see below.

From London to Leamington and Warwick by other roads, see Rte 32.

Railway Approaches. FROM LONDON (Paddington) *Stratford* (121½ m.) is reached viâ Leamington and Hatton in 2½ hrs.—From BIRMINGHAM, see Rte 33.—Travellers from LIVERPOOL or MANCHESTER reach Stratford viâ Birmingham.

Leamington is reached from LONDON (Paddington), 87½ m. in 1½–2 hrs, or from OXFORD, 42½ m., in ¾ hr; change at Leamington for *Warwick* (2 m.), both of which are easily reached from Birmingham (Moor St.).

A Leamington and Kenilworth

ROYAL LEAMINGTON SPA, a favourite inland watering-place and residential resort (45,000 inhab.), is situated on the Leam, an affluent of the Avon. Its chalybeate and saline springs first attracted attention at the end of the 18C and the first bath was opened in 1786, but its real prosperity dates from about 1840, when Dr Jephson was the leading physician.

Hotels in the Parade, Kenilworth Rd., etc.

Post Office at Victoria Bridge.—INFORMATION BUREAU at the Pump Room.

Buses from High St. to *Kenilworth* and *Coventry*; *Warwick* and *Stratford-upon-Avon*; etc.

Boats on the Leam at *Adelaide Bridge* and *Mill Garden*.
Golf Courses at Milverton (¾ m. N.) and at Whitnash (2¾ m. S.).—TENNIS in Jephson Gardens and Victoria Park.
Music. *Orchestra* daily in the Pump Room; also in the Town Hall.

The distinguished visitors to Leamington include Nathaniel Hawthorne, who wrote some of his English Notes at No. 10 Lansdowne Circus (N.E. of the Town Hall), and Mr Dombey, who was here presented by Major Bagstock to Mrs Skewton and Edith Granger. It was at Leamington that Cobden sought out John Bright three days after the death of his wife (1841), and called on him to lay aside his private grief and work for the repeal of the Corn Laws. The Manor House Hotel claims to be the site of the world's first lawn tennis club (1872).

In the middle of the town, where the Leam is crossed by the Victoria Bridge, are the gardens of the *Royal Pump Room and Baths* (including swimming-baths). To the N. extends the spacious Parade; to the S. is Bath St. (leading to the station), with the unusual 19C church of *All Saints*, outside which is the original *Old Well*. Facing the Pump Room Gardens are the beautiful *Jephson Gardens*, with the *Mill Garden* farther away, S. of the river; while in the other direction from the Pump Room the York Walk skirts the Leam for ¾ m. to the large *Victoria Park*. The *Art Gallery & Library* (adm. free; closed Sun morn.) is in Avenue Rd., off Bath Rd.

The following places of interest are within a radius of 5 m. from Leamington: *Warwick*, 2 m. W.; *Kenilworth*, 4½ m. N.; *Stoneleigh Abbey*, 3½ m. N.; *Offchurch* (3 m. E.), with a 13C church with Norman details and a Tudor manor-house (*Offchurch Bury*); and *Chesterton* (4½ m. S.E.), with a fine Perp. church (monuments of the Peyto family) and an imposing windmill (1632), ascribed to Inigo Jones but more probably by Nich. Stone, the sculptor of the monuments.

FROM LEAMINGTON TO KENILWORTH (4½ m.; bus every 15–20 min.). A 452 runs N., then N.W. Just beyond (2¾ m.) *Chesford Bridge* (Hotel), on the Avon, a road diverges on the right for *Ashow* and (2 m.) Stoneleigh Abbey (see below). In 1 m. more we reach *Castle End*, an outlying part of Kenilworth. The castle is about 1 m. N.W. (l.).

Kenilworth (Hotels) is a town of 20,100 inhab. with the scanty remains of an old priory (12C) and a fine Norman door (inserted) in the tower of a much-restored church. Its widespread fame is mainly due to Sir Walter Scott's romance, the first design of which is said to have been made in 1815 in a room shown at the King's Arms. *Kenilworth Castle (adm. daily, Sun in winter from 2; fee), the stately red bulk of which will hardly disappoint the visitor, is a magnificent feudal ruin in a charming setting.

It was founded, soon after 1120, by Geoffrey de Clinton, Treasurer of England, and the keep was probably erected by his son. Henry II, John, and Henry III visited it and the outer wall was built in 1203–16. In 1244 the castle was granted to Simon de Montfort, and in 1266 it was taken from his son, Simon, by Henry III's forces after a siege of nine months. Its possession then oscillated between the house of Lancaster and the Crown. John of Gaunt added the Strong Tower, the Banqueting Hall, and the southern rooms (1390 et seq.). From 1399 the castle continued to be a royal fortress until 1563, when Queen Elizabeth conferred it on Robert Dudley, Earl of Leicester. He improved and enlarged the building and entertained his sovereign here in 1565, 1568, 1572, and 1575, the lavish pageants of the last year being those so graphically described by Scott. In 1611 the castle reverted to the Crown. The process of destruction was begun by Col. Hawkesworth and the other Cromwellian officers to whom the pile was awarded in 1648. On the Restoration it passed into the hands of Lord Hyde, with whose descendants, the Earls of Clarendon, it remained until 1937, when it became national property. It has since been carefully restored.

Visitors enter the base-court or OUTER WARD by a gate on the N. side near *Leicester's Gatehouse* (1570; no adm.), the only part of the building still habitable. To the left are *Leicester's Stables*, and *Lunn's*, the *Water*, and *Mortimer's Towers*. On the other side are the main buildings enclosing the INNER COURT. To the right of the entrance to this is the so-called *Cæsar's Tower*, a massive Norman keep (1160–70), with walls 14 ft thick. It had at least two floors. Adjoining this on the same side are the scanty remains of the *Kitchens*, beyond which is the *Strong Tower* (c. 1390), the 'Mervyn Tower' of Scott, with Amy Robsart's room. The W. side of the Inner Court is occupied by the late 14C *Great Hall* (90 ft × 45 ft), with two fine oriels (one in the Sainteowe Tower) at its s. end. On the s. side of the court are the *White Hall*, or *Great Chamber*, and the *Second Chamber*, terminating John of Gaunt's work. In the S.E. angle are *Leicester's Buildings*, containing the rooms occupied by Queen Elizabeth in 1575. *Henry VIII's Lodgings*, on the E. side, have practically disappeared. The *Garden* was on the N. side of the keep, and to the w. of it were the *Pleasance* and the *Swan Tower*, near which Scott places the encounter of Amy Robsart and the Queen—although Amy died in 1560, five years before Elizabeth's first visit. Between Mortimer's Tower and the *Gallery Tower* is a causeway, 150 yds long, which served as a tilt-yard and also as a dam for the artificial mere which defended the s. and w. sides of the castle. This lake was drained by Hawkesworth in 1649.

About 3 m. E. of Kenilworth and 4½ m. N. of Leamington is **Stoneleigh Abbey**, a palatial Italianate edifice by Smith 'of Warwick' (1714–26), in a park famous for its huge oaks. Some Norman doorways (fine mouldings) of the original Cistercian monastery (1154) on the site still exist; also the old gatehouse and other 14C remains. The church of *Stoneleigh* has a Norman font and many Leigh monuments. In 1963 the Park became the permanent site for the Royal Agricultural Show (early July); here also takes place the International Dairy Event (Apr).

B Warwick

WARWICK, an ancient county town (18,300 inhab.), is situated on a rocky hill on the N. side of the Avon. Though founded in 914, it takes its character from the rebuilding after a fire in 1694, and has recently been relieved of much heavy traffic by a new by-pass. The best general view of the town, which contains many old houses, is obtained on the approach by the lower road from Leamington.

Hotels, mainly modest in size, near the centre.
Buses from Market Sq. to all destinations.
Racecourse (with golf links) w. of the town; meetings in Feb, Apr, Sept, Nov.— BOATS on the Avon.

The Coventry road and the Leamington road meet below the town to the E. Here, on the left, is the house known as *St John's*, a picturesque 17C building on an older foundation, opened in 1961 as a county and regimental museum (closed Tues and, in winter, Sun). Higher up, on the right, is the house where W. S. Landor (d. 1864) was born in 1775. Smith St. leads up to the *East Gate*, a relic of the old wall, crowned with a Gothic chapel of 1788. The dignified Jury St. leads past the *Pageant House* (l.), forming with *Court House* a fine group, now the Borough Offices, at the central crossing.

In Castle St. (l.) is the 16C house of Thomas Oken (d. 1573), now the *Doll Museum*, containing the Joy Robinson collection of dolls and toys (adm. 10–6, Sun 2.30–5; winter 2–4.30 Fri–Sun; fee).

Church St. leads to the right to the collegiate church of **St Mary**, the tower, nave, transepts, and aisles of which were rebuilt after the fire of 1694 by Sir William Wilson, with an interesting mixture of Gothic and Renaissance features. The tower (174 ft high) may be ascended on application (view; fee).

A cenotaph at the w. entrance is in honour of men of the Royal Warwickshire Regt. who fell in 1914–18; the regimental chapel, with good modern glass, is in the N. transept. The lofty chancel (1394) has a noteworthy vault. In the centre is a *Tomb with recumbent effigies of Thomas Beauchamp, Earl of Warwick (d. 1369), the founder of the choir, and his countess—a work that need not fear comparison with contemporary Italian sculpture. In front of the altar is a brass to Cecilia Puckering (d. 1636), with an anagram on her name. To the N. of the choir is the former chapter house, containing the ponderous tomb of Fulke Greville, Lord Brooke, who was assassinated in 1628. In the Norman crypt (adm. on application) is an old ducking-stool.

To the s. of the choir is the *Beauchamp Chapel (adm. fee), a wonderful example of the florid Perp. style of its period (1443–64). The Bear and Ragged Staff, the cognisance of the Warwicks, are much in evidence in the decoration. Outside the entrance (r.) is the brass of Thomas Beauchamp, Earl of Warwick (d. 1401), who finished the choir, and of his wife. In the centre is the tomb of the founder, Richard Beauchamp, Earl of Warwick (d. 1439), with a brass effigy surmounted by a herse of rare design. By the N. wall is the gorgeously painted monument of Robert Dudley, Earl of Leicester (d. 1588), and his wife Lettice (d. 1634). By the s. wall is the tomb of Robert Dudley (d. 1584), his infant son. To the s.w. of the founder's tomb is the altar-tomb of Ambrose Dudley, 'the good Earl of Warwick' (d. 1590). The windows contain contemporary glass and the stalls date from 1449, while over the w. door is a painted Last Judgment of 1678 (damaged in the fire). Between the chapel and the chancel is the so-called Little Chantry with rich fan-vaulting and niches and a curious wooden piscina.

Returning to the main thoroughfare, we follow the High St. past the *Aylesford Hotel* (1696) and the *Warwick Arms Hotel* (1790), the vista being closed by the *West Gate* (12C) with a prominent 16C chapel used for worship by the Hospital brethren. The *LORD LEYCESTER HOSPITAL (r.) is a fine 14–15C group comprising the buildings of three religious guilds converted by the Earl of Leicester in 1571 into an asylum for twelve poor brethren. It is bounded on the w. side by the great town wall.

The buildings (weekdays 10–6, fee), much restored, are picturesque from the court. The brethren, who are old soldiers and wear a black gown on state occasions, still retain the original silver badges of 1571. The Guild Hall of the s. range forms a museum containing part of a curtain said to have been worked by Amy Robsart, a 'Saxon' chair, and one in which James I sat in 1617. The Great Hall has a fine roof of oak (not chestnut). The Chaplain's Dining Hall is a regimental museum of the Queen's Own Hussars. A Malt House and the former Anchor Inn, both 17C, are now flats for the brethren.—Beyond the gate, at the foot of the hill, is a fine 17C timbered manor (now a restaurant).

To reach *Warwick Castle, which stands on the s. side of the town, overlooking the Avon, we return to the East Gate and follow Castle Hill, to the right. It is shown to visitors from 10 or 10.30 to 4 or 5.30 March–Oct; tickets are obtained at the shop opposite the lodge. The castle may be said to represent the transition period, when the formidable but dreary strongholds of early times were gradually being replaced by the more domestic type of fortified house. The exterior is a noble example of 14C fortification, while the interior is a magnificent 17–18C mansion.

It seems reasonably certain that Ethelfleda, daughter of Alfred the Great, erected a fortress of some kind here about 915, though the mound to the w. of the castle is probably a Norman motte. The fortress was strengthened by Earl Turchil at the behest of William the Conqueror. The outer walls were rebuilt and strong towers and gateways erected in the 14C. Large sums were expended by Fulke Greville (early 17C) in repairing it and making it "the most princely seat within these midland parts of the realm". During the Civil War it was regarded as of great importance, and in 1642 it made a successful defence against the Royalists. Extensive restorations were made after a disastrous fire in 1871.

From the *Porter's Lodge* (1800) a winding approach, cut in the solid rock for over 100 yds, leads to the *Outer Court* and the *Double Gateway* (portcullis) between the massive *Cæsar's Tower* (l.; 106 ft) and *Guy's Tower* (r.; 93 ft though apparently the higher). In the well-turfed *Inner Court*, the *Bear* and *Clarence Towers* are on the right, a castle-mound (see above) in front, and the domestic buildings on the left. The entrance to the State Apartments is near the farther end of the left-hand range. Visitors are conducted in parties.

The Great Hall is the largest of the series of communicating rooms overlooking the river (over 330 ft in total length; views). A good collection of arms and armour includes a helmet worn by Cromwell, the armour of Lord Brooke (killed at Lichfield in 1643), and a huge camp-kettle used by Warwick the King-maker. The other rooms shown (mostly decorated in 1770–90) contain interesting paintings, sculpture, furniture, china, and curiosities. Among the paintings are many portraits by Rubens (Loyola), Van Dyck (Charles I, Strafford, and Prince Rupert), Holbein, and Lely; and Frances, Countess of Warwick, by Carolus-Duran. Other noteworthy objects are a clock of Marie Antoinette in the Boudoir, the chimney-piece of the Cedar Drawing Room, the Venetian inlaid table in the Gilt Drawing Room, and portraits of Sibylla of Cleves, by Lucas Cranach, and Elizabeth of Bohemia, by Gaspard de Crayer. The Armoury Passage contains a fine collection of armour. In the *Gardens*, beyond the opposite side of the Inner Court, is a greenhouse containing the Warwick Vase (5½ ft high), found in Hadrian's Villa at Tivoli and believed to be a Roman work of Hadrian's time.—The extensive and attractive *Park*, through which the Avon runs, possesses many fine trees and peacocks.

From the castle gate Mill St., with some of the most attractive old houses, descends to the Avon, affording a view of the castle and of the broken 14C bridge.—The main Banbury road leads to the stone bridge (1790), 105 ft in span, which affords a better *View of the castle. On the left is the pleasant *St Nicholas's Park* (rfmts; swimming pool). Beyond the river is Bridgend with some timbered buildings and (l. in Myton Rd.) *Warwick School* for boys, in modern buildings but claiming a continuous existence since 1100.

The road to (4½ m.) *Kenilworth* (and Coventry) leads N. past a statue of Guy and the boar, by Keith Godwin (1964), to (1¼ m.) *Guy's Cliffe*, the romantic site above a pool of the Avon, of a 15C chantry with a gigantic statue of the knight. Here, says legend, Guy, Earl of Warwick, lived the life of a hermit after slaying the Dun Cow and the giant Colbrand and performing heroic deeds in the Holy Land. Near by is the picturesque *'Saxon Mill'* (Restaurant), often painted by David Cox and others.—To the left, a little farther on, rises *Blacklow Hill*, the spot where Piers Gaveston, the haughty favourite of Edward II, was beheaded in 1312 by "barons lawless as himself".—2¾ m. *Leek Wootton*. We join the route from Leamington at (3¾ m.) *Castle End*.

FROM WARWICK TO STRATFORD-UPON-AVON the direct distance by ROAD (A 46) is 8 m., but the most interesting route is 1½–2 m. longer. This route, beginning at the West Gate, at first follows the right bank of the Avon, and keeps to the left at (1½ m.) *Longbridge*. At (3 m.) *Barford* we cross to the left bank of the Avon.—4 m. *Wasperton* has a rebuilt church and an old hexagonal dovecote. At (4¾ m.) the fork we keep to the right.—5½ m. *Charlecote* has a rebuilt church, incorporated in which is the old Lucy Chapel (17C), with three handsome monuments of members of the Lucy family (17C). The road now skirts the E. and S. sides of *Charlecote Park* (N.T.), containing the noble Elizabethan mansion (1558; 'modernised' in 1847–67) of the Lucys (fine gatehouse; good pictures and furniture; Shakespearian relics; adm. May–Sept daily, except Mon unless BH, 11.15–5.45; fee). Tradition tells that the youthful Shakespeare was arrested for killing deer in Charlecote Park and brought before Sir Thomas Lucy (caricatured in 'Justice Shallow'). Most buses make the pleasant detour to *Wellesbourne Hastings* (Hotel), 1 m. S.E. of Charlecote. —7½ m. *Alveston*, a pretty village on the Avon, to the right.—8¼ m. *Tiddington*, with picturesque cottages.—9¾ m. *Stratford-upon-Avon*, see below.

From Warwick to *Birmingham* and to *London*, see Rte 32A.

C Stratford-upon-Avon

STRATFORD-UPON-AVON, a prosperous market town (19,400 inhab.) of great antiquity, is pleasantly situated, mainly on the right (w.) bank of the Avon. It owes its prosperity to the fact that Shakespeare was born here in 1564. Prior to 1769, when Garrick held the first Jubilee (attended by Boswell and all but ruined by bad weather), little interest seems to have been taken in the town on this account, but now it "stands in the position of an ancient shrine, drawing a pilgrimage of modern origin". Over 250,000 travellers visit the birth-house every year. The wide streets contain many good 18C houses as well as the half-timbered buildings for which they are renowned. Stratford still retains its ancient 'mop' or fair (12 Oct) and is commonly called 'on-Avon', though officially 'upon'.

Many excellent and picturesque **Hotels** and **Restaurants** in the town and by the river. Also innumerable *Private Hotels*, *Guest Houses*, and *Cafés*.

Car Parks near the Memorial Fountain, and Bridgefoot.

Post Office, Bridge St.—INFORMATION CENTRE, 20 Chapel St. (to be moved to Quiney House).—BRITISH COUNCIL CENTRE, Hall's Croft, Old Town.

Buses from Bridgefoot to *Warwick*, *Shipston-on-Stour*, *Birmingham*, *Leamington*, *Kenilworth*, *Coventry*, *Evesham*, etc.—PLEASURE BOATS may be hired from Clopton Bridge and (on the canal) at Wilmcote.

Golf Course, Tiddington Rd. (off Banbury Rd.).—SWIMMING POOL (river), Warwick Rd.

SHAKESPEARE'S BIRTHPLACE TRUST administers the following five properties: the **Birthplace, Anne Hathaway's Cottage, Hall's Croft, New Place**, and **Mary Arden's House**, for which an inclusive ticket may be obtained (cheaper than separate adm. to each). Opening hours: Apr–Oct, weekdays 9–6 or 7, Sun 2–6 (Birthplace and Cottage from 10); Nov–Mar weekdays only, 9–12.45, 2–4; Birthplace also Sun 1.30–4.30.

John Shakespeare, the son of Richard Shakespeare, a small farmer at Snitterfield (3¾ m. N.) and father of the poet, settled in Stratford c. 1551. According to varying accounts he was a glover, a woolstapler, a butcher, and a corn merchant, carrying on business in Henley St. In 1557 he married Mary, youngest daughter of Robert Arden, a substantial yeoman of Wilmcote (3 m. N.W.). In 1565 he became an Alderman, in 1568 High Bailiff. WILLIAM SHAKESPEARE, his third child and eldest son, was born on 23 April, 1564. Shakespeare is believed to have learned his "small Latin and less Greek" at the Grammar School between 1571 and 1577, and he seems to have married Anne Hathaway in 1582. There were three children of this union, Susanna (b. 1583) and the twins Hamnet and Judith (b. 1585). Shakespeare went to London soon after his marriage. The exact date of his return is not known, but it is probable that he attended Hamnet's funeral in 1596. Thenceforward his relations with his native town were uninterrupted, and he was formally described as 'of Stratford-on-Avon, gentleman'. He bought New Place in 1597, and in later days acquired considerable property in and near the town. He retired to live at Stratford in 1611, and died there on 23 April, 1616. His wife survived him seven and a half years. Both his daughters married, but Susanna's (Mrs Hall's) only child (first Mrs Nash and afterwards Lady Bernard) died childless, and the three children of Judith (Mrs Thomas Quiney) all predeceased their mother.

*Shakespeare's Birthplace (adm. see above) consists of two tenements now forming a detached half-timbered building on the N. side of Henley St., near the centre of the town. In 1847 this double house was purchased by public subscription as a national memorial of the poet and was vested in trustees. The W. part of the building is furnished in the manner of a family home of Shakespeare's day, while the E. part is presented as a museum, with a unique collection of books, manuscripts, pictures and objects illustrative of the life, times, and works of the poet.

Shakespeare inherited the double house on the death of his father, but left it to the occupation of his mother and sister. On the death of the latter in 1646 it passed to Mrs Hall (see above). Lady Bernard (see above) bequeathed it to Thomas Hart, grand-nephew of the poet, and it remained with his family till 1806. The w. house was at one time used as a butcher's shop, and the E. house was long an inn ('Maiden Head', then 'Swan & Maiden Head').

The door of the w. house or birthplace opens into the living-room and at the back are the kitchen and two other smaller rooms. An oak staircase ascends to the *Birth Room*. Scratched on the window-panes are the signatures of Scott, Carlyle, Henry Irving, and Ellen Terry.—The *Garden*, at the back, contains flowers, shrubs and trees mentioned in the plays.

The two coeval houses to the s. of the birthplace, given by Mr Andrew Carnegie in 1903, now serve as the office and library of the Shakespeare Birthplace Trust.—Likewise in Henley St. is the SHAKESPEARE CENTRE, opened in 1964 to house both the Birthplace Library and the Royal Shakespeare Library. The entrance has engraved glass panels depicting characters from the plays, by J. Hutton. On the opposite side, farther on, is *Tussaud's Shakespearian Waxworks* (fee).

Henley St. ends, on the s.e., at *High Street*, where, at the corner of Bridge St. (l.), stands the *Quiney House*, long occupied by Judith Shakespeare with her vintner-husband Thomas Quiney and now a snack bar with a 'crypt café' in the alleged old Town Jail. On the other side of the street (farther on) is *Harvard House* (9–1, 2–5.15, fee; members of Harvard Univ. free), a half-timbered edifice of 1596, so called as the early home of Katharine Rogers, who married Robert Harvard and became the mother of the founder of Harvard University. It was restored under the supervision of Marie Corelli, the novelist (d. 1924), and presented to the University in 1909, to serve as a rendez-vous for American visitors. The adjacent *Garrick Inn* and *Tudor House*, at the corner of Ely St., are pretty half-timbered dwellings (judiciously restored).

High St. is continued by Chapel St., at the corner of which (l.) is the *Town Hall* (1767). The statue of Shakespeare on the N. front was presented by Garrick in 1769. In Chapel St. are the picturesque *Shakespeare* (l.) and *Falcon* Inns (r.) and at the end, also to the left, beyond a shop in which the 'Shakespeare Head Press' functioned in 1904–30, is the **New Place Estate**, which includes the vacant site of Shakespeare's New Place and its garden and Nash's House (tablet on wall).

The original New Place, the largest house in Stratford, was built by Sir Hugh Clopton, c. 1483. Shakespeare bought it in 1597, and here he died. In 1756 it came into the possession of the Rev. Francis Gastrell, who tore it down in 1759 on account of a quarrel about assessment, thereafter leaving the town "amidst the rages and curses of the inhabitants".—Nash's House, next door, inherited by Shakespeare's granddaughter from Thomas Nash, her first husband, belongs to the Shakespeare Birthplace Trust (adm. p. 335). In this house furniture and other exhibits depict the background of Shakespeare's England, together with certain aspects of local history, including the Garrick Jubilee of 1769. Through Nash's House we obtain access to the site of New Place, containing the foundations of Shakespeare's house, in the rear of which is the Elizabethan Knot Garden. The *Poet's Great Garden* (entr. in Chapel Lane) is open to the public; in the central lawn is a mulberry tree grown from a slip of a tree planted by Shakespeare and cut down by the irascible Gastrell in 1756.

Opposite New Place, at the corner of Chapel Lane and Church St., is the *Guild Chapel*, with a nave rebuilt by Sir Hugh Clopton (1495), and a wall-painting of the Last Judgment (c. 1500) on the arch above the late 13C chancel. Adjoining this, in Church St., is the *Guildhall*, a half-timbered edifice, built in 1416–18 for the Holy Cross Guild to replace an earlier hall. It is usually assumed that the poet's interest in the drama may have been first aroused by the performances of strolling

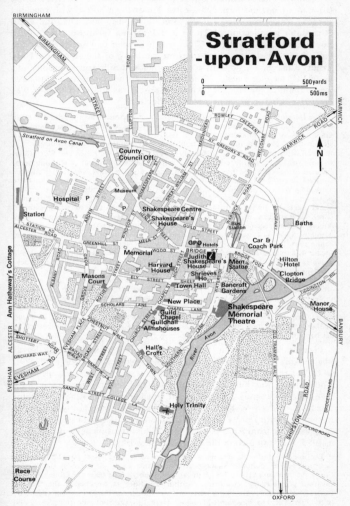

players here. It is now occupied by the *Grammar School* in which Shakespeare was educated (adm. in the Easter and Summer holidays 9–12.30, 2–4.30; fee).

Flight-Lieut. Warneford, V.C. (d. 1915), the first airman to destroy a zeppelin (at Bruges; June 1915), was a pupil of the school.—The adjoining *Almshouses* were originally maintained by the Guild. Farther on, the 18C *Mason Croft* is now the Shakespeare Institute of Birmingham University.

From the end of Church St. we follow Old Town to the left, passing (l.) *Hall's Croft* (adm. p. 335), a fine Tudor town house, with spacious garden, which belonged to Shakespeare's son-in-law, Dr John Hall. It contains a collection of Tudor and Jacobean furniture. Part of the house is used as a Festival Club, which is open to visitors. Near the end of this road, amid lime-trees on the bank of the Avon, is *Holy Trinity Church, a cruciform edifice with 13C tower and transepts, and early 14C nave and aisles. The chancel and the clerestory of the nave were rebuilt in the late 15C, when the porch was added. The spire was erected in 1763 in place of a wooden one.

The **Interior** (fee) is imposing and contains many monuments that deserve more attention than the Shakespearian pilgrim is usually willing to divert from the GRAVE OF SHAKESPEARE, who lies on the N. side of the chancel, covered by a slab with a doggerel inscription popularly ascribed to the poet himself. On the wall is his monument, consisting of a bust under an arch with two Corinthian columns of black marble, supporting a cornice and entablature. The monument, the colouring of which has been reproduced, was executed, soon after Shakespeare's death, by Garret (Gerard) Johnson of Southwark. The bust has little merit as a work of art and probably not much more as a portrait. The author of the epitaph is unknown. "Whatever their defects of style, the lines presented Shakespeare to his fellow-townsmen as the greatest man of letters of his time" (Lee). The adjacent window, representing the Seven Ages of Man, was erected by American admirers (1885). Close to the poet's grave are those of his wife, his daughter Susanna ("witty above her sexe") with her husband ("renowned in the healing art"), and Thomas Nash, first husband of her daughter. [Judith Shakespeare was buried in the churchyard, without a stone; the exact spot of Hamnet's grave is unknown; Lady Bernard is buried at Abington, p. 393]. The chancel contains also the tombs of its builder, Dean Balsall (d. 1491), and of Shakespeare's friend John Combe (d. 1614).—In the s. transept is another American window (1896), and a quaint polyglot epitaph to a 17C woollen-draper; also a memorial tablet, by Frampton, to actors who fell in 1914–18, with verses by Kipling. The *Clopton Chapel* (formerly the Lady Chapel), at the E. end of the N. aisle, contains monuments of the Cloptons. At the w. end of the N. aisle are the font in which Shakespeare was christened, and a case with the registers showing the entries of his baptism and burial.

Likewise on the Avon, fully ¼ m. N. of the church, is the **Royal Shakespeare Theatre**. The original MEMORIAL THEATRE (1877–79), where Sir Frank Benson produced all Shakespeare's plays except 'Titus Andronicus', was burned down in 1926 and was replaced by a more dignified building, by Elizabeth Scott, opened in 1932. It has five sculptured figures by Eric Kennington and includes a pleasantly decorated *Restaurant*, with terrace overlooking the Avon. Festival performances are given here from April to October. 'Titus Andronicus' was produced in 1955, thus completing the canon of the works.

The *Library* (adm. to students only weekdays 10–5, Sat 10–12.30), which escaped the fire, contains Shakespeariana (10,000 vols).—Upstairs is the *Picture Gallery & Museum* (10–1, 2–6, Sun Apr–Nov only, 2–6; fee), containing Shakespearian portraits and paintings. Authorities differ as to whether the 'Flower Portrait' of Shakespeare, hung here, was the model for the Droeshout engraving in the First Folio or was painted from it. Here, too, are Shakespeare's gloves, and a collection of relics of famous actors and actresses, including David Garrick, Sarah Siddons, Frank Benson, and Ellen Terry; paintings illustrating scenes from Shakespeare's plays; and commissioned portraits of actors associated with the Memorial Theatre. In the *Bancroft Gardens*, to the N. is a monument to Shakespeare, by Lord Ronald Gower.

The STRATFORD-UPON-AVON CANAL (25½ m. long) was completed in 1816 to connect the Avon with the Worcester and Birmingham Canal at King's Norton (p. 329). The long-neglected s. section, quitting the Avon by the Bancroft Gardens (yacht basin), was restored in 1961–64 for pleasure-craft (N.T.). It rises by 36 locks. [At (13 m.) *Kingswood* it is linked by a short branch with the Grand Union Canal (p. 316)].

The AVON has again been made navigable (after a century of disuse) by the Upper Avon Navigation Trust with nine new locks, and is open for pleasure-craft through to the Severn at Tewkesbury.

Above the theatre the Avon is crossed by the "sumptuous new bridge and large of stone" erected by Sir Hugh Clopton (view of town) and widened c. 1925. The adjacent footbridge of 1823 is the most conspicuous relic of a horse tramway that once linked Stratford with Moreton-in-Marsh.—*Bridge Street* leads w. into the town, passing (r.) the *Red Horse Hotel*, where 'Geoffrey Crayon's Throne and Sceptre' are still preserved in the room in which Washington Irving wrote his account of Stratford. Bridge St. is continued by Wood St. The *White Swan Hotel* here, containing a curious wall-painting (c. 1560) of the Story of Tobias, overlooks the broad Rother Market (Fri).

About 1 m. w. of Stratford, and reached by a pleasant footpath across the fields, is **Shottery**, the birthplace of Anne Hathaway, Shakespeare's wife. *Anne Hathaway's Cottage* (adm. pp. 335), picturesque half-timbered Elizabethan farmhouse with a thatched roof, is fully restored to its 'original state' since damage by arson in 1969, and contains original Hathaway furniture and relics, including a fine Elizabethan bedstead. The old-fashioned garden is attractive. From Shottery a lane leads N.W., crossing the Alcester road, to (2¼ m. more) Wilmcote (Hotel) with *Mary Arden's House* (adm. p. 335), the half-timbered Tudor farmstead where Shakespeare's mother was born. It contains Elizabethan farmhouse furniture and its barns accommodate a museum of Warwickshire bygones. The stone dovecote is attractive.

The ENVIRONS of Stratford are, of course, packed with interest for the lover of Shakespeare. Thus the enthusiast might arrange a trip of about 20 m. to take in the 'Eight Shakespearian Villages' mentioned in the following lines (ascribed to Shakespeare) and exercise his ingenuity in determining the fitness of the epithets:

> "Piping Pebworth, Dancing Marston,
> Haunted Hillborough, Hungry Grafton,
> Dodging Exhall, Papist Wixford,
> Beggarly Broom, and Drunken Bidford."

It was in the Falcon Inn at *Bidford* (still extant, though no longer an inn) that Shakespeare is reported to have taken part in the carouse that prompted the verse, and about 1 m. w. of it is shown the crabtree (or its successor) under which he slept off its effects. A Saxon cemetery (5–6C) discovered here in 1924 has yielded many important finds. *Temple Grafton* is one of the three claimants to be the scene of Shakespeare's wedding. *Wixford* has an interesting church with Norman details. Conveniently included in this drive are *Luddington* (2 m. s.w. of Shottery), the most generally accepted scene of the poet's marriage; *Welford*, a charming village, which has not been without a maypole for centuries; and *Abbot's Salford* (2 m. s.w. of Bidford), with the picturesque old mansion of *Salford Hall* (1602).—The visit to *Charlecote* (p. 334), 4 m. E., is more imperative.—*Snitterfield*, the home of Shakespeare's father, is 3¾ m. N. *Clopton House* (adm. daily 10–5, fee), long the manorhouse of the Cloptons, is 1 m. N. Just to the E. of this is *Welcombe* (where Shakespeare's friend and legatee, Anthony Nash, had property), with its lofty obelisk (120 ft) to Mark Philips (d. 1873), builder of Welcombe House.—*Clifford Chambers*, 1½ m. to the s., has an old church (with a wonderful chalice and paten of c. 1495) and a half-timbered vicarage. Michael Drayton (1563–1631) was a frequent visitor at the 16C manor-house ("the Muse's quiet port"; burned down in 1918).

Alcester (Motel), 8 m. w. of Stratford, an ancient little town of Roman origin, has a town hall of 1641 and an 18C Gothic church with a classical interior (by E. and T. Woodward, 1730). *Ragley Hall* (Marquess of Hertford), 1¾ m. s.w., is open 2–6 at Easter and in May–Sept on Tues, Wed, Thurs, Sat, Sun, and BH (fee; rfmts). Begun by Robert Hooke in 1679–83, it was altered and decorated by Gibbs

c. 1750 and provided with a portico by James Wyatt before 1794. The mansion, with a noble Great Hall, contains memorials of the Seymour family and fine paintings (*Rubens*, Holy Family; *Reynolds*, Four portraits; works by *Lely*, *Kneller*, *Hoppner*, *Morland*, and *Wootton*). The property, much beautified by the present marquess, includes a large park, with a lake for sailing, etc.—*Coughton Court* (N.T.; adm. 2–6, May–Sept, Wed, Thurs, Sat, Sun, & BH; Apr & Oct, Sat, Sun only; fee; teas), 2 m. N. of Alcester, is the early-16C house of the Throckmortons, famous as a recusant family. Behind the imposing Gatehouse (with wings of 1780) are the half-timbered N. and S. wings. The E. wing was destroyed by a mob in 1688. Within are some beautiful panelled rooms, with Jacobite and other relics and family portraits, some by Largillière. The staircase was brought from Harvington Hall in 1910. Adjoining are the Perp. parish church, adorned with many of its original furnishings and good 16C Throckmorton tombs, and a Rom. Cath. church of 1860.

From Stratford to *Birmingham*, see Rte 33; to *Banbury*, see p. 309 ; to *Oxford* and *London*, see p. 330; to *Warwick* and *Leamington*, p. 334.

35   BRISTOL TO BIRMINGHAM

ROAD (A 38), 85½ m.—To (34 m.) *Gloucester*, see Rte 17.—45 m. *Tewkesbury*.—59¼ m. **Worcester**.—66½ m. **Droitwich**.—72½ m. *Bromsgrove*.—85½ m. **Birmingham**.—MOTOR-COACH in 2 hrs.

A MOTORWAY (M 5) runs on the same general line as A 38.

RAILWAY, 88¾ m. (91½ m. viâ Worcester) in 1¾–2 hrs. Most direct trains stop only at (37 m.) **Gloucester** (Eastgate) and (43½ m.) **Cheltenham Spa**.—88¾ m. **Birmingham** (New St.).—Some trains diverge viâ (65½ m.) **Worcester** (Shrub Hill), where a change is necessary for (71 m.) **Droitwich Spa** and (77½ m.) *Bromsgrove*. (The main line has through trains between Plymouth and York or Liverpool.)

From Bristol to (34 m.) *Gloucester*, see Rte 17. A 38 leads N. in the Vale of Gloucester and at 42½ m. leaves on the left the road to Deerhurst (see below).

45 m. **TEWKESBURY** (good Hotels), an ancient borough (8700 inhab.) on the Warwickshire Avon, close to its confluence with the Severn, contains one of the most magnificent Norman churches in England and many interesting 16–17C houses, e.g. Tudor House and the Wheatsheaf Inn (now a coffee-house) both in High St. On both the Severn and Avon there is good boating. *King John's Bridge* (c. 1200) over the Avon has been widened (1964); the Severn Bridge is by Telford (1826).

Shakespeare refers to 'Tewkesbury mustard' ('Henry IV', Part II, ii, 4). The battle of Tewkesbury (comp. below) was fought in 1471 in the 'Bloody Meadow', ¼ m. S. of the town. Tewkesbury is the 'Nortonbury' of Mrs Craik's 'John Halifax, Gentleman' (*Tudor House*, the house of the 14 windows, is where Ursula March lived, and the Elizabethan *Bell Hotel* is the house of Abel Fletcher, the tanner), and Mr Pickwick once dined at the *Hop Pole* with Bob Sawyer and Ben Allen. The Abbey Mill, likewise associated with Fletcher, is now a restaurant.

The famous ***Abbey Church**, the successor of a Benedictine abbey founded in 715, was begun in 1092 by Sir Robert Fitzhamon (choir completed in 1123, nave and tower c. 1160); and, though neglect and frequent restoration have affected both exterior and interior, it is substantially as it was when reconsecrated after the battle of Tewkesbury. Internally it is 315 ft long, 71 ft wide, 122 ft wide across the transepts, and 58½ ft high. The **Central Tower* (148 ft; pinnacles added in 1660; restored 1936) is in colour, proportion, and arcading quite perfect. The rather later *North Porch* (impressive in its plainness), the unique *West*

Front, with its grand recessed arch, and the romantic cluster of *Choir Chapels*, added in 1330–50, are contrasting beauties of the exterior.

The INTERIOR has an even more varied range of architectural beauty. The great pillars of the **Nave*, though they dwarf the triforium and the later clerestory and vaulting (Dec.), justify their predominance by their grandeur. The vigorously carved bosses of the roof (regilt and coloured by Gambier Parry) should be noted. The tower vaulting has shields and dependent ornaments representing the 'glorious sun of York', triumphant over the Lancastrians in the 'Bloody Meadow' of Tewkesbury. A brass in the pavement beneath marks the traditional grave of the young Lancastrian Prince of Wales, slain in the battle or after. The *View from the top of the tower embraces the Vales of Severn, Gloucester, and Evesham and the surrounding hills. The *Transepts* are Norman, with 14C windows. In the beautiful s. arm is the apsidal *Lady Chapel*, in which is the Madonna del Passeggio, an original painting by Raphael, once in the possession of Madame de Pompadour. The transept contains a memorial tablet to Mrs Craik (1826–87).

The choir is surrounded by an *Ambulatory* with a sequence of chapels, including the elegant E.E. *St Margaret's Chapel* (with the tomb of Sir Guy de Brienne, 1390) and *St Edmund's Chapel*, with its appropriate bosses and the 15C Wakeman Cenotaph. Behind the high altar is the Clarence vault, where the murdered Duke of Clarence and his wife were buried in 1478. The truncated Norman pillars of the *Choir* support pointed arches and a lofty superstructure with a richly groined and bossed roof (14C). A few carved misericords survive. The brasses, the monuments, and the 14C *Windows of the choir commemorate the Fitzhamons, De Clares, Despensers, Beauchamps, and other lords of Tewkesbury in its great days. Finest of all is the exquisite *Beauchamp Chantry (1422), after which rank the adjacent *Founder's Chantry* (Fitzhamon; 1397), the *Despenser Monument* ('Hugo Tertius'; exquisite canopy; c. 1349), the tomb of Hugh le Despenser (1326), and the *Trinity Chantry* (1378), with its early fan-tracery and the unique kneeling figure of Edward le Despenser.

To the s. of the church is a *Cloister Walk*, with a fine 15C doorway. The *Abbey House* (15C and 18C; near the N. front) and the *Abbey Gate House* (w. of it), a 19C reproduction, are the only remains of the monastic buildings.

Deerhurst, with its two pre-Norman buildings, lies s. of Tewkesbury and may be reached thence by road (4 m.), or by a field-path (2½ m.). The *Church of St Mary belonged to a Saxon monastery with documentary history from 804. The lower half of the tower is of Saxon masonry, and later herring-bone work is visible in many parts of the exterior. The nave, with its E.E. arcades, incorporates the original choir (20 ft long), the Saxon apse of which, not rebuilt after a 15C fire, can be easily traced from without. In the E. wall of the tower is a curious two-light triangular-headed window, and below are a triangular opening (like others in the N. and s. walls) and a blocked door once leading to a w. gallery. A unique feature of the 15C brass of Sir John and Lady Cassey, in the N. choir-aisle, is the named figure of their dog 'Terri'. The ancient *Font has spiral ornamentation, probably earlier than the 9C. About 200 yards away, across the road and attached to a fine half-timbered house, is the so-called *Odda's Chapel, dating, according to an inscription stone now in the Ashmolean Museum at Oxford, from 1056. It was a memorial chapel for Odda's brother Ælfric.

Bredon, 3 m. N.E. of Tewkesbury, has a fine Norman and Dec. church and a large tithe-barn (14C; N.T.; adm. free). Above it is the rounded Bredon Hill (961 ft; *View), celebrated in song by A. E. Housman. The 16C manor-house of *Bredons*

Norton, 1½ m. N., is shown to visitors by courtesy of the owner; while on the N.E. flank of the hill is *Elmley Castle*, with an interesting church containing the sumptuous tomb of the 1st Earl of Coventry (d. 1699), by Wm. Stanton.

At *Stoke Orchard*, where the church has early-14C wall-paintings of the Life of St James, with four later overlays, is the research station of the National Coal Board. It lies c. 4 m. S.E. of Tewekesbury viâ (2½ m.) *Tredington*, with its little Norman church.

Our road ascends the Severn valley, passes beneath the Ross Spur (M 50), and enters Worcestershire. At 51 m., about 1 m. left beyond the river, is *Upton-on-Severn* (Hotels), the scene of an adventure of Tom Jones.—53 m. *Severn Stoke*. About 1½ m. E., beyond the M 5, is *Croome d'Abitot*, where Croome Court (1751; by 'Capability' Brown) is now a school (no adm.); the church contains 17C monuments of the Earls of Coventry and a graceful wooden font (1760). *Pirton* church, 1 m. to the N., has a 'magpie' tower.

59½ m. **WORCESTER,** an episcopal city and county town (73,400 inhab.), lies mainly on the left bank of the smoothly flowing Severn. At the time of Henry VIII "no towne of England made so many cloathes yearly as this town"; but its cloth trade has now given place to the manufacture of the renowned porcelain, of sauce, gloves, and other wares. Seagoing vessels ascend the Severn as far as Worcester Bridge. Though many old buildings survive, much of the centre has been robbed of character by recent planning in the interests of traffic flow (which has not conspicuously improved).

Railway Stations. *Shrub Hill* (Rfmts). *Foregate Street.* Both stations are used by main-line services and inquiry should be made on the spot.

Hotels (see plan).

Post Office, Foregate St.

Motor-Buses from Dolday.

Steamers in summer on the Severn from above the bridge. SWIMMING POOL in Sansome Walk; the river is dangerous.

Race Meetings in March, July, and Nov, on the *Pitchcroft*.

History. Traces (not altogether conclusive) of British and Roman occupation have been found at Worcester (*Vigornia*), but its real history may be begun with the foundation of a bishopric in the Saxon *Wigorna Ceaster* (c. 680). At the Conquest the town was important enough to be chosen as the seat of a Norman castle. It was the first city to declare for Charles I in the Civil War, and Prince Rupert won his first victory at Powick Bridge (1642), 3 m. w. of Worcester. It was the last rallying-point of the Royalists round the young Charles II, who were defeated before the city by Cromwell in 1651. A somewhat grandiloquent plaque at 56 Sidbury recalls this incident. For its fidelity to the monarchy the city bears the motto "Civitas in Bello in Pace Fidelis". Lord Nuffield (1877–1963), philanthropist and motor manufacturer, was born at Worcester; and Thomas Tomkins (1572–1656), the madrigalist, died here.

'Berrow's Worcester Journal', established most probably in 1690 as the 'Worcester Postman', and certainly existing in 1709, is the oldest unofficial English newspaper with a continuous history.

The ***Cathedral,** which stands near the river, is a cruciform structure (mainly E.E. and Perp.) with aisleless transepts and secondary choir transepts, and it has been somewhat excessively restored to the pitch of apparent newness. It is entered from College Yard, with its pleasant 18C houses.

HISTORY. The original church was dedicated to St Peter and served by secular canons. Bishop Oswald (961–92) rebuilt the cathedral and converted the secular foundations into a Benedictine monastery. St Wulstan (bishop 1062–95) pulled

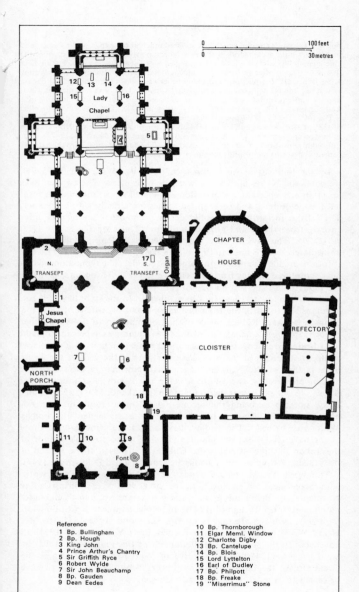

100 feet
30 metres

12 13 14
15 Lady 16
Chapel
5
3
2
17
N. S.
TRANSEPT TRANSEPT Organ

CHAPTER
HOUSE

1
Jesus
Chapel

REFECTORY

7 6
CLOISTER

NORTH
PORCH

18

19

11 10 9

Font
8

Reference
1 Bp. Bullingham
2 Bp. Hough
3 King John
4 Prince Arthur's Chantry
5 Sir Griffith Ryce
6 Robert Wylde
7 Sir John Beauchamp
8 Bp. Gauden
9 Dean Eedes

10 Bp. Thornborough
11 Elgar Meml. Window
12 Charlotte Digby
13 Bp. Cantelupe
14 Bp. Blois
15 Lord Lyttelton
16 Earl of Dudley
17 Bp. Philpott
18 Bp. Freake
19 "Miserrimus" Stone

Worcester Cathedral

down St Oswald's church, which had suffered much at the hands of the Danes, and in 1084–89 built a cathedral in the new Norman style, of which the crypt is the chief remaining part. In 1202 the cathedral was devastated by fire, but in 1218 it was dedicated after restoration, a splendid ceremonial attended by the young King Henry III, ten bishops, and many other ecclesiastics and nobles. Wulstan, at whose tomb miracles suddenly began to happen in 1202, was canonized in 1203; and the consequent influx of pilgrims necessitated (and paid for) the building of a Lady Chapel and the rebuilding of the choir (begun 1224). The nave was remodelled in the 14C. The Central Tower (196 ft; fee for ascent), which is the one rich feature of the exterior, was completed in 1374 and commands a fine view of the Malvern Hills (good chimes). The w. front is the design of Perkins (1857–73) who thoroughly restored most of the exterior.—The monuments throughout the cathedral deserve careful study (comp. *A. Macdonald*, 'Guide to the Monuments').

By the impressive *North Porch*, built by Bp. Wakefield (1375–94), we enter the NAVE, midway between its nine piers. The two w. bays (c. 1160) are remarkable illustrations of Trans. work; the capitals foretell foliage designs, and the pointed arches are already E.E. in manner. The lofty triforium is of peculiar design. The other seven bays differ entirely from these, and are not uniform. Those on the N. are Dec. (1317–27). The bays on the s. side are very early Perp., probably built immediately before the vaulting of the nave, completed in 1377. The triforium arcade also differs on the N. and s. side. The tympanum spaces bear sculptured figures from the Old Testament. Those on the s. side are modern. In the second bay of the *North Aisle* are a tablet and a memorial window to Elgar (not buried here). In the sixth bay of the N. arcade is the tomb of Sir John Beauchamp and his wife (c. 1400), and opposite is that of Robert Wylde of the Commandery (d. 1608). Farther E. opens the *Jesus Chapel*, one of the few remaining chapels in England so dedicated. Just beyond it is the curious tomb (not in its original place) of Bp. Bullingham (d. 1576). The lower part of the wall of the *South Aisle* is that of the Norman nave. Five Norman recesses face the present pier arches, two of them being filled with later monumental arches. In one of these is the tomb of Bp. Freake (d. 1591), by Anthony Tolly, notable as being the second-oldest signed tomb in England. The tomb of Bp. Thomas (d. 1689), farther E., is signed by Thomas White (see below). The two w. bays are of the same date as those of the nave (c. 1160). Bp. Gauden (1605–62), the probable author of the 'Eikon Basilike' attributed to Charles I, is buried at the w. end of the s. aisle. At the w. entrance lie the ashes of Lord Baldwin (d. 1947).

The WEST TRANSEPTS are a mixture of Norman and Perp. work, with inconsistent 19C restorations. In the E. wall of each arm is a fine Norman arch. Below this arch, in the N. arm, are Roubiliac's elaborate monument to Bp. Hough (d. 1743); and a plainer one to Bp. Stillingfleet (d. 1699); here too are tablets to Mrs Sherwood (1775–1851), to Mrs Henry Wood (1814–87), and to Francis Brett Young (1884–1954) all novelists. In the s. arm is the monument of Bp. Philpott (d. 1892) by Sir T. Brock (1847–1922), a native of Worcester. Here also is the Great Organ; the Little Organ (by 'Father' Smith; 1704), said to have belonged to Handel, is in the Lady Chapel.

*CHOIR. As a whole, the E. end of Worcester Cathedral is one of the most English of our cathedral choirs and second only to that of Beverley Minster as a work of the period (1220–60). Its beauty is best seen in the Lady Chapel (begun 1224; sculptured arcade, etc.) and the East

Transepts. The sculptures in the spandrels (often amusing) are worthy of study; one of them (E. end of s. aisle) is the 'Worcester Crucifix' with expressive figures of the Virgin and St John (restored 1862). Here the piers and arches are loftier than in the *Presbytery*, built over the Norman crypt, which raises the floor level considerably above that of the transepts and Lady Chapel. The detached shafts of Purbeck marble were added by Bishop Giffard (1268–1302). The *Stalls* are late Victorian,

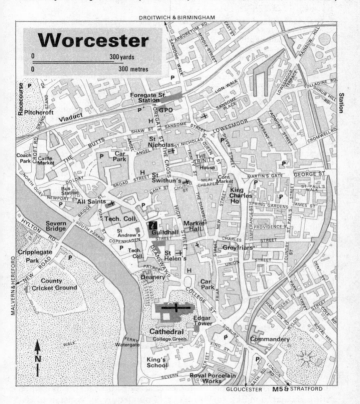

incorporating the medieval *Misericords; they replaced 17C stalls, part of which are now at Sutton Coldfield. The pulpit is of the 16C, the other furniture of the 19C. In the presbytery is the tomb of King John (d. 1216), of which the Purbeck marble effigy alone is of contemporary work. The lion biting the end of the sword is an alleged reference to the curbing of the royal power by the barons. The rest of the tomb is probably of the same date as the adjacent *Chantry of Prince Arthur*, erected in 1504, two years after his death at Ludlow. Within the screen-work below are two fine effigy tombs, probably of Bp. Giffard (d. 1302) and a kinswoman. In the *Lady Chapel* are the tombs of Bp. Cantelupe

(d. 1266) and Bp. Blois (d. 1236), and on the N. wall is a tablet to the second wife of Izaak Walton, with an epitaph by him (1662). To the left are a small alabaster Madonna (c. 1470) and a monument by Chantrey (to Mrs. Digby; d. 1820). The *N.E. Transept* is now St George's Chapel, dedicated to the Worcestershire Regt.; opposite is the tomb of Bp. de Cobham (d. 1327), who built the Jesus Chapel and began the 'new' nave (c. 1317); and in the *S.E. Transept* is the tomb of Sir Griffith Ryce (d. 1523).

The many-pillared *CRYPT (entered from the S.W. Transept; fee) built by St Wulstan in 1084, is the second in date of the four apsidal crypts in English cathedrals. Willis aptly calls it "a complex and beautiful temple", and both its complexity and its beauty must have been greater in its original and more extended form. The apsidal crypt of Canterbury is earlier, those of Winchester and Gloucester are later.

The CHAPTER LIBRARY, in a room over the S. aisle of the nave, contains some 4000 vols., including various rarities, and many MSS., particularly of canon law. Some charters and seals and other relics are displayed in the S. choir aisle.

The remains of the monastic buildings lie to the S., connected with the church by CLOISTERS (1374; restored), which are entered from the S. aisle of the nave. A second entrance on the S. side (from College Green) is by a richly moulded late-Norman door. The bosses of the vaulting are admirable. Those in the S. walk represent the ancestors of Christ. In the N. walk adoring angels turn towards the central boss, carved with the Virgin and Child. At the W. end of this walk is a tombstone inscribed 'Miserrimus', which inspired Wordsworth to a speculative sonnet. He was unaware that the epitaph is that of a Jacobite minor canon, unable to adjust himself to the rule of William III.

From the E. side of the cloisters, where a Norman slype leads to the ruined *Guest House*, we enter the CHAPTER HOUSE, a circular building of c. 1150, reconstructed externally in decagonal form about 1400. It is an early example of vaulting from a central shaft. Along the S. side of the cloisters lies the *Refectory* (1370), 120 ft long, with Norman vaulted cellars, and a magnificent though mutilated Romanesque *Majesty, probably from the W. front of the Norman cathedral, in a 14C frame. It has been restored, and is part of the King's School (adm. on application, when not in use).—*Edgar Tower*, the main entrance to College Green, was the Great Gate of the monastery. It may have been built in connection with the otherwise entirely destroyed *Castle*, the site of which is now the King's School garden. In return for the burial of King John, Henry III restored to the monks part of the outer bailey which had encroached upon their property. The tower got its name from its having held a statue supposed to represent King Edgar; the present statuettes date from 1909. The Water Gate leads from College Green to the Severn Bank, above which are the remains of the *Dormitory*.

George III attended the Three Choirs Festival (see p. 301) in 1788.

The *Diocesan Registrar's Office* (formerly *St Helen's Church*), in High St., preserves the marriage-contract of William Shakespeare and Anne Hathaway.

Just to the S.E. of the cathedral is the so-called *COMMANDERY (adjoining No. 79 Sidbury; shown morning and afternoon in business hours; fee), a rich example of domestic architecture and the most interesting secular building in Worcester. Founded by St Wulstan c. 1085 as a hospice for travellers, it remained a religious foundation until suppressed by Wolsey in 1524. Its prevailing character is Tudor.

In Severn St., 300 yds S.W., are the *Royal Porcelain Works*, which were founded in 1751 and have occupied their present site since 1840. Since 1768 they have been famous for elaborate and costly ware, notable for its perfect finish. The works are open 10–1, 2–5, Mon–Fri (fee), the *Dyson Perrins Museum* and showroom Mon–Sat (free; closed Sat in winter).

From the Commandery, Sidbury, Friar St., and New St., in all three of which stand picturesque timbered houses (17C), lead N. to the Old Cornmarket. The Worcestershire Archaeological Society's library adjoins the fine timbered *Greyfriars* (N.T.; adm. 2–6, first Wed in the month, May–Sept) in Friar St. In New St. are *Nash's House* (early 16C) and, at the Cornmarket end, the so-called *King Charles's House* (1577), now divided, where Charles II found momentary refuge after the battle of Worcester. Beneath the antique shop part is one of three 'bottle dungeons' in Britain.

In following HIGH STREET to the N. from the cathedral we pass (l.) the *Guildhall*, a handsome Queen Anne building by Thomas White, a Worcester pupil of Wren (1721). The statues of Charles I and Charles II, as supporters of Church and State (l. & r. of entrance), express significantly the politics of the 'Faithful City'. Inside are portraits of George III and Queen Charlotte by Reynolds, and a brass cannon used in the battle of Worcester. Beyond the ungainly *Market Hall* (r.) Church St. diverges for the church of *St Swithun*, by E. and T. Woodward (1733–36) apart from its Perp. tower, and preserving a remarkably complete set of 18C interior fittings, including a magnificent three-decker *Pulpit, with mayor's chair and sword-rest incorporated. In Trinity St., behind, is *Queen Elizabeth's House*, a restored 16C building.

High St. is prolonged by The Cross, at the end of which is the church of *St Nicholas* (1732; also by White), and by its continuation, The Foregate. In the latter is (l.) the *Berkeley Hospital* (1703), an almshouse with a typical founder's statue. In Foregate St., farther N., is the *City Museum and Art Gallery* (weekdays 9.30–5 or 6). The Roman finds and regimental relics are interesting.

DEANSWAY, leading from the cathedral to the Severn Bridge, passes the pictur- esque *Old Palace* (formerly the bishop's residence), the new *College for Further Education*, and the extraordinarily slender spire (245 ft high), erected in 1751, of *St Andrew's*, a demolished church. *All Saints'*, another of White's churches, furbished up by Sir Aston Webb, contains a Norman font from St Andrew's and a wrought-iron ornament from the mayor's stall. The *Severn Bridge* by John Gwynn (1771), but widened since, commands a good general view of the city. On the far bank, looking across to the cathedral, is the *County Cricket Ground*, traditional venue for Commonwealth touring teams of their first county match (May).

Sir Edward Elgar (1857–1934), the composer, was born at *Upper Broadheath*, 2 m. w., and died at Worcester. His cottage birthplace is now a memorial museum (adm. daily; fee), and contains interesting portraits, musical scores, etc.—*Stanbrook Abbey*, 3½ m. s. of Worcester, is the only house of Benedictine nuns in England (transferred from Cambrai in 1795; in the present abbey since 1838).—The gardens of *Spetchley Park*, 3 m. E. of Worcester, including a deer park, are open in Apr– Oct (weekdays exc. Sat 11–5; Sun 2–6; BH, 11–6; fee).

FROM WORCESTER TO WOLVERHAMPTON, 30 m. A 449 runs due N.—5¾ m. *Ombersley* has good black-and-white houses.—At (8¾ m.) Crossway Green (Hotel) a road bears left for *Stourport*, a picturesque canal town (17,900 inhab.), 2½ m. w., near an attractive reach of the Severn.—At (11¼ m.) *Hartlebury* is *Hartlebury Castle*, the residence of the Bp. of Worcester, founded c. 1268 but now mainly of 18C work.—14½ m. **Kidderminster**, an irregularly built town (47,300 inhab.) on the Stour, is noted for its carpet manufacture but lacks architectural interest. From 1641 till 1666 Richard Baxter (1615–91), the Noncomformist divine, was minister of the fine parish *Church*, which contains several good monuments. His pulpit is in the Unitarian chapel, while his statue stands outside the church. Another statue, beside the town hall, commemorates Sir Rowland Hill (1795–1879), the postal reformer, a native of the town. The 16–18C *Harvington Hall* (adm. daily exc. Mon, 2–6 or dusk; also Easter–Sept 11.30–1; closed Good Friday & Dec–Jan; fee; teas), with 17C wall-paintings and a number of 'priest-holes', lies 3 m. S.E., near *Chaddesley Corbett*, where the 14C church has a font of c. 1160. To Bewdley and

Ludlow, see p. 355; to Bridgnorth and Shrewsbury, see Rte 42; to Birmingham, see p. 329.

20 m. *Stewponey* (Hotel) is 1½ m. N.E. of *Kinver Edge* (N.T.), a natural moorland park. At *Holbeche House*, near (24 m.) *Himley*, Catesby and others concerned in the Gunpowder Plot made a desperate stand in 1605.—30 m. *Wolverhampton*, see Rte 41.

FROM WORCESTER TO TENBURY, 21 m. (A 443). 2½ m. *Hallow* (Restaurant).— At (6 m.) *Holt Heath* we quit the Severn Valley. Holt church (11–12C details) and the remains of the 14–16C castle (adm. May–Sept, Thurs 10–1, 2–5) lie to the right near the river. — 10½ m. *Great Witley* has an Italianate *Church, with a ceiling probably by Ant. Bellucci (brought from Canons, 1747) and a fine monument by Rysbrack to Lord Foley (d. 1733) and his wife.—At (12½ m.) *Abberley*, in pleasant hilly country, The Elms, a Queen Anne mansion, is now a hotel. We descend to the Teme valley.—21 m. *Tenbury*, see p. 355.

From Worcester to *Shrewsbury*, see Rte. 42; to *Malvern* and *Hereford*, see Rte 37; to *Oxford* (London), see Rte 31.

The Birmingham road (A 38) runs N.E. from Worcester, beyond (63 m.) *Martin Hussingtree* following a Roman alinement.—66½ m. **Droitwich** (Hotels), an ancient borough with 14,900 inhab., occupies a site known as *Salinae* to the Romans, who appreciated both the curative powers of the springs and their salt-bearing uses. Salt is still mined commercially, while the springs, rising from beds of rock salt 120–170 ft below ground, have radioactive properties and are useful in cases of rheumatism, neuritis, and general debility. They were exploited in the 19C by John Corbett, whose buildings give the town its characteristic brick and half-timbered style. The well-equipped *Baths*, the chief hotels, and the *Park* are in the upper part of the town. The *Raven* has a 16C core. The most interesting church is *St Peter's*, ½ m. s. of the centre where Edward Winslow (1595–1655), the 'Pilgrim Father', was baptized.

The *Hotel Impney* at Dodderhill, 1 m. N.E., was built (1869–75) as Corbett's château. Other points of interest are *Hindlip Hall* (3½ m. S.), where (in an earlier building) some of the Gunpowder Plot conspirators lay hid for a week; *Hanbury Hall* (N.T.), 2½ m. E., built in 1701, where the decorations by Thornhill are shown (2–6, Wed & Sat in Apr–Sept; fee); and *Westwood Park* (1½ m. w.), a fine 16–17C mansion.

We cross to the E. side of the M 5 motorway and, leaving *Stoke Prior*, with its salt-works, on the right, reach (72½ m.) **Bromsgrove** (Hotels), a town of 36,400 inhab., with gabled houses, a boys' school founded early in the 16C, and a handsome Perp. church. A headstone in the churchyard celebrates in verse two engine-drivers whose locomotive blew up in 1840 while climbing the Lickey Incline (comp. below). The *Avoncroft Museum of Buildings* (adm. Mar–Nov, daily 11–6 or dusk; closed Mon exc. BH & in Aug; fee; tea) brings together, 2 m. s., historic structures re-erected in an open setting.

A. E. Housman (1859–1936) was born at *Fockbury*, 1 m. N.W.—Near *Tardebigge*, 3 m. E., where the church has a graceful spire of 1776, the flight of 30 and 12 locks on the *Worcester and Birmingham Canal* is the longest in Britain. *Redditch* (40,800 inhab.; Hotel), 3 m. farther E., is a straggling town noted for the manufacture of springs, needles, fish-hooks, etc. It is becoming yet another receiving point of Birmingham's 'overspill' population.

The road now ascends between the *Clent Hills* (1036 ft; l.) and the *Lickey Hills* (900 ft). Near the top is (76½ m.) *Chadwich Manor*, an estate of the N.T. (1150 acres), favourite week-end resort from Birmingham. We pass between *Rubery*, with its large hospitals, and *Rednal* (r.) with the grave of Card. Newman.—82 m. *Selly Oak*, and thence to (85½ m.) **Birmingham**, see Rte 33.

36 GLOUCESTER TO HEREFORD AND SHREWSBURY

ROAD, 83 m. A 40. 16 m. *Ross.*—A 49. 30 m. *Hereford.*—43 m. *Leominster.*— 54 m. *Ludlow.*—70 m. *Church Stretton.*—83 m. *Shrewsbury.*

RAILWAY FROM HEREFORD TO SHREWSBURY, 50¾ m. in 1–1¼ hr. Stations: 12½ m. *Leominster.*—23½ m. *Ludlow.*—31 m. **Craven Arms**, junction for *Knighton* (12¼ m.). —38¼ m. *Church Stretton.*—50¾ m. **Shrewsbury.**

Gloucester, see Rte 30. A 40 crosses the Severn on Over Bridge, built by Telford, and runs due w.—At (7 m.) *Huntley* we reach the outskirts of the Forest of Dean (l.). On the right rises *May Hill* (969 ft; view).

A pleasant detour may be made to the s. viâ (2½ m.) *Longhope* (Hotel) and (4 m.) *Mitcheldean* (p. 302).

The road now enters Herefordshire. On the left are the fine tower of the church of (13¾ m.) *Weston-under-Penyard* (Hotel) and the woods of *Penyard Chase.* Just E. of Weston is the site of Roman *Ariconium*, once the focus of a thriving iron-smelting industry.

16 m. **Ross-on-Wye** (good Hotels), an attractive town with 6400 inhab., stands on a hill rising from the left bank of the Wye. Its most prominent building is the spacious Dec. and Perp. *Church* (poorly restored in 1743), from which and from the adjoining *Prospect* the horseshoe bend of the river is seen to special advantage. The E. window has glass of 1430. The monuments are numerous and excellent, notably those of the Rudhalls (1530–1651), while before the altar is the grave of John Kyrle (1637–1724), the 'Man of Ross' celebrated by Pope in his 'Third Moral Essay'. To him is due the creation of the Prospect Gardens. *Kyrle's House*, now a bookshop, in the market-place, is marked by a bust; in the garden, behind, is his curious summer house (adm. on application). In the Royal ⊙ak, Dickens and his biographer, Forster, decided in 1867 on the 'American Tour'. The adjacent red sandstone *Market House*, raised on open arches, dates from 1670.

The 'Ross Spur', part of the unfinished M 50 motorway to S. Wales, provides the quickest route to Birmingham viâ its junction with the M 5.—Descent of the *Wye Valley*, see Rte 38.

The direct road to Hereford (A 49) crosses the Wye by *Wilton Bridge* (1597; widened), with its 18C sundial, near the ruined *Wilton Castle* (12–16C), and, passing (20½ m.) the *Pengethley Hotel* (fishing), ascends over the flank (527 ft) of (26 m.) *Aconbury Hill* (Hotel). More attractive are the byways which keep closer to the river and are very little longer; either E. of the Wye passing near (23 m.) *Brockhampton Court* (Hotel), a country-house hotel, and (25½ m.) *Fownhope* (Hotel), between the Woolhope hills and the river; or w. of the river through (21½ m.) *Hoarwithy* (small Hotels), on a charming reach, and (27½ m.) *Holme Lacy*, with an interesting church (near the river) containing Scudamore monuments.

30 m. **HEREFORD**, an ancient county town (46,500 inhab.) and the seat of a bishop since 672 (when its see was detached from Lichfield), lies mainly on the left bank of the Wye. Its castle, once "high and

stronge, and full of great towres", as the proximity of the Welsh marches demanded, has almost totally vanished, and though many interesting old buildings remain, recent 'one-way' channelling of traffic through the medieval centre has disturbed the town and obscured its ancient plan. David Garrick (1717–79) is its most famous native, while Thomas Traherne was the son of a Hereford shoemaker. David Cox was a drawing-master here in 1814–26.

Hotels, see plan.
Post Office, Broad Street.
Buses from Commercial Rd. to most towns of the Marches, both sides of the Welsh border.
Boats for hire at *Wye Bridge*.—GOLF COURSE (18-hole) at *Tillington Common*, 5½ m. N.W. (bus).

The broad street known as HIGH TOWN is the commercial centre of Hereford. Here stands the *Old House*, a timbered house built in 1621 from the design of John Abell, to whom are due many fine timbered houses in Herefordshire. Formerly part of the Butchers' Row, it was restored in 1883 and now contains a small Museum (adm. weekdays, 10–1, 2–5.30, Sun in summer from 2; fee), with Jacobean and other old furniture. In High St. is the church of *All Saints*, with a distorted spire (212 ft) bearing an enormous weathercock, carved oak stalls (late 14C), a chained library, and the register of Garrick's birth.

Eign St. and Whitecross St. and Rd., continuing High St., lead past *Price's Hospital* (1655) to (1¼ m.) the *White Cross*, a hexagonal shaft erected by Bp. Lewis Charlton in 1361 in thanksgiving for the departure of the Black Death (stepped base alone original). The markets were held here during the plague.

From All Saints, Broad St. leads s. to the cathedral close, passing the *City Museum and Art Gallery* (adm. free, weekdays 10–6, Thurs & Sat 10–5). Here are a fine Roman altar and tessellated pavements from Castra Magna, interesting old farm and cider-making implements, and a good collection of English water-colours.

The *Cathedral, dedicated to SS Mary and Ethelbert, is a beautiful and interesting building, 342 ft long, illustrating many architectural styles. Visitors usually enter by *Bp. Booth's Porch*, on the N. side.

HISTORY. Legend has it that the ghost of St Ethelbert of East Anglia, murdered by Offa of Mercia in 794, demanded burial at Hereford; and in 825 a successor of Offa built over the miracle-working tomb of the saint what was probably the first stone church on this site. A later Saxon church was burned down, along with the town, in the Welsh invasion of 1056. The first Norman bishop, *Robert de Losinga*, began to rebuild the ruined church in 1079, but if, as tradition asserts, his church was circular, it must have been obliterated by *Bp. Reynelm* (1107–15), who is styled on his tomb 'founder of the church'. Yet the 11C character of parts of the E. end suggests that Reynelm's claim is excessive. *Robert de Bethune* (1131–48) completed the nave "with great solicitude and expense" and renovated the choir. *William de Vere* (1186–99) radically altered the plans of the E. end, and probably began the Lady Chapel (completed c. 1220), beneath which was constructed a lofty crypt. The N.W. Transept was rebuilt c. 1260, and the inner N. Porch was added by *Bp. Swinfield* (1283–1316). The dignified Central Tower (165 ft high), erected on the Norman piers and arches, and the Chapter House are due to *Bp. Adam of Orleton* (1312–27). *Bp. Booth* (1516–35) added the outer N. porch. The fall of the W. tower in 1786 afforded Wyatt an opportunity of pulling down the W. bay and destroying much Norman work in the nave and of erecting a new W. front after his own idea of Gothic. The latter was replaced in 1902–08 by a new façade in a florid Dec. style, by J. Oldrid Scott. The E. end and crossing were restored in 1843, the whole building in 1856–63. The removal in 1966 of Gilbert Scott's ornate screen of 1862 was greeted with mixed feelings.

Interior. The NAVE (12C), one of the richest Norman designs in England, though evilly treated by Wyatt (see above), who is responsible also for the present triforium, clerestory, and wooden vaulting, still preserves

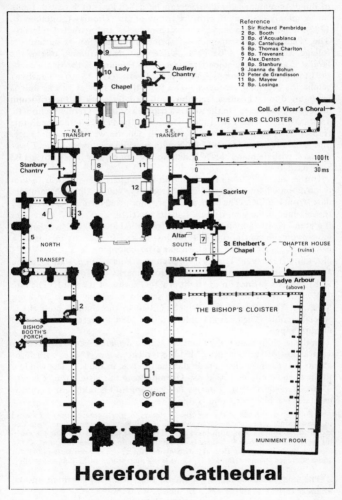

Reference
1 Sir Richard Pembridge
2 Bp. Booth
3 Bp. d'Acquablanca
4 Bp. Cantelupe
5 Bp. Thomas Charlton
6 Bp. Trevenant
7 Alex. Denton
8 Bp. Stanbury
9 Joanna de Bohun
10 Peter de Grandisson
11 Bp. Mayew
12 Bp. Losinga

Lady Chapel

Audley Chantry

N.E. TRANSEPT

S.E. TRANSEPT

Coll. of Vicar's Choral →

THE VICARS CLOISTER

0 — 100 ft
0 — 30 ms

Stanbury Chantry →

NORTH TRANSEPT

Sacristy

Altar

SOUTH TRANSEPT

St Ethelbert's Chapel

CHAPTER HOUSE (ruins)

Ladye Arbour (above)

BISHOP BOOTH'S PORCH

THE BISHOP'S CLOISTER

Font

MUNIMENT ROOM

Hereford Cathedral

its real grandeur in the eight massive piers, the main arches, with their rich carvings and the mouldings, and the noble arches that support the tower. The sculptured *Font* is likewise Norman. The *Aisles* are late-Dec., on Norman lower courses. Features of interest are the Jacobean oak pulpit and the monuments of Sir Richard Pembridge (d. 1375; s.

aisle) and Bp. Booth (d. 1535; N. aisle), the latter with its original grille.
—The *NORTH TRANSEPT, in a rich and unusual Dec. style (with some
15C glass), may have been built to receive the exquisitely designed tomb
of Bp. d'Acquablanca or d'Aigueblanche, called Peter of Savoy (d. 1268),
but is mainly associated with the shrine of Bp. Thomas Cantelupe (d.
1282), a saint whose remains worked miracles and attracted pilgrims.
The *Pedestal of his magnificent shrine is notable for its naturalistic
foliage, and figures of Knights. Under the great window, one of the
largest examples of Geometrical tracery in England, is the richly canopied tomb of Bp. Thomas Charlton (d. 1344).—The *SOUTH TRANSEPT
retains its Norman character. The primitive design of the E. wall is
probably due to Losinga (see above), with later work in the triforium
arch above the aisle. On the wall is a triptych of the S. German school (c.
1530). Bp. Trevenant (d. 1404), who made the Perp. alterations in this
transept, lies under the great s. window. On the w. side is a fireplace,
and beside it are a few 14C stalls with original canopies.—The *Tower
Lantern*, with its many shafts and curious gratings, was hidden by a 15C
roof until 1843.

In the solemn *CHOIR (dedicated in 1110) the rich Norman triforium
is surmounted by a graceful E.E. clerestory, which, like the vaulting,
dates from the 13C. The main arches are supported by massive piers, and
the capitals of the semi-detached shafts are richly carved. At the E. end
is a grand Norman arch (surmounted by a blind arcade) which originally
gave upon the central one of three low apses. In the axis of this arch
now rises a pier of the processional aisle belonging to Bp. de Vere's
alteration (1186–99). The *Choir Stalls* and *Bishop's Throne* date from the
14C. A marble slab opposite the throne marks the supposed spot of
St Ethelbert's shrine; on the right is a 14C statue of the saint. The late
12C chair to the left of the altar is said to have been used by King
Stephen. The brass of Bp. Trilleck (1360) in the chancel floor (l.) is
specially good. The organ (s. side), built in 1686–87, retains seven of its
original pipes.

In the N. choir aisle is the famous *Mappa Mundi*, executed on vellum
by Richard of Haldingham c. 1313, a typical medieval map, with Jerusalem in the centre and Paradise at the top (i.e. to the E.). The window
at the E. end contains 14C glass. Opening from this aisle is the *Chantry
of Bp. Stanbury* (1474), with rich fan-vaulting and heraldry, and curious
capitals; the bishop's tomb is opposite.

A door w. of it leads to the *Archive Chamber*, formerly entered only by a kind
of drawbridge, crossing the large window in the N.W. transept. The "genuine
monastic *Library" here (adm. weekdays, 11–1, 2–4; fee), said to be the largest in
the world, has nearly 1500 chained books in their original presses, including Celtic
Gospels (8–9C), a unique Breviary with plainchant of the Hereford use (1265–70)
and a Limoges enamel reliquary (13C) with the martyrdom of St Thomas Becket.

The EAST TRANSEPTS were built on the site of the Norman apsidal
chapels at the end of the 14C. In the s.E. transept is a bust by Roubiliac,
probably of James Thomas (d. 1757), and in the s. choir aisle are several
14C effigies of early bishops.

The E.E. *LADY CHAPEL (c. 1220), despite its interior want of height,
is beautiful, especially the clustered window-shafts and the E. end with
its five lancets (restored.) On the s. side is the 15C tomb of Precentor
Swinfield (with his 'swine' rebus); some of the windows contain 14C

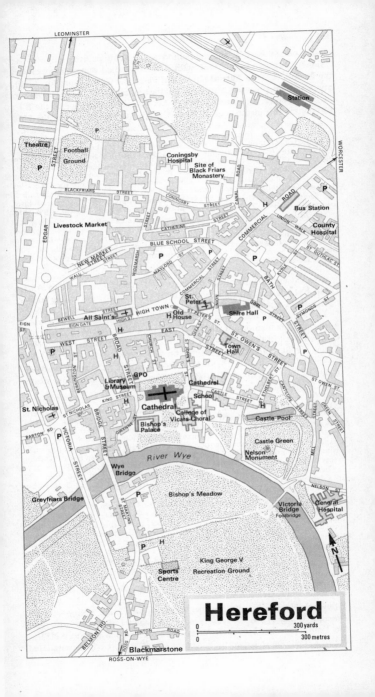

Hereford

LEOMINSTER

Theatre

P

EDGAR STREET

Football Ground

P

BLACKFRIARS STREET

Coningsby Hospital

Site of Black Friars Monastery

CONINGSBY STREET

CANAL ROAD

Livestock Market

NEW MARKET STREET

WALL STREET

WIDEMARSH STREET

CATHERINE STREET

BLUE SCHOOL STREET

MAYLORD ST.

COMMERCIAL STREET

COMMERCIAL ROAD

H

Bus Station

UNION WALK

County Hospital

ST. GUTHLAC ST.

BATH STREET

UNION STREET

Boat P

P

SYMONDS STREET

EIGN ST.

BEWELL STREET

All Saint's

HIGH STREET

HIGH TOWN

St. Peter's

ST. PETER'S ST.

Shire Hall

EIGN GATE

EAST STREET

Old House

H

WEST STREET

P

BROAD STREET

ST JOHN STREET

Town Hall

ST. OWEN'S STREET

ST. EBBETH ST.

CANTILUPE STREET

ST OWEN ST.

H

CHURCH STREET

GPO

Library & Museum

KING STREET

Cathedral School

CASTLE STREET

Castle Pool

GREEN STREET

MILL STREET

St. Nicholas

ST. NICHOLAS ST.

BARTON RD.

P

VICTORIA STREET

BRIDGE STREET

GWYNNE STREET

Cathedral

College of Vicars Choral

Bishop's Palace

Castle Green

Nelson Monument

River Wye

Wye Bridge

Greyfriars Bridge

P

ST MARTINS STREET

Bishop's Meadow

H

Victoria Bridge Footbridge

NELSON ST.

General Hospital

Sports Centre

King George V Recreation Ground

N

BELMONT RD.

HINTON ROAD

Blackmarstone

ROSS-ON-WYE

Station

WORCESTER ROAD

| 0 | 300 yards |
| 0 | 300 metres |

glass from St Peter's church. Behind a screen of painted stone is the
Audley Chantry (1492–1502), with a lierne-vaulted upper chamber. On
the N. side of the fine tomb of Sir Peter de Grandisson (d. 1358),
great-grand nephew of Cantelupe, and the monument of Joanna de Bohun
(d. 1327), under a painted arch. On this side is the entrance to the E.E.
CRYPT, the one instance of an English crypt founded later than the 11C.

A covered walk, with a finely carved oak roof, known as the *Vicars' Cloister*,
leads from the S.E. transept to the COLLEGE OF VICARS-CHORAL, built round a
quadrangle (1472). A second cloister, of two walks (Perp.), known as the *Bishops'
Cloister*, with vigorous grotesques and unusually elaborate tracery, is entered from
the S. side of the nave. In the E. walk is the doorway of a decagonal *Chapter House*,
the foundations of which may be seen in a garden between the two cloisters.
It was stripped of its lead in the Civil War, and used as a quarry in the 18C. The
square tower, with an upper chamber, at the S.E. corner, has always been called
the '*Ladye Arbour*'. On the W. side is the *Muniment Room* (1897), with the archive
cupboards (c. 1600–20) re-erected here in 1969.—Three Choirs Festival, see p. 301.

The *Bishop's Palace* stands to the S. between the cathedral and the river. It
contains a Norman hall with timber pillars. In Gwynne St., on the wall of the
bishop's garden, is a tablet marking the alleged birthplace of Nell Gwynne (or Gwyn;
1650–87). The *Cathedral School*, E. of the cathedral, dates certainly from the 14C but
probably had Saxon origins; it is now independent. In Berrington St. are some quaint
half-timbered alms-houses.

King. St and Bridge St. go on from the Cathedral to the *Wye Bridge*
(1490, but altered), which is relieved by the new Greyfriars bridge farther
upstream. A fine *Park* with river walks extends E. along the far bank.

To the S.E. of the cathedral close, on the river, is CASTLE GREEN,
preserving the memory of the old castle; the pool on its N. side was part
of the moat. In the middle is a column to Nelson. We return to High
Town viâ St Owen's St., passing the *Town Hall* (1904), the classical
Shire Hall (by Smirke, 1819), a statue of Sir G. Cornewall Lewis (d.
1863; by Marochetti), and *St Peter's Church*, which has a 13C steeple
and 15C stalls.

In Widemarsh St., which runs N. from High Town, is the *Raven Inn* (r.; formerly
the 'Angel'), where David Garrick was born in 1717. *Coningsby Hospital*, or *Black
Cross Hospital*, ¼ m. farther on, is an alms-house for old soldiers and servants,
erected in 1614 on the site of a commandery of the Knights Hospitallers, with a
chapel of c. 1200. The inmates (occasionally at least) wear a red uniform; the
visitor is shown round by the '*Corporal*' (gratuity). In the garden are a Preaching
Cross (c. 1370) and other relics of a monastery of Black Friars (c. 1322).

On Aylestone Hill, N.E. of the station, David Cox (see above) lived from 1817
in a 'picturesque cottage' in Parry's Lane, and from 1823 in Ash Tree House
(later called Berbice Villa), which he built for himself.

Kenchester (5 m. N.W.) occupies the site of *Castra Magna*, the Roman settlement
nearest Hereford, and *Dinedor Hill* (3 m. S.) has a British camp and a view. At
Madley, 6 m. W., the *Church has a 13C nave and a 14C apse covering a vaulted
crypt.—At *Kilpeck*, 7½ m. S.W., the well-restored *Church is one of the finest
remaining examples of enriched Norman work on a comparatively small scale.
The remarkable sculpture on the S. doorway and W. window, and the gargoyles,
showing Celtic influence, should be specially noticed. We may go on thence viâ
St Devereux to (11 m.) *Abbey Dore*, where the *Church consists of the choir and
transepts of a Cistercian abbey-church of 1147.

From Hereford to *Malvern* and *Worcester*, see Rte 37; to *Hay, Abergavenny*,
etc., see the 'Blue Guide to Wales'.

Beyond Hereford A 49 runs N., through the Lugg valley.—36 m.
Dinmore Manor (1¼ m. l.) preserves the 14C chapel of a commandery of
the Templars (adm. 2–6; fee). We go over the wooded Dinmore Hill to
(39 m.) *Hope-under-Dinmore*. *Hampton Court*, ¾ m. E., is a castellated

mansion built by Sir Rowland Lenthall with the ransom of prisoners taken at Agincourt (1415); *Bodenham*, 2 m. farther s.e., is charmingly placed on the Lugg.

43 m. **Leominster** (pron. 'Lemster'; Hotels), a town of 7100 inhab., once a famous wool market, celebrated by the poet Drayton, stands on the Lugg. Among many 16–17C houses, the *Talbot* and the *Royal Oak* hotels, both mainly Georgian, have earlier portions. The *Church of SS Peter & Paul, formerly part of a Benedictine priory, illustrates every style from Norman to Perpendicular. The present nave, added in 1239 as the church of the laity, is remarkable for its beautiful Perp. window, 45 ft high. The 14C s. aisle has fine ball-flower ornamentation. The ancient ducking-stool in the N. aisle was last used in 1809. In the park to the s. is *Grange Court*, a timber building erected in 1633 by John Abell, the 'king's carpenter', as the Market House, and from 1750 the Town Hall; it was removed to its present site in 1853. On the *Clarke Almshouses* (1736; rebuilt 1874) is a quaint effigy over a trenchant inscription in favour of thrift.

A 44 leads w. viâ (5 m.) *Eardisland*, with good half-timbered houses, and (7½ m.) *Pembridge* (Hotel), a large village with a rustic Tudor market hall and a 14C church with a detached timber *Belfry, to (14 m.) *Kington* (Hotels), a small town (with another good church) where Mrs Siddons made her début in a barn in 1772 or 1773. The golf course, on *Bradnor Hill* (N.T.; 1½ m. n.w.) is the highest in England (1284 ft). The return may be made through *Shobdon*, 3 m. n. of Pembridge, with a 'Gothick' church of 1755. Parts of its Norman predecessor, with carving recalling Kilpeck, have been erected on a hill to the north. Thence Leominster is regained viâ (2 m.) *Mortimer's Cross*, where the Yorkists defeated the Lancastrians in 1461. —*Weobley* (Hotels), 8 m. s.w., is notable for its half-timbered houses and a fine 13–14C church with a graceful steeple.

Or from Mortimer's Cross we may go on to Ludlow (11¼ m.) viâ (1 m.) *Lucton*, with its school of 1708, (2½ m.) Croft Castle, and (7¼ m.) Richards Castle. *Croft Castle* (N.T.; adm. 2.15–6, Easter–Sept, Wed, Thurs, Sat, Sun, & BH; Oct, Sat & Sun only; fee), a castle of c. 1400 altered in 1750, but preserving its corner drum-towers, shows good 17–18C decoration and stands in charming grounds. The little church beside it is notable for a fine monument (Sir Richard Croft; d. 1509). *Croft Ambrey* (¾ m. n. by footpath) is a large Iron Age fort.—*Richards Castle*, partly in Salop, has a Norman and 14C church with a detached tower, and a dilapidated motte-and-bailey castle, perhaps pre-Conquest.

The main road skirts the fine park of (46 m.) *Berrington Hall* (N.T.; adm. 2–6, Easter–Sept, Wed, Sat & BH; fee), built by Holland in 1778, with interesting plasterwork and painting. To the w. of it (1¼ m.) is *Eye Manor* (adm. 2.30–5.30, March–June, Sun, Wed, Thurs, Sat, & BH. Mon & Tues; in July–Sept, daily 2.30–5.30; fee), built in 1680 for Ferdinando Gorges, a West Indian slave trader. It has a fine 17–18C interior and a collection of 'corn dollies' and other crafts and adjoins an attractive church with a 14C porch of carved oak and 16C monuments.—At (50¼ m.) *Woofferton* (Hotel) we enter Shropshire and reach the valley of the Teme.

FROM WOOFFERTON TO KIDDERMINSTER, 23 m. (A 456).—5 m. Tenbury Wells (small Hotels) has mineral wells that enjoyed a brief vogue in the mid-19C. Timber-framed inns recall its position on an old posting road to Wales. The church contains interesting monuments including one to the parents of Lady Lucy of Charlecote. *St Michael's College*, founded by Sir F. Gore Ouseley as a school of church music, has an important library where the MS. treasures include Handel's 'Messiah'. Continuing E. we skirt *Wyre Forest*.—20 m. Bewdley (small Hotels), a quiet old town (7200 inhab.) on the Severn, here crossed by Telford's fine *Bridge (1801). In the canal era the town lost importance to Stourport and remains serenely Georgian. Severnside, by the river, Load St., with the Town Hall (1808) and Post Office (16C), and the High St. are all attractive. The church (1745) is by E. and T. Woodward. Earl Baldwin (1867–1947) was born at 15 Lower Park. At *Tickenhall Manor*, a former royal palace, Prince Arthur was married by proxy to Catherine of Aragon.—23 m. *Kidderminster*, see p. 347.

54 m. **LUDLOW**, finely "seated upon a hill at the joyning of the Teme and the river Corve", is an interesting and attractive old town (6774 inhab.), with many charming half-timbered houses.

Picturesque **Hotels** (coaching inns or older).
Post Office, Corve Street.
Golf Course (18-hole) at *Bromfield*, 2 m. N.W. *Horse Racing* also at Bromfield. —*Fishing* in the Teme and its tributaries; apply to National Provincial Bank, Bull Ring.—*Boating* on the Teme.

Entering the town from the s. we traverse the suburb of *Ludford*, with a 13C church (St Giles) and Ludford House (14C), and cross the Teme by Ludford Bridge (15C; *View). Thence Broad St., passing through Broad Gate, the only survivor of seven town gates, ascends, past some of the most interesting old houses in Ludlow, to the *Butter Cross* (1743), by Wm. Baker.

High St. leads w. to Castle Sq., in which is the Tudor *Castle Lodge*. The imposing *Castle (adm. 10.30–1, 2–4.30 or 7.30, Sun in winter on application) begun by Roger de Lacy in 1086, but with additions down to 1581, was long the seat of the Lords President of the Marches. It was taken by the Parliament in 1646 and partly dismantled, and in the 18C it was allowed to fall into ruin.

Over the 14C *Gateway* by which we enter the Castle Green (the Outer Bailey) were the rooms in which Samuel Butler (then steward of the Earl of Carbery) wrote a great part of 'Hudibras' (1661–62). In front is the 13C *Mortimer's Tower*, the alleged prison of Hugh de Mortimer, a sturdy opponent of Henry II. Beyond the inner moat is a 14C *Gateway*, with the arms of Elizabeth I and of Sir Henry Sydney (father of Sir Philip), President of the Court of the Marches. On the left of this is the Norman *Keep* (110 ft high; *View), the oldest part of the castle. In the Inner Ward stands an exquisite late-Norman *Round Chapel* (c. 1120), the chancel of which has disappeared. To the N. of this is a range of 13–14C buildings: at the w. end is the suite of rooms in which Prince Arthur, elder brother of Henry VIII, died in 1502, the year after his marriage with Catherine of Aragon; then come the *Great Hall* (now roofless) in which Milton's masque of 'Comus' was presented in 1634, after the Earl of Bridgewater had come to Ludlow to take up his appointment as lord-lieutenant of Wales; the *Banqueting Hall*; the *Armoury*; and the *Pendover Tower*, with the rooms occupied by the little Edward V and his brother in 1483, before their removal to London and their fate in the Tower.

The noble parish church of **St Lawrence** has a lofty 15C tower (130 ft), a remarkable E. window (15C glass), a 14C Jesse window in the Lady Chapel (s.), and a hexagonal porch. The reredos, misericords, and screens, and the monuments, in the chancel, of officials and lords of the Welsh Marches, all repay examination. The oldest tomb is that of Ambrosia (d. 1574), sister of Sir Philip Sidney. The ashes of A. E. Housman (1859–1936), the poet and scholar, lie in the churchyard beneath the N. wall.

Opposite the E. end of the church stands the picturesque *Reader's House* (adm. 9–7; fee), a half-timbered Tudor building with a Jacobean porch, incorporating some fragments of a much older stone 'church house', acquired in the 14 or 15C by the ancient Palmers' Guild. In the 18C it was the residence of the 'reader', an assistant to the rector of the parish.

From the Butter Cross there are excellent walks down the hill. King St. leads to the *Bull Ring*, a once broad street filled in down the middle in late-medieval times. The *Feathers Hotel, a notable Tudor hostelry, has Jacobean carving, plaster ceiling, and fireplaces. *Corve St.*, part Georgian, part Tudor, with *Foxe's Almshouses* (1593) in stone and many timbered houses, leads to Corve Bridge (18C). *Old Street* starts in the Bull Ring, then drops to the *Town Preacher's House* (1620), below which are fragments of the 13C Town Wall. *Broad St. ranks with the finest old streets in England. All the back lanes repay perambulation.

The surroundings are very attractive. Pleasant wooded walks skirt the Teme; while to the E. and N.E. rise the **Clee Hills**, best reached by the road to Bridgnorth (20 m.) viâ (10 m.) *Burwarton* (800 ft) and (11 m.) *Cleobury North. Titterstone Clee* (1749 ft; *View) rises to the S. of this road, *Brown Clee* (1790 ft) to the N.—A fine round may be completed by going on from Cleobury North to (13½ m.) *Ditton Priors* (758 ft) and thence, viâ *Abdon* and (18 m.) *Heath*, with its small but complete Norman church, descending by B 4368 *Corve Dale*, the broad valley between the Clee Hills and the long ridge of *Wenlock Edge* (800–950 ft). At *Aston Munslow* is the White House Museum of buildings and country life (adm. April–Oct, Sat & Wed, 2–5.30; fee).—A 4117 from Ludlow crosses the S. side of the Clee Hills and goes on to (11¾ m.) *Cleobury Mortimer*, a little town where the church has a Trans. Norman tower and some good 13C work

To the W. of Ludlow is (8½ m.) *Leintwardine*, with the tomb of Gen. Tarleton (1754–1833), who served in the American War of Independence. The return thence should be made by (12½ m.) *Wigmore*, with the huge ruin of the castle of the Mortimers (12–14C), and over *Bringewood Chase* (High Vinnals, 1235 ft), 3 m. S.W. of Ludlow.

56½ m. *Bromfield* preserves remains of a 12C priory in its parish church and elsewhere.—63½ m. *Stokesay Castle*, just beyond Telford's *Onny Bridge*, is the oldest and probably the finest example in England of a moated and fortified manor-house (adm. 9–6, winter 10–4.30, closed Tues; fee). It has a half-timbered gatehouse (1570) and two towers (1115 and 1291) flanking a great hall of 1284. It belonged to the Lords Craven in 1627–1869, but was built by Laurence de Ludlow, a clothier.— 64½ m. *Craven Arms* (Hotel) is important as the junction of the railway to Central Wales.

The Elizabethan *Shipton Hall*, 10 m. along the Wenlock road, is open on Thurs & BH, 2.30–5, in May–Sept (fee).

B 4368 leads W. to (8½ m.) *Clun* (Hotel), a remote little town with an old bridge and a poorly restored Norman church. The ruined castle, dating from the reign of Stephen, is sometimes identified with the 'Garde Doloureuse' of Scott's 'Betrothed'. Lord Clive bought the estate of *Walcot Park* (4 m. N.E. of Clun) in 1760.— *Bishop's Castle*, 11 m. N.W. of Craven Arms, is a tiny borough with quaint houses and shops, but no longer a castle.

70 m. **Church Stretton** (Hotels), a high-lying health resort, is well situated at c. 650 ft on the *Longmynd* (1696 ft; view), which rises to the S., and has a good golf course. The Church has much Norman work and a powerful 13C roof.

Attractive walks may be taken to *Cardingmill Valley*, N.W. of the town; to *Caer Caradoc* (1506 ft; 2 m. N.E.), with a British camp and Caractacus's Cave; to the top of the *Longmynd*, etc.—The line of the Roman Watling Street, between Leintwardine (Bravonium) and Wroxeter (Uriconium), lies E. of the railway.

75 m. *Longnor* has a Hall of 1670–90 (no adm.).—About 1 m. N.W. of (76½ m.) *Dorrington* is the 13C church of *Stapleton*, which prior to 1300 consisted of two stories (the lower one perhaps intended for a store), and 2 m. N.E. is *Condover*, where the church has a 17C nave, formed by throwing the early nave and N. aisle into one after the fall of the central tower (1660). The N. transept is late-Norman. The monuments, more

remarkable than artistic, include works by Roubiliac and G. F. Watts. *Condover Hall*, a fine stone house of 1598, is now a home for blind children (adm. free daily in Aug, 10–4).—83 m. **Shrewsbury,** see Rte 42.

37   HEREFORD TO MALVERN AND WORCESTER

ROAD, 30 m. (A 438 and A 449).—14½ m. *Ledbury.*—22 m. **Great Malvern.**—30 m. **Worcester.**—Worcester may be reached also (28 m.) by A 465 and A 44 viâ (14 m.) **Bromyard** (Hotel), with many timbered houses; or (26 m.) directly by A 4103 (poor road).—BUSES by the first two routes.

RAILWAY, 29¼ m. in 45–50 min. Intermediate stations: 13½ m. *Ledbury.*—17¾ m. *Colwall.*—20¾ m. **Great Malvern.**—21¾ m. *Malvern Link.*—28½ m. and 29¼ m. **Worcester** (Foregate Street and Shrub Hill).

Hereford, see Rte 36. The road traverses a rich country of orchards and hop-gardens; the wooded hills on the right (892 ft), centring on *Woolhope,* afford wide views.—8 m. *Tarrington* church has a fine 12C chancel arch.—14½ m. **Ledbury** (Hotels) is a busy little town on a hill slope. The 17C **Market House,* traditionally by John Abell, still rests on its sixteen original chestnut pillars. The *Feathers* and *Talbot* are both late-16C inns with fine interiors. The large *Church,* with a massive detached tower, is mainly of the 13–14C and contains good monuments, notably the Skynner Tomb (1631) and a rare 13C effigy of a priest (N. transept). In the churchyard lies Jacob Tonson (d. 1736), the publisher of Dryden and Pope. *Ledbury Park* (1590) is a fine gabled manor. Ledbury was the birthplace of the poets William Langland (1330?–1400?) and John Masefield (1878–1967), and many of the earlier narrative poems of the latter contain local allusions. The early years of Mrs Browning (until 1832) were spent at *Hope End,* a house 1¾ m. N.

About 2 m. s.e. is *Eastnor Castle* (open 2.15–6 on summer BH, and Sun in June–Sept; fee), a 'Gothick' edifice of 1810–17 by Smirke, with additions by Pugin, where the treasures, with the exception of the armour of Charles V's body-guard, are swamped by the hideous decoration. The Tewkesbury road goes on thence to (7 m.) **Birtsmorton Court* (no adm.), a delightfully unspoilt 12–16C moated manor. Here Wolsey was chaplain c. 1503–7, and Wm. Huskisson was born in 1770.—*Bosbury,* 3 m. N. of Ledbury, has many interesting old houses, notably the Crown inn (once the manor-house of the Harfords), with a panelled room dated 1571. The church contains two Harford tombs, one the oldest signed monument in England (by John Guldo, 1573). *Castle Frome,* 1½ m. farther N., has a magnificent **Font (c. 1150), with a vivid Baptism of Christ of the Hereford school of sculpture.—At **Much Marcle,** 4½ m. s.w. of Ledbury, is *Hellens,* a manor-house dating from the 13C (adm. Sun in June–Sept & BH; fee); attractive lanes lead N.W. over Marcle Hill to Woolhope (see above) and Hereford.—From Ledbury to Gloucester, see p. 302.

The railway tunnels through the Malvern Hills, but the road climbs to (18 m.) *Wynd's Point* (830 ft; Hotel), the pass between the *Hereford-shire Beacon* (1114 ft) and the main ridge.

The Beacon was once crowned by a huge and strong British camp, where, according to tradition, Caractacus was captured in A.D. 75. At Wynd's Point is the country-house long occupied by Jenny Lind (Mme Goldschmidt).

22 m. **MALVERN** (29,000 inhab.), a place of note in ecclesiastical history, attracts by the beauty of its situation and environs, the purity of its air, and medicinal quality of its springs. The name is shared by seven contiguous places at the base or on the slope of the MALVERN HILLS, a range of igneous rocks (8½ m. long, ½–1 m. wide) with about

twenty summits (1000–1400 ft), rising with unexpected charm out of the Severn plain. The town of **Great Malvern,** at the N. end of the chain, is the chief of the group, but pleasant quarters may be obtained in any of the villages. The whole region was once a royal chase.

Hotels (advance booking necessary in summer) at *Great Malvern* and (with fine views) at *Malvern Wells*; also at *West Malvern*, and at *Colwall* on the western side of the hills.
Buses to all destinations from Wells Rd., Gt. Malvern.
Amusements. *Theatre*, with annual dramatic festival in Aug, and *Winter Garden*, in Grange Rd.—GOLF COURSE at Malvern Wells.—RACECOURSE (steeplechases) at Colwall.—SWIMMING POOL, Grange Rd.—*Three Counties Agricultural Show*, below Malvern Wells, in June.
The medicinal properties of the springs were publicized in 1756; the spa, well established by 1820, reached the height of its fashion c. 1840–70, attracting (like Cheltenham) retired and affluent empire-builders. The many large hotels are characteristic, the Foley Arms of 1810–17 being the earliest.

Great Malvern possesses one of the chief springs, *St Ann's Well*, situated on the slope of the Worcestershire Beacon, 750 ft above the sea. The fine ***Priory Church** appears when viewed from without to be wholly a Perp. edifice of the 15C, but the interior reveals the Norman nave of the original 11C building. The tower recalls that of Gloucester Cathedral.

The church is notable for its 15–16C glass, the finest windows being those in the S.E. chapel (St Anne's), the E. window, the six high windows in the choir, and the N. transept window (with a portrait of Prince Arthur, son of Henry VII). The wall *Tiles (1453–58), set in the choir-screen, are of local manufacture, and the misericords and monuments deserve attention.—William Langland, author of 'The Vision of Piers Plowman', a famous poem in the Midland dialect, was probably educated in Malvern Priory, of which a restored Perp. gateway remains above the church.

Malvern College (1863), on the s. side of the town, ranks high among English public schools; in 1941–42 it was the training establishment for Free French cadets. In the *Cemetery*, near the station, lies Jenny Lind (1820–87).—At *Malvern Wells*, s. of Great Malvern, is the *Holy Well* (680 ft). At *Little Malvern*, still farther s., the church, rebuilt in the 14C, is a relic of a Benedictine priory of 1171 or earlier. Little Malvern Court, the former guest-hall (14C) is open Wed, May–Sept, 2.30–5.30. Sir Edward Elgar (1857–1934) is buried in the R.C. cemetery. *West Malvern* is the only one of the group which commands views towards the w. (Herefordshire hills). The *Royal Well* (1150 ft) is near it. *North Malvern* still has its old stocks and whipping-post.

The chief **Malvern Hills,** from N. to s., are *West Hill, North Hill, Sugarloaf Hill, Worcester Beacon, Herefordshire Beacon* or *Camp Hill, Swinyard Hill, Midsummer Hill, Hollybush Hill, Ragged Stone,* and *Gloucester Beacon* or *Chase* (or *Keys) End.* Most of their summits are accessible by easy paths, with benches.—*North Hill* (1307 ft) is ascended viâ the *Ivy Scar Rock* (½ hr; good view of Great Malvern and its church). *Worcestershire Beacon* (1395 ft), the highest (the "lonely height" of Macaulay), is ascended from Great Malvern in ½ hr. The *View includes 15 "fair counties", the cathedrals of Hereford, Worcester, and Gloucester, the abbeys of Malvern, Tewkesbury, Deerhurst, Evesham, and Pershore, the Wrekin (N.), and the Brecknock Hills (w.).—To the s. of this is the *Wyche Pass* (900 ft), beyond which we may follow the ridge to *Wynd's Point* and (3 m.) the *Herefordshire Beacon* (see above).

The Worcester road descends to the Teme valley, which it crosses at (27 m.) *Powick Bridge.*—30 m. **Worcester,** see Rte 35.

38 ROSS TO CHEPSTOW. THE WYE VALLEY

ROAD, 26¾ m. The road described below combines directness with easy accessibility to all the most famous beauties of the Lower Wye. A 40: 4¾ m. *Goodrich* (l.) and *Symond's Yat Rock* (6¼ m.).—6½ m. *Whitchurch* (for Symond's Yat village, 1¼ m. l.).—10¾ m. *Monmouth*. We turn l. on A 466.—21½ m. *Tintern.*—24½ m. Lane (r.) for the *Wyndcliff.*—26¾ m. Chepstow.

The *Wye* (Welsh *Gwy*, water) rises in Wales on the slopes of Plynlimon, only 2 m. from the headwaters of the Severn. It flows to the S.E. and E. viâ Rhayader, Builth Wells, and Hay to Hereford, then to the S., joining the Severn just below Chepstow after a course of 130 m. Walkers may spend a very pleasant week in following its whole course from source to mouth, but the majority of tourists will content themselves with a visit to the *Lower Wye*, which includes some of the loveliest river-scenery in Britain "a succession of nameless beauties". The most beautiful scenery is on the section between Gloucestershire and Gwent or Monmouthshire. The Wye, like the Severn, is a good salmon stream, and its fisheries are valuable.

Ross is the usual starting-point for a visit to the Lower Wye; but the trip is sometimes begun at Hereford, with a night halt at Ross or Monmouth. Parts of the river may be explored by boat (especially in the neighbourhood of Hereford, Ross, and Symond's Yat; see below), but the tidal reach (extending below Tintern) is less attractive at low water.

From *Ross* (see Rte 36) we cross the river and turn left on A 40. Beyond the pleasant grounds of (3½ m.) *Mount Craig Hotel*, a road on the left leads to *Goodrich* (¾ m.; Hotel). *Goodrich Castle* (adm. 9.30–4, 5.30, or 7; Sun from 2; fee), an imposing ruin finely situated above the Wye, was erected in 1101–2 and later became a seat of the Talbots. The existing keep dates from 1160–70, the rest from the 13–14C. Here Wordsworth met the little girl who inspired 'We are Seven' (1793). A farm near *Kerne Bridge*, ½ m. E., preserves some domestic remains of Flanesford Priory (1347). Below, the river makes a long loop and the scenery becomes more diversified.

The right bank now belongs to Herefordshire, the left bank to Gloucestershire (Forest of Dean). A road (B 4228) follows the latter past *Drybrook* (1½ m. from Goodrich; Hotel) to *Lydbrook* (3½ m.; Hotel).

We may continue on the Goodrich by-road, and diverge (l.) after 1 m. on to B 4432, which crosses the river by Huntsham Bridge and climbs to *Symond's Yat Rock* (473 ft). The famous hill rises between two reaches of the river which at their nearest points are but 500 yds apart. The summit, which forms part of the Dean Forest Park, has been discreetly equipped with a car park and a log cabin (rfmts). A footbridge across the road leads to an eminence (orientation table) commanding a wonderful *View* in which the serpentine loops of the river are framed in the rich pastoral and woodland landscape with charming effect. Below to the E. are the steep *Coldwell Rocks*, where the Wye makes a wide bend to the N.; while to the S.W. the river sweeps round the *Great Doward* (661 ft), crowned with an old encampment. Farther S.W. are the beautiful woods of *Lady Park*.—The ferry to the village (see below) may be reached on foot in ½ hr or by a narrow road.

The A 40 continues S.W., passing an alternative approach to Yat Rock (signposted 'Symond's Yat East').—At (6½ m.) *Whitchurch* (Hotel, with grounds), now just off the main road, P. Wilson Steer (1860–1942) lived in 1863–80 and from here attended Hereford Cathedral School. A road (B 4164, signposted 'Symonds Yat West'; bus) diverges for the popular village of **Symond's Yat** (1¼ m.; pron. 'Sim-'). The hotels lie near the water's edge at the foot of the precipitous rocks which here wall the Wye, mostly on the w. bank. A passenger ferry plies to the E. bank below Yat Rock (comp. above).

Beyond Whitchurch the main road skirts Great Doward and *Little Doward* (700 ft) on the left, then, entering Wales beyond the fine woods of (22¾ m.) *Wyaston Leys*, follows the river above a more open valley.

The historic border-county of **Monmouthshire**, though strongly Welsh in character, as its place-names testify, and largely peopled by Celts, was removed from the jurisdiction of the Lords Marchers and included among English counties by Henry VIII in 1535. Ecclesiastically, however, it remained part of Wales, and in 1974, when it was renamed **Gwent**, it was administratively confirmed to Wales. The portion E. of the Usk is undulating and rural; whilst that to the w. (by far the more populous) is mountainous (highest point 1905 ft), with valleys disfigured by ironworks and collieries. The county is more fully described in the 'Blue Guide to Wales'.

10¾ m. **MONMOUTH** (Hotels), perhaps on the site of the Roman *Blestium*, and until 1939 the county town (6500 inhab.), is finely situated on the w. bank of the Wye at the point where it is joined by the Monnow, and is surrounded by wooded hills. It preserves the street plan of a 15C market town. Henry V (1387–1422; 'Harry of Monmouth') was born in the castle, and his statue adorns the *Shire Hall* (1724) in Agincourt Square. In front of the hall is a bronze statue (by Goscombe John) of the Hon. C. S. Rolls, the aviator, accidently killed in 1910. The *Museum* (adm. April–Oct, weekdays; also Sun aft in July–Aug; closed Nov–March; fee), behind the hall, contains an exceptionally fine collection of Nelson relics and portraits and houses the *Local History Centre.* To the N.w. of the square are the remains of the Castle. The 12C Great Tower survives, and within the castle ward is *Great Castle House*, a mansion of 1673 now an officers' mess (adm. May–Sept, Mon, Wed, Fri, 2–5; ring), which has richly decorated plaster ceilings. As the senior regiment of the Territorial Army Volunteer Reserve, the Royal Monmouthshire Royal Engineers (Militia) takes precedence over all other units, directly following the Regular Army. *St Mary's* was originally the church of a Benedictine priory where Geoffrey of Monmouth (d. 1154), who was born in the town, may have been a monk; largely rebuilt in 1881 (by G. E. Street) it retains a graceful Dec. spire. In the Baptistery are some 15C tiles and a cresset stone from the earlier church (c. 1102). The 13C *Gateway* on the old Monnow bridge is a unique example in Britain of a fortified gateway actually standing on a bridge. Just beyond is the small over-restored *Church of St Thomas Becket*, which retains its Norman porches and chancel arch (c. 1185). The timber font and galleries are 19C. 'Monmouth caps' ('Henry V', iv, 7) were worn by soldiers and formed the town's principal manufacture in the 16–17C.

Just across the river is (c. 1 hr) *Kymin Hill* (850 ft; N.T.), with a 'temple' in honour of Nelson's admirals, commanding a *View over the Wye and Monnow. Another fine *View is obtained from the *Buckstone* (915 ft), a rocking-stone 1¼ m. farther E. A fine road (A 4136) climbs round the N. side of these to (3¾ m.) *Staunton*, on the edge of the Forest of Dean, with a church dating in part from 1100.

FROM MONMOUTH TO USK, 13 m. (more fully described in the 'Blue Guide to Wales'). 8 m. *Raglan* (Hotel). *Raglan Castle* (adm. daily; Sun in winter from 2), one of the most superb ruins in England, dating from c. 1435, was defended for 10 weeks in 1646 against Fairfax by the octogenarian Marquess of Worcester. Here his son, later second Marquess, invented and set up a 'water commanding engine', described in his 'Century of Inventions' (1663). Field-Marshal Lord

Raglan (d. 1855), of Crimean War fame, took his title from this town.—13 m.
Usk (Hotel) is a small town on the Usk, frequented by anglers, with a 13C castle
(adm. daily; fee) and church.

We cross the Wye and turn left on A 466. A 40 continues to Raglan
(comp. above). The valley contracts, and for the rest of the way road
and river keep close together.—13½ m. *Redbrook* tinplate works closed
in 1961 after 160 years of production.—At (16½ m.) *Bigsweir Bridge*, we
regain the w. bank.—18 m. *Llandogo* is beautifully situated in a fold
of the steep wooded hills.—Just below (20 m.) *Brockweir*, above which
(s.e.) are traces of Offa's Dyke, is *Tintern Parva* (Hotel), then, beyond
a loop, we reach (21½ m.) **Tintern** (Hotels).

*Tintern Abbey (adm. daily 9.30–4, 5.30 or 7; Sun from 2; fee), on a
strip of level river-margin, encircled by wooded hills, is the most romantic
Cistercian ruin in the country. It was founded in 1131, but most of the
church, which is notable for its beauty of composition and delicacy of
execution, dates from a rebuilding of c. 1220–87, though it was not
finally completed until c. 1320. The nave, which retains its clerestory on
the s., is mostly of the late 13C; the w. doorway comprises two trefoil-
headed openings enclosed by a moulded arch embellished by tracery,
while above it rises a great window of seven lights, likewise remarkable
for its fine tracery. The four large and beautiful arches of the crossing
formerly supported a belfry tower. The n. transept incorporates remains of the original 12C church, and retains the night stairs of the
monks and a six-light window with much of its tracery. The presbytery
has both n. and s. aisles; the great e. window covers almost the whole
of the wall. The domestic buildings (1220–70), on the n. side of the
church, are relatively unimportant.

The heights on the w. side of the Wye in the neighbourhood of Tintern are partly
contained in the *Tintern State Forest* (4890 acres).—The Wye is tidal below Tintern,
and between here and Chepstow it makes so many loops and bends as almost to
double the direct distance of 4 miles.

Beyond Tintern the road climbs above the Wye, of which delightful
views are obtained here and there. On emerging from the woods (24½ m.)
we turn back by a lane on the right for c. ¼ m. Hence a path on the right,
starting from a bend in the lane, leads in c. 15 min. to the top of the
*Wyndcliff (650 ft; the 'y' is pron. long), which displays one of the most
remarkable and beautiful views in Britain ("the grouping of the landscape is perfect"), over a wide bend of the Wye. To the s. the Severn is
prominent, and beyond it are the Mendips with the Cotswolds to the e.
We regain the road, when another ¼ m. brings us to (24¾ m.) *St Arvan's*
(Hotel). On the left is *Piercefield Park*, with the Chepstow racecourse,
in delightfully wooded country.

26¾ m. **Chepstow** (Hotels), the *Castell Gwent* of the Welsh and the
Striguil of the Normans, an old market-town (8000 inhab.) and formerly
an important port, stands on the w. bank of the Wye 2 m. above its
junction with the Severn. The *Castle (adm. daily, 9.30–4, 5.30 or 7,
Sun in winter from 2; fee), separated from the town by a ravine, is
of great extent and in tolerable preservation, highly picturesque in form,
and strikingly situated on a steep platform of rock washed by a broad
reach of the Wye. It is entered through an imposing gatehouse of two
drum-towers. Founded by William Fitz-Osbern, the castle is mainly of

Edwardian date (14C), but between the second and third of its four courts is, though much altered, the original Norman keep (1120–30). Henry Marten (1602–80), the regicide, was confined for 20 years in the fine s.e. drum-tower, and Jeremy Taylor also was imprisoned here in 1655. The church of *St Mary* (reached by a turning on the left from the top of Bridge St.), though vilely restored at various times, retains a considerable portion of Norman architecture (nave, w. door, etc.). The 13C *Port Wall*, which enclosed the medieval borough, may be traced throughout most of its course, and its w. gate still spans the main street. *Towngate Museum* (adm. Whit–Sept, weekdays exc. Wed, 2–4.30; fee (is a small museum of local interest.

The most popular short excursion from Chepstow is that to (2¾ m.) the *Wyndcliff* and (5¼ m.) *Tintern Abbey* (bus).—*Raglan* may be reached viâ Tintern (see above), viâ Monmouth, or by direct road (13 m.). *Mathern* (2¼ m.), *Caldicot Castle* (4¾ m.), and *Caerwent* (5 m.), all to the s.w., are likewise within easy reach.— About 1 m. s. of the town, beside the Wye, is the *Bulwarks Camp*, an early Iron Age cliff fort with a double rampart.—The region is more fully described in the 'Blue Guide to Wales'.

FROM CHEPSTOW TO BRISTOL, 17½ m. A spur from the A 48, just s.w. of the town, leads in 1½ m. on to the M 4 motorway, which crosses the mouth of the Wye and the Severn by the *Severn Road Bridge (toll). The bridge, opened in 1966 to replace the Beachley-Aust car ferry, has an overall length of 5240 ft and a central span between the 400-ft suspension towers of 3240 ft. It incorporates techniques learned from aircraft engineering in that the suspended structure has the shape of an aeroplane wing to reduce both weight and wind resistance. The distant views on the descending approach from the s. side are impressive, and a closer prospect of the graceful lines may be obtained from observation platforms at either end There is a passenger footbridge (cars may *not* idle or stop on the bridge).—At 8½ m. we join the unfinished M 5 and its continuation (A 4018) which, by-passing Westbury-on-Trym (p. 185), enters *Bristol* from the N.

From Chepstow to *Gloucester*, see Rte 30B.

39 LONDON TO CHESTER (LIVERPOOL, MANCHESTER)

ROAD, 180 m. A 5, A 51 (the old coaching route).—110 m. *Tamworth*.—116 m. Lichfield.—139¾ m. *Stone*.—160 m. Nantwich.—180 m. Chester.
A pleasant alternative (180¼ m.) leaves A 5 farther on, just beyond (133½ m.) *Weston-under-Lizard*, joining A 41 (comp. Rte 41).—MOTORWAY and other routes to Liverpool and Manchester, see pp. 539 and 548.

RAILWAY from Euston to Chester, 179¼ m. in 2¾ hrs; to Liverpool (Lime St.), 193½ m. in 2½–3½ hrs; to *Manchester* (Piccadilly), 188¾ m. in 2½–3½ hrs.—Principal Stations: 82½ m. Rugby.—97 m. *Nuneaton*.—110 m. *Tamworth*.—116½ m. Lichfield.—124½ m. *Rugeley*.—133½ m. Stafford, junction for Stoke-on-Trent (16 m.; through carriages from London), and some Manchester trains, etc.—158 m. Crewe is the point of divergence of lines to Chester, to Liverpool, to Manchester, and to the North. A change is sometimes necessary for Chester.
Alternative route to Chester, viâ Wolverhampton (change) and Shrewsbury, 198½ m. in 4 hrs (comp. Rte 41).

From London by A 5 to (69 m.) *Weedon*, see Rte 32B. The Chester road, part of the London to Holyhead turnpike beautifully engineered by Telford, follows the line of the Roman Watling Street, closely accompanied by the main Midland railway line, the Grand Union Canal, and the M 1 motorway.—72½ m. Near *Buckby Locks* the Roman settlement of *Bannaventa* was located in 1971. A mile farther N. we pass (l.) the junction of the two arms of the Grand Union, then cross the Leicester arm and the railway in the *Watford Gap*, with prominent motorway junction. The road leaves its Roman line for a few miles on either side of (75½ m.) *Kilsby*. About 2½ m. s. is *Ashby St Ledgers*, with the 16–17C manor-house of Robert Catesby (a meeting-place of the Gunpowder Plot conspirators) and a church containing 14C wall-paintings.

A detour of 4 m. to the left, viâ *Hillmorton*, with a Post Office wireless station and a church containing 14C effigies, leads to **Rugby** (Hotels), a town of 59,400 inhab., important as a railway junction and depot, for engineering, and for its school.

Rugby School, one of the leading public schools of England, was founded in 1567 by the bequest of Lawrence Sheriff, a member of the Grocers' Company, though the present buildings date only from the 19C. Matthew Arnold's poem 'Rugby Chapel' (1857) refers to the predecessor of the present chapel (by Butterfield; 1872), which has stained glass from Aerschot. Another chapel has been built as a war memorial (1920–23). A statue, by Brock, comemorates Thomas Hughes (1822–96), author of 'Tom Brown's School Days'. On the 'Doctor's Wall' is a tablet commemorating "the exploit of William Webb Ellis, who, with a fine disregard for the Rules of Football as played in his time, first took the ball in his arms and ran with it, thus originating the distinctive feature of the Rugby Game, A.D. 1823." The school first attained eminence under the headmastership (1828–42) of Dr Thomas Arnold, who revolutionized the whole system of public school teaching. Famous 'Rugbeians' include Sir Richard Temple, Landor, Dean Stanley, Matthew Arnold, Thomas Hughes, C. L. Dodgson ('Lewis Carroll'), Arthur Hugh Clough, Wyndham Lewis, and Rupert Brooke (1887–1915; born at Rugby). Sir Norman Lockyer (1836–1920), the astronomer and scientific journalist, was also a native of Rugby.

Bilton Hall, 2 m. s.w., was the residence of Joseph Addison from 1711 till his death in 1719 at Holland House in London.

FROM RUGBY TO PETERBOROUGH, 51 m. (A 427). The road at first follows the course of the infant Avon, which here divides Northamptonshire from Leicestershire.— 5 m. *Swinford. Stanford Hall* (1 m. r.), in a splendid park, is a dignified mansion of 1690 with additions by Smith of Warwick and containing Stuart paintings (adm. Easter–Sept on Thurs, Sat & Sun 2.30–6, also BH Mon & Tues only 12–6; tea; fee). P. S. Pilcher, a pioneer airman, was killed here in 1899 (replica of glider on show). *Stanford* church (early 14C), on the Northants bank of the river, contains fine old glass and good 16–17C monuments. The organ, brought from Magdalen College, Oxford, came originally from Whitehall Palace.— Beyond (11¾ m.) *Husbands Bosworth* we follow the course of the Welland.— 18 m. **Market Harborough**, see Rte 43.— 24 m. *Cottingham* is 1½ m s.w. of Rockingham (p. 408). To the s. and E. extends *Rockingham Forest*, once a royal deer-forest.— 27 m. *Corby* (Hotels) has developed since 1932 from a village to a town of 47,700 inhab., thanks to the exploitation of the ironstone quarries here and the erection of large steelworks operated by men moved *en bloc* from Scotland.— 31 m. *Weldon*. *Kirby Hall, 2 m. N., is a magnificent Renaissance mansion built in 1570–75 and altered in 1638–40 probably by Inigo Jones (adm. daily, Sun from 2; fee). Formerly the home of the Hatton family, it was already neglected in 1809 and derelict by 1828, but the shell is still remarkably complete. The s.w. wing has been restored (1967) and the garden replanted. A little to the E. is *Deene Park, the beautiful Tudor mansion (adm. Sun, May–July, & BH, 2–6; fee) of the Brudenell family; the church contains the memorial of the Earl of Cardigan (d. 1868), leader of the Charge of the Light Brigade at Balaclava.— 38½ m. *Oundle* and thence to (51 m.) *Peterborough*, see p. 394.

FROM RUGBY TO LEICESTER, 21 m. (A 426). The only place of interest on the way is (7½ m.) *Lutterworth* (Hotel), where John Wyclif was rector from about 1374 until his death in 1384. In 1414 his works were condemned by the Council of Constance, and his remains were disinterred, burned, and thrown into the little river Swift. St Mary's contains a number of alleged Wyclif relics, and also two fine wall-paintings.

From Rugby to *Althorp* and *Northampton*, see p. 393.

A 5 follows Watling Street, here the boundary between Warwickshire (l.) and Leicestershire for 18½ m.—82¼ m. *Caves Inn*, at the Roman station of Tripontium. At *Shawell* rectory (r.) much of Tennyson's 'In Memoriam' was written.—At (89½ m.) *High Cross* we cross the Foss

Way, and at 95 m. A 47 diverges left for Nuneaton (2 m.).—**Nuneaton** (Motel, Hotel), a thriving town (67,000 inhab.), manufactures bricks, woollen goods, and hats. *St Mary's* (1878) retains Norman piers and carving of the Benedictine nunnery church founded by the Earl of Leicester. *St Nicholas's* is a handsome E.E. and Perp. church. A memorial garden was opened in 1953 to George Eliot (1819–80) who lived just outside the town until 1841. Round the public *Library* (1962), designed by Frederick Gibberd, a new centre is developing.

Nuneaton, which now includes Stockingford ('Paddiford'), is itself the 'Milby' of 'Janet's Repentance'; and Lawyer Dempster's house was in Church St. (the 'Orchard St.' of the story).

FROM NUNEATON TO COVENTRY, 8 m. (A 444), we cross the 'George Eliot Country'.—1 m. *Chilvers Coton*, now a suburb of Nuneaton, is the 'Shepperton' of 'Mr Gilfil's Love Story'. George Eliot (born at South Farm, *Arbury*, 2 m. s.w.) was christened Mary Ann or Marian (Evans) in the church, which was destroyed in an air-raid in 1941 and voluntarily rebuilt by German prisoners in 1946. She was taken as an infant to (2½ m.) *Griff House*, her home until 1841 (comp. p. 321). Both were on the Newdigates' estate of *Arbury Hall* ('Cheverel Manor'), of which her father was agent. The 16C Hall, with 18C 'Gothick' alterations, contains period furniture and Newdigate letters (open Easter–Sept, Sun, & BH Mon & Tues following 2.30–6; fee).—3½ m. *Bedworth* (40,500 inhab.), a coal-mining centre. Corley Hall, a Jacobean farmhouse 4 m. w., has been suggested as the original of the 'Hall Farm' in 'Adam Bede.'—10 m. *Coventry* (p. 316).

To the N. of A 5, between A 447 (beyond Hinckley) and A 444 (the Burton road) are *Stoke Golding* (3 m.), with an early Dec. *Church, remarkable for the beauty of its detail, and *Market Bosworth* (6 m.), a tiny old town where Dr Johnson was usher at the grammar school. At *Bosworth Field*, 2 m. s., Richard III was defeated and slain by the Earl of Richmond (Henry VII) in 1485.

From Nuneaton to *Leicester*, see p. 329.

Beyond the Nuneaton turn A 5 passes (97 m.; r.) *Lindley Hall*, the birthplace of Robert Burton (1577–1640), author of the 'Anatomy of Melancholy'. Here is the testing-ground of the Motor Industry Research Association.—98 m. *Fenny Drayton* (r.) was the birthplace of George Fox (see below).—100 m. *Mancetter*, the Roman Manduessedum. At *Hartshill*, 2 m. s., Michael Drayton (1563–1631), the poet, was born.—101 m. *Atherstone* (Hotel) is an old market town with coaching inns. The remains of the Cistercian *Merevale Abbey*, 1 m. w., include the the 13–14C 'capella extra portam', now the parish church; it contains a plain Perp. screen, a mutilated Jesse window (14C), and an early 13C effigy.—Beyond (106½ m.) *Wilnecote* we turn r. on A 51.

A 5 goes on w. to (37½ m.) *Wellington* (Rte 42) viâ (20½ m.) *Gailey*, 4 m. s.w. of which is the 18C *Chillington Hall*, by Francis Smith and Soane (adm. 2.30–5.30, Thurs, May–Aug; fee).—27 m. *Weston-under-Lizard*, with *Weston Park* (adm. Easter–mid-Sept, daily exc. Mon & Fri, 2–6; fee; rfmts), the historic home of the Earl of Bradford. The mansion (1671) contains splendid furniture, tapestries, and silver, and a good collection of paintings.

110 m. **Tamworth** (Hotels), an ancient town (40,200 inhab.) on the Tame, the boundary between Warwickshire and Staffordshire, was, in Saxon times, one of the most important places in the Midlands. Offa had a royal palace here in the 8C and a mint; the castle-mound was perhaps raised by Ethelfleda, daughter of Alfred the Great, in 913. The fine old *Castle* (10–sunset, Sun from 2; closed on Fri in Nov–Feb; fee), now largely Jacobean, passed at the Conquest into the hands of the ancestor of the Marmion family. The light and spacious 14C *Church*, dedicated to St Editha, daughter of King Edgar, has a tower with a double spiral staircase and contains interesting monuments and pre-

Raphaelite stained glass. In the market-place is a statue of Sir Robert Peel (1788–1850), who lived at *Drayton Manor* (2½ m. s.w.) and is buried at *Drayton Bassett*. The *Town Hall* (1701) was built by Thomas Guy, of Guy's Hospital (London), who sat in Parliament for Tamworth (his mother's birthplace) from 1695 to 1707.

The meadows by the crossing of two Midland main lines have long been a haunt of railway enthusiasts; below the castle is an open-air swimming pool.

A pleasant road (A 513) descends the Tame valley to (15¾ m.) *Burton*, viâ (4½ m.) *Elford*, with a church famous for its monuments (14–16C), and (7½ m.) the Elizabethan *Croxall Hall*, frequently visited by Dryden when it belonged to his patron, the Earl of Dorset. Damaged by fire in 1942, it has since been partly rebuilt.

116 m. **LICHFIELD**, notable for its cathedral and its associations with Dr Johnson, is a peaceful old place (22,700 inhab.), whose inhabitants Johnson said were "the most sober, decent people in England —the genteelest in proportion to their wealth, and spoke the purest English."

Railway Stations. *Trent Valley*, on the main line, 1 m. E. of the city; *City*, off St John St., for Birmingham.
Hotels, with literary associations, near the cathedral and in Bird St.
Post Office, Bird St.
Bus Station, Birmingham Rd., for all destinations.

In the market-place are statues of Johnson, by R. C. Lucas, and Boswell, by Percy Fitzgerald. Edward Wightman, the last person burned for heresy in England, suffered here in 1612; and here in 1651 George Fox (1624–91), founder of the 'Society of Friends', walked barefoot crying "Woe to the bloody city of Lichfield". DR JOHNSON'S BIRTHPLACE, at the corner of Market St., is now a Johnson Museum (adm. weekdays 10–1, 2–4 or 5, exc. Mon; fee), with many interesting personal relics and a valuable library of Johnsonian literature. Samuel Johnson (1709–84) was born in the room over his father's bookshop, and his baptism is recorded in the register of *St Mary's Church* (rebuilt). The *Three Crowns Inn*, next door to the birthplace, where Johnson and Boswell stayed in 1776, is now offices. The next house was the birthplace of Elias Ashmole (1617–92; tablet).

In Dam St., the shortest route from the market-place to the cathedral, an antique dealer's occupies the dame school attended by Johnson and a tablet marks the house where Lord Brooke was killed during the siege of the close (see below), by a bullet fired from the cathedral tower by the deaf-and-dumb son of Sir Richard Dyott.—Bore St., with the *Guildhall*, the *David Garrick Theatre*, and a timbered Elizabethan house, leads to St John St., in which, opposite *St John's Hospital*, built in 1495 by Bp. Wm. Smyth, founder of Brasenose College, Oxford, is the old *Grammar School* where Ashmole, Addison, Johnson, and Garrick were pupils. The present school is at *Borrowcop Hill*, ½ m. S.E., where the quarry for the cathedral stone may be seen.

The best way from the market-place to the cathedral is by Market St. and Bird St., which we follow to the right. In Bird St. are the *George Hotel*, scene of Farquhar's 'Beaux Stratagem', the *Swan*, where Johnson and the Thrales put up in 1774, and the *King's Head Inn*, where the South Staffordshire Regiment was raised. Farther on, beyond a public garden with a statue of Capt. Smith, of the 'Titanic' (sunk in 1912), is the *Library & Museum* with local history collections (daily 10–4 or 6). The office next door occupies the site of the early home of David Garrick (1717–79; tablet). Farther on, to the right, is the house where Erasmus Darwin lived from 1756 to 1781 (tablet). We approach the cathedral from Beacon St. by the w. entrance of the quiet close, which commands a splendid view of the w. front.

The *Cathedral, dedicated to St Mary and St Chad, one of the smaller English cathedrals but one of the most beautiful, is built of red sandstone from Borrowcop Hill, to which it owes much of its charm.

It is mainly an E.E. and Dec. edifice of the 13C and 14C, and it is the only church in England with three *Spires (the 'Ladies of the Vale'). The central spire is a restoration (very uncertainly ascribed to Sir Christopher Wren) in the style of the older w. spires. The *West Front, a richly decorated screen of carving with a single large window, is almost entirely a modern, though careful, reproduction of the original, begun c. 1275 but not finished until c. 1320; of its 113 statues all but 5 (in the top row of the N.W. tower) are modern, like most of the rest of the exterior. The w. doors have fine metal-work.

HISTORY. The bishopric of Mercia was transferred from Repton to Lichfield by St Chad (d. 672), who, however, built his church at Stowe, 1 m. N.W. The first church on the site of the present cathedral was erected by Bp. Hedda (700), but there are no visible remains of this and only two doubtful remnants of the 12C Norman church that succeeded it. The earliest parts of the present cathedral are the three W. bays of the choir and the sacristy (1195–1208). These, like the transepts and chapter house (1240–50), are E.E., while the nave (1280) is early Dec. and the Lady Chapel (1320–36) and presbytery (1337) are in the full Dec. style. In 1643 the fortified close, garrisoned by the Royalists, was captured by the Parliamentarians under Lord Brooke (see above), after a three days' siege. It was again besieged in 1646, when the central spire was demolished and much damage was wrought in the interior. After the Restoration the work of reparation was completed by Bp. John Hacket (1662–69), who introduced many Perp. features. Lichfield did not escape the disastrous hand of Wyatt, and a thorough restoration, begun in 1842 by Sidney Smirke, was continued after 1856 under Sir Gilbert Scott. The summit cross was placed on the central spire in 1950.

The Interior is long in proportion to its width, but the general effect throughout is one of grace and unity, and the eye is carried along the unbroken vista of arches up to the famous stained glass in the Lady Chapel. The NAVE, built in the transitional period between E.E. and Dec., is richly ornamented. The finely carved capitals and all the stone bosses in the roof are unrestored work, though Wyatt substituted a wood-and-plaster groining for most of the original roof. The beautiful triforium, with dog-tooth moulding, is unusually large, and the clerestory windows are of a very uncommon design. In the N.W. chapel are tablets to Anna Seward (d. 1809), the 'Swan of Lichfield', with lines by Sir Walter Scott, and to Lady Mary Wortley Montagu (d. 1762). In the s. aisle are the monument of Dean Addison (d. 1703; w. end), father of the essayist, and two strange semi-effigies, said to represent canons.

The TRANSEPTS are earlier than the nave (c. 1220–40), but the stone-vaulted roofs date from the late 15C and are lower than the original roofs (the fine rose-window in the s. gable is thus invisible from the interior). The windows are either Perp. (Restoration period) or E.E. (modern). In the N. transept is the skeleton-monument of Dean Heywood (d. 1492). In the s. transept are busts, by Westmacott, of Johnson and Garrick (both buried in Westminster Abbey), a War Memorial chapel (1926), and the monument of Admiral Sir Wm. Parker (d. 1866), the last survivor of Nelson's captains. The window above contains some of the Herkenrode glass (see below).

The first three bays of the CHOIR (which has a deflection of 10° to the

N. of the line of the nave) are the oldest part of the cathedral (E.E.). The place of the triforium is here taken by high arcaded window-sills, with a passage through the piers. The tracery is of the Restoration period, with the exception of the fine Dec. window on the s. side. The canopied statues and angels on the piers date from c. 1860, as do the stalls by William Evans (a cousin of George Eliot but not the original of 'Seth Bede'). In the s. aisle is the charming 'minstrel gallery' (early 15C), probably intended for the exhibition of St Chad's head. This aisle contains a medallion to Erasmus Darwin (1731–1802), the grandfather of Charles Darwin and author of 'The Loves of the Plants'; the effigies of Bp. Hugh de Patteshull (d. 1242) and Bp. Walter de Langton (d. 1321); the curious effigy, naked to the waist, of a Sir John Stanley (d. 1515), who submitted to a public scourging as a penance; the tomb of Bp. Hacket (d. 1670); and, at the E. end, the *'Sleeping Children', by Chantrey (1817), the finest of his earlier works. The window above contains old Flemish glass representing the Trinity. In the adjoining piscina is a 14C fresco of the Crucifixion. The minstrel gallery forms the entrance to the SACRISTY, built at the same time as the E.E. choir, and now used as the consistory court, with Restoration stalls and Perp. tracery. The upper story is the chapel of St Chad (1225); restored by Dean Luckock in 1897.—The *LADY CHAPEL, a beautiful example of the Dec. style, has nine lofty windows resting on an arcade and a polygonal apse. In the seven eastmost windows is the famous *Herkenrode Glass (c. 1530–40; purchased in 1802), from the Cistercian abbey of Herkenrode, near Liège. The other two windows have old glass of the same period, acquired in 1895. On the s. are three small mortuary chapels, in one of which is the effigy of Bp. Selwyn (d. 1878) of New Zealand and afterwards of Lichfield.—At the E. end of the N. choir aisle is the monument of Bp. Ryder (d. 1836), one of Chantrey's last works, beneath a window with old Flemish glass (St Christopher). Farther w. is the effigy of Bp. Lonsdale (d. 1867), by G. F. Watts. Here also is a bronze bust of Bp. Woods (d. 1953) by Epstein.

The decagonal *CHAPTER HOUSE (for adm. apply to a verger) and its vestibule, with beautiful arcading and wonderfully undercut capitals, corbels, and bosses, were completed in 1249. The thirteen canopied stalls in the vestibule were most likely for the convenience of visitors attending the Chapter on business. In the upper story of the chapter house is the LIBRARY, in a simpler style; among its treasures, some of which are exhibited in the choir-aisles, are the Gospels of St Chad (Irish; end of 7C), a fine MS. of the Canterbury Tales, many rare Bibles, and a copy of South's Sermons (1694) used by Johnson in the compilation of his dictionary.

In the cathedral close the *Bishop's Palace* (1687), now the Choir School, was for over fifty years the home of Anna Seward (see above). She was visited here by the beautiful Honora Sneyd, who was wooed by Major John André and by Thomas Day but became the wife of Dr Edgeworth. The cathedral is well seen from the other side of the *Minster Pool*.

A pleasant walk may be taken from Dam St. to (1 m.) *Stowe*. On the way we skirt *Stowe Pool* (enlarged as a reservoir), by the side of which grows the successor of *Johnson's Willow*, while at the end is *St Chad's Church*, on the site of the church built by St Chad. The s. doorway (E.E.), the E. window (Dec.), the font (1455), and the screen at the w. end (1949), should be noticed. Within are buried Lucy Porter, Johnson's step-daughter, and Catharine Chambers, the servant of Johnson's parents. Adjoining is *St Chad's Well*.

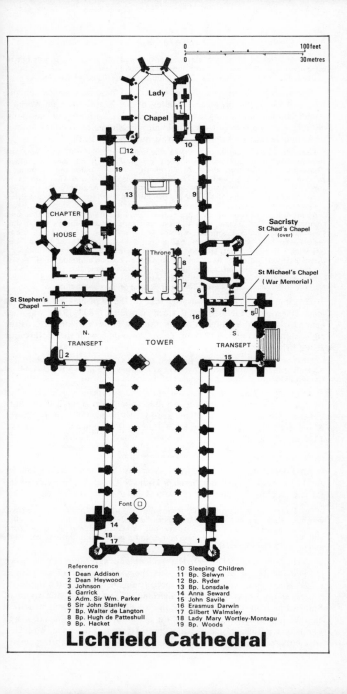

100 feet
30 metres

Lady

Chapel

11

10

□12

19

CHAPTER
HOUSE

13

9

Sacristy
St Chad's Chapel
(over)

Throne

8

St Michael's Chapel
(War Memorial)

7

St Stephen's
Chapel

6

3 4
16   5□

N.
TRANSEPT

S.

TOWER

TRANSEPT

2

15

Font □

14

18
17

1

Reference
1 Dean Addison
2 Dean Heywood
3 Johnson
4 Garrick
5 Adm. Sir Wm. Parker
6 Sir John Stanley
7 Bp. Walter de Langton
8 Bp. Hugh de Patteshull
9 Bp. Hacket

10 Sleeping Children
11 Bp. Selwyn
12 Bp. Ryder
13 Bp. Lonsdale
14 Anna Seward
15 John Savile
16 Erasmus Darwin
17 Gilbert Walmsley
18 Lady Mary Wortley-Montagu
19 Bp. Woods

Lichfield Cathedral

At *Edial Hall*, ¾ m. s. of the city, Johnson made an unsuccessful attempt to establish a school; one of his three pupils was David Garrick.

From Lichfield to *Burton* and *Derby*, and to *Birmingham*, see Rte 33.

The bracken-covered heights of Cannock Chase now appear on the left, and we reach the pleasant valley of the Trent.—123 m. *Rugeley* (small Hotels), a pleasant town (22,200 inhab.), with an interesting old church, was the scene of the wholesale poisonings of William Palmer (executed 1856). It is dominated by a huge power station.

Cannock Chase, stretching between Lichfield and Stafford, was once the hunting-forest of the Mercian kings, and is now noted for its coal and iron mines. There are still, however, about 25 sq. m. of delightful moorland including a permanent camping ground of 123 acres for Boy Scouts and Girl Guides in *Beaudesert Park*, the former estate of the Marquess of Anglesey. To the N.W. is the German cemetery (5000 graves) inaugurated 1967 for military casualties, who were formerly buried in scattered churchyards.

About 4 m. N. of Rugeley, in a fine park, is *Blithfield Hall*, the Elizabethan and Georgian seat of the Bagots, with a central courtyard and containing a carved oak staircase, Stuart relics, Georgian costumes, and a collection of toys. The house is open Easter–Sept on Wed, Thurs, Sat & Sun 2.30–6, also BH, 12–6 and Tues following 2.30–6 (fee; café). The road crosses Blithfield Reservoir for (6½ m.) *Abbot's Bromley* (Hotel), noted for its curious 'Horn Dance', held on a Monday (6–12 Sept). To the E. *Hoar Cross Hall* (adm. June–Aug. 2.30–6 on Sun; also BH; fee) has a collection of armour and a chapel by Bodley. Medieval banquets are held on Sat (Sept–May). Farther on extends *Needwood Forest*, a tract of oaks and hollies.

125½ m. *Wolseley Hall* was the seat of the Wolseley family for at least 800 years. Field-Marshal Lord Wolseley (1833–1913) was descended from a junior branch of this family. Here A 51 diverges to the right along the Trent.—127¾ m. *Great Haywood*, with the picturesque Essex Bridge.

At *Tixall Hall*, 1 m. w., Mary, Queen of Scots, was housed for a fortnight while Walsingham examined her papers at Chartley (see below) for evidence of treason. Only the imposing gatehouse of the old hall remains.

At (133½ m.) *Sandon* is *Sandon Hall*, the Jacobean seat of the Earl of Harrowby, with charming grounds (open Apr–July 2–7 on Sun) covering Great Sandon, a village abandoned in the 17C. In the church is the extraordinary monument of Sampson Erdeswicke (d. 1603).— 137½ m. *Stone*, see below.

———

An interesting alternative from Wolseley Hall (see above) follows A 513 to the left, past **Shugborough Hall** (N.T.), ancestral home of the Earls of Lichfield, birthplace of Adm. Lord Anson (1697–1762).

The *House* (fee) contains 18C furniture; the *Staffordshire County Museum* (free) occupies Park Farm. Admission Easter–Oct, daily exc. Mon unless BH, 11–5.30, Sun from 2. In the grounds are four 'Athenian' temples based on Stuart and Revett's 'Antiquities', a Chinese house, and a memorial to Anson's cat which accompanied him around the world.

132¼ m. **Stafford** (Hotels), the ancient and agreeable county town (54,900 inhab.) of Staffordshire, was the birthplace of Izaak Walton (1593–1683) and contains some interesting old houses. Its staple industry is bootmaking, whence Sheridan's toast: "May the trade of Stafford be trod under foot by all the world." Electrical and structural engineering are likewise carried on here. *St Mary's*, the large and handsome parish church, with a central tower, E.E. nave, and Dec. transepts, contains a bust of Izaak Walton, who was baptized in the

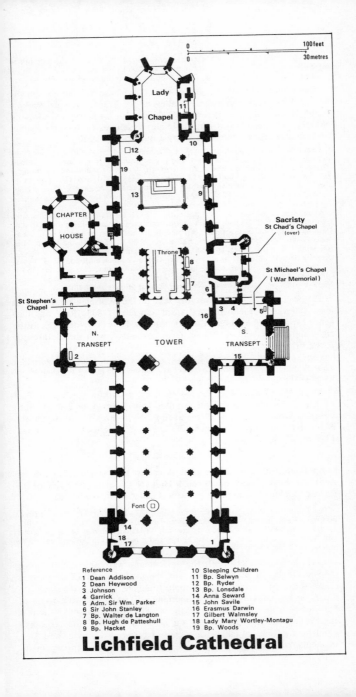

0 _____ 100 feet
0 _____ 30 metres

Lady

Chapel

☐12

□11

19

10

9

13

CHAPTER

HOUSE

Sacristy
St Chad's Chapel
(over)

Throne

8

St Michael's Chapel
(War Memorial)

7

St Stephen's
Chapel

6

16   3 4   5☐

N.

S.

2

TRANSEPT   TOWER   TRANSEPT

15

Font ☐

14

18

17   1

Lichfield Cathedral

Reference
1 Dean Addison
2 Dean Heywood
3 Johnson
4 Garrick
5 Adm. Sir Wm. Parker
6 Sir John Stanley
7 Bp. Walter de Langton
8 Bp. Hugh de Patteshull
9 Bp. Hacket
10 Sleeping Children
11 Bp. Selwyn
12 Bp. Ryder
13 Bp. Lonsdale
14 Anna Seward
15 John Savile
16 Erasmus Darwin
17 Gilbert Walmsley
18 Lady Mary Wortley-Montagu
19 Bp. Woods

At *Edial Hall*, ¾ m. s. of the city, Johnson made an unsuccessful attempt to establish a school; one of his three pupils was David Garrick.

From Lichfield to *Burton* and *Derby*, and to *Birmingham*, see Rte 33.

The bracken-covered heights of Cannock Chase now appear on the left, and we reach the pleasant valley of the Trent.—123 m. *Rugeley* (small Hotels), a pleasant town (22,200 inhab.), with an interesting old church, was the scene of the wholesale poisonings of William Palmer (executed 1856). It is dominated by a huge power station.

Cannock Chase, stretching between Lichfield and Stafford, was once the hunting-forest of the Mercian kings, and is now noted for its coal and iron mines. There are still, however, about 25 sq. m. of delightful moorland including a permanent camping ground of 123 acres for Boy Scouts and Girl Guides in *Beaudesert Park*, the former estate of the Marquess of Anglesey. To the N.W. is the German cemetery (5000 graves) inaugurated 1967 for military casualties, who were formerly buried in scattered churchyards.

About 4 m. N. of Rugeley, in a fine park, is *Blithfield Hall*, the Elizabethan and Georgian seat of the Bagots, with a central courtyard and containing a carved oak staircase, Stuart relics, Georgian costumes, and a collection of toys. The house is open Easter–Sept on Wed, Thurs, Sat & Sun 2.30–6, also BH, 12–6 and Tues following 2.30–6 (fee; café). The road crosses Blithfield Reservoir for (6½ m.) *Abbot's Bromley* (Hotel), noted for its curious 'Horn Dance', held on a Monday (6–12 Sept). To the E. *Hoar Cross Hall* (adm. June–Aug. 2.30–6 on Sun; also BH; fee) has a collection of armour and a chapel by Bodley. Medieval banquets are held on Sat (Sept–May). Farther on extends *Needwood Forest*, a tract of oaks and hollies.

125½ m. *Wolseley Hall* was the seat of the Wolseley family for at least 800 years. Field-Marshal Lord Wolseley (1833–1913) was descended from a junior branch of this family. Here A 51 diverges to the right along the Trent.—127¾ m. *Great Haywood*, with the picturesque Essex Bridge.

At *Tixall Hall*, 1 m. w., Mary, Queen of Scots, was housed for a fortnight while Walsingham examined her papers at Chartley (see below) for evidence of treason. Only the imposing gatehouse of the old hall remains.

At (133½ m.) *Sandon* is *Sandon Hall*, the Jacobean seat of the Earl of Harrowby, with charming grounds (open Apr–July 2–7 on Sun) covering Great Sandon, a village abandoned in the 17C. In the church is the extraordinary monument of Sampson Erdeswicke (d. 1603).—137½ m. *Stone*, see below.

An interesting alternative from Wolseley Hall (see above) follows A 513 to the left, past **Shugborough Hall** (N.T.), ancestral home of the Earls of Lichfield, birthplace of Adm. Lord Anson (1697–1762).

The *House* (fee) contains 18C furniture; the *Staffordshire County Museum* (free) occupies Park Farm. Admission Easter–Oct, daily exc. Mon unless BH, 11–5.30, Sun from 2. In the grounds are four 'Athenian' temples based on Stuart and Revett's 'Antiquities', a Chinese house, and a memorial to Anson's cat which accompanied him around the world.

132¼ m. **Stafford** (Hotels), the ancient and agreeable county town (54,900 inhab.) of Staffordshire, was the birthplace of Izaak Walton (1593–1683) and contains some interesting old houses. Its staple industry is bootmaking, whence Sheridan's toast: "May the trade of Stafford be trod under foot by all the world." Electrical and structural engineering are likewise carried on here. *St Mary's*, the large and handsome parish church, with a central tower, E.E. nave, and Dec. transepts, contains a bust of Izaak Walton, who was baptized in the remarkable Norman font. Outside the w. end lie the foundations of St Bertelin's chapel (c. 1000), excavated in 1954, and a replica of the wooden Saxon cross which lies buried beneath. *St Chad's*, in the main Greengate St. (largely rebuilt by Scott), has another noteworthy font. The Norman chancel-arch is decorated with five orders of moulding. In Greengate St. are a number of fine old buildings, including the half-timbered *High House* (1555), where Charles I and Prince Rupert were lodged in 1642; the *Swan Hotel*, at which George Borrow was ostler in 1825; and the *Post Office* (formerly *Chetwynd House*, occupied by the Duke of Cumberland in 1745 and by R. B. Sheridan, M.P. for Stafford in 1780–1806). The *William Salt Library*, 19 Eastgate St., in a beautiful 18C house, is a valuable collection of books and MSS. relating to Staffordshire (weekdays 10–5, exc. Mon).

FROM STAFFORD TO UTTOXETER, 14½ m. (A 518; bus). We cross (4 m.) *Hopton Heath*, where the Parliamentarians in 1643 fought an indecisive engagement with the Earl of Northampton, who fell on the battlefield, and pass (6¼ m.; r.) *Ingestre* church (1677), perhaps by Wren, with good furniture, and the *Hall*, the former seat of the Earl of Shrewsbury, now a residential arts centre.—8½ m. On the left are the ruined *Chartley Castle* (13C) and *Chartley Hall*, the successor of the moated mansion in which Mary, Queen of Scots, was confined for eight months in 1586, immediately before the final scenes at Fotheringhay.—14½ m. *Uttoxeter* and thence to *Derby*, see p. 402.

MOTORWAY M 6, which we may join 2 m. N. of Stafford, affords a rapid approach to the Potteries and the industrial districts of Lancashire (including Liverpool and Manchester), but, of course, avoids all places of interest *en route*.

A 34 runs due N. from Stafford and joins A 51 at (139¾ m.) *Stone* (Hotels), a pottery-making town of 11,000 inhab., in the churchyard of which is buried Lord St Vincent (d. 1823). Peter de Wint (1784–1849), the painter, was born here.

About 3½ m. s.w., close to *Norton Bridge* station, at *Shallowford*, is the farm of Halfhead, bequeathed by Izaak Walton to Stafford for charitable purposes, but since sold. The half-timbered cottage (adm. daily exc. Tues 10–4) where he was born is preserved as a Walton memorial. About 3 m. farther w. is *Eccleshall*, with the remains of a castle of the bishops of Lichfield and a fine E.E. church.

At (139 m.) *Darlaston* we leave the Manchester road (A 34); (see below) on the right. The Chester road (A 51) runs N.W., and, beyond (151 m.) *Woore*, enters Cheshire.—154 m. *Doddington Hall* was built by Samuel Wyatt in 1777–98. Of the original 14C castle, to the N., a single tower survives.

160 m. **Nantwich** (Hotels; 11,700 inhab.), once the second town of Cheshire and noted for its salt works, has a handsome 14C *Church*, with contemporary *Stalls, a rare stone pulpit, and a remarkable vault in the choir. *Churche's Mansion* (1577; fee; restaurant), in Hospital St., escaped the fire of 1583 and is a fine example of a 16C merchant's town house. Of many half-timbered houses dating from the Elizabethan rebuilding, the *Crown Hotel* and *Welsh Row* ('Cheshire Cat' restaurant) are notable. John Gerard (1545–1612), the herbalist, was born in Nantwich. *Dorfold Hall*, 1 m. N., a notable Jacobean house, is not open at the time of going to press (1975).

FROM NANTWICH TO CONGLETON, 17¼ m. (A 534), for the Peak District.— 4 m. **Crewe** (Hotels), a town of 51,300 inhab. and an important railway junction, owes its existence to the locomotive works of the old L.N.W.R. *Crewe Hall*, now the property of the Duchy of Lancaster, was rebuilt in the Jacobean style by

Edward Barry after a fire in 1866.—9¾ m. *Sandbach*, see p. 373—17¼ m. *Congleton*, p. 373.

165½ m. *Calveley*. *Bunbury*, 2¼ m. w., has a fine 15C collegiate church (St Boniface), founded c. 1388 by Sir Hugh Calveley (d. 1393). His recumbent effigy is noteworthy as are the original doors and a stone screen of 1527. About 2½ m. farther on is *Beeston Castle* (adm. daily, Mar–Oct, 9.30–5.30; Sun from 2); closed Sun morning Oct–Apr), built by the Earl of Chester in 1220 and dismantled in 1646. It is situated on a precipitous rock of red sandstone, and commands a magnificent view.—At (169½ m.) *Tarporley*, where the main street has distinguished-looking houses and the church has good 17C monuments, we cross A 49.—Beyond (175 m.) *Tarvin*, with an interesting church containing woodwork of the 14C, we join A 54 (Watling Street).—180 m. **Chester**, and thence to (198 m.) **Liverpool**, see Rte 40.

FROM STONE TO MANCHESTER, 45 m. A 34 ascends the industrial valleys of the upper Trent.—At (5 m.) *Trentham* are the fine gardens of Trentham Hall (demolished 1910), with a restaurant, ballroom and swimming-pool.— 8 m. **Newcastle-under-Lyme** (Hotels in the town, also on A 519, to the s.) is an old industrial town (77,000 inhab.), with a wide High St., from which the Duke of Newcastle takes his title. The interesting local *Museum & Art Gallery* (weekdays 10–1, 2–6) is in Brampton Park. *Keele Hall*, 2½ m. w. (bus), is the seat of the *University of Keele*, chartered in 1962; it was incorporated in 1949 as the University College of North Staffordshire, and accommodates c. 900 students. Here is housed a collection of c. 5 million air photographs (1939–46).

From Newcastle to *Whitchurch*, see Rte 41.

To the E. of our route lies the industrial district, c. 10 m. long and 2–3 m. broad, called **The Potteries**, devoted to the manufacture of pottery of every description, from the most artistic to the most utilitarian, together with a vast number of ancillary trades. Once a by-word for smoke and filth, the area has changed from coal to electric firing and is rapidly losing its characteristic smoke stacks and bottle kilns. The Potteries, known familiarly as 'The Five Towns', now consist of *six* large towns (from s. to N., Longton, Fenton, Stoke, Hanley, Burslem, Tunstall), besides several smaller ones, all united in 1910 into the borough of *Stoke on Trent*, now a city with 265,200 inhab. Rough brown pottery was made at Burslem before the end of the 16C, but the industry received its first great impetus from the introduction of purer clays from Devon and Cornwall in 1715. *Josiah Wedgwood* (1730–95) established a factory at Etruria, and, in the words of his epitaph at Stoke, "converted a rude and inconsiderable manufactory into an elegant art and an important part of national commerce". Other famous names of the late 18C are those of *John Davenport* of Longport (Burslem) and *Thomas Minton* and the *Spodes* and *Copelands* at Stoke. With the exception of marl for the saggars, practically all the requirements of the trade are brought from elsewhere: china clay from Cornwall and Devon, ball clay from Dorset, flints from Norfolk, felspar from Derbyshire. Visitors are usually admitted on application to see the various processes of manufacture at any of the 'pot-banks' of the district. The sturdy and intelligent character of the music-loving inhabitants of the 'Five Towns' is vividly described in the novels and stories of Arnold Bennett.

Stoke-upon-Trent (Hotels), Arnold Bennett's 'Knype', and the birthplace of Mrs Craik (1826–87), is the railway centre of the Potteries. *St Peter's* (1839), with a dado of glazed cenotaph-slabs, contains memorials to Josiah Wedgwood (d. 1795), with a medallion by Flaxman, and three Josiah Spodes (d. 1797, 1827, 1829). In the graveyard are some arches of the medieval church. The *Spode-Copeland Museum* (Mon–Fri, 10–4), in Church St., contains early collections and incorporates an old 'bottle oven'. Peter Terson's Victoria Theatre flourishes. Between

Newcastle and Hanley is *Etruria*, founded in 1769 by Josiah Wedgwood, and named by him under the erroneous impression that the classical vases which he copied came from Etruria. His residence, Etruria Hall (1770), is now used as the offices of an iron company, but his pottery works are still carried on by his descendants. The factory is now at *Barlaston*, 4 m. s. of Stoke; its Visitors' Centre including the *Wedgwood Museum*, with examples of 18–20C ware and of Josiah Wedgwood's experimental pieces, may be visited Mon–Fri 9–4; fee. The 17C Barlaston Hall is now an Adult College. Stoke is connected by bus with *Hanley*, *Burslem*, *Tunstall* (Hotel), and *Smallthorne*, where *Ford Green Hall* (16C) is open daily exc. Tues & Fri (10–4.30 or 6, Sun 2–5), on the N., and with *Fenton* and *Longton* (Hotel) on the s.

Hanley (Hotel), in the centre of the Potteries, is the most populous of all the 'Five Towns'. Arnold Bennett (1867–1931) was born here; his ashes are buried in Burslem cemetery; his early home, 205 Waterloo Rd., Cobridge, is shown on Mon, Wed, Thurs & Sat, 2–5. The city's famous collection of Staffordshire figures, the largest in existence, and other ceramics is housed in the *Museum and Art Gallery* (10–6 or 7, Sun 2.30–5) in Broad St., on the 1st floor of which are English water-colours. Good concerts are given at the Victoria Hotel.

At *Burslem* (Hotel), the 'Mother of the Potteries' and the birthplace of Josiah Wedgwood, is the Wedgwood Institute (1869), a school of science and art (where Sir Oliver Lodge and Arnold Bennett were students). To the N.E. on the Leek road is (4¼ m.) *Milton*, near which are the scanty remains of Hulton Abbey.

FROM STOKE TO LIVERPOOL, 49 m. A 50 leads N. through Burslem and Tunstall and crosses A 34 near Talke (see below).—At (5 m.) *Rode Heath* we bear left on A 533.— 12 m. *Sandbach* (Motel) is a quaint old place (13,300 inhab.). In the market-place are two Saxon *Crosses (pieced together in 1816), supposed to represent the conversion and marriage of Peada, son of King Penda.—17 m. *Middlewich*, a salt town (7800 inhab.).—24 m. *Northwich*, see Rte 42.—36 m. *Runcorn* is a port and busy chemical manufacturing town (36,000 inhab.) at the head of the Mersey estuary. A viaduct carries the railway over the Manchester Ship Canal and the Mersey, which are crossed also by a bridge (1082 ft span; 1961) which replaced the well-known transporter bridge. The remains of *Norton Priory* (c. 1200; 3 m. E. off A 558) have been excavated.— 37 m. *Widnes*, and thence to *Liverpool*, see Rte 61A.

From Stoke to *Derby*, see p. 402.

Going N. from Newcastle we traverse the N. Staffordshire coalfield. Beyond (12 m.) *Talke-o'-th'-Hill* we enter Cheshire.

On the right is the hill of *Mow Cop* (1091 ft; N.T.), crowned with an artificial ruin (1760); here, in 1807, under the leadership of Hugh Bourne, was held the first camp-meeting of the Primitive Methodists.

16 m. *Little Moreton Hall* (N.T.; adm. March–Oct, daily exc. Tues 2–6 or dusk; fee), on the right, is a magnificent specimen of an Elizabethan black-and-white timbered manor-house (1559–89).—18 m. *Astbury* has a noble 14–15C church with Jacobean pews and remarkable effigies in the churchyard.—20 m. **Congleton** (Hotel) is a yarn-manufacturing town of 20,300 inhab., with three old inns. It was the home town of John Bradshaw, the regicide. The *Town Hall* contains interesting relics. At the adjoining village of *Havanna* cigars were formerly made. At *Biddulph*, 4 m. S.E., are the ruins of *Biddulph Hall*, a Tudor mansion destroyed during the Civil War.—26½ m. *Capesthorne*, rebuilt by Blore in 1820, with a chapel of 1722, the earliest work of John Wood the Elder, has among its collections paintings by Marieschi and Joli and Attic pottery (6–4C B.C.).

The house is open Easter–Sept, Sun and BH, 2–5.30; also Wed from May, also Sat in May–Aug, 2–4; fee; café). Prominent from the fine park are the two radio telescopes (1957, 1964) of *Jodrell Bank* observatory, 3 m. w. on A 535 (open in summer; fee).

29¼ m. *Alderley Old Mill* (15C; N.T.; April–Oct, Wed & Sun, 2–7 or dusk; fee).—31 m. *Alderley Edge* (Hotels), a pleasant residential district.

The 'Edge' is a wooded sandstone cliff about 650 ft high and 2 m. long, commanding fine views (219 acres N.T.). Dean Stanley (1815–81) was born at the rectory.—32¾ m. *Wilmslow* (Hotels).

To the N.E. (1½ m.) is *Styal*, a late 18C village with contemporary cotton-mill, in the pretty Bollin valley (250 acres N.T.). At *Mobberley* (Restaurant), 4 m. N.W., the church has a superb timber roof (1450), a rood screen of 1500, and a memorial window to G. H. Leigh-Mallory (1886–1924), who died climbing Mount Everest.

34 m. *Handforth*, with the old hall of the Breretons (1562).—At (38 m.) *Cheadle* we reach the suburbs of Manchester.—45 m. **Manchester,** see Rte 60.

40 CHESTER

CHESTER (62,700 inhab.), the county town of Cheshire, is situated on the right bank of the Dee, 7 m. above its estuary, and is one of the principal 'gates' to North Wales. With its well-preserved walls, famous 'rows', timber houses, and fine cathedral, it is one of the most medieval-looking towns in England.

Hotels in the centre and near the Railway Station, ¾ m. N.E.—**Restaurants** at the principal hotels, otherwise mainly for lunch only.
Post Office (Pl. 7), St John St.
Bus Terminals at Town Hall Sq. for local and long-distance services, and Delamere St. for coach services.
Motor Launches from the Groves (Pl. 11) in summer to (3¼ m.) *Eccleston*.—**Boats** for hire.
Theatre. *Little Theatre*, Gloucester St.—**Horse Racing** on the Roodee (Pl. 10), see below.—**Golf Course** (18-hole), Curzon Park, w. of Grosvenor Bridge (Pl. 14).

History. Chester, the Roman *Deva* or *Castra Devana* (the 'camp on the Dee'), was for centuries after A.D. 60 the headquarters of the famous 20th legion ('valeria victrix'). It was known also as *Castra Legionium*, from which its Welsh name *Caerleon* and its Anglo-Saxon name Legaceaster, shortened to *Ceaster*, were derived. After the departure of the Romans (c. 380) the town was successively in the hands of the British, the Saxons, and the Danes, and in 908 was rebuilt by Ethelred of Mercia. In 973 Edgar here received the homage of eight British chieftains, who, according to the legend, rowed his barge on the Dee. Chester held out longer than any other English city against William the Conqueror, who in 1070 granted it, with as much land as he could win from his Welsh neighbours, as a country palatine to his nephew, Hugh Lupus. The earldom of Chester was united with the Crown by Henry III in 1237, and since 1301 has provided one of the titles of the eldest son of the sovereign. During the Civil War the town held out stoutly for Charles I, but after the battle of Rowton Moor (Sept 1645), fought about 3 m. S.E., it was starved into submission on 3 Feb 1646. William Lawes, the composer, was accidently killed during the siege. From the 13C to the 17C Chester was famous for its mystery-plays and pageants; the former have recently been revived. Chester had, until its closure in 1962, the only original Assay Office in England, outside London, for the hallmarking of gold and silver. Wm. Friese-Greene gave the earliest recorded public showing of a moving-picture film in Chester Town Hall in 1890.

The ancient *City Walls (12–40 ft high), of red sandstone, enclosing the old city in an irregular rectangle (c. 2 m.), are for the most part medieval with later alterations. On the N. and E. sides they follow the line of the Roman walls from near Pemberton's Parlour to the New Gate.

"The tortuous wall—girdle, long since snapped, of the little swollen city, half held in place by careful civic hands—wanders, in narrow file, between parapets smoothed by peaceful generations, pausing here and there for a dismantled gate or a bridged gap, with rises and drops, steps up and steps down, queer twists, queer contacts, peeps into homely streets, and under the brows of gables, views of cathedral tower and waterside fields, of huddled English town and ordered English county" (Henry James).

The main approach to the city from the E. is *Foregate Street* (Pl. 8), the ancient Watling Street, which is joined by City Rd. (Pl. 8) from the General Station, and leads to the *East Gate* (Pl. 7; 1769). Here we ascend the steps on the right.

At the top of the steps we turn to the right (N.), and on the left have a fine view of the cathedral. We cross the *Kaleyard Gate*, a postern at the end of Abbey St. (Pl. 7) leading to the kitchen-gardens of the abbot. The N.E. angle of the walls encloses the choir school playing-field. From the *Phœnix Tower* (Pl. 7; restored 1658) or *King Charles's Tower*, at the N.E. angle of the walls, Charles I witnessed the defeat of his troops at Rowton Moor (see above). The name refers to the crest of the Painters' and Stationers' Guild, which formerly occupied it. It now contains a small museum (adm. incl. the Water Tower; 10–6.30, Sun 2.30–6.30). The N. wall, part of which may be Norman work, is skirted by the Shropshire Union Canal, on the site of the old moat. Beyond the *North Gate* (Pl. 6; 1809–10), once used as the city prison, we pass a square watch tower overlooking a flight of locks and commanding a splendid view of the Welsh hills. St Martin's Gate was raised in 1966 to cross the Nicholas St. viaduct. We reach *Pemberton's Parlour* or *Goblin Tower*, a semicircular tower rebuilt in 1894, with an inscription recording the restoration of the city walls in 1701–8. *Infirmary Field*, where those who died of the plague were buried, is occupied by a new wing of the hospital. The N.W. corner of the walls is intersected by the railway. At the angle is *Bonewaldesthorne's Tower* (Pl. 6), connected by a projecting wall with the *Water Tower* (adm. as above), an outwork built in 1322 and once washed by the Dee. From Bonewaldesthorne's Tower the wall runs S. past the *Royal Infirmary* (1761), the *Queen's School* and Stanley Place with late 18C houses, to the *Water Gate* (Pl. 10; 1789). On the right lies the *Roodee* (Pl. 10), the beautiful but somewhat circumscribed racecourse (1 m. in circuit) on which the Chester Cup has been decided every May since 1540 (this portion of the wall is closed on race days). Near the S.W. angle of the walls the Dee is crossed by the *Grosvenor Bridge* (Pl. 14), a single stone arch 200 ft in span, built in 1832. The S. wall, which unlike the others, is irregular in outline, runs between the castle and the Dee. We cross the *Bridge Gate* (Pl. 11; 1782) near the Dee Bridge and later pass the *Recorder's Steps* (1700). At the S.E. angle of the walls are the *Wishing Steps* (Pl. 11; 1785) where, according to local belief, he who can run up and down, and up again without taking breath, will obtain the fulfilment of his wish. Farther up we cross the *New Gate* (Pl. 11; 1938) designed by Sir Walter Tapper to replace the narrow *Wolf Gate* (1768), just to the N. near the ruined *Thimbleby's Tower* (14C). In the *Roman Gardens* outside the gate (r.) are a hypocaust and some Roman columns (not in situ), also the reconstructed medieval High Cross; and, beyond the road, the remains of the S.E. angle-tower (A.D. 74–96) of the Roman fort. Farther off is the site of the *Roman Amphitheatre*, discovered in 1929, excavated in 1939 and since 1958. It dates from c. A.D. 100 and is the largest Roman building of its kind so far discovered in Britain (314 ft by 286 ft; with room for c. 9000 spectators). It covers an older wooden amphitheatre (c. A.D. 77). We go on N. to regain the East Gate.

The *Dee Bridge* (Pl. 15) is a picturesque structure of seven irregular arches, erected in 1280 and partly rebuilt in 1347–58 by Henry de Snelleston. The *Causeway* (Pl. 15), or weir, crossing the river diagonally to the E. of the bridge, is said to have been constructed by Hugh Lupus to provide power for the famous old *Mills of Dee*, which stood here until 1909.—The suburb of *Handbridge*, on the opposite side of the river, with a distinctive spire to the church (1887) of *St Mary-without-the-Walls*, is the seat of the Dee salmon-fishery, still of some importance (season, May–Aug).—The *Suspension Bridge* (Pl. 12; no cars) leads to the suburb of *Queen's Park*.

In the centre of the old part of the city with its many timbered houses, some of which are genuinely medieval, are the famous *Rows, galleries or arcades forming continuous passages along the first floor of the houses. Their existence is perhaps due to the presence of Roman ruins encumbering the site at street-level. A somewhat similar arrangement exists at Thun, in Switzerland. Several of the shops preserve medieval

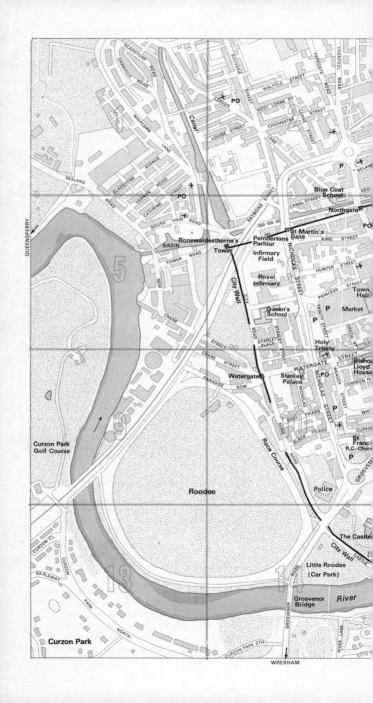

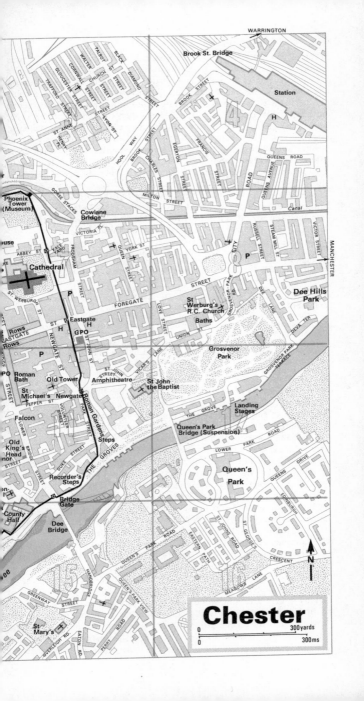

Chester

WARRINGTON

Brook St. Bridge

Station

WALTER STREET
TALBOT ST
CORNWALL STREET
GLOUCESTER STREET
TRAFFORD STREET
BLACK DIAMOND STREET
CHURCH STREET
YORK STREET

ST. ANNE STREET

HOOLE WAY
BROOK STREET
CHARLES STREET

EGERTON STREET
FRANCIS STREET
BROOK STREET

QUEENS ROAD
QUEENS AVENUE

ROAD
RUSSELL STREET
STEAM MILL ST
VICTOR STREET

MANCHESTER

Canal

Phoenix Tower (Museum)

GORSE STACKS

Cowlane Bridge

VICTORIA PL.

MILTON STREET

CITY

P

Dee Hills Park

DEVA TER.

ouse

ABBEY ST
TOWER ST
FROSDHAM STREET
QUEEN STREET
YORK ST.

Cathedral

P

ST. WERBURGH ST.
FOREGATE

STREET
LOVE STREET
UNION STREET

St Werburgh's R.C. Church
Baths

GROSVENOR PARK
DEE LANE

Grosvenor Park

Rows
EASTGATE
Rows

ST EASTGATE
H GPO
H

NEWGATE ST
ST JOHN ST.
ST. JOHN STREET

VICAR'S LANE

GROSVENOR PARK TERRACE

PO
STREET

Roman Bath
Old Tower
P

St Michael's Newgate
Falcon
TEPPER ST.
VOLUNTEER ST.
PARK STREET
Roman Gardens Steps

Amphitheatre

St John the Baptist

THE GROVE

Landing Stages

Old King's Head Manor

LOWER BRIDGE STREET
DUKE STREET
THE GROVES

Queen's Park Bridge (Suspension)

LOWER PARK ROAD

QUEENS DRIVE

Recorder's Steps

Queen's Park

Bridge Gate

County Hall

Dee Bridge

Dee

EASTERN PATH
ST. JOHN'S ROAD
ST. GEORGE'S
CRESCENT

EDINBURGH

N

15

GREENWAY STREET
HANDBRIDGE

QUEEN'S PARK ROAD
QUEEN'S PARK VIEW

16

MEADOWS LANE

St Mary's

OVERLEIGH RD.
EATON RD.
FERRY ROAD

0   300 yards
0   300 ms

crypts which are gladly shown; Brown's, in Eastgate Row (Pl. 7), uses a 13C vaulted crypt as one of its departments. At the Cross is *St Peter's Church*, the square plan of which is said to be due to its foundation on the site of the Roman Prætorium. Thence we follow BRIDGE STREET (Pl. 11) to the s., with rows on both sides and some particularly attractive houses on the right. At No. 12 is another vaulted crypt (c. 1230; adm. free). At No. 39, on the left, are the remains of a Roman bath, consisting of a hypocaust and a tank (adm. fee). Whitefriars (r.) has several good houses, notably No. 1 with pargeting (1658). We cross GROSVENOR STREET (comp. below), a busy thoroughfare leading to Grosvenor Bridge and North Wales, to reach Lower Bridge St. Here on the corner is the *Falcon*, dating mainly from 1626 (restored), where Handel stayed in 1741. Farther down are (r.) the *Old King's Head*, a good specimen of the early 17C style, and (l.) the *Tudor House* of the late 16C; the *Bear & Billet*, near the Bridge Gate, dating from 1664 was down to 1867 the town house of the earls of Shrewsbury.

Castle St. leads w. from Lower Bridge St. to the 14–16C church of *St Mary-on-the-Hill* (pl. 11) which has 17C monuments and a fine timber roof brought from Basingwerk Abbey in 1535. Farther on is the entrance to the **Castle** (Pl. 14), a group of classical buildings (1793–1820) by Thomas Harrison, whose home, St Martin's Lodge, still stands on Castle Parade. The group comprises a propylæum, the assize courts, the county gaol, the *County Record Office*, barracks, etc. The bronze equestrian statue of Field-Marshal Viscount Combermere (d. 1865), in front of the Grosvenor St. entrance, is by Marochetti. The Castle was founded c. 1070 by Hugh Lupus, but the only ancient part is the 13C Agricola Tower, containing the vaulted chapel of St Mary de Castro and the good *Museum* of the Cheshire Regiment (adm. 10.30–12.30, 2–4 or 5, closed Mon; fee).

In Grosvenor St., on the right, is the **Grosvenor Museum** (Pl. 11; adm. free, weekdays 10–5, Sun in summer 2.30–5.30), which has a valuable hoard of locally-minted Saxon and Norman coins and a fine collection of Roman incised stones. A gallery, illustrating the life and work of a Roman military station, has models of Roman Chester and of the station at Holt. Also displayed are charming 19C water-colours of the city, and Prehistoric, Bronze Age and Medieval collections.

From the Cross WATERGATE STREET (Pl. 10), with rows on either side, and three of the finest timbered houses in England, runs to the w. in continuation of Eastgate St. *God's Providence House* on the left, dating from 1652 but rebuilt to a more ornate design in 1862, derives its name from the pious motto under the gable: 'God's Providence is mine inheritance.' No. 11 has the finest medieval crypt in the city, dating from c. 1180, and gives access to another under (but unconnected with) No. 17, the unspoilt 16C *Leche House*, with a notable hall. No. 29, on the same side, is *Bishop Lloyd's House* (adm. on application exc. Sat aft. & Sun), built in 1615 and richly carved with scriptural subjects. At the corner of Weaver St. is the old *Custom House Inn* (1637). *Trinity Church* (Pl. 10; rebuilt 1865), opposite, contains the tombs of Matthew Henry, the commentator (d. 1714), and Thomas Parnell, the poet (d. 1718). Beyond Nicholas St. (which marks the w. line of the Roman wall) is *Stanley Palace* (adm. weekdays 10–12, 2–5 exc. Thurs aft.), built in 1591 and once the residence of the Stanleys, earls of Derby, with ornate gables (one added in 1935). It was presented to the city by the Earl of Derby in 1928 and is now occupied by the English Speaking Union.

In NORTHGATE STREET (Pl. 7), which runs N. from the Cross, the rows are mostly on the ground floor. Important Roman remains are visible in the basement of No. 23 (w. side; probably the Prætorium) and in Quaintways (E. side), beside the wine department, is part of a hypocaust. On the left are the newly rebuilt *Market* and the *Town Hall* (1869; adm. weekdays; paintings, charters, civic plate, etc.). Opposite, on the site of the abbot's lodging, a building by Blomfield (1876), formerly the King's School (removed to Wrexham Rd. in 1962) and now occupied by a bank and the Choir School, partly masks the w. front of the Cathedral. Farther on is the *Abbey Gateway* (14–15C), leading into the Abbey Square and Abbey St., with pleasant Georgian houses (c. 1760).

On the left, farther N. in Northgate St., are two interesting old houses: the Pied Bull Inn and the former Blue Bell Inn (15C timberwood), now a tiny shop standing on the kerbside. Beyond the North Gate is the old Blue Coat School.

The *Cathedral (Pl. 7) is a building of great interest and beauty. Built of New Red sandstone, it exhibits a variety of architectural styles ranging from Norman to late-Perpendicular.

HISTORY. The site of the cathedral was formerly occupied by a college of secular canons, dedicated to St Werburgh (d. about 700), senior abbess in Mercia, whose relics were transferred hither in the early 10C. In 1092 it was transformed into a Benedictine abbey by Hugh Lupus, with the assistance of St Anselm. The chief remnants of the Norman abbey church are to be found on the N. side of the cathedral. The rest of the cathedral, beginning with the Lady Chapel (1250–75), was built at various periods between the mid-12C and the Tudor period. The choir, the work of Edward I's military engineer, Richard of Chester, dates from the turn of the 13 and 14C, the arcades of the s. transept and the s. arcade of the nave from the mid-14C, the rest of the nave, the clerestory of the s. transept, and the top stages of the tower, from the end of the 15C. At the Reformation (1541) Henry VIII converted the abbey church into the cathedral of the new diocese of Chester. The title 'Bishop of Chester' frequently occurs at a previous date, the Mercian see of Lichfield having been transferred to Chester for a few years in the 11C.

Exterior. The w. front of the cathedral, in spite of its fine Perp. window, is somewhat lacking in dignity. The s.w. porch, with its upper chamber, was built in the Tudor period. The doorway inserted below the window at the s.w. corner of the huge s. transept was used as the entrance to the parish church of St Oswald (see below). The apsidal termination of the s. choir-aisle has a quaint conical roof, designed by Sir Gilbert Scott from indications in the old masonry. The best view of the E. end is obtained from the city wall.

Interior. From the w. end of the NAVE, raised a few steps above the rest of the pavement, we have a vista of great simplicity and beauty, enhanced by the warm red colour of the stone. The s. arcade of the nave is Dec., the N. arcade late-Perp. The place of a triforium is taken by a plain frieze; the clerestory is late-Perp. The glass in the w. window (1961) is by Carter Shapland. In the easternmost bay the arches are continued down to the ground without capitals (as are the great E. and w. arches below the central tower).

At the w. end of the late-Perp. s. aisle, in the base of an unfinished tower, is the *Consistory Court*, with Caroline furniture (1635). The wall of the N. aisle, now covered with mosaics of scriptural scenes (1886), is Norman; and at its w. end is the base of an unfinished Norman tower, now the *Baptistery*, with a font of Byzantine design (1885). From the E. end of the aisle a Norman doorway (c. 1100) leads into the cloisters.— The small NORTH TRANSEPT, over the entrance to which is the stone organ-loft, was part of the original Norman church. The windows and the roof are Perp. In the centre is a monument (1863) by Blomfield, to Bp. Pearson (1673–86), author of the 'Exposition of the Creed'. A mural tablet commemorates Randolph Caldecott, the artist (1846–86), a native of Chester. A Norman archway on the E. side opens into the *Sacristy*, in a transitional style, which replaces a Norman apse. Above is a small row of triforium arches of the earliest period. The SOUTH TRANSEPT (14C Dec., completed in 15C Perp.), with both w. and E. aisles, is as large as the choir and nearly as large as the nave. From the early 16C to 1881 it was used as the parish church of St Oswald. The great s. window (1887) is by Blomfield.

Among the flags of the Cheshire Regiment in this transept are two that were present at Bunker Hill (1775), and one that is said to have enwrapped the body of Wolfe after his victory at Quebec (1759). In a case against the s.w. pier are the two flags flown by H.M.S. 'Chester', the ship in which Boy Cornwell, R.N., won the Victoria Cross at the battle of Jutland (1916).

The CHOIR was built in the 13C and early 14C, the bays being early Dec. in character. Above is a beautiful triforium. The *Stalls* (c. 1390) are rivalled only by those at Lincoln and Beverley; the spired canopies, bench-ends, and misericords deserve careful examination. The SOUTH CHOIR-AISLE was lengthened to the E. about 1500, but the E.E. apsidal termination was restored by Scott. The third window from the w. is a fine example of Pugin's work (1850). Near the door lies Ranulf Higden (d. 1364), the author of 'Polychronicon'. The gates of both choir-aisles are of Spanish ironwork (1558). In the NORTH CHOIR-AISLE can be seen the bases of two Norman columns while a band of dark marble in the pavement marks the line of the Norman apse. This choir-aisle still retains its late-Perp. prolongation (c. 1500), now fitted up as St Werburgh's Chapel.—Thence we pass through a doorway occupying the place of one of the original windows into the LADY CHAPEL, which, though much restored, is a beautiful specimen of E.E. work. At the w. end, behind the high altar, are the reconstructed fragments of the *Shrine of St Werburgh* (c. 1330; not in its original position).

Precincts. The conventual buildings lie to the N. of the church, instead of occupying the more usual position to the s. From the N. transept of the E. walk of the cloisters we enter the *CHAPTER HOUSE, which, with its vestibule, is late 13C work at its best. It is rectangular in shape, like most of the early monastic chapter houses, and now contains the cathedral bookstall and a notable 13C cupboard. The graceful way in which the mouldings in the vestibule run up into the vaulting without capitals is an especially pleasant feature.—The CLOISTERS are Perp. In the s. walk and in part of the w. walk there is a double arcade. The wall of the s. walk is Norman, and here (and throughout the cloisters) the disregard of the later builders for earlier work is noticeable. At the end of this walk a late-Norman passage leads to the Song School. On the w. side of the cloisters a doorway leads to a large early-Norman UNDERCROFT, with two vaulted aisles, formerly the abbot's cellars; above was the guest-house. To the s., above the late-Norman passage, but entered from Abbey Sq., is the 12C *St Anselm's Chapel*, with a fine Caroline plaster ceiling. On the N. side of the cloisters lies the E.E. REFECTORY of the monks, entered by a fine doorway towards the w. end. Inside is a *Lector's Pulpit, with a staircase in the wall, the only other complete example of which is in England at Beaulieu. The hammer-beam roof dates from 1939. Outside, in the cloister, are the remains of the lavatorium. The vaulted building of two aisles at the N.E. corner of the cloisters was probably the COMMON ROOM of the novices. Between it and the vestibule of the chapter house is a passage or slype with an elaborate roof; it formerly led to the monks' infirmary.

From the cathedral we return viâ St Werburgh's St., passing (r.) the remains (visible in alley) of a chapel, originally built c. 1280, for the parish of St Oswald (see above), and serving later as a Wool Hall, and after 1773 as the Theatre Royal. Beyond the East Gate we turn right into St John St. to the site of the Roman Amphitheatre (see above). We bear left for ***St John's Church** (Pl. 11), finely situated above the Dee, the churchyard of which is a garden of rest. Built c. 1075, it was for about ten years the cathedral of the diocese of Mercia. The present building is little more than part of the nave of the Norman collegiate church. The N.W. tower, already rebuilt c. 1523, fell in 1573 and destroyed the w. end of the church; and in 1881 the lofty detached belfry erected on its site fell in its turn, crushing the beautiful N. porch. The

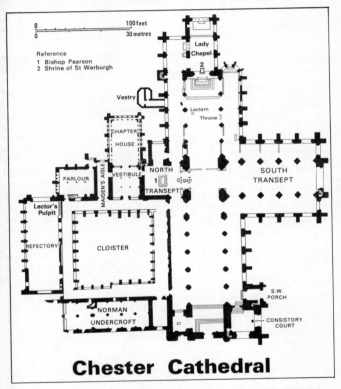

Chester Cathedral

belfry has been replaced by an incongruous erection on the N.E., but the porch has been restored in its original (E.E.) form. The interior is a fine example of stately Norman architecture. The massive pillars and arches are early-Norman, dating from c. 1095, but the charming triforium of four arches to each bay and the aisles are in the transitional style (c. 1200), while the clerestory above is E.E. The clustered pillars and bold arches of the crossing are mature Norman work. On the s. side is the Warburton Chapel, with a curious skeleton monument. In the N.W. corner is a group of Saxon crosses.

The picturesque ruins of the choir and Lady Chapel preserve some beautiful transitional Norman work. The 'crypt' is a fine 13C vaulted chamber; in a former residence built above it De Quincey (as a boy) lived for some time. By the s. wall of the churchyard is the *Hermitage*, to which, according to a curious legend, King Harold is said to have retired after the battle of Hastings.

Below St John's on the river bank are *The Groves* (rfmts) a shady promenade, with the boat landing-stages. To the E. extends *Grosvenor Park* (Pl. 12) with numerous re-erected medieval fragments. At 16 Dee Hills Park, farther E., Thomas Hughes lived during the last years of his life (1885–96).

Upton Zoological Gardens 2 m. N. (bus from Town Hall), with spacious enclosures, as at Whipsnade, provide natural surroundings for an important collection of animals; particularly notable are the polar-bears, sea-lions, pandas, leopards, and beavers, the ape house and the aquarium (adm. daily 9–dusk; fee, tropical house extra; rest.).

Eaton Hall, the magnificent seat of the Duke of Westminster, situated on the Dee, 4½ m. s. of Chester, is closed to the public. During the Second World War the Royal Naval College, Dartmouth, was accommodated here. The present hall, the third on the site, was built in 1869–82 to the designs of A. Waterhouse. In front stands a colossal bronze figure, by G. F. Watts, of Hugh Lupus, an ancestor of the duke. The 'Golden Gate' leading into the courtyard dates from the 17C.

FROM CHESTER TO LIVERPOOL DIRECT, 18 m. (A 5116, A 41), bus in 55 min. Railway in c. 50 min. (change at Rock Ferry). For the route viâ Hoylake, see p. 538 Both these routes traverse the WIRRAL, 'the dormitory of Liverpool', the peninsula between the Dee and Mersey estuaries.—A 5116 runs due N. from Chester and joins A 41. At 3½ m. A 5032 diverges r. for (3 m.) *Ellesmere Port* (61,600 inhab.), with large dyeworks, where the Ellesmere Canal joins the Ship Canal and the Mersey. At *Stanlow*, adjoining, is the Shell Chemical Plant (1949), the first in Britain for producing chemicals from petroleum.—9 m. *Eastham.* At Eastham Docks (1 m.), now enlarged for oil tankers of 30,000 tons, the Manchester Ship Canal enters the Mersey.—12¾ m. **Port Sunlight** consists of the extensive soap-works of Lever Brothers, Port Sunlight, Ltd., founded by Lord Leverhulme (1851–1925), and a model village occupied by the employees which is laid out with abundant open spaces for gardens and contains many public buildings. The *Lady Lever Art Gallery* (10–5, Sun 2–5) contains collections of porcelain and furniture and paintings by Reynolds, Turner, Gainsborough, Raeburn, Leighton, and other British masters, including Millais's portrait of Tennyson.— 14¾ m. *Rock Ferry* (Hotel).— 16 m. *Birkenhead*, and thence through the Mersey Tunnel to *Liverpool*, see Rte 59.

FROM CHESTER TO MANCHESTER VIÂ NORTHWICH, 40¼ m. (A 556). Railway to Manchester Piccadilly or Oxford Rd. in 1¼–1½ hrs.—We follow A 51 to (5 m.) *Tarvin*, then A 54 past (7¾ m.) *Kelsall*.—10½ m. *Delamere* is in the middle of *Delamere Forest*, with its quiet meres among pinewoods. On the left is *Eddisbury Hill*, with a well-preserved stronghold attributed to Ethelfleda.—13¾ m. *Sandiway* (Hotel).—17½ m. **Northwich**, a busy town of 18,100 inhab. (by-pass on the s.), is the centre of the once rich Cheshire salt-district. The brown rock-salt is now dug from only one mine, at *Winsford*, and the population is decreasing. White household salt is obtained from brine-springs by pumping the water into shallow iron evaporating pans. The constant pumping out of the brine has caused considerable subsidences in the town and its vicinity and much structural damage. *Great Budworth*, with an interesting 14–15C church containing 13C stalls and a good 15C font, lies 3 m. N., and *Vale Royal*, on the site of a Cistercian abbey founded by Edward I, is 3½ m. s.w.—Beyond (22½ m.) *Tabley Hall*, an 18C mansion, on the right A 5033 leads (r.) to *Knutsford* (2 m.).

Knutsford (good Hotels), a quiet town (13,800 inhab.), with several old houses, and a church of 1741, is the 'Cranford' of Mrs Gaskell (1810–65), who is buried in the old Unitarian graveyard, near the station. To the N. is *Tatton Park* (N.T.), the former seat of Lord Egerton, with fine gardens (2–6 or 6.30) and park (2087 acres) laid out by Repton. The mansion (by Samuel and Lewis Wyatt; adm. April–Oct daily exc. Mon, also BH, 2–5.15 or 5.45; fee), reached on foot in 2 m. through the park (open 11–6.30 or 8; winter 11–dusk), contains among the furniture and pictures, examples of Gillow of Lancaster, family portraits and two Canalettos. The church of *Rostherne*, a little to the N., on the bank of a lovely mere, contains the family monuments. About 3½ m. s. is *Peover Hall*, dating from the 16–18C, with a church containing fine Mainwaring tombs. The Hall was American 3rd Army H.Q. under Gen. Patton in 1944. The *Church of Lower Peover*, 2 m. w., built in the 13C, is an extremely rare black-and-white timbered church, constructed entirely of oak and plaster with the exception of the stone tower (c. 1500).—We cross M 6

and beyond (25 m.) *Mere* we join A 56 and reach the pretty valley of the Bollin.—
32 m. *Altrincham*, and thence to *Manchester*, see Rte 61A.

FROM CHESTER TO WARRINGTON, 20¼ m. (A 56). Railway in ½ hr; through trains
to Manchester (Victoria) in 1–1½ hr.—8 m. *Helsby* is well situated on a hill.—
10 m. *Frodsham*, in a similar situation overlooking the Weaver marshes, has a
partly Norman church. We leave the road to Runcorn on the left.—17½ m.
Daresbury was the birthplace of 'Lewis Carroll' (Rev. C. L. Dodgson; 1832–98),
author of 'Alice in Wonderland', who is commemorated in the church by a
window depicting the Caterpillar and the fish-footman.—20¼ m. *Warrington*, see
Rte 61A.

FROM CHESTER TO WREXHAM there are two roads (railway in 20 min.). The main
road (A 483; 12 m.) enters Wales beyond (5¼ m.) *Pulford* and passes (9 m.) *Gresford*
with its fine church tower.—A pleasanter road (B 5130; 15 m.) runs due s. viâ
(5½ m.) *Aldford* (Restaurant).—At (9 m.) *Farndon*, noted for its strawberries and
as the birthplace of the topographer John Speed (1552–1629), Edward the Elder
died in 924. Here the road crosses the Dee by a bridge of 9 arches (c. 1345) to
enter Wales at (9½ m.) *Holt*, with another good *Church. For *Wrexham*, see the
'Blue Guide to Wales'.

From Chester to *Birmingham*, see Rte 41; to *Shrewsbury*, see Rte 42; to *London*,
see Rte 39; to *Hawarden*, see the 'Blue Guide to Wales'.

41   CHESTER TO BIRMINGHAM

ROAD, 74½ m. A 41. 20 m. *Whitchutch.*—35 m. *Hinstock.*—41 m. *Newport.*—51½ m.
Albrighton.—59 m. **Wolverhampton.**—74½ m. **Birmingham**

RAILWAY, 73¾ m. viâ Crewe (change) in 1½–1¾ hrs. Principal Stations: 21½ m.
Crewe.—45¾ m. **Stafford.**—61 m. **Wolverhampton** (High Level).—66¾ m. *Dudley Port*
(for Dudley, 1½ m.).—73¾ m. **Birmingham** (New St.).

Alternative route (comp. Rte 39) viâ Shrewsbury (85½ m.) in 2¼–2½ hrs. (change at
Wolverhampton).

Chester, see Rte 40. A 41 (the by-pass) runs S.E. across the Cheshire
plain.—Near (11 m.) *Broxton* (Hotel) is *Carden Hall*, a beautiful
Elizabethan timbered mansion.—14½ m. *Hampton Heath*. *Malpas*,
1½ m. S.W., has a Perp. church with good ceiling and vaults, and was the
birthplace of Bp. Heber (1783–1826).—20 m. **Whitchurch** (Hotels) was
known in the 12C as *Blancminster*. In the church of *St Alkmund*
(rebuilt in a Grecian style in 1713) are the monuments of the first Earl of
Shrewsbury (1388–1453), Shakespear's 'Old John Talbot' ('Henry
VI', Part I), "who was so renowned in France that no man in that
kingdom dared to encounter him in single combat"; and of John
Talbot (d. 1550), founder of the grammar school. Sir Edward German
(1862–1936), the composer (E. G. Jones), was born at Whitchurch.

FROM WHITCHURCH TO NEWCASTLE-UNDER-LYME, 22 m. (A 525). Just to the N.
of (4½ m.) *Burleydam* is *Combermere Abbey*, a beautiful mansion on the site of a
Cistercian abbey, surrounded by fine woods and overlooking a large mere.—8¼ m.
Audlem.—22 m. *Newcastle*, see Rte 39.—From Whitchurch to Shrewsbury, see
Rte 42.

23 m. *Prees Heath.*—At (30 m.) *Ternhill* we cross the Shrewsbury–
Stoke road.

About 3 m. N.E. lies the ancient town of **Market Drayton** (16,800 inhab.; Hotel).
Here Lord Clive (1725–74; born at *Styche*, 2 m. N.W.), when a boy, achieved the
daring feat of lowering himself from the church tower to one of the gargoyles,
on which he sat astride. His alleged desk, with the carved initials 'R. C.', is preserved in the old grammar-school, and his grave is at *Moreton Say*, 2 m. S.W.—
At *Blore Heath*, c. 3 m. E., the Yorkists under the Earl of Surrey defeated the
Lancastrians under Lord Audley in 1459.

41 m. **Newport** (Hotel), with 6900 inhab., has an imposing *Grammar
School* of 1656. *Aqualate Mere*, the largest lake in Staffordshire is 2 m.

E. In the grounds of Lilleshall Hall, now a physical recreation centre, 3 m. s.w., are the beautiful remains of *Lilleshall Abbey*, founded in 1145 for Austin canons (adm. daily, Sun from 2; fee). The parish church has a Norman font.—46¾ m. We cross A5 near Weston Park (p. 365).

At (49 m.) *Tong* the *Church, an outstanding example of early Perp. work (c. 1410), has been described as a miniature Westminster Abbey on account of the number and beauty of its tombs (of the Pembruges, Vernons, and Stanleys). The epitaphs on the ends of the tomb (c. 1612) of Sir Thomas Stanley (d. 1576) are attributed to Shakespeare by Dugdale, the antiquarian (1664). The Golden Chapel (1515), on the s. side of the church, has fan-vaulting of beautiful design, with some remains of the gilding to which the name is due.

About 3 m. E. of Tong is *Boscobel House* (adm. daily, Sun from 2; fee), where Charles II, fleeing after the battle of Worcester, spent a day in an oak-tree and a night in a hiding-hole beneath the floor. The existing 'royal oak' grew from an acorn of the original tree. Close by are the Norman remains of the Cistercian nunnery of *Whiteladies* (adm. daily, Sun from 2; fee), an ancient wooden statue from which is preserved in the church of *Brewood*, 2 m. farther E.

Beyond (51½ m.) *Albrighton* we approach the 'Black Country', the busy iron and steel manufacturing district of S. Staffordshire, at night illumined by the glare of furnaces and foundries.—57 m. *Tettenhall*, with a large green and a Nonconformist college.

59 m. **WOLVERHAMPTON** (268,800 inhab.), on the verge of the Black Country, of which it is the 'capital', is a progressive industrial town, noted for its ironworks and its production of hardware of every description. Its locks and keys have been famous ever since the days of Elizabeth I. The name of the town is derived from Wulfruna, sister of King Edgar II, who endowed a collegiate church here in 994. John Wilkinson built the first steam-powered blast furnace (1756–57) at Bradley, S.E. of the centre.

Railway Stations. *High Level* and *Low Level*, at the N.E. end of Queen St.
Hotels in Lichfield St., Tettenhall Rd., Summerfield Rd., Compton, Goldthorn Park, Sedgley, and Tettenhall.
Restaurants in hotels, and Berry St.
Post Office, Lichfield St.
Buses from Cleveland Rd or from the Station.
Theatres. *Grand* (repertory), Lichfield St.—CONCERTS in the *Civic Hall*.

The large *Church of **St Peter**, with its stately tower, occupies a conspicuous position adjoining Queen Square.

The church is mainly an edifice of the close of the 15C, with remains of earlier work; the N. transept and tower are slightly later, while the present chancel and W. front date from c. 1865. In the interior are a finely carved stone pulpit, an octagonal font, and screens (all 15C); the W. gallery erected in 1610 for the boys of the grammar school; and a few stalls brought from Lilleshall Abbey (see above) in 1544. The tombs include those of Col. John Lane (d. 1667; by Jasper Latham) who aided the escape of Charles II after the battle of Worcester (N. transept), and a fine bronze statue of Adm. Sir Richard Leveson of Lilleshall (d. 1605), by Le Sueur (s. transept).

In the churchyard is the so-called *Dane's Cross*, an elaborately carved shaft c. 12 ft high, once associated with the defeat of the Danes near Tettenhall in 910, but probably a work of the 9C.

In Lichfield St., next the church, is the *Art Gallery & Museum* (weekdays 10–6) with pottery, Bilston enamels, and good water-colours. Behind the church are the *Wolverhampton & Staffordshire Technical*

College, and, in Stafford St., the modern *National Foundry College*. In North St. are the *Town Hall* and the good *Civic Hall* (1938). A 16C cottage, wrongly dated, survives at 19 Victoria St., to the s. The *Grammar School* (1875), founded in 1515, is in Compton Rd., to the w., where there remain, as also in Tettenhall Rd., many attractive early 19C houses.

Excursions may be made to *Wightwick Manor* (N.T.; adm. Thurs, Sat, & BH 2.30–5.30, closed Feb; also open Wed in May–Sept, 2–6; fee), 3 m. w., a remarkable example of work done under Pre-Raphaelite influence; *Moseley Old Hall*, 3 m. N., a refuge of Charles II after the battle of Worcester (adm. Wed, Thurs, Sat, Sun 2–6; BH Mon & Tues 2–6; closed Dec–Feb; fee); *Penkridge* (9½ m. N.), an old town, on the w. edge of *Cannock Chase*, where the large 13–15C church contains the tomb (1574) of Sir Ed. Littleton with the quaint figures of his 7 daughters; Bridgnorth (12½ m.); Lichfield (17 m.); etc.

About 6 m. E. of Wolverhampton and 10 m. N.W. of Birmingham lies **Walsall** (Hotel), a town (184,600 inhab.) engaged in making leather goods. A statue and a stained-glass window (St Matthew's Church) commemorate the devoted labours of 'Sister Dora' (1832–78), youngest sister of Mark Pattison. *Rushall Hall*, 1½ m. N. on the Lichfield road, has a fine 15C gateway.

From Wolverhampton to *Shrewsbury*, see Rte 42; to *Worcester*, see Rte 35.

The main road leads through a busy region of iron and steel works, the principal towns in which are (61¾ m.) *Bilston*, the birthplace of Sir Henry Newbolt (1862–1938), (64 m.) *Wednesbury*, and (67 m.) *West Bromwich* (Rest. in 13C moated manor-house), with 166,600 inhab., and skirts *Smethwick*, incorporated in the new county-borough of *Warley* (163,400 inhab.), before reaching (71½ m.) **Birmingham** (Rte 33).

The 15C *Oak House*, in West Bromwich, has 'period' furniture (open weekdays 10–4 or 5, Sun in summer 2.30–5; closed Thurs aft.).

An alternative road from Wolverhampton (A 4123, farther s., runs viâ (65¼ m.) **Dudley** (Hotels), a centre of the iron industry (185,500 inhab.), with a fine Town Hall (1928), Council House (1935), and Arts Centre (1947). Above it rises *Dudley Castle*, a ruin dating partly from the 14C, but mainly from the 16C. The grounds are occupied by a well-arranged open-air Zoo with a fine collection of animals. To the s. (2¾ m.) is *Old Hill*, with the public *Haden Hill Park*, a 'jewel of the Black Country', surrounding an old mansion.—74½ m. **Birmingham,** see Rte 33.

42 CHESTER TO SHREWSBURY AND WORCESTER

ROAD, 88 m. A 41. 20 m. *Whitchurch.*—A 5113. 29 m. *Wem.*—40 m. **Shrewsbury.** —A 458. 51½ m. *Much Wenlock.*—61 m. *Bridgnorth.*—A 442. 74 m. *Kidderminster.* —A 449. 88 m. **Worcester.**
RAILWAY. To Shrewsbury, 42 m. in c. 1 hr.

From Chester to (20 m.) *Whitchurch*, see Rte 41.—A 5113 runs thence nearly due s. through attractive country.

An equally attractive route, parallel to the main road on the E. diverges from the Wolverhampton road at (22 m.) *Warren House* and runs viâ (24½ m.) *Prees*, (31 m.) *Preston Brockhurst*, and (34 m.) *Hadnall. Hawkstone Park Hotel*, in fine grounds (incl. a golf course) beneath Hawkstone Hill (520 ft), 3 m. S.E. of Prees, was formerly the seat of Lord Hill (see p. 381), who is buried in Hadnall church. William Wycherley (1640?–1716) was born at *Clive Hall*, which is 1½ m. w. of Preston Brockhurst.—36½ m. *Battlefield* and (39 m.) *Shrewsbury*, see below.

27 m. *Edstaston* has a fine Norman church door.—29 m. *Wem*, a small

market town, gave the title of baron to Judge Jeffreys, and was long the home of William Hazlitt.—Beyond (34 m.) *Harmerhill* is *Lea Hall* (l.), a 16C house on the site of the earliest known home of the family of Robert E. Lee (no adm.).

40 m. SHREWSBURY (58,100 inhab.), pronounced 'Shrowsbury' by its natives (Salopians) and by pupils of its famous school, is the county town of Shropshire, and is strikingly situated on a peninsula of rising ground, encircled by the Severn on all sides but the the N. Its medieval remains—churches and timbered houses—its picturesque, quaintly named streets, its fine situation, and the beauty of its environs invest it with great interest for the tourist. It was England's fortress against Wales, as Durham against Scotland, and remains one of the principal gateways to the Principality.

Hotels in Wyle Cop, near the School, The Mount, Church St., beyond Longden Rd., and Mardol.
Restaurants at the hotels, and Abbey Foregate.
Post Office, Pride Hill.
Bus Station in Barker St. for all destinations.
Golf Course (18-hole) at *Meole Brace*, 1½ m. s.—*Fishing* in the Severn (particulars from the Town Clerk, Guildhall).—*Swimming Pool* (covered) in Quarry Park.

History. *Pengwern*, the British, and *Scrobesbyrig*, the Saxon name of Shrewsbury, may indicate its position in the centre of a wooded plain; 'Salop' is a corruption of the alternative *Sloppesbury*. After its foundation in the 5C it became the seat of the Princes of Powis, but it was conquered at the end of the 8C by Offa, King of Mercia. As a Saxon and a Norman town, Shrewsbury suffered many sieges and plunderings by the Welsh but under Roger de Montgomery (d. 1095) it was a cultural centre of some importance. Ordericus Vitalis (1075–1142), the chronicler was born and educated here. In 1215 and 1232 it was captured by Llewelyn the Great and in 1234 taken by the rebellious barons. Edward I made it the seat of his government during his subjugation of N. Wales (1277–83); and in 1283 Dafydd, the last Welsh royal prince, was here tried and executed. Richard II held a parliament here in 1388. At the battle of Shrewsbury in 1403 Hotspur was defeated and slain. Charles I made his headquarters here in 1642, but the town fell to the Parliament in 1645. Farquhar's 'Recruiting Officer' gives a picture of Shrewsbury under the Restoration.—Shrewsbury is noted for its cakes, ale, and brawn; comp. "A Shrewsbury cake of Pailin's own make" ('Ingoldsby Legends'; celebrated also by Congreve and Shenstone). Thomas Churchyard (1520?–1604), the Elizabethan poet, and Charles Darwin (see below) are natives and here also lived John Weaver (1683–1760), claimed to have introduced the pantomime to England.

Close to the *General Station*, on the neck of the peninsula (only 300 yds across) rises the CASTLE (adm. weekdays 9–12, 2–5; Sun, Mar–Oct, 2–5; fee), "builte in such a brave plott that it could have espyed a byrd flying in every strete" (Churchyard). Founded by Roger de Montgomery in 1070, and rebuilt by Edward I, it was modernized by Telford, and is now the borough council-chamber. Opposite the castle entrance is the *Museum and Library* (adm. weekdays, 10–6 or 8), occupying the old buildings (17C) of Shrewsbury School. It contains the cloak worn by Charles I at his execution. In front is a bronze statue of Darwin. Farther on to the left, is the fine half-timbered *Gateway* (1620) of the *Council House*, the meeting-place of the Council of the Marches, occupied by Charles I in 1642 and by James II in 1687, now the residence of the Roman Catholic Bishop of Shrewsbury. On the right stood the Raven Hotel, where Farquhar wrote 'The Recruiting Officer' (1705), dedicated to "all friends round the Wrekin". This was the first play ever acted in Australia (at Sydney, in 1789). Opposite the *Post Office* and on the site of an earlier cross where the body of Hotspur was hanged, drawn, and quartered, stands the modern High Cross (1952) by Laurence Gotch, presented by the school on its quatercentenary.

In St Mary's St., to the left, is *St Mary's, founded c. 970 as a collegiate church with a noble spire (222 ft). Of the Norman work, most notable is the sedile, a rare survival. The nave is E.E. work with a beautifully carved oak roof. The N. aisle was rebuilt or restored during the Commonwealth. The *Stained Glass includes a large 14C Jesse window at the E. end (from old St Chad's) and scenes from the life of St Bernard (1500; by the Master of St Severin of Cologne, 19 panels brought from the Abbey of Altenburg), in the E.E. triplet of the chancel and the S. nave aisle. In the 15C Trinity Chapel (16C glass from St Jacques, Liège) are an effigy of a 14C knight and alabaster carvings of the 14C; in the N. chapel is a tablet to Adm. Benbow (1653–1702), born at Coton Hill, N. of the town. In St Mary's Place, s. of the church, stands the half-timbered *Draper's Hall*, and opposite, in Church St., is *Jones's Mansion* (now a restaurant), where Prince Rupert once put up.

St Mary's St. is continued downhill by Dogpole, and that again by Wyle Cop with its old houses to the *English Bridge* crossing the Severn to Abbey Foregate. On the left in Dogpole we pass the *Guildhall* (1696) and the *Olde House*, occupied by Mary Tudor, and in Wyle Cop is the Lion Hotel, whose monthly concerts recall performances here in 1833 by Paganini and in 1849 and 1856 by Jenny Lind. Below the hotel is a half-timbered house in which Harry Richmond (afterwards Henry VII) lodged on his way to Bosworth Field (1485). The English Bridge was built by John Gwynn in 1769, and widened in 1927.

In Abbey Foregate once stood the Monastery of SS Peter and Paul (founded by Roger de Montgomery in 1083), now represented by the *Abbey Church, built of a deep red stone, with an imposing Dec. w. tower, the basement of which, however, with the doorway, is Norman. The statue above the magnificent w. window is said to represent Edward III. The two w. bays of the nave were rebuilt at the same time as the tower; the other bays are plain Norman work; the arch in the N. aisle is more elaborate. The transepts and chancel were built by J. L. Pearson in 1886–88. The monument of Speaker Onslow (d. 1571) in the N. aisle, was brought from Old St Chad's as was the 13C effigy of a lawyer. Opposite the N. door are the fragmentary remains of a chantry, with figures of SS Winefride, John the Baptist, and Beuno, recovered in 1933 from a garden in the town. In the s. aisle is a tomb assigned to the founder.

Almost the only relic of the monastic buildings is the elegant little *Reader's Pulpit* (14C) of the refectory, in an enclosure on the other side of the road. About 1 m. farther on is *Lord Hill's Column* (133½ ft), erected in 1816 in honour of Viscount Hill (1772–1842), the Peninsular veteran. Monkmoor Rd. diverges N., a little beyond the Abbey Church, to *Whitehall*, a fine stone mansion of 1582, with a notable dovecote, once belonging to Dr Butler (see below).

Returning to Wyle Cop we keep left, skirting the only surviving fragment of the 13C *Town Walls*, and passing the *Roman Catholic Cathedral* (built by A. W. Pugin in 1856, but still incomplete) and the only remaining rampart tower (15C; N.T.). We continue by Murivance to *New St Chad's*, a strangely planned circular church built by Telford (1792), with a Doric façade and tower. Below is the *Quarry (25 acres), a beautiful park in the loop of the Severn (two-day musical and floral fête in Aug).

On the brow of the hill, on the opposite side of the river, in Kingsland, reached viâ *Kingsland Bridge* (toll), is **Shrewsbury School**, founded in 1552 by Edward VI and now one of the leading public schools in England. The present buildings, by Sir Arthur Blomfield, were opened in 1882; the Speech Hall was added in 1911. The statue of Sir Philip Sidney was erected as a war memorial in 1923. Among pupils of the school were Sir Philip Sidney, Fulke Greville, Judge Jeffreys, Dr Burney, Charles Darwin, and Samuel Butler (of 'Erewhon'). Dr Butler, later bishop of Lichfield, was its headmaster for nearly forty years (1798–1836).

From the Quarry we may follow the path along the river bank to the *Welsh Bridge* (1795), the "reddie waye" to Wales, from the end of which Frankwell ascends to *Darwin House*, birthplace of Charles Darwin (1809–82). In Bridge St., is *Rowley's Mansion* (1618) now containing the *Viroconium Museum* (adm. weekdays, 10–1, 2–5) with Roman relics from Wroxeter, notably the fine Samian pottery, a 'time-expired' soldier's certificate, and a replica of a silver mirror, beautifully decorated. Here also are prehistoric and geological collections. In High St. are *Ireland's Mansion* (c. 1580) and *Owen's Mansion* (c. 1592), both splendid timber-framed houses. Off High St. opens The Square with the *Old Market Hall*, an Elizabethan building of 1596, and a statue (by Marochetti; 1860) of Lord Clive, M.P. for Shrewsbury and mayor in 1762.

From behind the Old Market Hall, Princess St. leads s.e. to *Old St Chad's* (14–15C; key from shop on corner of College Hill). Belmont, a street of pleasant 18C houses, leads towards the river. We turn to the N. viâ Milk St. and Fish St., passing *St Julian's* and *St Alkmund's*, two churches rebuilt in the 18C, with the exception of the towers. The line of Fish St. is continued by *Butcher Row*, which contains some of the most noteworthy 15C houses.

The ENVIRONS offer many attractive excursions. To the N. is (3½ m.) *Battlefield Church*, erected in 1408 to commemorate the battle of Shrewsbury, in which the rebel Earl of Northumberland, his son Hotspur, and the Earl of Worcester were defeated by Henry IV in 1403. Falstaff claimed to have slain Hotspur after a single combat lasting "a long hour by Shrewsbury's clock". The church contains an early 15C Pietà, in oak, probably from the chapel of the moated mansion of *Albright Hussey* (¼ m. w.).—To the N. (3 m.) above *Uffington* on the Severn is **Haughmond Abbey** (adm. daily, Sun from 2; fee), founded by William FitzAlan for Augustinian canons in 1135. Little is left of the church (12C), but the remains of the monastic buildings include the chapter house, the refectory (both 12C) and the large infirmary (14C). The ribbed oaken roof of the chapter house was added after the Dissolution. Behind the chapter house is the curious little Monks' Well (14 or 15C).—To the s.e. (4 m.) is *Atcham* (Hotel), with an ancient church containing some 16C glass, and a fine sandstone bridge of 1771 by John Gwynn. About 1½ m. farther on is **Wroxeter**, with the interesting remains of the Roman city of *Viroconium* (or Uriconium; adm. as for Haughmond), the capital of Britannia Secunda, founded before A.D. 70 and probably abandoned c. 400. The chief remains are the s. wall of the basilica, the public baths, and the forum. Wroxeter church, with a Saxon nave and a late 12C chancel contains many Roman stones. Just N. of Atcham is *Attingham Park* (N.T.), with a mansion of 1785 by George Steuart (partly occupied by an Adult College; adm. to state rooms and picture gallery, Tues, Wed, Thurs, Sun, & BH, Easter–Sept; 2–5.30; fee).—To the s. are (2½ m.) the *Sharpstones* (view), beyond which the walk may be continued past *Bomere Pool*, the 'Sarn Mere' of Mary Webb's 'Precious Bane', to (5½ m.) *Condover* (Rte 36). To the s. also is (6½ m.) *Pitchford Hall*, the finest half-timbered house in the county (1473); in the church is a remarkable wooden effigy of a knight (c. 1250). The beautiful E.E. church of *Acton Burnell*, 1½ m. farther, possesses the finest 14C *Brass in England (that of Sir Nicholas Burnell; 1382). Here also are the monuments of Sir Richard Lee (d. 1591) and Sir Humphrey Lee (d. 1632), collateral ancestors of Robert E. Lee. In the ruined manor-house, built by Bp. Burnell, Edward I's chancellor, was held the first Parliament to which the Commons were directly summoned (1283). *Langley Chapel* (fee), 1½ m. s., built by Bp. Burnell, was restored in 1601.—About 10 m. s.w. BY A 488 IS *Minsterley*,

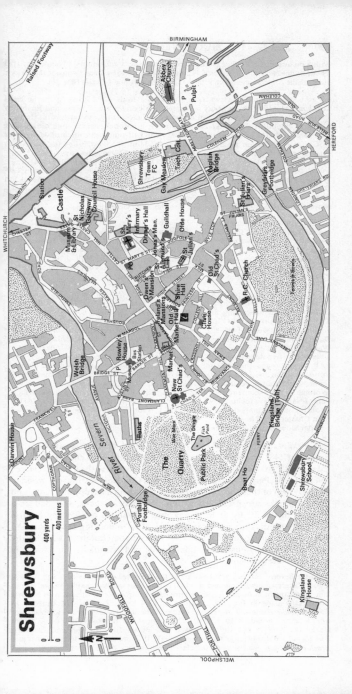

with a picturesque 17C brick church containing some 'virgin crants' ('Hamlet', v. 1). Thence a fine excursion leads s. viâ (1 m.) *Ploxgreen*, and by lanes alongside the rocky ridge of the *Stiperstones* (over 1700 ft) to (13 m.) *Bishop's Castle* (Rte 36).

FROM SHREWSBURY TO OSWESTRY, 17¾ m. A 5 leads N.W., crossing the Severn at (4½ m.) *Montford Bridge*, once a frequent parleying-place of Welsh and English. —8¼ m. *Nesscliff* lies at the foot of a wooded hill crowned by an earthwork. On the N. side of the hill is *Ruyton-XI-Towns*, formerly a borough, named from the eleven townships included in the manor; while the fine half-timbered church of *Melverley* (15C) lies 4 m. s.w. on the Severn.—Beyond (13½ m.; l.) *West Felton* the Oswestry road diverges l. from the main Holyhead road.—17¾ m. **Oswestry** (Hotel), an ancient border market-town, is named after St Oswald, slain here by Penda in 642. The church dedicated to him contains a Yale monument (1746). In the town were born Sir Walford Davies (1868–1941), the musician, and Wilfred Owen (1893–1918), the poet. *Old Oswestry*, 1 m. N., preserves a triple earth rampart.—*Ellesmere* (Hotel), 8 m. N.E. of Oswestry and 17 m. N.W. of Shrewsbury, lies among several of the small meres that characterize the Shropshire plain. See also the 'Blue Guide to Wales'.

FROM SHREWSBURY TO MARKET DRAYTON, 18¾ m. (A 53).—3 m. *Battlefield* (see above).—Beyond the Norman church and Air Navigation School of (3½ m.) *Shawbury* is *Moreton Corbet*, with a large ruined mansion begun in 1606 in the Italian style (adm. daily, Sun from 2; fee).—13 m. *Hodnet*, where Bp. Heber was rector for 15 years, has some good half-timbered houses. The Hall, a 19C mansion, is noted for its *Gardens of 60 acres (open April–Sept, weekdays 2–5, Sun & BH, 12–6.30; fee; teas).—18¾ m. *Market Drayton*, see p. 383.

FROM SHREWSBURY TO WOLVERHAMPTON, 30 m. We follow A 5, the Roman Watling Street, past Atcham and Wroxeter (see above).—11¼ m. **Wellington** (Hotel) is a manufacturing and market town (17,150 inhab.), with old houses. The *Preston Trust Homes* (1716), 4 m. N.E., are among the finest almshouses in the country. Capt. Webb (1848–83), the first man to swim the Channel, was born at *Dawley*, 3 m. S.E., now swallowed up in the new town of *Telford*, designated in 1965. The **Wrekin** (1334 ft; extensive view), an isolated extinct volcano 2 m. s.w., irreverently described by Arnold Bennett as a' swollen bump' is usually ascended from Wellington. "All friends round the Wrekin" is a famous Shropshire toast.—A 464 leads S.E. through *Oakengates* (16,700 inhab.) to (17½ m.) *Shifnal*, a little town with many half-timbered old houses, described by Dickens in 'The Old Curiosity Shop'. St Andrew's (Norman to Perp.) contains the Moreton Chapel, with numerous monuments. Bishop Percy is said to have found the MS. used for his 'Reliques of Ancient Poetry' (1765) in an old house in the market place. Tong is 3 m. E. About 7 m. farther on we join the road from Chester (see Rte 41).

From Shrewsbury to *Hereford*, see Rte 36.

The Worcester road (A 458) runs s.E. and turns s. away from the Severn at (48¼ m.) *Cressage*, ascending over the N.E. end of Wenlock Edge.—51½ m. **Much Wenlock** is a small town with a good *Church* (Norman to Perp.) and a half-timbered *Guildhall* resting on wooden pillars. Two of these bear wrist-fetters to fit them as whipping-posts, and the old stocks are preserved within. *Wenlock Abbey*, founded as a nunnery in the 7C by St Milburga, was refounded c. 1050, by Leofric and Lady Godiva, as a Cluniac priory. The interesting remains (adm. daily, Sun from 2; fee) include the ruins of the church (E.E.) and the Norman chapter house. The late Gothic and Norman priors' lodge is now a private residence.

On the Severn, 3 m. N., are the ruins of *Buildwas Abbey* (adm. daily, Sun from 2; fee), a Cistercian house founded in 1135, with a later vaulted chapter house. About 2 m. downstream is *Ironbridge*, the centre of the Shropshire coalfield, with the first iron bridge made in England, designed in 1774 by T. F. Pritchard and cast at *Coalbrookdale* (Hotel), ¾ m. N., 'the cradle of the iron trade'. Here is a museum of ironfounding (weekdays 10–5 or 6). The original old furnace (1708) of Abraham Darby (1677–1717) can still be viewed and Blists Hill area museum. *Coalport*, 2 m. S.E. of Ironbridge, was famous in the late 18C and early 19C for its china, and *Brosley*, to the s., had a name for clay pipes. Pottery was also made at *Madeley*,

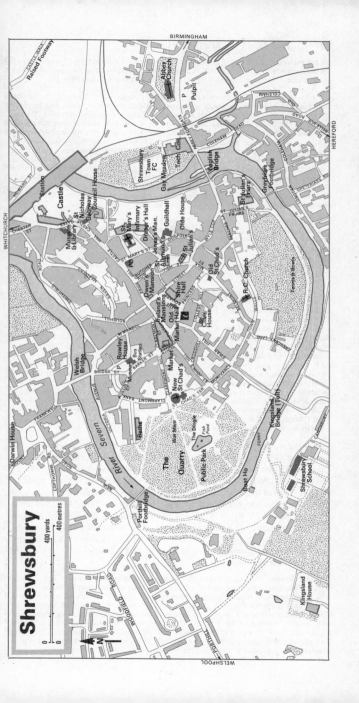

Shrewsbury

BIRMINGHAM

WHITCHURCH

HEREFORD

WELSHPOOL

400 yards
400 metres

N

River Severn

Abbey Church
Pulpit
P
Shrewsbury Town FC
Gay Meadow
English Bridge
Tech. Coll.
Coleham
St Julian's Friars
Greyfriars' Footbridge
Station
Castle
St Nicholas
St Mary's
Museum & Library
Gateway
Council House
St Mary's Infirmary
Draper's Hall
Guildhall
St James
Owen's Mansion
Mansion
Ireland's Mansion
St Chad's
Old St Chad's
R.C. Church
St Julian's
Old Market Hall
Shire Hall
Clive House
Rowley's House
Bus Station
Museum
P
New Market
St Chad's
The Dingle
Fish Pond
Baths
The Quarry
Public Park
Boat Ho
Kingsland Bridge (Toll)
Shrewsbury School
Kingsland House
Porthill Footbridge
Darwin House

Raised Footway
Castle Walk

with a picturesque 17C brick church containing some 'virgin crants' ('Hamlet', v. 1). Thence a fine excursion leads s. viâ (1 m.) *Ploxgreen*, and by lanes alongside the rocky ridge of the *Stiperstones* (over 1700 ft) to (13 m.) *Bishop's Castle* (Rte 36).

FROM SHREWSBURY TO OSWESTRY, 17¾ m. A 5 leads N.W., crossing the Severn at (4½ m.) *Montford Bridge*, once a frequent parleying-place of Welsh and English. —8¼ m. *Nesscliff* lies at the foot of a wooded hill crowned by an earthwork. On the N. side of the hill is *Ruyton-XI-Towns*, formerly a borough, named from the eleven townships included in the manor; while the fine half-timbered church of *Melverley* (15C) lies 4 m. s.w. on the Severn.—Beyond (13½ m.; l.) *West Felton* the Oswestry road diverges l. from the main Holyhead road.—17¾ m. **Oswestry** (Hotel), an ancient border market-town, is named after St Oswald, slain here by Penda in 642. The church dedicated to him contains a Yale monument (1746). In the town were born Sir Walford Davies (1868–1941), the musician, and Wilfred Owen (1893–1918), the poet. *Old Oswestry*, 1 m. N., preserves a triple earth rampart.—*Ellesmere* (Hotel), 8 m. N.E. of Oswestry and 17 m. N.W. of Shrewsbury, lies among several of the small meres that characterize the Shropshire plain. See also the 'Blue Guide to Wales'.

FROM SHREWSBURY TO MARKET DRAYTON, 18¾ m. (A 53).—3 m. *Battlefield* (see above).—Beyond the Norman church and Air Navigation School of (3½ m.) *Shawbury* is *Moreton Corbet*, with a large ruined mansion begun in 1606 in the Italian style (adm. daily, Sun from 2; fee).—13 m. *Hodnet*, where Bp. Heber was rector for 15 years, has some good half-timbered houses. The Hall, a 19C mansion, is noted for its *Gardens of 60 acres (open April–Sept, weekdays 2–5, Sun & BH, 12–6.30; fee; teas).—18¾ m. *Market Drayton*, see p. 383.

FROM SHREWSBURY TO WOLVERHAMPTON, 30 m. We follow A 5, the Roman Watling Street, past Atcham and Wroxeter (see above).—11½ m. **Wellington** (Hotel) is a manufacturing and market town (17,150 inhab.), with old houses. The *Preston Trust Homes* (1716), 4 m. N.E., are among the finest almshouses in the country. Capt. Webb (1848–83), the first man to swim the Channel, was born at *Dawley*, 3 m. S.E., now swallowed up in the new town of *Telford*, designated in 1965. The **Wrekin** (1334 ft; extensive view), an isolated extinct volcano 2 m. s.w., irreverently described by Arnold Bennett as a' swollen bump' is usually ascended from Wellington. "All friends round the Wrekin" is a famous Shropshire toast.—A 464 leads S.E. through *Oakengates* (16,700 inhab.) to (17½ m. *Shifnal*, a little town with many half-timbered old houses, described by Dickens in 'The Old Curiosity Shop'. St Andrew's (Norman to Perp.) contains the Moreton Chapel, with numerous monuments. Bishop Percy is said to have found the MS. used for his 'Reliques of Ancient Poetry' (1765) in an old house in the market place. Tong is 3 m. E. About 7 m. farther on we join the road from Chester (see Rte 41).

From Shrewsbury to *Hereford*, see Rte 36.

The Worcester road (A 458) runs S.E. and turns S. away from the Severn at (48¼ m.) *Cressage*, ascending over the N.E. end of Wenlock Edge.—51½ m. **Much Wenlock** is a small town with a good *Church* (Norman to Perp.) and a half-timbered *Guildhall* resting on wooden pillars. Two of these bear wrist-fetters to fit them as whipping-posts, and the old stocks are preserved within. *Wenlock Abbey*, founded as a nunnery in the 7C by St Milburga, was refounded c. 1050, by Leofric and Lady Godiva, as a Cluniac priory. The interesting remains (adm. daily, Sun from 2; fee) include the ruins of the church (E.E.) and the Norman chapter house. The late Gothic and Norman priors' lodge is now a private residence.

On the Severn, 3 m. N., are the ruins of *Buildwas Abbey* (adm. daily, Sun from 2; fee), a Cistercian house founded in 1135, with a later vaulted chapter house. About 2 m. downstream is *Ironbridge*, the centre of the Shropshire coalfield, with the first iron bridge made in England, designed in 1774 by T. F. Pritchard and cast at *Coalbrookdale* (Hotel), ¾ m. N., 'the cradle of the iron trade'. Here is a museum of ironfounding (weekdays 10–5 or 6). The original old furnace (1708) of Abraham Darby (1677–1717) can still be viewed and Blists Hill area museum. *Coalport*, 2 m. S.E. of Ironbridge, was famous in the late 18C and early 19C for its china, and *Brosley*, to the s., had a name for clay pipes. Pottery was also made at *Madeley*,

1½ m. N. of Coalport, in 1828–40, and earlier at *Caughley*, where the 'willow pattern' originated, 1½ m. s.w. of Broseley. *Benthall Hall*, 1 m. N.W. of Broseley, is a 16C house with good interior decoration (N.T.; adm. Easter–Sept, Tues, Wed, & Sat 2–6; fee).

Wilderhope Manor (N.T.), an Elizabethan house on Wenlock Edge, is 7 m. s.w. of Much Wenlock (now Youth Hostel; adm. April–Sept, Wed 2.30–5.30; fee).

57½ m. *Morville Hall* (N.T.; adm. by appointment), an Elizabethan house, converted in the 18C.—61 m. **Bridgnorth** (Hotels), an agricultural and carpet-making town, is picturesquely situated on the Severn, which divides it into a 'High Town' (right bank) and 'Low Town' (left bank), connected by steps and a steep inclined railway. In a public park at the s. end of the High Town is a leaning tower, the only fragment of the *Castle*, built in 1101 perhaps on the site of a Saxon fastness ascribed to Ethelfleda (c. 912) and blown up in 1646. The church of *St Mary Magdalene* (1792–97) is by Thomas Telford, the engineer. East Castle St., with the *Governor's House* (c. 1633), leads to the High St., in which is the *Town Hall* (1650–52) built on stone arches. *St Leonard* (N. end of the town), once served by Richard Baxter (1640; born at Rowton, 6 m. N. of Wellington), contains old cast-iron memorial tablets; near by is the little house (1641) where Baxter lived. The brick *Grammar School* dates from 1639, while the castellated *North Gate*, spanning the street, was rebuilt in 1740 and 1910. The house (1580) in which Bp. Percy of the 'Reliques' was born in 1729 stands near the bridge.

The *Severn Valley Railway Company* runs steam trains in summer on the picturesque former Great Western line to (12½ m.) *Bewdley* (50 min.; p. 355). It is hoped to resuscitate the continuation of the line to (16 m.) Kidderminster and operate a regular passenger service.

From Bridgnorth to *Ludlow* over the Clee Hills, see Rte 36.

We cross the Severn.—66 m. *Coton Hall* (1 m. E.), is an ancient home of the Lees of Virginia, ancestors of Gen. Robert E. Lee. It is a 15–16C house, refaced c. 1815, with a ruined chapel, some glass from which is preserved in *Alveley* church, 1½ m. s.w.—74 m. *Kidderminster*, and thence to (88 m.) **Worcester**, see Rte 35.

43 LONDON TO LEICESTER, DERBY, AND SHEFFIELD

ROAD, 156 m. To (38 m.) *Hockliffe*, see Rte 32B.—A 50. 64½ m. **Northampton.**— A 508. 82 m. *Market Harborough.*—A 6. 96 m. **Leicester.**—106½ m. *Loughborough.* —123 m. **Derby.**—145 m. *Chesterfield.*—156 m. **Sheffield.**

An alternative route to Northampton (4½ m. longer) keeps to A 5 as far as (53 m.) *Stony Stratford* (comp. Rte 32B); beyond the Great Ouse turn r. on A 508.— At (57 m.) *Grafton Regis*, on the edge of Whittlewood Forest, Edward IV in 1464 married Elizabeth Woodville, whom he had first met under the 'Queen's Oak' close by.—69 m. **Northampton.**

MOTORWAY M 1, passing w. of Newport Pagnell and Northampton, has exits (21) at 95 m., 3. w. of Leicester; (25) at 117 m., equidistant between Derby and Nottingham; and (33) at 155½ m., 5 m. E. of Sheffield.

RAILWAY from St Pancras viâ Bedford to Leicester (99 m.), hourly in 1½ hrs, or 2 hrs; to Derby (128½ m.) in 2 hrs (for intermediate stations, see Rte 44); viâ (152½ m.) *Chesterfield* to **Sheffield** (164¾ m.) in c. 3 hrs.—From Euston to North- ampton, 65¾ m. in 1½ hrs.

From London to (38 m.) *Hockliffe*, see Rte 32B. We leave A 5 for A 50.—40½ m. *Milton Bryan* (r.) is the birthplace of Sir Joseph Paxton (1803–65).—42½ m. *Woburn* (Hotels) is a quiet well-built market town. WOBURN ABBEY (adm. March–Oct, 11.30–5.45 or 6.15; Sun till ½ hr later; winter 1–4.45; fee; rfmts), the seat of the Duke of Bedford, was rebuilt by Henry Flitcroft in 1747 on the site of a Cistercian Abbey. The Sèvres family dinner service is admirably displayed.

The collection of paintings includes a magnificent series of works by Canaletto (not always on view; fee), and a portrait of Elizabeth I by Gower. The fine Park (adm. mid-March–Aug 10.30–5.45, Sun 10–6.15; Sept–Oct 11–5.15, Sun till 5.45; winter 12–3.30; fee; Safari Park daily 10–6), 12 m. in circuit with a road, footpaths and cable railway, contains c. 2000 head of deer (including the unique Père David herd), European and American bison, the Chartley herd of wild white cattle, and a huge 'Wild Animal Kingdom'.

We cross fine pine-woods to reach (45 m.) *Woburn Sands.*—51 m. *Newport Pagnell* (Hotel) is a town of 6300 inhab., with large motor works.—53 m. *Gayhurst* church, a fine building of 1728 with a good interior, stands beside an Elizabethan mansion (no adm.), the home of Sir Everard Digby (d. 1606) and birthplace of Sir Kenelm Digby (1603–65). *Tyringham House* (r.; now a clinic) with a fine gateway was designed by Soane (1793–7). To the left near (55 m.) *Stoke Golding-ton* is seen the tall steeple of *Hanslope* church. On the way in to North-ampton we pass a Queen Eleanor's *Cross, one of three survivors. Just beyond is (63½ m.) *Delapré Abbey* (16–19C; open Thurs & Sat 2.30–4.30 or 6), now the county record office. The park and gardens are open daily.

64½ m. NORTHAMPTON (125,600 inhab.), the capital of its county, situated on the N. bank of the Nene, is a manufacturing town, which (in Fuller's words) "may be said to stand chiefly on other men's legs", as by far its chief industry is shoemaking. More recent is the brewing under licence of Continental lager beers. First impressions are of an ugly and sprawling modernity amid which the few relics of its antiquity must be sought.

Hotels in Bridge St., Gold St., and at Weston Favell (2½ m. N.E.).
Post Office, St Giles's St.
Buses run from Derngate to most destinations, from Victoria Promenade to *Bedford*; from The Mayorhold to *Rugby*; *Leicester*; etc.
Canal Cruises in summer to *Banbury* and *Nuneaton*.
Theatres. *Repertory*, Guildhall Rd.; *New* (variety), Abington St.

History. The castle built at this ancient Saxon town soon after the Norman Conquest by Simon de Senlis became a favourite resort of the Norman and Angevin kings, and many great councils and parliaments were held here. It was the scene of the trial and condemnation of Thomas Becket in 1164, and Shakespeare laid the first scene of his 'King John' in the great hall. In 1460 one of the decisive battles of the Wars of the Roses was fought outside the town-walls, the Lancastrians being defeated and Henry VI taken prisoner. Northampton sided with Parliament during the Civil Wars, and one of the first acts of Charles II was to order its castle and walls to be razed. It suffered a disastrous fire in 1675.

From the *Castle Station*, which occupies the site of the vanished castle, Marefair leads towards the centre of the town. On the right is *ST PETER's, dating from c. 1160, one of the finest late-Norman parish churches in England. The chief features are the richly carved arch on the w. front and (in the interior) the massive w. tower-arch and the quaintly carved capitals of the piers. Within is a fine Saxon cross-shaft.

John Smith (d. 1742), the mezzotint engraver is buried in the church, and Wm. Smith (d. 1839), the geologist, in the churchyard.—In Doddridge St., on the left, is the *Independent Chapel* (1642) where Dr Doddridge ministered from 1729 to 1751.

Farther on in Marefair is the *Hazelrigge Mansion* ('H.M.'), a picturesque survival of the fire of 1675. Gold St. continues Marefair to the church of *All Saints*, rebuilt after the fire of 1675, with an Ionic portico, in the centre of which is a statue of Charles II in a toga and a flowing wig, by John Hunt (1712). On the opposite side of George Row is the *County Hall*, a good specimen of late Renaissance, completed in 1682. The two courts have beautiful plaster ceilings. The TOWN HALL or *Guildhall* (1864; enlarged in 1892), in St Giles's Sq., is a florid building, adorned with sculptures and statues of English kings. The borough records contain the names of 600 mayors (a roll unrivalled by any other municipality), including that of Laurence Washington (1532 and 1545). In Guildhall Rd. is the *Museum & Art Gallery* (weekdays 10–6, Thurs & Sat 10–8), with a fine archaeological collection, including early Iron Age antiquities from Hunsbury Hill (2 m. s.w.), a good geological collection, a unique section illustrating the history of foot-gear, and a display of English pottery and china.

St Giles's St. leads from the Town Hall to *St Giles's Church*, a cruciform Perp. building with Norman portions, restored and enlarged in 1857. Robert Browne (1553–1633), founder of the 'Brownists', the precursors of Congregationalism, died in Northampton Gaol and is buried here.—In Bridge St., leading s. from All Saints, is *St John's Hospital*, a somewhat decayed Dec. building; the chapel (now Rom. Cath.) has a fine Perp. w. window.

To the N. of All Saints is the spacious *Market Square* (markets on Wed and Sat), whence Sheep St. leads N. to *ST SEPULCHRE'S, one of the four round churches in England. The round part, with its eight Norman pillars supporting late 14C arches, dates from c. 1100–15, and was most probably built by the first Earl, Simon de Senlis, who was a fervent Crusader; it resembles its prototype, the Church of the Holy Sepulchre at Jerusalem, more closely than the other English round churches. The present nave is an enlargement (13–14C) of the original Norman choir; the choir dates from 1860–64. The tower and spire are late 14C. On the N. wall is the quaint Coles brass (1640).

Farther N., in Barrack Rd., is the *Roman Catholic Cathedral*, designed by A. W. Pugin, opened in 1864, and reconsecrated 1960.—Abington St., leading N.E. from the Market Square, past the *Public Library* (relics of John Clare, the poet) and a statue (by Tinworth) of Charles Bradlaugh (1833–91; M.P. for Northampton from 1880), is continued by Wellingborough Rd. to the *County Cricket Ground* (l.) and *Abington Park* (r.). In the manor-house here is *Abington Museum* (weekdays 10–12.30, 2–5 or 6; Sun in summer 2.30–5). It was the former residence of Lady Bernard, Shakespeare's grand-daughter (d. 1670), who was buried in the s. chapel of the old village church. *St Matthew's Church* (19C Gothic), in the Kettering Rd., contains a Madonna and Child (1944), in stone, by Henry Moore, and a painting (1947), 'Crucifixion', by Graham Sutherland.—*Gayton Manor*, 5½ m. s.w. (2 m. w. of the Towcester road at Blisworth; p. 316) is a 16C house of unusual plan (no adm.), on a ridge with a fine view.

A favourite excursion is by the Rugby road to (6 m.) **Althorp**, the 16–18C seat of Earl Spencer, which contains a large and famous *Collection of pictures, furniture, and china (conducted tours June–Sept, Sun, Tues & Thurs; May, Sun only; also BH, 2.30–6; fee) including works inherited from Sarah, duchess of Marlborough.

The collection is especially notable for portraits by *Van Dyck* (Earls of Bristol and Bedford, and others); *Lely* (Beauties of the Court of Charles II, with fine frames) in their original setting; *Kneller* (Duchess of Marlborough and others); *Reynolds* (eighteen portraits, notably Georgiana Countess Spencer and daughter, Lavinia Countess Spencer, Lady Anne Bingham, Viscount Althorp as a child, Countess of Bessborough); *Gainsborough* (four portraits); and most other great British portrait painters. Also: *F. Pourbus*, Duc de Chevreuse; *Mor*, Philip II; *Maes*, Tromp; *Walker*, Cromwell; and works by *Sacchi*, *Guido Reni*, *Guercino*, *Salvator Rosa*, etc.

On the w. side of the park is the church of **Great Brington**, which contains the

*Tombs of the Spencers (from 1522 onwards), and is interesting as the burial-place of the Washington brothers who removed from Sulgrave (p. 309) to this district. A wood board in the chancel floor covers the grave of Laurence Washington, "sonne and heire of Robert Washington of Soulgrave" and ancestor of George Washington, who lived at *Wicken* (3½ m. w. of Stony Stratford) from 1610 till his death at Althorp Park in 1616; and brasses in the central passage of the nave commemorate Robert Washington (d. 1622) and his wife who had occupied two houses at Great Brington since 1599. About 1½ m. N.W. of Althorp is *East Haddon*, where Anne, widow of Robert Washington of Sulgrave (d. 1620), lived from 1626 till her death in 1652; and 1½ m. N.E. is *Holdenby*, birthplace of Sir Christopher Hatton (1540–91), who in 1583 built *Holdenby House*, where Charles I was kept in the custody of Parliament for four months in 1647.   The old school (1668) at *Guilsborough*, 3 m. N. of E. Haddon, is a fine stone building. *Brockhall*, 3 m. s.w. of Gt. Brington, is an Elizabethan and 18C mansion (no adm.).

FROM NORTHAMPTON TO PETERBOROUGH, 40½ m. (A 45, A 510, A 604, A 605). The road keeps parallel to the Nene and affords access to an extraordinary number of interesting churches, culminating in Peterborough Cathedral. Cabin cruisers may be hired at Northampton, Oundle Marina, and Peterborough.—3½ m. *Great Billing* has a pretentious monument (1700) by Bushnell in its church. *Little Billing*, 1 m. s.w., has a remarkable Saxon font.—4½ m. *Ecton* was the home of the Franklin family for many generations, whence Benjamin Franklin's father emigrated to New England in 1685. His uncle, Thomas Franklin, is buried in the churchyard.—To the right, at 6½ m., is the church of *Earls Barton*, with its famous *West Tower, "by far the most noteworthy architectural monument of the Saxon period" (Prof. Baldwin Brown), dating from the late 10C. *Whiston* church, 1½ m. s.w., is an admirable specimen of late-Perp. work (1534). About 1½ m. farther s. is *Castle Ashby House* (Marquess of Northampton), an Elizabethan mansion with additions ascribed to Inigo Jones, and a 'lettered' balustrade (open Apr–Sept, Sun & BH; also Thurs, Sat, June–Aug; 2–5.30; fee), with a noted collection of Italian paintings, 17C furniture, etc. The church contains interesting monuments. To the s. extends *Yardley Chase.*—10 m. **Wellingborough**, see Rte 44.—At (14 m.) *Finedon* we cross A 6 (Rte 44).—18 m. *Twywell* (l.) has early-Norman features and Livingstone relics in its church.—20½ m. *Islip*, on the Nene, has a beautiful Perp. church, containing a tablet to the wife of Sir John Washington (d. 1624) and a chancel-screen presented by descendants of Mathias Nicoll (Mayor of New York in 1671). About 1½ m. farther N. is *Lowick*, the 15C church of which has a remarkable octagonal lantern on the *Tower, fine contemporary monuments, and good stained glass of the Dec. period. About 1 m. s.w. of Lowick is *Drayton House* (no adm.), a beautiful mansion of the 14–18C.—We cross the Nene into (21 m.) *Thrapston*, a small grain market.—23½ m. *Thorpe Waterville*. At *Aldwincle*, 1½ m. w., were born Thos. Fuller, historian (1608–61; in the rectory of St Peter's), and John Dryden (1631–1700; in the rectory of All Saints).—25½ m. *Barnwell* has the ruins of a 13C castle.

28 m. **Oundle** (Hotel) is a charming little town (3700 inhab.), with a well-known public school, a lofty church steeple (210 ft), and some of the best 17–18C houses in England, notably the White Lion Inn (1641). The front of the Talbot Inn was built with materials from Fotheringhay Castle (see below), whence came also the oak staircase, within. Fine misericords from the demolished choir of Fotheringhay are to be seen in the churches of *Benefield* (3 m. w.), *Hemington* (3 m. s.e.), and *Tansor* (2 m. N.E.). The Nene between Tansor and *Cotterstock*, nearer Oundle, is especially charming; and *Polebrook*, on the road to Hemington, has one of the finest churches in the district. About 1 m. s. of Benefield are the restored 'Old Building' (no adm.) and the shell of the unfinished 'New Building' at *Lyveden*, begun by Sir Thos. Tresham c. 1603, the latter (N.T.; adm. Mar–Oct, Wed, Thurs, Sat, Sun, & BH, 2–6; fee) adorned with 'Popish' sculptures and inscriptions.—The remarkable E.E. church of (31 m.) *Warmington* retains its original roof, groined in wood. Across the Nene, 2 m. N.W. by footpath, is *Fotheringhay*, the scene of the trial and execution of Mary, Queen of Scots, in 1587. Of the royal castle, where Richard III was born in 1452, almost the only trace is the mound of the great keep (no adm.). The collegiate church, with a noble lantern-tower, lacks the choir of the original building (1415); it contains two monuments erected by Queen Elizabeth in memory of Yorkist princes buried here.—32½ m. *Elton. Elton Hall* is a 15–19C mansion, noted for its collection of early Bibles, with charming gardens. At (35½ m.) *Kate's Cabin* we cross the Great North Road (comp. p. 428).—40½ m. *Peterborough*, see Rte 54.

From Northampton to *Olney* and *Bedford*, see Rte 44.

A 508 leads due N. past (70 m.) the Pitsford Reservoir, used by the Northamptonshire Sailing Club (trout fishing), to (71 m.) *Brixworth*, with the kennels of the Pytchley hunt. The *Church, built c. 680 with the bricks from adjacent Roman buildings, is a highly interesting example of Romanesque in which three distinct periods of pre-Norman architecture can be traced. *Spratton*, 2¼ m. w., has a Trans. Norman church containing the effigy of Sir John Swinford (d. 1371), with the earliest known example of the SS collar.—73½ m. *Lamport*, with the Hall of the Isham family, designed by John Webb in 1654 (adm. Easter–Sept, Sun & BH; also Thurs in June–Aug; 2.15–5.30; fee; teas).

Lamport is c. 5 m. s.e. of the battlefield of *Naseby*, where Charles I and Prince Rupert were decisively defeated by Fairfax in 1645. A column erected in 1936 marks the correct site.

We enter Leicestershire just before (82 m.) **Market Harborough** (Hotels), a town of 14,500 inhab. and a famous fox-hunting centre. In the market-place are the quaint grammar school (1614) and the Perp. church of *St Dionysius*, with its beautiful Dec. broach spire. Close by is the old house in which Charles I is said to have slept the night before the battle of Naseby (7 m. s.w.).

From Market Harborough to *Rugby* and *Oundle*, see p.364; *Rothwell* (p.408) is 6 m. s.e.

At (87½ m.) *Kibworth*, with some 17–18C houses and a post mill of 1711, Dr Philip Doddridge was a dissenting minister in 1723–25.

96 m. LEICESTER (283,500 inhab.), on the Soar, the ancient county town of Leicestershire, is a busy industrial city, long noted as the centre of the hosiery trade; more recently it has added light engineering to important manufactures of boots and shoes, elastic fabrics, etc., and many large undistinguished buildings to the centre. In 1919 its former city status was restored and it is now the seat of a bishop. The main interest for the visitor lies in its Roman remains, and the well-displayed Leicester Museums; an 'inner ring-road' makes a perambulation difficult.

Car Parks. Multi-story parks in St Peter's Lane (off Vaughan Way), and St Nicholas Circle, Lee Circle, Haymarket, etc.; also Abbey St., and Welford Road.

Railway Station, London Road.

Hotels in Granby St., and Abbey St.; and others less distinguished.

Post Office, Bishop St.—INFORMATION BUREAU, adjoining the Library, 12 Bishop St.

Buses from Northampton St., to *Market Harborough*; from St Margaret's (Abbey St.) to *Loughborough*; *Ashby* and *Burton*; *Oakham*; *Uppingham*; *Melton Mowbray* and *Grantham*; from Newarke to *Lutterworth*; to *Nuneaton* and *Coventry*; from Southgates to *Coventry* and *Birmingham*; also to *London, Cheltenham*, etc.

Theatres. *Haymarket*, Haymarket Centre; *Phoenix*, Newarke St., *Little*, Dover St.—CONCERTS at *De Montfort Hall* and the *City Art Gallery*.—EXHIBITIONS, roller-skating, etc., at Granby Halls—SWIMMING POOL, St Margaret's (Vaughan Way).

History. Leicester was the traditional residence of King Lear and his daughters. Under the Romans it was the fortified town of *Ratæ Coritanorum*. From 680 to 869 it was the seat of the East Mercian bishopric, but soon after it became one of the Five Boroughs of the Danelagh. It was recovered by Ethelfleda, the Lady of Mercia, in 918. After the Norman Conquest it fell to Hugh of Grantmesnil, who built the castle, and in 1239 to Simon de Montfort, Earl of Leicester, who was a great benefactor of the town. Under the Lancastrian kings the castle was an occasional royal residence, and three parliaments were held here in the 15C. Richard III, however, on his way to Bosworth Field in 1485, was obliged to sleep at an inn. In the Civil War Leicester was captured by Prince Rupert in 1645 after a three days' siege at which John Bunyan was present, but it was recovered by Parliament after the battle of Naseby. The modern prosperity of the city may perhaps be dated from the introduction of the stocking-frame about 1686. The confused medieval street plan, which survived the Victorian building, is fast being replaced by equally confusing highways and large blocks of mainly ugly buildings. The suffix 'gate' (except in East Gates) is the Danish 'street'. Leicester was the birthplace of Thomas Cooper, the Chartist (1805–92). Thomas Cook arranged the first railway excursion in 1841, from Leicester to Loughborough and back.

The former centre is now virtually closed to traffic and it is difficult to see the *Clock Tower* (1866), adorned with statues of Simon de Montfort and later benefactors of the city, as the hub of converging main roads which developed outside the Roman E. Gate. It is approached from the Station to the S.E., by Granby St., the principal shopping centre. From East Gates the Roman main street ran W. to the Soar bridge; the High St. follows the medieval line somewhat to the N. At the point where it intersects the old thoroughfare from N. to S. (Highcross St. and its continuation, in St Nicholas Circle) formerly stood the *High Cross.*

To the right Highcross St. leads past the site of the Free Grammar School (1573; plaque). Beyond, and isolated by the 'ring-road', are *All Saints*, a well-proportioned early-Dec. church (Norman W. doorway, outside clock of c. 1620, and E.E. font), and to the E., *St Margaret's*, with a noble Perp. tower and chancel and fragments of Anglo-Saxon masonry (E. end of the N. aisle). The fine *Great Meeting*, one of the oldest Nonconformist Chapels (1708), survives in East Bond St. behind St Margaret's Baths and Car Park on Vaughan Way.

The intrusive new St Nicholas Circle round a large hotel and multi-story car park preserves *William Carey's Cottage*, where the ministrations of William Carey (1789–94) and Robert Hall (1807–25) are commemorated. Excavations here in 1971 revealed part of the medieval walls. Across the Circle is the church of **St Nicholas**, the oldest in Leicester, built partly of Roman materials with an attractive early-Norman tower, a primitive Romanesque nave of the Saxon period, and an E.E. chancel. On the W. side of the churchyard rises the **Jewry Wall**, a mass of Roman masonry about 70 ft long and 18 ft high, with bonding-courses of brick. This relic, with its four arched recesses, may have been the W. wall of a basilica in the Roman Forum which extended to the E. and N., or part of later Roman Baths which may be seen in plan to the W. Beyond is the **Jewry Wall Museum** (weekdays 10–5.30, Sun 2–5.30).

A Museum of archaeology to the Middle Ages, it is specially noted for Roman exhibits, which include several tessellated pavements (notably the Peacock mosaic, and Cyparissus and his stag), large wall-paintings, a wooden bucket with bronze decoration, and milestones from the Foss Way, etc. The columns outside come from a colonnade in the Forum. The 'Blackfriars' mosaic is still *in situ* in Bath Lane (inquire at museum). The adjoining *Vaughan College* is the Department of Adult Education of the University of Leicester.—Beyond *West Bridge* over the Grand Junction Canal, St Augustine's St. leads to *Bow Bridge* over the Soar, where a plaque records the last resting-place of Richard III; according to tradition, his body, brought back from Bosworth for interment in the monastery of the Grey Friars, was thrown into the river on the suppression of the monasteries, but was afterwards reburied near here.

Castle St. leads out of the opposite side of St Nicholas Circle to ***St Mary de Castro** (key at vicarage), an interesting church with an unusual ground-plan; to the original Norman collegiate church were added a chancel in the richest late-Norman style (after 1150) and, in the E.E. period, a wide parochial nave, on the S. side, and a massive tower. The Norman N. doorway, arcading (N. aisle), windows, and sedilia,

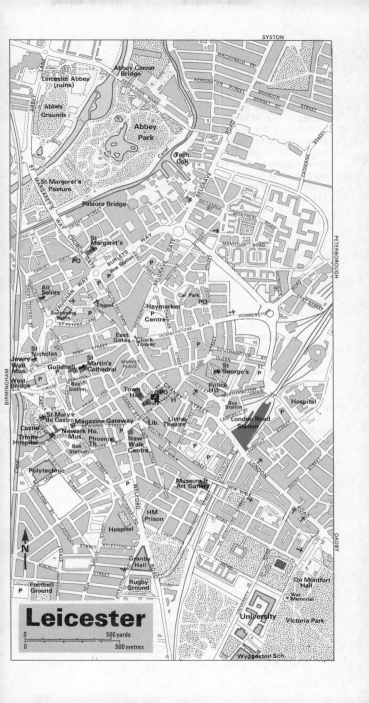

Leicester

SYSTON

BIRMINGHAM

PETERBOROUGH

OADBY

MACDONALD RD

KENSINGTON STREET

BRANDON
DORSET ST
STREET

ROAD

CATHERINE STREET

Abbey Corner
Bridge

Leicester Abbey
(ruins)

Abbey
Grounds

Abbey
Park

ST PARK ROAD

Canal

Tech
Coll

St Margaret's
Pasture

MONTREAL

ROAD

BELGRAVE

ST MARGARET'S WAY

BRITANNIA
ST

MANITOBA ROAD

Pasture Bridge

St Margaret's

FRIAR LANE STREET

CHURCHGATE

WAY

BELGRAVE GATE

GATE

PO

SANVEY GATE

BURLEYS
Bus Station

P

BRITISH ROAD

KENT STREET

All
Saints

VAUGHAN WAY

CATHERINE STREET

Chapel

HUMBERSTON

Swimming
Baths

ST PETERS LANE

SANDACRE STREET

Car Park
PO

P

Haymarket
Centre

CHARLES

East
Gates

HIGH STREET

Clock
Tower

HUMBERSTONE GATE

STREET

SOUTHAMPTON
ST

St
Nicholas

ST NICHOLAS

MARKET
PLACE

St
Martin's
Cathedral

QUEEN
ST

St
George's

P

Jewry
Wall
Mus.

Guildhall

Bus
Station

RUTLAND
STREET

HUMBERSTON

West
Bridge

CIRCLE

Bus
Station

FRIAR LANE

CHARLES STREET

Police
HQ

Hospital

CASTLE STREET

Town
Hall

GRANBY

GPO

Library

H

NORTHAMPTON

SWAIN

Bus
Station

CAMPBELL ST

London Road
Station

St Mary
de Castro

Magazine Gateway

Lib.

STREET

Newark Ho.
Mus.

NEWARKE STREET

Little
Theatre

Castle

Phoenix

WELLINGTON ST

LONDON

Trinity
Hospital

MARKET

Bus
Station

New
Walk
Centre

P

ROAD

CONDUIT STREET

SABY STREET

NEW WALK

Polytechnic

OXFORD STREET

WELFORD

REGENT

Museum &
Art Gallery

NEW WALK

ROAD

WATERLOO STREET

N

CATHERINE STREET

HM
Prison

ROAD

UNIVERSITY ROAD

LANCASTER

DE MONTFORT STREET

STREET

AYLESTONE ST

Hospital

Granby
Hall

WALNUT

STREET

WELFORD ROAD

Rugby
Ground

De Montfort
Hall

War
Memorial

University

Victoria Park

Football
Ground

Wyggeston Sch.

| 0 | | | 500 yards |
| 0 | | | 500 metres |

the Dec. roof in the original chancel, the E.E. sedilia and Perp. roof in the s. nave, and the 13C font should be noted. The few remains of the once famous CASTLE are approached by a timber gateway (1445) with the porter's lodge. *Castle House*, on the right, incorporates the domestic buildings. In the secluded Castle Yard, where Wesley used to preach, a façade of c. 1698 masks the late-Norman hall, divided in three in 1821 so that only the N. and s. ends are visible (still used for assize courts; open when not in use). A doorway from the hall can be seen in the w. wall of the church. Beyond the ruined *Turret Gateway* (1423), in Castle View, the Deacon Workshop (1771; re-created here in 1953) illustrates the art of a clock-making family of Barton in the Beans.

The gateway leads into the *Newarke*, added to the castle precincts in 1332, which includes the rebuilt *Trinity Hospital*, founded in 1331 by Henry of Lancaster and enlarged in 1354 by his son Henry, Duke of Lancaster (d. here 1361). Its partly original chapel (adm. on request) lies to the right. Here Mary Bohun, mother of Henry V, is buried (1394). To the left, the *Wyggeston Chantry House* (1512, damaged in 1940 and later rebuilt) and *Skeffington House* form the NEWARKE HOUSES MUSEUM (weekdays 10–5.30, Sun from 2). The rooms illustrate the social and industrial history of the city, with fine displays of shoes, clocks, and musical instruments. A plaque on the corner of Newarke recalls the bizarre practices of the 'Whipping Toms' here on Shrove Tuesday, a custom abolished by Act of Parliament in 1846. Beyond are various buildings of the Polytechnic. The splendid *Magazine Gateway* (c. 1400), isolated amid the traffic (reached by subway), houses the Museum of the Royal Leicester Regiment (weekdays 10–5.30, Sun from 2).

The old civic church of **St Martin**, the cathedral since 1926, is in Peacock Lane, approached by Southgates, or (more peacefully) by Castle St. It is mainly E.E. in style with a Perp. chancel. Adjacent (w.) is the **Guildhall* (weekdays 10–5.30, Sun from 2), a 15C–16C timber and plaster building, originally the hall of the Guild of Corpus Christi. The mayor's parlour contains a fine chimneypiece (1637), woodwork, and stained glass and the great hall is imposing. The Town Library, one of the earliest municipal free libraries, founded before 1587, has been here since 1632. A little to the E. lies the *Market Place* (recently covered; markets Wed, Fri, and Sat); the old Corn Exchange has a fine outside staircase (c. 1851). To the s. are the *Town Hall* (1875) and the *Central Reference Library*. Belvoir St., s. of the library, leads to King St., from which we reach NEW WALK, a long tree-lined footway (1785), with the *Museum and Art Gallery* (weekdays 10–5.30, Sun from 2).

The geology and natural history collections are well displayed as is church plate (1654) from Staunton Harold. The emphasis in painting and sculpture is on modern works. Notable are *Opie*, Boy with a Hoop; *G. V. Cole*, Thames Valley; *Lowry*, Industrial Landscape; *Laura Knight*, Three clowns; *Stanley Spencer*, Adoration of the Old Men; and works by *Duncan Grant* and *John Piper*. The muniment room contains the archives of the city, and the most valuable MSS., including the Codex Leicestrensis of the New Testament, from the Town Library.

From the end of New Walk, University Rd. leads to the right (passing Victoria Park, with *De Montfort Hall* and a *War Memorial Arch*, by Lutyens) to the University, which received its charter in 1957. The main building, once a hospital dates from 1837, and among the new buildings, the Engineering Block has a dramatic tower. Neighbouring is *Wygges-*

ton Boys' School, which can trace its origins to a charitable foundation in 1513.

Belgrave Gate leads N.E. from the clock-tower to Belgrave Rd. goods station, whence a road leads left to the *Abbey Park* (incl. a drive), with its lake, and to the remains of **Leicester Abbey**, whither Cardinal Wolsey, "an old man, broken with the storms of state", came to die, in 1530. His tomb has disappeared, and little remains of the rich Augustinian monastery except the conjectural foundations and the boundary-walls, the existing ruins being part of the Elizabethan *Cavendish House*. A *Museum of Technology* lies farther N. in a pumping station off Abbey Lane in Corporation Road. Farther on off Belgrave Rd., is *Belgrave Hall* (10–5.30, Sun from 2), built in 1709–13, with a charming garden, and now a period museum of coaches and agricultural equipment, etc.—*Quenby Hall*, in pastoral upland country, 8 m. E. of Leicester, is claimed to be the finest Jacobean mansion in the county (adm. Thurs 2–6, June–Sept, also BH; fee; teas).

Charming walks or drives may be taken from Leicester through the rugged Charnwood Forest, which extends to the N.W. Following A 50, we pass the new County Hall (2¾ m.; r.) and diverge left to (4¼ m.) *Groby* (Hotel). Here are the remains of the mansion of the Greys of Groby, where Elizabeth Woodville (afterwards Queen of Edward IV) lived with her first husband, Sir John Grey. A by-road leads N. (passing below A 50), skirting the attractive *Groby Pool*, and descending to (6½ m.) *Newtown Linford*. *Bradgate Park* (open daily to walkers; on Wed & Thurs in April–Sept, 2.30–8, for driving through), with the chapel (summer Thurs 2.30–5.30) and the ruins of the hall where Lady Jane Grey, the 'nine days' queen' (born here in 1537), was found by Roger Ascham reading Plato's 'Phædo' while the rest of the family were gone hunting.—About 2 m. N.W. of Newtown are the 14C remains of *Ulverscroft Priory*. The excursion may be extended to *Bardon Hill*, *Mount St Bernard*, *Grace Dieu* (see below), etc., or we may return viâ Cropston Reservoir, *Thurcaston*, birthplace of Bp. Latimer (1485–1555), and *Rothley*.

FROM LEICESTER TO BURTON, 25½ m. (A 50). The disused line to Swannington was Robert Stephenson's first railway (1832).—4½ m. *Groby* (see above). *Kirby Muxloe*, 2½ m. s., has a ruined and moated Castle (closed on Sun) built in 1480–84.—Beyond (10 m.) *Bardon Hill* (912 ft), on the right, a famous viewpoint, we enter the Leicestershire coalfield.—12 m. *Coalville* (28,300 inhab.) is a mining and brick-making town. The 13C manor-house at *Donington le Heath*, 1 m. s.w., has a fine oaken roof. About 2¾ m. N.E., in a remote position, is the abbey of *Mount St Bernard*, a Trappist monastery founded in 1835 and till 1955 the only 'mitred abbey' in England. The fine church was begun in 1839 by A. W. N. Pugin, and enlarged in 1934–39 by Albert Herbert (visitors welcome, but with the restrictions of a closed Order). Beyond Whitwick, 3½ m N., is *Grace Dieu*, with the scanty ruins of a 13C Augustinian nunnery (seen in a field skirted by A 512) and a manor-house, now part of a school, in which Francis Beaumont (1584–1616) was born.

17 m. Ashby-de-la-Zouch (Hotels) is a town of 8300 inhab. in pretty surroundings. The *Castle* (daily, Sun from 2; fee) is the extensive ruin of a fortress-house built by Lord Hastings in 1474–76 and incorporating much of a Norman (12C) and 14C manor. After a siege in 1644–46 it was slighted by the Parliamentarians in 1648. Mary, Queen of Scots, spent a night in it in 1569 and again in 1586, but it is more famous as the locale of several scenes in 'Ivanhoe'. The 'Tournament Field' lies about 1 m. N. of the town. In the well-sited church of *St Helen* (late-Perp.), are the tombs of the second Earl of Huntingdon (d. 1561) and of Selina, Countess of Huntingdon (d. 1791), Wesley's friend; a rare recumbent effigy of a pilgrim (15C); and a finger-pillory for delinquents in church. About 2 m. E. is *Coleorton Hall* (adm. by permit from the National Coal Board), in the grounds of which are memorials to Sir Joshua Reynolds and Beaumont (see above) and a garden designed in 1807 by Wordsworth, with the aid of his sister and Coleridge, for Sir George Beaumont (d. 1827). *Appleby Magna*, 5 m. s.w. of Ashby, has a moated house (15–16C); at *Appleby Parva*, ¾ m. farther on, is Sir John Moor's School (1693–97), by Sir Wm. Wilson. Between Ashby and Appleby is *Measham*, with the *Midland Motor Museum*.—From Ashby to *Derby*, see p. 402; to *Nottingham*, p. 402.—A 50 goes on past (20 m.) *Swadlincote*, in a colliery and fireclay-making district (20,200 inhab.).—25½ m. *Burton-on-Trent*, see p. 329.

FROM LEICESTER TO GRANTHAM, 30½ m. (A 607); railway to Melton Mowbray in 20 min.—At (4½ m.) *Syston* we diverge from the Foss Way to Newark and ascend the valley of the Wreak, in which are many villages with names ending in 'by', an evidence of Danish occupation.—5¼ m. (r.) *Queniborough* was the headquarters of Prince Rupert during the siege of Leicester.—7 m. *Rearsby*. *Gaddesby*, 2½ m. E., has a fine early 14C church.—8½ m. *Brooksby*, with a beautiful little Perp. church and an Elizabethan manor-house, the birthplace in 1592 of George Villiers, first Duke of Buckingham.—15 m. **Melton Mowbray**, see Rte. 44.—We cross the Leicestershire Wolds, for which (20 m.) *Waltham-on-the-Wolds* is a good centre.—*Sproxton*, 3 m. E., has a complete 10C cross.—30½ m. *Grantham*, see Rte 46.

Leaving Leicester by Belgrave Rd., we bear left and cross the Soar. —100 m. *Wanlip*. The church (½ m. r.) contains the brass of Sir Thomas Walsh (d. 1393), one of the finest in England.—At (101 m.) *Rothley* (Restaurant), to the left, is Rothley Court Hotel, an Elizabethan mansion (Rothley Temple) with the chapel of a preceptory of the Templars. Lord Macaulay (1800–59) was born here; the parish church has Babington monuments and (outside) a 10C cross. Here the Main Line Steam Trust has reopened a section of the Great Central Railway to Loughborough (steam service at weekends in summer).—We traverse the long street of *Mountsorrel*, with its neglected market cross of 1793. *Sileby* church, 1½ m. E., has a beautiful E.E. arcade.— 104 m. *Quorn* (or *Quorndon*) has good 16C tombs in the church.

The kennels of the famous Quorn hunt (pron. 'Corn') are now at *Seagrave* 4½ m. E., viâ (1 m.) *Barrow-on-Soar*, where the church has a fine Perp. wooden roof. —From Quorn B 591 goes W. to Charnwood Forest viâ (1½ m.) *Beau Manor* (no adm.), the beautiful home, until 1946, of the Curzon-Herrick family, of which Robert Herrick and Dean Swift were connections.

106½ m. **Loughborough** (Hotel), a thriving hosiery and engineering town (45,900 inhab.), has a large Dec. and Perp. church (*All Saints*) notable for its bold arches uniformly moulded. In the churchyard are some fine slate gravestones. The Old Rectory is open .May–Sept, Thurs 10–4.30. 'Great Paul' of London was cast in Messrs. Taylor's bell-foundry here. The *War Memorial Tower* (1923), in Queen's Park, has a carillon of 45 bells, one of the largest in the world. Loughborough College of Technology, founded 1909, achieved university status in 1964, and has extensive new buildings on the Leicester road.

At *Stanford Hall*, 3 m. N.E., a repertory theatre was founded in 1957. *Dishley Grange*, 1½ m. N.E., was the home of Robert Bakewell (1725–95), father of modern stockbreeding.

FROM LOUGHBOROUGH TO NOTTINGHAM, 14 m. (A 60). We cross the Soar and beyond (3 m.) *Hoton*, enter Notts.—5½ m. *Costock* has an old manor-house. A road on the left leads to *East Leake*, in the church of which is preserved a 'shawm', or long trumpet formerly used by the bass singer. About 3 m. N. is *Gotham*, famous for its 'Wise Men' who attempted to make a hedge round a cuckoo and went to sea in a bowl. Washington Irving bestowed this name on New York.— 7½ m. The attractive village of *Bunny*, rebuilt by the 'wresting baronet', Sir Thomas Parkyns (1664–1741), has a 14C church with a noble chancel.—14 m. *Nottingham*, see Rte 44.

A 6 descends the Leicestershire bank of the Soar past (111 m.) *Whatton* (gardens open Sun 2–7) to (112½ m.) *Kegworth*, an unusual village, with a late-Dec. church of a symmetrical and uniform design. The church of *Kingston-on-Soar*, on the opposite (Notts) bank, has a 16C chantry, profusely displaying the rebus (Babe-in-Tun) of the Babington family, to which Anthony Babington, the conspirator (executed in 1586), belonged.—113½ m. *Lockington* (l.) has fine wood-work in its church. We cross the Trent by the Cavendish Bridge (1957) and enter Derbyshire.—118½ m. *Elvaston Castle Country Park* (1½ m. r.; rfmts) has beautiful gardens open daily to pedestrians.

123 m. **DERBY** (pron. 'Darby'; 219,300 inhab.), the traditional capital of Derbyshire, though no longer its seat of administration, an episcopal see since 1927, the seat of extensive railway works, and an important manufacturing town with a great diversity of industries, is situated on the w. bank of the Derwent.

Car Parking, St Helen's St. (multi-story park).
Railway Station, Midland Rd.—**Airport** at *Castle Donington*, 10 m. S.E.
Hotels in Sadler Gate, London Rd., Midland Rd., and Macklin St.
Post Office, Victoria St.
Buses and **Coaches** from Bus Station (Morledge) to all parts.—TOWN BUSES from Market Place.
Theatre. *Playhouse*, Sacheverel St.—**Concerts,** Guildhall.—SWIMMING POOL and Sports Centre, More Lane, off Osmaston Park Rd.

History. The Roman station of *Derventio* was at Little Chester, on the opposite bank of the Derwent. Derby was one of the 'Five Boroughs' held by the Danes, and in the Anglo-Saxon period was a town of great importance. During the Civil War the town was held by Parliament. In 1745 Prince Charles Edward with his Highland army penetrated as far s. as Derby, but after two days he was forced to begin his retreat to Scotland, where the disaster of Culloden awaited him.—The first successful English silk-mill was erected in Full St. (now a power station) in 1718–21 by John Lombe (1694–1722), who stole the secret of the machinery from Piedmont, and in 1755 the Derby ceramic industry (comp. below) was established by Wm. Duesbury of London.—Joseph Wright, the painter ('Wright of Derby'; 1734–97), was born in Iron Gate, Herbert Spencer (1820–1903) in Exeter St., and John Flamsteed (1646–1719), astronomer-royal, at *Denby*, 6½ m. N.—Derby is the 'Stoniton' of 'Adam Bede'.

London Rd. runs direct to the centre of the town past the extensive British Rail Research Centre, with experimental laboratories. On the right Midland Rd., passing the Midland Railway War Memorial, leads to the Station; on the left is the *Royal Infirmary* (1891). Beyond the church of *St Peter's* (14–15C), Cornmarket (buses only) leads straight on to the Market Place (see below). Victoria St. diverges left to the Wardwick, with the *Library, Museum, and Art Gallery* (also entered from the Strand, behind; adm. 10–6, Sat 10–5).

The *Museum*, largely devoted to local industries, includes Derby ware and a good working model showing the development of the Midland Railway. There is the stone coffin of St Alkmund, and a fine cross-shaft, both 9C from the demolished church of St Alkmund. The committee room (glass doors) contains relics and oak panelling from Exeter House, where the Young Pretender lodged in 1745. The *Art Gallery* has a fine collection of paintings by Wright of Derby.—In Friar Gate is *St Werburgh's*, largely rebuilt by Blomfield and containing a font-cover by Bake-well. Here Dr Johnson was married to Elizabeth Porter on 9 July 1735. Drastic intrusions into the w. end of the nave are to provide a 'social centre' (1971).

We proceed N. by Bold Lane, and turn right into St Mary's Gate, with (l.) the *County Hall*, with an unusual façade of 1660, said to be the scene of Hetty Sorrel's trial ('Adam Bede'). At the end is the splendid Perp. *Tower (210 ft high) of *All Saints*, the cathedral of Derby, built in 1509–27 (closed for restoration, 1971). The church, rebuilt by Gibbs in 1722–25, with a spacious and light interior, has good ironwork screens by Robert Bakewell (d. 1752). It contains the tombs of 'Bess of Hard-wick' (1520–1608), the building Countess of Shrewsbury, and of Henry Cavendish (1731–1810), the chemist, and the unique wooden effigy of a canon (c. 1500), on the s. side; on the N. is the incised slab to sub-dean Lawe (c. 1450). At the bottom of the hill is the *Market Place*, with the *Guildhall* (1841), recently renovated to accommodate a concert hall, etc. Behind is the huge barrel-vaulted *Market Hall* (1864). On the E. side of the square a new Civic Centre is planned to incorporate the façade of the Assembly Rooms (1763–74; burnt in 1960).

Queen St. continues Iron Gate to *St Alkmund's*, rebuilt in 1846. To the left *Derby School*, founded in 1160 and chartered in 1554, occupies an 18C mansion; here Flamsteed was a pupil. On the right Bridge Gate, with the *Roman Catholic Church* (1838) by A. W. Pugin, leads to St Mary's Bridge, where the 15C chapel of *Our Lady of the Brigg* survives in isolation as work progresses on a new bridge to the s.

In Osmaston Rd. are the works of the *Royal Crown Derby Porcelain Company* (comp. above), open to visitors on written application. The present company was established in 1877 to revise the Derby porcelain industry, which had declined since the days of Duesbury.—Behind is the *Arboretum*, a pleasant park of 22 acres, containing a statue of F. H. Royce, the motor engineer, and the 'Headless Cross', in a hollow of which, filled with vinegar, the townsfolk used to place their money during the plague of 1665, when buying provisions from the country people. The famous *Rolls-Royce Works* are near Osmaston Rd., farther south.

About 4½ m. N.W. of Derby is *Kedleston* (Viscount Scarsdale; adm. Easter–Sept on Sun 2–6, also BH; tea), a classical mansion built from the designs of James Paine and Robert Adam in 1755–65, of which Dr Johnson said it would do ex-cellently for a town hall. The gorgeous interior, with plasterwork by Joseph Rose, is by Adam, also the bridge and fishing-house. The church contains tombs of the Curzons from the 13C, including that of Marquess Curzon (1859–1925) and his first wife, with effigies by Sir B. Mackennal.—Notable churches near Derby are: *Chaddesden* (c. 1375), 2 m. E. in a large suburb, with a beautiful screen and a wall-lectern, a local characteristic; *Breadsall*, 2½ m. N.E., rebuilt by Caroë but retaining its Norman doorway and splendid 14C spire; and *Morley*, 4 m. N.E., with *Monu-ments and 15C glass from the Premonstratensian *Dale Abbey*, one arch of which survives (7 m. E. of Derby).—It should not be forgotten that Derby is the 'Gateway of the Peak' (Rte 45).

The ROAD FROM DERBY TO NOTTINGHAM (A 52; 14 m.) by-passes (8 m.) *Sandiacre* (crossing the M 1), where the church has a fine 14C chancel, and (9 m.) *Stapleford*, a town manufacturing lead-pencils, with a fine Saxon cross-shaft near the church.

FROM DERBY TO ASHBY-DE-LA-ZOUCH, 14½ m.—5½ m. The long 14C *Swarkeston Bridge* over the Trent was the most southerly point reached by the advance guard of the Highlanders in 1745.—8 m. *Melbourne*, a pleasant small town where Thomas Cook, the first travel agent (1808–92), was born. The Church, restored by Scott, preserves a noble Norman interior, with might arcades. *Melbourne Hall* (16–18C; main façade to the s., overlooking a lake), with its delightful gardens and garden-sculpture by Nost (adm. May & June, Sun only; July–mid-Sept, daily exc. Mon & Fri; also BH; 2–6; fee; teas), was once the seat of Lord Melbourne, and here Baxter began his 'Saints' Everlasting Rest'.—At (11 m.) *Staunton Harold* (r.) is one of the few churches built during the Commonwealth, with curious inscriptions (N.T.; open Easter–Oct, 11–1, 2–6 or dusk, Wed, Thurs, Sat & Sun; services on Sun). Approached by a Baroque gateway (late-17C), it stands picturesquely beside the Hall (now a Cheshire Home), which has a fine classical façade (1763), and above a lake.—14½ m. *Ashby*, see p. 399.

FROM DERBY TO STOKE-ON-TRENT, 35 m. (A 516, A 50); railway in 50 min.—At (8½ m.) *Hatton* we join A 50, and thence follow the valley of the Dove.—On the Staffordshire bank, 1½ m. s., is *Tutbury* (Hotel; also at Rolleston, 2 m. s.w.), famous for its alabaster. The *Castle* belonged to the Ferrers family from 1070, but the existing remains are those of a late 14C mansion of John of Gaunt, with 15–16C additions, which Mary, Queen of Scots, as a prisoner visited in 1569, 1570, and 1585. The *Church* is the nave of a Benedictine priory founded c. 1086 and shows good *Norman work of the 12C.—12 m. *Sudbury* has a charming village street. The Hall (N.T.; adm. Easter–Oct, Wed–Sun & BH, 1–5.30; fee) is red brickwork of 1615–20 with fine Restoration interiors. The church of *Hanbury*, 3 m. s. claims to have the oldest alabaster effigy in England (Sir John Hanbury; d. 1303).—

19 m. **Uttoxeter** (Hotel), with 9000 inhab. is best remembered for the self-imposed penance of Dr Johnston, who stood bare-headed in the rain in the market-place to expiate his refusal, fifty years before, to attend his father's bookstall (bas-relief on the conduit). Mary Howitt was born here in 1804. The race-course is near the station. Hence to *Ashbourne*, see p. 415; to *Stafford*, see p. 371.—23½ m. *Checkley* has a fine *Church, with a Dec. chancel, much ancient glass, and three late-Saxon crosses.— From (25¼ m.) *Upper Tean* A 522 goes N. to Leek, viâ (2¼ m.) *Cheadle*, a pleasantly situated town with a Rom. Cath. church by A. W. Pugin (1846) and a 'Nature Reserve' on *Hawksmoor*, overlooking the Churnet.—29 m. *Blythe Bridge*, 1½ m. N. of which is *Caverswall Castle*, a massive Jacobean manor-house rebuilt in 1643 by Matthew Cradock, first governor of the Massachusetts Company. It is now a convent of Missionary Sisters.—We enter the Potteries at (32½ m.) *Longton.*—35 m. *Stoke*, see p. 372.

From Derby to the *Peak District* and *Manchester*, see Rte 45; to *Burton*, Birmingham, and the s.w., see Rte 33.

A 61 runs N.E. to (131½ m.) *Ripley.*—At (133 m.) *Swanwick* are held yearly conferences on religious and sociological topics.—134½ m. *Alfreton* and (140 m.) *Clay Cross* are colliery towns.

145 m. **Chesterfield** (Hotels), an iron-mining and engineering town (70,200 inhab.), has a fine parish church (c. 1350) with good window-tracery and elaborate 16C tombs. The spire (230 ft) is curiously twisted 8 ft out of the perpendicular, owing to the warping of the timbers beneath the leaden covering. George Stephenson (1781–1848), who lived at Tapton House, 1 m. N.E., is buried in Trinity Church beneath the communion table (his memorial). The *Stephenson Memorial Hall* now houses a civic theatre. The *Town Hall* (1938) is N.W. of the centre.

A 632 leads E. across the colliery-dotted *Scarsdale* to (6 m.) *Bolsover*, see Rte 44; while *Hardwick Hall* (6½ m.; see Rte 44) may be reached on A 617.
A 619 leads from Chesterfield to (15 m.) *Worksop* (Rte 46B) viâ (4 m.) *Staveley*, a centre of chemical and iron manufacture, 2 m. N. of which is *Renishaw*, the seat of the Sitwell family, with noted gardens (no adm.).

To the right of (146¾ m.) *Whittington Moor* is the old village of Whittington, with Revolution House (formerly an inn), where the plans for the overthrow of James II in 1688 were arranged.—150 m. *Dronfield* church has a fine 14C chancel with the brasses (c. 1390) of two brother priests upon a single slab (said to be a unique occurrence).—156 m. **Sheffield**, see Rte 61H.

44   LONDON TO NOTTINGHAM VIÂ BEDFORD

ROAD, 123 m., slow, but interesting. To (22½ m.) *St Albans*, see Rte 32B.—A 6. 33 m. *Luton.*—49½ m. **Bedford.**—74 m. *Kettering.*—A 6003. 87¾ m. *Uppingham.*—94 m. *Oakham.*—A 606. 104 m. *Melton Mowbray.*—123 m. **Nottingham.**
RAILWAY. From St Pancras to *Bedford*, 49¾ m. in 50 min.; to *Nottingham*, 126½ m. in c. 2 hrs. Principal Stations: 20 m. *St Albans.*—24¾ m. *Harpenden.*—30½ m. *Luton.*—49¾ m. *Bedford.*—65 m. *Wellingborough.*—72 m. *Kettering.*—83 m. *Market Harborough.*—99 m. *Leicester.*—111½ m. *Loughborough.*—126½ m. *Nottingham.*

From London to (22½ m.) *St Albans*, see Rte 32B.—A 6 continues N. to (27 m.) **Harpenden** (24,200 inhab.; Hotels) with beautiful trees and greens and a well-known school (*St George's*). *Rothamsted Experimental Station*, 5 min s.w., is noted for the agricultural experiments begun by Sir John Lawes and Sir Henry Gilbert in 1843 (adm. for technical visitors on application to the secretary; guide provided).

33 m. **Luton** (Hotels), with 161,200 inhab. and clothing factories, printing and motor-car works, and an international airport, is still famous for the hat-making industry which developed from the straw-plait manufacture introduced c. 250 years ago. To the N.E. of the station is the fine church of *St Mary*, with a 14C tower, good Dec. work in the interior, and several brasses. The stone tabernacled Baptistery was given by Philippa of Hainault, and the Wenlock Chapel (1461), in the N. transept, has a late-Perp. wooden screen and remarkable double arch. The tomb of William Wenlock (d. 1392), prebendary of St Paul's, is older than the chapel. On the S. side of the Presbytery is the tiny Barnard chantry (c. 1492). The *Museum* (adm. 10–5 or 6; Sun from 2), in Wardown Park, contains exhibits illustrating the straw-plait and lace industries, domestic crafts, local history, and the Tingrith coin hoard (4C). *St Andrew's Church*, 1 m. N.E. of the centre, off New Bedford Rd., is a striking building by Sir Giles Scott (1923).

Luton Hoo (Sir Harold Wernher; adm. April–Sept, Mon, Wed, Thurs, Sat, & BH, 11–6; Sun 2–6; fee; rfmts) lies 2 m. S. of the town in a fine park (1500 acres) by Capability Brown (entrance from A 6129: the Wheathampstead road). The house, built by Robert Adam in 1767–74 but completed by Smirke in 1816, was gutted by fire in 1843 and refashioned in 1903–7. It contains the *Wernher Collection of paintings, porcelain, bronzes, medieval ivories, Fabergé jewellery, and other art treasures. Outstanding among the many notable paintings are: *Bermejo*, St Michael; *Filippino Lippi*, Virgin and Child; and *Metsu*, Gallant Conversation.

At (41½ m.) *Silsoe* the gardens of *Wrest Park* (Nat. Institute of Agricultural Engineering) are open April–Sept, 10–5.30 or 7, Sat, Sun, & BH (fee). The imposing church, despite appearances, dates from 1819–21.— 42½ m. *Clophill* is 3 m. E. of **Ampthill** (Hotel), an old-fashioned town (5600 inhab.) in attractive country, which has been identified as Mark Rutherford's 'Cowfold'. The church contains the monument of Richard Nicholls (1624–72), first English governor of New York (1664–67), surmounted by the cannon-ball which is said to have caused his death at the Battle of Solebay (p. 449). *Ampthill Park* (1694) has a park (open to walkers) famous for its venerable pollarded oaks. A memorial cross with an inscription by Horace Walpole marks the site of *Ampthill Castle*, the residence of Catherine of Aragon in 1531–33.

To the E. of Ampthill Park, on a ridge to the N. of the town, are the ruins of *Houghton House*, built for the Countess of Pembroke, "Sidney's sister, Pembroke's mother", by John Thorpe and Inigo Jones (c. 1600). It is sometimes identified with Bunyan's 'House Beautiful'. About 2 m. N. is the church of *Houghton Conquest*, with a 14C wall-painting, fragments of good old glass, and brasses.— The embattled church of *Marston Mortaine*, 4 m. N.W. of Ampthill, has a detached belfry. At *Cranfield*, 3 m. farther on, is the Cranfield Institute of Technology, formerly the Royal College of Aeronautics.

48½ m. *Elstow*, John Bunyan's home, is now a suburb of Bedford, from which it is usually visited (see below).

49½ m. **BEDFORD**, a pleasant residential county town (73,100 inhab.) on the Ouse (good boating), with a successful one-way traffic system and some manufactures, is chiefly notable for its Bunyan associations and for its schools.

Railway Stations (1 m. apart). *Midland Road*, w. of the town, for the main line. *St John's*, s. of the Ouse, for Bletchley.
Hotels near the Bridge, and High St.

Post Office, Dame Alice St., near High St.— INFORMATION OFFICE at Town Hall.
Buses from All Hallows to all destinations.

Bunyan Sports Centre, Mill Rd.; *Newnham Pool* (open-air), near the river; *Robinson Pool* (covered) in Bedford Park.

The well-known SCHOOLS OF Bedford originated in the bounty of Sir William Harpur, a native of the town and Lord Mayor of London, who in 1556 endowed the "free and perpetual school" for which Edward VI had granted a patent in 1552. The Harpur Trust now controls four schools (with 3350 pupils): *Bedford School* (940 boys), in De Parys Avenue, on the N. of the town, the *Boy's Modern School* (970 pupils) in Manton Lane, the *High School* (610 girls) in Bromham Rd., and the *Dame Alice Harpur School* (830 pupils) in Cardington Rd., ½ m. S.E. of the centre. The Trust manages also a number of almshouses in Dame Alice St.

High St. runs N. from the Ouse Bridge (1813) through the centre of the town. In St Paul's Square (l.) are a statue of John Howard (see below), and *St Paul's*, the principal church (13–15C), containing a brass of Sir Wm. Harpur (d. 1573) on the s. wall, and the pulpit from which Wesley preached his assize sermon in 1758.

Behind are the *Town Hall* and *Civic Theatre*, and just to the N.W. in Harpur St. the façade (by Edward Blore, 1830) of the former Bedford Modern School now fronts a shopping centre.

The *Swan Hotel* (1784; staircase from Houghton House) stands at the Bridge. Upstream is the new *County Hall*, while *THE EMBANKMENT follows the tree-lined N. bank of the river downstream to Russell Park (¼ m.). The *Bedford Museum* (Tues–Sat, 11–5; Sun from 2), near the bridge, displays local bygones and bronze bowls from an Iron Age settlement at Felmersham. The castle-mound, in the gardens beyond, is the sole relic of the once-famous *Castle* which commanded the ford over the Ouse until its destruction in 1224. Adjoining is the *Cecil Higgins Art Gallery* (adm. Tues–Fri, 12.30–5; Sat from 11; Sun from 2; fee), an excellent 'private' collection of smaller works of art (especially *Glass and porcelain) and English water-colours and drawings. A bronze bust of Vaughan Williams, by Epstein, and alabasters from Chicksands Priory may be noted.

In Mill St., behind the museum, *Howard House*, belonged to John Howard (1726?–90), the prison reformer. Near by is the BUNYAN MEETING, built in 1850 on the site of the barn where John Bunyan used to preach. The panels on the bronze doors (1876) illustrate the 'Pilgrim's Progress'. In the adjacent *Bunyan Museum* (adm. Tues–Sat 2–4; fee) are the old prison door of the county gaol, many personal relics, and 200 translations of Pilgrim's Progress. The Frank Mott Harrison reference collection of Bunyan's books is in the County Library (Cauldwell St.).

John Bunyan (1628–88), born near Bedford (see below), served as a youth in the Civil War, on the side of Parliament. Later, at Elstow, he took up his father's trade of tinker or brazier, and in 1653 joined a Nonconformist body which had been founded in 1650 by John Gifford. He was elected pastor in 1672 and held that position till his death in 1688. Arrested in 1660 and committed to prison by Justice Wingate, he was indicted at the quarter sessions on the ground that he had "devilishly and perniciously abstained from coming to church to hear Divine service, and was a common upholder of unlawful meetings and conventicles". Though never legally convicted, he was kept in prison more or less continuously for twelve years, with possibly a short period of liberty in 1666, and after the first six months his treatment seems to have been rigorous. It is now established that his place of detention was the *County Gaol*, which used to stand at the corner of High St. and Silver St. Here he wrote 'Grace abounding to the Chief of Sinners' (1666) and other works. The first part of the 'Pilgrim's Progress' was written during a further term of imprisonment for six months in 1675–76, perhaps in the *Town Gaol* on the old bridge. He died in London and is buried in Bunhill Fields.

Near *St Peter's*, at the N. end of High St., "Bunyan's Statue stands facing where stood his jail". St Peter's has a Norman s. porch and tower incorporating Saxon work, and *St Mary's*, s. of the bridge, has another Norman tower.

About 1½ m. s. (turn right beyond the railway bridge) is **Elstow**, reputed birthplace of John Bunyan, who was really born at *Harrowden*, 1½ m. E. On the right as we enter the village is a cottage (much altered) said to have been occupied by him after his marriage in 1649.

While playing tip-cat on the village green one Sunday afternoon Bunyan was "put into an exceeding maze" by a vision which led to his conversion. The *Moot Hall* (c. 1500) on the green was used as the meeting-place and Sunday School of the Bunyan congregation until the opening of the Bunyan Memorial Hall in 1910. It contains a collection illustrating 17C life in England (open weekdays exc. Mon 11–5, Sun 2.30–5.30; fee). The over-restored *Church* consists of the nave and part of the chancel of the abbey church of a Benedictine nunnery, founded in 1078. Over the N. door is a Norman group of Christ between SS Peter and John. Within are the font in which Bunyan was baptized and the fine brasses of Abbess Elizabeth Hervey (d. 1524) and Lady Argentein (d. 1427). In the massive detached bell-tower hang five 17C bells (another was added in 1908), the ringing of which was Bunyan's favourite amusement as a young man, until a superstitious fear that a bell or the tower itself might fall on him drove him away. The ruins s. of the church are those of a vaulted 13C chamber, and a 17C manor-house.—The 18C mill at *Stevington*, 5 m. N.W. of Bedford, has been restored as a memorial to Bunyan; Joan, 'the Fair Maid of Kent', widow of the Black Prince, died here in 1385.

At *Cardington*, 2½ m. S.E. of Bedford, a house on the S.W. side of the churchyard was the home of John Howard (see above), after 1758. St Mary's has a black Wedgwood font and a memorial to the victims of the destruction of the airship R 101 in France (1930), who are buried in the churchyard; the airship hangars dominate the R.A.F. Station.

FROM BEDFORD TO HITCHIN, 16½ m. (A 600).—9½ m. *Shefford*. The 15C building known as Le Cokke was probably the guest-house of the Gilbertine Chicksands Priory just to the W. This is now marked by a gigantic R.A.F. aerial, likened by Pevsner to a steel Stonehenge. At *Southill Park*, 2 m. N., Adm. John Byng (1704–57), shot ("pour encourager les autres") for losing Minorca, was born, and is buried in the mausoleum. The house, rebuilt by Henry Holland for the Whitbread family, has a pleasant lake and gardens (open occasionally). At *Old Warden*, a quaint village 1½ m. farther N. where the 'Warden' pear originated, is the Shuttleworth College of Agriculture. The *Shuttleworth Trust Museum* (adm. daily 10–5), on a small flying-field, displays historic aircraft from 1909 (16 in flying trim), engines, cars from 1895, and bicycles from 1868. Exhibits include the 'Gull' (1932) flown by Jean Batten to Australia and the 1898 Panhard in which Edward VII drove to Ascot in 1901. At *Campton*, 1 m. s.w. of Shefford, is buried Robert Bloomfield (1766–1823), author of 'The Farmer's Boy'.—16½ m. *Hitchin*, see Rte 46.

FROM BEDFORD TO NORTHAMPTON viÂ OLNEY, 21 m. (A 428). 7½ m. *Turvey* has a church containing a painted *Crucifixion of the early 14C and fine monuments of the Mordaunts. *Clifton Reynes*, 3 m. W. on the Ouse, has 13–14C wooden effigies in its church.—Crossing the Ouse, we bear left off the main road.—11 m. **Olney**, a little bootmaking town pleasantly situated on the Ouse, at the N. extremity of Buckinghamshire, is famous for its associations with Wm. Cowper (1731–1800) and its 'pancake race' and 'pancake day'. In the market-place is the red brick house where Cowper lived with Mrs Unwin and her daughter in 1767–1786, now the *Cowper and Newton Museum* (open Tues–Sat 2–5; fee). Here the poet composed 'John Gilpin' and 'The Task'. The garden at the back, which still retains the poet's summer-house, communicates with the parsonage, the residence of the Rev. John Newton (d. 1807), perpetual curate of Olney, fellow-author with Cowper of the 'Olney Hymns'. The early-Dec. *Church* has a beautiful spire (185 ft). Newton's remains now rest in the churchyard, having been removed hither in 1893 from St Mary Woolnoth in London. At *Weston Underwood*, nearly 2 m. s.w., is the house occupied by Cowper and Mrs Unwin from 1786 to 1795. The church of *Ravenstone*, 1 m. farther on, is adorned by the splendid tomb (attr. to Catterns) of Lord Chancellor Finch, Earl of Nottingham (1621–82), who founded the adjoining almshouses

—From Olney we go on N.W. across *Yardley Chase*, a wide tract of moorland with fine oaks.—21 m. *Northampton*, see Rte 43.

FROM BEDFORD TO CAMBRIDGE, 28 m. (A 603). 4 m. *Willington* has a massive 16C pigeon-house and stable (N.T.; keys at near-by cottages) and, in the church, the fine Gostwick tomb (1615).—Beyond (7½ m.) *Sandy* (see Rte 46) we climb to a pleasant sandstone ridge.—11 m. *Potton*, 2 m. E. of which, among apple-orchards, is the church of *Cockayne Hatley*, containing 17C Flemish wood-carvings.—28 m. *Cambridge*, see Rte 55.

51½ m. *Clapham* has a Saxon church-tower.—55½ m. *Bletsoe* (r.), with some remains of the mansion of the Barons St John, is possibly the birthplace of Lady Margaret Beaufort (1443–1509), mother of Henry VII.—We enter Northants before reaching (62½ m.) *Rushden*, a boot-making town (20,200 inhab.), where the largely Dec. church has a 'strainer-arch' (comp. Finedon), a 15C screen, and alabaster Pemberton tombs. *Hinwick House* (adm. BH only, 2–5), 3½ m. S.W., dates from 1710. At *Hinwick Hall* the first school for spastic boys was opened in 1943.— 63¾ m. **Higham Ferrers** is a pleasant little stone town (4700 inhab.), where the **Church*, with a double nave, is in the E.E. and Dec. styles. A remarkable group of buildings erected in 1424 by Abp. Chichele (1362–1443) in honour of his birthplace includes the school-house and bede-house (Perp.), in the churchyard, and, 1½ m. N., the remains of his college in pleasant gardens near a beautiful 13C bridge over the Nene.

About 5½ m. w. of Rushden and Higham Ferrers is **Wellingborough** (Hotel, a fine 17C building), a shoemaking and ironworking town (37,600 inhab.) above the Nene with a fine park near the centre. It has a well-known grammar school, an old parish church (St Luke's) containing quaint misericords, and a church of 1908–30 (St Mary's) in a florid 15C Gothic style by Sir N. Comper.—To *Northampton* and to *Peterborough*, see Rte 43.

FROM HIGHAM FERRERS TO ST NEOTS, 18¼ m. (A 45). At (2 m.) *Chelveston* a road on the left leads to *Stanwick* (1½ m.), with an exquisite octagonal church-tower and spire, and to *Raunds* (2 m.), a shoemaking town of 6000 inhab., where the 13C church is likewise famous for its **Spire* (183 ft).—8½ m. *Kimbolton. Kimbolton Castle* (occupied since 1950 by the Grammar School; adm. Sun in Aug & BH, 2–6; fee), partly rebuilt by Vanbrugh, with an E. portico by Aless. Galilei (1719) and murals by Pellegrini, incorporates some of the old castle which was the residence of Catherine of Aragon in 1533–36, after her divorce. *Swineshead* church, 4 m. S.W., has a remarkable 14C choir, with misericords from a vanished priory; and at *Leighton Bromswold*, 6 m. N., the **Church* was rebuilt by George Herbert, incumbent in 1626–30; adjoining is the gatehouse of a vanished Jacobean mansion.—18¼ m. *St. Neots*, see Rte 46.

65½ m. *Irthlingborough* (5100 inhab.), beyond the Nene, has a detached bell-tower crowned by an octagon (14C).—68 m. *Finedon* has an excellent Dec. church (early 14C), with a 'strainer-arch' across the nave.— 70 m. *Burton Latimer* (5400 inhab.) has early 14C paintings of the story of St Catherine in its church. *Pytchley*, a village 3 m. w., gave name to a famous pack of foxhounds, removed to Brixworth c. 1818.

74 m. **Kettering** (Hotels), is an industrial town (42,600 inhab.) with boot and clothing factories and iron-works. The church, with its fine spire (177½ ft), is late-Perp., with an early-Dec. N. portal and E. end. The Art Gallery contains paintings presented to his native town by Sir Alfred East (1849–1913) and the Westfield Museum shows Roman finds and boot-making machinery. The Baptist Missionary Society, the first in England, was founded here in 1792 by William Carey, Andrew Fuller, and a few others in a house now known as the 'Mission House'.

Barton Seagrave, 1½ m. S.E., has an early-Norman and E.E. church, and 2 m. N.E. is *Weekley*, with early tombs of the Montagus and a charming almshouse

(1611) and school (1642); while *Warkton*, just to the E., has their later monuments (two by Roubiliac). *Boughton House* (adm. late-July–Oct, daily exc. Fri, 2–6; fee), close by, one of the seats of the Duke of Buccleuch, contains a fine art-collection; the beautiful park is noted for its avenues.— In the grounds of *Rushton Hall* (built by John Thorpe for Sir Thomas Tresham in 1595 and completed in 1630), 3½ m. N.W. of Kettering, is the singular 'triangular lodge'. The Hall, now a school of the Royal National Institute for the Blind (adm. 1st Thurs in the month, & daily in Aug 2–5), has a fine staircase. *Rothwell*, a shoemaking town of 4800 inhab., 4 m. w. of Kettering, has a Transitional church with some good misericords and a curious bone-crypt. The market-house, a Renaissance building begun by Tresham in 1577, was completed in 1896.

FROM KETTERING TO STAMFORD, 22¼ m. (A 43).—3 m. *Geddington*, once a royal manor, has a beautiful Eleanor's Cross, a 14C bridge and an interesting church with Saxon remains, a late-Dec. spire, and fine screens.—At (7½ m.) *Weldon* we cross the road from Corby to Oundle and then skirt Deene Park (see p. 364). About 1 m. beyond Deene a road leads r. for *Apethorpe Park* (6½ m.), built in part by Sir Walter Mildmay (d. 1589), founder of Emmanuel College, Cambridge.— 22¼ m. *Stamford*, see Rte 46A.

Our route follows A 6003 due N., past (78 m.) *Great Oakley*, with misericords from the vanished Pipewell Abbey, and leaves Corby on the right.—82 m. *Rockingham* (Restaurant) is a charming stone-built village.

Rockingham Castle (Cdr. Michael Watson) was royal property from the time of William the Conqueror until 1530. The great gateway is Norman, the great hall was built by Edward I, and the house was largely rebuilt after 1544. In the fine gardens are the remains of the Norman Keep. The house and gardens (fee) are shown, Easter–Sept, on Sun, Thurs and BH, 2–6.

We cross the Welland and enter Rutland.—87¾ m. *Uppingham* (Hotel), is a pleasant little town. Uppingham School, founded in 1587, attained its present position as one of the leading public schools of England under Dr Edward Thring (1853–87).

About 2 m. S.E. is *Lyddington*, with a beautiful 14C church and a Bede house (Apr–Sept daily), occupying a fragment of a palace of the Archbishops of Canterbury, and 2 m. S.W. is *Stoke Dry*, overlooking a large reservoir, with Digby monuments in its church. Sir Everard Digby (1578–1606), the gunpowder conspirator, was born here. *Morcott* church, 4 m. E., is mainly late-Norman.

90 m. *Preston* has a part-Norman church.—94 m. **Oakham** (Hotel) is the principal town (6400 inhab.) of Rutland and the headquarters of the Cottesmore Hunt. The chief relic of the *Castle* (adm. daily) is the unique late-Norman banqueting-hall, which contains a remarkable collection of horseshoes nailed to the walls, contributed, according to the custom of the manor, by royalties and peers of the realm on entering the lordship for the first time. Near the handsome church of *All Saints* (14C–15C) are the original building of *Oakham School* (founded in 1587), behind the churchyard, reconstructed as a Shakespearian theatre; the present school buildings, with a dignified War Memorial Chapel (by Streatfield); and the old *Butter Cross* and stocks. Sir Jeffrey Hudson, Henrietta Maria's dwarf (1619–82), and Titus Oates (1649–1705) were natives of Oakham. *Rutland County Museum* (closed Mon; s. of the library) houses Roman remains unearthed at Great Casterton.

Most notable of the neighbouring village churches are *Egleton*, 2 m. S.E. (footpath), with a striking Norman s. doorway; *Brooke*, 2½ m. S., with an unspoilt Elizabethan interior (1579); *Whissendine*, 4 m. N.W., a lovely 14–15C building with part of the old rood-screen (1516) from St John's College, Cambridge; *Teigh*, 4 m. N., which retains its furnishings of 1782; and *Exton*, 8 m. N.E., containing a rich group of monuments (14–18C) and standing in a fine park, amidst one of the largest ironstone extraction areas in Britain. The N. chapel of *Cottesmore* church (2 m. N. of Exton) was dedicated in 1949 as a memorial to the men of the British and American Air Forces stationed at the airfield here. The prominent mansion of *Burley-on-the-Hill*, on the way back to Oakham, was built in 1694 for the 2nd Earl of Nottingham.

A 606 leads N.E. entering Leicestershire before (104 m.) **Melton Mowbray** (Hotels), in summer a quiet country town (19,900 inhab.), and crowded with fox-hunters during the season. It is noted also for its pork pies and Stilton cheese. *St Mary's* (E.E. and Dec.), one of the finest parish churches in the county, has a beautiful effigy of a lady (c. 1400) in the s. transept. Opposite the church is a 17C *Bede House.*

About 4½ m. E., *Stapleford Park* (Lord Gretton) has an unusual wing built in 1500 and restored in 1633. The house (adm. May–Sept, Wed, Thurs, Sun, & BH, 2.30–6.30; also Tues in July–Aug; fee; rfmts), mainly 17C, has a sculptured exterior, Staffordshire pottery, and a miniature railway and lion reserve in its large park.

At *Willoughby-on-the-Wolds*, 2½ m. w. of (110 m.) *Upper Broughton*, are the tombs of the Willoughby family.—At (112¾ m.) *Widmerpool* we cross the Foss Way (A 46) from Newark to Leicester, see **p. 432.**

123 m. **NOTTINGHAM,** the capital (299,800 inhab.) of Nottinghamshire, a thriving industrial city making pharmaceutical chemicals, cigarettes, and bicycles, is especially noted as the centre of the lace and hosiery industry. It is situated nearly in the centre of England, on a rocky hill sloping down to the Trent. The steep streets retain much 19C industrial architecture, while new building progresses on an imaginative scale.

Car Parking. Trinity Square, Maid Marian Way.
Railway Station, Carrington St.
Hotels. Good new hotels in Derby Rd., across Trent Bridge, and in Granby St.; others in town centre.
Post Office, Queen St.—INFORMATION BUREAU, Milton St.
Buses from Mount St. to *Ilkeston*; *Derby*; *Chesterfield*; etc.; also from Huntingdon St. or Broad Marsh to *Mansfield* viâ Newstead Abbey; *Southwell*; *Ollerton*, *Worksop* and *Doncaster*; *Loughborough*; *Leicester*; *Melton Mowbray*; *Grantham*; etc.
Theatres. *Playhouse*, East Circus St.; *Theatre Royal*, Theatre Quadrant; *Arts Theatre*, George St.—CONCERTS. Albert Hall, off Derby Rd.—*Film Theatre*, Broad St.—SPORTS FACILITIES, Bilborough Park, Wollaton Park, University Park. *Notts County Cricket Club*, Trent Bridge. SWIMMING POOLS, Victoria, Gedling St. (Exhibition Hall in winter); Beechdale Baths, on by-pass, etc.— ICE STADIUM, Lr. Parliament St.—NATIONAL WATER SPORTS CENTRE (p. 431), 3 m. E.
History. The Saxon *Snotingaham* was occupied by the Danes in 868 and became the chief of the five boroughs of the Danelagh (the others being Derby Leicester, Lincoln, and Stamford). It was recaptured in 918 by Edward the Elder, who built the first bridge at the important strategical crossing of the Trent. After the Conquest a strong castle was built here, which became the key of the Midlands and a favourite royal residence. Henry II granted a charter to the town in 1155, and in the 14–15C Nottingham was famed throughout Europe for its alabaster carvings. In 1642, at the opening of the Civil War, Charles I unfurled his banner at Nottingham (on Standard Hill), but the castle was seized and held by Col. Hutchinson for Parliament, by whose orders it was finally demolished in 1651. The prosperity of Nottingham dates from the invention of the stocking-frame by the Rev. Wm. Lee of Calverton in 1589. Hargraves came to the town with his spinning-jenny in 1768, and in 1769 Arkwright erected his first spinning-mill here. The Luddite riots of 1811–16 broke out and were most violent at Nottingham. The *Luddites,* bands of starving weavers who saw a panacea for their evil plight in the wholesale destruction of machinery, are said to have taken their name from Ned Lud, a half-witted lad who had destroyed a couple of looms in an imbecile rage.

Of Lord Byron's three speeches in the House of Lords, the first was an impassioned appeal on behalf of the rioters. Among the famous natives of Nottingham are Col. Hutchinson (1615–64), Thomas and Paul Sandby, the artists (1721–98 and 1725–1809), Henry Kirke White (1785–1806), poet, General Booth (1829–1912; in Sneinton, the s.e. suburb), and Capt. Albert Ball, V.C., the airman (d. 1917; monument in the castle grounds). Richard Bonington (1801–28), the painter, was born at *Arnold*, 3 m. N.E. Lord Byron lived as a boy in Pelham St. and in St James St. (1798–99). William and Mary Howitt kept a chemist's shop at the corner of Parliament St. and Newcastle St.

Beneath the city are many caves, some used in the past as dwellings. Those under the Salutation Inn, the 'Trip to Jerusalem' Inn, and the Broad Marsh centre may sometimes be visited on application. Also, the remains of 'rock houses' may still be seen in Hollowstone, as well as near the Castle, and Mansfield Road.

The OLD MARKET SQUARE, an open space of 5½ acres, succeeds the former Saturday Market, from Norman times the focus of activity. On the e. side is the imposing classical *Council House*, by Cecil Howitt (1928), behind which Exchange Buildings boasts a gigantic shopping arcade. In the Shambles on the corner of King St., Kirke White was born, while in South Parade is the pargeted *Flying Horse Inn.* Several streets climb the hill out of the N. side of the square to Upper Parliament St. where the *Theatre Royal* has a classical façade of 1865.

Sherwood St., beyond, leads between the *Guildhall*, with the new City Treasury, and the *Trent Polytechnic* (1953–55), by Cecil Howitt. Its Victorian predecessor, behind, with the *Central Library*, and further extensions, face Shakespeare St., by which we may reach the *Arboretum*, a beautiful park with aviaries and a statue of Feargus O'Connor (1794–1855), the Chartist leader and M.P. for Nottingham in 1847–48. On the s. side is the *College of Art and Design*, with a statue of Bonington; on the N. the *High School* (founded 1513), beyond which is held the famous 'Goose Fair' (in 1st week of Oct), now given over to merry-making transferred from the Market Place in 1928.

To the e., Lower Parliament St. is crossed by a walk-way from the huge new *Victoria Centre*, which preserves the clock tower of the former railway station here. The present Market Hall, beyond, has kept its original fittings. To the s. the narrow streets retain their medieval courses and names. We may take Broad St., and its extension Stoney St., into the old 'Lace Market' area, with its characteristic red-brick mid-19C warehouses, to *St Mary's*, an imposing church of the late 15C which did not escape the too thorough hand of 19C restorers. It has a wide nave, rich Perp. windows, a massive central tower, and a Madonna by Fra Bartolommeo (N. aisle).

At the corner of Fishergate, a little to the e., is *Plumptre Hospital* (1825; founded 1392) for 13 poor widows.

In High Pavement are the *Shire Hall* (1770), and the former Judge's Lodgings, now the County Record Office (r.; façade of 1833), and the *Unitarian Chapel*, attended by Byron as a boy. Here S. T. Coleridge preached a charity sermon in 1796 and Bonington was baptized in 1802. Middle and Low Pavement continue w., south of *St Peter's* in Wheeler Gate, a church rebuilt in the 15C. Castle Gate crosses the new Maid Marian Way, at the corner of which is the attractive church of *St Nicholas* (1682), now on the edge of the new Broad Marsh development. To the N. is the 15C *Salutation Inn*. Approaching the castle, we pass (r.) *Newdigate House* (no adm.), where Marshal Tallard, taken prisoner at

Blenheim, resided in 1705–11, and is said to have taught allotment gardening to the citizens, and the *Severns* (l.), a 15C house removed from Broad Marsh.

The **Castle** (10–dusk), with pleasant grounds, crowns a precipitous rock 133 ft high. The bronze statues of Robin Hood and his men, outside the walls, are by James Woodford, a local sculptor (1952). The present building, in a heavy Italian style, was erected in 1674–79 by the first Duke of Newcastle, on the site of the Norman castle built soon after the Conquest by William Peveril, the sole relic of which is the Edwardian gateway. It was burned down by the Reform rioters in 1831, and was restored in 1875–78, when the corporation leased it from the duke's trustees and opened it as the first provincial **Museum and Art Gallery** (weekdays 10–4.45 or 6.45. free; Sun 10–4.45, fee; in course of slow rearrangement).

On the ground-floor are two Bronze Age canoes dredged from the Trent. The mezzanine floor exhibits classical antiquities from Nemi, S. Italy. Here also are two carriages of 1698; English glass, including the Bles punchbowl (c. 1685), pottery (good Wedgwood), and wrought iron; military relics, etc. Upstairs are *Works by Bonington, paintings by Italian artists of 16C, and by the Netherlands School (17–18C); local alabaster sculpture (14–15C); a bronze self-portrait by Epstein (1924); and modern paintings. Below is a textile gallery.—Outside the museum may be seen the entrance to 'Mortimer's Hole', a subterranean passage 100 yds long by which the young Edward III is said to have gained access to the castle in 1330 in order to arrest his mother Queen Isabella and her paramour Roger Mortimer. The quaint old '*Trip to Jerusalem*' *Inn* abuts on the entrance to another passage at the foot of the rock.

West of Old Market Square, the *Bell Inn* in Chapel Bar, has a pedimented façade, and, beyond, in Derby Road, is the Roman Catholic Cathedral, an early work with a good interior, by A. W. Pugin. Close by are the *Albert Hall*, built in 1909 by the Wesleyans, and the *Playhouse* (1959–63), by Peter Moro.

The pleasantest feature of the E. side of the town is *St Mary's Cemetery*, now a public park, with the solitary grave of 'Bendigo' (Wm. Thompson, 1811–80), the Nottingham-born prizefighter.

On the s. side of the town, 1 m. from the City Centre (bus 43, 46, 21, 14) is **Trent Bridge** (1869–71), which crosses the river (navigable below it for barges of 120 tons) to the famous *County Cricket Ground* (l.), and to the *County Hall* (r.) in *West Bridgford*. On the pleasant Victoria Embankment is a War Memorial Arch (1927). The grounds of Notts County and Nottingham Forest F.C. are on opposite banks of the river. Boats may be hired at the bridge, and small steamers ply downstream (E.) to *Colwick Park* (a popular resort, with a racecourse) and *Colwick Hall*, the home of Mrs Musters, Byron's Mary Chaworth (d. 1832), who is buried in the church.

About 2 m. w. of Nottingham by Derby Rd. (bus 45, 39) is *Wollaton Hall*, an ostentatious Renaissance mansion built by Robert Smithson for Sir Francis Willoughby in 1580–88, purchased by the city of Nottingham in 1925 and now containing a Natural History Museum (10–7 or dusk, Sun 2–5 summer, 1.30–4.30 winter). The large park has a golf course and a notable avenue of limes, and the first glass-house in England for the protection of plants is said to have been erected in the beautiful gardens (17C). The 18C stables are in severe contrast to the house. A two-mile long wagon railway laid here in 1603–04 may have occasioned the invention of the flanged wheel (which made the modern railway possible).

Castle Boulevard (bus 4, 5a) and its extensions lead w. viâ *Lenton*, which has a carved Norman *Font from a once famous abbey in its modern church, to (2 m.) *Highfields Park* (tennis, boating, etc.), presented to the city by Lord Trent in 1928 and occupied by **Nottingham University**, founded as University College in 1881 and incorporated in 1948. The buildings, well sited on sloping land with a lake above the city, were begun in 1922 with the Trent Building by Morley Horder. The Art Gallery stages public exhibitons.

About 1 m. farther on is *Beeston*, a manufacturing town, with Messrs. Boots' model factory for fine chemicals and toilet preparations. Clifton Bridge (rebuilt 1958) between Beeston and *Clifton* (s. bank) takes the new trunk road across the Trent.

In the industrial Erewash valley, 6 m. w. of Nottingham, lie *Ilkeston*, a mining and lace-making town (34,100 inhab.), with a stone screen and sedilia of the early

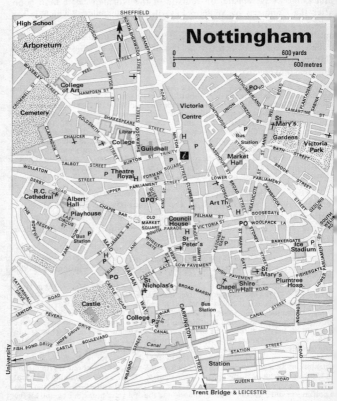

14C in its church; and *Eastwood* (10,900 inhab.), birthplace of D. H. Lawrence (1885–1930).—*Hucknall Torkard*, 6 m. N. of the centre, is a colliery town (25,300 inhab.), in the church of which Lord Byron rests beneath a slab of rosso antico presented by George I, king of the Hellenes. His mother and daughter also are buried here. *Linby*, 1½ m. N.E. of Hucknall, is unusual in having two village crosses, one (restored) with a medieval 7-sided base, the other 17C.

FROM NOTTINGHAM TO SOUTHWELL, 13½ m. (A 612). 5 m. *Stoke Bardolph* (1 m. r.; Inn) is a favourite riverside resort. The main road commands wide views across the Trent valley, which it follows as far as (10 m.) *Thurgarton*, where the fine church preserves a w. doorway and other remains of a 13C priory.—13½ m. *Southwell*, see Rte 46. An alternative route (A 60, B 6386) passes (6 m.) to the N.

of *Calverton*, with a modern colliery (1940), and through (8¼ m.) *Oxton*, where a tablet in the part-Norman church commemorates Robert Scothern, a fellow-emigrant of Wm. Penn.

FROM NOTTINGHAM TO ASHBY-DE-LA-ZOUCH (Birmingham), 22 m. (A 453). —Beyond (4 m.) *Beeston* (see above) is (8 m.) *Long Eaton* (33,700 inhab.) a lace-making town. At *Attenborough*, 2 m. E., is the house where Henry Ireton (1611–51) was born. On the left is *Trent College*, a well-known public school. Crossing the Trent, we enter Leicestershire.—12 m. *Castle Donington* has an electric power station and the ruins of a 16C paper-mill on the Trent adjoining *Donington Hall*, rebuilt in 1793. To the S.E. lies the Derby airport, with services to Paris, etc.— 16 m. *Breedon* has a fine church with a remarkable sculptured frieze and a cross-shaft from an earlier building (8C).—22 m. *Ashby*, see p. 399.

From Nottingham to *Grantham* and to *Newark*, see Rte 46; to *Derby*, see p. 402.

FROM NOTTINGHAM TO MANSFIELD AND WORKSOP, 27 m. At (9 m.) the *Pilgrim Oak* (bus No. 62 from Nottingham) is the entrance to *NEWSTEAD ABBEY (1¼ m.; pleasant walk or drive; the fine park and gardens are open daily 10–dusk; fee), the ancestral home of Lord Byron (1788–1824).

The original 12C Augustinian priory, founded by Henry II, was converted into a residence in 1540 by Sir John Byron of Colwick. During the poet's minority the place was let, but he resided at intervals here between 1806 and 1816, and in 1818 he sold it to Col. Wildman. In 1931 the abbey ruins and the Byron rooms were presented to the city of Nottingham by Sir Julien Cahn (adm. daily Easter–Sept, 2–6; fee). The cloister-square, containing the old chapter house (now a chapel), remains practically perfect, but virtually nothing of the church exists save the lovely late 13C w. front. Three 15–16C Byron tombs were brought here from Colwick in 1938. Among the most interesting rooms are the *Great Hall*, the *Prior's Dining Room*, with Byron's portrait by Thos. Phillips, the *Drawing Room*, with the Roe-Byron collection of relics and MSS., and *Byron's Bedroom*, which remains much as he left it. Near the N.E. angle of the house is buried his favourite retriever 'Boatswain'. Livingstone was a guest here in 1864–65 (plaque on staircase wall) and Stanley in 1872.—*Annesley Hall*, 3 m. S.W., was the early home of Byron's Mary Chaworth.

14¼ m. **Mansfield**, a busy town (57,600 inhab.) with hosiery mills and collieries, lies to the S.W. of Sherwood Forest. The *Church* (13–15C) has a beautifully proportioned interior. The *King's Mill* (rebuilt), associated with Henry II and the 'Miller of Mansfield', is 1 m. S.W.

Hardwick Hall (N.T.; adm. Easter–Oct, Wed, Thurs, Sat, Sun, & BH, 1–5.30 or dusk; rfmts; fee), c. 6½ m. N.W., is one of the noblest Elizabethan mansions in England, built by the celebrated 'Bess of Hardwick' in 1590–97. It is famous for its vast display of windows: "Hardwick Hall, more glass than wall". In the great *Picture Gallery* (166 ft long) are a famous full-length portrait of Mary, Queen of Scots (attributed to Richard Stevens), and other portraits, and here too are interesting tapestries and embroidery. Adjoining are the ruins of the early 16C mansion in which 'Bess' was born (1520).—To the N. lies the curious little church of *Ault Hucknall*, with early Norman details, in which is buried Thomas Hobbes (1588–1679), author of 'Leviathan'. At *Hardstoft*, 1½ m. w. of Hardwick, the first boring for crude oil in England was made in Oct 1918.

Bolsover (11,000 inhab.), which lies on the lip of a long ridge of magnesian limestone, c. 4 m. N. of Hardwick, commands extensive views westward to the distant Peak. *Bolsover Castle* (adm. daily; Sun from 2; fee), was originally built by William Peveril in the 11C, but the Norman keep was reconstructed, on the old foundations, by Sir Charles Cavendish (monument in the church) in 1613–17, and he also began the palace on the terrace (now in partial ruin). Here, in 1634, Charles I and his queen saw the repetition on a grander scale of the Welbeck entertainment (see below), with a 2nd version of Ben Jonson's 'Love's Welcome'. The keep, an interesting admixture of Gothic and Renaissance motives, contains some heavily decorated marble chimneypieces. The long gallery, partly ruined, and the riding school, were added c. 1620–30.

15¾ m. *Mansfield Woodhouse* (l.; 24,800 inhab.).—18¼ m. *Warsop*

(13,000 inhab.) has a good 12–13C church.—Beyond (21 m.) *Cuckney* we leave on the left a road through the picturesque ravine of *Cresswell Crags*, where the bone-caves have yielded the richest finds of early Stone Age art so far found in England, and reach an entrance to *Welbeck Park* (10 m. round), which provided timber for the roof of St Paul's.

Welbeck Abbey (no adm.), since 1953 a training school for the Army, occupies the site of a Premonstratensian abbey of the 12C, but the present house dates mainly from the early 17C, with later additions. The first version of Ben Johnson's antimasque 'Love's Welcome' was performed here in 1633 at an entertainment offered to Charles I by the Duke of Newcastle. Welbeck passed to the Bentincks, Dukes of Portland, in 1734.

The strangest feature at Welbeck is the extraordinary series of underground rooms and tunnels constructed at enormous expense by the disfigured fifth Duke (d. 1879). These include the *Ball Room* (159 ft by 63 ft), containing Reynolds's 'Angel in Contemplation', and the *Riding School* (nearly 400 ft long).

27 m. **Worksop**, see Rte 46B.

45 THE DERBYSHIRE PEAK

The hill region known as the **Peak District** (now a National Park) is constituted by the termination of the Pennine Chain. The Peak proper is comprised in the N. and N.W. portions of Derbyshire itself, but its characteristic scenery extends for a considerable distance into the 'Moorlands' district of Staffordshire, and also (to a lesser degree) into Cheshire. This famous scenery is divisible into two great types. The loftiest and wildest portion, attaining in three instances to a height of more than 2000 ft, is formed of the millstone-grit and Yoredale series, and consists of desolate, heather-clad moors, broken by cultivated valleys, the containing hills of which are often guarded towards their summits by low, black lines of crag locally known as 'edges'. The carboniferous limestone country, on the contrary, in the centre of the district, nowhere reaches an elevation of more than 1600 ft, and approximates more closely to an undulating plateau; heather is here replaced by a sweet, green turf, divided by loose stone walls (built without mortar) into an endless chequer of fields; and wood is almost wholly absent. The scenery is so far inferior to that of the millstone grit; but its monotony is redeemed by its intersection at frequent intervals by narrow ravines, in connection with the drainage of the Manifold, Dove, and Wye. In these ravines, which are often bounded (notably at Matlock, in Cheedale, and in Dovedale) by noble walls of gleaming white cliff, we find the unique characteristic of Derbyshire. The scale, of course, is diminutive; but in point of beauty these glens can vie even with the grand gorges of the Tarn, in Central France. The subterranean marvels for which Derbyshire is also famous are perhaps less striking than those of the Mendips and Craven.

The Peak, like other hill districts, is best explored on foot; but a superficial survey of what is best in it, natural and artificial, may be made by the motorist who follows the easy round, Derby–Matlock–Rowsley–Baslow–Hathersage–Castleton–Buxton–Bakewell–Ashbourne–Derby. Divergences, of course, will naturally be made to sites of interest a little off the route, such as Haddon Hall, Eyam, Chee Tor, Cratcliffe Tor, and Dovedale. Good walkers may explore the district pretty thoroughly by the following twelve-day itinerary. i. Matlock to Matlock, viâ Lea Bridge, Crich, Wingfield Manor, and Dethick (16 m.); ii. Matlock to Bakewell, viâ Bonsall, Winster, Cratcliffe Tor, Alport, and Lathkill Dale (15 m.); iii. Bakewell to Ashbourne, viâ Over Haddon, Youlgreave, Bradford Dale, Parwich, and Tissington (18 m.); iv. Ashbourne to Hartington, viâ the Dove (13 m.); v. Hartington to Buxton, viâ Longnor, Dove Head, Three Shire Head, and 'Cat and Fiddle' (18 m.); vi. Buxton to Edale, viâ Combs, Chapel, and Rushup Edge (13 m.); vii. Edale to Edale, round Kinder Scout viâ Edale Cross, Ashop Head, and Snake Inn (19 m.); viii. Edale over Lose Hill to Castleton and its caves (5 m.); ix. Castleton to Hathersage, viâ Hope, Win Hill, and Stanage Edge (18 m.); x. Hathersage to Baslow, viâ Abney, Eyam, and Stoney Middleton (11 m.); xi. Baslow to Bakewell, viâ Chatsworth and Haddon Hall (8 m.); xii. Bakewell to Buxton, viâ Ashford, Monsal Dale, and Chee Dale (16 m.).—*The National Park Information Centre* is at Edale.

A From Derby to Manchester viâ Leek

Road, 59½ m. (A 52, A 523; bus), skirting the Peak District on the s.w. and affording access to Dovedale and the Manifold valley.

Railway from Macclesfield to Manchester, 17¼ m. in c. ½ hr. Principal Stations: 8 m. *Bramhall.*—9½ m. *Cheadle Hulme.*—11¾ m. *Stockport.*—17¼ m. **Manchester** (Piccadilly).

Derby, see Rte 43.—2½ m. *Mackworth Hotel.*—4 m. *Kirk Langley* (Hotel), a pleasant village.—6¼ m. *Brailsford*, has a Saxon churchyard cross.—13 m. **Ashbourne** (Hotels) is an interesting town (5600 inhab.) with many good stone houses, on the s. verge of the wild limestone country of the Peak. The **Church* (13C) of St Oswald, with a lofty spire (212 ft), a beautiful s. arcade with notable **Capitals*, and double transepts, contains the touching memorial (by Banks) of a child (Penelope Boothby; d. 1791), the splendid medieval monuments of the Cokayne family (N. transept) and an interesting dedication-brass of 1241 (s. transept). Opposite the Tudor buildings of the *Grammar School* (1585), in Church St., is The Mansion, the home of Dr John Taylor, where he was often visited by his friend Dr Johnson. At Shrovetide a traditional game of football is played in the main street. Ashbourne is known for a special variety of gingerbread.

From Ashbourne to Uttoxeter, 11¾ m. (B 5032). We cross the Dove to Mayfield (see below) and turn left.—4¼ m. *Ellastone* is identified with 'Hayslope' the chief scene of 'Adam Bede', while *Norbury*, on the other bank of the Dove, is the 'Norbourne' and Ashbourne the 'Oakbourne' of the novel. The church of Norbury has an impressive chancel (14C) with blind arcading and striking tracery; notable also are the wealth of 14C glass, Fitzherbert monuments, and two 10C cross-shafts. The cottage where Robert Evans, father of 'George Eliot' and prototype of 'Adam Bede', was born, is shown at *Roston*, 1 m. s. of Norbury. His grave is in Ellastone churchyard. About 1 m. w. of Ellastone is *Wootton Lodge*, a Jacobean house (1615) in a lovely situation; thence the charming road goes on to Alton Towers (3½ m.).—6¼ m. *Denstone*, with a boys' school, is 2 m. s.e. of *Alton* (Shrewsbury) in the wooded valley of the Churnet. Perched on a lofty sandstone cliff are the scanty castle-ruins (c. 1175), in the grounds (adm. on previous application) of the Convent of the Assumption (French nuns), a picturesque building by the elder Pugin. On the opposite side of the glen is *Alton Towers* (a shell), with beautiful gardens and fine grounds.—At (7½ m.) *Rocester* the churchyard cross is in unusually good preservation. About 3 m. w. are the picturesque 13C ruins of *Croxden Abbey*, founded for Cistercians in 1178. The principal remains are those of the w. front and s. transept of the church (which had a fivefold apse) and of the chapter house and other buildings e. of the cloister.—11¾ m. *Uttoxeter*, see Rte 43.

From Ashbourne to *Dovedale* and *Buxton*, see Rte 45B.

At (15 m.) *Mayfield* (Hotel), on the Staffordshire bank of the Dove, is the cottage where Thomas Moore wrote most of 'Lalla Rookh'.—We ascend on to the moors, and at (20 m.) *Waterhouses* cross the Hamps, a tributary of the Manifold.

A fine footpath, 8 m. long, on the track of a disused light railway, descends the Hamps to (3½ m.) its junction with the Manifold, overlooked by the noble crag of *Beeston Tor*. It then ascends the Manifold viâ (4¾ m.) *Thor's Cave*, a striking cavern, below which the Manifold begins the subterranean course that ends at Ilam (Rte 45B).—8 m. *Hulme End*, see Rte 45B.

28 m. **Leek** (Hotel at Blackshaw Moor, 3 m. N.E.) is a town (19,400 inhab.), with important silk mills. The churchyard, in which is a fine Saxon cross of 10C Mercian type, commands a striking view of the

Roaches, a range of hills c. 5 m. N., perhaps the best example in the country of tumbled masses of millstone grit. About 1½ m. N. of Leek are the scanty remains of *Dieulacresse Abbey* (13C; no adm.).—32 m. *Rudyard Lake*, from which Kipling took his name, is a reservoir which has almost the charm of a natural lake (2 m. long; boating).—From (34¼ m.) *Rushton Spencer* we may visit *Swythamley Park* (3 m. N.E.) and the lovely scenery of the lower Dane valley, beyond which we enter Cheshire. This, with Ludchurch (**p. 418**), appears to be the scene of the principal events in 'Sir Gawain and the Green Knight'.—41 m. **Macclesfield,** an old-fashioned town (44,200 inhab.) is the chief seat of the silk industry in England. *St Michael's* (mostly rebuilt) contains the Legh and Savage Chapels, with recumbent effigies and an 'indulgence brass' of c. 1506.

A splendid walk may be taken across the wild *Macclesfield Forest* viâ the *Cat & Fiddle Inn* to (12 m.) *Buxton*. About 4 m. s.w. of Macclesfield is *Gawsworth*, with a beautiful half-timbered *Hall (Easter–Oct, daily 2–6; fee) and rectory and an interesting church with 17C monuments of the Fittons, including Mary Fitton (d. c. 1620), once thought to be the 'dark lady' of Shakespeare's sonnets.

43½ m. *Prestbury* (Restaurants), a pretty and sophisticated village, lies to the left. In the churchyard of St Peter's, the 13–15C mother-church of Macclesfield, stands a Norman chapel with a beautiful doorway; opposite the church is a half-timbered priest's house.—At (45 m.) *Adlington* is the fine half-timbered Adlington Hall (15–18C; adm. Easter–Sept, Sun & BH; also Sat in July & Aug; 2.30–6; fee; tea), home of the Legh family since 1351. The 15C Great Hall has a fine organ (c. 1670) probably played by Handel.—At (50 m.) *Hazel Grove* we join A 6.

About 2½ m. w. (1 m. E. of Cheadle Hulme station) is *Bramall Hall*, one of the finest specimens of black-and-white timber-and-plaster architecture in England. It dates in its present form from 1590–99, but has some earlier portions including the chapel. The hall, which is shown by a guide and contains a chapel, family portraits and old furniture, is open daily, exc. Thurs. 11–1, 2–7; winter 11–4 (fee); the lovely park of 62 acres is also open to the public.

53½ m. **Stockport** (139,600 inhab.; Hotels), principally engaged in cotton-spinning and hat-making, is situated on the slopes of the narrow valley of the Mersey. The high-lying parish *Church* (St Mary's), rebuilt by Lewis Wyatt (1814), retains its 13C chancel and a roof recalling that at Tarvin. A few old timbered houses have survived. In St Peter's Sq. (r.) is a statue of Richard Cobden (1804–65), M.P. in 1841–47. Stockport has a handsome *Town Hall*, a *War Memorial Art Gallery* (open weekdays 12–6, Sat 10–12, 2–6) with English water-colours and Epstein's head of Yehudi Menuhin, and a *Municipal Museum* (10–5 or 6, Sun 2–5; closed Sun Nov–Feb), in Vernon Park. Opposite the Town Hall is the *Grammar School* (1829–32), by Philip Hardwick. The huge railway viaduct of 22 arches is 1780 ft long and 108 ft high and dominates the town.—59½ m. **Manchester,** see Rte 60.

B From Ashbourne to Manchester (Dovedale, Buxton)

ROAD, 45 m. (A 515, A 5002, A 6; bus), mostly over high moorland.
RAILWAY, from Buxton only, 25¼ m. in c. 60 min. Principal stations: 5¼ m. *Chapel-en-le-Frith.*—9 m. *Whaley Bridge.*—19¾ m. *Stockport.*—25¼ m. **Manchester** (Piccadilly).

Ashbourne, see Rte 45A. The Buxton road leads due N. through (2½ m.) *Fenny Bentley*, with an old manor-house and, in the church, the unique Beresford tomb (c. 1550) showing two shrouded adult figures in alabaster, with 21 children below. *Bradbourne* church, 2½ m. N.E., has interesting Norman and pre-Norman stone carvings.—4 m. *Tissington*, an attractive village with a Norman church tower, and a Jacobean Hall, is noted for its ancient custom of 'well dressing' with pictures of flower-petal mosaic on Ascension Day. The disused railway line here is to be made into a public footpath (11½ m.).

A much more attractive way of reaching Tissington (4½ m.) is to descend across the Bentley Brook to (1½ m.) *Mappleton*, on the Dove, and then to ascend, past (3 m.) *Thorpe* (Hotel). Either of these villages is a starting-point for the s. end of ***Dovedale**, the narrow ravine (2¾ m. long) through which the Dove forces its way between Mill Dale and Thorpe.

The glen (path only) is beautifully wooded and guarded by fantastic limestone cliffs. No traveller is likely to deny its singular charm, even if he does not share Dr Johnson's opinion that "he who has seen Dovedale has no need to visit the Highlands". It passes for the 'Happy Valley' of 'Rasselas' and the 'Eagle Dale' of 'Adam Bede'. The entrance lies between the bare summits of *Thorpe Cloud* (E.; 942 ft) and *Bunster* (W.; 1000 ft). The National Trust owns over 2000 acres of land in the Dove, Manifold, and Hamps valleys, with covenants protecting c. 3000 more acres.

From the Peveril of the Peak hotel a direct path descends to the stepping-stones on the Dove (good trout fishing) in 10–15 min. A longer and prettier approach bears r. before *Thorpe Church* and leads across the river to (2 m.) the *Izaak Walton Hotel*, ½ m. S.E. of the stepping-stones. This hotel stands ½ m. E. of the village of *Ilam*, the church of which has a Norman font, the E.E. shrine of the local St Bertram, a group by Chantrey, and two Saxon cross-shafts in the churchyard. In the beautiful grounds of *Ilam Hall* (now a Youth Hostel) the Manifold comes to light from a long subterranean course (see p. 415). A path ascends its winding course to (4½ m.) *Beeston Tor* (*View).

From the stepping-stones the path ascends the E. or Derbyshire side of the Dove, crossing *Sharplow Point*, and passing the *Twelve Apostles* and the *Church* (l.), *Tissington Spires* (r.), and other fancifully named outcrops. Beyond the *Dove Holes* (caves) we reach *Mill Dale*, c. 2¾ m. from the entrance. Here Dovedale proper ends. Walkers with leisure should, however, continue up the Dove to (5 m.) *Hartington* (see below), traversing a succession of attractive glens, including *Wolfscote Dale* (N.T.), and *Beresford Dale*, last and most striking. At the exit of this is the classic fishing-house, built by Charles Cotton in 1674 as a memento of his fishing days with Izaak Walton. The 17C pew of the former is shown in the church of *Alstonefield*, his home, ¾ m. N.W. of Mill Dale.

6¼ m. *Alsop-en-le-Dale* (r.) has a partly Norman church. At *Parwich* 2½ m. E., the church-tower (Norman) has a striking tympanum. The road now climbs through a green limestone country, intersected in all directions by loose stone walls.—Beyond (9¾ m.) *Newhaven*, with a famous coaching inn, we leave on the right the Youlgreave and Matlock roads and (10¾ m.) on the left the Hartington road (see below).—12¼ m. *Parsley Hay*. Arbor Low, ¾ m. E. (adm. daily, Sun from 2; fee), is a circle, 250 ft in diameter, with the ditch within the vallum (c. 1700 B.C.). —20¼ m. **Buxton,** see below.

A more interesting route follows B 5054 at 10¾ m. (see above) for (12¾ m.) *Hartington* (Hotel), above Beresford Dale, where the Hall (1611) is a Youth Hostel. Beyond (14 m.) *Hulme End* (for path, see p. 409) we turn N. on B 5053.— 18½ m. *Longnor* is an excellent centre for the upper Dove and Manifold. The road reaches its summit-level at 1472 ft.—25 m. Buxton.

BUXTON (20,300 inhab.), a frequented holiday resort, once a famous watering-place, is the most loftily situated town of its size in the kingdom (c. 950–1100 ft). It is surrounded on three sides by wild green hills, while to the E. and S.E. extends an undulating and almost treeless limestone plateau. The old town (Higher Buxton) occupies the hill towards the s.; the new town (Lower Buxton), with some distinguished architecture of the 18C, lies in the shallow valley to the N. The two are separated by the attractively laid out *Slopes*.

Hotels in or near the Crescent, Grove Parade, Eagle Parade, and St John's Rd. Post Office, Quadrant.—INFORMATION BUREAU, opp. St Ann's Hotel.
Buses from the Market Place to various destinations.
Golf Courses at *Fairfield*, ¾ m. N.E.; *Cavendish Club*, ¾ m. W.—COUNTY CRICKET GROUND, Park Rd.
Theatres. *Playhouse*, St John's Rd. Concerts in the *Pavilion* in summer.—MUSIC FESTIVAL in August, and WELL DRESSING in July.

The waters of Buxton were known to the Romans (*Aquae Arnemetiae*), and in medieval times the town was a kind of English Lourdes, the Chapel of St Anne being rich in votive offerings. The *Thermal Springs* (28° C), the water of which is of a pretty bluish colour and is strongly charged with nitrogen, and the *Chalybeate Spring*, are no longer used for bathing. The last treatment in the thermal baths was given in Sept 1963.

At the high (s.) end of the Slopes is the *Town Hall*, near which is the Public Library with the *Museum*, a small but interesting collection (Mon–Fri 10–6, Sat 10–5) of prehistoric bones from bone-caverns, and a few local Roman antiquities, also Blue John ware, pottery from Stoke (1660–1860), and stoneware by Turner; the paintings include works by De Wint, Algernon Newton, and Brangwyn. In High St., s. of the Market Place, is the unobtrusive *Church of St Anne* (1625). Lower Buxton, with the baths and chief hotels, dates practically from the building of the striking Palladian CRESCENT, in emulation of those at Bath, by John Carr for the fifth Duke of Devonshire in 1779–84. At the s.w. end of this are the *Natural Warm Baths* for swimming, and at the other end the *Thermal Baths* (closed). Opposite is *St Ann's Well* (fee), above which ascend the Slopes. Beyond the Square (farther w.) are the *Pavilion Gardens*, with bandstand, café, and concert hall. To the N. of the Square is the parish church of *St John the Baptist* (1811), at the corner of St John's Rd., which leads to the *Serpentine Walks*, a pretty waterside park.—Behind the Crescent (and near St John's) is the other outstanding architectural feature of Buxton, the *Devonshire Hospital*, with a dome 154 ft wide, though only 118 ft in height. Originally a riding-school, it was converted by the sixth Duke of Devonshire in 1858.

ENVIRONS. Nearly 1 m. s.w. is **Poole's Hole,** a striking limestone cavern, near the source of the Wye (open daily, April–Oct; fee).—About 5 m. w. (pedestrians save about 1 m. by the old road from Burbage) is the *Cat & Fiddle* (1690 ft), one of the loftiest inns in England. The surrounding moorland is featureless and rather dreary; but the view is said to extend in clear weather to the Mersey. This walk may be extended across the wild moorlands of *Macclesfield Forest* to (7 m.) *Macclesfield* (Rte 45A). The old road from Burbage passes *Goyt's Clough* at the head of the Goyt valley. Part of the picturesque lower valley is submerged in a reservoir for Stockport.—Axe Edge (1810 ft), 2½ m. s.w., which, like Plynlimon, is a nursing mother of rivers—the Wye, the Goyt, the Dane, the Manifold, and the Dove—is the highest point in the immediate vicinity of Buxton. The summit is indefinite, and the view of the same character as from the 'Cat & Fiddle', though more extensive towards the s.e.—*Chee Tor* (p. 423) is 5 m. e.—*Ludchurch,* a narrow chasm in the millstone-grit, is 9 m. s.w. The whole of this neighbourhood, including the *Roaches* (Rte 45A) and the lower *Dane Valley,* is the most beautiful near Buxton, and should not be missed.—*Chatsworth, Haddon Hall, Castleton, Dovedale,* and *Eyam* are all easily reached from Buxton.

From Buxton to *Miller's Dale* and *Bakewell,* see Rte 45c.

Beyond Buxton A 5002 ascends to 1401 ft, with *Combs Moss* (1614 ft) on the right.—28 m. *Whaley Bridge* (5200 inhab.) with a fine Georgian inn, is at the mouth of the Goyt valley, beyond which B 5089 (mini-buses; no cars) ascends to Macclesfield (8½ m.).—30½ m. *New Mills* is a busy manufacturing town (9200 inhab.), whence B 6101 descends the Goyt valley, crossed at *Marple* (4 m.) by the restored aqueduct (1796–1801) of the Peak Forest Canal.—32 m. *Disley* (Hotel) is 2 m. N. of *Lyme Park* (N.T.; conducted parties only May–Aug, 1.30–6; Sept, Oct, March, & April, 2–5; Sun & BH, from 1; fee), a beautiful house, originally Elizabethan, but altered in 1726 (by Giacomo Leoni) and in 1817, with several Jacobean rooms, and with beautiful gardens. It is situated in a magnificent deer park of 1320 acres (open 8–dusk).—35½ m. *Hazel Grove,* and thence to (45 m.) **Manchester,** see Rte 45A.

C From Derby to Manchester viâ Matlock and Bakewell

ROAD, 44 m. (A 6, A 622, A 625; bus). This is one of the most beautiful and interesting roads in the kingdom, followed closely by the railway as far as Matlock. From Bakewell the direct Manchester road leads viâ Buxton, but the longer road through Castleton is more attractive.

RAILWAY. The old Great Central railway no longer operates between Matlock and Buxton. To Matlock, 17 m. in 35 min. (not Sun.). Principal Stations: 5½ m. *Duffield.*—7¾ m. *Belper.*—10¼ m. *Ambergate.*—15¼ m. *Cromford.*—17 m. **Matlock.** From Buxton to Manchester, see Rte 45B.

Derby, see Rte 43. A 6 ascends the Derwent valley. At (4½ m.) *Duffield* are the excavated foundations of a huge Norman keep (N.T.) razed to the ground in 1266, while at *Makeney,* 1 m. N.E. beyond the river, the completest Roman pottery kiln in Britain was discovered in 1964.

From Duffield B 5023 ascends the valley of the Ecclesbourne to (8 m.) Wirksworth, a small market-town (5200 inhab.), formerly important as the capital of the lead-mining district of the Low Peak, where well-dressing (comp. p. 410) is still carried out on Whitsunday. At the *Moot Hall* is preserved the Miners' Standard Dish (temp. Henry VIII). In the fine *Church,* mostly of the 13–14C, are a remarkable Saxon *Coffin-lid, the first bas-relief of a miner, and an incised stone of a forester of Duffield Frith; interesting also are the 16C monuments and two fonts (Norman; 1662). Wirksworth is probably the 'Snowfield' of George Eliot's 'Adam Bede'. Samuel Evans, original of Seth Bede, appears in the burial register (d. 1858), and his grave has been located. The novelist's aunt, Elizabeth Evans (d. 1849), who is supposed to have supplied the hint for 'Dinah Morris', is commemorated by a tablet in the Ebenezer Methodist Church, while her pulpit is preserved in the Bede Memorial Church.—The road to Ashbourne, 11 m. s.w. commands pleasant views.

7½ m. *Belper* (16,700 inhab.) has large stocking mills, founded in 1776 by Jedediah Strutt.—Beyond (10 m.) *Ambergate,* the valley increases in beauty.—12 m. *Whatstandwell* lies beneath *Crich Stand* (c. 2 m. N.E.; 955 ft; *View; war memorial to Sherwood Foresters), reached viâ the *Tramway Museum* (l.) in a quarry (open Sat, Sun, & BH).—On the right are the woods of *Lea Hurst,* residence of Florence Nightingale (d.1910). —15 m. *Cromford* has a 15C bridge with remains of a contemporary chapel. Here Richard Arkwright established the first cotton mill in

Derbyshire (1771), parts of which survive. Masson Mill, slightly later, survives intact and in use; and rows of his model workers' houses in North St. are preserved. *Willersley Castle*, built for him by William Thomas c. 1790, stands in beautiful grounds, and is now a Methodist guest-house (adm. on application to the Resident Secretary). About 2 m. E. is the 13C church of *Dethick*, with a good tower (1539).

16 m. **MATLOCK BATH** and (18 m.) **MATLOCK**. Under the general head of Matlock (19,600 inhab.) are comprised the village of *Matlock Bath* and the town of *Matlock*, both on the Derwent. Matlock itself consists of two distinct portions, i.e. *Matlock Bridge*, on the bank of the river, and *Matlock Bank*, on the steep hill above. Matlock, formerly famous as a watering-place, owed its reputation to the great water-cure establishments at Matlock Bank, the first of which was opened by Smedley in 1853. None of these remain, but the tepid springs (20°C) are used to feed a swimming pool. The town now has the county offices of Derbyshire.

Hotels in Matlock Bath.
Post Office, near Matlock station.
Buses to *Bakewell* and *Buxton*; *Derby*; *Wirksworth* and *Ashbourne*; *Rowsley* and *Edensor*; etc.
Golf Course, Matlock Moor, 1½ m. N.E. of Matlock Bridge.—SWIMMING-POOLS at New Bath Hotel.—'VENETIAN NIGHTS', a fortnight (Sept–Oct) of illuminations and fireworks.

Matlock Bath is situated in the depths of the narrow limestone ravine through which the Derwent forces its winding course between Matlock Bridge and Cromford. The noble line of precipices on the E. bank of the river is unsurpassed in extent and height by any similar crags in England. Conspicuous on the E., above sloping meadows, is *Riber Castle*, a mock-fortified building erected as a residence by Smedley and now visited for its zoo. On the opposite side are hanging woods and meadows, rising to the dome of Masson (see below). "My present impressions," wrote Nathaniel Hawthorne in 1857, "are that I have never seen anywhere else such exquisite scenery as that which surrounds the village." Unfortunately, indiscriminate building and untidy scraps of quarry have now greatly marred the landscape and in summer it is apt to be overrun by trippers. **Matlock** proper, at the N. entrance to the ravine, occupies an open and quite different situation.

In the narrow pass between Matlock Bath and Matlock, and overhanging the left bank of the river, is the noble rock pile of *High Tor (673 ft; view; fee). At its foot, and reached from the main road by a foot-bridge across the Derwent, is the *High Tor Grotto*, with remarkable crystallizations.—On the opposite side of the glen are the wooded **Heights of Abraham** (fee), the *Victoria Tower* on which commands a beautiful and extensive view. The walk may be continued (c. 20 min.) to the more commanding height of *Masson* (1110 ft), and the return made thence by Bonsall (see below).—The *Lovers' Walks* (fee), on the E. bank of the Derwent, are laid out beneath the limestone cliffs. Matlock Bath is famous also for its *Petrifying Wells* (fee; in the main street) and *Caves* (partly natural, largely abandoned lead-mines). The best and least artificial is the *Cumberland* (fee; visit ¾ hr), on the slope behind the New Bath Hotel. The large *Rutland Cavern* (fee; in the grounds of the Heights of Abraham) is said to have room for 10,000 men. It is believed to have been worked in Roman, Saxon, and Danish times. The *Fluor Spar Cave* is alleged to have been used as a place of refuge during the Pretender's invasion (1745).

EXCURSIONS. The distances are given from Matlock Bath. About 1¼ m. W., by footpath and lane, is the upland village of *Bonsall*, with a good market-cross. The church spire (14C) is surrounded by curious 'crowns'. The return may be made across the top of Masson (see above). Or from Bonsall we may continue by footpath to *Slaley*, and thence descend into the wooded *Via Gellia* (named after the local family of Gell), returning to Matlock by road (total round, c. 6 m.).

About 6 m. s.e. are the ruins of **Wingfield Manor** (no adm.) on a steep knoll above the Amber. It dates mainly from the second half of the 15C and has been described as "probably the most striking example of a later English manor-house with certain defensive features" (Hamilton Thompson). It was finally dismantled in 1646. Mary, Queen of Scots, was imprisoned here under the care of the Earl of Shrewsbury (1584–85).—Other points easily reached from Matlock are *Cratcliffe Tor* and *Robin Hood's Stride* (see below), 6 m. n.w.; *Ashover*, 5½ m. n.e., where the church has a 12C lead font and a splendid Babington tomb (16C); *Chatsworth* (see below); *Haddon Hall* (see below); and *Dovedale* (Rte 45b).

On leaving Matlock, we emerge from the narrow glen of the Derwent into its smiling upper vale.—19¼ m. *Darley Dale* is well-known to choristers and cricket enthusiasts. In the churchyard (1 m. left) is perhaps the oldest and finest yew in England (32 ft girth; at least 700 years old). The church possesses a stone parclose screen, an early 14C effigy of a knight, and two 16C incised slabs of the Rowsley family.

About 2¾ m. s.w., up a long hill, is *Winster*, with a 15–17C market-house (N.T.). About 1½ m. n., to the w. of the road to Bakewell, are the strange, castellated crags of *Robin Hood's Stride*, and the gritstone cliff of *Cratcliffe Tor*, with a remarkable rock-hermitage, carved on the side of which is a 14C crucifix.

21¾ m. **Rowsley,** at the junction of the Derwent and the Wye, has a hotel in a fine house of 1652. On *Stanton Moor*, to the s., are the 'Nine Ladies' and other prehistoric stones.

*Chatsworth House, the 'Palace of the Peak', is the vast Palladian mansion of the Duke of Devonshire in a large deer-park bounded towards the e. by moorland edges, and watered by the Derwent. Chatsworth lies 4 m. from Rowsley by road; on foot the pleasantest approach is by a path along the w. bank of the river (about 3½ m.).

Admission to house (April–Sept), Wed, Thurs, & Fri 11.30–4; Sat and Sun, 1.30–5; BH, 11–5; to gardens, Mon–Fri 11.30–4.30; Sat and Sun 11.30–5; BH, 11–5.30; fee. The *Theatre Gallery* (adm. as for house) contains a *Collection of Old Master drawings.

Chatsworth has belonged to the house of Cavendish since its purchase by Sir William Cavendish (d. 1557), second husband of the famous 'Bess of Hardwick' (p. 407). The house begun by him on the site of the old manor-house was completed by his widow; and it was this house that the captive Mary Stuart visited five times, between 1570 and 1581, in the custody of Bess's fourth and final husband, the Earl of Shrewsbury. The existing palace, designed by William Talman and Thos. Archer, was begun by William Cavendish, afterwards first Duke of Devonshire, in 1687 and completed in 1706. The n. wing, by Wyatville, was built in 1820–30.

The most striking features of the decoration are the pompous ceiling-paintings by *Laguerre, Verrio,* and others; and the *Wood-carving, formerly attributed to Grinling Gibbons, but now known to be largely the work of Samuel Watson (1663–1715), a local artist. Both features are seen to fine advantage in the sumptuous *Chapel. From the Ante-Library visitors catch a glimpse of the Great Library, with ceiling panels by Verrio, and pass into the Dome Room lined by rare books. The Dining Room contains portraits by *Van Dyck* and the Sketch Galleries portraits of the dukes and duchesses of Devonshire. Painted on a door in the Music Room is a fiddle, by *Vandervaart,* that often cheats the visitor into a belief in its reality. In the State Bedroom is the bed in which George II was laid out after dying in the adjacent room. The numerous works of art include 17C Mortlake tapestries, Henry VII's illuminated Prayer Book, miniatures of Edward VI (by Oliver) and of Cromwell (by Cooper), and a number of notable paintings, the arrangement of which is continuously changing; outstanding among them is *Rembrandt's* Portrait of an Oriental.

The GARDENS, which are entered from the Orangery, are somewhat formal in character. The *Grand Cascade* is merely a flooded staircase; but the *Emperor Fountain* throws a jet 267 ft high, rivalling the Eaux-Vives fountain in Geneva. In front of the house is the *Italian Garden*, and behind it the *French Garden*.

The *PARK is open to visitors, who may ascend (by privilege) to the *Hunting Tower* (temp. Elizabeth I) on the hill behind the house (view). Thence a beautiful walk is generally open along the crest of the hill (lovely views) to the farm of *Beeley Hilltop* (50 min.), whence we may return to Rowsley by road (c. 2½ m.). —Between Chatsworth House and Edensor (see below), on the right of the drive, is *Queen Mary's Bower*, said to have been frequented by the captive queen. This and the Hunting Tower are the two sole relics of the earlier Chatsworth.

On the extreme W. limit of the park is Edensor, a model village (1839), the churchyard of which is the burial-place of the Cavendishes. The church, rebuilt by Scott, with a graceful spire, contains the striking classical monument of the first Earl of Devonshire (d. 1626) and a brass inscription to John Beaton (d. 1570), steward to Mary, Queen of Scots. The E. window of the S. chapel is a memorial to Lord Frederick Cavendish (p. 608).—At the N. extremity of the park is Baslow (Hotel), a pleasant village on the Derwent.—Thence to *Sheffield*, see Rte 61H.

About 2 m. N.W. of Rowsley is ***Haddon Hall** (Duke of Rutland; adm. Apr.–Sept daily exc. Sun & Mon 11–6; BH, 2–6; fee, café), in a lovely situation on a slope above the sparkling Wye, and in itself "the most attractive and most thoroughly preserved of medieval houses".

The Norman lords of Haddon were the Avenell family, from whom it passed by marriage to the Vernons about the middle of the 12C. Towards the close of the 16C Dorothy Vernon married Sir John Manners, ancestor of the present owner, though the romantic story of her elopement is not now generally considered authentic.

The Hall consists of two courtyards on different levels, and is almost wholly domestic in nature. Among notable features of the interior are the *Chapel* (12–15C, with contemporary murals), the early 14C *Banqueting Hall*, with 17C the *Long Gallery*, added by Sir John Manners, and the *Ante-Room*, whence the picturesque flight of steps by which Dorothy Vernon traditionally eloped descends to the garden. Below the *Gardens* the Wye is crossed by a pack-horse bridge.

Rowsley (or Bakewell, see below) is the best starting-point for the picturesque limestone glens of the *Lathkill* and the *Bradford*, which unite at *Alport* (2¾ m. from Rowsley) and join the Wye below Haddon. The Lathkill should be explored to (4¼ m.) its source near *Monyash*, where it issues from the mouth of a cave.— About ¾ m. W. of Alport, and overlooking the glen of the Bradford, is the large village of *Youlgreave*, the church of which has a fine 15C tower, a curious miniature chest-tomb of 1488, and a font (12C) with a singular side-projection of much disputed use, perhaps intended as a chrismatory, or receptacle for consecrated oil.

Beyond Rowsley the road quits the Derwent, and proceeds up the green valley of the Wye, which winds along in a thousand shining curves.

25½ m. **Bakewell** (Hotels) is an attractive little town (4200 inhab.), in a situation of much quiet beauty, with a bridge of c. 1300 across the Wye. The *Church* (partly rebuilt; Norman w. doorway) contains an elaborate 14C font and Vernon and Manners monuments (s. transept; 15–17C), including those of Dorothy Manners (d. 1584) and of her father, Sir George Vernon (d. 1567), 'the King of the Peak'. In the s. aisle is the quaint tomb of Sir Godfrey Foljambe (d. 1377) and his wife. In the churchyard is a fine Saxon cross; and the s. porch is full of early gravestones (9–13C). 'Bakewell pudding' was first made at the Rutland Arms (1804); Market Hall and Holme Hall date from the 17C.

Bakewell is an excellent centre from which to visit Chatsworth and Haddon Hall (see above). Walkers can take the old Chesterfield road to (2½ m.) *Edensor*, visit *Chatsworth*, cross the hill by a somewhat intricate track to (3½ m.) *Haddon*, and return to (2 m.) Bakewell by path along the N. side of the Wye. The delightful round of 8 m. commands exquisite views.

FROM BAKEWELL TO CHAPEL-EN-LE-FRITH, 14½ m. To (1½ m.) *Ashford*, see below. We cross the Wye on B 6465, and turn left on A 623 at (5 m.) *Wardlow* (see below). —7 m. *Tideswell* is an old-fashioned town on the left of the road, with a large and beautiful 14C *Church (striking w. tower; stone screen behind the altar; *Brass of Bp. Pursglove, d. 1579). At *Wheston*, 1½ m. w., is a good 14–15C cross.—10½ m. *Peak Forest*, in a quarrying district, has a church (1657–66) dedicated to King Charles the Martyr. At *Tunstead*, 3 m. s., birthplace of James Brindley (1716–72), the canal-builder, is the largest limestone quarry in Europe.—14¼ m. *Chapel*, see Rte 45D.

In the opposite direction (E.) A 623 leads from Wardlow to Middleton Dale and Eyam (see below); while to the N.E. of Tideswell rises the abrupt Hucklow Edge (gliding) above the remote village of *Great Hucklow*, known for its village players (performances at full moon).

From Bakewell to *Sheffield* direct viâ Baslow, see Rte 61H.

FROM BAKEWELL TO MANCHESTER there are two fine alternative roads, viâ Buxton or viâ Hathersage and Castleton.

The BUXTON ROAD (A 6) skirts the Wye to (1½ m.) *Ashford-in-the-Water*, a pleasant village in the church of which are five old 'virgin crants' ('Hamlet', v, 1).—At (3½ m.) *Deep Dale* the road quits the river and ascends past the N.T. property of *Taddington Wood*.—8½ m. *Topley Pike* (see below).—12 m. *Buxton* (Rte 45B).

Almost every mile of the beautiful limestone **Ravine of the** Wye between Ashford and its source at Buxton should be visited, if possible on foot. Tantalizing glimpses only are obtainable from road or railway. About 2 m. may be saved between Ashford and Monsal Dale by taking the direct road over *Headstones Edge* ('surprise' *View of Monsal Dale).—Paths and lanes follow the stream through the retired and beautiful glen of *Monsal Dale* and thence through *Miller's Dale* (N.T.) to (6¾ m.) Miller's Dale station at the crossing of the Tideswell road. About 1½ m. up the Wye from Miller's Dale station (rough footpath) is the splendid crag of *Chee Tor* (c. 300 ft), in a narrow limestone ravine—the finest scene of its class in Derbyshire. The path joins the high road (10¾ m.) at the foot of *Topley Pike*, 3½ m. E. of Buxton.

The HATHERSAGE ROAD from Bakewell (A 622) joins the Edensor and Baslow route at (4¾ m.) *Calver*, and descends into the valley of the Derwent. To the left is Middleton Dale (see below); on the opposite bank rises *Froggatt Edge* (Restaurant).—7¼ m. *Grindleford Bridge* (Hotel) stands at the junction of a road to Sheffield on a lovely reach of the Derwent.

About 3½ m. s.w., by a hilly road commanding lovely views, is the large upland village of **Eyam** (pronounced 'Eem'), famous for its fearful devastation by plague in 1666, which carried off three-fourths of its 350 inhab., and for the heroic conduct of its rector, William Mompesson, and of the ejected minister, Thomas Stanley, who succeeded in isolating the parish and preventing the spread of the disease. Services for the terror-stricken villagers were held in the dell called 'Cucklett Church' (c. ¼ m. from the church). In Eyam churchyard is a fine Saxon cross (perhaps 9C). The Hall is dated 1676. Lead mining has practically ceased, but large fluorspar mines have been opened since the 1930s.—From Eyam the visitor should proceed through the rocky gorge of *Middleton Dale* to (1¼ m.) the curiously placed village of *Stoney Middleton*, whence he may return direct to (¾ m.) *Calver* (see above).

10½ m. *Hathersage*, and thence to Castleton, Glossop, and Manchester, see Rte 45D.

D From Sheffield to Manchester

ROAD. The route here described (44½ m.) follows A 625 to Whaley Bridge and thence reaches Manchester on A 6.—The direct route (A 57; 38 m.) runs viâ (11 m.) *Ladybower Reservoir*, (24 m.) *Glossop*, (30 m.) *Stalybridge*, and (31½ m.) *Ashton-under-Lyne* (see Rte 61G).

RAILWAY, 42½ m. in 1 hr. Intermediate stations (11¼ m. *Hathersage*, 19½ m. *Edale*, etc.) are served by local trains.

Sheffield, see Rte 61H. We quit the town beyond the suburb of (3 m.) *Ecclesall* and soon enter Derbyshire.—6½ m. The *Devil's Elbow*, once a notorious double corner, has been straightened.—8¼ m. *Fox House Inn*. On the moors, 1 m. N.W., is the striking *Carl Wark*, a British fort.

On the left (s.) as far as Grindleford station extends the *Longshaw Estate* (N.T.), over 1000 acres of woodland and moor, with a guest-house of the Holiday Fellowship. Sheep-dog trials are held here in September.

9½ m. *Millstone Edge Nick* commands a surprise *View of the upper Derwent valley that is probably unrivalled in the Peak. At (11 m.) **Hathersage** (Hotel), in a beautiful situation, the Bakewell road comes in on the left. In the churchyard, above the village, is the reputed grave of Robin Hood's lieutenant, 'Little John', a native of the place. The church is mostly 14C, with good 15C Eyre brasses. Hathersage is the 'Morton' and *North Lees Hall*, close by (adm. by appointment), is the 'Manor House' of 'Jane Eyre'.—At (13 m.) *Bamford* (r.; Hotel) we quit the Derwent, which flows down from the moorlands of N. Derbyshire.

To the N. of Bamford is the huge *Ladybower Reservoir* for Sheffield, Derby, Nottingham, and Leicester, built in 1937–39, which drowned the lower Ashop valley and part of the Derwent valley, including the village of Ashopton. From (11½ m.) the *Slippery Stones* (pack-horse bridge), higher up the Derwent beyond two other reservoirs, a fairly distinct track leads N.E. to (18 m.) *Langsett* (p. 557), across wild moors, the highest point of which, near the top of *Margery Hill* (1793 ft), commands a *View (s. and w.) unrivalled in England for savage desolation.—Langsett may be reached from Bamford by a road (16½ m.) less wild but very beautiful, viâ (7½ m.) the *Strines Inn*, (12½ m.) *Broomhead Hall*, and (15 m.) *Midhopestones*.—The road from Bamford to Glossop ascends past *Win Hill* (l., 1523 ft; view) and through the deep and narrow valley of the Ashop beyond the reservoir, with the savage N. escarpment of Kinder Scout to the left.—4½ m. *Alport Bridge* (see below).—6½ m. *Snake Inn* (1070 ft), ½ m. beyond which we have a striking retrospect of the craggy *Fairbrook Naze*, the noblest summit of Kinder Scout. We reach (9½ m.) the flat summit of the pass (1680 ft) between *Glossop Moor* (l.; 1785 ft) and *Higher Shelf Stones* (r.; 2039 ft), and then make the steep and winding descent to (13 m.) *Glossop* (see below).—From the Snake Inn a well-marked track leads s.w. across the moors to (6½ m.) *Hayfield* (see below), with fine views from the highest point (1670 ft).

Beyond Bamford we ascend the valley of the Noe, which flows from Edale. In front rise Mam Tor and the other hills round Castleton.—15¼ m. *Hope* has a churchyard cross (10C).

To the s. in an area of limestone quarrying, is the old lead-mining village of *Bradwell*, near which is the *Bagshaw Cavern* (fine stalactites; fee; 1½ hr). Between Bradwell and the main road is *Brough*, with scanty remains of the Roman *Navio*. To the N.W. is the green and open valley of Edale, bounded on the s. by Mam Tor and Lose Hill, and on the N. by the moorland edges of Kinder Scout.—19½ m. *Edale* (Hotel) is surrounded by the wildest scenery in Derbyshire. A good walking centre, it is also the beginning of the 'Pennine Way' (250 m.).

Kinder Scout (2088 ft), N.W. of the village, is the highest ground in Derbyshire. The summit is a plateau of deeply trenched peat-hag, and except from the broken edges the views are not good. The whole plateau is now open to ramblers, but the ascent should be attempted only in fine weather as it is easy to get lost. Good pedestrians may walk round it (about 21 m.). Crossing the neck between Kinder

Scout and Win Hill and descending to (5 m.) *Alport Bridge*, they proceed by road to
(2 m.) the *Snake Inn* (see above), whence they follow the track mentioned above to
(6½ m.) *Hayfield* (see below). Thence they regain (7½ m.) Edale by reversing the
route next described.—The walk w. from Edale to (7½ m.) Hayfield is one of the
easiest and prettiest mountain excursions in Derbyshire. We ascend Edale to
(2 m.) *Upper Booth*, about 1 m. beyond which, at *Edale Head House*, the lane ends.
Hence a path climbs steeply up Jacob's Ladder to (1 m.) *Edale Cross* (c. 1750 ft),
on the neck between Kinder Scout (r.) and *Brown Knoll* (l.; 1804 ft). We then
descend a charming moorland valley, past a picturesque farm, to (3 m.) *Hayfield*.

17 m. **Castleton** (Hotel) is an interesting village at the heart of the
subterranean marvels of Derbyshire (and consequently apt to be overrun by trippers). The ceremony of 'Riding the Garland', on the evening
of 29 May, commemorates Charles II's restoration. To the s., perched
on the summit of a splendid limestone crag, is the small late-Norman
keep (c. 1176) of *Peveril Castle* (part of whose enceinte wall remains;
adm. daily; closed Sun morning in winter; fee), originally founded here
by William Peveril in 1068. Scott's 'Peveril of the Peak' has little local
interest.

At the foot of this great precipice is the gaping mouth of the *PEAK CAVERN
(adm. daily Easter–Sept, 10–6; fee), which penetrates the limestone hill for c. ¼ m. At
least its spectacular mouth should be visited, used for over 400 yrs as a rope-walk, and
unrivalled for its dignity and mystery.—About ¾ m. w. is the artificial entrance to the
*SPEEDWELL MINE (adm. 9.30–6; fee; ¼–⅓ hr). We descend 104 steps, and then pass by
boat through a gallery nearly ½ m. long, originally driven in search of lead, which leads
to a natural subterranean pothole, the height and depth of which have never been
ascertained, though rockets have ascended 450 ft without revealing the roof. The effect
is gloomily impressive.—Immediately beyond the Speedwell Mine begins the abrupt
limestone ravine of the *Winnats* (Wind-gates; N.T.), through which the old road to
Chapel ascends steeply to the top of the mountain plateau (fine retrospect half-way up).
From the top (1¼ m. from Castleton) a footpath leads to the right (notice-board) to
(6 min.) the *BLUE JOHN MINE (adm. daily 10–6; fee), with the rare deposits of
amethystine spar ('bleu-jaune'; articles for sale), the finest of the Derbyshire caverns,
over 2 m. long, with 5 chambers 90–200 ft high. The near-by *TREAK CLIFF CAVERN
(adm. as above) likewise contains 'Blue John' deposits. All four caverns are open daily
throughout the year.—From the Blue John Mine we may return direct to (1½ m.)
Castleton by footpath and road or we may climb in 25 min. (no path, but route obvious)
to the top of *Mam Tor* (1700ft; N.T.), sometimes called the 'Shivering Mountain',
owing to the disintegration that is continuously taking place on its precipitous s. face
and has already partly destroyed the British camp upon its summit (view). Instead of
returning to Castleton direct (2 m.) we may continue E. along the narrow ridge between
the Hope valley (r.) and Edale (l.) to (1 hr) the summit of *Lose Hill* (1563 ft), and
descend either to Hope (2 m.) or Castleton (1 hr). This walk commands continuously
fine views.

The main road from Castleton curves uphill round the face of Mam
Tor and crosses the flank of *Rushup Edge*.—23½ m. *Chapel-en-le-Frith*
(Hotel), an old-fashioned town with market-cross and stocks, is 6 m.
N. of Buxton. The road to Manchester joins the road from Buxton
(Rte 45B) at (27 m.) *Whaley Bridge*.—44½ m. **Manchester,** see Rte 60.

FROM CHAPEL TO GLOSSOP, 8 m. (A 624).—From (4 m.) *Hayfield* excursions are
made to Edale and Castleton, round Kinder Scout, etc.—The church of *Mellor*,
3½ m. w., has a good Norman font and perhaps the oldest wooden pulpit in England
(14C.).—8 m. Glossop (24,100 inhab.) has cotton-mills and calico-printing works.
The near-by *Dinting Railway Centre* is open daily (locomotives in steam, summer Sun &
BH). For the direct road to Sheffield, see above. The main road goes on N.w. for 2½ m.
to join the Manchester–Barnsley road (Rte 61G) on the farther side of Longdendale.
From Chapel to *Bakewell*, see Rte 45C.

46   LONDON TO DONCASTER

A Viâ Stamford

ROAD, 163 m. (A 1). To (15 m.) *South Mimms*, see Rte 32B.—21 m. *Hatfield.*—23¾ m. *Welwyn Garden City.*—31½ m. *Stevenage.*—39 m. *Baldock* (these three with a motorway by-pass).—77½ m. *Norman Cross.*—90½ m. **Stamford.**—112 m. **Grantham.**—125 m. **Newark.**—140½ m. *Markham Moor.*—A 638. 145 m. *East Retford.*—154 m. *Bawtry.*—163 m. **Doncaster.**

The old GREAT NORTH ROAD, long notorious for its inadequacy, is now difficult to follow, passing as A 1000 through Barnet and Potters Bar to Hatfield and Welwyn, and B 197 thence via Stevenage and Baldock. In these southern parts A 1, improved almost throughout to dual-carriageway or motorway, no longer follows the old course; north of Biggleswade it still follows the traditional route to Markham Moor, though by-passing the towns on the old road. This in itself was a variation, remade in coaching days, of the Roman road to York viâ Ware and Huntingdon (now A 14; Rte 54), still followed by A 1 between Alconbury and Stretton, and continuing (as B 6403 and A 15) viâ Lincoln and the Humber ferry at Brough (p. 618).

RAILWAY. To Doncaster, 156 m. from King's Cross in 2–2½ hrs. This is part of the 'East Coast Route' to Scotland viâ York, Durham, and Newcastle. Frequent suburban service viâ Hatfield to (32 m.) *Hitchin.* Principal Stations: 58¾ m. *Huntingdon.*—76½ m. **Peterborough.**—105½ m. **Grantham.**—120 m. **Newark,** junction for *Lincoln* (15¾ m.).—138 m. *Retford.* On *Stoke Bank,* s. of Grantham, on 3 July 1938, 'Mallard' achieved 126 m.p.h., a world record for steam locomotives unlikely ever to be equalled.

From London to (15 m.) *South Mimms*, see Rte 32B.—21 m. **Hatfield** (by-pass; Hotels), an ancient Hertfordshire market town (45,000 inhab.), that has expanded towards the w. The old town stands on the old Great North Road, 1 m. E. In the church is the elaborate tomb of Robert Cecil, first earl of Salisbury (d. 1612), son of the great Lord Burghley; a small armoured effigy of c. 1200, by Maximillian Colt, and a monument by Nicholas Stone (1617).

In a fine park E. of the old town is *Hatfield House (Marquess of Salisbury)*, a majestic Jacobean mansion erected in 1607–11, after James I had constrained Robert Cecil to exchange the manor of Theobalds for that of Hatfield. The park is open daily (April–Sept) 10.30–8 (fee); the state rooms and gardens are open Easter–Oct daily, exc. Mon, but incl. BH, 12–5, Sun 2.30–5.30; rfmts (fee). The objects of interest include portraits by *Zucchero* and *Hilliard* of Elizabeth I, and others by *Van Dyck, Kneller, Mytens, Reynolds*, etc., the valuable collection of MSS. and state papers, and relics of Elizabeth I. The old Hatfield Palace was built in 1497 by Card. Morton and afterwards became a royal residence. Luncheon (not Sun) and tea may be taken in the surviving hall, where Elizabeth I held her first Privy Council. The future queen was living here in confinement when Queen Mary died; the oak in the park beneath which she received the news of her accession withered in the 19C and its remains were moved to the old riding school in 1978. In the park before Lloyd George and Kitchener in Jan and Feb, 1916, took place the successful trials of the first tank (built at Lincoln).

23¾ m. **Welwyn Garden City** (by-pass: pron. 'Wellin'), founded in 1920 as a 'satellite town' (40,000 inhab.) of London, is attractively planned in the manner of Letchworth (see below). A 1 passes close to *Brocket Hall* (l.) home in turn of Lord Melbourne (d. 1848), Lord Palmerston (d. here in 1865), and Lord Mount Stephen (d. 1921).

Queen Hoo Hall, near Tewin, 3½ m. N.E. of Welwyn Garden City, is a charming brick house of 1540–60, with contemporary *Mural paintings.

27 m. *Welwyn* (Hotel & Motel), where Edward Young (1683–1765), author of 'Night Thoughts', was rector. The railway crosses the graceful *Digswell Viaduct* 1 m. E.

A pleasant stretch of country, missed by the motorway, can be enjoyed by taking B 656 (l.) viâ (1½ m.) *Codicote*. At *Ayot St Lawrence*, 2¾ m. w., is *Shaw's Corner* (N.T.; open daily, exc. Tues 11–1, 2–6 or dusk; closed Dec–Jan; fee), home of George Bernard Shaw (1856–1950) from 1906 to his death. The contents of the house remain as in his lifetime.—4½ m. *Knebworth House* (r.), a much altered 16C mansion, has been the ancestral home of the Lyttons since 1492; here Bulwer Lytton (1803–73) wrote many of his novels. The house (adm. Easter–Sept daily exc. Mon unless BH; also Sun in Oct; 11.30–5.30; park 11–6; fee; restaurant in tithe-barn) contains MSS. and relics of Bulwer Lytton and a fine hall with portraits. In the adjacent church are 17C Lytton monuments. At *St Paul's Walden*, 3 m. farther N.W., the parish church has a *Choir by Hawksmoor. The Bury was the birthplace (1900) of Elizabeth, queen of George VI.—9 m. **Hitchin** (Hotel), an unspoilt market-town (28,700 inhab.) with narrow streets and old inns, has a fine parish church (12–15C) with good screen-work, a 15C font, and a fine brass of 1478. George Chapman (1559?–1634), translator of Homer, is said to have been born in Tilehouse St., which has numerous 16–18C houses and the *Salem Chapel* with a chair presented by John Bunyan.—By A 600 and A 6001, A 1 may be regained at (18 m.) *Biggleswade* (see below), viâ *Henlow*, with a large R.A.F. camp.

A 1 (here motorway) continues N. to by-pass Stevenage and Baldock.—31½ m. **Stevenage** (67,000 inhab.; Hotels), with a wide High Street, was developed to the E. in the 1950s as one of London's 'satellite towns'. Edward Gordon Craig (1872–1966) was born here. *St George's*, the parish church of the new town (1960), is by Mottistone and Paget.—39 m. **Baldock** (6300 inhab.; Hotel), at the crossing of the Icknield Way, has a church with a fine 15C rood screen, a broad High St., and many old corners. The town's name is a corruption of 'Baghdad', recalling its foundation as a 'bastide' by the Templars.

FROM BALDOCK TO LUTON, 13½ m. (A 505). 2 m. **Letchworth** (Hotels), the first 'garden city' in England (30,900 inhab.), was founded under the inspiration of Ebenezer Howard in 1903. Letchworth Hall (now a Hotel) is a Jacobean manor-house.—5 m. *Hitchin* (see above.)—8 m. **Great Offley** has several Nollekens monuments (1773) in the church.—13½ m. *Luton*, see Rte 44.

From Baldock to *Cambridge* viâ *Royston*, see Rte 54.

Ashwell, 4½ m. N.E. of Baldock, has a 14C church with a striking tower, within which is preserved a curious graffito of Old St Paul's. It also contains two fine tapestries by Percy Sheldrich, a local craftsman. The Town House, now a village museum (March–Dec, Sun 2.30–4.30), is one of many good houses in the attractive main street.

We enter Bedfordshire before reaching (46 m.) *Biggleswade*, now by-passed to the w. At *Ickwell*, 3 m. w., Thomas Tompion (1638–1713), 'father of English clock-making' was born, and a maypole ceremony is still performed.—At (50 m.) *Sandy* near the foot of a sandstone ridge we intersect the road from Cambridge to Bedford.—52½ m. *Tempsford* (Hotel). From the airfield, 1 m. E., the R.A.F.'s 'Moon Squadrons' operated in 1941–44, dropping secret agents into occupied Europe. The 18C Hasells Hall off its s. perimeter was used for briefing. We cross the Great Ouse.—57 m. *Eaton Socon* is 1½ m. s.w. of *St Neots* (10,300 inhab.; Hotels), on the E. bank of the Great Ouse, with a fine Perp. church tower.

A road connects St Neots with (9½ m.) *Huntingdon* viâ (3 m.) *Great Paxton*, where the church has a pre-Conquest w. end and a late-Norman chancel arch; and (8½ m.) *Godmanchester* (p. 482).

60½ m. *Diddington*. To the left an impressive embankment, 76 ft high and 5500 ft long, contains *Grafham Water* (1965) a reservoir on which boats may be hired for fishing (trout).—At (62 m.) *Buckden* are remains of a palace of the bishops of Lincoln (Aug–mid-Sept, daily 2–8; fee). Here Catherine of Aragon lived between the divorce and her retirement to Kimbolton.—65 m. A 604 leads E. viâ *Brampton* (1½ m.), the family estate of Samuel Pepys, and *Hinchingbrooke* (p. 482) to *Huntingdon* (3½ m.; Rte 54). At (69 m.) *Alconbury Hill* (Motel) A 1 is joined by A 14 from Huntingdon (Rte 54) and thence follows the line of the Roman ERMINE STREET.

About 5½ m. N.W. of Alconbury is *Little Gidding*, with a small partly 17C church, interesting as the scene of Nicholas Ferrar's 'Protestant nunnery' (1626), described in Shorthouse's 'John Inglesant'. Before the W. door is the tomb of Ferrar (d. 1637) and the brass font dates from his time.

To (76½ m.) *Stilton* (w. of the main road), 'Stilton' cheese (not made in the neighbourhood) was originally brought by waggon from Leicestershire to be carried to London by coach. Its sale at the Bell Inn (1642) ceased in 1964 after 170 years but is now carried on at the Post Office opposite.— 77½ m. *Norman Cross* (Motel) has a monument to the French prisoners who died in confinement, during the Napoleonic wars, at the barracks here (pulled down in 1816). A 15 diverges right for Peterborough (5 m.; see Rte 54)—We intersect the Peterborough–Oundle road at (81 m.) *Kate's Cabin*, and just beyond, at *Water Newton*, pass (r.) the important Roman station of *Durobrivae* where Ermine St. diverges w. from the earlier Roman 'King Street'.—At (85 m.) *Wansford* (Hotel), we meet A 47 from Peterborough, crossing the Nene a little below the 16C bridge. The Peterborough Railway Society here operates a 5 m. section (to Orton Mere) of the former Nene Valley line.— 87½ m. *Wittering* church (l.) has a Saxon arch.

90½ m. **STAMFORD**, an ancient town (14,500 inhab.) of unusual interest, is situated on the Welland, an ancient county boundary. Now bypassed to the w. by A 1, it retains an unequalled range of stone buildings, both domestic and official, mostly of the 17–18C. The almshouses, known as 'Callises' (from the wool-merchants of the great staple of Calais), are a feature of the town.

Car Parking, Bath Row.
Hotels in High St. St Martin, St Mary's St.
Post Office, All Saints' Place.—INFORMATION OFFICE, Town Hall.
Buses (local and long distance) from Central Bus Station, Sheepmarket.
Stamford is mentioned in a grant of c. 660, and became one of the Danelagh towns. For a time, after the arrival of seceding students from Oxford in 1333, it was a serious competitor of the older university, but of its medieval castle and town wall only fragments remain. Sir Malcolm Sargent (1895–1967) was born here, and is buried in the town cemetery.

Arriving from the s. or from the station, we cross the bridge and pass the *Town Hall* (1777) and a Norman arch-way into St Mary's Passage (l.), to reach the church of *St Mary*, with its noble E.E. tower (13C) surmounted by an early Dec. broach *Spire (163 ft high), in a dignified square. St Mary's St. leads w., with picturesque old lanes leading down to attractive meadows across the mill-stream, in one of which is a huge barn with a magnificent roof (now a restaurant). We turn right to *St John's* (Perp.; fine woodwork) and reach *All Saints*, mainly E.E. with Perp. insertions, a Perp. tower and spire (152 ft), and curious external arcading; the impressive interior contains some fine brasses.

All Saints St., and its continuation, St Peter's St. lead w. above the Bus Station with a 17C façade (removed from High St.), and past several callises, to the site of St Peter's Gate (plaque) dismantled in 1770 when more almshouses were built here.

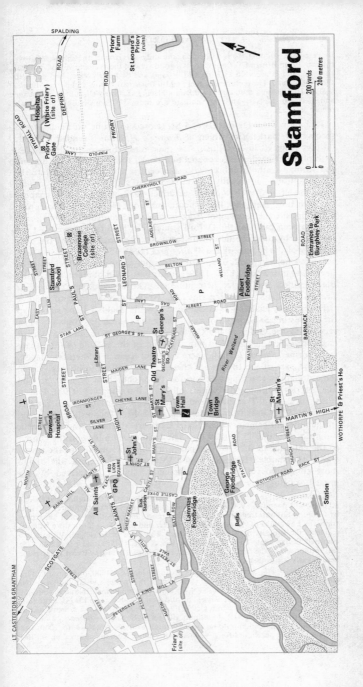

Stamford

SPALDING

N

200 yards
200 metres

Priory Farm

St Leonard's Priory (ruins)

RYHALL ROAD

Hospital

Priory (White Friary) (site of)

Priory Gate

DEEPING ROAD

PRIORY LANE

PRIORY ROAD

PINFOLD LANE

CHERRYHOLT ROAD

ADELAIDE ST

Brazenose College (site of)

STREET

Stamford School

EAST STREET

ELM STREET

ST PAUL'S STREET

LEONARD'S STREET

LANE

GAS LANE

BROWNLOW STREET

BELTON ST

WELLAND ST

Albert Footbridge

ALBERT ROAD

BARNACK ROAD

Entrance to Burghley Park

STAR LANE

ST GEORGE'S ST

Library

MAIDEN LANE

St George's Sq

ST GEORGE'S ST

Old Theatre

BLACKFRIARS ST

WHARF ROAD

River Welland

WATER STREET

NORTH STREET

BROAD STREET

IRONMONGER ST

CHEYNE LANE

SILVER LANE

HIGH STREET

ST MARY'S ST

St Mary's

St Mary's

Town Hall

Town Bridge

St Martin's

ST MARTIN'S HIGH

WOTHORPE & Priest's Ho

Browne's Hospital

BATH HILL

ALL SAINTS STREET

St John's

ST JOHN'S ST

RED LION SQUARE

RED LION ST

All Saints

GPO

PLACE

Bus Station

Sheep Market

CASTLE DYKE

BROAD ROW

ST MARY'S ST

CASTLE ST

STATION ROAD

George Footbridge

WOTHORPE ROAD

BACK ST

Station

SCOTGATE

BARN HILL

CASTLE LA

BATH ROW

ST PETER'S VALE

ST PETER'S STREET

KINGS STREET

AUSTIN ST

MILL LA

PETERGATE

Berfs

Lammas Footbridge

Friary (site of)

LT. CASTERTON & GRANTHAM

WOTHORPE ROAD

In Petergate, running N., is a Bastion, the only survivor of the city's defensive towers. From Rutland Terrace there is a good view of the Welland valley. Several charming old lanes, such as King's Mill Lane, and St Peter's Vale, lead down to the water-front. The picturesque King's Mill (restored) is now a childrens' home.

Barn Hill, leading N.W. out of All Saints Place, has some well-built Queen Anne and Georgian houses, while in Scotgate are more 17C almshouses (Snowden's rebuilt in 1823).

Red Lion St. leads into Broad St. (closed to traffic on Friday for a spectacular market), in which is *Browne's Hospital* (founded c. 1480; visitors ring, 10.30–3, 4–dusk), the most interesting of the almshouses, with pleasant gardens; the chapel and board room are shown. Beyond the Roman Catholic church with an eccentric tower, we turn s. into the less ambitious, but equally attractive St Paul's St.

To the left is *Stamford School* (founded 1532, with a 12–13C chapel), at which Lord Burghley, Bp. Ellicott, and Lord Northcliffe were pupils, with opposite the gateway of Brazenose Hall (demolished in 1688), said to have been built for the Oxford students in 1333 (see above). At the road fork by the hospital a little farther E. is an old gateway, the only remains of the House of the *Whitefriars* (1285–1539): Richard II held a council here in 1392. Opposite, a plaque commemorates the 'site of *Greyfriars* monastery (1220–1539); Joan, Fair Maid of Kent, wife of the Black Prince, was buried here in 1385. The Benedictine *Priory of St Leonard*, to the s.e., has remains of c. 1090, and a w. front of 1150.

High Street leads back to the centre, while Maiden Lane runs s. to the interesting *St George's Square*, where the church has some old glass relating to the Order of the Garter, dating from a rebuilding in 1449 (see description in Lady Chapel). Just out of the w. side of the square is the former *Theatre* (1768), where Edmund Kean and Sheridan played.

In the part of the town s. of the river are some almshouses (1597), the old George coaching inn, and the Perp. church of *St Martin*. The fine interior contains the tombs of Lord Burghley (1520–98), Queen Elizabeth's Lord Treasurer, and other members of the Cecil family; and late-15C *Glass from Tattershall and other Lincolnshire churches. In the adjacent cemetery lies Daniel Lambert (d. 1809), who attained a weight of 52 stone 11 lb (739 lb). The road goes on beyond the church to the entrance of the spacious park, in which (1¼ m. s.e. of the town) stands the stately **Burghley House** (Marquess of Exeter), one of the most sumptuous examples of Elizabethan building, erected by the great Lord Burghley in 1560–87.

It contains a large collection of paintings, chiefly works of the Italian and British schools, and portraits by Van Dyck, Holbein, and others; fine furniture; carvings by Grinling Gibbons; and many interesting relics. In the billiard-room hang portraits (by Lawrence) of the tenth Earl of Exeter and his wife, a Shropshire 'village-maiden', the subjects of Tennyson's ballad 'The Lord of Burleigh'. Visitors are admitted Easter–Sept, Tues, Wed, Thurs, Sat, & BH, 11–5; Good Fri & Sun 2–5; fee; restaurant).—The famous Burghley Horse Trials ('Three Day Event') take place here in early September.

At *Wothorpe*, 1 m. s.w., are the ruins of a mansion of c. 1600, once occupied by George Villiers, second Duke of Buckingham; 1 m. farther s.w. at *Easton on the Hill* is an early-16C Priest's House (N.T.; adm. by appointment); *Ketton* (famous for its cement) and *North Luffenham*, 3 m. and 6 m. s.w., have fine 13–14C churches. —*Colly Weston* (noted for roofing-slabs) and *Duddington*, on the s. bank of the Welland, are two of the best stone-built villages in England.—*Barnack*, 3 m. s.e., once famous for its building stone, has a *Church with a Saxon tower (c. 1000) and a beautiful E.E. porch and font.—*Little Casterton*, a Roman station 2 m. N., has an E.E. church.

Beyond Stamford we enter Rutland, now part of Leicestershire. The church of (94 m.) *Great Casterton* is unrestored 13C work, while that of (95 m.; l.) *Tickencote* has a rich late-Norman *Chancel arch of six orders and a vaulted choir with boss (c. 1160). The elaborate exterior arcading (restored 1792), 13C font, and wooden effigy of a knight (14C) should also be noted.— Beyond (100 m.) *Stretton* we re-enter Lincolnshire. The oolite of *Clipsham* quaries, 1½ m. E., has been famous as building-stone for 1000 years. Just to the left of (105 m.) *Colsterworth* is *Woolsthorpe Manor* (N.T.; adm. Apr–Oct, Mon, Wed, Fri & Sat 11–12.30 & 2–6; fee), where Isaac Newton was born on Christmas Day, 1642, and where he saw the 'gravitation apple' fall.— 109 m. *Great Ponton*, with its conspicuous church-tower (1509). *Boothby Pagnell*, 3¼ m. E., has a late 12C *Manor-house, the most complete remaining example of a Norman domestic building. A 1 by-passes Grantham to the w.

112 m. **Grantham** (Hotels in High St.), an ancient town (27,900 inhab.) on the Witham, is a railway and hunting centre. Beyond *St Peter's Hill* (with a statue of Sir Isaac Newton) is *St Wulfram's*, the parish church, a fine E.E. and Dec. structure (chiefly 13C), with a beautiful crocketed *Spire, 280 ft high (14C). The varied window tracery is a feature of the light and spacious interior. A library (1598) over the s. porch has chained books, and the 14C crypt, probably once the shrine of St Wulfram, retains its stone altar; both are well shown by the verger. To the N.E. of the church is the late-Perp. *King's School* (1528), of which Sir Isaac Newton (1642–1727) was a pupil; while to the E. is the 14–15C *Grantham House* (N.T.; adm. Wed & Thurs, April–Sept, 2–5; fee). In the market-place is an ancient *Market Cross*, re-erected here in 1910; and at the back is a curious old conduit-house (1597). The *Angel & Royal Hotel*, at the N. end of High St., is one of the very few medieval hostelries still remaining in England.

It was probably once the hall of the Lords of Grantham, and King John is said to have held a court here in 1213. Here Richard III signed the death-warrant of the Duke of Buckingham (1483). The date of the gateway (14C) is indicated by the heads of Edward III and Queen Philippa in the hood-moulding.—The *George Hotel*, nearly opposite, is praised in 'Nicholas Nickleby'. Newton boarded in what is now the N. wing. The *Blue Pig*, near the church, is a timbered inn.

About 7 m. s.w. of Grantham, viâ (3½ m.) *Denton* (13–15C church), is *Belvoir Castle* (pron. 'Beever'), the imposing seat of the Duke of Rutland, rebuilt by Wyatt in 1816 after a fire (adm. Easter–Sept, Wed, Thurs, Fri, 12–6; Sun 2–7; Good Fri & BH, 11–7; also Sun in Oct 2–6; Rest.). Besides one of the finest private picture galleries in England with notable examples of Rembrandt, Rubens, and most other Dutch and Flemish masters, the castle contains tapestry, armour, miniatures, and other objects of art, and the Regimental Museum of the 17/21 Lancers.

FROM GRANTHAM TO NOTTINGHAM, 22 m. (A 52). Railway in 40 min. At (7 m.) *Bottesford* the fine early-Perp. church has a lofty crocketed spire (210 ft) and its chancel is crowded with *Monuments of successive owners of Belvoir.—The church of *Orston*, 2½ m. N.W., has a striking Restoration font, carved after a medieval model.— 11¾ m. *Aslockton* (r.) was the birthplace of Abp. Cranmer (1489–1556; manor-house, now a farm).— 13 m. *Bingham* has an important church (E.E., Dec. & Perp.). Samuel Butler (1835–1902) was born in the rectory of *Langar*, 3¼ m. s.—From (17 m) *Radcliffe-on-Trent*, with a War Memorial park overlooking the river, a pleasant walk by the river may be made to *Stoke Ferry* (no ferry) and *Shelford*, where the church has Stanhope memorials.*Holme Pierrepont Hall* (adm. Easter–Sept, Sun & BH 2–6; also Thurs in June–July; fee) is an early Tudor mansion. Near by is the National Water Sports Centre.— 22 m. *Nottingham*, see Rte 44.

FROM GRANTHAM TO LINCOLN, 24½ m. (A 607). Railway viâ Newark in ¾ hr.— 2¾ m. *Belton House* (Lord Brownlow) is a creation of 1684–88, attractive both outside and in. The house is open Apr–Oct, Tues–Thurs 2–6; also Sun & BH, 12–6; fee; rfmts. *Belton Church* has some good monuments.—At (5 m.) *Honington* the Boston road diverges to the right. We now skirt the *Cliff* (r.), an oolite escarpment crowned by a series of interesting churches.—9 m. *Caythorpe* has an unusual Dec. church (partly rebuilt).—12½ m. *Leadenham*, with a good late-Dec. church. Sir Wm. Robertson (1860–1933), who rose from private to field-marshal, was born at (14 m.) *Welbourn.*— We pass the tall stump of an old windmill (l.) before (17 m.) *Navenby*, with the finest church on the Cliff (late-Dec. chancel with good sedilia and piscina; debased tower). King John of France was a prisoner in 1359–60 at *Somerton Castle*, whose foundations may be seen 2½ m. w.—24½ m. *Lincoln*, see Rte 58.

From Grantham to *Boston* viâ Sleaford, see Rte 58.

At (122 m.) Shire Bridge we enter Notts; the tall and graceful spire of *Claypole* is seen on the right. The by-pass diverges (r.).—125 m. **Newark** (Hotels), an ancient town (24,600 inhab.) noted for its Georgian houses, stands at the junction of the Great North Road and the Foss Way, and on a branch of the Trent. Near the river bridge is the Ossing-ton Coffee Palace (now offices), a copy of a 17C hostelry, erected in 1882 as a temperance hotel by Viscountess Ossington. The *Castle* (12–15C), with a fine Norman gatehouse tower, endured three sieges in the Civil War and was dismantled in 1646. King John died here in 1216. In the dignified cobbled *MARKET PLACE are the *Town Hall* (1773) by Carr of York with a fine Adam ballroom, the *Moot Hall* (1708; restored), and the *White Hart Inn* (14C), and in courts off it are interesting timbered buildings. Jeanie Deans spent a night at the Saracen's Head Inn (now a bank) on her way to London. The *Governor's House* was the residence of Prince Rupert at the time of his disastrous quarrel with Charles I. The Perp. church of *St Mary Magdalene* has an E.E. tower and Dec. spire (252 ft) and a Norman crypt. In the N. choir aisle is the large brass, in the Hanseatic style, of Alan Flemyng (d. 1363). The oaken rood-screen by Thomas Drawswerd dates from 1508; the choir-stalls from c. 1525; the Meyring (N.) and Markham (S.) chantry chapels, flanking the altar, from 1500 and 1506. The double squint and the small painting from the 'Dance of Death' in the Markham chantry should be noticed. In Appleton Gate is the well-arranged *Town Museum* (open weekdays; Sun aft. also in April–Sept); among local archaeological finds is a good collection of Anglo-Saxon urns. It occupies the former Magnus Grammar and Song School (now in Earp Av.) with the Tudor Hall (1529), where John Blow (1647–1708), the composer, received his early education. The *Beaumond Cross*, at the end of Carter Gate is thought to be a 15C wayside preaching cross. In Devon Park is the Queen's Sconce, a star-shaped earthwork built as a platform for cannon in the Civil War. Sir William Nicholson, the painter, was born at New-ark in 1872.

The church of *Hawton*, 2 m. s., has one of the finest *Easter Sepulchres in England, with sedilia and piscina to match (c. 1330). *Holme*, 3¾ m. N., has a church rebuilt in 1485 by John Barton, woolstapler of Calais, with complete con-temporary fittings and stained glass. At *Kelham* (2 m. N.W.) is a theological college with a striking chapel (1928) by Charles Thompson.

Newark is on the railway from *Nottingham* to *Lincoln*, with which it is connected also by the Foss Way (16 m.).—BUSES to *Southwell* and *Mansfield*; *Retford; Lincoln; Sleaford;* and *Grantham.*

FROM NEWARK TO SOUTHWELL, 7¼ m. **SOUTHWELL** (good Hotel; swimming pool), a pleasant little town, is noted for its noble Minster, which became a cathedral in 1884.

At Southwell Charles I, lodging in the *Saracen's Head* (then the King's Arms), a medieval timbered edifice with panelled rooms, surrendered to the Scots Commissioners in 1646. At *Burgage Manor*, on the Green beyond King Street, Byron spent the restless vacations of 1804–7 with his mother, occasionally taking part in amateur theatricals in the Assembly Rooms, now part of the Saracen's Head. Viscount Allenby (1871–1936) was born at *Brackenhurst Hall* (now Notts. College of Agriculture), 2 m. s. of Southwell, and was baptized in the minster.

*Southwell Minster finely illustrates three successive styles of architecture (12–14C). The two severe w. towers, flanking the large Perp. window above the fine w. door, the low central tower, and the nave and transepts, with circular clerestory windows, are Norman (early 12C), and on the N. side is a rare late-Norman porch, while the s. door is oddly encircled by the string-course. The choir is a beautiful example of E.E. (1234–50), while the Dec. chapter house (1295–1300) is the chief glory of the minster.

The church of St Mary is said to have been founded here c. 630 by Paulinus, first bishop of York, but the first authentic mention of a church on this site dates from c. 100 years later. The present church belonged to a college of secular canons (more or less under the wing of the Abps. of York), which, though temporarily suspended under Henry VIII and again under Edward VI, subsisted until 1841. In 1884 the new diocese of Southwell was formed, comprising the counties of Notts (previously in the see of Lincoln) and Derby (previously in the see of Lichfield; new see of Derby created 1926).

The interior of the NAVE, with its massive Norman piers and lofty triforium, and flooded with light from the Perp. w. window and Perp. windows inserted in the aisles, is remarkably impressive. The tower arches, with cable moulding, should be noted.—In the N. TRANSEPT are the tomb of Abp. Sandys (d. 1588) and a small door above which is immured a sculptured fragment, evidently dating from an earlier church. Steps descend to a chapel containing the *Airmen's Altar*, constructed of fragments of aeroplanes shattered in France during the First World War. In the S. TRANSEPT a Roman tessellated pavement has been exposed.—The graceful CHOIR is separated from the transept by a Dec. rood-screen (1335), the elaborate carving on which is said to include 220 miniature human heads (many restored by Bernasconi c. 1820). The capitals of the Norman arch above it are interesting, and under the stalls at the back of the screen are quaint misericords. The clerestory and triforium of the choir are ingeniously combined so as to add to the impression of height. Two heads on corbels on the N. side of the choir are supposed to represent Walter de Gray and Henry III, the archbishop and king under whom the choir was built. The E. window has two rows of four lancets (instead of the more usual three or five); the Flemish glass in the lower lights was formerly in the old Temple Church in Paris. The patchwork window in the s. aisle is of old glass, perhaps from the chapter house. The brass lectern (c. 1500) was discovered in the lake at Newstead Abbey, into which it had been thrown by the monks at the Dissolution, 200 years before. The sedilia on the s. side are in the same style as the screen and were likewise restored by Bernasconi. A short passage leads from the choir to the octagonal ****CHAPTER HOUSE**, the beautiful roof of which is not supported by the usual central pillar. The exquisite ***Carving** on the doorway of this chamber and on the arcading within will repay the closest scrutiny; the naturalistic foliage is the earliest sculpture of its kind in England.

To the s. of the minster are the remains of the *Palace* of the Archbishops of York (1400; hall restored 1880).—*East Stoke*, 4 m. s.e., beyond Fiskerton Ferry across the Trent, was the scene of the battle of Stoke, where the pretender Lambert Simnel was defeated and captured by Henry VII in 1487.—From Southwell to Nottingham, see Rte 44.

Beyond Newark we cross the Trent; the by-pass comes in on the right. —138 m. *Tuxford* is 3 m. N. of *Laxton*, a village with an interesting survival of the threefold system of cultivation, practised also in the Isle of Axholme. *Ragnall*, 5 m. N.E. of Tuxford, was the birthplace of Nicholas Hawksmoor (1661–1736), the architect.—At (140¼ m.) *Markham Moor* A 1 diverges w., coinciding with the Lincoln–Sheffield road before bending N. to join the Doncaster (motorway) by-pass just beyond Blyth. A 638 continues the old Gt. North Road, here described.— 145 m. **East Retford,** a brisk market town (18,400 inhab.), has a well-restored Perp. church. Retford is an important railway centre, with branch lines to Worksop, Gainsborough, and Lincoln. Road to *Ollerton*, etc., see Rte 46B. *North Leverton*, 5 m. E., has a working windmill of 1813.— 148½ m. *Barnby Moor* (Hotel). *Blyth*, with the early Norman nave of a Benedictine *Priory Church (two fine screens) lies c. 2½ m. N.W.; while *Mattersey Priory*, 4¾ N.E., preserves remains of a house of Gilbertine canons (1185; always open).

152½ m. *Scrooby* contains the scanty remains of a palace of the Abps. of York and (opposite) a manor-house (now a farm) occupied by William Brewster (1560?–1644), the 'Pilgrim Father'. Brewster was keeper of the 'post office' at Scrooby in 1594–1607. His pew is pointed out in the E.E. church.—At the old-fashioned little town of (154 m.) *Bawtry* (Hotel) we enter Yorkshire. *Austerfield*, 1¼ m. N.E. on the Selby road, with an interesting Norman church, was the birthplace of William Bradford (1590–1657), second governor of Plymouth in New England. The old manor-house of the Bradfords still exists.— 157½ m. *Rossington* (good Hotel). The church (l.) has a Norman doorway and chancel arch and a rich 15C pulpit.

163 m. **Doncaster,** see Rte 68.

B Viâ Sherwood Forest

ROAD, 164 m. (A 46, A 6097, A 614, A 616, A 6009, A 60). To (112¾ m.) *Widmerpool*, see Rte 44.—140 m. Ollerton,—149 m. Worksop.—164 m. Doncaster.

From London to (112¾ m.) *Widmerpool* see Rte 44. The Roman Foss Way (A 46) continues N.E.—116 m. *Owthorpe* (1 m. right), the residence and burial-place of Col. Hutchinson, the regicide (d. 1664).— 120 m. We cross A 52 from Grantham to Nottingham, see Rte 46A.— At (121½ m.) *Castle Hill* we diverge l. on A 6097 to cross the Trent at (123¼ m.) *Gunthorpe Bridge*, a riverside resort, beyond which our road intersects A 612 from Nottingham to Southwell (see p. 412).— 132 m. We join A 614 from Nottingham, and enter Sherwood Forest.

Sherwood Forest, an ancient demesne of the Crown, once occupied (roughly) the whole w. part of Nottinghamshire, and still covers an area fully 20 m. long and 5–10 m. wide. It was largely disafforested towards the close of the 18C, and its outlying parts have been spoiled in recent years by the eastward development of the Nottinghamshire coalfield. Certain (diminishing) tracts of lovely woodland in the N. part have, however, been preserved through their inclusion in the so-called 'DUKERIES', made up of the great parks of Welbeck (formerly Duke , of Portland), Clumber (N.T., recently Duke of Newcastle), Worksop (formerly Duke of Norfolk), and Thoresby (once Duke of Kingston), though these also are threatened with industrial invasion. The parks of Worksop and Welbeck and also that of Rufford are closed to the public, but those of Clumber and Thoresby are accessible; and within these and among the venerable oaks of Birklands and Bilhaugh, near by, are some of the noblest survivors of the ancient British forests.— Sherwood Forest is inseparably connected with the picturesque exploits of Robin Hood and his Merry Men, which may or may not rest on a basis of fact.

138½ m. *Rufford Abbey* (r.) incorporates a vaulted 13C undercroft, part of a Cistercian monastery founded in 1148 and colonised from Rievaulx in Yorks. The house, Elizabethan and Jacobean, is built of warm red sandstone, and belonged to the Savile family for 300 years until its sale in 1938. *Clipstone*, c. 2 m. w., has the scanty remains of '*King John's Palace*', once a house of the earls of Shrewsbury.

B 6034 leads l. to *Edwinstowe* (1½ m.; Hotel), where the church has a good 13C tower, with a later spire, and in the chancel is a dwarf pillar-piscina, a unique example of a detached E.E. pillar. We may rejoin our road 1¼ m. N. through the beautiful forest tract of *Birklands*, with the celebrated *Major Oak*, reputed to be 1400 years old.

140 m. **Ollerton** (r.; Hotels), an old market town recently much enlarged, is a centre for the exploration of Sherwood Forest.—We take A 616 N.w. through the lovely forest tract of *Bilhaugh*, and B 6034 (see above) comes in on the left. On the right, beyond, is the domain of *Thoresby Park (Countess Manvers), a mansion built from designs by Salvin (1864–71). The hall, decorated in the most lavish Victorian style, contains a portrait of Lady Mary Wortley Montagu (1689–1762), daughter of the first Duke of Kingston, who was born in an earlier house on this site. Adm. Easter–Sept, Sun 2–6, BH 12.30–6; also Wed, Thurs, & Sat 2.30–6; fee; Restaurant. There is a road (now used as a public path) through the *Park, which is the largest in the Dukeries (12 m. round) and claims to be the most beautiful deer-park in England.—Beyond (143 m.) *Budby*, a model village, we branch right on A 6009.—144½ m. A by-road (r.) leads viâ *Carburton* with its Norman chapel, to **Clumber Park** (11 m. round; N.T.), with a *Lime-Tree Avenue.

Clumber, once the seat of the Duke of Newcastle, was erected in 1770, largely rebuilt in 1879, and demolished in 1937. Adjoining the site of the house is the chapel of *St Mary* (N.T.; adm. Easter–Sept daily 12 or 2–7; winter 1–4), built for the Duke by Bodley and Garner in 1889. The interior, one of the most remarkable neo-Gothic creations in England, is of softly-tinted red Runcorn stone. The wood-carving is mostly by Belgian artists, the stained glass by Kempe.—Clumber spaniels are no longer bred here.

Welbeck Abbey (p. 414) lies c. 4 m. w. of the main road.

149 m. **Worksop** (Hotels), an industrial town (36,000 inhab.), stands on the verge of the coalfield. Of the *Augustinian Priory* established here in 1103 there remains the splendid Norman *Nave (140 ft long; c. 1150–60), the w. towers, the s. transept (partly of 1103), and the Lady Chapel (13C), restored in 1929 as a war memorial. The s. *Door, of Sherwood yew, has fine wrought-iron work of c. 1200. The N. transept and the crossing were rebuilt by Sir H. Brakspear in 1932–35 from the original stones of the priory which had been used for the erection of a mill and farmhouse after the Reformation. Outside the church is the 14C gatehouse.

Worksop Manor (no adm.), s.w. of the town, belonged in turn to the Duke of Norfolk and the Duke of Newcastle, but the huge original mansion was burned down in 1761.—*Steetley Chapel*, 1½ m. farther w., is one of the best examples in England, on a small scale, of enriched Norman work (mid-12C).—*Thorpe Salvin*, 4½ m. w. of Worksop, has an elaborate carved *Font in its Norman church, and a ruined manor-house of c. 1575.

From Worksop to *Mansfield* and *Nottingham*, see Rte 44.

A 60 leads N. to (155 m.) *Oldcotes*, where we cross A 634.

Roche Abbey, 2⅜ m. w. on A 634, was founded for Cistercians in 1147 (adm. daily; Sun from 2; fee). The beautifully sited ruins include parts of the transepts and chancel and the main gateway. Adjacent is *Sandbeck Park* (Earl of Scarborough). The church of *Laughton-en-le-Morthen*, 2¼ m. s.w. of the abbey, has a fine Perp. spire and a pre-Conquest N. doorway.

157½ m. *Tickhill* has a ruined Norman castle, a Perp. church (c. 1360), containing one of the earliest Renaissance monuments in England (1478), and a domed market hall.—164 m. **Doncaster**, see Rte 68.

IV EASTERN ENGLAND

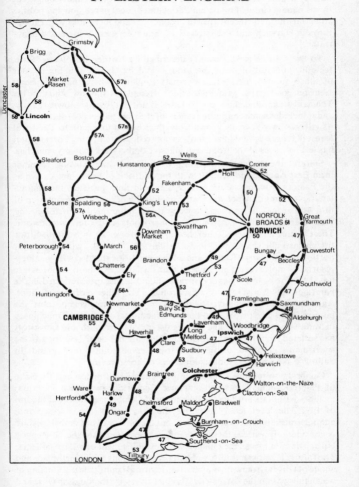

Eastern England, lying away from the great industrial trunk routes and having a long seaboard between Thames and Humber without deep-water harbours, has until recently been happily neglected by tourists and planners alike. Cut off from the rest of England until the railway age by the Lea marshes, Epping Forest, and the Fens, it has preserved in Norwich a true regional capital of great antiquity and a way of life largely agricultural in outlook. Though the southern half of Essex is now a dormitory for London, and a few seaside resorts—Southend, Clacton, Great Yarmouth, Skegness—attract a large summer holiday traffic, the tempo is still conducive to quiet sightseeing. The towns remain closely knit communities and dissent in religion and politics still flourishes. The recent growth of container and ferry links with Europe through Harwich and Felixstowe has, however, greatly increased heavy traffic.

To the s. lies **Essex,** a county described by Norden in 1594 as 'fatte, fruteful, and full of profitable things' and by George Gissing as 'one of those quiet corners of flat homely England, where man and beast seem on good terms with each other'. Except for the low lands on the Thames estuary and the E. coast, Essex is not flat, though nowhere hilly, and it includes some charming scenery of the rich, pastoral order. Some of its villages have scarcely grown since their Saxon foundation. The royal forest that once covered the county is now reduced to Epping Forest, but it has left its traces in the free use of massive timberwork in many churches.

Suffolk, the easternmost county of England, and **Norfolk** together form East Anglia and, usually with the addition of Essex, are known as the Eastern Counties. East Anglia is rich in fine churches, the characteristic features of which are their use of flushwork (i.e. a combination of flint and stone), their round towers (most numerous in Norfolk), and their elaborate and magnificent timber roofs and other woodwork. There are c. 50 thatched churches in Norfolk, c. 20 in Suffolk. Straw thatch lasts 30 years, reed thatch about 60. Norfolk, with the major portion of *Broadland* (Rte 51) and a long coast-line studded with summer-resorts, is more varied in scenery than Suffolk; but both counties are noted for the peaceful beauty of their inland landscapes, reflected in the paintings of Constable, Gainsborough, and the Norwich School. Agriculture is the chief industry in both, though printing is important; the poultry farms of Norfolk, and the manufacture of agricultural machinery in Suffolk may be noted. The herring fishing of Yarmouth and Lowestoft has suffered from foreign competition. Norfolk has been described as the sportsman's paradise, being the best-preserved county in England. In Suffolk is Newmarket, the headquarters of horse-racing.

Cambridgeshire since 1974 has incorporated Huntingdon and the Soke of Peterborough. The small, historic Cambridgeshire, rich in grain, includes within its borders the university of Cambridge and the cathedral of Ely. The level fens, including the *Isle of Ely* (once a separate administrative unit), cover its N. part; but the surface of S. Cambridgeshire is considerably varied, though its highest elevation is in the Gogmagog Hills. The county was the pioneer in the establishment of village colleges. The former **Huntingdonshire,** or **Hunts,** most famous as the birthplace and abode of Oliver Cromwell, is a small agricultural county the N.E. portion of which falls within the fen district. Its chief rivers are the sluggish Ouse and the Nene or Nen. Robin Hood figures in some later versions of his legend as Earl of Huntingdon, a title which in historical fact was borne by the Scottish kings from David I (1084–1153) until they lost their English possessions under Edward I. Since 1529 the title has been in the Hastings family. The Soke of Peterborough was transferred to Hunts from Northants in 1965.

Between the Wash and the Humber and thereby somewhat protected from long-distance through traffic, lies **Lincolnshire**, the second largest county in England, more noted for agricultural wealth, with acres of sugar-beet and potatoes, than for scenic beauty. The county was divided until 1974 into three 'Parts' or Ridings: *Lindsey*, the N. part, contains the chalk Lincoln Wolds and has a sandy coastline of 28 m.; *Kesteven*, in the s.w., presents a wooded, mid-England aspect; *Holland*, the s.e. quarter, is entirely fenland. The distinction between marshland and fen should be noted; the marsh, a coastline strip, was once under the sea and is chiefly grazing ground, the fen has mostly been reclaimed from swamp and makes splendid cornland. Lincolnshire was described by Henry VIII when the leaders of the 'Pilgrimage of Grace' were brought before him, as 'the most brute and beastly shire' in England. It is, however, the county of Sir Isaac Newton, John Wesley, and Alfred Tennyson. Though it contains but one large city, Lincoln, it is famous for its ecclesiastical architecture; churches of great beauty are to be found in nearly all the towns and in many villages, especially in Holland. During the Second World War the county was studded with airfields of Bomber Command, and Lincoln Cathedral served as a landmark for thousands of airmen returning to their bases. The formation in 1974 of the county of Humberside to the N. has removed the industrial Scunthorpe and the port of Grimsby from Lincs; but eventual completion of the Humber bridge may increase N.-s. traffic in the county.

47 LONDON TO COLCHESTER, IPSWICH, AND THE EAST COAST

ROAD, 124 m. A 12 (slow and congested to Chelmsford).— 16 m. *Gallows Corner.*— 31 m. **Chelmsford.**— 47 m. *Marks Tey.*— B 1408 serves (53 m.) **Colchester** (now avoided by A 12).— 70 m. **Ipswich.**— 78 m. *Woodbridge.*— 114 m. **Lowestoft.**— 124 m. **Great Yarmouth.**

Roads to Southend, Clacton, and Great Yarmouth should be avoided at week-ends; an alternative route to the E. coast is given in Rte 48.

RAILWAY to (68¾ m.) Ipswich, hourly, in 70–100 min.; more frequently to (29¾ m.) *Chelmsford*, in 35 min.; and to (51¾ m.) **Colchester** in c. 1 hr. At Ipswich a change is necessary for (117¾ m.) **Lowestoft**, viâ (79 m.) *Woodbridge.*— Branch lines run from Norwich (Rte 50) to **Yarmouth** (20½ m. in ½ hr) and *Lowestoft* (23½ m. in c. ¾ hr).

The old Roman road to East Anglia (A 118) traverses the East End of London, Ilford, and Romford. The main road, A 12 (Eastern Avenue) runs parallel to the N. through monotonous suburbs, to join A 118 at (16 m.) *Gallows Corner.*

A 127 here continues to Southend.—21½ m. *Prittlewell* has a fine 13C church and the refectory and prior's house of a 12C Cluniac Priory (now a museum; weekdays, 11–4.30 or 6, Sun 2.30–6). It is the 'south end' of this old village that has grown into the famous seaside resort of (22½ m.) **Southend-on-Sea** (Hotels), with 162,300 inhab. Standing at the mouth of the Thames, with a pier 1½ m. long (the longest in the world), Southend is largely patronized by excursionists from London. Its more select part is known as *Westcliff.*—AIRPORT, 3 m. N., for services to *Norwich, Channel Is., Le Touquet, Ostend, Rotterdam*, etc. (connecting bus to Rochford station).

To the E. of Southend the front extends past *Thorpe Bay* to (3½ m.) *Shoeburyness*, with a Norman church and an important gunnery school; to the w. is *Leigh-on-Sea*. Farther on is (2 m.) *Hadleigh*, with a Norman church and a castle, rebuilt 1359–70 as a residence of Edward III and the subject of a famous painting by Constable.— At *Foulness*, the flat deserted island to the N.E., is to be London's third international airport.

Rochford, 4 m. N. of Southend, has a Tudor mansion rebuilt by Anne Boleyn's father, and a fine brick church tower (c. 1500). *Great Stambridge* church, 1½ m. E., partly pre-Conquest, was the scene of the marriage of Governor Winthrop, of Boston, and Mary Forth (1605); and *Ashingdon*, 2 m. N., is the probable site of the battle of Assandun, in which Edmund Ironside was defeated by Canute (1016).

20 m. *Brentwood* (by-pass; Hotels) was the first staging-post on the old coaching road out of London, as the fine inn in the High St. testifies; opposite are some typical Essex weather-boarded houses. Brentwood School (1000 boys), founded in 1557, retains one block of 16C buildings. The Cathedral of the R.C. diocese of Brentwood was enlarged in 1974. The almost contiguous *Shenfield*, where the church contains a remarkable oak arcade, grew round the railway junction on another road to Southend (A 129; 21½ m.). This runs viâ (4½ m.) *Billericay* (p. 476), and (15½ m.) *Rayleigh*, with a good example of a Norman castle-mound (N.T.).

The brick towers and massive timberwork in the village churches are reminders of the absence of building-stone and of the great forest that covered Essex in the Middle Ages. 23¼ m. *Mountnessing* church has huge timber struts supporting the tower.—25 m. *Ingatestone* (by-pass). The church contains tombs of the Petre family, in whose fine 16C mansion, *Ingatestone Hall*, are displayed treasures from the Essex Record Office (open Tues–Sat & BH, in summer, 10–12.30, 2–4.30).—At (27 m.) *Margaretting*, the oak steeple and the 15C Jesse window are noteworthy.

31 m. **Chelmsford** (Hotel), the county town of Essex (58,100 inhab.), became the see of a bishop in 1914. *St Mary's*, now the *Cathedral*, was completed in 1424, but nearly the whole body of it collapsed in 1800 and had to be rebuilt. The chief features are the beautiful flintwork s. porch and the massive tower with its flèche spire (1749). In the N. wall of the chancel is a curious double or 'fan' arch (early 15C). The Mildmay monuments (1557–71) are interesting. The *Shire Hall*, by John Johnson, is an Ionic building of 1789–92.—Marconi developed his early wireless here and the town has a large electronics industry; it was the first town in England to be lit by electricity.

The Museum (weekdays 10–5, Sun from 2), in Oaklands Park at Moulsham, 1 m. S., contains Roman and other antiquities, and the Tunstill Collection of English drinking glasses.—Bus station, for all services, w. of the station.

FROM CHELMSFORD TO MALDON AND TO BURNHAM-ON-CROUCH—Beyond (5 m.) *Danbury*, which has a pleasant sandy common and a church with three 13C wooden effigies, the road forks. A 414 goes N.E. to (10 m.) *Maldon* (Hotels), a picturesque port and yachting resort (15,800 inhab.) on the Blackwater with important oyster-beds. The fine church (All Saints) has a triangular E.E. tower, surmounted by a hexagonal spire. Laurence Washington (see below), buried in the churchyard, is commemorated by a stained-glass window (1928). *St Mary's*, overlooking the attractive harbour, has remains of a 12C nave and a 17C brick tower. Attached to the 15C tower of *St Peter's* is the Plume Library. The *Moot Hall* has a quaint porch and tower. Maldon was the birthplace of the American Gen. Horatio Gates (1728–1806), who defeated the British under Burgoyne at Saratoga in 1777. Brihtnoth, ealdorman of Essex, was here defeated by the Northmen in 991, in a battle described in an extant Anglo-Saxon poem. *Beeleigh Abbey* (adm. Wed. 2–5), 1 m. w. by footpath, incorporates in the house (1536), the chapter house and dorter-vault of a Premonstratensian abbey (1180). At *Langford*, 1½ m. N.W. of Heybridge, beyond the river, is the only church in England with a w. apse. From *Heybridge* itself, with a massive church tower, a canal and footpath lead to (¾ m.) *Heybridge Basin*, frequented by yachtsmen and eel-boats.

From the Danbury fork B1010 leads S.E. At (9½ m.) *Purleigh* Laurence Washington, son of Laurence Washington of Brington and great-great-grandfather of George Washington, was rector in 1623–43. The church tower was

restored as a Washington memorial with contributions from America.—19 m.
Burnham-on-Crouch (4500 inhab.; Hotel) on the estuary of the Crouch, is a centre
for yachting and oyster breeding.—*Southminster*, 2½ m. N., has a large Perp.
church. *Bradwell-juxta-Mare*, 5 m. farther N., has a church with 14C details.
Bradwell Lodge (open April–Sept, Wed, Sat, Sun, & BH, 3–6; fee) is a 16C house
with an 'Adam' wing. On the coast, 2 m. farther N.E., is the chapel of *St Peter-on-the-
Wall*, erected by St Cedd in the 7C on the ruins of the Roman fort of Othona,
which was one of the castles of the 'Saxon Shore' (comp. pp. 452, 475). In striking
contrast is the nuclear power station.

33½ m. *Boreham House* (1728) shelters an institute of agricultural
engineering. To the l. of A 12 is (¾ m.) *Boreham New Hall*, now a convent, built by Henry VIII as the manor of Beaulieu.— 36½ m. *Hatfield
Peverel*, with a part-Norman church. *Terlin Place*, 2 m. N., the home of
Lord Rayleigh (1842–1919), was the scene of the experiments which
won him the Nobel Prize for Physics in 1904.— 39½ m. *Witham* (by-pass;
17,300 inhab.; Hotels) is an ancient town with a fine 13–15C church,
1 m. w., beyond the station. A plaque at 24 Newland St. marks the house
of Dorothy L. Sayers (1893–1957).—43 m. *Kelvedon* (by-pass) was the
birthplace of the Rev. C. H. Spurgeon (1834–92). The High St. has a wealth
of old houses from local weather-board to Georgian brick (more than
20 of the 17C).

B 1023 runs S.E. to the Blackwater. 3 m. *Tiptree* is famous for its jam.—7 m.
Tolleshunt D'Arcy, a pretty village, has a notable 16C moated hall, with bridge of
1585. At *Tolleshunt Major*, 2 m. w., by the church, is the brick gatehouse (16C)
and fortified wall of Beckingham Hall (house rebuilt in 18C).—9¼ m. *Tollesbury*
preserves some old sail-drying sheds.

At (47 m.) *Marks Tey* we are joined by A 120.—48 m. *Copford*
(Windmill) has a fine Norman *Church, 1 m. s., with an apse and a
magnificent series of mural paintings (c. 1150; restored) with Christ in
Majesty, the Raising of Jairus's daughter, signs of the Zodiac, and the
Virtues. The new Colchester by-pass swings A 12 to the left; B 1408
continues the Roman alinement into the city.

53 m. **COLCHESTER** (76,100 inhab.), a historic site and garrison
town as well as an agricultural centre, occupies a commanding ridge
above the Colne. Some two hundred Georgian houses and a greater
number still from earlier times show its abiding importance. The ancient
oyster fisheries on the Colne are famous, and Colchester nurseries (roses)
are noted.

Railway Station, 1 m. N. of the centre (bus). *St Botolph's*, s. of the town, a halt for
some trains to Clacton and Walton.
Hotels of historic character in the centre.
Post Office. Head St.—INFORMATION BUREAU, 4 Trinity St.
Theatre. *Repertory*, Albert Hall, High St.; *Mercury*, Balkerne Lane.
Bus Station, High St. (E. of Castle).

History. There was a Bronze Age settlement (c. 1100 B.C.) here, sited on the
ancient ridgeway, and the strategic placing of the site led Cunobelin (Cymbeline)
ruler of the Trinobantes to move his capital here in A.D. 40, from Verulamium
(St Alban's). The Emperor Claudius captured it in A.D. 44, and established the
Colonia Camulodunum, the first Roman colony in Britain. This was stormed in
A.D. 62 by Boadicea, queen of the Iceni, and at her defeat was re-established as a
Roman garrison. Tradition has it that here the Emperor Constantine was born.
On the departure of the Romans, it became the Saxon stronghold of *Colneceaster*.
William I built the castle, the keep of which is the largest in Europe. The ensuing
period of importance is attested by the seven surviving medieval churches within
the walls, and the remains of three abbeys. In the 14–17C the town was a centre of

the cloth trade, its prosperity boosted by the influx of Flemish and Dutch weavers as refugees in 1570. In the Civil War, the town was staunchly Royalist, holding out against Fairfax's siege for eleven weeks.—There is an 'Oyster Feast' to inaugurate the new season every year (20 October).

The *City Walls still form a rectangle nearly 2 m. in extent, and are best seen on the w. side.

The wall, probably begun in the time of Vespasian, though afterwards strengthened and extended, seems to have been over 20 ft high, and some parts are still over 10 ft. The w. section includes the ruined *Balkerne Gate*, most of which lies beneath the old Hole-in-the-Wall inn. *St Mary-at-the-Wall* retains only the tower of the church slighted by Cromwell. Near by is the obtrusive *Water Tower*, the dominant feature of the Colchester skyline, built in 1882, and affectionately known to the inhabitants as 'Jumbo'.

We turn N. by Head St., past the former King's Head Inn where the Royalists surrendered in 1648, to meet North Hill (a street of old houses ascending from the station) near the civic church of *St Peter*. Partly classicised in 1758, it retains 13C ironwork on its (blocked) s. door and unusual 16C brasses. The broad HIGH STREET runs W. and E. on the line of the ancient ridgeway and the Roman road. To the left is the *Town Hall* (1898–1902) by John Belcher; to the right the fine 15C *Red Lion Hotel*. On the left, farther on, is the entrance to the park surrounding the *Castle*, a Norman building constructed in part of Roman materials (adm. 10–5, Sun in summer from 2.30; visits to Roman vaults and 18C prisons 8 times daily; fee).

The massive keep (151½ ft by 110 ft), with walls 12 ft thick, is half as big again as the White Tower at London but lost its upper story in 1683. Built on the platform of a Roman temple, it contains a *Museum* notable for a fine collection of late Celtic and *Roman antiquities. The Castle Park includes a section of the Roman wall and affords a pleasant view of the Colne valley. An obelisk on the N. side of the castle marks the spot where Lucas and Lisle, the Royalist defenders of the town, were shot by Fairfax in 1648. Adjoining the park is *Holly Trees*, a mansion of 1718, now containing a good collection of 'bygones'. A *Natural History Museum* occupies an old church opposite (adm. to both as for Castle).

High St. now passes between the *Minories Art Gallery*, with the Batte-Lay bequest, and the pargeted *East Lodge*; its continuation, East Hill, descends past *St James's* (with a good monument of 1727) to the Colne. *Siege House*, occupied by Fairfax as headquarters, and the *Rose and Crown* inn are the most striking of the timbered buildings beyond the bridge.

Priory St., along the walls (or Queen St. opposite the Castle), leads to the ruined church of *St Botolph's Priory* (closed Sun morn.), an Augustinian foundation of c. 1100 built mainly of Roman brick. The arcaded w. front has three portals, the fine one in the centre receding in five orders. By Stanwell St. we reach St. John's Green, with *St John's Abbey Gateway* (Perp., c. 1415; restored), the stately relic of a Benedictine house.—We may now regain the centre of the town, crossing the line of wall by Scheregate steps. To the right is *Holy Trinity Church* (Trinity St.), with a Saxon tower built of Roman brick, and a Saxon doorway. A plaque marks the house, opposite, where John Wilbye, the composer, died in 1638; he lived for many years at Hengrave Hall (p. 458). *Tymperleys*, a fine half-timbered mansion next door, was the birthplace of Dr William Gilberd (1544–1603), 'father of electrical science'. In West Stockwell St., N. of High St., are the disused Dec. church of *St Martin* and many fine old houses, including one occupied by Ann and Jane Taylor, verse writers for children in the early 19C. *St Helen's Chapel* (no adm.), a little to the E., dates from c. 1290.

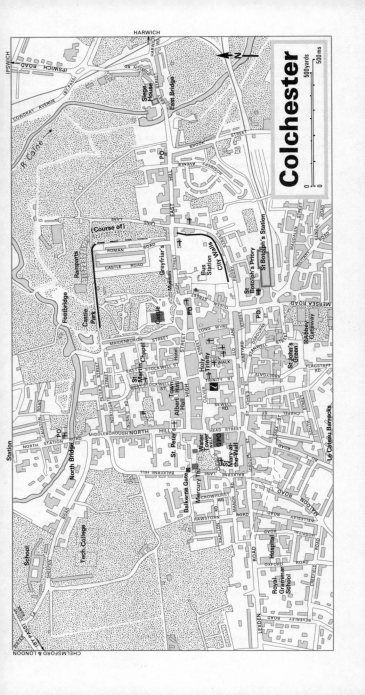

Colchester

HARWICH

N

500 yards
500 ms

IPSWICH ROAD

COWDRAY AVENUE

HARWICH RD

R. Colne

Siege House

East Bridge

PO

BROOK STREET

Ramparts

Course of)

ROMAN ROAD

CASTLE ROAD

EAST HILL

ROSEBERY AVENUE

Footbridge

Castle Park

Greyfriar's

Museum

Castle

Bus Station

City Walls

St Botolph's Priory

St Botolph's Station

MERSEA ROAD

MAIDENBURGH STREET

MAGDALEN STREET

KENDAL ROAD

MILITARY

Station

NORTH STATION ROAD

PO

North Bridge

MIDDLEBOROUGH NORTH HILL

St. Peter's

St. Martin

Chapel

St. Martin's

EAST STOCKWELL ST

STOCKWELL ST

Town Hall

Albert Hall

HIGH STREET

Holy Trinity

TRINITY ST

LONG WYRE STREET

QUEEN STREET

SHORT WYRE ST

EALD LANE

SIR ISAACS WALK

CULVER ST

VINEYARD ST

STANWELL ST

OSBORNE ST

ST JOHN'S

St John's Green

FLAGSTAFF RD

Abbey Gateway

CHAPEL RD

Le Cateau Barracks

SEWELL RD

HEAD STREET

GPO

Water Tower

St Mary's-at-the-Wall

Mercury Theatre

Balkerne Gate

BALKERNE HILL

BALKERNE LANE

CROWHURST RD

MANOR ROAD

PAPILLON RD

RAWSTORN ROAD

MALDON ROAD

WELLESLEY ROAD

OXFORD ROAD

HOSPITAL ROAD

CREFFIELD ROAD

Hospital

Royal Grammar School

BEVERLEY ROAD

LEXDEN

ST PETER'S STREET

PORTLAND RD

MUNN

School

Tech College

LEXDEN ROAD

NORTH STATION ROAD

ALBION ROAD

BY PASS

CHELMSFORD & LONDON

ESSEX

QUEEN ST

About 2 m. w., beyond the Royal Grammar School, is *Lexden*, possibly the site of Cymbeline's capital. The earthworks (of which considerable remains are still visible) effectually bottle up the peninsula between the Colne and the small stream known as the Roman River.—The *University of Essex*, founded in 1962, is in *Wivenhoe Park*, 2 m. s.e.—About 6 m. s.w. off B 1022, which passes Stanway Hall (Zoo), and 3 m. from Tiptree, is *Layer Marney Hall* (c. 1525; open April–Sept, Sun, Thurs; also Tues in July–Aug; 2–6, BH, 11–6; fee), the enormous entrance tower of which is interesting as "an example of the introduction of Renaissance ornament in the structure of an otherwise Gothic building". The adjoining church contains the *Tombs (c. 1525–30) of the Lords Marney, the first purely Renaissance tombs in England.

On the n.e. bank of the Colne estuary, below Colchester, are (4½ m.) *Wivenhoe*, with notable parget work in a street s. of the church, and, (10 m.) *Brightlingsea* with a good church (1 m. inland). This area was shaken in 1884 by the only serious earthquake in Britain in modern times. Opposite Brightlingsea, between the estuaries of the Colne and Blackwater, is the island of *Mersea*, with the yachting-resort of *West Mersea*, 9 m. from Colchester by B 1025. All these places are yacht-building centres. *Bourne Mill* (1591), with a wild extravaganza of gables, lies on B 1025, and a little farther on is *Cannock Mill*, still in working trim.

From Colchester to Clacton and Walton. Hourly trains to both. A 133 leads e. to (10 m.) *Weeley* and then s.e. to (16 m.) **Clacton-on-Sea** (many Hotels), one of the most crowded seaside resorts (37,900 inhab.) in Essex. To the e. and w. are the adjoining resorts of *Holland-on-Sea* and *Jaywick*, with a large holiday camp. About 4½ m. w. is the pleasant old village of *St Osyth*, where Osyth, Queen of the East Saxons, was murdered by the Danes c. 870. A *Priory (adm. May–Sept, daily 10–6; fee) on the site, preserves a fine 15C gatehouse, with a collection of paintings, and other monastic buildings with a pleasant garden. On the creek below are a tide-mill (restored) and a good boating-lake.

From Weeley (see above) B 1033 leads viâ *Thorpe-le-Soken* to (17 m.) Frinton and (17½ m.) Walton. Lord Byng (1862–1935) died at Thorpe Hall and is buried in *Beaumont* church, 1½ m. n.—**Frinton-on-Sea** (Hotels) is a fashionable and quiet bathing and golfing resort (with Walton 12,400 inhab.).—**Walton-on-the-Naze** (Hotel) a homely seaside and golfing resort, with a long pier (damaged 1978), lies near the headland called the *Naze*. Oysters are cultivated in the muddy creeks of Walton Backwaters, to the n.w.

From Colchester to Haverhill, 28½ m. From Lexden (see above), A 604 ascends the pleasant *Colne Valley viâ (10 m.) *Earls Colne* to (13½ m.) *Halstead*, p. 476.—16 m. *Sible Hedingham* church (l.) is the probable burial-place of Sir John Hawkwood (d. 1394 in Florence), the condottiere who was born here.—17 m. *Castle Hedingham*, to the right of our road, has a beautiful late-Norman church and a massive Norman keep (c. 1100) still used as a residence (adm. May–Sept, Tues, Thurs & Sat 2–6, also BH, 10–6; fee).—At (25½ m.) *Baythorn End* we join the road from Clare to Haverhill (see Rte 48).

From Colchester to Harwich, 19 m. (A 137, B 1352).—9¼ m. *Manningtree*, on the estuary of the Stour, is a gateway to the 'Constable Country'.—At (10 m.) *Mistley* the 'Towers' are a fragment of the only church in England built by Robt. Adam (1776).—17½ m. *Dovercourt* (Hotel), the bracing s.w. suburb of Harwich, is frequented for sea-bathing.—19 m. **Harwich** (Hotel) is a quiet old seaport and naval base (14,900 inhab.) on the broad estuary of the Stour and Orwell, with many 16–18C houses, among them, the red-brick *Guildhall* (1769), with an eccentric Gothick door. On the Green is the Naval Treadmill Crane (17C). The Low Lighthouse, in 'Chinese style', contrasts with the resplendent white brick High Lighthouse (1818). Nelson put up on several occasions at the Three Cups inn. Capt. Jones of the 'Mayflower' was married in Harwich and lived in King's Head St. The regular packet-boat service to the Hook of Holland succeeds that to Hellevoetsluis established at the Restoration; now equipped also as a car-carrier, it starts from *Parkeston Quay*, 1 m. n. of Dovercourt. Car ferries ply also to Ostend in summer, and steamers all the year to Esbjerg.

Ferry steamers (no cars) ply from Harwich Quay to *Felixstowe Pier* (2 m. from Felixstowe).—Through boat trains to London and the North.

A 12 leads N.E. from Colchester and at (59½ m.) *Stratford St Mary*, we enter East Anglia; the Perp. church with excellent flushwork, is an appropriate introduction to this area. The *North porch has an interesting window, and inside is a fine roof and 15C stained glass. There are some good 16C houses in the village. This pleasant pastoral and wooded region watered by the winding Stour is the CONSTABLE COUNTRY.

John Constable (1776–1837) was born at *East Bergholt* in Suffolk (house no longer extant), 3 m. N.E., and he has immortalized the whole district in his paintings. "I associate", he writes, "my careless boyhood with all that lies on the banks of the Stour; those scenes made me a painter." Among his favourite subjects were the water-mills of *Stratford St Mary*; *Flatford Mill (used as a field study centre), 1½ m. s. of Bergholt (presented, with *Willy Lott's Cottage*, to the nation in 1928); and the fine 15C tower of *Stoke-by-Nayland* church, 4 m. w. of Stratford. **Dedham** (Hotels), a dignified village, 1½ m. E. of Stratford, attracted both Constable and Sir Alfred Munnings, who lived from 1919 and died at *Castle House* (adm. mid-May–Oct, Wed, Sun & BH, also Thurs & Sat in Aug, 2–5; fee). The fine church was built in 1492–1520 and many houses of the 16–18C survive.—According to local legend, the church (15–16C) of East Bergholt was deprived of its steeple by the devil, and so its bells are hung in a timber cage (1531) in the churchyard.—*Nayland*, on the Stour, 1½ m. s. of Stoke, preserves some painted panels from a 15C rood-screen.

Little Wenham Hall, 1½ m. N. of (64 m.) *Capel St Mary*, is a very early example of Flemish brickwork (c. 1250).—At (67½ m.) *Washbrook* and *Copdock*, both with good churches, the Roman road (A 1100) swings N. towards *Venta Icenorum* (see p. 469). A 12 drops into the valley of the Orwell.

70 m. **IPSWICH**, the county town (122,800 inhab.) of E. Suffolk, stands at the head of the estuary. A thriving port and an important farming centre, with manufactures of agricultural and other machinery and printing works, it has too often torn down its past without putting much of worth in its place.

Hotels in the centre.
Post Office, Cornhill.
Local Buses from Tower Ramparts to the suburbs.—COUNTRY BUSES from Old Cattle Market (s. of Butter Market).
Theatre. *Wolsey,* Civic Drive.
History. At the ford beyond which the Gipping becomes navigable as the Orwell a prehistoric settlement grew up. It received its name *Gipeswic* from the Anglo-Saxons, was an important burgh at Domesday, and flourished for centuries as an agricultural centre and port. Chaucer's Merchant "wolde the see were kept for anything Bitwixe Middelburgh and Orewelle". It has more medieval parish churches than any English town of comparable size. Cardinal Wolsey (1475?–1530), the son of a butcher, was born at Ipswich. From the peak of its prosperity in the 18C it remained a busy market town, with an extensive port that handled much North Sea traffic and the great Thames barges.

The scale of Ipswich has been much altered by the building of a new Civic Centre to the w. of the old central square, CORNHILL, which contains the *Post Office* and the old *Town Hall* (1867), and closing to traffic the central shopping street. Tavern St. runs E. to the old *Great White Horse Hotel* (leaden sign), in which occurred Mr Pickwick's remarkable adventure with the lady in yellow curl-papers. Northgate St., with old houses and a 15C gateway, leads N. past the *Library* (important Suffolk collections) to St Margaret's Plain. To the E. (r.) is the noble flint church of *St Margaret*, with a double hammer-beam roof and a 15C clerestory.

In a pleasant park adjoining stands *Christchurch Mansion* (weekdays 10–5; Sun 2.30–4.30), built in 1548–50 and altered after a fire in 1675, and now housing an abundant collection (36 rooms) of local antiquities, paintings, and memorials of Edw. Fitzgerald and Thos. Woolner. Especially notable are the Pownder brass of 1525 (from St Mary-at-Quay; see below), part of a Tournai marble font, an early Tudor wing (re-erected here), and the Wingfield Room, with 16C panelling from an inn in Tacket St., once the house of Sir Anthony Wingfield (d. 1552).

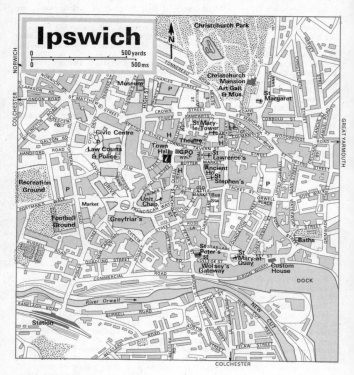

The Wolsey Memorial Art Gallery, added in 1931, contains works by Gainsborough and Constable.

From Northgate St. Oak Lane leads to the rebuilt civic church of *St Mary-le-Tower*, with a conspicuous spire (176 ft). Turning s., we see in Dial La., s. of Tavern St., the handsome tower of *St Lawrence's*. In Butter Market, hard by, is *Sparrowe's* or the *Ancient House* (1567), with its pargeted façade, a well-preserved specimen of Charles II ornamentation. It is occupied by a bookseller. Continuing s. past *St Stephen's*, we reach the Old Cattle Market. To the w., off Friars St., is the attractive *Unitarian Chapel* of 1699. St Nicholas St. and St Peter

St. lead to *St Peter's Church*, which contains a font of Tournai marble (c. 1100) and the Knapp brass of 1604.

Hard by stands *Wolsey's Gateway*, the sole relic of a college of secular canons built by Cardinal Wolsey in 1536, one of "those twins of learning, Ipswich and Oxford," that "fell with him, Unwilling to outlive the good that did it" ('Henry VIII', iv. 2). College St. leads E. past *St Mary-at-Quay*, now Boys' Brigade headquarters, and the fine classical *Custom House* (1844) by J. M. Clarke facing *Common Quay*. We continue to Fore St., where (r.) are the *Neptune Inn* and Lord's coal wharf (both 17C). In St Clement's Lane, to the W., Sam Weller saw Job Trotter coming out of the green garden gate. *St Clement's* has a slender Perp. tower. From the N. end of Fore St. Orwell Place leads into Tacket St. Here the Salvation Army Citadel occupies the site of the theatre where David Garrick made his début as an actor proper in 1741, under the name of Lyddal, and in the character of Aboan (in Southerne's 'Oroonoko'). A kiln discovered in 1961 in the near-by Cox Lane is believed to have manufactured the late-Saxon pottery known as 'Thetford ware'.

In High St., ¼ m. N.W. of Cornhill, is the *Ipswich Museum* (10–5, Sun 2.30–4), with important collections illustrating local geology and fauna, the prehistoric and Roman periods in East Anglia (including replicas of the Sutton Hoo and Mildenhall treasures now in the British Museum), etc. Adjacent is a small Art Gallery.

At *Holbrook*, 6 m. S., is the Royal Hospital School, transferred from Greenwich in 1933, at which c. 1100 sons of sailors and marines are trained for the Navy. On the way are seen the tall *Freston Tower* (c. 1640), and *Woolverstone Hall*, a boys' boarding school, beyond which, on the bank of the Orwell, 7 m. from Ipswich, is *Pin Mill*, a favourite mooring for yachts.

A 45 leads S.E. from Ipswich across *Nacton Heath*; a pleasant by-road, keeping nearer the Orwell, passes Nacton church; *Orwell Park*, the home of Adm. Vernon ('Old Grog'), now a school; and *Broke Hall*, the home of Adm. Sir Philip Broke (1776–1841), commander of the 'Shannon' in her memorable encounter with the 'Chesapeake' (1813).—11½ m. **Felixstowe** (Hotels), a pleasant and fashionable seaside resort (18,900 inhab.), is situated on a cliff between the Orwell and the Deben. It has an esplanade 2½ m. long and two golf links. This was the starting-point of the romantic swim described in Meredith's 'Lord Ormont and his Aminta'. Lord Allenby (1861–1936) lived at Felixstowe House.—About 2 m. S. is Felixstowe Dock with an oil-tanker terminal and container port, and a direct car-ferry service to Rotterdam; also a ferry to Harwich. Another passenger ferry crosses the Deben, 2 m. N., to *Bawdsey*, site of the first radar station (1936).

FROM IPSWICH TO SUDBURY, 21 m. (A 1071).—5 m. *Hintlesham Hall*, where a festival of music and the arts is held in summer.—10 m. **Hadleigh**, a well-built old centre of the woollen trade (5100 inhab.), has a large church (late 14C). The fine Deanery Tower (1495) was the gatehouse to the palace of Abp. Pykenham. The 15C Guildhall is open on Thurs 10–4 or 6. Thos. Woolner (1825–9⁊ sculptor and pre-Raphaelite, was born here. The Oxford Movement was founded by the rector of Hadleigh, Hugh Rose, in 1833. *Kersey*, 1½ m. N.W., one of the Suffolk weaving villages, gave its name to 'Kerseymere' ('Cashmere'). The pretty street with many fine timbered houses, dips down to a ford across the Brett. The *Church has a lovely flushwork s. porch and fine hammerbeam roof, and there are also remains of a 13C Augustinian priory. *Lindsey*, 1 m. farther w., another weaving village, gave its name to the cloth 'Linsey-woolsey'. The 14C church has a tie-beam roof, and wall-paintings. *St James's Chapel*, ¼ m. s., dates from the 13C, and has tiny lancet windows. Close by are the remains of a motte and bailey castle.—15½ m. *Boxford*, with pretty timbered houses, and a late-Dec. wooden porch to the church.—21 m. *Sudbury*, see Rte 53.

FROM IPSWICH TO NORWICH, 43 m. Leaving A 45 at (4 m.) *Claydon* (p. 458), we continue on A 140, following the line of the 'Pye Road', the Roman road from Colchester to Caistor St Edmund, to (10½ m.) *Earl Stonham* (see Rte 48). On the former airfield of *Mendlesham* (14½ m.; l.), is a memorial to the men of the U.S.A.A.F. (34th group). The Perp. church has a splendid flushwork tower. It contains a good collection of 15–17C armour, a Jacobean font cover and pulpit, and a brass to John Knyvet (1417). Hakluyt was the rector of *Wetheringsett* (¾ m. E. of our road) from 1590 till his death. The village has good timbered cottages.—At (19½ m.) *Yaxley* church is a 'sexton's wheel', used to determine voluntary fast days, one of only two in England (comp. below). Eye, 1½ m. E., is an attractive little town with a 16C timber-framed Guildhall. The church, with notable flintwork, particularly in the *Tower (101 ft), preserves a richly painted rood-screen (c. 1500). To the w. are the remains of the Norman castle of the Malets.—Crossing the Waveney, we enter Norfolk at (23 m.) **Scole**, which was an important staging-post, standing midway between Ipswich and Norwich at the crossing of the Great Yarmouth and Bury St Edmunds roads. The 'Scole Inn', correctly the White Hart, is a stately building of 1655 with Dutch gables. Remains of a Roman posting station (*Villa Faustina*), have been found at Scole House, and at Waterloo, on the Waveney. **Diss** (Hotel), 2½ m. w., is an attractive town built around a 6-acre mere. Among notable buildings are the Dolphin Inn and Saracen's Head, timbered with overhangs, and the Victorian 'Shambles'. The church has a tall flushwork tower with processional arches at its base. John Skelton (1460–1529), tutor to Henry VIII was given the living here in 1498, and held it until his death.

The *Bressingham Steam Museum*, 3 m. w. on A 1066, has a superb collection of locomotives, including the Royal Scot, and traction engines (adm. summer Thurs & Sun 1.30–5.30 or 6). *South Lopham*, 1½ m. farther w., has a good Norman tower. *Hoxne* (pron. 'Hoxen'), 2 m. E. of Diss is a pretty village, with Abbey Farm (to the s.), the traditional site of the death of St Edmund (for many years the patron saint of England), killed fighting the Danes in 869. The church has a fine tower and *Wall-paintings of St Christopher, the Seven Deadly Sins, and the Seven Works of Mercy.

At (28½ m.; l.) *Tivetshall St Margaret*, the church has a large Royal Arms (Elizabeth I). *Pulham*, c. 2 m. S.E., was the airship base to which the R34 returned after its double Atlantic crossing in 1919.—32 m. *Long Stratton* church contains a 'sexton's wheel' (comp. above), and a Jacobean font cover and pulpit. **Shelton* church, 2 m. E., is a fine Perp. building (1480) by Sir Ralph Shelton, with good brick-work. In the graceful interior is a well-carved Royal Arms (William III).—34 m. (l.) *Tasburgh*, a stronghold of the *Iceni*, has an iron age settlement and hill fort.— The bridge over the Tas at (35½ m.) *Newton Flotman* is part-medieval. *Saxlingham Nethergate* church, 1½ m. E., has fine 13C glass.—*Venta Icenorum* (p. 469), lies ½ m. N. of (39 m.) *Dunstan.*—43 m. *Norwich*, see Rte 50.

From Ipswich to *Bury* and *Newmarket*, see p. 458.

76 m. *Martlesham Heath*, the site of a famous pre-war airfield used for testing early radar systems at Bawdsey, is now destined as an industrial area and township. At the bottom of Martlesham Hill the Red Lion has a figure-head, captured from a Dutch ship at the battle of Sole Bay in 1672 (comp. p. 449). A by-pass avoiding Woodbridge diverges on the left. The old road, narrow and congested, descends to (78 m.) **Woodbridge** (Hotels), a charming old town on the Deben. The fine Perp. church has excellent flushwork and a famous peal of bells in the tower (108 ft). Within are a 15C font and Seckford monuments (Seckford Hall, s.w. of the town, is now a hotel). The Shire Hall (1575) and the Crown Hotel are among notable old buildings; and the walk along the Deben, with its yachts and old tide-mill, is pleasant. In New St. is a curious 18C steelyard, like that at Soham. To the left of the main road, farther on, is *Little Grange*, where Edward Fitzgerald (1809–93) spent his declining years.

Fitzgerald was born at *Bredfield House*, near *Boulge* (2½ m. N.), where he is buried. A thatched cottage occupied by him in 1838–53 still exists at Boulge, and though the rose-bush brought from Omar Khayyam's tomb in Persia and planted over his grave is dead its descendants still bloom here.—*Grundisburgh*, 3 m. w., is a village grouped round a green through which flows a small stream. Within the church beautiful *Roofs, double hammerbeam with a multitude of angels, cover the nave, s. aisle and chapel. There is also a 13C wall-painting of St Christopher.

From WOODBRIDGE TO ORFORD, 12 m. From Melton, 1 m. N.W. of Woodbridge, B 1084 crosses the Deben and traverses heathy country with very fine oak-woods. To the right (on B 1083, the Bawdsey road), beyond the golf course, is *Sutton Hoo* (no adm.), where a tumulus, excavated in 1938–39, yielded the remarkable ship-burial of a Saxon chieftain (c. 650–670) of the Wuffingas, who ruled E. Anglia at that time. The gold, silver, and enamel treasures from it are now in the British Museum.—8 m. *Butley* retains the notable 14C gatehouse (now a residence) of an

Augustinian priory, 1 m. s.; and in the Butley river oysters are bred.—12 m. **Orford** (Hotel) is a picturesque decayed seaport, with a massive castle keep (adm. daily, Sun from 2 in winter), built by Henry II in 1165–66, which, with its three towers, forms a polygon of 18 sides. The ruined chancel of the church has a double row of Norman columns. The 13C King's Head Inn has a noted restaurant. The river Ore here runs nearly parallel with the coast for 10 m., separated from the sea by a narrow shingly spit. At Orfordness in 1935 Robert Watson-Watt conducted the practical experiments that gave birth to radar defence.—Commanding a good view of the Alde estuary, 4½ m. N. of Orford, is the lonely church of *Iken*, whose elaborate thatched roof succumbed to a recent fire.

80 m. *Ufford* church (13C) has a superb tabernacled *Font-cover, and good benches with poppy heads and deep carving.—82 m. *Wickham Market*, where the Dec. church with a tall spire stands to one side of the pleasant little market square.—86 m. *Little Glemham* church has a Norman doorway. Just beyond, the road skirts the park of *Glemham Hall* (open April–Sept, Wed, Sun & BH, 2–6; fee), an 18C house on Elizabethan foundations, which contains good pictures, panelling and Queen Anne furniture, and has a fine garden.—91 m. *Saxmundham* is a small market town with a Dec. church (16C Flemish stained glass).

Beyond (95 m.) *Yoxford*, a road on the right leads viâ *Westleton* to (5½ m. E.) *Dunwich*, now merely an attractive coast-village, but once an important seaport, before the sea swept it away. It was the seat of the first East Anglian bishopric, established c. 630. Little is left of its ancient glory but the remains of a Franciscan friary (13C) and the ruins of a 12C chapel near the present church, which includes materials from the last surviving old church. Farther on A 144 diverges l. for Halesworth (see below), Bungay, and Norwich.—100½ m. *Blythburgh*, on the tidal Blyth, was once a bustling port, before the retreat of the sea and the silting up of the river closed it. It lies beneath one of the finest *Churches in Suffolk (1442–73), containing original woodwork and a painted tie-beam roof with fine angels, used as targets by William Dowsing's infamous crew of iconoclasts, but luckily fairly unharmed.—**Southwold** (2000 inhab.; Hotels), 4½ m. E., is a charming old town, seaside resort, and North Sea fishing port, with pretty colourful houses. Its harbour at the mouth of the Blyth is backed by open heathland, with golf course. The great Perp. *Church has a notable rood-screen, a panelled roof, and canopied stalls.

Walberswick, a village frequented by painters, with a half-ruined church (as large as Blythburgh and Southwold), is 1 m. s. across the ferry (no cars).—Excursions may be made from Southwold to *Dunwich* (4 m. by ferry and coast, 6 m. across the heath) and *Covehithe* (4½ m. N.; fine ruined church).—Offshore, in 1672, was fought the indecisive battle of *Solebay* (i.e. Southwold Bay) between the Dutch fleet under De Ruyter and the English and French under the Duke of York (James II).

The road running w. from Blythburgh leads viâ (2 m.) *Wenhaston*, with an interesting panel picture of the 'Last Judgment' in its church, dating from c. 1480, to (5½ m.) *Halesworth* (Hotel), where the Perp. church contains good 15C brasses. About 4 m. farther s.w. is *Heveningham Hall* (adm. Apr–Sept, Wed, Thurs, Sat, Sun & BH, 2–6; fee), built in 1777–80 by Taylor, decorated by Wyatt, and substantially unaltered. It was sold by the Vanneck family to the Nation in 1970. The park was laid out by 'Capability' Brown; the later formal garden has a crinkle-crankle wall.

A 12 now skirts the fine park of *Henham*, traverses the large villages of (106½ m.) *Wrentham* and (110 m.) *Kessingland*, and passes the church of *Pakefield*, rebuilt and rethatched after bomb-damage in 1941.

114 m. **LOWESTOFT**, the most easterly town in England is a favourite seaside resort, with a sandy beach, and a flourishing fishing-port and ship-building centre (52,200 inhab.).

Hotels on or near the S. Esplanade, and by Station.
Post Office, London Rd.—INFORMATION BUREAU, Esplanade.
Buses through the town from Pakefield (s.) to the Station and North Parade or Yarmouth Rd.; also from Gordon Rd (off High St.) to *Southwold, Yarmouth, Norwich, Beccles, Ipswich, Oulton Broad, Somerleyton*, etc.—STEAMERS in summer to Yarmouth; also on the Yare and Bure (for the Broads).
Theatres. *Arcadia* (repertory), London Road South; *South Pier Pavilion; Sparrow's Nest*, North Lowestoft.—GOLF COURSE at Pakefield (s.).—TENNIS COURTS at Kensington Gardens, on the Denes, at Normanston Park, and Oulton Broad; junior tournament in late August.

In the centre of the town are the railway station and the harbour, the latter protected by the *South Pier*. Suffolk Rd., opposite the station, leads to the *Fish Market* and the trawler basin. A swing-bridge beside the house of the Royal Norfolk & Suffolk Club leads to the s. part of the town, with the long *Esplanade* (miniature golf course; bathing stations, etc.) and the *Claremont Pier.*—In the old town to the N. (where a few old houses preserve their bright red pantiles) is the High St., whence several narrow lanes, called *Scores*, lead down towards the shore. Farther on beyond *Lowestoft Ness*, the dreary easternmost point of England (long. 1° 45′ E.), is the *North Light* (open weekday aft.); adjoining are *Bellevue Park*, with the Royal Naval Patrol Service memorial, and Sparrow's Nest (see above). The sandy strip bordering the N. beach is called the *Denes*.—The parish church of *St Margaret*, at the N.W. edge of the town, reached from High St. by B 1074 (the Somerleyton road), is a spacious 15C flint building, with an older tower.

The inner harbour, known as *Lake Lothing*, communicates by Mutford Lock with (1½ m.) **Oulton Broad** (Hotel), a favourite centre for boating and fishing with a yacht station. *Oulton* church, with a Norman chancel-arch, is 1m. N. of the Broad. George Borrow (1803–81) wrote most of his books at his home on Oulton Broad, but the house has been pulled down.

Blundeston, 3¼ m. N.W., is the 'Blunderstone' of 'David Copperfield', and was often visited by the poet Gray. The round-towered church has been restored as a Dickens memorial. At *Lound*, 1½ m. farther N., the Perp. screen is surmounted by a rood by Sir Ninian Comper (1914). From Blundeston we may go w. to (3 m.) *Somerleyton Hall* (open Easter–Sept, Sun, Thurs & BH, also Tues & Wed in July and Aug, 2–6; fee), built for the Victorian railway entrepreneur Sir Morton Peto by Thomas in 1844, around an old 17C manor. It has fine panelling and carving, and gardens (maze). The church and village were built at about the same time in an amusing eclectic style. Beyond are (4 m.) *Herringfleet*, with a part-Norman church and 17C hall and barn, and (6 m.) *Fritton Decoy* (see p. 452).

FROM LOWESTOFT TO SCOLE, 30 m. A 146 crosses the Waveney between Lake Lothing and Oulton Broad.—9¼ m. **Beccles** (Hotels), a town (8000 inhab.) on the Waveney (sailing and angling) noted for its crayfish, has a fine Perp. church with a detached tower (92 ft high). Chateaubriand, in 1794–97, lived at Beccles as an émigré and fell in love with the parson's daughter of Bungay. At *Gillingham*, 1½ m. N.W., is a pure early-Norman church divided into five parts—Galilee, towerspace, nave, chancel, and apse.—14½ m. **Bungay** (4000 inhab.; Hotel), with an octagonal market cross and two interesting churches (pre-Norman round tower), has a ruined Norman *Castle*, with remains of a keep and fore-building, built by Hugh Bigod, Earl of Norfolk, c. 1165, and a twin-towered gatehouse added in 1294.—About 2¼ m. S.E. of (19½ m.) *Homersfield*, at *South Elmham*, are the pre-Norman ruins called the Old Minster, claiming erroneously to mark the site of the E. Anglian cathedral of Elmham (comp. N. Elmham, p. 471). On a by-road that leads back thence to the little town of (22½ m.) *Harleston* (Hotels) is *Mendham*, birthplace of Sir Alfred Munnings (1878–1959). At *Wingfield*, 5 m. s.w. of Harleston, the *Church (1362) contains fine monuments of the Wingfield and De la Pole families, the owners of Wingfield Castle (1384), a fortified manor-house, now in ruins. *Fressingfield*, 4 m. s. of Harleston, has the 16C Fox & Goose inn, fine *Bench-ends, roof, and a Willis organ (from the Chapel Royal of the Savoy) in the church, and the grave of Abp. Sancroft (1616–93).— 30 m. *Scole*, see p. 448.

The Yarmouth road runs N. to (121½ m.) the seaside resort of *Gorleston* (Hotel), well situated on a low cliff at the mouth of the Yare facing the Fish Wharf of Yarmouth, of which town it is now part. The sands are broad and clean and the large Dec. church, inland, has a fine 15C font. From South Town, where Cotman lived as a drawing-master in 1812–23, we cross the Yare.

124 m. **GREAT YARMOUTH** (50,200 inhab.) is the chief town and the most popular holiday resort on the Norfolk coast. It lies on a peninsula between the sea and the Yare, N. of the narrow mouth through which the combined waters of that stream, the Bure and the Waveney enter the sea. The old town was severely damaged by German bombs in 1941–42, but a large number of old houses survived—often in unexpected quarters, where well-built flint cottages and 18C town houses stand side by side with banal Victorian terraces.

Railway Station. *Vauxhall*, on the N. side of Breydon Water.
Hotels near the sea (Marine Parade).
Post Office, Regent St.—INFORMATION BUREAU, Marine Parade.
Buses from the Town Centre (Regal Cinema) to the *Fish Quay*, *Gorleston*, *Caister*, etc.—From Wellington St. (behind Marine Parade) to *Lowestoft*; *Norwich* viâ Acle or Wroxham; *Stalham* viâ Ormesby and Potter Heigham; etc.
Amusements. *Britannia Pier*, with theatre, ballroom, and restaurant; *Marina* concerts, etc.; *Wellington Pier*, concerts and dancing. *Pleasure Beach and Boating Pool*, Marine Parade S.—GOLF COURSES at Caister and Gorleston.—STEAMERS from Hall Quay to *Gorleston*, up the Yare to *Norwich*, and up the Bure to the *Broads*.

Dickens stayed at the Royal Hotel in 1848, and readers of 'David Copperfield' will not forget the connection of Yarmouth with the Peggotty family. In the 1850s Borrow often visited No. 169 King St., there completing 'The Romany Rye' in 1857.

The fine QUAY on the Yare is approached by the rebuilt *Haven Bridge*. In the centre is Hall Quay, on which are the *Town Hall* and the *Star Hotel*, a restored Elizabethan house, once the residence of John Bradshaw, President of the Court of Commissioners for the trial of Charles I. The Town Hall contains perhaps the best authenticated portrait of Nelson, painted from life in 1801 by Matthew Keymer, a Norfolk artist. On South Quay, among many houses of great charm, No. 4 (N.T.), a refronted Tudor house, is the traditional scene of Cromwell's conference with his officers to decide the fate of Charles I. It contains a museum (June–Sept, Mon–Fri, 10–1, 1–5.30; fee).

The characteristic feature of the old town is the **Rows**, a series of extremely narrow lanes, all running at right angles to the river and sea and making of Yarmouth one vast gridiron. These suffered cruelly from bombing, but a number of them still remain intact between Hall Quay and the Market Place. In Row 117 the 17C *Old Merchant's House* (adm. Mon–Fri; Sun from 2) contains a collection of domestic ironwork (16–19C). The walls of the 14C *Tolhouse* or *Gaol*, in Middlegate St. (between S. Quay and King St.) have been incorporated in the local history museum; less remains of the 13C *Greyfriars Cloisters*, near by.— The large and animated *Market Place* was happily almost undamaged.

From its s. end the main KING STREET leads s. through the town, past *St George's*, an ingeniously planned church of 1714, with a pleasant cupola (key at Town Hall). At the N.E. corner of the Market Place are the interesting almshouses called *Fishermen's Hospital* (1702), and No. 26 Priory Plain, just beyond, was the birthplace of Anna Sewell (1820–78), author of 'Black Beauty'.

St Nicholas (236 ft long, 112 ft wide), one of the largest parish churches in England, was completely gutted in 1942. Though the exterior preserves its ancient appearance, with Norman tower (12C) and Early-English w. front, the interior was completely restored in 1957–61 by Stephen Dykes Bower, who reduced the number of nave arcades from eight to four each side and divided each choir aisle with a new arcade. The Norman font came from the deserted church of Highway (Wilts.), the pulpit from St George's. The ironwork and furnishing and the stained glass, by Brian Thomas, are noteworthy, as are the screens (1969) by Dykes Bower.

The adjoining *Priory Hall* (s. side), now a school, was originally the guesthouse of a Benedictine house established by Bp. Losinga with the church. A large section of the 14C *Town Walls* bounds the churchyard of St Nicholas; the *N.W. Gate* survives on North Quay, and the more interesting *S.E. Gate* may be seen in Blackfriars Rd., near the end of South Quay.

The fine *Marine Parade*, with the two piers and the usual amusements, is reached from Hall Quay by Regent St. and Regent Rd., crossing King St. at the Town Centre. At No. 25 is the *Maritime Museum for East Anglia* (June–Sept, 10–1, 2–8 daily; fee. Or by request at the Public Library.)

On the *South Denes*, s. of the town, is the *Nelson Monument*, a Doric column 114 ft high (view).—Adjacent, on the river, is the long *Fish Wharf*, busiest during the herring fishery of late autumn. 'Yarmouth Bloaters' are herring that have been subjected to one 'blow' or smoking.

About 3 m. w. of Yarmouth is **Burgh Castle**, a Roman fortress on the 'Saxon Shore' (c. A.D. 300); it commanded the large harbour at the confluence of the Yare and Breydon Water. The three remaining landward walls are impressive; the Roman mortar still holds them together though they lean at acute angles. The church to the N.E. has a Norman round tower, incorporating much Roman material from the castle.

The ROAD FROM YARMOUTH TO BECCLES traverses an area whose churches have characteristic flint round towers (11C) and lion fonts (15C). That at (7 m.) *Fritton*, with a beautiful Norman apse, overlooks the *Fritton Decoy*, the most charming of the East Anglian lakes.—7½ m. *St Olave's* has a ruined Augustinian priory (13C; adm. daily).—9½ m. *Haddiscoe* has a Norman s. portal and striking Saxon work in the tower.—15 m. *Beccles*, see p. 450.

From Yarmouth to *Norwich*, see p. 469; to *Cromer*, etc., see Rte 52.

48 LONDON TO ALDEBURGH

ROAD, 109 m. A 113.—21 m. *Ongar.*—B 184. 34 m. *Great Dunmow.*—B 1057. 49 m. *Steeple Bumpstead.*—B 1054. 52 m. *Wixoe.*—A 1092. 55½ m. *Clare.*—62 m. Long Melford.—66½ m. *Lavenham.*—A 1141. 70 m. *Monks Eleigh.*—B 1115. 80 m. *Needham Market.*—A 140. 84½ m. *Angel Hill.*—A 1120. 94 m. *Saxtead Green.*—B 1119. 96 m. *Framlingham.*—103 m. *Saxmundham.*—B 1121. 105½ m. *Friston.*—A 1094. 109 m. **Aldeburgh**.

This alternative to the A 12 (see Rte 47) passes by secondary roads through the finest parts of Essex and Suffolk to the E. coast. It is not for the hurried motorist.

We leave London through the E. suburbs, and at (7 m.) the Green Man, Leytonstone, take A 113.—11 m. *Chigwell* retains a village centre, with 15C church and 17C inn and grammar school.—21 m. *Chipping Ongar* ('Chipping' from the Anglo-Saxon, meaning 'market'), has a Norman church and Saxon castle mound. *Greensted-juxta-Ongar*, 1 m. w., has a *Church (c. 845) with a remarkable nave of split oak tree trunks set upright on a sill. The body of St Edmund rested here for a night in 1013 on its return from London to Bury St Edmunds, whence it had been removed in fear of the Danes. The brick choir dates from c. 1500.

Stondon Massey, 2 m. s.e. of Ongar, was the residence of William Byrd ('father of musick'), from 1595–1623. It has an early Norman church. *Blackmore*, 2 m. farther e., has a church with a fine timber tower, and Jericho House, built on the site of a favourite manor of Henry VIII.

We take B 184 from Ongar which follows the ridge above the valley of the Roding, an ancient trackway, known by its Saxon name of 'The Rodings' (or 'clearings', hence 'road').—23½ m. *Fyfield* church has a 12C font and unusual sedilia with sculptured heads. The parishes of *Willingale Doe* and *Willingale Spain*, 2 m. e. across the valley, have churches sharing one churchyard; St Andrew's is part-Norman, and St Christopher's has good brasses.—26 m. (½ m. l.) *Abbess Roding* church is 14C, with a Norman font and an 18C pulpit with fine tester.—At 27½ m. we turn r. on A 414 to (28 m.) *Leaden Roding* church with a weather-board belfry, and Norman nave and chancel. To the e. lie the Easters: *High Easter* church has a fine timber roof. B 184 turns n. and joins a Roman course (disused nearer London) on which stands (30½ m.) *High Roding*, with a 13C church (15C pulpit). *Great Canfield* church, 1 m. w., has a Norman chancel arch, and, above the altar, a 13C *Wall-painting of the Madonna and Child.— 34 m. *Great Dunmow*, a pleasant old market town, stands above the Chelmer. In the Doctor's Pond, Lionel Lukin, the inventor, tested the first lifeboat (1785).

At *Little Dunmow*, 2½ m. s.e., are the remains of *Dunmow Priory*, where by an old 'custom' a flitch of bacon could be claimed by any married couple who had "not repented them, sleeping or waking, of their marriage in a year and a day". The oath was originally taken kneeling before the Prior; the 'jury' of the present-day revival is an innovation. *Felstead*, 1 m. farther, a Jutish settlement, has a part-Norman church. In the Rich Chapel is the tomb by Epiphanius Evesham of the founder of the school (spelt Felsted), originally (1564) adjacent to the church. Here Richard Cromwell was a pupil.

A 130 leads N.w.—3 m. *Great Easton* has a motte and bailey castle. At *Little Easton* church, c. 1½ m. s.w., are *Wall-paintings of 12C–15C, German glass (17C), and fine Maynard and Bouchier monuments.—6½ m. *Thaxted*, a tiny town with old houses and a Jacobean *Guildhall* upon wooden pillars. It was the birthplace of Samuel Purchas (1575?–1626) of the 'Pilgrimes', and was once noted for its cutlery. The spacious *Church* (14–15C) has a fine crocketed spire (180 ft), pinnacled buttresses and grotesque gargoyles. The font, pulpit, N. and s. porches, timber roofs, and organ (1703; by John Harris) are noteworthy. While organist here in 1916, Gustav Holst composed 'The Planets', and a tradition of music-making survives. *Chickney*, 3½ m. s.w., has a primitive Norman church.

B 1057 winds N.e. through two notably attractive villages whose much publicized charms expose them to the risk of overcrowding. At (41½ m.) *Great Bardfield* a number of local crafts were revived in 1953. The church has a 14C stone rood-screen, said to be matched only at Stebbing, near by, and in Trondheim cathedral.—43 m. *Finchingfield* is well-grouped round a village green and duckpond below the squat Norman tower of the church, topped by an 18C cupola. At *Little Sampford*, 2½ m. N.W., is the beautiful little 15C manor-house of Tewes (adm. March–Nov, Thurs, Sun & BH, 2–6, or by appointment; fee).— 49 m. *Steeple Bumpstead* church has a good monument to Sir Henry Bendyshe (d. 1717) and his baby son. *Haverhill* (12,400 inhab.), now an 'overspill' town, lies 3 m. N.— We take B 1054, and join A 1092 to cross the Stour into Suffolk at (52 m.) *Wixoe*. Our road now follows the valley of the Stour to the pretty village of (53½ m.) *Stoke-by-Clare*, with a large Perp. church containing a pulpit (1498) and a wall-painting of 1550.— 55½ m. **Clare** (Hotels) preserves many beautiful houses, some pargeted. Remains survive of the Augustinian Priory founded here in 1248, in which was buried Lionel, first Duke of Clarence (d. 1368), son of Edward III; but only part of the keep still stands of the castle that was held by the semi-royal families of Strongbow, De Burgh, and Mortimer. The church is Perp., with much early Tudor work (all the glass was destroyed by the notorious Parliamentarian, William Dowsing); the N. chancel door has notable tracery.— 58 m. *Cavendish*, with a spacious green, has a church with a fine flint clerestory. It contains tombs of the Cavendish family, including Sir John (d. 1381), who built the chancel. Across the Stour is the church of *Pentlow*, with a round tower, opposite a timbered manor-house (c. 1500).

62 m. **Long Melford** (Hotels) has a main street over 2 miles long with many good buildings. The magnificent late-Perp. *CHURCH has 15C *Stained glass in the aisles (the devout donors), and the N. chapel (a beautiful Lily Crucifixion). The Clopton Chantry, off the N. aisle, contains fine monuments and brasses. In the nave is a seat from Granada Cathedral with the arms of Ferdinand and Isabella. The Lady Chapel, attached to the E. end of the church, has an ambulatory with a fine wood ceiling and sculptured corbels. To the E. of the attractive green, opposite a brick Conduit House, and entered through a brick gateway, is *Melford Hall* (N.T.; adm. April–Sept, Wed, Thurs, Sun, & BH, 2.30–6; fee), dating from 1545.

This was the house of Sir William Cordell, Speaker of the House of Commons and Master of the Rolls, who was visited here by Elizabeth I. Since the 18C it has belonged to the Hyde-Parker family, and contains good collections of Chinese porcelain, furniture, and paintings.— The moated *Kentwell Hall* (Apr–Sept, Wed, Thurs, & BH, 2–6; also Sat & Sun in July–Aug, 12–6; fee), part of the Hyde-Parker estate, lies ½ m. N., and has a mile-long avenue of limes planted in 1678, and a large brick dovecote.

By the timbered *Bull Hotel*, we take a by-road E. to (66½ m.) **Lavenham** (Hotel), which, like Long Melford, was one of the centres of the 15C Suffolk wool trade. The village is the most picturesque in Suffolk, with many streets of timbered houses, with carved angle posts and pargeting. The *CHURCH, with a tall tower and long, graceful nave, stands in a magnificent position. It was built (1480–1530) in friendly rivalry by the 14th Earl of Oxford and Thomas Spring, a wealthy clothier. It has a fine s. porch, and the *Spring Chantry (1523) and Oxford Chantry, and good misericords. In the Market Place is the *Guildhall (1529; N.T.; adm. daily, closed 12.30–2; fee), with a corner post representing the 15th Earl of Oxford. In the *Angel Hotel* is a 16C plaster ceiling, and 14C wall-paintings, and the *Swan Hotel* incorporates the old Wool Hall.

Acton church, c. 3 m. S.W., contains the *Brass of Sir Robert de Bures (d. 1302), one of the oldest and best in England, and a monument to Robert Jennens (d. 1722), aide-de-camp to Marlborough. *Little Waldingfield*, c. 2 m. E. of Acton, has a fine 15C church.

We take A 1141 to (68½ m.) *Brent Eleigh* where the church has 14C wall-paintings.—70 m. *Monks Eleigh* has good houses, a mill, and a large **Perp. church. Lindsey and Kersey lie 2 and 3 m. S.E., see p. 447.**

B 1115 continues eastwards to (71 m.) *Chelsworth*, an attractive village on the Brett (bridge of 1754). The church contains a decorated tomb recess and a wall-painting.—At (72 m.) *Bildeston*, with good timber cottages, we fork right on B 1078.—75½ m. *Great Bricett*, the church (Norman door) is all that remains of an Augustinian Priory.— 78 m. *Barking* has a Dec. church with an early tie-beam roof, and parclose and *Rood screens.—80 m. **Needham Market** is a pleasant town with old houses (some dating from the 14C), lining the High Street. The church contains a splendid *Roof, covered with angels, described as 'the culminating achievement of the English carpenter'.

At 81½ m. we turn left on A 140 to (84½ m.) *Angel Hill*. *Earl Stonham* *Church (½ m. w.) has a spectacular double hammerbeam roof with angels. The Jacobean pulpit has four hour glasses (for sermons from ¼ hr to 2 hrs). We follow A 1120 E. to (85½ m.) *Stonham Aspal* (large church with Dec. tower), and (92½ m.) *Earl Soham*, on an attractive green.—94 m. *Saxtead Green* has a windmill in full working trim (N.T.; open daily).

Dennington, 2½ m. N.E., has an impressive church with notable *Parclose screens. The benches have carved ends (including a 'sciapod', a one-legged man using his foot as a sunshade), and there is a rare pyx canopy, and the tomb of Lord Bardolph who fought at Agincourt.

We branch right on B 1119.—96 m. **Framlingham** (Hotel), grouped round the triangular Market Hill in front of the *Crown Inn* (16C), has an imposing ruined *CASTLE (adm. daily, closed Sun in winter till 2; fee), mainly of the time of Edward I, with a moat and 13 towers. Here Queen Mary found refuge with the Howards during the attempt to place Lady Jane Grey on the throne. Within the shell stands the *Poor House* (1636), and the towers are adorned with Tudor chimneys. The battlements look across the Meres to the *College*, Suffolk's memorial to Prince Albert (1864), on the opposing hill. The stately *CHURCH, Perp. with Dec. survivals, has a coved hammerbeam roof. It contains the magnificent *Monuments of Henry Howard, earl of Surrey, the poet, executed by Henry VIII in 1547; of Thomas Howard, 3rd duke of Norfolk (d. 1554), who escaped the same fate only by the king's sudden death; of Henry Fitzroy, natural son of Henry VIII, and his wife Lady Mary Howard; and of Sir Robert Hitcham (d. 1636), with fine supporting angels. In the Sanctuary is the Flodden Helmet, worn at that battle by the English Commander, the 2nd Duke of Norfolk. The organ has some pre-Commonwealth pipes.

103 m. *Saxmundham* (see p. 449).

B 1119 goes on to (4½ m.) *Leiston*, where the Garrett locomotive, which saw arduous service in many colonial and S. American countries, was produced. Richard Garrett built the model works and cottages, and commissioned the appropriate church by E. B. Lamb. The ruins of the Premonstratensian *Leiston Abbey* founded in 1183 (adm. daily, Sun from 2; fee), lie c. 1 m. N., and 1 m. farther on, *Theberton* church (thatched roof) has a rounded tower, and Norman doorway.

C. M. Doughty (1843–1926) of 'Arabia Deserta' was born at Theberton Hall. To the E. of Theberton, in a wild sandy area extending to the low sea cliffs, is the *Minsmere* nature reserve. *Sizewell* nuclear power station, a fine group of buildings, is on the coast, 2 m. E. of Leiston, and *Thorpeness* (Hotel) is 1½ m. s., a holiday village on the sea, with a pleasant 'Meare' used for boating.

We follow A 12 s. for ¾ m., then turn l. on B 1121.— 105½ m. *Friston*, with a post mill, has a church with an unusual w. tower. Beyond, we join A 1094 to (109 m.) **Aldeburgh** (Hotels), a seaside resort and fishing village (2800 inhab.). It was a favourite resort of Fitzgerald, and Meredith and Wilkie Collins resided here. The local atmosphere was tellingly evoked in 'The Borough' by the native poet George Crabbe (1754–1832), a memorial to whom is in the Perp. church. Since the production in 1945 of Benjamin Britten's opera 'Peter Grimes', based on an episode in 'The Borough', Aldeburgh has become a centre of musical activity (Festival in June); many of Britten's later works were composed for local performance. The *Moot Hall*, a half-timbered 16C building, now standing amid the encroaching shingle, was the town hall of the old town washed away by the sea. *Alde House* was long the home of Elizabeth Garrett Anderson (d. 1917), one of the first women doctors, and the first woman mayor (1908) in England. In 1967 the Maltings at *Snape* (c. 4 m. N.W.) were converted into an opera house for the Aldeburgh Festival, and restored in 1969 after a fire.

49   LONDON TO NEWMARKET AND NORWICH

ROAD, 109½ m. (A 11). 29½ m. *Bishop's Stortford*.—60½ m. **Newmarket** (by-passed to N.).—80 m. *Thetford*.—109½ m. **Norwich**.

MOTORWAY (M 11) from Wanstead/South Woodford to Stump Cross (1979), in construction to Cambridge. This is now the recognised route to Cambridge (c. 49 m.).

RAILWAY. To **Norwich** 115 m. from Liverpool St. Station (viâ *Ipswich*, see Rte 47), in 2–2½ hrs. To (55¾ m.) *Cambridge*, junction for **Newmarket** (14½ m. in 20 min) see Rte 54.— *Thetford*, *Attleborough*, and *Wymondham* are served by trains on the line from Ely to Norwich.

From London viâ Tottenham, Walthamstow, and Epping Forest to (16½ m.) *Epping*, see the 'Blue Guide to London'.— 23 m. **Harlow** (77,700 inhab ; Hotel). To the left of the old village the new town, planned by F. Gibberd, has an open market, an effective R.C. church, and a good swimming-pool, beside well-designed housing areas. Objects unearthed during building operations are displayed in the Civic Centre, the roof of which commands a view over the Stort, a tributary of the Lea. Navigable for cabin cruisers, this waterway, with a towpath (c. 10 m.), affords a quiet alternative way to Bishop's Stortford.—The church of (25½ m.) *Sawbridgeworth* contains good brasses.— 29½ m. **Bishop's Stortford** (22,100 inhab.; Hotels), in Herts, has a fine church (c. 1400) with contemporary woodwork, and a boys' public school. The old vicarage in South Road, where Cecil Rhodes (1853–1902) was born, is now the *Rhodes Museum* (daily, exc. Sun 10–4).

FROM BISHOP'S STORTFORD TO COLCHESTER, 32 m. (A 120; the Roman Stane Street). The road skirts the N. side of *Hatfield Forest* (N.T.; 980 acres), a woodland area with a boating lake. 3 m. s. beyond the forest is *Hatfield Broad Oak*, where the large church contains a fine mailed effigy of Robert de Vere, Earl of Oxford (d. 1221).—4½ m. *Takeley* church has Roman material in the walls and a decorative *Font cover. We continue through (9 m.) *Great Dunmow* (p. 453) and

(17 m.) *Braintree* (p. 476).—At (23 m.) *Coggeshall*, the church has good brasses to the Paycocke family. *Paycocke's House (N.T.; adm. April–Sept, Wed, Thurs, Sun & BH, 2–5.30) is a richly ornamented merchant's dwelling of c. 1500. Near the Blackwater, ¾ m. s., the remains of a Cistercian abbey (1140), perhaps the earliest medieval brick building erected in England, are incorporated in a farmhouse.— We join A 12 at (27 m.) *Marks Tey*, whence to (32 m.) *Colchester*, see Rte 47.

We re-enter Essex and reach (38 m.) *Newport*, a typical W. Essex town with a long street, an old Grammar School, and many 16–17C houses, some decorated with pargeting. Newport has a fine Perp. church; even better is the one at *Clavering*, a remarkably attractive village on the Stort, 4 m. w.—40¼ m. **Audley End** is the palatial Jacobean *Mansion begun in 1603, on the site of the Benedictine Walden Abbey, by Thomas Howard, Earl of Suffolk, reduced in size by Vanbrugh in 1721, and sold to the government by Lord Braybrooke in 1948. The principal state rooms, including the huge Great Hall with splendid wood and plaster work, and the great Drawing Room by Robert Adam with its original furnishings (lent by Lord Braybrooke), are open daily, exc. Mon, Apr–Oct, 10–5.30; Oct–March, Sat & Sun, 11–3.30 (fee). Hans Eworth's portrait of Margaret Audley (1562) is outstanding among the paintings.

The 16C Abbey Farm buildings are now restored as a home for retired clergy, known as the College of St Mark.

About 1½ m. E. is the charming little town of **Saffron Walden** (9900 inhab.; Hotel), with a fine Perp. church and some picturesque timbered buildings, including the *Sun Inn* (N.T.), a notable 15C house, with 17C pargeting, used as a headquarters by Cromwell and Fairfax. In the grounds of the interesting little *Museum*, which contains a pillory and a notable Anglo-Saxon sword, are the ruins of the 12C castle. The old *Grammar School* was the headquarters in 1941–45 of the 65th Fighter Wing of the U.S.A.A.F., in memory of whom a Sports Centre has been laid out.—At *Hempstead*, 6 m. E., Dick Turpin (1705–39), the highwayman, was born, and in the Harvey Chapel in the church lie William Harvey (1578–1657) and Sir Eliab Harvey (1758–1830), commander of the 'Temeraire' at Trafalgar.

43 m. (r.) *Little Chesterford* Hall is a rare 13C manor-house (no adm.). At *Great Chesterford* we curve sharply right across the Cam and enter Cambridgeshire, almost immediately joining the Romanized Icknield Way, on straight alinements all the way to Thetford. *Ickleton*, 1 m. w., has a church with Roman monolithic columns, late-Saxon details, and a 'sacring' bell outside the spire. At *Duxford*, a wartime airfield a little farther N.W., are displayed the Imperial War Museum's collection of aircraft and military vehicles (adm. daily Apr–Sept, 11–5).

At (44½ m.) *Stump Cross* A 130 bears left for (14½ m.) **Cambridge** (Rte 55) viâ *Sawston* (5 m.), with Sawston Hall (1557–84), the ancient home of the staunchly R.C. family of Huddleston (adm. 2.30–5.30, Sun & BH, Easter–Sept; also Sat, July–Sept; fee). Portions of the earlier house, where Mary Tudor took refuge in 1553, survived the fire started by her enemies.

We keep right on A 11, then cross in succession the line of the *Via Devana* (p. 500), *Fleam Dyke*, and, on Newmarket Heath, the *Devil's Ditch*. These are both parts of a rampart system raised by the Angles or the Mercians during the wars waged in the 6–8C for control of East Anglia.

60½ m. **Newmarket** (12,900 inhab.; large Hotels) is the headquarters of English horse-racing with the National Stud. Racing here, begun under James I, has been more or less regular since the time of Charles I. Part of the old Palace in the High St., built by Charles II, still exists, and the houses of 'Old Q' (Duke of Queensberry) and Nell Gwynne. The *Jockey Club* (1840) was restored by Richardson and Gill (1936). A serious fire at Newmarket in 1683 hurried away the royal party, thereby upsetting the Rye House Plot (see p. 480). The old railway station built in 1848 is a splendid piece of Victorian 'Baroque'.

The most important of the races decided on the famous racecourse on Newmarket Heath, 1½ m. s.w., are the 'Two Thousand Guineas' (spring), the 'Cesarewitch' (Oct), and the 'Cambridgeshire' (Oct). Special permission is necessary to visit any of the *Training Stables*, but the morning gallops on the Heath of the horses in training may frequently be witnessed.

At *Kirtling*, 4½ m. s., the church has a fine 12C doorway and monuments of the Norths, the gatehouse (1530) of whose mansion stands to the s.

FROM NEWMARKET TO IPSWICH, A 45 (41 m.); railway in c. 1 hr. As we leave Newmarket, the road forks right to (5 m.) *Kentford*, with a Dec. church (14C wall-paintings).—10 m. (l.) *Risby* church has a Norman round tower and chancel arch, a good screen, and an extensive series of wall-paintings. *Little Saxham*, c. 2 m. s., has a round church tower.—14 m. **Bury St Edmunds** (by-pass), see Rte 53.— 19 m. *Beyton* church has a Norman round tower, and (21 m.; r.) *Woolpit* church has a magnificent s. porch, and a fine double hammerbeam roof.—At 23 m. the road skirts the extensive *Haughley Park*, with a Tudor mansion and good gardens (open May–Sept, Tues 3–6; fee). At *Haughley*, 1½ m. E., is a church (timber roof), and the remains of a large moated motte and bailey castle.—27 m. **Stowmarket** (8700 inhab.; by-pass) trades in barley and manufactures chemicals and agricultural implements. The *Abbot's Hall Museum of Rural Life of E. Anglia* is open April–Oct, daily 11–5; Sun from 2 (fee). The *Church* has a wooden spire 120 ft high, above a square flint tower. At the old vicarage Milton used to visit his tutor Thomas Young (d. 1665). The neighbourhood is rich in interesting churches: at *Combs*, 1½ m. s.; and *Bacton* and *Cotton*, 5 m. N., with notable roofs.—The road follows the valley of the Gipping through (31 m.) *Needham Market* (p. 455) to (35 m.) *Claydon* (overshadowed by large cement works), and (41 m.) *Ipswich* (see Rte 47).

We cross the Lark at (69 m.) *Barton Mills* (Hotel), where the church has 14C stained glass, and a Jacobean pulpit. Just under a mile beyond the village, there is a five-way junction.

A 1101 goes w. to (1 m.) *Mildenhall* (26,600 inhab.; Hotel), a pleasant town with a Georgian High St., and a 15C timber market-cross. The *Church (St Mary and St Andrew), whose lovely E. window dominates the street, has a tower 120 ft high, and a Lady Chapel over the N. porch. The carved hammerbeam *Roof with angels, was preserved, it is claimed, from Puritan iconoclasts by divine intervention (since the timbers are peppered with shot holes, the immediate cause was poor marksmanship). The 'Mildenhall Treasure', a wonderful hoard of 4C Roman silver, now in the British Museum, was found in 1946 at Thistley Green.—A 1101 continues into Fen Country, joining (11 m.) A 10, between Ely and Downham Market (see Rte 56).

A 1065 leads N. passing (3 m.) *Lakenheath Airfield*, since 1941 an important U.S. base. The good church of Lakenheath (Norman and Dec.), w. of the airfield, contains a memorial to Lord Kitchener (d. 1916), some of whose ancestors (17–18C) lie in the churchyard. In Hockwold Fen, 3 m. N., the Roman town of *Camboritum*, overwhelmed by floods in the 2C, was discovered in 1961. Many military airfields were established hereabouts in 1939–45, and memorials to the men who fell in the war have been set up at *Elvedon* (p. 478), and *Feltwell* (R.N.Z.A.F.; Cross of Sacrifice), 1½ m. N. of Hockwold.—9 m. *Brandon*, and thence to Cromer see Rte 53.

A 1101 runs s.E. through (2 m.) *Icklingham*, with a large thatched church (Norman nave, Jacobean pulpit, 14C chest, and stained glass).—7 m. *Hengrave* church has a Norman tower, and is crammed with monuments to the Kytson family who built the adjoining *Hengrave Hall* (now a conference centre) completed in 1538 by Sir Thomas Kytson. The ornate bay window (by John Sparke) over the entrance doorway, is one of the finest of this date. Sir Thomas was brother-in-law to Laurence Washington; there is a window with the Washington arms surmounted by an eagle.—10 m. *Bury St Edmunds*, see p. 477.

A 11 now enters *Breckland*, the heath with firs and small meres described in 'Lavengro'. Although much of it has been altered by forestry or enclosed for military training and airfields, an abundant bird life still exists around the more isolated ponds and rushes.—76 m. *Elveden* church (with a U.S.A.A.F. memorial window), is a bizarre jumble of Gothick and Art Nouveau, perpetuated by the owners of *Elveden Hall*, originally the home of Adm. Keppel, who died here in 1786. In 1860 the Hall was purchased by the Maharaja Duleep Singh, as a seat near the Newmarket stables, who made of its interior a 'Moghul-Gothick' fantasy in Carrara marble, crowning all with a beaten copper dome. Extensions were added by Lord Iveagh in 1900.—The road now skirts the edge of Thetford Chase and enters Norfolk.

80 m. **Thetford** (Hotels), an ancient town (13,700 inhab.) on the Little Ouse, was the seat of the kings of East Anglia and of its bishops in 1075–94. It is now being artificially 'expanded' by the Greater London Council. It contains the scanty remains of a *Cluniac Priory* (founded in 1104; adm. daily, Sun from 2; fee), of a priory of the *Canons of the Holy Sepulchre* (12C), on the Brandon road, and of a *Dominican Friary* (1340), three of the five monastic establishments it possessed before the Dissolution. The Friary is behind the ancient *Grammar School*, which claims descent from a 7C choir-school. The library is the old schoolhouse where Paine attended. The *Castle Hill* (80 ft high, 1000 ft round), at the E. end of the town, is the finest castle-mound in the country, a Norman motte surrounded by Iron Age earthworks. Thomas Paine (1737–1809), author of 'The Age of Reason', was born in a cottage behind White Hart St. (tablet), near the *Ancient House Museum* (April–Sept, daily 2–5; Oct–March, Tues, Thurs & Sun 2–4; Sat from 10). A statue (1964), by Sir C. Wheeler, stands before the *Guildhall*, in which is the Duleep Singh Collection of Norfolk and Suffolk portraits (weekdays 10–5).

Euston Hall, 4 m. s.e., built c. 1670 by Henry Bennet, Earl of Arlington, one of the members of the Cabal, gave name to the famous London railway terminus (built on the estate of the Dukes of Grafton, then owners of Euston Hall). Open 2.30–5.30 on Thurs in May–Sept, the 18C house contains paintings by Stubbs and 17C portraits. The 14C church of *East Harling*, 7 m. E. of Thetford, has fine medieval Norwich glass and 15–17C monuments.

B 1110 leads N. for (22¼ m.) *East Dereham* viâ (12½ m.) Watton, and A 134 leads N.W. for (29½ m.) *Lynn*. Near Watton are *Wayland Wood* (2 m. s.), said to be the scene of the 'Babes in the Wood', and *Griston House* (2 m. s.e.), said to be the residence of their wicked uncle.

94½ m. *Attleborough* has a Norman and Perp. church with a magnificent *Rood-screen of 1475 surmounted by murals of similar date.—100¼ m. **Wymondham** (pron. 'Windham'; Hotel), an old market town (8500 inhab.), has one of the finest *Churches* in Norfolk, originally belonging to the priory (afterwards abbey) of SS Mary and Alban (1107). In 1349 the nave (mainly Norman) and N. aisle (Perp.) were assigned for the use of the parishioners, who added the w. tower about 1450. The E. tower and the original choir, of which only fragments remain, were retained by the monks. The nave has a hammerbeam roof with angels and large bosses; part of the ceiling has been removed to show the timbering. It has a terracotta monument to Elisha Ferrers. Outstanding among the many timbered houses is the *Green Dragon*.

The *Market Cross* is a timber building of 1616. A library occupies the 15C *Chapel of St Thomas Becket*. Robert Kett, the leader of the brief agrarian insurrection of 1549, was a tanner of Wymondham.

About 3½ m. w. is **Hingham**, where the fine Dec. *Church has a hammerbeam roof. The Morley *Monument, perfectly preserved, is a triumph of deeply carved 15C work, with statues of the family. The stained glass is German (c. 1500). There is a bust (1919) of Abraham Lincoln. Hingham was the home of Robert Lincoln (d. about 1540), generally accepted as the earliest known ancestor of Abraham Lincoln. Richard Lincoln of Swanton Morley (p. 471), buried in 1620 at Hingham, disinherited his son Edward, as a result of which his grandson Samuel emigrated from Hingham in 1637, to become the first American ancestor of the President. There was an Abraham Lincoln of Norwich (b. about 1685).

109½ m. **Norwich**, see below.

50   NORWICH

NORWICH (121,700 inhab.), the county town of Norfolk and the regional capital of East Anglia, is situated in a loop of the Wensum and commanded by its massive castle. It preserves an extremely irregular plan, inherited from its Saxon origins; possessing neither a main street nor a central square, and its continuous importance since the Middle Ages is everywhere reflected in surviving monuments. Famous for its beautiful cathedral, Norwich boasts in addition more than 30 pre-Reformation churches (many now disused and threatened) and many old buildings, both civic and domestic, the attraction of which has been enhanced of late by judicious restoration and the closing of streets to traffic.

The suffix 'gate', surviving in towns of Eastern England (comp. also York, Chesterfield, Lincoln), is from old Danish and means 'Street' (mod. Danish 'gade').

Car Parks in the old Cattle Market, and outside the Library; multi-story parks in St. Andrew St., Chapel Field Rd., Malthouse Rd.

Hotels (see plan), also at *Thorpe* on the river, 2 m. E.

Restaurants near the Cathedral and in London St.

Post Office, Bank Plain.—INFORMATION BUREAU, 24 Exchange St.

Buses from Castle Meadow (local); from Surrey St. to many parts of Norfolk and Suffolk.

Airport, Horsham St Faith. Services to *Edinburgh, Aberdeen, Southend,* and *Channel Is.*

Theatres. *Maddermarket, Theatre Royal.* CONCERTS at *St Andrew's Hall* and *Assembly House* (with Noverre Cinema; repertory). Also concerts and plays at the Univ. of East Anglia, Earlham Rd.—DANCING at *Samson and Hercules,* Tombland. —GOLF COURSES at Hellesdon, 2 m. N.W. and Eaton, 2 m. S.W.—BOATS on the Yare at Thorpe, 1 m. E.—SWIMMING-POOL (covered), Aylsham Rd.; also (open air) at Lakenham, 1½ m. S.

History. A settlement near the crossing of the Wensum (Fye Bridge) above its confluence with the Yare grew by 850 into a borough trading with the Rhineland. *Northwic* appears on coins minted for Athelstan I. In the Danish wars it was destroyed by Sweyn Forkbeard, but by the Conquest it had grown to be one of the largest boroughs in the kingdom, the fief of Gyrth Godwinsson, brother of King Harold, who was immediately replaced as Earl of East Anglia by a Norman. A large motte and bailey castle was built, driving a Norman wedge between the English areas. In 1094, when the see of Norwich was created, Bp. Losinga commandeered and razed much of the Anglo-Saxon borough to build his cathedral and moved the market site from Tombland to w. of the castle. By 1140 a large community of Jews lived here freely, not confined to a ghetto. Norwich acquired its charters in 1194 and 1256, and the circuit wall (2¼ m.) built of stone in 1294–1320 compares in extent with that of London. In the 14C an influx of Flemish weavers was attracted to the city which became the centre of the worsted trade. The city was occupied by the rebels during the Peasants' Revolt (1381) and social unrest continued (comp. the Paston Letters), so that again in 1549 many in Norwich sympathized with the insurrection of Robert Kett, paying the penalty with him on the castle gallows. The advent of the power loom, the banking activities of the Society of Friends, and the foundation of the Norwich General Assurance brought the city into the industrial era. With the coming of the railway the vast cattle market supplied more than half the meat for London. Sporadic air raids in the Second World War culminated in a series of destructive attacks in 1942. In post-war years the city has suffered changes in the cause of progress, while also fostering pioneer schemes of conservation and restoration. The University of East Anglia was established on the outskirts of the city in 1961.—Although one silk mill survives, the chief manufactures now are boots and shoes, mustard and starch, machinery and electrical equipment, pharmaceuticals, toffee, and beer. The city is known also for fine printing. The rearing of canaries, once a characteristic minor industry, is recalled by the popular name of the City footballers.—Among eminent natives, besides those mentioned below, are Robert Greene (1560–92), poet and dramatist, Harriet Martineau (1802–76), and Elizabeth Fry (1780–1845). The 'Norwich School' of landscape painters was founded by John Crome in the early 19C.

A visit to Norwich may conveniently start at the *Castle (Pl. 11), to the E. of which a large car park occupies the former Cattle Market. The castle mound was raised just after the Conquest, the great stone *Keep* being built by Henry I after the model of that at Falaise. It is unique among English castles in having an exterior decoration of blank Norman arcading; this was accurately reproduced in 1834–39, though in an alien stone, by Salvin.

The Museum (weekdays 10–5, Sun from 2.30; fee; rfmts.) is well laid-out, and has a fine collection of paintings by the Norwich School, by such masters as Crome, Cotman, Stannard, Stark, and Vincent. There are informative dioramas of the city at various periods, and collections of local antiquities, including the Iron Age hoard of gold and coins unearthed at Snettisham in 1948.

Below the castle, on the N.E., the Anglia Television Centre (Pl. 11) faces the Royal Hotel across the city's busiest traffic intersection. Bank Plain and its continuation Redwell St. lead N., passing (r.) *St Michael-at-Plea*, with a two-storied porch entered above by a Jacobean gallery. Within, the roof has carved angels and the font-cover is Jacobean.

Across Prince's St. is *ELM HILL, one of the finest medieval streets in England, still cobbled, each one of whose buildings repays attention. It was saved and restored by the Norwich Society and the Civic Trust. At the top is *St Peter Hungate*, rebuilt in 1460 by John and Margaret Paston, with a cruciform hammerbeam roof and 15–16C glass. It is now a Museum of Church Art (adm. daily, exc. Sun), with notable medieval woodwork, vestments, MSS., and bells. Beyond the bend is (l.) the *Stranger's Club* (the 'strangers' were the immigrant weavers), early 16C (with some 17C work), and (r.) *Pettus House*, and beyond (l.) the 17C *Flint House*. At the foot, on the corner of Wensum St., the church of *St Simon and St Jude*, aisleless with flint walls, and fine monuments to the Pettus family; it is now the headquarters of the Norwich Boy Scouts.

Wensum St. leads to the right past the Maid's Head Hotel to TOMB-LAND (Pl. 7), the old Saxon market-place displaced by the Normans. *Samson and Hercules House* (1657) takes name from the benign giants supporting the porch; the rest of the square is Georgian and pleasantly tree-shaded, with the lofty tower of *St George's Tombland* rising above the trees at the top. The 15C church has a good roof, and a relief and statuette (on the font cover) of St George.

The *Erpingham Gate* (1420), with sculpture beautifully preserved, leads into the cathedral CLOSE, spacious with many fine trees.

To the N.E. of the Erpingham Gate is *Norwich School*, refounded by Edward VI, including the Chapel of St John (c. 1316). Among its famous pupils were Lord Nelson (a statue of whom stands near the gate) and Rajah Brooke of Sarawak (1803–68). 'Old Crome' was for a time drawing master here. On the N. side of the Cathedral is the former *Bishop's Palace*, opened in 1962 as an extension of the School.—The Upper Close running E. from *St Ethelbert's Gate* (c. 1300; parapet modern), is continued by the Lower Close, leading to *Pull's Ferry*, the picturesque old water-gate of the Cathedral precincts (restored 1948; the line of the old canal that passed beneath it, and up which the barges brought the Caen stone to build the cathedral, can still be clearly seen).

The ***Cathedral** (Pl. 7; *Holy Trinity*) is a majestic building, mainly Norman in structure, 407 ft long, with a soaring spire 315 ft high, exceeded in height in England by that of Salisbury alone.

HISTORY. The see of E. Anglia, established at Dunwich c. 630 by Felix of Burgundy, was merged in that of Elmham in 956, and transferred to Thetford in 1075, and it was not till 1094 that it was permanently fixed at Norwich by Bp. Herbert de Losinga (d. 1119), who laid the foundations of Norwich Cathedral in 1096 and lived to complete the choir, transepts, E. end of nave, and lower stage of the tower. Bp. Eborard, his successor, finished the long nave (c. 1145). In 1272 the townfolk rose against the cathedral clergy and burnt the interior fittings and most of the domestic buildings. The clerestory of the choir was rebuilt in the Dec. style by Bp. Percy (1355–69). Bp. Alnwick (1426–36) altered the w. front and completed the cloisters (begun 130 years earlier). The present spire and the stone vault of nave and choir were built by Bp. Lyhart (1446–72) and Bp. Goldwell (1472–99). The cathedral, which suffered considerably at the hands of the Puritans, was repaired after the Restoration, and in 1930–32 the new E. chapel was added.

Exterior. The most striking features are the apsidal E. end (with its beautiful flying buttresses), the Norman arcading on the E. wall of the s. transept, and the Norman *Tower, surmounted by a 15C spire, the whole set off by the long unbroken line of the nave and chancel roof. The pinnacles, contemporary with the spire, are unsymmetrically placed. The large Perp. window in the w. front is flanked by Norman turrets.

Interior. In plan and structure the cathedral is still practically identical with Losinga's building. Viewing the finely proportioned church from the w. door, the eye is at once arrested by the majesty of the continuous lierne-vaulted roof of the 15C. The *Bosses tell the story of the Bible (both Testaments), and are well worth detailed study with binoculars (the Crucifixion and Harrowing of Hell in the 12th bay are outstanding). The NAVE consists of 14 bays, supported by massive Norman columns; its rhythmic unity is accentuated by the light colour of the stone and the absence of monuments. The arches of the triforium are (most unusually) the same size as those of the main arcade. The clerestory, set back within a wall-passage, has Norman lights. The circular opening in the central part of the roof was used for letting down a thurible or censer. The AISLES also are Norman. Two bays of the s. aisle (beside the pulpit) were converted into a Perp. chantry by Bp. Nykke (d. 1535). The *Monks' Door* and the Dec. *Prior's Door lead from the s. aisle to the cloisters. The two E. bays of the nave are included in the ritual choir and contain the fine 15C Stalls, with their curious misericords. The lower stage of the CENTRAL TOWER is Losinga's work, the upper stories are Norman of later date.

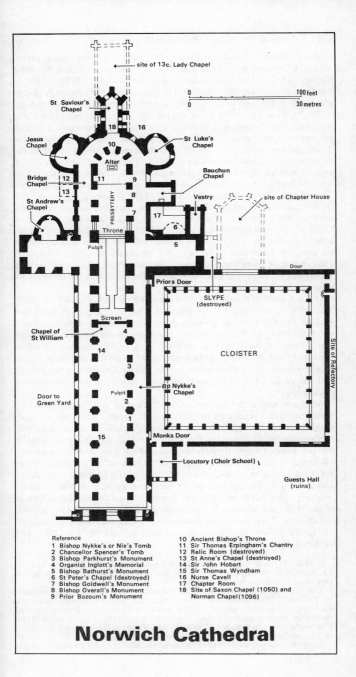

site of 13c. Lady Chapel

St Saviour's Chapel

Jesus Chapel

Bridge Chapel

St Andrew's Chapel

St Luke's Chapel

Bauchun Chapel

Vestry

site of Chapter House

Altar

PRESBYTERY

Throne

Pulpit

Door

Priors Door

SLYPE
(destroyed)

Screen

Chapel of
St William

CLOISTER

Site of Refectory

Bp Nykke's
Chapel

Pulpit

Door to
Green Yard

Monks Door

Locutory (Choir School)

Guests Hall
(ruins)

0 ——— 100 feet
0 ——— 30 metres

Reference
1 Bishop Nykke's or Nix's Tomb
2 Chancellor Spencer's Tomb
3 Bishop Parkhurst's Monument
4 Organist Inglott's Memorial
5 Bishop Bathurst's Monument
6 St Peter's Chapel (destroyed)
7 Bishop Goldwell's Monument
8 Bishop Overall's Monument
9 Prior Bozoum's Monument

10 Ancient Bishop's Throne
11 Sir Thomas Erpingham's Chantry
12 Relic Room (destroyed)
13 St Anne's Chapel (destroyed)
14 Sir John Hobart
15 Sir Thomas Wyndham
16 Nurse Cavell
17 Chapter Room
18 Site of Saxon Chapel (1050) and
   Norman Chapel (1096)

Norwich Cathedral

The TRANSEPTS resemble the nave. Off the N. arm is an apsidal chapel with 15C stained glass from the Deanery and a Madonna by John Skelton (1960). The monument to Bp. Bathurst (d. 1837), in the N. transept, is by Chantrey. In the S. Transept is an effigy originally placed above the N. transept door in 1100, representing probably Bp. Losinga.

The *CHOIR, beginning W. of the central tower, terminates on the E. in a semicircular apse, with ambulatory and radiating chapels, a French arrangement very unusual in English churches. The *Presbytery*, to the E. of the central tower, has been considerably altered, though the Norman ground plan remains unchanged. The early 15C lectern, with a pelican instead of the usual eagle, is notable. The ivory chair (1514) near the high altar may have belonged originally to the Abp. of Bavaria. The *Bishop's Throne* behind the altar is of the greatest interest, as, with its surroundings, it preserves the plan of the Christian sanctuary normal until c. 1000; the chair itself is 8C work and may have come from Dunwich. Bp. Herbert de Losinga (d. 1119) was buried before the high altar, and the top slab of a new monument erected to him in 1682 is let into the pavement. The beautiful clerestory was re-erected after 1362 in a style transitional between Dec. and Perp.; the stone vaulting was added between 1472 and 1499; and at the same time the main arches were redesigned in the current style.

In the S. aisle of the presbytery is the tomb of Bp. Goldwell (d. 1499). This aisle is adjoined by the *Bauchun Chapel*, founded in 1330 and vaulted in 1450 (notable bosses). Now the consistory Court, it has a window (1964), by Moira Forsyth, representing the Benedictine Order. The *Chapter Room* (1961), W. of this, contains Renaissance panelling, probably from St Benet's Abbey, and good 16–18C portraits of deans. At the E. end of the choir-aisles are St Luke's Chapel (S.; see below), and the *Jesus Chapel* (N.), each curiously formed of two segments of circles.

At the E. end is *St Saviour's Chapel*, erected in 1930–32 as a War Memorial. This is entered by two fine E.E. arches, a relic of the Lady Chapel erected by Bp. Walter de Suffield (d. 1257). Furnished in 1963 as the regimental chapel of the Royal Norfolk Regiment,. it contains fine 14C painted panels from St Michael-at-Plea. Even finer is the painted *Retable, in *St Luke's Chapel*, probably presented as a thank-offering for the suppression of the peasant revolt of 1381. Together they form a rare survival of masterpieces of the East Anglian School. The so-called *Bridge Chapel* in the N. aisle was probably used for the exhibition of relics. The vault above it has paintings of 1275. Also in the N. aisle was the chantry of Sir Thomas Erpingham (d. 1428), the "good old knight" of 'Henry V' (iv. 2). An adjoining window was filled in 1963 with medieval Norwich glass.

In May 1919, the body of Nurse Edith Cavell (shot by the Germans in 1915) was brought from Brussels and interred just E. of St Luke's Chapel. A bust in Tombland commemorates her heroism.

The *CLOISTERS, the only two-storied monastic cloister in England, were rebuilt in 1297–1425. The *Vault-bosses are even better than those in the nave; some have charming contemporary scenes. Notable also is the tracery of the cloister windows. At the S.W. corner are the Monks' Lavatories and on the E. side is the beautiful Dec. entrance of the vanished Chapter House. Ruins of the Infirmary and Refectory (S. side) and Guest Hall (W. side) may be seen from the Close.

Palace St., skirting the N. wall of the precincts, affords a view through an imposing gateway of c. 1430 (good bosses) of the new *Bishop's Palace* and of a surviving 14C porch of the old. Outside the gate stands the little church of *St Martin-at-Palace* with a 14C font and chandelier of 1726. Opposite is *Cotman House*, the home of J. S. Cotman. Farther on, in Bishopgate, is the **Great Hospital** founded in 1249 by Bp. Walter de Suffield. The original infirmary building (much altered, though the Gothic chancel roof survives) is still in use as wards (special permission necessary), but the attached church of *St Helen*, rebuilt c. 1480, may be visited. Other features include a 15C cloister and a two-storied range by Thos. Ivory (1752–53).—The 13C *Bishop Bridge*, at the foot of Bishopgate, is one of the oldest bridges in England still used for traffic. To the left is the brick *Cow Tower*, where the cathedral authorities collected river-tolls.

Farther N. is St James's Hill where there is a splendid view over the river valley to the Cathedral, Castle, and City Hall, and beyond, on *Mousehold Heath* is the best view of Norwich (eloquently described in chap. xiv of 'Lavengro'), overlooking the city on the N.E. Here Kett's followers encamped. The heath was a favourite subject of John Crome's brush, but the famous windmill was burned down in 1933.

From the cathedral we may return towards the Market Place by Queen St. Here *St Mary-the-Less* (13C; the 'French Church') hidden in a huddle of buildings gives a good idea of medieval conditions. A guild church, it was taken over in turn by Walloons, French Protestants, Swedenborgians, and the Scottish Apostolic Church, and is now a furniture store.

From Castle Meadow, to the N. of the Castle Hotel, Davey Place leads into the MARKET PLACE (Pl. 10). Expanded to its present bounds only in the last century, it is splendidly enclosed by civic grandeur of all ages, dominated by a great parish church, and filled with the colour and bustle of the stall market. The E. side is Gentleman's Walk, from which *Royal Arcade* runs through to Castle St. where it presents an Art Nouveau façade by Skipper.

Closing the s. side is *St Peter Mancroft, an admirable Perp. church with an elaborate tower (the turrets, crenellations, and flèche are additions by the Streets, father and son, in 1881–95). From this tower the first complete peal of 5040 changes was rung in 1715.

The light and lofty arches of the arcade and the arrangement of the clerestory are the epitome of Norfolk Perpendicular, though the double hammerbeam roof is hidden behind ornamental coving. Notable are the font-canopy, a 15C alabaster panel, good brasses, and a tomb chest with effigy of Francis Windham (d. 1592). In the chancel is a memorial to Sir Thomas Browne (1605–82), author of the 'Religio Medici', who is buried here. The E. window is filled with 15C *Glass. The sacristy contains admirable church plate and illuminated MSS. (13–14C). Outside the church is a statue of Browne who lived from 1637 to his death in a house near the Lamb Inn yard opposite.

The CITY HALL (1932–38, by James and Pierce) matches the scale of the square with a tower 202 ft high; the bronze lions are by A. Hardiman. The civic regalia is famous (adm. daily). To the s. is the *Central Library and Record Office* (1963) with an open court and memorial to men of the U.S. 8th Air Force lost from E. Anglian bases in 1941–45. The *Guildhall* (1407–13), of flint, was rebuilt in 1535 with a gable of chequered flush-work; the 16C council chamber within has contemporary panelling and fittings and much 15C stained glass.

By LONDON STREET, made pedestrian and tastefully embellished, and Bedford St. (l.) we reach Bridewell Alley. Here the *Bridewell*, a flint-faced house on a vaulted undercroft of 1325 built (c. 1370) by Bartholomew, father of Wm. Appleyard, first mayor of Norwich, houses a *Museum of local industries (adm. free weekdays). *St Andrew's Church* (1506), almost opposite, where John Robinson, pastor of the

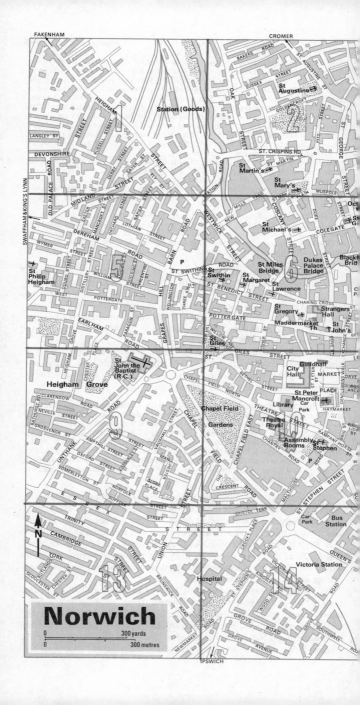

Norwich

| 0 | 300 yards |
| 0 | 300 metres |

MOUSEHOLD HEATH

MAGDALEN ROAD

SILVER STREET

MOUSEHOLD ST

BULL CLOSE ROAD

SILVER ROAD

CAVALRY ST

COWGATE

BARRACK

STREET

St James's

St Saviour

ST SAVIOUR

COWGATE

FISHERGATE

HILL

St James Hill

SPITALFIELDS

KETT'S HILL

Whitefriars Bridge

P

St Edmund

GATEGATE

St Martin at Palace

Cow Tower

PALACE STREET

EGYPTIAN RD

BISHOP BRIDGE RD

Meeting

St Clement

River QUAYSIDE

bridge

Palace

Gatehouse

Bishop's Palace

Great Hospital

BISHOPGATE

Bishop Bridge

GAS HILL

St Simon & St Judes

Maids Head

Norwich School

Cathedral

drew's II

St George's

St Peter's

TOMBLAND

Erpingham Gate

The Close

Deanery

Cricket Ground

ROSARY ROAD

St Michael's

QUEEN ST

UPPER KING ST

UPPER CLOSE

drew's

PRINCES

BANK PLAIN

ST FAITH LANE

Pulls Ferry (Watergate)

LOWER CLOSE

Royal

PRINCE OF WALES ROAD

ST FAITH LANE

RECORDER ROAD

ST MATTEW RD

Thorpe Hamlet

ATV

GPO

Castle

Shire Hall

Car Park

ROSE LANE

CHALKHILL RD

RIVERSIDE

ASPLAND RD

tle Gardens

ROSE AV

BELL AV

Car Park

P

RMENS AV

St John's

GOLDEN BALL

BALL

CATTLE MARKET STREET

MOUNTERGATE

ROSE LANE

Foundry Bridge

Library

THORPE

ROAD

ROAD

GT YARMOUTH

TRACEY RD

All Saints

11

St Peter Pamentergate

KING STREET

SYNAGOGUE ST

Norwich Station

12

LOWER CLARENCE ROAD

P

ROUEN ROAD

LANE

THORN

St Julian

RIVERSIDE ROAD

The Old Music House

BER STREET

CHAPELFIELD

St Etheldreda

ROAD

MARINERS

KING STREET

ROAD

15

16

Norwich City F.C.

ROAD

St John Sepulchre

FINKELGATE

Carrow Bascule Bridge

Boom Tower (Ruins)

STREET

GORDON RD

BURNABY RD

HALL ROAD

CITY ROAD

BRANCONDALE

Black Tower

CARROW HILL

CARROW ROAD

KING STREET

OLDWELL

LOWESTOFT

Pilgrim Fathers, was curate, contains the tombs of Sir John Suckling's mother and other ancestors of the poet. *Suckling House*, adjoining, is a fine 16C town house (open weekdays on request). **St Andrew's Hall** (Pl. 7; open weekdays), once the nave of a Dominican church of 1440–70, has been the city's place of assembly since the Dissolution. The chancel, now called *Blackfriars Hall*, served as the Dutch church in the 16–mid-19C. Together they constitute the only surviving Dominican church in England with notable Dec. and Perp. windows; the s. walk of the cloister endures and the vaulted vestibule of an earlier church (13C).

The Wensum (to the N.) is crossed by Blackfriars Bridge (1783; by Soane). Beyond, in the ancient 'Ward of Over-the-Water', stands *St George Colegate* (Pl. 6), a church built in 1459–1513 by rich local weavers. It retains 18C fittings. The painter John Crome (1786–1821; 'Old Crome') is buried here.

To the w. along Colegate is *St Michael-at-Coslany*, a fine church covered with flushwork tracery. Farther N., in St Mary's Plain, *St Mary-at-Coslany* has an Anglo-Saxon round tower; the 15C roof has been beautifully restored to show the diagonal bracing. *St Martin at Oak* in St Martin's Lane is now a parish hall. Farther N. still stands *St Augustine* with Perp. nave and chancel in flint and a brick tower (1687).

To the E. along Colegate is the *Octagon Chapel*, originally Presbyterian, now Unitarian, by Thomas Ivory (1755), with an impressive interior. A little farther on, a narrow alley leads to the **Old Meeting House* (1693) a fine old Congregational building, with a mellow exterior, and the interior perfectly preserved. At the end of the street, *St Clement* has a slender flint tower. It contains many tablets to the Ives and Harvey families, both of whom supplied Mayors for the city. To the left is MAGDALEN STREET (Pl. 3), the first to be comprehensively tidied up and beautified by the shopkeepers under the guidance of the Civic Trust. Along it is *Gurney Court*, where Elizabeth Fry and Harriet Martineau were born. *St Saviour* contains a Georgian w. gallery with organ, 15C font, and sword rests. Beyond, Anglia Square is an ambitious new shopping centre, with offices and a cinema. Farther E. is *St James Cowgate*, flint, with a brick tower perched on the w. roof, a sculptured font, a screen with painted figures (1505), and 15–16C stained glass. From here we may cross Whitefriars Bridge to Palace St. (p. 464), or branch right along Fishergate passing *St Edmund* (Perp.) now a store, to Fyebridge (1822), probably the oldest crossing place of the river, and so to Tombland.

From the Market Place, Dove St. leads N. to **St John Maddermarket*, as its name suggests the centre of the dyeing trade; the fine Perp. tower has the four evangelists on the top battlements. Within are a superb reredos (18C), many brasses, and monuments to Layers and Sothertons, mayors in the 16C and 17C. The *Maddermarket Theatre* is an 18C building reconstructed by Nugent Monck as an Elizabethan theatre with an apron stage. In Charing Cross is the *Strangers' Hall* (adm. weekdays, 10–5), a merchant's house with a 15C hall on a 13C under-croft. It was the centre for the immigrant weavers, then the assize judge's lodging, and is now a museum, founded in 1921 by L. G. Bolingbroke as England's first 'Folk Museum'.

Westwards along St Benedict St. are five churches. **St Gregory* has a sculptured font, a 'brass 'eagle' lectern (1496), a 14C Sanctuary knocker on the vestry door, and a 15C wall-painting. *St Laurence* has a tall Perp. tower with two reliefs over the w. door, and a 15C font. *St Margaret* (Dec.) has an 18C painted reredos above the s. door, and a brass to Anne Rede (d. 1577), which is a triple palimpsest. *St Swithin*, small, with a charming Victorian bell turret, is now a store. Turning s. up the narrow Three King Lane we can see the round tower (Norman) with a 15C octagonal upper stage of *St Benedict* (destroyed).

Across Pottergate is (l.) Cow Hill, where *St Giles* has the tallest of the Norwich towers (120 ft) which served as a beacon (fire basket in the church). The churchyard is beautifully planted with wistaria trees. The roof is an early hammerbeam with angels. The sword-rests, brasses and memorials to local doctors repay inspection.

Close by, in Willow Lane, is the house in which George Borrow spent his youth. St Giles St. continues w. to the R.C. church of *St John the Baptist* (Pl. 9), designed by Gilbert Scott in a convincing E.E. style with rich marbles and fine glass.— Farther w. lies (1½ m.) *Earlham Hall*, once the home of Elizabeth Fry, and since 1961 the administrative building of the University of East Anglia. The library includes the Coke collection from Holkham. The *Buildings by Denys Lasdun, with 'ziggurat' residence blocks, use to maximum effect the varying levels of this fine site in the Yare valley.

Chapel Field Gardens lead back to Theatre St. where is the *Assembly House*, the finest of the 18C buildings in the city, built by Thos. Ivory in 1754 on the foundations of the college of St Mary, now a restaurant and concert hall. Beyond, in Rampant Horse St.,**St Stephen* has a good flushwork tower and an impressive Perp. and Tudor interior with large clerestory windows. The E. window has 16C German stained glass. Among good memorials is one in Coade stone to Elizabeth Coppin (d. 1812), with a weeping putto. In Westlegate, across Red Lion St., is *All Saints*, in a rural setting. The font is carved with 24 figures of prophets and apostles. Just N. is *St John Timberhill* in whose churchyard those who died in the castle gaol were buried. The chandelier (1500) is German. Timberhill leads N. to the castle.

King Street (Pl. 7–16) runs s.e. from Prince of Wales Rd. Partly industrialized, it retains good old buildings including town houses of Anne Boleyn and the Howards. *St Peter Parmentergate*, in a shaded churchyard, has a carved 15C font, and the Berney tomb (1623; note the small boy in relief, asleep with his toy spade). The *Barge Inn* is 14–15C. *St Julian* (rebuilt) preserves three Anglo-Saxon windows in the N. wall. A Norman doorway (from the bombed church of *St Michael at Thorn*, to the s.) leads into the reconstructed cell of the anchoress Dame Julian. On the left is the *Old Music House* with Norman vaulting (crypt) and 15C timber roof, at one time (1633) the house of Lord Chief Justic Coke. *St Etheldreda* (now closed), in another lovely churchyard, has a round tower with a brick and flint octagonal upper stage. Farther on, King St. passes between the **Boom Towers* on either side of the river, and the *Black Tower* (r.) where the city walls follow Carrow Hill. Their line can be traced N.W. to Chapel Field Gdns. (see above). The direct return is along Ber St. where *St John de Sepulchre*, has a prominent Perp. tower, a two-storied N. porch, good flushwork, an E. Anglian 'lion' font, and a palimpsest brass. Thence to Timberhill, see above.

About 3 m. s. of Norwich (reached viâ King St.) lies **Caistor St Edmund**, or *Caister*, the Roman *Venta Icenorum*, the chief town in the territory of the Iceni. Within the 2C Roman enclosure (34 acres), which seems to have been burnt by the Saxons, is the parish church (Perp., with an E.E. chancel, containing a fine carved font of c. 1410, and a wall-painting of St Christopher).

FROM NORWICH TO YARMOUTH, 20 m. Railway in 30–40 min. A 47 at first skirts the Yare for 3 m.—7 m. *Blofield*. To the r., on the Yare, is the boating resort of *Brundall* (Yare).—11 m. *Acle*, with a round-towered 14C church, is a convenient starting-point for the Norfolk Broads (Rte 51). We keep to the right on A 1096, and skirt Breydon Water.—20 m. *Yarmouth*, see Rte 47.

FROM NORWICH TO CROMER, 27½ m. (A 140). Railway viâ Wroxham and North Walsham, in c. 50 min. The main road runs N. to (17 m.) *Aylsham*, an old market town with good 18C brick houses. In the churchyard of the Dec. church is a monument to Humphrey Repton (1752–1818), the landscape gardener, who lived at Sustead Hall, near by. B 1354 leads past the lovely Aylsham Old Hall (1689) to *Blickling Hall* (1½ m.). The gardens and state rooms (N.T.) are open April–Sept, daily exc. Fri, inc. BH, 2–6; from 11 in summer (fee). The park (4,500 acres) is open daily (no cars). The brick Jacobean house, built by Robt. Lyminge for Sir Henry Hobart in 1619–27, was altered by the Ivorys in 1765–70, about the time when it passed by marriage to the Marquess of Lothian. A fine 17C staircase leads up to the state rooms (family portraits); the Gallery (127 ft long) with a magnificent ceiling, is the chief architectural showpiece. In a previous house on the site Anne Boleyn spent her childhood. In the park is a mausoleum designed by Bonomi in 1793. The church contains Boleyn, Hobart, and Lothian monuments, and in *Erpingham* church, c. 3 m. N., is some 15–17C Flemish glass brought from the hall. To the w. is the 18C *Wolterton Hall* (Lord Walpole) open 2–5, Thurs in June–Sept (fee).—27½ m. *Cromer*, see Rte 52.

Another route from Norwich diverges from the Wroxham road by Constitution Hill (B 1150) and at (12¼ m.) *Coltishall*, a boating and angling centre with a picturesque lock, reaches the limit of navigation on the Bure. The attractive village has many good 18C houses, and the church has Saxon windows and a Norman font. The fine weather-boarded mill of *Horstead* stands across the river.—19½ m. North Walsham, a market town (6400 inhab.), is dominated by the ruined tower of the church, which contains a fine monument to Sir William Paston (d. 1610), who founded Paston School at which Nelson and Apb. Tenison were pupils. *Worstead*, 3 m. S.E., gave its name to a woollen fabric first manufactured here in the 12C by Flemish immigrants. The 14C church has good flushwork and 15C screens.—We bear left on A 149 for (23⅓ m.) *Gunton*, with a fine park (open to cars), and join A 140 2½ m. short of (27¾ m.) *Cromer* (Rte 52).

FROM NORWICH TO FAKENHAM, 25½ m. (A 1067). We ascend the Wensum valley, with the pleasant *Ringland* hills on the left. The church has a magnificent Perp. *Roof, a hammerbeam disguised by ribbed panelling with angels, and good stained glass. *Weston Longville* church, 2 m. N.E., has a fine 14C wall-painting of a Tree of Jesse.—On the right, beyond (8½ m.) *Attlebridge*, is *Great Witchingham*, where the *Norfolk Wildlife Park* (adm. daily from 10.30; fee) contains a notable collection of European mammals in their natural habitat, as well as exotic pheasants, etc.—We continue through the pretty hamlet of Lenwade and (13 m.; r.) *Sparham* with a 14C church (good roof) to (15 m.) *Bawdeswell*, the home of the Reeve, one of the Canterbury Pilgrims. The church (1955) is by Fletcher Watson. Near by are several fine churches. That of *Elsing*, 2¾ m. S., is a good Dec. building with the brass of its founder, Sir Hugh Hastings (d. 1347). The Aylsham road leads N.E. to *Reepham* (3½ m.). St Michael, with a tall Perp. tower dominates the market place; St Mary, connected by a vestry, has a Norman font and a fine monument to Sir Roger de Kerdiston (d. 1337). A third church is in ruins. The spectacular church of *Salle* (pron. 'Saul') lies 1½ m. farther N. It has a tall, decorated tower, two-storied N. and s. porches, an arch-braced roof with angels, good bosses in the transepts, finely carved stalls and misericords, and a 15C pulpit with Jacobean canopy. The church was built by the three local families of Brigge, Fontayne, and Boleyn; Anne Boleyn is reputedly buried here. *Cawston* church with another high tower and a superb *Roof, is 2 m. S.E. of Salle. It was built in the early 15C by Michael de la Pole, Earl of Suffolk.—At (18½ m.) *Twyford* is a Norman church. —25½ m. *Fakenham*, see Rte 53.

FROM NORWICH TO KING'S LYNN, 44 m. (A 47. A 17).—At (7 m.) *Easton* is the Norfolk School of Agriculture.—12¾ m. *Tuddenham* was the birthplace of Matthew Vassar (1791–1868), founder of Vassar College, N.Y.—16¼ m. East Dereham (9400 inhab.; Hotels), a market town has a fine parish church with painted Perp. ceilings in the N. and s. chapels, an 18C Flemish chest, and the tomb of William Cowper (1731–1800). Close to the unfinished belfry (16C) a ruined chapel covers the site of the tomb of St Withburga, foundress of the church. The site of Cowper's house, in the market-place, is occupied by the Cowper Memorial Church (Congregational). Bishop Bonner's Cottage (1502), with coloured pargeting, is now a museum (open in summer). W. H. Wollaston (1766–1828), the chemist, was born here; and George Borrow (1803–81) was born in *Dumpling Green*, 1½ m. s.—*North Elmham*, 5 m. N., was the seat of a bishopric founded in 673, the only see in East Anglia from 956 to 1075. Excavation in the extensive ruins behind the present church has revealed traces of a Saxon cathedral and bishop's castle. At *Swanton Morley*, a pleasant village 3 m. N.E. of Dereham, is the site (N.T.) of the house of Richard Lincoln, where he made the will that led to the emigration of his grandson Samuel, direct ancestor of Abraham Lincoln (comp. p. 460). The large E. window in the beautiful church (c. 1370) contains armorial glass commemorating the men of the adjoining R.A.F. station. At *Shipdham*, 5 m. s.w. of Dereham, the 13C church (two-stage lantern on the tower) contains a wooden *Lectern (c. 1500)—28¼ m. *Swaffham* and thence to (44 m.) *Lynn*, see Rte 56.

51 THE NORFOLK BROADS

Broadland, or the district of the **Norfolk Broads,** which are shallow lagoons among expanses of reed and fen, is a level tract of land in the form of a triangle, the apex of which is Norwich and the base the coast-line between Palling and Lowestoft. Within this area are about a dozen large 'broads' and twice as many smaller ones, and these together with the placid and sluggish streams, of which the chief are the *Yare,* the *Waveney,* and the *Bure,* all meeting ultimately in *Breydon Water,* provide about 200 m. of navigable water. The district has long been a favourite holiday resort for anglers and devotees of smooth-water sailing. The villages are often charming, with interesting churches; and there are many fine old manor-houses and a few ruined abbeys and castles.

A ROUND OF THE BROADS BY ROAD FROM NORWICH, 51 m.—Leaving Norwich by A 1151, which skirts Mousehold Heath, we pass through the suburb of *Sprowston,* where the 14C church has a brick tower and fine monuments, to reach Broadland at (7½ m.) **Wroxham** (Hotel), with a bridge over the Bure, crowded in holiday-time. Farther on a detour on the right should be made to (11½ m.) *Neatishead* and (12½ m.) *Barton Turf* (where the church has a good rood-screen), for a glimpse of Barton Broad. Returning to the main road, we cross the Ant at (16 m.) *Wayford Bridge* and traverse (17¾ m.) *Stalham* with the Maid's Head, a 14C inn (18C façade), and (19¼ m.) *Sutton.* Here a left turn leads to (20¾ m.) *Hickling* (Inn), connected by lane (¾ m.) with its broad.—From (24 m.) *Potter Heigham* (14–15C paintings in the church) we may return to Wroxham Bridge (8½ m.) viâ Ludham and Horning (see below).—A longer round follows the Yarmouth road across Heigham Bridge, on the Thurne, to (28¼ m.) *Rollesby Bridge* between *Rollesby Broad* (r.) and *Ormesby Broad.* On reaching (30¼ m.) *Ormesby* we turn right, then right again through (31½ m.) *Filby* and across *Filby Broad* to (36¼ m.) *Acle Bridge* (Inn). At (37½ m.) *Acle* (Hotel) we turn right on B 1140 for (40¼ m.) *South Walsham,* with two churches in one churchyard, and (41½ m.) *Ranworth,* with glimpses of broads on the right. Ranworth church contains a magnificent painted *Rood-screen and lectern and a fine illuminated choir-book (both early 15C). Thence viâ (44½ m.) *Salhouse* to Norwich.

Approaches. The chief gateways to the Broads are Norwich, Yarmouth, Lowestoft, Wroxham, Stalham, and Potter Heigham.—From *Norwich* we either descend the Yare, which communicates by 'dykes' with sundry small broads, or we may take train or bus to such points as Wroxham, Brundall, or Acle Bridge. *Surlingham Broad,* 6 m. w., is the nearest.—*Yarmouth* communicates directly with the Yare and Bure, and is a convenient starting-point for *Filby, Ormesby,* and *Rollesby Broads* (reached by road).—*Potter Heigham* may be reached by bus or viâ the Bure and Thurne. Viâ Breydon Water and the Waveney Yarmouth is linked with *Oulton Broad,* which is only 1 m. from *Lowestoft.*—*Wroxham* is the station for a whole series of broads adjoining the Bure.—*Stalham* connects with the Ant and *Barton Broad.*

Boats. Well-equipped *Yachts* or *Motor Cruisers* for holidays afloat on the Broads may be hired either in London (Messrs. Blakes Ltd., 47 Albemarle St., W.1, who have 20 boatyards on the Broads), at Geldeston, at Oulton Broad (Messrs. Hoseasons), or at any of the starting-points named above. A small rowing or sailing dinghy is usually included with craft from 32 ft upwards, which facilitates the exploration of the shallower waters. Boats without sleeping accommodation can be hired for day-trips. *Inns* are generally available for those who prefer not to sleep on board. The trading wherry, once the characteristic vessel of the Norfolk rivers almost disappeared from these waters, until in 1949, the Norfolk Wherry Trust saved the type from extinction.—Small *Excursion Steamers* ply on the Yare and Bure in summer.

Hamilton's 'Broads Navigation Charts and Index' (26th edn. 1971) is an essential practical companion.

Angling. The chief fish in the Broads and their connecting streams are bream and roach, but pike, perch, and rudd are also found. With the exception of Wroxham Broad (daily fee), most of the waters are free apart from the licence fee, but information should be obtained locally (e.g. from any of the boat-owners at the usual staithes; or direct from the Fishery Department, E. Suffolk and Norfolk River Authority, Norwich).

Perhaps the most characteristic series of broads are those strung along the river *Bure*, and *Wroxham Bridge* (comp. above) is a favourite starting-point for a tour (though the river is navigable up to *Coltishall*, to the N.W.). About 1½ m. below this a dyke on the right leads to *Wroxham Broad* (private moorings), sometimes called the 'Queen of the Broads'. On the right is *Salhouse Broad*; the *Hoveton Broads* on the left are private. Below these is (5 m.) *Horning* (Hotels). To the right are (6¾ m.) the entrance to *Ranworth Broad* (no adm. to inner broad; bird sanctuary) and (9½ m.) the *Fleet Dyke*, leading into *South Walsham Broad*. The tributary *Ant*, joining the Bure nearly opposite Fleet Dyke, leads viâ (¾ m.) *Ludham Bridge* and *Irstead* church, with good woodwork, to (4 m.) *Barton Broad*, a large but shallow lagoon (1½ m. long), with well-wooded banks. About 2 m. N. of this broad, reached viâ the Ant and a dyke, is *Stalham* (see above).—Returning to the Bure, we see, on its left bank, the ruins of *St Benet's Abbey* (founded in 1020) from which the Bishop of Norwich, the only abbot in the Church of England, takes the style of 'Abbot of St Benedict'. From (11¾ m. from Wroxham) *Thurne Mouth* we may ascend the Thurne (Hotel at *Thurne*, ¼ m. r.) to (3½ m.) *Potter Heigham Bridge*, much frequented in summer, and thence to (5 m.) *Heigham Sound*, communicating with the shallow *Hickling Broad*, the largest of all (3 m. in circumference), a noted bird sanctuary. At the N. end is *Hickling Staithe* (Inn). To the N.E. of Heigham Sound, and connected with it by Meadow Dyke, is (1½ m.) *Horsey Mere* (N.T.), 1½ m. s. of which is *Martham Broad*, on the opposite side of the Thurne.—A dyke, 1½ m. above the mouth of the Thurne, leads to (¾ m.) *Womack Water* and (1¼ m.) *Ludham*, with an interesting church.—The lower course of the Bure, from the mouth of the Thurne to (19½ m.) *Acle Bridge* (see above) and (31½ m.) Yarmouth, traverses duller country.

The Bure flows into the E. end of *Breydon Water* (beware of low tides); at the s.w. extremity, near Burgh Castle, is the mouth of the *Waveney*, the winding course of which may be ascended to (18 m.) *Beccles* and (21 m.) *Geldeston Lock*. It passes within 1 m. of *Fritton Decoy*. The *New Cut*, beginning near this point, connects it with the Yare at (3½ m.) *Reedham* (see below). *Oulton Dyke*, c. 5 m. above the New Cut, connects it with (1½ m.) *Oulton Broad* and so (comp. p. 450) with *Lowestoft*.

The *Yare* enters Breydon Water near the Waveney, and may be ascended all the way to Norwich. Beyond (6 m.) *Reedham*, with a fine 17C inn, we pass (1½ m.; l.) *Hardley Dyke*, the mouth of the *Chet*, which may be navigated to (4 m.) *Loddon*, a tiny old market town, with a very ancient alms-box in its 15C church. Near by are the churches of *Chedgrave* and *Heckingham*, with Norman work.—9 m. *Cantley Red House*, a favourite anglers' inn. About 1 m. farther on (l.) are the remains of *Langley Abbey* (c. 1200).—13 m. *Buckenham Ferry* (Inn), also frequented by anglers. A dyke on the left leads to (¾ m.) *Rockland Broad*, the reed beds of which harbour many wildfowl.—14½ m. *Coldham Hall* (Inn) is famous for its large 'baskets' of roach and bream. About ½ m. off is *Brundall*, and at 16¼ m. is the entrance (l.) to *Surlingham Broad*. The scenery to (21 m.) *Norwich* is very attractive.

52 GREAT YARMOUTH TO CROMER AND KING'S LYNN

ROAD, 88½ m., a devious but interesting way along the coast. The more direct road to Cromer (34½ m.; A 149) runs viâ Potter Heigham and North Walsham.

The main road leads N. from Yarmouth to (3¼ m.) **Caister-on-Sea**, with a moated *Castle* (adm. daily exc. Sat, May–Sept; fee), built c. 1432. It belonged to Sir John Fastolf (Shakespeare's 'Falstaff'), and subsequently to the Pastons (many of the 'Letters' were written here). It now contains a large motor museum. The Never Turn Back Inn contains relics of the lifeboat disaster of 1901. Caister was the site of a Roman harbour; parts of the town walls and a seamen's hostel remain (adm. daily, Sun from 2; fee).—Farther N. we keep to the right on B 1159 viâ *Hemsby* and (8¼ m.) *Winterton* (Hotel), with a fine 15C church tower (130 ft). We turn inland to (9½ m.) *East Somerton*, with a ruined church in woods, and *West Somerton* church, which has a Norman round tower and 14C wall-paintings.—At (12¼ m.) *Horsey*, near Horsey Mere (Rte 51), a huge barrier 4½ m. long has been erected against the sea to prevent a repetition of the floods of 1938. It has a fine drainage mill (adm. on request). Through (15¼ m.) *Waxham* and (16¼ m.) *Sea Palling* we skirt the sandy shore, and regain the coast again at (22 m.) *Happisburgh* (pron. 'Hazeburgh'), a pretty village with a lighthouse. The fine church with a high tower has a notable font, and a good Perp. screen.—At (25¾ m.) *Bacton* are the remains of *Bromholm Priory* (Cluniac; 1113), mentioned in Chaucer's 'Reeve's Taile' and in 'Piers Plowman'. This attractive village is now overshadowed by the terminal of the gas pipeline from the North Sea.—27¼ m. *Paston* is a name familiar from the 'Paston Letters' (15C). A fine flint *Barn (163 ft long) is all that remains of their manor. The thatched church contains Paston monuments.—29 m. *Mundesley* (Hotel) is a seaside resort with fine sands and cliffs.

Knapton *Church, 1½ m. inland, has a double hammerbeam roof with nearly 140 angels, and a fine font cover. *Trunch*, 1 m. w., has another good roof, a magnificent Perp. *Font cover (one of only four in England), and a good screen.

The road skirts the coast viâ (32 m.) *Trimingham*, with a notable painted choir-screen, and (34 m.) *Overstrand* (Hotel), another seaside and golfing resort.

36 m. **Cromer** (Hotels, mostly closed in winter), in a high but sheltered situation, is the most charming of the East Anglia seaside resorts (5300 inhab.). It became fashionable in Edwardian times, but retains

its fishing industry, famous for crabs. It has fine sands, high cliffs, a pier and esplanade, and excellent golf links. The church is a 15C building, notable for the height of piers and arches, and with a splendid tower 159 ft high (view; fee).

Just s.w. of the town is *Cromer Hall* (no adm.), the birthplace of Lord Cromer (1841–1917).—*Felbrigg* (N.T.; adm. April–Sept, Tues–Thurs, Sat, Sun & BH 2–6; fee), 2 m. s., is the fine country seat of the Wyndhams (c. 1620). The w. wing was added about 50 years later. In the park, by Repton, is a church with a series of *Brasses (1351–1608) and monuments by Grinling Gibbons and Nollekens.

The road continues through the *Runtons* above cliffs which have been mostly preserved from permanent building by 'Half Year Rights', the continuing medieval claim to common grazing; the rash of caravans are removed for the 6-month winter period. Beyond (38½ m.) *West Runton* (Hotel), where the delightful wooded Beacon Hill, or 'Roman Camp' (N.T.; shown in 1965 to be a telegraph station of the Napoleonic period), 1 m. inland, includes the highest ground in Norfolk, the coast-road passes the fine *Beeston Regis* church, on the cliff edge. The 13C Priory, to the w., is much ruined.—40 m. **Sheringham** (Hotels), another pleasant bathing and golfing resort (4700 inhab.). The 'Poppy Line', between Sheringham and Weybourne, is equipped with steam locomotives and open to the public from Easter to October. *Sheringham Hall* (open weekdays) is in grounds laid out by Humphrey Repton with magnificent rhododendrons.—At (43 m.) *Weybourne* (Hotel and Restaurant) are the ruins of an Augustinian priory next to the church. The high ground now recedes and the salt marshes begin, noted for their abundant bird life (and provided with 'hides' and dyke paths). A shingle barrier was built along the shore after the disastrous flood of 1953.—At (47 m.) *Cley* (pron. 'Cly'), once a busy port, is a fine windmill (N.T.), and an 18C custom house. The large 13–15C church, ¾ m. inland, has an elaborate clerestory and s. porch, and ruined transepts. It contains interesting brasses.

48½ m. **Blakeney** (Hotel with swimming pool) is a delightful sailing village (regatta in Aug). The *Church* has a slender beacon tower at the E. end, fine E.E. vaulting in the chancel, and a double hammerbeam roof in the nave. A steep High St. with charming houses leads down to the hard. The undercroft of the 14C *Guildhall* may be visited. *Blakeney Point* (N.T.; ferries from Blakeney or Morston, 1 m. w.), and the fore-shore to the N. are noted bird sanctuaries (1100 acres).

At *Langham*, 2 m. s., Capt. Marryat (d. 1848) wrote several of his novels.—B 1156 follows the Glaven viâ (1 m.) *Wiveton* (medieval bridge, and good Perp. church) to (2 m.) *Glandford*, a pretty village, with a shell museum beside the interesting church.

52½ m. *Stiffkey* is noted for its cockles ('Stewkey blues').—56 m. *Wells-next-the-Sea* (Hotel) is an attractive small seaport (2300 inhab.) with a rebuilt Perp. church. To Binham and Walsingham, see p. 479. —About 1 m. s. of (57½ m.) *Holkham* (Hotel) is ***Holkham Hall** (Earl of Leicester), a huge Palladian edifice of white brick by William Kent (1734–60), with an inscription over the door to the effect that it was "planned, planted, built, decorated and inhabited the middle of the 18C, by Thomas Coke, Earl of Leicester."

It contains very valuable collections of art (classical sculptures; paintings by Raphael, Veronese, Leonardo, Rubens, Van Dyck, Poussin, Claude, Reynolds, Gainsborough, etc.; and a copy of the lost 'Bathers' cartoon by Michelangelo), shown June–Sept, Thurs 11.30 or 2–5; also Mon in July–Aug 11.30–5; rfmts; fee. The *Park* (open daily; no cars) was laid out by Capability Brown. Holkham is well known in the history of agriculture for the work done here by 'Coke of Norfolk, the first farmer in England' (Thomas William Coke, 1st Earl of Leicester by the later creation, 1752–1842). His monument, a 120 ft column supported by four cows and crowned with a wheatsheaf, was erected by his tenants in 1845. The rebuilt *Church* contains good modern carving.

61½ m. *Overy Staithe* (Hotel) a pleasant little resort. Lord Nelson (1758–1805) was born in the old rectory (pulled down in 1802) of *Burnham Thorpe*, 1 m. s. The church contains the font at which he was christened and a lectern and rood made of wood from the 'Victory'; also the fine brass of Sir William Calthorp (d. 1420). About 1 m. s. of Burnham Thorpe is the ruined *Creake Abbey* (Augustinian; founded 1221) with a 13C chancel and 14C N. transept (adm. Wed, Thurs, Sat; fee). The churches of *North Creake* and *South Creake* are both interesting. *Burnham Market* is 1¾ m. s.w. of Overy Staithe.—62¾ m. *Burnham Norton* has a church with a lofty circular tower and vestiges of a Carmelite friary (1241).—The font at (64 m.) *Burnham Deepdale* has 11C carving (the 'Labours of the months').—65¼ m. *Brancaster* is a golfing resort, on the site of a Roman fort (Branodunum) guarding the 'Saxon Shore'. Offshore is *Scolt Head* (N.T.), a sandy and shingly island, with a famous ternery (strictly preserved).—The church of (69½ m.) *Holme-next-the-Sea* contains the earliest brass with an English inscription (c. 1400). Here the *Peddar's Way*, a prehistoric trackway, improved by the Romans, reaches the sea. It ran inland to Castle Acre and Ixworth (p. 478).

72½ m. **Hunstanton** (Hotels), facing w. across the Wash, is a favourite summer resort (3900 inhab.), with good bathing, a pier, swimming and boating pools, and coloured stratified cliffs surmounted by pleasant greensward. Just s. of the old lighthouse are the ruins of a chapel of St Edmund. At *Old Hunstanton*, 1½ m. N., with two golf courses, is *Hunstanton Hall* (mainly of 1500), which remained in the hands of the Le Strange family from the Conquest until 1949. The church contains a Norman font and Le Strange monuments, including a *Brass to Sir Roger (d. 1506).—In the church of (75 m.) *Heacham* is a portrait-medallion (1933) of Princess Pocahontas (1595–1617), wife of John Rolfe of Heacham Hall, whose parents are buried here.—77½ m. *Snettisham* and (80 m.) *Dersingham* (Hotel) both have fine churches, the former with a tall steeple. *Shernborne*, 2 m. E., is noted for its Norman font.

To the s. of Dersingham (1½ m.) is **Sandringham Hall,** the country home of the Queen. The 'Norwich Gates', at the main entrance to the grounds (open April, May & Sept, Tues, Wed & Thurs; June–Aug, Tues–Fri & BH; also Sun in July–Aug; 2–5; in the absence of the royal family), are of elaborate ironwork and were the wedding-present from the city of Norwich to Edward VII (1863). Among the chief points of interest are the *Rose Garden*, the *Dutch Garden*, the *Water Garden*, a Chinese bronze statue of Buddha (1698), and the *Kennels*. The *House* is usually open in summer. *Sandringham Church* (late-Perp.) contains memorials of Edward VII (including a silver altar presented by Rodman Wanamaker) and members of the royal family. George VI (1895–1952) was born at York Cottage in the grounds and died at the Hall.

At *Wolferton* (2¾ m. w.) the church contains some good screens.—At *Appleton House*, 1¼ m. s.e. of Sandringham Hall, Olav V of Norway was born in 1903.

84 m. **Castle Rising**, perhaps the most interesting of Norfolk villages, has a massive Norman *Castle* (c. 1150; adm. daily, Sun in winter from 2;

fee), with huge earthworks (covering over 12 acres), and a 12C Keep similar to that at Norwich. Also, a beautiful late-Norman *Church* (12C), and a Jacobean *Trinity Hospital* (adm. daily, exc. Sun), built by Henry Howard before 1614, a charity for ten elderly women, who still wear a quaint Stuart costume on Sundays.—86 m. *South Wootton* has a fine Norman font.—88½ m. **King's Lynn**, see Rte 56.

53 TILBURY TO BURY ST EDMUNDS AND CROMER

ROAD, 131 m. An interesting way to approach East Anglia from Kent or Southend airport. A 128, B 1007. 22 m. *Chelmsford.*—A 130, A 131. 34 m. *Braintree.*—48½ m. *Sudbury.*—A 134. 64½ m. **Bury St Edmunds.**—B 1106. 80 m. *Brandon.*—A 1065. 95 m. *Swaffham.*—109 m. *Fakenham.*—A 148. 131 m. **Cromer.**

Tilbury, opposite Gravesend (foot-ferry), see the 'Blue Guide to London'. We cross A 13, connecting with the Dartford–Purfleet tunnel. A 128 and B 1007 lead N. over the *Langdon Hills* (378 ft), a fine view-point for the Thames Estuary.—9½ m. *Laindon Church* has a unique 15C priest's house of timber against its w. end; the village has been engulfed by *Basildon New Town*, a vast suburban community with 129,000 inhabitants. We cross the main Southend road.—At (13¼ m.) *Billericay* is the Chantry House where the Pilgrim Fathers assembled before their embarkation.—22 m. **Chelmsford**, see Rte 47. We quit the town by the station and after 3½ m. N. on A 130, we turn N.E. on A 131. At *Pleshey*, 2¾ m. N.W. of the fork, the village is enclosed in an earthen rampart, with a huge motte and bailey on the s. preserving a brick arch bridge.—At (28 m.) *Great Leighs* is the Essex showground. *Little Leighs* priory (no adm.), ¾ m. w. of our road, preserves two gatehouses and part of a quadrangle of c. 1550.—34 m. **Braintree** (24,800 inhab.; Hotel), at the junction of two Roman roads, was a medieval wool town; it is now a centre of silk and rayon weaving. Nicholas Udall, the author of 'Ralph Roister Doister' was vicar here from 1537. A bronze fisherboy fountain (1938) adorns the centre. Bank St. leads past old houses and inns to *Bocking*, adjoining on the N., which has a good 15C church.

Black Notley, 1¾ m. S.E., was the birthplace of John Ray (1628–1705), the naturalist, who is buried in the churchyard. At *Cressing Temple*, 3 m. S.E., are two huge barns, one 15C, the other possibly partly of pre-Conquest date.—To Bishop's Stortford and to Colchester, see p. 456.

40 m. *Halstead* (7600 inhab.) in the upper valley of the Colne, has an unexpectedly steep High St. The mill set up by the Courtaulds in 1826 is by the stream. Blue Bridge House (1710–14) on the Earls Colne road is open June–Sept, Thurs–Fri, 2.30–5.30 (fee). *Gosfield Hall* (open May–Sept, Wed & Thurs, 2–4; fee), with a brick Tudor court and panelled long gallery, lies 2½ m. w. It was Louis XVIII's first English home in 1807–09. To Colchester and Haverhill, see p. 444.—42¼ m. *Little Maplestead* (l.) has the latest (mainly early-14C) and smallest of the four medieval round churches of England (circular nave 29 ft in diameter).—48½ m. **Sudbury** (8200 inhab.; Hotel) has three striking Perp. churches (*St Gregory*, *All Saints*, and *St Peter*) and some half-timbered houses from its prosperous days of silk-weaving. It was the birthplace of Thomas Gainsborough (1727–88), who is commemorated by a statue by Mackennal (1913) in Market Hill; his house in Stour St. is preserved (adm. daily exc. Mon,

10.30–12.30, 2–5, Sun from 2; fee). All three churches have notable woodwork, and the font-cover in St Gregory's rivals that of Ufford. In the vestry of St Gregory's is preserved the head of Simon of Sudbury, Abp. of Canterbury in 1375–81 (beheaded by Wat Tyler). The town is the 'Eatanswill' of the 'Pickwick Papers'.

Edwardstone, 6 m. E., was the birthplace of John Winthrop (1588–1649), first Governor of Massachusetts, and his son John (1606–76), Governor of Connecticut, was born at *Groton*, 1 m. farther, a village that has given name to a famous American school.

52 m. **Long Melford**, see Rte 48. The road viâ Lavenham (p. 454) comes in just s. of (60 m.) *Bradfield Combust*, the family home and burial-place of Arthur Young (1741–1820), agriculturalist and traveller, who was at school at Lavenham in 1748–58.

64½ m. **BURY ST EDMUNDS** (Hotels), the historic centre (25,600 inhab.) of west Suffolk, the seat of the bishop of St Edmundsbury & Ipswich since 1914, and the headquarters of the Royal Anglian Regiment, takes its name from the shrine of St Edmund, last king of East Anglia (d. c. 870), which was long a famous resort of pilgrims. The abbey (founded 945) rebuilt here in the 11C became one of the noblest and wealthiest in England, but it is now almost a total ruin.

The town (called by Cobbett 'the nicest town in the world') owes its grid-pattern to Abbot Baldwin (1065–97) who laid out round the precincts of the abbey the first planned town of Norman Britain, with Churchgate, the main street, in line with the high altar. Today it corresponds closely with Carlyle's description of it ('Past & Present') as a "prosperous brisk town beautifully diversifying, with its clear brick houses and ancient clean streets, . . . the general grassy face of Suffolk; looking out pleasantly . . . towards the rising sun," and having on its E. edge, "long, black, and massive, a range of monastic ruins." In 1214, in the abbey church, the barons, with Abp. Langton at their head, drew up the 'Petition of the Barons', the basis for Magna Carta. Humphrey Repton (1752–1818), the landscape gardener, and 'Ouida' (Louise de la Ramée; 1840–1908), were born at Bury. It is noted nowadays for sugar-beet processing and brewing.

The existing remains of the Abbey are approached from Angel Hill, on the E. side of the town, in which is the *Athenæum*, a building in the Adam style. Opposite the fine *Angel Hotel* (18C; 13C vaulted cellars), where Sam Weller first encountered Job Trotter, is the imposing *Abbey Gateway* (1327; rebuilt after fire in 1347), now the entrance to a well-kept public garden in which are the formless ruins of the refectory, the abbot's house, etc., and the *Abbot's Bridge* (13C) across the Lark. Beyond the river are the modern buildings of *King Edward VI School*, where Edw. Fitzgerald was a pupil. To the s. are the ruined E. end and transepts of the abbey church. The w. front is now incorporated into a row of houses. The *Norman Tower* is a magnificent example of early Norman work, executed with the axe and not with the chisel. Beside it is the *Cathedral of St James*, with a noble nave begun in 1438, and good 19C windows and roof; a new N.W. porch and cloister walk were dedicated in 1960–61 and a new chancel, by S. Dykes Bower, replaces that by Gilbert Scott. Across the huge graveyard is *St Mary's*, a beautiful 15C church, with a magnificent hammerbeam *Roof, and a fine waggon roof in the choir. In the s. aisle are the tomb (with skeleton effigy) and chantry-ceiling of John Baret (1467) and the brass of Jankyn Smith and his wife (1487), while s. and N. of the choir are the imposing Drury and Carew tombs (1536 and 1501). The N. or Notyngham Porch (1437) has an elaborate vault and pendant. In the N.E.

corner of the sanctuary is the grave of Mary Tudor (1496–1533), sister of Henry VIII.

The Queen Anne house (N.T.) at No. 8 Angel Hill contains the small but excellent *Gershom-Parkington Collection* of clocks and watches (weekdays, 10–1, 2–5). In Northgate St. is the ruined gatehouse of *St Saviour's Hospital*, where Humphrey, Duke of Gloucester, died in 1447.

Abbeygate St. (with Georgian shopfronts), or Churchgate St., in which is a notable Independent Chapel of 1711, lead to Corn Hill, the business centre of the town. In the Traverse is *Cupola House* (1693), a dignified town mansion, the best of many 17–18C houses in Bury. Many streets have earlier houses and inns. A little below the *Market Cross*, remodelled by Adam in 1774, is the 12C *Moyses Hall* (now a museum; weekdays 10–1, 2–5), which may have been a Jewish merchant's house. In Guildhall St., at the other end of Corn Hill, is the *Guildhall*, with a porch of c. 1480, and in Westgate St. is the *Theatre Royal*, by William Wilkins (1819; restored 1962–64).

Buses from Corn Hill or Angel Hill to all destinations.

Ickworth (N.T.), 3 m. s.w., a mansion of 1794–1830 designed by the Irish architect Francis Sandys, recalls by its unusual plan—a rotunda with flanking wings—the eccentricity of its builder, the Earl of Bristol and Bp. of Derry (1730–1803). Surrounded by a noble park (open daily), it may be visited on Tues, Wed, Thurs, Sat, Sun, & BH, 2–6, in April–mid-Oct (fee) and contains good furniture and paintings. *Great Saxham Hall* (1779), 4 m. w. of Bury, is by Adam and 'Capability' Brown.—Excursions may be made from Bury also to *Ampton*, 5 m. N., where Jeremy Collier was rector in 1679–84; and *Rushbrooke*, 3 m. s.e., with a charming little church.

The direct ROAD FROM BURY TO NORWICH (39½ m.) leads viâ (6½ m.) *Ixworth* where the main street may represent the start of the Peddar's Way (p. 475). The Abbey (adm. May–mid-Aug, Tues, Thurs, Sun & BH, 2–5; fee. Also by appointment) incorporates remains of a 12C priory. *Stowlangtoft* church, 2 m. S.E., contains fine carvings: *Bench-ends and misericords, and Flemish panelling at the E. end. At (19½m.) *Kenninghall* stood a palace of the Howards, dukes of Norfolk (demolished 1650). It was the birthplace of Henry Howard (1517–47), the poet earl of Surrey, and Mary I took refuge here in 1553 before going to Framlingham. *Quidenham* church, 1 m. N., has a memorial chapel to the U.S.A.A.F.—At (23½ m.) *New Buckenham* are the scanty remains of a Norman castle and a quaint market hall with a pillory, while *Old Buckenham* has a thatched church.—39½ m. *Norwich*, see Rte 50.

From Bury to *Hengrave* and *Icklingham*, see p. 458.

From Bury the direct road to King's Lynn (A 134) strikes N. through Thetford (p. 459). From it, at (66½ m.) *Fornham St Martin*, we take a minor road (l.) past *Culford School* (450 boys) and cross A 11 (Rte 49) at (77 m.) *Elvedon*.—80 m. **Brandon**, a small country town, was for long a centre of flint-knapping, one of the oldest trades in the world. It gives a title to the Dukes of Hamilton and Brandon.—We cross the Little Ouse into Norfolk.

Weeting, 1 m. N. on B 1106, has a 12C castle (adm. daily, Sun from 2), with a good keep and square moat. *Methwold* church, 5½ m. farther on, has a Perp. crocketed steeple (120 ft), and a brass to Sir Adam de Clifton (d. 1367).

We follow A 1065 across Thetford Chase.—At 82½ m. B 1108 branches r. to (1 m.) *Grime's Graves* (adm. daily, Sun from 2 in winter; fee), an area of ancient flint quarries (c. 2100 B.C.). Nearly 400 shafts and pits have been discovered closely clustered together, and several have been opened to allow visitors to descend to the galleries that radiate from the bottom of the shafts.—94½ m. **Swaffham** (Hotel), with 4300 inhab., a market town with good Georgian buildings. The elegant Rotunda, crowned with a figure of Ceres, was erected by the Earl of Oxford in

1783. The large Perp. church, traditionally built by a peddlar who found treasure under a tree in the town (and whose figure recurs several times in the church), is built of stone, with a double hammerbeam roof.

Oxburgh Hall (N.T.), 7 m. s.w. of Swaffham, a splendid 15C moated mansion still occupied by its founders, the Bedingfelds, has a castellated gatehouse adm. April–Sept, Tues, Wed, Thurs, Sat, Sun & BH, 2–6; fee) containing needlework panels signed by Mary, Queen of Scots, and Bess of Hardwick. The church contains Bedingfeld *Monuments (c. 1520) in terracotta.—At *Cockley Cley*, 3½ m. s.e. of Swaffham, is a Folk Museum.

98½ m. (l.) **Castle Acre**, with the picturesque remains of an extensive Cluniac *Priory* founded by William de Warenne in 1090 (adm. daily, closed Sun in winter till 2; fee). The chief feature is the beautiful late-Norman w. front of the church, but the prior's chapel and lodging, remodelled in Tudor times, the reredorter, and the Tudor entrance-gateway are also noteworthy. The *Castle*, the architectural remains of which are trifling, had the same founder and stood on enormous earth-works, probably of Roman origin. The N. gateway spans the village street. The *Parish Church*, between the castle and the priory, contains painted 15C woodwork (font-cover, pulpit, and screen-panels). The *Peddar's Way* (comp. p. 475) is well seen to the N.

South Acre church, just to the s., contains a brass to Sir John Harsick (d. 1384) and his wife, and the tomb of Lord Mayor Barkham (1621); also a 14C wooden effigy, and a delicately carved 14C screen. At *West Acre*, 2¼ m. w., the gatehouse and barn of another priory have survived near the church (with a wide 14C chancel arch). *Narborough* church, 2½ m. farther s.w., has a fine standing effigy of Clement Spelman, Recorder of Nottingham (d. 1679), as well as good brasses (one a palimpsest). A 14C gatehouse is the chief relic of the priory of *Pentney*, 1 m. beyond.

At (99 m.) is the tiny Saxon church of *Newton*, and beyond the elaborate churches of (103 m.) *Weasenham*, a by-road (r.) leads to (1 m.) *Wellingham* church, with a fine painted screen (1532).

The church of *Tittleshall*, 2 m. E., has striking *Monuments to Sir Edward Coke (d. 1634), by Nicholas Stone; to his wife, Bridget Paston (d. 1598); and to Thomas Coke, Earl of Leicester (d. 1759) and his wife, with bust by Roubiliac; and to other members of the family.

106 m. The road passes the lodge gates of *East Raynham Hall*, seat of the Marquess of Townshend (descendant of 'Turnip Townshend'), sometimes ascribed to Inigo Jones.—109 m. **Fakenham** (Hotels), a pleasant little market town, has a Dec. and Perp. church with a fine high tower, containing a notable font.—*Toftrees*, 2 m. s.w., and *Sculthorpe*, 2 m. N.w., have Norman fonts of local type.

B 1105 leads N. viâ (3 m.) *East Barsham*, with a fine early-Tudor manor-house, to (5 m.) **Walsingham**, or *Little Walsingham*, noted for the ruins of an *Augustinian Priory* (adm. Wed & BH, 2–5; also Sun in May–Sept, & Mon & Fri in Aug; fee), which onced owned the famous and wealthy shrine of 'Our Lady of Walsingham' commemorating the apparition of the Blessed Virgin to the lady of the manor (1061). The pre-Reformation pilgrimage was revived in 1921, and there are now two shrines: the Anglican church (1931, enlarged 1938), with a tall red brick tower, into which the image of Our Lady of Walsingham was transferred from the parish church in 1931; and the Roman Catholic *Slipper Chapel*, 1½ m. s., a 14C building reconsecrated in 1938 after being in secular hands since the Reformation. In the village are also the ruins of a late 13C *Franciscan Friary* (adm. Wed & Bank Holidays; fee), and the *Parish Church* (restored after a fire in 1961), containing a fine Perp. front. The church of *Great Walsingham*, 1 m. N.E., has good bench-ends.—

About 3½ m. N.E. are the remains of the Benedictine *Binham Priory*, the nave of which (1091) is now the parish church. The W. front is admirable E.E. work.

A 148 leads W. from Fakenham to King's Lynn.—9 m. *Harpley*. A mile N. is *Houghton Hall* (Marquess of Cholmondeley; adm. mid-Apr–late-Sept, Thurs, Sun, & BH, 2–5; fee), a vast Palladian edifice (façade 450 ft long), built in 1722–31 for Sir Robert Walpole (b. at Houghton village in 1676; d. 1745), who, like his son Horace (1717–97), is buried in the little church in the park. The house contains a fine collection of paintings. We cross the Peddar's Way (p. 475) which leads S. over the bleak *Massingham Heath* to Castle Acre.— 13 m. *Hillington*, with a manor-house of 1627, lies c. 3¼ m. s. of Sandringham.— 20½ m. *King's Lynn*, see Rte 56.

We take A 148 N.E. to (121 m.) **Holt** (Hotel), an attractive and colourful village, the birthplace of Sir Thomas Gresham (1519–79), Lord Mayor of London and founder of the Royal Exchange, who propounded 'Gresham's Law'. Gresham's School here was founded by his uncle in 1555. The elaborate Home Place was built by E. S. Prior in 1903.—At 125½ m., we pass the entrance to Sheringham Hall (see p. 474), and a by-road (r.) to (3 m.) *Baconsthorpe Castle* (adm. daily, Sun from 2; fee), the remains of a manor-house (1486) with a moat.—131 m. *Cromer*, see Rte 52.

54   LONDON TO CAMBRIDGE AND PETERBOROUGH

ROAD, 87½ m. A 10 crosses the N. Circular Rd. at (6 m.) *Edmonton.*—19 m. *Broxbourne.*—24½ m. **Ware** (both by-passed).—41½ m. *Royston.*—54½ m. **Cambridge.** Alternative route viâ Baldock, see Rte 46.—A 604. 68½ m. *Godmanchester.*—69 m. **Huntingdon.**—A 14. 73½ m. *Alconbury Hill.*—A 1. 82½ m. *Norman Cross.*—A 15. 87½ m. **Peterborough.**—Alternative route using motorway, see Rte 49.

RAILWAY to Cambridge, 55⅜ m. in 1¼–1¾ hrs, from Liverpool St. Principal Stations: 17 m. *Broxbourne* and *Hoddesdon*, junction for *Ware* (5¼ m.) and Hertford (7¼ m.), all by suburban service.—30¼ m. *Bishop's Stortford.*—55¾ m. **Cambridge.**

To Peterborough (76½ m. in 60–90 min.) from King's Cross viâ Hitchin and Huntingdon, see Rte 46.

Another route to Cambridge (58 m. in 1½ hr) from King's Cross leaves the main line at Hitchin and runs viâ *Royston* (where a change is made).

From London to (19 m.) *Broxbourne*, see the 'Blue Guide to London'. The old road (A 117) to the E. of the modern dual-carriageway (A 10) follows the line of the Roman *Ermine Street.* — 20½ m. *Hoddesdon* retains a fine Georgian High Street with spacious houses and inns, including the Golden Lion (c. 1600), with good timbering. John Loudon Macadam lived here in 1825–36 (tablets in High Street and Broxbourne church). To the east, astride the river Lea, is the area slowly becoming the *Lea Valley Regional Park* (6500 acres), as it is salvaged from the derelict land and gravel workings of 'the backyard of London', as a result of a plan prepared by the Civic Trust in 1964. Within the confines of the Park, 1 m. N.E. of Hoddesdon, is *Rye House*, where an abortive plot to assassinate Charles II and his brother James was hatched (1683; comp. p. 458); only the late-15C gatehouse now survives. The well-sited Power Station at *Rye Meads* is by Sir Giles Gilbert Scott.

A 602 leads N.W. to (4 m.) Hertford (see below) viâ (2 m.) *Hertford Heath*. Here *Haileybury College*, a boys' school founded in 1862, occupies the buildings (by Wilkins) of *East India College* established in 1805 by the East India Co. for its civil-service students but dissolved in 1858. In 1942 Haileybury was amalgamated with the *Imperial Service College*. Earl Attlee was a pupil at Haileybury.

B 180 leads N.E. viâ (6¾ m.) *Widford*, with Blakesware Park, the 'Blakesmoor' of Lamb's Essays, to (c. 9 m.) the long Georgian street of *Much Hadham*, for 900 years a manor of the Bishops of London, with a partly 15C 'Palace' and many good 16–18C houses.

23 m. *Great Amwell.* Below the church (r.), with its Norman apse, in a romantic setting beside one of the springs of the New River, is a monument (1800; by Robert Mylne) to Sir Hugh Myddelton, its creator.— 24½ m. **Ware** (14,700 inhab.) is reverting to its old character since the by-pass opened. In High St. is the *Priory* (Council Office), the remains of a 15C Franciscan foundation (17–18C additions). The river Lea is lined with pleasant houses. The church (over-restored) has a tablet to Chas. Chauncey, the vicar, who became President of Harvard College in 1654. Off East St. in *Bluecoat Yard* are the old Bluecoat School buildings; the original Manor House is 15C with 16–17C alterations. The row of cottages (1698) were used until 1761 for the younger Christ's Hospital boys and their 'nurses' (see below). Among many fine 17–18C industrial buildings are Canons Maltings, and Albany Corn Stores. The Grammar School occupies *Amwell House* (c. 1730), originally the home of John Scott, the Quaker poet; his 'Grotto' is in Scott's Rd. Ware was the limit of John Gilpin's unwilling ride.

The main A 10 passes between Ware and Hertford on an elevated and windy bridge across the valley.

About 3 m. w. of Ware (and now almost joined to it) is **Hertford**, an ancient country town (20,400 inhab.) on the Lea, with a fine old inn (c. 1600), and a *Shire Hall* (1769) by James Adam. The scanty remains of a famous *Castle*, where King John of France was imprisoned in 1359, include a Norman motte and a gatehouse of 1461–65, 'beautified' in c. 1800. On the Ware road are the interesting buildings of *Christ's Hospital School*, with a gateway of 1695 and (l.) a long building of 1778 (the original girls' school).

Now devoted exclusively to girls, the buildings were originally intended for the younger boys and their 'nurses', but after a rebuilding in 1695 the little girls were brought here from Hoddesdon and (1697–1761) the boys from the old school at Ware (comp. above). In 1780 the older girls were transferred here from Newgate St. in London. Coleridge found himself "very happy on the whole at Hertford". Coloured figures of boys (1721) and girls adorn the street front and another boy (from Ware) the School Hall entrance. The fine bust of Treasurer Lockington (c. 1716), on the Dining Hall front, was brought from a demolished London church.

At *Bengeo*, in a secluded site on the N. bank of the Lea, is a small apsidal Norman church.

A 414 rises above the Lea valley (an alternative road, B 158, passes below the *County Hall* of 1939 and keeps nearer the river).—5½ m. *Hertingfordbury* (Hotel) is a pretty village with a church containing Cowper monuments and one to Anne (d. 1622), wife of Lord Baltimore, the founder of Maryland. Near the Lea, 1 m. s., is *Roxford*, where Haydn rested in 1791 with his banker-friend Nathaniel Brassey. —11 m. *Hatfield*, see Rte 46.

A 602 goes on from Hertford to Stevenage (12½ m.), passing (5 m.) *Patchenden* and *Woodhall Park* (r.), now a school, joining the Great North Road (comp. p. 424).

Beyond Ware the A 10 regains the old alinement. Beyond (26¼ m.) *Wadesmill*, a roadside obelisk commemorates Thomas Clarkson (1760–1846), who at this spot in 1785 resolved to devote his life to the abolition of slavery.—27½ m. *High Cross* church has a surprising w. window of 1893.— At 30 m. a by-road (r.) leads to (¾ m.) *Standon* church with an impressive w. porch and detached tower. The chancel is raised above the nave under a fine arch (restored in the 19C). The good *Brasses include one of John Field (d. 1474), a merchant of the Staple.—At (30½ m.) *Puckeridge*, we keep left.

An alternative route from Puckeridge (B 1368; 1 m. shorter) runs viâ *Braughing*, an important Roman road junction, (34½ m.) *Little Hormead* (l.), where the church has 12C *Ironwork on its N. door, Barkway, and (40½ m.) *Barley*, where the inn-sign spans the roadway, and joins the main road 2 m. S. of Trumpington.

34½ m. *Buntingford* has a brick church of 1614–26, and a long street of 17–18C houses, notably Ward's Hospital, an almshouse founded in 1684 by Bp. Seth Ward (1617–39) of Salisbury, a native.—At (41½ m.) *Royston* (Hotels), we leave the line of Ermine Street. The hooded crow (*Corvus cornix*), known also as the Royston crow, is said never to winter s. of Royston.

Ermine St. (A 14) continues N. to (20 m.) *Huntingdon*, viâ (6 m.) *Arrington*, which adjoins the park of *Wimpole Hall*, a mansion built in 1638–40, with a noted avenue of elms 2½ m. long and 300 yds wide. Gibbs added the wings in 1713–21, and Flitcroft altered the house in 1740. Here in 1721 Matthew Prior, the poet, died while on a visit to his patron Robert Harley, Earl of Oxford. In the church of *Croydon*, 1 m. w., is buried the founder of Downing College (p. 493; d. 1749).— At (14 m.) *Papworth Everard* (l.) is the *Village Settlement*, a successful colony founded for the treatment, training and employment of tubercular men and women, with c. 1200 residents.—Thence viâ Godmanchester to Huntingdon, see below.

We bear N.E. and enter Cambridgeshire.—44½ m. *Melbourn* church (13C) has an early-16C rood screen.—49½ m. *Harston* has an imposing flint church.—At (50 m.) *Hauxton*, a pretty village, the church has a Norman nave and chancel, and a 13C painting of Thomas Becket.— 52 m. *Trumpington* (p. 500).

54½ m. **Cambridge**, see Rte 55.

We leave Cambridge by A 604, which takes the line of the Roman Via Devana, passing Girton College.—At (59½ m.) a by-road (r.) leads to (2 m.) St Michael's, the reed-thatched church at *Longstanton.*— 64½ m. *Fenstanton* was the home of Capability Brown from 1767 to his death in 1793.— 68½ m. *Godmanchester* was a Roman settlement on Ermine Street, and recent excavations have found the E. and W. gates and the baths. It received its charter in 1214; the large church (13C) is built of cobbles, with a 17C stone tower. It contains a 13C mass dial and good 15C misericords. The medieval Causeway has excellent houses. The Chinese Bridge (1827) spans the river on to islands. The main *Bridge (14C) over the Great Ouse was built from both banks at once (reputedly without consultation), which accounts for the misalinement in the centre. On the N. bank stands **Huntingdon** (Hotels), the former county town (16,500 inhab. with Godmanchester) of Hunts and the birthplace of Oliver Cromwell (1599–1658). In the church of *All Saints* (late-Perp.; restored), in the High St., is preserved the register of the demolished church of St John, with the record of Cromwell's birth and baptism, and the later gloss (now scored out) "England's plague for 5 years". The *Cromwell Museum* (Tues–Sat 11–1, 2–5; Sun 2–4) is in the former Grammar School where the Protector and Samuel Pepys (1633–1703) were educated, which incorporates the w. end of the old Hospital of St John (founded by David I of Scotland, 1084–1153). To the N.W. the High St. passes *Cromwell House*, incorporating the house in which Cromwell was born. In the other direction the street leads past the house where Cowper lived with the Unwins in 1765–67 (tablet) to *St Mary's* (tower rebuilt in 1620).

George St. leads s.w. past the station to *Hinchingbrooke*, the palatial seat of the Earl of Sandwich, built on the site of a suppressed nunnery. From 1538 to 1627 it belonged to the ancestors of Oliver Cromwell, and it has now become a grammar school (adm. Sun in March–May, July–Aug, also BH 2–5; fee).

The Great Ouse (boating) between Huntingdon's pleasant meadows and St Ives (p. 507) is charming, especially at *Houghton Mill* (17C; Y.H.) and the pretty village of *Hemingford Grey*. It is navigable for cruising upstream to Bedford and out to the Wash at King's Lynn.

A 14 continues past the *Stukeley* villages with their airfields to (73½ m.) *Alconbury Hill* where we join A 1 (see Rte 46).—At 80 m., B 660 leads r., passing N. of *Wood Walton Fen*, a nature reserve on the last relic of the great shallow meres that covered this district until c. 1850, to *Ramsey* (9 m.; 5600 inhab.). It has a part-Norman church and the ruined gate-house (N.T.; late-14C) of an important Benedictine abbey (969), the 13C Lady Chapel of which is now incorporated in the Grammar School. —At (82½ m.) *Norman Cross* (Motel) we diverge right from Ermine Street on to A 15 through an area of brickfields, the worst scars of which are to be removed by an excellent scheme of landscaping.—83½ m. *Yaxley*, a pretty village with timbered buildings and brick and tile cottages, has a church with a tall Perp. steeple, medieval wall-paintings, and a 15C chancel screen.—86½ m. *Old Fletton* is now an untidy suburb of Peter-borough on the s. bank of the Nene.

87½ m. **PETERBOROUGH** (Hotels; 70,000 inhab.), an ancient city, once known as *Medeshamstede*, grew around a great monastery founded c. 656 (see below) and has been a bishop's see since 1541. Here was the birthplace of William Paley, of the 'Evidences'. Owing its 19C development to railway works and its large brickfields, mainly in the suburb of Fletton, it became a thriving industrial town with steel works. The city is undergoing a 'planned expansion' to double its size. Thomas Cook moved to new headquarters here in 1977.

Bridge St. leads from the Nene Bridge (1933) to the market place, passing the *Town Hall and County Buildings*, by Berry Webber (1929–33). In Priestgate, opposite, is a *Museum* (weekdays, 10–1, 2–5; Mon from 2) interesting for its Roman remains, objects found in Whittlesey Mere, and *Articles made by French prisoners at Norman Cross (see above). Notable also are the earliest known portrait of a judge in robes (1547), and the relics of John Clare. From the market place, with the 17C *Guildhall*, Cowgate leads w., passing the Perp. church of *St John Baptist* (1401–7).

On the other side of the square the *Western Foregate* (late 12C but much altered) admits to the *Minster Close*, in front of the w. façade of the cathedral. The *King's Lodging* (13C), to the right, is now a bookshop. To the left, the chancel of the *Becket Chapel* (late-Dec.; c. 1370) is now the song-school. On the right (s.) of the close is the *Abbot's Gateway* (c. 1302), leading to the *Bishop's Palace*. The figures are probably Edward I, Abbot Godfrey of Croyland, and his prior. *Abbot Kirkton's Gateway* (1515), to the left, admitted to the Abbot's Park.

The *Cathedral (dedicated to SS. Peter, Paul, and Andrew) is one of the most important Norman buildings in England, with a notable 13C w. front.

HISTORY. Peterborough Cathedral belongs to that splendid series of Saxon foundations—the monasteries of the Fen District. Founded by Peada, sub-king of Mercia (d. 656), the monastery, with its first church, was destroyed by the Danes in 870. It was rebuilt in the 10C. This second Saxon church was burned down in 1116, and the present building was begun the following year. The E. limb was completed, the transepts and tower piers carried some way up, and the nave begun before 1155. In that year William de Waterville took up the work. He completed the transepts, the piers and arches of the crossing, and the central tower, and did a good deal of work in the nave, especially on the s. side. All this grand early Norman work, except the tower, remains. In 1177 Abbot Benedict added two w. bays, making ten in all, completed the aisles, vaulted all but the tenth bay of the aisles, and (probably) ceiled the nave. This work, finished in 1199, completed the original design, adhered to by successive builders. In the West Transept, which Benedict began, pointed arches show the departure from the old style. This transept was finished by Benedict's successor, Abbot Andrew (1195–1200), who built also the N. tower, and began a rich and spacious porch to the central portal; the corresponding s. tower remains incomplete. The next abbot, Acharius (1200–10), probably designed the unique and splendid *West Façade, which is the most striking feature of the exterior, though masking the Norman front. A magnificent Lady Chapel (pulled down in 1651) was added c. 1270. In the 14C the central Norman tower was replaced by one lower and lighter (rebuilt on the original lines, 1884–86), and the lovely s.w. spire was added. In the 13C and 15C larger windows were substituted for the Norman ones. The fan-vaulted retro-choir was built c. 1496–1509. The interior (glass, woodwork, sculpture, monuments) suffered wholesale sacking by Cromwell's soldiers. The 19C repaving of the presbytery, new stalls, and the replacement in 1949–59 of statues on the w. front, by Alan Durst, complete the history of the fabric.

Interior. The grand Norman *NAVE is entered from the parvise porch, a rich early-Perp. addition (1370), with a remarkable central boss of the Trinity. On either hand opens a chapel, with noble pointed arches under the w. towers. Other impressive features of the nave are the finely vaulted aisles, the dignified triforium and clerestory, and the expanse of painted ceiling, dating from c. 1220 (repainted c. 1750 and 1834), which is unique in England. The 13C font, with a bowl of local marble, stands in the N.W. transept. The s.w. chapel, now the *Chapel of St Sprite*, contains a beautiful double piscina. To the N. of the w. door is an 18C copy of a curious portrait of Old Scarlett (d. 1594), who "interd two queenes within this place" (see below); and on the 6th s. nave-pier a tablet commemorates Nurse Cavell, who was at school in Peterborough. —In the s. transept wall is a tombstone of two Saxon bishops, discovered in 1888 in the foundations of the early Saxon church which may be seen beneath the s. transept. The N.E. chapel of the s. transept contains part of a watching-loft, probably for a shrine of St Oswald. The screens on the E. side of the transepts are of the 15C. The timber ceiling of the transepts (restored) is the only original Norman ceiling extant. That in the nave was given sloping sides in the 14C. The choir furnishings are Victorian with the exception of the late-15C brass lectern.

The *SANCTUARY is the oldest part of the building, but the wooden roof is Perp., with groining ribs springing from the Norman shafts, except over the apse, where the flat roof is retained (painted 1855). This apse stands within the 'new building', i.e. the procession path and chapels added late in the 15C, which have fine fan-vaulting (restored 1936). In the N. choir aisle is the fine tomb-slab of Abbot Benedict (d. 1192), and, farther E., beneath the standard of Castile and Aragon, is the grave of Queen Catherine of Aragon (d. 1536), demolished by the Puritans. At the end of the s. choir-aisle is the 'Monks' Stone', traditionally the memorial of the monks who perished at the hands of the Danes in 870, and certainly not less old than that date. The effigies of 12–13C abbots, removed here from the ruins of the chapter house, are claimed to be the finest series of Benedictine memorials in England. To the right a slab, beneath the Scottish flag, marks the supposed burial-place of Mary,

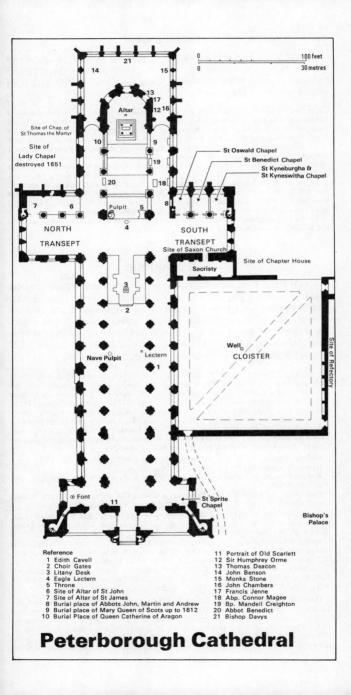

21

14   15

13 17
Altar 12 16

Site of Chap. of
St Thomas the Martyr

Site of
Lady Chapel
destroyed 1651

10   9

19

20   18

St Oswald Chapel

St Benedict Chapel

St Kyneburgha &
St Kyneswitha Chapel

7   6   Pulpit   5   8

4

NORTH
TRANSEPT

SOUTH
TRANSEPT
Site of Saxon Church

Site of Chapter House

Sacristy

3

2

Well
CLOISTER

Site of Refectory

Nave Pulpit   Lectern

1

⊕ Font

11

St Sprite
Chapel

Bishop's
Palace

0   100 feet
0   30 metres

Reference
1 Edith Cavell
2 Choir Gates
3 Litany Desk
4 Eagle Lectern
5 Throne
6 Site of Altar of St John
7 Site of Altar of St James
8 Burial place of Abbots John, Martin and Andrew
9 Burial place of Mary Queen of Scots up to 1612
10 Burial Place of Queen Catherine of Aragon

11 Portrait of Old Scarlett
12 Sir Humphrey Orme
13 Thomas Deacon
14 John Benson
15 Monks Stone
16 John Chambers
17 Francis Jenne
18 Abp. Connor Magee
19 Bp. Mandell Creighton
20 Abbot Benedict
21 Bishop Davys

Peterborough Cathedral

Queen of Scots, buried in the church in 1587 but in 1612 transferred by her son, James I, to a more stately tomb in Westminster Abbey. Tablets to the two queens, subscribed for by 'Catherines' and 'Marys', have been placed near their graves.

On the s. side of the cathedral are the ruins of the cloister, with 14C *Lavatory* bays on the s. side. From the s.e. corner a passage with a blind arcade (once vaulted) leads to the two fine E.E. arcades of the Infirmary (now incorporated in more recent buildings).—On the banks of the Nene is a public park (swimming pool).

At *Longthorpe Tower* (closed Sun until 2; fee), 2 m. w. of Peterborough, a remarkable series of early 14C domestic *Murals has been discovered; *Castor*, 2½ m. farther w., has a beautiful church (1124), dedicated to St Kyneburga, daughter of Penda, king of Mercia. It has a richly decorated central tower and a 14C wall-painting of St Catherine.—Excursions may be made also to *Thorney*, 6½ m. N.E. (on A 47), the site of a great Benedictine abbey founded in 972, where the nave of the church (1108) has later sculptures on its w. front; and to *Whittlesey*, 5 m. E., an old town (10,500 inhab.), with a fine 15C church tower and spire.

To *Fotheringhay* and the unique series of churches on the way to *Northampton*, see Rte 43; to *Crowland*, see Rte 57.

55   CAMBRIDGE

CAMBRIDGE (98,500 inhab.), on the Cam or Granta, is famous as the seat of one of the great English universities. It lies, nowhere more than 50 ft above the sea, on the s. margin of the Fen Country, and owes its attractiveness mainly to its series of stately colleges admirably set off by groups and avenues of trees. Building for building, it is hard to award the palm between the sister universities, and if Cambridge has no High Street, the greenery of its 'Backs' is unparalleled at Oxford.

CAMBRIDGE UNIVERSITY has 25 colleges (incl. *Homerton*, incorporated in 1976, and *Robinson*, not yet finished). There are 118 professors, about 71 readers and 500 lecturers, approx. 1000 fellows and over 10,000 students. The women's colleges (admitted to full status in 1948) are *Girton College* (1869), *Newnham College* (1875), and *New Hall* (1954). All but four of the former men's colleges now take women; Girton is to take men after 1979. Not incorporated with the University are six foundations for postgraduates: *Hughes Hall*, *Darwin College*, *St Edmund's House*, *Wolfson College*, *Lucy Cavendish College*, and *Clare Hall*, as well as four theological halls: *Westminster College*, *Ridley Hall*, *Westcott House*, and *Wesley House.*

Railway Station. 1¼ m. S.E. of the centre of the town (Bus No. 101).

Hotels in Regent St., by the river, in Trinity St., etc.

Restaurants and tea rooms in or near King's Parade, St Andrew's St., Bridge St., and Northampton St.

Post Office, St Andrew's St.—**Information Office,** City Reference Library, behind Guildhall, weekdays, 9–7.—**English Speaking Union,** 8 Pembroke St.

Buses run from the station to Petty Cury and Chesterton, and from Market St. to the suburbs; also from Drummer St. to *Ely*, *Saffron Walden*, *Newmarket*, *St Ives*, *Huntingdon*, *Bedford*, etc.

Boats, preferably punts or canoes, for the Backs, may be hired at Magdalene bridge and in Mill Lane; for the upper river at the foot of Mill Lane to the left. BATHING (river) near Fen Causeway, s. of the town (indoor heated), Mill Rd.

Theatres. *Arts*, Peas Hill; *A.D.C.* (performances usually only during term), Park St.—A Music and Drama Festival and a Folk Festival are held at the end of July. CONCERTS in Guildhall, College chapels, etc., at frequent intervals.

Hints to Visitors. The remarks on p. 263 as to the escort of a member of the University, the vacations, and the admission to the college buildings apply also to Cambridge, although the regulations for morning visits are less stringent. The liveliest time to visit Cambridge is the so-called *May Week* (actually c. 10 days in June) at the end of the Easter term, when the College Boat Races are held, followed by a series of balls, concerts, and other entertainments. On the Tues after the races there is a *Congregation* for prize exercises and the conferring of honorary degrees.—The Lower River is the scene of the College Boat Races in late Feb ('Lents') and early June ('Mays'). These, decided as at Oxford by 'bumping', begin at *Baitsbite Lock*, 3 m. downstream.

The UNIVERSITY SYSTEM of Cambridge and Oxford is described on pp. 264–265. To obtain any adequate idea of Cambridge, the visitor must devote several days to it. The day's walk described below will, however, show him at least the outside of the buildings of chief interest. The points which most imperatively demand attention include *King's, St John's, Trinity, Queen's,* and *Jesus Colleges,* the *Round Church,* and the *Fitzwilliam Museum.*

History. Excavations in the castle hill on the N. side of the town have revealed three successive pre-Roman phases of occupation, and Roman remains confirm a Roman settlement indicated by the name of the transpontine suburb, Chesterton. Early names of the river were Rhee and the more frequent Granta (now usually applied to the two branches of the river above Cambridge), which gave the forms Grantebrycge (Grantabridge) and (later) Cantebrigge, eventually softened into Cambridge. The present name of the river Cam was derived from the town, not the other way about. The situation of Cambridge must always have been important, but the significance of town and castle was speedily eclipsed by that of the University. This, according to myth, was founded by Prince Cantaber of Spain in the year of the world 4321; as a fact it probably grew up around the religious establishments of the early 12C. It is recognized as an important seat of learning in a writ of Henry III (1231). Peterhouse, the first college properly so called, dates from 1281–84. Friction between the University and the Town culminated in the riot of 1381, when the townsmen sacked several colleges and destroyed many important documents. Cambridge attained a European reputation with the advent of Erasmus in 1510. Its wealth and well-being were increased rather than lessened by the great religious change of the 16C; it lost little during the Civil War except the plate melted down for the war chest of Charles I. For Americans Cambridge must always have a special interest as the main fount of higher education in the United States, the stream flowing through John Harvard, President Dunster, and many other graduates of this university. The most famous native of Cambridge is Sir Jack Hobbs (1882–1963). The status of city was granted by charter in 1951 and confirmed in 1974.

In the centre of the city *Petty Cury* (perhaps 'petite curye' or 'little cookery') leads w. to *Market Hill,* in which are (l.) the *Guildhall* (rebuilt 1937–39) and (r.) Bacon's tobacco shop, immortalised by Calverley (bust and inscription on the façade). **St Mary's the Great** is an imposing Perp. church rebuilt between 1478 and 1608, when the tower (fee) was finished. It is a parish church but is used also by the University (service on Sun at 2.30). The nave has elegant, tall arches, a good roof (after 1505), and fine galleries (1735). The organ, by Father Smith, was brought, with its case, from St James's, Piccadilly, in 1697. Opposite the church is the dignified *Senate House (normally open daily Easter–Sept 3.30–4.30; otherwise Sat & Sun only), the scene of the chief public functions of the University, and corresponding to the Sheldonian Theatre at Oxford. It was built by James Gibbs in 1722–30, and contains statues of Pitt (by Nollekens) and the 6th Duke of Somerset, Chancellor of the University for nearly 60 years (1689–1748; by Rysbrack). At the back of Senate House Yard stand the former **Old Schools** (i.e. lecture rooms) and the old court of King's College, occupied by the University Library from 1829 to 1934, and now housing the offices of the Senate and the University Registry. The oldest part, lying between the picturesque Cobble Court and the West Court, dates from c. 1350–1473, the main E. facade was finished in 1758, the N. side (by C. R. Cockerell; 1837–40) houses various libraries.

Senate House Passage, passing the Gate of Honour of Caius College (p. 500), leads to **Trinity Hall,** founded in 1350 by William Bateman,

Bp. of Norwich, with special provision for students of law. It is the only college that retains the name of 'Hall'.

The first court was remodelled by Sir James Burroughs in 1730–45, but the *Library* (10–2 in term) dates from c. 1600 and retains chained books of a still earlier period. In the *Ante-Chapel* are three 16C brasses. The pretty *Fellows' Garden* has some fine chestnuts.

FAMOUS MEMBERS: Tusser (author of '500 Points of Good Husbandry'), Holinshed, Bp. Gardiner (Master), Lord Fitzwilliam, Lord Chesterfield, Bulwer Lytton, Chief Justice Cockburn, F. D. Maurice, Sir Leslie Stephen, Prof. Fawcett, and Ronald Firbank.

To the s. of Trinity Hall is **Clare College**, founded in 1326 as University Hall and refounded (1338) by Lady Elizabeth de Clare, and thus junior to Peterhouse alone. The buildings, mainly by Robert Grumbold, a local craftsman, are an admirable example of their period (1638–1715). The chapel was added in 1763–69.

The w. range opens on to Clare Bridge (1640; *View), perhaps by Thomas Grumbold, leading over the Cam to the beautiful *Fellows' Garden* (fine limes) and to the 'Backs' (see below).

FAMOUS MEMBERS: Abp. Tillotson, Bp. Latimer, Whiston (translator of 'Josephus'), Hervey ('Meditations among the Tombs'), and Peter II of Yugoslavia. Tradition connects Chaucer with Clare Hall and identifies it with the 'Solere Hall' of the 'Reeve's Tale'.

Those who have not time to walk along the whole length of the *BACKS OF THE COLLEGES (i.e. the tree-shaded grounds on the left bank of the river) will get a good idea of them by crossing Clare Bridge and entering King's College from behind. An avenue leads from Clare Bridge to the fine *New Court of Clare* (by Sir Giles Scott, 1924–29), with an imposing War Memorial Arch; in the garden is a bronze Unknown Warrior, by Henry Moore.

In Burrell's Walk, behind this court, is the **University Library** (recently extended), also by Scott (1930–34), with a lofty tower. The library (open weekdays 9.30–6.30, Sat 9–1, to visitors accompanied by a graduate; weekdays at 3 to unaccompanied visitors), with c. 3,000,000 books, c. 500,000 maps, and over 14,000 MSS., ranks next in order to the British Museum and the Bodleian. Among its principal treasures, a large number of which are usually on exhibition, are a magnificent collection of Caxtons, including his 'Historyes of Troye', 1475–76, the first book printed in English, and the only perfect copy of his 'Golden Legend' (1483); a Mazarine Bible (Mainz, c. 1456) and the first dated Bible (Mainz, 1462); the Book of Deer, a 10C Gaelic MS.; the Codex Bezæ, of the 6C, one of the five great uncial MSS. of the Gospels.

Farther s. are a hostel for King's, and their Choir School (across the playing fields). We turn back towards the river along West Road, past new University buildings (see p. 489), and the interesting *Harvey Court* (1962), of Caius, by Martin and St J. Wilson, with terraced rooms overlooking a garden and a surrounding 'cloister'.

Opposite the E. entrance of Clare is the beautiful but unfinished 15C gateway of the original court of King's College, which stood on this site until 1836. **King's College** (The King's College of Our Lady and St Nicholas), adjoining on the s., was founded by Henry VI in 1441 and re-established on a roomier site and in connection with Eton College four years later. The street frontage consists of a lodge and stone screen of 1828 by William Wilkins.

On the s. side of the *Great Court*, with its fountain, is the *Hall*, by Wilkins (1824–28); on the w. side is the gracious *Fellows' Building* (1724), by Gibbs, with a wonderful lawn, sloping to the river and bounded on the s. by the *Library* and *Bodley's Building* (1894, completed 1928), and on the N. by Clare. Fine *View from the bridge.

FAMOUS MEMBERS: Christopher Tye (chorister), Walsingham, Phineas and Giles Fletcher, Orlando Gibbons (chorister and member), Edmund Waller, Sir Robert and Horace Walpole, Sir William Temple, 'Turnip' Townshend, Lord

Stratford de Redcliffe, Rupert Brooke, Lord Keynes, Roger Fry, and E. M. Forster (fellow).

On the N. side of the Great Court is **King's College Chapel**, a late-Perp. building of 1446–1515, begun by Henry VI and continued by successive sovereigns to Henry VIII. It is regarded as the crowning glory of the University, mainly on account of its perfect interior, a "Sursum Corda done into stone", which inspired three noble sonnets by Wordsworth (open usually weekdays 9–4; Sun from 2; choral service on Sun at 10.30 & 3.30 and on weekdays at 5.30 p.m.). It is 289 ft long, 40 ft wide, and 80 ft high. The design of the interior is bold and simple, the ornamentation rich but not excessive (including the Tudor rose and portcullis; the rose and crown motif is probably also the 'Rosary' and 'Corona' of Our Lady). The outstanding features are the 25 magnificent *Stained Glass Windows (all of the 16C except that by Clayton & Bell at the w. end), the *Fan vaulting, the stalls, and the wooden organ screen (1533–36) and case (1688). The altarpiece is the *Adoration of the Magi, by Rubens, donated anonymously by Alfred Allnatt in 1959, which greatly impairs the effect of the lovely E. window.

Each of the chantries, opening between the buttresses, contained an altar; the chantry at the S.E. corner is a War Memorial Chapel with Flemish glass of 1530; that at the N.E. corner, with its lierne vault, was completed before 1461.

The passage nearly opposite the main gate of King's leads to the church of *St Edward the King* (12C and 14C; the nave arcade with fine slender piers), where Latimer preached the Reformation. The chancel was enlarged after 1446 to provide chapels for Clare College and Trinity Hall.

In Bene't St., opposite the s. range of King's, is (r.) *St Bene't's* (i.e. *Benedict's*) *Church*, which retains its Saxon tower and tower-arch. A gallery of finely toned red brick connects the church with Corpus Christi, of which it was the original chapel.

Corpus Christi College, on the E. side of Trumpington St., was founded in 1352 by the united Guilds of Corpus Christi and the Blessed Virgin, and was long known familiarly as Benet College.

The *Old Court* (reached from the N.E. corner of the front court) is the earliest example in England of a complete medieval academic quadrangle. The *First Court*, by Wilkins (1823–27), facing on to Trumpington St., includes the *Library* (adm. weekdays 2–4 or 5), containing a priceless collection of MSS. bequeathed by Abp. Parker, Master from 1544 to 1552, and the Lewis Collection of Coins and Gems. In the *Hall*, with richly repainted roof, are paintings by Reynolds, Romney, Poussin, Kneller, etc. The *Chapel* has early 16C Rhenish glass.

FAMOUS MEMBERS: Sir Nicholas Bacon, Robert Browne, Christopher Marlowe, John Fletcher, Abp. Tenison, John Robinson (Fellow, 1598), and Gen. Braddock.

Opposite Corpus Christi is **St Catharine's College**, founded in 1473 by Robert Wodelarke, Provost of King's, rebuilt in 1674–1757 by Robert Grumbold and James Essex, and extended in 1932–51. The rich colour of the old brick is notable. A joint development for King's and St Catharine's, known as King's Lane Courts (by Fello Atkinson; 1968), blends with the college frontages on King's Parade.

Abp. Sandys and Bp. Lightfoot, the oriental scholar, were Masters of St Catharine's; John Bradford, the Reformer, and James Shirley, the playwright, were members.

Behind St Catharine's, in Queens' Lane, is the imposing main gateway of *Queens' College*, founded in 1448 by Andrew Dokett, under the patronage of Margaret of Anjou, wife of Henry VI, and refounded in 1465 by Elizabeth Woodville, wife of Edward IV. It is, perhaps, the most picturesque of Cambridge colleges.

The 15C red brick *First Court*, well restored, includes the *Hall* (w.), remodelled in 1732–34 (roof repainted 1961), the *Old Chapel* (no adm.) with a sundial on the wall, and the *Library* (N.; Jacobean bookcases). To the w. of this is the charming **Cloister Court*, whence the 'wooden bridge' leads to the *College Gardens* and to *Fisher Court* (1936), flanked by a 17C brewhouse. On the N. side of the cloisters is the **President's Lodge* (c. 1537), with a beautiful panelled gallery of the 16C. In the small *Pump Court*, s. of the Cloister Court, is the *Erasmus Tower*, above the rooms occupied by Erasmus, who taught Greek in this college (1510–13). To the N. of the main court are the *Walnut Tree Court* (1617–19) and another court, with the large *Chapel* by Bodley between them. Almost opposite the chapel is the *Erasmus Building* by Basil Spence (1959–61), built in russet brick and stone and raised on pillars.

FAMOUS MEMBERS: St John Fisher (President), Thomas Fuller (who removed to Sidney in 1628), Abp. Whitgift, and Sir Charles Stanford.

On the s. Queens' is bounded by Silver St., which continues beyond the Cam, past Newnham Grange, a former home of the Darwin family and now the nucleus of *Darwin College*, founded as a graduate college in 1964 by Caius, St John's, and Trinity colleges. Sensitive new buildings (1968) for the College have been added to the Hermitage and Old Granary extending up to the corner of Newnham Rd. Sidgwick Av. goes on w. past *Ridley Hall* (Anglican; l.), and **Newnham College**, established in 1875 as the second women's college. The new buildings have effective, colourful brickwork. Opposite are the striking new buildings of the *University Arts Faculties*, including Lady Mitchell Hall and the Marshall Library of Economics, by Casson and Conder (1959–64) and, beyond the English quadrangle raised on pillars, the glass History Faculty building, by Stirling and Gowan (1968). At the end of the road is **Selwyn College**, originally incorporated in 1882 for Church of England students 'willing to live economically'. Across Grange Rd., down an avenue, is the Victorian *Leckhampton House*, extended in 1954 by the good new *Thompson building* (by Philip Dowson; the pleasant garden has a statue by Moore), for graduates of Corpus. To the s. is *University College* founded in 1965, the first mixed college for graduates.

We now return to Trumpington St. along Silver St., opposite the end of which is *St Botolph's Church* (chiefly Perp., with a 15C painted rood screen). To the right, as we proceed s., is the *University Press*, or *Pitt Press*, with its conspicuous tower (1831–33), popularly known as the 'Freshman's College' from an alleged common mistake of the unsophisticated. The building was erected with the aid of the surplus of a fund subscribed for the erection of a statue of William Pitt in London. A new printing-house (1963) flanks the railway line to London. To the left, almost opposite, stands **Pembroke College**, founded by the Countess of Pembroke in 1347, but largely modernized or rebuilt.

The *Chapel*, which contains a chair said to have been Bp. Ridley's, was Wren's first major work (1663–65); it was lengthened in 1880. The *Old Library* (in the first court, to the l.), with a fine plaster ceiling of 1690, was originally the first college chapel in Cambridge (1366). *Ivy Court* (c. 1614–59) was restored in 1964; to the s.e. is *Orchard Court* (1957).

FAMOUS MEMBERS. Pembroke has been called the 'Collegium Episcopale' from the number of bishops it has produced (Ridley, Grindal, Whitgift, Andrewes, etc.); it might also be called the 'College of Poets', for Spenser, Crashaw, Gray (see below), and Mason were among its members. The younger Pitt, Sumner Maine, and Sir G. G. Stokes were Pembroke men.

Farther along Trumpington St. stands **Peterhouse**, properly *St Peter's College*, founded by Hugh of Balsham, Bp. of Ely, in 1281. This is the oldest college in Cambridge.

In the first court is the *Chapel*, an attractive example of Laudian Gothic (1628–32), connected with the main buildings by galleries (1709–11). The E. window retains its original glass and in the reredos is a 15C Pietà of wood. On the r. is the dignified *Fellows' Building*, by Burrough (1738–42). On the left are the *Library* (c. 1590; extended in 1633) and the *Hall* which, though much altered in 1868–71, is substantially the original hall of c. 1290. It contains portraits, and stained glass by Madox Brown, Burne-Jones, and William Morris, who likewise designed the windows of the *Combination Room* (1460). Beyond the Hall a path leads to the *Garden*. From the second, or *Gisborne Court* (1825), a passage (r.) leads to the quaint old building called 'Noah's Ark'. At the back is *Fen Court* (1939), by Hughes and Bicknell. The *Master's Lodge*, a fine Queen Anne house of 1702, and a building of 1928 are on the other side of Trumpington St. An eight-story block (1964), by Martin and St John Wilson (beyond the Museum), has features of interest.

FAMOUS MEMBERS: Card. Beaufort, the poet Gray, Chas. Babbage, Clerk-Maxwell, and Lord Kelvin. Gray's rooms in the Fellows' Building may be identified by the iron bars placed by the poet for use in case of fire. Induced to use his rope-ladder by a false alarm of fire, he left Peterhouse in dudgeon at the practical joke and became a member of Pembroke.

The church of *St Mary the Less* (14C, but considerably altered), adjoining Peterhouse on the N., served as the college chapel before 1632. Its flowing Dec. tracery is exquisite. Near the entrance is the tomb of Godfrey Washington (d. 1729) with the family arms.

Just beyond Peterhouse is the *Fitzwilliam Museum (open weekdays 10–5; Sun from 2.15, paintings only), a massive classical building by George Basevi and C. R. Cockerell (1837–47), erected for the valuable collections bequeathed to the University by Viscount Fitzwilliam in 1816.

The original building was completed in 1875 by E. M. Barry, who designed the entrance hall; and since 1924 the Marlay Galleries, on the s. side, and the beginning of a new quadrangle (by Smith and Brewer) have been added, to house extensive recent bequests. Further extensions are in progress.—In the main rooms are exhibited furniture, ceramics, drawings, etc., associated with the period of the paintings, which combine to create a particularly charming atmosphere.

From the entrance hall the staircase ascends to the large ROOM III, devoted to English works, notably portraits by *Highmore* (Illustrations to 'Pamela'), *Eworth* (*Mary Tudor), *Hogarth*, *Romney*, *Reynolds*, *Wright of Derby* (Lord Fitzwilliam, aged 19), *Lawrence*, and *Raeburn*; and landscapes by *Constable*, *Turner*, *Bonington*, and *Richard Wilson*. Here, too, are a bust of Wm. Pitt, by *Nollekens*; and cases of *Miniatures (by *Hilliard*, *Oliver*, *Samuel Cooper*, *Cosway*, and others), and illustrations by *Blake*. Beside the door is a clock by *Thomas Tompion* (c. 1700). The gallery above contains prints and water-colours.—ROOM II (r.) has 19–20C English works, by *Millais*, *Madox Brown*, *Stanley Spencer* (Self-portrait), *Graham Sutherland* (Deposition), *Paul Nash* (November Moon), *Augustus John* (Thomas Hardy), *P. W. Steer* (Children paddling), *Sickert*, *Gilman*, *Sargent*, *Whistler*, and *Alma Tadema*. Also, small bronzes by *Epstein*, *Moore*, and *Elizabeth Frink*.—ROOM I contains the fine Broughton collection of flower paintings by 17–19C European artists. In the table-cases is an interesting collection of literary autographs by past members of Cambridge colleges, including Keats's 'Ode to a Nightingale', as well as musical autographs.

In ROOM IV (beyond R. III) are represented the French Schools, with impressive works by *Oudry*, *Vouet*, *Poussin* (Deposition, Landscape), *Corot* (La Chataigneraie, Dutch landscape, The Dyke), *Delacroix*, *Géricault* (wounded soldiers in a cart), *Rousseau*, and *Decamps*; also a terracotta statuette of Voltaire by *J. A. Houdon*.—Cases in the corner (l.) contain the finest illuminated MSS. in the collection, including the *Metz Pontifical, produced for a Bishop of Metz at the beginning of the 14C, the most sumptuous French liturgical MS. of its date; and the *Psalter and Hours of Isabella of France, sister of St Louis (Paris, before 1270).—French painting is continued in ROOM V, with examples of *Boudin, Fantin-Latour, Degas* (*Au Café), *Renoir, Monet, Signac, Cézanne, Gaugin, Pissarro, Sisley, Matisse,* and *Rouault;* also bronzes by *Degas, Rodin,* and *Medardo Rosso.* The cases contain fine drawings by *Millet, Delacroix,* and *Ingres.*

From R. IV opens the UPPER MARLAY GALLERY (R. VI) devoted to Italian paintings, with particularly fine works of the 13–16C Florentine, Sienese, and N. Italian Schools. *Simone Martini,* *SS. Ambrose, Michael and Augustine (3 panels of a polyptych of 1322); *Botticini,* Virgin in adoration; *Zuccaro,* The Three Kings; *Lorenzo di Credi,* *Martyrdom of St Sebastian; *Mazzolino,* Christ before Pilate; *Dom. Veneziano,* *Annunciation; *Giov. dal Ponte,* Four Saints; *Lorenzo Monaco,* Virgin enthroned; also reliefs by Dom. Rosselli and Desiderio da Settignano. —COURTAULD GALLERIES. R. VII. Italian Schools: *Cima,* St Lanfranc and Saints; *Tintoretto,* Nativity; *Seb. del Piombo,* Adoration of the shepherds; *Iac. Bassano,* Shepherds, Journey to Calvary; *Guido Reni,* Ecce Homo; *Palma Vecchio,* *Venus and Cupid; *Titian,* *Venus, *Tarquin and Lucretia; *Sassoferrato,* Holy Family, *Veronese,* Hermes, Herse and Aglauros; in the cases, *Drawings by *Leonardo, Michelangelo, Parmigianino, Titian, Tintoretto,* and *Tiepolo.*—R. X. Flemish School: *Rubens,* *Oil sketches; *P. Brueghel the Younger,* Village Fête; *Heemskerck,* Self-portrait; *Joos van Cleef,* Madonna.—R. XI. Dutch School: *Landscapes by *Hobbema* and *Ruisdael,* and Portraits by *Rembrandt, Franz Hals, Cornelius Johnson,* and others.—The Print Room, beyond, usually displays temporary exhibitions.

Returning to R. VII we enter R. VIII, with Spanish paintings, notably St John the Baptist with the Pharisees, by *Murillo.*—The Octagon and Water-colour Room display a varying selection of works.

The GROUND FLOOR galleries (closed on Sun): at the foot of the stairs is the small WEST ASIATIC GALLERY, with superb Assyrian reliefs (9–5C B.C.). To the right, the EGYPTIAN COLLECTION is housed in two rooms: *Room I* has well-displayed exhibits from the pre-Dynastic period to the Coptic period, including the shrine of the goddess Nekhbet, and a granite head of Sesostris III, King of Egypt, 1878–1843 B.C.—*Room II* contains the *Gayer-Anderson collection, the sarcophagus of Nekhtefmut (early 9C B.C.), Roman mummy-portraits, and the huge *Sarcophagus lid of Rameses III, King of Egypt, 1198–1166 B.C.—The GREEK ROOM contains representative examples of pottery, seals, bronze and terracotta statuettes, Attic stelae, and the fine gravestones of Theokles, and of Hegemon, and a colossal caryatid head from the Inner Propylaea at Eleusis (1C B.C.)—Among the fine exhibits in the ETRUSCAN AND ROMAN ROOM are: the Pashley sarcophagus, Head of Antinöus (A.D. 110–130); a child's sarcophagus (early 2C A.D.); mosaic fountain niche from Baiae (c. A.D. 50); *Cinerarium of Helia Postumia (A.D. 25–50); exquisite *Seals and engraved gems.—The LOWER MARLAY GALLERY contains fine collections of porcelain, glass, silver, and watches, and a display of coins from the adjoining COIN ROOM.—At the end is the GLAISHER ROOM with European stoneware and earthenware.—Beyond (r.) are the CHINESE COLLECTIONS (ceramics and jade), and in the adjoining room, are textile displays.—Returning through the Glaisher Room, we come to the ISLAMIC COLLECTIONS, and, beyond, the HENDERSON COLLECTION OF ARMOUR (note Henry VII's hearse cloth).—The adjoining Small Henderson Room contains the MEDIEVAL COLLECTION, miscellaneous but of high interest, notably ivories and enamels, church plate, and ancient scientific instruments. Also, paintings of the early 15C E. Anglian School, an exquisite capital (c. 1150) from Avignon, a stained-glass fragment of 1500, and a head of Mary Magdalen in wood (Italian, late 15C).—The rich LIBRARY is notable for its collection of autographs,

prints, and historical documents. The musical treasures include the Fitzwilliam
Virginal Book and many autograph scores (notably those of Handel).

Opposite the Museum is a building of 1737, formerly occupied by *Fitzwilliam
House* (now in Huntingdon Rd., see p. 496).

Beyond *Addenbrooke's Hospital*, Trumpington St. ends at *Hobson's Conduit*,
transferred hither in 1856 from its original site in Market Hill, where it was
erected in 1614, partly at the expense of Thomas Hobson (d. 1631), "carrier
between Cambridge and London, and a great benefactor to this University and
town". Hobson is the subject of two short poems by Milton, and the phrase 'Hobson's
choice' embalms his rule of letting out his 'forty good cattle' in strict
rotation. In Lensfield Rd. (l.) is the *Scott Polar Research Institute* (1935), with an
interesting museum (weekdays, 2.30–4) of polar equipment and relics.—In
Trumpington Rd., a few yards farther on, is the *Leys School*, a Methodist public
school founded in 1875 (on a pasture called St Thomas's Leys), beside which Fen
Causeway leads to the *Engineering Laboratories*, etc. In Bateman St. (l.) is
the entrance to the *Botanic Gardens* (weekdays, 8–dusk; houses 2–5), founded in 1696.

Fitzwilliam St., opposite the Fitzwilliam Museum, leads E. to Tennis
Court Rd., which we follow to the left.

The part of Tennis Court Rd. to the right skirts the grounds of **Downing College**
(main entrance in Regent St.), which was founded in 1800 with the proceeds of
estates devised by Sir George Downing (d. 1749). The classical design of its three
ranges of buildings, surrounding a huge court, is due to Wilkins, whose work on the
E. and w. ranges was carried out in 1809–20; the N. portions of these ranges were
completed in 1875 by E. M. Barry; while the N. range begun by Sir Herbert Baker
(end wings; 1930–31) was completed with the chapel, by A. T. Scott (1951–53).
A new combination room (1970) at the s.w. corner (off Tennis Court Rd.) has a
blending design in pre-stressed concrete.

FAMOUS MEMBERS. Hon. T. R. Keppel (original of Mr Midshipman Easy) and
C. M. Doughty.

The New Museums is the name given to the group of museums,
laboratories, and lecture-rooms, lying N. of Downing St., while to the s.
others form the 'Downing Site'. Here are mainly science faculty buildings.

Perhaps the most generally interesting is the *Archaeological and Ethnological
Museum* (weekdays 2–4). Also important is the *Sedgwick Museum of Geology*
(weekdays 9–1, 2–5; Sat 9–1). Both are on the s. side. On the opposite side of Downing
St., in a crowded and depressing medley, is the *Zoology Museum.*—To the w. are the
Cavendish Physical Laboratory (famous for the work of J. J. Thomson, Rutherford,
Chadwick and Cockcroft), the *Mond Physical Laboratory*, a remarkable little building
by H. C. Hughes (1935), and the *Chemical Laboratory.* The *Examination Rooms*,
adjoined on the E. by the *Arts School*, are entered from Benet St.
Corn Exchange St. leads (l.) from Downing St. between the Corn Exchange and the
Lion Yard precinct, with a new Central Library, to the Guildhall and Benet St. In Corn
Exchange St. is the *Whipple Museum of the History of Science*, housed in the original
hall of Perse School (17C).

Downing St. ends opposite **Emmanuel College**, which was founded
in 1584 by Sir Walter Mildmay. "I have set an acorn," he replied to
Queen Elizabeth's charge of Puritanism, "which when it becomes an
oak, God alone knows what will be the fruit thereof." It occupies the
site and incorporated the buildings of a 13C Dominican priory.

The main court, with its attractive garden front, is substantially the original
construction by Ralph Symons (1584–89), though the entrance wing and the Hall
(l.) were transformed by Essex (1760–75), while the *Westmorland Building* (r.) is
a notable work of 1719–22 (restored 1964). Facing the entrance is the *Chapel*
(1677), designed, with the accompanying arcade, by Wren. It contains an altarpiece by Amigoni (1734), a good plaster ceiling, and a memorial window to John
Harvard. To the s. extends the *Brick Building* of 1633–34, with the Harvard room.
The smaller court to the N. is original, except for the N. range (1825), and there are
further buildings (1914) beyond the gardens and (reached by a subway) on the other
side of Emmanuel St. The extensive *Gardens* contain a large pond.

FAMOUS MEMBERS: Abp. Sancroft, Bp. Percy (of the 'Reliques'), Sir William Temple, William Law (of the 'Serious Call'), John Harvard, and some of the Pilgrim Fathers.

To the s. of Emmanuel, and bounded by Regent St., is *Parker's Piece*, an open space named from Edward Parker, cook of Trinity College, to whom it was leased in 1587. Still farther s. is the *University Cricket Ground*, known as 'Fenner's'.

Following St Andrew's St. towards the N., we next reach **Christ's College**, established in 1505 by Lady Margaret Beaufort, Countess of Richmond (1443–1509), mother of Henry VII, largely at the instance of St John Fisher, then chancellor. It absorbed *Godshouse*, a small college founded by William Byngham in 1436 on the site of King's College Chapel, and refounded on the present site in 1448.

The original first court (with Tudor arms on the gatehouse and a fine oriel in the Master's lodge) was refaced in 1758–69 and the *Hall* was rebuilt in 1876. The small *Chapel* (l.) may retain some walls from the days of Godshouse. Panelled in 1701, it contains the fine monument, by Joseph Catterns (1684), to Sir John Finch and Sir Thomas Baines. High up on the s. wall is the window of Lady Margaret's oratory, now in the Master's lodge. The *Fellows' Building*, in the second court, dates from 1642 and is ascribed to Thomas Grumbold; the third court dates from 1911 and 1949, with a startling addition, to the N., by Denys Lasdun. In the large **Gardens* (10.30–12.30 and 2–4 on weekdays) is an old mulberry tree associated (somewhat doubtfully) with John Milton.

FAMOUS MEMBERS: Denzil Holles, Milton, Edward King ('Lycidas'), Sir Walter Mildmay, Quarles, Leland, Paley, H. W. Betty (the 'Infant Roscius'), Darwin, Calverley, Seeley, Walter Besant, J. C. Bose, and Smuts.—John Milton, admitted as a pensioner in 1625 at the age of 16, occupied a first-floor room on the first stair on the N. side of the first court, and here wrote the 'Hymn on Christ's Nativity' as a college exercise.—The earliest certain use of stage scenery in England was at a play in Christ's hall in 1551.

St Andrew the Great, opposite Christ's, contains a memorial to Capt. Cook, his wife, and his six children. We follow Sidney St., leading N., past *Holy Trinity*, where Jeremy Taylor was baptized and Chas. Simeon (d. 1836) was vicar for 54 years (relics shown by verger). **Sidney Sussex College**, farther on, was established on the site of a Franciscan convent, under the will of Frances Sidney, Countess of Sussex (d. 1589).

The original buildings, by Ralph Symons, were completed in 1598, but the present Gothick appearance of the college is the work of Sir Jeffry Wyatville (1831–32), who spared only the old oriels on the garden front. A court overlooking the garden was added by Pearson in 1890, and the *Chapel*, with a painting by G. B. Pittoni, was attractively refitted and enlarged in 1912 by T. H. Lyon, who likewise built the block behind it. A covered way skirts the beautiful Master's garden to an impressive new extension (1970).

FAMOUS MEMBERS: Oliver Cromwell (entered as a fellow commoner in 1616) and C. T. R. Wilson. In the well-restored *Hall* hangs a famous portrait of Cromwell, attributed to Sam. Cooper, though it has been suggested that this is the portrait by Lely, in which the Protector charged the painter to include "all these roughnesses, pimples, and warts". After many vicissitudes, Cromwell's severed head found a resting-place in the precincts in 1961.

Beyond Sidney Sussex we pass the Whewell's Courts of Trinity (l.; being transformed in 1971), and turn r. into Jesus Lane. In Park St., on the left, beyond the classical portico of the *Pitt Club*, are the *Amateur Dramatic Club* ('A.D.C.'), founded in 1855 by Francis Burnand, and, opposite, the fine 'Little Trinity' guest hostel (early 18C). Following Jesus Lane we pass *Wesley House* (l.; being extended, 1971), by Aston Webb (1925), and reach ***Jesus College**, founded in 1496 by John Alcock, Bp. of Ely, on the site of the suppressed Nunnery of St Radegund.

Architecturally this is one of the most interesting colleges in Cambridge, since it retains part of the old conventual buildings.

We enter by a fine tower gateway by Alcock. From the first court (17–18C) an ogee doorway with Alcock's badge leads (r.) into the charming cloister court (early 16C), which occupies the site of the nuns' cloister. On the E. side is the beautiful old entrance to the Chapter House (c. 1210). The cruciform *Chapel (open all day), on the S. side, represents the conventual church, though the W. part of the nave is incorporated in the Master's lodge. It is an admirable piece of E.E., well restored, with traces of Norman (N. transept) and with Perp. additions by Alcock. The stained glass is by Pugin and Hardman, Madox Brown, Burne-Jones, and Morris. On the N. side of the cloister is the *Hall* (Alcock) from the vestibule of which a stair ascends to the quaint *Old Library*. The *Grounds* are extensive. The buildings behind the chapel are by Waterhouse (1870) and Morley Horder (1929–35). *North Court*, attractively sited in the extensive grounds, was added in 1965, to designs by David Roberts.

FAMOUS MEMBERS: Cranmer, Sterne, Coleridge, Malthus, and Quiller-Couch (Fellow).

Opposite Jesus College are *Westcott House* (Anglican), and the church of *All Saints* (by Bodley, 1865). Farther on we turn to the left across *Midsummer Common* to (½ m.) the river Cam, which we cross by the New Bridge near the *University Boat Houses*.

In the suburb of *Chesterton*, a little to the N.E. on the left bank of the river, beyond a fine old manor-house, is the singular *Chesterton Tower* (14C), believed to have been the residence of the rector, whose appointment was for 300 years in the hands of the Italian abbey of Vercelli.

Jesus Lane is continued E. by Maids' Causeway and Newmarket Rd. through the industrial quarter of *Barnwell* to (1 m.) *Stourbridge Chapel*, the little Norman chapel of a hospital for lepers (before 1199). The ancient fair formerly held here in September used to last five weeks and was described by Defoe as the greatest in the world.

After crossing the river, we turn to the left and follow Chesterton Rd. to (fully ½ m.) the CASTLE HILL, an artificial mound, beside which William the Conqueror built his castle (1068), never of much importance. Close by is the church of *St Giles*. The chancel arch (S. Aisle) and doorway (N. Aisle), of c. 1200, remain from the earlier church pulled down in 1875. Below the children's church of *St Peter's* (Norman doorway and font) is the *Cambridge and County Folk Museum* (adm. 10.30–1, 2–5, Sun 2.30–5.30; closed Mon; fee), in the former White Horse Inn (16C), with an interesting collection of local 'bygones'.

Northampton St. leads w. to Madingley Rd., passing on the left the entrance to *Merton Hall*, formerly a Norman manor-house (partly mid-12C); the name 'School of Pythagoras' has been given for obscure reasons to the oldest part of the building. The estate, in the possession of Merton College, Oxford, from 1270 to 1959, has been acquired by St John's, and the new Cripps building lies to the S.E. At the corner of Madingley Rd., is *Westminster College* (see p. 486), a Presbyterian training school (1899).

The N.W. quarter of Cambridge is changing as the new colleges rise. In Storey's Way off the Madingley Rd. is **Churchill College** (named after Sir Winston Churchill), founded in 1960 to promote research and teaching in the sciences and technology in particular. As at Trinity, the Master is appointed by the Crown. The low brick and wood buildings, by Richard Sheppard and Robson, follow the traditional Cambridge plan of courts, with a notable element of spaciousness. The barrel-vaulted hall is hung with copper strip-lighting. An *Archives Centre* will house the papers of Sir Winston and other 20C statesmen.—Farther w. is the *University Observatory* (1822–23; open 8–10 p.m. first Sat in month to visitors accompanied by a member of the University).

Castle St. is prolonged by Huntingdon Rd., where since 1964 is situated (l.) New Hall, founded in 1954 at the third women's college. The stark white buildings (completed in 1966) by Chamberlin, Powell and Bon, include a domed hall approached by four staircases. Beyond is **Fitzwilliam College** (formerly in Trumpington St.), established in 1887 as a centre of the corporate life of members of the university who are not members of one of its colleges, but incorporated into the university in 1966. The long low brick buildings (by Denys Lasdun; 1966) are divided in three by stone string-courses. The hall, with its glass 'clerestory' and concrete canopy, provides in contrast a striking vertical emphasis.

Farther on are the *National Institute of Agricultural Botany* (r.) and the *University Farm* (l.), and (2 m.; r.) **Girton College**, a college for women, founded by Emily Davies at Hitchin in 1869 "to avoid scandal" but transferred to Cambridge in 1873. Built way out to discourage male visitors, it is planning to admit men students from 1979.

From the castle we go s.e. to **Magdalene College** (pron. 'Maudlen'), founded by Lord Audley in 1542 on the site of a hostel of Benedictine monks established after 1428 by the four great Fenland abbeys of Crowland, Ely, Ramsey, and Walden, and later known as Buckingham College (c. 1480–1539).

Though considerably altered, the *First Court*, entered through a gateway of 1585, preserves much of the original monastic fabric, especially on the s.e., or river, side. The *Hall* (c. 1519; refitted 1714) has an unusual double staircase, and the *Chapel* retains its late-15C timber roof. At the e. end of the second court is the *PEPYSIAN LIBRARY (adm. Mon–Sat in term, also mid-July–Sept; 11.30–12.30, 2.30–3.30), containing the collection of books bequeathed by Samuel Pepys (d. 1703). The great treasure is the cypher MS. of the immortal 'Diary', but there are many other valuable MSS. and incunabula. The books are kept on their original shelves exactly as arranged by Pepys. The building, probably by Robert Hooke, dates from c. 1679; the date on the front refers to the installation of the books. The *Garden* (1–5 or 6.30) affords a good view of the Library. Other buildings are by Aston Webb and Ingress Bell. *Mallory Court*, on the other side of Magdalene St., was reconstructed from old buildings by H. Redfern, while *Benson Court*, adjoining, is by Lutyens (1935). The medieval buildings fronting on Magdalene St. have been carefully restored by David Roberts.

FAMOUS MEMBERS: Henry Dunster (first President of Harvard), Pepys, Charles Kingsley, Parnell, and A. C. Benson (Master).

We now recross the Cam and follow Bridge St., in which (l.) is *St Clement's Church*, E.E. but much altered. On the same side stands the highly interesting *Church of the Holy Sepulchre, one of the five medieval round churches in England, the circular part dating from c. 1130. The chancel was added in the 15C, also probably, the 'angel roof' of the N. aisle and choir. The whole was ruthlessly restored in 1842.

Behind is the building of the **Union Society**, containing a debating hall, a dining-room, and a large library. Founded in 1815 in a room behind the Red Lion inn in Petty Cury, it acquired the present site in 1866.

Opposite, in St John's St., is *St John's College, founded in 1511 by Lady Margaret Beaufort (see p. 494) and replacing the 13C Hospital of St John.

The FIRST COURT, entered by a fine *Gateway*, with a statue of St John, the Beaufort 'yales' supporting the royal arms, and the Tudor rose and portcullis, was built in 1510–16 under the direct supervision of St John Fisher, executor of the foundress. The s. side was rebuilt in 1772. On the N. side is the large *Chapel*, built by Sir Gilbert Scott (1864–69) in an early Dec. style (open 9.30–12.30 & 2–4). Between the first and second courts is the *Hall*, a fine panelled room with a hammerbeam roof. Its many portraits include one of Wordsworth, by Pickersgill. —The *SECOND COURT, an admirable example of Elizabethan brickwork (1598–1602; by Ralph Symons), practically unchanged and of a lovely plum-colour, justifies Ruskin's praise of it as the most perfect in the University. On the N. side is the *Combination Room*, one of the finest panelled galleries in England (rich plaster ceiling; interesting portraits).—The THIRD COURT was in building between 1623 and 1674. On the N.E. side is the *Old Library* (11–1 in term), on the first floor, Jacobean in its fitting up and containing many valuable autograph letters, MSS., and early printed books, including Lady Margaret's Book of Hours (French; early 15C), and a vellum copy of Cranmer's or the 'Great' Bible (1539).—From this court the Gothick NEW COURT (1826-31), by Rickman and Hutchinson, is approached by their picturesque 'Bridge of Sighs', crossing the Cam. Thence we may reach the *Cripps Building*, by Powell and Moya (1966), paid for by a single benefaction to the college of £1 million. It uses the river and its inlet to great effect. The beautiful College Grounds provide a good approach to the 'Backs'. We return to the Third Court by Robert Grumbold's lovely *Old Bridge* (1696; completed 1712).—Behind the chapel (and reached from the Second Court) is CHAPEL COURT (partly Victorian), extended in 1939 by Sir Edward Maufe, with *North Court*, facing Bridge St., beyond. The sculptures are by Eric Gill (Chapel Court) and Vernon Hill (N. Court), the stone beasts by A. P. Hardiman (St John's St. gate) and Charles Wheeler (Bridge St. gate).

FAMOUS MEMBERS: Sir Thomas Wyatt, Roger Ascham, Lord Burghley, Robert Greene, Thos. Nashe, Ben Jonson (doubtful), Strafford, Lord Falkland, Fairfax, Herrick, Stillingfleet, Matthew Prior, Bentley, Sir John Herschel, Chas. Churchill, Erasmus Darwin, Horne Tooke, Wilberforce, Wordsworth (inscription in College Kitchen), Palmerston, Kirke White, Samuel Butler, Sir Edward Appleton, Sir John Cockcroft, Louis Leakey, and many bishops and archbishops.

Next to St John's is ***Trinity College**, the largest college in the sister Universities (820 students). It was established in 1546 by Henry VIII, who incorporated the earlier foundations of King's Hall and Michael-house (going back to 1317).

The undergraduates wear gowns of a darker blue than those at Caius. The Master is appointed by the Crown, a practise now followed at Churchill College. The **Great Gateway* (1518) bears statues of Henry VIII (E. face), James I, Anne of Denmark, and Charles I (when Prince) (all on the inside). It leads into the spacious GREAT COURT, in the centre of which is a fountain erected by Thomas Nevile, Master from 1593 to 1615. On the s. side (l.) is the *Queen's Gate* (1597), with a statue of Elizabeth I. On the N. side stands the *Chapel* (open always), a Tudor building (completed 1561), with good 18C woodwork. In the ante-chapel are statues of *Newton (by Roubiliac), Bacon (by Weekes), Barrow (by Noble), Macaulay and Whewell (by Woolner), and Tennyson (by Thornycroft). To the w. of the chapel are the quaint little *King's Hostel* and *King Edward III's Gate* (1428-32), re-erected on this site by Nevile. The **Hall* (w. side of court; 1604-5; usually open 1.30-3), 100 ft in length, contains many interesting portraits, including one of William Fredk., Duke of Gloucester (at the age of six), by Reynolds. To the s. is the enormous *Kitchen* (1605).—We now enter NEVILE'S or CLOISTER COURT, a Jacobean work of c. 1605-12, extended to the library in 1681. The **LIBRARY* (w. side; 150,000 vols.), built by Wren in 1676-95, is of a singularly appropriate design, best seen on the river-front. The four statues on the parapet (Divinity, Law, Physics, and Mathematics) are by C. G. Cibber (1681). In the dignified and harmonious interior (190 ft long; weekdays 1-4), which has few rivals among libraries in England, are bookcases, finely carved by Grinling Gibbons, and busts of Newton, Bacon (both by Roubiliac), Tennyson (by Woolner), and other eminent members of the college. The **Statue of Lord Byron*, at the s. end, by Thorvaldsen, was meant for Westminster Abbey but was refused admission. The curious stained-glass window above it is an example of a lost 18C process. The glass cases contain illuminated MSS., autograph writings of Milton, Thackeray, Tennyson, Byron, and Houseman, and relics of Newton.—To the s. of Nevile's Court is the NEW COURT, built by Wilkins in 1825, to the E. of which is *Bishop's Hostel*, a separate building of 1670-71. From its w. side we enter the beautiful **College Grounds*. The view from the bridge (1764-68) is charming.—Just outside the Great Gateway is *Angel Court* (1959), and opposite are the two dark *Whewell's Courts* (1860).

FAMOUS MEMBERS (besides those particularly mentioned, some 50 bishops, and several Nobel prizewinners): Essex, Coke, Herbert, Cowley, Marvell, Dryden, Judge Jeffreys, Porson (Fellow), Melbourne, Thirlwall, Kinglake, Edward Fitzgerald, Arthur Hallam, Galton, Clerk-Maxwell (Fellow), Farrar, Lord Acton (Fellow), Balfour, F. W. Maitland, Stanford (Organist), Sir James Frazer, A. E. Housman (Fellow), Baldwin, Rayleigh, Rutherford (Fellow), Eddington, Jeans, Gowland Hopkins, Pandit Nehru, G. E. Moore, Wittgenstein, Clive Bell, Vaughan Williams, Bertrand Russell, and Vladimir Nabukov. Also members of the royal family, including Edward VII, George

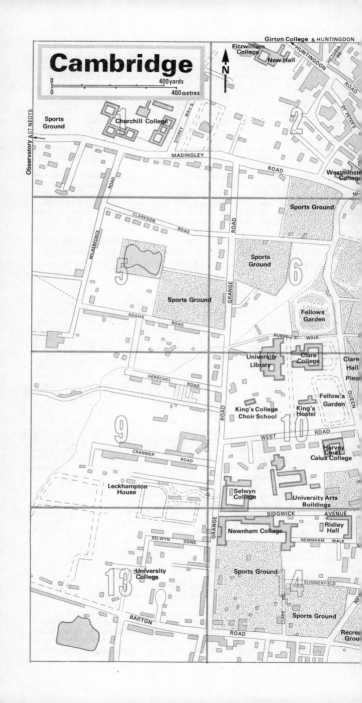

Cambridge

0   400 yards
0   400 metres

Girton College & HUNTINGDON

Fitzwilliam College

New Hall

HUNTINGDON

VICTORIA RD

ST PETER'S

N

Observatory & ST NEOTS

Sports Ground

Churchill College

STONEY

M.A.'s

MADINGLEY   ROAD

Westminster College

CLARKSON   ROAD

WILBERFORCE

Sports Ground

ROAD

Sports Ground

5

GRANGE

6

Fellows Garden

ADAMS   ROAD

BURRELL'S   WALK

University Library

Clare College

Clare Hall

Piece

HERSCHEL   ROAD

ROAD

King's College Choir School

King's Hostel

Fellow's Garden

QUEEN

9

CRANMER   ROAD

WEST   ROAD

10

Harvey Court

Caius College

Leckhampton House

Selwyn College

University Arts Buildings

GRANGE

SIDGWICK   AVENUE

Newnham College

Ridley Hall

NEWNHAM   WALK

SELWYN   GDNS.

13

University College

12

Sports Ground

4

SUMMERFIELD

BARTON   ROAD

Sports Ground

Recreation Ground

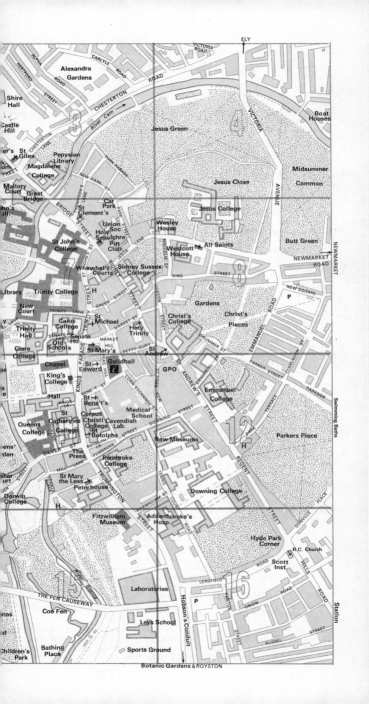

VI and H.R.H. Prince Charles. Thackeray (like Henry Esmond) occupied the ground-floor rooms on the N. side of the Great Gateway and Newton those on the first floor. Macaulay had the ground-floor rooms next the chapel. Byron is said to have 'kept' in Nevile's Court (on the first floor of the central staircase on the N. side, next the Library), Hallam had rooms in the New Court (first floor, central staircase, s. side), but his friend Tennyson did not live in college. Among celebrated Masters of Trinity were Abp. Whitgift, Bp. Pearson, Dr Isaac Barrow, Richard Bentley, William Whewell, Montague Butler, J. J. Thomson, and G. M. Trevelyan.

To the s. of Trinity, opposite the restored 14C church of *St Michael*, stands **Caius College** (pronounced 'Keys'), properly Gonville and Caius, founded by Edmund Gonville in 1348 and refounded by Dr Caius in 1557.

Second and third year students at Caius are still known as 'Junior' and 'Senior Sophs', i.e. 'Sophomores', an old Cambridge term for such students that has been adopted in American universities. The undergraduates wear blue gowns with black facings.

We pass through a modern gateway occupying the site of the small *Gate of Humility* (now preserved in the Master's garden) into TREE COURT (1868–70), by Waterhouse. From this court the *Gate of Virtue* (w.) gives access to the CAIUS COURT, the exit from which, opposite the *Chapel*, is the *Gate of Honour* (1575), a charming little Renaissance gateway leading to Senate House Passage. At the restoration of 1959 two of the sundials and four obelisks were replaced after 300 years. On the right of Caius Court is GONVILLE COURT, refaced in 1753. The *Hall* (1853) contains interesting portraits. In the *Chapel* (1375; modernized 1718) are quaint monuments to Dr Caius (d. 1573), Dr Legge (d. 1607), and Dr Perse (d. 1615).—On the other side of the street is *St Michael's Court*.

FAMOUS MEMBERS: Gresham, Harvey, Jeremy Taylor, Wharton, Thurlow, Hookham Frere, Seeley (Fellow), Chadwick (Master), and J. E. Flecker.

The favourite short excursion is to **Grantchester** (2½ m. s.w.; tea-gardens) either by river or footpath. This village, affectionately sung by Rupert Brooke, is often wrongly identified with Grantebrycge. The church has a resplendent chancel and a Norman font. 'Byron's Pool' here was named after Lord Byron. Walkers should go on to (3½ m.) *Trumpington*, which still retains its village character in the centre. The Green Man Inn has a fine timbered roof. In the early-14C church (much restored) is a *Brass to Sir Roger de Trumpington (d. 1289), said to be the second oldest in England. The War Memorial Cross is by Eric Gill (1921). The successor of the mill of Chaucer's 'Reeve's Tale', supposed to have inspired Tennyson's 'Miller's Daughter', was burned down in 1928. Thence Cambridge is 2 m. N. by a pleasant road (bus).

Madingley (3½ m. N.W.), a pretty village, has a rebuilt windmill, and the Tudor mansion occupied by Edward VII while keeping his terms at Cambridge (now a University hostel); on the way is the beautifully laid out *American Memorial Cemetery* (1944). Other points of interest are *Cherry Hinton* church (3 m. s.E.), with an E.E. chancel; *Fulbourn*, 4½ m. s.E., with a church showing a curious mixture of E.E., Dec., and Perp. (good brasses); *Impington Hall* (3 m. N.; 16C), for 300 years in possession of the Pepys family and frequently mentioned in the famous 'Diary'; the churches of *Barton and Kingston* (3 m. and 7 m. s.w.), the latter with mural paintings (13–15C); *Bourn*, 1½ m. beyond Kingston, with a fine church containing a mizmaze, and the oldest dated windmill in England (1633); and the *Gogmagog Hills* (the 'Gogs'; 222 ft), with *Wandlebury Camp* (4 m. s.E.), traversed by the disused but conspicuously Roman '*Via Devana*'.

FROM CAMBRIDGE TO HAVERHILL, 19 m. (A 604). Hills Rd. starting beside the large *Rom. Cath. Church* at the end of Regent St. (p. 494) leads s.E. past the 'Gogs' (see above), and the new buildings of *Perse School*, founded in 1615 in Free School Lane by Dr Stephen Perse of Caius.—*Balsham*, 3½ m. N. of (10½ m.) *Linton*, has a Dec. and Perp. church with two 15C brasses. At *Hadstock*, 2 m. s. of Linton, the church has important early 11C portions, ascribed to Canute, including a unique door.—19 m. *Haverhill*, see Rte 48.

FROM CAMBRIDGE TO MILDENHALL, 22 m. We follow the Newmarket road (A 45) leaving on the left (4½ m.) *Quy*, the name probably a corruption of 'Cow Ey' (island). Just beyond, the road forks, and we take B 1102 left.— 6 m. *Anglesey Abbey* (N.T.; house open April–early-Oct, Tues, Wed, Thurs, Sat, Sun & BH, 2–6;

gardens daily; fee). The crypt (1236) of an Augustinian Abbey is incorporated into the 17C house. *Bottisham* church (early-Dec.) with fine screens, is $1\frac{1}{4}$ m. s.e.—$7\frac{1}{2}$ m. *Swaffham Bulbeck* has an E.E. church with carved bench-ends, and good 16–17C houses clustered round the green; the *Commercial End* built on a tributary of the Cam is a 19C development, dominated by the Merchant's House.—$8\frac{1}{2}$ m. *Swaffham Prior* has two churches in the churchyard; the earlier one has a Norman octagonal tower, and the derelict one (restored in 1809) has a good Perp. tower. Baldwin Manor is an early-16C timbered hall.—11 m. *Burwell* was a 'long street' village, and as at Long Melford the chief glory is the late-Perp. *Church (with a Palimpsest brass of c. 1542). *Burwell Fen* and *Wicken Fen* (N.T.), 2 m. and 3 m. N. are untouched fenland areas reserved as a sanctuary for the characteristic insects and flowers (visitors must sign an undertaking to abide by the rules of preservation). Celery-growing is locally important.—15 m. *Fordham* church has an interesting two-storied Lady Chapel on the N. side. *Isleham* church, 3 m. N.E., has a good roof, eccentric Jacobean Communion rails, and a charming brass to Thomas Peyton (d. 1484) and his two beautiful wives. *Landwade* (1445), 2 m. s.w., remotely situated and practically unrestored, has Cotton monuments. *Chippenham*, $2\frac{1}{2}$ m. s.e., is a 'model' village built by the Thorpes of Chippenham Park in the 17C, and here is another undrained fen (also N.T.), strictly preserved. The church has ancient wall-paintings.—22 m. *Mildenhall* (see p. 458).

56 CAMBRIDGE TO ELY AND KING'S LYNN
A Viâ Downham Market

ROAD, 45 m. A 10.—16 m. Ely.—34 m. *Downham Market.*—45 m. King's Lynn.
RAILWAY, $41\frac{1}{4}$ m. in c. 1 hr, viâ ($14\frac{3}{4}$ m.) Ely and ($30\frac{1}{4}$ m.) Downham.

The Ely road leaves Cambridge by Magdalene Bridge, immediately turning right.—4 m. *Milton* church has a Norman chancel arch, 17C altar-rails, and monuments by Flaxman and Chantrey.—At ($5\frac{1}{2}$ m.) *Waterbeach* we cross a section of the *Car Dyke*, the Roman canal dug to transport the fenland corn to the garrisons of Lincoln and the north, then join for 2 m. the conspicuous alinement of the Roman Akeman Street.—7 m. (r.) *Denny Abbey*, founded in 1160 and taken over by the nuns of St Clare in 1342. Fragments of the church remain, and the refectory building.—$10\frac{1}{2}$ m. *Stretham* is a well-preserved village with a 15C cross, 16–18C houses, and a Dec. church. To the s.e. of the village, on the Old West River, is a fine Pumping House, with the original Butterly Beam Engine.

16 m. **ELY** (Hotel and Restaurant) deriving its name ('eel island'), according to Bede, from the eels in the river, is a small city (10,000 inhab.) situated on an eminence rising from the left (w.) bank of the Ouse.

The old '*Isle of Ely*' (7 m. by 4 m.) was surrounded by marshland crossable only by the 'Fen-slodgers' who knew the firm tussock paths. On this island Hereward the Wake, the 'Last of the English', held out against the Norman invaders until 1071 when a road was constructed, floated on bundles of faggots, to bring the army across the wastes. Nowadays the name is applied to the whole of the North part of the shire.

The *Cathedral (dedicated to the *Holy Trinity*), one of the longest and most varied churches in England, is a huge cruciform structure representing an architectural history of four centuries.

HISTORY. The first edifice was a Benedictine abbey established by St Etheldreda (or Audrey), Queen of Northumbria, who took refuge here in the home of her girlhood and became abbess in 673. The present structure was begun in 1083 by *Abbot Simeon*; the transepts and E. end were completed by 1106, three years before the church was raised to cathedral rank. The Norman nave seems to have been finished c. 1189, and the Galilee or w. porch was added by Bp. *Eustace* (1198–1215). *Bp. Hugh of Northwold* (1229–54) lengthened the choir by six exquisite bays in the E.E. style. In 1322 the fall of the central tower wrecked the Norman choir and gave *Alan de Walsingham* (1322–28) and his team of craftsmen the opportunity of erecting the lovely and original Dec. octagon and the three w. bays of the present choir. They designed also the Lady Chapel. The chantries at the E. end of the church belong to the Perp. period (1486–1533). The N.W. transept was perhaps never finished.

EXTERIOR. The most prominent part is the *West Front*, including the castellated *West Tower*, the *Galilee Porch*, and the *South-West Transept*. With the exception of the octagonal top and turrets (Dec.), the whole of the striking tower belongs to the Transition Norman period (1174–89), though the lack of the N.W. transept robs the façade of its full measure of dignity. The unique *Central Octagon* is one of the marvels of medieval building. The timber lantern was restored by G. Gilbert Scott.

INTERIOR. The E.E. *Galilee Porch* consists of two simply vaulted bays, with blind arcades. The doorway leading into the nave is almost too richly moulded. From the w. end of the church we obtain a most impressive vista of its full length, the architecture increasing in richness as the eye travels on to the stained glass of the E. end lancets. The interior of the *West Tower* (adm.; parties at 11.30 & 3; also at 4 in summer), with its arcaded galleries, has a 19C painted roof. The *S.W. Transept*, in the Norman Transition style, has richly arcaded walls, triforium, and clerestory. It is adjoined by the semicircular *Chapel of St Catherine* (rebuilt 1848).

The narrow *NAVE* of twelve bays (1106–89), more or less contemporaneous with that of Peterborough, is an imposing example of late-Norman work. The triforium arcade is very nearly equal in height to the main arcade, both in nave and transepts. Massive though the piers are, they are light in comparison with the earlier work of the transepts or of Durham and Gloucester. The old unadorned roof has been replaced by a 19C painted ceiling, but the s. aisle vaults in the four E. bays retain their original 12C colouring. The windows in the N. aisle are Perp. insertions, those in the s. aisle have been restored to their original Norman form. In the s. aisle is the *Prior's Doorway* (c. 1140; closed in winter) with rich external ornament, and near it is the fragment of a *Saxon Cross*, erected to Ovinus, principal 'housethegn' of Etheldreda. The *S. Doorway*, also richly decorated outside, at the E. end of the aisle, was the monks' entrance from the cloisters. Near the w. end of the nave lies Prior Alan de Walsingham, under a marble slab from which the brass has disappeared.

The lower parts of the GREAT TRANSEPTS, which have aisles on both sides, show the oldest work in the cathedral (1083–1107). In the E. aisle of the N. arm is the *Chapel of St Edmund*, with a 14C screen and a 12C wall-painting of St Edmund's Martyrdom. The adjoining *Chapel of St George* was restored as a War Memorial by Sir Guy Dawber. The bronze group 'Christ and Mary Magdalene' in the s. arm is by David Wynne (1963).

The great **CENTRAL OCTAGON** has been described as "perhaps the most beautiful and original design to be found in the whole range of Gothic architecture". The sacrist Alan de Walsingham (with, probably, his carpenter William Hurley), "alone of all the architects of Europe, conceived the idea of getting rid of the narrow, tall opening of the central tower, which, though possessing exaggerated height, gave neither grace

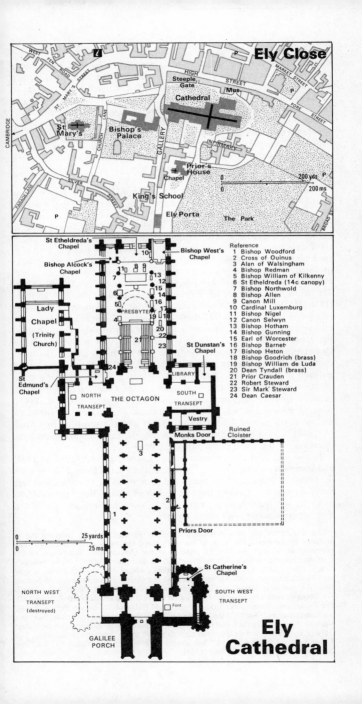

Ely Close

WEST FEN ROAD
ST MARY'S STREET
HIGH STREET
Steeple Gate
Cathedral
Mus
MARKET STREET
FORE STREET
CAMBRIDGE
St Mary's
Bishop's Palace
CHURCH LANE
GALLERY
INFIRMARY
SILVER STREET
Prior's House
Chapel
King's School
PREBEND LANE
Ely Porta
The Park
BROAD ST

0 ——— 200 yds
0 ——— 200 ms

Ely Cathedral

St Etheldreda's Chapel
Bishop Alcock's Chapel
Bishop West's Chapel
10
11 8 9
7
13
6 15
5 14
PRESBYTERY 16
Lady Chapel (Trinity Church)
4 19 17
18
20
21 22
23
St Dunstan's Chapel
St Edmund's Chapel
24
LIBRARY
NORTH TRANSEPT
SOUTH TRANSEPT
THE OCTAGON
Vestry
Monks Door
Ruined Cloister
Priors Door
3
2
1
St Catherine's Chapel
NORTH WEST TRANSEPT (destroyed)
Font
SOUTH WEST TRANSEPT
GALILEE PORCH

0 ——— 25 yards
0 ——— 25 ms

Reference
1 Bishop Woodford
2 Cross of Ouinus
3 Alan of Walsingham
4 Bishop Redman
5 Bishop William of Kilkenny
6 St Etheldreda (14c canopy)
7 Bishop Northwold
8 Bishop Allen
9 Canon Mill
10 Cardinal Luxemburg
11 Bishop Nigel
12 Canon Selwyn
13 Bishop Hotham
14 Bishop Gunning
15 Earl of Worcester
16 Bishop Barnet
17 Bishop Heton
18 Bishop Goodrich (brass)
19 Bishop William de Luda
20 Dean Tyndall (brass)
21 Prior Crauden
22 Robert Steward
23 Sir Mark Steward
24 Dean Caesar

nor dignity to the principal feature. Accordingly, he took for his base the whole breadth of the church" (Fergusson). The octagon is formed by four larger and four smaller arches. The wooden lantern is set in such a manner as to have its angles opposite the faces of the stone octagon below. All England was searched to find oaks of sufficient size for the corner-posts (63 ft long). The weight of the lantern is distributed by a wooden framework (on the principle of the hammerbeam), out of sight behind the vaulting. The roof forms "the only Gothic dome in existence". The details are admirable. The best general view is from the s.w. angle, near the door of the Vergers' Vestry.

The *Choir is separated from the Octagon by a 19C screen. The division between the E.E. and Dec. portions is very sharply marked. The clerestory windows in the E.E. part are triplets, set flush with the outer wall. The details of the three w. bays "are equal to anything in Europe for elegance and appropriateness" (Fergusson). The upper stalls date from the 14C, but the other furnishings are of the 19C. On the high altar a cross (1964) by Louis Osman stands between candlesticks of 1661. The most interesting monuments (beginning in the s. aisle) are those of Bp. William de Luda (Louth; 1290–98), Bp. Barnet (1366–73), John Tiptoft, Earl of Worcester (beheaded 1470), Bp. Hotham (1316–37), Bp. Hugh of Northwold (1229–54), Bp. William of Kilkenny (1255–56), Bp. Redman (1501–5), and Dean Cæsar (d. 1636). The monument next to Bp. Northwold's tomb is probably the canopy of Bp. Hotham (see above). An inscribed slab of slate marks the site of Queen Etheldreda's Shrine.—At the E. end of the N. aisle is the over-elaborate *Chantry of Bp. Alcock* (d. 1500), and in the corresponding position to the s. is the *Chantry of Bp. West* (d. 1533), a graceful combination of classical and medieval styles. In the *Chapel of St Etheldreda*, between these, is the monument of Card. de Luxembourg (d. 1443), Abp. of Rouen and Bp. of Ely. Behind the altar-screen are the black marble tomb-slab of Bp. Nigel (1133–74) and the tomb of Bp. Allen (d. 1845), with a slab of Alexandrine mosaic, made of materials once intended for the tomb of Napoleon at Paris.

To the N.E. of the N. transept is the *Lady Chapel, started in 1320, and completed in 1335–53. It served as the Parish Church from 1566 to 1938. It is elaborately decorated, but most of the statuettes are badly damaged, a fault of the soft clunch of which they were made, as much as the depredations of the Lord Protector Somerset (in 1547). The complex lierne vault spans 46 feet.

The Cloisters are now represented mainly by the E. walk, forming the s. entrance to the nave. To the E. of the s. transept are parts of the *Infirmary* (fine examples of Norman work). The remains of the Conventual Buildings, to the s. of the cloisters, include also the *Prior's House* and the exquisite *Prior Crauden's Chapel (Dec.; 1321–41), with a 13C undercroft, which, like the Ely Porta, is now used by the *King's School*, refounded in 1543 but claiming an uninterrupted descent from the monastic school at which Edward the Confessor (d. 1066) was a pupil. The chapel is open always; other buildings in the July–Aug holidays (10–4, Mon–Fri). The *Deanery* was constructed from the old Guest Hall and retains some of its 13–14C work and remains of the 12C monks' kitchen. The cathedral precincts (s. side) include a pleasant *Park*. Thence the *Great Gateway* (*Ely Porta*) of the monastery leads out to the Gallery, by which street we may turn right to regain the w. front of the cathedral. The *Bishop's Palace* (l.) is mainly 18C, but retains wings built by Bp. Alcock and the Long Gallery built by Bp. Goodrich (d. 1554).

The *Church of St Mary*, a little w. of the palace, dates from 1215.
The vicarage, adjoining the churchyard on the w., was a residence of
Oliver Cromwell.—The course of the Cambridge trial eights is on the
Cam near Ely, and is used by the University crew for practice in the Lent
term.

FROM ELY TO NEWMARKET, 13½ m. Railway in ½ hr. A 142 runs S.E. across the
Fens.—1½ m. *Stuntney* was a Bronze Age settlement, and a timber trackway of
that period connecting it with Ely has been traced.—5 m. *Soham*, a large and
attractive village of brick houses, was the site of a cathedral built by St Felix,
the 'Apostle of East Anglia' (d. 634). The present church is 12C, with a Perp. tower
and good flushwork. There are still many windmills in this area (mostly derelict).
—8½ m. *Fordham* (p. 501).—We enter Suffolk near (11½ m.) *Exning* (r.), a pleasant
old village and the mother-parish of Newmarket.—13½ m. *Newmarket*, p. 458.

A 10 runs N.E. from Ely.—21 m. *Littleport* (Perp. church with 19C
additions).—At (25 m.) *Brandon Creek* we enter Norfolk.—31 m.
Hilgay church has a brick tower (1794).—33 m. *Denver* with a 13C
church, has a fine tower-mill, and a series of sluices; the Old Denver
Sluices (1825) are by Rennie. Dorothy Sayers (1893–1957) used the
name of this village for the ducal family of her detective, Lord Peter
Wimsey, and the Fenland atmosphere is brilliantly evoked in 'The Nine
Tailors'.—34 m. **Downham Market** (3600 inhab.), is a compact market
town; the E.E. church has a high tower, and an excellent peal of bells.

A 1122 runs E. from Downham Market.—4 m. *Stradsett* church (good German
stained glass of 1540) is set in the grounds of the Hall, which is Elizabethan with
a Georgian façade.—5½ m. *Fincham* has a Perp. church with a Norman font.
Fincham Hall (16C) has a famous garden with one of the largest collections of
plants in the country (open Sun in June and early July).—Just before (10 m.)
Swaffham (p. 478), the road crosses the Devil's Dyke.

36 m. *Stow Bardolph* (Hare monument in the church).—39½ m.
Tottenhill.

A by-road (l.) leads viâ Magdalen Rd. Stn. to (2½ m.) the Ouse, across which is
the attractive and lonely village of *Wiggenhall St Mary Magdalen* with a Perp.
church and 13C tower, containing good painted screens, benches, and Jacobean
panelling. *Wiggenhall St Mary the Virgin* lies c. 2 m. N.W. in beautiful country,
and has a brick church with excellently carved early-16C benches and a good eagle-
lectern (1518). On the E. bank of the Ouse lies the church of *Wiggenhall St German's*
(also with good benches), where the village has large 16–18C houses. Just to the s.
is *Wiggenhall St Peter* with an impressive ruined Perp. church standing at the 'Eau
Brink'.

45 m. **KING'S LYNN** (30,100 inhab.; Hotels) is an ancient port on
the Great Ouse, 3 m. above its outflow into the Wash. The original
parish of St Margaret grew up round the Saturday Market, and a new
town was laid out by Bp. Turbus across a creek to the N. in c. 1160,
with the church of St Nicholas and the Tuesday Market. There remains
a splendid townscape of buildings, domestic, industrial, and official,
from the 14C to the early 19C, only a few of which can be mentioned
here. An affinity with the Netherlands is everywhere apparent.

The church of **St Margaret* in the Saturday Market Place was founded
c. 1100 by Bp. Losinga, and rebuilt in the 13C. Within are 14C screens,
misericords, an early-Georgian pulpit, an organ by Snetzler (1754), and
two of the most elaborate *Brasses in England, Flemish or German in
origin; the Walsoken brass (Adam de Walsoken, d. 1349) has a border
of country scenes; that of Robert Braunche (d. 1364) is known as the
'Peacock Brass' from the scene of the feast that Braunche gave for

Edward III. Opposite the church, and towards Queen Street, are a fine group of buildings; the *Gaol* of 1784, the *Guildhall*, built in 1421, beautifully chequered in flint and stone, with an Elizabethan addition in the

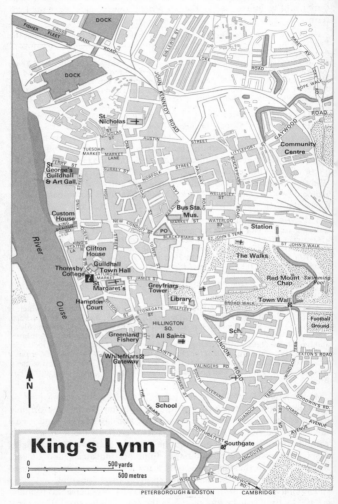

same style to the left, and the *Town Hall* (1895). The Corporation plate and regalia includes the 14C King John's Cup, a mayoral chain made from 15C Waits' collars, and the 16C Nuremberg Cup. In St James St. is the Perp. *Greyfriars Tower*.

From the Saturday Market, Queen St. and King St. lead to the Tuesday Market. In Queen St. are *Thoresby College*, a 15C monastic house with 17C front, and *Clifton House*, a unique 16–17C merchant's house with a tall brick watch-tower, a façade remodelled by Bell in c. 1708, and a 14C crypt. In King's Staithe Lane leading to the Quay are fine 16–17C warehouses and 17–18C houses, and in King's Staithe Sq., the 18C *Bank House*, with a statue of Charles I. On the Quay stands the **Custom House* (by Henry Bell, 1683), perhaps the most graceful composition among the buildings of Lynn; the statue is of Charles II. King Street has a wealth of good houses, including *St George's Guildhall* (N.T.; 1410), used as a theatre in the 18C, and now restored to this purpose (adm. daily, exc. Sat aft. & Sun; 10–12.30, 2.30–5; fee). The Market Square beyond is spacious and dignified with two notable hotels; the Duke's Head is by Henry Bell. *St Nicholas* was built as a chapel of ease in 1146. It has a splendid Perp. s. porch, good benches, a 15C brass lectern, and a tie-beam roof. In the neighbouring streets are many excellent domestic buildings.

The old streets s. of the Saturday Market Place are equally interesting, especially Nelson St., Bridge St., and Friars St. In the first is *Hampton Court*, a monastic building of c. 1400 considerably altered, and in Bridge St. is the restored *Greenland Fishery*; the local history museum formerly here is now in Market St. (weekdays 10–5). Farther on is the *South Gate* (1437), and in The Walks, a park s. of the station, are some remains of the *Town Wall* and the *Red Mount Chapel* (1482), an octagonal brick building probably for the use of pilgrims to Walsingham.—Fanny Burney (1752–1840) and George Vancouver (1758–98) were born at Lynn, the latter in a Tudor house behind the Friends' Meeting House in New Conduit St., and Arthur Young was married here in 1765. Eugene Aram was an usher in the grammar school here at the time of his arrest.—Lynn is a good centre for visiting the famous Marshland churches (comp. below). A Festival of Music and Drama is held here at the end of July.—At *Middleton*, c. 3 m. s.e., is the Tower, a moated mansion with a brick gatehouse (15C) 60 ft high, and a walled aviary garden.

FROM KING'S LYNN TO SPALDING, 25 m. A 17 leads westwards through an area with particularly fine churches.—6 m. *Terrington St Clement* *Church (Perp.) one of the finest in the marshland, with many interesting details. The inscription on the font-cover refers to the manifestations of the Holy Trinity at the baptism of Christ. The lovely church of *Walpole St Andrew* lies 2½ m. s.w., and near by, **Walpole St Peter*, with beautiful Perp. tracery and ornament. It has a tie-beam roof, 17C screens, misericords, and a pulpit of 1620. Under the chancel is a richly groined passage, a public right-of-way.—10 m. *Sutton Bridge* is a small river port on the Nene which here divides Norfolk from Lincolnshire. To the N. is the WASH, a wide shallow bay, gradually being silted up by the rivers that flow into it (the Nene, the Ouse, the Welland, and the Witham). It was near here that King John, while marching across the flats, was overtaken by the tide, losing his baggage and treasure (1216).—13 m. *Long Sutton* (Hotel), a lovely little market town whose *Church has one of the oldest lead-covered spires (E.E.) in the country, and a a 15C porch.—14½ m. *Gedney* has a fine E.E. *Church; the tower has a Perp. spire. Inside is 14–15C stained glass. The two-storied s. porch has a turret stair, and coloured alabaster monuments to the Welby family. Over the s. door is an ivory plaque of the Crucifixion.—15½ m. *Fleet* church (14C) has a detached tower and spire and a Perp. w. window.—17¼ m. Holbeach (Hotel), a market town since the 13C, is the centre of the bulb-growing district of Lincolnshire. The Trans. church has a tower and spire which dominate the surrounding country.—19½ m. *Whaplode* *Church has a Norman chancel arch, and a fine Irby monument (c. 1620). The 12C tower stands at the E. end of the s. aisle. *Moulton*, ½ m. s., has an early Perp. rood-screen, and steeple 160 ft high (c. 1380).—22 m. **Weston* church is E.E. with 14C transepts, and a Perp. tower; the s. porch is notable. About 1½ m. N. are the ruins of *Wykeham Chapel* (early Dec.).—25 m. Spalding, p. 509.

B Viâ March and Wisbech

ROAD, 61 m. To (16 m.) Ely, see Rte 56A.—A 142, A 141. 36 m. **March.**—47 m. **Wisbech.**—A 47, 61 m. **King's Lynn.**
RAILWAY, see Rte 56A to (14¾ m.) Ely, the junction for **March** (15¾ m. in c. 20 min.).

To (16 m.) *Ely*, see Rte 56A.—A 142 runs w. to (22½ m.) *Sutton* which stands on a ridge above the Fens surrounded by orchards. It has a large and light Dec. church of c. 1370.

From Sutton a road leads s.w. to (5 m.) *Earith*, the point from which the New Bedford River and the Old Bedford River were cut to Denver. On their smooth waters, with floating objects lined up at 3 m. intervals, experiments in the 17C demonstrated the curvature of the earth's surface. A disused railway line near by is to be used as a test-run for a hover-train.—A 1123 continues w. to (10 m.) St Ives (7100 inhab.; Hotels) which ascribes its foundation to St Ivo, a Persian missionary-bishop (6C). It was Sterne's first curateship. On the old bridge spanning the Ouse is a chapel of the 15C (partly rebuilt in 1689). Oliver Cromwell (statue in the market place) lived here for five years. *All Saints'* is a good 15C church. A 14C tithe-barn, N. of the town, is known as *Cromwell's Barn.*—14 m. *Huntingdon*, see Rte 54.

The road turns N.W. to (23½ m.) *Mepal* where it crosses the Bedford rivers (see above).—At (28 m.) *Chatteris* (5600 inhab.), the road from Huntingdon is joined; farther on, this crosses the Forty Foot Drain, dug in the 17C by Cornelius Vermuyden.— 32 m. *Doddington* church (13C) has 15C windows with stained glass by Morris and Rossetti, and a Dutch carving of Christ and the Women of Samaria.— 36 m. **March** (14,300 inhab.; Hotel) has been an important Fen town since Roman times, when it stood on the river Nene. This was diverted after the 15C, direct from Peterborough to Wisbech, but the market town flourished again in the 19C as a railway junction. The *Church* (St Wendreda), mixed Dec. and Perp. with the tower topped by a fine spire, has a double hammerbeam *Roof with triple ranks of angels, admirably carved.

47 m. **Wisbech** (17,000 inhab.; Hotels) developed when the new cut of the Nene made it the port for Peterborough. The *Church* was enlarged by the addition of a second N. aisle; it contains 15C stained glass, some good monuments, and a brass to Thomas de Braunstone (d. 1401), over 7 ft long. By the Nene quay are fine old warehouses, and, reflected by the river, *North Brink* and *South Brink*, two fine Georgian streets along either bank, recall the tranquil townscapes of the Netherlands. In North Brink is *Peckover House* (N.T.; adm. April–Sept, Wed, Thurs, Sat, Sun & BH, 2–6; Oct 2–5; fee. Or by previous arrangement with custodian), built in 1722, with a splendid rococo interior. The garden has a large maidenhair tree and orangery with exotic trees. *Walsoken* church, in the Norfolk suburb, has one of the finest Norman interiors in E. Anglia (also some notable 17C sculptures).

West Walton church, 1½ m. farther N., has an E.E. interior, with beautifully carved capitals and arcades echoing those at Lincoln. The Prayer board (17C) asks for delivery from floods, and the detached bell-tower to the s. of the church dates from the 13C.—*Emneth* church, 2¼ m. s.E. of Wisbech, is Norman, E.E., and Perp.; while *Leverington* church, 2 m. N.W., built of clunch has an impressive E.E. tower, a 14C porch, and a 15C Jesse window. The tomb of Goldsmith's Tony Lumpkin is in the N.E. corner.

A 47 runs N.E. across the Fens passing (54 m.; l.) *Terrington St John*, where the 14C church is connected to a later tower by a series of rooms,

a staircase, and passages. The font cover dates from 1632.—57 m.
Tilney All Saints (l.), 12C with much Norman work, has a fine Dec.
hammerbeam roof, misericords, and two fonts. We cross the Great
Ouse into (61 m.) **King's Lynn** (Rte 56A).

57 PETERBOROUGH TO GRIMSBY
A Viâ Louth

ROAD (83 m.) A 47, A 1073. 8 m. *Crowland.*—17½ m. **Spalding**. Thence A 16 viâ
(33½ m.) **Boston** and (66½ m.) **Louth** to 83 m. **Grimsby**.
RAILWAY. To *Grimsby*, viâ Newark or Retford or Doncaster (comp. p. 426), in
2½–3½ hrs; a change is generally necessary.—To *Boston* (60¾ m.), viâ Grantham
(change) and Sleaford, in 2 hrs. From London viâ Peterborough (no additional
change) in 1½ hr more, in both cases.—To *Spalding* (19¾ m.), viâ March (poor
connection) in c. 1–1½ hr, or direct (only 3 times daily) in 20 min.

From Peterborough we take the Lynn road and turn left at (3¼ m.)
Eye.—8 m. **Crowland**, or *Croyland*, a pleasant town, with wide tree-
planted streets, is noted for its *ABBEY, built c. 716 by King Ethelbald
over the cell of the hermit St Guthlac, which became a centre of learning
and is said to have supplied some of the earliest teachers at Cambridge.
It was sacked by the Danes in 870, burned in 1091, and the E. portion
pulled down in 1540. The nave and s. aisle were wrecked by Cromwell's
bombardment in 1643. Of the Norman church of Abbot Joffrid (1109–
70) there remains the lofty arch of the central tower, the w. fronts of the
aisles, and the attached font. The N. aisle (now the parish church; c.
1400) contains a parclose screen of 1413. The Perp. w. tower (fine bells)
and the five reliefs of the life of St Guthlac over the 13C central door
should be noted. Standing high and dry in the middle of the little town
is a *Triangular Bridge*, dating from c. 1350. The curious stone effigy
on it is a figure of the Saviour which once crowned the w. façade of
the abbey.—The road next traverses the fertile *Bedford Level*, one of the
great fen areas, taking its name from the reclamation operations of the
Earl of Bedford and the Dutch engineer Vermuyden (d. 1677) in 1650–53.

14 m. *Cowbit* (pron. 'Coubbitt') is a great centre for fen-skating in
winter, and the championships are often decided here.—17½ m. **Spalding**
(Hotels), an ancient market-gardening town (16,950 inhab.) stands on
the Welland (here navigable for vessels of 80 tons). This produces a
tranquil atmosphere of reflection and space more characteristic of the
Low Countries than of England. From the Market Place there are
walks to the river, where the banks are lined with fine Georgian houses.
Ayscoughfee Hall, a 15C mansion, much altered, by the river, was the
residence of Maurice Johnson, founder of the still existing 'Gentlemen's
Society of Spalding', the oldest scientific and literary association in
England (1710). The beautiful garden, with fine yew hedges, is a public
park. It is an excellent centre for the bulbfields or for visiting the
Lincolnshire churches. The *Church of SS Mary & Nicholas*, founded in
1284, has been much extended and the tower, with its early Perp. spire,
is somewhat small for the double-aisled church.

Spalding lies in the heart of the **Fen District**, formed by the gradual silting up of a
large bay (now reduced to the Wash) and extending 70 m. from N. to S. and 35 m.
from E. to W. Drainage was first carried out by the Romans, but after their departure much of the area was reflooded. Important works were instituted under

Charles I and continued by Vermuyden under Cromwell and Charles II, but complete drainage and reclamation were not accomplished till the beginning of the 19C. Many of the deep drains and sluices constructed for this purpose may be seen in the neighbourhood of Spalding. The efforts at reclamation often met with considerable resistance from the 'Fen Slodgers', who gained their living by fowling and fishing. The reclaimed land is very fertile, and huge quantities of bulbs are grown round Spalding. The daffodils and tulips make a great show in April–May; at all seasons the sunsets are fine owing to the flat surface and the watery air. The Fens afford good wildfowl shooting and the best skating in England. The Fenland churches are famous. The pumping stations and other drainage works throughout the area are of great interest; *Pode Hole Pumping Station* (2 m. w. of Spalding) still uses the original *Boulton and Watt Beam Engines.

19¾ m. *Pinchbeck* has a large church with a 14C tower, and much Perp. and Dec. work; the good E. window is a 19C restoration by Butterfield. The alloy known as 'pinchbeck' (copper; 'false-gold') is named, not from this village, but from Christopher Pinchbeck a London watchmaker who invented it c. 1720. There is a beam-engine of 1833 in the *Pinchbeck Marsh* pumping station.—23¾ m. *Gosberton* has another fine early-Perp. church.

Donington, 3½ m. N.W., was the birthplace of Matthew Flinders (1774–1814), the Australian navigator, of whom there is a memorial in the fine late-Dec. and early-Perp. church.

The churches of (27¾ m.) *Sutterton*, of *Algarkirk* (¾ m. E.), and of (30 m.) *Kirton-in-Holland* are all of interest.

33½ m. **Boston**, i.e. 'St Botolph's Town' (Hotels), a seaport and market town of 26,000 inhab., near the mouth of the Witham, was the second port of the kingdom in the early 13C, and a town of the wool staple, when the Hanseatic League maintained their own depot here. It is the mother-town of a great namesake.

John Foxe (1517–87), the martyrologist, Jean Inglelow (1820–97), the poetess, and John Conington (1825–69), the translator of Virgil, were natives of Boston, and John Taverner, the musician, lived here from 1537 to his death in 1545, as Cromwell's personal agent dissolving the four local priories. Paul Verlaine in 1875 took his first English schoolmaster's job at *Stickney*, 8 m. N., and gave French lessons in Boston.

The church of *St Botolph, one of the largest parish churches in England, is an almost pure example of the richest period of flowing Dec., with only a few Perp. additions besides the lofty Perp. tower (288 ft), which is crowned by a beautiful octagonal lantern, forming a sea and land mark for 20–30 m. round. The nickname of 'Boston Stump' may come from its truncated appearance when seen from a distance, or from the assumption that a spire was always intended to crown the lantern. The oldest part of the present edifice is the lower section of the tower (1309), in which a tablet commemorates George Bass, surgeon of this town (born in 1771 at *Aswarby*, 4 m. s. of Sleaford), and other Lincolnshire men who bore a gallant part in the exploration of Australia. In the interior the tower vault is 137 ft above the floor. There are fine misericords, a pulpit (1612), and several interesting tombs, including the fine slab of a Hanse merchant (1340), brought from the destroyed Franciscan church, an effigy of a knight from the church of St John, and one of a lady with charming puppies playing round her feet (early 14C). The s.w. chapel was restored in 1857 by New England Bostonians in memory of John Cotton (1584–1652), who was vicar here

(1612–33) before he went to America. The streets and houses of the town make a most agreeable perambulation; they are redolent of the sea, with warm brick and bright paint-work (there is a 'flood-step' in front of many of the doors). In South St., leading from the market-place towards the port, are *Shodfriars Hall*, a timbered 16C building, part of a 13C Dominican friary, which has been restored as a theatre; and the *Guildhall* (15C; gratuity), with the court (much altered) in which Brewster and other 'Pilgrim Fathers' were tried in 1607 for seeking to flee the country, the cells in which they were confined, and a notable old kitchen. Adjoining is *Fydell House* (1726), now occupied by Pilgrim College, an adult training centre (weekdays, 9–12, 2.30–4.30). The *Grammar School*, farther on, preserves its original hall of 1567. *Hussey Tower* behind is a relic of a mansion of c. 1500. Small lanes lead to the Sea Bank, from which the views extend far over the Wash and inland to a superb panorama of church towers.

The marsh villages near Boston are noted for their fine churches. That of *Skirbeck*, 1 m. S.E., has an Elizabethan pulpit. Here, too, dyer's woad (Isatis tinctoria) was last grown in England; the old mill for grinding it stopped work in 1932. *Fishtoft*, 1½ m. beyond, has its village stocks and traces of Norman work in the chancel of its church. The church at *Freiston*, 3½ m. E., is the nave of a priory church of the 12C.

FROM BOSTON TO LINCOLN viâ HORNCASTLE, 39¼ m. The road runs due N. across the Fens to (11¼ m.) *Revesby*, the 'model' village attached to Revesby Abbey (long the home of Sir Joseph Banks), named after the Cistercian house that was founded here from Rievaulx in 1142. The present house is Victorian and little remains of the abbey church. *East Kirkby* church, 2¼ m. E., has fine Dec. and Perp. details.—At (16 m.) *Scrivelsby* is the late-Perp. gatehouse, the last intact remnant of *Scrivelsby Court*, the ancient home of the Dymokes who succeeded the Marmions as lords of the manor, a position carrying the right to serve as King's Champion. The church contains memorials of the Marmions and Dymokes.—18 m. **Horncastle** (4100 inhab.; Hotel), stands on the site of the Roman *Banovallum*, at the junction of the rivers Bain and Waring, at the foot of the Wolds. Part of the walls of the fort have been incorporated into the new *Library*. In the church of *St Mary* are the brass of Sir Lionel Dymoke, King's Champion (1519), and the monument of Sir Ingram Hopwood, "who paid his debt to nature . . . in the attempt of seizing the arch-rebel [Cromwell] in the bloody skirmish near Winceby" (1643). The scythe blades and hay knives over the door are said to have been fastened to staves for use in the battle. There was a famous August horse fair here (see Borrow's animated description in 'Romany Rye'). The old rectory at *Somersby*, 6 m. N.E., was the birthplace of Tennyson (1809–92). The church contains a memorial to him, and has a remarkable churchyard cross. *Bag Enderby* church, ½ m. E., has a notable font; and there is another, and good monuments, at *Harrington*, 1 m. farther.
The shortest road to Lincoln runs w., crossing the Witham at (29 m.) *Bardney*, where excavations have laid bare the ground-plan of the once wealthy Benedictine abbey and brought to light pillar-bases, tomb-slabs, and other relics. St Oswald (d. 642) was buried here. The church of St Lawrence has an old altar-slab with seven crosses.—35 m. *Branston* has a late-Saxon church tower.—As we approach (39 m.) *Lincoln* (p. 515) from the s. there are fine views of the cathedral standing over the Fens.

Beyond Boston, the Grimsby road runs N. across the Fens, then the attractive S. Lincolnshire Wolds, with access to the 'Tennyson country'. —38 m. *Sibsey* has a Norman church with E.E. tower.—50 m. **Spilsby** was the birthplace of Sir John Franklin (1786–1847) whose statue adjoins the Market Cross. The 14C *Church* contains Franklin's flag and monuments of the Willoughby de Eresby family.

Halton Holgate, 1½ m. E., has a spacious Perp. church, and *Gunby Hall*, 4 m.

farther on, is a fine mansion of 1700 (N.T.; open April–Oct, Wed 2–6, Thurs, Fri & BH, 2.30–5.30; fee). At *Bolingbroke*, 4 m. w. viâ *Mavis Enderby*, only a few mounds remain of John of Gaunt's Castle.

51¾ m. *Partney*, with a pleasant church, was a favourite haunt of Dr Johnson when staying with his friend Bennet Langton at the Elizabethan *Langton Hall* (2 m. N.W.).—At (55¼ m.) *Ulceby Cross*, A 1104 leads N.E. to *Alford* (3 m.), a small town (2300 inhab.) with a good Dec. church, and thence to the seaside resort of Mablethorpe (9 m.; see Rte 57B).

Markby, 2¾ m. N.E. of Alford, has a thatched church, and *Willoughby* (3 m. s.) was the birthplace of Capt. John Smith of Virginia (1580–1631). In the lovely park of *Well Vale*, 2 m. farther s.w., (gardens open mid-April–mid-Sept, daily 2–6; fee. House by appointment only), is a charming little mid-18C church.

66½ m. **Louth** (11,700 inhab.) is dominated by its **Church*, with one of the most beautiful steeples in England (1501–15; 295 ft). The interior is well-proportioned with a magnificent high tower arch. It contains paintings, and the 'Sudbury Hutch', a chest of c. 1500 with portraits of Henry VII and Elizabeth of York. The centre has good buildings of the 17C, 18C, and 19C, harmoniously grouped, especially in Westgate, with a lovely series of 18C doorways, and Upgate, 16C, with additions from every succeeding century. John Smith (of Virginia) and Sir John Franklin, as well as Tennyson and his brothers, were educated at the grammar school here (rebuilt), and the 'Poems of Two Brothers' (by Alfred and Charles Tennyson) were published in 1827 by a Louth bookseller. The village churches in the neighbourhood are worth inspection; but only scanty traces remain of *Louth Park Abbey* (Cistercian; 1139), 1½ m. E. At *Manby*, 5 m. E., is the R.A.F. Flying College (1950).

The road follows the edge of the Wolds N.—83 m. **GRIMSBY** (95,700 inhab.; Hotels), or **Great Grimsby**, the premier fishing port in Britain, lies on the s. bank of the Humber. Formerly in Lincolnshire, it now adheres to Humberside. The animated *Fish Market* is the chief attraction. The town has been a fishing and trading port since the 11C, obtaining its charter in 1202, but dwindled to decay before Tudor times. *St James's Church* is a much-altered E.E. edifice (13C), in which the most notable feature is the curious combination of clerestory and triforium. The *Royal Docks* built during the early 1850s are dominated by the Victoria Flour Mill (1906) and the Dock Tower (1852), a copy of the tower of the Town Hall in Siena.

Grimsby carries on a very important trade in coal, grain, timber, etc.—The *Fishing Fleet* consists of c. 150 trawlers and c. 100 seiners; the catch of fish in 1970 was nearly 163,250 tons. Danish and Icelandic fishermen regularly use the port. The landing of the catch, the dressing of the market, the fish auctions, the dispersal of the fish, and the clearance of the huge market for the following day offer scenes of great interest and activity.

Clee, 1 m. s., has a restored church of which the w. tower is a fine example of the Saxon style, while the nave and font are Norman.

The deep-water dock of *Immingham*, 6 m. farther up the Humber, is an oil port equipped with storage facilities, which also has large chemical industries, and is the terminus of a car-ferry to Gothenburg. A monument at *South Killingholme Haven*, to the N., marks the site of the Pilgrim Fathers' embarkation for Holland in 1609.

Ashby-cum-Fenby lies 6 m. s., a pretty village with an E.E. church (good Dec. windows, and screen). *East Revendale*, 1 m. s.w, has the remains of a Premonstratensian Priory, and 2½ m. w. of Ashby is *Hatcliffe*, beautifully situated above a valley.

B Viâ the Coast

ROAD, 98 m. To (33½ m.) *Boston*, see Rte 57A.—A 52. 49 m. **Wainfleet.**—54¼ m. **Skegness.**—71 m. *Mablethorpe*. B 1031.—98 m. **Grimsby**. A 52 is congested in summer because of the many holiday camps on the coast, but at other times this route between the soft line of the Lincolnshire Wolds and the coastal flats is recommended alike for its characteristic atmosphere and its superb series of churches.

RAILWAY. To (60¾ m.) *Boston*, see Rte 57A. This branch line continues to (79½ m.) **Wainfleet** and (84½ m.) **Skegness.**

To (33½ m.) Boston, see Rte 57A.—A 52 leads N.E. from Boston through a series of small villages with fine marshland churches: (38½ m.) *Benington*, (39½ m.) *Leverton*, Perp. with good exterior tracery and a Dec. interior, (41 m.) *Old Leake*, with Norman arcading, and (42 m.) *Wrangle*, Perp. with good 14C glass.—45½ m. (l.) *Friskney* church is Perp., with some Norman work, and later additions. It has a Jacobean pulpit, 14C wall-paintings, and, in the graveyard, a 17C Cross and graveside shelter.—49 m. **Wainfleet**, a pleasant large village, was the birthplace of William of Waynflete (1395–1486), Bp. of Winchester and founder of Magdalen College (Oxford). He built the *Magdalen School* here, a fine brick building of 1484 (with Victorian additions), as a 'feeder' for his college. **Croft* church (Dec.), 2 m. N.E., contains an early-17C pulpit, good screens and benches, a fine lectern, and 13C memorial brasses (some of the earliest in England).

54¼ m. **Skegness** (13,600 inhab.; Hotels), a popular seaside resort, is favoured for its fine sands. The pier was wrecked in 1978. Its huge holiday camps continue up the coast past (59 m.) *Ingoldmells*. A 52 here turns inland to (62 m.) **Hogsthorpe** (E.E. church), and (66½ m.) **Huttoft**, with a fine windmill and tall granary. The church, with a 13C tower, has good corbels, a richly carved Perp. font, and a 14C chest.—69 m. *Sutton-on-Sea* and (71 m.) *Mablethorpe* are holiday resorts, less brash than Skegness, with fine sands and golf courses.

75 m. (l.) *Theddlethorpe-All-Saints* church is built of colourful stone, with traces of every period from early-Norman. Among its interesting contents are a funerary helm (comp. Framlingham, p. 455). The three *Saltfleetby* villages lie c. 1½ m. N., on the banks of the Great Eau, all with fine churches.—At (79 m.) *Saltfleet*, the Manor House has been identified as Tennyson's "Locksley Hall, that in the distance overlooks the sandy tracts", but it is more likely to have been the house so named in (82 m.) *North Somercotes*, where the road turns inland to another series of fine churches: (85 m.) *Grainsthorpe*, Perp., with a brick floor, 18C gallery, and panelling made from the old pews, (86½ m.) *Marsh Chapel*, (91 m.) *Tetney*, with a high Perp. limestone tower, and (94 m.) *Humberston*, 18C brick, with Perp. stone tower.—97 m. **Cleethorpes** (35,800 inhab.; Hotels), now a suburb of Grimsby, was a Victorian seaside town that grew up round the railway station (1863) built on the front. It has a fine sea-wall, and promenade, a good beach, pier and pier-gardens, a golf course, and other attractions.—98 m. **Grimsby**, see Rte 57A.

58 PETERBOROUGH TO LINCOLN AND DONCASTER

ROAD, 86 m.—A 15. 15½ m. *Bourne.*—48 m. *Lincoln.*—A 57. 55½ m.—A 156.
66 m. **Gainsborough.**—A 631. 77 m. *Bawtry.*—A 1. 86 m. *Doncaster.*

RAILWAY, to Lincoln in c. 1 hr 10 min, to Doncaster in c. 1 hr 20 min. Principal
Stations: 39 m. **Grantham.**—53¾ m. *Newark* (North Gate). Junction for **Lincoln**
(15¼ m.).—72½ m. *Retford.* Junction for **Gainsborough** (10½ m.).—89¾ m. **Doncaster.**
Junction for *Hull* (40¾ m.). From Sleaford to *Lincoln* (21¼ m. in c. ½ hr) and
Doncaster (58 m. in c. 2½ hrs).

We leave Peterborough by A 15.—5½ m. *Glinton. Peakirk*, 1½ m.
N.E., is worth visiting for the 14C wall-paintings in the church of St
Pega. The *Waterfowl Gardens have a large collection of birds in
wooded grounds, and a 17C decoy still in use for catching and ringing
ducks. *Helpston* (3 m. w.) was the birthplace of John Clare (1793–
1864).—After (7 m.) *Northborough*, which preserves much of its 14C
manor-house (adm. 2–6, May–Sept; fee), we cross the Welland into
Lincolnshire.—8½ m. *Market Deeping* has some fine old houses, but no
longer a market, and a 12–13C church. The rectory is the oldest inhabited
parsonage in England, dating from the 13C (altered in succeeding
centuries; adm. on request). Robert Fayrfax (1464–1521), the composer,
was born here. At *Deeping St James*, to the E., the church was part of a
Benedictine Priory, a cell of Thorney. It has a fine 12C nave, Norman font,
and a graveside shelter. The R.C. church near the 17C bridge over the
Welland at *Deeping Gate* has two good sculptures: a 14C Crucifixion and a
15C Virgin.— 15½ m. **Bourne** (Hotel), a typical Lincolnshire market town
(6500 inhab.), is the apocryphal birthplace of Hereward the Wake. In the
Priory, Robert Mannyng (Robert of Brunne; fl. 1300) made his translations from the Norman that laid the foundations for the English
language. Lord Burghley (1520–98) was born here (house now the
Burghley Arms), as was Monsieur Charles F. Worth of Paris (1825–95).
The *Priory Church* has Norman arcades. The *Town Hall* (1821) has an
unusual exterior staircase. In South St. are good 17C cottages and the
Tudor *Red Hall.*

At *Edenham*, 3 m. N.W., the church has a fine roof and monuments of the Bertie
family, and 2 m. farther is *Grimsthorpe Castle* (Earl of Ancaster), a huge building
of various dates, containing some fine Holbeins and other works of art (shown by
special permission only). The church of *Irnham*, 3½ m. farther N.W., has a 14C
Luttrell tomb combined with an Easter Sepulchre, rivalling that at Hawton (p. 432).

20 m. (r.) *Rippingdale* has a church with good Geometric windows
(14C) and a rare effigy of a deacon.—24 m. *Folkingham*, once a town of
some importance with its own quarter-sessions, has an imposing old
coaching-inn, Perp. church with notable oak screen, and the remains of
the local House of Correction. At *Pickworth*, 2½ m. w., the church has
14C wall-paintings.

To the E. are (2½ m.) *Billingborough* church with a tall tower and splendid flying
buttresses, and florid windows, and (1 m. N.) *Harbling*, a Georgian village with
interesting church, and a votive well. *Sempringham*, 1½ m. s. of Billingborough,
was the birthplace of St Gilbert (d. 1189), founder of the only English order of
monks and nuns; a Norman doorway and the nave remain of their church.

At 26 m. we cross A 52. *Threekingham*, 1 m. E., has a Norman
church with a fine spire and decorated windows.—31 m. *Silk Willoughby*
church (Dec.) has good pews and bench-ends, and a Norman font.—

32½ m. **Sleaford** (8000 inhab.; Hotels) is an old and thriving market town. The *Maltings*, over 1000 ft in length, is one of the finest industrial buildings in the country of c. 1900. The *Church* (St Denis) is noted for its Dec. window tracery and ornamentation and a 15C screen with a rood by Comper (1918). It stands on one side of the bustling *Market Place* in an harmonious group of buildings: the 15C *Vicarage*, the *Sessions House* (1831), the fine Georgian *Bristol Arms*, and the *Corn Exchange* (1857).

Rauceby, 4 m. N.W., has a conspicuous church with a fine tower and broach spire (13C). *Ancaster*, 6 m. W. on the Grantham road, has a few traces of its occupation as a Roman fortified station (Causennae) on Ermine Street.

FROM SLEAFORD TO BOSTON, 17 m. (A 17, A 154). Railway in c. 30 min.— 5 m. *Heckington* has a mill with eight sails. The *Church is a fine example of pure late-Dec. (1345–80), with exquisite flowing tracery, a magnificent Easter Sepulchre, and a fine E. window. *Ewerby*, 3 m. N., has a noteworthy 14C church, with a broach spire, and *Helpringham*, 2½ m. s., likewise has a fine Dec. steeple.— 11¼ m. *Swineshead*, where we turn left from the Lynn road, has an interesting church, the old stocks, and the base of the market cross. *Swineshead Abbey*, where King John stayed in 1216 after crossing the Wash, lay 1 m. E.; a few remains are incorporated in a farmhouse.— 17 m. *Boston*, see Rte 57A.

FROM SLEAFORD TO HORNCASTLE, 23½ m. (A 153). We cross the Fenland, through (4½ m.) *Anwick* and (9 m.) *Billinghay*, both with notable steeples. *South Kyme*, a remote fen village s. of the road, has a 13C keep, while the church is a fragment of a 12C priory. We cross the Witham.— 13½m. **Tattershall** has the keep of a *Castle (N.T.; 11–6.30, Sun 1–6.30 or dusk; closed 1–2, Oct–March; fee) built in 1440 by Baron Cromwell, Lord High Treasurer to Henry VI, which is perhaps the best example of a fortified dwelling in England, and notable for its brickwork. The walls are in part 16 ft thick. The large collegiate church (late Perp.) contains many 15–16C brasses, much glass of c. 1500 in the E. window, and a stone choir-screen. The village cross dates from the 15C.— 14 m. *Coningsby* is supposed to have furnished Disraeli with the title of his well-known novel. The church has a processional path under its 15C tower. About 4 m. N. is **Woodhall Spa** (Hotels), with bromo-iodine springs situated amid pines and firs. At *Kirkstead*, 2 m. s., is a fragment of a Cistercian abbey (13C) and the *Chapel of St Leonard (now the parish church), a gem of E.E. architecture with a choir-screen of 1210.— At 15 m. the road passes close to *Waterloo Wood* planted from acorns immediately after the battle; the monument to Wellington was erected in 1844.— 23½ m. *Horncastle*, see Rte 57A.

36 m. By-road (l.) for (1 m.) *Cranwell*, with the *Royal Air Force College*, founded in 1920. The church has an interesting bell-cote. *Temple Bruer*, 2 m. N., with a massive Norman tower, is all that remains of a preceptory of the Knights Templar.—Our road now ascends a long ridge to (45 m.) *Bracebridge Heath*. *Dunston Pillar* (now ruined) was erected by Sir Francis Dashwood in 1751 as a land lighthouse. The lantern was replaced in 1810 by a statue of George III.

48 m. **LINCOLN** (74,200 inhab.) dominated by its superbly situated cathedral, lies mainly on a hill rising from the Witham, at the N.W. point of the flat fen district, but it spreads also over the lower ground and beyond the river, which is navigable by barge. It is one of the most ancient towns in the realm, and, though important industrially, is rich in historic interest.

Car Parking. Flaxengate (multi-story) below the Cathedral, Saltergate, and Cattle Market.
Railway Stations. The *Central Station*. High St., is ¼ m. from *St Mark's*.
Hotels near the cathedral and Central station.
Post office, Guildhall St.—INFORMATION OFFICE, Saltergate.
Buses from Bus Station to most destinations. Town Buses from outside Central station, services also from Unity Sq., and Thorn Bridge.

Amusements. *Theatre Royal.*—BOATING, TENNIS, and SWIMMING-POOL at Boultham Park, 1 m. s.w.—MOTOR-LAUNCH in summer from Brayford down the Witham canal.

History. The pre-Roman settlement guarding the gap in the oolite cliff was occupied by the Romans in A.D. 47, and c. 80–86 it became a colony under the name of *Lindum Colonia.* The Saxons also have left their traces, and a little later it became one of the Danelagh towns. Christianity was reintroduced by St Paulinus in 627; the bishopric dates from 1072, when Remigius transferred his bishop's stool from Dorchester-on-Thames to Lincoln. At the time of the Norman Conquest London, Winchester, and York alone outranked Lincoln in importance among the cities of England, and in the 13C it was the fourth 'seaport' of the realm. The castle, built by William I was captured about 1140 by Stephen, whose conflict with Matilda surged round the city. Henry II had a second coronation here in 1158. The Civil War found Lincoln loyal to Charles I, but it had to yield to the Parliamentarians in 1644, after a stout resistance. William Byrd (1543–1623), the composer, was a native of Lincoln. Peter de Wint (1784–1849), the painter, lived for many years at Hilton House, Drury Lane (tablet).

Lincoln is important for its heavy engineering works and for agricultural machinery. In the First World War (1916) it was the birthplace of 'tanks'.

Queen Eleanor of Castile, wife of Edward I, died at *Harby,* 8 m. w. of Lincoln, in 1290 (memorial statue on the church tower). The successive stages of the funeral procession that bore her body, after embalming at the Gilbertine nunnery of St Katherine of Lincoln, to Westminster Abbey were marked by the beautiful ELEANOR CROSSES, erected between 1291 and 1294. The list of these varies, but there seems to have been crosses at Lincoln, Grantham, Stamford, Geddington, Northampton, Stony Stratford, Woburn, Dunstable, St Albans, Waltham, and at Cheapside and Charing in London. The only survivors are those at Geddington, Northampton, and Waltham.

A visit should start on CASTLE HILL (car parking). The **Castle** (adm. daily, Sun from 2; fee) is one of the eight known to have been founded by William the Conqueror himself. It was started in 1068 and the walls have the herring-bone masonry typical of early-Norman works built near Roman remains (comp. the tower of St Alban's). The plan has the unusual feature of two mottes incorporated into the bailey wall.

We enter through the *Eastern Gate,* a massive 14C work on top of a Norman tunnel vault; on the right is a delicate oriel window brought from a house which stood in the High Street, popularly, but erroneously known as 'John of Gaunt's Palace'. The walls enclose a pleasant garden of 6½ acres; on the lawn is preserved a fragment of an Eleanor cross. To the left is the *Observatory Tower* on its motte (Norman base with 14C upperworks and 19C turret). Steep ladders inside lead to the roof from which there is a *View. On the second and later motte beyond, the *Lucy Tower,* a shell keep, has the graves of prisoners from the brick *City Prison,* in use from 1787 to 1878 (now courts and Archives Repository). The prison *Chapel* retains a powerful atmosphere, with coffin-like stalls. The N.E. tower *Cobb Hall* is 13C and vaulted on two levels; this was the place of execution until 1868. Smirke's *Assize Court* (1826) stands in the western part of the castle grounds, behind which is the *West Gate* (no adm.), beside the w. gate of the Roman fortress.

We descend between the fine *Judge's Lodgings* (1810) and a good timbered house at the corner of Bailgate to *Exchequer Gate,* the 14C entrance to the cathedral precincts. Passing through the gateway we stand under the w. front of the **Cathedral,** which has many claims to rank as the foremost church in England, especially if its fine situation be taken into account as well as its beautiful design. The fabric is undergoing extensive repair. The bells are rung on Thurs evening.

HISTORY. Of the original early-Norman church, erected by Remigius (see above) about 1072–90, there remain the central portion of the w. front (with its three recesses) and part of the first bay of the nave. The three w. doorways (with the intersecting arcade above), the three lower stages of the w. towers, and their N. and s. gables are ascribed to the late-Norman restoration of Bp. Alexander after a fire in 1141. The Norman cathedral was shattered by an earthquake in 1185

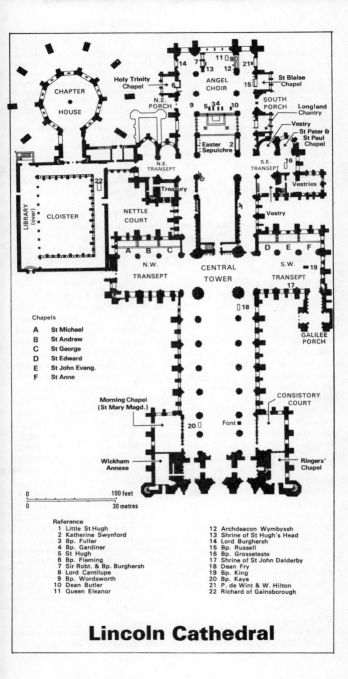

Lincoln Cathedral

CHAPTER HOUSE

Holy Trinity Chapel

N.E. PORCH

ANGEL CHOIR

14 7
13   11 8
12

St Blaise Chapel

15

9   5 3 4   10

SOUTH PORCH

Longland Chantry

Easter Sepulchre   2

Vestry
St Peter & St Paul Chapel

N.E. TRANSEPT

S.E. TRANSEPT   16

LIBRARY (over)

CLOISTER

22

Treasury

NETTLE COURT

Vestries

Vestry

A B C

D E F

N.W. TRANSEPT

CENTRAL TOWER

S.W. TRANSEPT

19

17

18

GALILEE PORCH

Chapels

A	St Michael
B	St Andrew
C	St George
D	St Edward
E	St John Evang.
F	St Anne

Morning Chapel (St Mary Magd.)

CONSISTORY COURT

20

Font

Wickham Annexe

Ringers' Chapel

0 _____ 100 feet
0 _____ 30 metres

Reference

1 Little St Hugh
2 Katherine Swynford
3 Bp. Fuller
4 Bp. Gardiner
5 St Hugh
6 Bp. Fleming
7 Sir Robt. & Bp. Burghersh
8 Lord Cantilupe
9 Bp. Wordsworth
10 Dean Butler
11 Queen Eleanor
12 Archdeacon Wymbyssh
13 Shrine of St Hugh's Head
14 Lord Burghersh
15 Bp. Russell
16 Bp. Grosseteste
17 Shrine of St John Dalderby
18 Dean Fry
19 Bp. King
20 Bp. Kaye
21 P. de Wint & W. Hilton
22 Richard of Gainsborough

and Bp. Hugh of Avalon ('St Hugh of Lincoln'; 1186–1200) at once began to restore and extend it. The choir and E. transepts were his work, and the five-part vault of his choir is the earliest example of the use of ribs for purely decorative purposes—"the beginning of late Gothic" (Kidson). As the whole cathedral, except the Angel Choir and part of the w. transepts, is in the main of his design, Bp. Hugh deservedly ranks as one of the greatest names in the history of English architecture. The nave and w. transepts were completed and the chapter house, Galilee Porch, and upper part of the w. façade added by 1250. The presbytery or Angel Choir belongs to the transitional period between 1258 and 1280, the cloisters to the end of the same century. The upper part of the central tower dates from 1307–11 (Geometrical Dec.); the w. towers are late-Dec. (c. 1380). The only Perp. work in the cathedral is the w. window of the nave (1436–49) and the chantry chapels (1400–1500).

Exterior. The imposing *West Façade* consists, roughly, of a block of Norman work encased in a larger surface of lancet work. Above the richly moulded central doorway are eleven statues of kings, from William I to Edward III. The curious band of carved panels (c. 1145) is very probably derived from an Italian series at Modena cathedral. Those on the s. have Old Testament scenes (the expulsion from Eden, Cain and Abel, Noah building the Ark, and the Deluge, etc.); those on the N. are from the New Testament (Lazarus, the Wise Virgins, Harrowing of Hell, and a Doom). The s.w. turret is surmounted by a statue of St Hugh (see above), the other by the so-called 'Swineherd of Stow', who gave all his savings to St Hugh.—The *West Towers* are 206 ft high; the magnificent *Central Tower*, in which hangs 'Great Tom of Lincoln', a bell weighing $5\frac{1}{4}$ tons, is 271 ft (fine view). In walking round the building by the s. side, we come to the *Galilee Porch*, affording entrance to the s.w. transept. Farther on, between two Perp. chantries, is the *Judgement Porch*, the deeply recessed arch of which has a remarkable representation of the Last Judgment and other rich carvings; the head of the Christ and the figure of the Madonna are modern. Among the interesting gargoyles of this part of the edifice is one known as the 'Devil looking over Lincoln' ("with a torve and tetrick countenance", according to Fuller). The figures on the buttresses are believed to represent Edward I and his two wives, Queen Eleanor and Queen Margaret (the head is 19C).—The clear space beyond this affords a good view of the E. end of the cathedral, with its noble window, its deep buttresses, its lines of arcading, its enriched gable, and its crocketed pinnacles. At the top of the gable is a group of the Virgin and the Infant Saviour.—Near the N.E. buttress is the old *Well*, with its recently restored covering, while beyond is the *Chapter House*, with its great flying buttresses. The building farther w. is the *Library* (over the cloisters).

Interior. The nave is striking in its unusual width, and the correspondingly wide spacing of the arcades. The view from the w. end is spoilt by the organ, which is placed above the rood-screen. The general proportions are harmonious and imposing; the clustered columns, the arcading of the aisles, and the beautiful triforium all demand admiration. The chapels opening off the w. end of the nave, called the *Morning Chapel* (St Mary Magdalene; N.) and the *Consistory Court* (s.), are of a little later date than the nave itself. Of the chapels below the towers that on the s.w. is known as the *Ringers' Chapel*. The fine late-Norman font, in the second bay of the s. side, is one of the seven in England of Tournai marble.

The CENTRAL TOWER is supported by four enormously massive pillars bearing lofty arches. The GREAT or WEST TRANSEPTS were begun by

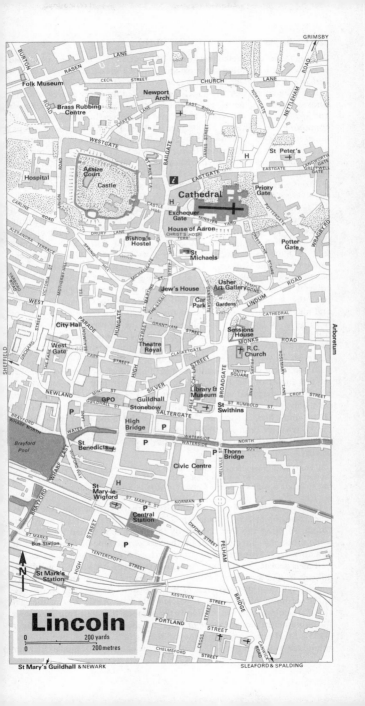

GRIMSBY

BURTON
RASEN LANE

Folk Museum
CECIL STREET
CHURCH LANE
NORTHGATE
NETTLEHAM ROAD

Brass Rubbing Centre
Newport Arch
HAZEL LANE
EAST BIGHT
JAMES STREET

WESTGATE
BAILGATE
EAST BIGHT

St Peter's
EASTGATE
LANGWORTH GATE
GREYWELL GATE
GREYWELL GATE

Hospital
Assize Court
Castle
H
EASTGATE

BURTON ROAD
UNION ROAD

CARLINE ROAD

Cathedral

Priory Gate

CASTLE HILL
H
Exchequer Gate
MINSTER YARD
POTTERGATE

ALEXANDRA TERRACE

DRURY LANE

Bishop's Hostel
House of Aaron
CHRIST'S HOSPITAL TERR

Potter Gate

SPRING HILL
VICTORIA STREET
MICHAELGATE
St Michaels

WEST
VICTORIA STREET
MOTHERBY HILL
EE
Jew's House
THE STRAIT
STEEP
Usher Art Gallery
TEMPLE GDNS
LINDUM ROAD

City Hall
PARADE
HUNGATE
Car Park
Gardens
CATHEDRAL ST
MONKS ROAD

West Gate
THE PARK
Theatre Royal
GRANTHAM STREET
Sessions House
ROSEMARY LANE
DICKSON ROAD

NEWLAND
PARK STREET
HIGH STREET
CLASKETGATE
R.C. Church
UNITY SQUARE
BEAUMONT FEE

SHEFFIELD

MINT ST
SILVER STREET
FREE SCHOOL LANE
BROADGATE
PRIORY LANE
CROFT STREET

GPO
Guildhall
Stonebow
Library & Museum
St Rumbold St
CROFT STREET

BRAYFORD WHARF NORTH
WATER LANE
GUILDHALL ST
SALTERGATE
St Swithins

High Bridge
P

Brayford Pool
VICTORIA WAY
WATERSIDE
WATERSIDE
NORTH
SOUTH

St Benedicts
P
Thorn Bridge

BRAYFORD WHARF EAST
P
Civic Centre
MELVILLE ST

H
St Mary-le-Wigford
ST. MARY'S ST
NORMAN ST
OXFORD STREET
PELHAM

ST MARKS ST
Bus Station
P
Central Station

St Mark's Station
HIGH STREET
TENTERCROFT STREET

N

Lincoln

0   200 yards
0   200 metres

KESTEVEN STREET
PORTLAND STREET
CHELMSFORD STREET
CROSS STREET
BRIDGE
CANWICK ROAD

St Mary's Guildhall & NEWARK
SLEAFORD & SPALDING

Arboretum

St Hugh and completed between 1200 and 1235. The beautiful rose windows, still retaining their original stained glass, are known as the *Bishop's Eye* (s.; Dec., c. 1325–50) and the *Dean's Eye* (N.; E.E., c. 1220). The six transeptal chapels are enclosed by richly carved screens. Those on the N., recently decorated, are called the *Services Chapels* and are devoted to the Army, Navy, and Air Force. In the last are books containing the names of 22,000 men of Nos. 1 and 5 Bomber Groups, killed in 1939–45. The double arcading in the Army chapel and in those on the s. side is an interesting feature. In the S. Transept are the remains of the shrine of the sainted bishop, John Dalderby (d. 1320), and a vigorous statué of Bp. King (1885–1910; grave in the cloister). In 1961 a dozen windows (in the great transepts and the E. end of both choir-aisles) were filled with old stained glass.

The fine E.E. CHOIR, begun in 1192, is separated from the nave by a Dec. stone *Screen* (c. 1300), richly decorated with diaper work and flanked by elaborately carved doorways. We enter by the door of the s. aisle, in which are the remains of the shrine of '*Little St Hugh*', once said to have been crucified by the Jews in 1255. The magnificent canopied *Choir Stalls* (early Perp.; c. 1380), with elaborately carved bench-ends and misericords, rank among the finest in England. The subjects range from Alexander carried to Heaven by eagles to scenes from the Arthurian Legend, as well as more strictly Christian carvings, and medieval parables such as the fox preaching to the geese (w. end of N. range). To the left of the high-altar are the *Easter Sepulchre* and the tomb of Bp. Remigius; to the right is the monument of Katherine Swynford (1403), third wife of John of Gaunt, and their daughter, the Countess of Westmorland (1440).

In the N. choir aisle is a tablet to William Byrd, organist in 1563–72. At the angles of the EAST or LESSER TRANSEPTS are very remarkable piers with detached crocketed shafts. The former *Dean's Chapel*, on the w. side of the N. arm, with mural paintings, by Vinc. Damini (1728) and Giles Hussey, of four bishops above the door, now houses the *TREASURY (adm. weekdays, Easter–mid-Sept 2–4, other times by appointment). The irregular vault and the fine Purbeck shafts are note-worthy.

It contains a magnificent collection of plate from churches in the diocese, chalices and patens from the tombs of three 13C bishops (including Grosseteste) and an original copy of Magna Carta, formerly in Longland's chantry.

In the s. arm is the plain tomb of Robert Grosseteste, the great scholar-bishop (1235–53; comp. p. 264).—The **PRESBYTERY or ANGEL CHOIR, forming the five E. bays of the choir, was added in 1255–80, when Gothic architecture had reached its acme. One of the loveliest of human works, "it exhibits in every part a refinement and elegance, as well as a delicacy of finish in its minutest details, to which it would be difficult to find a parallel" (Sharpe). The name is taken from the thirty winged figures in the spandrels of the triforium. The carved stonework at the springing of the arches is particularly fine. At the top of the last complete column on the N. side is the famous 'Lincoln Imp'. Among the monuments here are those of Bishop Fuller (1675), Bishop Gardiner (1705), St Hugh (above the site of the saint's original burial-place, behind the E. end of the 12C choir), and the cenotaph of Queen Eleanor

(d. 1290), destroyed in 1644 but reproduced in 1891. Here, too, are the *Chantries of Bp. Fleming* (N.: 1431) and *Bp. Russell* (s.; 1494), or *Chapel of St Blaise*, with mural paintings by Duncan Grant (1959); while off the s. aisle opens the *Chantry of Bp. Longland* (1547), completed in the very year when chantry masses were abolished. At the N.E. corner is the *Burghersh Chapel*, and in front of it the battered *Shrine of St Hugh's Head*, of the 14C, despoiled in 1540 and further damaged in the Civil War. Opposite are the tombs of Lord Cantilupe (14C) and Archdeacon Wymbyssh (d. 1460); and in the s.E. corner that of Peter de Wint (d. 1849). The great *East Window* is one of the finest English examples of Geometrical tracery (glass modern). The three sculptures of Christ, the Virgin, and St Nicholas are by J. R. Skeeping, and originally stood in King's College Chapel, Cambridge.

We enter the 13C CLOISTER from the N.E. Transept. In the E. walk is the entrance to the graceful 13C *CHAPTER HOUSE*, with vaulting springing from a central shaft. Several of the earliest meetings of the English parliament took place here (temp. Edward I and Edward II). Fine views of the cathedral are obtained from the N. walk (rebuilt for Dean Honywood by Wren c. 1674) in which is the original 'Swineherd of Stow' (see p. 518). Above it is the *Chapter Library* (open usually on Tues and Fri 11–1, 2–3.30; entr. in N.E. corner), with one bay of the medieval library burned in 1609, but mainly built by Wren to house Dean Honywood's remarkable and varied collection, largely acquired during exile in the Netherlands. In the s. walk is the tomb of Richard of Gainsborough (1300), perhaps the builder of the Angel Choir.

Léaving the cathedral by the Galilee Porch, we enter the CLOSE or MINSTER YARD and see, at the corner nearly opposite, the *Cantilupe Chantry House* (14C). Below and behind this is the arched entrance to the *Old Bishop's Palace* (no adm.; founded in the 12C), with 13–15C additions. Next comes the gatehouse of the *Vicars' Court*, built for a college of priest-vicars between 1300 and 1380, beyond which Greestone Place descends steeply, through the precinct wall, to the lower city. To the E. of the cathedral are the *Chancery* (14–15C) and the *Choristers' House* (17C); farther N. is the *Priory Gate*, an arch on the site of the old gateway destroyed in 1815. On the green stands a statue of Tennyson, by Watts. On the N. side are several other old houses, including the present *Bishop's Palace* and, in James St., *Deloraine Court*, once a prebendal residence, and the dilapidated *Burghersh Chantry House*.

BAILGATE, the centre of the Roman town, leads N. from the square. Circles mark the spots where bases of Roman pillars were found, and at the corner of Westgate is the 19C church of *St Paul*, on the site of that of St Paulinus (A.D. 628). Bailgate ends at *Newport Arch*, the N. gate of the Roman city. It dates probably from the early 2C. In Burton Rd, to the N.W., is the *Museum of Lincolnshire Life* (daily exc. Mon 2–5).

Returning, we may follow East Bight to the left. This reveals a portion of the *Roman Wall*, bends round to the right, and leads to Eastgate. To the left, in front of the Eastgate Hotel, foundations of a tower of the Roman *East Gate* have been exposed. Descending beyond this, we pass through the Priory Gate (see above) and the early 14C *Potter Gate* and reach the busy Lindum Rd. On the right, well sited, is the Usher Art Gallery (daily, Sun from 2) by Blomfield (1927), containing watches, miniatures, porcelain, a Tennyson collection, and pictures by Peter de Wint.

Monks Rd., to the left farther on, runs hence to the main entrance of the *Arboretum*. Farther on (r.) is *Monks Abbey*, a small park, with the remains of an E.E. chapel (with Perp. windows), a 'cell' of St Mary's Abbey at York.

From the s. end of Lindum Rd. Broadgate leads s. to the City and County Museum (weekdays 10–5, Wed 10–1, Sat to 5.30; Sun 2.30–5), which occupies the *Grey Friars Priory* (13C) and contains a fine collection of local antiquities; the upper room has a fine 'barrel' roof. Thence Melville St. goes on to *Pelham Bridge* (1958), a fine by-pass route avoiding the notorious level crossings in High Street.

Turning down St Mary's St. we come to the church of *St Mary-le-Wigford* in High St. It has a Saxon tower, on the outside of which is a Roman memorial slab with a later Saxon inscription. The nave, chancel, and N. aisle are E.E. (c. 1225). *St Mary's Conduit*, in front of the church, was built in the 16C with the stones of the White Friars monastery.

In High St. just to the s., in Akrill's Passage, is a 15C timbered house. Farther on (l.) is an interesting Norman building (12C), the *Hall of St Mary's Guild* (now a storehouse). Just beyond is the church of *St Peter-at-Gowts*, with a Saxon tower resembling that of St Mary-le-Wigford and a Romanesque font. About ⅓ m. farther on stood the *Bar Gate*, the s. entrance to the medieval city, near which rose an Eleanor Cross.—The road goes on to *Bracebridge* (1½ m. s.), which has an early tower (restored) of the same type as those of St Mary and St Peter.

High St. leads N., passing the church of *St Benedict*, with a low 11C tower and a rustic 13–14C interior, to the *High Bridge*, one of the few bridges in England on which houses still stand. The original ribs can be seen from the riverside path (l.) which leads to *Brayford Pool*, with its old quay. A short way beyond the High Bridge is the *Stonebow, a fine 15C town gate, the upper room of which is used as the Guildhall. Just beyond the 15C *Cardinal's Hat* High St. ends at the STRAIT, ascending to the right. At the top of this (l.) is the *Jew's House*, one of the oldest examples of domestic architecture in England (Norman; early 12C). STEEP HILL continues the ascent, and a 'step' across it forms the so-called *Mayor's Chair*. Above this are *Harding House* and other timbered houses; and (r.) the *House of Aaron the Jew*, a late-Norman building with a round-headed window. To the left is the *Bishop's Hostel*, occupied by theological students. Michaelgate and Danesgate are interesting old streets.

The Roman walls of the city were extended down the hill almost to the river in the 3C A.D. In 1971, the massive *West Gate was discovered, and can now be seen in The Park (see Plan; footpath at the end of Guildhall St.). Further remains of the wall have been located to the N. in Motherby Hill (footpath), on the site destined for a new police station.

FROM LINCOLN TO GRIMSBY, 37 m. (A 46). Railway viâ Market Rasen and Barnetby (44 m.) in 1¼–1¾ hr.—8½ m. *Snarford* church contains fine monuments of the St Poll family.—Under 1 m. w. of (10½ m.) *Faldingworth* lies *Buslingthorpe*, the church of which contains one of the earliest brasses in England (c. 1290).—Near (16 m.) *Market Rasen* many traces of Roman and pre-Roman occupation have been found.—24½ m. *Caistor* occupies the site of a Roman camp and possesses an interesting church. *Pelham's Pillar*, on top of the Wolds above Caistor, commemorates an extensive plantation scheme by the Earl of Yarborough (1840).—37 m. *Grimsby*, see Rte 57A.

FROM LINCOLN TO KINGSTON-UPON-HULL, 38 m. A 15 leads due N. from Lincoln, arrow-straight across the Fens, following the line of the Roman *Ermine Street* to just before (17 m.) *Redbourne*.

A much more interesting route (B 1398; 3 m. longer) runs parallel, clinging to the crest of the *Cliff*, a limestone escarpment commanding wide views across the Trent valley. Of the villages lying below it the most interesting are (11 m.) *Glentworth*, which has an 11C church tower, and (18 m.) *Kirton-in-Lindsey*, a large village with a fine E.E. church tower, 2 m. w. of Redbourne.

23 m. *Brigg* (Hotel) is a small market town (4800 inhab.) which grew prosperous with the draining of the Fens. At *Broughton*, 3½ m. N.W., the

church has a Saxon 11C tower. *Barnetby*, 4 m. N.E., has a remarkable leaden font (late-Norman).

The road to Doncaster (A 18) runs W. passing just S. of (9¼ m.) **Scunthorpe** (70,900 inhab.; Hotels), the centre, with *Frodingham*, of an iron-smelting district. Frodingham Vicarage is now a museum (weekdays; Sun from 2) with prehistoric and later collections (fine enamelled bowl, 7C) and mementoes of John Wesley. An important Belgic site has been excavated at *Dragonby*. Farther on we cross the Trent and enter the peaty levels of the 'island' of Axholme. At (23 m.) *Hatfield* (p. 617) we join the Doncaster–Hull road, 7 m. short of Doncaster.

A 15 crosses the M 180 (unfinished) and climbs the northern spur of the Wolds before dropping down to (32½ m.) *Barrow-on-Humber* and (35 m.) *New Holland* with the ferry to **Hull** (p. 640).

Goxhill lies 2½ m. E. of Barrow-on-Humber. The church has a fine Perp. tower, and contains a cross-legged effigy in chain armour of c. 1300. The so-called Goxhill Priory, ¾ m. farther E., is an old stone building with vaulted rooms.
A 1077 leads S.E. to (2 m.) *Thornton Curtis*, where the Norman and E.E. church. contains a Tournai marble font. The remains, 2 m. W., of **Thornton Abbey** (adm. daily, Sun from 2), founded in 1139 for Austin Canons and rebuilt after 1264, include a magnificent brick *Gatehouse (1382) preserving five of its original statues, its oaken doors, and, inside, a charming oriel; two bays of the chapter house (1282–1308); and foundations of the church and claustral buildings.—At (7¾ m.) *Brocklesby*, the church has monuments of the Pelhams, Earls of Yarborough (whose seat is at Brocklesby Hall). In the park near the village is the circular Mausoleum (1787–94), by James Wyatt. About 2 m. farther on is A 18 the main road from Doncaster to Grimsby.

Barton-upon-Humber, with 7500 inhab., a market town and decayed port, 3 m. w. of Barrow, is chiefly interesting for its two churches. *St Peter's* possesses one of the earliest church towers in England with the characteristic Saxon arcading and panels divided by strips of stone. The narthex or w. porch is of the same date (c. 1000) and its circular lights retain fragments of the original Saxon oak shutters. The rest of the church is of the Dec. and Perp. periods. *St Mary's*, close by, is mainly E.E., with some Transition work. It contains a fine brass to Simon Seman, Sheriff of London in 1433. The controversial, costly, and unfinished *Humber Suspension Bridge* is designed to join the two parts of the county of Humberside.

A 57 runs N.W. out of Lincoln, past the *Racecourse* (with a good grandstand of 1826), where the first race meeting of the year is held. The road follows the *Foss Dyke* cut by the Romans to connect the Trent with the Witham. *Doddington*, where the Hall of 1593 was refitted inside in the 18C (adm. May–Sept, Wed & BH 2–6; also Sun in July–Aug; fee), lies 3½ m. s. of (54½ m.) *Saxilby*.—At 55½ m., we branch right on A 156 to (59 m.) *Torksey* where the Foss Dyke joins the Trent. There was a Saxon mint here. At (61 m.) *Marton*, we cross Till Bridge Lane, a branch from Ermine Street. The church tower has early-Norman herring-bone work, and in the chancel is a 13C crucifixion. *Stow church, 2 m. E., is one of the largest and oldest pre-Conquest churches in England, with huge 10C crossing-arches. It contains an E.E. font, and 13C wall-paintings. *Cotesby-Stow church, 2 m. farther E., has a fine rood-loft.—At (63 m.) *Knaith*, Thomas Sutton, founder of Charterhouse (p. 106), was born in 1532.— 64 m. *Lea* church has 14C glass, and a 15C Crucifixion.

66 m. **Gainsborough** (Hotel) is an old market town (17,400 inhab.) and river-port on the Trent (crossed by a fine bridge of 1787). It has been identified as the 'St Ogg's' of the 'Mill on the Floss'—a "venerable town with red-fluted roofs and broad warehouse gables." Here in 1014 Sweyn Forkbeard, king of Denmark, died after conquering England.

The *Old Hall* (adm. daily 2–5, exc. Sun in winter), rebuilt in 1480–1500, has a contemporary kitchen, a fine roof, and a good oriel at the N.E. end. The 18C church of *All Saints* has a late-Perp. tower, 90 ft high.

The *Congregational Church* (1897) commemorates John Robinson (1576?–1625), pastor of the Pilgrim Fathers at Leydon, probably born at *Sturton-le-Steeple*, 4½ m. s.w. The 'eagre', or tidal wave on the Trent, ascends above Gainsborough.

FROM GAINSBOROUGH TO GOOLE, 33 m. Turning N. off A 631 at (3 m.) *Beckingham*, our road runs N. through the alluvial **Isle of Axholme**, an outlying part of Lincolnshire, which was drained by Vermuyden and his Dutch workmen (1626–28). Much of the land has been reclaimed by the flooding process known as 'warping'. Near (11½ m.) *Haxey*, which has a dignified 14C church, the system of strip-cultivation is much in evidence. Here on 6 Jan the 'Haxey Hood', a traditional game, is played in costume.—14½ m. *Epworth*. The old rectory here (burned in 1709) was the birthplace of John and Charles Wesley (1703 and 1707); adm. daily.—16 m. *Belton* church has an effigy of a knight (14C) made from an Anglo-Saxon gravestone.— Beyond (21½ m.) *Crowle*, where the church has Norman traces (good doorway), and an Anglo-Saxon Cross shaft, we enter Yorkshire.—33 m. *Goole*, see p. 617.

A 631 runs through the N. corner of Nottinghamshire, passing (71 m.; r.) *Gringley-on-the-Hill*, which commands a fine view.—We join A 638 at (77 m.) *Bawtry* (see Rte 46A) and, now in Yorkshire, continue to (86 m.) **Doncaster**, p. 617.

V NORTHERN ENGLAND

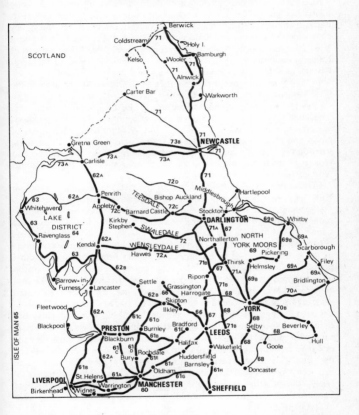

The counties of Northern England offer, perhaps, the greatest contrasts in the country: on the one hand the densely populated manufacturing regions either side of the Pennines, and the shipbuilding, mining, and petro-chemical industries of Teesside and Tyneside; on the other hand the pastoral beauties and rocky grandeur of the Lake District, the lovely Yorkshire Dales and more severe scenery of the North Yorkshire Moors, and the bleak empty spaces of the Border Country. All these four regions have been designated as National Parks in an attempt to protect them from the further encroachment of industry. The new county boundaries segregate the industrial from the rural, seemingly the opposite of the avowed intention in the s. of integrating the formerly independent centres with their hinterlands.

The historical **Yorkshire** was the largest county in England (c. 6000 sq. m.). It was divided from Anglo-Saxon times to 1974 into three *Ridings* (i.e. 'thridings' or thirds), which met near the city of York: the West Riding (the largest with most of the industry), the East Riding, and the North Riding. A South Riding never existed, save in fiction. York itself had been a county of its own since 1396. Yorkshire was always noted for the scenery of its dales, its moors, and its coast; and, in another direction, for the sturdy character and well-marked dialect of its natives. It is unusual if some bluff Yorkshire sporting hero is not making controversial headlines. No part of England contains more important monastic remains; those of the great Cistercian abbeys are unequalled in Europe.

In 1974 Yorkshire lost territory in the s.w. to Greater Manchester, in the w. to Lancashire, in the N.w. to Cumbria, in the N. to Durham, in the N.E. to the newly created Cleveland, and most of the East Riding to Humberside. The remainder was carved into three new counties: SOUTH YORKSHIRE, surrounding Sheffield and Doncaster and incorporating small areas of Notts and Derbyshire (administered from Barnsley); WEST YORKSHIRE, surrounding Leeds and Bradford (administered from Wakefield); and NORTH YORKSHIRE, including York and parts of all three Ridings (administered from Northallerton).

Humberside, extending either side of the riverine estuary, centres on Hull, its principal port, but has its administrative centre at Beverley.

Cleveland, extending either side of the Tees has petro-chemical industries, though the last of the ironstone mines for which it was once known closed in 1964.

Lancashire, to which both Liverpool and Manchester belonged, was one of the richest counties in England, and, apart from London, the most populous. South Lancashire, with its commerce, its coal-mines, its cotton industry, and its engineering works, has been divided between the new counties of **Merseyside** and **Greater Manchester,** while the area round Warrington has been added to Cheshire. The loss of Furness to Cumbria has been compensated by territory astride the Ribble from Yorkshire, but the area of Lancashire has been reduced by a third; it is now predominantly rural with moors rising towards the Pennines. The coast is flat with wide estuaries exposing vast sandy areas at low water. The level region between the estuaries of the Wyre and the Ribble is known as the *Fylde.* Lancashire has been a county palatine since 1351, but on the accession of Henry IV (1399) the palatine rights were vested in the Sovereign as Duke of Lancaster. Lancaster the traditional county town has now been displaced in favour of Preston.

Cumbria, an amalgamation of the former counties of WESTMORLAND and CUMBERLAND with the addition of the district of *Furness*, extends from the Irish Sea to the Pennines and embraces the *Lake District.* The w. end of the Roman Wall and the Borderlands of romance occupy the N. part; farther s. the vale of the Eden flows between mountains or rolling hills.

The old county of **Durham** was conterminous with the diocese, 'the patrimony of St Cuthbert'. Like Cheshire and Lancashire, Durham was a county palatine, and until the death of Bp. Van Mildert in 1836, when the palatine rights were vested in the Crown, the bishops, as counts palatine, exercised rights of sovereignty within its limits, like the king in his palace. In 1974 it lost the mouths of both its river boundaries, the Tees to Cleveland and the Tyne to Tyne and Wear, with its most heavily populated industrial areas. There remains in the valleys of the Derwent, Wear, and Tees, striking and pastoral scenery of great beauty, while in the w. is a wild and bleak region of high moors.

Tyne and Wear combines the former industrial areas of Durham (Gateshead, Jarrow, and Sunderland) and of Northumberland (Newcastle) into one small heavily populated county.

Northumberland, the most northerly county in England, having shed the busy Tyneside in 1974, is one of the most unspoilt and sparsely populated. Its administrative centre remains paradoxically in Newcastle. From the sandy coast, off which lie the *Farne Islands* and *Holy Island*, the land rises gently through an attractive pastoral belt to the mountainous moors of the Middle Marches, culminating in the Cheviot (2676 ft) to the N.W. The lonely upper reaches of Coquetdale and Redesdale, now partly afforested, are characteristic. The county, which, owing to its proximity to the Scots, is rich also in remains of medieval fortifications, is crossed in its s. part by the *Roman Wall.*

59   LIVERPOOL AND BIRKENHEAD

LIVERPOOL (606,800 inhab.), the second seaport of England, and an episcopal see since 1880, is situated on the gently rising north bank of the estuary of the Mersey, which at the Landing Stage, 3 m. from the open sea, is ¾ m. wide. This broad stretch of tidal water and the position of the docks in the heart of the city give Liverpool its character. Rebuilding in the 19C left few vestiges of the past and, while the city was endowed with unusually grandiose buildings, these bore little relation to the street plan. The heavy bombing of 1940–41 tore great holes in the central area, but, in the monumental replanning still in progress, traffic flow has so far taken precedence over visual improvement. The chief imports are cotton, timber, grain, provisions, fruit, and tobacco; the chief exports the textiles, metals, and machinery of the hinterland and West Midlands. The city population is steadily decreasing while adjacent dormitory areas of Merseyside expand.

Railway Stations. *Lime Street* (Pl. 3; Rfmts), for London and most destinations.—*Central* for *Southport*; also low-level station for the Mersey Railway.

Airport at *Speke*, 6 m. s.e. (coach service from Lime St. station and Adelphi Hotel). Booking Offices: *B.A.*, 3 Bold St.; *Cambrian Airways*, 8 Cotton Exchange. Services to London, Isle of Man, Belfast, Dublin, etc.

Hotels, large, near the stations; less expensive accommodation is better sought outside the centre (Waterloo, Blundellsands, Toxteth).

General Post Office (Pl. 2), Victoria St.—INFORMATION OFFICE, Municipal Buildings, Dale St.

United States Consulate, Cunard Building.

Bus Station at the Pierhead (Pl. 5). For the Cathedral (from the centre of the city) bus Nos. 72, 73, 80, 86 or 87 to Rodney St.

Mersey Railway. Electric trains c. every 5 min. from the *Central* (*Low Level*) and *James Street* stations viâ the Mersey Tunnel (1 m. long; constructed in 1866) to Birkenhead (*Hamilton Square* station), and thence either to *Rock Ferry* (junction for Chester) or viâ *Birkenhead Park* to *West Kirby* or *New Brighton.*

Ferry Steamers ply from George's Landing Stage (Pl. 5) every 10 or 20 min. to *Birkenhead* and *Seacombe*; every 30 min. in summer to *New Brighton* (perhaps to be suspended).—**Car Ferry** to Dublin from terminal ½ m. N. of Pierhead.—TOUR OF THE DOCKS from Bootle.

Steamers from Prince's Dock on weekdays to the *Isle of Man* (Sun in summer),

Belfast and *Dublin*; also 2 or 3 times weekly in summer to *Llandudno*.—ATLANTIC LINERS berth at Prince's Landing Stage.

Amusements. THEATRES. *Neptune*, Hanover St. (Pl. 6); *Playhouse* (Pl. 7; repertory), Williamson Sq.; *Empire*, Lime St.; *Everyman* (repertory), Hope St.—CONCERTS of the Philharmonic Society on Tues and Sat evenings, at the *Philharmonic Hall* in Hope St. (Pl 12); concerts on Mon evening in winter at the Walker Art Gallery; lunch-hour recitals alternate Thurs at St Nicholas (Pl. 1). Organ recitals (monthly) at *St George's Hall* (Pl. 3).—GOLF COURSES at *Allerton* and *Bowring* (municipal), *Woolton*, *Childwall*, *Blundellsands*, *West Derby*, etc.—LIVERPOOL SHOW at Wavertree in mid-July (3 days).

History. Liverpool, a name of doubtful etymology, is first mentioned in the early 12C. King John here built a castle and founded a settlement to serve as a point of departure for Ireland, and for centuries this seems to have been its main function. In 1644 it held out for twenty-four days against Prince Rupert; in 1648 arrived its first cargo from the Americas. As an extension of its trade with the plantations of Virginia and the West Indies (sugar, tobacco, cotton, rum), Liverpool (like Bristol) engaged largely in the slave traffic between Africa and America, the profits from which financed its 18C growth. The first dock was opened in 1715, and after 1734 further docks spread into the neighbouring town of Bootle until they stretched 7 miles in an unbroken line. This enterprise and the wider river enabled Liverpool to inherit Bristol's position as premier seaport on the w. coast after the abolition of the slave-trade and the introduction of steam. Though much of its world-wide passenger traffic has been lost in the 20C to aircraft and to Southampton, its system of docks, recently expanded in the direction of the sea, handles nearly 30 million tons a year.—Liverpool is the birthplace of Jeremiah Horrocks (1617?–41), astronomer, George Stubbs (1724–1806), William Roscoe (1753–1831), Felicia Hemans (1793–1835), A. H. and Anne Clough (p. 531), W. E. Gladstone (1809–98), and W. S. Jevons (1835–82). Richard Mather (1596–1669), father of Increase and grandfather of Cotton Mather, was minister of the *Ancient Church* (Unitarian), in Park Rd., Toxteth Park. John Watson ('Ian Maclaren'; 1850–1907) was pastor of Sefton Park Presbyterian Church for 25 years.—Francis Bacon was member of Parliament for Liverpool in 1588–92. Matthew Arnold died here in 1888.

The finest view of Liverpool is from the Mersey, from which the waterfront is dominated by the large mercantile palaces and pinnacled steeple of St Nicholas; behind them the city rises to a skyline crowned with the two cathedrals. The LANDING STAGE (Pl. 5), the world's largest floating quay, 2534 ft long and 80 ft wide, is connected to the river wall by ten hinged bridges and an inclined roadway, 550 ft long. The downstream half, where passenger vessels are moored, is known as *Prince's Landing Stage*, the upstream half, or *George's Landing Stage*, is used by the ferry steamers. The upper deck of the bus station and ferry terminal buildings provides a fine view of the busy river scene. The 'Royal Iris' makes luncheon cruises daily at noon.

The open space behind the Terminal, known as PIERHEAD, occupies the site of the former St George's Dock; behind rise three great blocks of offices. The *Royal Liver Building* (1910) has two towers (295 ft) surmounted by the legendary 'Liver' birds (pron. 'lye-ver'), which are supposed to have given their name to the city and which support its arms. Next is the former Cunard Building (1912–16), now the *Custom House*, then the *Dock Board Offices* (1907; with later additions) in a Renaissance style. Also notable, behind these offices, are the ventilating building and shaft (rebuilt 1951, after war-damage) of the Mersey tunnel.

The ***Docks**, probably the finest system of the kind in the world, are, with those in Birkenhead, under the control of the *Mersey Docks and Harbour Board* (constituted in 1858). They are mostly the work of Jesse Hartley (Dock Engineer, 1824–64), who built the massive river wall and the huge boundary wall; starting it with cut blocks, he soon changed to a cyclopean construction, piercing the wall with gates and lodges of colossal proportions. The *Albert Dock* (Pl. 9), built in 1841–45, is the finest, with five-storied warehouses supported on massive pillars forming a colonnade round the basin. Many of the docks farther upstream are going out of use.—The imposing bonded warehouses farther downstream, difficult of close access, are well seen from Great Howard Street.

Overlooking Pierhead in a memorial garden stands the church of St Nicholas (Pl. 1), the original parish church of Liverpool, founded in 1360 as a chapel-of-ease to the mother-church at Walton. Destroyed, except for the tower (1815; by Thos. Harrison), during an air-raid in 1941, it has been rebuilt (1952), and contains good woodwork, designed by the architect, E. C. Butler. Opposite the church is the Dock Entrance to the Mersey road tunnel (see below).

From the Cunard Building Water St. ascends to the **Town Hall** (Pl. 2), designed by John Wood the elder (1749–54) and enlarged by James Wyatt and John Foster after 1789. Somewhat dwarfed by the surrounding buildings, the Town Hall is crowned with a dome (1802) and has a dignified façade with a Corinthian portico (1811). It may be viewed on application to the City Estates Surveyor, Municipal Buildings.

The quadrangle behind, known as the 'Exchange Flags', was the busy resort of cotton-brokers before the opening of the Cotton Exchange (see below). In the centre is the Nelson Monument, by Westmacott.

From Tithebarn St. (Pl. 2), in which is the *Exchange Station*, Old Hall St., beginning opposite Derby House, leads past the Renaissance *Cotton Exchange* (Pl. 1; 1906), with a double colonnade, to the *David Lewis Northern Hospital* (Pl. 1; 1902) and the *St Paul's Eye Hospital* (1911), noted for its pioneer work in the cure of infantile ophthalmia.—CASTLE ST., opposite the Town Hall, is lined by bank buildings among which C. R. Cockerell's *Bank of England* (1848) and Norman Shaw's *Westminster Bank* (1899) are the most notable. Beyond Brunswick St. (r.), with the *Corn Exchange* (1957), is Derby Square, on the site of King John's castle (pulled down in 1659); here stands a statue of Queen Victoria (Pl. 6) beneath a dome. South Castle St. goes on to Canning Place (Pl. 6), occupying the site of the first dock, constructed in 1715 and filled up in 1829.

From the Town Hall Dale St., with the imposing *Municipal Buildings* (Pl. 2; 1866), or the parallel Victoria St., to the E., leads to the vast open space from which *Queensway* threads the first **Mersey Tunnel** beneath the river to Birkenhead. Begun in 1925 and opened in 1934, this road tunnel cost c. £7½ million. It is 2⅝ m. long and the main tunnel (36 ft wide) takes four lines of traffic. Two narrower branches serve the dock quarters on either side of the river. The tunnel was built by *Sir Basil Mott* and *J. A. Brodie*, engineers, and *H. J. Rowse*, architect. A second tunnel (comp. p. 538) now relieves its former congestion. Facing the tunnel entry are *St John's Gardens* (Pl. 3), overlooked on the E. by St George's Hall and on the N. by an imposing series of public buildings in the classical style, in William Brown St. (Pl. 3).

At the lower end are the *Technical School* (1902), by Mountford, and the *Horseshoe Gallery* (1906) of the City Museum. Next is the **Merseyside County Museum & Library** (1860), by John Weightman, erected at the expense of Sir Wm. Brown; the interior of this building, destroyed by bombs in 1941, has been rebuilt (adm. free 10–5, Sun 2–5). The galleries are still being arranged but contain displays selected from the *Mayer Museum of Archaeology and Ethnography* and the *Derby Museum* of zoological, mineralogical, and botanical specimens. Part of the *Bryan Faussett Anglo-Saxon Collection* is on view, including the *Kingston Brooch (7C), one of the finest examples known of cloisonné work of its period. The superb *Sassoon Collection* of ivories is so far represented by only a few pieces. Special galleries are devoted to the history of Liverpool and there are a

Planetarium, Aquarium and *Vivarium*, and a *Transport Museum.*—The **Brown Library**, rebuilt 1961 with six floors, comprises a lecture room, the Art and Music Libraries with prints and music MSS. on view, and various other specialized collections including Commonwealth and American Libraries, and the Record Office with local history exhibits. Adjoining is the circular *Picton Reading Room* (1879), with a Corinthian peristyle (after the Temple of Vesta at Tivoli), designed by C. Sherlock, containing an important reference library. Communicating with the reading room is the *Hornby Library* of fine-art books, prints, and autographs; below the Picton Library is the International Library. The next building, the gift of Sir A. B. Walker, is the ***Walker Art Gallery** (adm. free 10–5, Sun 2–5; café), by C. Sherlock and H. H. Vale (1874–77), the home of one of the most important collections of paintings in the provinces. The Roscoe Collection of Old Masters of the early Italian and Flemish Schools is outstanding.

The gallery, though enlarged in 1893 and 1933, has insufficient rooms to exhibit all its treasures. A selection of the paintings, arranged chronologically on the 1st floor, is given below.—In the hall is a large Flemish tapestry (16C) typifying Fortitude. In the 1st floor foyer are displayed the 18C marbles from the *Ince Blundell Collection*, presented to Liverpool in 1959. The antiquities from the collection are displayed in the museum.

ROOM 1 (almost the farthest from the Foyer). **Italian Primitives.** *Simone Martini*, Holy Family; *Ercole de' Roberti*, Pietà; *Master of Forlì*, Christ on the Cross; *Studio di Perugino*, Birth of St John the Baptist; *Giov. Mazone*, St Mark enthroned; *Cosimo Rosselli*, St Lawrence; works by *Bart. di Giovanni* and *Spinello Aretino*.—ROOM 2. **15–16C Italian, German, and French Schools.** *Giov. Bellini*, Young Man; *Girolamo da Santa Croce*, Resurrection; *Fr. Granacci*, Life of St John the Baptist; *Isenbrandt*, Madonna; *Lucas Cranach*, Nymph at fountain; *Florentine School*, Madonna; *Vecchietta* (?), St Bernardino preaching; *Palmezzano* (?), Virgin and Child with saints; *Signorelli*, Madonna; *Master of Aachen*, Scenes from the Crucifixion (triptych); *Master of Frankfurt*, Holy Family; *Master of the Virgo inter Virgines*, Entombment; *Mostaert*, Portrait of a man; *French School*, Portrait of a lady with a parakeet.—ROOMS 3–5. **Foreign Schools (17–18C).** *P. Bor*, Magdalen; *Sch. of Dom. Tintoretto*, Court of Heaven; *Procaccini*, Marriage of St Catherine; *Studio of Veronese*, Finding of Moses; *Bonifazio Veronese*, Holy Family; *Vinc. Catena*, Madonna; *Hans Baldung Grien*, Mercenary love; *Solimena*, Birth of St John the Baptist; *Ciro Ferri*, Rest on the flight into Egypt; *Pittoni*, Solomon and Queen of Sheba; *Sch. of Miereveld*, Duke of Brunswick; *N. Poussin* (?), Landscape; *Fragonard*, Head of old man; *Carel Fabritius*, Portrait; *Mengs*, Self-portrait; *Flinck*, Portrait of an Oriental; *Van Schuppen*, Guitar player; *Rembrandt*, *Self-portrait (c. 1629); *Van Dyck*, Infanta Isabella (one of several versions); *S. van Ruysdael*, River scene; *Horst*, The betrothal; *Rubens*, *Madonna with St Elizabeth and St John (formerly in the collection of the Duke of Devonshire); *Rosso Fiorentino*, Portrait of a young man; *Murillo*, La Vierge Coupée (temporarily removed). This picture was cut in two during the Peninsular War and the two parts were not reunited till 1862, one part having been brought to England, while the other part remained in Marshal Soult's collection until sold by his heirs.

The **British Schools** (16–19C) are displayed in Rooms 6–9. ROOM 6. *School of Holbein*, Henry VIII; the 'Pelican' portrait of Queen Elizabeth (after *Nicholas Hilliard*); portraits by *Allan Ramsay*, *Hogarth* (Garrick as Richard III), *Reynolds*, *Gainsborough*, *Zoffany* (Family group), *Van Somer*, also *Cornelius Johnson*, *Richardson*, and *Devis*; works by *Richard Wilson* (Welsh landscapes), *Stubbs*, *Gawen Hamilton*, *Wm. Dobson* (Executioner with the Baptist's head), *Kneller* (Charles II), *Romney*, and *Lely*. Here also is the Wavertree Collection of Sporting Trophies (17–19C silver).—ROOM 7. Portraits by *Raeburn*, *Lawrence*, *Hoppner*; works by *Turner*, *Constable*, *David Cox*, *Ibbetson*, *Morland*, also *Stubbs*, *Joseph Wright of Derby*, *Jas. Ward*, and *Fuseli*.—ROOMS 8–9. Pre-Raphaelites are well represented, with works by *Millais*, *Holman Hunt*, *Madox Brown*, *Burne-Jones*; also *Maclise*, *Poynter*, *Watts*, *Yeames* ("And when did you last see your father?"), etc.—In the remaining rooms are shown the later schools, including examples of *Sickert*, *John*, *Roger Fry*, *Paul Nash*, *Lowry*, *Matthew Smith*, and *Lucien Freud*, of the Camden Town Group (*Bevan, Ginner, Conder, Spencer*) and the Newlyn School, also a selection of 19–20C French works (*Monet, Matisse, Degas, Courbet, Cézanne, Vuillard, Derain, Vlaminck, Seurat*).—Among the sculpture are interesting examples of the 16–18C and works by *Epstein, Rodin, Barye, Gaudier-Brzeska, Renoir* and *Henry Moore* (Falling Warrior).—For the *Sudley Art Gallery*, see p. 537.

Finally, at the end of the long row of buildings, comes the *County Sessions House* (1884), by J. D. Holme.

In Lime St. is the main façade of *St George's Hall (Pl. 3; adm. as for Town Hall, see p. 529), a noble building 500 ft long and 170 ft wide, designed by Harvey Lonsdale Elmes in 1839 at the age of twenty-four. On Elmes death in 1847 the building was completed by Sir Robert Rawlinson, with interior decoration by C. R. Cockerell. It is the finest modern example in England of the classical style, though it has lost Cockerell's pedimental sculpture. The Great Hall, 151 ft long, 73 ft wide, and 83 ft high, has a tunnel vault of hollow blocks and contains a huge organ; in the bays are statues of local celebrities by Chantrey, Noble, Spence, and Fontana. Off the Great Hall are assize courts, and above the N. entrance a Concert Room with a fine balcony supported by caryatids.

In front of the Hall are a Cenotaph, by *L. B. Budden*, and statues of Queen Victoria and Prince Albert, by *Thornycroft*, and Beaconsfield, by *C. B. Birch*. To the N. is the Wellington Column, 115 ft high, by *Lawson*. Facing the hall is Lime Street Station, by Waterhouse (1870), a Victorian 'cathedral of steam', with its hotel now used as offices; when built the cast-iron span of the train shed was the largest in the world. To the S. the square is closed by the new shopping area of *St John's*, dominated by a tower (450 ft; copied from that at Rotterdam), functionally a flue, with a revolving restaurant at the top.

Lime St. continues E. to Ranelagh Place (where Lewis's store is adorned by Epstein's "Adventure"). Thence Brownlow Hill ascends beside the *Adelphi Hotel* to the University (see below) and Ranelagh St. leads past *Central Station* to Bold St., a quiet shopping street. The busy Church St. (Pl. 6) is prolonged s.w. by Lord St. towards the river. In Church Alley, off Church St. (l.), is the *Athenæum*, a news-room and library founded by Wm. Roscoe and others. At the end of the Alley is the attractive building of the former *Blue-coat School* (1716–17) now a centre of the arts. Bold St., in which is the *Lyceum* (by Harrison, 1802), an institution similar to the Athenæum, leads viâ *St Luke's* (1831; burnt 1941) towards the Cathedral (see below). Leece St. ascends to Rodney St., the 'Harley St.' of Liverpool, with its dignified 18C houses. At No. 9 were born A. H. Clough (1819–61) and Anne Clough (1820–92); at No. 62, W. E. Gladstone (1809–98).

Conspicuously situated on St James's Mount is the Anglican *Cathedral (Pl. 11) completed in 1978 after continuous work since 1904 when the foundation stone was laid by King Edward VII. Though the concept may seem a pretentious anachronism for the 20C, the execution is superbly realized in a highly original Gothic style that does not conform strictly to any of the recognized periods. The red sandstone of which the cathedral is built is quarried within the city boundary at Woolton. The *Vestey Tower* (331 ft), the dominant feature of the church, rests, unusually, on the outer walls of the building. The church is placed N. and S., but in the description the points of the compass are used in the ecclesiastical sense.

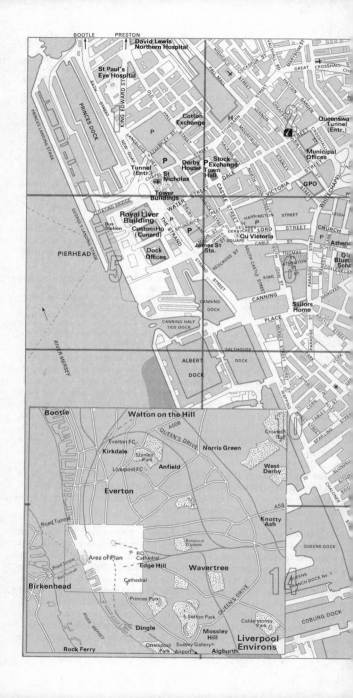

BOOTLE PRESTON

David Lewis
Northern Hospital

St Paul's
Eye Hospital

Cotton
Exchange

Queensway
Tunnel
(Entr.)

Municipal
Offices

GPO

P

P

Derby
House

Tunnel
(Entr.)

Stock
Exchange

Town
Hall

St Nicholas

Tower
Buildings

PRINCES LANDING STAGE

PRINCES DOCK

KING EDWARD ST

NEW QUAY

HALL ST

LANCELOTS

FAZAKERLY ST

CHAPEL

BATH STREET

OLD HALL ST

TITHEBARN

MOORFIELDS

STANLEY

VERNON

DALE

NORTH JOHN ST

CASTLE STREET

VICTORIA

WATER

STREET

WHITECHAPEL

HIGHFIELD

PALL MALL

COCKSPUR ST

MARYBONE

VAUXHALL RD

GREAT

CROSSHALL

HATTON

GARDEN

GILDARD

Royal Liver
Building

Custom Ho
(Cunard)

Dock
Offices

Bus
Station

LOADING BRIDGE

GEORGE'S LANDING STAGE

PIERHEAD

James St
Sta.

THE STRAND

BRUNSWICK ST

DRURY LANE

JAMES

SQUARE

CABLE

LORD

STREET

CHURCH

HARRINGTON   STREET

GEORGES

DERBYCRES

Qu Victoria

SOUTH CASTLE STREET

KING

STRAND STREET

REDCROSS ST

SOUTH JOHN ST

JAMES ST

ATHERTON

PARADISE

COLLEGE LA

HANOVER

THOMAS
ST

Athena

Old
Blue
Schl

LEIGH

SCHOOL

CANNING

DOCK

CANNING

PLACE

Sailors
Home

CANNING HALF
TIDE DOCK

RIVER MERSEY

SALTHOUSE

ALBERT

DOCK

DOCK

MERSEY STREET

HURST

PARK

PARADISE

ARGYLE STREET

STANHOPE

YORK

CORN

TABLEY ST

STANLEY

SPARLING

WAPING

Bootle

Walton on the Hill

A508

QUEEN'S DRIVE

Croxteth
Hall

Everton FC

Kirkdale

Stanley
Park

Liverpool FC

Anfield

Norris Green

West
Derby

Everton

A58

Knotty
Ash

Road Tunnel

Road Tunnel

Rail Tunnel

Area of Plan

RO
Cathedral

Edge Hill

Cathedral

Botanical
Gardens

QUEENS DOCK

Wavertree

Birkenhead

RIVER MERSEY

Princes Park

Sefton Park

Sudley Gallery

QUEEN'S DRIVE

Calderstones
Park

QUEENS
BRANCH DOCK No 1

COBURG DOCK

14

Dingle

Mossley
Hill

Liverpool
Environs

Rock Ferry

Otterspool
Park

Airport

Aigburth

Liverpool

0   400 yards
0   400 metres

The architect, *Sir Giles Gilbert Scott*, was chosen as a result of a public competition when he was still in the early twenties, but the actual building bears little resemblance to his original design, owing to changes introduced at the architect's suggestion as the work progressed.

The Cathedral is the largest church in the country and exceeded in Europe only by St Peter's at Rome, and Seville and Milan cathedrals. The first part to be finished was the Lady Chapel, consecrated in 1910 (reopened in 1955 after war damage); the Choir, Eastern Transepts, and Chapter House were consecrated in 1924, the Central Space under the Tower and the Western Transepts in 1941. The Vestey or Central Tower and the N. and s. porches were completed in 1949. The West Front has been completed more simply than was originally planned; the completion of the last bay of the Nave was marked by a rededication in the presence of H. M. The Queen in 1978. The Tower (ascent in summer by lift; fee) contains 13 bells of which the bourdon ('Great George') weighs 14½ tons.

The principal entrances open into the Under-Tower through triple doorways leading from the *Welsford* (N.) and *Rankin* (S.) *Porches*, adorned with sculptured figures by E. Carter Preston. The ordinary entrance is by the Rankin Porch and thence into the Baptistery.

The plan is unique, the outstanding feature being the rectangular *Central Space* (203 by 73 ft), comprising the Under-Tower and the two Transept Crossings. This area, entirely unobstructed by pillars, has room for 4000 people.

CENTRAL SPACE and W. TRANSEPTS. The most striking feature of the interior is the tremendous height of the arches (107 ft) of the *Under-Tower* with its superb vaulting, the apex of which is 175ft above the floor. The *Windows, by James Hogan, form two groups of triple lancets 69½ ft high surmounted by a rose. In the *S.W. Transept*, beneath an elaborately carved oak baldacchino (39 ft high), is the font of Languedoc marble, carved by Carter Preston, with a tabernacled oak cover.—The first bay of the NAVE, with the Bishops' and Scholars' windows, is spanned by the *Dulverton Bridge*, an arch supporting a musicians' gallery.

CHOIR and E. TRANSEPTS. The lofty *Choir* (116 ft high) of three bays has a triforium but no clerestory; the oak stalls are noteworthy. The reredos, with carved panels by W. Gilbert and L. Weingartner, is part of the E. wall, an unusual feature. The E. window is the largest in England (76 by 44 ft), the subject of the glass being the Te Deum. The *N.E. Transept* is a War Memorial Chapel, with a Cenotaph and Colours of the King's (Liverpool) Regiment. Next is the *Chapel of the Holy Spirit*, with an alabaster reredos and a 15C polychrome Madonna. The *S.E. Transept* contains a bronze effigy (by Scott) of the 16th Earl of Derby (d. 1908). The *Choir Aisles*, above the w. ends of which are the two parts of the great organ, are connected by an Ambulatory off which opens on the N.E. the octagonal *Chapter House*. In the S. Choir Aisle is buried Sir Robert Jones (d. 1933), the surgeon; here also are memorials (designed by Scott) to the first two bishops of Liverpool—Ryle (d. 1900) and Chavasse (d. 1928), and to the first dean, Dr F. W. Dwelly (d. 1957; by Carter Preston). In the N. Choir Aisle is a splendid Cope Chest, wholly medieval in concept and of superb 20C craftsmanship.

The *LADY CHAPEL, on a lower level S.E. of the choir, is entered from the s. choir aisle. The windows commemorate famous English women.

In *St James's Cemetery*, which is picturesquely laid out in an old quarry E. of the Cathedral, is the mausoleum of Wm. Huskisson, the statesman (1770–1830), killed at the opening of the Liverpool & Manchester Railway. Some remains of

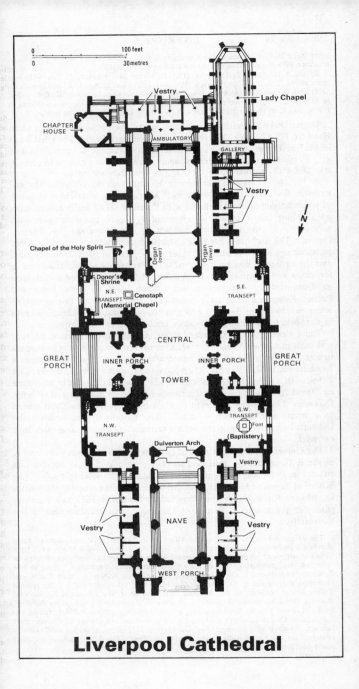

Liverpool Cathedral

early track laid on stones without sleepers are still visible in a coal-yard to the E., together with the portal of the tunnel leading to the Docks.

To the N.W. descends Duke St. (Pl. 11), where Mrs Hemans (1793–1835) was born at No. 118, and Hawthorne's 'Mrs Blodgett' lived at No. 153. In Cornwallis St. (l.) are the workshops of the *School for the Blind*, the oldest of its kind, founded in 1791 and now removed to Smithdown Rd., Toxteth Park.—Georgian streets to the N. and E. of the Cathedral extend towards Abercromby Sq. (see below).

Upper Duke St., with a rewarding view of the Cathedral, brings us to HOPE ST. (Pl. 12) in which is the *Liverpool Institute*, founded by Huskisson in 1825 and now comprising five different schools, including a school of art. Farther on (r.) is the *Philharmonic Hall*, built in 1937–38 to replace the 'Old Phil' burned down in 1933; its acoustics are noted.

At the end of Hope St, crowning Mount Pleasant, rises the METRO-POLITAN CATHEDRAL OF CHRIST THE KING (R.C.), a circular skeleton of sixteen concrete trusses, faced with Portland stone and white mosaic, with sloping buttresses and surmounted by a glass-panelled tower with a 'crown' of pinnacles, soon dubbed by the irreverent the 'Mersey funnel'. The architect, Frederick Gibberd, evolved a scheme for rapid construction after the abandonment of the plan of Sir Edwin Lutyens, and the cathedral was built in 1962–67. Through a porch, decorated in ferocious and daunting vein by William Mitchell, is entered a vast open pavilion, riotously lit by abstract stained glass by John Piper and Patrick Reyntiens. The nave encircles a central altar (a 19-ton slab of white marble from Skopje) and sanctuary, while the chapels, sixteen in number, form an irregular outer circle between the buttresses.

The CRYPT (1933–58), entered from the opposite corner, is all that was built of Lutyens' original design for an immense building to surpass in size St Peter's, Rome, abandoned after the war. Built of brick in a Renaissance style, it has massive pillars, cavernous vaults, and maze-like aisles, with a series of chapels, one of which shelters a notable Madonna by David John, and another the tombs of Abp. Whiteside and of Abp. Downey. The roof of the crypt forms a piazza (where the choir would have been) with an open-air altar.—The basement area beneath the Gibberd building is equipped with a refreshment room, lavatories, and car park.

The **University,** on either side of Brownlow Hill, extends to N. and E. of the R.C. cathedral. Founded in 1881 (comp. p. 546), it received its charter in 1903, and its faculties are strong on the scientific side. The School of Tropical Medicine, founded in 1899, is the earliest in the world. In 1948 the Royal Institution, founded by Roscoe in 1817 as a meeting-place for the learned societies of Liverpool, was incorporated in the University.

The original *Victoria Building*, by Alfred Waterhouse (1890; a Liverpool man) stands on Brownlow Hill, surrounded by buildings (mostly since 1950), each by a different architect, showing neither remarkable individuality nor any attempt at cohesion, and prompting the accusation from one unkind critic of "trying to live down to Waterhouse". On the opposite corner is the *Student's Union*, the N. end charmingly designed by Sir Chas Reilly (1910–12). Of some note are the *Harold Cohen Library* (1938), by H. A. Dod and, next to it, the *Electrical Engineering Building* (1963, by Yorke, Rosenberg, and Mardall); the *Civil Engineering Building*, by E. Maxwell Fry, in Brownlow St.; Sir Basil Spence's *Physics Block*, facing the Lawn; and Denys Lasdun's striking *Sports Centre* on the corner of Abercromby Square. The not very distinguished Georgian (1815) of the square is inoffensively matched on the fourth side by the *Senate* building. The *Music School* occupies some pleasant houses.

In 1895 and 1902 the boundaries of the city of Liverpool were extended to include a number of once separate villages that had become suburban. These now stretch from *Everton*, in the N., noted for its toffee and its football team (Goodison Park), to *Garston*, with B.R. docks and *Speke* airport, to the S. (see Plan inset). For Speke Hall see p. 550. The only contiguous township that has escaped amalgamation is Bootle (see below). Liverpool is well provided with parks and open spaces, all at some distance from the centre. These and many suburban points of interest can be combined into an easy drive (c. 15 m.). From the Cathedral Princes Road leads shortly to *Prince's Park*, Paxton's first independent commission (1842), and the much larger **Sefton Park* (269 acres), to the S.E., with a lake, palm house, and an aviary. Beyond, on reclaimed ground, is the attractive *Otterspool Park*, with a mile-long promenade along the Mersey (*Views). Behind the park in *Aigburth* starts the QUEEN'S DRIVE, a handsome boulevard 7 m. long and 84 ft wide, encircling the city. In Mossley Hill Road (r.), opposite the parish church, is the **Sudley Art Gallery** (10–5, Sun 2–5) with a good collection of British paintings including fine works by Gainsborough and Turner. On the E. side of Mossley Hill, the new *Botanic Gardens* with greenhouses (adm. 2–4, fee) at Hart Hill (E. of Sefton Park) adjoin *Calderstones Park* (94 acres) called after a prehistoric passage grave, the remaining stones from which have been taken to the Museum. Within the circuit of Queen's Drive lie *Wavertree Playground*, venue of the Liverpool Show (mid July), and *Newsham Park* (147 acres), with a boating lake; while to the r. at West Derby and 5 m. N.E. of the centre is *Croxteth Hall* (Earl of Sefton), a Jacobean mansion altered in 1702, with a park of 850 acres. In *Anfield*, to the left, are Liverpool's football ground ('Spion Kop') and *Stanley Park* (90 acres), commanding fine views. Beyond Walton Hill Park (r.) Queen's Drive meets the road leading out to Liverpool racecourse at *Aintree*, 5 m. N. Here the 'Grand National', the premier event of the steeplechase season, has been run in March since 1839.

FROM LIVERPOOL TO SOUTHPORT, 20 m. (A 565). Frequent trains in 40 min. from Central Station.— 3 m. *Bootle*, a borough of 74,200 inhab., containing the newest and largest of the Mersey Docks, adjoins Liverpool on the N.—At (4 m.) *Seaforth*, site of a new 'container' port, the church (1815) was built by Sir John Gladstone, in whose house here his son W. E. Gladstone spent part of his boyhood. Beyond are a number of pleasant residential suburbs on the sandhills near the mouth of the Mersey.— 5 m. *Waterloo* (Hotel) was founded in 1815.— 6½ m. *Great Crosby*, with the Merchant Taylors' Schools for boys and girls, adjoins *Blundellsands* (Hotel).— 12½ m. *Formby* (l.) has a fine golf course, 2 m. E. of which is *Altcar*, noted as the venue of the Waterloo Cup (usually held in Feb), the premier event of the coursing world.— 20 m. **Southport** (Hotels) is a well-built seaside resort and residential town (84,300 inhab.), invaded in summer by excursionists from the North and the Midlands. It has a fine boulevard (Lord St.) with early 19C villas, gardens, good sands, and a long pier, and is abundantly provided with the usual attractions. Notable among its golf courses is the *Royal Birkdale*. The old parish church at *North Meols*, 1½ m. N.E., contains magnificent woodcarving (c. 1704) from the demolished church of St Peter, Liverpool. *Scarisbrick Hall*, now a school, 4½ m. S.E., on the Ormskirk road is an astonishing exercise in the Gothic revival, by A. W. and E. W. Pugin (1836–70). *Halsall*, 1½ m. S. on A 567, near the attractive Leeds and Liverpool Canal, has a good church (mainly early 14C) with a notable N. door and doorway.

From Liverpool to *Manchester*, see Rte 61A; to *Preston, Blackburn, Burnley*, and *Halifax*, see Rte 61B; to *Chester*, see Rte 40 and below; to *Carlisle*, see Rtes 62 and 61B; to *London*, see below.

Birkenhead

Birkenhead is reached from Liverpool by ferry steamer, by the Mersey Railway (see p. 527), or by the **Mersey Tunnel** (p. 529), which emerges in Birkenhead at King's Sq., or at Rendel St. (N. branch), for the Docks.

Birkenhead (Hotels), a seaport with 137,700 inhab., is situated on the w. or Cheshire bank of the Mersey opposite Liverpool, of which to all intents and purposes it is a part. Though a Benedictine priory was established here about 1150, Birkenhead was even in 1810 an insignificant village of 110 inhab., and it owes its modern importance to its *Docks* (182 acres water area and 10 m. of quays), opened in 1847, which, after a period of intense rivalry, were amalgamated with Liverpool docks in 1858. The first iron vessel in England was built in 1829 at Messrs. John Laird & Co.'s shipbuilding yards and engineering works, and in 1862 was launched the famous Confederate privateer 'Alabama', for the depredations of which Great Britain had to pay over £3,000,000 to the United States. Close to *St Mary's Church* (1821), in Church St., are the remains of the *Priory*, with a chapter house (now a chapel) and a ruined refectory and crypt.

The *Williamson Art Gallery & Museum* (10–5 or 9; Sun 2–5), in Slatey Rd., has watercolours, a fine portrait by Raeburn, the Knowles Boney Collection of Liverpool and other porcelain, and a gallery of shipping. *Birkenhead Park*, the upper part of which was laid out by Sir Joseph Paxton, is 180 acres in area.

P. Wilson Steer (1860–1942), painter, and J. L. Garvin (1868–1947), journalist, were natives of the town, as was F. E. Smith (Lord Birkenhead; born at 8 Pilgrim St.). Wilfred Owen lived in Birkenhead from 1900, and Baden-Powell officially inaugurated the Boy Scout movement at Grange Road Hall in 1908.—From *Birkenhead Park* station (N. of the park) the Wirral railway, coming from Liverpool Central underground, runs to (7½ m. in 20 min.) West Kirby or (4 m. in 11 min.) New Brighton.

From Birkenhead to *Chester* and to *London*, see below.

To the N. of Birkenhead, and separated from it by the Great Float, is the borough of **Wallasey** (97,100 inhab.), comprising the townships of New Brighton, Wallasey, Egremont, Seacombe, Liscard, and Poulton.— *Seacombe* (Hotel) and *Egremont* are pleasant residential suburbs on the Mersey, connected with New Brighton by a riverside promenade 3 m. long, and with Liverpool by ferry steamer (see p. 527).

In July–Sept 1962 an experimental Vickers hovercraft service (the first fare-paying service of its kind in the world) carried passengers between Wallasey and Rhyl (N. Wales; 19 m. in 25 min.).
The second Mersey Tunnel, named KINGSWAY. was opened in 1971 to link Wallasey to Liverpool. Costing £29 millions, it is 5½ m. long including approaches, and emerges in Liverpool N. of Exchange Stn. to connect with Scotland Road.

New Brighton (Hotel), at the mouth of the Mersey, with an amusement park, is patronized in summer by thousands of townsfolk from the industrial North. Here Sibelius's music, conducted by the composer, was first publicly heard in England (1899).

FROM BIRKENHEAD TO CHESTER viâ HOYLAKE, 29½ m. (A 553, A540).—Above (2 m.) *Bidston* is Bidston Hill, a favourite viewpoint.—To the N. of (3½ m.) *Moreton* is *Leasowe Castle*, a curious building erected by the Earl of Derby in 1593 for the sake of the fashionable horse-races formerly held here. It contains oak panels from the Star Chamber and is now a Railwaymen's Convalescent Home.—8 m. **Hoylake** (Hotels), at the mouth of the Dee, is a bracing resort (32,200 inhab.) with a famous golf course. Here William III embarked on his way to the Battle of the Boyne (1690).—9½ m. *West Kirby* (Hotel) is a more sheltered resort with fine sands. Off the coast are the *Hilbre Islands*, once important as a telegraph station and noted for bird life.—Between West Kirby and Neston (see below) the former coastal valley railway track affords a fine walk through the Wirral Country Park.—11½ m. *Thurstaston*, with 180 acres of N.T. heathland. Arrowe Park 2½ m. N.E., was the site of the first Boy Scouts' world jamboree in 1929.—15 m. *Heswall* (Hotel).—18½ m. *Neston*, ¾ m. r., was the birthplace of Emma Lyon (1763–1815), Lady Hamilton. Her cottage survives in the hamlet of Ness, to the s. On the coast adjoining is *Parkgate* (Hotel), once the starting-point of the Dublin packet, by which Handel sailed in 1741 to give the first performance of 'Messiah'.—29½ m. *Chester*, see Rte 40.

Routes from Liverpool to London

ROAD. *A.* MOTORWAY, 211 m.—We quit Liverpool by Edge Lane and take M 62 to join M 6 at (20 m.) *Fearnhead* (Junction 21A) for the s. (comp. Rte 62).

B. Viâ the Shakespeare Country, 214½ m. From Liverpool to (54 m.) **Stafford,** see above. Thence we take A 513 and A 51 to (83 m.) **Lichfield**. Thence we take A 446 to (98 m.) *Coleshill,* and A 452 to (111 m.) *Kenilworth.* Thence to (214½ m.) **London,** see Rte 34.

C. Viâ the Mersey Tunnel and Birkenhead, 205 m. (A 41 and A 5).— 18 m. **Chester.**—38 m. *Whitchurch.*—59 m. *Newport,* beyond which we join A 5.—124 m. *Kilsby* and thence to London, se Rte 46.

RAILWAY, see Rte 46.

From Liverpool to *Manchester* and other Lancashire towns, see Rte 61.

60   MANCHESTER

MANCHESTER, situated on the E. bank of the river Irwell, at its confluence with the insignificant Irk and Medlock, is an important commercial city (541,500 inhab.), an episcopal see, and long the capital ('Cottonopolis') of the great cotton-manufacturing district of S.E. Lancashire, one of the most densely populated areas in Europe. **Salford,** on the w. bank of the Irwell, is still anomalously a separate city (130,600 inhab.), while the suburbs extend in all directions to meet, without a break, those of a dozen surrounding towns (Bolton, Oldham, Rochdale, Ashton, Stockport, etc.). Thus, though the populations of both Manchester proper and Salford are steadily decreasing, one million people live within 5 miles of the centre, and 2½ million within ten miles. For this sprawling conurbation, administered by some 50 local authorities, Manchester is the financial, business, and entertainment centre. The city suffered severely from air attack in 1940–41 and wholesale demolitions have followed the closure of huge railway yards, but the new development schemes have so far produced little of architectural note. A characteristic atmosphere of bluff friendliness pervades the city.

Airport at *Ringway*, 10 m. s., between Altrincham and Wilmslow, the principal airport of N. England, with services to London, to most European capitals and resorts, to N. America, etc.—*Air Terminus* in Royal Exchange.

Railway Stations (Rfmts at all). *Piccadilly* or *Oxford Road* for London (Euston) viâ Crewe; Buxton; Birmingham and the s.w.; Chesterfield, Derby, and St Pancras London; Sheffield; Liverpool viâ Warrington; Chester.—*Victoria* for Yorkshire; Huddersfield, Leeds, York, and Newcastle; Liverpool; Chester and N. Wales; the Lake District and the N. (Scotland).

Hotels in St Peter's Sq, in Piccadilly, and elsewhere, including the suburbs; Hotel Reservation Bureau.—Good RESTAURANTS between King St. and the Cathedral.

Post Office (Pl. 7), Spring Gardens.—INFORMATION OFFICE, Town Hall, Albert Square.—WEATHER CENTRE, 56 Royal Exchange.

United States Consulate, Arkwright House, Parsonage Gdns., off Deansgate (Pl. 6).

Bus Stations.—LOCAL BUSES start from Piccadilly (Pl. 11) and Chorlton St. (Pl. 11); buses 41, 42, 97 for the *Whitworth Art Gallery*; 161 for *Didsbury*; 62, 75 (from Albert Sq.) for *Heaton Hall.*—LONG-DISTANCE BUSES from Lower Mosley St. (Pl. 14).

Amusements. THEATRES: *Opera House* (Pl. 9), Quay St.; *Palace* (Pl. 15), Oxford St.; *Library* (Pl. 10), St Peter's Sq.; *Royal Exchange*, St Ann's Sq.—CONCERTS. **Hallé Concerts* in the Free Trade Hall, Peter St. (Pl. 10), on alternate Sundays, Wed, and Thurs evenings in winter, a great social institution, founded by Sir Charles Hallé.—

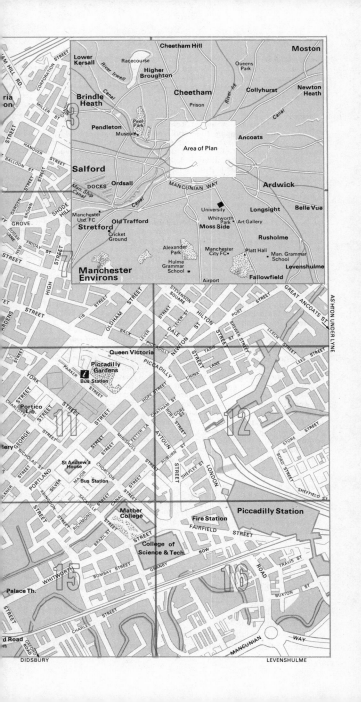

Area of Plan

Cheetham Hill
Moston
Lower Kersall
River Irwell
Racecourse
Higher Broughton
Queens Park
Collyhurst
Newton Heath
Cheetham
Brindle Heath
Prison
River Irk
Canal
Pendleton
Peel Park
Museum
Ancoats
Salford
Ordsall
Man. Ship Canal
DOCKS
MANCUNIAN WAY
Ardwick
Canal
University
Longsight
Belle Vue
Manchester Utd. FC
Old Trafford
Whitworth Park
Moss Side
Art Gallery
Stretford
Cricket Ground
Rusholme
Alexander Park
Manchester City FC
Platt Hall
Man. Grammar School
Manchester Environs
Hulme Grammar School
Levenshulme
Airport
Fallowfield

CORPORATION STREET
HAM HILL RD
ria
on
MILLER ST
HANOVER STREET
BALLOON ST
SHODE HILL
STREET
STREET
3
SHODE HILL
GORDON
BROWN
FRIDAY ST
GROVE
CEDAR
LANE
STREET
HIGH STREET
GARDENS
STREET
TIB STREET
OLDHAM STREET
BACK
STREET
LEVER
DALE
STEVENSON SQUARE
HILTON ST
PORT STREET
GREAT ANCOATS ST
ASHTON UNDER LYNE
LEVER ST
NEWTON ST
TARIFF
LANE
CHINA
BREWER STREET
LEECH STREET
LEES STREET

Queen Victoria
PICCADILLY
Piccadilly Gardens
i
Bus Station
PARKER STREET
YORK STREET
CHARLOTTE STREET
GEORGE STREET
Portico Lib.
NICHOLAS ST
11
PORTLAND STREET
STREET
MINSHULL ST
CHORLTON ST
HOPE STREET
ORMATHAM ST
BRIBI GORE
STREET
AYTOUN STREET
12
STREET
PORT STREET
STORE STREET
STREET
SHEFFIELD ST

St Andrew's House
SILVER STREET
ABINGDON STREET
SACVILLE STREET
CANAL STREET
STREET
ATBURN STREET
SHEPLEY ST
LONDON ROAD
Bus Station

Mather College
RICHMOND STREET
BRAZIL ST
STREET
Fire Station
FAIRFIELD STREET
Piccadilly Station
PALKER
gallery
STREET
College of Science & Tech
BOMBAY STREET
GRANBY ROW
15
WHITWORTH
16
ROAD STREET
TRAVIS ST
BUXTON ST
Palace Th.
STREET
STREET
CHARLES STREET
MANCUNIAN WAY
d Road
n
OXFORD ROAD
DIDSBURY
LEVENSHULME

Tuesday Mid-day Concerts (1.10 to 2 p.m.), Lesser Free Trade Hall, Peter St.—BELLE
VUE GARDENS (buses 57, 77, 210; adm. 10–dusk), with *Zoological gardens, boating-
lake, amusement park, firework displays, boxing, etc.—GOLF COURSE at *Heaton Park*
(municipal), and in many other suburbs.—COUNTY CRICKET GROUND at *Old Trafford*
(see Plan inset).

History. Though the Manchester of today is in the main a creation of the 19C,
its origins are ancient. A walled Roman castrum (possibly the *Mancunium* or
Mamucium of the Antonine Itinerary) stood at the confluence of the Irwell and
Medlock, on the military road from Chester to York. A fragment of its wall
survives in a yard in Collier St. off the Knott Mill End of Deansgate (Pl. 13),
near the old Liverpool Rd. station (1830). The later Saxon town (garrisoned against
the Danes in 923) lay farther to the N. at the junction of the Irk and Irwell, near
the present cathedral. Manchester's industrial prosperity has its beginnings in
Edward III's settlement of Flemish weavers here in 1375. During the Civil War
Manchester successfully withstood a siege by the Royalists in 1642; but in 1715
and again in 1745 (when Prince Charles Edward Stuart occupied the town) it gave
evidence of warm Jacobite sympathies (comp. Shenstone's ballad, 'Jemmy
Dawson'). Though cotton was imported into Manchester from the Levant as early
as the 17C, the rise of the Lancashire cotton industry, fostered by the moist climate,
a convenient coal supply, and improvements in machinery, dates from the middle
of the 18C. The first cotton mill in Manchester was opened in 1781 and Arkwright's Mill (1783) in Miller's Lane was the first cotton mill to use steam power.
The evils of the factory system were aggravated by the distress caused by the
Napoleonic wars, and in 1819 occurred the famous 'massacre' of Peterloo, when a
mass meeting of protest was dispersed by the sabres of the yeomanry with the loss
of eleven lives. Manchester, until then "the largest village in the country" (150,000
inhab.), obtained parliamentary representation in 1832 and a charter of incorpor-
ation in 1838; in 1853 it became a city. The Lancashire cotton famine, due to the
failure of the cotton-crop during the American civil war, caused great distress
here in 1864–65.

In the first half of the 19C Manchester was a stronghold of the reform agitation
that led to the Reform Act of 1832 and the repeal of the Corn Laws in 1846. The
'Manchester School', led by Cobden and Bright, advocated the policy of *laissez-
faire* or unrestricted competition, free trade, and non-intervention in foreign affairs,
and the 'Manchester Guardian' newspaper was founded in 1821 to press for
constitutional reform and support the cause of Liberalism. With the opening in
1894 of the Ship Canal (p. 548) Manchester became the first major inland port in
the world; today in terms of tonnage, it is the third port in England. Manchester is
noted for its love of music, and as the headquarters of the temperance and vegetar-
ian movements has been styled "the home of living causes". Among its eminent
natives are Thomas De Quincey (1785–1859), who passed his boyhood here and
wrote his 'Vision of Sudden Death' in a Manchester tavern; Harrison Ainsworth
(1805–82), the novelist; Frances Hodgson Burnett (1849–1924), who was born at
141 Cheetham Hill Rd., and spent her early years at 19 Islington Sq., Salford;
David Lloyd George (1863–1945; b. at 5 New York Place, Chorlton-on-Medlock);
and John Alcock and Arthur Whitton-Brown, the aviators. Ann Lee (1736–84),
foundress of the American Society of Shakers, was a Manchester factory hand.
George Bradshaw (1801–53), creator of the first general railway time-table, born
at Pendleton, had his office at 27 Brown St.—Manchester factory life is described
in *Mrs Gaskell's* 'Mary Barton' (1848) and 'North and South' (1855) and in
Dickens's 'Hard Times' (1864); here also "the condition of the working classes"
inspired from Engels a classic of a different kind. *Louis Golding's* 'Magnolia
Street' (1932) delineates the life of the Jewish community and *Walter Greenwood's*
'Love on the Dole' is set in Salford. George Gissing (1857–1903) and Francis
Thompson (1860–1907) were students at Owens College.

The Midland Hotel, outside the former Central Station stands at the
s.w. corner of *St Peter's Square* (Pl. 10), whence Mosley St. runs N.E.,
Oxford St. S.E., and Peter St. W. In the square is a war Cenotaph by
Lutyens and on the left is the Rotunda of the **Central Library**, by E.
Vincent Harris (1934). This is the largest municipal library in the
country, with a reading-room second in size to that of the British
Museum. Among the nine specialized libraries it houses is the *Henry*

Watson Music Library, with the Flower and Aylesford collections of Handelian MSS. PETER ST., lined with theatres and cinemas, leads towards Deansgate (p. 544); on the left are the headquarters (1910) of the *Y.M.C.A.* with a swimming pool, and the large *Free Trade Hall* (Pl. 10), home of the Hallé concerts. Sufficient of the Italianate façade of 1856 escaped the fire-bombs of 1940 to be restored in the rebuilding.

The hall stands on Peter's Field (scene of the Peterloo 'massacre' in 1819), presented by Cobden to the Anti-Corn Law League. In a previous hall on this site Cobden and Bright delivered their speeches against the Corn Laws.

We follow South St, opposite the Free Trade Hall to ALBERT SQUARE. On the E. side rises the dominant **Town Hall**, a Gothic pile designed by Alfred Waterhouse in 1867 and completed in 1876. Recent cleaning has revealed much of the fine detail. The great hall (adm. on application to the Superintendent) has a hammerbeam roof; the walls are adorned with mural paintings by Ford Madox Brown, illustrating the history of Manchester. The tower (281½ ft) contains a fine peal of 21 bells, with a line from canto 106 of 'In Memoriam' on each. The extension, connected to it by bridges over Lloyd St., is by Vincent Harris (1938).

The busy Cross St. (Pl. 10) leads N. to the Royal Exchange, intersecting King St., which, on the right, is bordered by insurance offices and banks. On the left is the beginning of the best shopping area. In St Ann St. to the left is *St Ann's* (Pl. 11), a dignified Renaissance church of 1712, with contemporary pulpit and font, where De Quincey was baptized; here also is Carracci's "Descent from the Cross", transferred hither from the vanished churches of St Peter and St James. On the right of St Ann's Square, with its statue of Richard Cobden (1804–65), is the **Royal Exchange** (Pl. 11), a 19C cotton exchange, transformed (1976) into a theatre and restaurant.

A 16C half-timbered house, the *Wellington Inn*, survives in Market Place (Pl. 6). Here was born John Byrom (1692–1763), author of 'Christians Awake' and inventor of a system of shorthand.

Victoria St. (Pl. 10) continues N. and, beyond the statue of Oliver Cromwell (by Matt. Noble), reaches a huge area of reconstruction. Here, recently cleaned, and contrasting with its dingy surroundings, the **Cathedral** (Pl. 10) faces across the grimy waters of the Irwell to Salford and the disused Exchange Station. The old parish church ('t'owd church') of Manchester, was made collegiate in 1421 by Thomas de la Warr (who was both lord of the manor and rector), and raised to its present dignity in 1847. The church, in the Perp. style and dating mainly from 1422–1520, is only 220 ft in length, with a disproportionate width of 112 ft. The square tower (130 ft high) was resurfaced and heightened in 1868, when the building was much restored; an air-raid in 1940 caused damage. Reglazing in colour has been started.

The NAVE has double aisles, the outer aisles having originally accommodated chantries for Henry V, the founder, etc. The arch opening into the tower is a relic of an earlier church. Angels with musical instruments support the principals of the 15C roof; likewise of the 15C is the beautiful pulpitum. The CHOIR contains superb *Stalls (1505–9), considered by some to be the finest in Europe, with quaint misericords.

These, and the splendid panelled roof (15C), suffered from blast in 1940 and have since been well restored. Noteworthy also are the fine brass of Warden Huntington (d. 1458), the 18C ironwork, and a chandelier of 1620. In the retro-choir the *Lady Chapel*, destroyed in 1940 and rebuilt by Sir Hubert Worthington, is entered by a screen of c. 1440 (restored); on the exterior is a Madonna by Sir Charles Wheeler. To the s. of the choir is the CHAPTER HOUSE, rebuilt as an octagon in 1485; the tracery over the entrance is filled with paintings of the Beatitudes (in modern dress) by Carel Weight (1963). Adjoining on the w. is the *Jesus Chapel*, with a 16C screen, beside which hangs the royal charter of 1421, the earliest of three here displayed. The *Chapel of the Manchester Regiment* (N.), built in 1513 by Bp. Stanley and long known as the Derby Chapel, was shattered by bombs in 1940 and has been carefully restored (1951); the roof has carvings by Alan Durst, but parts of the 16C screen survive, also the founder's altar tomb. The font is of the 18C. Near the N. door is a seated figure of Humphrey Chetham (see below), by Theed.

Beyond the cathedral is *Chetham's Hospital* (Pl. 2), originally built in 1422 by Thomas de la Warr as a residence for the warden and fellows of his collegiate church (see above). Under Elizabeth one of its wardens was Dr Dee, the famous astrologer. In accordance with the will of Humphrey Chetham (1580–1653), here was founded in 1653 a charity school, for the maintenance and education of 40 poor boys; in 1969, after a long period as a grammar school (which always supplied the choristers of the cathedral), it became an independent school for young musicians, teaching 350 boys and girls, with entry by audition. The fine collegiate buildings, with 15C refectory, screens passage, and musicians' gallery, are in use by the school; the old dormitory wing is occupied by the *Library*, also of the foundation. This claims to be the oldest free public library in England; its books were chained until 1740; it now comprises 70,000 volumes (90 incunabula) and many MSS. (open Mon–Fri 9.30–5, Sat to 12). The Reading Room contains the 17C portrait of Chetham on which Theed's sculpture (com. above) is based, a Jacobean gate-legged table, and the desk used by Marx and Engels, both regular readers.

Opposite Chetham's Hospital begins CHAPEL STREET (Pl. 5), the main thoroughfare of **Salford**, an independent city, but to all intents and purposes a part of Manchester, from which it is separated only by the narrow Irwell. Among its buildings are the Rom. Cath. *Cathedral of St John* (1848), in Chapel St., and *St Philip's Church* (1825) by Sir Robt. Smirke. At the entrance to *Peel Park* is the *Art Gallery*, with a head of Tagore by *Epstein*, a collection of paintings by *L. S. Lowry*, and a model 19C 'street'. *Ordsall Hall*, a 15C timber house, is also open (10–5, Sun from 2) as a museum. For *Joule House*, see p. 546. Salford Docks on the Ship Canal are important (comp. p. 548).

From Cromwell's statue DEANSGATE (Pl. 10), an important thoroughfare, runs s.s.w. towards (½ m.) the *Central Station*. On the right is the *John Rylands Library* (Pl. 10; 1890–99), an admirable structure in the late-Gothic style by Basil Champneys, built and endowed by Mrs Rylands in memory of her husband, and opened in 1900. In the recently cleaned entrance-hall the watermarking of the red sandstone is remarkable. The library (adm. Mon–Fri 10–6, Sat to 2) contains over 700,000 vols, including the Althorp Library of 40,000 vols collected by the 2nd

Earl Spencer (d. 1834) and part of the Bibliotheca Lindesiana purchased from the 25th Earl of Crawford (d. 1913), also c. ¾ million documents and charters. These comprise a superb collection of early printed books, among which is the block-print 'St Christopher' (1423), the earliest dated piece of European printing extant; Bibles in over 300 languages; works on art and architecture, voyages and travels; scarce engravings; and fine bindings. The 16,000 MSS. include the 'St John Fragment' (c. A.D. 150), the earliest piece of New Testament writing extant, and the 'Deuteronomy fragment' of the same date, both recovered from a mummy wrapping from Fayûm. Also on view are the Grafton portrait of (?) Shakespeare, discovered in 1907, and a selection (changed periodically) of rare books.

Hardman St., on the right, leads to the new *Law Courts* (1961), by Leonard Howitt. Farther on is Quay St., the *County Court* (Pl. 9) in which was the residence of Richard Cobden and later (1851–73) the first home of Owens College (see p. 546). St John St., also on the right of Deansgate, is the 'Harley St.' of the city and a "genuine relic of mid-Victorian Manchester".

We return by Peter St. to St Peter's Sq. and follow Mosley Street. On the right is the severely classical *City Art Gallery (Pl. 11; open free 10–6, Sun 2.30–5) built for the Royal Manchester Institution by Sir Charles Barry in 1825–29, often described as Manchester's finest building. It houses the principal collections of paintings, sculpture, silver, and pottery, which are supplemented at the branch galleries (comp. below) administered by the City Corporation.

The arrangement of the paintings is apt to be altered owing to the numerous temporary exhibitions, but is normally chronological, beginning with the works of Old Masters (14–16C) and Foreign Schools of the 17–18C; then showing the development of British painting from the 17C to the 20C, with a small group of 19C French pictures breaking the sequence.

ENTRANCE HALL AND BALCONY. *Constable*, Landscapes; *Turner*, Pas de Calais; *Etty*, Self-portrait; *Blake*, Heads of the Poets; *Maclise*, A Winter Night's Tale. Modern sculpture: *Zadkine*, Diana; *Butler*, Torso; *Rodin*, Eve, The Age of Bronze.

ROOM 1. *Follower of Bernardo Daddi*, Virgin and Child with the Goldfinch; *Attr. Jan Soens*, Holy Family with St John the Baptist; *John Souch*, Sir Thomas Aston at the deathbed of his wife.—R. 2. *Baciccia*, St John the Baptist; *P. F. de Grebber*, Holy Family; *Dom. Fetti*, Portrait of a Musician; *G. Poussin*, Landscape.

R. 3. Portraits by *M. Wright*, *Lely*, *Highmore* (Earl of Leicester), *Hogarth* (also represented by the Pool of Bethesda; oil sketch); *Dandridge*, The Ladies Noel; oil sketches by *Mengs*, and *Thornhill*.—R. 4 Portraits by *Romney*, *Hoppner*, *Reynolds*, *Gainsborough* and *Kauffmann*. Landscapes by *Wootton*, *Lambert*, *Wilson*, *Gainsborough*, *Ibbetson*, *Crome*; *Morland*, Farrier's Forge.—R. 5. Pre-Raphaelite paintings and sculpture, a comprehensive display, including *F. Madox Brown*, Work; *Millais*, Autumn Leaves; *Holman Hunt*, Light of the World, The Scapegoat, The Lady of Shalott, The Shadow of Death, Hireling Shepherd; *D. G. Rossetti*, Astarte Syriaca, Bower Meadow.—R. 6. Landscapes by *Troyon*, *Corot*, *Courbet*, *Pissarro*, *Sisley*, *Gauguin*, *Boudin*.

R. 7. *John*, W. B. Yeats; *Orpen*, Homage to Manet; *Steer*, Summer at Cowes; *Sickert*, portraits and interiors; works by *Bevan*, *Ginner*, *Gilman*, *J. D. Fergusson*.—R. 8. *W. Lewis*, *Etchells*, *Bomberg*, *B. Nicholson*, *Sutherland*, *Paul Nash*, *Giacometti*, *Piper*, *Pasmore*, *Henry Moore*, Two Forms (1969).—R. 9. *Vaughan*, *Bratby*, *Sutton*, *Redpath*, *H. Cohen*, *John Hoyland*, *Kidner*, *Tyzack*, *Jack Smith*, *Roy Ascott*, *Brian Kneale*.

The **Athenaeum Annexe Museum** (adm. as above) in Princess St., occupies another building by Barry (1839) and contains further displays of pottery and porcelain from late medieval to the 19C including 18C English porcelain, Wedgwood Jasper and Basalt ware, tin-glazes, lead-glazes and salt glazes from the Greg

Collection and enamels from the Raby Collection. Other important collections are distributed among several branch galleries: *The Gallery of English Costume*, **Platt Hall**, Rusholme, 17–20C (in a fine country house of c. 1764); **Heaton Hall**, Heaton Park, a mansion of 1772 by James Wyatt, with splendid plasterwork, fresco decorations, contemporary paintings, sculpture (including *Thorvaldsen's* Shepherd Boy and Dog) and furniture (Samuel Green organ, 1790); **Wythenshawe Hall**, Northenden (16–17C and later, timber-frame country house with 17C furniture, paintings, Royal Lancastrian pottery and Local History Collection); **Fletcher Moss Museum**, Didsbury, an old Parsonage in a charming garden—now housing the principal English watercolours and drawings, 18–20C, **Queen's Park Art Gallery**, Rochdale Road, Harpurhey, Museums of the 14th–20th King's Hussars and Manchester Regiment; Egerton Collection of oriental Arms and Armour; British Painting and Sculpture 1860–1914. Admission: November to February: 10–4; Sun 2–4; May to August: 10–8; Sun 2–8. Other periods: 10–6; Sun 2–6. Free in each case. See Plan inset.

Farther up Mosley St. is the *Portico Library* (adm. by arrangement, daily, 10–5), with rare first editions, opened in 1806 as a social and literary institution and mentioned by De Quincey. No. 36 George St. (Pl. 11) is the headquarters, rebuilt in 1960, of the *Manchester Literary and Philosophical Society*, founded in 1781. Among its famous members were John Dalton (d. 1844), whose experiments led to the enunciation of the atomic theory, and James Prescott Joule (1818–89), who first determined the mechanical equivalent of heat; his experimental apparatus and other relics may be seen at *Joule House*, 1 Acton Sq., Salford (Mon–Fri 9–5 on application).

Mosley St. brings us to PICCADILLY (Pl. 11), with its garden (only too rare in this city), now backed by a series of new buildings, including the Hotel Piccadilly and two towering office blocks. The busy Market St. (Pl. 7) leads (l.) to the Exchange.

PORTLAND STREET (Pl. 11), which runs s.w. from Piccadilly to Oxford St., is lined with new office buildings, of which the Bank of England building (r.) and St Andrew's House (l.) are conspicuous.—In Whitworth St. (Pl. 15), leading from Piccadilly Station to Oxford St., is the *College of Science and Technology*, founded as a mechanics' institute in 1824, rebuilt, largely through the munificence of Sir Joseph Whitworth, in 1902, and now being greatly enlarged (comp. below).

OXFORD STREET (Pl. 14), leading s.e. from St Peter's Sq., is continued by OXFORD ROAD, the chief thoroughfare of South Manchester, to the University quarter; it is crossed by the Mancunian Way, an elevated section of the city ring road. To the left, in Grosvenor St., is the *North-Western Museum of Science and Industry* (open 10–5 weekdays).

Manchester University, officially the *Victoria University of Manchester*, occupies as its central premises a characteristic building (1873; since enlarged) by Waterhouse, in Oxford Rd., 1 m. from St Peter's Square. Additional buildings have been erected in the neighbourhood, while with the University various other institutions, including the College of Science and Technology and seven theological colleges, are associated.

A scheme is envisaged for a University "precinct" involving considerable re-building, rerouting of thoroughfares, and the addition of new buildings, eventually to join up with those of the College of Science and Technology.

Manchester University has developed out of Owens College, founded under the will of John Owens (d. 1846), a Manchester merchant, opened in 1851 in Quay St. (Pl. 9), incorporated in 1871, and removed to the present building in 1873. The Victoria University was founded in 1880, with Owens College as its seat, and the University College at Liverpool (1884) and the Yorkshire College at Leeds (1887) were admitted as the other constituent colleges. Liverpool, however, obtained a separate university in 1903 and Leeds in 1904, while Owens College was incorporated in 1904 within the Victoria University of Manchester, and its old name finally disappeared. The *University Library* displays in its permanent exhibition editions of Francis Thompson and George Gissing (both students) and of Mrs Gaskell, who lived locally. Inside the new main entrance hall of the Institute of Science and

Technology is a vast mural by Victor Pasmore.—The *Christie Library* of scientific subjects is open to all who obtain an order from the Librarian.

Much research work has been done on atomic physics, including the later work of Rutherford, Chadwick, and Cockcroft.

The *Manchester Museum* (adm. free, weekdays 10–5), on the right of the entrance to the university, contains natural history, ethnographical, and archaeological collections, among which the Egyptian antiquities found by Flinders Petrie (1853–1942) and the mollusca are notable.

No. 84 Plymouth Grove (leading to the Stockport road), to the E., was the residence of Mrs Gaskell (1810–65). It is now a club for overseas students. Charlotte Brontë, who visited her future biographer here three times after 1850, began 'Jane Eyre' in lodgings at 59 Boundary St. (since demolished), off Oxford Road.

Farther on in Oxford Rd., on the left, is the *Royal Infirmary*, founded in 1752 and removed hither in 1908. Opposite is the **Whitworth Art Gallery** (adm. free, weekdays 10–5), a bequest of Sir Joseph Whitworth (d. 1887) and since 1958 part of the University. It contains a collection of the first order of English *Watercolours from the 18C to the present day, and drawings by Old Masters and of the 19C and 20C French Schools. The early foreign prints if not on view may be seen on request. The collection of ancient *Textiles, brilliant in colour and wonderful in design, is superb. These include Coptic robes and cloths (1–10C) collected by Flinders Petrie, a 15C German altar frontal, Spanish, Italian, and Near-Eastern embroideries of the 16–18C, and Far-Eastern work of the 18–19C; also English embroideries (16–17C), and English and French printed cottons (18–19C).

In Birchfields Av., Rusholme, on the left of Wilmslow Rd., the continuation of Oxford Rd., is *Manchester Grammar School*, one of the leading schools of the North, founded in 1515 by Hugh Oldham, Bp. of Exeter. Here were educated John Bradford, Humphrey Chetham, De Quincey (who ran away in 1802 because he felt his time was being wasted), and Harrison Ainsworth. The school was moved from beside Chetham's Hospital in 1931; the buildings are by P. S. Worthington and Francis Jones.

Wilmslow Rd. goes on to (c. 1 m.) *Platt Hall* (see p. 546) adjoining *Platt Fields Park*, in which is a replica (1919) of Barnard's statue of Abraham Lincoln in Cincinnati. Here, at *Fallowfield*, is Hollings College, a strikingly original building (1963).—At *Moss Side*, farther w., is *Alexandra Park* (60 acres), on the s. side of which is the *Hulme Grammar School*, founded in 1881 and endowed by funds bequeathed by Wm. Hulme (d. 1691). *Slade Hall* (no adm.), in *Longsight*, to the E., dates from 1585. Farther out are *Whalley Range*; *Chorlton-cum-Hardy*; *Withington*, once a wealthy German colony, with *Hough End Hall*, a gabled house of 1596 (poorly restored), and the notable church of St Christopher, by B. A. Miller (1935); and also viâ the Wilmslow Rd. (5 m.) Didsbury, a well-to-do suburb above the Mersey, with the *Fletcher Moss Museum* (p. 546) and a fine park; in the *Church of St James* is a fine monument to Sir Nicholas Mosley (d. 1612), Lord Mayor of London.

On the farther bank of the Mersey is *Northenden*, w. of which is *Wythenshawe Hall*, Tudor with Georgian additions (com. p. 546), standing in a beautiful park. *Baguley Hall* is a timber 14C building with one medieval brick wing and another of the 17C. The *Wythenshawe Estate*, developed by Manchester Corporation after 1931 from a design by Barry Parker, is well laid out and has two outstanding churches: St Michael's, Orton Rd, built in 1937 by Cachemaille-Day and Lander, and the *William Temple Memorial Church*, Simonsway (1965), by G. G. Pace.

The *Manchester Ship Canal, 35½ m. long and 28 ft deep, with a minimum bottom width of 120 ft, was constructed in 1887–94 at a total cost of nearly £17,000,000, and connects Manchester with the Mersey at Eastham (p. 382), running viâ Warrington and Runcorn. Steamers up to 15,000 tons trade regularly from Manchester to all parts of the world. There are locks at Mode Wheel (Manchester), Barton, Irlam, Latchford, and Eastham. The *Manchester Docks* (c. 700 acres; water-area 179 acres) are reached by Chester Rd., the continuation of Deansgate, and Trafford Rd. (r.) in *Salford*; Chester Rd. goes on past the *Old Trafford Cricket Ground. Trafford Park*, the former estate of Sir Humphrey de Trafford, has been converted into an industrial area.

The **Bridgewater Canal**, which now belongs to the Ship Canal Co., was the first cross-country canal in England. It was constructed, in face of enormous difficulties, in 1758–72 by James Brindley for the third Duke of Bridgewater, and earned the latter a princely fortune. The first portion, from Worsley to Manchester, of which the chief feature is the aqueduct over the Irwell at Barton, brought cheap coal to Manchester, while the extension to Runcorn (with an aqueduct over the Mersey at Stretford) brought cheap food. The canal provides the only link apart from the tidal Trent between the N. and s. canal systems.

From Manchester to *Chester*, see Rte 40; to the *Peak District* (*Macclesfield, Derby, Buxton, Sheffield*), see Rte 45; to *Liverpool, Warrington, St Helens, Widnes*, and *Altrincham*, see Rte 61A; to *Bolton, Blackburn, Clitheroe*, and *Settle*, see Rte 61C; to *Bury, Burnley*, and *Skipton*, see Rte 61D; to *Rochdale, Halifax*, and *Bradford*, see Rte 61E; to *Oldham, Huddersfield*, and *Leeds*, see Rte 61F; to *Penistone* and *Sheffield*, see Rte 61G.

Routes from Manchester to London

ROAD. *A.* 201 m. We quit Manchester by Chester Road and take A 56 to (8 m.) *Altrincham.*—A 556 to the junction of M 6; thence to (201 m.) **London** as on p. 539.
B. 190 m. The most attractive road is viâ *Buxton*. We leave Manchester by London Rd. (Pl. 16) and follow A 6.—At (25 m.) **Buxton** we take Á 515 (or keep to A 6 viâ *Matlock* for Derby).—At (46 m.) *Ashbourne* we take A 52 for (59 m.) *Derby.*—87 m. **Leicester**, beyond which we join M 1 for (190 m.) **London**.
Or motorists may keep to A 6 at Leicester (118½ m.; comp. Rte 43).—15 m. *Market Harborough.*—26 m. *Kettering.*—50 m. **Bedford**, and thence to (101 m.) **London**, see p. 403.
C. Viâ the Shakespeare Country, 190 m. We quit Manchester by Oxford Rd. (Pl. 15) and follow A 34 to (36 m.) *Newcastle*, beyond which we join A 51 at (45 m.) *Stone.*—67 m. **Lichfield**. Thence to (95 m.) *Kenilworth* and (190 m.) **London**, comp. Rte. 34.

RAILWAY viâ *Crewe* (188¾ m. in c. 2¾–3¼ hrs), or viâ *Stoke-on-Trent* (187½ m. in 2¾ hrs.), from Picadilly Station to Euston.

61 THE MANUFACTURING DISTRICTS OF LANCASHIRE AND YORKSHIRE
(Merseyside, Greater Manchester)

This densely populated region is not in the special sense a tourist district, but as an important source of England's industrial wealth and prosperity from the Industrial Revolution it is profoundly interesting, and it offers some characteristic aspects of the English social order. Though its industrial activity scarcely makes for beauty, it has attractive interludes and fringes of fresh and picturesque country. The towns, largely of 19C growth and mostly in the course of redevelopment, offer a wealth of 'industrial archaeology'; their handsome public buildings are typical of British civic architecture and many of them have museums and art-collections of more than merely local importance. The summary routes given in this section are merely a selection from the innumerable routes that a close network of busy roads makes possible, aided by a widespread system of bus services. The hotels are comfortable and many of them have excellent restaurants.

A From Liverpool to Manchester

The Direct Road or East Lancashire Road (A 580; 32 m.) is a modern by-pass from Queen's Drive, the Liverpool ring road, at Walton, to Irlams-o'-th'-Height, where it joins A 6 to Manchester.—The Motorway (M 62; 34 m.) runs farther s. from Knotty Ash, crossing the M 6 N.E. of Warrington; at present its spur (M 602) joins A 57 at Salford.— The following roads serve the intervening towns:

I. Viâ Warrington direct

Road, 36 m. (A 57).—Railway, 34½ m., from Lime St. Station to *Manchester* (Piccadilly) in 50 min. hourly viâ Widnes and Warrington Central.

A 57 quits Liverpool by London Rd. and Prescot St.—8 m. *Prescot*, an old watchmaking town (12,600 inhab.), has a church with a classical exterior (1729) and a Jacobean roof (1610). To the N. extends *Knowsley Park*, enclosing within its 12 mile wall the princely seat of the Stanleys (Earls of Derby; no adm.) and a Safari Park of African animals (open daily;fee) with a dolphinarium.—At (10 m.) *Rainhill* (Hotel) we cross the original Liverpool and Manchester Railway (comp. below). Here the trial of locomotives, won by Stephenson's 'Rocket', took place prior to the opening; in commemoration this was the first stop made by the last scheduled steam passenger train to run in Britain (Liverpool to Carlisle) in 1968. *St Bartholomew's*, a R.C. church (1840) in the form of an Ionic prostyle temple, has a rich interior.— 10 m. **Warrington** (66,300 inhab.; Hotels), a town of ancient foundation, on the N. bank of the Mersey, is noted for its foundries, chemicals, and soap-works. Cromwell, whose statue stands by the bridge, lodged in the town after here defeating the Duke of Hamilton in 1648. The *Town Hall* has since 1872 occupied a mansion built by Gibbs in 1750. *Holy Trinity* was rebuilt in 1760, also probably by Gibbs. *St Elphin*, the parish church farther E., was virtually rebuilt in 1859–67 by F. and H. Francis with a tall spire (281 ft) which is among their best work. It contains a fine monument to Sir John Butler (d. 1463) and a War Memorial window by Hugh Easton. The *Museum & Library*, by John Dobson (1857), was the first rate-supported library in England.

Tablets mark the residence of Joseph Priestley (in 1761–67) and the site of the house in Bridge St. where John Howard lodged when printing his work on prison reform (between 1777 and 1789). *Warrington Academy*, founded in 1757 as a place of higher education for sons of Dissenters, numbered Priestley among its tutors, and Malthus among its pupils. It was dissolved in 1783, and its building is now a school. Warrington was the place of origin of both Independent and Primitive Methodism, and the first total abstinence society was established here in 1830 (comp. p. 551).

From Warrington to *London*, and to *Preston* and the North, see Rte 62. Bank Quay station, on the N.–S. line, is ¾ m. from Central station.

Beyond Warrington we cross M 6 and skirt the s. side of *Chat Moss* (comp. below), now reclaimed.—Beyond M 62 is (31 m.) *Patricroft*, with the Britannia Iron Foundry, established by James Nasmyth (1808–90), inventor of the steam-hammer.—32¼ m. *Eccles* (38,400 inhab.) is noted for its 'cakes', now mainly made in Manchester.—34 m. *Salford*.— 36 m. **Manchester**, see Rte 60.

II. Viâ St Helens

ROAD, 33½ m. (A 57, A 58, A 572).
RAILWAY, 31 m. from Lime St. to *Manchester* (Victoria) in ¾–1 hr c. hourly,
viâ (14 m.) *Earlestown*.—This line in its original form was completed in 1825–30
by George Stephenson. The chief difficulty was the carrying of the railroad across
the spongy surface of Chat Moss, a morass 4 m. wide, which was effected by the
construction of a floating embankment of compressed turf.

From Liverpool to (8 m.) *Prescot*, see above.—A 58 keeps left for
(11½ m.) **St Helens** (104,200 inhab.; Hotels) one of the chief centres in
the world of the glass industry, founded here in 1773. A **Glass Museum*
(1964) in the premises of Pilkington Bros. illustrates the history, manufacture, and technology of glass in all forms (adm. free, Mon–Fri 10–5,
Sat & Sun 2–4.30). There are also large iron and brick manufactures,
and coal is worked in the district. Sir Thomas Beecham (1879–1961)
was born here.

From St Helens A 58 goes on to (5 m.) *Ashton-in-Makerfield* (26,300 inhab.),
noted for its locks and hinges, s. of which is *Haydock Park* racecourse. Thence
it continues viâ (9 m.) *Hindley* (24,300 inhab.) to (15 m.) *Bolton* (Rte 61c).—Ashton
is also on A 49, the old N.–S. road through Lancashire (Rte 62); 4 m. N. along this
road is Wigan.
    Wigan (Hotel), possibly occupying the site of Roman *Coccium*, has long been a
prosperous manufacturing town (81,300 inhab.); coal-mining, bell-founding,
pewter and brass have now given way to plastics, coach-building, and canning.
The rebuilt church of *All Saints* has a partly 13C tower. *Mab's Cross*, at the top
of Standishgate, is mentioned in Scott's 'The Betrothed'. Heinz's factory at
Lambehead Green is an excellent example of modern industrial design. *Haigh
Hall* (1832–34), 2¼ m. N.E., formerly a seat of the Earl of Crawford, now belongs
to the town.

Beyond (16¼ m.) *Newton-le-Willows* (22,400 inhab.), with diesel-
electric works, we cross A 49 and M 6; and beyond (21¼ m.) *Leigh*, a
colliery and cotton centre (46,100 inhab.), we skirt the N. side of Chat
Moss (see above).—26½ m. *Worsley*, with 18–19C houses of the Bridgewater and Ellesmere estates, is the start of the Bridgewater Canal; near
the church the old canal basin, and the tunnel entrance to the mines.—
28½ m. *Patricroft*, and thence to (33¼ m.) **Manchester**, see above.

III. Viâ Widnes and Altrincham

ROAD, 40 m. (A 562, A 50, A 56).
We leave Liverpool by Princes Rd. and Sefton Park. *Allerton Hall*, the home of
Wm. Roscoe in 1799–1816, 1 m. s.w. of (6 m.) *Woolton*, was presented to Liverpool in 1925.—7½ m. *Speke* (r.), with the Liverpool airport. **Speke Hall* (N.T.),
built in 1598 by Sir Edward Norris, is one of the finest timbered manor-houses in
the country and is noted for its carved wainscoting (adm. weekdays 10–5 or 7,
Sun from 2; fee).—In the churchyard of (10 m.) *Hale* (r.) is buried John Middleton
(1578–1623), the 'Childe of Hale', reputed to have been 9 ft 3 in. in height.—13 m.
Widnes (56,700 inhab.), the chief seat of the alkali industry, with numerous chemical factories, is situated on the N. bank of the Mersey, opposite Runcorn (p. 373).
    20 m. **Warrington**, see above. We cross the Mersey on A 50, and at (21 m.)
Latchford cross the Ship Canal and join A 56.—25¼ m. *Lymm* (Hotel, a pleasant old
town, has a quaint market-cross and stocks.— 32 m. **Altrincham** (Hotels), a pleasant
'dormitory' town (40,800 inhab.), is noted for its market-gardens. The adjoining town
of *Bowdon* (Hotel) has a late-Perp. church with interesting monuments and was the
birthplace of John Ireland (1879–1962), the composer. *Dunham Massey*, 2 m. w., is the
seat of the Earl of Stamford (park open).—We enter the suburbs of Manchester and
beyond the twin towns of (35 m.) *Ashton-on-Mersey* and *Sale* recross the Mersey.—
Urmston, to the w. of (36¼ m.) *Stretford*, was the birthplace of 'Tim Bobbin' (John

Collier; 1708–86), dialect author and painter, a famous Lancashire 'character'. We enter (40 m.) **Manchester** through the suburb of Old Trafford.

B From Liverpool to Preston, Blackburn, Burnley, and Halifax

ROAD, 72½ m.—A 59 viâ Ormskirk and Preston to (34 m.) *Samlesbury*.—A 677 to (40½ m.) *Blackburn.*—A 679 to (51½ m.) *Burnley.*—A 646 to (73 m.) *Halifax*.
RAILWAY (viâ Ormskirk) to *Preston*, 27¾ m. in 70 min. A slow service connects Preston with Blackburn, Accrington, and Burnley.

We leave Liverpool by Scotland Rd. (A 59) and *Walton*, and pass (5 m.) *Aintree* (p. 537). To the left at 6½ m. is the 15C church of *Sefton*, with notable early monuments and magnificent 16C screens and stalls.— 12½ m. **Ormskirk** (27,600 inhab.) is an agricultural market town. The *Church*, mainly Perp. with Norman remains, has a tower and spire side by side, and contains the burial-chapel of the Stanleys (earls of Derby), whose seat, *Lathom House* (3 m. N.E.), was finally demolished in 1960.— 18 m. *Rufford*. The Old *Hall (N.T.; adm. Tues–Sat and BH, 12–6 or dusk, Sun from 1; fee; closed Dec & Jan), the home of the Heskeths till 1936, is an early Tudor building of timber and plaster, with wings added in 1662 and 1821. The great hall is notable for its hammer-beam roof, and contains fine arms and armour; in the newer wings is the Ashcroft 'Village Museum'.

30½ m. **Preston** (Hotel), long an important centre of Roman Catholicism, is an engineering and cotton-weaving town, with the county offices of Lancashire, a perplexing road pattern and docks on the Ribble. It has a pleasant late-Georgian quarter, large mills (many now put to other uses), many early 19C churches, and the largest bus station in Europe.

Its strategic position on the Ribble, astride the lowland route from Scotland, has made it important since Roman times. Once the capital of the ancient duchy of Lancaster, 'Proud Preston' was sacked by Robert Bruce in 1323, captured by the Parliamentary forces in 1643, and occupied by the Old Pretender in 1715 and by the Young Pretender in 1745. Arthur Devis (1711–87), the painter, Sir Richard Arkwright (1732–92), and Robert Service (1874–1958), the 'Canadian Kipling', were born here. The teetotal movement may be said to have started at Preston about 1830, under the advocacy of Joseph Livesey (1794–1884; but see p. 549).

The *Harris Museum and Art Gallery* (weekdays 10–5), an imposing building by James Hibbert (1882–93) in classical style, contains 19–20C British paintings (*James Gunn*, Pauline in the yellow dress) and works by the Devis family. Between Friargate and Fishgate extends an attractive shopping centre (1964), free of wheeled traffic.

About 6 m. S.E., beyond *Walton Bridge*, where Cromwell defeated the Duke of Hamilton in 1648, is *Hoghton Tower* (pron. 'Haw-ton'; adm. 2–5, Sun, Easter–Whitsun and mid-June–Oct; also Thurs & Sat and BH, mid-June–Sept; daily in Easter and Whit weeks; fee), a fortified 16C mansion, where James I is said to have knighted the loin of beef ('sirloin').
Ribbleton Lane (B 6243) ascends the N. side of Ribblesdale viâ (7 m.) *Longridge* and (10 m.) *Hurst Green* (Hotels) to (16 m.) *Clitheroe*, passing near Stonyhurst College (Rte 61c).—On B 6245 to the r. beyond Longridge, is *Ribchester*, on the Ribble 8 m. above Preston, with the well-defined Roman station of Bremetennacum (N.T.; weekdays 2–5.30; adm. fee, incl. museum; closed 1st week in Oct & Fri in winter). The 13–15C church is attractive, as is the old White Bull Inn. The fine bridge (1774) is 1½ m. upstream; while at *Stidd*, ¾ m. N., are a small Norman chapel and early 18C almshouses.
From Preston to *Blackpool* and to *Lancaster*, see Rte 62; to *Bolton*, see Rte 61c.—A car-ferry plies six times weekly from Preston to Larne (Ireland).

We leave Preston by New Hall Lane and cross the Ribble and M 6.—
35½ m. *Samlesbury Old Hall*, partly of the 16C, now contains a collection
of furniture. It was built by the Southworth family, best known of whom
is John Southworth (1592–1654), a Jesuit, and one of the 'English
Martyrs' canonized in 1970. Beyond an airfield A 59 bears left for
Clitheroe; we follow A 677.—From (40½ m.) **Blackburn** (Rte 61c)
A 679 leads E. to (45½ m.) **Accrington** (36,800 inhab.), a town engaged in
manufacturing cotton and bricks. It possesses in the *Haworth Art
Gallery* (free daily 2–5; also 6–8 Sun in summer) an unusual collection
of Tiffany glass, the invention of L. G. Tiffany of New York (d. 1933).—
A 646, by-passing the centre of (51½ m.) **Burnley** (Rte 61D), ascends
through moorland country and enters Yorkshire at (56¼ m.) *Cornholme.*
—At (61 m.) *Todmorden* (Hotel), a cotton-spinning town (15,150 inhab.),
the Post Office occupies the 17C Todmorden Hall. Sir John Cockcroft
(1897–1967), pioneer of radar and atomic energy was a native. We
descend the upland Vale of Todmorden, watered by the Calder.—
65 m. **Hebden Bridge** is a typical West Riding mill town, jammed into
the bottom of a narrow valley. The community of weavers from which
it sprung was at *Heptonstall* on the shoulder of the moor above; the
two are still connected by a steep pack-horse way. In Hebden Vale, 3 m.
N.W., are *Hardcastle Crags* in N.T. woods.

We climb out of the valley and pass above *Sowerby Bridge.*—73 m.
Halifax, see Rte 61E.

C   From Manchester to Bolton, Blackburn, and Settle

ROAD, 53 m. A 6 and A 666 viâ Bolton and Blackburn to (31 m.) *Whalley.*—
A 59 to (42 m.) *Gisburn.*—A 682 to (52 m.) *Settle.*
RAILWAY from Victoria Station to *Blackburn*, 24½ m. in ¾–1 hr. viâ Darwen;
to *Bolton*, 10¾ m., more frequently in 17–30 min.

The Bolton road leaves Manchester by Chapel St., Salford, and at
(3¼ m.) *Irlams-o'-th'-Height* bears right (A 666) towards the Irwell
valley.

11 m. **Bolton** (Hotels), one of the oldest seats of the woollen trade
(154,000 inhab.), is now the chief centre of the fine cotton-spinning
industry and has engineering and chemical works. Here Richard Arkwright, who was a barber in Church Gate, invented his water-frame in
1768, and Samuel Crompton (1753–1827), born at Firwood near by,
brought out his spinning-mule in 1779. These machines, and Hargraves' spinning-jenny may be seen at the *Textile Machinery Museum*
(weekdays, 9.30–7.30; closed Wed at 1, Sat at 5.30), in Tonge Moor Rd.
(A 676; N.E.). The imposing classical *Town Hall* was opened in 1873;
the near-by *Civic Centre*, completed in 1939, contains a Museum and
Art Gallery (free weekdays, 10–5.30, 6, or 8).

The town was sacked in 1644 by Prince Rupert and the Earl of Derby, and
when the latter was captured at the battle of Worcester seven years later he was
sent to Bolton and beheaded opposite the 'Man & Scythe' in Church Gate.
Bolton School was founded in 1524. About 2 m. N. (bus 46) is *Hall-i'-th'-Wood*,
a half-timbered house in which Crompton lived in 1758–82 and invented the
spinning-mule. It was bought by the first Lord Leverhulme (1851–1925; b. in
Bolton), restored, and presented by him to the town. It is now open as a museum
(weekdays 10–6 exc. Thurs; Sun 2–6 in summer) with 16C furnishings and Crompton relics.—Another interesting old manor-house is *Smithills Hall*, 2½ m. N.W.—

Turton Tower, 4½ m. N. of Bolton, 16C and older, contains a museum of old furniture and weapons (adm. Wed & Sat, 2–dusk; fee).—A fine moorland road (A 675) leads N.W. to Preston (18¾ m.) viâ Belmont and Hoghton (see Rte 61B).

FROM BOLTON TO CHORLEY AND PRESTON, 19 m. (A 673, A 6).—3 m. *Lostock* preserves the gatehouse (1591) of its demolished hall. Above (5¾ m.) *Horwich* (16,400 inhab.), with locomotive works and paper-mills, are the *Rivington Reservoirs*, supplying Liverpool, and the conspicuous *Rivington Pike* (1190 ft; fine view). On the slope of the Pike is the splendid *Lever Park* (400 acres), with the 18C Rivington Hall and barn; in the village is a good 16–17C church and a Unitarian chapel of 1703.—10 m. **Chorley** (Hotel) is a cotton-weaving and engineering town (31,600 inhab.), the birthplace of Henry Tate (1819), sugar refiner and donor of London's Tate Gallery. *Duxbury Hall*, demolished in 1955, the probable birthplace of the doughty Myles Standish (1584–1656), stood 1½ m. s. *Astley Hall*, ¾ m. N.W., an Elizabethan mansion in fine grounds, contains Cromwellian furniture and 17C Flemish tapestries (adm. daily, Apr–Sept 2–8; Oct–March 12–5). *Euxton*, on the main Wigan–Preston road, 1½ m. farther W., has an important arsenal, and at *Leyland* (23,400 inhab.), 2 m. N.W. of Euxton, are commercial motor works.— 19 m. *Preston*, see Rte 61B.

Beyond (15 m.) *Egerton*, where the 19C church has a 15C Spanish altarpiece, the road crosses bleak moors, diversified by ravines.—19 m. *Darwen* (28,900 inhab.) has cotton mills, paper mills, and chemical and paint works.

24 m. **Blackburn** (Hotel) is perhaps the greatest cotton-weaving centre in the world (101,700 inhab.). Since 1926 it has been the see of a bishop, and the parish church (1819–31), now the cathedral, is being greatly enlarged; the rebuilding of the crossing and transepts was begun in 1937 and completed in 1950. *Blackburn Museum* (weekdays, 9.30–8, Sat to 6) has historical and military collections and good coins. The *Lewis Textile Museum* (adm. free, weekdays 10–5, Wed & Fri to 7.30), in Exchange St., contains a series of period rooms illustrating the development of the spinning and weaving industry. James Hargraves (d. 1778), the inventor of the spinning-jenny, was a Blackburn weaver, but, his house and machinery being destroyed by the mob, he set up his works at Nottingham. Another famous native was Viscount Morley of Blackburn (1838–1923).

From Blackburn to *Preston*, and to *Burnley* and *Halifax*, see Rte 61.

Beyond Blackburn we leave the industrial district and emerge into the pleasant valley of the Ribble.—31 m. *Whalley* has the remains of a once splendid Cistercian abbey and an interesting church (Dec. and Perp.), where the fine woodwork, includes 15C stalls from the abbey with notable misericords, and there are three Anglian churchyard crosses (early 11C).

Whalley Abbey (adm. daily 10–dusk; fee) was transferred from Stanlow in Cheshire in 1296. Its 17th and last abbot, John Paslew, was hanged in 1537 on the pretext of complicity in the 'Pilgrimage of Grace'. Of the church (1330–80) little more than the foundations survive; and the chief remains are the fine N.W. gatehouse (1320), on a public road, the N.E. gatehouse (1480), by which we enter, and the cloister (c. 1375–1440). The W. walk, with the lay-brothers' and cellarer's quarters, now serves as a hall for a Rom. Cath. church; the E. walk preserves the entry to the octagonal chapter house. Behind it are some remains of the abbot's lodge, most of which, altered to form a dwelling-house by the Asshetons, is now a diocesan conference house (no adm.).

John Mercer (1791–1866), textile chemist and inventor of 'mercerising', was born at *Dean*, 1¾ m. s.—To the N.W. of Whalley, viâ *Great Mitton*, with the 14–18C hall and monuments (16–18C) of the Shireburns, beautifully situated above the junction of the Hodder and Calder wîth the Ribble, is (4 m.) *Stonyhurst*, a famous Roman Catholic school for boys, founded by the Jesuits at St Omer in 1593 and transferred hither in 1794. In amalgamation has recently come the senior part of Beaumont School, though the Preparatory school remained at Old Windsor. The nucleus of the extensive buildings is the Elizabethan mansion built by Sir Richard Shireburn in 1594–1606. The library includes copies of Froissart's 'Chronicles' and Caxton's 'Golden Legende', and other early works; among the curiosities are Mary Stuart's Horæ and More's hat and seal. Among the historic vestments in the Church is Henry VII's cope, worn by Henry VIII at the Field of the Cloth of Gold.

35 m. **Clitheroe** (13,200 inhab.; Hotel), the farthest N. of the cotton towns, retains the shell of a Norman castle, commandingly situated on a limestone rock. To the E. rises *Pendle Hill* (1831 ft; *View), associated with the 'Lancashire Witches' and with George Fox's mission of 1652.

A fine moorland road (B 6243) leads w. across the Ribble (here the boundary between Lancs and Yorks) to (8 m.) *Whitewell* (Hotel), and thence to (10¼ m.) *Dunsop Bridge*, where it joins the road through the Trough of Bowland from Lancaster (see Rte 62).—Another good hill-drive (B 6478) leads N. viâ (1½ m.) *Waddington* and (3¼ m.) the *Moorcock Inn* to (6½ m.) *Newton*, 1½ m. s.w. of *Slaidburn* (p. 570).

About 1 m. E. of (37 m.) *Chatburn* is the pretty village of *Downham*, with its Tudor manor-house. We enter Yorkshire before (38½ m.) *Sawley Abbey*, a ruined Cistercian house (l.) founded in 1148.—From (42 m.) *Gisburn* (Hotel) a road leads (l.) to the charming village of *Bolton-by-Bowland* (3 m.). We turn left for (49½ m.) *Long Preston*, 3½ m. s. of **Settle**, see Rte 62B.

D   From Manchester to Bury, Burnley, and Skipton

ROAD, 42 m. (A 56).—RAILWAY, to *Bury*, 24½ m., from Victoria Station, every ½ hr in 24 min. (not Sun). *Accrington, Burnley*, and *Colne* are served by slow trains from Preston; from Manchester, change at Blackburn.

A 56 follows the Bury New Road.—8½ m. **Bury** (Hotel), with 67,800 inhab., manufactures woollen yarn, and has paper-making, dyeing, and engineering works. Calico-printing was introduced into Lancashire by Robert Peel, whose grandson, the prime minister (1788–1850), was born at Bury and is commemorated by a statue in the market-place. A monument in Kay Gardens commemorates John Kay (1704–64), inventor of the fly-shuttle (1743), who was mobbed by his townsmen and died a pauper in France. The *Art Gallery & Museum* (free weekdays, 10–6, Sat 10–5) contains the Wrigley Collection of 19C paintings, watercolours, and engravings. A new *Town Hall* was opened in 1954 and some good Victorian buildings survive. Kay's cottage, at Park, 4 m. N., has recently been restored.

The road now ascends the narrowing valley of the Irwell, "the most long-suffering stream in the Kingdom".—At (12½ m.) *Ramsbottom* (l.) were the printing works of Messrs. Grant, the originals of the Cheeryble Brothers in 'Nicholas Nickleby'. We leave on the left a road to Accrington viâ *Haslingden* (2½ m.), the centre of the cotton-waste trade, and ascend through the *Forest of Rossendale*, a moorland district. From (16½ m.) *Rawtenstall* A 681 leads E. to Bacup (4 m.), a town in the heart of Rossendale, noted especially for its felt slippers as well as for cotton-spinning and weaving, and to *Todmorden* (Rte 61B).

23½ m. **Burnley** (Hotels), situated in a pretty district blackened by its industries, is the centre of cotton-weaving (76,900 inhab.) and has also spinning and dyeing works, engineering works, and collieries. The parish church contains the monument of Charles Towneley (1737–1805), the collector of the Towneley Marbles at the British Museum. *Towneley Hall* (free weekdays 10–5 or 5.30; Sun 1 or 2–5), in a large public park 1½ m. s.E., is a medieval mansion rebuilt in the 18C when the late-15C chapel was removed to its present site. It contains notable plaster-work, paintings (Charles Towneley, by Zoffany), and ceramics. The Brew House displays local crafts. The Jacobean *Gawthorpe Hall* (1600–5), 2⅔ m. w. near *Padiham* (which has a font from Whalley Abbey in its church), is built round a pele tower, the home of the Shuttleworths from c. 1300. The house (N.T.) with the Kay-Shuttleworth Collection of printed textiles, etc., may be seen Tues, Wed, Sat, Sun & BH, 2–6, mid-March–Oct; fee.

At *Hurstwood*, 3½ m. E. of Burnley, Spenser is said to have written 'The Shepheard's Calendar' (1579), and there are several 16C manor-houses on the moors to the E. To *Preston* and to *Halifax*, see Rte 61B.—27½ m. *Nelson* (31,200 inhab.).—

29½ m. **Colne** (18,900 inhab.) is an ancient textile centre, with a well-restored church and 'mobile stocks'. A museum devoted to the British in India (adm. Sat & Sun 2–5, May–Sept; fee) occupies a converted sweet factory in Sun St. To the w. rises Pendle Hill and to the E. extend the Haworth moors.—Beyond (31½ m.) *Foulridge* we enter Yorkshire.—42 m. *Skipton*, see p. 610.

E From Manchester to Rochdale, Halifax, and Bradford

Road, 39 m. A 664 to (13 m.) *Rochdale.*—A 58 to (31 m.) *Halifax.*—A 647 or 6036 to (39 m.) *Bradford.*—MOTORWAY, M 62, see Rte 61F.

RAILWAY from Victoria Station, frequent service to *Rochdale* in ¼ hr; hourly to *Halifax* (c. 1 hr) and *Bradford* (c. 1¼ hr). Intermediate Stations: 10½ m. **Rochdale.**—13¾ m. *Littleborough.*—19¼ m. *Todmorden.*—24 m. *Hebden Bridge.*—29 m. *Sowerby Bridge,* junction for Wakefield.—32½ m. **Halifax.**—40½ m. **Bradford** (Exchange).

We leave Manchester by the Rochdale Road and the suburb of *Blackley,* with the public park of Boggart Hole Clough (188 acres).—7½ m. *Middleton,* formerly a silk and cotton town (53,400 inhab.) now has plastics and chemical industries. The commanding church has a curious tower and contains a 16C screen, brasses of the Asshetons, and a stained-glass window commemorating Flodden (1513).

13 m. **Rochdale** (Hotels), with 91,300 inhab., is noted for its blankets, calicoes, and flannels and for many other industries. The baronial *Town Hall* (1866), by W. H. Crossland, near the Parish Church, stands in pleasant grounds. John Bright (1811–89), the son of a mill-owner, was born, lived, and is buried (in the Friends' graveyard) at Rochdale and is commemorated by a statue. The co-operative movement originated at Rochdale in 1844 with the foundation of the Society of Equitable Pioneers (shop in Toad Lane now a museum). The moors to the E. and N.W., with many reservoirs, are still attractive.

From (16½ m.) *Littleborough* the road climbs to the moors. Just before the summit (1269 ft), where we cross the Pennine Way, a *Roman road carries straight over *Blackstone Edge*; a long stretch of paving retains the central gutter in which turves gave the horses added foothold on the hill. We enter Yorkshire, descending from Rishworth Moor by the beautiful *Vale of Ripponden* to (28½ m.) *Sowerby Bridge,* on the Calder.

31 m. **Halifax** (Hotels) rises steeply on the slopes of the Hebble valley. The cloth trade moulded the town (91,200 inhab.) which is dominated by its mills. The vast *Piece Hall* (1779) was the old cloth market; some of its 300 rooms opening from a colonnaded court display textile machinery (open 11–5 or 7; Sun 2.30–5). The low-lying parish church of *St John* (15C) contains a quantity of old oak, a life-size wooden beggar ('Old Tristram') by the poor-box, and a monument to Bp. Ferrar (d. 1555), the martyr, born at Midgley 4½ m. w. More conspicuous is the (burnt) *Congregational Church* (1857) with its lofty spire (235 ft). The *Town Hall* is an Italianate work by the Barrys, father and son (1862). *Bankfield Museum,* in Akroyd Park, has a collection of costume and fabric.

All Souls' (1859), in Haley Hill (A 647), was considered by Sir Gilbert Scott to be his best church. Higher up, in Ackroyd Park, *Bankfield Museum* (adm. free weekdays, 11–5 or 7; Sun 2.30–5) contains good textile exhibits (Balkan, Burmese, etc.), silver, natural history collections, etc., and a model of the celebrated Halifax Gibbet (base preserved on Gibbet St.), the precursor of the guillotine, by which stealers of cloth of a value greater than 13½d. were summarily executed down to 1650 ("From Hell, Hull, and Halifax, Good Lord, deliver us!"). Here also is the museum of the Duke of Wellington's Regiment.—Laurence Sterne was at school in

Halifax (1723–31) and Sir Matthew Smith (1879–1959) was a native. Here in 1934 Percy Shaw invented reflecting road studs ('cats eyes').

Just E. of Halifax, in an attractive park with a lake in the valley below, is **Shibden Hall**, a 15–17C house, partly timber-framed, containing period furniture and late 16C wall-paintings in the dining-room (shown on request). The fascinating *West Yorkshire Folk Museum, in its outbuildings and barn with superb woodwork, includes craft workshops, a brewhouse, agricultural implements, and a collection of carriages. Adm. Apr–Sept, weekdays 11–7, Sun 2–5; Oct and March, weekdays 11–5, Sun 2–5; in Feb Sun only; closed Nov–Jan.—The road, ascending steeply, goes on to Bradford.

Luddenden, in a steep valley 2 m. N.W. of Halifax, preserves the cobbled streets, mills, and cottages of a typical weaving village.

On Good Friday the 'Pace Egg Play' is acted at *Midgley* (see above), and other points in the Calder valley, by boys of Calder High School.

From Halifax to *Todmorden, Blackburn*, etc., see Rte 61B.

39 m. **BRADFORD** (293,800 inhab.) stands in a broad basin on a tributary of the Aire. Though it remains the great traditional centre of the worsted trade, engineering is now nearly as important and industry generally diversified. It became a cathedral city in 1920 and its Institute of Technology was raised to university status in 1966. Bradford was the first and last place in Britain to operate trolley-buses (1911–72). Frederick Delius (1863–1934), the composer, was born here. Sir Henry Irving died suddenly in a Bradford hotel (1905) after a performance of 'Becket'.

Railway Stations. *Exchange*, Leeds Rd. and Bridge St., for main line trains. *Forster Square* for Ilkley, Keighley, etc.

Hotels, with traditional comforts, near the stations.

Post Office, Forster Square.

Theatre. *Alhambra*, Victoria Square.—CONCERTS in *St George's Hall*, Bridge St.— WINDSOR SWIMMING-BATHS, Gt. Horton Road.

Bus Station, Chester Street; for local buses, near Town Hall.

Airport (Leeds–Bradford) at *Yeadon*, 6½ m. N.E.; services, see p. 563.

Bradford has little antiquarian interest, but the stone commercial buildings of the Victorian era lend a dignified air to the city in contrast with the modern structures in the 'redeveloped' squares. The *City Hall* (1873; cleaned), with a campanile 200 ft in height, and the *Wool Exchange* (1867), are both by a local firm in the Gothic style. Above Forster Square is the **Cathedral** (*St Peter's*), the former Parish church (14–15C), which has been greatly extended by Maufe (1951–63). Within, noteworthy are the beautiful 15C font-cover, the modern woodwork, and the stained glass by Morris (1862) in the Lady Chapel (1961–63).

The *Grammar School*, refounded by Charles II in 1662, is in the Keighley road, c. 1½ m. N.W. (viâ Cheapside). In *Lister Park* (53 acres), opposite, is the ornate CARTWRIGHT MEMORIAL HALL (*Art Gallery and Museum*, 1904), presented by Lord Masham in honour of Edmund Cartwright (1743–1823), reputed inventor of the power-loom, with a good collection of British and a few foreign paintings, drawings and studies (these shown on application), and sculpture; also an interesting collection of model engines (adm. free, weekdays 10–5, 7 or 8).

Bolling Hall, a manor-house (15–18C), 1 m. s. of the centre (bus 60 from behind City Hall), was the ancestral home of Edith Bolling, wife of President Woodrow Wilson. It now contains a good collection of old furniture and domestic objects (adm. as above).

At *Thornton*, 4 m. w. of the centre of the city on a bus route to Haworth, is the house where Charlotte, Emily, Anne, and Branwell Brontë were born (in Market

St., a turning off High St.; tablet).—At *Fulneck*, 4 m. E. (1 m. S. of *Pudsey*), is the oldest Moravian church in England (c. 1742–50).

Bradford is 9½ m. W. of *Leeds* (by A 647) and 3 m. S. of *Shipley*, in Airedale (see Rte 61H).

F From Manchester to Huddersfield and Leeds

ROAD, 40¼ m. (A 62).—RAILWAY from Victoria Station, express service every 2 hrs to (7¾ m.) *Stalybridge*; (25½ m.) *Huddersfield* in 40 min.; and (42¾ m.) *Leeds* (City) in 70 min.—A MOTORWAY (M 62) crosses the Pennines S. of Rochdale, passes over the holding dam of Scammonden Reservoir, S.E. of Ripponden, and runs N. of Huddersfield, serving Bradford and Leeds by spurs.

Oldham Rd. runs N.E. through dreary suburbs.—7 m. **Oldham** (Hotels) is an old-established cotton-spinning town (105,700 inhab.) set on a hill, and is noted also for textile machinery. The *Town Hall* (1841, enlarged 1880) is derived from Stuart's drawing of the 'Temple by the Ilissos' in Athens (since destroyed). It stands at the top of Yorkshire St., opposite the *Parish Church* (1827–30) by Richard Lane. The famous 'Oldham Wakes' begin on the penultimate Sat in June. Winston Churchill was first elected M.P. at Oldham in 1900.

A 62 enters Yorkshire beyond Oldham and gradually ascends towards the head of the Tame valley. *Delph* and *Dobcross*, N. and S. of the road, were once important centres of clothmaking, and retain old cobbled streets and weavers' stone houses. The summit of the moors is reached on (14½ m.) *Standedge* (1271 ft), beneath which is the Standedge Tunnel (3 m. 63 yds; completed 1849), the fourth longest in England, alongside the tunnel of the Huddersfield Canal (3½ m.; built 1811).—17½ m. *Marsden* and (20 m.) *Slaithwaite*, in the Colne valley, afford access to fine moorland scenery to the South.

25½ m. **Huddersfield** (Hotels), a strikingly placed town (131,000 inhab.) with wide streets, is the third of the Yorkshire 'cloth towns', widely known for the music of its choral society. The *Railway Station* (1847) is successfully classical in style. In *Ravensknowle Park*, 1½ m. E. on the Wakefield road, are a shelter made from the old *Cloth Hall* (1766) and a hypocaust from Slack (the Roman Cambodunum, 3½ m. w.); also the *Tolson Memorial Museum* (adm. free 10.30–5, or 7, Sun 2–5), with good collections of local antiquities and exhibits showing the development of the cloth industry. A 17C barn, ¼ m. downhill, houses old farming implements and industrial tools (key with the curator).

In the pleasant environs are *Castle Hill* (2 m. S.), with an Early Iron Age camp, surmounted by a 19C tower; and, to the S.E., *Almondbury* (2 m.), with a good late Perp. church; the Tudor *Woodsome Hall* (now a golf club); and *Kirkburton* (5 m.), with an early 13C church containing remains of a 9C cross. *Skelmanthorpe* church, 2½ m. farther on, has an 11C font. The area is dominated by the fine television tower (900 ft) by Ove Arup on *Emley Moor*.

FROM HUDDERSFIELD TO SHEFFIELD, 26 m. (A 616).—Railway, 27¾ m. in c. 1 hr.— From (3½ m.) *Honley* a branch road ascends (r.) to the grim town of *Holmfirth* (2½ m.), and thence over bleak moors to Woodhead (10½ m.).—Beyond (10½ m.) *Hazlehead Bridge*, on the Don, we cross the Manchester–Barnsley road at (11½ m.) the *Flouch Inn* and descend viâ (12½ m.) *Langsett* and (14½ m.) *Midhopestones* (to the Derwent Valley, see Rte 45D).—At (17¾ m.) *Deepcar* we reach the attractive *Wharncliffe Woods*, which may be visited also from (21¼ m.) *Oughtibridge*. About 1½ m. N. of the last is *Wharncliffe Lodge*, in which Lady Mary Wortley Montagu lived for some time after her marriage. A shallow rocky recess below the natural terrace extending along the *Wharncliffe Crags* (view) is pointed out as the den of the fabled 'Dragon of Wantley' (perhaps a corruption of 'Wharncliffe').—26 m. *Sheffield*, see Rte 61H.

28½ m. *Cooper Bridge*. To the left is *Kirklees*, with some remains of a Cistercian nunnery (incorporated in a farm) and the alleged grave of Robin Hood.

To the right is A 644, which traverses the principal seats of the West Riding heavy woollen industry.—At *Mirfield* (1½ m.; 16,900 inhab.) is the Community of the Resurrection, a large theological college.—4½ m. **Dewsbury** (51,300 inhab.) has a *Museum* in Crow Nest Park and a rebuilt *Church*, in which are fragments of a 9C cross and some 13–14C stained glass. **Batley** (42,000 inhab.), 1½ m. N. on A 652, where the manufacture of shoddy was invented, has a 13–15C church. *Thornhill*, 2¼ m. s. of Dewsbury, has a church with much 15C stained glass, monuments of the Savile family (15–20C), and Saxon cross-fragments.

The main Leeds road goes on to (31 m.) *Heckmondwike* (9400 inhab.), a centre of the blanket industry, and (33 m.) *Birstall*.

This is the district described in Charlotte Brontë's 'Shirley': 2 m. s.w. of Heckmondwike is *Roehead*, with Miss Wooller's school, where Charlotte was a pupil in 1831–2 and a teacher in 1835–8; at *Hartshead*, 1 m. N. of this, is 'Nunnely Church'; *Birstall* is 'Briarfield'; the Red House at *Gomersal*, ½ m. w. of Birstall, is ''Briarmains'; and the Elizabethan *Oakwell Hall*, ¾ m. N.W. of Birstall, is 'Fieldhead'. The last, with period furniture, is open weekdays (exc. Mon), 10–5 or 6; Sun, summer only, 1–5. *Morley* (44,300 inhab.), another woollen-cloth town, 3 m. N.E. of Birstall, was the birthplace of Lord Asquith (1852–1928).

40½ m. **Leeds**, see Rte 61H.

G From Manchester to Penistone and Sheffield

ROAD, 39½ m. A 57 to (9½ m.) *Mottram*.—A 628 to (26½ m.) *Penistone*.—A 629 thence to *Sheffield*. From Manchester to Sheffield viâ the Peak District, see Rte 45D.

RAILWAY from Piccadilly Station, 42¼ m., in 1 hr.

The Hyde road runs E. from Manchester and, beyond (5½ m.) *Denton* (38,100 inhab.), crosses the Tame.— 7 m. *Hyde* (37,100 inhab.) is one of a group of cotton-manufacturing and coal-mining towns in the once beautiful Tame valley.

Oldest and most important of these is (2 m. N.) **Ashton-under-Lyne** (48,900 inhab.), 6 m. E. of Manchester, which retains some magnificent *Glass of c. 1500 in its church. *Stalybridge* (22,800 inhab.) and *Dukinfield* (17,300 inhab.), adjoining Ashton, were formerly in Cheshire; and farther upstream are (7½ m.) *Mossley* (10,100 inhab.), and (11 m.) *Saddleworth* (20,500 inhab.), noted for its fine woollen cloth. At Stalybridge a tablet on the New Market Inn records the writing here in 1912 of the famous song 'Tipperary'.

9½ m. *Mottram* has a fine Perp. church. We enter *Longdendale*, watered by the Etherow and almost filled with reservoirs, leaving A 57 (for Glossop) on our right.—Beyond (16½ m.) *Woodhead*, a deserted site where the moor-road to Huddersfield bears left, we see the mouth of the Woodhead Tunnel (3 m. 66 yds), which pierces the hard millstone grit of the Pennine Chain, or 'backbone of England', and emerges in Yorkshire. The digging of the first tunnel (1840–46), one of the great feats of Victorian building, cost a toll of 32 'navvies' killed and 250 injured. This tunnel is disused; the second twin tunnel (1847–52) has been reopened to carry electricity cables. A new twin-track tunnel has carried the railway since electrification in 1954.—A long descent, past (23 m.) the *Flouch Inn* (Rte 61F), brings us to the rocky valley of the

Don and to (26¼ m.) **Penistone**, a bleak little town (7300 inhab.) with steel works and a fine Dec. church.

The Barnsley road, diverging to the left, passes through a beautiful district which is also one of the richest coalfields in England. Its centre is (3 m.) *Silkstone*, with a church containing fine woodwork, a monument to Sir Thos. Wentworth (d. 1675), and a memorial to Joseph Bramah (1748–1814), the hydraulic engineer. Adjoining the charming village of *Cawthorne* (c. 2 m. N.), where the church has two fonts (11C and Perp.), are the grounds of *Cannon Hall* (adm. free; 10.30–5, Sun 2.30–5), built mainly in the 18C by Carr and now a museum of interesting furniture and pictures.—7¼ m. *Barnsley*, see Rte 61H.

To the s.w. of (31 m.) *Wortley*, with a forge of 1711, are the Wharncliffe Woods (p. 557).—39½ m. **Sheffield**, see below.

H Sheffield, Leeds, and Airedale

SHEFFIELD (519,700 inhab.), the chief centre in England for the production of high-quality steel, and seat of a bishop and of a university, is the largest town in Yorkshire. It is situated at the confluence of the river Sheaf with the Don, in a naturally beautiful position at the foot of the Derbyshire hills, and, though once "one of the foulest towns in England in the most charming situation", as Horace Walpole wrote in 1760, it now claims the cleanest air of any manufacturing city in Europe. The residential suburbs and the neighbouring country to the w. are very attractive, and the Peak District is within easy reach (comp. Rte 45D). Good planning and architecture are beginning to transform the centre of the city.

Railway Station. *Midland.*
Hotels in the centre, and in the suburbs.
Post Office, Fitzalan Sq.—INFORMATION SERVICE, Central Library, Surrey St.
Bus Station in Pond St.
Theatres. *Crucible,* Arundel Gates; *Library Theatre,* Tudor Place.—CONCERTS at City Hall.
Swimming-Baths in Glossop Rd., etc.—GOLF COURSES at Beauchief and Tinsley Park (municipal), also several clubs.—COUNTY CRICKET GROUND at Bramall Lane.
History. The manor of *Hallam,* or *Hallamshire,* a term now embracing Sheffield and the neighbouring localities where the cutlery industry is carried on, belonged at the time of the Conquest to Earl Waltheof, the 'last of the Saxon barons', beheaded in 1075. In 1406 the estates came to the Talbots, earls of Shrewsbury, and in the 17C to the Howards, whose descendant, the Duke of Norfolk, is still the chief landowner in the city. Mary, Queen of Scots, spent most of her captivity from 1570 to 1584 in the custody of the Earl of Shrewsbury at Sheffield, partly in the Norman castle and partly in the Manor Lodge. The castle was wholly destroyed after its capture by the Parliamentarians in 1644.—Since the time when the miller in Chaucer's Canterbury Tales bore "a Sheffield thwitel in his hose", the town has been famous for its cutlery, and its present production of steel and tools of all kinds is enormous. Coal and water-power are abundant in the neighbourhood, but the iron ore is nearly all imported, mainly from Sweden. The great steel works now stretch in an unbroken line down the valley of the Don, N.E. through the suburbs of *Attercliffe, Brightside,* and *Tinsley* to Rotherham. In 1740 Benjamin Huntsman invented the crucible process of steel production, and in 1742 Thomas Bolsover discovered that silver could be bonded to copper and then rolled into sheets, producing the famous 'Sheffield plate', now superseded by electroplate. Born at Attercliffe were Joseph Locke (1805–60), the railway engineer, and John Stringfellow (1799–1883), who flew the first heavier-than-air machine.

From the *Midland Station* Pond Street ascends past the *Sheffield*

Polytechnic (left) to FITZALAN SQUARE, with the *Post Office* (pedestrians may follow an alternative sign-posted route from the station to the city centre). In Waingate is the ingenious *Castle Hill Market* (1960–65, by J. L. Womersley). High St. leads w. across Church Sq. to Church St. with Fargate opening on the left. In Church St. is the **Cathedral** (*SS Peter & Paul*), of the bishopric founded in 1914, a building dating back to the 14–15C, with a crocketed spire. The *Shrewsbury Chapel*, added prior to 1538 on the s. side of the 15C chancel, contains the interesting monuments of the earls of Shrewsbury, including that of the sixth Earl, Queen Mary's keeper, with an epitaph composed by Foxe. In the chancel is a monument by Chantrey, perhaps his first work (comp. below). The nave was partly rebuilt in 1805; on the N. side is the Chapel of the Holy Spirit (1949), by Sir Charles Nicholson, who was responsible also for the chapter house (1939).

To the N. of the cathedral lies Paradise Square, a quiet oasis of Georgian houses, at No. 24 of which Chantrey lived in 1802; Wesley preached to his largest weekday congregation here in 1779 (plaque). On the opposite side of Church St. stands CUTLERS' HALL, a 'Grecian' building of 1832, containing a few busts and portraits. The Company of Cutlers, incorporated in 1624, though shorn of many of its ancient privileges, still possesses the right of granting trade marks. An annual feast is given by the Master Cutler in March.

The TOWN HALL, at the end of Fargate, is a gabled Renaissance building by E. W. Mountford (1897), with St Paul's Gardens on its s. side. The tower, 210 ft high, is crowned with a 7 ft bronze statue of Vulcan. Facing Barker's Pool, farther w., is the Corinthian portico of the **City Hall**, a dignified classical building by E. Vincent Harris (1932), decorated by G. Kruger Gray.

In Surrey St. is the large building of the **Central Library**, opened in 1934, which includes an important technology department and the Wentworth Woodhouse muniments; the Burke papers, presented in 1949 by Lord FitzWilliam, are accessible to students. The *Graves Art Gallery (adm. 10–8, Sun 2–5), due mainly to the munificence of J. G. Graves (d. 1945), of Sheffield, occupies the top floor.

Owing to the lack of space in which to show the whole of the 1500 paintings in the possession of the gallery, each room is hung afresh every six weeks, and the collection is therefore shown in successive groups. Bona-fide scholars and interested visitors are, however, given access to any picture not exhibited, provided application (preferably in writing) is made to the Director. The collection contains the 'Ruskin Madonna' by *Verrocchio*, possibly partly by the young *Leonardo da Vinci*, and includes works by *Clouet, Rubens, Gainsborough, Turner, Constable, Whistler, Cotman, Richard Wilson*, and *Epstein*, and the *Grice Collection* of Chinese ivories. The watercolours of the British School are among the best in the country.

The **University** of Sheffield, incorporated in 1905, occupies a series of important buildings in Western Bank, a continuation west of Broad Lane. It had its origin in *Firth College*, founded in 1879, and the Sheffield School of Medicine, founded in 1828. The list of faculties includes arts, pure science, law, medicine, metallurgy, engineering, mining, and glass technology. The large new *Library* dates from 1953–59, the *Arts and Economics Building*, 225 ft high, from 1963–65. Just beyond is the beautiful *Weston Park* (bus 52), which contains an observatory and a statue of Ebenezer Elliott, the 'Corn Law Rhymer' (born

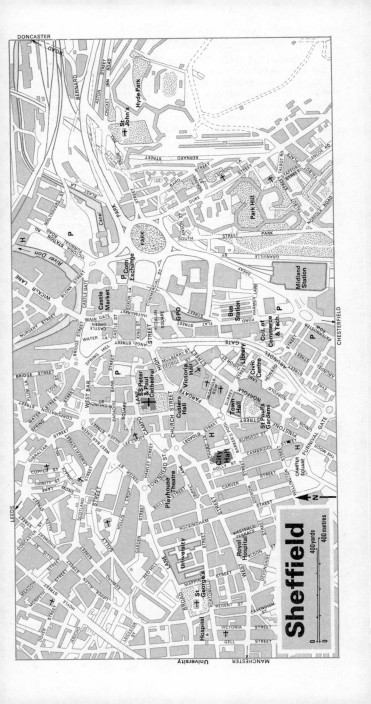

Sheffield

400 yards
400 metres

at Masborough in 1781). The *City Museum* (10–5 or 8.30 in summer; Sun from 2), in the park, includes the most extensive collection of Sheffield plate in existence, cutlery, and other metal-work, porcelain and silver, and archaeological and geological collections. The *Mappin Art Gallery* adjoining (adm. as above), houses permanent and loan exhibitions from the Graves Art Gallery.—*St Mark's*, Broomfield Rd., the university church, has been rebuilt by George Pace with a w. window by Piper and Reyntiens (1960).

The spectacular *Hyde Park* and *Park Hill* estates, by J. L. Womersley, rising up the steep slope above the river Sheaf, E. of Midland Station, are important examples of new high-density housing, with raised streets; while at *Gleadless*, 2 m. s., on the Chesterfield Rd., the low houses have been set into the hill-side.

A 10-mile perambulation of the city viâ paths, parks, and farms in the ownership of the Corporation may be followed (information at the City Library).

Abbeydale Rd., branching to the right from London Rd., forms the main approach to the pleasant s.w. suburbs of Sheffield. The chapel of (4 m.) *Beauchief* (bus 61, 63), to the left, with its 14C tower and arches, is a relic of a Premonstratensian abbey (1183). To the N. of this are the pleasant *Whirlow Brook Park* and the fine *Botanical Garden* (bus 50), with three greenhouses built in 1836. One mile farther N. in Whiteley Woods, beside the Porter beck, is the *Abbeydale Industrial Hamlet* (adm. 11–5 or 8 in summer; fee) with 18C crucible kilns and the last working example of a 'little mester's' grinding wheel.—At (6 m.) *Totley* is the mouth of the Totley Tunnel (3½ m.), the second longest in England. Thence the road goes on to (13½ m.) *Baslow*, in the Peak District (see Rte 45C).

Norfolk Rd. leads out S.E. to the public *Norfolk Park*. To the E. are the remains of *Manor Lodge*, a 16C mansion occupied occasionally by Queen Mary during her captivity. Wolsey spent 18 days here in 1530 on his way to Leicester.—At *Norton*, 3½ m. s., an obelisk commemorates Sir Francis Chantrey (1781–1841), who was born and buried here. Several of his works may be seen at *Oakes Park*, ½ m. E.

The road from Sheffield to Doncaster (A 630; 18 m.) traverses (6½ m.) **Rotherham** (Hotel), a murky colliery and iron-working town (84,600 inhab.) on the Don. On the altered 15C bridge is an ancient chantry. *All Saints*, with its crocketed spire, is one of the finest Perp. churches in the North, with a Jacobean pulpit, and fine bench-ends in the choir. The *Museum and Art Gallery* (weekdays exc. Fri, 10–5 or 6, Sun 2.30–4.30; Thurs 10–8) in *Clifton Park* is housed in a charming 18C residence, and contains antiquities from the Roman fort at *Templeborough* to the s.w. (now obliterated by steel works), and a notable collection of Rockingham china, the kiln for which was near *Swinton*, 3 m. N. About 4 m. N. is *Wentworth Woodhouse* (no adm.), the magnificent mansion built by Flitcroft for the first Marquis of Rockingham.—13 m. *Conisbrough*, and thence to Doncaster, see Rte 68.

The Lincoln road from Sheffield (A 57; 45½ m.) runs viâ (17 m.) *Worksop* and (27 m.) *Markham Moor;* the railway viâ Worksop and Retford.

From Sheffield to *Manchester* viâ the Peak District, see Rte 45D; viâ *Penistone*, see Rte 61G; to *Nottingham* and *London*, see Rte 44.

From Sheffield to Leeds and Skipton

ROAD, A 61 viâ (23½ m.) *Wakefield* to (32½ m.) *Leeds*; A 657 from Leeds to (11 m.) *Shipley*; A 650 from Wakefield to (14 m.) **Bradford**, (17½ m.) *Shipley*, and (25½ m.) *Keighley*; A 629 thence to (9 m.) *Skipton*.

RAILWAY from Sheffield to *Leeds*, 41 m. viâ *Barnsley* and *Wakefield* (Kirkgate) in 1½ hr; 39 m. viâ *Rotherham* and *Wakefield* (Westgate), in 65–70 min. Leeds to *Skipton*, 26¼ m. in c. 40 min. Except by occasional through trains from Nottingham to Carlisle, a change is necessary at Leeds.

A 61 leads nearly due N. from Sheffield through a colliery district.—13½ m. **Barnsley** (Hotels), a busy and cheerful town (75,300 inhab.) that has earned the epithets of 'bleak' and 'black', is the centre of a rich coalfield and has two early 19C churches by Rickman. The *Cooper Art*

Gallery (open weekdays, 11.30–5), in Church St., contains a good collection of English watercolours (19–20C) and of *Isabey's* works.

Cannon Hall (p. 559) lies 4½ m. N.W. off A 635.—At *Royston* (3½ m. N.) the 15C church tower preserves a pentagonal oriel, while at *Woolley* (4½ m. N.W.) the church has interesting bench-ends.—About 2 m. N.E. on the Pontefract road are the remains of *Monk Bretton Priory*, a Cluniac foundation of 1153, with a 14C gatehouse (adm. daily, Sun from 2; fee).

From Barnsley to *Penistone* (Manchester),· see Rte 61G.

23½ m. **WAKEFIELD** (Hotel), an ancient city (59,630 inhab.), standing above the Calder, is the county town of West Yorkshire as it was of the W. Riding, and has been the seat of a bishop since 1888. It was for long the centre of the cloth trade in Yorkshire; many prosperous Georgian houses survive (e.g. in S. and W. Parade), and woollen factories still abound. The Cathedral, a handsome church dating mainly from 1470, was restored in 1858–74 by Sir G. G. Scott, and has a large E. extension (by J. L. Pearson; 1901–5), including an undercroft chapter house reached from the N. choir-aisle. The conspicuous crocketed spire (247 ft) is the tallest in Yorkshire. The chief features of the interior are the fine Caroline screen (1635) in the chancel, the church plate by Lamerie (1739; in N. choir-aisle), and the windows by Kempe (1872–1900). In Wood St. are the *Court House* (1810), the *Town Hall* (1880), by Collcutt, and the *Museum*, mainly of local history (open 11–6, Sun 2–5.30). The *Bridge Chapel* (St Mary's), almost entirely rebuilt in 1847 by Gilbert Scott, was originally erected c. 1350, about the same time as the bridge (s. of Kirkgate). The Battle of Wakefield (1460), when Richard, Duke of York, was slain by the Lancastrians, was fought near Sandal Castle (1¾ m. s.).

Among distinguished natives of Wakefield are Dr John Radcliffe (1652–1714) and George Gissing (1857–1903; tablet at 30 Westgate).

About 6 m. S.E. (A 638; bus) is *Nostell Priory (N.T.; adm. Easter–Oct, Wed, Sat, & Sun 2–6; daily in Aug 2–6; BH, 11–6; fee; tea), the Georgian mansion of the Winn family, begun in 1733 by James Paine and continued in 1765–80 by Robert Adam. The *Interior*, with its splendid decoration, is superbly furnished, and contains a first-class collection of paintings, including Holbein's famous picture of Sir Thomas More and his family, and works by Van Dyck, Breughel, Hogarth, and Claude Lorraine, and a full range of Chippendale furniture (the accounts survive, as at Harewood). Chippendale was for years the estate carpenter, and may have worked on the exquisite miniature furniture for the dolls' house which is here displayed. The collection of Etruscan and Attic pottery is ranked as fourth best in the country. The grounds, with three lakes. are extensive. Within the park the church of *Wragby*, where Paine was married in 1741, contains a wealth of Swiss glass (1514–1751). The Norman font came from *Auburn* church (E. Riding), overwhelmed by the sea before 1830. Nearly opposite is the site of the original priory (Augustinian) founded c. 1119.

At *Heath*, 2½ m. E., the Hall (1753), by Carr, is open occasionally in May–Sept (2–5; fee; tea); Heath House is by Paine (1744). *Normanton*, 2¾ m. farther on, is a grimy town (17,700 inhab.), with a large 14–15C church.—*Horbury*, 3 m. s.w. is the birthplace of John Carr (1723–1807), who was buried in the classical church of his own design (1791–93).

32½ m. **LEEDS** (495,000 inhab.) is a thriving industrial town, the centre of the ready-made clothing trade, with large engineering works and textile mills, built across a basin of the river Aire. The industries are concentrated on the flat ground s. of the river, while the residential suburbs are on the heights that ring the city to the north.

Railway Station. *City* (for London, the Midlands, Sheffield, Manchester, etc.)
Airport at .*Yeadon*, 8 m. ׀ N.W. Direct .services׀ to׀ Heathrow, ׀Glasgow, Belfast,

Dublin, Bristol, Edinburgh, Aberdeen, Norwich, Jersey, Brussels, Amsterdam, etc.
Hotels, near the station.
Post Office, City Square.—INFORMATION BUREAU, Central Library.
Bus Station, New York St., for almost all country services.
Theatres. *Grand,* New Briggate; *Civic,* Albert Hall; *City Varieties,* Swan St. (off
Briggate).—CONCERTS in the Town Hall, and at lunch-time on Wed in the Art
Gallery.— International Concert Pianists' competition.
Golf Courses at Temple Newsam (2 courses), Roundhay Park, Moortown, etc.—
COUNTY CRICKET GROUND at Headingley.—SWIMMING POOL, Westgate.

History. The monks of Kirkstall Abbey began a trade in wool, which was
consolidated by Flemish workmen in the reign of Edward III, and by 1730 the
Leeds cloth market was the finest in the country. The city centre today is witness
to its continued prosperity, which has always encouraged indiscriminate new
building to replace the old.—Charles I was confined in Red Hall, formerly in
Upper Headrow, during his journey s. in 1647. Tablets commemorate Phil May
(1864–1903), the caricaturist, born at 66 Wallace St., New Wortley (near the Pudsey
Rd.); and Louis le Prince (1842–90), pioneer of the cinema, on the site of his workshop, 160 Woodhouse Lane. The s.w. suburb of Farnley Moor was the birthplace
of J. C. Ibbetson (1759–1817).

Several busy streets radiate from CITY SQUARE, in the centre of which
is a bronze equestrian figure of the Black Prince, by Brock, eight
'flambeaux' by Drury, and statues of Dr Priestley, James Watt, John
Harrison (see below), and Dean Hook. On the E. side, overshadowed by
new tower blocks, is the Gothic *Mill Hill Chapel* (rebuilt in 1847), where
Dr Priestley was minister in 1767–78. Boar Lane leads E. to the classical
church of *Holy Trinity* (1727) and, beyond Briggate, the old *Corn
Exchange* (1863) by Cuthbert Brodrick. To the N. is *Kirkgate Market,*
rebuilt in 1904 in an extravagant Baroque style.

From City Sq. the busy PARK ROW leads N. to The Headrow (see
below) in which, to the left, is the *Town Hall,* an imposing classical
structure by Brodrick (1853–58), with a tower 225 ft high. The Leeds
Triennial Music Festival (which Sullivan conducted in 1883–98, and
which heard the first performance of Walton's 'Belshazzar's Feast' in
1931) is held here in the spring (next in 1981). A tablet commemorates
Joseph Aspdin (1799–1855), a Leeds bricklayer, one of the inventors of
Portland cement. The **City Art Gallery** (adm. 10.30–6.30, Sun 2.30–5),
near by, contains a fine collection of paintings (interchangeable with
Temple Newsam; see below).

These include works by *Guido Reni* (St John the Baptist), *Boudin, Renoir,
Bonnard, Derain, Courbet,* and *Gainsborough*; and sculpture by *Henry Moore* and
Barbara Hepworth (both of whom trained at the Leeds College of Art under Jacob
Kramer), also *Arp, Rodin, Gaudier-Brzeska,* and *Reg Butler.* The SAM WILSON
COLLECTION is housed in a separate gallery and includes Brangwyn's huge panels
for the 1905 Venice Biennale, a massive fireplace and overmantel by Gilbert, and a
collection of early-20C Academic paintings by Orpen, Knight, W. W. Russel,
Heyman, Senior, etc. The magnificently representative *COLLECTION OF ENGLISH
WATERCOLOURS is particularly strong in the works of Cotman, and there is a
notable collection of Leeds Pottery (from 1760).—*Park Square,* off Westgate
farther w., is a relic of Georgian Leeds.

Adjoining is the *City Museum* (adm. weekdays 10–6.30), containing
well-arranged geological and zoological exhibits, and the important
Saville collection of Roman antiquities from Lanuvium (near Rome).
In Cookridge St. are *St Anne's Cathedral* (Rom. Cath.), by J. H.
Eastwood (1904), and the *Albert Hall* (1868), now the Civic Theatre;
and in Calverley St. are the *Civic Hall,* by E. Vincent Harris (1933), a

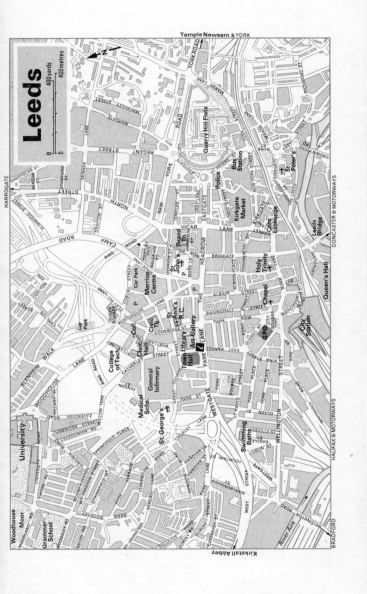

Leeds

400 yards
400 metres

HARROGATE

Temple Newsam & YORK

Woodhouse Moor

University

Grammar School

Kirkstall Abbey

BRADFORD

HALIFAX & MOTORWAYS

DONCASTER & MOTORWAYS

Quarry Hill Flats

Bus Station

Police

Kirkgate Market

Corn Exchange

Leeds Bridge

Holy Trinity

Chapel

Queen's Hall

City Station

GPO

Swimming Baths

St. George's

Medical Schs.

General Infirmary

College of Tech.

Civic Hall

Coll

Town Hall

Art Gallery

Library

St. Ann's R.C.

St. John's

Grand Th.

Merrion Centre

Car Park

Car Park

St. Peter's

Woodhouse Walk

Blenheim Walk

classical building with a fine reception hall and council chamber, and the huge *Central Colleges*, begun in 1953.

In Queen Square, off Claypit Lane, No. 16 houses the *Thoresby Society's Library*, with MSS., books, and relics of old Leeds (Tues and Thurs 10–2).

The HEADROW, a broad E. to w. thoroughfare (80 ft wide), prolongs Westgate eastward across Briggate to Vicar Lane. **St John's**, in New Briggate, is a fine example of a 'Laudian' church, built by John Harrison, a Leeds merchant, before 1634. Most of the superb woodwork (*Screen, pews, pulpit) has survived. Beyond Vicar Lane, Eastgate prolongs The Headrow to *Quarry Hill Flats* (1935–41), by R. Livett, a monumental solution to the housing problem. In Kirkgate, hidden behind the railway embankment, stands the parish church of *St Peter's*, rebuilt in 1839–41 in a Perp. style by the efforts of Dean Hook (1798–1875), the 'Apostle of the West Riding'. It contains a restored 11C *Cross and the cenotaph of Dean Hook (by Scott). Here S. S. Wesley was organist in 1842–49. The choir maintains a fine tradition of 'cathedral' music. Commercial St. and Bond St., the central shopping areas, have been closed to traffic (except buses).

The **University**, in Woodhouse Lane, received its charter in 1904, and devotes itself especially to science and technology. It grew out of the Leeds School of Medicine (1831) and the Yorkshire College of Science (1874), and for a time was affiliated to the Victoria University (p. 596). The circular *BROTHERTON LIBRARY, erected by the generous gift of Lord Brotherton (d. 1935), contains, among the 500,000 vols. of the University collection, the Brotherton Collection (the private library of Lord Brotherton), notable for its early editions and MSS. of English literature, including Caxtons, and all four Shakespeare folios (adm. by appointment with the Librarian). New buildings include the large Parkinson Building (1951), designed by T. A. Lodge, with an impressive assembly hall, and the Department of Textile Industries (1956).

The chief residential quarters of Leeds lie to the N. of the city, in the neighbourhood of *Headingley*, *Chapel Allerton*, and *Roundhay*. On the way to Headingley is *Woodhouse Moor*, partly laid out as a public park. *Leeds Grammar School*, s. of the moor, was founded in 1552. About 2¼ m. N. of Headingley is **Adel**, the beautiful little Norman *Church of which has interesting sculptures on the s. porch and chancel arch.—In Roundhay Road, the approach to *Roundhay Park* (775 acres), one of the finest public parks in the country, is *St Aidan's*, a remarkable Romanesque church (1894) with splendid mosaics by Brangwyn and a Madonna by Josef Heu.

Buses run from the Headrow or Wellington St. to *Kirkstall Abbey, 3¼ m. N.W. in a park in the valley of the Aire, a Cistercian house founded in 1147 by Henry de Lacy, and now the property of the city of Leeds. The ruins, chiefly in the transitional Norman style, are perhaps more perfect than those of any other Yorkshire abbey, with the exception of Fountains, which they closely resemble. The chief remains are the chapter house (late-Norman and E.E.), which is almost intact; the impressive church, with its collapsed Perp. tower; and the abbot's lodging, a splendid example of early 13C architecture. In the restored gatehouse, N. of the road, is the *Abbey House Museum* (adm. weekdays 10–5 or 6, Sun from 2; fee), with historical and folk collections including toys and games, and an attractive reconstructed street with shops and an inn. In the park is an interesting *Geological Garden*.—*Temple Newsam* (adm. daily 10.30–6.15 or dusk, Wed till 8.30 in summer; fee), 4¼ m. E. of Leeds (bus No. 22 from New York St.), was the birthplace of Lord Darnley in 1545 and the original of 'Templestowe' in 'Ivanhoe'. The existing house, built after 1622 by Sir Arthur Ingram, ancestor of Lord Halifax, and altered in the 18C, was bought by Leeds in 1922. On the ground floor the Great

Hall has 16–17C furniture, and adjoining rooms contain English satinwood furniture, French and English jewelled snuff boxes, and Chinese carvings in semiprecious stones. Upstairs, the Gallery in the N. wing (108 ft long) has medallion portraits of George II and his family in the ceiling and the original furniture, and the rooms in the W. wing are splendid examples of mid-Georgian decoration with appropriate paintings including two Venetian scenes by *Guardi*. In the stables is a licensed restaurant.

FROM LEEDS TO DONCASTER, 28½ m. (A 639). Railway in c. ¾ hr viâ (10 m.) Wakefield.—Crossing Leeds Bridge we bear to the left.—5 m. *Oulton.* The *John o'Gaunt Inn*, 1 m. N.W., is said to mark the spot where the last wolf in Yorkshire was killed by John of Gaunt.— 7½ m. *Methley* church contains interesting tombs with recumbent effigies (15–17C) of the Waterton and Savile families, and a lectern with an elaborate 16C base.— 10 m. *Castleford*, at the junction of the Aire and the Calder, was an important Roman station, but is now a grimy colliery and bottle-making town (38,200 inhab.). It was the birthplace in 1898 of Henry Moore, the sculptor.— 13½ m. **Pontefract** (formerly pron. 'Pomfret'), a market-town (31,300 inhab.), has a well-known racecourse. In the Norman *Castle*, Richard II (1367–1400) was either murdered by Sir Piers Exton ('Richard II', v. 5) or starved to death, and here James I of Scotland, and Charles, Duke of Orleans, after his capture at Agincourt, were held. The castle was razed to the ground after its capture in 1648; one wall survives in the corner of the recreation ground which now covers the site. 'Pomfret cakes' are lozenges made of liquorice. At *Ackworth*, 2¼ m. S., an important school of the Society of Friends, founded in 1778, occupies buildings of a Foundling Hospital of 1758. *Ackworth Park* was the residence of John Gully (1783–1863), the prize-fighter, afterwards M.P. for Pontefract.—At (20 m.) *Barnsdale Bar* we join the Great North Road, 8½ m. N. of *Doncaster* (see Rte 68).

FROM LEEDS TO SELBY, 22 m. (A 63). Railway in c. ½ hr (through trains to Hull). The road traverses the ancient district of *Elmet*, extending N.E. towards Tadcaster, and crosses A 1 near (15 m.) *Monk Fryston* (p. 645). In the church of (4 m.) *Whitkirk* John Smeaton (1724–92), the engineer, is buried; near by is *Austhorpe Lodge*, where he lived.

From Leeds to *Skipton* viâ *Ilkley* (Wharfedale), see Rte 66; to *Harrogate, Ripon*, and *Stockton*, see Rte 67; to *Huddersfield* and *Manchester*, see Rte 61F; to *Bradford, Rochdale*, and *Manchester*, see Rte 61E; to *York*, see Rte 68; to *Settle* and *Carlisle*, see Rte 62B.

The road (A 657) ascending industrial Airedale from Leeds joins the direct route from Sheffield viâ (37½ m.) Bradford (A 650) at *Shipley* (28,400 inhab.), 11 m. from Leeds, and practically continuous with Bradford.—44½ m. *Saltaire* is named after the river and Sir Titus Salt, the first manufacturer of alpaca fabrics, who established a model factory here (the first in Britain) with sturdy terraced housing in 1853. The result remains as a monument to enlightened Victorian enterprise.—47 m. *Bingley* (26,500 inhab.; Hotel) with the five-rise staircase of locks on the Leeds & Liverpool canal and (51½ m.) **Keighley** (pron. 'Keethley'; 55,300 inhab.; Hotel) are likewise manufacturing towns. *East Riddlesden Hall* (N.T.; adm. Mar–Oct, 11 or 2–6 exc. Mon, but open BH; fee), on the main road 1¼ m. N.E. of Keighley, is the 17C manor-house, furnished in period of the notorious Murgatroyds, with a medieval tithe barn.

The Todmorden road runs s.w. to (3¾ m.) **Haworth** (Hotel), a bleak village on the shoulder of the moors, imperishably associated with the Brontë family. The cobbled main street climbs precipitously to the tiny square by the church. The parsonage, whither the Rev. Patrick Brontë brought his family in 1820, is now the *BRONTË PARSONAGE MUSEUM (adm. 11–4.45 or 5.45, Sun from 2; fee), containing Brontë MSS. and relics, including the Bonnell collection from the U.S.A. The church, rebuilt in 1879–81, with the exception of the tower, contains the tomb of Charlotte Brontë (1816–55) and Emily Brontë (1818–48). The Black Bull inn was the haunt of the unfortunate Branwell Brontë. Walks may be taken across the moors, which exercised such an influence on the sisters, to the *Brontë Waterfall* (2 m. w.) and *Far Withens* (perhaps 'Wuthering Heights'; 3 m.); or to *Ponden House* (the 'Thrush-cross Grange' of 'Wuthering Heights'; 2½ m.), *Wycoller Hall* (the 'Ferndean Manor' of 'Jane Eyre', now in ruins; 6½ m.), and *Colne* (10 m.).

The *Worth Valley Railway*, a privately owned company, running from Keighley to Oxenhope, has a museum of locomotives and carriages at Haworth.

56½ m. *Kildwick* has a stone bridge dating from Edward II and a long Perp. church containing good pews. Charlotte Brontë was governess in 1839 at *Stonegappe*, the 'Gateshead Hall' of 'Jane Eyre', c. 2 m. w.— 60½ m. **Skipton**, see p. 610.

62 LONDON TO CARLISLE
A Viâ Lancaster

ROAD. 296½ m. From London to (145½ m.) the Potteries, see Rte. 39.—The old main road diverges from Rte 39 at (149½ m.) *Talke-o'-th'-Hill.* Thence we follow the Liverpool road viâ (160½ m.) *Holmes Chapel* and (168½ m.) *Knutsford* to (180½ m.) **Warrington.** Then A 49 leads through industrial Lancashire (Rte 61) to (192½ m.) **Wigan** and (209½ m.) **Preston.**—Thence A 6: 231½ m. **Lancaster.**—252½ m. *Kendal.*— 278½ m. *Penrith.*—296½ m. **Carlisle.**

MOTORWAY (M1, M6) to Preston (223 m.), Lancaster (244 m.) and Carlisle (310 m.), with spur to Blackpool. This is to be recommended for all through journeys between Warrington and Preston.

RAILWAY FROM EUSTON, 299 m. in c. 4 hrs. Principal Stations: To (158 m.) **Crewe**, see Rte 39.—182 m. *Warrington* (Bank Quay).—193¾ m. *Wigan.*—209 m. **Preston**, junction for *Blackpool* (18 m.), *Lytham*, etc.—230 m. **Lancaster**, junction for *Morecambe* (4 m.); also for *Barrow-in-Furness* (Rte 63).—249 m. *Oxenholme*, junction for **Kendal** (2 m.) and **Windermere** (10½ m.).—281½ m. *Penrith for Ullswater*, bus connection with **Keswick** (18¼ m.).—299 m. **Carlisle.**

From London, on the old road, to (137½ m.) *Stone* and (149½ m.) *Talke-o'-th'-Hill*, see Rte 39. Thence A 50 closely paralleled by the M 6 motorway, leads across the Cheshire plain to (180½ m.) *Warrington* (Rte 61A). A 49 then leads N. through (185 m.) industrial *Newton-le-Willows* to (192½ m.) *Wigan* (Rte 61A), and on viâ (199½ m.) *Charnock Richard* to (205½ m.) *Bamber Bridge*, where it joins A 6.—209½ m. **Preston,** see Rte 61B. This route, traversing Lancashire from S. to N., gives an excellent idea of the varied character of the county.

FROM PRESTON TO BLACKPOOL and FLEETWOOD. Frequent service of trains either viâ Poulton to Blackpool North (bus connection to Fleetwood) or viâ Lytham and St Annes to Blackpool South. The broad direct road (A 583; 17 m.) runs to Blackpool by-passing (8½ m.) *Kirkham*; while A 584 diverges left after 4 m. and reaches Blackpool (20 m.) viâ (12 m.) Lytham. These roads cross the *Fylde*, the level region between the estuaries of the Wyre and the Ribble, and a continuous esplanade, 18 m. long, joins Blackpool with Lytham and Fleetwood.

Lytham St Annes (Hotels at St Annes), is a quiet residential seaside resort (40,000 inhab.) stretching along the shore from Lytham, facing S. at the mouth of the Ribble estuary, to the more open St Annes, with first-class golf links, looking S.W. *Lytham Hall* is an imposing building by Carr (1764), who added Grecian embellishments to the Jacobean house.

Blackpool (many Hotels on N. and S. promenade, and near the centre), a modern and enterprising town (151,300 inhab.), is one of the most popular resorts in the country. Crowded in summer by myriads of excursionists from all parts of the industrial North and Midlands, it draws over 8 million visitors a year. The manifold attractions include three piers; the Tower (520 ft high; 1891–94), with a ballroom; the Pleasure Beach, with many side-shows and bathing pool, both on the S. Shore; the Derby Baths, on the N. Shore; Stanley Park (nearly 300 acres), with a boating lake, tennis courts, etc., and superb gardens and conservatories; four golf courses, etc.

AIR SERVICES from Squire's Gate to the *Isle of Man* and *Jersey*. Buses run along the shore s. to (5 m.) St Annes and (8 m) Lytham, and trams N. to (9 m.) Fleetwood, passing (4 m.) *Thornton Cleveleys* (Hotel) and (5 m.) *Rossall Hall*, a public school founded in 1844, where Sir Thomas Beecham was a pupil. **Fleetwood** (Hotels), a seaside resort at the mouth of the Wyre, looking N. across Morecambe Bay, is one of the largest fishing ports in England (28,600 inhab.). A passenger ferry plies across the Wyre to *Knott End* (connected by bus with Lancaster).

The road from Fleetwood to Preston (A 585; 22½ m.) passes near (6 m.) *Poulton-le-Fylde*, a little market town with an old cross and stocks and an 18C church.

Beyond Preston A 6 runs N. through pleasant country, with the *Bleasdale Moors* on the right, and crosses the Wyre below (219 m.) *Garstang* (Hotel).—After the crossing of M 6 we pass (229 m.; r.) *Bailrigg*, the attractive site of Lancaster University (see below).

231½ m. **Lancaster** (Hotel), for centuries the county town (49,500 inhab.) of Lancashire until the rise of Preston, is on the tidal Lune, here crossed by *Skerton Bridge* (1788), the work of Thos. Harrison. The Lancaster Canal, which runs N. to Kendal, crosses the Lune on a fine aqueduct (1797) by Rennie.

Dr. William Whewell (1794–1866) and Sir Richard Owen (1804–92) were born here and educated at the grammar school (founded in 1472). In the 18C Lancaster was famous for its cabinet-makers, notably the Gillows. The old furniture factory of Waring and Gillow had been adapted as the nucleus of the University (see above).

The CASTLE, standing high above the river on the site of a Roman castrum and occupied by the law-courts and a prison, is open from Easter to Oct on weekdays 10.30–12, 2–3.30 or 4 (conducted parties every 20 or 30 min; fee). The Norman *Keep* (1090), damaged by Robert Bruce in 1322 (when the town was burnt), was strengthened by John of Gaunt and restored c. 1585. One of its turrets is known as 'John of Gaunt's Chair'. The *Great Gate* (1403) is not open to the public. The so-called *Hadrian's Tower* dates from 1200 and contains a miscellaneous collection of prison equipment. The buildings were extensively altered in 1788–1823 by Harrison and J. M. Gandy. The splendid *Shire Hall* (1796) is adorned with Royal arms and those of the Constables of the Castle and High Sheriffs. Assizes have been held in the castle since 1176.

"Old John of Gaunt, time-honoured Lancaster," son of Edward III, succeeded to the Lancaster estates in right of his wife Blanche, and became Duke of Lancaster in 1362. This title now belongs to the Sovereign, one of whose ministers bears the title of 'Chancellor of the Duchy of Lancaster'. George Fox was imprisoned in the castle in 1664.

To the N.E. of the castle is the *Priory Church of St Mary*, which in 1094 became a cell of the Benedictine Abbey at Sées and in 1431 passed under the jurisdiction of the Bridgettines of Syon. The church (mainly 15C), entered by a doorway of 1180, preserves its Saxon doorway (at the w. end) and exquisitely carved oak *Stalls (c. 1340) said to have come from Cockersand (see below). On the floor of the choir is marked the site of the apse of the Roman basilica, discovered in 1912. The rebuilt tower (1759) was designed by Henry Sephton.

From the w. end there is a fine view (and a path) down to St George's Quay, with the *Old Custom House* (1764) by Richard Gillow and Georgian warehouses recalling 18C trade with the West Indies.

Fine Georgian houses, still a feature of the town generally, mark Castle Park and Castle Hill. At their junction the *Storey Institute* (1891) is open occasionally for art exhibitions. At the top of Church St., the *Judge's Lodging* (1675) contains Gillow furniture and a Museum of Childhood (Apr–Oct, weekdays 10 or 2–5; also Sat & Sun aft. in summer) with the Barry Elder doll collection. The old centre, to the s.e., largely closed to traffic, is well documented (with models of the town in 1610, 1778, 1881) in the Museum (adm. free 10–5, weekdays & BH). Occupying the Old Town Hall (1781–83), in Market Square, it has a well-arranged collection of antiquities and the *Museum of the King's Own Royal Regiment*. Among the exhibits are Roman pottery (1–4C) and fragments from Cockersand. To the n.e., near the Bus Station, is the church of *St John* (1754) with a tower added by Harrison in 1784. In Dalton Square farther s. are the *Town Hall* (1909) by E. W. Mountford, and the Information Bureau, to the e. of which is the *Roman Catholic Cathedral* (1859). Surmounted by the conspicuous Ashton Memorial (by John Belcher), *Williamson Park*, farther e., commands an extensive view.

The Golf Club in Ashton Park lies c. 2½ m. s.w. on A 588. Beyond (4 m.) *Conder Green* B 5290 (r.) goes to *Glasson Dock* (¾ m.), an 18C dock on the Lune estuary, where salmon are taken by 'wammelling' with the drift-net, or by the stationary haaf-net. The next right-hand turning leads in c. 3 m. to a farm on the coast, beside which, sadly neglected, is the finely vaulted 13C chapter house of *Cockersand Abbey* (locked), with a few fragmentary remains near by.

A 589 runs n.w. from Lancaster to (3½ m.) Morecambe and (5½ m.) Heysham.— **Morecambe** (Hotels), named after its bay, long noted for shrimps, is a seaside resort (10,000 inhab., incl. Heysham), with good sands and a golf course, and an 'oceanarium' (dolphins). For the walk across the bay, see p. 575.—**Heysham** (pron. 'He-sham') was once the starting-point of the night mail-steamers to Belfast and has a service to Douglas, Isle of Man. The old village has some interesting houses and a 12–14C church, with a carved 'hog-backed' gravestone and a fragment of a Saxon cross in its churchyard. On the promontory above is the ruin of St Patrick's chapel (?9C); near by are some early Saxon rock graves with holes for a post or cross.

From Lancaster to Kirkby Lonsdale, 17 m. (A 683 on the s. bank of the Lune, a salmon river).—2½ m. *Halton* (n. bank) preserves in its churchyard a *Cross (early 11C) depicting episodes from the saga of Sigurd the Volsung.—We now enter the *Crook o' Lune* (Hotel), the loveliest part of the green valley of Lonsdale, immortalised by Turner.—9 m. *Hornby* (Hotel), a good centre for anglers. The castle has a 13C pele tower with additions by Sir Edward Stanley ('Mounteagle'; d. 1523), who also built the octagonal tower of the church as a thank offering for his safe return from Flodden Field. Thence a pleasant alternative route to Kirkby Lonsdale, viâ Whittington, crosses Loyn Bridge to *Gressingham*.—At (11 m.) *Melling* (Hotel) the 15C church has a raised chancel.—About 1½ m. beyond (13 m.) *Tunstall* (p. 574) is the site of a Roman fort (l.; ? Galacum).—17 m. *Kirkby Lonsdale*, see Rte 62b.

From Lancaster a fine moorland road leads s.e. to the Yorkshire border at (12 m.) the *Trough of Bowland* (1000 ft), the pass between the Bleasdale Moors (r.) and the Forest of Bowland, and thence into the Hodder valley at (15½ m.) *Dunsop Bridge* (to Clitheroe, see Rte 61c).—Farther on is (20 m.) *Slaidburn*, a remote village in beautiful country, with a splendid Jacobean screen in its church. Thence roads lead either e. to (29 m.) *Gisburn* (Rte 61c) or n.e. (B 6478) to (30 m.) *Long Preston* (Rte 62b).

234½ m. *Slyne* lies ¾ m. e. of *Hest Bank*, the s. end of the 'road' across the sands of Morecambe Bay (see p. 575).—From above (235¾ m.) *Bolton-le-Sands* a good view of the bay is enjoyed.—238 m. *Carnforth* (Hotel). The station yards and sheds (car park; adm. daily, fee) display steam locomotives (British and Continental) preserved as a memorial to one of the last homes of steam (closed 1968 but reopened as the base for summer excursions on the Cumbrian Coast line). We enter Cumbria.

A road runs N.W. to (1½ m.) *Warton*, with the Washington arms on its church tower, (4½ m.) *Silverdale*, where Mrs Gaskell did some of her best work, and (8 m.) *Arnside* (Hotel), once a busy port, and now a quiet resort on the sandy estuary of the Kent. Arnside Knott (N.T.), 1 m. s., affords good views of Morecambe Bay and the Lake mountains.—*Leighton Hall* (adm. May–Sept on Wed, Sun, & BH, 2.30–5; fee), in a fine park 1½ m. N. of Warton, has a Neo-Gothic façade and contains furniture by the Gillow family, who lived here after 1823.—*Borwick Hall*, 3 m. N.E. of Carnforth, is mainly Elizabethan.

244¼ *Beetham* (Hotel), has a fine old bridge.—245½ m. *Milnthorpe*. Here the railway begins a long ascent of 24 m. to Shap Summit (1000 ft), climbing for the first 13 m. almost without a break (average gradient 1 in 130); thence the line descends practically all the way to Carlisle, falling 850 ft in 31 m.—At (247¾ m.) *Levens Bridge* we pass (l.) Levens Hall (see below), just short of the road junction with A 590, and, farther on, Sizergh Castle (see below).

252½ m. **Kendal** (Hotels), an old Westmorland town (21,600 inhab.) pleasantly situated on the Kent, is still noted for its snuff, although the making of woollen cloth (established here perhaps by Flemings c. 1330) now takes second place to the manufacture of shoes. 'Kendal Green' was a heavy kind of serge. A number of narrow 'yards' or alleys lead off the long main street (traffic northbound only). Catherine Parr (1512–48) was born in the ruined *Castle* on the hill to the E., and her prayer-book is preserved in the Town Hall. Also in the Mayor's Parlour (shown on application) are several portraits by Romney. In the *Parish Church* is a memorial tablet to Romney, and (Bellingham Chapel), a 13C coffin lid with a foliated cross, sword and shield. Overlooking the river is *Abbot Hall* (adm. 10.30–5.30, Sat & Sun 2–5; fee), built in 1759 notably by Carr. Carefully restored in 1962, it now contains an interesting collection of 18C furniture and paintings, including works by Romney, Reynolds, de Wint, Devis, Highmore, and Daniel Gardner (see below). Exhibitions of Lakeland life and industry are held on the first floor.

Daniel Gardner (1750–1805) and Sir Arthur Eddington (1882–1944), astronomer, are natives of Kendal. Romney lived here in his youth till 1762, returning in 1798 to die in a house at the s. end of the town (near the bridge). Close to the station is a *Museum* (weekdays 10–4.30) with a natural history collection, etc.— In 1847 Wordsworth made a vociferous protest (in a sonnet) against the building of the railway between Kendal and (8½ m.) *Windermere*. Nowadays buses run to all points.—*Scout Scar* (713 ft) to the s.w. commands a fine view.

*Sizergh Castle (N.T.; adm. April–Sept on Wed & Sun, 2–5.45; also Thurs in July–Aug; fee), c. 3 m. s. of Kendal, consists of a magnificent 14C pele tower (in excellent condition), a Tudor hall (much altered), and Elizabethan additions with decorated barge-boards. Since 1239 Stricklands have resided continuously at Sizergh. Visitors are permitted to wander unhurriedly through the castle and garden. Among the interesting collection of portraits (Huysmans, Wissing, early and late Reynolds, and Romneys) are examples by Rigaud of James II and his family, with whom Sir Thomas and Lady Strickland shared exile. The delicate Elizabethan panelling and fine 16C chimney-pieces should be noted. In the pele tower, with its original floors, are relics given to the family by the Stuarts. A direct ancestor of George Washington married Joan Strickland of Sizergh in 1292.—**Levens Hall** (adm. May–Sept, Tues, Wed, Thurs, & Sun 2–5; fee; tea), c. 2 m. farther (bus), an Elizabethan house built on to a 14C pele tower, is famous for its topiary *Garden (open daily 10–5.30), laid out by Beaumont. The house, with splendid plaster and woodwork, Cordova leather wall-hangings (1690), and 17–18C furniture (pieces by Gillow of Lancaster), is, with the surrounding dales, the scene of Mrs Humphry Ward's 'Helbeck of Bannisdale'. An outbuilding houses models of steam-engines.

Windermere (Rte 64c) is reached in 8½ m. by the main road (A 591) viâ (5 m.) *Staveley*, from which a by-road ascends the Kent to *Kentmere* (4 m. N.), with a pele tower and 16C church.—A pleasant alternative from Kendal follows B 5284 to (8 m.) *Bowness*.

It is recommended to ascend the steep road opposite the Town Hall, which, enjoying marvellous views, runs due w. to (3½ m.) *Underbarrow* and (6 m.) *Crosthwaite*. Thence the road, crossing the Levens Bridge–Bowness road, strikes s.w.; beyond (8 m.) *Bowland Bridge* the road climbs and an unexpected *View appears before the descent to (13 m.) *Newby Bridge* (Rte 64c). The turning on the left beyond Bowland Bridge leads in 1 m., above the charming Winster valley, to the church of St Anthony (c. 1504) at *Cartmel Fell*, containing good woodwork, a pre-Reformation Crucifixion (mutilated), a three-decker pulpit, and 15C *Glass perhaps from Cartmel Priory.

From Kendal to *Sedbergh, Hawes*, and *Northallerton*, see Rte 72a; to *Ingleton, Skipton, Leeds*, etc., see Rte 62b; to *Brough* (Teesdale), see Rte 72c.

Beyond Kendal A 6, increasingly intertwined with M 6, begins the long climb up Shap Fells (1 in 10 to 20), reaching (263 m.) the summit at 1304 ft. The road is as notorious for winter snows as the railway was in days of steam for the necessity of 'banking' locomotives and 'double-heading'. To the right at 265 m. is Shap Fells Hotel. Beyond the granite works we pass B 6261 (r.), a moorland road leading to Tebay. As we descend to (268 m.) *Shap* (Hotel), there are views (l.) of the High Street range and, later, of Saddleback.

Keld Chapel (N.T.), in the Lowther valley 1 m. s.w., is a small 16C monastic building (key at cottage opposite), and ½ m. downstream are the 13C and 16C remains of *Shap Abbey*, of which only the w. tower still stands. A fine road leads from Shap to (10 m.) Pooley Bridge viâ (3½ m.) *Bampton Grange*, 2 m. from Haweswater, and the charming village of (7 m.) *Askham* (Hotel).—About 5 m. e. of Shap is *Meaburn Hall*, a pele-tower manor, the home of Miss Lowther (afterwards Duchess of Bolton), the betrothed of General Wolfe.

To the N.w. of (273½ m.) *Hackthorpe* is *Lowther*, where the church (1½ m. w.; altered 1686) lies near the remains of Lowther Castle (demolished in 1957) in its fine park (European wild life).

278½ m. **Penrith** (Hotels), an old Cumberland market town (11,300 inhab.), has a ruined *Castle* (temp. Edward IV) in the park opposite the station. The agricultural market buildings are likewise of reddish stone. Outside the church of *St Andrew* (1722) are two ancient graves (?10C) and the old grammar school (16C). In Great Dockray the *Gloucester Arms Inn*, perhaps a residence of Richard of Gloucester, has fine panelling and the *Two Lions Inn* (once the town house of the Lowthers) has a notable plaster ceiling. *Hutton Hall*, in Friargate, incorporates a 15C pele tower.

Penrith Beacon (937 ft), N.E. of the town, commands a magnificent view.—*Brougham Castle* (pron. 'Broom'; adm. daily, Sun from 2; fee), 1½ m. s.e. (bus), with the ruins of a keep of c. 1170 and other later buildings, occupies the site of the Roman station of *Brocavum*.—At *Edenhall* (3½ m. N.E.; Hotel) the church contains armorial glass of 1660–1700 and monuments to the Musgraves, who lived at the Hall (now demolished) for nearly 500 years. The old glass goblet whose legend has been made familiar by Longfellow's translation of Uhland's ballad on 'The Luck of Eden Hall' is now in the Victoria and Albert Museum.

FROM PENRITH TO KESWICK, 18 m. A 66 leads w. to (9 m.) Troutbeck; a more interesting route (B 5288; 2 m. longer) runs viâ *Greystoke*, a pleasant village with a rebuilt castle. St Andrew's, founded as a collegiate church in the 14C, preserves its oak stalls and 15C *Glass (with a rare 'Red Devil').—At *Troutbeck*, A 5091 runs s. to Ullswater (p. 568).—10 m. To the right a lane leads to (2 m.) *Mungrisdale*, whence a track goes on to (3 m.) *Mosedale* for *Carrock Fell* (2174 ft; hill-fort), climbed in 1857 by Dickens and Wilkie Collins.—12 m. *Scales* is the starting-point of the usual ascent of *Saddleback*, which rises to the N. (p. 585).—13¾ m. *Threlkeld* has in its churchyard a memorial to over forty "noted veterans of the chase", all natives of the parish. To the left opens the Vale of St John.—Beyond (15¼ m.) the

Naddle Beck a lane on the left leads to the *Castlerigg Stone Circle* (p. 585). We descend the valley of the Greta beneath Skiddaw.—18 m. *Keswick*, see Rte 64B. From Penrith to *Patterdale* (Ullswater), see Rte 64A.

The direct road (A 6) goes N. to (296½ m.) **Carlisle**, viâ (290½ m.; l.) *Wreay* church built in 1842 on a basilican plan, with good carving by the local mason William Hindson. A more attractive route from Penrith follows A 686 N.E., passing near Edenhall (see above) and crossing the Eden at (5 m.) *Langwathby*, where we turn left. (A 686 goes on across the moors to Alston, 14½ m. N.E.)—Less than a mile beyond (6¾ m.) *Little Salkeld* are the monolith and stone circle known as *Long Meg and Her Daughters* (64 stones, 27 of which are still upright; *Little Meg*, ½ m. N.W., is a circle of 11 standing stones).—11 m. *Kirkoswald*, beautifully situated, has scanty remains of a castle and a church with a detached tower. The College has a fine entrance of 1696.

Over 1 m. s.w. is *Lazonby* (Hotel, 1 m. w.), reached by a fine bridge (1763) over the Eden. The church of the attractive village of *Great Salkeld*, 2 m. farther s., has a 14C fortified tower and a 12C doorway.

Beside (12½ m.) the Croglin Water are the enchanting Nunnery Walks. —At (15¾ m.) *Armathwaite* (Hotel) we cross a lovely stretch of the Eden. —26¼ m. **Carlisle**, see Rte 73A.

B Viâ Leeds and Skipton

ROAD, 309 m. To (161 m.) *Sheffield* and (193½ m.) *Leeds*, see Rtes 43, 61H. Thence to (219½ m.) **Skipton**, see Rte 66. We follow A 65: 234½ m. **Settle.**—245 m. *Ingleton.*—265 m. **Kendal**, and thence to **Carlisle**, see Rte 62A.—The industrial district may be avoided by following the Great North Road (A 1) to (191½ m.) *Bramham*, and turning left on to A659 at the cross-roads 2 m. N. Thence it is 28½ m. to Skipton.

RAILWAY (now no through trains; change at Sheffield or Leeds). Leeds is reached from King's Cross viâ Doncaster (Rte 46) and Wakefield in 2¾–4½ hrs. Principal Stations: to (158½ m.) *Sheffield*, see Rte 43; thence to (197¾ m.) *Leeds*, see Rte 61H.— 208½ m. *Shipley.*—214¾ m. **Keighley.**—223¾ m. **Skipton.**—233¾ m. **Hellifield.**— 235½ m. *Long Preston*, junction for Giggleswick, Clapham, and Carnforth.—239 m. *Settle.*—279¾ m. **Appleby.**—310¾ m. **Carlisle.**

From London to *Leeds*, see Rtes 43, 61H. Thence viâ *Otley*, and *Ilkley* to (219½ m.) *Skipton*, see Rte 66.—At (224 m.) *Gargrave*, where the Malham road bears right, we leave Airedale, and soon cross the 'backbone of England' into Ribblesdale.—At (231¼ m.) *Long Preston* begins the Bowland route to Slaidburn and Lancaster (see Rte 62A).— 234½ m. **Settle** (Hotel), a curious little town with a local style of 17–18C building. It possesses a market charter 700 years old, and is an excellent centre for exploring the wild surrounding country. Here (at Townhead) is a *Museum* illustrating the geology and history of the Craven caves. The 17C 'Folly Hall' contains a fine staircase. George Birkbeck (1776–1841), founder of the eponymous College and initiator of mechanics' institutes, and Benjamin Waugh (1839–1908), who founded the N.S.P.C.C., were born at Settle. About ¾ m. w., on the opposite bank of the Ribble, is *Giggleswick*, with a boys' public school founded in 1512, the domed chapel of which is the masterpiece of Sir Thomas Jackson (1901–2). Archdeacon Paley and Sir Matthew Smith were pupils here. About 1 m. N.W., under Giggleswick Scar, is the *Ebbing & Flowing Well*, celebrated in Drayton's 'Poly-Olbion'. In Langcliffe Scar, above

Settle to the E., is the *Victoria Cave*, the best and most accessible of many
caves in the local limestone, which, with the near-by *Jubilee Cave*, has
yielded traces of occupation from Mesolithic to Roman times.

FROM SETTLE TO HAWES, 22¼ m. This moorland road (B 6479), following the
main railway line (here protected by snow-screens), crosses the wildest corner of
Yorkshire.—2½ m. *Stainforth* (Y.H.), with a 17C single-arch bridge (N.T.) over the
Ribble.—3¾ m. Helwith Bridge Inn.—5½ m. *Horton-in-Ribblesdale*, with a mainly
Norman church, lies at the foot of *Penyghent* (2273 ft), on the W. side of which is
the deepest pot-hole in England (c. 525 ft), discovered in 1949. On the left are
Ingleborough (see below) and, farther on, *Whernside* (2414 ft).—12 m. *Ribblehead*
is 2 m. N.E. of Weathercote Cave (see below). The railway crosses *Batty Moss* by
a great viaduct, but we turn to the right, leaving on the left before (16 m.) Newby
Head Inn the road to Dentdale and Sedbergh (Rte 72A), and then descend Widdale.
—22¼ m. Hawes, see Rte 72A.
From Settle to *Malham*, see p. 610.

241 m. **Clapham** (Hotel), at the S. foot of Ingleborough, is a good
starting-point for numerous fine excursions in this attractive limestone
district. About 1½ m. N. of the village is *Ingleborough Cave* (adm.
10.30–6.30 Sat, Sun & BH, also Mon–Fri in June–Sept; fee), a series of
chambers and passages 800 yards in length, filled with glittering stalactites and stalagmites.

Farther up the hillside is (1 m.) the mouth of *Gaping Gill*, a vast cavern 350 ft
deep, into which a beck flings itself. Thence it is an easy ascent of 1½ m. to the top
of Ingleborough (2373 ft; *View), the most striking though not the highest of the
Yorkshire hills. On the level summit is an Iron Age fort, with part of the walls still
standing, and the foundations of circular huts of the 1C. The descent may be made
N. to (2 m.) Chapel-le-Dale or S.W. to (3 m.) Ingleton.

245 m. **Ingleton** (Hotel), is situated at the junction of two streams, and
noted for its *Glens' Walk* (fee), a round of c. 4 m. with charming waterfalls.

About 2 m. N.E., beside the Hawes road, are *White Scar Caves* (fee), a fine series
of caverns. Thence we may go on to (4½ m.) *Chapel-le-Dale*, with the birthplace of
Daniel Dove (in Southey's commonplace book 'The Doctor'; "about a bow-shot"
E. of the church), and *Weathercote Cave*, a rocky chasm with a waterfall.—
Yordas Cave in Kingsdale, 4½ m. N., was discovered in the 18C.

We traverse a strip of Lancashire and, passing (249 m.) *Cowan Bridge*
(see below), then enter Cumbria just before crossing the Lune below the
Devil's Bridge (?15C).— 252 m. **Kirkby Lonsdale** (Hotels), finely situated
and commanding beautiful views, has good Norman work in its church and
a Thursday market, and is the 'Lowton' of 'Jane Eyre'.

At *Cowan Bridge* in 1824–25 Charlotte Brontë was a pupil in the Clergy
Daughters' School, described in 'Jane Eyre' under the name of 'Lowood'. Part of
the old school (tablet) remains N. of the bridge over the Leck; but in 1833 the
institution was removed to *Casterton* (1 m. N. of the Devil's Bridge), the Old Hall
at which was the former residence of the Rev. Wm. Carus-Wilson (the 'Mr
Brocklehurst' of the story). From Cowan Bridge "an exposed and hilly road"
leads S.W. to (2½ m.) *Tunstall* ('Brocklebridge' in the novel), with the church attended by the pupils of the school. Thence to *Lancaster*, see p. 570.
A beautiful road (A 683) ascends Lonsdale *viâ Casterton* (Hotel) to (10¾ m.)
Sedbergh (Rte 72A).

265 m. **Kendal**, and thence to (309 m.) **Carlisle**, see Rte 62A.

63 FURNESS AND THE CUMBRIAN COAST

ROAD FROM KENDAL TO WHITEHAVEN, 78½ m. A 6 to (5 m.) *Levens Bridge* then A 590 viâ *Lindale* (for Grange and Cartmel) and *Newby Bridge* (Windermere) to (30½ m.) *Dalton*, for Barrow-in-Furness, 13¾ m. s. A 595 rounds the Duddon estuary and then follows the coast N. to (78½ m.) *Whitehaven*.

RAILWAY FROM CARNFORTH TO WHITEHAVEN viâ BARROW-IN-FURNESS, 74¼ m. in c. 2½ hrs.; through carriages to *Barrow* from London and Manchester. Principal Stations: *Carnforth*, see Rte 62B.—9 m. **Grange.**— 13¼ m. *Cork & Cartmel.* — 18¾ m. *Ulverston.*—23½ m. *Dalton (for Furness Abbey).*—28½ m. **Barrow.**— 40 m. *Foxfield.* — 44½ m. *Millom.*—57½ m. *Ravenglass* (for Eskdale).—61½ m. *Seascale.*— 69¾ m. *St Bees.*— 74½ m. **Whitehaven.** Steam-hauled excursions in summer.

Kendal, and thence to (5 m.) *Levens Bridge*, where we turn right, see Rte 62A.—A 590 crosses the Winster and enters Furness just before (11½ m.) *Lindale.*—B 5277 on the left leads in 2 m. to **Grange-over-Sands** (Hotels), a pleasant seaside and golfing resort (3600 inhab.) on Morecambe Bay.

At *Kent's Bank* 2 m. w., is the N. end of a 'roadway' across the sands of More-cambe Bay to (9 m.) Hest Bank (p. 570). The Cartmel monks guided travellers along this route, which was later used by coaches as a short-cut across the Bay; it is now a popular walk (apply to the guide at Guide's Farm, Cart Lane, Grange). **Cartmel** (Hotel.—Steeplechases at Whitsun), a charming little town 2 m. w. of Grange, has a beautiful 12C *Priory Church, crowned diagonally with a tower in the 15C, at which period were built the powerful nave, and fine E. window. Note-worthy are the *Tomb of Sir J. Harrington (d. 1347) and the oak stalls (1450) with misericords beneath an exquisite canopied screen (1620). A memorial (by Woolner) to Lord Frederick Cavendish (p. 608), in the N. aisle. In the vestry is a curious umbrella, upwards of 200 years old. The *Gatehouse* (N.T.; adm. weekdays, fee) dates from the 14C.—About 2 m. s.w. IS *Cark Hall* (1580), where George Fox, founder of the Society of Friends, spent a night in 1663. *Holker Hall* (pron. 'Hooker'; adm. daily exc. Sat, Easter–Sept, 11–6; fee, café), ½ m. N., a seat of the Cavendishes with lovely gardens and park (deer), was partly rebuilt in 1871.

From Lindale the main road ascends to (13½ m.) *High Newton* and goes on N.W. to the Leven valley at (17 m.) **Newby Bridge** (Hotels), near the foot of Windermere (Rte 64C). It then descends the river, crossing it before (19 m.) *Haverthwaite*. A steam railway runs in summer to Lakeside, connecting with Lake Windermere steamers to Bowness. From (22 m.) *Greenodd* an attractive route to *Coniston* (10½ m.) ascends the Crake valley viâ *Torver* (8 m.); while A 5092, quitting the valley at *Lowick Green* provides an alternative road to *Broughton* (8½ m.) with fine views.— 25¼ m. **Ulverston** (11,900 inhab.; Hotels) is a market town with a charter granted in 1280 and a weekly cattle auction (Thurs). In the early 19C it was the maritime centre of Furness with a canal to the sea. Now it produces penicillin. Here Stan Laurel (1890–1965) the film comedian, was born Arthur Stanley Jefferson.

On *Hoad Hill* (435 ft) is a memorial to Sir John Barrow (1764–1848), founder of the Royal Geographical Society, who was born at Dragley Beck (s.). *Swarth-moor Hall* (¼ m. s.; adm. mid-March–mid-Oct, Mon, Tues, Wed, & Sat 10–12, 2–5; or by appointment), an Elizabethan house, was at one time the residence of Judge Fell whose widow, Margaret, married George Fox (1624–91). Swarthmore College in Pennsylvania takes its name from this house. Here Fox built the meeting-house in 1668.—A pleasant coast road (A 5087) runs s. to (13 m.) *Piel* (see below) viâ *Baycliff* (Hotel; 6 m.) and *Aldingham* (7 m.) with an ancient church dedicated to St Cuthbert within its own sea-wall, and the 14C ruins of *Gleaston Castle* (1¼ m. w.).

About 1 m. beyond (30¼ m.) *Dalton-in-Furness*, where George Romney ('pictor celeberrimus'; 1734–1802) was born and is buried, a lane on the left of A 590 descends to *Furness Abbey*. In the main street is the 14C Dalton Tower (N.T.; key at 18 Market Place), once the court of the abbots (restored).

Hidden away in the 'Vale of Deadly Nightshade' are the important and attractive red sandstone ruins of *Furness Abbey (adm. daily, Sun from 2, Oct–Apr; fee). Visits during the holiday season should be avoided, if possible, at the popular hours. Founded in 1124 by Stephen of Blois (afterwards King) for Benedictines from Savigny in Normandy, who in 1147 adopted the Cistercian rule, the abbey soon attained a wealth and importance little inferior to Fountains and its abbot enjoyed feudal powers over the whole district of Furness. Little remains of the Norman nave. The transepts, with a fine N. doorway, are late Norman and E.E. work with 15C windows; the beautiful sedilia and piscina (in the choir) are Perpendicular, likewise the W. tower. The E. cloister wall is pierced by rich arches of 1230, and the elegant chapter house is E.E. The two effigies of Norman knights in armour in the vaulted 14C Infirmary Chapel are perhaps the oldest in England. Among the other interesting remains is the 12C gatehouse near the inn.

From Dalton A 590 goes on to (3¾ m.) **Barrow-in-Furness** (Hotels), a town (64,000 inhab.) founded on the iron and steel industry, and planned in 1847–65 by James Ramsden, a locomotive engineer It now has diesel-engine and armament works (Vickers-Armstrong's), with important docks and shipbuilding yards. In 1964 the keel of the first British Polaris submarine was laid here. A bridge near the docks leads to *Vickerstown*, a suburb on the long *Walney Island*, which shelters the harbour and has a nature reserve and lighthouse at its S. end (5 m.).—At *High Cocken*, 1½ m. N., is the house in which the youthful George Romney (see above) lived for upwards of ten years.—To the S.E., reached by A 5087, are (3¼ m.) *Rampside* and (4 m.) *Piel*, off which is Piel Island with the ruins of the castle (1327) where Lambert Simnel held a brief court in 1487.

From Dalton A 595 runs N. and makes a wide loop round the Duddon Sands.—At (41½ m.) *Broughton-in-Furness* (Hotel) a charming road to Coniston bears to the right. *Broughton Tower* (1744) incorporates a 14C pele. We cross the Duddon and leave on the right the Ulpha road and (44¾ m.; l.) the road to *Millom* (4 m. s.), with 19C iron-works, an interesting church and remains of its 14C castle.

The road sweeps round the base of *Black Combe* (1970 ft) and runs parallel to the sandy coast, crossing the Esk just below (59½ m.) *Muncaster Castle* (adm. Easter–Sept, Tues–Thurs, Sun, & BH, 2–5; fee), the seat of the Penningtons, remodelled by Salvin in 1866, with the 'Luck of Muncaster' (an old enamelled glass bowl; comp. p. 572), Elizabethan chimneypieces, and 16–17C furniture.

The grounds and bird garden are open from 12 and the Garden Centre from 8; the terrace commands perhaps the finest view in Cumbria overlooking the Esk. Henry VI was given refuge at the castle in 1464 after fleeing from Hexham; a monument on the hill to the N.E. marks the alleged spot where he was found wandering.

61 m. (l.) *Ravenglass* (Hotel), at the junction of the Esk, the Mite, and the Irt, has some remains of a Roman fort (Glannaventa).

Near Ravenglass is a large *Gullery* (best visited by boat), where many thousands of terns and black-headed gulls breed.—In summer a miniature railway (15-in. gauge) ascends the Mite and then the Esk to (4½ m.) *Eskdale Green* and (6¼ m.) *Dalegarth*, for upper Eskdale (see Rte 64D).

Crossing the Mite and then the Irt we reach (63½ m.) *Holmrook* (Hotel), 1¼ m. E. of which is *Irton*, which has a fine churchyard cross (9C).

To the left is the road to (3¼ m.) *Seascale* (Hotels), a seaside and golfing resort, and a good starting-point for motorists for the western Lake District.—Buses to *Gosforth* and *Whitehaven*, and to *Ravenglass* and *Millom*.

66¼ m. *Gosforth*, with the interesting *'Viking Cross', 14½ ft high, in the churchyard, showing a singular mixture of Norse saga and Christian lore in its decoration (10–11C).—Near (69 m.) *Calder Bridge* (Hotels), on the right, is *Calder Abbey*, a Cistercian ruin (adm. Fri 10–4; fee), founded from Furness Abbey in 1134, while to the s. are the atomic energy plants of *Calder Hall* and *Windscale*.

Of the abbey church the w. door (1180) and the N. arcade (1220–40) survive, with part of the s. transept. In the book-closet just outside the last is preserved a cresset-stone of 16 cups, the largest in England.

At (73 m.) *Egremont* the ruined castle (12–13C), on a high mound, retains its 12C gatehouse (comp. Wordsworth's 'Horn of Egremont Castle'). The Crab Fair, with sports and games, is held on the Sat nearest 18 Sept.

About 2½ m. N.W., lies *St Bees* (Hotel), named from St Bega, a 7C Irish maiden, and now frequented for its sandy beach. It has an interesting collegiate church (c. 1170), with a fine but weather-beaten w. doorway, and a boys' school, founded by Abp. Grindal in 1583. *St Bees Head*, to the N.W., attains a height of 462 ft.

78½ m. **Whitehaven** (Hotel), a seaport (26,700 inhab.) once trading with Virginia, is surrounded by coal-mines, some of which extend under the sea. The Georgian church of *St James* has a good interior with galleries, a fine ceiling, an elegant pulpit, and an altarpiece by Giulio Cesare Procaccini. A tablet in the churchyard of *St Nicholas* (burnt 1971) records the burial of George Washington's grandmother (d. 1701). John Paul Jones, who served his apprenticeship on a Whitehaven vessel, made an abortive raid on it in 1778, and its bombardment by a German submarine in 1915 was equally futile. At *Rosehill*, 2 m. N.E., is a small theatre (1959) where first-class plays and concerts are performed (Sept–June).

From Whitehaven to Keswick, 26½ m. We follow A 595 N.E. through (4 m.) *Distington*, beyond which we emerge from the colliery district and reach the Derwent valley.— 13½ m. **Cockermouth** (Hotel & Motel), is a little town (6400 inhab.) at the junction of the Cocker and the Derwent. William Wordsworth was born here in 1770 and his sister Dorothy in 1771; their father is buried in the church. *Wordsworth's Birthplace* (N.T.; adm. April–Oct daily exc. Thurs & Sun, 10.30–12.30, 2–5; fee), built in 1745, in the main street (w. end), has its original staircase and fireplaces. In 1648 the Roundheads slighted the 13–15C *Castle* of the Percys. Fletcher Christian, the 'Bounty' mutineer, was born in 1764 at *Moorland Close*, 1½ m. s.w. *Eaglesfield*, ¾ m. farther on, was the birthplace of John Dalton (1766–1844), chemist and physicist, and of Robert de Eglesfield (d. 1349), chaplain to Queen Philippa of Hainault and founder of Queen's College, Oxford. *Bridekirk* church, 2¼ m. N., incorporates two 12C doorways, and a *Font of c. 1140, a remarkable example of North English sculpture introducing Norse motifs, signed by the artist in Runic letters.—The main road (A 594) goes to Keswick viâ *Bassenthwaite Lake* (comp. p. 589); an alternative route (B 5292) runs s.e. and over Whinlatter Pass.

The direct road (A 595) from Cockermouth to (26 m.) *Carlisle* runs N.E., passing (10½ m.) *Mealsgate* and (14½ m.) *Red Dial*, which is just s.w. of the Romano-British town of *Olenacum*, mistakenly known as 'Old Carlisle'. From Mealsgate a pleasant alternative and hilly route follows B 5299 (r.) to (1¾ m.) *Boultongate* church with an unusual stone-vaulted nave (15C). The road goes on e. viâ (3 m.) *Sandale* (*View from fell above) to (8 m.) *Caldbeck*, in the churchyard of which is the grave of John Peel (d. 1854), the fox-hunter, whose home was close by. The famous song in his honour was composed by J. W. Graves in 1828. Thence we strike N.E. over the fells viâ *Dalston* to (20 m.) *Carlisle*, see Rte 73.

From Whitehaven to Carlisle viâ Maryport, 42 m. Railway, 40½ m. in 1¼ hr. Beyond (4 m.) *Distington* (see above) we bear left on A 596.— 8 m. *Workington* (Hotels) is a seaport (28,400 inhab.) at the mouth of the Derwent, with steel and wood-pulp works. Mary, Queen of Scots, landed here on her flight to England

after the battle of Langside (1568), and was escorted hence to Carlisle Castle.—
14½ m. *Maryport* (Hotel) is a decayed coal and iron port (11,600 inhab.). A road
(B 5300) goes on along the coast to Silloth (13 m.; see Rte 73) viâ *Allonby* (5 m.),
a fishing village and seaside resort. The Carlisle road turns inland.—30½ m.
Wigton (Hotel) is an old market town (with tweed factories) with an 18C church,
and a market fountain with fine reliefs by Thomas Woolner (1871).—42 m.
Carlisle, see Rte 73A.

64 THE LAKE DISTRICT

The **English Lake District**, popularly so called, is a tract about 35 miles square,
in the centre of Cumbria. Nowhere else in England is such a wealth and diversity of
natural beauty concentrated in so limited an area; and the comparatively small size of
its lakes and mountains is no index to the wildness and even grandeur attained at places
by its scenery. *Windermere*, the largest of the lakes, is but 10½ m. long; *Scafell Pike*, the
loftiest summit, is only 3210 ft high. The botanist and geologist will find the district a
happy hunting-ground. The vast forests that once covered a great part of the district
have largely disappeared, but reafforestation by the Forestry Commission is
conspicuous in several areas. Traces of Norwegian influence (dating from the 7C and
8C) still linger in the place-names and in the dialect and customs of the dales. The hardy
Herdwick sheep are the local breed; ram fairs are held in late September or early
October at Keswick, Boot, Wasdale Head and elsewhere.

The comparative lack of historical interest in the district is compensated by a
wealth of poetical and literary association. It was the spiritual home of the 'Lake
School'—Wordsworth, Coleridge, Southey, and their literary associates. Gray,
Wordsworth, and Harriet Martineau are among those who have written accounts
of the Lake District, which has inspired many volumes, down to the works of
Canon Rawnsley (1851–1920), and the 'Herries' saga of Sir Hugh Walpole (1884–
1941). See also 'Lake District History' and 'The Lake Counties' by *W. G. Collingwood*. A large and increasing number of the most beautiful sites and those most in
danger of disfigurement have been acquired by the National Trust (80,000 acres).

Visits to the Lake District should be made when possible in spring (when daffodils are abundant), early summer, or autumn, for the serenity of the landscape is
disturbed in July and August by the influx of holidaymakers. Views in the evening
light are particularly rewarding. Accommodation in the high season should be
reserved in advance. Coach parties will very often be found at many of the larger
hotels.

Plan of Tour. The great majority of visitors begin with Windermere, thus
progressing from the quieter to the wilder scenery. ONE DAY in the Lake District
may be well devoted to one of the whole-day tours (the *Wastwater Round* or
Ullswater Round), or to the *Buttermere Round* from *Keswick* described on p. 585,
which reveals some of the most exquisite scenery. The *Tour of the Langdales
from Ambleside* ranks with this. For a visit of Two DAYS the most serious rivals
to the trips just mentioned are the *Ambleside and Coniston Round* and the *Ullswater
Trip from Pooley Bridge to Patterdale*, continued over the Kirkstone Pass to
Windermere, and the drive from *Windermere to Keswick* through the Wordsworth
country. No thorough exploration of the Lake District, however, can be made
except on foot, and the following WEEK'S WALKING TOUR should be well within
the compass of the average pedestrian. 1st Day. From *Penrith* to (6 m.) *Pooley
Bridge*, and steamer thence up *Ullswater to Patterdale* (8 m.).—2nd Day. From
Patterdale to *Thirlspot*, over the top of *Helvellyn*, 3½–4½ hrs; thence to (5¾ m.)
Keswick, perhaps by bus.—3rd Day. From Keswick to *Buttermere* viâ *Borrowdale*
and *Honister Hause*, 14 m.—4th Day. From Buttermere viâ *Gatesgarth* to *Scarth
Gap*, and thence across *Upper Ennerdale* to the *Black Sail Pass* and *Wasdale Head*
(4–4¾ hrs); or viâ *Scale Force* and the *High Stile* ridge to Scarth Gap, and thence as
above (8–10 hrs in all).—5th Day. From Wasdale Head to *Dungeon Gill* viâ *Esk
Hause*, 3–4 hrs (with the ascent of *Scafell Pike*, 2 hrs more).—6th Day. From
Dungeon Gill to *Windermere* viâ *Grasmere* and *Ambleside*, 16 m. (last part by
steamer, if desired). Those who wish to get back to Penrith will be repaid by the
walk over the *Kirkstone Pass* to Patterdale (9 m. from Ambleside).

Motoring. M 6 now skirts the E. boundary of the Lake District; during summer
and holidays the exits from the motorway are often congested, and delays are
frequent. Parking in towns is extremely limited. The chief roads in the Lake
District, though rather twisty, have good surfaces, and ample width. The road

(unclassified) over the Wrynose Pass and Hardknott Pass, however, is steep and narrow with sharp bends. Passing is difficult and motorists must be prepared for reversing some distance on occasion.

Walks. In fine weather these will present no difficulty to a pedestrian of any experience; but, as some of the routes are not well marked, and as sudden mists are not uncommon, a good map and a compass, as well as a little food, should always be carried. Walkers not using well-marked routes should notify their hotel before setting out. Strong fell boots with formed soles, and weatherproof clothing are desirable.

Sport. GRASMERE SPORTS, held on the Thurs nearest 20 Aug, are the chief athletic festival in the Lake District, with the best wrestling (Cumberland and Westmorland style), fell-running, and hound-trailing. Interesting sheepdog trials are held in every dale; the best are at Rydal Park and on Applethwaite Common, E. of Troutbeck (p. 583), in August.—FOX HUNTING, the dalesman's favourite sport, is done on foot and demands great physical endurance. The chief packs are at Threlkeld, Patterdale, Ambleside, Eskdale, and Lorton.—ANGLING. Salmon, trout, and char are taken in the lakes, the best months being May, June, Aug, and Sept. The salmon-fishing in the Derwent and Eden is excellent, but the waters are now nearly all occupied by private owners or clubs.—*Gurning* is perhaps the oddest 'sport' in the district; at the Egremont Fair a prize is awarded to the person pulling the ugliest face with his head through a horse-collar.

Climbing. The most famous rock-climbing 'courses' are found on *Pillar Rock*, *Great Gable*, *Scafell*, *Gimmer Crag* (on the Langdale Pikes), *Pavey Ark*, *Dow Crag*, in *Borrowdale*, and round *Buttermere*. Many new routes, some of extreme technical difficulty, have been opened up in Borrowdale, Gillercombe, Deepdale, and Dovedale. The sport is organized locally by the *Fell & Rock Climbing Club*, which issues a number of handbooks describing the climbs in detail. Particulars of first-aid and mountain rescue stations are given in a booklet obtainable (free, with supplements) from the Mountain Rescue Committee, Hill House, Cheadle Hulme, Stockport, Cheshire.

Lake District National Park. The area was designated a National Park in 1951. The Park Guide published by H.M.S.O., and the one-inch tourist map of the area are invaluable to the visitor. The National Park Centre is at Brockhole, Windermere; while the Park Information Centre is at District Bank House, High Street, Windermere (Tel. No. 2498). During the summer other offices are opened at Ambleside, and the main centres, and a mobile information centre tours the Park. The English Lake Counties Travel Association is at Ellerthwaite on Windermere.

Glossary of Local Terms. *Band*, elevated terrace or ridge between two lower tracts; *Beck*, stream; *Combe*, hollow; *Dodd*, lower spur or foothill, generally rounded; *Fell*, mountain; *Force*, waterfall; *Gill*, *Ghyll*, mountain torrent, narrow ravine; *Hause*, top of a pass (French 'col'); *Holme*, island; *How*, *Howe*, low rounded hill; *Knott*, rocky knob; *Nab*, projection, promontory; *Pike*, peak; *Pitch*, steep ascent; *Raise*, top of a ridge; *Scar*, *Scarth*, rocky face; *Scree*, steep slope of loose stones; *Stickle*, sharp peak; *Tarn*, small lake; *Thwaite*, clearing; *Trod*, sheep-path; *Wyke*, bay.

A   Ullswater and Patterdale

Penrith (Rte 62A) is the gateway for the Ullswater part of the Lake District.—Through express trains from London (Euston) to Penrith in c. 4 hrs.

FROM PENRITH TO PATTERDALE BY ROAD AND BOAT. Buses, in connection with the trains, from Penrith (railway station or Sandgate) to *Pooley Bridge*. The direct route to Pooley Bridge is viâ the M 6 junction, thence A 66, and l. on A 592, passing *Dalemain* (r.) an old Georgian-fronted house (adm. daily exc. Fri, 2–5.15, Easter–Sept; fee); but we follow A 6 to *Eamont Bridge*, 1 m. s. of Penrith, where we turn r. on B 5320 between *King Arthur's Round Table* (l.) and *Mayburgh* (r.), two ancient circular earthworks.—2 m. *Yanwath Hall*, where we cross the railway, has an old pele tower, overlooking the 'barmkin' or inner bailey.—3 m. *Tirril*

(Hotel), c. 1½ m. beyond which is *Barton* church (r.) with double arches (12C and 14C) to its 'central' tower.—6 m. **Pooley Bridge** (Hotels), at the foot of Ullswater.

On the site of the 13C *Dacre Castle* (now a private house), 2 m. N., the kings of England, Scotland, and Cumberland are said to have met c. 927.

*Ullswater (476 ft; i.e. 'Ulf's Water'), the grandest of English lakes in scenery and the second in size, separates Cumberland (w. bank as far as Glencoyne) from Westmorland (E. bank and head). It is 7½ m. long and ¼–¾ m. wide, and consists of three reaches, the bends of which prevent any general view of the lake as a whole. Its scenery increases in beauty as we near its head.

A good road skirts the entire w. side of the lake, but the road on the more rugged E. bank, passing (2 m.) Sharrow Bay Hotel (closed in winter) turns inland at (4 m.) *Howtown* (Hotel) for *Martindale* with its tiny church (1¼ m.; 1633) and for the lakeside hamlet of *Sandwick* (2 m.; see below).

A MOTOR-YACHT service operates in summer from Pooley Bridge to (70 min.) Glenridding thrice daily (incl. Sun) and four times on weekdays in July and Aug, calling at Howtown and (weekdays only) Aira Force. At the head of the first reach, 3 m. in length, lies (l.) *Howtown* (see above). Passing *Skelly Neb* (r; 1434 ft) we enter the second reach (c. 3¼ m. long). On the left is *Sandwick*, at the mouth of *Martindale*, enclosed between *Hallin Fell* (l.; 1271 ft) and *Sleet Fell* (1179 ft). On the right are *Gowbarrow Park* and *Fell* (1578 ft; see below), and beyond the Aira Force pier *Glencoyne Park*. Catstycam, the N.E. spur of Helvellyn, becomes prominent at the end of the reach, with the main summit to its left. The last *Reach, running N. and s., is about 1¼ m. long and presents a striking "blend of wild overhanging mountain and rich homelike foreground". To the right is the finely wooded *Stybarrow Crag* (N.T.), to the left the steep side of *Place Fell* (2155 ft). The pier at *Glenridding* is ¼ m. from the head of the lake and 1 m. from *Patterdale* (see below), dominated by the imposing St.Sunday Crag.

FROM PENRITH TO PATTERDALE BY ROAD. To (6 m.) *Pooley Bridge*, see above. A 592 follows the N.W. bank of Ullswater (Hotels), affording increasingly fine views across it, and skirting (10 m.) *Gowbarrow Park* (main entrance at 11 m., the foot of the Dockray road, A 5091).

Gowbarrow Park (inseparably associated with Wordsworth's 'Daffodils') includes the whole Ullswater side of *Gowbarrow Fell* (1578 ft; N.T. 754 acres), together with Aira Force, reached by a path (¼ m.) ascending from the entrance. To the right stands *Lyulph's Tower*, a small shooting-lodge, the name of which is supposed to go back to the same Baron de l'Ulf after whom the lake itself is named (the 'Ulfo's lake' of Scott's 'Bridal of Triermain'). Red and fallow deer roam the fell. *Aira Force, one of the most beautiful waterfalls of the Lake District, is 65 ft high and romantically situated in a deep winding glen. The scene of Wordsworth's 'Somnambulist' is laid here. A path ascends the left bank, above the fall, to (1¼ m.) *Dockray*, passing another pretty little fall named *High Force*.

Our road continues to skirt the lake, below *Glencoyne Park* (N.T. 2692 acres; 17C farmhouse), then passes under *Stybarrow Crag* (view), above which are the ancient oaks of *Glencoyne Wood* (N.T.).—13½ m. **Glenridding** (Hotel), with a pier (boat trips), is at the mouth of the valley of that name. We pass a well (r.), with misty traditions of baptisms by St Patrick, and cross the mouth of Grisedale.

14½ m. **Patterdale** (Hotel), a good centre for excursions, is a tiny village, charmingly situated at the head of Ullswater and the foot of the dale of its own name ('Patrick's Dale').

EXCURSIONS. The walk to (5 m.) *Howtown* (returning by boat) by path skirting the S.E. bank of the lake, viâ *Sandwick* and *Hallin Fell*, may be recommended. Walkers may return to Patterdale (c. 2 hrs) viâ *Boardale* and *Boardale Hause* (1250 ft; view), while from the Hause the top of **Place Fell** (2154 ft; view) is easily reached in ¾ hr. Another pleasant walk may be taken to (1–1½ hr) *Angle Tarn* viâ (½ hr) Boardale Hause.

ASCENTS. ***Helvellyn** (3113 ft), the third in height and one of the finest in form of the Lake District mountains, is ascended from Patterdale by one or other of three routes. *a*. For the RED TARN ROUTE (2¼–2¾ hrs; steeper but more interesting) we follow the Grisedale lane (see below) for ¾ m. and then (finger-post) turn right and cross the stream. A few minutes later the well-marked path turns to the left and ascends over the fell towards a conspicuous gateway on *Striding Edge*, about 2 m. ahead of us. Striding Edge may be followed to the top. In mist, gale, or snow it should be treated with caution, but otherwise it presents no difficulty to the steady-headed. Those who wish to avoid it keep to the right, pass to the N. of *Red Tarn* (2356 ft), the highest in the Lake District (ground here rather boggy), and mount to *Swirral Edge* (2500 ft) and (¾ hr) the summit.—*b*. By the GLENRIDDING ROUTE (3¼–4¼ hrs) we leave the road opposite the Ullswater Hotel and ascend the left bank of the beck to (1½ m.) the *Greenside Smelting Mills*. Thence, avoiding both the cart-track to the right and the path to the left, we follow the pony track straight on, along the main beck. Just short of (½ hr) *Kepplecove Tarn* (1825 ft) the track (not easy to find) zigzags up to the right, at the brow of the hill bending to the left. On reaching (½ hr) the top of the ridge (c. 2800 ft) we turn sharply to the left for (½ hr) the summit.—*c*. For the GRISEDALE ROUTE (2¾–3¼ hrs; viâ Grisedale Tarn), see below.—The *View from Helvellyn is extensive but less varied than from some other peaks. Windermere, Esthwaite Water, and Coniston Water are visible to the S., with the Irish Sea beyond them; Ullswater is conspicuous to the N.E. In the extreme N.W. are the Solway Firth and the Dumfriesshire hills. Among the most prominent peaks are Scafell Pike and Great Gable (S.W.), Skiddaw and Saddleback (N.), St Sunday Crag and High Street (S.E.), and Fairfield (S.). To the E. are the long rolling ridges of the Pennine Chain. At our feet lies Red Tarn, between Striding Edge and Catstycam. Near the top of Helvellyn are memorials of Charles Gough (whose death here from exposure in 1805 and the fidelity of whose dog have been sung by Scott and Wordsworth), and of the first aeroplane to land on the summit. The descent may be made to *Grasmere*, *Thirlspot*, or *Wythburn* (p. 589). —**St Sunday Crag** (2756 ft; 1½ hr; view) is ascended by a zigzag track (l.) beginning about 200 yds beyond (1½ m.) the farm of *Elmhow* in Grisedale, or (better) by a track starting behind Patterdale post office and ascending through *Glenamara Park* and along the side of *Birks* (2040 ft). The descent may be made viâ Deepdale. —**Fairfield** (2863 ft) and its N. spur *Cofa Pike* are other good viewpoints (comp. below).

FROM PATTERDALE TO GRASMERE (8½ m. in 3–3½ hrs). The route, ascending *Grisedale*, between Striding Edge, Dollywaggon Pike, and Seat Sandal, on the right, and St Sunday Crag and Fairfield, on the left, is easy to follow. Leaving the road a little W. of the church we follow the right bank of Grisedale Beck to (½ hr) the farm of *Elmhow*. The track crosses the stream about ¼ hr farther up, turns r. and then l., crosses a side-stream, and reaches (20 min.) a mountain hut about ½ hr below *Grisedale Tarn* (1768 ft). We keep to the l. of the tarn and reach (¼ hr) the top of **Grisedale Pass** (1929 ft), between *Seat Sandal* (2415 ft; r.) and *Fairfield* (2863 ft), where we pass through a gap in the wall. Fine views of Coniston Water and Grasmere are disclosed as we descend the winding pony track to (1¼ hr) the main road, where we turn left for Grasmere.—Robust walkers may easily combine the 'traverse' of St Sunday Crag or Fairfield, or both, with this route.

FROM PATTERDALE TO KESWICK BY THE STICKS PASS, 11 m. (last 5 m. by road). This route is now rarely used. To (1½ m.) the *Greenside Smelting Mills*, see above. About ¼ m. farther on we leave the Helvellyn bridle-path and ascend the steep zigzag cart-track to the right, viâ (¼ hr) the *Greenside Lead Mine* (disused) and the N. end of *Greenside Reservoir*. From (½ hr) the top of the **Sticks Pass** (2420 ft; view), named from upright stakes planted in the ground which have now disappeared, the path descends in zigzags to (¾ hr) the farmhouse of *Stanah* and to the Vale of St John road just short of A 591, 4¾ m. from *Keswick* and ¾ m. from *Thirlspot*.

From Patterdale to Keswick viâ Troutbeck, 18 m. by road. From Patterdale to (3½ m.) the divergence of the Dockray road, see above. The road (*Retrospects) ascends between *Glencoyne Park* (l.) and *Gowbarrow Park* and *Fell*. [Walkers in either direction should do the bit between the lake and Dockray viâ Gowbarrow Park and Aira Force.] From (5¼ m.) *Dockray* a fine high-level walk leads through Glencoyne Park. Beyond (6½ m.) *Matterdale End* the road reaches its highest point (1124 ft), to the w. of *Great Mell Fell* (1760 ft).—9 m. *Troutbeck*, and thence to (18 m.) *Keswick*, see Rte 62A.

From Patterdale to Hawes Water. The easiest route starts from *Howtown* (comp. above). The walk thence takes 3¾–4 hrs. We ascend by a track on the banks of the *Fusedale Beck*. After about ½ hr we incline to the left (little or no visible path) and cross a tributary stream. To the right is the Martindale deer-forest, almost the last refuge of the indigenous red deer that used to range over the Pennine and Lake mountains. In ½ hr we reach *Wether Hill* (2174 ft), the top of the ridge, affording a fine view s. and w. (Coniston Old Man s.w.). We descend in the same general direction (s.e.), follow (½ hr) the *Measand Beck*, and soon reach the path descending the w. bank of Hawes Water (r.) to (½ hr) *Burn Banks*, below the foot of the reservoir. Thence it is ½ hr more either to Bampton (p. 561) or to the hotel on the e. bank.—A longer, but more interesting walk is to turn due s. at Wether Hill and follow the ridge over *Red Crag* (2328 ft), *Raven Howe* (2358 ft) and *High Raise* (2634 ft) to Kidsty Pike, where we join the path to Riggindale. A ridge walk, with excellent views, this follows the line of the old Roman road (see below).—The direct route from Patterdale to Haweswater (4½–5½ hrs; for good walkers) diverges (l.) from the Windermere road at (2 m.) Brothers Water. We pass through the hamlet of *Low Hartsop*, cross (¾ m.) the *Hayeswater Gill* (route to the obvious pass on the right to be avoided), and in ½ m. more recross the beck and pass a little to the n. of the foot of *Hayes Water* (1383 ft). A zigzag track, keeping to the left of the *Knott* (2423 ft), ascends to (¾ hr) the top of the ridge. The direct route to Mardale passes through a gateway in the wall and then drops very steeply for 1 hr to the foot of *Riggindale*, whence a path (l.) follows the w. bank of the reservoir for Bampton (1½ hr), while another (r.) rounds the head of the reservoir and reaches the hotel on the e. bank in 1½ hr. [Little time is lost by inclining to the left and including *Kidsty Pike* (2560 ft), from the shoulder of which a slanting track leads down to the foot of *Riggindale*.] Those who wish to combine the ascent of **High Street** (2719 ft; view) with this route diverge to the right at the top of the ridge and follow it to the s. (1 hr). The descent to (1¾ hr) *Mardale* leads viâ *Long Stile* to the foot of *Blea Water* (1584 ft), whence the path to the dale is distinct (not very easy). High Street derives its name from an old Roman road that ran from the camp at the head of Windermere to Brocavum (Brougham) over High Street, past Rampsgill Head, and High Raise; traces of it are visible near the top of High Street; and it may be followed along the ridge s. of Wether Hill (see above).

Haweswater (789 ft; 4¼ m. long, ⅛–½ m. wide; Hotel) was in 1937 converted into a reservoir for the water-supply of Manchester by the construction of a 90 ft dam near *Burn Banks*, at the foot of the lake. Every house in the dale was submerged and the village of *Mardale Green*, near the head, including the old church, was demolished. The Haweswater Hotel, half-way along the afforested e. bank, takes the place of the old Dun Bull Inn. The lake has lost most of its charm, but the mountain group at its head is fine (Harter Fell, High Street, Kidsty Pike, Welter Crags).—Active walkers may reach *Windermere* from Haweswater Hotel viâ *High Street* and the *Troutbeck Valley* (5¼–6¼ hrs), or viâ the *Nan Bield Pass* (2050 ft), *Kentmere* and the *Garburn Pass* (1450 ft; 4¾–5¾ hrs); or by a good but little-used route viâ the *Gatescarth Pass* (1900 ft), *Sadgill* (2½–2¾ hrs; the highest hamlet in Long Sleddale), *Kentmere* and the *Garburn Pass* (5¼–5¾ hrs).—*Kendal* may be reached viâ the *Gatescarth Pass* and the beautiful valley of *Long Sleddale*, the 'Long Whindale' of 'Robert Elsmere' (5¾–6¾ hrs).

From Patterdale to Windermere, 12½ m. (bus). The road (A 592) ascends through Patterdale, crossing (1 m.) the Deepdale Beck and (1¾ m.) the Goldrill Beck. It next turns to the right, and skirts the e. side of *Brothers Water* (520 ft; N.T.), popularly supposed to be named

from the drowning of two brothers (more probably a corruption of
'Broader' Water; retrospect of Place Fell). From (3¼ m.) Brotherswater
Hotel the road mounts rapidly (1 in 4–10) to (6 m.) the top of **Kirkstone
Pass** (1489 ft), between *Caudale Head* (1474 ft; left; overtopped by
Stony Cove Pike, to the E.) and *Broad End* (1871 ft; right; wide view).
About 200 yds short of this point (r.) is the stone after which the pass is
named, from its supposed resemblance to a church (*View). At the
Kirkstone Pass Inn (1476 ft; rfmts.) the direct road (1 in 4½–6) for
Ambleside diverges on the right down the *Stock Gill* valley. The main
road (1 in 6) trends to the left, then descends above the beautiful
Troutbeck valley. Just before (9 m.) the Queen's Head Inn a road on the
right for Ambleside (4 m.) leads through the village of *Troutbeck*
(Hotels), at the s. end of which is *Townend* (N.T.; adm. April–Oct,
daily exc. Sat & Mon; Wed in March, 2–6; fee), the yeoman residence of
the Brownes (c. 1626), whose furniture and possessions are preserved,
with a finely timbered barn. The main road runs straight on to (9¾ m.)
Troutbeck Church (with a window by Morris, Madox Brown, and
Burne-Jones), beyond which the road ascends again to the *Borrans*
(view).—12½ m. *Windermere*, see Rte 64C.

B Keswick, Derwentwater, and Buttermere

Penrith (Rte 62A) is the gateway for this section of the Lake District also. Road
thence to (18 m.) *Keswick*, p. 572.

KESWICK (280 ft; 5200 inhab.), on the Greta, c. ½ m. from Derwentwater, lies in a sheltered position beneath Skiddaw. At Easter and in
summer an invasion of holidaymakers transforms the character of the
town, and in winter ski-ing in the surrounding fells is becoming increasingly popular.

Numerous Hotels, caravan, and camping sites.
Post Office, Main St.; *Information Office*, Moot Hall.—GOLF COURSE at
Embleton, 9½ m. N.W.
Buses throughout the county.
Motor Launches on Derwentwater (50 min. for a round trip), call at Ashness
Gate, Lodore, High and Low Brandelhow, and *Hawes End* (for Catbells).

The main streets converge on the narrow market-place, with the quaint
Moot Hall (1813). At the corner is the Royal Oak Hotel, where Scott
wrote part of the 'Bridal of Triermain'. Thence Station Street, traversing
the delightful *Fitz Park*, bounded by the river, passes the *Museum*
(adm. weekdays 10–12, 2–5; fee). Notable among its collections are
MSS., letters and personal relics of Southey and Hugh Walpole (Head
by Epstein), two MSS. of Wordsworth, a loving cup (1858) made of
silver from the Goldscope Mines, a geological collection, and early rock
harmonicons, as well as a model of the Lake District (1834), and works
by Brangwyn. To the s.w. of Moot Hall rises *St John's* church (by
Salvin; 1836) with a conspicuous spire. The churchyard, in which is
buried Sir Hugh Walpole (s.w. corner), commands a marvellous view.

To the right of Main Street (beyond the Post Office) lies *Greta Hall* (now part
of Keswick School), the residence of Coleridge from 1800 to 1803 and of Southey
from 1803 till his death in 1843. Near Greta Bridge (l.) is an *Exhibition Room*
(adm. Mon–Fri, 9–12.30, 1.30–5) illustrating the methods of pencil-making in
Keswick from 1558 (with graphite) to the present day. The plumbago or 'wad'

mine at Seathwaite (p. 588) has long been closed, and Keswick gets its black-lead from other sources.

Crosthwaite church (c. ½ m. farther on), on the site of a church built by St Kentigern in 553, dates mainly from 1553 and has (unusually) twelve 'consecration crosses' on its outside walls. Within are a brass to Sir John Ratcliffe (d. 1527) and a monument (by Lough) to Southey (inscription by Wordsworth), whose grave is in the churchyard. Canon H. D. Rawnsley (1851–1920) was vicar of Crosthwaite in 1883–1917.—Shelley lived at Keswick for a short time in 1812 (in a cottage on Chestnut Hill), soon after his marriage to Harriet Westbrook.

*Derwentwater (244 ft; Hotels on s.e. shore), one of the most absolutely satisfying in its loveliness of all the lakes of England, is 3 m. long, 1 m. wide, and 10–70 ft deep. Its banks present a wonderful blending of abrupt crag, green fell, and wooded slopes, while the final charm is lent by the islets dotting its surface. The mountain background, especially Skiddaw (to the N.), is very imposing. To the s. opens the romantic Borrowdale. The chief islands (all N.T.) are *Derwent Island* (originally Hertholm), with a house on it; *Lord's Island*, once the site of Lord Derwentwater's mansion; the smaller *Rampsholme*; and *St Herbert's Island*, the site of the retreat of St Hereberht, a disciple of St Cuthbert. The *Floating Island*, a periodic appearance near Lodore, is a tangled mass of weeds made buoyant by marsh gas. The N.T. own 562 acres of the lake itself, as well as large stretches of its beautiful shore.

Southey maintained that the best view of Derwentwater was obtained from "the terrace between Applethwaite and Millbeck". To reach this point we may follow the Greta N.W. through Fitz Park to A 591, where we turn right, cross the railway and keep right for (1½ m.) *Ormathwaite* (once visited by Benjamin Franklin) and then bear left for (2 m.) *Applethwaite*.—A much closer view of the lake is enjoyed from (¾ m.) **Friar's Crag* (N.T.), purchased in 1922 as a memorial to Canon Rawnsley, a founder of the N.T., with *Calf Close Bay* (¼ m. s.). It is reached by following Lake Rd. past *Cockshott Wood* (N.T.). On the crag is a memorial to John Ruskin (1819–1900).—The best view is perhaps that from ***Castle Head** (529 ft; N.T.), a wooded hill ½ m. s., just to the E. of B 5289 (see below). The top commands a view of the whole lake, at the s. end of which are the 'Jaws of Borrowdale', apparently filled up by the conical Castle Crag. The background just to the right of this is formed by Great End, Scafell Pike, and Scafell. Beyond the next gap come Scawdel Fell and Maiden Moor, the latter sloping (N.) towards Cat Bells, over the shoulders of which peer Hindscarth and Robinson. Farther to the right are High Stile and Red Pike, rising over Newlands Hause. To the N. (r.) of this depression are the prominent butt of Causey Pike, Sand Hill, and Grisedale Pike.— Other good views of Derwentwater are afforded by *Walla Crag* (see below), *Latrigg* (1203 ft; N.E.), the terrace of *Cat Bells* (1481 ft; s.w.), and *Swinside* (803 ft; above Portinscale).

*ROUND DERWENTWATER BY ROAD (10 m.; bus to Borrowdale). Leaving Keswick by B 5289 (s. of the Moot Hall), we pass through the *Great Wood*, with *Walla Crag* (1234 ft; view) rising to the left. Beyond it is *Falcon Crag* (1050 ft).—2 m. the lane on the left leads to Watendlath (p. 575). In the grounds of *Barrow House* (l.), now a Youth Hostel, are falls with a descent of over 100 ft, and 1 m. farther on, are the FALLS OF LODORE (fee) which (in spite of Southey's rhapsodic verses) are disappointing except after heavy rain.—We cross the Derwent by a couple of bridges for (4½ m.) **Grange** (Hotels, closed in winter), a charming village greatly frequented in summer.—5 m. *Manesty*. Walkers should here choose the path to the right (from which a path for Newlands diverges after ¼ m.), as it affords more open views of the lake. On the left beneath the ridge of *Cat Bells* (1481 ft) are the N.T. estates of *Manesty Park* and *Brandelhow Park*, and *Brackenburn*, the home of Sir Hugh Walpole (1884–1941).—Beyond (7½ m.) Swinside Lodge

Hotel, where the Buttermere road comes in on our left, the lake is mainly hidden by trees.—At (8¾ m.) *Portinscale* (Hotels) we cross the Derwent for (10 m.) *Keswick*.

ASCENTS FROM KESWICK. The ascent of Skiddaw (3053 ft; up and down 4½–6 hrs) offers a safe and easy day on the fells. We pass under the railway to the right of the station and then follow (¼ m.) *Spoony Green Lane*, the second turning on the right, which works round the w. and N. side of *Latrigg* (see below) and ends (1¼ m.) at a gate opening on a road from Applethwaite. There is another gate about 50 yds to the right (E.) through which we pass on to the open hillside. The track leads to the left along a wall to (¾ m.) a hut. The next ½ hr is the steepest part of the route (good retrospects). At the angle of the wall the track bears to the left and becomes nearly level (cairn). We keep a little to the right of the highest part of the *Little Man* (2837 ft), the s. extremity of the main ridge (view better than from the summit), and pass through (¼ hr) a fence. We reach the *High Man* or top in less than ½ hr more. The panorama is extensive. Among the most prominent points in the "turbulent chaos of dark mountains" to the s. are Helvellyn (S.E.), the Scafells, the Borrowdale peaks, and Coniston Old Man (in the distance). Bassenthwaite is conspicuous to the w. with the Isle of Man behind; to the N.W. are the hills of Galloway. A shorter (but steeper) descent leads viâ *Carl Side* (2400 ft) and *Millbeck*.—*Latrigg* (1203 ft; 1½–2 hrs up and down), the s. 'cub' of Skiddaw, commands a better view than that from Skiddaw itself.

Saddleback or Blencathra (2847 ft), E. of Skiddaw, is a more difficult and more remunerative climb. The best plan is to proceed by A 66 to (6 m.) *Scales* (p. 552) and follow the whole ridge of the mountain from E. to w., with descent to *Threlkeld* (4–5 hrs in all) or to Keswick (5–6 hrs). The route, keeping to the left (s.) of *Scales Tarn*, is fairly obvious. The view of Thirlmere and the Vale of St John is charming; other features are seen much as from Skiddaw.

Helvellyn (3113 ft) may rank among the Keswick mountains, though the actual ascent (marked by cairns and whitened stones) begins on the Grasmere road either at (5½ m.) *Thirlspot* (1½–2¼ hrs) or at (8 m.) *Wythburn* (1¼–1½ hr). (a) The track from Thirlspot begins behind the King's Head Inn and after 1¼–1½ hr is joined on the left by the Keppelcove Tarn track from Ullswater. A sharp climb hence brings us to (¼ hr) the *Low Man* (3033 ft) and (10 min) the *High Man* or summit. (b) The well-marked track from Wythburn leaves the road by the church. About half-way up there is a patch of soft ground where the track is a little less clear. 40–50 min Spring (l.), the highest in England. In 5 min more we join the Grasmere track (r.) ½ hr below the top. View and descent to Patterdale, see Rte 64A; descent to Grasmere, see p. 596.

FROM KESWICK TO THIRLMERE BY CASTLERIGG CIRCLE AND VALE OF ST JOHN (7¼ m. to Thirlspot). We follow the Penrith road, then take the right-hand turning immediately beyond A 591. Passing (1½ m.) a lane on the right, we reach (r.) the *Castlerigg Stone Circle* (N.T.; 100 ft in diameter), consisting of 38 stones, the tallest nearly 8 ft high; within the circle (E. side) is a rectangle of 10 stones. We rejoin A 66 ½ m. farther on, near the Naddle Beck, and take the next turning on the right which, crossing (3½ m.) the St John's Beck, joins B 5322 in the *Vale of St John*, flanked on the left by the *Wanthwaite Crags* and the *Dodds of Helvellyn*. Ahead rises the *Castle Rock* (c. 1000 ft), familiar from Scott's 'Bridal of Triermain'. At (6½ m.) the fork we may either keep left for (7½ m.) *Thirlspot*, or right for (7 m.) the dam at the foot of Thirlmere beyond the main road.

FROM KESWICK TO WATENDLATH, 5 m. due s., a road affording delightful views. We diverge to the left from the Borrowdale road, a little short of (2 m.) *Barrow House* (p. 584). After ½ m. we cross the Barrow Beck by *Ashness Bridge* (*View). Thence we ascend through wood, most of the way skirting the Watendlath Beck. *Watendlath*, on a small tarn (847 ft), is the scene of much of Sir Hugh Walpole's 'Judith Paris'. Just N. of the hamlet is the *Churn* or *Devil's Punchbowl*. Walkers may follow the track (s.w.) to (1½ m.) *Rosthwaite*, on the Borrowdale road; or they may go on from Watendlath over the fells E. to (1½ hr) *Thirlmere* (see below).

*FROM KESWICK TO BUTTERMERE viâ Borrowdale and Honister Hause, returning viâ Newlands. This round of 22 m. is certainly one of the finest in Britain.—From Keswick to (4½ m.) *Grange*, at the entrance to Borrowdale, see above. Here we keep straight on, following the right

bank of the Derwent, with *Grange Fell* (1363 ft; N.T.) on the left. From
a slate quarry (l.) about ½ m. farther on a track ascends to (7 min.) the
Bowder Stone (N.T.), a marvellously balanced mass of metamorphic
rock (estimated to weigh c. 2000 tons) fallen from the adjacent cliffs.
Its top (26 ft) is reached by a ladder. Immediately opposite is the wooded
Castle Crag (900 ft; N.T.; view). Farther s. over Rosthwaite rise
Glaramara (see below) and (w. of that) Great End, the N. buttress of
the Scafell group. The road clings to the river until suddenly the valley
opens out. *Borrowdale is the most beautiful valley in the Lake District,
with its level green floor enclosed by picturesque and multi-coloured
crag and fell. "A truly secreted spot is this, completely surrounded by
the most horrid romantic mountains that are in this world of wonders."
—6 m. The village of **Rosthwaite** (Hotel) is attractively situated on the
Stonethwaite Beck.

A bridle-path leads N.E. from Rosthwaite to (1½ m.) *Watendlath*, whence we may
reach (5 m.) *Keswick* as described above (a charming route).

Rosthwaite, or Seatoller (see below), is the starting-point for the ascent of
*Great Gable (2949 ft), the finest in form of all the Lake mountains, either via
the Sty Head Pass (2¼–3½ hrs) or viâ Honister Hause, *Grey Knotts* (2287 ft),
Brandreth (2344 ft), and *Green Gable* (2603 ft). Owing to the central situation of
Great Gable the *View is magnificent. It includes Skiddaw, Helvellyn, the Butter-
mere peaks, the Scafells, the Pillar, Wastwater, Ennerdale Water, Crummock
Water, and a strip of Windermere. The Isle of Man is visible and sometimes
even Snowdon. Bronze map on the summit, see p. 588. Great Gable is supposed
to have been in Carlyle's mind when he described the mountain-ascent in 'Sartor
Resartus' (ii. 6). The descent may be made to Wasdale Head viâ Sty Head, or viâ
Beck Head, between Great Gable and *Kirk Fell* (2631 ft).—*Glaramara* (2560 ft),
ascended in 2–2½ hrs, affords an exquisite view of Borrowdale and Derwentwater.

About ½ m. beyond Rosthwaite, near the church, the route to *Stonethwaite* and the Stake Pass (p. 595), dominated by the finely shaped
Eagle Crag, diverges to the left, while to the right, beyond the Derwent,
is *Longthwaite*, a youth hostel. At (7¼ m.) the hamlet of *Seatoller* we
begin the steep ascent (1 in 4 in parts) to (8¾ m.) the top of **Honister
Hause** (1190 ft; youth hostel), with a noble *Retrospect of Borrowdale.
To the left rises *Honister Crag* (1750 ft), somewhat defaced by its slate
quarries. The descent, abrupt at first (1 in 5–9) traverses wild and bleak
country; but beyond (11 m.) the farmhouse of *Gatesgarth*, at the foot of
the pass, where the Scarf Gap path leads to the left towards Ennerdale,
the verdant beauty of Buttermere is suddenly revealed. Our road skirts
the N.E. bank of Buttermere, passing (12 m.) *Hassness*, a Ramblers'
Association guest house, to (13 m.) the village of **Buttermere.**

*Buttermere (329 ft; 1¼ m. long, ⅓ m. wide, and 94 ft deep near its S.E. end)
and its N.W. neighbour **Crummock Water** (321 ft; 2½ m. long, ¾ m. wide, 144 ft
deep), connected by a stream ¾ m. in length, fill a trough-like valley about 5 m. long
and ¼–¾ m. wide. Both lakes belong to the National Trust. On the w. mountains fall abruptly to the water's edge. At the N.W. corner of Buttermere, opposite
the village, are the thread-like cataracts of *Sour Milk Gill*, descending from
Bleaberry Tarn.—In a small ravine s.w. of Crummock Water is *Scale Force
(N.T.), a striking waterfall with a sheer leap of at least 120 ft, reached from
Buttermere (2¼ m.) by crossing the stream connecting the two lakes (path usually
wet).—The visit to Scale Force may be extended by a not very attractive route to
(1¾ m.) *Floutern Tarn* and (2½ m.) *Ennerdale Water*, or it may be combined with an
ascent of *Red Pike* (2479 ft). The direct route for the latter (1½–2 hrs), however, is
up Ruddy Beck, the stream flowing into the s.w. corner of Crummock Water. The
*View includes Ennerdale Water and many other lakes and tarns. The descent may
be made viâ *Bleaberry Tarn* (see above). A fine ramble goes on s. along the ridge
over *High Stile* (2644 ft) and *High Crag* (2443 ft) to the Scarth Gap path, returning

by it to Gatesgarth and Buttermere.—*Fleetwith Pike* (2126 ft), of which Honister
Crag (see above) is part, is likewise ascended from Buttermere (2–2½hrs) and affords
a fine though limited view.—*Buttermere How* or *Moss* (1725 ft), E. of the village,
easily ascended in 1 hr, is a good point of view. From Buttermere along Crummock
Water to (3½ m.) *Scale Hill*, see below; to *Wasdale Head* viâ *Scarth Gap*, see p. 588.

The return route to Keswick ascends steeply from Buttermere (good
retrospect) to (14¼ m.) *Newlands Hause* (1096 ft), between *Robinson*
(2417 ft) on the right and *Whiteless Pike* (2159 ft) and *Wanlope* (2533 ft)
on the left. A short steep descent brings us to the high-lying *Keskadale*,
with an ancient mountain oak-wood on the left. At (16¾ m.) *Gillbrow*,
whence a road leads r. to *Newlands Church* (½ m.), we begin our descent
through the lovely valley of **Newlands**.

The name of the *Goldscope Mines* in this valley may possibly be a corruption of
Gottesgab ('God's gift'), the name used by the German (chiefly Bavarian) miners
imported by Elizabeth I c. 1566. Some local patronymics trace back to the same
source.

At (18¾ m.) a fork we keep to the right (left for Braithwaite, see below),
and beyond (19½ m.) *Swinside* we join the road from Grange and turn
left for (22 m.) *Keswick*.

FROM KESWICK TO BUTTERMERE VIÂ THE WHINLATTER PASS, 14½ m. (bus). The
road (A 66) runs w., crossing the Derwent at (1 m.) *Portinscale*. Just before (2½ m.)
Braithwaite (Motel), at the entrance to *Coledale* (see below), A 66 strikes off r.
Our road (B 5292) winds up in steady ascent (steep at first), with a glimpse of
Bassenthwaite Lake, to (5 m.) the top of the Whinlatter Pass (1043 ft), between
Lord's Seat (r.; 1811 ft) and *Grisedale Pike* (2593 ft). We traverse Thornthwaite
Forest of the Forestry Commission. About 3 m. farther we turn left and left
again to join B 5289 in the *Vale of Lorton* which we follow to the left. At (10 m.)
the fork B 5289 bears left for *Lanthwaite Green* and runs along the E. bank of Crum-
mock Water to (14½ m.) *Buttermere*; while the right-hand fork leads to (10¾ m.)
Scale Hill (Hotel, closed in winter), ½ m. from the foot of Crummock Water. The
Scale Hill Hotel may be made the starting-point of walks viâ *Mosedale* and *Floutern
Tarn* (pron. 'Flootern'; 1250 ft) to (6 m.) the *Angler's Inn* (p. 598) at the foot of
Ennerdale Water or of a drive viâ (1½ m.) **Loweswater** (397 ft; N.T.) a little-visited
lake 1 m. long, and (6 m.) *Lamplugh* to (11 m.) the *Angler's Inn*. Between Scale Hill
and the N. end of Crummock Water are pleasant woods (N.T.), and at the N.W.
shoulder of the lake is the curious fortified hill of *Peel*, once an artificial island.

A fine route from Keswick to Buttermere for good walkers (6 hrs) is the mountain
walk over the summits of *Cat Bells* (1481 ft), *Maiden Moor* (1887 ft). From here
there is a fine ridge walk s. along *Narrow Moor*, over *High Spy* (2143 ft) along the
Eel Crags and down the spur to a small tarn under the *Dale Head* crags, where there
is a steep ascent to the summit of *Dale Head* (2473 ft). We may proceed N.W. along
another fine ridge, with excellent views, to *Robinson* (2417 ft), whence a good track
runs westerly to Buttermere. A pleasant circular walk from Keswick can be made
by taking the above route to *Dale Head*, then after ½ m. on the Robinson path,
branching N. down the ridge of *Hindscarth* along *High Crags* to *Scope End*, and
thence to Keswick along the Newlands Valley. At places the going is stony and the
ridges are narrow, but there is nothing sensational. The bogs can (even in wet
weather) be avoided by keeping strictly to the watershed.

Another route from Keswick to Buttermere (4½ hrs) viâ Braithwaite and up
Coledale to *Coledale Hause*, thence s.w. by the ridge of *Whiteless Pike* (2159 ft;
fine view), may be combined with the ascent of **Grasmoor** (2791 ft). The descent of
Gasgale Gill, N. of Grasmoor (for Lanthwaite or Lorton), is steep in places but not
difficult.

*FROM KESWICK TO WASDALE HEAD VIÂ THE STY HEAD PASS (14 m.).
Driving is practicable to Seathwaite, whence the walk to Wasdale Head
takes 1¾–2¼ hrs—To (7½ m.) *Seatoller* (bus), see p. 586. We ascend the
valley of the Derwent, crossing the river.

A gate on the right, just short of the bridge, leads to what remains of the
Borrowdale Yews, the 'fraternal four' of Wordsworth. The girth of the largest

was 22 ft. We may follow up the same path, past the old plumbago mine (comp. p. 583), and rejoin the main route by crossing a foot-bridge to Seathwaite.

9 m. *Seathwaite* (N.T.) has a rainfall of 130 in. per annum (at the Sty Head, see below, the average is 170 in.). Hence the footpath ascends on the right bank of the stream. To the right rises *Base Brown* (2120 ft), to the left *Glaramara* (2560 ft). The imposing mountain generally visible ahead of us is Great End. At (9½ m.) *Stockley Bridge* the path crosses the Grain Gill and turns to the right (the path ascending Grain Gill provides a short but uninteresting cut to Esk Hause and Scafell Pike). Beyond (10 m.) *Taylor Gill Force* (r.; fine retrospect of Borrowdale and Derwentwater) we keep to the left, cross (10½ m.) the Sty Head beck, and reach (10¾ m.) the *Sty Head Tarn* (1430 ft), a sombre little lake in the heart of some of the wildest scenery England has to offer. Ahead of us (from l. to r.) are Great End, Scafell Pike, and Lingmell; to the right are Great Gable and Green Gable, with the depression known as *Aaron Slack* between them. Just beyond the tarn the track leading viâ *Sprinkling Tarn* (1960 ft) and *Esk Hause* to Langdale diverges to the left. From (11 m.) the top of the **Sty Head Pass** (1600 ft; cairn), the track (steep and stony) descends to the right, s. of Great Gable. From (12¾ m.) *Burnthwaite Farm* a lane (l.), practicable for cars, leads to (13¼ m.) the church and a field-path (r.) to (14 m.) the hotel at *Wasdale Head* (p. 599).

The fells on both sides of the Sty Head (incl. Great Gable, Green Gable, Kirk Fell, Glaramara, Allen Crags, Great End, and Lingmell) were bought in 1923 by the Fell and Rock Climbing Club as a war memorial to fallen members, and are now vested in the National Trust, together with other acquisitions of land on both sides of Ennerdale (from Great Gable to Steeple and Haycock), and Scafell and Scafell Pike above the 2000-ft line (bronze relief map on the summit of Great Gable).

FROM KESWICK TO WASDALE HEAD VIÂ SCARTH GAP AND THE BLACK SAIL PASS (19 m.). We may drive to (11 m.) *Gatesgarth* viâ Honister Hause or Newlands (see above), whence the walk to Wasdale takes 3–3½ hrs. From Gatesgarth the Scarth Gap track crosses a beck near the head of Buttermere and mounts the open fell to (1 hr) the top of **Scarth Gap** (1410 ft), the saddle between *Haystacks* (l.; 1750 ft) and *High Crag* (2443 ft; retrospect of Buttermere). As we begin the rough descent we have *Kirk Fell* (2630 ft) in front of us, with *Great Gable* (2949 ft) on its left and *Pillar* (2928 ft) on its right. On the N. or Ennerdale slope of the last is the famous *Pillar Rock*, a mightly pile of precipices, first ascended in 1826 by John Atkinson, an Ennerdale cooper. This rock is no place for the inexperienced. On reaching (¼ hr) the green floor of *Ennerdale* at a youth hostel, the bridle-path turns to the left along the bank of the Liza; it then (½ m.) crosses the stream and ascends, between two becks, to (½–¾ hr) the **Black Sail Pass** (1825 ft), flanked by Kirk Fell (l.) and Pillar (r.). [Note that we keep to the right of Kirk Fell.] The *View here is one of great austerity and savage grandeur. Behind us (from l. to r.) are High Crag (with Grasmoor in the distance), Haystacks (with Fleetwith Pike peering over it), Brandreth, and Great Gable. In front lies *Mosedale*, with another *Red Pike* (2629 ft) to the right and *Yewbarrow* (2058 ft) to the left. Our path winds down along a beck, trending to the left after c. ¾ m. and revealing a sudden *View of Scafell. The hotel at *Wasdale Head* (p. 599) soon comes into sight, and our path descends to it (c. 1½ m.) along the left bank of the Mosedale Beck.

The MOTOR ROUTE from Keswick to Wasdale makes a long detour viâ the *Whinlatter Pass* and the coastal plain. From Keswick to *Scale Hill* and (17 m.) *Lamplugh*, see p. 587. The road then runs s. to (3½ m.) *Ennerdale Bridge*, diverging to the right (s.w.) for (9¾ m.) *Egremont*; hence to (15¼ m.) *Gosforth* and (25 m.) *Wasdale Head*, see p. 599.

FROM KESWICK TO COCKERMOUTH there are three alternative routes. A. VIÂ A 66 (13 m.; bus). To (2½ m.) *Braithwaite*, see p. 587. Thence we skirt the foot of the fells of Thornthwaite Forest. Opposite (4 m.) the Swan Hotel is the *Barf* (1536 ft) with the rock known as the 'Bishop of Bart' (generally painted white). We soon reach the w. shore of **Bassenthwaite Lake** (223 ft; 4 m. long, ¾ m. wide). The view of Skiddaw, opposite, is imposing.—Beyond (7½ m.) the Pheasant Inn B 5291 diverges right for Carlisle, while we bear left for (13 m.) *Cockermouth* viâ (9¼ m.) *Embleton* with its golf course.—B. Viâ A 591 (14 m.; bus). Crossing Greta Bridge we follow A 591 (r.) beneath the w. slopes of Skiddaw.—At (7¼ m.) a lane on the left leads to a pleasant footpath to Ouse Bridge (see below).—5¼ m. Ravenstone Hotel.—At (7¼ m.) Castle Inn we turn left on B 5291, passing (8 m.) Armathwaite Hall Hotel in fine grounds. We cross the Derwent by the Ouse Bridge (view) and soon join A 66 (see above) for Cockermouth.—C. VIÂ LORTON and the WHINLATTER PASS, 14 m. see p. 587.

From Keswick to *Dungeon Gill* and *Ambleside*, see Rte 64c; to *Patterdale*, see Rte 64A.

FROM KESWICK TO GRASMERE, AMBLESIDE, AND WINDERMERE, 21 m. (several buses daily). We leave Keswick by St John's Rd. running s.e. from the Moot Hall and ascend to (1½ m.) the top of *Castlerigg* (702 ft) after joining A 591. Helvellyn ('Low Man') appears in front. At 4 m. a road on the right leads to the Thirlmere dam.

It is pleasant to diverge here and follow the road along the w. bank of Thirlmere, beneath *Raven Crag* (1400 ft), opposite the great dam, *Fisher Crag*, 2½ m. farther on and, beyond Launch Gill (½ m.) with its perched boulder, waterfalls, and carpet of stag's horn moss, *Bull Crag* (200 ft), with the 'New Nick' at its foot (½ m.). The road rejoins the main road about ½ m. s. of *Wythburn*.—From Thirlmere a rough track, starting 1 m. s. of Raven Crag, leads across *Armboth Fell* (1650 ft) to (1½ hr) *Watendlath*.

We cross St John's Beck, just beyond which the road through the Vale of St John diverges on the left. On the same side rises the Castle Rock (comp. p. 585). To the right the wooded *Great How* (1092 ft) cuts off the view of the foot of Thirlmere. Opposite is the *Dale Head* post office, also the path to the Sticks Pass. Just beyond (5½ m.) **Thirlspot** we ascend (retrospect of Vale of St John) and come in full view of **Thirlmere** (569 ft), a narrow sheet of water nearly 4 m. long, formerly known as *Brackmere*.

Thirlmere belongs to the Corporation of Manchester and is the chief source of the water supply of that city (aqueduct nearly 100 m. long). Its level has been artificially raised 50 ft by a large dam at its foot, but this has rather improved its appearance than otherwise. The dam, which is 260 yds long and 100 ft high, is traversed by a road connecting the roads on the E. and w. banks. The plantations with which the reservoir is enclosed frequently restrict the views from the roads.

The road skirts the w. base of Helvellyn (ascents, see p. 585), shrouded in conifers. Beyond (8 m.) *Wythburn* church the road ascends to (9½ m.) the top of *Dunmail Raise* (782 ft; retrospect of Thirlmere), the dip between *Seat Sandal* (l.; 2415 ft) and *Steel Fell* (r.; 1811 ft). The wall here divides Westmorland from Cumberland, and the cairn to the right is said to mark the grave of Dunmail, last king of Cumbria, whose defeat here in 945 made Cumberland a dependency of Scotland for over a century. As we begin the long descent on the s. side of the pass we enjoy a good view of the vale and lake of Grasmere, with Helm Crag conspicuous to the w. (r.). To the right runs the Rothay. A gate on the left, before we cross (11¼ m.) Tongue Gill, opens on the path to Grisedale Pass and the top of Helvellyn.

At (12 m.) the foot of the pass is the Swan Hotel, where the right-hand road leads to (12½ m.) **Grasmere** village (p. 595). The Ambleside road runs straight on to (12¾ m.) the Prince of Wales Hotel and skirts the E. bank of *Grasmere*, with a fine retrospect of the vale of Grasmere, backed (right to left) by Great Rigg, Seat Sandal, Steel Fell, and Helm Crag.

The old Rydal road, diverging (l.) short of the Prince of Wales Hotel passes *Dove Cottage* (Wordsworth's house; p. 595) and *White Moss*, whence walkers should follow the road (l.) and the path along the s. slope of *Nab Scar*, finally descending by the steep road passing Rydal Mount (see below).

Near (13¼ m.) the end of the lake, backed by Loughrigg Terrace, we sweep to the left and come in sight of (13¾ m.) *Rydal Water* (181 ft), a charming lakelet, 3¾ m. long and ¼ m. across, connecting with Grasmere and Windermere by the Rothay. The road skirts its N. bank, passing (l.) *Nab Cottage*, where De Quincey lived in 1806 and Hartley Coleridge from 1840 till his death in 1849.— 14¾ m. **Rydal** (Hotel), a hamlet near the E. end of Rydal Water, was the home of Wordsworth from 1813 till his death in 1850. His house, *Rydal Mount* (behind the church), with charming gardens, is open daily 10–4 or 5.30 (closed Feb & 12.30–2 in winter).

Beyond the church (with memorials to Thomas and Matthew Arnold) to the right of the main road *Pelter Bridge* crosses the Rothay and a narrow road follows its right bank to (2 m.) *Clappersgate*. At the foot of Loughrigg Fell, near the road, are *Fox Gill* (r.) and *Fox How* (l.), the homes of W. E. Forster (1818–86), the statesman, and Dr Thomas Arnold (1795–1842) of Rugby.

The main road skirts the park of *Rydal Hall*, a Georgian seat of the Le Flemings, now a diocesan guest-house, and passes the mouth (l.) of the glen of the Scandale Beck. To the right is the *Knoll*, once the residence of Harriet Martineau (1802–76). We then cross the Stock Gill and pass through (16¼ m.) **Ambleside** (see p. 593) and (17 m.) *Waterhead*, the starting-place of the steamers at the N. end of Windermere. We then skirt the E. bank of this lake with a view of the fells, from the Coniston Old Man (l.) to the Langdale Pikes (r.). To the left, on the slopes of *Wansfell*, is *Dove Nest*, for a time the home of Mrs Hemans (1793–1835).—18 m. Low Wood Hotel (closed in winter). Farther on is a hilly road leading to the attractive village of *Troutbeck* (Rte 64A). Beyond the Langdale Chase Hotel, our road turns somewhat away from the lake, and at (19¾ m.) *Troutbeck Bridge* it is joined by another charming road from Troutbeck. To the right stands *Calgarth Park*, once the home of the tree-planting Bp. Watson of Llandaff (1737–1816). At the cross-roads the left-hand branch leads to Patterdale by the Kirkstone Pass, while the right goes to Bowness. We keep straight on, passing the grounds of *Elleray* (see below) for (21 m.) *Windermere Station*, see below.

C Windermere, Ambleside, Grasmere, and Coniston

Windermere, if not necessarily the best, is undoubtedly the most popular starting-point for a visit to the Lake District. It is approached by rail either viâ Oxenholme and Kendal (Rte 62A; through-expresses from London, Liverpool, Manchester, etc.), or viâ Carnforth and Lake Side (Rte 63; summer only) with steamer connection.—ROAD, A 591 from Kendal to Windermere, 8¼ m.; B 5284 to (8 m.) *Bowness*, or a hilly by-road viâ Bowland Bridge to (13 m.) *Newby Bridge* (comp. p. 575) and thence along Windermere (see below), are pleasant alternatives from Kendal.—From *Levens Bridge* A 590 leads to (12 m.) *Newby Bridge* (Rte 63); at (1½ m.) Sampool Bridge A 5074 diverges right for (10 m.) *Bowness*.

Windermere ('Winand's lake'; 130 ft above the sea), the largest of England's lakes, is 10½ m. long and so narrow (¼–1¼ m.) as almost to resemble a river. Its greatest depth is 220 ft. It drains, through the Leven, into Morecambe Bay. Its banks are beautifully wooded and of moderate elevation, except near its head, above which rises a circle of imposing fells. On the E. bank are Windermere and Bowness, but the w. bank is unspoilt. Sailing and water ski-ing may be enjoyed on its waters; because of the volume of traffic, strict rules are enforced (set out in a booklet available with a chart of the lake from the Nat. Park Information Office).

On Windermere in 1930 Sir Henry Segrave perished in breaking the record for speed-boats with a speed of 98¾ m.p.h., and in 1966 the world water speed record was broken here by Norman Buckley and Albert Redmen with a speed of 75.9 m.p.h. covering 227 m.—In 1958 Cdr. C. G. Forsberg, R.N., swam Windermere both ways in 12 hrs 58 min.; in 1960 Helge Jensen made a record swim (one-way) in 4 hrs 50 min., while the women's record of 5 hrs 33 min. was set up by Miss Ruth Oldham in 1964, and that of the youngest swimmer, by Jean Wilkin, aged 14, in 1969.

Steamers (several times daily, mid-May to mid-Sept). It is preferable to take the steamer from Lake Side pier for the sake of the view. From Lake Side (see below) to *Bowness* in 35 min., to *Waterhead* in 1½ hr, up and down the lake in 2½ hrs. The steep wooded w. bank from the ferry N. to Wray Castle is N.T. property. Approaching Bowness we steer E. of the wooded *Belle Isle* (⅜ m. long), with a circular house by John Plaw (1774–75). It is open at Easter and Spring BH to Sept, Sun, Mon, Tues, & Thurs, 10.30–5; fee (boat from Bowness).— 6¼ m. *Bowness*, also the pier for *Windermere*, see below. Passing the N. end of Belle Isle and clearing *Ladyholme* (N.T.) and other islets, we emerge into the beautiful upper reach of Windermere. The mountains at the head of the lake now assume their full value. Immediately in front is Fairfield, with a peep of Helvellyn over its w. (l.) shoulder; far to the left of it are the Langdale Pikes, Bowfell, and the Scafell Range, ruggedly imposing; to the right are Red Screes, High Street, and Ill Bell; to the w. are Coniston Old Man and Wetherlam. To the l. (9¼ m.) appears *Wray Castle* (c. 1850; a school for Merchant Navy cadets).— Beyond (9¾ m.) *Low Wood* (r.) Bowfell and Scafell Pike are seen to the left of the Langdales, with the distant Great Gable rising over the top of Esk Hause. To the left opens *Pull Wyke*. — 10¾ m. *Waterhead* is ¾ m. from Ambleside (bus) and 5 m. from *Grasmere* (bus). Opposite Waterhead the Brathay enters the lake just after receiving the waters of the Rothay.

Windermere (400–500 ft; Hotels), the terminus of the railway from Kendal, lies partly on the s.w. slope of Orrest Head and is now contiguous with the older Bowness, 1 m. s.w. of the station, the two forming one town of 8000 inhabitants.

The best general *View of the lake is obtained from *Orrest Head* (784 ft), just N. of the station. The second gate on the right, at the foot of the drive to the Windermere Hotel, brings us to the track ascending through the woods of Elleray to (20 min.) the summit (mountain indicator). Keeping to the right in descending we pass *Elleray*, for forty years the country home of John Wilson ('Christopher North';

1785–1854), and reach the Troutbeck road, but the return then has to be made along the main road. From the cross-roads Rayrigg Rd. leads to Bowness viâ *Millerground* (bathing) and *Queen Adelaide's Hill* (259 ft; N.T.) on the lake shore.

BOWNESS-ON-WINDERMERE (135–340 ft) is situated on an attractive bay on the E. side of Windermere and is the chief place on the lake (very congested in summer).

Hotels near the lake, beside the church, on Biskey How, on the Crook Rd., etc.
Buses from Windermere station to Bowness Pier; also to main towns.
Steamers on the lake in summer and boats to Belle Isle (see above).—*Sailing School* at Storrs Hall (see below).
Swimming-Pool at Millerground; *Water ski-ing;* underwater swimming.—Also facilities for pony-trekking, tennis, fishing, etc., in and near the town.
Golf Course (18 holes) on the Crook road (2 m. S.E.).

About 100 yds from the pier is the parish church of *St Martin,* consecrated in 1483. The greater part of the beautiful E. window is made up of late 15C stained glass from Cartmel Priory, together with earlier fragments including a Virgin of c. 1260 and the arms of John Washington (fl. 1403). In the S. aisle is a memorial to Bp. Watson (see above) by Flaxman, also two 16C chained books. *Biskey How* (300 ft), E. of the church, affords a pleasant view.

FROM BOWNESS TO LAKE SIDE BY ROAD (8½ m.; A 592), a well-wooded route keeping fairly close to the shore.—2 m. *Storrs Point* (Hotel) was the scene of a regatta held in 1825 in honour of Sir Walter Scott's 54th birthday, and witnessed by Wordsworth, Wilson, Canning, and Southey. Storrs Temple, on the lake, was built in 1804 in honour of Admirals of the Fleet, Duncan, St Vincent, Howe, and Nelson.—3½ m. Beech Hill Hotel. We pass beneath (5 m.) *Gummer's How* (1054 ft), a splendid viewpoint.—We join A 590 at (7¾ m.) *Newby Bridge* (Hotels), just beyond the foot of Windermere, immediately turning right again across the old bridge.—8½ m. **Lake Side,** with the steamer pier. Thence we may go on to (6 m.) *Far Sawrey* (see below).

FROM BOWNESS TO CONISTON viâ HAWKSHEAD, 10 m. We leave Bowness by the 'Low Road', which runs S. to (1 m.) the *Ferry Nab* (footpath shorter).

The ferry (⅓ m.; fee) runs every 20 min. (¼ hr in busy period) from 7 a.m. (Sun 10) to 8.40 or 9.40 p.m.

From Ferry House, on the W. shore, now the laboratory of the Freshwater Biological Association, the road (B 5285) ascends, skirting *Claife Heights* (N.T.), to (2½ m.) *Far Sawrey.* At (3¼ m.) *Near Sawrey* is *Hill Top* (N.T.; adm. Easter–Oct, weekdays 11–5.30, Sun from 2; fee), a small 17C house, the home of Beatrix Potter (1866–1943) with a collection of her illustrations. Our road runs along the E. side of (4 m.) *Esthwaite Water* (1½ m. long and ¼–⅜ m. wide) and passes the pool known as the *Priest Pot.*—5¾ m. **Hawkshead** (Hotel) is a quaint little town with alleys and courts, greatly frequented in summer. The old grammar school (fee), founded in 1585 by Abp. Sandys of York, who was born at Esthwaite Hall in 1517, contains an interesting library of ancient books. Wordsworth was a pupil here from 1778 to 1783 and his name is carved on one of the oaken desks. *Ann Tyson's Cottage,* where the poet lodged, is in the lane leading out of Red Lion Square. On a hillock (view) the 15–16C *Church*, with plain low-arched arcades and 17–18C murals, contains the effigies of Abp. Sandys's parents and two monuments, removed in 1878 from St Dionis Backchurch, London, to Daniel Rawlinson (d. 1679), founder of the library, and of his son Sir Thomas (d. 1708), Lord Mayor of London.—We join the road from Ambleside at (6¼ m.) *Hawkshead Courthouse* (N.T.; April–Sept, adm. daily, exc. Mon & Thurs; 2–5; fee), once the property of Furness Abbey, a 15C gatehouse in which the manor courts were once held. Beyond (7 m.) *Hawkshead Hill*, where a road leads right to Tarn Hows (p. 597), we reach *High Cross* (647 ft), the highest point of the route. As we descend we enjoy a marvellous view of Coniston Water. We keep right at the fork.—10 m. Coniston, see p. 597.

Another way of reaching Coniston from Windermere is round the head of the lake (a drive of 13 m.), see p. 595.—For walkers an agreeable route (3–4 hrs) to *Coniston* follows the w. bank of Windermere from the ferry to *Belle Grange* and thence viâ *High Wray*, *Outgate*, and *Tarn Hows* (views).
A pleasant drive s. from Hawkshead runs through the Grizedale Forest to (6 m.) *Satterthwaite*. Grizedale Hall (now ruined) was a prison camp for German officers in the Second World War and the scene of Von Werra's first escape. The Forestry Commission have opened a fine nature trail from Satterthwaite car park N.E. to the Windermere Ferry.

From Windermere to *Ambleside*, *Grasmere* and *Keswick*, see Rte 64B; to *Patterdale* (Ullswater), see Rte 64A; to *Kendal*, see p. 571.

AMBLESIDE, a little town much frequented in summer, is pleasantly situated in the vale of the Rothay, ¾ m. from the head of Windermere (not visible) and at the foot of Wansfell Pike.

Hotels in the town, and on the lake at Waterhead.
Buses to *Windermere Station* and *Kendal*; *Bowness* and *Newby Bridge*; *Grasmere* and *Keswick*; *Coniston*; *Hawkshead* and *Sawrey*; *Dungeon Gill*.
Steamers (pier at Waterhead, ¾ m. s. of the town) to Bowness and Lake Side.—
BOATS for hire at Waterhead—*Water Ski-ing.*
Golf Course (9 holes) on Loughrigg Fell (see below).—The Ambleside Sports and International sheep dog trials are held in Aug.

The church of *St Mary* (1854), by Gilbert Scott, contains a memorial chapel to Wordsworth, and a large mural painting, by Gordon Ransom, representing the rush-bearing festival, held on the last Sat in July. This is thought to originate either in a medieval cleansing ceremony when the churches were prepared for winter, or in the Roman 'Floralia', a forerunner of the Harvest Festival. Over the Stock Gill, on the Rydal road is a tiny 17C bridge-house, now an information centre of the National Trust. J. C. Ibbetson, who married at Ambleside in 1801, lived here and at Troutbeck in 1799–1805. Harriet Martineau died at Ambleside in 1876, having spent her last years at the Knoll.

A lane behind the Salutation Hotel ascends to (¼ m.) the charming *Stock Gill Force*, a fall of c. 70 ft.— Near Waterhead is the *Borrans Field* (N.T.), with traces of the small Roman fort of Galava, finds from which may be seen in the Armitt Library, in Lake Rd. (Mon–Fri 10–5, Sat 10–1).—*Jenkin Crag* and *Kelsick Scar* (N.T.), c. 1¼ m. s. of Ambleside, afford admirable views.

ASCENTS. *Loughrigg Fell (1099 ft; views), s. of Grasmere and Rydal Water, may be ascended direct from *Miller Bridge*, w. of St Mary's Church, viâ *Brown Head Farm*, in less than 1 hr. A slightly longer route is by the path ascending from *Clappersgate* (see below). The descent (steepish) may be made to Loughrigg Terrace (see below) and Grasmere.—About ⅓ m. beyond the entrance to Stock Gill (and 200 yds beyond a gate) a stile (r.; finger-post) gives on to a distinctly marked path leading to the summit of Wansfell Pike (1851 ft; *View), E. of Ambleside

(¾–1 hr). The descent may be made by a marked path on the s.e. slope to (1½ hr) *Troutbeck* (p. 583).—*Nab Scar* (c. 1000 ft), the s. buttress of Fairfield, is ascended viâ Rydal in 1¼ hr. We follow the road passing Rydal Mount, take a path to the left between walls, and (¼ hr from the road) reach the open fell by a stepped stile. From Nab Scar we may follow the ridge N. to (1–1½ hr) the summit of *Fairfield* (2863 ft), but this fell is better ascended from Grasmere.—To the *Langdale Pikes*, see below.

TOUR OF THE LANGDALES, 19½ m. We follow A 593 across *Rothay Bridge* and skirt the s. base of Loughrigg Fell. At the hamlet of (1 m.) *Clappersgate* the Hawkshead road crosses *Brathay Bridge* (l.), but we keep to the main road. About 1 m. farther on a lane (r.) leads viâ *Loughrigg Tarn* (N.T.) and Red Bank to Grasmere (see below). Just short of (3 m.) *Skelwith Bridge* (Hotel) the easy road to Great Langdale diverges right. We, however, cross the bridge [about 300 yds upstream is *Skelwith Force*] and, keeping to the main road, turn right at 4 m. just beyond the top of the hill. We descend rapidly to *Colwith Bridge*, where we turn sharp left, passing *Colwith Force*. We ascend through the valley of *Little Langdale*, separated from Great Langdale to the N. by *Lingmoor Fell* (1530 ft), c. 550 acres of which belong to the N.T.—5½ m. *Little Langdale*. Beyond *Little Langdale Tarn*, near *Fell Foot* farm, the road forks, the left branch going over *Wrynose Pass* (p. 589). We take the right branch, which begins to cross the w. slope of Lingmoor towards Great Langdale and becomes narrow and steep. A sudden and striking *View of the Langdale Pikes opens out in front. On the left lies *Blea Tarn* (612 ft). —7½ m. *Blea Tarn Farm* is still "the one abode, no more" of the scene as it was when occupied by the 'Solitary' of Wordsworth's 'Excursion'. From the top of the pass (c. 770 ft) the abrupt descent brings us to *Wall End Farm*, beyond which lies (9 m.) the Old Dungeon Ghyll Hotel, at the foot of the Langdale Pikes (bus to Ambleside). We now follow B 5343 to (9¾ m.) *Millbeck*, with the New Dungeon Ghyll Hotel.

*Dungeon Gill Force, 1 m. from the Old Hotel and ½ m. from the New Hotel, has a vertical descent of 65 ft and is framed by the perpendicular walls of a picturesque gorge. Above the fall a natural bridge is formed by two rocks wedged in the narrow ravine.—Ascents from Dungeon Gill, see below.

In returning from Dungeon Gill our route runs at first to the E. through *Great Langdale, a verdant valley N. of Lingmoor Fell, with c. 1000 acres of N.T. land. Its beck drains into Elterwater and the Brathay. Fine retrospects of the Pikes. Just short of (2 m.) *Chapel Stile*, where the fells are defaced by slate-quarries, the road forks. [The branch to the right, leading direct to (5½ m.) Ambleside, passes the *Langdale Estate*, a holiday centre, and the village and tarn of *Elterwater* (187 ft; Hotel) and rejoins the outward route beyond (2½ m.) *Skelwith Bridge*.] The left-hand road (very hilly) leads past *Langdale Parish Church* and reaches (3¼ m.) *High Close* (N.T.; 523 ft; view), the top of the depression between Loughrigg Fell and Silver How. [A footpath on the left, a little short of the summit, shortens the route to Grasmere by ½ m.] We descend *Red Bank* (steep) and enjoy a lovely glimpse of Grasmere. [A still finer view is obtained from *Loughrigg Terrace* (c. 300 ft), reached by a path to the right.] The road skirts the s.w. margin of Grasmere to (4¾ m.) *Grasmere Village*. Hence to (8¾ m.) *Ambleside*, see Rte 64B.

ASCENTS FROM DUNGEON GILL. The ascent of the **Langdale Pikes** (*Harrison Stickle* 2403 ft, *Pike o' Stickle* 2323 ft), which requires 3–4½ hrs, hardly fulfils the promise made by the striking outline of the Pikes, as the view is much limited by the higher fells around. The best ascent is by the winding bridle-path to the left of Dungeon Gill. The two peaks are separated by a gully, and climbers are advised to make a detour to the left, round Loft Crag (whether they actually climb to the top of Pike o' Stickle or not), and approach the summit of Harrison Stickle from the N.W. The view includes Skiddaw and Saddleback, Helvellyn and Fairfield, the Coniston Fells, Bowfell, Great Langdale, and Windermere. The descent may be made over *Pavey Ark* (N.E.; fine crags) and thence round *Stickle Tarn* (1540 ft) to *Mill Gill*. An alternative descent to (2 hrs) Grasmere leads N.E. from the tarn to the top of *Blea Rigg* and thence down to the right of *Easedale Tarn*.—*Bowfell* (2960 ft; N.T.) may be ascended from the Old Dungeon Ghyll Hotel in 2–2½ hrs viâ *Stool End Farm* and the shoulder known as the *Band*. The attractive view includes Skiddaw, the Scafell range, the Langdale Pikes, Windermere, Esthwaite Water, Devoke Water (s.w.), and the Solway Firth.

FROM AMBLESIDE TO KESWICK VIÂ DUNGEON GILL AND THE STAKE PASS (c. 22 m.; driving practicable to Dungeon Gill, 7½ m., and from Stonethwaite to Keswick,

7 m.; walk across the path from Dungeon Gill to Stonethwaite, 3–4 hrs).—From Ambleside to (7½ m.) the Old Dungeon Ghyll Hotel, by Elterwater and Great Langdale, see above. The road ends here and we ascend the bridle-path up *Mickleden*, keeping to the right of the beck. To the left rises the *Band* (see above). Beyond (9¼ m.) a sheep-fold the path bears to the right (Esk Hause path to the left), and zigzags up to (11¼ m.) the **Stake Pass** (1576 ft; view of Skiddaw), the saddle between *Rossett Crag* (l.) and *Pike o' Stickle* (see above). At (12 m.) the foot of the pass we cross the Stake Beck and descend (rough path) along the right bank of the Langstrath Beck, crossing to the left bank in ¾ m. more. 15 m. *Stonethwaite*. About ½ m. farther on we join the Borrowdale road. 16 m. *Rosthwaite*, and thence to (22 m.) *Keswick*, see Rte 64B.

From Ambleside to Coniston viâ Barn Gates, with return by A 593 (16 m.).— At (1 m.) *Clappersgate* (see p. 594) we turn left off the main road, cross *Brathay Bridge* into Lancashire, and pass *Brathay Hall* (l.). Leaving the Hawkshead road on our left, we follow the left bank of the lovely Brathay and ascend to (3½ m.) *Barn Gates* (425 ft). In 1¾ m. a road diverges right for *Tarn Hows* (p. 597) viâ the Tarn Hows Hotel.—At (5½ m.) *High Cross* (647 ft) we turn right on to B 5285 for (7½ m.) *Coniston* (comp. p. 593). The return-route follows the attractive main road through *Yewdale*, passing *Yewdale Crag* (1050 ft) on the left and, farther on, a small tarn. Beyond (3½ m.) the top of *Oxenfell Pass* (526 ft) there are fine views of the Langdale Pikes. We descend, with the road for Little Langdale on our left, to (5¼ m.) *Skelwith Bridge*. Hence to (8¼ m.) *Ambleside*, see above.

From Ambleside to Wasdale Head. For this route, we may go to (7½ m.) *Dungeon Gill* and proceed thence (3½–5 hrs) by the track (comp. above) up *Rossett Gill* and over *Esk Hause* (2370 ft), near the summit of which meet the passes from Langdale, Wasdale, Eskdale, and Borrowdale. The highest point of the hause (2490 ft) is just to the left. The topography of the col, standing at the junction of many valleys, is confusing, and care is needed in finding the correct path; in bad weather, map and compass should be consulted.

From Ambleside to *Patterdale* (Ullswater), see Rte 64A; to *Windermere* and to *Grasmere* and *Keswick*, see Rte 64B.

*Grasmere (208 ft; 75 ft deep), barely 1 m. long and fully ½ m. wide, with a green islet in the midst, is the roundest of the lakes. The main village of **GRASMERE** lies c. ¼ m. N. of the lake, a little w. of the Keswick road, on the E. side of which is *Town End* with Dove Cottage, long the home of William Wordsworth (1770–1850), who has left unsung but few points in the beautiful environs.

Hotels on the lake, and in the village.
Buses to *Ambleside*, *Windermere* (connections for Bowness and Newby Bridge), and *Kendal*; and *Keswick*.
*Sports on Thurs nearest 20 Aug (first held in 1852); guides' race up and down Butter Crags, wrestling (Cumberland–Westmorland style), hound trail, etc.— Rush-bearing Service in the church on the Sat nearest 6 Aug (St Oswald's Day).— Grasmere is noted for a special variety of gingerbread.

Part of the church of *St Oswald*, which is "for duration built, not raised in nice proportion", may date back to the 13C. Wordsworth is buried in the churchyard and commemorated in the church (head by Woolner). His wife (d. 1859), his sister Dorothy (d. 1855), and Hartley Coleridge (d. 1849) likewise lie in the churchyard, where there is also a memorial to A. H. Clough (d. at Florence in 1861). Church Stile, opposite, is a 16C cottage owned by the N.T., and used as an information centre. From 1799 to 1808 Wordsworth lived at *Dove Cottage* (adm. weekdays 10–5.45; winter 10–4.15; closed mid-Jan–Feb; fee), about 200 yds N.E. of the Prince of Wales Hotel. A collection of relics and local 'bygones' is housed in the *Wordsworth Museum* (adm. as above), opposite. Wordsworth removed in 1808 to *Allan Bank*, N.W. of the church, and in 1811 to the *Parsonage*, which he quitted for Rydal Mount in 1813. Thomas De Quincey (1785–1859) succeeded Wordsworth at Dove Cottage, which remained his headquarters until 1835.

The so-called *Wishing Gate*, on the old road, less than ½ m. s. of Dove Cottage, commands a favourite view of Grasmere.—*Tongue Gill Force*, a very pretty little waterfall, 1¾ m. N.E., is reached by a slight digression (r.) from the route up Helvellyn (comp. below).—*Helm Crag* (1299 ft), N. of Grasmere, is ascended (c. 1 hr) less for its view than for the curious crags described by Wordsworth as the "Astrologer, sage Sidrophel", and an "Ancient Woman cowering beside her rifted cell". Crossing the Easedale Beck by Goody Bridge, we turn left but soon ascend the steep slope of Helm Crag; the summit is rough and broken and the E. cliffs and screes should be avoided.—*Walk round Grasmere* (4 m.). We follow the road on the w. bank to (1½ m.) *Red Bank* (view), and there take a lane to the left, leading to *Loughrigg Terrace* (c. 300 ft; views). We descend to the foot-bridge across the Rothay between Grasmere and Rydal Water (2 m.), and return by the road on the E. bank of the former (2 m.) or by the old road (higher). Or we may continue along the terrace and make a circuit of Rydal Water (2 m. more). *Loughrigg Fell* is ascended from High Close (above Red Bank) in ½ hr—*Easedale Tarn* (915 ft) is 2½ m. N.w. of Grasmere. After following the left bank of the Easedale Beck (see above), we soon recross the beck. About 1 m. higher up we see the white *Sour Milk Force*, c. ½ m. beyond which lies the tarn. This walk may be continued to (3½ m.) *Dungeon Gill* viâ *Stickle Tarn*.—*Silver How* (1292 ft), ¾ hr from the Red Lion Hotel viâ *Allan Bank* (see above), commands a view of half a dozen lakes. It may readily be combined with the Easedale Tarn trip; or we may descend s. to Langdale Church viâ Meg's Gill.—From Grasmere to *Patterdale*, see p. 581.

ASCENTS. Grasmere is the most frequent base for the ascent of Helvellyn (3113 ft; 3½–4 hrs). From Grasmere to (2½ hrs) *Grisedale Tarn*, see p. 581. Beyond the tarn we diverge to the left from the Patterdale track and ascend in zigzags to (½ hr) *Dollywaggon Pike* (2810 ft), the s. end of the Helvellyn ridge. The incline hence to (½ hr) the main summit is comparatively slight. *View, see p. 581. Descent to *Patterdale*, see p. 581; to *Keswick*, see p. 585.—**Fairfield** (2863 ft) is ascended from Grasmere in 1½–2 hrs, from near Dove Cottage viâ *Alcock Tarn* (N.T.) and *Great Rigg* (2513 ft). Or (better) we may diverge from the Helvellyn route (see above) at the top of *Grisedale Hause*. Helvellyn dominates the view.— The **Langdale Pikes** (see above, 3–3¾ hrs) may be ascended either viâ *Dungeon Gill* or viâ *Easdale Tarn* and *Stickle Tarn* (comp. above).

FROM GRASMERE TO BORROWDALE VIÂ EASEDALE (to Rosthwaite 3½–4½ hrs). From Goody Bridge (see above) we keep to the left bank of Easedale Beck and follow the pony-track up *Far Easedale Gill*. After about 1 m. we cross the beck by *Stythwaite Steps*. The track ascends along the beck to (3 m.) the head of the Easedale Valley (c. 1600 ft). We cross the head of the *Wythburn Valley* (descending to the right; usually very wet), and re-ascend to (4 m.) *Greenup Edge* (2081 ft; view), between *High Raise* (l.; 2500 ft) and *Ullscarf* (2370 ft). In descending we turn to the right (N.; route indicated by small cairns on big rocks). Below *Lining Crag* the path again becomes clear, descending along the right bank of *Greenup Gill*. Borrowdale is now in view. At (6 m.) *Stonethwaite* we cross the beck. Hence to (7 m.) *Rosthwaite*, see p. 595.—From Grasmere to *Keswick*, by road, see Rte 64B. Keswick may be reached also viâ *Dunmail Raise*, *Harrop Tarn* or *Armboth Fell*, and *Watendlath* (4–4½ hrs). A rather more strenuous walk continues N.w. from Helm Crag (see above) on a curved ridge that goes over *Gibson Knott* (1379 ft), Pike of Carrs, and under the Calf Crags, to the head of Easedale.

Coniston Water (143 ft), formerly known as *Thurston Mere*, lies wholly within Lancashire, parallel with and 5 m. w. of Windermere. Just over 5 m. long and ¼–½ m. wide, it presents a less imposing version of that larger lake. The N. end, overlooked by Coniston Old Man and other fells, is the finest part; but the view down the lake (especially from near Tarn Hows, see below) is very attractive also.

Here in 1959 Donald Campbell set up a world water speed record of 260.35 m.p.h. He was killed attempting to raise the record in 1967 when his jet-powered speed-boat somersaulted (memorial at Lakeside).

The village of CONISTON (Hotel), a good centre, is beautifully situated at the foot of the Old Man and Yewdale Crags, ½ m. from the w. bank of the lake at its N. end. Coniston is as closely associated with John Ruskin (1819–1900) as Grasmere is with Wordsworth. Ruskin is buried in the N.E. corner of the churchyard, under an Anglo-Saxon cross. About 100 yds N. of the church is the *Ruskin Museum* (adm. daily, 10–6; fee), containing drawings and MSS. by Ruskin, minerals collected by him, a 'rock harmonicon' (a dulcimer of 3 octaves made for Ruskin of Skiddaw stone), photographs, books, and personal relics from Brantwood (see below).

BUSES run to *Ambleside*, with connections for Windermere and Keswick, and to *Ulverston*; also to *Foxfield* (comp. Rte 63).

TOUR ROUND THE LAKE, 13¾ m. The Old Man, to the N.W., is the dominant feature throughout the drive. Keeping the church on our right, we reach the head of the lake. At 1½ m. (r.) is *Tent Lodge* where Tennyson once sojourned. About 1 m. farther on (l.) is *Brantwood*, now a centre of the *Council of Nature*. It was the home of Ruskin from 1871 until his death in 1900; a selection of his paintings and personal relics is shown (Mon–Fri 10–4.30; Sat from 2.30). *Coniston Hall* (nearly opposite), a farmhouse, was built in the late 16C by the Le Flemings. The banks lower down are beautifully wooded. About ½ m. beyond (6¾ m.) *High Nibthwaite*, at the foot of the lake, we turn r. to cross the Crake and join the road from Greenodd (Rte 63; buses). The view up the lake is superb, backed by Helvellyn and Fairfield. At (11¼ m.) *Torver* (p. 575) we join the charming Broughton road.— 13¾ m. *Coniston*.

SHORT WALKS. To reach *Tarn Hows (2½ m.), the best point of view near Coniston (4520 acres of N.T. land, running w. to the Duddon Valley), we follow the Hawkshead road to (1¼ m.) Monk Coniston Hall (r.). Hence we ascend to the left through a woody dale, to (2 m.) *Tarn Hows Farm* (l.). At (2½ m.) the top of the hill we come suddenly upon the tarn, set in a delightful hollow, the loveliness of which causes it to be overcrowded in the season. The high ground on the opposite side of the valley commands a beautiful *View. From this point we may either descend to the Hawkshead road at *High Cross*, or retrace our steps until we come upon a steep path descending (r.) through Tom Gill into *Yewdale*.—The route to (2½ m.) *Tilberthwaite Gill*, a romantic little rocky glen, traversed by a series of footbridges, wooden galleries, and planks, is indicated below. At the top of the gorge is a pretty little waterfall. The return may be varied by striking direct from the waterfall to Coniston (path rough and muddy), or by a track descending N. of the gorge to Tilberthwaite Farm, with fine downward views into the cleft.

ASCENTS. The *Coniston Old Man (i.e. *Allt Maen*, steep or high rock; 2635 ft) is ascended in 1½–2 hrs. Its sides are disfigured by copper-mines and slate quarries, and many different tracks lead to the summit. The best route is by a track above and left of the *Church Beck*, eventually bending to the left towards a slate quarry near *Low Water* (1786 ft). Thence we climb to the s., passing another quarry. The *View is one of great variety and charm. To the N. are Skiddaw, Saddleback, the serrated ridge of Helvellyn, and Fairfield; High Street (N.E.); in the foreground Coniston and Esthwaite Waters, part of Windermere; the Yorkshire hills (in the distance); Morecambe Bay and the sea (s.), Snowdon (s.w.; in very clear weather), Devoke Water (w.) with the sea and the Isle of Man beyond it; and the Scafell group (N.W.). Immediately to the w. is the precipitous *Dow Crag* (2555 ft), with *Goat's Water* at its foot (not visible from the summit). The descent may be made w. and s.w. over Dow Crag to the *Walna Scar Pass* (see below); to the N.W., viâ *Seathwaite Tarn* (1210 ft; now a reservoir), to the *Duddon Valley* (see below); or to the N. to *Wrynose Pass* (p. 601; 2–2¼ hrs), viâ *Brim Fell* (2611 ft), *Great How Crags* (2625 ft), *Swirl How* (2630 ft) and *Little Carrs* (2250 ft) down *West Side Edge* to the Pass. In misty weather walkers should take care to follow the left fork on this edge, as the right path leads along the curved ridge to Rough Crags down into Greenburn and Little Langdale. A favourite round for good walkers is to keep eastwards along the ridge from Swirl How, over *Black Sails* (2443 ft) to Wetherlam, and descend thence to *Little Langdale* (p. 594; 3 hrs).—*Wetherlam* (2502 ft) is ascended from Coniston viâ Church Beck; from the disused mines, a well-marked path goes along the Lod Stanes ridge to the summit. The view (particularly of the Old Man) is good.

FROM CONISTON TO DUNGEON GILL, 8 m. Following the Ambleside road we take the first turning on the left and ascend *Tilberthwaite Glen*. To the right are Raven Crag, Ivy Crag, and Holme Fell. *Tilberthwaite Gill* (another approach to Wetherlam, see above) diverges to the left 1 m. above the fork. Beyond (2¼ m.) *High Tilberthwaite Farm* we pass through the gate on the left. After passing some slate quarries we descend, keeping roughly to the w. (l.) to cross the Brathay below (4¼ m.) the farm of *Fell Foot*. Hence viâ Blea Tarn to (8 m.) *Dungeon Gill*, see p. 594).

FROM CONISTON TO THE DUDDON VALLEY viâ Walna Scar Pass, a walk of c. 2 hrs (motorists must make the detour viâ Broughton).—We cross Church Beck and follow (w.) the Walna Scar cart-road, which reaches the open fell at (1 m.) a point where five tracks meet. We keep straight on and pass the tiny *Boo Tarn*. After 1 m. the track to Goat's Water, Dow Crag, and Coniston Old Man diverges to the right. Good retrospects as we ascend to (3½ m.) *Walna Scar Pass* (1990 ft; *View). In fine weather, the right-hand path may be followed to the top of *Brown Pike* (2237 ft), where the view is even better towards the N.; the ridge walk thence to *Dow Crag* is exhilarating, but only for the experienced walker in good weather. The descending route bears first to the left and then to the right, soon skirting *Long House Gill*. At (5 m.) *Long House* we bear to the left, join (5½ m.) the Duddon valley road (r. for Cockley Beck, see below), and follow it s. to (6 m.) *Seathwaite* (Inn). In the churchyard is the grave of 'Wonderful Walker', rector and benevolent despot of the parish for 67 years (1735–1802), "a Pastor such as Chaucer's verse portrays", who, with a stipend of less than £50, brought up and liberally educated a large family, besides leaving a fortune of £2000.—Buses run on Tues, Thurs, and Sat to Broughton (and Ulverston).

The *Duddon Valley*, which we have now reached, is described in Wordsworth's series of charming sonnets with singular fidelity to nature. The river descends, in a wonderful series of bends and water-breaks, from the sterile ridges of Wrynose Pass to the stony levels near *Cockley Beck* (Y.H., ½ m. s.w.), the deeply graven cleft at *Birks Bridge*, and the fine gorge just above Seathwaite. The N.W. bank below Cockley Beck, on the slopes of *Harter Fell*, is now largely covered by *Dunnerdale Forest*; several farms belong to the N.T. Farther down the scene becomes tamer, till the stream sleeps through its last marsh to its junction with the sea.

From Seathwaite the Broughton road leads down the valley to (3 m.) *Ulpha*, where the road to *Eskdale Green* diverges to the right over *Birker Moor*. From Ulpha to (8 m.) *Broughton* (Rte 63) we may follow either bank of the Duddon.

D   Ennerdale, Wasdale, Scafell, and Eskdale

This w. section of the Lake District is most conveniently approached from the road or railway between *Ravenglass* on the s. and *Whitehaven* on the N. (see Rte 63; through-carriages from London). It communicates with other parts of the district by various passes.

From Whitehaven the road goes viâ (3 m.) *Cleator Moor*, an industrial town no longer devoted to mining, whence it is 3½ m. to *Ennerdale Bridge* (the churchyard of which is the scene of Wordsworth's 'The Brothers') and 1¾ m. more to the *Anglers' Inn*.—A bus runs from Whitehaven to Ennerdale Bridge on Mon, Tues, Thurs, and Sat, also Sun in summer.

Ennerdale Water (368 ft; Hotel), the northernmost lake in this section, is about 2½ m. long and ½–¼ m. wide; several farms and over 2000 acres along its shore are owned by the N.T. The lake and its dale deserve a visit, though the lower slopes have been afforested up to the 1250 ft contour. The character of the lake is stern and solemn, and the mountains encircling it vie in grandeur with any in the district. The Steeple and Pillar group forms a specially fine combination beyond its head.

FROM ENNERDALE TO WASTWATER (9¼ m., in 3–3½ hrs). From the Anglers' Inn we follow the N. bank of the lake (views). Beyond (2½ m.) its head we ascend on the right bank of the river Liza (cart-road), with the Steeple and Pillar towering on our right. Beyond (3¾ m.) *Gillerthwaite Farm* a path crossing a small bridge to the right ascends to the foot of the famous *Pillar Rock* (p. 588). About 2½ m. farther on our path joins the route from Buttermere at the foot of the Black Sail Pass

(Y.H.). Thence to (9¾ m.) *Wasdale Head*, see p. 588.—From the Anglers' Inn to *Scale Hill, Crummock Water*, and *Buttermere*, see p. 587.

*Wastwater (200 ft), the most grim and savage of all the lakes, is just over 3 m. long, ½ m. wide, and 260 ft deep. The most characteristic feature of the imposing landscape is the almost perpendicular series of the *Screes on its S.E. bank, culminating in *Illgill Head* (1983 ft). Around the head of the lake rise Yewbarrow, Kirk Fell, Great Gable, Lingmell, Scafell Pike, and Scafell—a magnificent group. The timber near its foot makes a splendid foreground. The lake is subject to sudden squalls from the s.

Wastwater is best approached from the w. The Whitehaven bus (Thurs & Sat) to *Nether Wasdale* connects at Gosforth with a bus from Seascale (Rte 63), a convenient starting-point. From Seascale we cross the main road at (2½ m.) *Gosforth* (p. 577) and then bridge the Bleng and (after a steep climb) descend to (6¾ m.) *Nether Wasdale*, 1 m. from the s. end of *Wastwater*. Thence the road runs along the N.W. bank (*Views) to (12¼ m.) *Wasdale Head*. A narrow road on the left, ½ m. short of Nether Wasdale, passes close to Windsor Farm (Y.H.) and the prominent crag of *Buckbarrow* and in 2½ m. joins the lakeside road 3½ m. from Wasdale Head.—Wasdale Head may be reached from *Ravenglass* (Rte 63) by taking the miniature railway to (7 m.) *Dalegarth*, and walking thence (6¼ m. more) viâ *Boot* and *Burnmoor Tarn* (see below).

Wasdale Head (Hotel), in a deep and mountain-girt hollow, 1 m. from the N.E. end of Wastwater, is the headquarters for many fine ascents and excursions and the chief centre of English rock-climbing. The great rock-faces are on Scafell, Great Gable (N. front; Napes Ridges on s. side), and Pillar (Pillar Rock on N. side), but there are scores of other interesting courses in the gills and upper crags. A good deal of snow and ice work is done at Christmas and Easter. The quaint church is one of the smallest in England (42 ft by 16 ft). William Ritson (1807-90), landlord of the hotel, was a typical Cumberland 'statesman' or yeoman farmer, famous for his yarns, and forming a link with the Wilson and Wordsworth group.

WALK ROUND WASTWATER (12 m.). The route recommended is to descend along the N.W. bank and return to Wasdale Head viâ the top of the Screes (fine and varying views). We ascend to the s. end of the Screes viâ *Hawl Gill* and descend to Wasdale Head viâ the *Burnmoor Tarn* track (see below).

ASCENTS. The Scafell Mountains, S.E. of Wasdale Head, form the most imposing group in the Lake District. The top of Scafell Pike the highest summit in England, was presented in 1920 by Lord Leconfield to the National Trust as a War memorial, and in 1925 all Scafell above 2000 ft was added to this gift. Though the usual routes are quite safe in good weather, great care should be exercised in mist.—
*Scafell Pikes (3206 ft) is the most repaying climb (2–3 hrs). The usual route is viâ Lingmell Gill. We cross (¼ m.) the *Lingmell Beck* and ascend towards the s. round the base of *Lingmell* (2649 ft), which rises to the left. Higher up we cross another wall and the *Lingmell Gill*, reaching the foot of (½–¾ hr) *Brown Tongue*. The fine rocks in front are part of Scafell. We ascend the tongue, in c. ½ m. bearing to the left, and after ½ hr, in the dip between Lingmell and Scafell Pike, we turn to the right. Hence to the top, ¼–⅓ hr. A finer and harder route ascends viâ (½ m.) *Burnthwaite*, following the general course of the Lingmell Beck. After ½ m. more our path diverges to the right from the Sty Head track just before its steep rise. We bend to the right and ascend, keeping well to the left of the chasm of *Piers Gill* (see below). In ¾–1 hr more we join the above-described route in the hollow between Lingmell and the Pike. Another good route goes s. from Sty Head following a track (the *Corridor Route*) under *Long Pike* and Round How, and running due s. along a broad ridge to the summit. The *View includes Skiddaw and a bit of Derwentwater (N.), Helvellyn and Fairfield (N.E.), the High Street range (E.), Ingleborough (in the distance) and part of Windermere (S.E.), the Coniston Old Man (S.S.E.), Black Combe and the Duddon estuary, and Snowdon (S.), the sea,

the Isle of Man, and (at times) the Mourne Mountains in Ireland (s.w. and w.). The descent may be made to *Dungeon Gill* or *Rosthwaite* (marked paths).

Scafell (3162 ft) also may be ascended from Wasdale Head, either viâ *Brown Tongue* (see above) or viâ *Burnmoor Tarn* (p. 601), with about the same expenditure of time and energy as Scafell Pike. This, however, is not recommended to those who have climbed the latter summit. It is much better to combine the two (1 hr extra) by passing from one to the other by the *Mickledore* ridge (not difficult in good weather). From Scafell Pike we descend to the s.w. to (¼ hr) the ridge, cross it, turn to the right, and follow a grassy terrace (between Scafell and its screes) to (¼ hr) the foot of *Lord's Rake*, a steep scree slope. The way thence to (½ hr) the summit is unmistakable. The view is similar to that from the Pike, but more of Wastwater is visible. The direct descent (steep and laborious) is on the w. side, viâ *Green How* and *Hard Rigg*, to (1 hr) the Burnmoor Tarn track above *Wasdale Head Hall* (c. 2 m. from the Wasdale Head hotel).—The *View from Great End (2984 ft), the N.E. massif of the Scafell group, is even finer than that from Scafell Pike (Derwentwater and Borrowdale are marked features). It is easily reached from Scafell Pike in ¾ hr. The most direct descent is by its N. ridge to Sty Head.— *Lingmell* (2649 ft), the grassy w. member of the Scafell group, is sometimes ascended (no difficulty) *en route* to Scafell Pike (similar but less extensive view).—*Great Gable (2949 ft) is one of the finest ascents from Wasdale Head (viâ Sty Head Pass; 1 hr). *Kirk Fell* (2631 ft; viâ Black Sail Pass) and *Yewbarrow* (2058 ft; *View of Wastwater) may also be ascended.—*Piers Gill*, a chasm on the E. side of Lingmell, 2 m. E. of Wasdale Head, is a fine thing for the ordinary tourist to look at but not enter.—From Wasdale Head to *Ambleside*, see Rte 64c; to *Boot*, see below; to *Ennerdale*, see p. 598; to *Keswick*, see Rte 64B.

Eskdale, descending s.w. to the coast from between the Scafell range on the w. and the fells stretching s. from Bow Fell on the E., has (like the Duddon Valley) no lake on its floor. Its mountains and waterfalls, however, repay a visit.

The narrow-gauge railway mentioned on p. 576 brings us in summer from *Ravenglass* viâ (4½ m.) *Eskdale Green* to (6½ m.) *Dalegarth*, half-way up the dale, while *Esk Hause* forms the approach from other parts of the district to its head. A narrow road, on the line of the old Roman road, connects it with the Duddon Valley and the Langdales.

Boot, ¼ m. above the terminus of the railway, is a small village on the beck descending from Burnmoor Tarn, 250 yds N. of the main road and ½ m. from the Esk.

The chief attraction near Boot is *Stanley Force, which though not very high (60 ft), is from its setting deservedly regarded as the finest waterfall in the Lake District. It is reached by a road leaving the main road ⅓ m. below Boot, crossing the Esk, and passing *Dalegarth Hall*, a quaint old farmhouse. The gate for the fall is on the left, a little higher up (1¼ m. from Boot). Fine view from the open fell ¼ m. above the fall.

To see something of **Upper Eskdale** (3328 acres N.T.) we follow the road to the E. to a point about 1½ m. beyond the Woolpack Inn (near the foot of the Hardknott Pass). Here we diverge to the left, pass the farm of *Brother Ilkeld*, turn to the right, and ascend along the left bank of the Esk to (2 m.) the small but charming *Esk Falls*. We may follow the Esk hence to (1½ hr) *Esk Hause* (N.W.), or the *Lingcove Beck* (N.E.) to *Three Tarns* (s. slope of Bow Fell) and (2 hrs) *Dungeon Gill* (p. 594), but clear weather is desirable.

ASCENTS. Scafell (see above) is ascended in 4–5 hrs. We diverge to the left from the main road, ¾ m. E. of the Woolpack, and follow a lane (finger-post) to *Bird How* and (¾ m.) *Taw House*. After ¾ m. more the track crosses a bridge, with a small waterfall on each side of it, beyond which it ascends to the left in zigzags. It then turns to the right and curves round towards the N. (not always very clear), passing to the right of *High Scarth Crag* (1458 ft). In about ¾ hr we reach *Cam Spout*, descending from the *Mickledore* ridge (see above). We ascend to the right of the beck, turn to the left, and reach (¾ hr) the top. A less interesting route diverges from the Burnmoor Tarn track at *Gill Bank* and ascends the long slope to the right (passing *Eel Tarn* and *Stony Tarn*) until it joins the path described above.—The route up Scafell Pike (see above) coincides with that described above

as far as Cam Spout. The direct route thence (20–30 min; laborious) is to climb to
the top of Mickledore and turn to the right.

FROM BOOT TO AMBLESIDE viâ Hardknott Pass and Wrynose Pass (16 m.; a
walk of at least 5 hrs). Motorists should take note that the road (1 in 3½–5;
adequate surface) over Hardknott is narrow with sharp zigzags. For those un-
accustomed to this type of driving, it is perhaps advisable to reverse the route
(comp. p. 582). From Boot to (2¾ m.) the beginning of the Hardknott route, see
above. Our road ascends to the E. to (3¾ m.) **Hardknott Pass** (1290 ft), between
Harter Fell (2129 ft; r.) and *Hard Knott* (1803 ft). Fine view of Eskdale and Scafell.
Just to the left of the road, at the head of the first steep rise from Eskdale, is
Hardknott Castle, an interesting Roman fort (Mediobogdum; c. A.D. 100) built by
Agricola and partly reconstructed since 1954 with the original stones. We now
descend into the upper part of the Duddon Valley. At (5 m.) *Cockley Beck*
(p. 586) our road begins the ascent to Wrynose Pass, while the road to the right
descends along the Duddon. 7¼ m. **Wrynose Pass** (1270 ft), with the 'Three Shire
Stone' (2700 acres N.T.), where Cumberland, Lancashire, and Westmorland meet.
As we descend, *Pike o' Blisco* (2304 ft) rises to the left and Little Langdale opens up
in front. A ridge walk runs viâ Pike o' Blisco and Red Tarn to *Cold Pike* (2259 ft),
and thence N.W. along a ridge to the **Crinkle Crags** (2816 ft). From here, to cross
the plateau and ascend straight up the summit of Bow Fell, is most rewarding.
This magnificent walk may be extended along *Esk Pike* (2903 ft), dropping to *Esk
Hause* (2490 ft) and up over *Allen Crags* (2572 ft). The great sweep of ridge continues above High House Tarn, to Pinnacle Bield then over the summit of
Glaramara (2560 ft); we keep N. along the top of Raven Crags to *Capell Crag*
(1775 ft). Finally down Thornythwaite Fell to Combe Gill and Borrowdale.

FROM BOOT TO WASDALE HEAD viâ BURNMOOR TARN, 6 m. The track ascends
N. along the Whillan Beck, passing (¾ m.) the farm of *Gill Bank*. It reaches (3 m.)
its culminating point (977 ft) beyond (2½ m.) *Burnmoor Tarn* (832 ft). It then descends (views) to (6 m.) the hotel at *Wasdale Head*.

FROM BOOT TO ULPHA (DUDDON VALLEY), 7 m. We follow the road up the glen
of *Stanley Gill* and pass (2 m.) the farm of *Low Ground*. Just beyond this the road
forks. Walkers may keep straight on to (2½ m.) *Birkethwaite*, beyond which a
somewhat blind path crosses *Black Moor* and rejoins the road 1¼ m. farther on.
The driving route (rough) takes the right branch at the fork, passes (2½ m.) *High
Ground*, and ¼ m. farther on joins the Eskdale–Ulpha road, where we turn left.
[The high-lying *Devoke Water* (765 ft) is ½ m. straight ahead.]—7 m. *Ulpha*, see
p. 598.

65 THE ISLE OF MAN

The ISLE OF MAN (227 sq. m.; 56,250 inhab.), situated in the Irish Sea,
midway between England and Ireland (c. 30 m. from both) and 19 m. s. of
Barrow Head in Scotland, is 33 m. long and 12 m. broad. In summer the
more accessible pleasure-resorts and beauty spots are overcrowded and
casual accommodation hard to find; but farther afield the island,
mountainous except in the extreme N., has a wealth of attractive scenery in
its wooded glens and cliff-bound coast that well repays exploration and is
rarely overcrowded. The townscapes are neat, orderly, and prosperous.
With a mild climate, the island is surprisingly little visited out of season.
The inhabitants still preserve some ancient customs, though the Manx
language (akin to Gaelic, with a Scandinavian flavour, especially in
proper-names) now survives only in ceremonial (see p. 605). Of the
antiquities the most important are the *Crosses, decorated with interlaced
patterns and Norse runes; the churches, though of ancient foundation, are
mostly 19C rebuildings.—The roads are excellent, cars for hire are
plentiful at moderate charges, and the Isle of Man Road Services control a
comprehensive service of buses to all parts of the island.—The Manx cat is
a tailless variety of the domestic cat. The bird life is abundant.

History and Administration. *Ellan Vannin* or *Mannin* (perhaps 'middle isle'), where the place-names are mostly of Norse or Celtic origin, has no very authentic early history, though archaeology has proven its occupation since prehistoric times. In the 9C it was conquered by the Norwegians, and became subject to the Norse kings of Dublin. In 1079–95 'Orry the Dane' (Godred Crovan) ruled over Man and the Western Isles of Scotland, but in 1265 Man became subject to Scotland by purchase. Edward I of England, however, intervened, and from 1333 it has been under English overlordship. Its first viceroys, the Montacutes, earls of Salisbury, called themselves 'Kings of Man' and were crowned in Peel Cathedral. In 1406 Henry IV bestowed the island upon the Stanleys, earls of Derby, the fourth of whom changed his title in 1505 to 'Lord of Man', on the ground that he would rather be a great lord than a petty king. During the Civil War the island was held for the king by the 7th or 'great' Earl of Derby, but after his execution in 1651 it was surrendered by the receiver-general, William Christian, the Illiam Dhône ('brown-haired William') of Manx history. In 1765 the Duke of Atholl, descendant and successor of the earls of Derby, sold his sovereignty to the Crown, which in 1829 acquired also the manorial and other rights by purchase. The regular steam-packet service from Liverpool started in 1830. The chief industries of the island are agriculture and catering for visitors.

The Isle of Man remains constitutionally separate from the United Kingdom. The COURT OF TYNWALD, the legislative and executive authority, consists of the *Lieutenant-Governor*, the *Council*, and the *House of Keys*, one of the oldest legislative assemblies in the world, with 24 elected members. The Council includes the bishop, the two deemsters or judges, the attorney-general, all appointed by the Crown, two nominees of the Lieut.-Governor, and four members elected from the House of Keys. British Acts of Parliament do not apply to the Isle of Man, unless it be expressly so enacted, but the laws of Tynwald require the approval of the Crown, and must be proclaimed on the Hill of Tynwald (p. 605).—The use of the well-known 'three legs' device dates before 1265; the motto 'Quocunque jeceris stabit' appeared on the earliest known Manx coinage (1668). The island government issues its own notes for £10, £5, £1, & 50p, and coins (though English, Scottish, and Irish monies are equally accepted); but Man has its own postal authority, rates, and stamps (U.K. stamps not valid). Customs duties and VAT are, however, in line with Westminster.—The Bishop of Sodor and Man takes the first part of his title from the 'Sudreyjar' (i.e. the Hebrides as distinct from the Nordreyjar, or Orkney and Shetland), within the diocese until the 14C.—Scott's 'Peveril of the Peak', Wilkie Collins's 'Armadale', and several novels by Hall Caine refer to the Isle of Man.—The *Tourist Trophy Motor Cycle Races*, or 'T.T.', held every June in Man since 1907, attract many competitors and thousands of visitors.

Steamer Services (tickets from travel agents or main railway stations). MANX INFORMATION CENTRE, 14 Dover St., London W.1. To DOUGLAS services (mostly by Car Ferry) are maintained by the Isle of Man Steam Packet Co. from *Liverpool* on weekdays (2–3 times daily in summer; 70 m.; 3½ hrs). Day excursions also from Liverpool, Fleetwood, and Llandudno (no cars) to Douglas.—In addition there are services in summer from *Ardrossan* to Douglas 2 or 3 times weekly (6 hrs); from *Belfast* to Douglas; and from *Dublin* to Douglas. Trailer-caravans are not allowed on the island.—Intending visitors to the island may obtain the current time-tables from the Steamer Co.'s head office (Imperial Buildings, Douglas).

Air Services. The airport is at *Ronaldsway*, 1½ m. N.E. of Castletown. Services by British Airways from *Heathrow*, daily, direct or viâ *Liverpool*; from *Manchester*; by British Island Airways from *Blackpool*; from *Gatwick* (3 times weekly); also from *Belfast* and from *Dublin*. Increased service in July–Aug (also by Dan-Air from other regional airports); less frequent in winter.

DOUGLAS, the chief town (c. 19,000 inhab.), is finely situated on a wide bay on the E. coast, backed by a range of hills, just below the confluence of the Awin Dhoo and Awin Glass (i.e. dark and light rivers). During the summer months it is inundated by excursionists, for whom every variety of entertainment is provided, including the characteristic huge dancing-halls. The port of Douglas was the first in the world to be controlled by radar (1948).

Sea Terminal Building (with Rest.) opposite *Victoria Pier*, where steamers moor.—
Railway Station (summer only). North Quay, ½ m. w. of the landing-place.

Hotels mainly along the Promenade, best towards the centre and N. end.—CHINESE RESTAURANTS in Strand St.

Post Office. Regent St. (Sun 9–10.30 a.m.).—INFORMATION OFFICE, 13 Victoria St.

Bus Station in Lord St. (¼ m. w. of Victoria Pier) to the Airport, and to main towns c. every hour.—HORSE TRAMWAY in summer from the pier to Derby Castle. STEAM LAUNCH from the Pier to Douglas Head.

Pleasure Resorts. *Casino*, Central Prom.; *Gaiety Theatre*, Harris Prom.; *Palace Lido Ballroom* and *Coliseum*, Central Prom.; *Solarium* and covered fun-fair in construction at Derby Castle; *Villa Marina*, Harris Prom., with concert-hall and dancing. Also at *Onchan Head* and *Douglas Head* (see below).

Golf Courses at Howstrake, 2½ m. N.E., near Groudle Glen, and Pulrose, ¾ m. w. TENNIS COURTS, Noble's Park.—SWIMMING, Derby Castle Baths (heated sea water), Queen's Prom. (sauna, etc.).—SEA FISHING from the piers (free).

In the oldest part of Douglas, w. of Victoria Pier, are the chief public buildings, including the *Town Hall* (1899) and the *Legislative Buildings* (1894), with the Keys Chambe, Tynwald Court, and Government Offices. A little s.w. is *St George's*, the ceremonial church of the diocese. The terraces of opulent Victorian houses are unsurpassed, but the chief attraction of the town is the splendid sea-front, a promenade 2 m. long. In the bay rises the Conister Rock, on which is a *Tower of Refuge* for shipwrecked mariners (1832). The *Castle Mona Hotel* was built as the residence of the Duke of Atholl, the last Lord of Man. The **Manx Museum** (adm. free weekdays, 10–5), in Crellin's Hill, above the junction of the Loch and Harris Promenades, has an informative Archaeological Gallery which contains a singular *Crucifixion (?Celtic) in low relief, from the Calf of Man, a chalice of 1521, from Jurby, and other Manx antiquities; a good local natural history collection; memorials of T. E. Brown (1830–97), the Manx poet, maps, local history, folk life and costume. Farther N. in Upper Douglas is *Noble's Park*, with an aviary and a cattery.

On *Douglas Head* (view), reached by ferry (see above) or by the swing-bridge at the end of Parade St., are a lighthouse, a war memorial cross, Port Skillion bathing-creek, an open-air theatre, etc.; also the Fort Anne hotel, once the home of Sir William Hillary (1771–1847), founder of the Royal National Lifeboat Institution. Here begins the *Marine Drive*, which runs along the picturesque rocky cliffs to (3½ m.) *Port Soderick*, another popular resort with a pretty glen.—Services in the meadow beside the new church at *Kirk Braddan* (Sun 10.45 a.m.), 1½ m. N.W., are attended in summer by thousands of visitors. The 18C church has an earlier tower and a number of runic crosses. John Martin (1789–1854), the artist, is buried in the churchyard.—The N. suburb of *Onchan* is reached by bus viâ *Government House*, the official residence of the Lieut.-Governor. The church (1833), with its pretty spire, likewise attracts visitors on Sundays. In its predecessor in 1781 Bligh of the 'Bounty' was married.—About 4 m. w. of Douglas is *Braaid* (motor-bus to Mount Murray, see below, 1½ m. S.E.), with two prehistoric monuments known as *St Patrick's Chair* and the *Stone Circles*.

FROM DOUGLAS TO PORT ERIN

14¼ m. BUS in 1 hr; to *Port St Mary* in 65 min.; to *Castletown* in 35 min. RAILWAY (steam trains) in 50 min.; to (10 m.) *Castletown* in 35 min.

3¾ m. *Mount Murray* (450 ft; Hotel) commands splendid views.— 5½ m. *Santon* (l.; Hotel), for *Port Greenaugh*, a pretty bay on the coast 1 m. s.—At (7¾ m.) *Ballasalla* are the unimportant ruins of *Rushen Abbey*, a Cistercian offshoot of Furness Abbey, founded by Olaf I in 1135, and dissolved in 1540. It is now part of an inn-garden. Over the mill-dam is the *Monks' Bridge* or *Crossag* (13C). The road skirts the

Isle of Man Airport (Ronaldsway) on the edge of which stands *King William's College*, founded in 1668, the chief school on the island. Here were educated Dean Farrar (1831–1903) and T. E. Brown (see above).

9¾ m. **Castletown**, the capital of the island until 1869, is a compact old town (c. 1500 inhab.) with a tidal harbour. *Castle Rushen* (adm. daily, 10–7; fee), dating perhaps from the time of Magnus (1252–65), or somewhat earlier, was gallantly defended against Parliament by the Countess of Derby after the execution of her husband in 1651. It was afterwards used as the island gaol and as the seat of the legislature and still contains a courthouse. In Bridge St. is an interesting *Nautical Museum* (adm. in summer 10–1, 2–5; fee), which incorporates an 18C armed yacht and her original boathouse. The *Witches' Mill* (restaurant) in Arbory Rd., to the N.W. contains a museum of witchcraft (adm. daily).

On the E. side of the town is *Hango Hill*, where William Christian was "shot to death" in 1663 for his surrender of the island. Farther on is *Derbyhaven* (Hotels), a small village at the neck of *Langness*, the promontory forming the E. boundary of Castletown Bay, with a golf course.

11½ m. *Balladoole*, where (at Chapel Hill) a remarkable Viking boat-grave of the 9C was discovered in 1945 above earlier Christian Celtic graves.—12¾ m. *Colby* (r.), for the pretty *Colby Glen*. About 5 m. N. rises *South Barrule* (1585 ft), with a fine view of the s. half of the island.—At the fork (13 m.) we bear right for Port Erin (see below), and left for (14 m.) **Port St Mary**, a fishing village and golfing resort on the w. side of *Poolvash Bay*, with a harbour and a breakwater 400 yds long.

This is the starting-point for a coast walk to (7 m.) *Port Erin*, round the *Mull Promontory*, the s.w. extremity of the island, with its splendid cliffs and rock scenery, viâ *Perwick Bay*; *Noggin Head*, with its perpendicular cliffs and fine caves; the remarkable series of fissures known as the *Chasms*; *Black Head* and *Spanish Head*, where the cliffs rise to a height of 400 ft; and *Calf Sound.*—On the direct road to Calf Sound is (1½ m.) *Cregneash*, with the *Manx Village Folk Museum* (adm. 10–1, 2–5, mid-May–Sept; fee), a group of characteristic old Manx houses, centred on the cottage of Harry Kelly (d. 1934), a crofter who was one of the last persons to speak Manx as his mother-tongue. *The Calf of Man* (N.T.), an island of 616 acres, is reached by boat from Port St Mary or Port Erin. It is noted for its bird life (landing fee; closed during breeding season, May and June). About ¾ m. s.w. of this island is the *Chickens Rock*, with a lighthouse (visible 16 m.).

14¼ m. **Port Erin** (Hotels), one of the oldest and most attractive towns in the island, with excellent bathing and golfing, is situated amid fine scenery on a square bay protected by a ruined breakwater. The aquarium of the *Marine Biological Station* here is open on weekdays in summer (10–5).

On the N. side of the bay is (2 m.) *Bradda Head*, crowned with the Milner Tower (view).—A boat should be hired in fine weather to enjoy the magnificent coast scenery, as far as *Fleshwick Bay* on the N. and the Calf of Man on the s. (experienced boatman necessary).

The interesting road which runs N. from Port Erin to (14 m.) *Peel* (see below) passes near *The Stacks* (3½ m.; surprising cliff-view from a viewpoint to the left), the *Round Table* (6 m.; 1000 ft), *Dalby* (9 m.), and *Glen Maye* (11 m.).

FROM DOUGLAS TO PEEL

9½ m. BUS in 40 min.

Beyond (4 m.) *Crosby*, on the slopes of *Greeba Mountain* (1383 ft) to the right, are *Greeba Castle*, the residence of Sir Hall Caine (d. here in 1931), and the ruins of *St Trinian's Church*.—7½ m. *St John's*.

On the right, is Tynwald Hill, an artificial mound, "Still marked with green turf circles narrowing stage above stage," where on 5 July (Midsummer Day, O.S.), in accordance with ancient Scandinavian custom, new laws are promulgated (in Manx and English) and officers are appointed for the ensuing year.

9½ m. **Peel** (Hotel), at the mouth of the Neb, the most attractive town (c. 2500 inhab.) on the island, consists of the old fishing village and a visitors' quarter and is the chief centre for curing Manx kippers. A Viking festival (1st week in July) commemorates the invasion of A.D. 798.—On *St Patrick's Isle*, united by a causeway with the w. arm of Peel harbour and reached also by a ferry from the pier opposite, stands *PEEL CASTLE (adm. daily, May–Sept, 10–5 or 7; Sun 2–6; fee), a group of ruins within a stout 16C wall.

To the right, beyond the *Keep* and the *Guard Room*, is the roofless CATHEDRAL, dedicated to St Germanus, a disciple of St Patrick. It was founded by Bp. Simon (1230–48) and the existing remains date from the 13C and 14C; it was unroofed in 1727 to build the governor's stables in Castletown. A scheme is on foot to reroof the cathedral and restore it to full use.—We visit also the *Old Palace* of the bishops, with a banqueting hall; *Fenella's Tower*, whence Fenella is said to have leapt into the boat in 'Peveril of the Peak'; the *Round Tower*, resembling those in Ireland; and the roofless little *St Patrick's Chapel* (c. 9C).

A good walk from Peel leads s. along the cliffs, viâ *Corrin's Folly* and *Contrary Head*, to (4 m.) *Glen Maye*, a delightful wooded spot with pretty cascades. A bus runs viâ *Knockaloe*, site of a huge German internment camp in 1914–18, and Glen Maye to (5 m.) *Dalby*, a quiet village, for (5½ m.) *The Niarbyl*, on the shore, commanding the best coast-view in the island. Thence to *Port Erin*, see above.— A road follows the disused railway above the w. coast, which has fine rock-scenery and a number of caves, to (7 m.) *Kirk Michael* (p. 606). Buses run infrequently from *Castletown* and *Port Erin* viâ *Foxdale*, with disused silver and lead mines, passing beneath *South Barrule* (1585 ft) crowned with a huge Iron Age hill-fort.

From Douglas to Ramsey

A. Viâ LAXEY. By the narrow-gauge *MANX ELECTRIC RAILWAY, 18 m., in 1¼ hr; to *Laxey*, 7½ m. in ½ hr. Magnificent views on both sides.—The hilly coast ROAD (16½ m.; bus in 65 min.) follows much the same route.

The line runs from Derby Castle viâ *Banks Howe* (393 ft) to (2½ m.) *Groudle Glen* (adm. fee), the most picturesque part of which is the *Lhen Coan*. About ½ m. N.E. of the glen is the old church of *Lonan*, with two runic crosses.—4¼ m. *Garwick Glen* (adm. fee) is a pretty hollow, with the prehistoric *Cloven Stones*. On the beach (¾ m.) are some interesting smugglers' caves.—7½ m. **Laxey** (Inn) is a little bathing resort and centre of rural industry, with the *Laxey Glen Gardens* (adm. free) and the *Big Wheel* (1854; 72½ ft in diameter) of the old lead mines.

From Laxey the SNAEFELL ELECTRIC RAILWAY (average gradient 1 in 12) ascends to (5 m. in ½ hr) the top of Snaefell (2034 ft), the highest mountain in the island. The line crosses the mountain road from Douglas to Ramsey at (3½ m.) the *Bungalow* (1400 ft), at the junction of the road to Sulby Glen (see below). The *View from the top (Restaurant) comprises the whole of the island and, in clear weather, the peaks of the Lake District in England, the Mull of Galloway in Scotland, the Mourne Mountains in Ireland, and the Snowdon group in Wales.

The Ramsey line returns to the coast along the N. side of the valley, leaving on the left 'King Orry's Grave' a megalithic chambered cairn of c. 2000 B.C. We then obtain a superb *View of *Bulgham Bay*, 400 ft below.—10½ m. *Dhoon Glen*, Devonian in character, with a waterfall (130 ft in two leaps).—12¼ m. *Glen Mona*, with a pretty little fall.—14 m.

Ballaglass Glen, quite unspoilt, with pretty cascades.—On the left appears *North Barrule* (1860 ft), on the right *Maughold Head* (373 ft).— 18 m. *Ramsey* (see below).

B. BY MOUNTAIN ROAD (15 m.), a laborious ascent as far as Snaefell.

We diverge to the left from the Laxey road at (1½ m.) *Governor's Bridge* and ascend to (4½ m.) *Keppelgate* (magnificent views) and (8 m.) the *Bungalow Restaurant* (comp. above), at the foot of Snaefell. Here is the extensive *Motor Cycle Museum*. Hence we may descend to the left through *Sulby Glen* (see below) and join the 'Long Drive' at (15 m.) *Sulby*; or we may follow the mountain road to the right which crosses the E. face of Snaefell and the W. slopes of North Barrule. By the former route Ramsey is 20 m. from Douglas, by the latter 15 m.

C. By BUS viâ Kirk Michael, 23¼ m. in 1–1½ hr, a much more circuitous route than the Manx Electric Railway.—This route and Rte B, above, in reverse, constitute the Tourist Trophy Course (37¾ m.).

Fom Douglas to (7½ m.) *St John's*, see p. 605. We diverge to the right at the *Ballacraine Inn* and ascend in an enclosed valley past the mouth of (9½ m.) **Glen Helen* (r.), with charming woods, a hotel, a chalet-restaurant, and the *Rhenass Fall* (25 ft). Joining a steep mountain road from Snaefell, we descend towards the coast (view).— 13½ m. *Kirk Michael*, where the coast road from Peel is joined, is a little summer resort ½ m. from the sea, with good bathing. At the conspicuous parish church are preserved eight runic crosses. *Glen Wyllin*, to the s., is a popular resort.—About 1 m. N. of Kirk Michael is *Bishopscourt*, the residence of the bishop, with a theological college and a chapel which is the official pro-cathedral.— 16½ m. *Ballaugh* (pron. 'Baláff'). The old church (17C), 1½ m. N., has an 11C cross and a curious font. On the left is the CURRAGH WILD LIFE PARK (adm. 10–6; car park free), where the partially drained marsh harbours wild orchises, yuccas, and a multitude of bird species, and otters play.— 18½ m. *Sulby Glen*, whence a road runs up the narrow **SULBY GLEN*, the 'Manx Switzerland', to the *Tholt-y-Will Inn*, which has beautiful grounds of 200 acres with waterfalls (adm. free).— 19½ m. *Sulby Bridge*, a favourite anglers' resort (excellent trout-fishing).— 21½ m. *Lezayre* church contains a runic cross.

23¼ m. **Ramsey** (Hotels, Restaurant), a somewhat undistinguished town of c. 3800 inhab., situated on a magnificent bay, is the second holiday-resort on the island, quieter than Douglas. It has an excellent sandy beach, an indoor swimming pool and a pier 2160 ft long. Beyond a small tidal harbour with Norwegian undertones is *Mooragh Park*, with its marine lake and tennis courts.

The environs of Ramsey, with its background of mountains, are very attractive. Pleasant walks may be taken to (1 m.) the *Albert Tower* (view); and viâ *Glen Auldyn* or over *North Barrule* and along the ridge to (c. 4 m.) *Snaefell* (see above).

Buses run along the coast s.e., viâ Ballure Glen and Port Lewaigue, to (3½ m.) *Maughold* (pron. Mack'ld; Inn), where the churchyard contains a rare medieval cross (14C) and many runic crosses; also viâ (4½ m.) *Bride* (*Thor Cross in the churchyard) to (7½ m.) the *Point of Ayre*, the barren N. extremity of the island, with a lighthouse (1815; tower open 1–dusk); and to (4 m. N.W.) *Andreas* (noted restaurant), which has some inscribed tomb-slabs, including *Sandulf's Cross, with beasts and inscriptions.

Other Viking crosses may be seen at *Jurby*, 8 m. w. of Ramsey (2 m. N. of Ballaugh, see above).

66 LEEDS TO ILKLEY AND SKIPTON. WHARFEDALE

ROAD, 26¼ m. A 660. 11 m. *Otley*.—14 m. *Burley*.—A 65. 17 m. Ilkley.—19¾ m. *Addingham* (r. for Bolton Abbey and Wharfedale, B 6160).—26¼ m. Skipton.—An alternative route (A 65) to (12 m.) *Burley* runs viâ Kirkstall and (9 m.) *Guiseley* (see below).

RAILWAY to *Skipton*, 26¼ m. in 35–55 min.; to (16¼ m.) *Ilkley* in c. ½ hr; also service from Bradford, viâ *Guiseley*, similar.

A 660 quits Leeds viâ Headingley and Adel. Beyond (6 m.) the Parkway Hotel lies the Golden Acre Park.—At (8 m.) *Bramhope* is a Puritan chapel of 1649 with contemporary fittings.—11 m. **Otley** (13,300 inhab.; Hotel), an industrial market town on the lower Wharfe, was the birthplace of Thomas Chippendale (1711–79), the cabinet-maker. The restored Perp. church contains 17C monuments of the Fairfax and Fawkes families, and fragments of Anglo-Saxon crosses (8–11C). In the churchyard is a memorial (in the form of a scale model of the tunnel portals) to the 'navvies' killed driving the Bramhope Tunnel (1845–9). To the s. rises the *Chevin* (924 ft), affording a good view of the Wharfe valley and the hills to the N.W.

About 1½ m. N.E. is *Farnley Hall* (G. N. le G. Horton-Fawkes, Esq.; adm. on written application), a mansion of 1581 with an imposing wing of 1790 by Carr of York. It contains a collection of watercolours and other works by Turner, who frequently visited his friend Walter Fawkes here, pictures by Reynolds and other masters, and various historical relics. Guy Fawkes was a scion of the Farnley family.—On the E. of Farnley Park is *Leathley*, with its early-Norman church tower and village stocks. Beyond Farnley a pleasant drive ascends the Washburn valley to (7 m.) *Blubberhouses*, on the Harrogate–Bolton Abbey road. In the valley (l.) are the reservoirs of the Leeds Waterworks. *Fewston Reservoir*, the largest of these, has submerged the hamlet of *Thackray*, said to be the home of W. M. Thackeray's ancestors.

Guiseley, 2½ m. s. of Otley, with a gabled rectory (1601), has a part-Norman church, dedicated to St Oswald (pageant on the Sat after St Oswald's Day, 6 Aug). Here Charlotte Brontë's parents were married in 1812; and in the churchyard lie many generations of Longfellows, ancestors of the poet.

Denton Park (rebuilt by Carr in 1778), the birthplace of Gen. Fairfax (1612–71), is seen to the right, on the other side of the Wharfe, beyond (14 m.) *Burley*.

17 m. **ILKLEY** (Hotels), identified with the Roman fort *Olicana*, is a residential town (21,800 inhab.), noted for its position (highest point 750 ft) on the s. bank of the Wharfe, surrounded by moors.

The late Perp. parish church of *All Saints* has three Anglian crosses in the churchyard. Behind it, the *Manor House Museum* (on the site of Olicana) is a collection illustrating local history, including many Roman finds (adm. daily, 10–5, 7, or 8; free). To the N. of *St Margaret's Church*, in the s. part of the town, is a singularly fine example of a rock with 'cup and ring' markings. The old bridge across the Wharfe is now used for foot-traffic and cycles only.

Ilkley is an excellent centre from which to make excursions in Wharfedale and on the breezy moors that adjoin it. The pleasant road on the N. side of the Wharfe passes the golf course and leads to Bolton Abbey (5½ m.) viâ *Nesfield* and *Beamsley*. —Among the points of interest near by are the *Cow & Calf Rocks*, to the S.E. (above Ben Rhydding; view of Wharfedale); the *White Wells*, ¾ m. S; and the *Twelve Apostles*, 1 m. farther S. on Burley Moor, a fine Bronze Age stone circle. South-west of Ilkley are *Heber's Ghyll*; the *Swastika Rock*, an Iron Age incised rock on Addingham High Moor; and the *Panorama Rocks*. The track to (6½ m.) *Keighley* crosses the highest part of *Rombald's Moor* (1321 ft), 2 m. s.

*Wharfedale challenges Wensleydale for natural beauty and is among the loveliest valleys in England, with its ideal combination of water, wood, hill, crag, castle, and abbey. At the height of summer (and at Easter and Whitsun) the dale becomes crowded and accommodation is difficult to secure. Bolton Abbey in particular is a favourite rendezvous of the neighbouring townsfolk.

At (19¾ m.) *Addingham*, with the small shaft of a late-Anglian cross in its church, the main road goes on to **Skipton** (p. 610). We bear right (B 6160) and ascend the Wharfe to (22 m.) *Bolton Bridge* (Hotel), where we cross the Skipton–Harrogate road.

Beamsley Hospital, ¾ m. E. on A 59, founded by the Countess of Cumberland in 1593, is a unique group of almshouses for old women, with seven living-rooms opening directly off the little circular chapel. Across the valley of the Kex Beck rises *Beamsley Beacon* (1314 ft), a good viewpoint.

Bolton Abbey or (more accurately) *Bolton Priory*, an Augustinian foundation of c. 1120, was removed from Embsay, near Skipton, to its present beautiful site on the Wharfe in 1151, by Lady Alice de Romilly, daughter of the founder. The legend (comp. Wordsworth's 'Force of Prayer') that this was in consequence of the death of her son at the Strid (see below) is a fabrication. The nave (E.E.) of the *Church* has been used as a parish church since c. 1170 and was not destroyed at the Dis-solution. The roof and E. end, and the former rood-screen, were last restored in 1875–80 by G. E. Street. The Perp. w. front (intended as the base of a w. tower which was never completed) was added in 1520 by Prior Moon, whose inscription and rebus it bears; it masks the 12–13C front. At the end of the aisle was the Mauleverer Chantry (with a rare seated altar-stone), where the Mauleverers and Claphams were popularly supposed to be buried upright—an unfounded tradition, adopted by Wordsworth in his 'White Doe of Rylstone'. The choir (large E. window) and transepts remain in ruins, but the monastic buildings to the s. are razed practically to ground-level.

In the churchyard is a cross commemorating Lord Frederick Cavendish, assassinated in Phoenix Park, Dublin, in 1882. To the s. is the picturesque *Rectory*. To the w. of the church is BOLTON HALL, a residence of the Duke of Devonshire, a 19C building incorporating the priory gatehouse. To the E. of the abbey the Wharfe is crossed by a footbridge and a long row of stepping-stones.

The road goes on to *Barden Bridge* (2¾ m.), but a visit to Bolton Woods is highly recommended, particularly in spring, as well as the walk to the bridge (c. 2 hrs there and back). Near the *Cavendish Foun-tain* (¼ m.; view) a drive descends to *BOLTON WOODS (adm. daily 10–7; fee), with a car-park (fee; rfmts) and to the *Wooden Bridge* (1 m.), beyond which a road ascends the left bank of the Wharfe (view). Walkers enter the woods and hug the right bank of the river beside an enchanting stretch of water. Beyond the *Meeting of the Waters* we reach (2 m.) the *STRID, where the water boils through a rocky channel 50 yds long and c. 12 ft wide. Here the 'Boy of Egremont' is supposed to have been drowned, missing his leap because his dog hung back on the leash. It is prudent not to approach too near the edge, as the rocks are often wet and slippery, and the force of the water is vicious. A few minutes later we cross the Barden Beck and pass under an aqueduct.— 3 m. *Barden Bridge*. BARDEN TOWER (i.e. 'boarden'), high up on the left, was rebuilt by Henry, Lord Clifford, the 'Shepherd Lord', after 1485 and used for alchemical studies; it was restored by Lady Anne Clifford in 1658–59. The farmhouse (rfmts) in the courtyard, on 13C foundations, extends into part of the tower of the little parish church.

The return route to (3½ m.) Bolton Abbey by the left bank takes c. 1¼ hr recrossing the river by the Wooden Bridge, or, lower down, by the stepping-stones or footbridge. A charming detour may be made by ascending (2 m.) the Posforth Beck, with its waterfalls, to the *Valley of Desolation*.

Upper Wharfedale, above Barden Bridge, is likewise superbly beautiful and well worth exploration on foot or by car. The direct road, with superior views, ascends the w. bank of the river. To the right rises *Simon Seat* (1529 ft; view). Near (5½ m. from Bolton Bridge) *Appletreewick*, on the E. bank, is the striking gully of *Troller's Gill*. High Hall was the home of Sir Wm. Craven (d. 1618), Lord Mayor of London and father of the Earl of Craven, the loyal supporter of Elizabeth of Bohemia. —7 m. **Burnsall** (Hotels), with an interesting church (Norman font, and Jacobean pulpit) and the old Grammar School (1602), is on a lovely reach of the Wharfe.—9½ m. *Linton* (l.) is a pretty village with a packhorse bridge and an old clapper bridge over the stream, and Fountaine's Hospital (1721) in the style of Vanbrugh. The church (partly 12C), with a 10C brass Crucifix, stands ¾ m. N.E. beside the Wharfe.— We cross the river to (10½ m.) **Grassington** (650 ft; Hotels), a little town with a tiny square on a hill.

Ghaistrills Strid, ¼ m. upstream, is reached by a river-path beginning at the E. end of the bridge.—B 6265 crosses the Wharfe to *Threshfield* and leads s. to (9½ m.) Skipton viâ Linton and (3¼ m.) *Cracoe*.
From Grassington B 6265 traverses the moor E. with remains of Roman lead mines, to (10½ m.) Pateley Bridge viâ (1¾ m.) *Hebden* and (5½ m.) *Stump Cross Caves* (adm. daily Easter–Sept; fee) with fine stalactite formations.

13½ m. *Conistone*, with an ancient church (restored 1957) containing pews by Thompson of Kilburn, lies to the w. of a fine limestone gorge.— Recrossing the Wharfe we reach (14½ m.) *Kilnsey*, at the base of the overhanging *Kilnsey Crag*, part of the 'Craven Fault' (comp. p. 611). The crag, where the overhang is at its greatest, is a notorious obstacle for rock-climbers.

FROM KILNSEY TO MALHAM TARN. Beyond Kilnsey a road (l.) follows the Skirfare (fishing) up Amerdale to (3¾ m.) *Arncliffe* (725 ft), a charming little village. Thence a moorland road (l.), steep in parts (1 in 4), leads to *Malham Tarn* (p. 611). 5 m. s.w.—Another road ascends the l. bank of the Skirfare, through *Littondale* to (4½ m.) *Halton Gill*; thence it runs s.w. beneath Penyghent to (12 m.) *Stainforth*.

We cross the Skirfare.—17½ m. **Kettlewell** (700 ft; Hotel), a large village on the E. bank of the Wharfe, is a good centre for anglers and walkers.

To the E. of Kettlewell rises *Great Whernside* (2310 ft; view).—The rough and steep road from Kettlewell viâ *Coverdale* to (16 m.) *Leyburn* (see p. 667) skirts the

N. flanks of Great Whernside and *Little Whernside* (1984 ft) and offers some fine views. It attains a height of 1652 ft.

Continuing to ascend the Wharfe above Kettlewell, we next reach (19¼ m.) *Starbotton* (730 ft) and (21 m.) *Buckden* (780 ft; Hotel), where B 6160 bears right for Aysgarth (see below). Our road crosses the Wharfe and continues up the dale, here called *Langstrothdale*. The dialect of this dale agrees more nearly than any other with Chaucerian English as used (e.g.) in the 'Reeve's Tale'.—22½ m. *Hubberholme* has a small 12C church, containing one of the only two rood-lofts in Yorkshire (1558, bearing the arms of the Percy family; comp. p. 637); the stalls are by Thompson of Kilburn.—At (25 m.) *Deepdale* we cross to the left bank. At (26 m.) *Beckermonds* (970 ft) two streams unite to form the Wharfe. The cloudberry (Rubus chamaemorus) is so abundant on the hills here that its berries redden the ground. Our road turns sharply to the right and ascends to (29 m.) the summit of *Fleet Moss* (1934 ft). The road then descends rapidly to (32½ m.) *Hawes*, in Wensleydale (Rte 72A).

FROM BUCKDEN TO AYSGARTH. The road ascends rapidly along the Cray Beck (retrospective view) to (1½ m.) *Cray* (1050 ft). About 1½ m. farther on a track (unsuitable for cars) diverges left for Semer Water (p. 667) and (10½ m.) Bainbridge viâ the *Stake Pass* (1832 ft). Our road climbs to c. 1392 ft before the descent to *Bishopdale*. Beyond (5 m.) *Newbiggin* is (r.) the attractive village of (6½ m.) *West Burton* with a large green.—8 m. *Aysgarth* (Rte 72A).

From (19¾ m.) *Addingham* (p. 608) A 65 ascends N.W. out of Wharfedale and crosses the watershed into Airedale.—26¾ m. **Skipton** (Hotel), a fine old market town (12,400 inhab.), with a wide main street is the capital of the limestone district of CRAVEN, which extends from the sources of the Wharfe and the Ribble to the borders of Lancashire and contains some of the wildest and most picturesque scenery in Yorkshire. From the 12C to the 15C most of it was divided between the two great houses of Percy and Clifford. *Skipton Castle*, the home of the Cliffords, afterwards Earls of Cumberland, and their descendants, from 1307 to 1955, consists of an older part (open daily 10–6 or dusk, Sun from 2; fee; conducted parties hourly), dating from the reign of Edward II but much altered by Lady Anne Clifford in 1657–58, and a Tudor portion (1536) built by the first earl. Over the gate is a 'lettered' balustrade with the Clifford motto 'Désormais'. The Conduit Court, due mainly to Lady Anne, is particularly charming. The great defensive strength of the castle allowed it to withstand three years of siege by the Parliamentary troops during the Civil War. The parish *Church* contains Clifford tombs, notable for their heraldry, and a fine screen (1533). The *Craven Museum*, in the public library, illustrates local prehistory and history (adm. daily, exc. Tues, 2–5, Sat 10–12, 1.30–4.30).

FROM SKIPTON TO MALHAM (bus). We follow A 65 to (4½ m.) *Gargrave*, where we turn right.—9¾ m. *Kirkby Malham*, the birthplace of the Parliamentarian general John Lambert (1619–83), has an interesting church (Perp.). A narrow road (*View) ascends N.W. over the moor (1272 ft) to Settle (4½ m.), passing *Scaleber Force* (3¼ m.), a beautiful waterfall.—11 m. **Malham**, among wild hill scenery, is an attractive and popular hamlet on the Aire, overcrowded during summer week-ends and Bank holidays.

About ¾ m. N. is *Malham Cove*, a striking precipitous amphitheatre of rock, 300 ft in height, from the foot of which issues the Aire, a full-grown stream, from

a subterranean course; and 1¼ m. N.E. is *Gordale Scar*, where the collapse of the subterranean cavern roof has formed a deep ravine also c. 300 ft in height, with waterfalls. Energetic walkers may climb the rocks by the side of the falls to reach the upper valley. Both these features lie on the escarpment created by the 'Craven Fault' which stretches from Kirkby Lonsdale to Wharfedale, a distance of 22 miles. A narrow road passing close to Malham Cove ascends nearly to (2¼ m.) *Malham Tarn* (N.T.), a secluded upland lake. The stream that drains the Tarn to the s. can be followed until it disappears into the ground to reappear as the Aire in Malham Cove. The scenery of the early chapters of Charles Kingsley's 'Water Babies' derives from the moors of this part of Yorkshire. Tarn House, on the N. shore, is a field-study centre. At the cross-roads (w. of the Tarn) the w. fork leads to (5 m.) Settle, the N. fork to (5 m.) Arncliffe, and a fine walk (E.) crosses the moors to (6½ m.) Kilnsey by an old drove road (Mastiles Lane).
    From Skipton to *Colne, Burnley*, etc., see Rte 61D.

67 LEEDS TO HARROGATE, RIPON, AND TEESSIDE

ROAD, 62 m.—A 61. 15 m. **Harrogate**.—26 m. **Ripon**.—37½ m. *Thirsk*.—A 19. 62 m. **Teesside**.
RAILWAY. To (15 m.) **Harrogate** in c. ½ hr, continuing to (22½ m.) *Knaresborough* (and York). To Teesside viâ York (direct) and Northallerton, see Rte 71.

A 61 runs N. from Leeds through *Chapel Allerton*, and ascends to (5 m.) *Alwoodley*, passing near the famous *Moortown* golf links.— 8 m. **Harewood**, a model village by John Carr (1760), built outside the walls of *Harewood House* (open daily Easter–Sept, Sun in Oct, 11–6; fee), an 18C mansion by Carr and Robert Adam, with additions by Barry (1843). The house is noted for its ceilings, Chippendale furniture, Sèvres porcelain and Chinese ceramics, and *Paintings, including works by *Bellini, Tintoretto, Veronese, Turner,* and *El Greco*. The formality of the terraces and garden to the s. (by Barry and Nesfield) contrast with the Park (damaged in a gale in 1962) laid out by 'Capability' Brown which extends to the N. (skirted by the main road). It contains a superb Bird Garden, the ruins of *Harewood Castle*, a tower-house of c. 1367, and the Perp. *Church* containing a fine series of tombs, including that of Chief Justice Gascoigne, who is said to have committed the Prince of Wales for contempt of court ('Henry IV', Pt. II, v. 2).— We cross the Wharfe by a fine bridge (1729).

15 m. **HARROGATE**, on a plateau 400–500 ft above sea-level. Its clean air and mineral springs made it the chief inland spa and holiday resort (62,300 inhab.) in the North of England. Although the waters are no longer taken, the large hotels have given the town a new importance as a conference centre. *The Stray*, a common of 200 acres, reaches in to the centre of the town from the s. Harrogate has attractive shops and gardens and is an excellent centre for excursions.

Numerous large **Hotels**, many with spacious grounds.
Post Office, Oxford St.—INFORMATION BUREAU, Parliament St.
Bus Station, adjoining the Station (E. of War Memorial), for country services.
Amusements. *Royal Hall*, Ripon Rd. (concerts, ballet, exhibitions, etc.); *Opera House*, Oxford St. (repertory); *Valley Gardens*, orchestra daily (July–Sept).— GOLF COURSES at Pannal (s.), Starbeck (E.), and Oakdale (w.).—SWIMMING BATHS (April–Sept) in Skipton Rd. and at Starbeck. GREAT YORKSHIRE AGRICULTURAL SHOW every July (s.E. of town). Annual *Festival of Arts and Sciences* in Aug.
History. The springs seem to have been used locally in much earlier times, but the history of the spa begins with the rediscovery of the Tewit Well by Sir William

Slingsby in 1571. Its vogue in the 18C is reflected in 'Humphry Clinker'. The springs to which Harrogate owes its reputation are 88 in number and of remarkable variety, being either sulphurous or chalybeate. More than thirty of them lie within the limited area of the *Bogs Field* (Valley Gardens), where the geological structure is such that sulphur and iron wells occur close together and yet are quite distinct.—Harrogate has long been noted for its toffee, and now synthetic fibre and rubber industries have research centres here.

West Park runs N. from *The Stray* to the centre of the town. Facing Crescent Gardens are the old *Royal Baths* (closed in 1970), the treatment establishment and pump-room, erected in 1897 (with later additions). To the w. is the *Royal Pump Room* (1842), now an interesting *Museum* of local history (adm. weekdays 11–7, Sun 2–5) with the Holland Child Collection of Yorkshire china, also toys, costumes, etc. Here, too, is the old sulphur well (fee). Farther w. are the *Valley Gardens*, attractively laid out with a path to (1 m.) *Harlow Car Gardens* (45 acres; adm. daily, fee), the ornamental gardens and woodlands of the Northern Horticultural Society, with *Birk Crag* to the N.

Alms Cliff Crag (750 ft) lies c. 4 m. s.w. of Harrogate; while 2½ m. s.E. (off A 661) is *Rudding Park* (adm. to gardens only, daily June–mid-Sept, 10–dusk; fee), a charming Regency house in a park laid out by Repton. *Spofforth*, c. 2 m. farther on, has a ruined 14C castle of the Percys (adm. daily, Sun from 2; fee).

The route to **Nidderdale**, the attractive valley of the Nidd, follows the Ripon road to (4 m.) *Ripley* (see below), then bears left on B 6165.—11 m. *Summer Bridge*, 2 m. N. of which are *Brimham Rocks* (adm. in summer; fee), grotesque and fantastically-named crags of millstone grit, scattered over 60 acres.—14 m. *Pateley Bridge* (Hotel, ¾ m. s.E.), is a quaint little town amid beautiful scenery. Once the centre of the Roman lead mining industry, it has the remains of a Roman camp. The ruined church has extensive views. To Grassington, see Rte 66.—Between *Wath* and (18¼ m.) *Ramsgill* is the Gouthwaite Reservoir of Bradford Corporation. Eugene Aram (see below) was born at Ramsgill and kept school at *Gouthwaite Hall*, now submerged.—Above (20¼ m.) *Lofthouse*, near the *How Stean* gorge and caves (fee), and (21 m.) *Middlesmoor* rough roads (no cars) go on to the head of the dale, 6 m. farther on, at Angram Reservoir beneath Great Whernside.

A 59 runs N.E. from Harrogate viâ (1½ m.) *Starbeck* to (3½ m.) **Knaresborough** an old-fashioned town (11,900 inhab.) with 18C houses, attractively situated on the Nidd, which here flows through a deep glen (excellent boating). The *Church* (E.E. to Perp.) contains monuments of the Slingsby family. High above the river in Castle Gardens (*View) are the remains of John of Gaunt's *Castle*, where Richard II was imprisoned in 1399, the best preserved part being the 14C Keep (adm. daily 1–6; parties only; fee), which (uniquely) served also as a gatehouse between the outer and inner wards. The bridge and the station show the finest characteristics of 19C railway design. On the right bank of the Nidd, above the Low Bridge are the *Dropping Well* (fee), famous for its petrifying properties, and *Mother Shipton's Cave*, where the Yorkshire prophetess is said to have been born at the end of the 15C; a delightful woodland walk leads to High Bridge, the main entrance (car-park). Thence charming walks go upstream, opposite the public park of Conyngham Hall (zoo; fee). On the other bank, below Low Bridge, is *Crag Chapel* (fee), a cave carved in the limestone cliff in 1409, with a roughly carved figure of a knight at its entrance. About 1 m. downstream, near Grimbold Bridge, is *St Robert's* or *Eugene Aram's Cave*, where Aram concealed the remains of his victim Daniel Clark (1745). At *Farnham*, 2 m. N., the church has a Norman apse.—For the continuation of A 59 to *York*, see Rte 68.

The road from Harrogate to (16½ m.) *Bolton Abbey* (A 59) runs over the moors viâ (9½ m.) *Blubberhouses* (525 ft), in the Washburn Valley (see p. 607).

A 61 crosses the Nidd just before (19 m.) *Ripley*, built in 1827 by the local squire, and modelled on an Alsatian village. In the churchyard is the remains of a singular 'kneeling' cross (? 13C). *Ripley Castle* (adm. May–Sept, Sun 2–6; also BH; fee), home of the Ingilbys since the 14C, has a tower of 1550 and gatehouse of 1450, and here James I stayed, and Cromwell passed the night after Marston Moor.—21½ m. *South Stainley* (Restaurant).

26 m. **RIPON** (Hotels and Restaurant) is a pleasant little cathedral city (11,000 inhab.). It stands on the Skell, a tributary of the Ure, which is spanned by a medieval bridge.

At Ripon, the *Inhrypum* of Bede, a monastery dependent on Melrose was founded c. 660. About 10 years later St Wilfrid build a church here, and for a short time (681–6) Ripon was a bishop's see (resuscitated in 1836). Ripon thus ranks with York and Beverley as one of the three original Christian centres of Yorkshire. The ancient custom of blowing a horn every night (9 p.m.) at the market cross and in front of the house of the mayor (anciently the 'Wakeman', i.e. watchman) is still observed.

In the spacious MARKET PLACE is an obelisk 90 ft high, surmounted by the town arms (1781). Here also are the *Town Hall* (1801), with the city's motto, and the 13C *Wakeman's House*. Kirkgate descends to the **Cathedral,** or Minster (dedicated to SS Peter and Wilfrid), which, though small (270 ft long), is interesting by reason of its multiplicity of styles. It celebrated its 1300th anniversary in 1972.

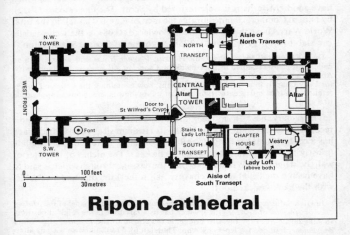

Ripon Cathedral

HISTORY. The crypt of the Saxon church of St Wilfrid (634–709) survives, as does that of its 10C successor; but the main existing structure was begun by Abp. Roger of York (1154–81) as a church for secular canons. His plan, unique in England, included an aisleless nave, an aisled choir, transepts with E. aisle only, and a central tower. The existing w. front, with its twin towers, is probably due to Abp. Walter de Gray (1215–55). The E. end of the choir is a Dec. reconstruction of the last quarter of the 13C; and the E. and S. sides of the central tower were rebuilt, after their collapse in 1450, in the Perp. style of the 15C. Finally, the nave was enlarged, by the addition of aisles, in the first quarter of the 16C.

The best external feature is the lancet w. front, which is the single E.E. example of a twin-towered façade of its kind in England (at Wells the towers stand clear of the aisles), but is disappointingly flat and lifeless. The central tower is "probably unique in being divided vertically between two different styles of architecture". The whole external aspect of the church undoubtedly suffers from the lowness and uniform height of its triple group of towers. The effect was probably better before the central leaded spire fell in 1660, and before the spires of the w. towers were taken down in 1664.

Interior. On entering by the w. door visitors will be struck by the great width (87 ft) of the NAVE and AISLES, a feature in which Ripon is excelled by York (104½ ft) and Winchester (88 ft) alone among single-aisled, medieval English churches. Part of Roger's work still survives at both the w. and E. ends, and in the N. aisle is a pillar-base from the 10C cathedral. The Pulpit is a remarkable work of 1913. The TRANSEPTS retain Roger's design in fair completeness; but the s. and E. arches of the central tower were recast in the Perp. style (15C), and the unfinished appearance of the crossing is due to the fact that the other arches were not thus rebuilt. The Gothic pulpit, in the N. transept, was originally above the rich stone screen (c. 1480; with carved figures of kings and clerics by Esmond Burton, 1948) through which we enter the *CHOIR, where work of three periods (Trans., Dec., and Perp.) is curiously interwrought. "Ripon choir alone, of English cathedrals, possesses a glazed triforium" (Bond). The tracery of the E. window, and the naturalistic foliage of some capitals in the two E. bays, are finely characteristic of the Dec. period. The roof retains some remarkable bosses (c. 1300). The splendid 15C stalls, which have good *Misericords, were restored by Scott. The fine reredos (1922), by Ninian Comper, commemorates the men of Ripon who fell in the First World War. Above the tomb of Dean Fowler (d. 1608), in the s. choir aisle, is a slab to Robt. Porteous (d. 1758), a cousin of George Washington.

On the s. side of the choir are the Norman *Chapter House* and *Vestry*, with an undercroft below, restored in 1948–60 as the *Chapel of All Souls* and a choir vestry. Above, and approached by steps from the s. transept, is the Dec. *Lady Loft* (or Lady Chapel; in a very unusual position), now containing the *Chapter Library*, refounded in 1624 and recently restored. Visitors are shown these rooms on application to a verger.

The remarkable *CRYPT (fee), one of the half-dozen Saxon crypts now recognised in England, was built, like its Hexham sister, by Wilfrid. Each has a central chamber for the exhibition of relics. Here is displayed plate (mostly 17–18C) from churches of the diocese. The niches of the interior walls held lights. 'St Wilfrid's Needle', the passage through which is said to have been a medieval test of chastity, is (in fact) the old credence-table, with the back knocked out.

In High Saint Agnesgate, below the cathedral, is the ruined chapel of the *Maison Dieu* or *Hospital of St Anne* (15C), which has its altar-stone in the original position. In Magdalene St., near the Ure bridge, is the chapel of the *Hospital of St Mary Magdalene*, founded for lepers by Abp. Thurstan (d. 1140), likewise with its altar-stone *in situ* (key at the almshouses opposite).

FROM RIPON TO STUDLEY ROYAL AND FOUNTAINS ABBEY, 4 m. Cars may use the drive direct to the West Lodge or may proceed viâ Studley village to the East Lodge (car-park and rfmts). If walking, we leave Ripon by Westgate and Park St. (l.), and keep left. Farther on, after crossing the Laver, we take B 6265, whence in c. 3 m. a wicket on the left leads into a field path (r.), affording a short cut to the centre of *Studley Roger* village. Here we cross the road, taking a footpath immediately opposite. We soon enter the park of *Studley Royal (Mr Henry Vyner), with its splendid timber, and, following the footpath which crosses the fine lime avenue diagonally, approach the sumptuous *Church*, built in 1871 (Burges). Before reaching the church we turn to the left down a beech avenue leading to the little river Skell, here formed into a lake, beyond which we reach (c. 1 hr) the *East Lodge* of the private pleasure-grounds (adm. see below). The grounds are among the finest examples of Italian and Dutch formal gardening. They preserve, in the main, the design from 1720 onwards of the then Lord of the Manor, John Aislabie. The Skell, canalized, and supplying a series of ponds, passes between terraced banks with trimmed hedges. Small temples and statuary complete a stately pleasance. The drive forward from the East Gate is the most direct way to Fountains Abbey, but a better route is to cross the stream (l.) by stepping-stones. Beyond the *Temple* *of Piety* we bear to the left, then diverge left again to ascend to an arbour affording a sudden *View of Fountains Abbey upstream, on the opposite bank of the Skell. Descending, and continuing on the right bank of the Skell, we pass *Robin Hood's Well*, one of the traditional sites of the encounter in which that glorious outlaw was beaten and thrown into a brook by the 'Curtal Friar'.

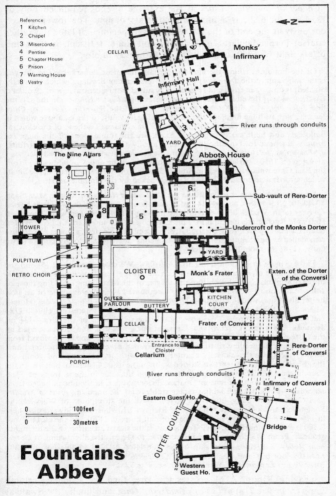

Reference
1 Kitchen
2 Chapel
3 Misercorde
4 Pentise
5 Chapter House
6 Prison
7 Warming House
8 Vestry

Fountains Abbey

*Fountains Abbey (adm. daily, from 9.30; fee incl. Fountains Hall; café), founded 1132 for Benedictines, but taken over by the Cistercians in 1135, is one of the largest and best-preserved monasteries in England. The buildings are of four principal periods. To the first (1135–47) belong the nave and transepts of the church; to the second (1147–79), the gradual reconstruction of the domestic buildings; to the third (1220–47), the rebuilding of the E. end; and to the fourth (1498–1526), the erection of the tower. The *Nave*, of 11 bays (complete to ceiling height), is a grand example of austere Cistercian building; while the *Chapel of the Nine Altars* at the extreme E. end, paralleled only at Durham (p. 652), is a miracle of delicate design. The tower, placed curiously at the end of the N. transept, is a specimen of late (and rather coarse) Perpendicular. In the vestry, off the S. transept, is the tomb of a knight (c. 1300) of the Percy or Mowbray family.

Of the buildings round the cloister, perhaps the most remarkable (on the w.) is the sub-vault of the *Dormitory of the Conversi* or Lay Brothers, which (formerly divided) is now open from end to end, and vaulted from a central row of 19 pillars. On the E. side of the cloister garth is the interesting *Chapter House.* On the S. is the fine *Refectory*, with the *Kitchen* to the W. of it and the *Warming House*, or *Calefactory*, with its huge fireplace and still retaining its vault, to the E., above which is the *Muniment Room*, reached by the Monks' Day Stairs. To the E. of the cloistral buildings, and built partly across the Skell, are the foundations of the huge *Infirmary*, intended for both the sick and the aged.—Outside the *West Lodge* (rfmts) is *Fountains Hall* (open 10–4 or 6; adm., see above) a perfectly preserved Jacobean mansion (c. 1610), with contemporary furniture and the abbey muniments. From the East Gate walkers may regain Studley Roger by the track descending the Skell, which affords a splendid *View of Ripon, backed by the Hambleton Hills.

Likewise within easy reach of Ripon are *Markenfield Hall* (adm. Mon in May–Sept, 10–12.30, 2.15–5; fee), an early 14–16C manor-house, 2 m. S.W.; the woods of *Norton Conyers* (adm. Wed & BH 2–6, mid-May–mid-Sept; fee), identified with 'Thornfield Hall', Mr Rochester's mansion in 'Jane Eyre', 3½ m. N.; and (3 m. S.E.) *Newby Hall* (adm. Easter–mid-Oct, Wed, Thurs, Sat, & Sun, and BH, 2–6; fee), a Queen Anne house remodelled by Adam, noted for its superb Gobelins tapestries and lovely gardens (open daily, 11–6; tea-room in the orangery).

FROM RIPON TO LEYBURN, 19¾ m. (A 6108). We cross the Ure at (5½ m.) the pleasant village of *West Tanfield*, in which stands the Perp. gatehouse of the castle of the Marmions. The church contains effigies of the Marmions, including those of John Marmion (d. 1387) and his wife, surmounted by a fine example of an iron herse; also good wood-carving by Thompson of Kilburn.—9 m. *Masham* (Hotel), where J. C. Ibbetson died, has a huge market-place and interesting church (12–16C) with Danby tombs. We now ascend the right bank of the Ure.—13½ m. **Jervaulx Abbey** (pron. 'Jervo', i.e. Urevale; open 9–6, exc. Sun; fee), founded by the Cistercians in 1156. The ruins, overgrown with flowers, appear confused from the entrance; proceeding N. to the church, levelled practically to its foundations, we may recognize the cloister, chapter house (with its columns and tombs of the abbots), and the dorter (two-storied wall), in the usual Cistercian pattern. In the church, the S.W. doorway is well-preserved, and the altar in the N. transept. The stones reveal a variety of masons' marks. Prior Aylmer, in 'Ivanhoe', hailed from Jervaulx.—17 m. *Middleham* has racing stables and the imposing ruins of *Middleham Castle* (adm. daily, Sun from 2; fee), once the stronghold of Warwick the Kingmaker and a favourite residence of Richard III, whose son Edward died here in 1484. The space between the large Norman keep (c. 1170) and the curtain wall (13C) is extraordinarily narrow. To the S.W. is the site of an earlier castle on higher ground. From Middleham we may walk S.W. to (1¾ m.) the slight ruins of *Coverham Abbey*, a Premonstratensian house translated c. 1212 to this beautiful site near the foot of *Coverdale*. Thence to *Kettlewell*, see Rte 66.—We cross the Ure for (19¾ m.) *Leyburn* (for Wensleydale), see Rte 72A.

Leaving Ripon, A 61 crosses the Ure, then the Roman Leeming Lane (A 1; Rte 71B) at (30 m.) *Baldersby Gate*, and finally the Swale at (32½ m.) *Skipton-on-Swale*.—37½ m. **Thirsk**, see Rte 71A. Here we turn left on A 19, skirting the foot of the Hambleton Hills (*Black Hambleton*, 1257 ft).—At (49 m.) the Cleveland Tontine Inn, A 172 bears right for Whitby.

About ¼ m. E. of the road lies *Mount Grace Priory (N.T.; adm. Tues–Sat and BH all day, Sun from 2; fee), founded in 1398, the most perfect Carthusian monastery in England. The ground plan consists of two large courts with the church between them. Each monk had a house and garden off a court. Part of the domestic buildings were converted into a private house in the 17C.

58 m. *Yarm* is a quaint little town on a loop of the Tees, with a broad High Street. It was an important stage on the coaching route to the N., with 16 inns; the oldest is the 17C Ketton Ox, with a cockpit in a second-floor room. At the George and Dragon the first meeting of the promoters of the Stockton and Darlington Railway was held (comp. p. 646). We cross the river by a 14C bridge to *Egglescliffe* and enter the Durham industrial area.—62 m. **Teesside**, see Rte 71B.

68 DONCASTER TO YORK

ROAD, 34 m. (A 19).—RAILWAY, 32 m. in 30–40 min. This is part of the main line from London to Edinburgh.

DONCASTER (Hotels S.E. of the centre, and near the station; prices raised during the races), a thriving town (82,500 inhab.) on the site of the Roman *Danum*, with coal mines in the vicinity and locomotive works, lies on the Don. The parish church (*St George's*), built in 1854 by Gilbert Scott, the previous church (13C) having been burnt down, has a fine tower 170 ft high. The *Mansion House* (1745–48) is by Paine, his only surviving public building. The *Museum* (10–6, Sun 2–5) contains interesting Roman material, etc. Doncaster, a racing centre since 1615, is most familiarly known as the scene of the *St Leger*, the oldest 'classic' race, established in its present form in 1778 and named after Col. St Leger; the earliest grandstand dates from 1776 (by John Carr). It is run on the Town Moor in the second week of September; and 'winter comes in with the tail of the last horse in the Leger'. Here in Oct 1909 were held the first air races in England.

At *Sprotborough*, 3 m. w., the interesting church, with good woodwork, preserves an unusual stone seat (? 14C), perhaps a sanctuary chair. Francis Washington, rector in 1668–78, lies beside the altar. About 2 m. N. is *Cusworth Park* (1740–67), by Platt and Paine, containing characteristic painting and plasterwork in its chapel.

Conisbrough, in the Don valley 4½ m. s.w. (bus), possesses a Norman castle (c. 1190; adm. daily, Sun from 2; fee), the home of Athelstane in 'Ivanhoe', with perhaps the finest circular *Keep in England, probably built by Hamelin (1163–1202), half-brother of Henry II. The church has fine capitals and a carved tomb-chest of the 12C. Thence A 630 goes on to (12 m.) *Rotherham* and (19½ m.) *Sheffield* (Rte 61H).

FROM DONCASTER TO HULL, 46 m. (A 18, 614); railway in 1–1¼ hr.—7 m. *Hatfield* (good church of the 12–15C) is in *Hatfield Chase*, part of the district known as the 'Levels', most of which was under water until drained by Cornelius Vermuyden (see p. 524) in 1626.—10¼ m. *Thorne* is a small town with a church of c. 1300, on the w. edge of a great peat moor. At *Fishlake*, 2 m. w., the large church has a s. *Doorway with notable Romanesque carving of c. 1170.—We skirt the Don, canalized lower down by Vermuyden as the Aire and Calder Navigation, and touch the Aire at (17¼ m.) *Rawcliffe*.—20¼ m. **Goole** (18,100 inhab.; Hotel), a seaport since 1826, with large docks, is situated at the junction of the Ouse and the Don, not far from the point where the Ouse unites with the Trent to form the Humber. The Aire and Calder Navigation Company built the conspicuous church in 1843. Steamers ply hence to various Continental ports.—The best route to Hull avoids Goole, turning left at 19 m. off A 614 viâ *Airmyn*.—21 m. *Boothferry Bridge* across the Ouse.—23 m. *Howden*, and thence to *Hull*, see below.

From Doncaster to *London*, see Rte 46; to *Wetherby* and *Berwick*, see Rte 71B; to *Worksop* and *Ollerton*, see Rte 46B; to *Lincoln*, see Rte 58; to *Scunthorpe* and *Brigg*, see Rte 58.

After crossing the Don we bear right on A 19, and continue N. across a system of rivers and canals to (18½ m.) *Brayton*, where the 14–15C church has a fine tower, chancel arch and s. doorway with notable carving of c. 1150.

20 m. **Selby** (Hotel), a market and manufacturing town (11,600 inhab.), lies on the right bank of the tidal Ouse, navigable for tugs and barges up to York. In the open Market Place is the *ABBEY CHURCH (dedicated to the Virgin and St Germanus; begun c. 1097), which, despite a disastrous fire in 1906, remains one of the most perfect monastic churches in England (306 ft long). The Benedictine abbey to which it belonged was founded in 1069.

The w. front, the lower part of which is Transitional, has a fine recessed doorway of five orders. The w. towers were raised a story in 1935. The nave is notable as representing five different periods of building. Norman work (1097–1123) occurs in the four E. bays on the N. side of the nave and two on the s. side, and the four tower-arches. At the w. end the architecture becomes Transitional, with pure E.E. in the s. triforium and both clerestories. The slender vaulting-shafts on the s. side of the nave are unusual. The *Choir is Dec. throughout, though of more than one period, with remains of rich sculpture (note the charming carved balustrade of the N. Gallery). The blind arcading and sedilia are also remarkable. Some old stained glass remains in the choir and War Memorial chapel (s. of choir) in which is an alabaster *Deposition. The great *East Window, a 'Jesse window', has a fine 'Doom' in its beautiful Flamboyant tracery. The Washington arms appear in a window of the s. choir clerestory. In 1912 a new s. transept was built on the site of the old one, ruined by the fall of the central tower in 1690. The N. porch enshrines a magnificent Norman doorway.

Buses run s.e. to (6 m.) *Drax*, dominated by a vast power station, with a part-Norman church, notable for its carved figures and bench-ends, and a grammar school founded in 1669, and past *Carlton Towers* (by Pugin and J. F. Bentley), the Yorkshire home of the Duke of Norfolk (adm. daily exc. Mon & Fri, 1–5, in late-May & June; fee), to (7½ m.) *Snaith*, where the 13–15C church contains Dawnay tombs; also N. to *York* viâ (4½ m.) *Cawood*, with the gateway to the palace of the Abps. of York, where Wolsey was arrested in 1530; (7½ m.) *Stillingfleet*, where the church has a fine Norman s. door with ironwork showing Viking influence, and the well-preserved effigy of Sir Robert de Moresby (1286–1336); and (9½ m.) *Bell Hall* (1680; adm. by appointment), near Escrick.

FROM SELBY TO HULL (A 63), 34 m. Railway, 31 m. in 40–60 min.—5½ m. *Hemingbrough*, 1½ m. s.e. of its station. The church (12–15C), with its tall *Spire (120 ft), has old bench-ends and woodwork by Thompson. At *Wressell*, to the left beyond the Derwent bridge, are the ruins of a 14C castle, where the Percys, earls of Northumberland, once kept regal state.— 10 m. **Howden**. The important *Church of *St Peter* (mainly Dec., but of different dates) was made collegiate in 1267. The *West Front (14C) is a very beautiful composition, and the tower (135 ft high), completed in the 15C, is one of the finest in Yorkshire. The nave and crossing are used as the parish church. The Saltmarshe Chapel contains family tombs from the 14C to the 20C. The choir (14C) and chapter house (early Perp.) are in ruins but retain many beautiful details. Roger of Hoveden (d. 1201?), the chronicler, was rector of Howden, and his statue stands in front of the market hall. Here in 1923 Nevil Shute, the novelist (1899–1960), worked with Barnes Wallis on the design of the R100, Britain's last successful airship. *Eastrington*, 3 m. N.E., has an interesting church. Near the foot of the Wolds we bear s. To the r. is (24 m.) *Brough*, the site of the Roman station of *Petuaria*, one of the few in England identified by an inscription (now at Hull) found on the actual site. The fort guarded the ferry by which Ermine Street crossed the Humber.— 34 m. *Hull*, see Rte 70B.

From Selby to *Leeds*, see Rte 61H.

The York road crosses the Ouse (toll-bridge) and runs N.—At (32¼ m.) *Fulford*, in the suburbs of York it crosses the York ring road.

34 m. **YORK** (104,500 inhab.), famous for its stately minster and its
medieval city walls, is situated on the Ouse. It is one of the most interesting
of ancient English cities; many of its streets retain the narrowness and
irregularity of medieval times; and its churches present an array of stained
glass that makes it prominent even among the cities of Europe. The
Archbishop of York bears the title of Primate of England, and his sway
extends over the N. Midlands and the N. of England (14 dioceses). York is
the headquarters of the N. military district and an important railway
centre. Like its French 'twin' Dijon, it is also famous for chocolate.

Good **Hotels** at the station, outside Micklegate Bar, near the Minster, and s.w. of the
town at Dringhouses, and in Tadcaster Rd. (Motel).
Restaurants mainly in the Hotels.
Post Office (Pl. 6), Lendal.— INFORMATION BUREAU, De Grey House, Exhibition Sq.
Buses from Rougier St. (Pl. 9) to *Tadcaster* and *Wetherby* or *Leeds; Scar-
borough; Pickering* and *Whitby;* from Toft Green (Pl. 9) to *Boroughbridge* and
Ripon; Knaresborough and *Harrogate;* from the Station (Pl. 9) to *Thirsk;* from
Piccadilly (Pl. 11) to *Selby* and *Doncaster; Beverley* and *Hull; Bridlington;* from
the Art Gallery (Pl. 2) to *Coxwold* and *Helmsley.*—**Motor Launches** from Lendal
Bridge (Pl. 5) upstream and King's Staith (Pl. 10) downstream.
Theatre. *Royal* (repertory), St Leonard's Place (Pl. 6).—Triennial Festival of the
Arts (1979).
Racecourse on the Knavesmire, 1 m. s.

History. York, the British *Caer Ebrauc*, attained to great importance as the
Eboracum of the Romans. It was garrisoned by Q. Petilius Cerealis, nephew of
Vespasian, in A.D. 71, and subsequently became the headquarters of the 6th Legion, and
capital of the province of Britain. The first emperor to visit York was Hadrian (A.D.
121), the first stone wall was built c. 108, and Severus and Constantius Chlorus both
died here (211 and 306). Constantine the Great was proclaimed emperor here on the
death of the last, but was probably born elsewhere. Under the Saxons *Eoforwic* played a
prominent part in the spread of Christianity through N. England, and when Alcuin
(734–804) was 'Magister Scholarum' here it was one of the chief centres of European
learning. Charlemagne made Alcuin Master of the Palace School at Aachen in 782. For
some time York was an important settlement of the Danes, who gave it the name of
Jorvik. William the Conqueror built the two castles. Here Alexander II of Scotland
married Joan, sister of Henry III, in 1221, and at York 30 years later Alexander III
married Margaret, Henry's daughter; here also in 1328 Edward III married Philippa of
Hainault. Strafford, the last President of the Council of the North, was executed in
1641, and the city surrendered to the Parliamentary forces after the Battle of Marston
Moor in 1644. Guy Fawkes (1570–1606), John Flaxman (1755–1826), William Etty
(1787–1849), and J. A. Hansom (1803–82) are natives of York. Robinson Crusoe, "of
York, mariner", was "born in the year 1632, in the city of York, of a good family,
though not of that country". Laurence Sterne lived at Stonegate and at the Treasurer's
House, and 'Tristram Shandy' was published by John Hinxman "at the sign of the
Bible" in Stonegate, Isaac of York, in 'Ivanhoe', dwelt in the Castlegate, Dick Turpin's
famous 'ride to York' was in fact made by Swift Nick (Wm. Nevison) in the 17C and has
been added to the Turpin tradition.

*York Minster (Pl. 2), the *Cathedral Church of St Peter*, the largest
of English medieval cathedrals (60,952 sq. ft) and correspondingly
stately in effect, affords a coherent and typical view of architectural
development during three periods: E.E. (transepts), Dec. (nave and
chapter house), and early and late Perp. (choir and towers). It lies in the
N. corner of the old city and the best view of it is from the city walls. It is
open daily from 7.30 to dusk; adm. to chapter house and crypt on
application to a verger; to the central tower (11–3; fee); to the Undercroft
(10.30–4; fee).

HISTORY. The building covers the site of a wooden chapel put up for the baptism
of Edwin, King of Northumbria, and his court by Paulinus, first Bishop of York,
on Easter Day, 627. This was soon replaced by a stone church, which served as the

basis for reconstruction until burned down in c. 741. A magnificent second stone church (180 ft long, and 55 ft wide), begun by Abp. Albert (767–80), was ruined, with the city, in the troubles following the Norman Conquest. Thomas of Bayeux, first Norman archbishop, began rebuilding (c. 1080). His church, the choir of which had been rebuilt by Abp. Roger of Pont-l'Evêque (1154–81), was gradually replaced by the present edifice. The s. transept was first rebuilt by Abp. de Gray (c. 1220–41); then the N. transept (1241–60). The new nave was founded in 1291, and, together with the chapter house and vestibule, was in process until c. 1345. Roger's Norman choir was displaced by the present one between 1361 and 1405. The erection of the central tower (1400–23) and of the w. towers (1433–74; 202 ft high) completed a labour of nearly 250 years. Much damage was caused by fires in 1829 and 1840, in choir and nave, respectively.

In 1967 investigations revealed that the central tower and w. end were in danger of collapse, due to fatigue and water erosion in the building material. Extensive engineering works were necessary to strengthen the fabric; new foundations were cast in reinforced concrete and repairs undertaken in the w. towers. The eroded statues and pinnacles on the exterior were extensively restored in 1965.

The finest parts of the **Exterior** are the *West Façade*, particularly the great window and finely sculptured portal (in the N. tower hangs 'Big Peter', a 10¾-ton bell); the *North Transept*, especially the façade and 'five sisters' window; the octagonal *Chapter House*; and, above all, the great *Central Tower*.

Interior. The glory of York Minster is the extensive series of **Stained-Glass Windows, mainly the product of a well-defined local school. It includes some of the earliest glass in England, a masterpiece of E.E. grisaille glass, a great range of splendid Dec. windows, and superb Perp. glass. The priceless glass, removed during the Second World War, carefully restored under the direction of Dean Milner-White (1884–1963), and still being replaced, is augmented by acquisitions from other churches in the diocese.

The entrance by the s. transept door reveals an unequalled aspect of the interior, culminating in the perfect five-lighted lancet window in the N. transept. The visitor should, however, begin his detailed inspection at the w. end.

The effect of the NAVE is less impressive than we should expect from its exceptional height and breadth but defects in proportion, such as the over-wide spacing of the piers and the practical suppression of the triforium, are due perhaps to the aim of giving the utmost space for stained glass. The design, moreover, presupposed a stone vaulting which was never built. The present wooden roof (1841; part of Sydney Smirke's restoration), painted to resemble stone, perpetuates an earlier sham. The detail throughout the nave is good, if timid, and the tracery of the large clerestory windows and the Flamboyant tracery of the *West Window (1338; glass being replaced) are admirable. The unusually wide aisles (30 ft), stone-vaulted, achieve the lofty effect missed in the nave. The w. windows here have fine glass, and the second window from the w. in the N. aisle contains a panel of the oldest glass in England (c. 1150). Besides the 14C glass elsewhere in the aisles, the remains of 12–13C glass in the clerestories should be noted. All round the nave and choir, below the triforium, are painted stone shields of Edward II and the barons who met in parliament at York in 1309–10. An oak pulpit to the memory of Abps. Lang and Temple was dedicated in 1948; the Garbett Throne (1959), by Sir Albert Richardson, is a memorial to Abp. Garbett.

The *TRANSEPTS are most important, having aisles on the w. side as

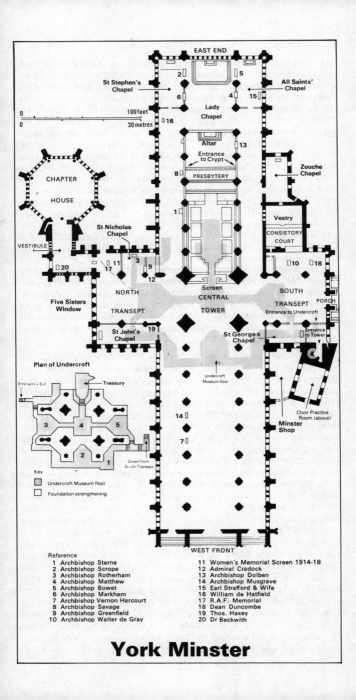

EAST END

St Stephen's Chapel

All Saints' Chapel

2   5

6   4   15

Lady Chapel

16

Altar

CHAPTER HOUSE

Entrance to Crypt

13

8   PRESBYTERY

Zouche Chapel

VESTIBULE

St Nicholas Chapel

1

Vestry

CONSISTORY COURT

20   17   11   3

9

10   18

12

Five Sisters Window

NORTH TRANSEPT

SOUTH TRANSEPT

PORCH

CENTRAL TOWER

Entrance to Undercroft

St John's Chapel   19

St Georges Chapel

Screen

Entrance to Tower

Plan of Undercroft

Treasury

Undercroft Museum floor

Emergency Exit

3   4   5

Choir Practice Room (above)

2

14

Minster Shop

1

7

Down from South Transept

Key

Undercroft Museum floor

Foundation strengthening

WEST FRONT

0 ___ 100 feet
0 ___ 30 metres

Reference
1 Archbishop Sterne
2 Archbishop Scrope
3 Archbishop Rotherham
4 Archbishop Matthew
5 Archbishop Bowet
6 Archbishop Markham
7 Archbishop Vernon Harcourt
8 Archbishop Savage
9 Archbishop Greenfield
10 Archbishop Walter de Gray
11 Women's Memorial Screen 1914-18
12 Admiral Cradock
13 Archbishop Dolben
14 Archbishop Musgrave
15 Earl Strafford & Wife
16 William de Hatfield
17 R.A.F. Memorial
18 Dean Duncombe
19 Thos. Haxey
20 Dr Beckwith

York Minster

well as on the E. The lantern is the largest medieval example in England, and the impression of magnitude in this part of the church is hardly marred by the obtrusive triforium, and consequent meanness of the clerestory, or by the unsatisfactory (though original) wooden vault. In the N. Transept the vault (oak ribs with cedar infilling) dates from 1934–51, with many ribs and bosses from the 15C ceiling. All the detail is worth notice. The terminal wall of the N. Transept, incorporating the lancet lights of the *'Five Sisters', with their wonderful 13C grisaille glass, is far finer than that of the S. Transept, with its rose-window. The 'Five Sisters' window was releaded in 1925 (with medieval lead found at Rievaulx Abbey) as a memorial to the women who gave their lives in 1914–18; an oak screen in the E. aisle bears their names. Here also are an astronomical clock (Pl. 17) designed by Richardson (1955) as a memorial to airmen based on N.E. England who died in the Second World War; the fine brass of Abp. Greenfield (Pl. 9; 1306–16); and a memorial (by F. W. Pomeroy) to Adm. Cradock (killed at Coronel in 1914). The tomb of Abp. de Gray (Pl. 10; 1215–55) is in the E. aisle of the S. transept.

A new undercroft, formed by the excavations made for the central piers, houses a *MUSEUM in which extensive remains of Roman York lie exposed. Among the relics preserved here are the 'Horn of Ulf', most probably an 8C S. Italian work, Abp. Scrope's mazer bowl, architectural relics of all periods, and magnificent church plate and domestic silver. The undercroft connects with the early-Norman WESTERN CRYPT beneath the W. bays of the Choir.

The *CHOIR is separated from the nave by an elaborate late-Gothic *Rood Screen* (1473–1505) with life-size statues of English kings, from William I to Henry VI (the last modern); the central boss of the vaulted entrance has a high relief of the Madonna (c. 1150), Byzantine in manner. The *Glass in the great E. window (78 ft × 31 ft), by John Thornton of Coventry (1405), is still almost intact and forms the largest sheet of medieval glazing in England, and probably in the world. The soaring windows of the *East Transepts* (properly transeptal bays) contain 15C glass depicting the lives of SS William and Cuthbert (replaced after restoration). All the woodwork in the choir was lost in 1829, in a fire started by a madman; the present stalls are an accurate reproduction by Sir Robert Smirke; while the archbishop's throne is by Thompson of Kilburn. The miracle-working shrine of St William of York, canonized in 1230, is believed to have stood behind the high altar. The altar Screen, the work of John Scott (1831), is a free copy of its predecessor of c. 1475. In the N. choir-aisle are the Tudor monument of Abp. Savage (Pl. 8; 1501–7), with a restored chantry above, and the damaged but finely wrought effigy tomb (c. 1370–80; with a new base by Sir Chas. Peers, 1947) of William of Hatfield (Pl. 16; d. 1336), the young son of Edward III. In the *Lady Chapel* is the splendid tomb of Abp. Bowet (Pl. 5; 1407–23). Opposite is the plain (restored) monument of Abp. Scrope (Pl. 2), beheaded in 1405 ('Henry IV', Part II). On the S. side of the choir is the *Zouche Chapel* (1352), reserved for private prayer; while in the S. choir-aisle are monuments of Abp. Dolben (d. 1686), of Abp. Lamplugh (d. 1691), an unsuccessful work by Grinling Gibbons, and of Wm. Burgh (d. 1808) by Westmacott.

The late-Norman EASTERN CRYPT, entered from the choir-aisles, has archaeological as well as architectural interest. The structure shows the extent of Roger's choir, with carvings of the Virgin and Child and the Harrowing of Hell, and includes foundations of the work of Abp. Thomas; a trap-door reveals the base of a pillar of the Roman Praetorium.

A *Vestibule* leads from the E. aisle of the N. transept to the *CHAPTER HOUSE. Both are among the supreme examples of Dec. work, and both preserve in traceries of inventive beauty contemporary glass of rare quality. The chapter house suffered renovation in 1845, but little damage was done to the beautiful and spirited details which enrich a building not unduly vaunted in the inscription on the doorway, "Ut rosa flos florum, sic est domus ista domorum." The roof is original and of unique construction.

Despite its designation, the minster was a foundation of the secular clergy, and has, therefore, no monastic outbuildings. In the Dean's Park (open daily, 10–5), on the N., is a fragment of a cloister belonging to the Norman *Archiepiscopal Palace* of Abp. Roger; the building used since 1811 as the *Chapter Library* (open Mon– Fri 10–5) was built by Abp. de Gray after 1233 and recently enlarged. This contains about 8000 vols. (some of great rarity and interest), valuable MSS., and the Hailstone Collection of Yorkshire books and prints.

Immediately E. of the minster is *St William's College* (Pl. 3; adm. weekdays, fee), founded in 1461 to house the chantry priests attached to the minster, in the one-time house of the Prior of Hexham. Much altered in 17C and later, it is now used as the House of Convocation for the province of York. It has a fine timbered roof and some Gothic and later furniture. To the left in Minster Yard is the *Treasurer's House* (Pl. 3; N.T.), a 17C building on 12C foundations (adm. April–Oct daily 10.30–6; fee). It contains good 17–18C furniture.

Opposite the s. transept of the Minster stands a restored Roman column from the H.Q. building of the 6th Legion, excavated from the s. transept and incorrectly erected (base over apex) in 1971. The late Perp. church of *St Michael-le-Belfrey* (Pl. 6), just to the w., has some magnificent stained *Glass (13C and 16C), and its registers contain the entry of the baptism of 'Guye fauxe' (1570), who was probably born behind the house in Petergate that is now Young's Hotel. Stonegate, near by, a pretty street with fine shops (pedestrians only from 10.30 a.m.), has the remains of a Norman dwelling (behind No. 50).— *Holy Trinity* (Pl 7), in Goodramgate, is York's quaintest church, a 14C building, with box-pews and a fine E. window of 1472. The mid-14C houses of Lady Row, Goodramgate, are the oldest dwellings in York.

The *City Walls (c. 3 m. in circuit), with their frowning 'bars' or gates, are among the finest surviving examples in Europe of medieval city-fortification and have been well restored. As they now stand they date mainly from the reign of Edward III (1327–77), and at their N.W. angle follow the line of the Roman wall. The visitor should walk along at least part of their circuit.

Goodramgate (see above) leads N.E. to *Monk Bar* (Pl. 3), probably so called from an adjoining monastic house. This is the tallest of the four main gates, and, like the others, has a Norman core, encased later in the Dec. period, when the portcullises were added. We here mount the wall and follow it (l.) round its N.W. angle, enjoying a good view of the minster, to *Bootham Bar* (Pl. 2). Here we quit the wall, cross *Lendal Bridge* (Pl. 6), and regain the wall beyond the river (good retrospect of the minster). Farther on is *Micklegate Bar* (Pl. 13), the chief of the

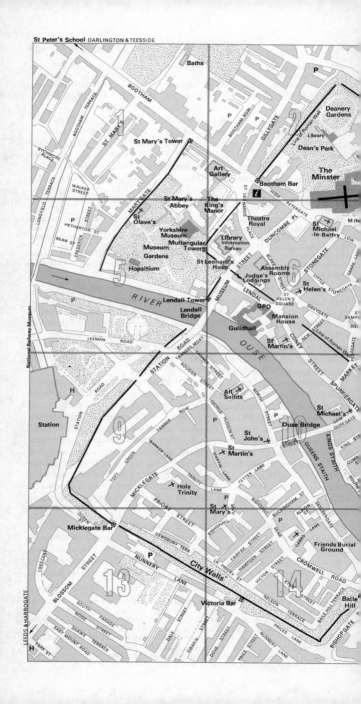

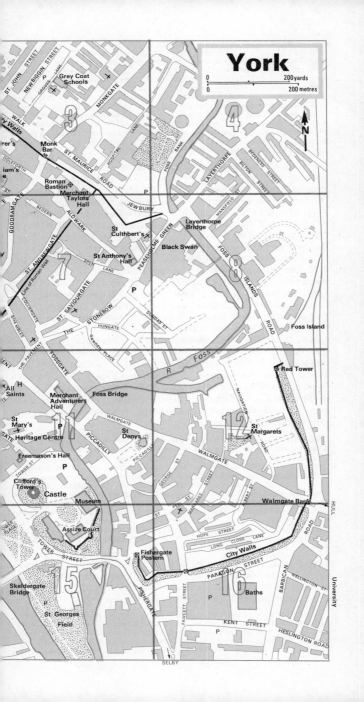

York

	200 yards
0	
0	200 metres

N

ST. JOHN STREET

NEWBIGGIN STREET

Grey Coat Schools

GROVES LANE

MONKGATE

...y WALK

...ry Walls

Monk Bar

ST. MAURICE ROAD

HOSPITAL LANE

FOSS BANK

LAYERTHORPE

RYDENESS STREET

BILTON STREET

...er's

OGLEFORTH

...iam's

...e

Roman Bastion

Merchant Taylors Hall

JEWBURY

P

Layerthorpe Bridge

MANSFIELD

GOODRAMGATE

BEDERN

ALDWARK

St Culthbert's

Black Swan

PEASEHOLME GREEN

ST. ANDREWGATE

St Anthony's Hall

SPEN LANE

Line of Roman Wall

FOSS ISLANDS ROAD

Foss Island

COLLIERGATE

ST. SAVIOURGATE

THE STONEBOW

P

DUNDAS ST.

SHAMBLES

THE PAVEMENT

HUNGATE

GARDEN PLACE

R. FOSS

...ENT

FOSSGATE

All Saints

H

Merchant Adventurers Hall

Foss Bridge

Red Tower

St Mary's

WALMGATE

St Denys

NAVIGATION

Heritage Centre

PICCADILLY

St Margarets

...ATE

Freemason's Hall

PIC... ...LLY

WALMGATE

Clifford's Tower

P

GEORGE ST.

PEEL ST.

MARYGATE STREET

ALBERT ST.

Castle

Museum

Walmgate Bar

HULL

...N PLACE

Assize Court

HOPE STREET

LONG CLOSE LANE

BARBICAN

WELLINGTON ST.

University

TOWER STREET

Fishergate Postern

City Walls

PARAGON STREET

Baths

Skeldergate Bridge

P

FISHERGATE

FAWCETT STREET

P

St Georges Field

KENT STREET

HESLINGTON ROAD

SELBY

3 4 7 8 11 12 15 16

four original gates, where Richard of York's head was exposed in 1460–1 and those of Jacobite rebels in 1746. Beyond the 19C *Victoria Bar* (Pl. 14) we skirt (l.) the old *Baile Hill* (Pl. 14), site of William the Conqueror's first castle. We cross the river by the iron *Skeldergate Bridge* (Pl. 15), pass the *Castle* (Pl. 11; see below), cross the Foss or canal, and regain the wall at *Fishergate Postern* (Pl. 15). Thence we follow the top of the wall, past *Fishergate Bar*, to *Walmgate Bar* (Pl. 12), which still retains its barbican or outwork. The stretch between the *Red Tower* (Pl. 12). built of brick in the 16C, and *Layerthorpe Bridge* (Pl. 8) was never walled, as the city was protected here by a marsh. At the bridge we remount the wall; on the left, beyond the *Merchant Taylors' Hall* (Pl. 3), is the foundation of the Roman E. bastion, which is approached from beside Monk Bar.

In Lendal (Pl. 6) the *Judges' Lodgings* occupy a fine mansion of c. 1720, while close by are the MUSEUM GARDENS (Pl. 5; adm. 8–dusk, Sun in summer from 1), containing the ruins of St Mary's Abbey (comp. below). On the right, as we enter the grounds, are the remains of *St Leonard's Hospital*, built by Abp. Thomas (d. 1114) to replace a hospital founded by Athelstan c. 940. The ruins (ambulatory and chapel) probably date from the 13C. Beyond it, at the corner of the City Wall, is the *Multangular Tower*; the lower part of this and the adjoining wall is Roman.

To the w. is the **Yorkshire Museum** (weekdays 10–5; Sun from 1; fee), with natural history and antiquarian collections, including Roman inscriptions and tomb reliefs; the 8C silver-gilt Ormside *Bowl of Viking origin; embossed tiles of c. 1200 (from All Saints, Pavement); 13C Limoges candlesticks; and statues from the façade of the abbey church. The ruins of **St Mary's Abbey**, founded in 1089 by Stephen of Lastingham for the Benedictines, and enlarged by William Rufus, in fact lie all around. In the adjoining basement are the Warming House (with original hearth), part of the Cloister and the Chapter-House Vestibule of the abbey, with part of St William's shrine (reconstructed), late 15C alabasters, and a notable Trajanic inscription from the Roman s.e. gate. The ruins of the *ABBEY CHURCH, built by Abbot Simon of Warwick, begun in 1259, consist chiefly of the N. wall of the nave and part of the w. front. The foundations of the E. end of the original Norman church, with seven apses, have been partly excavated.

Through the N. door of the nave we see (in St Olave's churchyard) the grave of William Etty. The *Abbey Gatehouse*, now a private residence, adjoins *St Olave's Church*, with some 15C glass. The *Hospitium* or *Guest House* (adm. Easter–Sept 10.30–12.30, 2–5), at the bottom of the garden, contains Roman antiquities, including tesselated pavements. Adjoining is a fragment of the *Water Gate*.
To the N.E. of the gardens is the **King's Manor** (Pl. 6), originally the abbot's house, but after the Dissolution assigned to the Lord President of the Great Council of the North. Founded c. 1270, but dating mostly from an enlargement of 1485–90, it was visited by Henry VIII and Charles I and II and was occupied by Strafford in 1628–40. Francis Place (1647–1728), artist and engraver, lodged here, and Dickens and 'Phiz' stayed here with the cathedral organist on their way back from Teesdale (p. 670). It has been beautifully restored (1962–64) as a hall of residence of the University of York.

Next door is the CITY ART GALLERY (10–5, Sun from 2.30), completely transformed in 1955 by the Lycett Green gift, mainly of Old Masters. There is also a notable collection of the British School, in which the native painter William Etty is well represented.

Among the foreign paintings (ground floor) may be mentioned: *Bachiacca*, Agony in the Garden; *Bellotto*, View in Lucca; *Fiorenzo di Lorenzo*, Madonna; *Parmigianino*, Portrait; and some good early Florentine and Sienese works. *Baburen*, Caritas Romana; *B. Fabritius*, The centurion Cornelius; *J. van Goyen*, Peasants and Horsemen; *Scorel* (?), Portrait; *J. van Streek*, Vanitas; *Corn. de Vos*,

Portrait. *Valdés Leal*, A Jesuit conversion; *Alonso Cano* (?), Female martyr. *J. F. Millet*, The Nobleman of Capernaum; *Watteau*, Le Défilé; *Gravelot*, The reader. The British paintings, mostly in the side room and on the first floor, begin with the early 16C Leake Panels, apparently a rood-screen from St Lawrence's chantry, Leake (Lincs.); among many interesting portraits of the 16–17C are Ferdinando, Lord Fairfax, by *Edw. Bower*, Daniel Goodricke (1634), and Mrs Lamplugh (1664); Lady Charlotte Fitzroy, daughter of Charles II and Barbara Villiers, a charming work by *Lely*; works by *Reynolds* and *Morland*; and a fine *Turner*. The collection of works by *Etty* includes many portraits and landscapes. Among more recent paintings those of the Barbizon School are notable; *Théodule Ribot* and *J.-E. Blanche* are well represented; also *Whistler* (Nocturne), *Greaves*, *Conder*, *Wilson Steer*, *Pryde*, and *Roderic O'Conor*. Likewise the London Group and their successors; *L. S. Lowry*, *Sickert*, *Stanley Spencer*, and *Gwen John*.— Dean Milner White's bequest of ceramics (first floor) may be viewed on application.

High Petergate, with the house (No. 9) where Sir Thos. Herbert died in 1681, leads from the Minster to Bootham Bar.—*St Peter's School*, in Clifton, the N.W. extension of Bootham (beyond Pl. 1), claims a continuous history from its foundation as a choir-school by Alcuin in 718.

Across St Leonard's Place are the De Grey Rooms with the Tourist Information Centre, and the *Theatre Royal* (Restaurant) granted its patent in 1769. The 12C vaulted crypt of St Peter's Hospital, founded by Athelstan and rebuilt by William II, is incorporated into the building. The theatre was rebuilt in 1882–90 and a foyer added in 1968.

In Blake St. (Pl. 6) are the *Assembly Rooms* (adm. weekdays on previous application), built by the Earl of Burlington (1731–32; restored 1951). The finest of the rooms is the Egyptian Hall, 112 ft by 40 ft, with double rows of columns; the Rotunda is adorned with mural paintings of Roman York. *St Helen's* church (Pl. 6) preserves some 15C glass. The *Mansion House*, in St Helen's Square facing the church, dates from 1725–26. The *Guildhall*, behind, built on the river in 1447–53, has been rebuilt on the old lines since the bombing of 1942 (adm. free weekdays 9–5.30; Sat till 5 or, in winter, 12).—Coney St., passing the late-Perp. *St Martin* (Pl. 6; under partial reconstruction), is continued by Spurriergate, where, sadly truncated in 1967, is the 12–15C church of *St Michael* (Pl. 10), with fine medieval glass. In Coppergate (l.) new excavations into Viking levels were open to view in 1978 (fee). Castlegate continues E. past the redundant 13–15C church of *St Mary* (Pl. 11), opened in 1975 as an architectural heritage centre (adm. daily 10–5, Sun from 1). It has a Saxon dedication-stone (within, w. of the organ), medieval glass in the s. aisle, and a fine Perp. tower and spire.

The **Castle** (Pl. 11), William I's second fortification, is now mainly replaced by John Carr's *Assize Courts* (1773–77) and the Museum. *Clifford's Tower* (adm. daily, closed Sun in winter till 2; fee), with its remarkable quatrefoil ground-plan, was erected early in the 14C and stands on the mound thrown up for the Conqueror's wooden keep. In 1190 when surrounding buildings were set on fire in riots, Jews crowded into the castle for sanctuary, and when it, too, was burnt, 150 were killed. The *Castle Museum (adm. daily, 9.30–7.30, Sun from 2; closed at 4.30 in Oct–March; fee), housed in the former Female Prison, a dignified building by John Carr (1780), and the old Debtors' Prison (1705; the centre block), grew out of the private collections of Dr J. L. Kirk of Pickering (d. 1940).

The outstanding feature is the cobbled 'street', with hansom cab, lined by old shops complete with wares, illustrating the life of the city in the 18–19C. Here too are 17–19C interiors, exhibits illustrating the development of trades; musical and scientific instruments; agricultural implements; silver, etc.—In the Debtors'

Prison is the condemned cell where Dick Turpin and Eugene Aram were confined;
also craftsmen's workshops; an Edwardian street with a gipsy caravan and a
sheriff's coach; costumes and toys; and a military collection with notable arms and
armour, and uniforms and silver of the Yorkshire regiments.

To the N., in High Ousegate, is the 15C church of *All Saints* (Pl. 11),
partly rebuilt, with an elegant octagonal lantern on its square tower and
a curious brass knocker on the N. door. In The Pavement (Pl. 11) is the
half-timbered Jacobean house where Sir Thomas Herbert (1606–82),
Cavalier and traveller, was born. From The Pavement diverge, on the left
(N.), Parliament St., the only wide street in York, and the Shambles, one of
the narrowest and quaintest. The former leads to St Sampson's Sq., where,
in the basement of the *Mail Coach Inn*, a Roman bath may be seen on
previous application. From the E. end of The Pavement opens Fossgate, in
which No. 40 is the entrance to the *MERCHANT ADVENTURERS' HALL (Pl.
11; adm. weekdays 10–12.30, 2–4 or 5.30; fee). The fine hall of 1357–68 is
noted for its splendid timber-work. Beneath is the 'hospital', occupied
until 1900 by pensioners of the guild, with massive wooden piers and a 15C
chapel, altered in the 17C, in which an annual service is held (Fri after
Michaelmas). Behind is a pleasant garden.

The company, which supported the northern cloth-export trade for 300 years
(15–17C), no longer has a commercial function, but holds four courts a year.
In Walmgate, the continuation of Fossgate, are the churches of *St Denys*
(Pl. 11), with good 14C glass and a Norman S. doorway, and *St Margaret* (Pl. 12),
with an elaborate *Porch (c. 1160), brought from the demolished church of St
Nicholas.

St Anthony's Hall (Pl. 7), partly of the 15C, the headquarters of a guild founded
before 1435, houses the Borthwick Institute of Historical Research (adm. Mon–Fri
9–1, 2.30–5). Opposite is the *Black Swan*, a good timbered inn. Close by is *St Cuthbert's*
church, rebuilt c. 1500. Aldwark leads back to the cathedral, passing the *Merchant
Taylors' Hall* (Pl. 3; adm. free week-days 10–5), another guild hall with a late 14C roof,
well restored, a smaller hall adjoining, and almshouses of 1728–29.
Some of the churches on the W. side of the Ouse are interesting. *St John Ousebridge*
(Pl. 10) is now the institute of Advanced Archaeological Studies. *All Saints, North
Street* (Pl. 10; late 12–15C), has windows (in the N. aisle) depicting the Fifteen Last
Days, in illustration of the 14C poem 'The Pricke of Conscience', and the Seven
Corporal Acts of Mercy, besides other glass of great beauty. The angel corbels have
been finely restored. In Micklegate (Pl. 10) are *St Martin-cum-Gregory*, with one 15C
window, and another *Holy Trinity*, partly of the 12C. *St Mary*, Bishophill Junior (Pl.
10), has an 11C tower. In the old *Friends' Burial Ground* (Pl. 14) is buried John
Woolman (1720–72), the Quaker diarist and opponent of slavery. The stones of St Mary
Bishophill Senior have been used to build a new church (by G. Pace) in the N.W. suburb
of *Acomb*. In Skeldergate is the York Model Railway (open 10–5.30).

To the W. of the station, approached by Leeman Road (Pl. 5; signposted;
car park) is the *National Railway Museum (adm. free, 10–6, Sun from 2;
rfmts), opened in 1975 as a department of the Science Museum (London).
Occupying the former North Motive Power Depot at the side of the main
line, it brings together a wealth of railway relics formerly in York,
Clapham, Kensington, and elsewhere. The main hall displays, round two
turntables, *Locomotives* (mainly steam 1829–1960), restored in their
original liveries (including the record-breaking 'Mallard') and *Rolling
Stock* (from 1797) with emphasis on Royal carriages (Q. Adelaide's &
Victoria's and Edward VII's). This is overlooked by a balcony with smaller
historical exhibits, models, etc. The front gallery shows domestic arts
associated with railway use.

The University of York, opened in 1963, has its centre at *Heslington Hall*, an
Elizabethan mansion 1½ m. S.E. of Walmgate Bar. In addition to the buildings

in the park here, the university will possess a number of halls of residence in the city, as well as the research institutes already there.

The *Knavesmire*, 2 m. s.w. on the Leeds road, is part of the ancient common lands of York (called Strays). Until 1801 it was the site of the 'three-legged mare', or gallows, for the city where Dick Turpin was hanged in 1739 (buried in St George's churchyard). The site of horse-racing since 1731, it now has one of the finest racecourses in the country. The Corporation has, over the years, acquired the rights to all the Strays in the city.

Bishopthorpe, the residence of the archbishop since 1226 (now also a conference house), was rebuilt c. 1769 but retains a 13C chapel. It is 2¾ m. s. by road (bus), but is preferably reached by boat (see above).

FROM YORK TO HARROGATE, 21½ m. (A 59). Railway in 35 min. To the s. of (8 m.) the Skip bridge stretches *Marston Moor*, the battlefield on which Cromwell won his decisive victory over the Royalists in 1644. To the left, just beyond the river, is *Kirk Hammerton* (Hotel), the Saxon church of which forms the s. aisle of a 19C church. *Nun Monkton*, 3 m. N.E. at the junction of the Ouse and the Nidd, has a beautiful little conventual church (Trans. and E.E.) and a maypole on the green.—At (13 m.) *Allerton Park* we join A 1 for about a mile.—15½ m. *Goldsborough Hall* (l.; now a school) was the first home of Viscount Lascelles (later Earl of Harewood) and Princess Mary. *Ribston Hall*, 2 m. s., gave its name to the Ribston pippin, introduced from Normandy in 1709.—18 m. *Knaresborough*, and thence to *Harrogate*, see Rte 67.

FROM YORK TO LEEDS, 24 m. (A 64). Railway viâ Church Fenton, 25½ m. in 30–45 min.—9¾ m. *Tadcaster* (Hotel) is a brewing town on the Wharfe, 3½ m. N. of the bloody battlefield of *Towton*, where the Lancastrian cause was defeated in 1461. *Bolton Percy*, 4 m. s.E., has a good church (1411–23), with fine 15C glass in the E. window, and an Elizabethan sundial in the churchyard. Gen. Fairfax (d. 1671) died in his manor-house (rebuilt) of *Nun Appleton* on the Wharfe, 1½ m. farther s.E. His tomb is preserved in the church (1873) of *Bilbrough*, 4 m. N.E. of Tadcaster.

12½ m. We pass (l.) *Hazlewood Castle*, where Mass has been said without a break in the chapel of c. 1290 (with Vavasour tombs) since its foundation.—At (13½ m.) *Bramham Moor* we cross A 1.—At 15½ m. a road leads left to *Barwick-in-Elmet* (1¾ m.) with some remarkable mounds (probably early Norman), including the *Hall Tower Hill* (30 ft high; 200 ft in diameter).—24 m. *Leeds*, see Rte 61H.

From York to *Bridlington*, *Beverley*, and *Hull*, see Rte 70; to *Scarborough* and *Whitby*, see Rte 69; to *London*, see above and Rte 46; to *Durham*, *Newcastle*, and *Berwick*, see Rte 71; to *Selby* viâ Cawood, see p. 618.

69 YORK TO SCARBOROUGH AND WHITBY: THE NORTH YORK MOORS

A To Scarborough

ROAD, 41 m. (A 64; bus).—RAILWAY, 42 m. in 50–65 min. Principal Stations: 21¼ m. *Malton*.—39½ m. *Seamer*.—42 m. **Scarborough**.

We leave York by Monkgate (Pl. 3) and cross the level plain of York.— 10½ m. *Barton Hill* lies 1 m. s.E. of *Foston*, of which Sydney Smith was rector from 1809 to 1829. The old Rectory, which he built in 1813–14, is open on Sun in June–Sept by appointment only. The by-road going N. from Barton Hill is prolonged by the five-mile avenue of ***Castle Howard**, the magnificent seat of the Howard family.

The mansion designed by Vanbrugh (with the assistance of Hawksmoor) and built in 1700–37, with a later w. wing (1753–59) by Sir T. Robinson, is open Easter–Oct daily, 1–5 (grounds and Rest. from 12); also BH, 11–5; fee. The interior has decoration by Pellegrini and Bagutti, and contains a collection of paintings (including works by Reynolds and Dom. Feti), notable furniture, statuary, and china, and Soho tapestries (1714). The chapel, with Pre-Raphaelite stained glass, contains a Sansovino bas-relief. A splendid Gallery of Costume, with exhibits from the 17C to the present day in contemporary settings, is housed in the 18C Stables, by Carr. In the beautiful park are the family *Mausoleum, by Hawksmoor, the *Temple of Four Winds*, by Vanbrugh, and lake of 65 acres; these, with the magnificent avenue, the obelisks, and the gatehouses, complete an ideal 18C landscape.

The ruins of *Sheriff Hutton Castle* (c. 1381), a stronghold of the Neviles, are 4 m. w. of Foston. The church here contains effigies of the 14–15C, one of which is probably that of Edward, son of Richard III (1471–84; if so, the only monument of a Prince of Wales in a parish church), and the brass of two babies (1491).— *Howsham Hall*, with Jacobean front and 18C interior, is in a beautiful position on the Derwent, 2½ m. S.E. of Barton Hill.

11¾ m. *Whitwell-on-the-Hill* (274 ft). Attractively situated below (r.), on the opposite bank of the Derwent, are the scanty ruins of *Kirkham Priory* (adm. daily, Sun from 2; fee), an Augustinian house founded in 1122 by Walter l'Espec. The chief remains are the sculptured gatehouse and the exquisite *Lavatorium in the cloister, both late 13C, and the Romanesque doorway of the refectory. In *Westow* church, 1½ m. E., is a Saxon cresset stone.—To the left farther on is another road to Castle Howard (3 m.; see above) viâ Welburn.

17½ m. **Malton** (Hotels), the Roman station of *Derventio*, is a market town (4000 inhab.) on the Derwent, with two partly 12C churches and an important cattle trade; the museum in the Market Place (adm. daily, exc. Thurs, 2–5; Fri only in winter, 2–4; fee) has a Roman collection. At *Old Malton*, 1 m. N.E., survive the beautiful w. front and aisleless nave of a Gilbertine priory (founded c. 1150), now the parish church (late-Norman and E.E.).

From Malton, Castle Howard (see above) is reached viâ (3 m. w.) *Easthorpe Hall*, the home of Charles Smithson (d. 1844), the friend of Dickens, who wrote part of 'Martin Chuzzlewit' here.

Between Malton and Driffield (20 m. S.E.) is some of the finest wold country. At (4½ m.) *North Grimston* and at *Cowlam* (2½ m. N.E. of Sledmere) are two of the crudely carved 12C fonts for which this district is noted; while at (12½ m.) *Sledmere* is the splendid park of the Sykes family, to whom the Wolds owe their agricultural prosperity. The mansion (adm. April, Sun only; May–Sept, daily exc. Mon & Fri 1.30–5.30; also BH; fee) has a fine library 100 ft long (1790–96). In the grounds laid out by 'Capability' Brown is the parish church (1898, by Temple Moore), and in the village, a memorial to the Yorkshire Waggoners, the regiment raised by Sir Mark Sykes in 1912. *Garton Hill*, 2½ m. S.E., is topped by a huge spire in memory of Sir Tatton Sykes (fine view over the Wolds).

From Malton to *Helmsley*, and to *Pickering* and *Whitby*, see Rte 69B.

We quit Malton by the suburb of *Norton* (5400 inhab.) and the escarpment of the Wolds appears on the right.—Beyond (22 m.) the attractive spire of *Rillington* we skirt the park (l.) of *Scampston Hall* (1803), by Thos. Leverton.—At (27½ m.) *East Heslerton* the church (by Street) is adorned by statues of the Four Latin Fathers, rejected as un-Protestant from the N. porch of Bristol Cathedral (1876).—31½ m. *Ganton* has a noted golf course.—Beyond (33¾ m.) *Staxton* the road to Filey and Bridlington diverges on the right; we turn N. through *Seamer* (Motel).

41 m. **SCARBOROUGH** (44,400 inhab.), the most popular seaside resort in the N.E. of England, is splendidly situated with two fine sandy bays, separated by a rocky bluff crowned with the ruins of the castle. The sea-front is laid out with pleasant irregularity, and the cliffs of both bays are covered with delightful gardens.

Hotels in the town, on South Cliff, and on North Cliff.
Post Office, Aberdeen Walk, off Westborough.—INFORMATION OFFICE, St Nicholas Cliff.

Buses from Valley Bridge or Northway to all destinations.—STEAMER CRUISES along the coast.

Cliff Lifts at St Nicholas Cliff (two), the South Cliff, and Alexandra Gardens (see below).

Amusements. *The Spa*, see below; *Opera House* (repertory drama), St Thomas St.; *Open Air Theatre*, Northstead Manor Gardens; *Floral Hall*, Alexandra Gardens, North side; *Futurist Theatre*, South Bay; *Library Theatre*, Vernon St.—BATHING POOLS on N. and S. sides.—GOLF COURSES on the N. Cliff, S. Cliff, and at Ganton (see above).—TENNIS COURTS in Filey Rd. (national championships) and Northstead Manor Gardens.—CRICKET GROUND (festival early Sept), North Marine Rd. —HOCKEY FESTIVAL (Easter) and REGATTA (Aug).

The headland at Scarborough on which the town's history centres, has borne in turn an Iron Age settlement, a Roman beacon, Saxon and Norman chapels, and the castle, built in a seemingly impregnable position 300 ft above the sea. As a watering-place it dates from the discovery of mineral springs in 1620, and it was frequented for sea-bathing as early as 1767 (comp. Smollett's 'Humphrey Clinker' and Sheridan's 'A Trip to Scarborough'). Lord Leighton, P.R.A. (1830–96) and Dame Edith Sitwell (1887–1964) were natives of the town.—On 16 Dec 1914, it was bombarded by a German battle-cruiser squadron.

The main street, known as Westborough, Newborough, and Eastborough, descends N.E. from the Station to *South Bay* and the *Harbour*, which, with its fishmarket and varied craft, is always a scene of great interest. Facing the harbour, a café occupies a house, built c. 1350, where Richard III is reputed to have stayed. To the N. the broad *Marine Drive* sweeps round the base of the castle hill, to be continued by the *Royal Albert Drive* to (1½ m.) the quieter NORTH BAY, with *Northstead Manor Gardens*. Above are *Alexandra Gardens* and *Peasholm Park*, with a boating lake and glen.

A member of Parliament may voluntarily vacate his seat by accepting the stewardship of the Manor of Northstead, 'an office of profit under the Crown' (comp. p. 307).

Immediately above the harbour, where the quaint 'old town' is rapidly disappearing, the steep streets climb towards Castle Rd. Here stands the parish church of *St Mary* (c. 1180), with four vaulted chapels (14C) opening off the s. aisle. The choir and N. transept were destroyed during the siege of the castle in 1645. Anne Brontë (1820–49) is buried in the detached part of the churchyard, E. of the church. Of the ruined **Castle** (adm. daily, Sun from 2 in Oct–Aug; fee), the chief remains are the keep (1158–64) and the 13C barbican by which it is approached across the moat. On the cliff are foundations of the Roman signal-station.

Piers Gaveston was besieged and captured in this castle by the Earl of Pembroke in 1312. It suffered two sieges during the Civil War and was twice surrendered through starvation to the Parliamentarians (in 1645 and 1648). George Fox, the Quaker, was confined here in 1665–66.

On the SOUTH BAY, along St Nicholas Cliff, are the pretty *St Nicholas Gardens*, at the top of which (cliff lift), in St Nicholas St., is the *Town Hall*, a converted mansion (1852), by H. J. Wyatt. Farther s. Valley Road, with its attractive park, divides the town from South Cliff residential quarter.

The elegant Crescent contains the Art Gallery, Medical Baths, and the Natural History Museum (weekdays 10–1, 2.30–5; Sun also in summer, 2–5) which was the Sitwells' 'Woodend'. In the Valley is the Rotunda built by Sharpe in 1829, to house the *Museum* founded by the geologist, William Smith (1769–1839).

Restored in 1953, the museum (open weekdays 10–1, 2.30–5) contains pre-historic antiquities (including finds from Star Carr, 6 m. s.), early engravings of the town, and copies of Cayley's aeronautical models (see below). The Valley leads to the Grand Hotel, a swaggering building by Cuthbert Broderick (1867).

Near the sea the valley is spanned by the *Spa Bridge* with an entrance to the SPA and its gardens, a popular rendezvous, situated on a terrace at the foot of the South Cliff (cliff lift). It includes a concert hall, a theatre, a restaurant, and a ballroom. The SOUTH CLIFF is reached direct from Westborough by the lofty Valley Bridge. The well laid out *South Cliff Gardens* (views) and *Holbeck Gardens* occupy the face of the cliffs. The church of *St Martin-on-the-Hill* by G. F. Bodley (1862) has a superb organ case by him, and a notable Lady Chapel. The reredos, pulpit panels, and windows, are by Burne-Jones, Rossetti, Ford Madox Brown, and Morris.

Farther s., off the Filey road, *Oliver's Mount* (500 ft), surmounted by the War Memorial (an obelisk 75 ft high), commands wide views.—Fine walks may be taken from Scarborough along the cliffs or sands (beware of the tide): s. to *Cornelian Bay* (pebbles), *Cayton Bay*, *Gristhorpe Bay* (fossils), and (8 m.) *Filey* (see below); and N. to (4½ m.) *Cloughton Wyke* and (6½ m.) *Hayburn Wyke* (see below).

To FORGE VALLEY and HACKNESS, a charming inland drive (14½ m.). We climb Stepney Brow (B 1262) and descend to (4½ m.) *Ayton*. We now ascend the wooded *Forge Valley*, watered by the Derwent, from the end of which (6½ m.) 'Lady Edith's Drive' (r.), leads back to Scarborough (4½ m.). We continue along the Derwent, past (7½ m.) *Everley* (Hotel) to (8½ m.) *Hackness*, beautifully situated at the junction of several valleys. [The left-hand road leads through charming country to *Langdale End* (2½ m.).] Hackness Church (r.; Norman and E.E.) has a font-cover of 1480, a monument by Chantrey and fragments of an Anglian cross (? 8C) with a unique inscription in Latin, Ogams, and Runes. This was the site of a Saxon monastery between 680 and 869. The road ascends past *Hackness Hall* (Lord Derwent) to (9½ m.) *Suffield* (534 ft) and then descends, with a superb view, to (11½ m.) *Scalby*, whence we return to (14½ m.) Scarborough on A 171.

From Ayton (see above) A 170 goes on w. to (17¾ m.) *Pickering* (Rte 69B) viâ (6 m.) *Wykeham*, with a church by Butterfield, and (7½ m.) *Brompton*, where Wordsworth was married to Mary Hutchinson in 1802. The Hall was the home of Sir George Cayley (1773–1857), the 'father of the aeroplane'.—About 2 m. beyond (9 m.) *Snainton* (Hotel) is *Ebberston Hall*, a charming house by Colen Campbell (1718).—From (14½ m.) *Thornton-le-Dale* (Hotels) a drive may be taken up the pretty valley viâ *Ellerburn* (1 m.), with a primitive church, and thence by forest road to (11½ m.) *Langdale End* (see above), passing near the *Bridestones* (7 m.; N.T.), six great gritstone rocks.

FROM SCARBOROUGH TO HULL, 44½ m. (A 165). Railway, viâ Filey, Bridlington, Driffield, and Beverley, 53¾ m. in c. 1½ hr. [An alternative road (1½ m. shorter) runs inland viâ *Langtoft*, with a 12C *Font from the disused church of *Cottam*, and *Driffield* (21 m.; see p. 636)]. The Filey road affords good sea views on the left. —7 m. Filey (Hotel) is a pleasant bathing and golfing resort (5300 inhab.) on Filey Bay, with a good sandy beach extending N.E., below the cliffs, to (1 m.) *Filey Brigg*, a low rocky spit, c. ¼ m. long. At one time the boundary between the East and the North Riding separated the town from its interesting church (St Oswald's; Norman and E.E.), now both in the East Riding. The small rude figure on the wall of the s. aisle is probably not St Oswald (who was a king, not a cleric). Charlotte Brontë stayed in 1845 in a house in Belle Vue St. Filey is on the *Cleveland Way*, a 100 m. footpath along the border of the National Park, and is the starting-point for the projected Wolds Way Walk to (67 m.) North Ferriby, on the Humber foreshore. *Hunmanby*, 3 m. s.w., is a large and attractive village where the church has Norman features and remarkable heraldry.—Above (11½ m.) *Reighton*, where the church has a fine Norman font, the road to Flamborough Head (8½ m.; B 1229) diverges viâ *Speeton* and *Bempton*. Both are noted for their lofty chalk cliffs (400 ft sheer drop), the breeding-places of innumerable sea-birds. The fine cliffs may be followed s.e. to the North Landing (p. 637).—17½ m. *Bridlington*, and thence to Hull, see Rte 70B.

FROM SCARBOROUGH TO WHITBY, 20 m. (A 171, very hilly).—5 m. *Cloughton*. Here a road leads viâ *Hayburn Wyke* (1½ m.; Hotel), a wooded dell laid out with a labyrinth of walks, and over *Staintondale Moor* to *Ravenscar* (5½ m.; 600 ft; Hotel), a holiday resort at the N. end of a fine range of cliffs, and the terminus of the Lyke Wake Walk across the moors from (40 m.) Osmotherley.—From Cloughton the Whitby road ascends over *Fylingdales Moor*, now largely requisitioned as a military training ground with the conspicuous globes (140 ft diameter) of the Ballistic Missile Early Warning Station (1963).—From (17½ m.) *Hawsker*, a road on the right (B 1447) leads in 2½ m., by a steep descent, to **Robin Hood's Bay** (Hotel, closed in winter), a quaint irregular fishing village on a steep slope.—20 m. *Whitby*, see Rte 69B.

B   To Whitby; The North York Moors

DIRECT ROAD, 47 m. (A 64, A 169) viâ (17½ m.) *Malton*, (see Rte 69A) and (26 m.) *Pickering*. The longer and more interesting route (58 m.) viâ (23¾ m.) *Helmsley*, (30¾ m.) *Kirkbymoorside*, and (37 m.) *Pickering* is described below.

This route lies mainly in the **North York Moors National Park**, designated in 1949, which includes the upland area 20 m. N.E. of York, from the coast to the plains at the foot of the Hambleton and Cleveland Hills, and from the edge of the plains in the s. to Cleveland in the N. From the central hills (c. 1400 ft), the drainage has run off in parallel valleys, long to the s., where all the streams eventually join the Derwent; short to the N., where they flow into the Esk. It is a superb walking area; the 2½ in. Ordnance Survey map, and H.M.S.O. Guide to the Park are useful.

Leaving York by Gillygate (Pl. 2), B 1363 leads due N. to (8¼ m.) *Sutton-on-the-Forest*, whose name recalls the royal *Forest of Galtres*, now completely vanished. Sutton Park (adm. Apr–Sept, Tues, Wed, Thurs, & Sun, 2–6; fee) dates from 1730. Laurence Sterne was vicar from 1738 and in 1743 acquired also the living of (10½ m.) *Stillington*.—We ascend to (15¾ m.) the summit of the *Howardian Hills*, and then drop down to (18¼ m.) *Gilling* (or *Gilling East*), with a castle (now a school) built on Edwardian foundations. The great chamber, with its Elizabethan panelling, glass, and heraldic and decorative painting, may be seen on weekdays (10–12, 2–4; best in Aug).—At (20 m.) *Oswaldkirk* we enter the North York Moors National Park.

A by-road leads w. under the limestone escarpment of the Hambleton Hills to (2 m.) *Ampleforth*, where there is a Benedictine Priory (founded 1802), with a well-known boys' public school.— 5 m. **Byland Abbey** (adm. daily, Sun from 2; fee), a Cistercian foundation of 1147 (Benedictine 1134) transferred from Old Byland, 5 m. N., in 1177; the chief features are the façade and s. transept of the church, which contains fine 12–13C *Tiles, and an arch of the gatehouse, a little w.—6½ m. *Coxwold* (Inn), a delightful village whose Perp. church has an unusual octagonal tower. Here Sterne, whose pulpit still stands, was perpetual curate in 1760–68, and he is buried in the churchyard. He wrote part of 'Tristram Shandy' and 'A Sentimental Journey' in the house now called *Shandy Hall* (w. end of village). The Hall dates from c. 1450, and is open (2–6, Wed in June–Sept) as a memorial to the writer. At *Newburgh Priory*, just s.E., the headless body of Oliver Cromwell is said to be preserved in a vault by his descendants the Wombwells. The house is open 2–5.30, Wed in mid-May–mid-Sept (fee). *Kilburn*, 2½ m. N.W., beneath Roulston Scar, is noted for the village workshop of Robert Thompson (d. 1955), whose beautiful wood-carving ('signed' with a mouse) adorns many churches.

B 1257 leads E. from Oswaldkirk to (12½ m.) *Malton* (Rte 69A) viâ (4½ m.) *Hovingham* (Hotel), a pleasant village, with a tiny 8C (?) carving in its church. *Nunnington Hall* (N.T.; adm. May–Sept, Wed and Sun, 2–6; fee), 2½ m. N. is a large 16–17C manor-house with a panelled hall and staircase.—Farther on are (6½ m.) *Slingsby*, with a fine ruined Caroline country house, and (8 m.) *Barton-le-Street*, where the rebuilt church has good Norman carving.

23 m. **Helmsley** (pleasant Hotels), a small market town, stands at the foot of the s. slopes of the Cleveland Hills, and is a good centre for the

moors. The ruined 12C *Castle* (adm. daily, Sun from 2; fee), with later additions, is surrounded by extensive earthworks, and adjoins *Duncombe Park*, the gardens of which are open in May–Aug on Wed (10–4; fee). Beautifully situated in *Rye Dale*, 2½ m. N.W., are the extensive remains of *Rievaulx Abbey* ('Reevo'), the earliest Cistercian house in Yorkshire (adm. daily; Sun from 2 in Oct–Aug; fee), founded by Walter l'Espec in 1132. The mainly E.E. ruins include the lower walls of the nave with its chapels, the *Choir and transepts of the church; the chapter house with its apse, a unique feature in an English Cistercian house, and remains of the shrine of the first abbot (1148); the sub-vault of the dorter (c. 1175); and the refectory (13C). Rievaulx Terrace (fee), above to the s., commands a magnificent *View of the dale and the ruins.

A charming lane ascends w. to the main Helmsley–Thirsk road a little short of (4 m.) the top of *Sutton Bank* (car park). with a wide and sudden *View extending across the Plain of York to the Pennines. The descent to Thirsk is very steep (1 in 4 or 5). Walkers may follow the old Drove Road N. from *Cooper Cross* on the main road near Sutton Bank viâ *Hesketh Dyke* and many earthworks and standing-stones, to *Osmotherley* (c. 10 m.).

Beyond Rievaulx the fine road (B 1257) skirts Rye Dale on the E., and continues up *Bilsdale*, at the head of which *Urra* earthwork runs along the crest of the hill for c. 3 m. We cross the Cleveland Hills to (20 m.) Stokesley (p. 624). At 1½ m. a side road (l.) descends across the valley to (4½ m.) *Hawnby*, at the E. foot of the Hambleton Hills.

At Helmsley A 170 turns right (E.) for (26½ m.) *Nawton* and (30¾ m.; l.) *Kirkbymoorside* (Hotel), where the 2nd Duke of Buckingham died in 1687 as the result of a hunting accident.

On a by-road to the left (¾ m.) between these two villages is the church of *Kirkdale* (l.) with a noted sundial recording the rebuilding of the church in the days of Edward the Confessor, and two Anglian crosses in the porch. The famous Kirkdale Cave can be seen in the quarry face by the ford; discovered in 1821, it yielded a rich haul of lion, hyena, rhinoceros, and mammoth bones of the pre-glacial period.

From *Gillamoor*, c. 3 m. N. of Kirkbymoorside, a road (one-way, and congested in spring) ascends *Ferndale*, noted for daffodils, and now a nature reserve; the return may be made down the E. side of the valley to *Hutton-le-Hole*, a charming village (crowded in summer). John Richardson, friend of William Penn, lived here at Quaker Cottage (1695). *Lastingham* (Hotel), c. 2 m. E., another pretty village beneath Spaunton Moor, has an interesting church (Trans. and E.E.) with an aisled Norman crypt (c. 1080), forming practically a lower church (also the remains of a large Saxon cross). *Appleton-le-Moors*, 2 m. s. of Lastingham, retains its medieval plan; while *Cropton*, 2 m. s.E., has a ruined castle with a view of Rosedale.

35½ m. *Middleton* church has three 10C wheel-head crosses.—37 m. **Pickering** (Hotel), a plain little town (4500 inhab.), with a *Castle* where Richard II was confined for a time after his abdication, and which had two wards and a shell keep, recast in the 14C but probably with a Norman core. The *Church* (Norman & Dec.) contains a Norman font, but its chief interest is the remarkable series of mural paintings (c. 1450) in the nave, too drastically restored in 1889.

On the N. choir wall is a monument to Nicholas and Robert King (d. 1812 and 1817), surveyors of the city of Washington; brasses beneath it commemorate the Anglo-American alliance and W. H. Page (1855–1918), U.S. ambassador in London. The choir panelling (1929) is a memorial also to Anglo-American friendship and to J. H. Choate (1832–1917), likewise ambassador.

About 4 m. s.w. is *Kirby Misperton Hall* with the Flamingo Park Zoo (open

daily; fee; café).—Cawthorne Roman Camps lie c. 4 m. N.; a Roman road ran N.
to Grosmont, part of which is preserved (see below).—to *Scarborough*, see p. 632.

The North Yorkshire Moors Railway ascends the narrow and wooded
Newton Dale. It was built by George Stephenson in 1836, and part of it is
now privately owned (regular summer service to Grosmont with connection to Whitby). The road (A 169) climbs on to the open moor, passing
1½ m. w. of the Bridestones (p. 632).—To the left are the moorland
villages of *Lockton* and *Levisham*, affording unusual views of the deep
dales below them. Levisham church, with a Saxon chancel arch, lies in the
Beck (footpath).—45¼ m. *Saltersgate Inn* stands on the old pack route by
which salt from Whitby was taken to Pickering market for distribution
throughout Yorkshire, and near the head of the *Hole of Horcum*, a
depression in the moors eroded by the springs that rise on its slopes.—
Beyond (47¾ m.) *Eller Beck Bridge* a road on the left leads in 2¾ m. to
Goathland (Hotels), in a charming moorland situation and noted for its
waterfalls (Mallyan Spout, etc.). In the village, set round a large green, a
tradition of folk dancing by the Plough Stotts (sword-dancers) survives,
and performances, with a large repertory, are frequent. It is an excellent
centre for walking. On *Wheeldale Moor*, 3 m. s.w., over a mile of a *Roman
road has been exposed.—A long, steep descent (views, with Fylingdales
radar-domes conspicuous to the E.) leads to (53¾ m.) *Sleights*, whence a
pleasant walk of 3½ m. may be taken s.E. up the Little Beck to *Falling Force*,
a waterfall 40 ft high, in a woodland setting.—We cross the Esk and ascend
to join A 171 beside a pillar recording the shooting-down of the first
German air-raider in the Second World War (3 Feb 1940).

58 m. **WHITBY** (Hotels on W. Cliff), with a busy harbour and 12,700
inhab., consists of the picturesque old red-tiled fishing town on both
banks of the Esk (which here makes its way to the sea between tall cliffs)
and the popular seaside resort on the West Cliff. 'Whitby jet' ornaments
are still made here, and the characteristic cobles may be seen in the
harbour.

Capt. Cook (1728–79) made his first voyage around the world in Whitby-built
ships; and William Scoresby (1789–1857), another famous navigator, was a native.
Whitby is the 'Monkshaven' of Mrs Gaskell's 'Sylvia's Lovers'.

The road from York passes *Pannett Park*, in which is a *Museum* (adm.
9–1, 2–5.30, Sun 2–5; in winter 10.30–1, and also on Wed, Sat, Sun 2–4; fee)
containing a good local fossil collection, an Anglian comb (with runes),
relics of Capt. Cook, ship models, etc. The *Art Gallery* adjoining contains
good water colours. On the r. is the 16C *Bagdale Hall* (adm. as above).
Thence Baxtergate descends past the Post Office to the swing-bridge
spanning the Esk, the mouth of which is protected by two stone piers. We
cross the bridge to the old fishermen's quarter. To the right opens Grape
Lane, in which stands a house (No. 16; dated 1688) where Capt. Cook
served as an apprentice. From the N. end of Church St., the main
thoroughfare, a flight of 199 steps ascends to *St Mary's Church*, containing
a curious array of 18C galleries and box-pews, a three-decker pulpit, and
some portions of Norman work (chancel and s. doorway). The Cholmley
Pew (c. 1700) is a gallery in front of the chancel arch, and in the chancel is
the tomb of Sir Richard Cholmley (1631). A cross (1898) in the churchyard
commemorates the poet Cædmon (d. c. 680), who was a monk of Whitby

Abbey. Close by are the beautiful ruins of **Whitby Abbey** (adm. daily, Sun from 2 in Oct–April; fee), which was founded in 657 by St Hilda for monks and nuns, and was long the chief school of learning in the North.

Destroyed in 867 by the Danes, the abbey was refounded for the Benedictines by William de Percy. The ruined church, in a commanding situation on the exposed cliff 200 ft above the sea, dates for the most part from the E.E. period (12–13C), with Dec. work towards the w. end. The w. front, battered by a naval bombardment in 1914, was restored in 1922. The s. side of the nave and the central tower have disappeared. The N. front and the E. end, with its three tiers of triple lancets, are especially fine. The axis of the choir is deflected 9 ft from the line of the nave. The plan of an earlier Norman church is marked out within the existing walls. No domestic buildings remain. The ruined mansion s. of the Abbey was built by Sir Hugh Cholmley, temp. Charles II.

On the WEST CLIFF is the so-called *Spa* (concert-hall, restaurant, etc.) and the modern holiday quarter. The promenade overlooks a good sandy beach (lift; fee). The bronze statue of Capt. Cook, at the E. end, is by Tweed.

Although the beauty of the landscape round Whitby is threatened with the intrusion of petrochemical fertilizer plants, numerous pleasant excursions may be made. There are walks to *Ruswarp* (1½ m. s.w.), on the Esk (boating); to *Cock Mill*, in a pretty glen, 2 m. inland; N. to (3 m.) *Sandsend* and (4 m.) *Mulgrave Castle and Woods* (see below); s. to (7 m.) *Robin Hood's Bay* along the cliffs, viâ *Saltwick Nab* (N.T.), ¾ m. E. of the Abbey. The routes to Guisborough, Pickering, and Stokesley provide opportunities for fine walks along the coast and among the moors and dales. An interesting local feature is the series of moor crosses (probably marking boundaries).

FROM WHITBY TO TEESSIDE, 43¾ m. The road (hilly and meandering) ascends the Esk valley and gives access to the wild moorland scenery of *Cleveland*. Railway to Middlesbrough, 35 m. in 1¼ hr.—7 m. *Grosmont*, junction with the North York Moors Railway, preserves an ancient font in its church.—Near (9 m.) *Egton Bridge* is an ornate Rom. Cath. church (1866). It was the parish of Father Postgate, executed for his faith in 1679 at the age of 83. We cross the defile of *Arncliffe Woods* near the 'Beggar's Bridge' (1619), at the w. end of it.—10½ m. *Glaisdale*, at the mouth of a beautiful side-valley (fine moor walks).—We cross the Esk at (13 m.) *Lealholm* to reach (16 m.) *Danby*, with the North York Moors National Park centre. To the N.E. rises *Danby Beacon* (988 ft); to the s.E. lies the ruined *Danby Castle* (c. 1300), once the home of the Latimers, near the medieval Duck Bridge.—17½ m. *Castleton*, a good centre for moorland walks. The church (1924) has fine carvings by Thompson of Kilburn. *Commondale*, c. 3 m. N.W., is also a good starting-point for walks. Fine roads lead s. across the moor to Kirkbymoorside or Pickering viâ (4½ m.) *Ralph's Cross* (18C) and either Blakey House or (9¾ m.) *Rosedale* (Hotel), with the scant remains of a Cistercian abbey. The track of the old Ferndale railway s.w. of the Cross may be followed over the moor to the Cleveland Hills.—We then proceed w. to (23¾ m.) *Kildale*, where we leave the Cleveland Hills, and (25½ m.) *Easby. Ingleby Greenhow* church, 2 m. s., is Georgian, with Norman fragments.—29¼ m. *Stokesley*, a little market town with a fine wide street and packhorse bridge of 1648. On the Guisborough road, 3 m. N.E., is *Great Ayton* (Hotel), the base for the ascent (¾ hr) of the conical *Roseberry Topping* (1057 ft). Capt. Cook attended the old village school here and his cottage, removed to Melbourne, Australia in 1934, is replaced by an obelisk of Australian granite, on Easby Moor. He stayed as a boy at Airy Holme Farm, c. 1 m. N. of the Moor.—We turn N. on B 1365 to join A 174.—39 m. *Teesside*, see Rte 71.

FROM WHITBY TO SALTBURN AND MIDDLESBROUGH, 32 m. (A 174). There is another road (30½ m.; A 171) across the moors viâ Guisborough.—3 m. *Sandsend* is a small seaside resort. *Mulgrave Castle* (Marquess of Normanby), in a wooded valley 1 m. w., has beautiful woods and the scanty ruins of an 11C castle.—4 m. *Lythe* has a superb view s. over Whitby and the bay, and a church with many Anglo-Saxon fragments.—9 m. *Hinderwell*, for *Runswick* (1 m. s.E.), a fishing village on *Runswick Bay* (good bathing).—10½ m. *Staithes*, another fishing village, partly at the bottom of a deep ravine reached by a precipitous descent, was once notorious for smuggling. Capt. Cook served here as a lad in a huckster's shop. To the w. rises *Boulby Cliff* (666 ft), said to be the highest cliff on the English coast, while inland runs a singular pair of parallel wooded glens, near the head of which (c. 4 m.) is *Grinkle Park Hotel*, reached viâ Easington.—14½ m. *Loftus* is a beautifully situated but grimy town (7700 inhab.) with ironworks.—At (17 m.) *Brotton* A 173 bears left for (22½ m.) *Guisborough*; A 174 keeps right for (19 m.) *Saltburn* and *Middlesbrough*, see Rte 71.

70   YORK TO BRIDLINGTON AND HULL

A To Bridlington

ROAD, 41½ m. (A 1079, A 166) viâ (29½ m.) *Driffield*.

Leaving York by Walmgate and A 1079, we bear to the left on A 166 at (2¾ m.) *Grimston*.—8 m. *Stamford Bridge*, over the Derwent, was the scene of the victory of Harold of England over Harald Hardrada of Norway on 25 Sept 1066. Farther on we ascend the escarpment of the undulating chalk Wolds. The roads N. and S. to Malton and Pocklington run through out-of-the-way country, with unspoilt villages, many with interesting Norman work in their churches, e.g. at *Bishop Wilton* (1 m. S. at 13 m.), a charming village in a hillside combe, and at (18 m.) *Fridaythorpe* on the top of the Wolds.—29½ m. *Driffield* (correctly *Great Driffield*; Hotel, also at Nafferton, 2 m. N.E.), an agricultural town (7900 inhab.), has a fine 15C church tower, and a remarkable private museum of local archaeology.

About 3 m. S.W. is the Norman *Church of *Kirkburn*, with rich carvings; a Norman font; and a curious, and perhaps unique, tower staircase (c. 1200). *Bainton*, c. 2 m. farther S.W., has a notable church (1335) with the elaborate tomb of Sir Edmund de Mauley (d. 1314).—About 5½ m. S., off the Beverley road, is *Watton Priory*, an Elizabethan mansion incorporating some remains of the largest Gilbertine priory in England (12C), including an exquisite oriel window. The priory was dual, the canons and canonesses each having a church of their own.

At (35¼ m.) *Burton Agnes* are an interesting church, containing the extraordinary monument of Sir Henry Griffith (d. 1654), and the splendid red brick Elizabethan *Hall (1601–10), with its turreted gatehouse, by Smithson. The house (adm. daily exc. Sat 1.45–5, May–mid-Oct, Sun till 6; fee; tea) contains a remarkable oak staircase, fine chimneypieces, furniture, and 19C French paintings. Close by is its Norman forerunner, altered in the 16C (adm. daily always).

41½ m. **Bridlington** (Hotels), a popular summer resort (26,700 inhab.) with fine sands and a small harbour (regatta in Aug), is situated on the wide sweep of *Bridlington Bay*. It was formerly called *Burlington*. William Kent (1685–1748) is a native. In the old town, to the N., is the imposing nave of the old *Priory Church* (E.E. to Perp.), founded for Augustinian canons in the reign of Henry I, and now used as the parish church; notable features are the W. façade, the N. porch, and the elegant arcades. The neighbouring *Bayle Gate* dates from c. 1388.

Flamborough Head is reached from Bridlington by road or footpath. The road (bus) runs N.E. past (2 m.) *Sewerby Hall*, a Georgian mansion (adm. in summer; fee) in a fine public park, and crosses (3½ m.) the misnamed *Danes' Dyke*, the best example in England of a late Neolithic (or early Bronze Age) 'promontory fort'.—4½ m. *Flamborough* church, partly Norman and E.E., has a 16C *Rood-Loft, one of only two in Yorkshire (comp. p. 610).—6¼ m. **Flamborough Head**, a bold chalk headland with sheer cliffs descending to the sea, is a sanctuary for sea-birds during the breeding season. The finest scenery (stack rocks, caves, etc.) is on the N. side, beyond the *North Landing* (p. 632). It was off Flamborough Head that in 1779 Paul Jones, the American privateer, in the 'Bonhomme Richard' captured the British ship 'Serapis' after a bloody fight; his own ship sank next day.

To the w. of Bridlington are (3½ m.) *Boynton Hall.* where Henrietta Maria took refuge in 1643 when bombarded in Bridlington by the Parliamentarian Adm. Batten, and (6½ m.) *Rudston,* with an early Norman church tower, and, in the churchyard, a huge menhir, 25 ft high. The Roman pavements, discovered here in 1933 (c. 1 m. s.w.) are now in Hull Museum.

From Bridlington or Flamborough to *Filey* and *Scarborough,* see Rte 69A.

B To Hull

ROAD, 37½ m. (A 1079) viâ (29¼ m.) *Beverley.*—RAILWAY viâ *Selby,* 44¾ m. in c. 1 hr.

We leave York on A 1079.—At (10¾ m.) *Barmby* B 1246 diverges left for *Pocklington* (2 m.; Hotel), a small town with a boys' school where Wm. Wilberforce was a pupil. The fine 13–14C church contains a 14C cross-head.—19¼ m. *Market Weighton* (pron. 'Weeton'; Hotel) is at the foot of the Wolds.

About 1¼ m. N.E. is *Goodmanham,* the 'Godmundingaham' of Bede, where the 12C church probably occupies the site of the heathen temple destroyed by the high priest Coifi after the Great Council of 626. The Church is noteworthy for its chancel arch and two fonts, one possibly Saxon, the other of c. 1525.—*Nunburnholme,* 4¾ m. N., has an interesting mid-10C churchyard-cross. *Kipling Cotes,* 3¾ m. E., is noted as the starting-point of the oldest and longest horse-race in England, run yearly since 1519 on the third Thurs in March (at midday). The present course, extending 4 m. N.W., has been used since 1667.

29¼ m. **BEVERLEY** (Hotel), an old-fashioned market town (17,100 inhab.), until 1974 the county town of the E. Riding of Yorkshire, and now the administrative centre of Humberside, was incorporated in 1129 by Abp. Thurstan of York, and possesses two splendid churches and many attractive houses. Bp. John Fisher (1459–1535), the martyr, was born here. Within the red brick *North Bar* (1409; restored), the sole survivor of the five town gates, is *ST MARY'S CHURCH, with a Dec. chancel and Perp. nave, and a fine 15–16C central tower.

Among the most striking features of the exterior are the w. front, a notable example of the transition from Dec. to Perp. (c. 1380–1411) and the great s. porch, with an outer E.E. arch (perhaps not *in situ*), surmounted by a Dec. canopy, and an inner Norman arch. The panelled ceiling of the chancel. the earliest part of the interior, is adorned with painted figures of English kings (1445; restored 1939, when that of George VI was inserted). The N.E. chapel (1330–49) is elaborately vaulted, and has flowing window-tracery. The rood screen and misericords (c. 1445) deserve attention. The nave was carefully restored by Sir Gilbert Scott, and its roof was renewed in 1937. The N. aisle arcade was destroyed in 1520, when the tower collapsed, and on its pillars are angles with shields recording the names of those who contributed to the rebuilding in 1524. The rich sculpture throughout is well preserved (and includes a rabbit which inspired Lewis Carroll to create the 'White Rabbit').

In Saturday Market, the principal square, is the charming *Market Cross* (1714), whence the main street leads towards the minster, passing on the right the *Guildhall,* with a Georgian court-room (1762; good ceiling).

**Beverley Minster (interior length 334 ft, width 64 ft, across the transepts 168 ft), dedicated to St John the Evangelist, is one of the few great English churches with a double set of transepts, and in size and splendour it is more than the equal of some English cathedrals. It is especially noteworthy for the purity and loveliness of the E.E. work (13C), and the splendour of the Perp. w. front.

John of Beverley (d. 721), Bishop of Hexham and of York, died and was

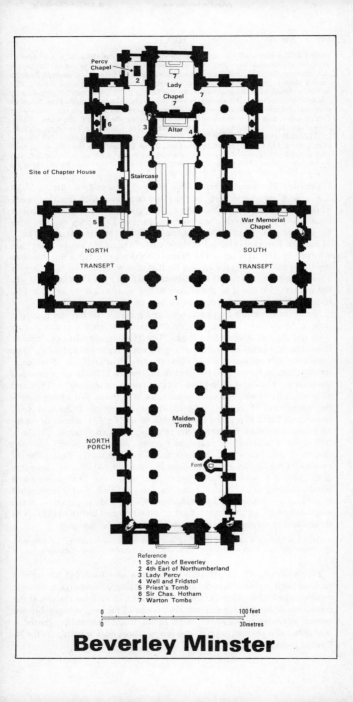

Percy
Chapel

2

Lady
Chapel
7

7

6

3

Altar

4

Site of Chapter House

Staircase

5

War Memorial
Chapel

NORTH

SOUTH

TRANSEPT

TRANSEPT

1

Maiden
Tomb

NORTH
PORCH

Font

Reference
1 St John of Beverley
2 4th Earl of Northumberland
3 Lady Percy
4 Well and Fridstol
5 Priest's Tomb
6 Sir Chas. Hotham
7 Warton Tombs

0   100 feet
0   30 metres

Beverley Minster

buried at the monastery founded by him at Beverley on the site of a chapel of St John the Evangelist. Miracles supposedly wrought at his tomb led to his canonization in 1037, and kings, from Athelstan to Henry V, conferred benefits on the church, in gratitude for victories won after pilgrimages to his shrine. The minster, rebuilt after its destruction by the Danes in 866, was much disfigured by fire in 1188; and in 1213 the central tower fell down. Though much of the Norman core was preserved, its restoration during the next two centuries was mainly on Gothic lines; and the blending of styles that makes the church, the work of centuries, appear of single design is soon apparent. The Choir and Transepts are E.E. (c. 1220–60), the Nave mainly Dec. and Perp.; the Perp. *Façade (with slender twin towers, 163 ft high) is the finest of its kind in England. In the 18C the church was saved from ruin by restoration under Hawksmoor, and a further restoration was carried out in 1866–68 by Sir Gilbert Scott.—The towers may be ascended on weekdays (10–4.30; fee).

Interior. The usual entrance is by the N. Transept door. In the NAVE E.E. (two E. bays) and Perp. (w. bay) are combined with fine Dec. work of the first half of the 14C. In the s. aisle, which is the earlier and better in detail, are the massive late-Norman font of Frosterley marble, with an elaborate cover of 1726, and the canopied 'Maiden Tomb' (Dec.). St John of Beverley is buried at the E. end of the nave. The w. doors are adorned by 18C carving.—The *GREAT TRANSEPT (E.E.) is notable (like the transepts at York) for having both E. and w. aisles. In the s. arm is a painting (temp. James I) of Athelstan making a grant of sanctuary to the minster (938), and in the E. aisle of the N. arm is a remarkable 14C tomb with the effigy of Precentor Gilbert de Grimsby (d. 1306).

We enter the choir by the N. aisle and pass on the left the beautiful double *Staircase (13C; a very rare feature) formerly communicating with the chapter house (destroyed). The *CHOIR, a perfect example of E.E., has a wealth of wood-carving in the *Stalls (c. 1520–24). The collection of misericords (68 in all) is the largest in England. The Snetzler organ dates from 1769, restored in 1880 when Gilbert Scott designed the screen. The front of the Dec. altar-screen was renewed in 1826 and adorned in 1897 with statues and mosaics. On the N. side of the altar is the magnificent *Percy Tomb (c. 1350) to the memory of Idoine, wife of the second Lord Percy, the masterwork of the English school of sculptors (best seen from the top of the reredos; apply to verger). On the s. side is the 'Fridstool', or peace chair (temp. Athelstan), which afforded inviolable sanctuary until the Reformation.—The lovely RETRO-CHOIR, or *Lady Chapel*, has an E. window (inserted in 1416) containing fine glass (13–15C), some collected from other windows. The vaulting and blind arcading at the back of the reredos (c. 1340), with Flamboyant tracery, are notable. In the small *Percy Chapel* (15C), to the N., is the mutilated tomb of the fourth Earl of Northumberland (d. 1489). The stone carving throughout the minster repays careful attention.

At the s. end of Lairgate (w. of the minster) is *Lairgate Hall* (1770–80), now municipal offices, with a Chinese room containing handpainted wallpaper.

37½ m. **HULL**, officially the city of *Kingston upon Hull* (285,500 inhab.) ranking third in point of cargo tonnage among English seaports, is situated on the N. bank of the Humber (here 1 ¾ m. wide), 20 m. from the sea, at the confluence of the little river Hull. Hull is one of the largest vegetable oil-extracting centres in the world, and is an important flour-milling centre. It is a timber and petroleum port, and is now also a busy transit port for N. Europe from the North.

Railway Stations, *Paragon; Corporation Pier*, for the ferry (see below) to *New Holland*, whence trains run to Grimsby, Lincoln, etc.

Hotels in Ferensway and Paragon St.; also in Beverley Rd., Anlaby Rd., and Jameson St.

Post Office, Lowgate.—INFORMATION CENTRE, Central Library (Albion St.).

Bus Station in Ferensway.—FERRIES from Corporation Pier c. every hr to *New Holland* (cars also).

Steamers ply regularly to *Gothenburg*. CAR FERRY SERVICE daily to *Rotterdam*.

Theatres. *New*, Kingston Sq. *Arts Centre*, Spring St.—CONCERTS, etc., at the City Hall, and Middleton Hall (University).

History. Hull was deliberately selected and laid out as a seaport by Edward I (1293–99)—an origin different from that of any other town in England. The port contributed ships to fight the Armada and was noted for its warships in the 18C; the Lord Mayor ranks as 'Admiral of the Humber'. The refusal of Sir John Hotham, the governor, to admit Charles I to the town in 1642 (though he had been hospitably entertained in 1639) was the first overt act of rebellion in the Civil War; and in 1643 and 1644 the town resisted sieges by the Royalists. Andrew Marvell, who was member of Parliament for Hull from 1658 till his death, received 6/8d.

a day during session for his services, and is often cited (perhaps erroneously) as the last paid borough member before the resolution of 1911 established the present payment of members. William Wilberforce (1759–1833) was a native of Hull.—Some of the streets preserve their quaint old names, e.g. 'Land of Green Ginger' and 'Rottenherring Staithe.'

Remains of the medieval walls have been excavated in North Walls, s. of the Technical College. The Castle, one of the last defensive works carried out by Henry VIII (1541), has been excavated on the E. bank of Hull river (now the Victoria dock area); part of the site may be opened to the public.

From the *Railway Station*, opposite which is the City War Memorial, the broad and attractively planted Paragon St. leads E. to QUEEN VICTORIA SQUARE, with *City Hall* and the *Town Docks Museum*. The Court Room of the former Docks Board survives and there are displays of whaling, trawling, and other fishing activities. On the s. side is the **Ferens Art Gallery** (adm. weekdays 10–5.30, Sun 2.30–4.30; rfmts). The exhibits are frequently rearranged; works not on show may be seen on request. The collection includes: *Bonington*, *Seascape; Rubens*, Triumph of Hope; *Hanneman*, Andrew Marvell; portraits by *Joos van Cleve, Frans Hals*, and *Gheeraerts the Younger; William Dobson*, Portrait of a Musician; *Richard Wilson*, Crow Castle; *Cesare D'Arpino*, Transfiguration; *José Ribera*, Portrait; *Guercino*, David and Goliath (fresco); and sculpture including works by *Foggini, Nollekens, Epstein*, and *Moore*.

Farther E. the spacious square, called QUEEN'S GARDENS, laid out on the site formerly occupied by the Queen's Dock (1778; filled in 1930–34), is slowly being surrounded by new administrative buildings. On the N. side are the *Custom House* (1964) and the headquarters of the *City Police*, between which will be erected the Central Museum; at the E. end is the Wilberforce Monument (1834), backed by the *College of Technology*, and (l.) the *College of Commerce*. The *Nautical College* is rising in George St., behind a multi-story car park, and the skyline to the N. is dominated, at present, by the tower of Kingston House.

From Queen Victoria Square, Whitefriargate leads s.E. to the oldest part of the town, which, despite its decay, has more character and interest for the visitor than the area to the N. with its wide featureless thoroughfares. Parliament St., on the left, preserves some 18C façades. We follow Trinity House Lane (r.) past *Trinity House* (rebuilt 1753), a 14C foundation for the relief of distressed mariners and, since 1787, for the training of seamen. Just beyond is *Holy Trinity, an exceptionally long parish church (272 ft). The transepts and choir were begun c. 1291, the nave just a century later.

This church is noteworthy for the early use of brick (introduced from the Low Countries) in the chancel and transepts, for its fine central tower (150 ft high), and for its variety of window-tracery. A tomb in the s. choir-aisle is supposed to be that of Sir William de la Pole (d. 1366), first mayor of Hull and ancestor of the earls and dukes of Suffolk. The font (c. 1370) and the modern glass are noteworthy. In the choir are some bench-ends of c. 1370, and in the retro-choir a fine but over-charged communion table of 1770.

The open-air market (held on Tues, Fri, and Sat), backed by a group of trees and the great brick church, strongly suggests a Netherlandish influence. To the s.w. of the church is the old *Grammar School*, rebuilt in 1583, where Marvell and Wilberforce were educated. The E. end of the church gives upon Market Place with a gilt statue of William III. From the statue Queen St. runs s. to *Victoria* or *Corporation Pier*, where the ferry boats start. Near by is a statue of Sir William de la Pole (see above), whose house was excavated in 1971, at 34 High St. (across car park). Lowgate continues Market Place to the N., past (l.) the Market Hall and Hepworth's Arcade, an art nouveau work. Beyond, the tower of the Perp. church of St Mary (enlarged 1863) projects over the pavement. The narrow Bishop Lane leads to *High Street*, parallel with Lowgate, now a mere back-lane, retaining its wood-block surface, and several fine merchants' houses (with access to the harbour). *Maister House* (No. 160), built in 1743, contains a *Staircase, decorated by Joseph Page, with a balustrade by Bakewell. It is now owned by the N.T. (adm. Mon–Fri 10–5, staircase only). Opposite in the old Corn Exchange, is the Mortimer **Archaeological and Transport Museum** (adm. daily, 10–5; Sun 2.30–4.30) with a good collection of horse-drawn vehicles and motor-cars. The prehistoric, Roman, and Saxon antiquities include the Roos Carr Images (late Bronze Age), the important Roman finds from Brough-on-Humber, and the splendid Roman mosaic pavements from Rudston; the pavement from Brantingham will not be on view until the archaeological collections are removed to the new Central Museum (see above). Farther on is ***Wilberforce House** (adm. as above), the Elizabethan house (with a charming garden) where the great abolitionist was born in 1759 and where Charles I was entertained in 1639. It contains a *Historical Museum* (with period rooms), a model of part of the N. walls excavated in 1969 (see above), Hull silverware, part of the Swine hoard of coins, relics of Wilberforce, and a collection referring to the abolition of the colonial slave-trade. The museum extends into the adjoining Georgian houses (Nos. 23 and 24), both beautifully restored, with collections of costumes, arms, and relics of past industries. We may return to the centre along Alfred Gelder St. past the imposing *Guildhall* (by Sir Edwin Cooper), and *Law Courts*.

To the s. of the station, in Osborne St., is the *Danish Church*, built in 1954 to replace the church bombed in 1941. Thence Porter St. and Hessle Rd. lead through a largely rebuilt area to (2¼ m.) *Pickering Park*. Here the *Maritime Museum* (adm. 10–5, Sun 2.30–4.30) illustrates the shipping and fisheries of Hull, including the Greenland whale-fishery, for which Hull was until 1865 an important centre.—In Cottingham Rd., 2¼ m. N.W. of the centre, is the University, founded in 1927 as University College by T. R. Ferens and raised to its present dignity in 1954. The red-brick buildings blend well, and include *Middleton Hall* (1967), with the University Art Collection consisting of English art (1890–1940), and the *Gulbenkian Building* (1969), an audio-visual centre.—Farther w. is the old village of *Cottingham*, where the fine church (Dec. and Perp.) contains the over-restored brass of Rector Nic. de Luda (d. 1383), who built the chancel. Cottingham, with Anlaby and Hessle, forms the district of *Haltemprice*.

Apart from the older Town Docks, the Docks at Hull extend along the river frontage for nearly 7 m. and have an aggregate water-area of about 200 acres. The *King George Dock* (53 acres; 1914), modernized in 1964, is the largest dock on the N.E. coast and from that and from the *Alexandra Dock* steamers maintain services to all parts of the world.

To the E. of Hull lies the flat corn-growing district of HOLDERNESS, noted for its churches and for the bathing resorts of *Hornsea* (18¼ m. N.E.), and *Withernsea* (20½ m. E.). A public footpath (c. 5 m.) encircles Hornsea Mere, a sanctuary for birds. The pottery is open to visitors. On the main road to Withernsea (A 1033) are (6 m.) *Hedon*, a famous port before Hull was dreamt of, and (16 m.) *Patrington*, each with an unusually striking church. *Hedon Church, known as the 'King of Holderness', has a Dec. nave, E.E. choir and transepts, and a noble Perp. tower. The tracery in the windows of the three E. bays of the nave is exceptionally fine. *Patrington Church, the 'Queen of Holderness', with a central spire 189 ft high, is a beautiful example of the Dec. style; the w. window, the vaulted Lady Chapel (s. transept), the Easter Sepulchre, and the exquisite capitals, should be noted.

Andrew Marvell (1621–78) was born in the rectory of *Winestead*, 1½ m. N.W. of Patrington.—From Patrington a road goes on to (6 m.) *Easington*, beyond which the coast ends (c. 13 m. from Patrington or Withernsea) in *Spurn Head*, a causeway of sand and pebbles overgrown with sharp-pointed rushes and marked by two lighthouses. The last 4 m. of the road (cars adm. on sufferance, fee) runs through a nature reserve, with a bird-migration observatory. No trace has survived of the port of *Ravenspur*, where Bolingbroke landed in 1399 ("upon the naked shore of Ravenspurg" and Edward IV in 1471 on his return from exile, nor of *Ravenser* (the 'Hrafnseyrr' of Icelandic saga), its Danish predecessor, whence Olaf, son of Harald Hardrada set sail for Norway in 1066 after his father's defeat and death at Stamford Bridge. The medieval cross of Kilnsea, another eroded village, still stands at Hedon.—The road (B 1238) from Hull to Hornsea runs viâ (8 m.) *Sproatley* and (12 m.) *Aldbrough* (Restaurant). *Burton Constable*, an impressive mansion of 1570, altered in the 18C, with work by Adam, Carr, and Wyatt in the interior, is 1½ m. N. of Sproatley. The house is open Whitsun–Sept, daily exc. Mon & Fri 1–6 (grounds from 12; fee; rfmts). Beyond Hornsea the Bridlington road goes on to (5½ m.) *Skipsea*, with a large Norman motte-and-bailey castle.

From Hull to *Selby*, see p. 618; to *Lincoln*, see Rte 58.

71   YORK AND DONCASTER TO BERWICK

A   From York

ROAD, 145½ m.—A 19. 23 m. *Thirsk*—A 168. 32 m. *Northallerton*—A 167. 50 m. **Darlington**. Thence to Berwick, see Rte 71B.

RAILWAY, 147½ m., part of the main line from London to Edinburgh. To Darlington in 40–60 min.; to Newcastle in c. 1½ hr; to Berwick in c. 2½ hrs.— Principal stations: 22¼ m. *Thirsk*.—30 m. **Northallerton**, junction for *Stockton, Hartlepool*, etc.—44 m. **Darlington**, junction for Middlesbrough, Redcar, and Saltburn, and for *Bishop Auckland* (Rte 72D).—66½ m. **Durham**.—72 m. *Chester-le-Street*.—80½ m. Newcastle, for *Tynemouth, South Shields, Sunderland*, etc., and for *Hexham* (Rte 73).—147½ m. **Berwick**.—Only a few trains stop at (97 m.) *Morpeth*, and (115¾ m.) *Alnmouth*.

We quit *York* (Rte 68) by Bootham.—4 m. *Skelton* has a beautiful little church of 1247. About 3 m. N.W. is *Beningbrough Hall* (N.T.; adm. Apr–Oct, Wed–Sun & BH, 2–6; fee) an early 18C mansion notable for its woodwork and grounds (open from 11), with an American arboretum.— 13 m. *Easingwold* (Hotel) has a large and pleasant green. In the church is the old parish coffin, formerly used to convey the bodies of the poor to the grave. *Raskelf*, 2 m. N.W., has the only wooden church tower in the county. At *Alne* (4¼ m. S.W.) the church doorway (1160) is carved with animals (named) from the medieval bestiary. The 'Sterne Country' lies to the E. (see Rte 69B).

23 m. **Thirsk** (Hotel), 1¼ m. E. of its station, has a good Perp. church and a racecourse. Here was born Thomas Lord (1755–1832) of the Cricket Ground. The town makes a useful centre for exploring the North Yorkshire moors.

32 m. **Northallerton** (8750 inhab.; Hotel), the county town of North Yorkshire, has a fine church (mostly 12–13C) with a striking Perp. tower. About 3 m. N. near the main road was fought the *Battle of the Standard* (1138).

From Northallerton to *Wensleydale, Hawes*, and *Kendal*, see Rte 72A.

At (46½ m.) *Croft* (Hotel), where we cross the winding Tees and enter County Durham, the old rectory was the boyhood home of 'Lewis Carroll'.

Byron spent his honeymoon at *Halnaby Hall* (now demolished), 3 m. S.W.—

Sockburn, 5 m. s.e., with its ruined church containing Anglian fragments, is attractively placed on the Tees.

50 m. **Darlington,** and thence to Berwick, see Rte 71B.

B From Doncaster

The MAIN ROAD (A 1), greatly improved in recent years, by-passes a large number of the towns and villages (including Doncaster) that lined the former Great North Road, and crosses many of the transverse roads by means of fly-overs or underpasses. Beyond Scotch Corner a short section of the old alinement is designated Motorway, but beginning with the Darlington by-pass, the motorway thereafter follows a new alinement to beyond Durham, while the old road is re-numbered A 167. A 1 (M) then diverges E. to cross the Tyne by tunnel below Jarrow, rejoining the old alinement at Seaton Burn. Though avoiding Newcastle, this is considerably longer. The present description is for the most part of the old road, on which lie most of the points of interest.

ROAD, 175 m.—16 m. *Brotherton.*—32 m. *Wetherby.*—44 m. *Boroughbridge.*— 71½ m. *Scotch Corner.*—79½ m. *Darlington.*—98 m. *Durham.*—112½ m. Newcastle. —127 m. *Morpeth.*—146 m. *Alnwick.*—175 m. *Berwick.*—RAILWAY, see Rtes 68 and 71A.

Doncaster, see Rte 68. A 638 leads N.W. across the Don.—4¾ m. *Adwick-le-Street* (½ m. r.) has a 12–16C church with the tomb of James Washington (c. 1580).—At (6 m.) we reach the end of the Doncaster by-pass and turn right on A 1, while A 638 continues W. to Wakefield.— At (8½ m.) *Barnsdale Bar* A 1 quits the Roman line, which runs to the w. as A 639 and A 656 through Pontefract and Castleford (p. 567). *Robin Hood's Well* (rebuilt by Vanbrugh), 1 m. s., marks the centre of the former forest of Barnsdale, reputedly a favourite haunt of the outlaw.—11 m. *Wentbridge* (Motel, Hotel) is by-passed to the E. by a superb *Viaduct (1962).—12½ m. *Darrington* church has a remarkable Lady Chapel with a small gallery above its entrance and 15C stained glass.—At (15 m.) *Ferrybridge* A 1 crosses the Aire by a new bridge, leaving Carr's bridge of 1789 for foot traffic. We enter an unattractive industrial area, dominated by the eight huge cooling towers of (16 m.) *Brotherton*, three of which fell in a gale in 1965. Particularly unpleasant are the stagnant scummy pools used for chemical settlement.

Here A 162 diverges on the right for Tadcaster and York. It traverses the ancient district of *Elmet*, passing (2¾ m.) *Monk Fryston* (where Monk Fryston Hall, 1 m. E., is now a hotel) on the Selby road.—5¾ m. *Sherburn-in-Elmet*, where the part-Norman church contains the halves of a 14C *Cross-head, foolishly divided when it was rediscovered c. 1850. *Steeton Hall*, 1½ m. s.w., has a 14C gatehouse. The *Church of *Birkin*, 3½ m. E. of Brotherton, is an unspoilt little late-Norman building of c. 1140, with a remarkable doorway and capitals, and a vaulted apse.— To the left, 2¾ m. N.W. of Brotherton, a road leads to (¾ m.) *Ledsham* and (3½ m.) *Kippax*, both with early 11C churches. *Ledston Lodge*, N. of the former, is a striking example of a 17C hunting-lodge.

At (24 m.) *Aberford*, ¼ m. w. on the Roman line, Parlington Park has an arch, dated 1783, celebrating 'liberty in North America triumphant'. *Lotherton Hall* (1 m. E.; open daily), with the Gascoigne art collections (Batoni portrait), 18C silver race cups, and costume galleries, was presented to the City of Leeds in 1968.—We cross the Leeds–York road at (26¼ m.) *Bramham Moor. —* 28 m. *Bramham* is 1½ m. N.E. of *Bramham Park* (adm. Easter–Sept, Sun, Tues, Wed, Thurs, & BH, 1.15–6; fee), a Queen Anne mansion in beautiful grounds in French classical style.— 32 m. *Wetherby* (Restaurant), a market town on the Wharfe, can be by-passed.

At *Walton*, 3 m. E. beyond the racecourse, is the *National Lending Library for Science and Technology*, the largest collection in the country of literature in these fields, with a public reading-room.

Bardsey, 4¼ m. s.w., on A 58, was the birthplace of William Congreve (1670–1729) and has a late Norman church with a Saxon tower. To *Harrogate*, see Rte 67.

At (35¼ m.) *Walshford* we cross the Nidd.—The new by-pass, bridging the river, has diminished the importance of (44 m.) **Boroughbridge** (Hotels), where the traffic of six roads crossed the Ure, among them the Roman road, rejoining its N. line after diverging viâ York. Here the Duke of Lancaster was defeated by Edward II in 1322; at the Crown, then the Tancreds' manor-house, the pro-Catholic 'Rising of the Northern Earls' came to an abortive end in 1569. About ¼ m. s.w. of the village are the *Devil's Arrows*, three gritstone monoliths, c. 20 ft high.

Aldborough, ¾ m. E., with a 14–15C church (large 14C brass), was the Roman city of *Isurium*, an early headquarters of the IX Legion. In the garden of the *Aldburgh Arms Inn* can be seen two tessellated pavements (apply to publican). Farther up, a MUSEUM (adm. daily, Sun from 2) occupies the site of the s. gate; in the grounds behind, is a section of city wall.—*Newby Hall* (p. 616), c. 2½ m. N.W., is reached viâ Skelton.

Beyond the Ripon road on the left we pass Dishforth airfield (r.).—60½ m. **Leeming Bar** (Motel), for Wensleydale (Rte 72A), is by-passed to the w., as is also (66½ m.) *Catterick*, with a good 15C church.— 67½ m. *Catterick Bridge* (Hotel), on the Swale, has a racecourse and a large military camp, 'the Aldershot of the North' (3 m. w.). The bridge dates from 1425 and some traces of the Roman *Cataractonium* are visible on the left of the road leading to the camp.

Kiplin Hall, 4½ m. s.e. of Catterick Bridge, was built in 1616 by Lord Baltimore, founder of the state of Maryland.—For *Richmond* and *Swaledale*, see Rte 72B.

At (71½ m.) *Scotch Corner* (Hotel) A 66 diverges N.W. for Greta Bridge (10 m.), Teesdale, Appleby, etc. (see Rte 72C). The A 1 becomes a motorway and 1½ m. farther N. bears right, while the Roman road continues as B 6275 viâ Piercebridge (p. 670) to Bishop Auckland. Three miles farther on we quit the motorway by a spur, and crossing the Tees enter County Durham.

79½ m. **Darlington** (Hotels), with 85,900 inhab., the location of large iron and steel works and a centre of engineering, notably bridge-building, owes its rapid industrial growth to the institution of the railway (see below). W. T. Stead was editor here (1870–80) of the 'Northern Echo', the first of the halfpenny papers. The *Church of St Cuthbert (formerly collegiate) is a fine E.E. structure of 1180–1220. The spire was added in the 14C. Inside are a curious stone rood-screen (added to strengthen the central tower), stall work of the time of Card. Langley (1406–37), and a 17C Gothic font cover. Church Lane, to the N., is a quaint relic of old Darlington.

The opening in 1825, through the joint exertions of George Stephenson and Edward Pease, of the 'Stockton & Darlington Railway', the pioneer passenger line in England, laid the foundation of Darlington's heavy industry. The No. 1 Locomotive, which drew the first train at a rate of 10–13 m. per hour, is exhibited at North Road Station Railway Museum; here, too, is the Derwent engine (1845).— Ben Jonson bought a new pair of shoes at Darlington on his way to Hawthornden to see Drummond in 1618

From Darlington to *Swaledale*, see Rte 72B; to *Teesdale*, Rte 72C; to *Weardale*, Rte 72D.

FROM DARLINGTON TO STOCKTON, MIDDLESBROUGH, AND SALTBURN, 28¼ m.

Railway to Stockton in c. ½ hr; to Middlesbrough in ½ hr and Saltburn in 1 hr—A 66 runs due E. viâ (1½ m.) *Haughton-le-Skerne*, with an attractive green and a Norman church containing good woodwork (c. 1660).—At 9 m. we reach the county borough of **Teesside** (395,500 inhab.), constituted in 1965 to include Stockton, Thornaby, Billingham, Middlesbrough, and Redcar.—11 m. **Stockton** (Hotel), with ship-repairing yards and ironworks, is also the birthplace of Thomas Sheraton (1751–1806). In the wide High St., a characteristic of Teesside (comp. Yarm), are the parish church (1710) and the Town Hall of 1736; at No. 59 in 1827 John Walker invented and sold the first practical matches. *Preston Hall*, 2¼ m. s.w. (off A 19), contains a museum of arms and armour, local bygones, etc. (adm. free, Apr–Sept, weekdays, 10–6). To the N.E. of Stockton, on the Hartlepool road, *Norton* (2 m.) retains much of its character as a prosperous village with 18C houses; here the mother-church of Stockton has Saxon stonework and knightly effigies. *Billingham* (Hotel), farther on, where the church, enlarged in 1938, has a fine 10C tower, is a modern industrial town, the seat of the huge works of Imperial Chemical Industries, including petrochemical and fertilizer plants. It was the first town in England to have a central hot-water system (1965). The 'Forum' (1967) incorporates a theatre, two swimming pools, an ice rink, squash courts, and restaurants.

Leaving Stockton we cross the Tees to (12 m.) *Thornaby* (Hotel).—15 m. **Middlesbrough** (Motel, Hotel), on the s. side of the Tees estuary, is the chief place in the Cleveland steel and iron district and the see of a Roman Catholic bishop. Founded in 1830, it grew with enormous rapidity and has an important college of technology and a modern theatre (1957). The *Dorman Museum*, with natural history and local antiquities, and the *Art Gallery* are in Linthorpe Rd. (adm. weekdays 10–6). The Tees is crossed by the *Transporter Bridge* opened in 1911 (toll), N.E. to *Port Clarence* (for Hartlepool) and the *Newport Bridge*, N.W. to Billingham, opened in 1934, with a vertically lifting roadway between steel towers 182 ft high, and a main span of 270 ft. About 3 m. S.E. is *Ormsby Hall* (N.T.; adm. May–Sept on Wed & Sat 2–6; fee), with 18C plasterwork, 1½ m. w. of which lies *Marton* (Hotel), the birthplace of Capt. James Cook (1728–79). The Birthplace Museum, in Stewart Park, was opened in 1978. A monument close by marks the site of the cottage of his birth.—23½ m. **Redcar** (Hotels) is a popular seaside resort. At *Kirkleatham*, 2¾ m. s., is an almshouse of 1676 with a museum containing a boxwood *Carving of St George and the Dragon (15C). Our road skirts the dunes to (25 m.) *Marske-by-the-Sea* (Hotel), then turns inland.

28½ m. **Saltburn** (Hotels) is a pleasant seaside resort (19,000 inhab. with Marske), with good public gardens, and golf links. To the E. rises the prominent *Huntcliff* (549 ft). To Whitby, see Rte 69B.—The return to Middlesbrough may be made viâ (2 m.) *Skelton*, where the 18C castle was a favourite haunt of Laurence Sterne and the 'Demoniac' club, and (5½ m.) *Guisborough* (Hotel), a pleasant residential town (13,900 inhab.), with the scanty but charming ruins (12–14C) of an Augustinian priory, founded by Robert de Bruce in 1119 (adm. daily, Sun from 2; fee), at the foot of the Cleveland Hills.

From Stockton (see above) A 19 and A 689 (r.) lead to (11 m.) **Hartlepool** (Hotel; also at Seaton Carew, 1½ m. s.), one of the chief exporting centres (96,900 inhab.) of the Durham coalfield which developed after 1845. Here was born Compton Mackenzie (1883–1972). The town was shelled by German cruisers in 1914. The *Gray Art Gallery and Museum* (10–5.30, Thurs 10–1, Sun 3–5), in Clarence Rd., contains Chinese porcelain, exhibits of local industries, English water-colours, and marine paintings. The original and much more interesting settlement, N.E. of the docks, dates from the foundation of a Saxon convent by St Hieu c. 640. St Hilda became abbess in 649 and raised the house to great eminence, but it was destroyed by the Danes in 800. A headstone of St Hilda's time is preserved in the parish church of *St Hilda (late Norman and E.E.; 1188–91), which has a heavily buttressed tower. Towards the sea there remains a section of the 13C *Town Walls*, including the *Sandwell Gate*.

From Stockton to *Durham*, see p. 653; to *Sunderland* and *Newcastle*, p. 661.

The old road runs N. as A 167.—84½ m. *Aycliffe*, on the Skerne, just beyond our crossing of the A 1, has a 13C church and two Saxon crosses (one with St Peter, head downwards). To the N.W. extends *Newton Aycliffe*, one of the least successful of the earlier 'new towns'.—88½ m. *Rushyford* (Hotel).—91 m. *Ferryhill* is on the S.E. edge of a coalfield, the centre of which is *Spennymoor.*—Beyond (94 m.) *Croxdale* (Hotel) we cross the

Wear (view). We then bear right on A 1050 to enter Durham by New Elvet. Or we may continue on A 167 to (97 m.) *Neville's Cross*, commemorating the battle of 1346, in which the Scots were decisively defeated and David II taken prisoner. Turning right there, we enter Durham by Crossgate and pass *St Margaret's* church (partly late-Norman).

98 m. **DURHAM** (24,700 inhab.) is built on a bold peninsula almost surrounded by the Wear, the most dramatic city site in England. On the summit of a richly wooded bank that rises abruptly from the river, tower, side by side, the great Norman cathedral and the castle of the prince-bishops. The university, first concentrated near the cathedral, has recently much expanded on the other bank of the Wear.

Hotels, inadequate in number, in Old and New Elvet.
Post Office, Claypath.
Buses from North Rd.
Boats on the Wear (hired below Elvet Bridge).

History. Durham grew up, somewhat like St Albans, round the nucleus of a cathedral that arose on virgin soil in 995 (see below). As count palatine the bishop held his own courts of law and ruled with the powers of a petty sovereign, in return for defending the N. marches of the kingdom, so that the city had, almost from the first, a curiously complex aspect—"half church of God, half castle 'gainst the Scot".

There is a magnificent view of the cathedral and castle from the Railway Station, which stands high above the city. North Road, below the impressive railway viaduct (1857), descends to the Wear at *Framwelgate Bridge* (famous *View), rebuilt c. 1400 by Bp. Skirlaw and widened in 1856. We ascend rapidly to the triangular MARKET PLACE, with the church of *St Nicholas* (rebuilt 1858), the *Town Hall* (1851), and a vigorous equestrian statue of the third Marquess of Londonderry (d. 1854). Hence the shortest ascent to the cathedral follows Saddler St. (r.; see below).

Those arriving by road will find convenient multi-story car parks by Milburngate Bridge or Elvet Bridge. The ancient *Elvet Bridge*, originally built by Bp. Puiset and widened in 1805 though retaining a few old bridge-houses, ascends to Saddler St.

On the farther side is the 18C 'suburb' of *Elvet*. Old Elvet, lined by several fine houses, leads to the *Courthouse* (1809–11), near which is an unexpected view of the cathedral. We follow New Elvet (r.), where a new Arts building has been erected, and pass *Kingsgate Bridge* (1963), a footbridge by Ove Arup, beside which is *Dunelm House* (1965), the Students' Representative Council building. Hallgarth St. (l.) leads to the Prison, adjoining which are 15C tithe-barns now used as a social club. We go on by Church St. to *St Oswald's*, a late 12C–15C church, partly rebuilt 1834, with the w. window by Ford Madox Brown. A path, crossing the churchyard, affords a magnificent *View of the cathedral and continues beside the river through the delightfully laid-out 'Banks'. We descend (¼ hr from Elvet) to *Prebends' Bridge* (1772–78; *View), from which a track leads N. to the *Old Fulling Mill* with local archaeological finds (open Wed & Fri), and another (l.) mounts steeply to the cathedral viâ College Green and the cloisters.

Those who ascend direct from Saddler St. cross the delightful Palace Green, passing on the right the *Castle* and the University Library, and on

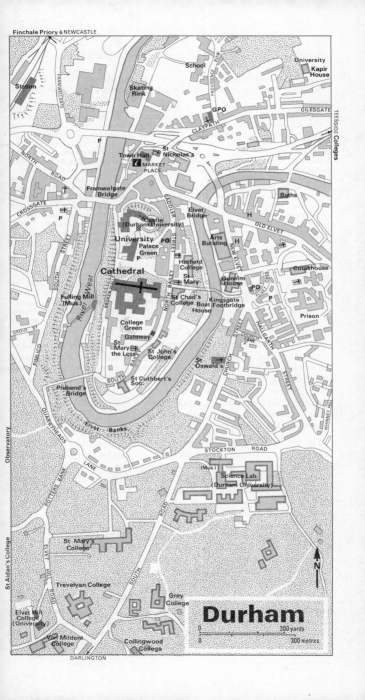

Durham

0   300 yards
0   300 metres

Finchale Priory & NEWCASTLE

Station

School

University Kapir House

GPO

GILESGATE

TEESSIDE Colleges

Skating Rink

PROVIDENCE ROW

CLAYPATH

FRAMWELLGATE

Town Hall

St Nicholas's

MARKET PLACE

NORTH ROAD

CROSSGATE

Framwelgate Bridge

Baths

Elvet Bridge

SADDLER STREET

Castle (Durham University)

University

Palace Green

Arts Building

OLD ELVET

NEW ELVET

Cathedral

Hatfield College

St Mary

Courthouse

Dunelm House

PO

Fulling Mill (Mus.)

River Wear

BROKEN WALK

St Chad's College

Kingsgate Footbridge

Prison

SOUTH STREET

GROVE ST

College Green

Gateway

NORTH BAILEY

Boat House

HALLGARTH STREET

CHURCH STREET

PIMLICO

St Mary the Less

St John's College

SOUTH BAILEY

St Oswald's

CHURCH LANE

TINY WHINN?

St Cuthbert's Soc.

Prebend's Bridge

Elvet Banks

QUARRYHEADS LANE

STOCKTON ROAD

Observatory

POTTERS BANK

(Mus.)

Science Lab. (Durham University)

St Aidan's College

ELVET HILL ROAD

St Mary's College

SOUTH ROAD

Trevelyan College

Grey College

N

Elvet Hill College (University)

Van Mildert College

Collingwood College

DARLINGTON

the left *Bp. Cosin's Hall* with a rich 17C doorway and *Almshouses* of 1666 (now a café).

The ****Cathedral,** dedicated to Christ and the Blessed Virgin, is one of the largest and most important of English churches and has few rivals in situation.

HISTORY. The see of Bernicia, originally founded at Lindisfarne by St Aidan in 635, followed the body of St Cuthbert (d. 687) to Chester-le-Street in 883, and thence, under Bp. Aldhun, to Durham in 995. Of the Saxon cathedral then erected there is no trace. The present great Norman church was begun by Bp. William of St Carilef in 1093, the choir and transepts being first put in hand, and the nave being completed by Bp. Flambard (1099–1128). The whole church was designed to be vaulted, and the ribbed vault of the N. choir-aisle (before 1096) is perhaps the oldest in England; the main choir vault was renewed early in the 13C. The Galilee, at the w. end, was added as a Lady Chapel by Bp. Puiset (or Pudsey; 1153–95), while the two w. towers (144½ ft) were probably built between 1150 and 1226. The original church terminated in three apses to the E.; but the present Chapel of the Nine Altars, in the shape of an E. transept and paralleled only at Fountains Abbey, was substituted (1242–78) by Bp. Farnham and his successors. The great central tower (218 ft) was rebuilt in the latter half of the 15C. The interior was damaged by the Scottish prisoners confined in the church after the battle of Dunbar (1650). Much of the Renaissance woodwork, misguidedly 'cleared up' by Salvin in 1845–47, has been recovered and replaced.

The Exterior remains bold and imposing, surviving its barbarous treatment in 1795 by Wyatt, who pared down the wall (N. side, E. end, W. towers) for a depth of 4 inches, thus ruining the proportion of the detail. The N.W. porch was spoilt by the removal of its upper story, and by recasting in its present form. The famous mid-12C *Sanctuary knocker is a reminder that Durham was a place of sanctuary throughout the Middle Ages. The figure of a cow at the N.E. perpetuates the legend that a woman seeking a dun cow acted as guide to Bp. Aldhun in choosing the site for his church.—The tower may be ascended on weekdays (fee).

Interior. The uninterrupted view up the church produces an impression described by Dr Johnson as one of "rocky solidity and indeterminate duration". No other great English church, save perhaps Peterborough and Norwich, retains its original Romanesque bulk so comparatively untouched; no Norman work elsewhere is so strongly individualised (an effect due largely to the great circular columns, with their remarkable incised ornament, and to the profusion of zigzag moulding); and none is on the whole so admirably proportioned.

The *Nave is built on the system of alternate single circular columns and clustered piers. The quadripartite ribbed vaulting is designed for single bays. The pointed transverse arches (finished in 1133) are probably the earliest pointed arches in a high vault anywhere in Europe. In the pavement between the second pair of piers from the w. is a cross of Frosterley marble beyond which, in accordance with the Benedictine rule, no woman was permitted to advance. The Renaissance font, removed as 'inappropriate' in 1845, was brought back from Pittington in 1935; its towering tabernacle is part of the magnificent woodwork with which Bp. Cosin (1660–72) endowed his cathedral. The existing w. window is an insertion of c. 1346. Part of the s. aisle was formerly screened off as the *Neville Chantry*, and two battered Neville effigies remain in the s. arcade. Farther w. is the case of the organ built by Father Smith (1683) to stand on the choir-screen.

The *GALILEE, entered from the w. end of the nave, is a remarkable example of Trans. work, begun by Bp. Puiset in 1176, but altered by Card. Langley (d. 1437), who built his altar-tomb (Pl. 7) in front of the w. door. It contains the simple 16C tomb of the Venerable Bede (Pl. 8; d. 735 at Jarrow; remains transferred hither in 1020); the inscription

('Hâc sunt in fossâ Bædæ venerabilis ossa') was cut in 1831. Here are preserved two reliefs (the Resurrection and Transfiguration; c. 1150–60) of the original nave screen. Above the arcade of the inner N. aisle are 13C wall-paintings of the Passion; those in the recess in the E. wall

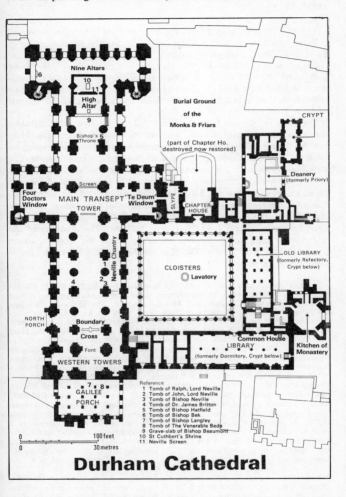

Durham Cathedral

Reference
1 Tomb of Ralph, Lord Neville
2 Tomb of John, Lord Neville
3 Tomb of Bishop Neville
4 Tomb of Dr. James Britton
5 Tomb of Bishop Hatfield
6 Tomb of Bishop Bek
7 Tomb of Bishop Langley
8 Tomb of The Venerable Bede
9 Grave-slab of Bishop Beaumont
10 St Cuthbert's Shrine
11 Neville Screen

(SS Cuthbert and Oswald) date from the late 12C. The same saints are depicted in modern windows by Hugh Easton in the nave.

The original Norman ends of the GREAT TRANSEPTS were altered in the 14C (N.) and 15C (S.) by the insertion of the present windows, but the vaulting of the N. transept is original (1104). The crossing is surmounted by an open lantern of unusual height and dignity. The statue of Bp. Barrington is by Chantrey. At the end of the S. transept is Prior Castell's Clock (c. 1500), the case of which, dismantled in 1845, was restored in 1938.

The *Choir is separated from the crossing by a light, open screen of coloured marbles by Sir Gilbert Scott, replacing the former screen of Bp. Cosin, removed in 1845. Cosin's fine stalls, however, survive. On the S. is the *Bishop's Throne*, the "highest in Christendom", the lower part of which, with a fine recumbent effigy, serves also for the monument of Bp. Hatfield (1345–81), who erected it. The magnificent stone *Altar Screen*, with its lofty open pinnacles, dates from 1372–80, the gift of John, Lord Neville.

The *Chapel of the Nine Altars (1242–78) harmonizes admirably, though wholly different in style, with the massively Romanesque choir; but the tracery of the great E. rose window is neo-Gothic tampering by Wyatt (1795). The slender polished shafts are of Frosterley marble. The rich *Bede Altar*, in the central chapel, was designed by S.E. Dykes Bower (1935). The fine 13C stone cross, to the S., came from the vanished abbey of Neasham, near Darlington. Behind the High Altar stood the *Shrine of St Cuthbert*, destroyed in 1540. The saint's body still rests below, notwithstanding the tradition, quoted in 'Marmion', that its secret burial-place is known to none "save of his holiest servants three". The candlesticks and tester were designed by Sir Ninian Comper and the wooden screen preserves four 17C panels. The plan of the original Norman apse is outlined on the floor.

Durham, as re-established in 995, was a secular church; but Bp. St Carilef made it monastic in 1083, by transferring hither the monks from the revived Benedictine houses of Jarrow and Monkwearmouth. The **Monastic Buildings** are clustered round the Cloister (c. 1388–1418), S. of the nave. Both doorways from the church are noteworthy, especially the Monks' Door (W.) with splendid ironwork of c. 1130. The w. range consists of the *Monks' Dormitory* (adm. weekdays; fee), built by Bp. Skirlaw (1388–1405) over a 13C undercroft and retaining its original timber roof. The walls are lined with book-presses; in the centre are displayed fragmentary 7–11C sculptured crosses. The undercroft contains a restaurant, bookshop, and the *Treasury. Here are shown Cathedral plate, the carved wooden *Coffin of St Cuthbert, made before 698 (restored), in which his body was carried on its famous wanderings, and the relics (including a fine pectoral cross of the mid-7C) and embroidered stoles (early 10C) found within it in 1827. Here also are illuminated MSS, a fine collection of seals (including early ones of the Washington family, and vestments. The *Kitchen* (no adm.), at the S.E. angle of the dormitory, is an octagonal chamber (1368), by Lewyn, with a vault recalling Moorish work. It now serves as a muniment room.—The *Refectory*, on the S. side, was rebuilt c. 1684 as the Chapter Library (adm. to scholars only). The *Prior's House* is now the *Deanery*.—In the E. range the Chapter House, completed under Bp. Geoffrey Rufus (1133–40) but partly destroyed in 1796, was restored in 1895.

From the cathedral cloisters we cross College Green to the *Gatehouse* (c. 1500), beyond which, in both North and South Bailey, are attractive houses and the churches of *St Mary-le-Bow* (1685), with a screen of 1707, and *St Mary-the-Less* (rebuilt), containing a fine 13C Majesty.

To the N. of the cathedral, on the opposite side of Palace Green, and placed so as to guard the exact neck of the peninsula, is the stately *Castle of the bishops, used by Durham University since 1836. Founded by the Conqueror in 1072, it was probably originally a mere system of defensive earthworks of the 'motte-and-bailey' type, and this plan has been retained through all subsequent mutations. The castle (fee) is open on weekdays in April (exc. last week), July–Sept 10–12.30, 2–5; rest of year, Mon, Wed, & Sat 2–4 (5 in May–June).

Passing through the 12C *Gatehouse* (much altered), we cross the courtyard and enter the castle by Bp. Cosin's Ionic portal. Visitors are conducted first to the *Kitchen*, with its huge fireplaces, recast by Bp. Fox in 1499 from Bp. Puiset's building. The *Great Hall*, dating from the late 13C, with a fine roof (c. 1350), was also altered by Fox. We ascend the splendid Renaissance staircase, added in 1662 by Cosin, to *Bp. Tunstall's Gallery* (1530–59) at the end of which is a *Chapel* (c. 1542) containing some good woodwork. A *Doorway "which may fairly be called the most magnificent example of late-Norman Romanesque art in England" leads from the gallery to the *State Rooms* (shown only on application to the Master), converted from the Lower Hall of Bp. Puiset, with 16C Flemish tapestries. We ascend next to the *Norman Gallery* of Puiset, once the upper or 'Constable's Hall', remarkable for its open wall-arcades. We finally descend a spiral staircase to the striking Norman *Chapel, on the ground floor, the earliest existing portion of the castle (c. 1072). The 14C *Keep*, on the ancient motte, was rebuilt in 1840 (not shown).

Durham University was founded in 1832 by Bp. Van Mildert, the last episcopal count palatine, who gave up the castle and part of his princely revenue for the purpose, thus endowing both a continuity of tradition and a position in the heart of the city. The University, much enlarged, consists of *University College* (occupying the castle), *Hatfield College* (in North Bailey), and *St Cuthbert's Society* (in South Bailey); also *Grey College* and *Van Mildert College*, for men; and *St Mary's College* (by Vincent Harris) and *St Aidan's College* (by Sir Basil Spence), for women—all these s. of the river. *St John's College* (in South Bailey) and *St Chad's College* (in North Bailey), Church of England theological colleges, are constituent colleges of the University. In 1937–63 King's College, Newcastle (comp. p. 659), was part of Durham University.

The GULBENKIAN MUSEUM (adm. weekdays 9.30–1, 2.15–5; Sun from 2.15; closed Sat & Sun aft Christmas–Easter & BH; fee), 1½ m. s. on Elvet Hill below St Aidan's, has notable *Collections of oriental art and archaeology.—*Neville's Cross College* is a training college for teachers, associated with the University, so also are *Bede College* (men) with a fine chapel (1939) by Mottistone and Paget, and *St Hild's College* (women), both s. of Gilesgate. Here, high above the river, is the church of *St Giles*, with early and late 12C work and an unusual 16C effigy.— Views of the cathedral and castle from the University Observatory, near Neville's Cross College, and from the upper end of South St. are worth seeking out.

The wooded banks of the Wear, both above and below the city, afford charming walks.—Of *Kepier Hospital*, ¾ m. N.E., on the right bank, originally founded in 1112 by Bp. Flambard, little remains save a 14C gatehouse.—*Sherburn Hospital*, 2½ m. E., retains the contemporary gatehouse of the hospital founded by Bp. Puiset in 1181.—*Ushaw College*, 4 m. W., was founded in 1808, in direct succession to the dispossessed seminary for Rom. Cath. priests at Douai. Visitors are admitted on Tues and Thurs (2–4) to the chapel and library.

*Finchale Priory (pron. 'Finkle'; adm. daily; Sun from 2; fee), 4 m. N. of Durham by lane and footpath, is charmingly situated on the left bank of the rocky Wear. It was founded as a cell to Durham Priory by a natural son of Bp. Puiset in 1196 on the site of the hermitage of St Godric, whose stone coffin was unearthed here in 1928. Most of the remaining buildings are of the 13C, the cloisters and undercroft 14C. The nave has sculptured capitals.—About 4½ m. s.w. is **Brancepeth**, where the *Castle* (no adm.), mostly rebuilt in the 19C, was the seat, prior to 1569, of the princely house of Neville. It now houses the research division of the Pyrex glass company. In the grounds stands the church of *St Brandon* (12–14C) with remarkable Neville monuments and *Woodwork by John Cosin (rector in 1626–44).—For *Weardale* and *Teesdale*, see Rtes 72c, and 72D.

FROM DURHAM TO SUNDERLAND, 13 m., A 690.—About 1 m. right at 4 m. is *Pittington*, where the church has an interesting N. arcade of c. 1175.—At (7 m.) *Houghton-le-Spring*, with good 16–18C houses, the fine 13C church contains the tomb of Bernard Gilpin, 'the Apostle of the North' (d. 1583).—From Houghton a longer route goes N. (A 182) to (11½ m.) **Washington** (Hotel), an expanding colliery 'new town', where the *Old Hall* (1610) incorporates fragments of the medieval house of the Washington family (N.T.; adm. daily exc. Tues 1–6; Nov–Feb, Wed, Sat & Sun only, 1–dusk; fee). Across the Wear is *Penshaw Monument*, a Doric temple erected to Lord Durham in 1844. We go on to (18 m.) Sunderland viâ (16 m.) *Hylton Castle* (adm. daily; Sun from 2; fee), a 15C gatehouse-keep with the arms of the Washingtons on its front.

FROM DURHAM TO STOCKTON, 19 m., A 177.—We cross the Wear near (1½ m.) *Shincliffe*.—5½ m. *Coxhoe Hall* (l.) was the birthplace of Elizabeth Barrett Browning (1806–61).—10½ m. *Sedgefield* (Hotel) has a church with a Perp. tower and a good 17C screen and stalls in Bp. Cosin's manner.—15¼ m. *Thorpe Thewles* is 1¾ m. S.W. of *Wynyard Park* (Marquess of Londonderry).—19 m. *Stockton*, see p. 647.

FROM DURHAM TO NEWCASTLE BY THE DERWENT VALLEY, 29¼ m. A 691, 694.— 8 m. *Lanchester* has a good 12–13C church with Roman columns in the N. arcade and a Roman altar (A.D. 244) in the porch, and (½ m. S.W.) remains of the Roman *Longovicium.*—12¼ m. At the cross-roads A 691 turns left for *Consett* (2 m.), with its huge steelworks (35,400 inhab.), and A 692 runs N.E. to *Tantobie* (3 m.) with Stanley Zoo. We go straight on, following the Roman road.—15 m. *Ebchester*, the burial-place of Surtees, stands on the site of the fort of *Vindomora* above the Derwent, and has Roman stones in its church tower. We turn E.— 16½ m. *Hamsterley*. At *Hamsterley Hall* (1770), c. 3 m. S.E., R. S. Surtees (1803–64), creator of 'Jorrocks', spent much of his life.—A 694 crosses the river for (20 m.) *Rowlands Gill*. On the S. bank, in the grounds of the dismantled *Gibside*, are a beautiful chapel, begun in 1760 by James Payne and completed in 1812 (with a three-decker pulpit), and a distinctive Column of Liberty, 140 ft high (1757). The church of *Tanfield* (2¼ m. S.E.) has 14C Marmion tombs. Causey Arch, near by, is the oldest railway bridge in the world (1727) built for a mine tramway.—28 m. *Newcastle*, see below.

We leave Durham by A 177 past the Durham Light Infantry Museum and County Hall and, at (99½ m.) *Framwellgate Moor*, rejoin A 167.— 104¼ m. *Chester-le-Street* (l.; Hotel), a colliery town (20,500 inhab.), lies on the site of Concangium, a Roman fort. Hither in 883, after eight years of wandering, the monks of Lindisfarne brought the body of St Cuthbert, and here it rested until the see was removed to Durham in 995. The church is remarkable for its spire (156 ft), its anchorite's cell, and the fourteen Lumley monuments in its 'Aisle of Tombs' (mostly Elizabethan forgeries).

About 1 m. E. is *Lumley Castle (Earl of Scarborough), a fine example of the local type of 14C castle (courtyard with angle-towers), altered by Vanbrugh. In 1946–70 it was the hall of residence for Durham University. Farther N., beyond the Wear, is the turreted *Lambton Castle* (19C), with a lion park.—At *Beamish* 3 m. W., is the North of England Open Air Museum (adm. Easter–Sept, Tues–Sun and BH 10–6; Mon in May, June, July & Aug; Oct–March, reduced hrs). Devoted to how the people of the North East lived and worked late last century, it contains a station, a colliery, a farm and an exhibition of bygones in Beamish Hall. An urban area is planned.

The old road continues N. as A 6127 through (107½ m.) *Birtley*, beyond which it crosses relics of the Bowes Railway, a rope-hauled standard-gauge colliery line (1826). At *Springwell*, on B 1288 to the E., a 1¼ m. section is preserved with a stationary haulage engine.—At (112 m.) **Gateshead** (Hotels), an industrial town (94,500 inhab.), the centre has yet to be freed from traffic. Grouped about Saltwell Park are the Library, Shipley Art

Gallery, a Theatre and Shipcote Swimming Baths. *St Mary's Church*, overlooking the Tyne, has fine 17C pews.—The road enters (112½ m.) Newcastle by the Tyne Bridge.

NEWCASTLE UPON TYNE, the county town of Northumberland, as well as of Tyne and Wear, itself of county rank in 1400–1974, stands on a steeply sloping site on the left bank of the Tyne, about 9 m. from its mouth. It has been the see of a bishop since 1882 and, with 222,200 inhab., is the chief city of N.E. England. The sarcasm 'to carry coals to Newcastle' is a tribute to the magnitude of its former principal industry, the export of coal, for which it was for generations famed. Steel and petro-chemicals are now more important; shipbuilding and electrical and marine engineering are also carried on on a very large scale. Richard Grainger (1798–1861), a speculative builder, aided by John Dobson (1787–1865) and other architects, is largely responsible for the dignified appearance of the centre of Newcastle, most of which will survive unchanged the present extensive alterations. The city is unusually well provided with covered markets, arcades, and public clocks.

Car Parks. *Manors* (multi-story), near N. end of Tyne Bridge; Claremont Rd (Town Moor), free, near the University; etc.

Good Hotels at and near the Station; in Grey St.; in Jesmond; etc: advanced booking is advisable.

Post Office (Pl. 14), St Nicholas St.—INFORMATION SERVICE, Central Library, New Bridge St. (Pl. 10); also at Tyne Commission Quay.

Town Buses. From the railway station to all parts of the city and suburbs; COUNTRY BUSES from Haymarket (Pl. 6) to *Whitley Bay*; *Rothbury*; *Alnwick* and *Berwick*; *Alnmouth* and *Bamburgh*; from Worswick St. (Pl. 10) to *Durham*; *Jarrow*; *Sunderland*; *Darlington*; etc.; and from Marlborough Crescent (Pl. 13) to *Hexham* viâ Corbridge; *Allendale*; *Carlisle*; etc.

Steamers from *Tyne Commission Quay*, 8¼ m. downstream, to N. European ports *(Oslo, Bergen, Esbjerg, Gothenburg)*.

Airport at *Woolsington*, 6 m. N.W. Services to *London, Belfast*, and *Dublin; Liverpool; Cardiff*, and *Bristol; Isle of Man; Rotterdam, Amsterdam*, and *Düsseldorf; Bergen*.

Theatres. *Theatre Royal* (Pl. 10), Grey St.; *University Theatre*, Barras Bridge; *People's* (beyond Pl. 4), Stephenson Rd., Heaton.—CONCERTS in the City Hall, in the Lit. and Phil. Soc., and at King's Hall in the University.—TOWN MOOR FESTIVAL, held in Race Week (3rd in June).

Sports Centre, *Lightfoot Stadium.*—SWIMMING BATHS, Northumberland Road; at Scotswood; Jesmond, etc.—GOLF on *Town Moor* and at *Gosforth*.

History. Newcastle, under the name of *Pons Ælius*, was a station on the Roman Wall, the line of which through the city has been traced. The foundation of the present city is due to the building here of a castle by Robert Curthose (eldest son of the Conqueror) on his return from his incursion into Scotland in 1080. The city suffered more than once (e.g. in 1342 and 1388) from the unfriendly proximity of the Scots, and it held out against them for ten weeks in 1644 on behalf of Charles I. Two years later Charles was here surrendered to the English Parliament by the Scots. The Royal Grammar School, now at Jesmond, was founded by Henry VIII. The locomotive industry, founded here by Robert Stephenson in 1823, closed its works in 1960.—Duns Scotus (d. 1308?) is said to have become a Franciscan monk at Newcastle. Notable among its natives are Mark Akenside (1721–70), the poet, Adm. Collingwood (1750–1810), Lord Eldon (1751–1838), Lord Armstrong (1810–1900), and John Forster (1812–76), the biographer of Dickens.

The **Cathedral** (*St Nicholas*; Pl. 10) stands in Mosley St, midway between Tyne Bridge and the Central Station. Formerly one of the largest parish churches in England, it was raised to its present dignity

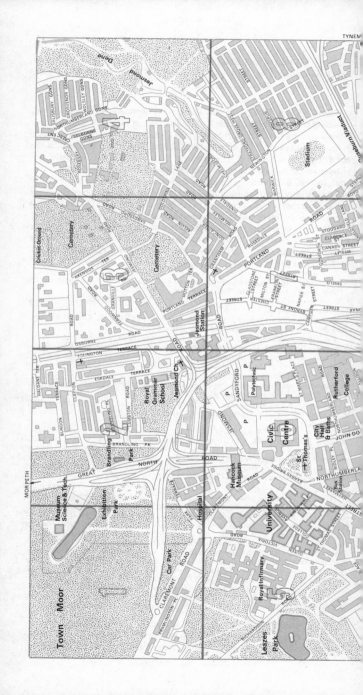

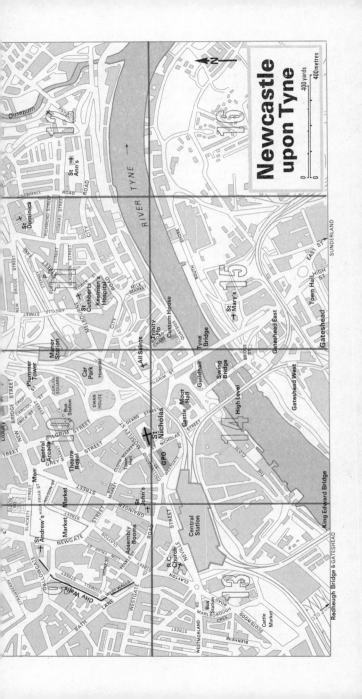

Newcastle upon Tyne

0   400 yards
0   400 metres

in 1882. Externally the main feature of note is the w. tower, crowned by a famous *Spire (194 ft) supported in the air by flying buttresses. This is the earliest (c. 1442) and best example of the 'crown spire' in Britain (since rebuilt), and almost certainly served as a pattern for St Giles's, Edinburgh.

The interior (1330–60) is noteworthy for the absence of capitals. Beneath the striking lierne vault of the tower stands the font, with a superbly carved *Canopy (c. 1500), likewise remarkable for its exquisite vault with a boss of the Coronation of the Virgin. Close to the font is a bust of Adm. Collingwood, who was here baptized and married. In St Margaret's Chapel, which interrupts a series of low-arched recesses in the s. aisle, is a medallion of 15C glass. The lectern dates from c. 1500. The upper part of the organ case survives from the original Harris organ of 1676. The crypt has 14C ribbed vaulting and a small internal 'wheel' window. In the s. choir-aisle are the magnificent German *Brass of Roger Thornton (d. 1429) and his wife, and a good 'thanksgiving' window of 1945. The so-called 'Hexham' Bible (1220), in the vestry, is shown on request.—Thomas Bewick, the engraver, had his workshop at the s.w. corner of the churchyard.

From the cathedral St Nicholas St. leads s. to the interesting remains of the *Castle (Pl. 14), the site of which is intersected by the railway. Restoration work was proceeding in 1971.

The *Black Gate*, a barbican of 1247 (named for a person not its colour), is one of the most remarkable examples of its kind in England. The upper part (added in 1618) houses the library of the Newcastle Society of Antiquaries. The noble though not very large *Keep*, on the other side of the railway, was built by Henry II in 1172–77 (adm. Tues–Sat 10–4 or 5, Mon from 2; fee). An external stairway over a fore-building containing the chapel mounts to the restored entrance (1848) at second-floor level. This arrangement, paralleled only at Dover, was probably the work of the same mason, one Maurice. From the *Hall*, which occupies the whole interior space of the keep, stairways descend to the beautiful *Chapel* (c. 1175–80), and the so-called *Garrison Room*, with its central pillar; and ascend to the rebuilt *Battlements*. Chambers and passages in the thickness of the walls can also be explored.

We cross Castle Garth and, passing the *Moot Hall* (1812) on our left, go through the s. postern gate to descend the steep Castle Stairs to the river. The *Swing Bridge* (1876), occupying the site of the Roman and medieval bridges, commands a fine view of the river and its bridges. Upstream, the *High Level Bridge*, by which the railway crosses from Gateshead, with a roadway at a lower level, was erected in 1845–49 by Robert Stephenson and Dobson. In Sandhill (l.) handsome 16–17C houses rise to four and five stories. A tablet on No. 41 marks the window through which Bessy Surtees eloped in 1772 to marry the future Lord Chancellor Eldon. Opposite is the *Guildhall* (shown on request at the Civic Centre), rebuilt by Robert Trollop in 1658 but later classicized, the rounded E. end being the work of Dobson (1823).

The Mayor's Parlour, panelled with paintings from the 17C Mansion House (demolished), has a splendid plaster ceiling. Opening out of the Great Hall, the rebuilt *Merchant Adventurers' Court* preserves a sumptuously carved chimneypiece of 1636. On the stairs is a statue of Charles II, originally on the old Tyne Bridge swept away in 1771.

The conspicuous *Tyne Bridge* (1925–28) has a single steel arch 531 ft in span and 193 ft above high water; the road level of 94 ft is reached by lift from the quay (closed Sat & Sun aft.). Quayside (with a Sun morn. market) leads E. past the *Custom House* (1766), altered c. 1840 by Sydney Smirke, and affords a fine view (l.) of *All Saints' Church* (in 1971 closed and difficult of access), rebuilt by David Stephenson in

1786–96 with a striking steeple and an elliptical nave. In Broad Chare, farther on, is *Trinity House* (adm. to court only), a foundation of 1492 with 18C hall and almshouses, the chapel of which has good Jacobean woodwork. Milk Market leads into City Road.

Across the busy thoroughfare are *The Keelmen's Hospital* (1701), a Dutch-style building of brick, and the *Sallyport* or *Well Knoll Tower*, at the crossing of Hadrian's Wall and the town walls.—*St Ann's Church* (1764–68), to the E. is by Wm. Newton.

Narrowly confined between City Road and the Swan House round-about stands *Holy Jesus Hospital*, an arcaded and Dutch-gabled alms-house of 1681–83, beautifully restored in 1971 to house the JOHN GEORGE JOICEY MUSEUM. The first floor is arranged chronologically with local history exhibits and the second has 'period' rooms, while the adjacent Austin Friars Tower (15C) displays armour. Below the monumental *Swan House* (1970), into which Dobson's Royal Arcade (1831) has been skilfully incorporated, pedestrian passages lead, viâ a court commemorating Sir Jos. Swan (p. 661), to Mosley St. On the corner of Pilgrim St., which leads N. from Tyne Bridge, is the Bank of England building. Mosley St. descends to GREY STREET (Pl. 10), the finest street in the city, a noble curve of buildings (1835–39) gently ascending in continuation of Dean St. (with its notable gabled façade of 1901) from the Swing Bridge. Grey St. is Dobson's masterpiece, though the *Theatre Royal* is by Benjamin Green. At the top is a *Column* (164 steps; Sat, Easter–Oct) to the second Earl Grey (1764–1845).

New Bridge St. leads E., passing the new Pearl Building at the N. end of Pilgrim St. Farther on the new John Dobson St. runs N. between the *Central Library*, by Sir Basil Spence, and the *Laing Art Gallery* (week-days 10–6, or 8 on Tues & Thurs; Sun 2.30–5.30), which includes among its collections English water-colours and Newcastle glass and silver, notably the Sawley flagon (1670).

In Croft St., opposite, is the *Plummer Tower* (adm. free, 10–1, 2.30–6), a relic of the medieval wall altered in 1742 and now containing exhibits of the city's archives.

Northumberland St., a shopping street with restricted vehicle access, continues the line of Pilgrim St. N. to Barras Bridge (Pl. 6), where Dobson's church of *St Thomas* (1825–30) forms a focal point between the Civic Centre and the University.

The *Civic Centre (1960–68), designed by George Kenyon and opened by King Olav V of Norway, has a quasi-monastic plan, cruciform with a central tower and an arcaded cloister garth enclosed by the administra-tive wings. A *Ceremonial Way*, lined with tall flambeaux and dominated by a huge bronze symbolizing the Tyne, leads to the elliptical *Council Chamber*. A pool in the garth is adorned with *Swans in flight, another bronze also by David Wynne, reflecting Newcastle's ties with the five Scandinavian lands. At the N. end extends the *Banqueting Hall*, plain and massive (124 ft by 47) in Clipsham stone, with deep-set slit windows. The *Tower* (250 ft) has a copper lantern, adorned with sea horses and crowned by the gilded three castles of the city's arms; it houses a carillon that plays traditional Tyneside tunes.

Opposite extends the **University of Newcastle upon Tyne**, formerly *King's College*, but granted its own charter in 1963 after being incorpor-ated with Durham University since 1937; its medical faculty, founded in 1834 as the College of Medicine, was amalgamated in 1937 with Armstrong College (1871), a noted school of engineering. Among the new buildings (1958–61) are the Library Extension, by Easton and Robertson, and the Physics Laboratories (1961), by Spence. King's Walk leads through a double gateway. Inside (l.) is the *MUSEUM OF ANTIQUITIES (adm. free; weekdays 10–5) constructed in 1960 to house the fine collection of the Society of Antiquaries of Newcastle and other items on permanent loan from Alnwick Castle.

The GROUND FLOOR is devoted to Roman altars, inscriptions, and relief sculpture, and a reconstruction of Carrawburgh Mithraeum.

The FIRST FLOOR, excellently displayed, includes the Whittingham sword (late Bronze Age); Iron Age finds from Ryton; the Æsica brooch (Celtic; A.D. 75–80) from Hadrian's Wall, and other similar brooches; a gladiator and the *Bear cameo, both from South Shields (3C), and a set of Roman military cooking-vessels (bronze; 2C) found near Ponteland; an Anglo-Saxon hanging bowl (the most northerly in England); the Falstone Latin/Runic inscription (8–9C); and part of a 10C cross from Alnmouth. Notable also are scale models of Hadrian's Wall; original and reconstructed Roman body armour; and a facsimile of the Corbridge lanx (p. 664). The *Hatton Gallery* in the Department of Fine Art contains 16C–18C Italian paintings.—The Department of Classics has a *Museum* of Greek and Etruscan art and archaeology.

Beyond the University is the *Hancock Museum* (Pl. 6; adm. weekdays 10–5; also Sun 2–5 Easter–Sept; fee), with collections of natural history and geology (including fossils from the coal-measures), as well as an important series of water-colours and wood engravings by Bewick (see above). Farther N. is the extensive *Town Moor* (Pl. 1), part of which is *Exhibition Park*, with the *Museum of Science and Engineering* (adm. summer 10–6 or 8. Sun 2.30–5.30; winter 10–4.30, Sun from 1.30; fee), an interesting collection of models, drawings, etc., illustrating the industries of N.E. England. Noteworthy are Stephenson's locomotive (built 1826); Armstrong's first breech-loading gun and first hydraulic engine; and the 'Turbinia', Sir Charles Parsons's first turbine-driven vessel (1894).

Beyond the little *Brandling Park*, in the E. side of the Great North Rd. (subway), stands the *Royal Grammar School.*—About 1½ m. N.E. of BARRAS BRIDGE is Jesmond **Dene** (Pl. 4), an attractive dell with steep wooded banks and ornamental grounds, presented to the city by Lord Armstrong.

To the s.w. of the University, overlooking the pleasant *Leazes Park* (Pl. 5), is the dignified Leazes Terrace (1829), designed by Oliver Thomas and being gradually restored. Adjoining is the St James's Park ground of Newcastle United F.C.

From Barras Bridge the busy Percy St. leads s.w. past Haymarket (bus stn). To the left the area as far as Blackett St. and Eldon Sq. is being redeveloped with covered markets. Beyond Gallowgate, in Newgate St., is *St Andrew's Church* (Pl. 9), with a good chancel arch (1175) and a 15C font-cover, marvellously carved.

In the churchyard begin the surviving *City Walls* (1265–1307; restored), with towers and rampart-walk, continued along West Walls and Bath Lane to Westgate Road.—In Fenkle St. (Pl. 9) are the *Assembly Rooms* (1776) by Wm. Newton, and farther N.W., viâ Low Friar St. and Monk St. are the scanty remains of the *Blackfriars Monastery* (founded before 1239), later occupied by city guilds.

Streets on the left lead to *Grainger Market*, a covered shopping precinct of 1835 situated between Clayton St. and GRAINGER STREET, an important thoroughfare running s.w. from the Grey column (see above).

From its junction with Newgate St., Bigg Market, with stalls (Tues, Thurs, & Sat), descends to the old *Town Hall* (to be replaced by a new Exhibition Hall), beside which Cloth Market (with Balmbras music-hall) continues to Mosley St. and the Cathedral. Hence Collingwood St., passing *Lloyd's Bank* (1891) and the Grecian *Literary and Philosophical Society* (1822–25), leads to Lough's statue of George Stephenson at the busy junction of Westgate Road and Neville St. (comp. below).

Grainger St. passes the church of *St John the Baptist* (14–15C), with a Jacobean pulpit and a beautiful 15C font-cover beneath the tower-vault, then joins Neville St. opposite the *Central Station* (Pl. 13), an impressive building by Dobson (1846–50), opened by Queen Victoria.

Just to the w. rises Pugin's *Roman Catholic Cathedral* (1844) with a spire (222 ft) by Hansom. Farther on is the large cattle market (Mon).

FROM NEWCASTLE TO SOUTH SHIELDS, 10½ m. (A 184, A 185). Railway, 11 m. in ½ hr.—From Gateshead the road skirts the s. side of the industrial Tyne.—7 m. **Jarrow** (28,800 inhab.), whose name recalls unemployment and the hunger marches of the 20s, has ship-repair yards and oil installations, and is connected with Willington by the *Tyne Tunnel* (1967; toll). Part of the basilica founded here by Benedict Biscop in 684 survives as the chancel of *St Paul's Church*, with its 11C tower, at the E. end of the town. Within, above the tower arch is the dedication stone; and in the N. porch are fragments of pre-Conquest sculptured stones of great interest. The Venerable Bede was an inmate of the adjacent monastery from 682 until his death in 735. In the chancel is a chair reputed to be his.

10½ m. **South Shields** (Hotels) is a seaport and seaside resort (100,500 inhab.) on the site of the Roman station of *Arbeia*. Excavations in 1952 on the Lawe, a hill near the sea-front, revealed remains of the *Fort*, mainly 3C, now adjoined by a *Roman Museum* (adm. free 10–4 or 7.30; closed Sat aft. and Sun in Oct–Apr; entered from Baring St.), with a splendid collection of inscribed stones and a decorated *Sword similar to one at Oslo University. The principle of the lifeboat was perfected by Henry Greathead of South Shields in 1790; in the *Central Museum* (adm. 10–7, Sat 10–5), Ocean Rd., is a model of a rival lifeboat designed in 1789 by Wm. Wouldhave. Ernest Thompson Seton (1860–1946), author and naturalist and the first chief scout of America, was born here, but went to Canada at the age of five.

FROM NEWCASTLE TO STOCKTON, 38 m. Railway, 41¾ m. in 1¼ hr. A 184 leads E. from Gateshead to (7 m.) *East Boldon*, beyond which it joins a 19.—10½ m. *Monkwearmouth* is an unattractive suburb of Sunderland. St Peter's Church preserves a porch, the tower, and the west wall of the church of a monastery founded by Benedict Biscop in 674. The Venerable Bede (see above) entered the monastery in 680, at the age of 7. The Wear bridge (1929) replaces one of 1793–96, then the boldest iron bridge of its time (236 ft span). To the N.E. of Monkwearmouth are the seaside residential quarters of *Roker* (Hotel) and *Seaburn* (Hotel). Roker has a pleasant park and a church by E. S. Prior (1906) with tapestries by Burne Jones and Morris and tablets by Eric Gill.—11½ m. **Sunderland** (Hotels), an industrial town (216,900 inhab.) at the mouth of the Wear (s. bank), with a theatre, has shipyards and exports coal. The *Museum* (adm. 9.30–6, Sun 3–5), in Mowbray Park, contains Saxon glass, excavated in 1962 at Monkwearmouth, Sunderland glass and pottery, English silver, and ship models. *Holy Trinity*, the parish church (1719), and *St Michael's*, rebuilt by Caröe (1935), in High St. West, are worth seeking out. Sir Henry Havelock (1795–1857) and Sir Joseph Swan (1828–1917), inventor of the incandescent electric lamp (before Edison; 1878), were born in Sunderland; and here Henry Irving made his first stage appearance in 1856. To *Durham* viâ Washington, see above.—At (14½ m.) *Ryhope* we leave on the left the road to *Seaham Harbour* (2½ m.), a coal-port (23,400 inhab.); at *Seaham Hall* (¾ m. N.) Byron and Miss Milbanke were married in 1815.—At (20¾ m.) *Easington*, with a 13C church, the Hartlepool road bears to the left, passing the new mining town of *Peterlee*, founded in 1948, with a distinguished parish church (1957) by D. McIntyre —35 m. *Billingham*, and thence to *Stockton*, see p. 647.

FROM NEWCASTLE TO TYNEMOUTH AND WHITLEY BAY, 11 m. Railway, 10 m. in 25 min.—The best road is A 1058. The route below (A 695) links up the industrial towns on the N. bank of the Tyne.—3½ m. **Wallsend** (45,800 inhab.), so called from the E. end of the Roman Wall, which here rested on the Tyne. The fort, *Segedunum*, is being excavated in 1978. We cross the N. approach to the Tyne Tunnel (see above) and leave (r.) the road to Tyne Commission Quay.—7¼ m. *North Shields*, a coal-port, is connected by ferry (toll) with South Shields.—8½ m. **Tynemouth** (68,900 inhab. with N. Shields; Hotels) is a bathing resort with good sands and a residential suburb of Newcastle. The ruins of the *Priory* and *Castle* (adm. daily; Sun from 2 in Oct–Apr; fee), a foundation of perhaps the 8C, re-established in 1090, on a prominent cliff at the mouth of the Tyne, consist chiefly of the 14C fortified gatehouse, the E.E. presbytery, and the 15C Percy Chapel at the E. end.—10 m. *Cullercoats* (Hotel), once a fishing village.—11 m. *Whitley Bay* (Hotels) a popular seaside resort (37,800 inhab., including the adjoining residential suburb of *Monkseaton*). The road (A 193) to *Blyth* (7 m.; see below) follows the coast N. viâ (3½ m.) *Seaton Sluice*, a derelict port. **Seaton Delaval Hall** (adm. May–Sept, 2–6 on Wed, Sun & BH; fee), c. 1 m. E., was built by Vanbrugh in 1720–29 and, though partly gutted by fire in 1822, still ranks as one of his masterpieces. The inhabited w. wing, the stables (E. wing), the gardens, and the tiny Norman church are of outstanding interest.

FROM NEWCASTLE TO CARTER BAR, 45½ m., a good road (A 696 and A 68).—7½ m. *Ponteland*, with an interesting church (late 12–14C).—13 m. *Belsay Castle* (l.) comprises a Georgian house and a 14C pele-tower. *Bolam*, 3½ m. N., has a Norman church with a Saxon tower.—17 m. *Shaftoe Crags* (r.), where Lord Derwentwater lay hid before the Jacobite rising of 1715. At *Capheaton Hall* (1 m. l.), a beautiful house of 1668 by Trollop of Newcastle, the young Swinburne spent much time with his grandfather.—17½ m. *Kirkharle* was the birthplace of Lancelot ('Capability') Brown (1716–83). To the right (2 m.) is **Wallington** (N.T.; adm. daily to grounds; to house, Easter–Sept 2–6, exc. Tues; also Sat & Sun in Oct, 2–5). In the house (built in 1688) are pictures by Reynolds and Gainsborough, and one of the best private collections of china in England; the woods and gardens are among the finest in the north.—21 m. *Kirkwhelpington*, on the edge of the wild Northumbrian moors.—30 m. **Otterburn** (Hotels) was in 1388 the scene of the defeat of the English under Hotspur (who was captured) by the Scots under Douglas (who was slain). The battle is the subject of the English ballad of 'Chevy Chase' and of the Scottish ballad of 'The Battle of Otterbourne'.—At (32½ m.) *Elishaw* we join A 68 (the Roman Dere Street from Corbridge), then ascend the wild valley of *Redesdale*, past (35 m.) *Rochester* with the Roman station of *Bremenium* (¼ m. r.), and (41 m.) the *Catcleugh* reservoirs of the Newcastle waterworks, to (45½ m.) *Carter Bar* (1371 ft) between England and Scotland on the site of the 'Raid of the Reidswire' (1575), the last Border battle. Thence to Edinburgh or Glasgow, see the 'Blue Guide to Scotland'.

From Newcastle to the *Roman Wall* and to *Carlisle*, see Rte 73.

Beyond Newcastle A 6125 skirts the Northumberland coalfield. At *Killingworth*, to the E. of (117 m.) *Gosforth Park* racecourse, George Stephenson constructed his first locomotive in 1814. At (120 m.) *Seaton Burn* the Tyne Tunnel road joins from the right and A 1 continues N.— 127 m. **Morpeth** (Hotels; by-pass), a pleasant small town (14,100 inhab.) on the Wansbeck, has a 14C *Church*, with a contemporary Jesse window (restored), and the remains of a *Castle* (15C gatehouse). The *Town Hall* (1714), by Vanbrugh, was altered in 1870. The *Town Belfry* survives from the 15C in Oldgate. At *Mitford*, 2 m. up the pleasant Wansbeck, and at *Bothal*, 3 m. downstream, are ruined castles and interesting churches.

Roads run S.E. from Morpeth to (5½ m.) *Bedlington*, famous for its terriers, and (9½ m.) the colliery and shipbuilding port of *Blyth* (34,600 inhab.; Hotel), and E. to (9½ m.) *Newbiggin* (Hotel) a small seaside resort.—To the s.w. the very winding road to *Corbridge* (26 m.) passes (6 m.) *Whalton* and (16 m.) *Stamfordham*, two good villages enhanced by their long greens. Whalton church contains good 13C work.

FROM MORPETH TO COLDSTREAM, 45½ m. About 2¼ m. N. of Morpeth we turn left on A 697.—At (9 m.) *Weldon Bridge* (Hotel) we cross the Coquet (B 6344 on the left for Rothbury, see below) and beyond (11 m.) *Longframlington* ascend over the moors of Rothbury Forest.—19 m. *Bridge of Aln Inn.* The church of *Whittingham* (pron. 'Whittinjam'), 1½ m. w., has traces of Saxon work.—*Callaly Castle* (adm. 2.15–5.30, Sat, Sun & BH June–Sept; fee), 2 m. s.w., is a mansion of the 17C and later, built round a pele-tower.—At (21 m.) *Glanton* (l.) is a Bird Station (adm. daily in Aug, 2–6; fee).—From beyond (22½ m.) *Powburn* we may ascend the valley of the

Breamish to (7 m.) the ancient British village of *Greaves Ash* and (8 m.) the fall of *Linhope Spout*, in the heart of the desolate Cheviots.— 31 m. **Wooler** (Hotels) is a small, grey market town on the N.E. edge of the Cheviots. About 6½m. S.E. is *Chillingham Castle* (Earl of Tankerville) built in the 14C. In the small church is the elaborate table-tomb of Sir Ralph Grey (d. 1443). At the warden's cottage tickets (weekdays, exc. Tues, 10–5, Sun 2–5) are obtained to view the last wild *Cattle in England, involving a walk of at least ½ hr. The cattle, always pure white, are peaceable but must not be approached; they have been emparked here for 700 years. *Humbleton Hill*, where the Scots were defeated in 1402, rises 1½ m. w. of Wooler. *The Cheviot* (2676 ft; wild desolate view), the highest point of its group, is ascended in c. 2 hrs from *Langleeford*, 5½ m. S.W. (rough road). The descent may be made by the wild gorge of *Henhole* and the fine *College Valley* to (c. 9 m.) Kirknewton (see below).— From (33½ m.) *Akeld* a road (l.) ascends the valley of the Glen, passing *Yeavering Bell* (l.; 1182 ft; *View), above the site of a 7C Saxon palace. Beyond *Kirknewton* (2¾ m.) it crosses the College Burn and goes on up the Bowmont Water to *Yetholm* (11 m.) In Scotland. The main road descends the valley of the Till with *Ford Castle*, partly 14C, on the opposite bank.— 40 m. *Crookham*. About 1½ m. w. is the battlefield of *Flodden*, where the Scots under James IV were disastrously defeated in 1513 by the English under the Earl of Surrey. A monument 'To the Brave of Both Nations' stands near *Branxton* church on the spot where James is supposed to have fallen.— 44 m. *Cornhill* and (45½ m.) *Coldstream*, see p. 666.

After Morpeth we cross the Coquet at (137 m.) *Felton*. About 7½ m. E. by B 6345 *Warkworth* stands on a beautiful reach of the Coquet above a bridge of 1379. The pleasant village, with a largely Norman church, occupies a loop of the river below the castle. *Warkworth Castle (adm. daily, Sun from 2 in Oct–Apr; fee), which belonged to the Percys from 1332 to 1922, is mentioned by Shakespeare in 'Henry IV'. It is now a magnificent ruin, largely 13C, but with a very unusual 15C keep.

Other notable features are the Lion Tower, the gatehouse, the Carrickfergus Tower, the Great Hall, and the dungeon beneath the keep. About ½ m. up the Coquet (adm. daily in summer, Sun from 2, fee; footpath and ferry), in the cliff, is a remarkable *Hermitage* (probably excavated in the 14C), the subject of one of Bp. Percy's ballads.—At the mouth of the Coquet, 1½ m. S.E., is the coal-exporting town of *Amble*, and c. 1 m. offshore is *Coquet Island*, the site of a Benedictine house, with a lighthouse.

From Felton B 6345 runs w. to (4½ m.) *Longframlington* (see above), then descends into the Coquet valley. About ½ m. E. of the junction with B 6344 is the late 12C Augustinian church of *Brinkburn Priory* (no adm.).—11½ m. **Rothbury** (Hotel), an attractive market town, is frequented for the beautiful moorland scenery on the Coquet. The church font incorporates part of a 9C cross. To the E. are the attractive grounds of *Cragside* (Lord Armstrong; adm. daily, Easter–Sept; fee) best seen in June. To the S.W. rise the heather-clad *Simonside Hills* (1447 ft).—A beautiful road ascends *COQUETDALE to (9 m.) *Harbottle*, with the remnants of a late 12C castle, and (10½ m.) *Alwinton*, beyond which it reaches the boundary of the vast Redesdale Artillery Range. The road (closed during firing practice) continues to (19½ m.) *Blindburn*, 3 m. from the Roman Camp of *Chew Green*, on Dere Street, near the Scottish border. Another road (B 6341), diverging S. from this in 4 m., runs to (15 m.) *Otterburn* (see above), passing (12 m.) the curious motte-hills and the fortified parsonage at *Elsdon*.—Near *Holystone*, 2 m. S.E. of Harbottle, is a well (N.T.) in which Paulinus is said to have baptized 3000 Northumbrians in 627.

146 m. **Alnwick** (pron. 'Annick'; Hotel; by-passed to the E.) an ancient and unspoilt town (7100 inhab.) above the Aln, is entered by the 15C *Hotspur Gate*, which, with the *Pottersgate*, near the church, is the only relic of the medieval walls. *St Michael's Church* contains notable capitals and effigies (14–15C) and a fine Flemish chest in the vestry. *ALNWICK CASTLE (Duke of Northumberland; adm. daily, exc. Fri & Sat, in May–late-Sept, 1–4.30; fee), the principal seat of the Percys, though much restored, is one of the most imposing examples in England of medieval fortification. The

enceinte walls, strengthened in 1309–15, when the towers were added, were probably erected by Eustace Fitzjohn (d. 1157). The outer ward is entered by a striking *Gatehouse* (c. 1440), preceded by a barbican. The inner ward retains its 14C gatehouse, enshrining a Norman arch and covering its original dungeon; the rest, apart from the old well, is mostly reconstructed (1854). Within are shown the *Library*, with the Sherborne Missal (1400), the Northumberland Household Book (1512), and a Caxton's 'History of Troye'; the *Music Room* and *Drawing Room* (interesting paintings); and the *Dining Room*, in which are the Celtic Witham sword (2C A.D.), from that river, and the Corbridge *Lanx, a massive sculptured silver dish unearthed at Corstopitum in 1734, perhaps made in Delos c. 400 B.C. The 14C *Postern Tower* houses a collection of Roman and British antiquities. In the *Stables* is a magnificent state coach (1825). The grounds were laid out by Capability Brown contemporaneously with his work for the Northumberlands at Syon Park.

Of *Alnwick Abbey*, founded in 1147 beyond the Aln for Premonstratensian canons, nothing remains save a late 14C gatehouse.—*Hulne Priory*, situated above the Aln, 3 m. N.W. of Alnwick, is reached by a beautiful road through *Hulne Park* (no motors; adm. pass obtained at Alnwick Castle). Hulne Priory is possibly the earliest example of a Carmelite friary in England (c. 1240), and the ruins are the most perfect of their kind. *Brizlee Tower* (1781), 1 m. farther on, commands a fine view.—**Alnmouth** (Hotel), 4½ m. E., on the estuary of the Aln, is a pleasant seaside resort with excellent golf links. A road leads N. thence to (4½ m.) Earl Grey's beautiful gardens at *Howick Hall* (adm. daily 2–7 in summer; fee) and to (6 m.) *Craster*, with its medieval tower and tiny harbour, 1 m. s. of Dunstanburgh (see below).

The direct road from Alnwick to (160½ m.) *Belford* (Hotel) is not interesting, and the detour nearer the coast, described below, is recommended. On a deserted stretch in the parish of Kyloe stands *Grizzly's Clump*, scene in 1685 of Grizzel Cochrane's hold-up of the King's Messenger; here she relieved him of her father's death warrant, thus gaining time for the arrival of a reprieve.

The road (B 1340) running N.E. from Alnwick leads to (7½ m.) Christon Bank. About 2 m. E. is *Embleton* (Hotel), with a 14C fortified vicarage. On a rocky headland 2 m. E. (1 m. from the road-end) are the striking ruins of *Dunstanburgh Castle* (adm. daily, Sun from 2; fee), begun by Thomas, earl of Lancaster in 1314 and extensively altered in 1380–84 by John of Gaunt. One of the largest of the Border castles, it changed hands twice during the Wars of the Roses, hastening its ruin. The *Gatehouse (afterwards the keep) and the Lilburn Tower are the principal remains; the view is extensive. Just N. of Christon Bank is *Fallodon Hall*, famous as the home of Lord Grey of Fallodon (1862–1935). From (13 m.) *Beadnell* (Hotels, closed in winter), with its sandy bay, we follow the coast N. to (15 m.) *Seahouses* (Hotels), a popular resort, the nearest port for the *Farne Islands* (boats daily at 10 and 2, weather permitting, from May to Sept).

The *Farne Islands (N.T.; landing fee; passes must be obtained before leaving mainland), a bird-sanctuary and a breeding-place of the grey seal, are a scattered archipelago of about 28 small islands, the nearest and largest of which, *Inner Farne*, is 1½ m. from the coast. Hither St Aidan (see below) often withdrew for contemplation and prayer; and here from 676 to 684 St Cuthbert lived in a hermitage (the site of which is marked by a 14C chapel), returning to die here in 687. The *Longstone Lighthouse*, on one of the remotest islands, was the scene in 1838 of the rescue by Grace Darling (1815–42) and her father of the survivors of the 'Forfarshire'.

16½ m. **Bamburgh** (Hotels) was the Saxon capital of Bernicia and even (for a time) of united Northumbria. The imposing *CASTLE (adm. daily, Easter–Sept, 2–8; fee), on a precipitous basalt crag, was for generations a royal fortress, and is sometimes identified with the 'Joyous Gard' of Lancelot.

The property of the Armstrong family, it was too freely renovated in 1894–1905, though the magnificent Norman keep is a genuine structure of the mid-12C and much of the curtain walling dates from before 1250. The choir of the *Church*, on the opposite side of the village, is admirable work of the 13C. St Aidan died here in 651. In the churchyard is the tomb of Grace Darling, and her boat is preserved in the *Memorial Museum* of the RNLI opposite (donation; Apr–mid-Oct, weekdays 11–7, Sun 2–6).

We rejoin the main road at (22 m.) Belford (see above).

---

167 m. (by direct road) *Beal* is the starting-point for (4¾ m.) Holy Island. Motors may be hired here or by writing or telephoning beforehand to the post-office (Tel. 201) at Holy Island. The sands are never wholly dry, but motorists and pedestrians may cross them (2¾ m.) by causeway from 3½ hrs after to 2 hrs before high tide (tide-table; care required).

Lindisfarne, or **Holy Island** (c. 200 inhab.; small Hotels), is separated from the mainland by a channel covered at high tide. St Aidan (d. 651), a missionary from Iona, was consecrated first bishop in Lindisfarne in 635, and under him and his successors the island became a lamp of Christianity. A shining proof in the form of the 'Lindisfarne Gospels' (c. 698) can be seen in the British Museum. St Cuthbert (see above) was made bishop in 684, and was buried on the island. When the Danes descended on Holy Island in 875, the monks fled with his body (see p. 654). In 1083 a Benedictine *Priory was founded here as a cell to Durham, and to this belong the existing ruins (adm. daily; fee), described in 'Marmion'. Built mostly of red sandstone the church affords an admirable example of Norman work, very like the mother-house at Durham, and is remarkable for its fortified character. The domestic buildings are of the 13C and 14C; a small museum preserves stones of the Anglian and Danish periods. The *Parish Church*, adjacent, dates mainly from the 12C and 13C, with a massively buttressed bell-tower; the little *Castle* (adm. Apr–Sept, daily exc. Fri, 11–12.30, 2–5; fee), on its steep-faced rock, was built c. 1550, garrisoned until 1820 and restored by Lutyens after 1903.

At (173¾ m.) *Tweedmouth* (Hotels), we cross the Tweed on a high concrete bridge (1928) with a main span of 361½ ft, supplementing the 15-arched Old Bridge (1611–34). To the left is Robert Stephenson's Royal Border Bridge (1847) of the railway, 126 ft high and 2000 ft in length.

175 m. **Berwick-upon-Tweed** (Hotels), a seaport and fishing town (11,600 inhab.), lies at the mouth of the Tweed, on the N. bank.

This ancient border town, alternately English and Scottish for centuries, was finally surrendered to England in 1482. As a bastion against the Scots it was then organized as a kind of extra-territorial community, with a government of its own; this autonomy was recognized till the 19C, but Berwick is now administered as part of Northumberland.

The *Ramparts, begun in 1555, are among the earliest examples in northern Europe of the new military engineering pioneered in Italy and afterwards developed by Vauban. The N. front was complete in 1569; the remainder is a later extension, not finished until 1747. They enclose a much smaller area than Edward I's wall, only traces of which survive. The fine *Barracks* (1719) are perhaps by Vanbrugh. Of the *Castle*, in the Great Hall of which Edward I delivered judgment in 1291 in favour of the claims of Baliol to the Scottish crown, only fragments survived its demolition to make way for the railway station. *Holy Trinity* (1648–52) is one of the few churches built during the Commonwealth; the outside is marred by 19C turrets, but the inside has good woodwork and a reredos by Lutyens. The church-like *Town Hall* was completed in 1754 and the interesting street pattern antedates its predominantly 18C buildings.

At *Halidon Hill* (537 ft), 2 m. N.W., a Scottish army under the Regent Archibald Douglas, endeavouring to raise the siege of Berwick, was defeated with great slaughter by the English in 1333.

A 1 crosses the Border at *Lamberton Bar*, 3 m. N. of Berwick, where the toll-keeper performed the same good offices for runaway couples as the Gretna Green blacksmith.

FROM BERWICK TO KELSO, 22¼ m. (A 698, B 6350), ascending the s. bank of the Tweed.—6½ m. **Norham** lies 1¾ m. N,W. The ruined *Castle* (adm. daily, Sun from 2; fee) was the Border stronghold of the prince-bishops of Durham and is celebrated in Scott's 'Marmion'. The fine Norman keep dates from Bp. Puiset (c. 1160). In the *Church* (Norman chancel) Edward I opened the fateful Convention in 1290 to weigh the contesting claims of Bruce and Baliol.—9¾ m. We cross the deep glen of the Till by the 15C *Twizel Bridge* (Hotel, with fishing), over which the English vanguard passed unmolested before the battle of Flodden. The 'castle' above is a ruined 18C folly.—At (13 m.) **Cornhill** (Hotel) we join A 697, which crosses the Tweed to (14½ m.) *Coldstream* in Scotland. Adm. Duncan, the victor of Camperdown, died at Cornhill in 1804.—B 6350 goes on along the s. bank. At (15½ m.) *Wark-on-Tweed* are the scanty remains of a once formidable castle, defended against David II by the Countess of Salisbury. Edward III hastened to its relief and, according to Froissart, fell in love with its beautiful defender.—Beyond (17¼ m.) *Carham* we enter Scotland 5 m. short of (22¼ m.) *Kelso*.

72   WENSLEYDALE; SWALEDALE; TEESDALE; WEARDALE

These dales, the first two in Yorkshire, the third between Yorkshire and Durham, and the last in Durham, with their picturesque and varied scenery, can be thoroughly explored by the active walker only, although their main points are accessible by car or bus. The Yorkshire Dales National Park covers much of this area. Most of the inns in the dales, though small and simple, are clean and comfortable.

A From Northallerton to Kendal. Wensleydale

ROAD, 62 m. (A 684); motor-bus to Leyburn and thence to Hawes (in summer to Kendal, one bus daily).

From Northallerton A 684 runs s.w., crossing the Swale and, at (6 m.) *Leeming Bar*, the Roman road to the North (Rte 71B).—7¾ m. *Bedale* has a good church (mainly 13–14C) with a defensive tower and fine Fitzalan tombs. The Georgian hall (adm. March–Sept, Tues 2–4.30) contains a local craft museum. About 3 m. s. are the important remains of *Snape Castle* (15–16C), a stronghold of the Nevilles and the Cecils.—11¼ m. *Patrick Brompton* church has a beautiful 14C chancel.

*Wensleydale, the upper valley of the Ure, begins at Kilgram Bridge, below Jervaulx Abbey (4½ m. s.w.), and extends thence to the border of Westmorland. Its scenery, mostly pastoral without any approach to grandeur, is inferior only to that of Wharfedale among the Yorkshire dales, and the passes out of it on the N. and the lateral valleys on the s. are well worth exploration on foot or by car. The well-known Wensleydale cheese is no longer made exclusively in the dale farms.

18¼ m. **Leyburn** (675 ft; Inns), an old market town high up on the N. bank of the Ure (views), is the best centre for excursions in E. Wensleydale.

A footpath which begins just N. of the Bolton Arms leads w. to (¼ m.) the *Shawl, a green terrace running along the N. side of the valley and commanding an exceptionally fine view of Wensleydale. About half-way along the walk is the *Queen's Gap*, where Mary, Queen of Scots, is said to have been stopped during an attempted flight from Bolton Castle (see below).—The direct road from Leyburn to (9 m.) *Richmond* (Rte 72B) crosses *Hipswell Moor*, on which, 1 m. beyond (3½ m.) Halfpenny House, is *Hartleap Well* (l.), the scene of Wordsworth's poem; but it is better to diverge to the left at Halfpenny House and reach Richmond viâ the Elizabethan *Walburn Hall* and an attractive stretch of Swaledale (bus).—Road to *Kettlewell* (Wharfedale), see Rte 66; to *Middleham*, etc., see Rte 67.

20 m. **Wensley** has a 15C bridge and an interesting 13C church containing a Flemish *Brass of a priest, Sir Simon de Wenslaw (1395), choir-stalls (1527), and fragmentary mural paintings. The Bolton pew (E. end of N. aisle) incorporates an old parclose (1506–33) from the Scrope chantry at Easby Abbey, and near the door is a unique wooden reliquary (? of St Agatha), also from Easby. *Bolton Hall* lies in a lovely park (no adm.), 1 m. w.—From Wensley roads ascend both sides of the dale. Keeping above the N. side we pass below (22½ m.) *Scarth Nick* (*View) and descend to (23½ m.) *Redmire*. About 1 m. N.W. is *Bolton Castle* (late 14C; adm. daily 10–6; fee), the grim, well-preserved stronghold of the Scropes, Wardens of the Western Marches from the time of Richard II down to the Commonwealth. Mary, Queen of Scots, was detained here for six months after her flight to England (1568). The Great Hall contains a folk museum devoted to the crafts of the Dale.—At (26½ m.) *Carperby* we turn left to cross to the s. bank by the picturesque *Aysgarth Bridge*, built in 1539. The Ure here falls over a fine series of flat limestone ledges, forming the *Upper Force* (above the bridge) and the *Lower Force* (½ m. below). The church, near by, has a superb late-Dec. rood-screen.—28¼ m. **Aysgarth** (Hotels).

The road from Wensley on the s. bank passes through the pretty village of *West Witton* and under *Penhill* (1792 ft; view). To the s. open the *Walden Valley* and the pleasant *Bishopdale*. *Buckden* in Wharfedale (Rte 66) may be reached by a good road through Bishopdale or a rough track from Bainbridge (see below).

32¼ m. **Bainbridge** (Hotel), at the foot of the flat-topped *Addlebrough* (1564 ft), is a pleasant village with an extensive green and a Roman fort on Brough Hill (E.). A horn is sounded here every night at 9 from Holy Rood (28 Sept) to Shrovetide to guide travellers benighted on the fells.

Semer Water (816 ft), with its tradition of a submerged village, lies 3½ m. s.w. below *Countersett*, beautifully situated at the foot of *Raydale* (see above).—To the N. of Bainbridge a bridge crosses the Ure for *Askrigg* with an old market cross and a fine hall of 1678. *Nappa Hall*, 1¼ m. farther E., was built in 1484. Fell road to *Muker*, see Rte 72B.

36 m. **Hawes** (800 ft; Hotel), noted for its sheep sales, is a grey little town in Upper Wensleydale, with the Duerley Beck cascading through

its E. end. About 1½ m. N. is *Hardrow Force* (key at the Green Dragon), a fine waterfall c. 90 ft high.

From Hawes to *Wharfedale*, see Rte 66; to *Settle* and *Ingleton*, see Rte 62B; to the *Buttertubs* and *Muker*, see Rte 72B.

At (41 m.) the *Moor Cock Inn* A 684 quits the Ure, which descends from Lunds Fell, to the N.

B 6259 leads N. to (10 m.) *Kirkby Stephen* (Rte 72C), passing (2¾ m.; r.) *Hell Gill*, the striking gorge in which the Eden rises, and descends *Mallerstang*, the green valley of the upper Eden, between *Wild Boar Fell* (2324 ft; l.) and *Mallerstang Edge* (2328 ft). Between road and river is *Pendragon Castle*, built according to tradition by Uther Pendragon, father of Arthur.

The main road descends *Garsdale*, while a moorland road on the left leads into the parallel *Dentdale*, affording a pleasant detour to Sedbergh viâ *Dent*, with narrow cobbled streets, once famous for its cottage knitting industry. Adam Sedgwick (1785–1873), the geologist, was a native of Dent, and is commemorated in the village street by a large boulder with a drinking basin. The fine fells on the left culminate in *Whernside* (2419 ft; *View); to the N. of Garsdale is *Baugh Fell* (2216 ft).—51 m. *Sedbergh* (Hotels), in a beautiful mountain site (congested in summer), has a public school founded in 1525 by Roger Lupton, Provost of Eton. We cross the Lune and enter Westmorland.— 62 m. **Kendal**, see Rte 62A.

B From Darlington to Kirkby Stephen. Swaledale

ROAD, 43 m. (A 1, A 6108, B 6270); bus to Keld.

The Darlington by-pass (motorway) runs S.W. to (8 m.) *Scotch Corner* (Rte 71B), beyond which we turn right on A 6108.—12½ m. **Richmond** (Hotels), a charming old town (7200 inhab.), is strikingly situated above the foaming Swale. At *Trinity Church*, in the large market-place, a curfew bell is rung daily at 8 p.m. and 8 a.m. The Perp. *Tower* N. of the market-place is the sole relic of the Grey Friars' monastery, founded in 1258. On the edge of a precipice sheer above the river rises the *CASTLE (daily, Sun from 2 in Oct–April; fee), originally built c. 1071 by Alan Rufus, first Norman Earl of Richmond, to whom are due Scolland's Hall and the little Chapel of St Nicholas. William the Lion of Scotland was probably imprisoned in 1173–74 in the Robin Hood Tower. The magnificent keep was erected over the Norman gatehouse in 1171–74. Henry VII, who derived the title of Richmond from his father Edmund Tudor, transferred the name to his new palace at Sheen in Surrey. The *Georgian Theatre* (adm. Easter–Sept, 2.30–5.30), built in 1788, and reopened in 1962 after 100 years' disuse, is the second oldest theatre in the country. The restored *Parish Church* contains Perp. choir-stalls (from Easby Abbey) and the Green Howards' memorial chapel. Lewis Carroll was a pupil at the Grammar School.

A pleasant quiet riverside walk leads hence (l. bank) to (1 m.) the beautifully situated ruins of *Easby Abbey (adm. daily; Sun from 2; fee), founded in 1155 for Premonstratensian canons and dedicated to St Agatha. The ground-plan of the ruins is extremely irregular. Very little remains of the church, where the Scropes of Bolton Castle were buried, but the refectory, chapter house, guests' solar, and gatehouse (to the S.E.) are interesting. The little parish church, adjacent, contains 13C wall-paintings, an early Norman font (c. 1100), and the cast of a 9C cross, one of the finest in the North.

The *Racecourse*, where horse-races have been held for over 200 years, on the hill 1½ m. N.E. of the town, commands a wide *View.—Other pleasant walks may be taken to *Hudswell*, on the Swale, 2 m. w. and to *Willance's Leap*, on *Whitcliffe Scar*, 2½ m. w. (obelisk).

Richmond is the starting-point for the exploration of *Swaledale*, the deepest, wildest, and one of the most beautiful of the Yorkshire dales, the first part of which is protected by N.T. covenants. The inn accommodation is limited.—4½ m. The picturesque *Downeholme Bridge* crosses the river to (6 m.) *Marske Hall*, the seat of the Hutton family.—The road to Leyburn (A 6108) now ascends on the left. We continue by B 6270, passing (7¼ m.) the scanty ruins of *Ellerton Priory* (Cistercian) and those of *Marrick Priory* (Benedictine nuns; founded between 1154 and 1181), 1 m. farther, on the opposite bank.—At (9¼ m.) *Grinton*, where we cross the river, is the mother-church of Upper Swaledale (Norman to Tudor), with 15C parclose screens.—10½ m. *Reeth* (650 ft; Hotels) affords good quarters. A hilly road diverging right here ascends the side valley of *Arkengarthdale*, with disused lead mines, and crosses the moors viâ (11 m.) *Tan Hill Inn*, the highest licensed house in England (1730 ft), to (20 m.) *Brough* (Rte 72c). From it another road, diverging to the N.E. 4 m. from Reeth, leads viâ the *Stang* (1677 ft; view) to (15 m.) *Barnard Castle* (Rte 72c).

The main valley, although still unexpectedly populous, now grows wilder and the road (on the N. bank) becomes hilly.—14 m. *Feetham.*—We cross the river at (16½ m.) *Gunnerside*. At *Ivelet*, 1 m. farther on, are pretty falls.—19 m. *Muker*, a quaint village in a beautiful situation. Wensleydale (Rte 72A) may be reached hence by a road across the fells (1633 ft) to (6 m.) Askrigg, or (better) by the steep road (*Views) past the *Buttertubs* (four deep holes in the limestone) and viâ the *Buttertubs Pass* (1726 ft) to (8 m.) *Hawes.*—The road quits the Swale at Muker and runs through the valley of the *Muker Beck* to (20½ m.) *Thwaite* and (22½ m.) *Keld*, where it rejoins the Swale. Walkers may follow the track on the w. bank of the Swale past *Kisdon Force*, ½ m. below Keld, in a most romantic site. The head of Swaledale beyond Keld is much less impressive, but the road thence to (32½ m.) *Kirkby Stephen* (see below) commands a fine view of the Eden valley from the top of the pass at (28¼ m.) *Hollow Mill Cross* (1698 ft).

C From Darlington to Penrith. Teesdale

ROAD. A 67 from Darlington to (16 m.) *Barnard Castle* and (20½ m.) *Bowes*; thence A 66 viâ *Brough* and *Appleby* to (55 m.) **Penrith.**—B 6277 from Barnard Castle through Teesdale to (30½ m.) *Alston*.

From Darlington A 67 runs w. up the valley of the Tees.—5¼ m. *Piercebridge* (Hotel) lies within the Roman fort on the old road across the Tees to the North. The remains of a drainage system (N.W. of the green), and some mounds of the walls, may still be seen.—8 m. *Gainford* has a good 13C church beautifully situated above the Tees.—10 m. *Winston* is 2¼ m. s. of Staindrop (see below), and has a fine bridge of 1763.

At *Stanwick*, 4 m. S.E. of Winston and 3½ m. S.W. of Piercebridge, is the site of a large British tribal 'capital' (1C A.D.), first explored in 1951.

16 m. **Barnard Castle** (520 ft; Hotel), is a small and attractive market town (5200 inhab.) with wide streets, in a lovely situation on the N. bank of the stony Tees (here crossed by an ancient bridge). Dickens stayed at the 'King's Head' in 1838, on a flying trip with 'Phiz' to investigate the condition of the Yorkshire schools, when a little watchmaker's shop nearly opposite suggested his 'Master Humphrey's Clock'. Below the quaint *Market House* (1747) is a good 16C house. Through the yard of the 'King's Head' we reach the ruined CASTLE (adm. daily; Sun from 2; fee), strikingly placed above the Tees.

The castle, founded in 1112–32 by Bernard Baliol, was confiscated in 1295 on the revolt of John Baliol. The chief features of the ruins are 'Baliol's Tower', a circular 'juliet' 50 ft high (not earlier than Edward II), erected on the wall of an older shell keep which has a curious flat vault to its first story, and (l. of this) 'Richard III's Window', bearing his badge (a boar).

Off Newgate, E. of the town is the *Bowes Museum (adm. weekdays, 10–4, 5, or 5.30; Sun 2–4 or 5; fee; teas), a handsome building in the style of a French château, erected in 1869–85 by the Countess of Montalbo and her husband, John Bowes of Streatlam. It contains a good collection of pictures, in particular the Spanish School (El Greco, Goya), and of porcelain, notably Chantilly, as well as a fine display of French 18C furniture and works of art.

To EGGLESTONE ABBEY, ROKEBY, AND GRETA BRIDGE, a 10½-m. round. Crossing to the suburb of *Startforth*, we descend the Yorkshire bank of the Tees to (1¾ m.) the picturesque E.E. ruins of Egglestone Abbey (adm. daily; Sun from 2; fee), founded c. 1195 for Premonstratensian canons.—2 m. The *Abbey Bridge* (1773) commands a lovely view in both directions. About 1 m. farther on a lane (l.) leads to the *Meeting of the Greta and Tees, painted by Turner and Cotman, and *Mortham Tower*, a restored 15C bastel-house.—To reach (3¼ m.) *Greta Bridge* (Hotel) we skirt *Rokeby Park*, visited in 1809 and 1812 by Scott, who has celebrated the beauties of the district in his 'Rokeby'. A pleasant walk ascends the Greta valley viâ *Brignall Banks* to *Bowes* (7½ m.; see below).—The return to Barnard Castle may be made viâ *Whorlton Bridge*, 2½ m. N.E. of Greta Bridge and 1 m. w. of *Wycliffe*, where the church has 13–14C glass and whence the family of John Wyclif may have derived its name, though the reformer himself was probably born at *Hipswell*, near Richmond.

FROM BARNARD CASTLE TO BISHOP AUCKLAND, 14½ m. (A 688).—2¾ m. *Streatlam Castle* (l.), refaced c. 1720 and now a ruin, was long a seat of the Bowes and Bowes-Lyon families, and was often visited by the Queen Mother.—At (5¾ m.) *Staindrop* the interesting *Church (11–14C) contains monuments of the Neville and Vane families. Close by is the entrance to *Raby Castle (Lord Barnard; adm. Easter–Sept, Wed, Sat, Sun, & BH; daily exc. Fri in Aug; 2–5; fee), the magnificent seat of the Nevilles and later of the Vanes, "the most perfect example of a 14C fortalice". It was reconstructed and modernized in 1768–88 by John Carr of York. Visitors should note the Neville Gateway, the Keep, and the magnificent Barons' Hall (136 ft long).—14½ m. Bishop Auckland, see Rte 72D.

Barnard Castle is the chief centre for excursions in *Teesdale, which extends from the junction of the Tees and Greta, 3 m. below the town, to Caldron Snout, 20 m. above. The best road (B 6277) ascends the Yorkshire bank of the river, leaving *Deepdale* on the left.—4½ m. *Cotherstone*, a Quaker village at the foot of *Baldersdale*, had a school of the 'Dotheboys Hall' type, at which Cobden was a pupil in 1814–19.—6 m. *Romaldkirk* is an attractive village with the mother-church (12–15C) of the Yorkshire side of Teesdale.—Beyond (8 m.) *Mickleton* we cross the foot of *Lunedale*. By taking the Brough road to *Grains o' th' Beck* (7 m.) we may ascend (c. 3 hrs) to the headwaters of the Lune and the summit of *Mickle Fell* (2591 ft; view), the highest hill in Yorkshire.—We cross the Tees to (10¼ m.) **Middleton-in-Teesdale** (750 ft; Hotel, 1½ m. N.), once a lead-mining town. The buses go on in summer to (15 m.) High Force Hotel, below which, at *High Force*, perhaps the noblest waterfall in England, the copious Tees hurls itself over a basalt cliff, 72 ft high, into a richly wooded glen.—From (17¾ m.) the *Langdon Beck Inn* (1268 ft) a cart-road (2 m.) and a walk of 1½ m. bring us to *Caldron Snout*, the junction of three counties, where the Tees descends a wild ravine in a series of cascades. Mickle Fell (see above) rises to the s.; and in fine weather walkers may cross the fells (no track), to the w. of Caldron Snout, to (5 m.) *High Cup Nick*, a savage defile between basalt cliffs, and descend thence to (9 m.) *Dufton* or (12½ m.) *Appleby* (see below).—Beyond Langdon Beck Inn the main road, one of the highest in England, leaving on the right a road to St John's Chapel in Weardale (Rte 72D), goes on over (24½ m.) *Yad Moss* (1962 ft) to (29 m., l.) *Garrigill* and (32½ m.) *Alston* (Rte 73A).

Leaving Barnard Castle by A 67, we cross the Tees into Yorkshire and join A 66 at (20½ m.) *Bowes* (950 ft), the Roman fort of *Lavatræ*, with a ruined Norman keep (c. 1170; adm. daily, Sun from 2) within it. The reputed original of 'Dotheboys Hall' in 'Nicholas Nickleby' is at the w. end of Bowes.—The road follows the line of the old Roman road along the upper valley of the Greta and traverses the desolate waste of *Stainmore Forest*, attaining its summit level (1436 ft) and entering Westmor-

land beyond (26 m.) the Roman camp of *Rey Cross*. A magnificent
*View now opens across the rich vale of Eden to the distant mountains
of the Lake District, and the road descends rapidly.—33½ m. *Brough*
(Hotel) has a ruined castle (adm. daily, Sun from 2; fee), built c. 1170
within the Roman fort of *Vertera* and restored in the 17C by Lady
Anne Clifford.

FROM BROUGH TO KENDAL, 28¼ m. (A 685).—4½ m. Kirkby Stephen (Hotel),
a pleasant town on the Eden, has a church containing the effigies of Sir Richard
Musgrave (d. 1409) and Lord Wharton with his wives, and an 11C stone showing
Satan in bonds. It is connected by moorland road with Swaledale. About 1¾ m. s.
is *Wharton Hall*, the 16C seat of the profligate Duke of Wharton (d. 1731).—9½ m.
Ravenstonedale (pron. 'Rassendale').—Beyond (16½ m.) *Tebay* we cross the Lune.—
28½ m. *Kendal*, see Rte 62A.

41¾ m. **Appleby** (Hotels) is the charming former county town (1900 inhab.)
of Westmorland, with a steep High Street. The castle, rebuilt in the 17C
retains its fine Norman keep (no adm.). In the church are a monument to
Lady Anne Clifford (d. 1676) and an organ (restored 1977) moved here in
1684 from Carlisle Cathedral. The annual gatherings of gipsies in June and
Sept (on the Dufton road) are extraordinary. To High Cup Nick, see
above.

We descend the beautiful valley of the Eden, with the Lake District
fells in the distance on the left, and on the right the Pennine chain, with
Cross Fell (2930 ft), its highest summit, ascended in c. 4½ hrs from
(48¼ m.) *Temple Sowerby* (Hotel), near which is *Acorn Bank*, a 16–18C
manor-house (N.T.; adm. to garden only Easter–Oct, daily, 2–5.30; fee).
Beside (53½ m.) *Brougham Castle* (Rte 62A) we cross the Eamont and
enter Cumberland.—55 m. **Penrith**, see Rte 62A.

D Bishop Auckland and Weardale

Bishop Auckland is reached by railway or bus from Darlington and Durham,
or by bus from Barnard Castle.

Bishop Auckland, a colliery town (33,300 inhab.), has been a seat of
the bishops of Durham from the 12C. *Auckland Castle* is largely of the
early 16C, but its beautiful *Chapel* (adm. on application) was built in
the late 12C and recast by Bp. Cosin (d. 1672), who is buried here. The
attractive Bishop's Park, entered by a gatehouse of 1760, is open to the
public.

About 1¼ m. S.E. is the 13C mother-church of *St Andrew Auckland*, which contains a fine Northumbrian cross (9C), reconstructed from fragments, a piscina
made from a Roman altar, and 14C brasses. The small and simple 7C *Church of
Escomb* (3 m. W.), one of the earliest in England, is built partly with stones from the
Roman station of *Vinovia*, at *Binchester*, 1½ m. N. of Bishop Auckland.
FROM BISHOP AUCKLAND TO ALSTON, 38½ m. We cross the Wear and keep as
close as possible to its N. bank.—4½ m. *Witton-le-Wear*, on A 68, is an attractive
village, with a striking (though altered) castle of 1410 on the S. bank of the river.
With 800 acres of its fine grounds it is now a caravan and camping centre.—12 m.
Wolsingham, on B 6293.—15 m. *Frosterley*, noted for its marble.—17½ m. Stanhope,
the centre of a quarrying district, is the best headquarters for walks over the moors
bounding Upper Weardale, of which it is the capital. The church dates mainly
from the 13C. Bp. Joseph Butler, author of the 'Analogy', was rector here in 1725–
40.—from (25¼ m.) *St John's Chapel*, a charming place, a steep fell road leads S.
to (5½ m.) *Langdon Beck* in Teesdale.—28 m. *Cowshill*. B 6293, surrounded by
lofty bleak hills, goes on N.W. over (32½ m.) *Killhope Cross* (2056 ft, the highest
main road in England; fine views) to (38½ m.) *Alston* (Rte 73A) in Cumberland;
while B 6295 leads N. to (11 m.) *Allendale* (Rte 73A) in Northumberland.

73 NEWCASTLE TO CARLISLE

ROAD. A 69 (57½ m.; bus) runs viâ (7¼ m.) *Heddon-on-the-Wall* (16½ m.) *Corbridge*, and (20½ m.) *Hexham*; A 695 follows the s. bank of the Tyne to (20½ m.) Hexham. The direct route, by the old Military Road (55½ m.), keeps closer to the line of the Roman Wall and joins A 69 at (38 m.) *Greenhead*. The two alternatives given below take in all the points of interest.

RAILWAY, 60¼ m. in 1¾–2 hr. Principal Stations: 4 m. *Blaydon*.—10½ m. *Prudhoe*.—13¼ m. *Stocksfield*.—17¾ m. *Corbridge*.—20¾ m. **Hexham**.—21½ m. *Haydon Bridge*.—32½ m. *Bardon Mill*, for Housesteads (3½ m.).—37¼ m. *Haltwhistle*.—49¼ m. *Brampton*, 1¾ m. from the town.—60¼ m. **Carlisle**.

A Viâ Tynedale and Hexham

Leaving Newcastle by Scotswood Rd. (Pl. 13) we follow A 695 through (1½ m.) *Elswick*, with the huge Vickers-Armstrong works, and cross the Tyne on a bowstring-arch bridge at (3 m.) *Scotswood*. The valley here is part of the coalfield.—7½ m. *Crawcrook* is 1½ m. S.E. of *Wylam*, on the N. bank of the Tyne, where George Stephenson was born in 1781 (tablet on cottage).—10 m. *Prudhoe* has a ruined castle on a cliff (small Norman keep). *Ovingham* (pron. 'Ovinjam'), ¾ m. N.W., across the Tyne, has an E.E. church with a Saxon tower at the foot of which lies Thomas Bewick, the engraver (1753–1828; b. at *Cherryburn*, 1 m. S.W.). We quit the coalfield and the valley becomes attractive.—Opposite (13 m.) *Stocksfield* is *Bywell*, a beautifully situated village with a 15C gatehouse, two fine 11–13C churches, one with a Saxon tower (950–1066), and an 18C Hall by James Paine.—From (15 m.) *Riding Mill* (Hotels) A 68 ascends S. for Darlington. R. S. Surtees was born in 1803 at The Riding near by.

17¾ m. **Corbridge** (Hotels), a pleasant old town, lies above the N. bank of the Tyne, to the right, approached by a bridge of 1647. The church, rebuilt in the 13C, retains a Saxon 'porch-tower' and window (8C) and a 12C S. doorway. The fortified priest's house (13C; Information bureau) preserves a 15C iron yett. Like the tower-arch of the church, it is built of stones from *Corstopitum*, ½ m. N.W., a Roman garrison town that grew from a 1C fort guarding their main crossing of the Tyne. The *Remains (adm. daily; Sun from 2 in Oct–Apr; fee) comprise the supply-depôt with its granaries and fountain, military compounds, built round earlier temples (the rippling subsidence may be due to an earlier road), the H.Q. building with a strong room like that at Chesters, and an unfinished storehouse with rusticated masonry, one of the largest Roman buildings surviving in Britain. The first-class collection in the Museum includes, notably, the 3C Corbridge *Lion and a model of the Tyne bridge based on the still visible abutment. *Aydon Castle*, 1½ m. N.E. (footpath), is a manor-house of 1305.

From Corbridge A 68, roughly on the line of the Roman Dere Street, runs N. through lonely country, crossing the Wall at (2¾ m.) *Stagshawbank*.—11½ m. *Tone Inn*.—At (16½ m.) *West Woodburn* (Hotels) we cross Redesdale near the Roman fort of *Habitancum*.—22½ m. *Elishaw*, see p. 662.—From Corbridge to *Morpeth*, see p. 662.

20 m. The ruined *Dilston Castle* (l.), on the Devil's Water, was the original seat of the earls of Derwentwater, of whom the last was executed for his part in the Jacobite rising of 1715.

20½ m. **Hexham** (Hotels), an ancient and attractive place (9800 inhab.), is intersected from E. to W. by one long street, the different sections of which are known as Priestpopple, Battle Hill, and Hencotes. Abutting on the Market Place, with the 18C *Shambles*, is the magnificent *PRIORY CHURCH, the "text-book of E.E. architecture", larger than some cathedrals.

Of the first church here, erected by St Wilfrid in 674, the foundations of the apse, some fragments of the nave, and the important *Crypt or *Confessio* (resembling that at Ripon; closed during excavations in 1978) survive in the present building. Inscribed Roman incised stones from Corstopitum should be noted in the crypt walls. Between 681 and 821 this church was the cathedral of a Saxon bishopric. It was succeeded by an Augustinian priory (1114–1536) and to the canons is due the erection (c. 1175–1225) of the existing beautiful choir and transept, the latter distinguished for its disproportionate length (c. 153 ft) and for its almost unique retention (s. end) of the canons' night-stair from the dormitory. The nave, destroyed by the Scots in 1290, was rebuilt in 1908. Among the rich furnishings of all periods, of special interest are the remarkable wooden *Pulpitum* (1491–1524); the stone Saxon *Bishop's Chair*, which afterwards served as a sanctuary-stool (comp. p. 640); the 15C *misericords*; the 7C chalice in the s. choir-aisle; the 15C *Leschman* and *Ogle Chantries*, respectively N. and s. of the chancel, the latter containing its triptych altarpiece; the fine 15C *Portraits* of seven bishops of Hexham; the four surviving panels of a *Dance of Death*; and (s. transept) the monument of *Flavinus*, a Roman standard-bearer, and the famous *Acca Cross* of c. 740; also (N. transept) a Descent from the Cross (Flemish; early 16C). There are remains of priory buildings (partly restored) to the s., and ruins of the late 12C gateway in Market St. (N.W.).

The 15C *Moot Hall*, E. of the Market Place, was the tower-house of the bailiff of the Abp. of York, lord of the Regality of Hexham prior to 1572. Still farther E. are the *Manor Office*, the medieval prison of the regality (built in 1330), perhaps the only example of its class in England, and the *Grammar School* (1684). Fore St. and Market St. are rewarding.

Hexham is a good centre for the Roman Wall (Rte 73B) for walkers, who can take the train or bus hence to various points near it.

B 6306 runs S.E., crossing the Devil's Water above the gorge of Swallowship Hill and the Dilston Woods, and passes near (2½ m. S.E.) the site of the battle of Hexham (1464), in which the Lancastrians were defeated by the Yorkists. Thence the road ascends across the moors to (10 m.) **Blanchland** (Hotel), a charming village in the secluded valley of the Derwent. The parish church preserves the choir and N. transept of the church of a Premonstratensian abbey founded in 1165. By the late-15C abbey gateway we enter the unusual village square, the centrepiece of an 18C model village built by Lord Crewe covering parts of the conventual buildings.—A hill road leads s. to (4 m.) *Dalton*, on the Rowley Burn. Near here ('Heavenfield') St Oswald defeated the heathen King Cadwalla, in 634.—*Allendale* (780 ft; Hotels), 10¾ m. S.W. viâ B 6305, is a small summer resort, whence we may explore the lovely pastoral dales of the East and West Allen. The bus from Hexham goes as far as (18 m.) *Allenheads* (Hotel), a delightfully secluded village, but the road goes on to (21¾ m.) *Cowshill* (Rte 72D).

FROM HEXHAM TO BELLINGHAM, 17 m. (bus). The road (A 6079) crosses the Tyne by an 18C bridge and, beyond (4 m.) *Wall* (Hotel), the Roman Wall, after which we turn left across the N. Tyne for (5¼ m.) *Chollerford* (Rte 73B). Here we bear right for (5¾ m.) *Humshaugh* (pron. 'Humshalf') and ascend the beautiful wooded vale past (6⅓ m.) *Haughton Castle* (in part 13C). Quitting the river, we keep right on B 6320 and pass (9½ m.) *Nunwick House* (1760). Farther on, on the opposite bank, is *Chipchase Castle*, a 14C tower-house attached to a mansion of 1621, reached by a bridge from (11¾ m.) *Wark-on-Tyne* (Hotel), with its motte-hill. Ascending, we have a view of the wild *Redesdale*, and then cross the N. Tyne for (17 m.) *Bellingham* (pron. 'Bellinjam'), where the church has a remarkable stone-vaulted nave (17C).—Hence B 6320 leads N. for 9 m. to Otterburn on the Newcastle–Jedburgh road, or we may follow the roads up the lonely valley of the N. Tyne, which rises on the desolate slopes of *Peel Fell* (1975 ft). *Kielder Forest*, at the head of the N. Tyne, together with those of *Redesdale* (N.E.) and *Warke* (S.), makes up the largest afforested area in Britain. About 2 m. S.E. of Kielder a cottage has been fitted up as the *Border Forest Park Museum* (2–5, summer weekends; daily in Aug). About ½ m. beyond (36½ m.) *Deadwater* we enter Scotland, joining the Carlisle–Jedburgh road at (40¼ m.) *Saughtree*.

23½ m. *Warden* (¾ m. r.), at the meeting of the N. and S. Tynes, has a Saxon church tower with a Roman arch.—At (28½ m.) *Haydon Bridge* a tablet marks the birthplace of John Martin (1789–1854), the artist. On the Alston road (A 686; l.) is *Langley Castle* (1½ m.; adm. Wed 2–7, May–Sept), a large and striking mid-14C tower-house. We cross the S. Tyne, which is joined farther w. by the Allen, descending through a wooded glen (N.T.).—32¾ m. *Bardon Mill* is 3½ m. s. of Housesteads (Rte 73B).—37¼ m. *Haltwhistle*, a pleasant little town with a good E.E. church, is the centre of a small detached coalfield.

Featherstone Castle (3¼ m. s.w.) should be visited for the sake of its situation by the side of the stony S. Tyne. *Unthank Hall*, 2 m. s.e., was the birthplace of Bp. Ridley (1500–55).

We quit the S. Tyne and join the military road (Rte 73B) at (40¾ m.) *Greenhead*, c. 2 m. s. of Gilsland.—47 m. (r.) Road for Naworth and Lanercost (Rte 73B).—49¼ m. **Brampton** (Hotels) is an old-fashioned market town, with good bathing and boating at *Talkin Tarn*, 2 m. s.e. (Hotel at Talkin, 1 m. farther).

About 10½ m. N. of Brampton, by a moorland road, is the remote church of *Bewcastle*, built on a Roman fort, with a remarkable Anglian *Cross of the late 7C (14½ ft high), and adjoining an Edwardian castle-ruin.

B 6292 (bus) leads s.e. from Brampton, viâ (1½ m.) *Milton*, ro the upper S. Tyne valley and (19½ m.) *Alston* (Hotels), the highest market town in England (c. 950 ft). It is a good starting-point for the ascent of *Cross Fell* (c. 4½ hrs; p. 671). A 686 runs s.w. to (19 m.) Penrith viâ (5¾ m.) *Hartside Cross* (c. 1900 ft; *View); good hilly roads go s.e. to *Weardale* and *Teesdale* (Rte 72).

58½ m. **CARLISLE** (71,500 inhab.), celebrated as 'merrie Carlisle' in many a Border ballad, and long the county town of Cumberland (now of Cumbria), has been the seat of a bishop since 1133. Notwithstanding its age and chequered history, it is, on the whole, of modern aspect, and its present importance centres in the fact that it is the meeting-place of six great railway lines.

Hotels near the Station and in English St.
Post Office, Warwick Rd.
Buses from Lowther St., to all destinations.

History. Carlisle was not exactly on the Roman Wall, which ran slightly to the N., through the suburb of *Stanwix* (*Petriana*), but it was an important military centre during the earlier Roman occupation. It later became a small town, called *Luguvallium*, which survived into Saxon times. Its re-foundation was due to William Rufus, who began the castle. Carlisle, as an important Border fortress, was repeatedly attacked by the Scots, but without any lasting success, though they were ceded the city in 1136–57. During the Civil War it surrendered to the Scots under Gen. Leslie after a siege of nearly nine months in 1644–45. In 1745 the Young Pretender entered Carlisle, mounted on a milk-white steed and preceded by 'the hundred pipers' of the well-known Jacobite song, but a few weeks later the city was retaken by the Duke of Cumberland.

Thomas Woodrow, grandfather of President Wilson, was pastor in 1820–35 of the Lowther St. Congregational Church (tablet; at that time in Annetwell St.). Sam Bough (1822–78), the painter, was the son of a Carlisle shoemaker. The 'Carlisle Experiment', an essay in state ownership of licensed premises, inaugurated during the First World War to control sales of liquor to munition workers, seems likely to end shortly.

From Court Sq., outside the *Citadel Station*, we enter the city by

ENGLISH STREET, passing between the two huge drum-towers of the *County Buildings* and *Court House* (1808–12), designed by Telford and Smirke, but incorporating part of the ancient *Citadel*, founded by Henry VIII. At the end of English St. is the spacious MARKET PLACE, with the *Market Cross* (1682) and the somewhat rustic-looking 18C *Town Hall* (Information Centre), beside which is the Tudor *Guildhall* (now a restaurant). Castle St. leads hence to the beautiful E. end of the cathedral, passing the house (No. 81) where Miss Charpentier stayed before her marriage to Walter Scott in the cathedral (1797).

The *Cathedral, though one of the smallest in England since the six w. bays were destroyed by Leslie's Scots in 1645 (to repair the town walls), has many points of interest. The church of an Augustinian Priory founded here in 1093 and completed in 1123 became a cathedral in 1133, and was the only Augustinian church in England that was also the seat of a bishop. Ascent of tower and clerestory, fee.

The surviving two bays of the NAVE are plain Norman work of 1123; they are fitted up as a memorial chapel to the Border Regiment. The distortion of the arches is due to settlement at the time of building. The window over the N. door contains fragments of old glass. The small S. TRANSEPT is of similar date, and contains a Runic inscription; but the N. TRANSEPT was rebuilt by Bp. Strickland c. 1390. The short original Norman presbytery began to be replaced by the beautiful existing CHANCEL c. 1225, and the vaulted aisles and arcade arches date from this period. The choir was completely destroyed by fire in 1292, and the triforium and clerestory were subsequently restored in the Dec. style by Bp. Halton in 1292–1324. The E.E. arcade piers (though not the arches) were reconstructed at the same period; their interesting carved capitals represent the employments of the twelve months. The special glory of this choir is the magnificent late-Dec. *East Window*, which excels in design the West window of York Minster. The tracery lights have glass of 1380–84 (a 'Last Judgment'); the main lights are a successful work by Hardman (1861). Below the window is a monument to Archdeacon Paley (1743–1805), author of 'Evidences of Christianity', who is buried in the N. choir-aisle. The *Stalls*, with misericords, date from 1413–33. Their backs are painted (1484–1507) with the Apostles and legendary scenes from the lives of SS Anthony and Cuthbert (N.) and St Augustine (s.). The lovely Flamboyant screenwork in *St Catherine's Chapel* (w. end of s. choir-aisle), the Renaissance *Screen erected by Prior Salkeld in 1542 on the N. side of the chancel and the splendid carved 16C *Pulpit (Flemish), brought from the church of Cockayne Hatley (Beds.) in 1964, deserve attention; also two recumbent effigies of bishops (13C and 15C) in the N. aisle, and the brass to Bp. Bell (d. 1496) in the centre of the choir.

There are some remains of the monastic buildings to the s.w. of the church, in the precincts called 'The Abbey', including the *Prior's Lodging* (now the *Deanery*), the *Gateway* (1527), and the *Refectory* (now the *Chapter Library*; rebuilt 1482), with its 14C undercroft (adm. on application).

Farther on in Castle St. is the *Tullie House Museum* (weekdays 9–5 or 8; Sun 2.30–5 in June–Aug), in a mansion of 1689, with a fine collection of local antiquities, notably Roman, but covering the whole period from the 1C to the 19C; here, too, are modern paintings and a natural history collection. Abbey St, behind, has Georgian houses. A pedestrian subway leads below Castle Way to the **Castle**, the outer gates of which open on to a strip of ground bounded by the ancient *City Walls*. The castle, founded in 1092, includes two wards, the outer entered through the impressive *Ireby Tower*, the inner by the 14C *Captain's Tower* (adm. by guide only). The barrack blocks include Alma (1819). In the inner ward is the massive Norman *Keep (adm. daily; Sun from 2 in Oct–Apr; fee), one of the finest examples of its kind in England, though likely built under the Scottish occupation of King David. It was originally entered by a doorway on the first floor, over a fore-building, the foundations of which can be seen. On the second floor are 14–15C carvings made by prisoners.

Between 300 and 400 Scottish prisoners were confined here and in the cathedral after the rebellion of 1745 ('Fergus MacIvor', in 'Waverley', was one of these). The restored remnant of *Queen Mary's Tower* (14C), also in this ward, recalls the imprisonment here of Mary, Queen of Scots, for nearly two months in 1568. The famous rescue from this stronghold of Kinmont Willie by the 'bold Buccleuch' took place in 1596. The ramparts of the inner ward command a fine view. Within them is also the *Museum of the Border Regiment.*

Returning to the outer gate, we turn left, and then take the footway (l.) that leads round *Castle Bank*. This completely encircles the outer N. wall of the castle (at this point identical with the city walls), and commands pleasant views (r.) of *Victoria Park*, beyond which are the Eden and the suburb of *Stanwix*.

Returning viâ the subway and turning right into Annetwell St., near the site of the Irish Gate, we may follow the city wall, past the deanery, to the church of *St Cuthbert* (l.; rebuilt 1778). Here the only English tithe-barn (1490) inside a city wall has been restored as the parish hall.

Excursions may be made from Carlisle to *Dalston Hall* (4 m. s.w.), incorporating a pele-tower, and *Rose Castle* (7 m.), the country seat of the bishop (13–17C); *Netherby* (11 m. N.), whence young Lochinvar carried off his bride; and *Wetheral* (Hotel), 5 m. E. on the Eden (good fishing), with the gatehouse of a Benedictine priory of 1106, opposite *Corby Castle*. This 17C house built on to a 13C pele-tower was enlarged in 1812–17 by Peter Nicholson. It was a seat of Howards from the time of 'Belted Will' (1611) until 1934.—About 1¼ m. N. of *Burgh-by-Sands* (pron. 'Bruff'), 5 m. w. of Carlisle, is a monument marking the spot where Edward I died in 1307, on his way to crush the rebellion of Robert Bruce.—The *Lake District* (Rte 64) is approached from Carlisle viâ *Penrith* (A 6), or viâ *Cockermouth* (A 595).

FROM CARLISLE TO SILLOTH, 22½ m. The direct road follows the Maryport road to (11½ m.) *Wigton* (p. 578), beyond which it turns r. for (18 m.) *Abbey Town*. The parish church here occupies part of the nave of the Cistercian church of *Holme Cultram*, an abbey founded in 1150 by Henry, son of David I of Scotland. The original work includes the w. door, the massive clustered pillars, and the newel stair; here, too, is the tomb of Abbot Rydekar (d. 1434).—22½ m. **Silloth** (Hotels) is a bathing and golfing resort on the Solway Firth. For the coast road thence to Maryport, see Rte 63.

FROM CARLISLE TO LONGTOWN, 8 m. A 7 traverses the plain between the Eden and the Esk, crossing the diminutive river Lyne at (5½ m.) *Westlinton*.—8 m. *Longtown* (Hotel) is an ancient Border town on the Esk, s. of which is the early 17C parish church of *Arthuret*.—Beyond the Esk lies the 'Debatable Land', a Border tract c. 8 m. long by 4 m. broad extending N. to the Sark, which was long disputed by England and Scotland. Here, at *Solway Moss*, 3 m. w. of Longtown, the crushing defeat of the Scots in 1542 is said to have hastened the death of James V. The existing boundary on the Sark was agreed upon in 1552.

The Solway Firth, an estuary fed by the Eden, Esk, Annan, and Nith, is notorious for its dangerous tides, which sometimes rise with extraordinary rapidity, forming a bore 3 or 4 ft high. Strangers should remember the caution given to Darsie Latimer (in 'Redgauntlet') that "he who dreams in the bed of the Solway will wake up in the next world". A barrage from Annan to Bowness is projected to create from the Solway Firth a freshwater reservoir and an area of industry.

From Carlisle to *Penrith*, *Kendal* and the South, see Rte 62A; to *Whitehaven*, *Barrow*, etc., see Rte 63; to *Gretna*, *Edinburgh*, *Glasgow*, etc., see the 'Blue Guide to Scotland'.

B Along the Roman Wall

Buses from Newcastle to Carlisle follow A 69 (see above). In late-July–Aug service 690 runs between Hexham and Haltwhistle via the Military Road and Once Brewed Inn (car park; information centre). Hence a 'Park and ride' service serves the sites at Steel Rigg, Housesteads, and Vindolanda.

The finest sections of the Wall itself lie between Chollerford and Lanercost, but the Vallum is visible throughout the greater part of the distance. The scenery is striking throughout. The greatest antiquarian interest is in the military fortresses and settlements at Corbridge, Chesters, Housesteads, and Vindolanda. In high summer site car parks are often full.

*Hadrian's Wall and **Vallum** form a zone of fortification extending across England for 73½ miles, from Wallsend to Bowness-on-Solway. The Wall was intended to form an obstacle, an elevated patrol line, and a base for sorties against barbarians from the north. It lay behind a ditch c. 27 ft wide, and was constructed of stone, being c. 15 ft high and 7½–9 ft thick. It was patrolled from so-called "milecastles" (c. 1620 yds apart), between which were smaller turrets at every 540 yds, and was garrisoned by infantry and cavalry in 17 large forts.

The Wall was built under the governorship of Aulus Platorius Nepos (A.D. 122–126) after the evacuation of Inchtuthil on the Tay and the abandonment of Scotland beyond the Tay. The portion w. of Gilsland (where limestone was not readily to hand) was originally of turf, replaced in stone before 132; for 2 m. w. of Birdoswald (see below) the turf and the stone walls run on different lines. The Vallum lies always s. of the wall, at a short but varying distance; it is a flat-bottomed ditch 20 ft wide, running between mounds 80 ft apart. It was built to control access to the military zone from the south but abandoned after free Britons became Roman citizens (c. 214). A military road (called *Stanegate* by the Saxons) ran between it and the wall. This had been built under Agricola in A.D. 79–80 to provide lateral communication between the two main garrisoned roads to the N. outpost. The wall was prolonged s.w. by a line of coastal signal towers (at 540-yd intervals) as far as St Bees Head, but these seem to have been abandoned in the 2C after the frontier had been advanced again into Scotland. Extensive reconstructions were undertaken after the Scottish campaigns of Septimius Severus to make good the damage done by the barbarians during the troubled period when Albinus bid for the Empire, and again by Constantius Chlorus after Allectus' bid for power (296). A final restoration was made by Theodosius after the defeat of the Barbarian conspiracy of 367.

The brief itinerary below will sufice for a superficial visit using a car; a proper exploration of the wall should be made on foot, for which purpose the 2 in. to 1 m. map (special series) of the Ordnance Survey is recommended. The standard authorities are the late Sir Ian Richmond and Prof. Eric Birley.

Leaving Newcastle by Westgate Rd. (Pl. 9), we follow A69.—At (2 m.) *Benwell* (*Condercum*) are the foundations of a small apsidal temple and a causeway (the only one now visible) crossing the Vallum.—We pass fragments of the Wall beyond (3 m.) *Denton Burn* (with a turret) and just before (7¼ m.) *Heddon-on-the-Wall*, which has Norman work in its church. Here the military road (B 6318) along the Wall diverges right. It was constructed, largely on the Wall, in 1751 after its predecessor had proved inadequate to bear Wade's artillery during the '45 Rebellion; Wade quarried the Wall, leaving standing only those portions distant from his chosen alinement.—8½ m. Site of *Vindovala* (*Rudchester*); to the left, Beyond some reservoirs, is the pele-tower of *Welton*.—15½ m. Site of *Onno* (*Halton Chesters*). To the s. is the Border stronghold of *Halton Tower*.— 16¼ m. *Stagshawbank* (Inn), at the crossing of A 68, on the Roman Dere Street, is 2½ m. N. of Corbridge (p. 672); extensive *Views.—A cross (r.)

near (19¼ m.) *Planetrees* marks the site of Oswald's camp before the battle of 634 (p. 673).—On the left, in the grounds of (20½ m.) *Brunton House*, is a fragment of the Wall, with an excellent example of a turret.

At (21 m.) *Chollerford* (Hotel) we cross the N. Tyne. About ½ m. s. of the present bridge the *Abutment of the Roman bridge may be seen; also (when the river is low) the bases of some piers.— In the park of (21½ m.) **Chesters** (adm. 9–4, 5, or 5.30; Sun 2–4 or 4.30; fee) are the excavated remains of the fort of *Cilurnum, claimed to be the best surviving example of a cavalry fort in the whole Empire. The Headquarters building has a well, protected by a carved phallic stone; the strong-room preserves its vaulted roof (its wooden door disappeared after description in 1840). Near the river is a well-preserved *Bath-house. The museum has a collection of *Antiquities from the Wall, including a bronze corn-measure and the facsimile of a diploma, or discharge tablet. The church of *Chollerton* (Hotel, 1 m. N.W.), 1½ m. N.E., has Roman columns (s. arcade) and a Roman altar converted to a font.— 25 m. Site of *Brocolitia* (*Carrawburgh*), where ¼ m. s. of the unexcavated fort a temple to Mithras (3C) was uncovered in 1950. Here also the Well of Coventina yielded up many ex-voto offerings to its dedicatory nymph.

For the next 15 m. the Wall runs just inside the s. boundary of the NORTHUMBER-LAND NATIONAL PARK, a huge area of wild and secluded border land, comprising the central Cheviot Hills and the upper valleys of the Rede, the Coquet, and the North Tyne. The N. part is almost roadless, though skirted by A 697 N. of Wooler (p. 663); the central area is approached by Otterburn (p. 662) or Bellingham (p. 673). H.M.S.O. publish a detailed guide to the Park and there are Information Centres at Ingram in the Cheviots (turn left off A 697 N. of Powburn) and at Once Brewed hostel on the Roman Wall.

Before (28 m.) the farm of *Sewingshields* the military road quits the Wall, which is henceforth fairly continuous, mounting the crest of the Whin Sill and commanding views of wide extent and grandeur. The Vallum diverges considerably to the s.— 29¾ m. *Housesteads, or *Vercovicium*, has considerable excavated remains (N.T.; adm. daily, Sun from 2 in Oct–Apr; fee) of a fort containing a praetorium, granaries, and hospital. The drainage system is impressive. A small museum houses finds. A little farther on (½ m. walk along the wall-top; precipitous cliff) is a well-preserved milecastle; to the N. are the small *Northumbrian Lakes*, in a moorland setting of extreme desolation.— 31½ m. *Crag Lough.* — 32½ m. *Once Brewed Inn* (Information Centre with Y.H. adjoining). The well-preserved Roman fort of **Vindolanda** (*Chesterholm*), with a Roman milestone on the Stanegate, lies 1 m. s.w. of the road to Bardon Mill. The most interesting excavations (1970–continuing) are however in the civil settlement outside the walls, including an inn (mansio) and work-shops for bronze and iron. A full-scale reconstruction has been built of the Wall. The *Museum, in pleasant gardens, contains writing tablets, leather boots, and textiles from pre-Hadrianic times, and replicas of Roman transport.— 34 m. *Cawfields* milecastle (½ m. r. of road) has a picnic site. *Winshields Crag*, where the Wall reaches its highest point (1230 ft), rises to the E.— 35¾ m. Site of *Æsica* (*Great Chesters*), with excavated remains.—We traverse the broken basalt cliffs known as the *Nine Nicks of Thirlwall* with a good stretch of the Wall at *Walltown*, including an unusual signal-turret.— 39 m. *Carvoran*, the site of *Banna* (no. adm.).—Near (40 m.) *Greenhead* we rejoin the main road, but leave it there for B 6318 (r.).— 42 m. *Gilsland*

(Hotel), in the Irthing valley, was once a spa. It was here that Walter Scott first met Miss Charpentier (comp. p. 675), and he celebrated the neighbourhood in 'Guy Mannering'. About 1 m. w., beyond the farm of *Willowford*, is an abutment of the bridge by which the Wall crossed the Irthing; 2 m. w., on the N. bank, are the remains of *Camboglanna* (*Birdoswald*; key at adjoining farmhouse), one of the largest forts on the Wall. *Over Denton* church, ½ m. s., has an ill-fitting chancel arch of Roman stones.—47 m. *Banks*, with a good turret, is 3½ m. N.E. of Brampton (Rte 73A). Of the remaining part of the Wall, to *Bowness* on the Solway, there is very little to see.

***Lanercost Priory** (adm. daily; Sun from 2; fee), in the Irthing valley, 1 m. beyond Banks on the descent towards Brampton, was founded for Austin Canons by Robert de Vaux c. 1144. The choir and transepts (with the Dacre tombs) and the cloister are ruinous, but the E.E. nave is the parish church. The w. front is particularly beautiful, and part of the gateway and the guests' solar (now the village hall) remain. Beyond the Irthing (medieval bridge r. of road), 1½ m. s., is ***Naworth Castle** (Earl of Carlisle; no adm.), which passed from the Dacres to the Howards in 1577 by the marriage of the heiress to 'Belted Will Howard' (comp. 'The Lay of the Last Minstrel'). It dates from c. 1335, and is built round a central courtyard.

INDEX

Topographical names are printed in **bold type**, names of persons in *italics*, other entries in Roman type. The works of architects, artists, and sculptors have not been indexed. *Saints* are indexed under that title.

The following abbreviations occur in the index: